THE LETTERS OF KINGSLEY AMIS

Kingsley Amis was a brilliant and frequently outrageous correspondent. In his love letters and letters to intimate friends – in particular Philip Larkin and Robert Conquest – he wrote with a freedom and frankness impossible in work intended for publication. As a result the more than eight hundred letters in this volume contain some of his wittiest, most acerbic and most painfully revealing pages.

Spanning over fifty years, the letters open with Amis as an undergraduate at Oxford, energetically advising a fellow recruit not to abandon the Communist Party, and end with him as one of the country's pre-eminent men of letters, with a public image – not altogether accurate, but not discouraged by Amis himself – as an arch-conservative. Along the way they trace the frustrations and discontents of his life as penniless research student and lecturer (dazzlingly recreated in his first novel, *Lucky Jim*, which earned him his early reputation as 'redbrick' novelist and 'angry young man'; his lifelong enthusiasms for jazz, whisky, science fiction, limericks and the English language; his frequently savage opinions of the merits of other writers, alive and dead; his womanising and the breakdown of his two marriages; and the day-to-day workings of his life as a professional writer.

Above all, *The Letters of Kingsley Amis* provide a moving, scandalously funny, warts-and-all self-portrait of one of our finest, most influential and most-missed writers.

SIR KINGSLEY AMIS was born in South London in 1922, and educated at the City of London School and St John's College, Oxford. From his fictional debut in 1954 with *Lucky Jim* to his death in 1995 he published twenty-five novels and numerous works of non-fiction, verse collections, volumes of short stories and anthologies of poetry and prose. He was also a prolific critic and polemicist in newspapers and periodicals, writing widely on politics, education, language, books, films, jazz records, restaurants and drink. In 1981 he was awarded the CBE and in 1990 he received a knighthood.

ZACHARY LEADER is Professor of English Literature at the University of Surrey Roehampton. He is the author of *Reading Blake's Songs* (1981), *Writer's Block* (1991) and *Revision and Romantic*

Authorship (1996), and co-editor, with Ian Haywood, of *Romantic Period Writings 1798–1832: An Anthology* (1998). He is also a regular contributor to the *London Review of Books* and *The Times Literary Supplement*. He is currently writing the authorised biography of Kingsley Amis.

THE LETTERS OF KINGSLEY AMIS

EDITED BY

Zachary Leader

HarperCollins*Publishers*

HarperCollins*Publishers*
77–85 Fulham Palace Road,
Hammersmith, London W6 8JB

The HarperCollins website address is:
www.**fire**and**water**.com

This paperback edition 2001
1 3 5 7 9 8 6 4 2

First published in Great Britain by
HarperCollins*Publishers* 2000

ISBN 0 00 638783 7

Set in PostScript Linotype Minion by

Printed and bound in Great Britain by
Omnia Books Limited, Glasgow

CONTENTS

ILLUSTRATIONS

INTRODUCTION

Throughout his life, in addition to writing poems, novels, short stories, essays, critical studies, radio and television adaptations and programmes, reviews, and editing anthologies, Kingsley Amis was a prolific and inventive letter-writer. He was fully aware of the value of his correspondence. 'What a feast is awaiting chaps when we're both dead and our complete letters come out,' he writes to Philip Larkin on 24 September 1956, after a 'sodding good day' reading over Larkin's letters to him. When in 1955 an attack on Laurie Lee in the *Spectator* generates a heated correspondence, Amis imagines its likely afterlife in a letter of 22 August to Robert Conquest: 'It's nice to think that our exchange of views on the Laurie question will almost certainly appear, say about 1990 – you know, a book of about 50pp. costing 8/6: *Spanish Fly* a literary exchange: the Amis-Conquest correspondence edited by John Wain, O. M., published by Hartley and Tomlinson.' Several letters reflect on the proper idiom or style for the correspondence. 'I think your letters are very good, too,' he writes to Larkin on 22 April 1947. 'I see what you mean about formality and content; I think so too sometimes, but I enjoy the capital-&-underlining stuff so much. I think whag ramsh what you say apl lambsh applies chiefly to descriptions and scenarios.'

'Ramsh' and 'lambsh' here (one begetting the other, as it were) catch 'whag' and 'apl' (typos for 'what' and 'applies') and are just the sort of intricate foolery Amis enjoys. The correspondence with friends is meant to entertain, and is sometimes worked at with fanatical ingenuity, even when its subjects are boredom or business. 'I wrote you a letter a couple of days ago,' he writes to Larkin on 18 September 1979, 'but tore it up because when I read it through it turned out to be full of whining self-pity. I mean nothing wrong with self-pity but I don't want you thinking when a letter arrives Oh fuck what'll he be on about this time.' (What Larkin in fact thought was just the opposite: 'The obsessively-neatly typed address and Hampstead postmark sets me chuckling in advance,' he declares in a letter of 16 January 1981.) Self-pity in this instance derives in part from the tedium of more routine correspondence:

> I've just written a lot of turdy letters to strangers. Do you get that much? Find yourself writing things like unable to accept your kind invitation to address the Literary Soc– any merit. However this is only one man's opinion and your poems give up all debating, especially on facetious motions. I hope you away from my typewriter. So I will just wish the festival all the charity already and feel I should not 'spread myself too thin,' or secretary recently and can only assume the previous one failed to sorry about the delay which was due to please accept my apologies. No I *wouldn't* mind if they all stopped writing.

Even the sorts of letters Amis is parodying here, though, have their moments, as when he informs the Secretary of the Eton Literary Society, in a letter of 30 December 1970, that 'if I ever (these days) gave a talk anywhere, it would be at Eton, what with it being such a haunt of the Establishment and the ruling class and all,' or when he accepts a minuscule rights fee on the grounds that 'even chickenfeed has some nourishment value' (in a letter to Liz Calder, Publicity Manager at Gollancz, 1 May 1974). Amis, I am arguing, took his duties as a correspondent seriously (once he got around to them), especially when least serious, often when the duties themselves were most mundane. The letters matter, as a result, because they are so good, the best of them as funny and perceptive as anything he ever wrote.

They also matter because they tell us much about the man and his work: as novelist, poet, critic, anthologist, polemicist and teacher. From the start Amis was a figure of controversy: at the heart of the pre-eminent poetical grouping of post-war Britain, the Movement; the earliest of redbrick novelists and Angry Young Men. These labels he mostly resisted, but he did so in letters that reveal much about their origin and meaning. Politically, he was also high-profile (a phrase he wouldn't much like): an outspoken Communist at Oxford in the early 1940s; a vocal opponent of capital punishment in the 1950s; a defender of United States policy in Vietnam in the 1960s; an arch-conservative (anti-Soviet, anti-educational reform, anti-Common Market, anti-government subsidy) from the mid-1960s onwards. The private letters are often more nuanced and tentative – also cruder – about social and political issues than are the public letters, products of what he calls, in a letter to Larkin of 9 November 1952, 'the awful neurotic write to the papers fit'. They also show him as an enthusiastic, if intermittent, conspirator and campaigner, eager to orchestrate and sway public debate.

But the writing – of novels and poems, that is – always comes first. 'Work holds up my letter writing, speeds yours,' Amis explains to Conquest in a letter of 13 December 1977. 'Unlike you,' he writes on 3 July 1978, after another lengthy silence, 'I shy away from personal letters till my desk is clear.' When caught up in work, or late with it, Amis simply ignored correspondence, and most everything else. 'He's so *exhausted* at the moment with over work that as you see he can't even put pen to paper,' apologises his first wife, Hilly, in an undated letter of 1962 to Edmund and Mary Keeley (now among Edmund Keeley's papers in the Princeton Library). As she explains later in the letter:

> he really does mean to do these things but is so shagged to buggery. I spend all my time ringing up people [. . .] the day *after* we should have been there trying to explain the whole thing laughing (up your bum) away & isn't it cute that K never gets round to answering invitations & doesn't even discover them till 24 hours after the event was supposed to take place, & I can't spell or write, but so lucky I can count & phone up sometimes, pretty soon no one will ask us any more & our problems will be over.

In a number of letters, mostly to Larkin or sympathetic researchers, the work itself takes centre stage. Early in their friendship Amis and Larkin read each other's unpublished poems, novels and stories, offering detailed suggestions and criticisms. They also collaborated on poems and stories in the 1940s and later (see, for example, the 'Ron Cain' parodies in Appendix B, printed here for the first time). In several letters, Amis calls on friends or family for background information. 'As regards the literary mission you've kindly said you'd do for me,' he writes in a letter of 20 June 1962 to William Rukeyser, an ex-student from Princeton, 'this is what I would ideally like' (he is at work on *One Fat Englishman*, set in the United States):

> What my hero Roger Micheldene would notice in Greenwich-Village-type-surroundings at night – both in the street and in a bar or two – and in the morning.

> Short description of modest but not squalid apartment in the nearby area.
>
> Anything at all about $50,000-a-year house and grounds located anywhere between 30 and 60 miles from Manhattan, out in the country rather than in small town, though either would do [. . .]
>
> As an Englishman Roger would have his eye and ear open for oddities, but as you know for the author's benefit nothing is more helpful than simple details of lay-out of rooms, size of hallways etc., such as will help the author to visualise the thing in general terms.

A similar request to Martin Amis (while the father was at work on *Girl, 20* (1971), and before the son had published anything) results in a detailed description of a London discotheque. The son knows exactly what the father needs:

> You go down pink-light-bulb-light stairs, through glass doors to what looks like a small bar without any drinks or glasses where a Greek takes your money (usually between 15/- and 30/-). The Greek manager sometimes hangs around here and if you're a girl and you go there a lot he comes out and kisses you (might be useful). Then you go through more glass doors into an ante-room where there are more Greeks. There is apparently no way out of here except to the lavatories or to an alcove where you give in your overcoats etc. There is however a huge wardrobe in the far corner with mirror doors. When you have handed him your slips of paper a Greek will open one of these doors which leads into the club itself [. . .]

The description goes on for four pages, with diagrams (it can be consulted at the Huntington Library, in San Marino, California), and most of its details are incorporated in Chapter 3 of *Girl, 20*, with particular attention paid to the mirrored wardrobe.

Amis the private man is recognisably Amis the public man, but the letters also reveal a range of unfamiliar or unexpected character traits: insecurity, fearfulness, patience, regret, generosity, tact. Though much of what he writes about women will be deplored, the love letters printed here (all to Elizabeth Jane Howard) are warm, open, tender, even abject in their expression of feeling. Though often malicious about friends, Amis could also be loyal and loving, though in a way peculiar to Englishmen of his background and age. The letters reveal almost no social snobbery, and relatively little in the way of racial or religious prejudice. Readers must judge for themselves whether the several anti-Semitic and racist epithets in the letters make Amis an anti-Semite or a racist, labels he would have rejected – 'not really my style, I hope' (Amis to Thwaite, 24 March 1991).

This book is a selected edition of Amis's letters, and the picture of the man that emerges from it is subject to several forms of distortion, mostly a product of lost or unrecoverable correspondence. The earliest letters, those from the period 1941 to 1954, the year *Lucky Jim* was published and became an immediate success, are predominantly to Larkin, by far the most important correspondent of Amis's life. Five hundred and thirty-one letters to Larkin survive (in the Bodleian Library, Oxford, MSS. Eng.c. 6044–54), of which I have printed almost half. Most of these letters come from the period of their closest friendship, in the 1940s and 1950s. That I have printed fewer than a dozen letters to Larkin from the 1960s reflects a falling-off in the relationship; its revival in the 1970s and 1980s (Larkin died in 1985) accounts for the increase in numbers from those decades (almost seventy). Larkin saved all Amis's letters, which he kept, oddly for a librarian, in a ring binder, with resulting damage. I have found no letters to school friends, nor, with the exception of those to Bruce Montgomery, to any of the several dozen Oxford contemporaries mentioned in the *Memoirs*, in Eric Jacobs's authorised biography, or in the correspondence with Larkin. The ninety letters to Montgomery that survive (also deposited in the Bodleian) cannot be inspected until the year 2035.

There are no letters to Amis's parents, though in the *Memoirs* and elsewhere he presents himself as an outwardly dutiful and obedient son, and must have written to them regularly, not only from school (in 1939 the City of London School was evacuated to Marlborough College, in Wiltshire) but later from Oxford, the army and Swansea. Nor are there many letters to his extended family. Amis was an only child and wrote infrequently to his relatives. According to Robert Foster, an American cousin, Amis initiated a correspondence in the mid-1930s with his paternal aunt Gladys, Foster's mother, which extended into the 1950s. 'None of it survives,' Foster reports, adding that the extended Amis family 'was not much in the way of sentimentalists' (personal communication, 9 November 1997). After Amis's mother died in 1957, his father took up with several of what his son calls 'lady friends'. To one of them he left all his possessions, including, it seems, all personal papers. As Amis records in the *Memoirs*, she 'refused to let any of them go, even claiming back the watch and wallet Hilly had passed on to Philip and Martin'.

The preponderance of letters to Larkin at the beginning of this book produces the impression of a man who will reveal himself totally. As Amis writes on 19 June 1946, in terms that apply as much to their correspondence as to their private conversation:

> I enjoy talking to you more than to anybody else because I never feel I am giving myself away and so can admit to shady, dishonest, crawling, cowardly, brutal, unjust, arrogant, snobbish, lecherous, perverted and generally shameful feelings that I don't want anyone else to know about; but most of all because I am always on the verge of violent laughter when talking to you, and because you are savagely uninterested in all the things I am uninterested in.

When Amis contemplates the eventual publication of his letters to Larkin he is well aware of the reactions they will provoke in some readers. In a letter of 18 January 1951 he writes to Larkin to enquire about a common friend: 'Not that I care a 4d fart really, of course, but I like to be thought the sort of man who does, if it doesn't inconvenience me at all.' This admission he then footnotes, in the manner of an editor:

> This sentiment, which is typical of many in the *Letters*, should not of course be taken at its face value. In common with many men of great reserve, sensitivity and disinterestedness, Amis hated the appearance of sentiment, even when it was most strongly and truly felt, perhaps especially then. No reader of his work can fail to be struck by the unmistakable sincerity of his affections; he was pre-eminently 'the sort of man' who cared, and cared deeply, for the least member of the circle of which he was the centre. We may be sure that Larkin understood this.

That Larkin understood and trusted his friend is clear from the frankness of his own letters, called by Amis 'the above-water, visible part of a vast, sunken continent of self-nourished, fantastically amusing malice' (29 December 1945). The two friends egged each other on in the correspondence, and recognised ensuing distortions. 'I must say here, by the way, how much funnier than RGP is our conception of old Rodge,' writes Amis in a letter of 30 August 1948, of a common friend from Oxford, later a relation. 'Not that it's a "wrong conception", it's just much funnier, that's all.' Comparable distortions attend Amis's correspondence with Robert Conquest, who several times remarks on the dangers of confusing the writer, whether of letters or novels, with the man. 'Marriage bloody good,' he informs Amis in a letter of 7 October 1980, 'though no one reading passages in The Egyptologists, Peach Key, The Tit Man etc. written at other periods would expect the author ever to utter such sentiments.'

A second feature of the early letters to Larkin – aside from their complete candour – is their difficulty, a product of numerous private jokes, allusions, obscure abbreviations, associational leaps and word games. Most books, records, poems and songs, for example, are referred to by the first and last words in their titles, as in 'A Time' for *A Dance to the Music of Time*. Some are identified by the first letters, or first few letters, of their first and last words, as in 'GB' for *Goodbye to Berlin*, or 'Appara' (an editor's nightmare, this) for *Appointment in Samarra*. Often the letters proceed associationally: 'I love the *persistent mis-spelling* of authors' names,' declares Amis in a letter of 25 May 1947, 'it's amazing how it lowers the tome wainsh the tone. Talking of Wainsh . . .'.

Misspellings are of several sorts. Some derive from typos (all of which have been retained, even when most obvious), as in 'teh' for 'the', or 'thiknign' for 'thinking' (which to Amis 'sounds really extraordinary – a character in Ibsen? Pastor Thiknign?'); others are laboriously crafted, as in 'methsleevs' for 'themselves', or 'darts B. A.' for 'bastards'. Then there are phonetic spellings, often parodies of the sort of prim, suburban pronunciation mocked in the fiction: 'ab8' for 'about', 'hay' for 'how', as in Chapter 4 of *Lucky Jim*, where Margaret comments of Christine after their first meeting: 'Pity she's so refained, though.' (The most memorable phonetic spellings in the novels occur in *Girl, 20*, with its meal of 'Ham and Russian salad and sweep pickle tim peaches and plung cake and lots of cups of char'.) The intent of the misspellings is often subversive. 'Seriously though', for obvious reasons, is treated with special violence: when not typed upside down and backwards (an astonishing visual joke), it becomes 'Esoursyl htuohg', a comparably effortful undermining. Readers who tire of this sort of playfulness will be pleased to discover its gradual diminution in later letters.

The letters to women pose problems of another sort. When Eric Jacobs asked Amis who he thought might have letters from him, Amis replied 'women', adding immediately, in Jacobs's reconstruction (recorded in a note in the Huntington), 'that the trouble with that was that I might find some, then he would not want them published – for whatever reason – and then the women in question might be upset'. The only such letters to women printed here were written to Amis's second wife, Elizabeth Jane Howard. Hilly Amis (Lady Kilmarnock), his first wife, burned all his letters in 1963, the year their marriage collapsed. Though she does not remember how many there were, the figure must have been high. When the couple were separated for a month in October 1949, for example, he wrote daily. The letters to Hilly that survive, those written after 1963, are mostly notes about money and arrangements for the children. They are chastened, considerate, affectionate, but in no way convey the variety and depth of Amis's feelings for her over the years. After the break-up of his marriage to Elizabeth Jane Howard, Amis became clearer (or at least more public) about Hilly's importance to him: leaving her, he claimed, was the single biggest mistake of his life. In the fiction, the biographical writings and the poetry, his feelings for her are carefully pondered; in the extant letters they figure only rarely, or in passing. His feelings for Elizabeth Jane Howard, by contrast, are amply documented. Amis deeply loved her in the early years of their relationship, gradually grew apart from her during their marriage, and detested her after its break-up, with a ferocity as obvious in the correspondence as in the (related) misogyny of the later fiction. None of the letters I have seen to her is anything but warm and loving; but I have seen no letters from the period after she left him.

A final distorting absence concerns Amis's children. Philip, his older son, kept no letters. His daughter Sally has letters, but does not want them printed. Martin ('savage little Mart', in one letter) could produce only a single birthday postcard, though he remembers in its entirety one other card written in the period 1976–79, when he was literary editor of the *New Statesman* (the original is deposited in the *New Statesman* archive at the University of Sussex Library). It is undated and reads:

Note
whiskey – US and Irish.
whisky – others
Jolly good luck
Dad

Martin remembers parts of other, fuller letters, but they have not survived; nor were the children's letters to their father saved. The dozen or so Martin Amis letters deposited in the Huntington Library survive because they were also addressed to Elizabeth Jane Howard, whose papers the library also possesses. These letters mostly date from 1967 when Amis and Howard spent four months in Nashville, Tennessee, where Amis was a visiting Professor of English at Vanderbilt University. From the evidence of Martin's letters, those of his father seem to have been tolerant and good-humoured, even when responding to requests for money, a flat of his own, permission to quit a summer job. The father's tone can also be conjectured from several letters addressed to the 'Blokes', the collective name he and Howard gave to the male inhabitants of their household, including Philip, Martin, Colin Howard (Elizabeth Jane Howard's younger brother) and Colin's friend the painter and jazz musician Sargy Mann. These letters are affectionate and extremely funny, which is how the children remember Amis as a father – though they also remember him as often disengaged, not wanting to be bothered. That few of the letters Amis wrote to his children survive, I suggest, says little, or little for certain, about their relations.

Over eight hundred letters are printed in this selection, from a trawl of several thousand. Soon after I was asked to edit the correspondence I was given Amis's last address book, and wrote in search of letters to everyone listed in it. I also tried to contact all possible recipients listed in the *Memoirs*, in Eric Jacobs's biography, and present at the memorial meeting for Amis held at St Martin-in-the-Fields on 22 October 1996. A number of interesting letters, mostly to fans, resulted from requests for correspondence, or information about correspondence, placed in British and American newspapers and literary periodicals. In addition to the letters to Larkin in the Bodleian, I have printed letters now deposited in over twenty other university libraries and research institutes in Britain and North America (they are listed in the Acknowledgements). The most important of the collections still in private hands are those of Robert Conquest and Anthony Powell. After each letter I provide the location of the original, where it exists. Doubtless many Amis letters survive which I have not seen, and I would be grateful if readers who have such letters, or know of their whereabouts, would contact me through the publishers, perhaps for the inclusion of new material in an eventual complete letters.

I have tried to print letters from all periods of Amis's life and to a range of his correspondents. As well as letters to friends and fellow writers (Brian Aldiss, John Betjeman, William Cooper (Harry Hoff), Robert Graves, Anthony Powell, Edith Sitwell, C.P. Snow, John Wain and others), I have included letters to publishers, editors, agents, critics, academics, importunate research students, fans (according to Amis's secretary Susan Allison, all fan mail was scrupulously answered), radio and television producers and newspapers. From the time he resigned his Fellowship at Peterhouse, Cambridge, in 1963, Amis supported himself and his family as a novelist and freelance writer. The letters show how he did it. They also offer a wealth of literary (and musical) insights, interpretations and judgements. These judgements are often intemperate, iconoclastic, instrumental (that is, they serve Amis's own needs and habits as a writer). That Amis found it hard to finish his son Martin's novels puts the son in good company; Amis also had trouble with Proust, Joyce, Lawrence, Updike, Bellow and Nabokov. Towards the end of his life, he told Martin, the only books he could finish were thrillers, the sort that began 'A shot rang out' or 'A scream rent the air.'

The shape of the life as revealed in the letters will be familiar to readers of Amis's novels and biographical writings. *You Can't Do Both* (1994), the most autobiographical of the novels, explicitly links the hero's excesses, notably his compulsive philandering, to the restrictions of his upbringing – a linking the letters echo. What is less clear is the precise ebb and flow of these excesses, as with his drinking (always heavy, though heavier at some periods than others) or his neurotic fears and phobias. It is not possible to tell from the correspondence, for example, that Amis several times consulted therapists in the period 1946 to 1959 (according to Eric Jacobs, in a note in the Huntington). The major turning points in his life occur with the publication of *Lucky Jim* in 1954 and the break-up of his marriages in 1963 and 1980. His political shift to the right can be variously dated: after the war he ceased to be a member of the Communist Party; the Soviet invasion of Hungary in

1956 turned him into a firm and total anti-Communist; his support for the Vietnam War in the mid-1960s reflected (and accelerated) a conservatism that had been building since the end of the 1950s.

As for the inevitable narrowing that comes with age, though obvious in the letters, it is nowhere near as dispiriting as that in the letters of Larkin (for all the comedy or self-consciousness of late Larkin's gloom). Amis's late letters, like his late novels, remain alert to the temptations of self-caricature; something that seems not always to have been true of Amis in life (that is, in the life outside work, after the morning session at his desk). In 'Coming of Age', a poem from *A Look Round the Estate* (1967), this temptation is clearly anticipated. The poem concerns a man who 'played his part so well/That he started being it from then on./His trick of camouflage no longer a trick.' As for Amis's capacity for outrage – at pretension, stupidity, mean-spiritedness, bloody-mindedness in all its forms – this remains undimmed. Though there is little mellowing in the letters, no 'growth into wisdom', there is also little diminution of energy, insight, comic aggression. Going gentle into that good night, to quote Dylan Thomas, a poet he both deplored and served (as literary executor), was not Amis's way.

My criteria for selection were straightforward. When two letters make the same general points, observations, jokes, or transmit the same news, I print what I think is the livelier or stronger letter. When material is repeated in the letters I have chosen, I mostly omit it (all editorial excisions are marked by square-bracketed ellipses). I also omit detailed references to letters (either by Amis himself or his correspondents) that have not survived, a frequent occurrence in the correspondence with Larkin, for whom we have no letters to Amis for the period April 1947 to June 1967 – a gap which also accounts for the occasional unexplained reference or allusion in the letters to Larkin of this period. Some omissions within letters, especially to Larkin and Robert Conquest, may look like censorship, but they occur because it is impossible to make sense of what is omitted without both sides of the correspondence (though in a very few instances material has been omitted at the request of Amis's estate). Whole pages in the early letters to Larkin consist of detailed comments and enquiries about jazz records, many of which I have cut. For a taste of the sort of jazz rant omitted or abbreviated elsewhere, see the letters of 15, 24 and 31 December 1945, the last of which (it is not atypical) is accompanied by twenty-nine footnotes. A few otherwise undistinguished letters (mostly short and about business) have been included because they provide interesting biographical details or shed light on Amis's character.

A word or two about editorial procedures. I have annotated for non-British as well as British readers, and for readers of future generations. So I explain what *Woman's Hour* is, and the Suez Crisis. I have also tried to give dates wherever possible, even for well-known figures such as, to pick at random, John Dryden and Harold Wilson. When the nationality of jazz musicians and songwriters is not specified it is American; when the nationality of writers and politicians is not specified it is British. I have silently omitted a number of Amis's small drawings (though by no means all) and interpolated manuscript additions; when marginal manuscript additions are retained they are printed in the footnotes, so as not to clutter the page. I have also moved postscripts written at the tops of letters (because of lack of space) to the ends.

When the abbreviations 'TLS' (typed letter signed) or 'ALS' (autograph letter signed) are missing, and no provenance is given, it means that I am printing a published letter of which no original exists. When provenance alone is missing, it means I have been unable to discover where the original is, and am working from a photocopy (these photocopies, left behind by Amis after his death, are now in the Huntington). Dates in square brackets are conjectural or, in the case of undated postcards, taken from postmarks. The dates of all letters to editors of newspapers or journals are those on which the letter was published. The letters are printed in order of composition or publication, and their contexts should be clear from the footnotes, though I also provide a detailed Chronology at the beginning of the book, as well as Notes on Recipients. Recipients not listed in the Notes on Recipients are identified more briefly in the footnotes. There are few conjectured readings, all in square brackets (Amis's hand is an editor's dream). When in the footnotes I quote from Amis's published books, page numbers are taken from the paperback editions, if they exist. I have tried throughout to consider the reader's needs and pleasures, in the manner of Amis himself.

ZACHARY LEADER
London, November 1999

PREFACE TO THE PAPERBACK EDITION

I am grateful to the following people for offering corrections and additions to the footnotes which appeared in the hardback, especially those who praised the book and its editing before informing me that they were, for example, still alive, or named 'Edwin' rather than 'Edward': Oliver Andrew, Muriel Barton, Alan Bell, Daniel G. Berwick, Kate Bucknell, Robert Conquest, Fr Toby Forward, Timothy Garton Ash, Lynn Glynn, Selina Hastings, Donald Hawes, Christopher Hitchens, P.R. Jeffreys-Powell, Sargy Mann, Allan Massie, Tom Miller, John Mole, Robin Oakley-Hill, G.A. Parish, William Rukeyser, John Russ, James Silvester, Peter Sims, Beth Staffell, Edwin Tarling, Anthony Thwaite, James Trainer, Simon van Heyningen, Alan Watkins and B.J. Whyatt. Special thanks to the astonishingly generous and erudite Tom Deveson, who spotted dozens of allusions I had missed.

I have included two previously unpublished letters, both to Robert Conquest (*see Appendix I*). The originals of these letters, dated 8 January 1958 and 6 December 1960, are probably in Conquest's possession, but he cannot put his hands on them. They were not among the letters he photocopied for me in 1997 when I first began work on the book, but they were among those he photocopied for Eric Jacobs for use in his *Kingsley Amis: A Biography* (1995). These photocopies Jacobs has deposited among the Amis papers in the Huntingdon Library in San Marino, California. I am grateful to the Huntingdon and to Conquest for permission to print them here.

CHRONOLOGY

1922 16 April, Kingsley William Amis born in a nursing home on the edge of Clapham Common, the only child of William Robert Amis (1889–1963) and Rosa Annie Lucas (Peggy) (1891–1957). Amis's father was an employee in the London office of J. J. Colman and Co., the mustard manufacturer. The family lived at 16 Buckingham Gardens, Norbury, London SW16, a ward of the borough of Croydon.

1927 Attends St Hilda's primary school, not far from his home in Buckingham Gardens; then a second local primary, Norbury College, where he produces his first poetry and fiction: a ninety-line poem in blank verse on the miracle of St Sophia (a set topic) and a three-hundred-word story, 'The Sacred Rhino of Uganda', published in the school magazine (the story does not survive, but the poem can be consulted in the Harry Ransom Humanities Research Center in Austin, Texas).

1932 After a five-shilling 'flip' in a small aeroplane at the Croydon Aerodrome, Amis is put off flying for the rest of his life.

1934 Enters City of London School.

1935 Wins scholarship to City of London School.

1939 In August, City of London School evacuates to Marlborough College in Wiltshire.

1940 The Amis family moves from Norbury to Berkhamsted in Hertfordshire, within commuting distance of London.

1941 Arrives in Oxford in April, to read English as an Exhibitioner at St John's College. Meets Philip Larkin in first week. Joins the Communist Party in June. Attends summer term Communist Party study group on 'Colonialism'.

1942 Openly recruits undergraduates, at St John's and elsewhere, for membership in the Communist Party; attends meetings of the People's Convention, a peace campaign with strong communist links; sings in the University Labour Club choir; edits the club's *Bulletin* for a term.

1942–1943 Joins the army in July 1942, reporting to Catterick Camp in Yorkshire. Basic training for two months, then posted to Royal Signals unit for officer-cadets, 152 OCTU, also at Catterick. After twenty-six weeks' training, commissioned as second lieutenant. Postings: to Southern Command Signals at West Farnham near Salisbury; to High Wycombe, Buckinghamshire (where he begins a two-year affair with a married woman, Elisabeth Anne Simpson); back to Catterick (by August 1943) for an advanced wireless course; to Headington Hall in Oxford, where in November 1943 joins Second Army Headquarters Signals.

1944 Arrives in Normandy with Second Army HQ Signals on 30 June. Runs an office on eight-hour shifts, first at Main Headquarters, later at Rear Headquarters, dispatching and receiving messages by wireless, line, or dispatch rider. After several weeks on the move, constantly setting up and dismantling Rear Headquarters (in Banville, Vaux sur Seulles, Bazouches near Falaise, Joué sur Erdre and Amiens in France, then Pepingen and Holsbeek in Belgium), settles with his unit for five months in November in Sonnis in Belgium. Attempts first adult fiction, 'Who Else is Rank', a projected 80,000-word novel, jointly written with E. Frank Coles, a fellow officer. It was unfinished, but survives in portions (in the Henry E. Huntington Library in San Marino, California). In November promoted to lieutenant.

1945 Headquarters moves to Aarle in March. On 22 May war ends. Amis is sent to a reinforcement holding unit (RHU) at Minden in Westphalia. Some time after 25 June the whole Second Army disbanded. In August Amis is sent to another RHU in Bruges. On 22 August Larkin writes a letter welcoming him back to England. Demobilised and returns to Oxford in October.

1946 In January meets Hilary (Hilly) Bardwell in Oxford. Stays with Larkin in Leicester (where a brief visit to the senior common room inspires *Lucky Jim*). In July stays with Hilly's family at their home, Abbey Timbers, in Harwell, not far from Oxford. Holiday in France from end of August until mid-September with Hilary and Oxford friend Christopher Tosswill.

1947 Publishes first collection of poems, *Bright November*, with Fortune Press in London. Moves out of college into Miss Butler's lodging house at 19 St John's Street in June. In July stays with Hilly's family at Abbey Timbers. In October moves to 55 St John's Street. On 6 December writes to Larkin that Hilly is pregnant. Works on a novel, 'The Legacy' (completed September 1948 but never published). Takes Examination Schools at end of Michaelmas term (December); awarded First Class Honours degree. Begins work on B. Litt. thesis on 'English Non-Dramatic Poetry 1850–1900 and the Victorian Reading Public'.

1948 Marries Hilly on 21 January in Oxford registry office. Lives with Hilly in one-bedroom flat at 14 Norham Road in North Oxford; on 23 June moves to three-bedroom Marriner's Cottage in village of Eynsham, twenty-minute bus ride from Oxford. Philip Nicol William Amis born on 15 August. Completes 'The Legacy' in September.

1949 Longmans and other publishers turn down 'The Legacy'. Co-edits annual anthology *Oxford Poetry* with James Michie. Martin Louis Amis born on 25 August. Family leaves Eynsham, moves in with Hilly's parents at Abbey Timbers. Gets job as Lecturer in English, University College of Swansea, in October; begins work immediately. Hilly and boys move to Swansea in November.

1950 By February has written 250 pages of *Lucky Jim* (working title 'D & C', for 'Dixon and Christine'). Completes B.Litt thesis in May. Examined orally on the B.Litt in November and his thesis is failed. At the end of the year, writes librettos for two operas by Bruce Montgomery (the novelist Edmund Crispin), a friend from Oxford.

1951 In January, after Hilly receives a small legacy, buys a house in the Uplands district of Swansea, at 24 The Grove; acquires a room of his own for writing. Visits Larkin in Belfast in mid-April. Writes to Larkin in November announcing completion of 'D & C'.

1952 Meets Robert Conquest at PEN Club party to celebrate publication of *New Poems 1952*, the first of a series of yearly anthologies (it contains poems by Amis, Larkin, Conquest and others).

1953 In March settles on title of *Lucky Jim* for the much revised 'Dixon and Christine'. On 26 April an extract from *Lucky Jim* is broadcast in the first programme of the radio series *First Reading*, produced by the novelist John Wain. Several days later Gollancz accepts the novel for publication. Writes libretto for Bruce Montgomery's Coronation Ode *The Century's Crown*, performed in June by the Glasgow Choral Union and the Scottish National Orchestra. Gollancz sells American rights to *Lucky Jim* to Doubleday in November. Publishes a selection of poems, *A Frame of Mind*, in a Reading University series of limited editions at end of the year.

1954 Sally Myfanwy Amis born on 17 January. *Lucky Jim* published 25 January. *Kingsley Amis: No. 22, The Fantasy Poets* (Fantasy Press) also published in January. By February, *Lucky Jim* into its fourth printing (7,500 copies in print by mid-February; 12,000 by the end of the year, in sixteen Gollancz-style mini-impressions). Film rights sold to the Boulting Brothers.

1955 Wins Somerset Maugham Award in late March for *Lucky Jim*. Goes to Portugal on 23 June, staying in Estoril, then Monchique, in the Algarve. Attacks Laurie Lee, Peter Mayne and other travel writers in 'Is the Travel-Book Dead?', in 17 June issue of *Spectator*. Second novel, *That Uncertain Feeling*, published in August (Gollancz; Harcourt Brace, 1956). Returns to Swansea in September.

1956 Publishes *A Case of Samples: Poems 1946–1956* (Gollancz; Harcourt Brace, 1957). Poems also appear in D. J. Enright's anthology *Poets of the 1950s* (Tokyo: Kenkyusha), published on 14 January and often considered the first 'Movement' anthology, and in *New Lines*, ed. Conquest (Macmillan). Publishes two short stories: 'Court of Inquiry' in *Spectator*, and 'Interesting Things' in *Pick of Today's Short Stories 7* (Putnam); both later included in 1962 collection *My Enemy's Enemy*. Edits *Oscar Wilde: Poems and Essays* (Collins). In April begins reviewing jazz records for the *Observer*, at first monthly, then more frequently (until autumn 1958). Marches in protest against Anglo-French-Israeli invasion of Egypt. Soviet suppression of Hungarian uprising (begun on same day, 4 November, as UN Suez resolution) converts Amis to firm and total anti-communism.

1957 Release of film of *Lucky Jim*, adapted by Jeffrey Dell and Patrick Campbell, directed by John Boulting, starring Ian Carmichael as Jim

Dixon. Amis's mother dies of a stroke in March; after a trip to visit relatives in the United States, father moves in with the Amis family in Swansea. Amis writes BBC radio play *Touch and Go*. Publishes pamphlet for Fabian Society, *Socialism and the Intellectuals.*

1958 Appointed Visiting Fellow in Creative Writing at Princeton University, Princeton, New Jersey. In early September sets sail to America on the *Queen Elizabeth* with wife, children and father. Rents a house in Princeton at 271 Edgerstoune Road. Publishes short story, 'Moral Fibre' (John Lewis from *That Uncertain Feeling* is its narrator), in *Esquire* (later collected in *My Enemy's Enemy*, 1962). Publishes third novel, *I Like it Here* (Gollancz and Harcourt Brace). Begins reviewing foreign films for *Esquire* in column called 'The Art of the Cinema'. In November debates 'Is there a Beat Generation?' at Young Men's Hebrew Association in New York with Jack Kerouac, Ashley Montagu and James Weschler, editor of the *New York Post.* Publishes short story, 'The 2003 Claret', in *The Compleat Imbiber*, vol. 2 (Putnam), later appears in *Collected Stories* (Hutchinson, 1980). Lectures on recent British writing at Swarthmore, Yale, Vassar, University of Illinois at Champaign-Urbana and Library of Congress, Washington DC.

1959 Gives Christian Gauss Seminars in Criticism at Princeton in the spring (six lectures on science fiction, later to become *New Maps of Hell: A Survey of Science Fiction*, published by Harcourt Brace, 1960; Gollancz, 1961). Returns with family to England in July, on the *Liberté*, a ship of the French Line.

1960 Publishes *New Maps of Hell: A Survey of Science Fiction* (Harcourt Brace; Gollancz, 1961). *Take a Girl Like You* published (Gollancz; Harcourt Brace, 1961). Attends writers' conference in Copenhagen in September. Publishes two short stories: 'Something Strange', in *Spectator*, later published in *Pick of Today's Short Stories 12* (Putnam, 1961), *The Magazine of Fantasy and Science Fiction* (1961) and *My Enemy's Enemy* (Gollancz, 1962); and 'Hemingway in Space', in *Punch*, later published in *Collected Stories* (1980). Writes afterword to Samuel Butler's *Erewhon* (New American Library). In October, becomes science fiction reviewer for the *Observer*, until May 1965.

1961 In April, offered Fellowship in English at Peterhouse, Cambridge (making him the college's first Fellow and Director of Studies in

English; the appointment was officially confirmed in May and formal election was in June). Attends Albert Hall anti-capital punishment rally, also in April. Holiday in Sitges in Spain in August before moving to Cambridge to look for house. Family moves to The Mill House in West Wratting, a few miles from Cambridge, for two months, then to 9 Madingley Road, Cambridge. Begins five-year stint co-editing *Spectrum: A Science Fiction Anthology*, with Robert Conquest (Gollancz, 1961–65; Harcourt Brace, 1962–67).

1962 Publishes short story, 'All the Blood Within Me', in *Spectator*, later in the year included in *My Enemy's Enemy*. Publishes *The Evans Country* (Oxford: Fantasy Press), a sequence of six poems (expanded to eleven when it appears in subsequent volume, *A Look Round the Estate: Poems 1957–1967*, Cape, 1967). Appears in *Penguin Modern Poets 2* (with Dom Moraes and Peter Porter). From 12–21 August visits Robert Graves on Majorca, partly on holiday with family, partly to write profile for *Show* magazine. Release of *Only Two Can Play*, film version of *That Uncertain Feeling*, adapted by Bryan Forbes, directed by Sidney Gilliat, starring Peter Sellers. Attends seminar on 'Sex in Literature' at the Cheltenham Literary Festival on 4 October and begins affair with Elizabeth Jane Howard, the festival's artistic director. In December, resigns Peterhouse fellowship to pursue full-time writing career (though teaches two more terms, until the end of the academic year).

1963 Goes with Hilly during spring vacation to Majorca, to scout out a house to live in for a year; finds one in Soller. Father dies of cancer, 18 April. Hilly discovers Amis's affair with Elizabeth Jane Howard (henceforth Jane); in June Amis announces his intention to take Jane on a three-week holiday in Spain, before moving with family to Soller. In early summer he and Hilly attend science fiction fair in Trieste. Leaves Cambridge for holiday in Spain on 21 July, Hilly's birthday. Hilly and family move to Soller in August while Amis is on holiday; he returns to Cambridge in September to discover they have moved without him. Moves in to Jane's flat in Maida Vale in London (where her brother Colin also lives) instead of joining family in Soller. Moves with Jane to a flat in Basil Mansions, near Harrods, in Knightsbridge. In mid-November Philip and Martin (aged fifteen and fourteen), encouraged by Hilly to pay a brief visit to London, fly by themselves from Majorca and arrive unannounced at the Basil Mansions flat. After the visit, Amis and Jane return to live with Colin

Howard in the flat in Maida Vale. *One Fat Englishman* published.

1964 In January begins work on *The James Bond Dossier* (Cape and New American Library, 1965), which he finishes in May. Hilly and the children return to Britain in January, staying briefly in a flat in Ovington Gardens, in Knightsbridge, then in a rented house in the Fulham Road in Chelsea, where they stay for just over a year. From August to November works on *The Egyptologists*, beginning while on holiday in Majorca with Jane, Colin Howard and, after Colin's departure, Robert Conquest and his wife Caroleen. Publishes short story, 'The Friends of Plonk', in *Town*, later reprinted in *Collected Stories* (1980). Writes television play, *A Question About Hell*, a modern version of *The Duchess of Malfi*. After return from Majorca, moves, with Jane and Colin Howard, to a small rented flat in Keats Grove in Hampstead.

1965 Moves to five-bedroom house at 108 Maida Vale, acquired by Jane on a ten-year lease. Publishes *The Egyptologists*, co-written with Robert Conquest (Cape; Random House, 1966), *The James Bond Dossier* (Cape and New American Library) and *The Book of Bond, or Every Man His Own 007* (under the pseudonym Lt. -Col. William ('Bill') Tanner) (Cape). Divorce from Hilly and marriage to Jane Howard, on 29 June. In July Hilly moves to a house in Wivenhoe in Essex; Sally goes to boarding school and the boys move in to 108 Maida Vale, visiting their mother at weekends. August-September, on holiday with Jane in Venice and Greece. Works on outline for a film based on an original Fleming idea (for George Willoughby).

1966 January to March, trip to Jamaica with Jane to visit their friends Bobby and Dolly Burns, who have a house on Montego Bay. Publishes *The Anti-Death League* (Gollancz and Harcourt Brace). Votes for the Anti-Common Market candidate in the March general election (his first non-Labour vote). Travels in spring to Czechoslovakia with Jane for six-day visit, at the invitation of the Czech Embassy; lectures at Prague University.

1967 Quits Gollancz for Cape after the death of Victor Gollancz in February. Publishes *A Look Round the Estate: Poems 1957–1967* (Cape; Harcourt Brace Jovanovich, 1968). Publishes article entitled 'Why Lucky Jim Turned Right' in *Sunday Telegraph*, 2 July (reprinted in *What Became of Jane Austen? and Other Questions*, Cape, 1970;

Harcourt Brace, 1971). Involved in long and acrimonious correspondence in the press supporting United States policy in Vietnam. Appointed Visiting Professor of English, Vanderbilt University, Nashville, Tennessee (October to mid-January), an appointment arranged by Russell Fraser, the new Chairman of English at Vanderbilt and a friend from Princeton; delivers thrice-weekly lectures on modern British writing. While at Nashville works on *I Want it Now* (Cape, 1968; Harcourt Brace, 1969). On 21 November, Hilly marries David Shackleton Bailey (1917–99), Fellow of Gonville and Caius College, Cambridge, and University Lecturer in Tibetan.

1968 On 18 January, travels with Jane to Mexico to meet Princeton friends Edmund and Mary Keeley, and tour the country. In February begins four-week stay in San Miguel de Allende, two hundred miles north-west of Mexico City, visiting the science fiction writer Mack Reynolds; finishes *I Want it Now*. After visiting Princeton, sails from New York to Southampton on 14 March, arriving 20 March. Returns to 108 Maida Vale. Purchases large house with Jane, Lemmons (formerly Gladsmuir), on Hadley Common in Barnet, Hertfordshire, in May (but does not take possession until August, moving in on 25 November). Publishes *Colonel Sun* (as 'Robert Markham') (Cape and Harper and Row), *I Want it Now* (Cape; Harcourt Brace, 1969) and *Lucky Jim's Politics* (Conservative Political Centre). Hilly and Shackleton Bailey move with Sally to Ann Arbor, Michigan (where Shackleton Bailey is Professor of Latin); Hilly opens fish and chip shop called Lucky Jim's.

1969 Publishes *The Green Man* (Cape; Harcourt Brace, 1970). Contributes two articles (one with Robert Conquest) to the 'Black Papers on Education', in *Critical Survey 4*, ed. Brian Cox and A. E. Dyson.

1970 Publishes *What Became of Jane Austen? and Other Questions* (Cape; Harcourt Brace Jovanovich, 1971). Contributes third article (with Robert Conquest) to the 'Black Papers on Education', in *Critical Survey 5*, ed. Brian Cox and A. E. Dyson. Release of film of *Take a Girl Like You*, adapted by George Melly, directed by Jonathan Miller, starring Hayley Mills as Jenny Bunn. On 18 June, Amis's first Tory vote in a general election. In summer, on holiday in Europe, Hilly and Shackleton Bailey separate; Hilly meets the writer and teacher Alastair Boyd (b.1927) in Ronda, in southern Spain; after brief stay in Seville, settles in Ronda in 1971, eventually moving in with Boyd and later (in 1977, after divorce from Shackleton Bailey) marrying him. (Boyd first moved to Ronda in 1957 and ran a language school there.)

1971 Publishes *Girl, 20* (Cape; Harcourt Brace Jovanovich, 1972). Writes television play entitled *The Importance of Being Hairy*. In September, on holiday in Albufeira, Portugal. Starts *The Riverside Villas Murder* (Cape and Harcourt Brace Jovanovich, 1973).

1972 On 27 January Hilly gives birth to a son, Jaime, her child with Alastair Boyd. Amis publishes three short stories: 'Too Much Trouble', in *Penguin Modern Stories II* (Penguin); *Dear Illusion* (Covent Garden Press); and 'Mason's Life', in *Sunday Times*, later in *Collected Stories* (1980). Publishes *On Drink* (Cape; Harcourt Brace Jovanovich, 1973). Edits *G. K. Chesterton: Selected Stories* (Faber). Cecil Day-Lewis, an old friend of Jane's, moves in to Lemmons; ill with cancer, he dies there on 22 May.

1973 Publishes *The Riverside Villas Murder* (Cape; Harcourt Brace Jovanovich, 1973) and *Ending Up* (Cape; Harcourt Brace Jovanovich, 1974). Also publishes *Wasted, Kipling at Bateman's* (London: Poem of the Month Club), a limited-edition printing of two short poems, only the former of which is included in *Collected Poems 1944–1979* (Hutchinson, 1979; Viking, 1980). Edits *Tennyson* (in Penguin Poet to Poet series). In May, elected a member of the Garrick Club.

1974 Adapts his short story 'Dr Watson and the Darkwater Hall Mystery' for television. Writes episode of television police series *Softly, Softly* (*See What You've Done*). On 1 June, goes on holiday to Rome with Jane.

1975 February, *Paris Review* interview. Has lunch with the Queen at Buckingham Palace on 26 March. Writes episode of television series *Against the Crowd* (*We Are All Guilty*). Publishes *Kipling and his World* (Thames and Hudson; Charles Scribner's Sons, 1976). Publishes 'The Crime of the Century' as a summer-holiday serial in *Sunday Times* (six episodes, beginning 13 July).

1976 Publishes *The Alteration* (Cape; Viking, 1977). In July, moves from Lemmons to Gardnor House, in Flask Walk, Hampstead. After 'various difficulties had arisen between us' (*Memoirs*, p. 117), he and Jane consult several sex therapists. In November, finishes 'A Reunion', his longest poem, the first in two and a half years.

1977 Hilly marries Alastair Boyd, who in 1975 had become Lord Kilmarnock (the seventh holder of a barony created in 1831, though with aristocratic forebears reaching back to the thirteenth century); they return to London. Amis edits collection of pieces from *New Statesman* and *Spectator* entitled *Harold's Years: Impressions from the New Statesman and Spectator* (Quartet).

1978 Edits *The Faber Popular Reciter* and *The New Oxford Book of Light Verse*. Publishes *Jake's Thing* (Hutchinson and Viking) and a limited edition of the short story 'The Darkwater Hall Mystery' (Edinburgh: Tragara Press).

1979 Publishes *Collected Poems 1944–1979* (Hutchinson; Viking, 1980), *An Arts Policy*? (London: Centre for Policy Studies) and the short story 'The House on the Headland', in *The Times*, later in *Collected Stories* (1980). At end of September announces to Larkin 'total loss of sex drive'.

1980 Publishes *Russian Hide-and-Seek* (Hutchinson) and *Collected Short Stories* (Hutchinson; reissued in 1987 with the addition of two stories, 'Investing in Futures' and 'Affairs of Death'). Judges Arts Council National Book Award in April. Meets Mrs Thatcher at reception at 10 Downing Street. He and Jane go on two-week Mediterranean cruise with Anthony and Violet Powell and Paul and Betty Fussell; then stay with friends in the Dordogne; then on to Edinburgh Festival. Starts novel with homosexual narrator (the aborted 'Difficulties with Girls') in October. Jane 'bolts' on 13 November, after planned ten-day visit to health farm; refuses to return to Amis until he promises to give up drinking totally.

1981 Awarded CBE in New Year's Honours List. Edits *The Golden Age of Science Fiction* (Hutchinson). Puts Gardnor House on the market in February, the month Jane files for divorce (on grounds of 'unreasonable behaviour'). In August, Gardnor House sold and Amis moves to temporary flat around the corner, at 19 Jeffrey's Place, which he shares with Hilly and Alastair (Lord and Lady Kilmarnock) and their son Jaime, an arrangement originally suggested by Philip Amis.

1982 Moves with the Kilmarnocks to small house in Kentish Town, 186 Leighton Road, in early January. In March, breaks leg (tibia and fibula) after stumbling when getting out of the bath; is hospitalised for three weeks following an operation at the Royal Free Hospital in Hampstead. Housebound for nine weeks. Stops smoking entirely and gives up drink for almost six months (starts again in September, on holiday in Swansea). Starts a column on drink in *Daily Express.*

1983 Divorced from Jane. Publishes collection of *Daily Express* columns as *Every Day Drinking* (Hutchinson).

1984 Invited by *Daily Mirror* to be its poetry editor, choosing and introducing a poem a day, Monday to Friday (the column lasts a year, and the poems and introductory notes are subsequently reprinted as *The Pleasure of Poetry*, Cassell, 1990). Publishes *How's Your Glass?* (Weidenfeld and Nicolson) and *Stanley and the Women* (Hutchinson; Summit, 1985), his first novel in four years (the longest gap between novels in his career).

1985 In July, moves with the Kilmarnocks to a house at 194 Regent's Park Road, Primrose Hill. Honorary fellowship from Swansea. Gives up 'Difficulties with Girls' (the novel begun in 1980 and narrated by a homosexual; not the 1988 novel of the same title). On 21 November, ill with throat cancer, Larkin dictates his last letter to Amis; Larkin dies on 2 December; Amis and Hilly attend the funeral in Hull on 9 December.

1986 Wins Booker Prize for *The Old Devils* (Hutchinson; Summit, 1987). Publishes short story, 'Investing in Futures – A Story', in Cyril Ray, ed., *The New Compleat Imbiber* (Collins). Edits *The Great British Songbook* (with James Cochrane) (Pavilion/Michael Joseph). Writes introduction to G. K. Chesterton, *The Man Who Was Thursday* (Penguin). Appointed an executor of Dylan Thomas's literary estate by his friend Stuart Thomas (no relation to the poet), who was himself a trustee and lawyer to the estate.

1987 28 January to 4 March, broadcasts six-part series on jazz, *Blues with a Difference*, on BBC Radio 3. In February sells his papers (483 catalogued items) to the Huntington Library in San Marino, California, for $90,000. Publishes *The Crime of the Century* (Dent, 1987; Century-Hutchinson, 1989). Reissues *Collected Short Stories*, including two stories not in the 1980 edition: 'Investing in Futures' and 'Affairs of Death' (Hutchinson).

1988 Publishes *Difficulties with Girls* (Hutchinson; Summit, 1989) and *The*

Amis Anthology (Hutchinson), described in the introduction as 'a collection of my favourite poems'.

1990 Knighted in June Honours List. Publishes *The Pleasure of Poetry* (Cassell), reprinting *Daily Mirror* poetry columns; *The Folks that Live on the Hill* (Hutchinson and Summit); and *The Amis Collection: Selected Non-Fiction 1954–1990*, with an introduction by John McDermott (Hutchinson). In September, appointed restaurant reviewer, *Harpers and Queen*.

1991 Publishes *We Are All Guilty* (Viking), a novel for young adults (based on his 1975 script for the ITV television series *Against the Crowd*).

1992 Publishes *The Russian Girl* (Hutchinson; Viking Penguin, 1994) and *Memoirs* (Hutchinson and Summit).

1993 Publishes *Mrs Barrett's Secret and Other Stories* (Hutchinson).

1994 Fired after three columns as restaurant critic for *The Oldie* magazine. Publishes *You Can't Do Both* (Hutchinson).

1995 Publication of *Kingsley Amis: A Biography* (Hodder and Stoughton) by Eric Jacobs, Amis's authorised biographer. Publishes *The Biographer's Moustache* (HarperCollins). At work on a new novel, the unfinished 'Black and White' (the manuscript can be consulted in the Huntington Library, San Marino, California). In late August, while staying in Swansea with Michael and Virginia Rush, has a fall and suspected stroke; moved into Chelsea and Westminster Hospital on 31 August; recovers sufficiently to return home to Regent's Park Road, 6 September; enters University College Hospital, 20 September; moved to St Pancras Hospital, 12 October; contracts pneumonia, 14 October; dies on morning of 22 October; cremated 31 October, funeral service, St Mark's Church, near Regent's Park Road.

1996 Memorial meeting, St-Martin-in-the-Fields, 22 October.

1997 Posthumous publication of *The King's English: A Guide to Modern Usage* (HarperCollins).

NOTES ON RECIPIENTS

Brian Aldiss (b. 1925) Novelist, critic, science fiction author and editor. Born in East Dereham, Norfolk, and educated at Framlingham College. Served for four years in the army (1943–47), including a period in India (awarded the Burma Medal). Then worked as a bookseller (1947–56); as Literary Editor, *Oxford Mail* (1957–69); and as Editor of Science Fiction, Penguin Books (1961–64). Has written over thirty works of fiction, more than a dozen non-fiction books, and numerous collections of stories. Has also edited over thirty science fiction collections. Since publication of his first science fiction novel, *Non-Stop*, in 1958, has received many major awards in the field, including a Hugo Award for *Hothouse* (1962), a Nebula Award for *The Saliva Tree* (1966), a John Campbell Memorial Award for *Helliconia Spring* (1982) and a James Blish Award for excellence in science fiction criticism. His autobiography, *Twinkling of an Eye*, was published in 1998. Aldiss first met and became friends with Amis in 1956, after a talk Amis gave at Oxford.

Hilary Amis (*née* Bardwell) [*Hilly, Hilary Boyd, Lady Kilmarnock*] (b. 1929) Born in Kingston upon Thames and educated at Bedales School, Dr Williams's School for Young Ladies in North Wales, and Ruskin School of Art in Oxford. She and Amis met in Oxford in January 1946, were married on 21 January 1948, and their first child, Philip, was born on 15 August 1948. A second son, Martin, was born on 25 August 1949, and a daughter, Sally, on 17 January 1954. In the early years of their marriage she took on occasional part-time work to supplement Amis's income as an Assistant Lecturer at the University College of Swansea. The marriage was stormy from the beginning but lasted until the summer of 1963, when Amis refused to break off an affair with Elizabeth Jane Howard, who would become his second wife. After living briefly on Majorca, Hilly and the children returned to London in January 1964. In London she took in boarders and worked for a time at the Battersea Park Zoo. The marriage was formally dissolved in 1965, the year she moved to a house in Wivenhoe in Essex. In 1967 she married David Roy Shackleton Bailey (1917–99), Fellow and Bursar of Gonville and Caius College, Cambridge. In 1968

Shackleton Bailey accepted a professorship at the University of Michigan and Hilly and Sally accompanied him to Ann Arbor (where she opened a fish and chip shop called Lucky Jim's). In the summer of 1970, while on holiday with Sally and Shackleton Bailey in Spain, she decided not to return to Ann Arbor. Instead she stayed on in Ronda, in southern Spain, where she formed a relationship with Alastair Boyd (b. 1927), who ran a language school in the Palacio de Mondragon. They moved to Seville for a year, where Hilly worked as matron at the International School, at which Sally was a pupil. On her return to Ronda with Boyd, she helped with expenses by running a bar and taking in paying guests. In 1972 she gave birth to a son, Jaime Boyd, and in 1977, at last able to obtain a divorce from Shackleton Bailey, she and Boyd married and returned to London. This was also the year in which Boyd became Chief of Clan Boyd and seventh Baron Kilmarnock (with a family history stretching back to the thirteenth century) and she became Lady Kilmarnock. In 1981, after the break-up of Amis's marriage to Elizabeth Jane Howard, he and the Kilmarnocks set up home together, first in Kentish Town, then in Primrose Hill, an arrangement in which Amis paid most of the bills and the Kilmarnocks ran the household. In 1998, three years after Amis's death, she and Lord Kilmarnock returned to live in Ronda.

John Amis (b. 1922) Singer, broadcaster and music organiser. Amis's first cousin (son of James Amis, the younger brother of William Amis, the novelist's father), born in London and educated at Dulwich College. London Music Critic, *Scotsman* (1947–63); Concert Director of the Royal Philharmonic Orchestra (1948–49); Secretary of the Dartington Summer School of Music (1948–81); organiser of, and performer at, Hoffnung Music Festivals in the 1950s; Editor, BBC television music programmes; Presenter, BBC Radio 3 programme *Music Now*; panellist on the BBC Radio 4 programme *My Music*. Author of the autobiographical volume *Amiscellany* (1985).

Kingsley Amis [see also *Bill, Binks, Binky, Bunny, Kingers, Pud, Rabbit*]

Martin Amis (b. 1949) Novelist. Born in Oxford and educated at schools in Swansea, Princeton, Cambridge, Majorca, London and at Sussex Tutors in Brighton. Read English at Exeter College, Oxford; worked as an Editorial Assistant (1972–74), then Fiction and Poetry Editor (1974) on *The Times Literary Supplement*; Assistant Literary Editor (1974–76) and Literary Editor (1976–79), *New Statesman*. His first novel, *The Rachel Papers* (1973), won the Somerset Maugham Award (as had his father's first published novel, *Lucky Jim*). He is the author of eight other novels: *Dead Babies* (1975), *Success* (1978), *Other People* (1981), *Money: A Suicide Note* (1984), *London Fields* (1989), *Time's Arrow* (1991), *The Information* (1995) and *Night Train*

(1997). He has also published two collections of short stories, *Einstein's Monsters* (1987) and *Heavy Water and Other Stories* (1998), and two volumes of collected journalism, *The Moronic Inferno and Other Visits to America* (1986) and *Mrs Nabokov and Other Excursions* (1993). In 1984 he married the philosopher Antonia Phillips, with whom he has two sons: Louis (b. 1984) and Jacob (b. 1986). The marriage was dissolved in 1997, the year he married the writer and literary journalist Isabel Fonseca, with whom he has two daughters: Fernanda (b.1996) and Clio (b.1999). A third daughter, Delilah Seale (b.1976), he came to know in 1995.

Philip Amis [*Pinetop*] (b.1948) Painter and graphic designer. Born in Oxford and educated at schools in Swansea, Princeton, London and at the Friends' School, Saffron Walden, as well as at the Camberwell School of Art. After art school worked for some twenty years as a professional graphic artist (the Rebel Yell whisky label was designed by him), but at forty decided to pursue his own art and has exhibited abstract watercolours, flower paintings and collages at several London galleries.

John Betjeman (1906–84) Poet, freelance writer, broadcaster. Born in London and educated at Highgate School, Marlborough College and Magdalen College, Oxford. Worked briefly as a schoolmaster and published his first volume of poems, *Mount Zion: or in Touch with the Infinite*, in 1931, when he also began writing articles for the *Architectural Review*. Among his subsequent volumes of verse were *Continual Dew: A Little Book of Bourgeois Verse* (1937), *Old Lights for New Chancels* (1940), *New Bats in Old Belfries* (1945), *A Few Late Chrysanthemums* (1954), *Collected Poems* (1958, expanded 1962), *A Nip in the Air* (1972) and *High and Low* (1976). He published a blank-verse autobiography, *Summoned by Bells*, in 1960. Throughout his life, Betjeman broadcast and wrote books and articles on architecture and topography. He was knighted in 1969 and was appointed Poet Laureate in 1972, in succession to C. Day-Lewis. Amis was an early admirer of Betjeman's verse, began corresponding with him in 1954 when *Lucky Jim* was published, but only got to know him well in the early 1960s.

Bill see *Kingsley Amis*

Binks [*Binky*] see *Kingsley Amis*

Bird see *Elizabeth Jane Howard*

Blokes The collective name for the male inhabitants of the Amis-Howard household, primarily Sargy Mann and Colin Howard, but also, when living there, Martin and Philip Amis.

Bunny see *Kingsley Amis*

Robert Conquest [*Ol' Bob, O'B, O. Bob, Victor Gray, Ted Pawker*] (b. 1917) Anglo-American poet and historian. Born in Great Malvern in Worcester, educated at Winchester and Magdalen College, Oxford. Served as an infantry officer in the army (1939–46), worked as a diplomat in the Foreign Office (1946–56), was Sidney Webb Research Fellow at the London School of Economics (1956–58), then took up a number of visiting appointments to universities and research institutes in the United States. He is currently a Senior Research Fellow at the Hoover Institution at Stanford University in California. In 1955 he published *Poems*, his first collection of verse. In 1953 he co-edited (with Michael Hamburger and Howard Sergeant) the PEN Club anthology *New Poems 1953*, which contains poems by both Amis and Larkin, and in 1956 he edited the first of two *New Lines* anthologies (in which both Amis and Larkin again figure). From 1962–63 he was Literary Editor of the *Spectator*. Among his many books on the history and politics of the Soviet Union are *The Great Terror* (1968), *Lenin* (1972), *Kolyma* (1978), *The Harvest of Sorrow* (1986) and *The Great Terror Reassessed* (1990). Conquest first met Amis in 1952 and their correspondence (consisting of over a hundred letters on Amis's part) was spread over four decades. He and Amis collaborated on a number of projects, including a novel, *The Egyptologists* (1965), five volumes of the science fiction anthology *Spectrum* (1961–66) and countless limericks. His latest books are *Reflections on a Ravaged Century* and a book of poems, *Demons Don't*, both 1999. He was awarded an OBE in 1955 and made a CMG (Companion, Order of St Michael and St George) in 1996. He has been married four times: to Joan Watkins in 1942 (diss. 1948); Tatiana Mihailova in 1948 (diss. 1962); Caroleen Macfarlane in 1964 (diss. 1978); and Elizabeth Wingate (previously Neece) in 1979.

Brian Cox (b. 1928) Literary critic and academic. Born in Grimsby and educated at Wintringham Secondary School and Pembroke College, Cambridge. Lecturer in English, University of Hull (1954–66); Professor of English Literature, Manchester University (1966–76); John Edward Taylor Professor of English Literature, Manchester University (1976–93); Dean, Faculty of Arts, Manchester University (1984–86); Pro-Vice-Chancellor, Manchester University (1987–91). He is the author of three volumes of poems, *Every Common Sight* (1981), *Two-Headed Monster* (1985) and *Collected Poems* (1993); several studies of modern poetry and fiction; an autobiography, *The Great Betrayal* (1992); and two books on the English curriculum in higher education (1991, 1995). In 1959 he was founding co-editor, with A. E. Dyson, of the literary periodical *Critical Quarterly* (1959–); he and Dyson were also founding co-editors of *Critical Survey*, a periodical aimed at teachers of English. *Critical Survey* was the publishing site of the 'Black Papers on Education' (1969–77), which opposed current educational trends, and to which Amis and Robert Conquest contributed articles. In 1990 he was made a CBE.

John Davenport (1908–66) [*Uncle, Uncle John*] Literary journalist and critic. Born in London and educated at St Paul's School and Corpus Christi College, Cambridge, where he read History (he matriculated in 1928, but was not awarded a BA until 1937; MA, 1938). After Cambridge employed as tutor to the novelist Malcolm Lowry, then moved to Hollywood where he worked briefly as a screenwriter. Returned to England and taught English for a year at Stowe (1941–42), where his pupils included the journalist Peregrine Worsthorne and the singer and critic George Melly. Worked as a broadcaster for BBC radio (1943–47) and as a literary critic on the *Spectator* and other magazines, and then on the *Observer*, where for a ten-year period from the mid-1950s he was lead fiction reviewer. Also worked briefly as Literary Editor, *Vogue*, and Drama Critic, *Queen* magazine. Co-author, with Dylan Thomas, of *The Death of the King's Canary*, a spoof murder-mystery mocking contemporary poets. Began corresponding with Amis in 1955 in connection with Amis's *Spectator* article 'Is the Travel-Book Dead?' (17 June 1955).

D. J. Enright (b. 1920) Poet, novelist and critic. Born in Leamington, Warwickshire, and educated at Leamington College, Downing College, Cambridge, and the University of Alexandria (D. Litt., 1949). Spent over twenty years teaching English literature abroad, in Egypt, Japan, West Germany, Thailand and Singapore. Returned to England in 1970 and was co-editor of *Encounter* (1970–72); worked for several years for the publisher Chatto and Windus, joining their board of directors in 1973. The first of his many verse collections, *The Laughing Hyena and Other Poems*, was published in 1953; his first novel, *Academic Year*, was published in 1955. In 1956, while in Japan, edited the Movement anthology *Poets of the 1950s*, which contained poems and introductory statements by Amis and Larkin. *The Terrible Shears: Scenes from a Twenties Childhood* (1973) is an account of his youth in a working-class family; *Paradise Illustrated* (1978) and *A Faust Book* (1979) are comic reworkings of the biblical tale of the Garden of Eden and of the Faust legend. Among his several works of literary criticism are *The Apothecary's Shop: Essays on Literature* (1955) and *Conspirators and Poets* (1966). In 1981, the same year his *Collected Poems* was published, he received the Queen's Gold Medal for poetry. Amis first began corresponding with Enright in the mid-1950s, in connection with *Poets of the 1950s*.

Paul Fussell (b. 1924) American critic, essayist and academic. Born in Pasadena, California, and educated at Pomona College in California (BA, 1947) and Harvard University (MA, 1949; Ph.D., 1952). Before university, Fussell served in the army as an infantryman and was wounded in action in France (he received the Bronze Star and two Purple Hearts). He began his career as an academic at Connecticut College (1951–54); then at Rutgers

University, in New Brunswick, New Jersey (1955–83), where in 1976 he was appointed John DeWitt Professor of English Literature. In 1983 he moved to the University of Pennsylvania as Donald T. Regan Professor of English Literature. Among Fussell's many books of literary and cultural criticism and social history are studies of eighteenth-century writing, the literature of the First and Second World Wars, travel and social class. He is also the author of *The Anti-Egotist: Kingsley Amis, Man of Letters* (1994). Fussell first met Amis in Princeton some time in 1958–59, probably through their mutual friend Edmund Keeley.

Jack Gohn (b. 1949) American lawyer, author of *Kingsley Amis: A Checklist* (1975). Born in London and educated at the University of Pennsylvania (BA, 1971), the Johns Hopkins University, in Baltimore, Maryland (Ph.D., 1975), and the University of Maryland (JD, 1981). Gohn first wrote to Amis in early 1974, in connection with his doctoral dissertation on Amis's fiction. He also interviewed Amis several times in London in July. The dissertation was accepted the following year, but the only part of it to be published was an expanded version of the bibliography, *Kingsley Amis: A Checklist* (Kent, Ohio: Kent State University Press, 1976). Gohn went on to publish academic articles on Shakespeare and Shelley and to write book reviews for the *Baltimore Sun* and the *Washington Post*. He then trained for the law, qualifying in 1981. He is now a partner in the law firm of Gohn, Hankey and Stichel, LLP, of Towson and Baltimore, Maryland.

Victor Gollancz (1893–1967) Publisher. Born in London and educated at St Paul's School and New College, Oxford. After serving briefly in the army and teaching at Repton School (1916–17), Gollancz entered publishing in 1921, for Benn Brothers Ltd. He was Managing Director, Ernest Benn Ltd, from 1923 to 1927. In 1927 he founded his own firm, Victor Gollancz Ltd, which began by publishing fiction and books of general interest. In the 1930s the firm also published many books and pamphlets advocating left-wing and humanitarian causes; in 1936 it founded the mail-order Left Book Club. Gollancz was knighted in 1965. In 1919 he married Ruth Lowy, who helped with the running of the business (as a director, and as co-designer of the firm's distinctive book jackets). Livia Gollancz (b. 1920), their daughter, joined the firm in 1953 as an Editorial Assistant and typographer, became a member of the board in 1954, and took over from her father as director of the firm in 1965. Gollancz published Amis's first six novels (excluding *The Egyptologists*, which was co-written with Robert Conquest and published by Cape), his first volume of short stories, *My Enemy's Enemy* (1962) and *New Maps of Hell* (1961), a study of science fiction.

Gouger see *John McAndrew*

Robert Graves (1895–1985) Poet, novelist and prose writer. Born in London and educated at Charterhouse and St John's College, Oxford (1918–20). He joined the army in 1914 and published his first volumes of poetry – *Over the Brazier* (1916) and *Fairies and Fusiliers* (1917) – while serving in the First World War. In 1926 he taught briefly in Egypt, as a professor of literature, then lived and worked on Majorca and in Brittany with the American poet Laura Riding. After a spell in England during the Second World War he returned permanently to Majorca with his second wife Beryl Hodge. Though Graves saw himself primarily as a poet, he wrote many volumes of essays, novels, biographies and works for children. His best-known prose works are the autobiographical *Goodbye to All That* (1929), the historical novels *I, Claudius* and *Claudius the God* (both 1934) and *The White Goddess: A Historical Grammar of Poetic Myth* (1948). His last volume of *Collected Poems* appeared in 1975. Graves was professor of Poetry at Oxford from 1961–66. Amis first corresponded with him in 1954 and later (in 1962) interviewed him on Majorca for a profile in the American magazine *Show*. After resigning his fellowship at Peterhouse in December 1962, Amis planned to spend a year with his family in Deyá on Majorca, where Graves lived, a plan aborted by the break-up of the Amis marriage.

Victor Gray Pseudonym of *Robert Conquest*

HFD Horse Faced Dwarf, Larkin's nickname for *Anthony Powell*

Colin Howard [*Monkey, Monk*] (b. 1934) Designer of sound systems, younger brother of Elizabeth Jane Howard. Born in London and educated at Radley College and Trinity College, Cambridge. National Service in the Air Force (1953–54). Howard lived with Amis and Elizabeth Jane Howard from 1963–80.

Elizabeth Jane Howard [*Bird, Jane, Min, Minnie, Piney, Pineytop, Tiny* and *Wog*] (b. 1923) Novelist. Born in London and educated at home until age sixteen. From 1939–46 took up a series of part-time jobs as a model, publisher's reader and newsreader at the BBC. In 1947 employed as a secretary at the Inland Waterways Association. In 1942, aged nineteen, married the naturalist and painter Peter Scott (1909–89), son of the explorer Captain Robert Scott of the Antarctic. Her daughter Nicola, her only child, was born the same year. The marriage was dissolved in 1951. Howard began writing soon after her marriage to Scott, and her first novel, *The Beautiful Visit* (1950), won the John Llewellyn Rhys Memorial Prize. Her second novel, *The Long View*, was published in 1956, and her third, *The Sea Change*, in 1959. In 1959 she married James Douglas-Henry, an Australian broadcaster; this marriage also ended in divorce, in 1964. She met Amis in 1962, when she was already separated from her second husband. Amis and Howard were married in 1965. From 1965 to 1982 she published five novels, including *Something in Disguise* (1969), which was filmed for television in 1982, and *Getting it Right* (1982), which won the *Yorkshire Post* Prize and was turned into a film in 1985. Howard left Amis in 1980 and the marriage was dissolved in 1983. Since the break-up of her marriage to Amis she has published five novels.

Samuel Hynes (b. 1924) American author and academic. Born in Chicago and educated at the University of Minnesota (BA, 1947) and Columbia University (Ph.D., 1956). Taught English at Swarthmore College (1949–68), where he met and befriended Amis, who came to lecture in 1958; Professor of English, Northwestern University, Evanston, Illinois (1968–76); Professor of English, Princeton University (1976–90). Author of critical studies of Hardy (1961), William Golding (1964), Edwardian culture (1968, 1972) and the Auden generation (1976). Has also written two highly acclaimed accounts of wartime experience and culture: *Flights of Passage: Reflections of a World War Two Aviator* (1988) and *A War Imagined: The First World War and English Culture* (1990). He is the editor of *The Complete Poetical Works of Thomas Hardy*, 4 vols (1982–85).

Jane see *Elizabeth Jane Howard*

Edmund Keeley [*Mike, Stud*] (b.1928) American author, translator and academic. Born in Damascus, Syria, came to the United States in 1939. Educated at Princeton University (BA, 1949) and Oxford (D. Phil., 1952). Taught English at Brown University, Providence, Rhode Island (1952–53) and at Princeton (1954–), where he was appointed Professor of English and Creative Writing (1970); also Co-Chairman, Program in Comparative Literature (1964–65); Director, Program in Creative Writing and Theater (1971–73); and Director, Hellenic Studies Program (1989–). Has had numerous visiting fellowships to Greece and has translated the poems of a number of modern Greek poets, including George Seferis (1967), C. P. Cavafy (1972, 1975, 1992) and Yannis Ritsos (1985). His wife, Mary Keeley (b. 1925), who was educated at the French Lycée in Alexandria and St Hugh's College, Oxford, has also published translations from modern Greek into English. The latest of Keeley's many books on modern Greece and Greek culture is *Inventing Paradise: The Greek Journey 1937–47* (1999). The Keeleys met and befriended the Amises at Princeton in 1958.

Philip Larkin (1922–85) Poet and novelist. Born in Coventry and educated at King Henry VIII School, Coventry, and St John's College, Oxford (1940–43), where he met Amis in April 1941. Graded C3 (for poor eyesight) in army medical examination in January 1942 and therefore found unfit for military service. Appointed Librarian, Wellington, Shropshire, in December 1943; Assistant Librarian, University College of Leicester,

September 1946; Sub-Librarian, Queen's University, Belfast, September 1950; and Librarian, University of Hull, March 1955. His early poems appeared in *Poetry from Oxford in Wartime* (1945) and *The North Ship* (1945), the latter published by the Fortune Press. His first novel, *Jill*, was published in 1946 by the Fortune Press, and his second, *A Girl in Winter*, in 1947, by Faber and Faber. In 1951 *XX Poems* was printed privately in Belfast and in 1954 five of his poems were published in Oxford as *The Fantasy Poets No. 21. The Less Deceived*, his second major verse collection, was published in 1955 by the Marvell Press, and his work figured prominently in several influential Movement anthologies, including Robert Conquest's *New Lines* (1956). Two other volumes of verse, *The Whitsun Weddings* (1964) and *High Windows* (1974), both published by Faber and Faber, established his reputation as one of England's foremost poets. *All What Jazz*, a collection of record reviews originally published in the *Daily Telegraph* (1961–70), appeared in 1970. He edited *The Oxford Book of Twentieth Century English Verse* in 1973, and published a collection of essays, *Required Writing*, in 1983. Larkin was made a CBE in 1975, a CH (Companion of Honour) in 1985, and was awarded numerous prizes, honorary fellowships and degrees. His correspondence with Amis was by far the most extensive and important of Amis's life. Anthony Thwaite, one of Larkin's literary executors, edited the *Collected Poems* in 1988 and the *Selected Letters* in 1992.

John Lehmann (1907–87) Editor and writer. Born in Buckinghamshire and educated at Eton and Trinity College, Cambridge, where he met and befriended Julian Bell, nephew of Virginia Woolf. It was through Bell that he became associated with the Hogarth Press, of which he became a partner (1938–46). Wrote several volumes of poems but was best known as an editor, broadcaster and publisher. From 1936–40 he edited the book-periodical *New Writing*, which in 1940 was retitled *Folios of New Writing*, and in 1942 became *New Writing and Daylight* (under which title it lasted until 1946, in association with Penguin Books). *New Writing* published the early work of Auden, Spender, Isherwood and V.S. Pritchett, among others. In 1946 Lehmann founded his own publishing house, John Lehmann Ltd, which he directed until 1952. In 1954 he founded a literary monthly, the *London Magazine*, which he edited until 1961 (when Alan Ross succeeded him as Editor). As a broadcaster he was best known for the 1952 BBC radio series *New Soundings* (succeeded in 1953 by John Wain's *First Reading*, which broadcast a pre-publication excerpt from *Lucky Jim* in its first programme). Lehmann's *Collected Poems 1930–1963* were published in 1963. He wrote three volumes of autobiography (1951, 1960, 1966) and several volumes of reminiscence and biography, including portraits of the Sitwells

(1968), the Woolfs (1978) and Rupert Brooke (1980). His sister was the novelist Rosamond Lehmann (1901–90). Amis met Lehmann in the early 1950s and contributed to the *London Magazine*.

Jean McAndrew (d. 1998) and **John McAndrew** [*Gouger*] (1912–62). Neighbours of the Amises in Princeton, New Jersey. John McAndrew was born in Youngstown, Ohio, trained as a lawyer and began practising law with firms in Milwaukee, Wisconsin and then Youngstown. Married Jean in 1941; served in the army (1942–45). After the war, according to Jean McAndrew (personal communication, 15 March 1997), John 'did not want to start in law for the third time. He got a job in sales, and we moved to New Jersey. In the mid 1950s, he switched to the advertising company in New York City that he had been working with in his capacity as sales manager for a fine china company. Work in advertising is seasonal, like coal mining. When the company you work for loses a big account, they cut back their work force, and you're out of a job, and he was unemployed part of the year, 1958–1959, that we came to know the Amises so well, and so there was quite a lot of free time to play.' The McAndrews had five daughters: Linda (b. 1942), Karen (b. 1944), Shelagh (b. 1947), Megan (b. 1949), who went to school with Martin Amis, and Maura (b. 1955), a playmate of Sally Amis. The McAndrews lived at 235 Edgerstoune Road and the Amises lived at 271.

John Hamilton McCallum (b. 1911) Publisher. Born in the Philippines and educated at Harvard. After Harvard taught at the Buckley School in New York City. Joined Harcourt Brace and Co. in 1938, where he was involved in college textbook selling and editing. In 1953 became Vice-President of the company and head of its college division, briefly helping to manage the company in a triumvirate including James Reid, Editor-in-Chief for both college and school publishing, and William Jovanovich, head of the school department (an arrangement which lasted until late 1954 when Jovanovich became sole President of the company). In 1955 was appointed Executive Vice-President, occupied mainly with trade (general) books and college textbook publishing, and between 1955 and 1964 made several trips to Britain as a Trade Editor. He retired from Harcourt Brace, and all further full-time employment, in 1964. As Trade Books Editor, McCallum helped establish Harcourt Brace's fiction list, which numbered among its authors Virigina Woolf, E.M. Forster, Eudora Welty, Mary McCarthy, William Golding, Arthur C. Clarke and C.S. Lewis, as well as Amis. He began corresponding with Amis in 1956.

John McDermott (b. 1948) Critic and teacher. Born in Wigan and educated at St John Rigby College in Wigan, University College London and the University of Birmingham. After teaching English at St Michael's Convent

Grammar School in London (1971–73) he returned to Wigan as Head of English at his old school (1973–83). From 1983–90 was Senior Vice-Principal, De La Salle College, Salford, then Principal, from 1990–96. Taught summer courses in English (organised by *Critical Quarterly*) at Manchester University (1984–92) and since 1996 has been Tutor in the English Department at the University of Birmingham. From 1990–95 he wrote a weekly column on language in *The Times Educational Supplement*. He is also the author of *Kingsley Amis: An English Novelist* (1989), *Punctuation for Now* (1993) and *A Hopkins Chronology* (1997), as well as articles on Francis Thompson and Catholic writing of the Victorian period. He began corresponding with Amis in 1980 and later assisted in the compilation of *The Amis Collection: Selected Non-fiction 1954–1990* (1990), for which he wrote the introduction. His wife Ann McDermott was also born in Wigan (in 1961), and was educated at St John Rigby College, the University of Birmingham and Manchester University. She is Lecturer in English, University of Birmingham, and Director, University of Birmingham Johnson Dictionary Project. Her edition of *Samuel Johnson's Dictionary on CD-ROM* appeared in 1996.

Sargy [Martin] Mann (b. 1937) Painter. Born in Hythe in Kent and educated at Dartington School, Oxford Technical College and the Camberwell School of Art, where he taught painting and drawing from 1969–99. In addition to painting, teaching and publishing a book (1991) and several catalogues on Bonnard's drawings (also co-curating a Bonnard exhibition at the Hayward Gallery in 1994), he has worked part-time as a jazz drummer since the 1950s. In 1967, the year Amis and Elizabeth Jane Howard were in Nashville, Howard suggested to Mann that he move into 108 Maida Vale to help his friend Colin Howard with the running of the household. He stayed on after Amis and Howard returned, helped with the move to Lemmons, in Barnet, Hertfordshire, in 1968, and remained at Lemmons until 1976, the year he married the painter Frances Carey. In 1988, after a period in which his eyesight deteriorated, he was declared officially blind, though he retains a little peripheral vision in one eye. He continues to paint, and his most recent exhibition was held in London in the spring of 1999.

Tom Maschler (b. 1933) Publisher. Born in London and educated at Leighton Park School. Began his career in publishing as Production Assistant, André Deutsch (1955–56); then Editor, MacGibbon and Kee (1956–58); Fiction Editor, Penguin Books (1958–60); Editorial Director, Jonathan Cape (1960–70); Chairman (1970–91); Publisher, Children's Books, Jonathan Cape (1991–); Director, Random House (1991–). Maschler was Elizabeth Jane Howard's editor at Cape and became Amis's editor in 1966.

Karl Miller (b. 1931) Editor, critic, academic. Born in Edinburgh and educated at Royal High School, Edinburgh, and Downing College, Cambridge. After brief stints at HM Treasury (1956–57) and BBC Television (1957–58), embarked on a career in literary journalism: as Literary Editor, *Spectator* (1958–61); Literary Editor, *New Statesman* (1961–67); Editor, *Listener* (1967–73). In 1974 he was appointed Lord Northcliffe Professor of Modern English Literature, University College London, a post he held until 1992. While at UCL he founded and edited the *London Review of Books* (1979–92). Among his books are *Cockburn's Millennium* (1975), *Doubles and Authors* (1985) and two volumes of autobiography, *Rebecca's Vest* (1993) and *Dark Horses* (1998). Miller first met Amis in 1958, in connection with the *Spectator*.

Mike see *Edmund Keeley*

Min [*Minney*] see *Elizabeth Jane Howard*

Monkey see *Colin Howard*

Bruce Montgomery [*RBM, Edmund Crispin, Crippen, Crips, Crip, Creep-in*] (1921–78) Novelist and composer. Born in Chesham Bois in Buckinghamshire and educated at Merchant Taylors' School in London and St John's College, Oxford, where he got to know Larkin and Amis. Published his first Edmund Crispin crime novel, *The Case of the Gilded Fly* (1944), while still an undergraduate; at the same time also established himself as a composer and musician (pianist, organist, conductor). His earliest published music was a choral *Ode on the Resurrection of Christ* (1947), written in memory of Charles Williams (1886–1945), the Oxford poet, novelist and theological writer. In 1953 he collaborated with Amis on a Coronation Ode, performed in Glasgow; they also collaborated on two operas, *Amberley Hall*, extracts from which were broadcast on radio in 1952, and the unfinished *To Move the Passions*. From the early 1950s to the mid-1960s composed music for films. Amis's letters to Montgomery (ninety survive) are held in the Bodleian Library in Oxford but cannot be consulted until 2035.

P.H. Newby (1918–97) Novelist and broadcaster. Born in Crowborough, Sussex, and educated at Harley Castle Grammar School and St Paul's College, Cheltenham. Joined the Talks Department of the BBC in 1949, became Controller of the Third Programme (1958–69), then Director of Programmes, Radio 3 (1971–75), then Managing Director, BBC Radio (1975–78). In the 1960s he broadcast new work by Tom Stoppard, Harold Pinter and Dennis Potter. Newby wrote over a dozen novels, the first of which, *Journey to the Interior*, was published in 1945; *Something to Answer For* (1969) won the newly-established Booker Prize. He began corresponding with Amis shortly after the publication of *Lucky Jim* in 1954.

Ol' Bob [*O'B, O. Bob*] see *Robert Conquest*
Ted Pawker Pseudonym of *Robert Conquest*
Pinetop see *Philip Amis*
Piney [*Pineytop*] see *Elizabeth Jane Howard*
Anthony Powell [*Tony, A.P., Horse Faced Dwarf, HFD*] (1905–2000) Novelist. Born in London and educated at Eton and Balliol College, Oxford. Served in the Welch Regiment and the Intelligence Corps in World War II. Published his first novel, *Afternoon Men*, in 1931; best known for the twelve-volume novel sequence *A Dance to the Music of Time* (1951–75). Published four volumes of memoirs, under the general title *To Keep the Ball Rolling* (1976–82), two volumes of criticism, *Miscellaneous Verdicts* (1990) and *Under Review* (1992), three volumes of journals (covering the years 1982–92 and published 1995–97) and several novels not included in the *Music of Time* sequence. Created a CBE in 1956 and CH (Companion of Honour) in 1988. Married Lady Violet Pakenham in 1934. Amis got to know Powell in the summer of 1953, frequently visited Powell's house near Frome in Somerset, reviewed a number of his books, interviewed him several times on radio and in the press, and corresponded with him throughout the following decades.
Pud see *Kingsley Amis*
Rabbit see *Kingsley Amis*
Theo Richmond [*Son*] Documentary film-maker, journalist, writer. Born in London and educated at St Albans Grammar School and the London School of Economics (1949–52). Worked as a journalist and in the film business until 1987, when he embarked on a work of historical non-fiction, *Konin: A Quest*, which was published in 1995 and won the Royal Society of Literature's Heinemann Award and two other literary prizes. He was working for the Boulting Brothers, a producing-writing-directing team, when they bought the film rights to *Lucky Jim*; he and Amis became friends in 1956 when he was sent to Swansea to meet Amis before filming began. Their friendship included a collaboration in 1962, at Richmond's suggestion, on a screen treatment of Amis's story 'Moral Fibre' (from the 1962 collection *My Enemy's Enemy*). The film was never made. Richmond is married to the novelist Lee Langley.
Christopher Ricks (b. 1933) Literary critic and academic. Born in Kent and educated at King Alfred's School, Wantage, and Balliol College, Oxford (1953–56). Fellow of Worcester College, Oxford (1956–68); Professor of English, Bristol University (1968–75); Professor of English, University of Cambridge (1975–86); Professor of English, Boston University (1986–). The author of critical studies of Milton (1963), Tennyson (1972), Keats (1974), T.S. Eliot (1988) and Samuel Beckett (1993), as well as two volumes of

essays, *The Force of Poetry* (1984) and *Essays in Appreciation* (1996). He has edited a number of volumes of poetry, including the standard edition of Tennyson's poems (1969, rev. edn 1989), *The New Oxford Book of Victorian Poetry* (1987), the poems and prose of A.E. Housman (1988) and T.S. Eliot's poems of 1909–17 (1996). In 1980 Ricks and Leonard Michaels edited a collection of essays, *The State of the Language*, which contains Amis's essay 'Getting it Wrong'. Ricks first corresponded with Amis in the early 1950s (the correspondence, about Amis's poetry, has not survived); they did not meet until much later (Ricks cannot remember the date), at a dinner party in London.

Hilary Rubinstein (b. 1926) Literary agent. Born in London and educated at Cheltenham College and Merton College, Oxford. He entered publishing in his uncle's firm, Victor Gollancz Ltd, as an Editorial Director (1952–59). Rubinstein had known Amis slightly at Oxford and wrote to him in 1952 asking to see the novel he was working on. The novel was *Lucky Jim*, and Rubinstein remained Amis's publisher until he left Gollancz in 1963 to become Special Features Editor, *Observer* (1963–64), then Deputy Editor, *Observer Magazine* (1964–65). In 1965 he joined the literary agency A. P. Watt Ltd, as Partner and Director (1965–92), then Chairman and Managing Director (1983–92). He was founding editor of *The Good Hotel Guide* (1978–97) and in 1992 started his own literary agency, Hilary Rubinstein Books.

William Rukeyser (b. 1939) Journalist. Born in New York City and educated at New Rochelle High School (New York), Princeton University (1957–61) and Christ's College, Cambridge (1962–63). Worked at the *Wall Street Journal* (1961–67); then as writer and Editor, *Fortune* magazine (1967–72); Managing Editor, *Money* magazine (1972–80); Managing Editor, *Fortune* magazine (1980–86); and Editor in Chief and Executive Vice-President, Whittle Communications, Knoxville, Tennessee (1991–). Has also worked as a commentator on *Good Morning America*, ABC-TV (1978–85) and on CBS Radio (1979–86). He is currently Editorial Director, *Corporate Board Member*, a magazine/website (1998–), and is a director, officer or trustee of numerous charitable organisations in Knoxville. Rukeyser first met Amis in 1958 at Princeton, as a student in Amis's Creative Writing seminar. He kept in touch while he was at Cambridge, married the sister of one of Amis's students at Peterhouse, and after returning to the United States (in 1967) corresponded regularly.

Dale Salwak (b. 1947) Critic and academic. Born in Greenfield, Massachusetts, and educated at Purdue University in Indiana (BA, 1969) and the University of Southern California (MA, 1970; Ph.D. 1974). Has taught at Citrus College, Glendora, California, since 1973, where he is Professor of English.

His many publications include three books on Amis: *Kingsley Amis: A Reference Guide* (1978), *Kingsley Amis in Life and Letters* (1990) and *Kingsley Amis: Modern Novelist* (1992); and studies of John Braine (1979), A.J. Cronin (1983), Philip Larkin (1989), Barbara Pym (1991), Carl Sandburg (1988), Anne Tyler (1994) and John Wain (1981). He has also edited *The Literary Biography: Problems and Solutions* (1996) and *A Passion for Books* (1999). In 1985 he was awarded a National Endowment for the Humanities grant and in 1987 received a Distinguished Alumnus Award from Purdue University. He first corresponded with and met Amis in 1973 while at work on a doctoral dissertation on Amis's fiction.

Edith Sitwell (1887–1964) Poet and essayist. Born in Scarborough in Yorkshire, the sister of the poets and writers Osbert Sitwell (1892–1969) and Sacheverell Sitwell (1897–1988). She and her brothers championed Modernist writing over the writing of the Georgians; from 1916–21 she edited the anti-Georgian annual *Wheels*, which first published the poems of Wilfred Owen. After the success of *Façade* (1923), a Modernist 'entertainment' for voice and orchestra (with music by William Walton), she became a public figure, as famous for her eccentric dress and manner (and sensitivity to criticism) as for her writing. The first of her many published volumes of verse was *The Mother and Other Poems* (1915); her most acclaimed volumes – *Street Songs* (1942), *Green Song* (1944), *The Song of the Cold* (1945), *The Shadow of Cain* (1947) – were published during the war and took as their subjects the horrors of poverty, the blitz and the atom bomb. Her *Collected Poems* were published in 1954. Amis met Edith Sitwell in 1954, after an anonymous contribution to a debate about modern verse in the letters pages of the *Spectator*. She was created DBE (Dame of the British Empire) in 1954.

C.P. Snow (1905–80) Novelist and scientist. Born in Leicester and educated at Alderman Newton's School in Leicester and the University College of Leicester. His early non-writing career was devoted to scientific research (at Christ's College, Cambridge, where he took a Ph.D. in physics and was a Fellow and Tutor in science from 1930–45). During the war he served as a scientific adviser and from 1945–60 as a Civil Service Commissioner. He was knighted in 1957 and became Parliamentary Secretary to the Ministry of Science and Technology in 1964, when he was also created Baron Snow of Leicester. His first novel was a detective story, *Death Under Sail* (1932), but his literary reputation rests on the eleven-volume novel sequence *Strangers and Brothers* (1940–70), of which *The Masters* (1951) is probably the best-known volume. His Read Lecture on *The Two Cultures and the Scientific Revolution* (1959) generated an acrimonious public debate with the literary critic F.R. Leavis. In 1950 he married the critic and novelist

Pamela Hansford Johnson (1912–81), best known for the 'Dorothy Merlin' trilogy of novels, *The Unspeakable Skipton* (1959), *Night and Silence, Who is Here* (1962) and *Cork Street, Next to the Hatter's* (1965). Amis got to know Snow and his wife in 1953 after his editor at Gollancz, Hilary Rubinstein, sent Snow a proof copy of *Lucky Jim*, and Snow produced an admiring quotation for the jacket.

Son see *Theo Richmond*

Stuart Thomas (1914–94) Solicitor. Born in Swansea, where he lived all his life, excluding military service, educated at Swansea Grammar School and the University of Wales, Aberystwyth. Served in the army from 1939–45, stationed in India and Burma. Entered his father's firm of solicitors, D.O. Thomas and Co., specialising in marine law, after the war. Became a trustee of the literary estate of Dylan Thomas, his friend since schooldays, in 1953, appointing Amis a co-trustee in 1987. Married Eve Davies in 1945. The Thomases and the Amises became friends soon after Amis arrived in Swansea as an Assistant Lecturer in 1949. When the Amises left Swansea in 1961, and separated in 1963, the friendship with both Amises was maintained. For some years in the 1960s the Thomases kept a flat in South Kensington and were frequent visitors to London. After the break-up of his second marriage in 1980, Amis regularly spent two or three weeks with the Thomases in August and September, when the Garrick Club shuts for its summer holiday.

Anthony Thwaite (b. 1930) Poet and editor. Brought up in Yorkshire and educated at Kingswood School and Christ Church, Oxford, where he read English and, as Secretary of the Oxford University Poetry Society, first corresponded with and got to know Amis. Taught English literature in Japan (1955–57) and Libya (1965–67). Worked as a radio producer for the BBC (1957–62); Literary Editor of the *Listener* (1962–65) and the *New Statesman* (1968–72); co-editor of *Encounter* (1973–85). His first verse collection was *The Fantasy Poets No. 17: Anthony Thwaite* (1953), a pamphlet in a series which was later to include both Amis (No. 22, 1954) and Larkin (No. 21, 1954). Among Thwaite's subsequent collections of poetry are *Home Truths* (1957), *New Confessions* (1974), *Victorian Voices* (1980) and *Selected Poems 1956–1996* (1997). He is one of Philip Larkin's literary executors, along with Monica Jones and Andrew Motion, and has edited *Larkin at Sixty* (1982) and Larkin's *Collected Poems* (1988) and *Selected Letters* (1992). He has been married to the biographer and writer of books for children Ann Thwaite since 1955. In 1990 he was awarded an OBE.

Uncle [*Uncle John*] see *John Davenport*

John Wain (1925–94) Poet, novelist and critic. Born in Stoke-on-Trent, educated at Newcastle-under-Lyme High School and St John's College, Oxford, where he met Amis and Larkin. He was Fereday Fellow at St John's (1946–49), and Lecturer in English Literature, Reading University (1947–55). After resigning his lectureship at Reading in 1955 he took up a career as a freelance novelist, poet, critic, broadcaster and dramatist. He was Professor of Poetry at Oxford from 1973–78. In 1951 published *Mixed Feelings*, his first volume of poems, in a series he was helping to edit for the School of Fine Arts at the University of Reading (Amis's *A Frame of Mind*, 1953, was also published in the series). His first novel, *Hurry on Down*, was published in 1953, a year before *Lucky Jim*, with which it is frequently compared. As a poet Wain was associated with the Movement and contributed to the influential Movement anthology *New Lines* (1956), edited by Robert Conquest. Among his other novels are *The Contenders* (1958), *A Travelling Woman* (1959) and *Strike the Father Dead* (1962). His several volumes of verse were collected in *Poems 1949–79* (1981). A volume of autobiography, *Sprightly Running*, was published in 1962.

Wog see *Elizabeth Jane Howard*

ABBREVIATIONS

The following abbreviations and short titles are employed in the notes and for the provenances given at the foot of each letter.

AL	Autograph letter
ALS	Autograph letter signed
BBC	BBC Written Archives Centre, Caversham Park, Reading, Berkshire
Biography	Eric Jacobs, *Kingsley Amis: A Biography* (London: Hodder and Stoughton, 1995)
BJLH	Brynmor Jones Library, the University of Hull
Bodleian	Bodleian Library, Oxford
Bristol	University of Bristol Library
Buffalo	The Poetry/Rare Books Collection, University Libraries, University of Buffalo, State University of New York
Checklist	Jack Gohn, *Kingsley Amis: A Checklist* (Kent, Ohio: Kent State University Press)
Columbia	Rare Book and Manuscript Library, Butler Library, Columbia University, New York, New York
CP	Kingsley Amis, *Collected Poems 1944–1979* (London: Hutchinson, 1979)
Edinburgh	Edinburgh University Library
Eton	Eton College Library
Gollancz	Victor Gollancz Ltd
Harcourt	Harcourt Brace and Company, Orlando, Florida
HEHL	Henry E. Huntington Library, San Marino, California
Hoover Institution	Hoover Institution, Stanford University, Stanford, California
HRHRC	Harry Ransom Humanities Research Center, The University of Texas at Austin

Indiana	Lilly Library, Indiana University Library, Bloomington, Indiana
Leeds	Brotherton Collection, Leeds University Library
Life	Andrew Motion, *Philip Larkin: A Writer's Life* (London: Faber and Faber, 1993)
LCP	Anthony Thwaite, ed., *Larkin: Collected Poems* (London: Faber and Faber, 1988)
LL	Anthony Thwaite, ed., *Selected Letters of Philip Larkin* (London: Faber and Faber, 1992)
Manchester	The John Rylands Library, University of Manchester
Memoirs	Kingsley Amis, *Memoirs* (London: Century-Hutchinson, 1991)
NGDJ	Barry Kernfeld, ed., *The New Grove Dictionary of Jazz*, 2 vols (London: Macmillan, 1988)
NOBLV	Kingsley Amis, ed., *The New Oxford Book of Light Verse* (London: Oxford University Press, 1978)
OUP	Oxford University Press
Pennsylvania State	Rare Books Room, The University Libraries, The Pennsylvania State University, University Park, Pennsylvania
Princeton	Manuscript Division, Department of Rare Books and Special Collections, Princeton University Library
Reading	The Library, University of Reading
Reference Guide	Dale Salwak, *Kingsley Amis: A Reference Guide* (Boston: G.K. Hall, 1978)
Sussex	Manuscripts Collection, The University Library, University of Sussex, Brighton
Syracuse	The George Arents Research Library for Special Collections, Syracuse University Library, Syracuse, New York
TL	Typed letter
TLS	Typed letter signed
Victoria	McPherson Library, University Archives and Special Collections, University of Victoria, Victoria, British Columbia
Warwick	Modern Records Centre, University of Warwick Library, Coventry

THE LETTERS

TO JOHN RUSSELL LLOYD[1] – 5 NOVEMBER 1941

3 Highfield Road, Berkhamsted, Herts[2]

My dear John,

I was more than pleased to get your letter and am replying with a speed unusual to me. Now, really, you know, this won't do at all, leaving the Party like that. Tut, tut, John. I am seriously displeased with you. The trouble is, you underestimate your capabilities. Obviously your mental equipment is more than enough to fit you for the Party, even without the 'high standard' you mention. Most party members join without any knowledge, some, it is whispered, without any intelligence. I think you can, without undue conceit, give yourself marks above the average for knowledge and intelligence. After all, when you read in "World News & Views"[3] (that is if you read it) that "260 people joined the Party at an open air meeting held at —" do you suppose that any, let alone many, of those 260 are expert Marxist theoreticians? No, sir, they are not. So rejoin the Party right away. Not the YCL[4] – that is only a bleeding kindergarten, or, an excuse for getting to know lascivious young ladies – as if that needed an excuse anyway.

As the so called Smash Hitler Fund (I should be interested, too, to

---

1. Lloyd came up to Oxford in April 1941 (during the war the university allowed undergraduates to matriculate at the beginning of the Hilary or Trinity terms), as did Amis, whom he met in a study group on colonialism organised by the Communist Party. It was Amis who convinced Lloyd to join the Party, around the time the Soviet Union was attacked by Germany on 22 June 1941 (when Amis joined as well, according to his friend George Blunden). By the time of this letter Lloyd had begun to have second thoughts about the Party: 'I was too young to take such a drastic step; besides, my father would have been horrified' (personal communication, 10 April 1997). He wrote to Amis saying he wanted to leave, and Amis responded with this and the following letter. After Oxford, where he read Politics, Philosophy and Economics, Lloyd (1923–97) worked as a bookseller in Wimbledon and Brighton.

2. In the summer of 1940, Amis's family moved from Norbury in South London, where he was born and grew up, to Berkhamsted in Hertfordshire, a small town within commuting distance of London and (unlike Norbury) outside the flight path of German bombers. See 'Berkhamsted' in *Bright November* (1947).

3. Published fortnightly by the Communist Party of Great Britain.

4. Young Communist League.

know where that ten grand is going to be spent)[5] will have closed by the time you get this I would suggest that (if, indeed, you have not already done so) you go & put yourself at the disposal of the small woman at the Oxford Bookshop[6] – I hope you know where it is – it's near the station and is ornamented, adequately if somewhat inappropriately, with dazzling (at the moment) green paint.

Your reference to the wangling of Party members onto committees, is, as you justly remark, a commonplace to the initiated, among whom, however, it is technically known as "the selection of the best and most representative candidate by free discussion before the votes are actually cast." This bears an interesting (though superficial) resemblance to elections in the Soviet Union.

I don't know exactly what you mean by "good works". I have been doing just *below* the minimum amount of academic work, I have been doing a satisfactory quantity of Party and Russia Today[7] (Party) work, I am shortly to have a white clad friend drilling, and moreover yanking out, my teeth, I have been listening to the gramophone, I have been drinking a small quantity of gin & smoking not enough cigarettes to assuage my craving for them: but (most important) I have been becoming increasingly intimate (but not intimate enough. Yet) with a charming and romantically-minded young woman. I will tell you all about her, and everything, when I see you. After an apology for my writing, (and for my writing in pencil) nothing remains but for me to subscribe myself (with a cordial invitation to come and see me as soon after I come up as is compatible with convenience)

KINGSLEY

[ALS: Private collection, Altadena, California]

5. The fund was set up by the British Communist Party, 'for maximum help for the Soviet Union, for the full mobilisation of the British people, and for the creation of the Second Front' (*World News and Views*, 18 October 1941). Its target figure was £10,000; the final total raised was £14,938. 'You may rest assured good use will be made of the money,' declared Party Secretary Harry Pollitt (*World News and Views*, 25 October 1941).

6. See *You Can't Do Both* (1994), partly set in wartime Oxford, in which the heroine lives 'across the river in a part of town rarely visited by members of the university, apart from those visiting the communist bookshop there, whether to buy or to confer' (p. 101).

7. A forerunner of the British-Soviet Friendship Society, it ran both a book club and a journal.

TO JOHN RUSSELL LLOYD – 13 JANUARY 1942[1]

3 Highfield Road, Berkhamsted, Herts

Dear John,

Many thanks for your long and informative letter. I'm afraid I shan't be able to spread myself in an equally long and informative reply, as I should have liked, partly because there's so little, political and other, going on here (I'll have something to say to you on this point when I see you); and partly because I'm at present engaged in a feverish effort to get some work done at the last minute before I come up.

I don't know whether I entirely agree with your remarks about the "Russian sit." It seems to me, that although the Russian offensive is purely local in character at the moment, there are signs (e.g. Hitler's assumption of command, and especially the weak protestations of Lord Haw-Haw) that this may develop into a real attack on German territory.[2] I don't think this is being unduly optimistic; I suppose we're so used to bad news that when some really good news comes along at last we're unduly suspicious.

I was sorry to hear about your Cert. 'A', but you'll get this all right next time. I hope the JRB turns up trumps.[3] Your party-contact experiences are really awful; knowing the sort of thing, I can fully sympathise.

---

1. The letter is dated '13.i.41', but '42' is evidently meant, since Amis and Lloyd only entered Oxford in May 1941. Amis was mostly reliable about dates, but getting the year wrong is a common mistake in January.

2. By December 1941 German troops were twenty kilometres from Moscow. The Red Army's Moscow counter-offensive began on 6 December, and by the sixteenth the Germans were in retreat. Hitler appointed himself Commander-in-Chief of the German Army on 18 December. 'Lord Haw-Haw' was the pseudonym of William Joyce (1906–46), a British fascist executed for making propaganda broadcasts from Germany.

3. Certificate 'A' was a qualification entitling students to be considered for vacancies in Officer Cadet Training Units (OCTUs). Most undergraduates (Amis among them) were awarded Cert 'A' in school. Those who were not (like Lloyd, presumably) could earn it at university. Undergraduates were recommended for commission by the Joint Recruiting Board (JRB) of their university, to which they applied in writing. JRBs were set up 'to ensure that the best use is made, in the interests of the State, of the services of resident graduates and undergraduates who offer their services' (printed notice of 1939, Oxford University Archives).

Before we get off the subject; I'd be very obliged if you'd tell Saul Rose[4] that a) I've scoured the shack for things for the LC rooms[5] & can't find anything suitable b) I can't come up early because I'm suffering under dental treatment & have got appointments right up to Wednesday afternoon. Thanks in anticipation! But tell him I shall be at the EC[6] meeting on Thursday afternoon if I can.

I quite agree with what you say about the country. Though my parents are all for it, I must say it leaves me cold – bloody cold on occasion. I too hanker after the company of young men and maidens – especially, let me hasten to add, of young men and maidens.

I'm afraid that as our lit. sec. might just as well be stone dead for all one ever hears of him, I don't know anything about recent pamphlets, but I want to see some. I'll leave you with a few questions to work out answers to, which you, as a man who reads "World N[ew]s & V[iew]s", should find easy:

a) what is CP policy towards the punishing of Germany for atrocities, oppression & general war-guilt? b) What is the CPSU (b)[7] policy on this question; if it is not the same as our CP's, how does it differ? c) if we disagree with the government on this question, what action, if any, should be taken?

d) if you disagree with each or any policy, if the above are not identical, why & how far do you disagree & what is your own view?

I heartily agree with you about our relations with the town. I'll support you when you raise the matter.

4. Saul Rose (1922–92), a friend of Amis's from the City of London School, admitted to New College, Oxford, in Michaelmas term 1940, to read Moderations; returned to New College as fellow and bursar (1963–88).

5. Labour Club rooms. Amis edited the Oxford Labour Club *Bulletin* for a term in 1942. He also led the Labour Club choir, according to the December 1941 'Oxford Letter' of the *City of London School Magazine*, in which he is described as 'very red and very musical' (p. 133). Larkin, in the introduction to the revised edition of his novel *Jill* (1964, originally published 1946), speaks of 'visiting the [Labour] club's social room in the High once or twice for coffee after closing time' (p. 16).

6. Executive Committee (of the Labour Club, or Communist Party). Or possibly English Club.

7. Communist Party of the Soviet Union (Bolshevik).

I must shortly submit to dental (and mental) torture, so cheerio. Looking forward to seeing you.

Yours

Kingsley ← I shall have to develop this

[ALS: Private collection, Altadena, California]

TO THE SECRETARY, JUNIOR COMBINATION ROOM, ST JOHN'S COLLEGE, OXFORD – C. APRIL 1941–JUNE 1942[1]

Sir,

The fact that potatoes have jackets is no excuse for their being largely black inside. And the cooks do something to the jackets that makes them taste like brown paper. When I have potatoes in their jackets at home their jackets are worth eating. Here jacket and potato are fucking awful. What is wanted is not necessarily *no* potatoes-in-jackets, but *better* potatoes-in-jackets.

Yours considerately,
K. W. Amis

[ALS: St John's College, Oxford]

1. An entry from an undated St John's College Junior Combination Room Suggestions Book. Larkin, a student at St John's from 1940 to 1943, asks in another entry in the same volume: 'What has happened to the first page of this book?' In other volumes, the first page gives the term and the year. Amis came up to St John's in April 1941 and left for the army in July 1942; hence the dating. The suggestions book records no answer.

TO PHILIP LARKIN – C. 26 OCTOBER–6 NOVEMBER 1943[1]

No 2 Mess, Helles Lines, Catterick Camp, Yorks

Dear Philip,

I was extra pleased to receive your letter because I had just come back from three days in London, where we were all taken round to be shown things. Now I *hate* being taken round to be shown things, especially when they are things I do not want to be shown. A spectacular enemy success, involving the failure to tell me I was wanted on the phone until too late, meant that I did not meet Betty[2] on the Saturday before we left, and she came to see me off at Darlington. I liked this because I want to take her trousers down, but I didn't like it because I couldn't then. We arrived in London during a fog that lasted all the time we were there. On two evenings we went out to try and find a nice place where they drink. But all the places were nasty. There was one enormous place near Victoria Station, just like a station bar, absolutely crammed with foreign soldiers and passée whores. There was a nasty man there, who told me not to put my glass down on the snack bar with all the rapid, efficient insolence of Henry.[3] On the third evening

---

1. Amis entered the army in July 1942, reporting to Catterick Camp in Yorkshire for basic training and then for twenty-six weeks' further training at the Royal Signals unit for officer-cadets (152 OCTU), earning his commission as second lieutenant early in 1943. After postings to South Command Signals at West Farnham near Salisbury and to High Wycombe, he returned to Catterick to take an advanced wireless course. This letter dates from the end of the course and responds to a letter from Larkin of 24 October 1943, in Anthony Thwaite, ed., *Selected Letters of Philip Larkin* (London: Faber and Faber, 1992; henceforth cited as *LL*); Larkin replied in a letter of 24 October 1943 (in the Brynmor Jones Library at the University of Hull, henceforth BJLH).

2. Mrs Elisabeth Anne Simpson, a married woman with whom Amis had a two-year affair. A thinly fictionalised account of the affair is presented in 'Who Else is Rank', an unfinished and unpublished eighty-thousand-word autobiographical novel Amis co-wrote with E. Frank Coles, a fellow officer, in 1944–45, when the two were stationed in Belgium and Germany. It is now part of the Amis Collection at the Henry E. Huntington Library in California (henceforth HEHL). The relevant chapters are entitled 'Rhapsody' and 'Ecstasy'. See also 'Letter to Elisabeth' and other poems in Amis's first published volume of poetry, *Bright November* (1947), bearing the dedication 'For Elisabeth'.

3. Henry Payne (d. 1948), a porter at St John's; see Larkin to Amis, 12 October 1943, on the *dramatis personae* of *Jill*: 'There are no artists, or dons, or nice friendly girls, or comic scouts. I have rather a nasty porter, but not Henry' (*LL*, p. 75); see also John Wain's poem 'In Memory of Henry Payne', *Mixed Feelings* (1951).

we went and saw an awful revue "Get a load of this" (get a load in the crup*hawse*): you know, where they come down into the audience and talk to you, and *you don't want to talk to them.*

We spent the days being driven round in an ex-Green Line Bus by an old army driver who seemed as if he had been commandeered with the bus. We were shown over sets[4] and things. They all seemed just the same. Sometimes I would be standing half-listening to the man talking ("Nah, 'ere's the sender, gentlemen, inside, we got the pahr supply. Over there, we got the line equipment. Over 'ere, the switchboard" ah ahrs swor ahs sw ahrghs*ghwoighl*) and a terrific pang would hit me in the stomach, as if I were suddenly randy, and I realised it was a stab of boredom.

This letter does not seem to be going very well. The reason is that I have got a fucking cough, a slight headache and intermittent toothache, and to-day we had half of our final exam (questions like: "You are in charge of . . . . what would you do?") and to-morrow we have the other half and I don't know anything about any of it.

I think the most poignant single word in all Betty's harrowing narrative was "Morpeth",[5] I am glad you singled it out and thank you for enquiring after "Radio Pictures." No, it *wasn't* anything to do with Jack Oakie.[6] It was all about the radio pictures in your newspaper: "Air Raid Devastation in Hamburg". (Picture by radio from Stockholm). Yes, I talked about it. For three-quarters of an hour. That was one of the times when I would rather have been talking to *Mrs. Sharrock.*[7] Almost, anyway. Don't take it too hard about the torments of a commissioned officer: Y'see, kid, the world's in one hell of a mairss. And – wal, yer know I ain got no time for this pehtriotism . . . guff, but – wal, it kinda seems to me that it's – our dooty; yeah! our *dooty* as human beings, to – go out there 'n' – see what we kin do aboud ut. Maybe I cain't do merch, but . . . I kin do *somethun*', 'n' as long 's I got the strength to do ut, wal, I guess that's the way it'll always be. I hate it, you know, Philip. I hate it more when I read that the Germans say that 1,000,000 people have been killed in air raids in Germany.

4. Of wirelesses.

5. A market town in Northumberland.

6. Jack Oakie (1903–78), American film star and comedian.

7. Gertrude Elizabeth Adams Sharrock. Her husband Roger Sharrock (1919–91) was Larkin's tutorial partner in English at St John's, later a literary academic and author.

Since you ask, Betty was terrifically flattered at being given the Brwhoredway Fook.[8] I expect she is studying it hard, poor little bastard "Runs howling to his art . . . *howling* . . . m'm. I wonder why it's . . . (I wish I liked this. I ought to) . . . I'd better ask Bill [Amis]. That will please him."

I think Kuno[9] says it too, but I can't remember.

Pattern conversation.[10]

"It was awfully nice of you to come and see me to-night, darling, when you've got all that work to do."

"Don't say that. I wanted to." (Liar)

"It's been awful this week. I've missed you so much."

"It hasn't been nice for me, either, I've missed you too." (Liar)

"You know, Bill . . . it's just like having . . . pins and needles . . ."

"You'll have to get used to being without me, you know." (Bastard)

"Yes, I know."

"Never mind, May.[11] I shall never forget you." Yes, I really said that.

I hope you will try and come and stay with me for a day or two during my leave, which starts on Thursday: that is if you think you can give

8. 'Broadway Book'; that is, the *Broadway Book of English Verse*, ed. William Bowyer Honey (London: Routledge, 1940). The line Amis alludes to concludes W.H. Auden's poem 'Journey to Iceland', the last in the anthology (pp. 463–5): 'Tears fall in all the rivers. Again the driver/Pulls on his gloves and in a blinding snow storm starts/Upon his deadly journey; and again the writer/Runs howling to his art.'

9. Baron (Kuno) von Pregnitz, a wealthy homosexual who commits suicide at the end of Christopher Isherwood's *Mr Norris Changes Trains* (1935). For what Amis thinks he says, see Larkin to Amis, 24 October 1943 (in BJLH): 'I have got two [girls' school stories], which are charming in their way – "Niece of the Headmistress" by Dorothy Vicary, and "Two Thrilling Terms" by Nancy Breary. Jolly good. I feel like Kuno – "this is a work of genius, I find" – or have I said that to you before?' In a note to this passage, Larkin adds: 'I think I mean Natalia Landauer: "Read. It's beautiful, I find."' Natalia Landauer is a character in Isherwood's *Goodbye to Berlin* (1939). The quotation in question, though, comes from Kuno, commenting on a prized volume from his 'small library of stories for boys' (see Christopher Isherwood, *The Berlin Stories* (New York: New Directions, 1963), p. 117).

10. Defined as 'a typical conversation between young man & young woman showing how y.w. could twist y.m. round her little finger' (Amis to Anthony Thwaite, 5 May 1991). But see also Larkin to Amis, 16 September 1943, in *LL*, p. 70: 'these "pattern conversations" are the last word, and I simply adore them. The anonymous interlocutor is so facelessly vile – "No, I shan't. Tell me." – This of course isn't meant to be insulting, as you will understand.'

11. An ATS (Auxiliary Territorial Service) soldier Amis met and pursued at Catterick (see Larkin to Amis, 12 October 1943, in *LL*, p. 76).

yourself a holiday for the time.[12] I hate to bring blackmail into this, but at the *mew*ment it is very likely that in six weeks or so I shall be on the banana boat, ole boy, bound probably for India, which I shall not like. I am told that all the boys (and women) there have syphilis. And it is very hot there too. So try and accept this never-to-be-repeated offer.

Betty said she would ring me up to-night and she hasn't yet. This fills me with disproportionate and resented anxiety.

I also deprecate the kind of blues riff; dah deedle dardle dah (ooch!) dah deedle dardle dah (ooch!) dah *dee*-dah dah (ooch!) dah dee-*dah* dah (ooch!) dădă <u>dee</u>dah dah (ooch!) dah dada dāh . . . . (ooch!)

26 Shrublands Road, Berkhamsted Herts.,[13] *6 November*

Yes, I'm home on leave now. I've left this letter for a disgracefully long time, I'm afraid; the reason is that I was very busy during my last few days at Catterick, packing and all that, you know. I go back (where I do not know yet) on the 19th. During that time you can surely come over here for *two* or <u>three</u> days. Please try. It is very nasty here on one's own. My parents would be very glad to have you, if you see what I mean. I think they regard you as a "stabilising influence" on me ("Does Philip care for girls much?" "Well, not an awful lot; he likes them, though." Silent registration of approval). If you come, bring all your obscene stories and things, especially Willow Gables.[14] It's no use bringing any records, because my gramophone is still broken. Don't

12. From job applications. Larkin was exempt from military service (graded C3 in his army medical examination, because of poor eyesight). After coming down from Oxford in June 1943 he was rejected by both the Civil Service and the Foreign Office, and at the time of this letter was living with his parents in Warwick and looking for work. In December he would take up a post as librarian, Wellington, Shropshire.

13. This was the third and final Amis family home in Berkhamsted. When they first moved to the town in 1940 they stayed briefly at the flat of Amis's father's secretary, then at a house which Amis described as 'a sort of workman's cottage' (Eric Jacobs, *Kingsley Amis: A Biography* (London: Hodder and Stoughton, 1995), p. 62; henceforth cited as Jacobs, *Biography*), then they settled at the Shrublands Road house.

14. From Autumn 1942, partly at Amis's urging, Larkin had begun a series of jokey and scurrilous soft-porn texts under the pseudonym Brunette Coleman. By October 1943, according to Andrew Motion, *Philip Larkin: A Writer's Life* (London: Faber and Faber, 1993; henceforth cited as Motion, *Life*), p. 86, these included two novels, one of 143 typed pages, entitled 'Trouble at Willow Gables', and an Oxford sequel of 143 handwritten pages, entitled 'Michaelmas Term at St Bride's'; six poems, collectively titled 'Sugar and Spice'; and a fragment of autobiography, 'Antemeridian'. 'Willow Gables' is Larkin's name for the fictional

forget, ole boy: any time, we're always deligh'ed to see you. Name your own time.

The other day I heard a programme on the wireless: Jazz in miniature or something, records by Armstrong.[15] Several things struck me; the archaic sound of the 1927 records compared with the Teschmaker[16] sides: Hines's[17] first solo phrase in West End Blues; and Bechet's[18] phrase after Armstrong's second pronouncement of 'You take the T & P, I'll take the L.M.N,' or whatever it is, in 2.19 Blues[19] (or "two one nine" blues, as the announceress called it). I wonder if you heard it (You didn't).

My parting with Betty was heart-breaking, because we love each other, or so we say. I think we do, too. We certainly want to make the beast with two backs, eh? Yesh. Do you mind the name Betty, by the way? I'm indifferent to it myself. Her full name is Elisabeth Anne, which I like, and her married name is Simpson, Mrs. E.A. Simpson. . . . This is funny. I didn't say good-bye to May.

On Thursday I also heard Hari-Pari,[20] for the last time, as I always say. They had a "famous British trumpeter" with them, Archie Craig[21] I think his name was. He made wrong sounds when he blew into his trumpet with his mouth and pressed the valves down with some of his fingers.

Now it's time for me to go out on some futile shopping expedition

girls' school in Mallerton, Wiltshire, in which the texts are mostly set; it is also the name John Kemp makes up for Jill's school in *Jill*. James Booth is shortly to publish an edition of Larkin's early fiction provisionally titled *Philip Larkin and 'Brunette Coleman': Unpublished Fiction 1941–1951*.

15. Louis ('Satchmo', 'Pops', 'Dippermouth') Armstrong (c. 1898–1971), trumpeter and singer.

16. Frank Teschemacher (1906–32), clarinettist, alto saxophonist and violinist.

17. Earl ('Fatha') Hines (1903–83), pianist and bandleader.

18. Sidney ('Pops') Bechet (1897–1959), clarinettist and soprano saxophonist.

19. In 1940 Louis Armstrong recorded '2:19 Blues', a straightforward twelve-bar blues, for a United States Decca 'New Orleans' album. It contains the couplet: 'The 2:19 took my baby away/But the 2:17 will bring her back some day,' followed by a couplet referring to two railway lines, the 'T and P' and the 'L and N').

20. Harry Parry (1912–56), Welsh clarinettist and bandleader. See Larkin to Amis, 24 October 1943 (in BJLH): 'At 3:30 pm this afternoon the paper says "Jazz Jamboree" will be broadcast, and I am curious to find out what it is. I expect its some ghastly business at the London Palladium with Victor Feldman and Max Bacon and . . . Hari-Pari's sextet playing cunning little riff numbers called "Thrust & Parry" and "Parrylitic".'

21. Archie Craig (1914–88), a Glaswegian trumpeter, never recorded with Harry Parry, but seems to have played with him on this broadcast; a member of the Squadronaires, the RAF big band.

or something. How I hate Berkhamsted. What a place to spend a leave.

Please forgive my delay in writing and reply soon. I've nothing whatever to do here, so my next letter will be speedy–

Kingsley

PS. I should think Buddy Featherstonehaugh's head wobbles when he plays, *just* like Frank Dixon's.[22]

[ALS: Bodleian]

TO PHILIP LARKIN – 25 NOVEMBER 1944

Lt K W Amis R Signals HQ Second Army Rear B L A[1]

+o+o+o+o+o+o+o+o+o+o+o+o+o+o+o+o+o+o+o+o+o+o+o+o+o+

My dear Philip I was very glad to hear from you after what also seemed to be a long silence. I wrote unprovoked words only yesterday but I will write some more, provoked, to-day. I am glad you liked the Gailstorms.[2] I like them too. The extraordinary lack of reticence is even more marked in the latest example. She is not, howver, (you know the word) what one usually understands as not of the educated classes: she talks with a more refined accent than I do and has obviously had a quasi-public-school education, is a parson's daughter. The last letter is rather funny and contains some absolute jewels of middle-class morality at *the same time* as being the most shameless yet. Here are some extracts:

"I have thought it over an awful lot and have decided that I cannot come away with you when you come home ...... I have been brought up very strictly and have been taught to look on it as something rather despicable. It is too sordid registering as Mr and Mrs and wearing a

22. Buddy Featherstonhaugh (1909–76), English tenor and baritone saxophonist; Frank Dixon, undergraduate at Magdalen, previously at school with Larkin, a clarinettist and leader of the Oxford University Jazz Band, the Bandits.

---

1. British Liberation Army. In November 1944 Amis's unit was posted for five months to Sonnis (Bourg Leopold) in Belgium, from which this letter was presumably written.

2. No letters from Larkin to Amis survive for 1944, and I have found no other references to Gail/Gabrielle. Presumably 'the Gailstorms' are passages from, or accounts of, Gail/Gabrielle's letters to Amis.

wedding ring, and being terrified of meeting someone who knows you. Birth control is not infallible. Someday I hope to get married, and I should feel bound to tell my husband, and that would start married life under a stain ...... We should probably end by hating each other ...... Don't think I don't want you because my God I do, so much so that at times it torments me ...... Maybe if you tried to persuade me, I should change my mind ...... I am the type for a home and children, not for a mistress ...... My cunt is small owing to the fact that I am a virgin and my hymen is not intact. The hair extends about an inch behind my cunt and several inches in front. My clitoris is warm and soft ...... In spite of all I have said I still want you to make love to me. I want to stroke your cock and feel your hands on my cunt and feel our naked bodies pressed together ......"[3]

I quite agree; I don't believe it either. But it's true all right. A very subdued and anxious letter followed to-day, with no pornography at all, asking what I thought of her decision, and explaining that she has been talking to a friend of hers who got into the same bed as a man was who had not had any words said over him when she was with him, and when she finally had words said over her and another man, her previous affair hung over her like a tword of Damocles, and she is "very unhappy". This is amusing because not perturbing: in this letter too she says how much she wants me to get into the same bed as she is, and I think that that is going to happen alright artschartschartsch*aaah*. Yes, of course you are right; I am returning comparable information. It is nice to be able to write the words 'I want to fuck you' in a letter and send the letter off without qualm. What do you think of all this?

I am grateful for your qualified liking of my poem. I was disappointed that you could not find a poem for me. I was reduced to rollin' with fackin' laughter, ole boy, by your bit about the landlady's butter and buttocks – mmm Yacks bugg but bugter *butter*. What do you mean by the "relevant" parts of my letter? And why did it make her "mad"? Poor little thing I should like to vbghtysddy578egd8e ...... I am experiencing a febrile and *drastic* desire for evacuation. If I try to suppress it any longer I shall start to fail and that is bad thing to do.

3. Amis here adds a handwritten asterisk and at the bottom of the page writes: '*I forgot the two most excruciating ones: ". . . some wizard invitations to parties . . ." ". . . what I suggest is that when you come home, we get to know each other really well . . ." The thought of this positively *unmans* me.'

But I will be back before very long. *Christ*! I want to see the *MAAAAA*-aaajor . . .

I know exactly what you mean about Eric Portman's voice.[4] I have always viewed him as a very attractive person. It would be nice to write an amorous letter to him, I think. Yes I want to reread Hamlet; that is a good idea. I love the dumbness of Ophelia (balls): "Belike this show imports the argument of the play." I think a horse-pissing of it would be rewarding, too.[5] When I think of the expression "Horse-pissing" and the entirely unamused way we used to utter it, I want to burst out laughing. I think I will start a dream-book: your results sound delightful. The trouble is that my batman so often remembers to come and wake me in the mornings and so the ideal time for writing the things down is occupied with saying good morning and what sort er bloody day is it to-day – when you come to thinko fart think of it not so very different from "Good-morning, sah" – "Morning, Owen" – "Twen-nty minnuts to eight, sah" – "Thank you".

[Del.] wondering if it would be a good idea to go back to Oxford after the war. It would provide a base for us to meet, which is one heavy advantage; knowing so much more now about sex it would be good "fun"; and, most supreme of all thoughts, I shaould *rrts* be able to have Elisabeth to stay and Gail to stay and *John Simmons*[6] to stay, and see how two halves of my life fit together. Can you imagine showing Elisabeth to Costin?[7] Or introducing Gail to Freddy Hurdis-Jones?[8] Or John Simmons to Chitra?[9] The thought of it makes me *scream*. Oh yes I know half the people will have gone down; but one of the good things about Oxford is that its vessels of corruption are always being

4. Eric Portman (1903–69), stage and film actor.

5. 'Horse-pissing' means connecting the epithet 'horse-piss' with works of literature; or, more generally, mocking the literary through a process of 'denigration-by-obscene-accretion' (Amis to Larkin, 15 December 1959). See, for example, Larkin to Amis, 16 January 1981, in *LL*, p. 638: 'Surely you hated literature more than I did. How about 'I have gathered up six slender basketfuls _OF HORSEPISS_"? "I hop alwey behinde" _TRYING TO BUGGER HIM EH_.'

6. John Simmons appears nowhere else in the correspondence.

7. W.C. Costin (1893–1970), Tutor and Lecturer, Modern History (1922–57), St John's College, Oxford; later Vice President (1930–57), President (1957–63), St John's.

8. Reading Moderations at Magdalen College, Oxford (1941–42); he did not take his degree.

9. Chitra Rudingerova: 'Czech. On committee of student CP during war . . . I pursued her slightly but unavailingly' (Amis to Thwaite, 5 May 1991). She read History at St Hilda's (1940–43) and got a second; in the same year as Larkin, who called her 'a strange, magnetic, fool of a girl' in letter to Amis, 20 August 1943 (in BJLH).

replenished. It is a thought more moving and exciting than any dreams of illicit and satyriacal bliss. I really have half a mind to do it. You will come up a lot, won't you? Nick will be back too I suppose.[10] Oh ecstatic thought: oh the beer and the croaking clarinets and hating the Sharrocks and the suppers and the necking parties and the Labour Club which I shall *crap* on to revenge myself for the months I wasted in its service and the river and Laybourne[11] oh oh oh imagination is drunken at the thought.

It is funny that you put Don't say Ye in your letter when I put it in the last letter I wrote without knowing that you had done it too. It is a pity that there will be no Bone[12] to introduce Elisabeth to. I wonder if I shall re-seduce Elizabeth if she comes back. My greatest linguistic feat has been to translate the words of When You're Smiling into French: "er – quand vous er – souriez tout le monde sourit avec vous ..... Continuez à sourire ......"

I will let you know of any more Gabrielliana (I told you her real name was Gabrielle,[13] didn't I? – shit). Now I will stop; I should like to have some soon backwords.

I am ill at these numbers.[14]

Kingsley

PS – Mr Moore would like to see you at a quarter past nine.[15]
PPS – Thanks very much.

10. Nick Russel (b. 1922), reading English at St John's (1941–42, 1946–48), later went into publishing; one of 'The Seven', a loose group of college friends, also including Amis, Larkin, Norman Iles, James Willcox, Philip Brown and David Williams (see Jacobs, *Biography*), pp. 70–1).

11. G.J.E. Layborn (1923–48) read Modern Languages at St John's (1941–42, 1946–47) and was kitchen secretary (1942). See Larkin to Amis, 21 or 28 July 1942: 'You will be glad to know there is a Henryist agent here – a coastguard. When you stroll along the beach he comes out of his little shed on the sand dunes and stares at you like Henry in the lodge with a laybornian intensity' (*LL*, p. 38). Also Amis to Larkin, 12 January 1948, with news of Layborn's death.

12. Gavin Bone (1907–42), Fellow, Tutor and Lecturer in English, St John's College, Oxford (1931–42), specialist in Old English poetry, died of cancer during Amis's first year in the army.

13. Presumably Gail of 'Gailstorms'.

14. See Hamlet to Ophelia: 'O dear Ophelia, I am ill at these numbers' (II.ii.119).

15. W.G. Moore (1905–78), University Lecturer in French (1931–72); Fellow, Tutor and Lecturer in Modern Languages at St John's College, Oxford (1934–78), also Dean and Senior Tutor (1940–43); see Larkin to Norman Iles, 13 December 1942: 'Moore called me into his room for a little straight talk on the evils of drinking' (*LL*, p. 49).

Isn't this nice paper?
PPPS. Did you find you could train yourself to remember your dreams without difficulty? If so, how long did this training take?[16]

K. W. Amis

[TLS: Bodleian]

TO PHILIP LARKIN – 16 JANUARY 1945[1]

[. . .] One *very* good thing has happened and that is that I have got hold of a quite good portable wireless set which is now in my room. The only disadvantage so far is that the broadcasting stations do not make many noises that make me feel happier when I hear them. But it is the first time in my life that I have had a wireless set all to myself with nobody to say they do not like the noises that I like and to turn themm saul off and put on noises that they like I don't.

You sound rather as if you would like to know more about my Christmas than I told you in my last letter. All right. Here is

MY 3RD XMAS IN KAHKI – SOMWHERE IN BELGUIM

On Xmas Eve three of the sergeants and I got into my jeep and I drove us away. We were going to a party, one of them said, where there sure to be lots of girls and drink. The only reason they asked me was that they wanted a jeep to go in. There is no door on my jeep where the driver sits and I was very soon very cold and this made one of my teeth start to hurt. When we had gone about twenty miles we stopped to make sure we were on the right road. We weren't. So we went back about eight miles and eventually found the house we were looking for. As I told you in my last letter there were not enough girls and not enough drink which made the sergeant who had brought us there very unpopular: our hosts can hardly have been unaware of this and its

16. MS addition. Here and henceforth all MS additions are italicised.

1. The beginning of the letter is missing, but according to the last paragraph it was written twenty-three days after the Christmas Eve episode related in the previous paragraph, which means 16 January 1945. Among other details, the final paragraph's unannounced segue into soft porn identifies Larkin as the recipient (for Jennifer and Marsha see Amis to Larkin, 5 February 1946, note 2).

cause. After about two hours of this I got sick of it and we wnt away. After another freezing drive we found two shutting cafes and one that was shut but they let us in. I wish they hadn't done that. The girls in it were ugly and one of them wasn't a girl at all; she was one of them's mother and old too. None of them spoke English or French and none of us spoke Flemish, so the conversation was limited to "Cognac, ah! Nix good, nijn, no, nix good. Vijf frank, Tommee", on their side, "I could do her a bit of no good", on the sergeants', and "What's the Flemish for fuck off?", on mine. Even the sergeants got sick of this before long and we went back to the camp and drank two bottles of whisky before going to bed, which happened at half-past three or so. I sat up in bed and made the window stop still before going to sleep, which happened at about four o'clock. Three hours later a different sergeant came in and woke me up, telling me to get up and help serve tea to the men. I did not want to do this at *all*, but it was so cold that it was too cold even to stay in bed, so I got up shivering and reeling because of the whisky which hadn't had time to wear off, and feeling very ill. I met the sergeants in the kitchen and we took the tea round. Someone took his accordeon out and started to play a tune; some people wanted me to sing, but not many, and I did not have the pleasure of refusing. One of the sergeants had brought a bottle of whisky with him, and to avoid having to drink any of this I began to get the fire ready for lighting, but as everything was covered with coal-dust I very soon gave this up. After wanting to go and have breakfast for a long time I at last thought it was decent to go away, and did. Not very long after breakfast some of the sergeants came into the officers' mess and drank, which except at Christmas is never done, and we all got drunk again, in my case as usual in the Army, painfully, slowly and sickly. Then I went off with some of the officers and some of the sergeants and we served Xmas dinner to the men, who like it for some reason. I went to sleep in the afternoon and on duty at six o'clock until two o'clock on Boxing afternoon, when I ate my Christmas dinner alone and feeling very and legitimately sorry for myself and wishing I had an audience who would appreciate the pathos of it all, but I hadn't. Then I went to sleep again and read a not book in the evening and went to bed at half-past ten, nearly crying with depression. But the next morning there were a lot of letters including yours and one from Elisabeth and one from Elizabeth and one from Nick and one from Gail, and the one from Elisabeth had a nice photograph of her charming face in it, which made me feel a little happier. And that is all there was of Christmas and of New Year there was nothing at all.

No signs of my having developed syphilis have appeared yet, and this is the twenty-third day, so I am feeling a bit more hopeful. When I have finally decided I have not got it, or when I have come out of hospital after having it, I will tell you how I spent my 48 in Brussels. I am beginning to wonder if all this is worth while, said Marsha, turning towards the window with her head drooping slightly, so that the evening sun gave her flaxen hair a rosy sheen. Jennifer made as if to move towards her, then spoke instead: "You sound very disillusioned, darling," she said softly. The younger girl reacted instantly. She whirled round, ran to the back of Jennifer's chair, and flung her arms round her neck, so that the prefect's head rested on her breast. "No, no, no," came her voice muffled by Jennifer's thick hair; "I didn't mean that, dearest; I was only thinking how we never seem to be able to get far enough away from other people; all I want is to be close to you, but somehow we never seem to be close enough to one another." For answer, Jennifer pulled her on to her lap and held her mouth in a long, shuddering kiss. Marsha flexed her slim body and pressed herself to her. And then there was nothing but their closeness as the shadows lengthened and the sunlight paled and dusk swam into the still, silent room, and Barbara, passing by in the chilly garden, stooped and picked a furled rose from the flower-bed beneath their window. All this is so beautiful and so sincere that I shall, with your help, have to write it all down some day.

Let it be soon, I said, trembling; oh God, please let it be soon; as soon as it can be; make it happen soon, I said, soon, yes; yes, God, let it be soon; you made me wait for the other but that was all right, only let this be soon, please God, as soon as you can. And that is all, but only for the moment.

Kingsley

'Yes, sir, you're on; two till four.'

K. W. Amis

[TLS: HEHL]

TO E. FRANK COLES – 12 JULY 1945

Lieut K W Amis R Sigs, 91 Tele-Op Section,
1 Indep Adm Coy R Sigs, B L A[1]

My dear Frank,

But I *have* written by now. I posted a letter three days ago, addressed to 30 Corps of course. Your two packets got here the night before last; I didn't get them till yesterday morning. I enclose –

1 The Parting – stephens teil)
2 Francis in Sackcloth)) returned
3 Ecstasy – parts 1 to 4 & a bit)
4 Parting – frans teil 2 parts) for retention[2]
5 Supper Relief – 3 parts)

So your discreditable suspicions that I had been idle were unfounded. I quite liked F in Sckclth except that it only half as long as it should be. Look at the lovely long one I did about you! And there isn't anything about what I look like. If you do put in something about what I look like I insist on seeing it first. One more thing – 'F still thought that an opinion, if it was erroneous, was dangerous and must be combated.' That's very nice if it means what I hope it means, but if it means 'F would never let pass any statement, however trivial, with which he disagreed ('Nice day to-day' – 'I don't agree with you at all; I think it's too windy')' then I want it cut out. But if it does mean what I hope it means, then I think it'll have to be changed a little to make clear it doesn't mean what I hope it doesn't mean. See? I'm not quite so keen on The Parting; did you do it in a hurry? Since writing the last sentence I've read it through again and can't really see why I didn't like it: the

---

1. Second Army HQ was closed down on 25 June 1945, and Amis was sent to a reinforcement holding unit (RHU) at Minden in Westphalia, from which this letter was presumably written. He was posted to a second RHU in Bruges 'around August' (Jacobs, *Biography*, p. 98).

2. According to a 'survey of work complete and incomplete' accompanying the surviving manuscript of 'Who Else is Rank', which Amis was co-writing with Coles, the novel was to have thirty-five chapters, fourteen of which were already 'wholly or partly written'. It was composed pseudonymously: Coles was 'Stephen Lewis', Amis was 'Francis Archer', the name also given to the protagonist of several stories Amis published in the 1950s about army life ('Court of Inquiry', 'I Spy Strangers'). The novel's title comes from *Julius Caesar*, III.i.151: 'I know not, gentlemen, what you intend,/Who else must be let blood, who else is rank.'

OCTU board is delightful, the best possible farewell to God's Adj.[3] I think all I meant was it needs polishing, but I'm sure you realise that. The last § but 1 – 'I went on ahead' struck me as a bit wonky. And what happened after you took the house in Kanalstraße?

Ecstasy I think is all right – anyway you ve seen most of it already. Fran's angle on Parting isn't bad – it's what happened too. Do you like the bit about the serviettes?[4]

Supper Releif is a bit unfinished and hurried and even dull in places, but we've got to put the reader in the picture old boy. I think the Interlude will fit all right, don't you? And I like the bit abojt Harris.[5] In retrospect I can't think how we ever put up with that amn for 5 minutes. I have told you quite a lot about this place in my previous letter which you may have got by now. The only new thing is that I have been appointed officer i/c french letters, thus demonstrating my superior knowledge of them, which you remember was denied by Raleigh.[6] You must work that in somewhere. David Ross says the unit is reforming in Enger in a few weeks' time.[7] There is a Russian barbed wire entanglement round the unit in Potsdam, with only one gate and a Russian guard. When the unit put a guard on on the inside of the

3. 'God's Adjutant' is the title of the novel's first chapter, in which the adjutant is Captain Bill York. This was also the name of one of Amis's real-life adjutants, with whom he did not get on. In 'The Parting' the adjutant in question is Captain Gilbert Lang, who also had a real-life prototype, identified as 'Milner' in a list of 'Aliases' provided at the bottom of the 'survey of work complete and incomplete'. Eric Milner (later Colonel Eric Milner, OBE, TA), served with Amis and Coles in Rear Army HQ. Sometime after VE Day, Milner reported, 'many of us were posted to 21 Army Group Signals, I as their new Adjutant, Bill [Amis] I think went as well' (letter to Eric Jacobs, 15 August 1993, in HEHL). See Amis to W.Y. McNeil, 12 November 1988: '[Milner] wasn't my favourite man in the old days but seems to have mellowed since, or perhaps I have.'

4. See 'The Parting', from 'Who Else is Rank': 'I spent most of the day sitting on the veranda of the third-rate hotel where the section were billetted . . . The hotel's entire stock of paper serviettes, of superb texture, had thoughtfully been transferred to the "Damen" compartment.'

5. A captain who lands Archer/Amis with unwanted duties.

6. In Chapter XI of 'Who Else is Rank' Major Raleigh denies Archer/Amis's knowledge of contraceptives, eliciting the following response: 'I think you're wrong about that, sir (none of us ever omitted the "sir"; I dont think there was another field officer in the British army who attached so much importance to not having the Sir left out),' which recalls Jim Dixon on Professor Welch in *Lucky Jim* (1954): 'No other Professor in Great Britain, he thought, set such store by being called Professor' (p. 7). In the stories Raleigh is vicious as well as pompous.

7. 'David Ross' is not mentioned in 'Who Else is Rank'. In 'The Parting', Archer/Amis is drunkenly referred to as the 'member for Enger, and former member for Headington, Southampton, Bayeux, Amiens, Horst, Dingden and all the rest'.

gate, the Russians doubled theirs on the outside. No body can leave the camp without Russian authority. I like that.

Rose Macaulay's nephew lives in our mess.[8] He writes poetry and thinks DH Lawrence wrote pornography. He is having a book published by Chatto, a poetry book – but 'most of the stuff has already appeared.' – 'Where?' 'Blackwood's and the Strand.' That!s right. He let me read one. No. Please type your next letter. I can't read your handwriting.

I am going on leave on the 16th, and *hope* to see Elisabeth, but it was all very sudden and she may not have time to arrange things. I hope she does. There is a bullshit parade here on Saturday and officers will attend. A regular soldier in the mess thinks Kipling is bad. But he likes Rupert Brooke.

Bidgood is Honeywill.[9] Don't ask me why.

I will write again soon. Don't forget to acknowledge this MS.

Yours
Bill

[TLS: HEHL]

TO BERT WOOTTON – 11 AUGUST 1945[1]

My dear Wootton,

I was very sorry to leave here without saying good-bye to you in person, but I've a feeling that the War Office wouldn't have let me wait till your return. So it's got to be like this. I should like to thank you most gratefully for looking after me so well during my stay with the section. And I valued you not merely as a batman (though you were all right at that) but as a person whom I felt I had come to know. I may see you "out there" – *if* either of us go, or perhaps as I rather hope in civvy life, though not in the Sigs Memorial Club. Meanwhile, thanks again for everything, and I should like to hear from you: I shall

8. Rose Macaulay (1881–1958), novelist, essayist and travel writer.

9. Not mentioned in the 'Aliases' list.

1. Bert Wootton appears as 'Waller' in 'Who Else is Rank'. For his relations with Amis see the chapter entitled 'Jeeps': 'it was only rarely that Francis's jeep was ever with his section and more rarely still that his batman permitted him to drive it.'

be writing to the section from time to time. The marks are a very inadequate return for your services but they are all I have to give.

All the best, Bert: I hope we meet again.

Yours sincerely
K.W. Amis

[ALS][2]

TO PHILIP LARKIN – 10 SEPTEMBER 1945[1]

L[t] K.W. Amis R. Sigs, 53 RHU BAOR

My dear Philip

Got 3 of your letters a day or 2 ago. Will agree to any of:

a) I stay with you

b) you stay with me

c) We both stay somewhere else – Oxford. Leaving here – tk Xt – tomorrow. Getting to *UK* (*a*oh) abt Thursday or Friday, 28 days leave from Sat or Sun. Class B release[2] now about an even chance; if I get out may be in time for Oct term at Oxford. Which I think I sh[d] like, rather, all for now, de boy – in haste. I don't like any of those phrases, very jealous an angry about the Nwhoreth Ship – congratulations.[3] EAS's [Elisabeth Anne Simpson's] husband still away. She is getting impatient at my stay here. Sent for you yesterday and here you come to-day.

Kingsley

2. A photocopy of this letter was found among Amis's papers after his death and is now deposited in HEHL.

---

1. The date '1945' is a MS addition. In a letter of 22 August 1945 Larkin welcomed Amis 'back to England' (*LL*, p. 107), the location, presumably, of '53 RHU BAOR [British Army of the Rhine]'.

2. As in the story 'I Spy Strangers' (1962), reprinted in *Collected Short Stories* (1980): 'Mr Archer showed me a letter from the head of his college in Oxford, the Master I think he called himself. It said they were arranging his release from the Army . . . Yes, I know it seems strange, Mr Archer getting out so soon, but apparently this is something called the Class "B" Scheme' (p. 83).

3. *The North Ship*, Larkin's first volume of poems, had been published in July 1945 by the Fortune Press.

Saw *Jackson* the other day. 'Have you heard aboud Briad Groob?'[4]

[ALS: Bodleian]

TO PHILIP LARKIN – 15 DECEMBER 1945

26 Shrublands Road, The Bad Town [Berkhamsted], Herts.

My dear P.

I seem to have two letters of yours to reply to, which I am rather sorry about, because it means that I shall not hear from you so often unless I write some words out of season, and it is easier to reply to words out of season than to initiate them. However I will try: that is if you approve of this non-stop writing. I do not only because I like hearing from you but because writing to you is one of the two things I like doing here: the other is playing jazz records but I can't do that much because the noise of them gets on my mother's nerves. For similar reasons this letter is being written with a pen that I am holding in my hand, instead of being made on a wordmaking machine. I don't know why it is, but being at home has got much worse than it ever was before. I think in my book ['Who Else is Rank'] that there will have to be a lot about being at home and not liking it.

I too heard Spike Hughes[1] on Tuesday with the result that Ballin' the Jack is now on my turntable. I too like this outfit (bwbwbwbwbw), but they *do* sound best on first hearing. However, I think you are much too hard on the Deutero-Russell[2] who is after all the most interesting

4. Arthur Jackson, a Mathematics scholar at St John's, whom Amis seems to have run into in the army, is reporting some unrecoverable piece of gossip about a fellow St John's student, Brian F. Groom, reading Modern Languages. Groom is 'Groob' in imitation of Jackson's presumably adenoidal voice (hence also 'aboud'); see Larkin to Amis, 13 September 1945 (in BJL): 'Well, and what has happened to Brian Groob? Has he got a wubbud to wayk [wagk?] hidse [hilse?].' Groom did not return to Oxford after the war and never completed his degree.

---

1. Spike Hughes (1908–87), English double-bass player, composer, jazz writer and critic.

2. A clarinettist on the recording of 'Ballin' the Jack' by Victor Lewis and His Jazzmen, first heard by Amis on the radio. Lewis (b. 1919) was an English bandleader, guitarist, singer and cornettist. Larkin, in a letter of 14 December 1945 (in BJLH), had said of this recording that it 'contains the first English Russell-disciple solo: really extraordinary: just as bad and derivative . . . as you or I would be if we could play the clarinet "a little". Russell, here, is Pee Wee Russell (1906–69), and Amis calls his unnamed English disciple 'Deutero-Russell'

part of the record. I *like* it being derivative: it's more like 1945 Russell than any Russell we can get (except? There'll Be Some Changes Made?). If you do get a copy, note the last very quiet half-bar or so with which he finishes his first 8 bars, especially the last note of all; it will repay attention. No, I must say I like the solo very much. Also deserving honourable mention was the tpt on both sides, though that fucking "ten" and "ds" want shagging.[3] I agree with what you say about Dippermouth.[4] I have the Spanier[5] version and it is an excellent discing hukh hukh hukh. I also liked the 2 Pinetop[6] sides, though I should have preferred more points of difference between them than that he talks on one & sings on the other. The trouble is, of course, that all good b.w. [boogie-woogie] is the same b.-w. – Pinetop's Blues = P's b.-w. = Cleo Brown's[7] b.-w. = Honky Tonk etc. It's only when you come to pseudo- or quasi-b.-w. (Preachin' Blues) that you can tell the difference. That is one of *my* heresies. Before we leave the Jass Music, be sure to bring the numbers of those Commodore[8] records when you come. I don't want any thing to go *wrong* about that if *I* can avoid it. *Nor do you.*

The last week-end of my vac is January 12th et seq. (or *ff.*) I shall be very pleased to see you then though I wish you c[d] have come twice, as the a said to the b.[9] On Monday I will find eight from the Inquiry Bureau at Euston Station (Please Make Your Requests as Short as Possible) all abt y[r] train. I will then slip the gen across to you ole boy woof woof. I like 'Beowuff' by the way.

because he comes second or follows. He is probably Derek Hawkins (see Amis to Larkin, 21 February 1946, note 3).

3. That is, Amis disapproves of the tenor saxophone ('ten') and drums ('ds').

4. The song 'Dippermouth Blues' (not Louis Armstrong, sometimes known as 'Dippermouth'), also on the Victor Lewis recording; Larkin had praised it in his letter of 14 December 1945 (in BJLH).

5. Muggsy Spanier (1901–67), cornettist.

6. Pine Top Smith (1904–29), singer and pianist. The sides were 'Pinetop's Boogie'/ 'Pinetop's Blues'. Barry Kernfeld, ed., *The New Grove Dictionary of Jazz*, 2 vols (London: Macmillan, 1988; henceforth cited as NGDJ), 2, p. 274, calls 'Pinetop's Boogie-Woogie' 'probably the most influential and widely imitated of all blues recordings'. For Amis's views on the NGDJ see 'All the Boys in All the Bands', reprinted from the *Spectator* review of 11 February 1989, in *The Amis Collection: Selected Non-Fiction 1954–1990*, intro. John McDermott (London: Hutchinson, 1990), pp. 377–9.

7. Cleo(patra) Brown (b. 1909), pianist and singer, recorded a series of tunes for United States Decca in 1935–36; her specialty number was 'Pinetop's Boogie Woogie', which is listed simply as 'Boogie Woogie' in the catalogue.

8. A New York record company and label, established 1938, specialising in Chicago jazz.

9. 'As the actress said to the bishop.'

What are the best of the Spl. List Wallers? I am ordering Ridin' but W. (and Serious Thing, F. Drazey, Shag, When S Thinks Y Wond, NKTWIFTM).[10] What's the 12th Honeysuckle R[ose]. Blue Turning G[ray] like? Thank you for your remarkson the other jass pieces, by the way. I haven't begun work yet; Gower, Chaucer, Langland, you see. I can see another session in the offing: Bill Langland and his Plowmen of Rhythm (Somer Sesoun Drag/Half-acre Stump: Perkyn's Blues/Wikked Weye Jump).[11]

I find it very hard not to write to Gillian.[12] You are right abt. me not being logical abt. her but then I don't *feel* l. abt. her. I haven't found an Xmas axmas ammas ammons armans armsn ars*awl* card for her yet. My prophecy abt. your Christmas card may not turn out to be correct, after all.[13]

Do you know that epigram abt. naked Truth and naked Ruth?[14] 'A's 'Azel Amis, Eh?[15]

I can't understand why Greta[16] being away – the poor little Devil, no symphathy for other's you haven't got, not much Eh Ah! Ah! – means you can't write letters on a wordmachine. Why do your capital G's (BUGGERY) make me laugh? This letter is more than usually scrappy, but there is one more thing that doesn't fit in with anything else: I opened a Children's Encyclopaedia to day and there were annotations by you – Oh Christ – Shakespeare letting a fart – Milton reads

10. The 'Special List Wallers' were those Fats Waller recordings found on the HMV Special List, a twelve-to-sixteen-page leaflet issued free in the 1930s which included perhaps two to three hundred titles, all jazz. The full titles from Amis's selection are 'Ridin' but Walkin'', 'That's a Serious Thing', 'Feelin' Drowsy', 'Shag' (which is a variation on the chords of 'I Got Rhythm'), 'When Somebody Thinks You're Wonderful' and 'Nobody Knows the Way I Feel this Morning'.

11. The first of many such literary discs, combos and sessions to appear in the Amis–Larkin correspondence (see, for example, 30 January and 6 February 1947). 'Bill' Langland (c.1330-c.1386) wrote *Piers Plowman* (c. 1367–79), an allegorical poem of the Middle English Alliterative Revival, from which all four titles on these 'discs' come. See A.V.C. Schmidt, ed., *William Langland: The Vision of Piers Plowman: A Complete Edition of the B-Text* (London: Dent, 1978), Passus 1, line 1 and Passus 6, lines 1–4.

12. Gillian ('Jill') Williams, an Oxford girl Amis was attracted to, not a student at the university.

13. The prophecy was that Larkin wouldn't be getting a Christmas card from him; it wasn't correct. These Christmas cards were elaborate, hand-crafted affairs. See Amis to Larkin, c.16–18 December 1946.

14. A reference to Ruth Bowman, Larkin's girlfriend in Wellington, later his fiancée.

15. Hazel Amess (pronounced Amis), a friend of Ruth Bowman's (see Amis to Larkin, 11 January 1946, note 1).

16. Larkin's assistant in the library at Wellington.

filthy stories in Braille – wd you 2 boys like to be made happy? And I laughed eight laid. It was done at the height of the craphace[17] craze.

I am so glad you are coming down to see us*, Phil.

Kingsley Agonistes

Did you know *Golding*[18] at school? Was he *homo*? *Never mind why I'm asking.*
*No. Only ME.

[ALS: Bodleian]

TO PHILIP LARKIN – 24, 27 DECEMBER 1945

26, Shrublands Road, Ferkhamsted, Ferts, Xmas eve bwbwbwbwbw 1945[1]

My dear Philip,

It was very nice to hear from you to-day, while I was in bed recovering from a bout of 'flu that looked as if it might have kept me in bed for Christmas, but it didn't. I don't know that I have an awful lot to say right now, but it is good to keep the thing going anyway. Never think I am not going to like you saying a lot about the Jass music; I am only afraid *you* won't like *me* saying it.

Borlin' the J. I see what you mean. *Bert* the whole thing now strikes me as very rehearsed, lacking spontaneity. The solos are all very well but don't hang together. You're probably right about the Russell solo. It is the abject *entreaty* of the second phrase and the first half of the 3rd phrase that gets me. But something too much of this.[2]

Dippermaith. I still like it. It is more of a whole than B le J. I like the sop, especially when the start of his second cho looks like becoming Rompin' and doesn't. And the tmb. And the tpt, especially the one Spanier-inspired high note 2nd cho I think last note of 6th bar. Like a lark shot while on the wing.

17. Craphouse.
18. John Golding, reading medicine at St John's (1944–50).

---

1. '1945' is a MS addition.
2. Hamlet's words to Horatio (III.ii.72).

Pinetop's BWbwbwbw. Nor am I.[3] Is your copy shagged on the Blues side, by the way? Mine makes a noise like Christopher[4] breathing while using the chamber-pot. Honestly, these bloody Brunswicks.[5]

Go(u)lding.[6] Can't be the same one. I ask because *I* think he *is*.

Very funny and annoying about JILL.[7] Oh yes you are proud to be having yr first novel abt to be printed. Your ability to write and get it published is a constant source of irritation and gloom in me, who can't put pen to fucking paper; so much so that you forfeit all claims on my sympathy for everything – or you would if I weren't such an unwordly fool, a vagabong christ – bond of the heart with its red blood my only guerdon and unavailing is our solid tear WOOF WOOF

27 December

Oh well it is all over now and thank Xt too. The presents I got were – as always – far inferior in every way to the ones I gave, and that is annoying. The parties I went to didn't have any nice young ladies at them, and everybody had a much smaller brain than mine. And last night the *craning* horror – those awful songs; do your parents sing them? Until & Homing & Onaway Awake Beloved & Xtopher Robin is Saying his Prairs?[8] Well last night there were a lot of those.

Because God made thee mine I'll cherish
thee. No.
Through light and darkness for all time
to be. No.
And pray his love will make our love
divine. No.
Because God made thee mine. No-*o*.[9]

I've decided I don't like Christmases much.

3. As impressed as on a first hearing? See Larkin to Amis, 28 December 1945 (in BJLH): 'P-T's Bwbwbwbw I have learnt to like a little.'

4. Tosswill, reading Physics at Queen's College, Oxford (1941–42, 1946–47).

5. Records released under the Brunswick record company label.

6. See Amis to Larkin, 15 December 1945, note 18.

7. Larkin had complained that the MS of *Jill* had been 'BLUE-PENCILLED. Heavily and senselessly' by the publisher (see LL, p. 112).

8. The songs in question – 'Until' (cf. similar titles: 'Nevertheless', 'Because'), 'Homing' (that is, 'Over the Sea to Skye'), 'Onaway Awake Beloved' and 'Christopher Robin is Saying his Prayers' (made popular in the 1930s by Gracie Fields) – are all sentimental ballads.

9. Lines from 'Because' (1902), a much-recorded sentimental ballad, popularised by Enrico Caruso, then Perry Como and Mario Lanza.

While I remember it –
WILLOW GABLES AT OXFORD
ILLOW GABLES AT OXFORD W
LLOW GABLES AT OXFORD WI
LOW GABLES AT OXFORD WIL
OW GABLES AT OXFORD WILL
W GABLES AT OXFORD WILLO
GABLES AT OXFORD WILLOW
ABLES AT OXFORD WILLOW G
BLES AT OXFORD WILLOW GA
LES AT OXFORD WILLOW GAB
ES AT OXFORD WILLOW GABL
S AT OXFORD WILLOW GABLE
T OXFORD WILLOW GABLES A
OXFORD WILLOW GABLES AT
XFORD WILLOW GABLES AT O
FORD WILLOW GABLES AT OX
ORD WILLOW GABLES AT OXF
RD WILLOW GABLES AT OXFO
D WILLOW GABLES AT OXFORD[10]
WILLOW GABLES AT OXFORD

What a wonderful record the Waller 'Baby Brown' is. The other day I played it twice without removing it from the turn-table which is good for a record I have had for four years. And the other side would be as good but for that *bastard* celeste[11] cho coming where it does.

The first letter from Gillian has duly arrived ('We had all been anxiously awaiting it'). It is a – well, the ink isn't blue or green, but a sort of luminous intermediate clour fxfx clobls c o l o u r that suggests she's been using a blue pen in green ink or something. I didn't have to write a letter to get it. Pattern extracts:

'. . . fickle . . .'

'Thank you very much for the Christmas Card, it stands out as much the nicest on the whole mantle-piece.'

'. . . eating buns! . . .'

'. . . poetry . . .'

'. . . be happy . . .'

10. MS addition: Amis has written 'ars*awl*' in the right margin, with an arrow pointing to the top of the D of OXFORD.

11. Keyboard instrument, like a small upright piano.

Yes, it seems it will all fall pat as I told you.[12]

I think I'm going to try and get some other records beside those Commodores, like 'Mean Old Bed-Bug Blues', played by Billy Banks[13] and his Orchestra. With vocal refrain. They are available in America, no?

I don't understand what you are getting at about the naked truth,[14] old man.

I have just read this letter through and think it is very dull.

DONT YOU HATE PEOPLE ASKING YOU ABOUT OXFORD WHAT A DEGREE IS AND WHY YOU TAKE THEM AND WHAT SUBJECTS YOU STUDY AAOH AOH AAOOH WOOF WOOF BILLY BARLEY BUB BWBWB WBWBWBWBWBWBWBWBWBWBWBWBWBW

Kingsley Ikonoklastes
Kingsley

P.S. Shite-horse[15]

[TLS: Bodleian]

TO PHILIP LARKIN – 31 DECEMBER 1945

26, Shrublands Road, Berkhamsted, Herts,
New years' Eve bwbwbw 1945[1]

PM 3/1/46[2]

My dear Philip,

It was nice (as it always is) to hear from you *once* again – why can't I *stand* people who say once again, as if when other people said again

12. See *A Midsummer Night's Dream* (v.i.184–5): 'You shall see it will fall pat as I told you: yonder she comes.'

13. Billy Banks (1908–67), singer; described in Amis's *Memoirs* (1991) as 'a sort of counter-tenor, not very jazzy perhaps by some standards but fascinating to me, especially in the words he sang. I had not known then [1941] that such singers would have in their memory several hundred blues verses which, in their allotted minute or so, they would sing a few of more or less at random. I thought Banks was performing connected songs or poems of a kind of awesome surrealism' (p.67).

14. That is, Ruth (Bowman, Larkin's girlfriend).

15. MS addition.

1. MS addition.

2. MS addition.

they menat bollabolla meant "twice again" or "three times again" when what they mean is A G A I N. Rather like 'He looked at his watch: the time was *precisely* eight-and-a-half minutes past six' (my – 's). You can say 'the time was precisely three o'clock' *to show you dont mean* 'the time was about 3' but the 'precisely' in 'precisely 8½ mins past 6' means *P R E C I S E L Y* fuck-*orl*. Sorry to lose my temper like that, but I am a little distrait these days.

I have just got your second letter and it excited me (don't look like that). But I'll just speak right on. I am going to say a lot about the jass music in little bits, each one on a fresh line:

Yes isn't it funny how nobody can bear Shavers.[3] I can. He is good on 29th & D[earborn] and Blue D[ilemma] though not on R[oyal] G[arden] B[lues]. It's a pity he got in with that Bailey-Procope-Kyle gang,[4] all of whom suffer from not being able to play their instruments properly. Allen[5] is a *marvellous* tptr and anybody who can't see that is a navel-obsessed moron. I suppose by the 'various' he[6] means the Bland[7] sides Who Lock/Someone Horn and ?/?[8] on the same session (what are they, by the way?)

I have listening lately to quite a lot of Ladnier[9] (Baby/Jelly-Roll, Lay Yr Rkt/U To-Nite, R the B's/J-D) and I am coming relentlessly to the decision that he cant play

who's bunk johnson[10]

3. Charlie Shavers (1917–71), trumpeter and arranger.

4. Members of the John Kirby sextet: Buster Bailey (1902–67), clarinettist; Billy Kyle (1914–66), pianist; and Russell Procope (1908–81), alto saxophonist and clarinettist.

5. Henry ('Red') Allen (1908–67), trumpeter and vocalist.

6. 'He' is the unnamed author of a book about jazz, with photographs, recommended to Larkin by Amis in a missing letter of December 1945 (see note 14 for a possible identification). Larkin refers to it in a letter of 28 December 1945 (in BJLH): 'I bought the little book you mention and scanned it rapidly . . . I HATED THE PHOTOGRAPHS.'

7. Jack Bland (b. 1899), guitarist and banjoist.

8. 'Who Stole the Lock (from the Henhouse Door)'/'Someone Stole Gabriel's Horn' and 'Shine on Your Shoes'/'It's Gonna be you' were recorded in 1938 by Jack Bland's Rhythmakers, a group brought together for the recording and comprising most of the personnel from Billy Banks' Rhythmakers, including Henry 'Red' Allen on trumpet and vocals, Pee-Wee Russell on clarinet, Happy Cauldwell on tenor sax, Tommy Dorsey on trombone, Frankie Froeba on piano, Eddie Condon on banjo, Jack Bland on guitar and Pops Foster on bass.

9. Tommy Ladnier (1900–39), trumpeter; the full titles of the Ladnier sides are 'I Found a New Baby'/'I Ain't Gonna Give Nobody None of my Jelly Roll', 'Lay Your Racket'/'I Want You Tonight', 'Really the Blues'/'Ja-Da'.

10. Bunk Johnson (1889–1949), trumpeter.

Anybody who underestimates Harry James[11] (except Bl Md/Bl Md & B-W/W-W) is probably right about doing that thing

Bix.[12] Why is it that so many otherwise reasonable people get all silly in their heads when they start talking about Bix? They think all jass tpts shd be like Armstrong and Allen. I shouldn't mind much if they were but god damn christ people can play the tpt in different ways from Ar & Al and still play the jass music. Anyway, listen to S My B Gal T Me D and Jass Me Blues/ – though *not* /Royal Gdn B's – and then come back and tell me that Bix doesn't play jass. I know you will, but at least you'll have heard two good records.

I haven't the Bumpet in Jass[13] (I wonder if the MacCarthy who wrote it is the MACSHITEMacCarthy who is supposed to run the Marble Arch Mus Shop but doesn't?) and from what you tell me of it it seems as if I shall not mind not doing that It seems to be a characteristic of jass books that as soon as the thing's gone to the printers nobody cares any more. Did you notice the record numbers in oozoo in jass?[14]

Yes werent those foatoes *sodomitical* except for hazel scott[15]

Do you know anything about Hello Little Devil/Barefoot Boy, a recent Brunswick, by the Harlem Hamfats? I mention this because as you know they accompany Rosetta (Yule Be *Har*bour Noff*long*ngngng) Howard[16] on If You a Viper, and I like the tpt, Morand[17] by name, and he is on this Litl Devl recd he *sings* on it so the label says now if he plays his tpt to, thats' good, do you no if he does, or what its' like, I expect so, somtimes I think you no evrything (*ARGH*'m the queen of avry*theng*) Its not krupas[18] *off* beat bashing on the *symbol* I mind; its

11. Harry James (1916–83), trumpeter and bandleader; the full titles of the James recordings were the double-sided 'Blue Mood' and 'Boo-Woo'/'Woo-Woo'.

12. Leon ('Bix') Beiderbecke (1903–31), cornettist. The full titles of the songs Amis mentions later in this paragraph are 'Since My Best Gal Turned Me Down' and 'Jazz Me Blues'.

13. *The Trumpet in Jazz* (1945) by Albert (John) McCarthy.

14. *Yearbook of Jazz: An Illustrated Who's Who of Jazz Personalities* (1945) by Peter Noble.

15. Hazel Scott (1920–81), pianist and singer.

16. Rosetta Howard (1914–74), singer. The Harlem Hamfats was a septet formed in the 1930s by J. Mayo Williams (1894–1980), the record producer. Accoring to *NGDJ*, 'Their unique sound . . . was a precursor of rhythm-and-blues' (p. 485). 'Hello Little Devil' is actually 'Mellow Little Devil', and the line from 'If You'se a Viper' alluded to parenthetically is 'You'll get high but not for long if you'se a viper'.

17. Herb Morand (1905–52), trumpeter and singer.

18. Gene Krupa (1909–73), drummer and bandleader.

his *non*beat bashing on the base *drum* All right, clever; what *is* I GSfx M H L?[19]

Now 'm gonna *pick this* pian'

It's no use asking me to hear hodes[20] records. I've been trying to hear a Russell record for two months now and I can't. All right, I'll try.

At this moment I can hear a lot of men called Glenn Miller[21] and his Orchestra playing some notes called 'Take the "A" Train' put down by a man called 'Duke' Ellington,[22] I wish I weren't doing that

It is now January 2nd. Later on New Years Eve I went to the Police Dance with a young lady whom I only like at *all* when I am actually fixing her up old boy and not much even *then* so you can imagine that I didn't enjoy myself *much*. I wanted to get too pissed to *care*, but I couldn't do that because there was no bar at the dance, and then of course at midnight the band stopped – there were *two* gtrs in it, one an electric gtr played for rhythm only, the two moving as if on one spindle and giving a terrific beat which the rest *ignored* – but those two were splendid; if they had recorded the 'Georgia' they played Edgar Jackson[23] would have written about it 'Burns[24] (alt) with E. Condon[25] (bjo). Remainder of personnel unavailable that's enough about that – and everybody joined hands and the band leader talked through a microphone ('Is everybody happy? No *sir*') oh dear oh dear and I realised the year of Elisabeth was over and wouldn't come again and sure I'm enjoying myself I said I'm having a wonderful time.

You shall see gillians letter and shes going to have a copy of jill

19. See Larkin to Amis, 28 December 1945 (in BJLH): 'Well, of course you are a deviationist abt Teshc frtss Tesche: Oh Baby is the better side and I quite like the final cho. and I like Krupa's solemn offbeat bashing on the cymbal. While Sullivan's solo is very good indeed and second only to the I F A N B and I G S M H L. ("Work that one out" – "Work it yourself").' 'I F A N B' is 'I Found a New Baby', 'I G S M H L' is 'I'm Gonna Stomp Mr Henry Lee', both with piano solos by Joe Sullivan.

20. Art Hodes (b. 1904), pianist, broadcaster and writer; 'Philip Larkin remarked of him that he sounded as if he had three hands and didn't know what to do with any of them' (Amis, *Memoirs*, p. 70).

21. Glenn Miller (1904–44), bandleader and trombonist.

22. Duke Ellington (1899–1974), composer, bandleader and pianist.

23. Author of jazz reference books and discographies, including *'His Master's Voice' Swing and Hot Rhythm Records* (n.d. [?1941]) and, with L. Hibbs, *Decca, Brunswick, Vocalion Encyclopedia of Swing* (1941); reviewed jazz records for the monthly magazine *The Gramophone*.

24. Bob Burns (b. 1923), a Canadian alto saxophonist, settled in London in 1937.

25. Eddie Condon (1905–73), banjoist and guitarist.

sorry abate the digs old boy[26] I got a card from hilary[27] too oh ergh and one from nick cookfook crookes[28] told me abt golding that he was at yr school I mean not that hes homo thats just my idea what about willow gables at oxford you flaring ballock you god I must cræp I thought it was that sweet man of mine making his 4-day cræp whats a 4day creep did we ever do "wswswswswsws"? well its the same as bwbwbwbw or achachachachacharch thats yer arch eye thats yer eye yer archeye bald thats yer bald yer eyebald yer archeyebald ars thats yer ars yer bald arse yer eyebaldarse yer archeyebald arse ole thats yer ole yer arsole yer baldarsole yer eyebaldarsole yer archeyebaldarsole I was certain I'd told you that, but no. If your train stops at Harrow I can meet you there otherwise I will meet you at Euston. Going back you can bus to Potford (½hr) & pick train up there. All for now. Be happy.

archibald anus
Kingsley

bring the bumpet in jass[29]

[TLS: Bodleian]

TO PHILIP LARKIN – 5 JANUARY 1946

26 Shrublands Road, Berkhamsted, Herts

[. . .] This could really wait till you come but I must have something to talk about when I go into the gramophone shop here and find my records aren't in, something to prevent the nice, smiling, *hopelessly incompetent* old lady there from telling me *again* (she has told me three

26. Larkin's landlady needed his room back for her own use, something she told him just after Christmas (see Motion, *Life*. p. 140).

27. Hilary Morris (1922–59) read Natural Sciences at St John's College, Oxford (1941–42, 1946–48); he and his wife died in an aeroplane accident in 1959.

28. Kenneth Burchell-Crookes attended the King Henry VIII School in Coventry from 1934–44 (Larkin was there from 1930–40), before going up to St John's to read Mathematics (1944–47). His nickname at school was 'Tilly', not 'Nick'. Neither Oxford University nor the King Henry VIII School has a listing for 'Nicholas Crookes'. Since Amis has been leaving out punctuation in this paragraph, it is likely that 'cookfook' begins a new sentence; 'Nick' is probably Nick Russel (see Amis to Larkin, 25 November 1944, note 10).

29. MS addition.

times already) that 80% of Brunswick records are going for export and that is why I can't have georgiabobo or iwoulddoanythingforyou or earlymorningblues or sweetpatootie or georgewettlingsifoundanewbaby[1] – which I ordered to prevent her telling me for the fifth time that my needle–sharpener wasn't repaired yet [. . .]

Conversation I don't want to have again:

'Why didn't you see me home last night?'

'It didn't occur to me.'

'I see.'

'I'm sorry.'

'Not much use being sorry now.'

'I hope you don't think I . . .'

'I know what it is. We're through, that's what you want to say, isn't it?'

'Don't be silly. Of course we aren't wswswswswswswswbwbwbwbw bwachachachachawoofwf

I think I should like to meet Ruth

I know I shouldn't really

I will be on the right platform at 2045 hrswsws on the 12th inst ownst odes [del.] des ards arsls ar*sawl*

Dont laugh at me in brane clothes what a rotten job youve got why dont you get another eh

I look forward too.

kingsley hamfat
Kingsley

TO PHILIP LARKIN – 11 JANUARY 1946

26, Shrublands Road, Berkhamsted, Herts.

My dear Lurkin,

So nice of you to write to me and tell me all the news oh farks. There isn't really much for me to say at now: I must have been pist when I said I wanted to see Ruth, yes I must. Perhaps I could take her

1. George Wettling (1907–68), drummer.

to the Pickarso exhibition, what do you say cham. I hope my pretty little namesake ergh comes along too.[1]

Your letter came too late no' your fau' o' boy I 'precia'e tha' to be of use to me in my wanderings round the record shops, but I have the following to report [. . .]

You are being very *tiresome* about this train on Sunday *NO THE TRAIN I MEAN ISN'T THE 2.13 FROM WATFORD TO BROAD STREET IT'S THE 2.50 FROM WATFORD TO EUSTON AN EXPRESS YES WE COULD GET THE 2.3 BUT THAT MEANS LEAVING HERE AT ONE O'CLOCK AND HAVING LUNCH AT ABOUT 12.30 WHICH MY MOTHER WON'T LIKE BUT I WILL ASK HER AND I DON'T GIVE A POODLE'S PUKE FOR YOUR LOUSY OLD BRADSHAW*[2] *YOU FLARING BALLOCK YOU*

ACHACHACHACHA HACHA HACH HAC HA A ACHACHACHACH-ACHACHA Don't you *ever* go *near* a film called confidential agent[3]

Look forward to see in flesh

kingsley blue boy
Kingsley

[TLS: Bodleian.]

---

1. Larkin's trip to London, before going on to Amis and his family at Berkhamsted, was in connection with the publication of *Jill* by the Fortune Press. Ruth Bowman, Larkin's friend, had begun a course in English at King's College, London, in October 1945, and Amis was to meet her while Larkin conducted his business with the shadowy R.A. Caton of the Fortune Press (for Caton see Amis to Larkin, 18 January 1946, note 1). See Larkin to Amis, 8 January 1946 (in BJLH):

> I don't think you *really* want to see Ruth but you said you did.
>
> *I* benefit by this tiresome trip to London insofar as I remove this obstacle to the publication of JILL without having to make a special journey and pay a special 29/4d WHICH I CANNOT AFFORD. YOU benefit insofar as you meet Ruth and therefore have an item of information about me which no one else bar Bruce [Montgomery] has. RUTH benefits insofar as she sees me and sees you: she has had a surfeit of you over the last three months and now wants to see very much what you are like.

Amis's 'namesake' was Ruth's friend from King's College, London, Hazel Amess, who had no connection with the Amis family. She was in the same year as Ruth but read Modern Languages, not English. For R.A. Caton, see Timothy D'Arch Smith, *R.A. Caton and the Fortune Press* (1983).

2. The famous British railway timetable, published monthly from 1841 to 1961.

3. *The Confidential Agent* (1945), starring Charles Boyer and Lauren Bacall, adapted from the Graham Greene novel (1939) by Robert Buckner, directed by Herman Shumlin.

TO PHILIP LARKIN – 18 JANUARY 1946

St. John's College, Oxford.

My dear Pee,

It was very nice to get back to the old place and to find your letter waiting for me. You raise several interesting points:

i Yes I enjoyed your week end enormously. My mother and father thought you very nice ('whoever you've got your cynical views from, it isn't from him').

ii Thank you for doing that to the FP.[1] But it's gon' to be a *farkle* getting those poems together. I had a look at some of them the other day and they nearly made me craep

iii wuck-*wuck*-WUCK-*WUCK-WUCK!!!*[2]

I'm glad Ruth likes me. *Bert* one or two of those extracts[3] make me feel a wee bit narked, ole boy:

'unnatural vice' what had you said to her[4]

'much better-looking than you had led me to suppose' now I don't fancy myself as a young adonis ole boy, but *WHAT HAD YOU LED HER TO SUPPOSE???*[5]

And how do you *mean*, "stroking me"? uuuurgh oorgh uff-uff er *beeeeeaaoorghgh*

Graham[6] is sitting here now writing a letter to one of his young

---

1. In December 1945 Amis had sent a collection of his poems entitled *Bright November* to R.A. Caton of the Fortune Press, but it was not accepted for publication until May 1946. Amis may be thanking Larkin for having praised the collection or urging its publication on Caton. R.A. (Reginald Ashley) Caton (1897–1974) was in property as well as publishing, and at the time of his death owned ninety-one houses in his home town of Brighton. In 1924 he founded the Fortune and Merriman Press, later the Fortune Press, which specialised in such soft-porn titles as *Bachelor's Hall, Boys in their Ruin* and *Chastisement Across the Ages.* He also published a number of distinguished poets, including Dylan Thomas, Roy Fuller, C. Day-Lewis and Larkin, and several influential anthologies, including the first gathering of 'The New Apocalypse' poets in 1940. From 1930 to 1970 he published over six hundred titles. He was a shadowy and elusive figure, and Amis was not alone in complaining about his methods. See Timothy D'Arch Smith, *R.A. Caton and the Fortune Press* (1983); also Amis to Larkin, 16 July 1948, note 2; Amis to Gollancz, 27 February 1955, note 1; and Amis to Larkin, 10 April 1956, note 2.

2. The last '*WUCK!!!*' typed in red.

3. Taken from a Larkin letter which has not survived.

4. 'What had you said to her' typed in red.

5. '*WHAT HAD YOU LED HER TO SUPPOSE???*' typed in red.

6. Graham Parkes (1924–98), a fellow jazz enthusiast from St John's, reading Moderations (1942, 1946–47), previously a contemporary of Larkin's at King Henry VIII School.

ladies. What a nice person he is; nothing to offend. He sends his love. Last night he & Mervyn[7] and I went out and found a pian' in a pub, which M played while G and I blue-blew and sang. M wants to make a record. It's not a bad idea uh? "King – I'm no oil painting beeeeoooooouuyygh sley's Blues" (Amis): Amis (kazoo, voc) with M. Brown (reeds), G. Parkes (pno), J. Silvester (bs), R. Partington (bjo), et al.[8] Sounds all right eh? The piano was called 'Kingsley' too, which made us all laugh [. . .]

Oh Christ I've got to write a bleeding essay all about that sodding old bore Langlad gland I mean there you know what sort. But I've discovered the way to my tutor's heart – he likes all those shags like Pickarso (the exhibition of whose works Philip[9] liked very much) and Klee (the exhibition of whose works Philip didn't think was very good) so I say things like 'blue period' and 'delicate colour sense' instead of things like 'Saga-like' and 'piling-on of images'; and instead of things like 'Blue arseholes' and 'frothy whorls of menstrual fluid'.

Oh and 'Egyptian Fantasy'/'Shoe Shine Swing' Bechet with Allen and Higgy:[10] HYDROCEPHALIC EEL'S TESTICLES[11] Records like that belong to Mervyn, who has a lot of *bad* records: lots of Bix and Hawkins[12] and Ellington and Ma*no*ne,[13] but NO Yellow Dog [Blues] and *NO* Spider Crawl.[14] If I hear a record of his which I have got too, it makes me wonder straightaway if I was wise to get it.

I must stop now and start this fworking essay.

Bacwords and love to Ruth dont look like that

kingsley famous chicagoan
KINGSLEY[15]

[TLS: Bodleian]

7. Brown (b. 1923), read Modern History at St John's (1941–42, 1946–48); subsequently a diplomat; knighted (1981).

8. For Silvester and Partington, fellow undergraduates, see Amis to Larkin, 16 June 1947, note 4, and 15 July 1946, note 7.

9. Brown (b. 1923), reading medicine at St John's (1940–46), one of 'The Seven'; 'called "little Philip" to distinguish him from big Philip' (Motion, *Life*, p. 40).

10. J.C. Higginbotham (1906–73), trombonist. According to *NGDJ*, 1, p. 523, Higginbotham 'recorded with numerous small groups, especially ones whose music had a New Orleans flavor, including those led by Sidney Bechet and Henry "Red" Allen, and a group of his own. During these years Higginbotham was considered one of the best of the swing trombonists.'

11. 'HYDROCEPHALIC EEL'S TESTICLES' typed in red.

12. Coleman Hawkins (1901–69), tenor saxophonist.

13. Wingy Manone (1900–82), trumpeter, singer and bandleader.

14. 'NO' and '*NO*' typed in red.

15. A further page of jazz and other queries, after the signature, has been omitted.

TO PHILIP LARKIN – 5 FEBRUARY 1946

Coll: Di: Io: Bapt:[1] *Oxon wswswswswswsws*

My dear Philip,

Thank you for your mewst amewsing card. I newt with some distaste your habit of writing cards; no of course silly of me – the last one was a letter wasn't it? and a very nice one too. I hope you had a nice time in London with your young lady, get your end away you old bugar eh, don't look like that. What on earth did you *do* all the time? You don't have to tell me you know, said Marsha, standing on tip-toe to peg a newly-washed pair of stockings on the line that ran from the picture-rail above their bed to the corner of the wardrobe. Jennifer lay back and watched lazily, breaking into silent laughter as the pin on the picture-rail came out and line and stockings fell to the floor. O blast! cried Marsha wrathfully, bending and picking them up. A wisp of yellow hair fell across her brow and one of the straps of her slip dropped from her shoulder, revealing[2]

You are very right of course about how good we are, especially me, and how nice it would be to be here together, but things like that don't happen, as Elisabeth[3] used to say. She was always right about that. Talking of young ladies once more, I have told Gillian[4] I am fed up, and *all* the reasons why, especially that she *just doesn't know what to do* about young chaps. So it's all over. I don't mind this much but I feel rather let down; nobody as *lovely* as she in the particular way that she was lovely had any right to be as *S T U P I D* as she turned out to be in the particular way that she was stupid.[5] Ah, soul. I am not, nor I cannot come to good.[6] Yes, I was *very* nasty to her the last time we met. I liked that.

---

1. As opposed to St John the Divine.
2. Marsha and Jennifer are characters in the 'untitled long story' outlined in an enclosure accompanying this letter and eventually called 'I Would Do Anything for You', a title taken from the 1932 song co-written and popularised by the pianist and bandleader Claude Hopkins (1903–84) and his band (also twice recorded by Billy Banks and His Rhythmakers, with vocals by Billy Banks).
3. Simpson; see Amis to Larkin, c.26 October-6 November 1943, note 2.
4. Williams; see Amis to Larkin, 15 December 1945, note 12.
5. 'In the particular way that she was lovely', '*STUPID*' and 'in the particular way that she was stupid' typed in red, with '*STUPID*' underlined in alternating red and black.
6. See *Hamlet*, I.ii.158: 'It is not, nor it cannot come to good.'

Tell Ruth to ask Geraldine Cunninghame[7] – (aagh! naaagh! I can't er ar aawwwr ooooo er *beeeeeuuuyyyhar* it) if she has sisters called Patsy, Helen May, Angela and Molly. 'Cos if she has, I fell in love with all of them twelve and a half years ago. Don't forget to tell her. I have secured 3/1 for her.[8] gogges bones its a bad word.

We had a good week-end with Nick,[9] though I cdn't spend as much time with hime pissipiss him as I shd have liked. Phonograph discs were played and a lot of beer was drunk. It was delightful seeing him again; he is the least changed of any of us, though of course he had least need to change. He asked about you and said he hopes to see you next term when he comes up. I made him your excuses, and he laughed

By the way – how about
Stompin' at the Heorot/Monster's Blues
Dragon Crawl/Bright-Dane Boogie, by
Winnie Hrothgar and his Hot Hallthanes. Personnel:
Hrothgar (tpt, voc); Theo Beowulf (reeds); 'Sleepy'
Sigemund (tmb); 'King' Higelac (bjo); Lil Wealhtheow
(pno); 'Pops' Wulfgar (bs); Joe 'The Monster' Grendel
(ds). Recorded under the supervision of Hal Drihten at the Heorot Saloon, 5 Feb, 946. (V)[10]

I must go now and see Slade[11] for not telling him that Nick was going to stay another night. No, I wasn't paying. Yes, the room was vacant in any case. No, there wasn't time to tell Slade. Yes, Slade is a oogh ogh aw 'r e-beeeeuuuyyygh

Kingsley Yorkshire Scholar[12]
Kingsley

7. Geraldine Cunninghame, Ruth Bowman's friend, also reading English at King's College, London. Ruth Bowman [Siverns] recalls her as 'a strikingly handsome girl, pleasant but reserved' (personal communication, 26 January 1999).

8. A record, with 'Three . . . [something]' on one side and 'I . . . [something]' on the other; untraceable.

9. Russel (see Amis to Larkin, 25 November 1944, note 10).

10. This 'personnel' is drawn from *Beowulf*, the eighth-century Anglo-Saxon poem: 'Heorot' is the Hall of Hrothgar, King of the Danes (it is threatened by the monster Grendel, whom Beowulf defeats); Sigemond is conqueror of the dragon Fafnir; Higelac, Beowulf's uncle, was King of the Geats; Wealtheow was Hrothgar's Queen, Wulfgar his chamberlain.

11. Edwin Slade (b. 1903), Fellow, Tutor and Lecturer in Law, St John's College, Oxford (1928–70), also Senior Dean (1932–40, 1945–57), St John's College.

12. The Yorkshire Scholar was one of several Oxford stereotypes developed by Amis, Larkin and their circle. Amis claimed he appeared in Larkin's *Jill* as the character Whitbread

untitled long story

Phase I. *1 week*[13] The idyllic life of Jennifer and Marsha, two art students in Oxford. They spend their time playing old jazz records out of curiosity, and painting each other. One evening Jennifer brings home the wrong easel, and Mady, a young half-caste girl, calls round to reclaim it. She likes the look of Marsha, but neither of the others suspect this as yet.

Phase II. *2–3 weeks* Mady keeps calling on Marsha when Jennifer is out at a bi-weekly lecture. Eventually she seduces Marsha, who loves her very much. One day Jennifer unexpectedly stays in, and when Mady calls grasps the reason for the recent change in Marsha's behaviour. Mady goes soon, and a quarrel between Jennifer and Marsha ends in Marsha going to share Mady's new digs.

Phase III. *2 weeks* Now Mady has 'got' Marsha, she is no longer considerate to her and treats her with increasing brutality. Marsha becomes disillusioned, and when at a party she overhears Mady arranging for Marion to call when Marsha will be out, she has a furious quarrel with Mady in pyjamas. Marsha leaves and returns to Jennifers digs about half-past two in the morning. Jennifer, who in Marsha's absence has had an unsuccessful affair with Bobbie, receives her because she loves her, and they plan a holiday together while the dawn breaks and Marsha's favourite record plays.

Marsha: Age 17. 5'6". Small bones, sturdy. Golden-bronze hair. Tawny eyes, slightly slanting. High cheek-bones. Speaks in slightly breathless voice.

Jennifer: Age 20. 5'9". Strongly built, dark hair and blue eyes. Fresh complexion. Deep clear voice. Serious.

(see 'Farewell to a Friend', in Dale Salwak, ed., *Philip Larkin: The Man and his Work* (Iowa City, University of Iowa Press, 1989), p. 3). See also Larkin's introduction to the 1964 reprint of *Jill*: 'We quickly invented "the Yorkshire Scholar", a character embodying many of our prejudices, and conversed in his flat rapacious tones in going to and from our tutor, Gavin Bone. "You're getting the best education in the land, lad." "Ay, but you must cut your coat according to your cloth." "Had tea wi' t'Dean on Sunday – I showed him I'd been reading his book." "Never lose a chance to make a good impression." "What play have you written about?" "*King Lear*. You see, I've DONE *King Lear*." "Ay." "AY"' (p. 13).

13. MS addition, as with succeeding italicised phrases.

Madeleine: Age 20. 5'8". Half-caste. Slim and strong. Black hair, dark skin. Large brown eyes, full lips. Rich, reckless, promiscuous, athletic.

Bobbie: Age 16. 5'4". Petite. Milk-white skin, red hair green eyes. Wears bangle. Tarts with men or women (expects a tip).

Marion: Mary Morris type. Age 18.

Notes on Scenes.

Phase I: Finding jazz records – art school life & Mady – washing up – Jennifer's school friends – Marsha's washing – they get pissed.

Phase II: Mady lonely – 'don't tell Jennifer' – Mady talks of her life and to her own surprise Marsha reveals her life with Jennifer they kiss – establish physical relationship – Marsha admires Mady.

Phase III: Jennifer-Bobbie episode precedes secondary night-piece.

4 Incidents are i) J & Marsha painting ii) Mady seduces Marsha iii) J & Bobbie iv) secondary night-piece Mady-Marsha.

[TLS: Bodleian]

TO PHILIP LARKIN – 10 FEBRUARY 1946

St John's College Oxfx.

My dear Philip,

I can see I shall have to apologise for all sorts of things about this letter: its shortness its inaccuracy its nasty paper isnt it? But I'm in a hurry and a very bad temper indeed: because I have been getting ready some of those rotten old poems of mine for the fortune press and I find there aren't enough because (i) a lot of them seem without *any* merit at *all* now and (ii) because I seem to have lost a lot of them. You haven't by any chance got a copy of a poem of mine about Brussels, have you?[1] I thought not. It looks as if I shall have to write to June[2] – aaoh aoh aaooh – and ask her for copies of the ones which – jaycee knows why – she insisted on my giving her. I shan't like any of that and I can't write any more to put in the collection as I thought I could until I tried and that is why I am in a bad temper and *that* is why this letter will be unsatisfactory. I'm sorry but *there's nothing I can do about it bockcxs.*

I am sorry you are getting yourself into such a mess old boy, with Ruth. Mind you dont go puting her up the Spout or braeking her little Haert you old bugar. I think you are wrong about love or at least I don't agree with you. The people *I* love I love beacuse of all the things you mention, but chiefly because, they would be glad, and are glad, to get into the same bed, as I do, when I do and because, of what I feel, when I am, in bed, with them. So there. [. . .]

Bruce[3] is up this week-end, just as nice as ever, thank God. I wish I could say the same for 'Holy Disorders'[4] which by a coincidence I had been reading. I don't like all those silly literary allusions, and some of the funny bits are funny but not many, and the blend of fantasy and detective novel isn't done skilfully enough, and there is a lot of pointless facetiousness and sheer bad writing.

> " . . it appears larger than is really the case."
>
> What case?
>
> ". . . What he is actually *recorded to have said* is . . ."
>
> ". . . smarting not only with physical pain (this had by now *considerably* abated), but also with a *considerable* mental irritation . . .
>
> ". . . It occurred to Geoffrey that she probably got an innocent enjoyment out of pretending to be wicked (aaoh aoh aaooh). He greatly doubted, *at all events*, if she actually was."
>
> ". . . It was not, he reflected, entirely a lie, at that"

---

1. Perhaps 'Belgian Winter', from *Bright November* (1947).
2. An old girlfriend, whom Amis first mentions in a letter to Larkin of 11 December 1945 (in Bodleian): 'I told June I was too much in love with EAS [Elisabeth Anne Simpson] to carry on with her. Though this is not quite true, it is not quite untrue either.'
3. Montgomery. See Notes on Recipients.
4. Edmund Crispin (Bruce Montgomery), *Holy Disorders* (1946).

At what?

"... Unlike parallel lines, it was inconceivable that
their views should ever meet, even at infinity..."

Nominative absolute and sheer wuck-wuck.

Sorry to take up all that space; what I say is largely inspired by envy and I can't write *at all*, but I felt I had to tell somebody about it. Bruce says he doesn't like it much either. But what an intelligent and charming person he is, and how I wish he were up here still. How nasty for you, being without him up there.

Must stop nay; have some of those rotten old Queynterbarey Tales to pulp into an essay. Any news of Gerry?[5]

Looking forward to seeing your Ugly mugg next Satuday therll be a Hot time in the old Town then eh Ah!Ah!

Kingsley Oxford Grey
Kingsley

You are wrong-about mr roderick cless,[6] but not altogether wrong. Mervyn[7] wd like Sat Nite Funk. AA[8] I like very much tho' I agree as a performance by a jass band it's a non-starter, old boy. Jaycee knows abt bob casey.[9] Nick[10] isn't coming *back* next term; only up for a visit. Sorry I misled you. K.

TO PHILIP LARKIN – 21 FEBRUARY 1946

S. John's Cge Woop

My dear Philip,

This probably won't be as long as you would like it to be or have any right to expect (wuck-wuck), but the alternative is a rather short

5. Geraldine Cunninghame (see Amis to Larkin, 5 February 1946, note 7).

6. Rod Cless (1907–44), clarinettist.

7. Brown, a saxophonist, was the only member of Amis's jazz-loving circle at Oxford who could read music.

8. There are nine citations for Rod Cless in Charles Delaunay, *New Hot Jazz Discography: The Standard Directory of Recorded Jazz* (New York: Criterion, 1948), none of them for tunes whose titles can be abbreviated as 'AA'; 'Sat Nite Funk' (i.e. 'Saturday Night Function') is a tune by Duke Ellington.

9. Bob Casey (1909–86), double-bass player.

10. Russel.

letter nay or a full-length one in abait three days' time so I am writing the shorter one now; oh doesn't it take a long time to explain even the simplest things. I have a tut on a rotten old book this morning otherwise I wd spend much longer on this.

I now possess Wipe off/In Blues. I like them both. Who is it on W 'E O? A funny and I think not right jass book I have seen says it's Ed Allen cnt (that's right) Cecil Scott clt? Clarence Williams voc Cyrus St Clair (Sinclair?) tuba.[1] And unknown others. How is that extraordinary farting noise produced, by the way? It doesn't sound like a tuba to me. I like the determinedly unimaginative way the on-beat is stressed all through. Didn't you say it was Waller once?

Glad you liked Jill.[2] I think she has elements of Ingrid Bergman in her too. She has been heard – not by me – to shout 'Yeah' during a drum-break by the Vic Lewis band (in this programme, *which I was told about afterwards*, there were 6 Derrick Hawkins-Russell soli)[3] Graham[4] has kissed her. I am sorry about that. He said she didn't respond. I didn't mind that so much. Mervyn[5] is going to penetrate Cynthia in a day or two (I hate the way he keeps *talking* about it) and I have discovered that Hilary,[6] so far from being 22, is 17, younger than Jill, and hence not nearly so depraved as I had hoped. But she has 8 Cleo Brain[7] sides and some early 5 Penis[8] records, which may contain Russell – I haven't seen them yet. So I am prepared to carry on until I get some records or fin bocqs find that she won't sell. *BUT NO LONGER THAN THAT.*

---

1. The sides Amis refers to here are 'Wipe 'em Off'/'In the House Blues'. 'Wipe 'em Off' was recorded by the Seven Gallon Jug Band, with Ed Allen (1897–74), trumpeter; Cecil Scott (1905–64), clarinettist and baritone and tenor saxophonist; Clarence Williams (1898–65), pianist and vocalist; Cyrus St Clair (1890–1955), sousaphone player. 'In the House Blues' had vocals by Bessie Smith.

2. Gillian Williams.

3. Derek Hawkins (b. 1918), English saxophonist, clarinettist; perhaps the 'Deutero-Russell' mentioned in Amis to Larkin, 15 December 1945, since his playing is like that of Russell (as suggested by 'Derrick Hawkins-Russell soli').

4. Parkes.

5. Brown.

6. The first mention of Amis's future wife, Hilary Bardwell, in the correspondence. See Notes on Recipients for biographical details.

7. Cleo Brown.

8. Five Pennies, a recording group of the late 1920s led by Red Nichols (1905–65), cornettist and bandleader.

I was terribly amused by Ruth's accaint of the conversation with Gerry[9] ('terribly' is literal here – 'When Criseyde greets him with her terrible "Fux that ye been!"')[10]. And I think the phrase 'I could not forbear to laugh in rath *hoax* rather an evil way' shows real literary ability – unless she read it somewhere or you told it to her, which I shouldn aawwwwwghrr think somehay. But there mustn't be any more of[11] this nonsense about not telling her about what I told you to tell her to tell her. Jerrie must be told all those things. After all, it isn't as if Ruth will be drawn into participating in the nastiness that went to their creation. Tell her I shall be awfully angry if G isn't told by Monday and keep on at her till she does tell her. I'm quite thrilled (so are you) by the idea of Gerry being an incestuous puerorum amatrix. Jimmy can't be more than 14 at the most. Oh I do like that, said Marsha.

Have begun It[12] – what did we say we were going to call it? – but not enough to send yet. I love it. It was funny when I went into the shop to buy an envelope for it. I kept saying I wanted a state one and only wanted one and so on until the women looked at me as if she thought I wanted it to send my french letters to the wash each week in. Yes don't they cost a lot? Of course now they're scarce there's a blak market in them – Durex as I think I told you are sending all theirs to troops.

Chain it up. Keep it still and mend it. Nobody thinks that ain't two lovely frivolous abstractions.

Kingsley Church Street sobbin'
Kingsley

Josh[13] asked to read your letter – I didn't let him – saying 'He never writes to me now'. I pass this on to you for what it isn't worth.

[TLS: Bodleian]

9. Geraldine Cunninghame.
10. See Geoffrey Chaucer, *Troilus and Criseyde* (written between 1372–1386), Book 3, line 1565; Criseyde addresses Pandarus: 'Fox that ye ben, god yeve youre herte care!'
11. This 'of' is the last word on the first page of the letter, which, with two exceptions, has been typed entirely in red. The exceptions, both in the preceding paragraph, are '*afterwards*', in the phrase '*which I was told about afterwards*' and '*BUT NO LONGER THAN THAT*', underlined in alternating red and black.
12. The 'untitled long story' outlined in Amis to Larkin, 5 February 1946.
13. Nickname of Noel Hughes (b. 1921), friend of Larkin's from King Henry VIII School and St John's; subsequently journalist, publisher.

TO PHILIP LARKIN – 25 FEBRUARY 1946

Siant knx St John's college oxford

My dear Philip,

I am writing back quickly not because I have the time to spare but because I have to do a nasty old essay for my tutor to read to-day and it is better that I reply now than in two days' time. I'm sure you understand all this. There are one or two things in you letter that cd be answered; it was a funny and nice and long one, by the way.

I laughed a lot at Yeah I think. She has produced two *dicta* since then that I regard as inalienably amusing:

I. I pick up a photograph of a dog's face from the mantelpiece by her bed, and 'I could not forbear from laughing in rather an evil way.'[1] She says: 'Ooh, don't laugh; that's the only thing I love mm.' (The 'mm' is a tiny self-deprecatory giggle.)

II. She has washed her hair. There is a tremendous amount of it. I say, Haven't you got a lot of hair, Jill? She says, No mm.

Sinthia has got mumps now, which I pretend to be very sorry about, I have told Mervyn (who hasn't had them) about orchitis.[2]

Hilary is much more brainful than H J M.[3] She has said

'I can't stand Ellington after about 1930.'

'After that I worked at some kennels with some dreadful women, two of them. They were lesbians. (Me; "Did they lezz with each other or with other people?" – geuss Who I maent eh you old Bugar I know my sort) With each other and with the dogs too. It was rather sordid.'

'Sex, sex, sex, nothing but sex all day long.'

She is seventeen. I like that. Oh yes, and one other thing. She brought some of her records in the other day. One of them was 'Georgia On My Mind', by Hoagland ('Hoagy') Carmichael.[4] That's right. On HMV magenta label. B6133. With Ellington's mystery song on the back. No, I don't mind that. Yes, she has sold it to me. For 7/6 (the price of a front and rear cycle lamp). Yes, I am glad I've got it. No, I don't suppose

1. See previous letter, Amis to Larkin, 21 February 1946.
2. Inflammation of the testicles; Mervyn is Mervyn Brown, boyfriend of Cynthia.
3. 'Hilary' is Hilary Bardwell; 'HJM' is Hilary Morris, a student at St John's.
4. Hoagy Carmichael (1899–1981), songwriter, singer, pianist, bandleader.

you are. Yes, she has got some others, nearly all cut-out and collector's items. Armstrong 'Melancholy'/Henderson 'Hot Mustard', Br. 02001 8 – eight – Cleo Brown sides: You're Thing/The Mellow, B-W/P S, Latch On/*SLOW POKE*, Love Degree/My Mezzanine.[5] Do you think I ought to buy any of those? She has some more which she is bringing in to-day.

Yes, I like hearing about Ruth and Gerry. Go on about them. G. does sound an awful little shit, but amusing too, don't you think? You do. *Has Ruth passed on my message yet*? How I hate all this Puddy talk. *YOU KNOW MY NAME'S KINGSLEY REALLY DON'T YOU*?[6] And as for us having bad effects on Ruth and G not liking us, I think G ought to know how p e r v e r t e d we both are when she would probably like us more, which I might like. Yes, I think you ought to see her. So ought I, come to that. *Bum* to that.

I suppose I ought to be glad to hear that Norman[7] has got off, and in a way I am, but only in an abstract way, insofar it is good for *anybody* not to go into the army. But I don't like thinking how pleased he and Philip[8] will be about it. And one more thing – for gods sake dont like his poems that would spoil everything. While we are being spiteful about our friends, let me record how right you were about Mervyn & the anticipating of that sort of intercourse.

I bought Queenie Leavis[9] eventually and she is sodding good.

About It[10] – I am dreadfully sorry, I know how much you are looking forward to it, but I haven't had time to finish it yet. It shd be with you by Thursday though. It isn't as good yet as I had hoped, but I'm sure it will get better. I like the jass bits.

5. Henderson is Fletcher Henderson (1897–1952), pianist and bandleader. The full titles of the Cleo Brown songs are: 'You're a Heavenly Thing'/'The Stuff is Here and it's Mellow', 'Boogie Woogie'/'Pelican Stomp', 'Love in the First Degree'/'My Gal Mezzanine', 'Latch On'/ 'Slow Poke' (addressed to the singer's eponymous dog). Amis has typed '*SLOW POKE*' in red.

6. Amis has typed this underlined, capitalised phrase in red.

7. Norman Iles (b.1922), Larkin's tutorial-mate in English at St John's College (1940–42), one of 'The Seven', who in 1945 registered as a conscientious objector 'on anarchistic and humanitarian grounds' (*LL*, p.xxix); since 1949 he has been variously employed as a social worker, teacher and lecturer in Further Education colleges in Nottingham and Lancashire.

8. Brown, also a conscientious objector.

9. *Fiction and the Reading Public* (1932) by Q.D. Leavis (1906–81), literary critic, wife of F.R. Leavis (1895–1978), a key influence on Cambridge English.

10. The untitled long story Amis and Larkin were collaborating on, later titled 'I Would Do Anything for You'.

What do you know of Snub Mosely's Blues at High Noon/Art Tatums Lonesome Graveyard Blues?[11] It sounds good.

whats gretas operation

I'll tell Josh.[12]

Kingsley potato head
Kingsley

I roared at *Maddy's* YES.[13]

[TLS: Bodleian].

TO PHILIP LARKIN – 12 MARCH 1946

St. John's College, Oxford.

My dear Philip,

Thank you for your letter which arrived this morning and for your forbearance about me being so nasty about replying to the one bf woof before that one. I am feeling a little low at the moment, chiefly because I have got to go to one of those dances at the Rand-olf[1] to-night, with Hilary (who has got a new evening dress), and it has cost me 12/6, and I don't really want to go, very much, at all. But you will know why I am going: the quasi-Ruth implications[2] of this business are coming out and I want to push them back again but cant quite see how I am going to do that, you see.

How funny about those dance records of Bill Elliot's.[3] I hope they do bring out those ones you say, though I can't see why the fucky *nell*

11. Snub Mosley (1905–81), trombonist, slide saxophonist, singer, bandleader, composer; Art Tatum (1909–56), pianist.

12. Noel Hughes.

13. Ms addition.

---

1. The Randolph Hotel in Oxford.

2. A product of Hilary's age (she was only seventeen, a year older than Ruth Bowman when she first met Larkin).

3. Bill Elliot was a journalist on the staff of the *Melody Maker*, at the time a musical trade magazine, editing its jazz section. Under the magazine's auspices he helped to set up a number of Rhythm Clubs in England (where jazz records would be played and raffles held). The University Rhythm Club in Oxford was founded by Elliot and others in 1945, and at its first meeting at the Taylorian attracted over two hundred undergraduates; Oxford was the first university in Britain to form such a club.

they can't do reissues. I should have thought it wd have been cheaper for the gramophone company. What's EMI? No, I don't know Newton's The Sunrise, but I think Indiana was one of the Coleman sides.[4] It is worth buying though not sensational. Have you ever heard of a band called Boots and his Buddies, by the way? There was a side by them in Drawda for 1/6 and I got it:[5] 'Riffs' (they aren't); big-band stuff very noisy but apparently genuine, with some goodish solos, and a really respectable trumpet. No?

Anna feels rather guilty about It.[6] She has been so busy this week with her various girls that she hasn't had much time. She hopes to get the next instalment off by the week-end. Fosdick,[7] I am alarmed to learn, is ME. When she found Marsha had taken number sixty-nine she nearly broke a shoulder-strap with laughter.

Graham has got mumps and gone off to the isolation hospital about them. Jill wrote him a letter which he got this morning before going to the hospital. She and Cynthia gave him a pair of brushes, wire, drummers', for his birthday. At the party Jill broke Oh Peter, Pigfoot, and Shight Like Pis, and cracked Some Heart/There'll Made.[8] Norman and the male Hilary came up that week-end and showed up at the party. Jill liked Norman a lot. His hair is even longer. He is getting all religious and talked of becoming a lay preacher. He says I have a bad conscience which will prevent me from being happy in a wrong job however much money they pay me. I do not think he isv wop is very

4. Frankie Newton (1906–54) and Bill Coleman (1904–81), trumpeters.

5. Boots and His Buddies recorded forty-two titles in San Antonio, Texas between 1935 and 1938; its leader was the drummer Clarence 'Boots' Douglas (b.1908); 'Drawda' was Drawda Hall, a bookshop in Oxford which also sold records, opposite University College.

6. The story, later titled 'I Would Do Anything for You', which Amis and Larkin were collaborating on; 'Anna Lucasta' was the authorial persona Amis adopted for the story, to match Larkin's 'Brunette Coleman'. Amis described the story as follows: 'it was about two beautiful lesbians in something like Oxford. The interest was divided between jazz and lesbianism. In their digs there was a mysterious cupboard full of jazz records Philip and I had heard of but never heard. It was Mr So-and-so who had left them there and might come back for them one day. We were especially interested in Wild Bill Davison, whom we'd read about, and one of the girls – Marsha, who went in for avowals of love – found "On a Blues Kick". Philip admired it so much he said he'd rather she found anything but that, and wrote in the next paragraph, "As the heavy steel needle, which they never changed, clumped into the first groove"' (from an interview with Andrew Motion, quoted in *Life*, p. 86).

7. Presumably a character in the story, which has not survived.

8. The records broken were 'Oh Peter' (Billy Banks), 'Gimme a Pigfoot' (by Bessie Smith, recorded in 1933), the much-recorded 'Tight Like This' and 'Some Day Sweetheart'/'There'll be Some Changes Made'.

right about that. His manners are much better and he was almost inoffensive. But not quite. Hilary was stupider and more boring than ever. But I was telling you about Jill's letter. I read it. It started 'Hello Graham!' and contained the sentence 'Did you get the rythem brushes alright.' Yes, that is all right, thank you.

I must go and have a bath and then get tight enough not to mind this horrid dance so much. Oh yes, and Jill's letter ended 'Yours Gillian (I think!)'.

Hilary (the young lady) is having her portrait painted in the nude. That's right. No, not by me. She said, Did I think she was right to agree to having it done? I said, Yes, I thought she was. I'm sorry to have to tell you this, but it's a man who's doing the painting.

Kingsley Jumped a Rabbit

Mervyn is going to marry Sinthia[9]

[TL: Bodleian]

TO PHILIP LARKIN – 18 MARCH 1946

as from St John's Clge, Oxford.

My dear Philip,

Thank you for your two letters and postcard especially the postcard which made me laugh very much oh and especially the pin up which both Anna and I liked very much, especially Anna. For your own information, by the way, Anna's surname is Lucasta.

I am living up in this town for another week because I do not want to go to the town where is my home, and Hilary's term goes on for another week after ours ends. H looks as if she is going to be sensible about things, which is a great comfort. I am having a nice time, drinking, smewking (I have taken it up again because it is so nice: 10 a day), and making (at present) unconsummated love. And if only I cd do some writing, then I wd do some writing. The F[ortune] P[ress], by the way, are silent. Is this a good or a bad sign? Next term I am having a collection[1]

9. The marriage never took place.

1. College examination.

on a fine old relic of Anglo-Saxon culture; that remarkable survival of the civilisation from which our own, in however indirect a fashion, is derived; I refer of course to the anonymous, crass, purblind, infantile, *featureless* HEAP OF GANGRENED ELEPHANT'S SPUTUM, 'Barewolf'.[2] i dont like that

I was very interested by Ruth's account of the Cuninghame visit. I don't relly *focks* really think that all the sisters can be as nasty as hx she says. And since Jimmy[3] can't have been more than about 3 when I saw him last, and I wasn't homo then (What?), I don't see how I can be said 'still' to be likely to like Jimmy. And I don't like gold teeth. A Polish whore I knew had them, and I didn't like them then, eether. (In answer to your unspoken query, no, I didn't, an' I din't min') [. . .]

I met Costin[4] in the street the other day when I was with H and he raised his hat. Or perhaps he merely caught it when his erection had already knocked it off.

Graham and I have made up 'Jill's Blues' of which the last verse is:

My man's gone down to the river Lord (/baby)
he's standing on the brink
Whos the woman made him do it Lord? it's me, I think.

Pattern conversation with H:

'Haven't you ever slept with a woman?'

'Yes.'

'Good, good; yes yeah.' (She was saying 'yes yeah' *before* she heard me say it)

Send It to John's soonest.

Kingsley Round My Bed
Kingsley

[TLS: Bodleian]

2. Beneath this word Amis has added in pen: 'aaoh! ach! aaooh!' The words 'crass, purblind, infantile, *featureless* HEAP OF GANGRENED ELEPHANT'S SPUTUM' have been typed in red.

3. Jimmy Cunninghame, younger brother of Geraldine and her four sisters.

4. See Amis to Larkin, 25 November 1944, note 7.

TO PHILIP LARKIN – 24 MARCH 1946

26, Shrublands Road, Berkhamsted, Herts.

My dear Philip,

Here I am then, in the bad town and not liking to be in it at all. And there is nothing that has happened that you would be liking to be being told about about it. But I will do my best. I don't know whether you want to get your job in Saithampton, but if you do, then I hope you get it. What is the job about exactly? Will you have to talk to men and ladies with your voice? The last time that I had to do that, I was wearing a brown suit, and I found, that I didn't like, having to do that, at all. [. . .]

I have perused It with a good deal of discreditable avidity since arriving home. Anna had to change her undies after reading it. She syas byas myers mares mezz *says* that if that is whanging the gold then let it be whanged like that, then. She suggests:

1. She now gets on with *VI*, which would be the painting plus oddities like description of Early Morning Blues – Marsha's favourite record – and something abt. Jennifer's sketches, all this to end Phase I.

2. Brunette does V, which would comprise Mady's visit about the easel and Jennifer's school-friends.

3. There ought to be more satire on rotten old painters: Mister Graham Sutherland[1] and *Pickarso* – oh ergh jaycee *wept* – were too good not to be followed up. *Much* too good.

Anna is a little worried about how far she is to go in the painting. I told her not to worry and go as far as she wants to. She is also wondering what to call you-know-what. I suggested 'crotch', but though she laughed at this she said it gave the wrong associations. And when I said she could probably get round it by euphemism or periphrasis, she went red and stamped her foot, and said that I was stupid. She wants to know what Brunette thinks about this. I said I would ask you.

The jass music is spreading like a great benign tumour over our little social circle. Cynthia has conceived a passion for Mezz; Jill said 'Billy Banks and Billie Holiday; which is the man and which is the woman who sings like a little girl?' To hear her mention the name 'Billy

---

1. Graham Sutherland (1903–80), British artist.

Banks' seems to me to represent a victory of some kind, though I'm not sure what. And Hilary, of course, is continually giving evidence of appreciation. She liked Good Berlin, and I wd lend her Mr Trains[2] if I had it. Moreover, she keeps showing that she would be interested in things to do with notes and words and celluloid whth *bucks* whether I were there or not, which I must say that I rather like. And I think she will, too, if you see what I mean. (You do.)[3] [. . .]

[TL: Bodleian]

TO PHILIP LARKIN – 29 MARCH 1946

26 Shrublands Road, Berkhamsted, Herts.

My dear Philip,

Thank you for your letter which entertained me a lot in different sorts of ways. *For*-ne-*kay*-shon & *hore*-mung-ger (the double g) made me laugh a lot. Abt staying: the outlook seems black at the moment, since various people are coming to stay and the week-end before Easter my parents, and not I, want us to go away to the sea-coast. But if we don't, could you come then? I will let you know what looks like going to happen here. [. . .]

Ref It:[1] it will have to hang fire for a few days I fear. Anna has begun VI, which focks[2] contains among other things an account of Mr. Davis. She agrees about In and says she can probably manage it. Brunette is awfully right abt Madynmarsha.

I have had two letters from Hilary.

". . . vaguely trying to solve the problem of existence, we had tea at lions . . .

". . . thankyou so much for the Fats record . . ."

". . . 'The Map of Love' . . ."

". . . went up on the downs on my pony befor breakfast . . ."

2. The Christopher Isherwood novels *Goodbye to Berlin* (1939) and *Mr Norris Changes Trains* (1935).

3. The letter is incomplete.

---

1. In the absence of the manuscript of the story it is impossible to identify references to episodes and characters (e.g. 'VI', 'In', 'Mr Davis').

2. A response to the uneven typing of 'which', caused by a slip of the paper.

Yes yes yes yes yes yes yes yes yes

Somebody once told me, that Dorothy Parker,[3] was good, at writing, short stories The other day I bought a book of hers for a shilling, and I am sorry now. It is not only that the stuff is TOO OBVIOUS AND ELEMENTARY TO BE WORTH SAYING AT ALL, nor that THE DIALOGUE THINKS IT IS SO FUCKING GOOD AND IS THE SORT OF THING YOU REJECT IF SOMEBODY WANTS TO PUT IT IN THE SCHOOL MAGAZINE, nor that YOU JUST DON'T *CARE*; no, not only that; there are a lot of *F L A T L I E S* in it too:

"they hate you as soon as they are sure of you" (men–women) NOOOOOOOOOO.

"yes here we are, she said; aren't we?" NO, we are NOT.

When I had finished looking at the book, and had closed it up again, I went and looked into the lavatory-pan.

I am sorry this is short and not-very-good, but I have not much time. It shd reach you next Thursday if all goes well

Kingsley whatdyoucallem
Kingsley

Tomorrow we are taking Jill to the boat-race[4]

[TLS: Bodleian]

TO PHILIP LARKIN – 1 APRIL 1946

26 Shrublands Rd, Bad Town, Herts. April Tools' Day[1]

My dear Philip,

Thank you for your letter and the *redolent* whore's-piss thing which I have only read once but think is marvellous and must read again. I am a little pissed-up, you understand (pay no attention for me), and so this is porbably quite a good time to write a let- bwhaggs[2] -ter to

3. Dorothy Parker (1893–1967), American humorist, story writer, poet.
4. MS addition.

1. '*April Tools' Day*' is a MS addition.
2. Amis has drawn arrows from this word to the preceding typo 'porbably', which he has presumably just caught.

you. I doe-noe that there is actually much to dfs say, but I will only speak right on. Right on er-hw*aaaart*? [. . .]

I know *exactly* what you mean about getting bored with Ruth when you cannot etc. When these things have reached a certain stage they must be completed. Why don't you have it all out with her (that's right)? I really think it might be a good idea. I certainly don't think there is anything even a little wrong with you in feeling bored; all wrong-thinking people will agree with me. I know so well what you mean because I had a similar experience with June, though it went even farther without than I hope for your self-respect that you have gone without. And however fond I am of a young lady I like to do things away from her occasioanally fx which is only the same sort of thing as playing other records than Spider Crawl when Sp. C. is still one's favourite record. Let her be cross abt week-end. I still dont know whether it is all right but I will let you know. What I want to know is: did she ever tell Gerry what I said about her and those wucking parents of hers? Because she should have done so . . . I was amused and even a little flattered to hear I haunt your meetings, though I can well imagine that she is neither.

Anna is awfully sorry about It. She doesn't think she can do it till next week now, though when she does she promises a real rip-snwhoreter.

I *saw* the bleeding boat race on Saturday. So did Graham and so did Hilary and so did Jill. An African gentleman held her up to see. I liked that.

We had an elction *corks*[3] too. No Labour candidates got in.

Teddy Grace[4] has a brown skin. I have heard the Teagarden ones and you are right.

Now I must go to bed, and read myself to sleep with Richard Churchurchurchuuurrrgh[5]

meanest kind of kingsley
Kingsley

[TLS: Bodleian]

3. 'Caucus'. In March 1946, in a by-election for the English Universities constituency, the Conservative candidate defeated the incumbent independent. In the nation at large, Attlee's Labour government, fresh from its landslide victory of 26 July 1945, was laying the foundations of the modern welfare state.

4. Teddy Grace (1905–92), vocalist.

5. Richard Church (1893–1972), poet, biographer, autobiographer, novelist, publisher (at J. M. Dent, where Dylan Thomas was among his writers).

TO PHILIP LARKIN – 6 APRIL 1946

26 Shrublands Road, Berkhamsted, Herts.

My dear Philip,

Unsolicited words: it is a beautiful day and I think I will write. Anna is really responsible for this: she is afraid Brunette is angry about her delay with It and asks me to assure B. that she wants to get on with It but can't – VI is not an easy episode, is half-finished, is going to be good, will be long, thorough. Marsha tells Jennifer about Davis in it, by the way, so Brunette can put the idea of doing it out of her mind if it was there at all. Anna was humble about all this and kept talking about circumstances she wasn't able to alter. [. . .]

My parents aren't here now, and so I can't ask them what's happening next week-end, but I will tell you as soon as anything is known.

I wish that man had burned the manuscript of Barewolf.

Give my love to Ruth. Do something about it, man. If I were in your shoes, I would . . . An efficient Elephant can undress in fifteen seconds.

kingsley why don't you leave me alone?
Kingsley

[TLS: Bodleian]

TO PHILIP LARKIN – 11 APRIL 1946

Darling Brunette –

You must hate me for being such a perfect *age* with the thing, but my dear you've just no conception of what it's been like here for the past ten days. The house has been absolutely *over-run* with young men – nasty friends of Kingsley's, and I just haven't had a minute to call my own. Anyway, the point is that after the most *immense* labour I've somehow managed to finish VI. I am going to persuade Kingsley to bring it up with him on Saturday, though he looked very cross when I mentioned it and asked what would happen if he were knocked down in the street and they found it among his belongings. I can understand what he means, because it's really rather *hot*, if you know what I mean. But you shall judge of this. I must say the bit I liked most in it was Marsha's reverie while she is being painted; so much so that it was almost an effort (though not quite, darling) to do the other bit. I hope you'll like it.

The bits I liked best in IV were:

'"pig's ears"'

Fosdick – especially 'uncomfortably hot surface'

'it makes me feel so cheap' (I *loved* that)

Picasso (Kingsley had to go and laugh in the lavetry*)

A bientot.

All my love, dearest,

Anna.

* Of course I can spell "lavatory". Really darling there's no need to try and make me like you more – surely you know that?

[TLS: Bodleian]

TO PHILIP LARKIN – 18 APRIL 1946

The Wrong Town, Herts

My dear Philip,

This is not going to be very long I am afraid as I have got to go out to tea with a young lady; so charming ('Like a picture, Herr Issyvoo')[1], whom I met this morning at her mother's instigation. Somehow I don't feel we are going to get along all that well: it was betrayed that I had literary ambitions, to which she remarked: 'I love arty people' er *awr* . . . ah-eeh mmm ooooh er-beeeeeeeeeeeeeeeeeee.[2]

I didn't have a lot of enjoyment on my birthday. There was a copy of Alun Spweis *bunks* Spewis[3] from Hilary: 'Ha Ha Among the Trumpets'

---

1. Herr Isherwood; a locution of Fräulein Schroeder, the plump landlady in Christopher Isherwood's *Goodbye to Berlin* (1939).

2. The last eight of these 'e's have been typed in red.

3. Alun Lewis (1915–44), Welsh poet and short-story writer; *Ha! Ha! among the Trumpets*, a volume of poems, was published posthumously in 1945, after Lewis died on active service in Burma.

(nim-fo-ma-*ni*-er-c'l eck-*sess*-is) with a message written on half the back of a blank telegram form – 'Darling I do hope you havent got this. Is it nice being 24 yrs.' In the afternoon we saw 'The Horn is Green'[4] with Bette Davis (*saf*-fic le-*ay*-zo(ng)), which you must never permit yourself to visit. The nastiest part was pretending to my parents that I liked it. It was American-Welsh, with miners' choirs, examinations for Oxfawd *fook* you to goodness, and the poetry of daily life unspoiled by civilisation (*kar*-nal con-*cew*-piss-ents).

I have finished pride and prejudice now and think it rather nasty on the whole though not as nasty as you think it is.[5]

Did you hear that pno programme last night? yancey sullivan shearing smith ('selected by the British Hot Record Society in 1928') and tony short;[6] who is he?

It was nice of you and Ruth to send me that bellygramme; I got it on returning from London that awful to-day he *can't* be twenty-*four* mummy *can* he it just isn't *pos*sible is it doesn't look a *day* over twenty wswswswswswswswswswswswswswswswswswswswswswswswswswsws wswswswswswswswswswswswswswswswswswswswswswswswswswsws wswswswswswswswswswswswswswswswswswswswswswswswswswsws wswswswswswswswswswswswswswswswswswswswswswswswswswsws

kingsley low down dirty shame
Kingsley

[TLS: Bodleian]

4. *The Corn is Green* (1945), directed by Irving Rapper; based on the play by Emlyn Williams.

5. For Amis on Jane Austen see the title essay in *What Became of Jane Austen? and Other Essays* (London: Jonathan Cape, 1970), pp. 13–17.

6. The pianists Amis refers to are Jimmy Yancey (1894–1951), Joe Sullivan (1906–71), George Shearing (b. 1919) and Pine Top Smith. Tony Short appears in neither *NGDJ* nor John Chilton, *Who's Who in Jazz: Storyville to Swing* (London: Macmillan, 1972).

TO PHILIP LARKIN – 24 APRIL 1946

Meanest Kind of Town

My dear Philip,

You are a bit of a scēaȝ-bēaȝ,[1] not writing to me like this, but I expect Ruth and Easter have a lot to do with it. Tommorow I go to the good town for notes and words, and shall become happier like that. For the last many days I have been 'doing' Beowulf and this has made me unhappy. I am not caring very much about the men in those words, and I can't *stand* Wheelthyow.[2] But I have 'Poet of Spring', by Richard Beech-Burch,[3] as my bedside book now. I don't like Henry Green[4] much, by the way: it takes me too long to understand what he means by the things he says, and Hilary's nickname is Hilly. I will send it back to you soon. [...]

I'm sorry but this cannot go on any longer now, as I have to swot up the gen on the knotty spots of old man Beowulf fockqxs Time you dropped me a line, old son. The young heart-throb sugars off to the Big City to-day, I trow? Hope I haven't dropped one. Must close down now; shall I see you among the old dreaming spires next semester? yer hawrabble pawcksy sponk-aiyed busturrrd[5]

kingsley with a feelin'
Kingsley

[TLS: Bodleian]

---

1. 'Middle English' (Amis is parodying the West Midlands dialect of *Sir Gawain and the Green Knight*) for 'shag-bag'.

2. Wealtheow, wife of Hrothgar, King of the Danes and builder of the great hall of Heorot, in *Beowulf.*

3. Untraceable, probably a joke about Richard Church (see Amis to Larkin, 1 April 1946, note 5); James Booth notes that one of the schoolgirls in 'Trouble at Willow Gables' was initially called Mary Burch, before becoming Mary Beech (personal communication, 8 February 1999).

4. Henry Green (Henry Vincent Yorke) (1905–73), novelist and businessman; among his best-known novels are *Living* (1929), *Party Going* (1939) and *Loving* (1945).

5. 'Yer hawrabble . . . busturrrd' in red.

TO PHILIP LARKIN – 29 APRIL 1946

The Good Town

My dear Philip,

Thank you for your two letters and your card. Now it has been my turn to be a bit of a schaeg-baeg, and I am sorry, but I have had things to do: a collection paper on Beowulf ('Though unsatisfactory as narrative, the poem often shows great descriptive power' bum bum bimma bomma bum bum *bum*), the usual start-of-term scouring of the no-record shops, drinking, smewking, and cetera. Now however I am feeling better after handing in my paper and being about to light a cigarette. [. . .]

I am sorry about Ruth,[1] though I don't see what else could have happened. I should think that you are right in what you say, and there will be some shouting (There'll be some crying out when he's come there). Well better luck with a Capetal f next Time you hav a go, shuld hav thuoght a Blocke with yor iddeas wuld hav been beter at Pickin them, still, you nevre no til you try, thats what I allways say. I think the most pornographic sentence on your postcard (which I enjoyed a lot) was 'From Teen-Age to Maturity'.

Twelve Bad Men:
1. The Author of Beowulf (capt.)
2. The Head of the Fortune Press
3. Moore
4. Chaucer
5. Ladnier
6. Warwick Deeping
7. The Man Who Wrote 'A Tree Grows in Brooklyn'
8. Woody Herman
9. Henry (wicket-keeper)

---

1. For Larkin's problems with Ruth Bowman at this period see his letter to J.B. Sutton, 7 April 1946, in *LL*, p. 116: 'I find that once I "give in" to another person, as I have given in not altogether voluntarily, but almost completely, to Ruth, there is a slackening and a dulling of the peculiar artistic fibres . . . Time and again I feel that before I write anything else at all I must drag myself out of the water, shake myself dry and sit down on a lonely rock to contemplate glittering loneliness. Marriage, of course (since you mentioned marriage), is impossible if one wants to do this.' See also Amis to Larkin, 5 May 1946.

10. Mr. Cunningham
11. Milton

Twelfth Man: To be selected from George Gershwin, John Heath-Stubbs, Browning, Arthur Koestler, Jimmy Lunceford, John Redwood.[2]

I see that H C Bailey has written a book called 'The Wrong Man'.[3] Nancy is the girl in Berkhamsted I told you about in my letter: the one who couldn't believe I was really 24.[4] She's quite nice. eh

Now I must go away and clash my teeth in some food. Tell Brunette to get on with I You. Backwords will be quickly backworded as I haven't got a tut till Friday. Gimme all the service you got.

kingsley galore
Kingsley

[TLS: Bodleian]

TO PHILIP LARKIN – 5 MAY 1946

The Good Town

My dear Philip,

Thank you for your long and funny letter and I wish I had written sooner but there. I'm glad you're so pleased about my poems. You won't feel like that when you read them. Some of them are so dreadful

2. Among the 'Twelve Bad Men': 'Moore', probably W.G. Moore, of St John's; Tommy Ladnier (1900–39), trumpeter; Warwick Deeping (1877–1950), popular novelist (discussed in 'Pater and Old Chap', in *What Became of Jane Austen? and Other Questions*, pp. 37–41), best known for *Sorrell and Son* (1925); 'The Man [sic] Who Wrote "A Tree Grows in Brooklyn" ', the novelist Betty Smith (b. 1904), though the 1945 film version (the novel was published in 1943) was co-written by a man and a woman, Frank Davis and Tess Slesinger; Woody Herman (1913–87), clarinettist, saxophonist, bandleader and singer; Henry, a porter at St John's (see Amis to Larkin, c. 26 October–6 November 1943); Mr Cunningham, mentioned nowhere else in the correspondence (perhaps another porter, or Geraldine Cunningham's father); John Heath-Stubbs (b. 1918), poet, first published in Sidney Keyes and Michael Meyer, eds, *Eight Oxford Poets* (London: Routledge, 1941), which excluded Larkin; Jimmy Lunceford (1902–47), bandleader; John Redwood (b. 1923), reading medicine at St John's (1941–47).

3. *The Wrong Man* (1946) by H.C. Bailey (1878–1961), English author and journalist.

4. See Amis to Larkin, 18 April 1946.

and senseless[1] that I can hardly bear to be in the same room as them. Now I am feverishly trying to get 'enough for a volume' written and finding the going tough. I don't know what I'm going to call it. 'Last Poems' would fit as well as anything (I can't write, very much, at all, now) but it's been done before as far as I remember. I roared at the old scag.

I think about Ruth (none o' my business o' boy bu' i's f' y' own good) that the 2 things (lack of *kernt* and objections to sharing) acted on one another: if these things are successful on the physical plane (*mass*-ter-*bay*-shee-oh per *ay*-n'm) one wants to share all one has, for a little while anyway. I suppose that is a further objection to it. I didn't know about that when I met Elisabeth: that one wants to share all, etc. I do now. To revert: I feel sorry for her about this, but her attitude asked for defeat (wēan āhsodon) as women's always do, or seem to. Somehay I can't see myself appearing to lunch with her & Jerrie, but you never know (Oh yes you do).

To-day I saw Teddy Simpson[2] in the quad: he has returned from war-service.

'Good morning, Teddy.'

'*Christ*, er –'

'Amis.'

'*Jesus* yes. Hallo.'

What was the other hawrubble thing? You only mentioned the trip to Swissland. I loved the birth control thing: 'spirituo-sentimental' exactly describes the tone of these silly, ecstatic, *wrong* books. There will be a parody.

What has happened to It? Anna is always asking me about it, and gets pettish when I tell her it'll be here any day now. I loved the Bad men; as far as I can see there are two organisations we have to deal with: Henry Paine Ltd, Inc. (identical with the International Society of Bad Men), and the affiliated but discrete body, the World Federation of Nasty Friends (headquarters, Oxford, Eng.).

One nice thing has happened: I can take 5 schools papers instead of 9, being a sex-service man. I shall do Beowulf, becos I've done so

1. 'Senseless' typed in red.

2. Teddy Simpson (b. 1922) read medicine at St John's College (1940–44, 1946–49); see *LL*, p. 189n, quoting Amis: 'Bit of a prototype for Christopher Warner in *Jill*, in his apparently sneering superior manner that is.'

much work on it, and Chaucer Spenser & Milton for similar reasons, and 2 modern papers, but I shall *leave out* The Owl and the Shitingale[3] and its friends, and I shall *leave out* Shakespeare, and I shall L E A VE O U T[4] philology, and this makes me *pochkqxs* vairy happy. Don't forget about It. I get a funny feelin runnin da-arn mar *sparn*.

kingsley stack o'
Kingsley

[TLS: Bodleian]

TO PHILIP LARKIN – 13 MAY 1946

colldiiobaptoxon

My dear Philip,

Thank you for your two lots of words. The reason why I have been long this time is chiefly Hilary. We have been arguing for the past week about sleeping in the same bed as each other. First she said no, and I said she would have to say yes, then she said yes, and I said I had forced her into it and what she meant was no, then she said no, and I feel hurt and angry and disappointed and am trying to make her say yes, and there for the moment the matter rests. It has absorbed more of my attention and energy (which should have gone into singingwords) than I think is right and this increases my bitterness. If only one could be ruthless about these things! Which brings up Monsr. Montherlant.[1] Though his feelings are our feelings, it occurs to me that what is interesting is not that that is what we think, but that that is what we do not say. Women appear to me as basically dull, but as basically pathetic too

3. *The Owl and the Nightingale*, anonymous Middle-English poem (early thirteenth century).

4. '*Leave out*' and 'L E A VE O U T' typed in red; Amis has drawn two arrows from '*pochkqxs*' in the next line to 'VE' (because of the missed spacing).

---

1. Henri de Montherlant (1896–1972), French novelist and dramatist, introduced to Amis by Larkin. For Larkin's view of de Montherlant, see 'The Girls', in *Required Writing: Miscellaneous Pieces 1955–1982* (London: Faber and Faber, 1983), pp. 260–2: 'The four novels collectively known as *Les Jeunes Filles (or The Girls)* written by Henri de Montherlant in the 1930s . . . mount a colossal barrage against women. They are naturally inferior, haters of reality ('I don't want to think of it'); they cling and make a virtue of suffering; they get everything second-hand' (p. 260).

(vide poor little Greta's[2] letter, which nearly made me crar), and while this makes us annoyed, it still doesn't allow us to say rude things to them, about them. It is one's very indifference to their feelings that turns one's anger into pity a-bim a-bom a-bem-bammy-bum. I liked a lot hearing about Jeri and Hazel Ems and Mary Hill.[3] I should like to meet some of those young ladies with myself on one day.

The other morning a lot of old dance records came into Taphouses[4] from a man who had got tired of them and wanted 2/6 each for them, fibre played. Hilary, who met me with the Venuti-Lang A Y G/F B[5] under her arm (that didn't make me like her better) led me and Mervyn to the scene and Mervyn got a lot of red nickles and Goodman, and *I* got

Venuti-Lang B S B/S S – an *un*shagged copy

Swing 8, by Hy. Allen Jr[6] – not Feelin' Drazey, though; there's some Carmichael nastiness on the back. I like it quite a lot.

Beale St by the Charleston Chasers,[7] feechering Teagarden and Goodman

Davenport Blues, by Rollini,[8] which is a tune I adore, feechering Teagarden and Goodman.

Ridin' Walkin'/Won't Please,[9] which I like, especially R B W, feechering Teagarden.

Bugle Call Rag (Voc S. 12); not good but it was the record that was warped in Bruges, and I got it for old times' sake kracqxs,[10] feechering Teagarden and Goodman

2. Larkin's assistant in the library at Wellington.

3. Geraldine Cunninghame, Hazel Amess and Mary Hill, another friend and fellow student of Ruth Bowman's at King's College, London, remembered by her as 'moody and unpredictable but at her best a wonderfully entertaining and sardonic companion' (personal communication, 26 January 1999).

4. A music shop in the Cornmarket, Oxford.

5. 'Venuti-Lang' refers to a long-standing musical partnership between Joe Venuti (1903–78), violinist, and Eddie Lang (1902–33), guitarist. The Venuti-Lang sides referred to here and below are 'After You've Gone'/'Farewell Blues' and 'Beale Street Blues'/'Someday Sweetheart'.

6. Henry 'Red' Allen.

7. The name given to various groups recording on the Columbia label between 1925 and 1931, most often led by Red Nichols.

8. Art Rollini (b. 1912), tenor saxophonist, brother of Adrian Rollini (1904–56), bass saxophonist; Art played in the band of the clarinettist and composer Benny Goodman (1909–86) from 1934 to 1939; Jack Teagarden (1905–64), trombonist, singer.

9. 'Ridin' but Walkin''/'Won't You Get off it, Please'.

10. Amis has typed 'kracqxs' in red.

Tailefpynne Blves,[11] I like; Mervyn saw it first, played it over and gave it to me, feechering Teagarden.

I was gladdened by this as you can guess. H. gave me Doin' the Voom Voom – did you say once that you *liked* this? – and a Spk Hghs negrorch record – Firebird/Donegal Cradle Song,[12] with some good Hawkins THATS WHAT I SAID. She gave me those records yesterday when Christopher[13] and I went to tea with her father,[14] an extraordinary old man like a music-loving lavatory attendant. They have a nice house but apart from H. seem to be a family of ruffians.

Talking of Hilary, the other one[15] came here over the week-end, invited himself to tea, slept on my couch, messed up my room, ate my chocolate biscuits without asking, bored and irritated me beyond all measure, and announced his attention of coming up next term. He is getting £50 a month for doing sweet fuck-all, and wears a bomb-disposal badge he isn't entitled to. The reason I mind the last thing is that I am a coward, and the bomb men were not cowards, and Hilary is no less of a coward than I am. Christopher hated him at first sight. He said he found humour which consisted of contradicting what others said annoying to him. That is trueish. Also appearing next term, as I've told you I think, are Walter Widdowson, Layborn, Dai Williams, Ian Davie, and Nick, and Denis Frankel.[16] The Type[17] will be by then a formidable quasi-military organisation. One thing about Hilary I forgot; I told

11. 'Tailspin Blues', recorded in 1929 by Red McKenzie (1899–1948), singer, entertainer, promoter, and the group he founded in 1924, the Mound City Blue Blowers, with McKenzie on paper and comb and Teagarden on trombone. The Elizabethan 's' of 'Tailefpynne' is created by typing a 'j' over an 'f'.

12. 'Spk Hghs negrorch' is Spike Hughes and his Negro Orchestra (later All American Orchestra), which included Henry 'Red' Allen and Coleman Hawkins.

13. Tosswill.

14. Leonard Sidney Bardwell (1886–1967), an official in the Ministry of Agriculture.

15. Hilary Morris.

16. All undergraduates at St John's. J.B. Widdowson (b. 1922) read Moderations (1941–42, 1946–48), served as printer of the Oxford University Labour Club *Bulletin* when Amis was its editor (1942), later became a public-school headmaster in Gloucester; for Layborn, see Amis to Larkin, 25 November 1944, note 11; Dai Williams was Idris David Glyn Williams (1923–75), at St John's 1941–42, 1946–48, and one of 'The Seven' (he read law and eventually became a barrister); Ian Davie (b. 1924) read Theology (1942–43, 1946–49), wrote poetry (he won the Newdigate Prize in 1949), and later became a schoolteacher; Dennis Frankel (1925–72), described by Amis as 'arty . . . fancied by Costin', read PPE (1942–43, 1947–48), became a solicitor, and died of cancer aged forty-seven (see Amis to Thwaite, 5 May 1991).

17. This is the only reference to 'The Type' in the correspondence; neither Thwaite nor Motion nor Amis's surviving friends from St John's (at least those I have consulted) know what it was.

Philip[18] he (H) wanted to see him (P) and he (P) said *tuckles* he (P) didn't want to see him (H), which made me laugh. Norman is on the land and looking very healthy, according to Hilary.

Graham said the other day that he thought Hawkins's Body and Soul (3 solid choruses of glucous, suppurating toss) was better than the Banks sides. I said I didn't think so, at all, really. You must write hima sht letter and tell him not to be such a wrong man about that.

People's jazz tastes are funny, though. Mervyn thinks that the three jazz kings are Armstrong, Goodman and Hawkins; Graham thinks that Hawkins is better than Freeman;[19] Roger [Partington] thinks Allen's Body and Soul is good (I don't). Did you hear Huddie Leadbetter,[20] by the way? They all called him Hewdie, wch annoi'd mee, in spite of the fact that he called himself Huddie on one of the records. He reminded me a bit of Sleepy Jno. Incestes[21] but the prog had a lot too much to do with folk music, reminding me at times of Indian music, and I didn't like his 15-bar way of singing a blues. Did you hear it?

I am back on Chaucer now. Do you know, I don't believe I like that man very much? There was never anybody who so unswervingly refrained from doing what his admirers are unanimous in declaring he did do. But we know what we think about that, don't we, old boy? Yes, old boy, we do. *J.* Maclaren-Toss;[22] I like him. Hilary's favourite record is Oh Peter (You're so nice) *and she says the best parts are the piano solo and the clarinet solo.*[23]

I have been doing this for a long time now and shall have to cease. Tell Brunette not to be such a lazy little cat about Iwdafy (a Welsh girl?). Poor little Greta: I am very big made (or bonny) . . . I should like my clothes to make me look slimmer than I am, – *poor* little *bleeder*. Anna enjoyed the pin-up, but asks whether it isn't perhaps the weeniest bit *vulgar*?

kingsley vibraphone
Kingsley

[TLS: Bodleian]

18. Brown.

19. Bud Freeman (1906–91), tenor saxophonist.

20. Huddie Ledbetter ('Leadbelly') (1885–1949), singer.

21. Sleepy John Estes (1899–1977), singer.

22. Julian Maclaren-Ross (1912–64), author of novels, short stories, translations; the model for the doomed literary dandy X Trapnel in Anthony Powell's *Books Do Furnish a Room* (1971).

23. 'Oh Peter' was a 1932 recording by Billy Banks and his Rhythmakers; the piano solo was by Joe Sullivan and the clarinet solo by Pee Wee Russell.

TO PHILIP LARKIN – 15 MAY 1946

St jhns cllg

My dear Philip,

In response to your swift and welcome letter I am writing again now, though I don't think I shall be able to find as much to say as I did larse time. Not very much has happened, you see. This week I am writing another eſsaie on Chaucer (G.): 'The levels of C's art as shown in the Cuntherbelly Tails.' If I say, that I am of the opinion, that the levels, of his art, anywhere, are all, of the same level, as the level, of the big pipe, that takes away, the waste matter, from a public lavatory, when men, have been there, to let, waste matter, out of the holes, in the backs, of their bodies, with their trousers down, which is, what I think, then, I am sure, the man, who teaches me, will, be quite sure, that I am, trying to be funny, and will not, like it, at all, THE SODDING OLD *FOOL*.[1]

Is Greta attractive – sorry: Would she still be attractive if she weren't 17? She can't be as big as ME. Sri I seem to have got Mr Motherland wrong; tho (aaoh naaoh) I still say most people couldn't say that; and I doubt if he could. The cutting was good, though I'm sorry one of them had to pay for her sin. I liked thinking about them, VERY MUCH INDEED.

Yes thats what I think about HJM[2] too. I remember hearing you say you could never think of anything to say to him. I find that more and more every time I see him. His inclusion in the circle was, as I remember, all Philip's fault. I didn't think him attractive till Philip said he was. Christ knows what's going to happen next term; thank Xt I shall be in digs. I think the really exasperating thing about him is his self-conscious, satisfied, *baseless* eccentricity: the way he walks rapidly across a room, with a *false* air of decision, his mouth pouting and his eyes half-closed, to put a lump of sugar in his mouth or go for a piss. Have I made clear what I mean? And his laugh when he farts; yes Mis' music man, keep him 'way from mah do'.

---

1. 'THE SODDING OLD *FOOL*' typed in red.
2. Hilary J. Morris.

As regards your coming up, do please come I said. I'll see Slade[3] myself. It looks as if they are charging us twice for you as there is 15/– on my battels for guest chmbr. Do come. Bring some records. When you come be ready to play.

I said this wouldn't be very long and it isn't. Anna is getting annoyed with Brunette about Iwdafy. Is she tired of doing it, she asks, lowering her long lashes and looking at me in a way that makes me wonder what she is referring to. Get crackin. You ain't no preacher, you' a good old soul.

kingsley weary
Kingsley

[TLS: Bodleian]

TO PHILIP LARKIN – 18 MAY 1946

St John's Coll Oxon
Tell Brunette Anna cried about Iwdafy last night[1]

My dear Philip,

[. . .] Leishmann[2] has pronounced himself 'very pleased' with my essay on the levels of Cah warrggh Chaucer's fart. He kept on talking about Chaucer's humour and I could hardly keep myself from BREAKING WIND IN HIS FACE. Tell me: surely you couldn't get a laugh out of the old rape-lust either, could you? I thought not.

I see what you mean about your words. Don't be angry if I say I'm glad I've stopped writing like that now, though whether the way I write now is any less *sogging* is uncertain. I wrote some words the other day too, for my buck;[3] they are about Bayou Woof, and go

3. See Amis to Larkin, 5 February 1946, note 11.

---

1. MS addition.
2. J.B. Leishman (1902–63), Fellow, Tutor and Lecturer in English, St John's College, Oxford (1948–63), University Lecturer in English (1946–60), a specialist in Shakespeare and metaphysical poetry.
3. *Bright November* (1947).

So, bored with dragons, he lay down to sleep
Locking for the last time his hoard of words
(Thorkelin's transcript B[4]), forgetting now
The hope of heathens, muddled thoughts on
fate.

Councils would have to get along without him
The peerless prince had taken his last bribe
(Zupitza's reading[5]); useless now the byrnie
Hard and hand-locked, fit for a baseball
catcher.

now
Consider ~~king~~ what this king had not done:
Never was human, never lay with women
(Weak conjugation), never saw quite straight
Children of men or the bright bowl of heaven

Someone has told us this man was a hero.
But do we want him? do we want to follow
His tedious journey to his ancestors
(An instance of Old English harking-back)?[6]

I enjoyed writing that a good deal. Do you think anybody would mind if I dedicated it to Professor Bollkeen?[7]

We go down on 22nd June. Come up bifaw then. Whats rilegoin mean? sorry I see nay. Love to Rewth (strewth). Theres no college dance.

4. G.K. Thorkelin (1752–1829), a Danish scholar, made two copies (transcripts A and B) of the damaged *Beowulf* MS in the Cotton collection, reconstructing many missing letters and words. In 1815 he brought out the first printed edition of the poem, with a parallel Latin translation.

5. Julius Zupitza (1844–95), a German scholar, translated and edited *Beowulf*; also Chaucer and other works of Medieval English.

6. This first draft was altered both for *Bright November* and *Collected Poems 1944–1979* (London: Hutchinson, 1979; henceforth *CP*).

7. J.R.R. Tolkien (1892–1973), Merton Professor of English (1945–49), author of critical and philological studies of *Beowulf* and other Old English texts, as well as fantasy novels such as *The Hobbit* (1937) and *The Lord of the Rings* trilogy (1954–55).

Sorry to hear from Josh abt your novel.[8] Hilary is going to do her hair in plaits when the weather gets hot.

Kingsley uptown cafe

[TLS: Bodleian]

TO PHILIP LARKIN – 22 MAY 1946

St. John's College Oxford.

My dear Philip,

Sorry to write to you on this blue-suited paper,[1] but I have no other. As regards the american men sides, I don't *think* the man will be taking them away from here for quate a tame, as he hasn't got a gramophone and isn't likely to get one; anyway, I *think* I can guarantee to borrow them for you to hear when you come up. The Russell solo on 'Mammy o' Mine' moved me to tears the other day, which is a thing that sort of thing doesn't do often. In one place he breaks away from external

8. Larkin may have complained to 'Josh' (Noel Hughes) about delays in the publication of *Jill*, or a 'not-very-hopeful letter from "my agent" about *The Kingdom* [*of Winter*, later retitled *A Girl in Winter*]', as he did to J.B. Sutton in a letter of 15 May 1946 (*LL*, pp. 117–18).

---

1. The paper is headed 'Royal Air Force' (below an insignia), with the address 'No. 31 Royal Air Force Depot, Moncton, N.B., Canada'. 'ACHACHACHACHA' (for which see Amis to Larkin, 31 December 1945, and 25 November 1944, with its almost identical-sounding 'artschartschartsch*aaah*') is typed in red.

characteristics (*or*-to-i-*ro*-tick fick-*say*-shun) and breaks into the realms of pure music (*mew*-tew-al fel-*lar*-tee-oh).

Of course, my dear boy, I understand *only too well* about you and 'the mistress of your heart' (!!). Though I have been past *les affaires du coeur* for longer than I care to think of, yet still there remain 'in my memory locked' the lost hours of my life when I was at the mercy of every wind that blew, and the least look or word from my 'fair charmer' *whoever she happened to be at the moment!!!* – could lap me in bliss or plunge me into the blackest despair. Ah youth! But an 'old fogey's' idle reminiscences must be boring you, I fear me. As the Americans say, "go right on ahead, big boy" – *for that is what you are now*!!!!

Serously thuohg old Sun you are in a natsy Spot & no mistaek. *I* don't know what you are to do. When one's affection is exactly balanced by one's irritation there is nothing much one can do. The only thing would be to have a tremendous ray, but of course you can't do that. If you cd convice sckhocqs convince Ruth she might meet someone else like you some time, *or* that she doesn't really want anyone like you – oh xt no I date whether that wd help. I'm sorry to be unable to advise you; all I can say is 'I understand' which you probably don't believe and in any case won't make you feel any better.

You are *right* about Leishmann and Roger Sharrock.[2] I hate a man who is *such* an ANUS. He says he likes my work though. That's because I say I enjoy reading and Chaucer and like the Wife of Bath – WHO IS SOMEBODY AT THE BACK OF CHAUCER'S MIND WE NEVER GET TO KNOW AND IF HE HAD BEEN ABLE TO TELL US ABOUT HER WHICH HE *W A S N' T*[3] WE SHOULD NOT WANT TO KNOW

Anna and I are very sorry about Iwdafy. How long is the halt likely to last? I suppose it is due to all these great intension nastinesses you are learning. I would much rather we adhered to our plan and you kept it for a long time until you were able to finish it. How is that?

I am feeling a little better nay than I have been for some time. This is because a Hilary has yielded and b because I have sent my 2nd lot of songwords off to the FP, giving them I hope 'enough for a volume'. Now I suppose there will be a VERY LONG DELAY before anything happens about my book. When you read those poems, Philip, get a

2. See Amis to Larkin, c. 26 October-6 November 1943, note 7.
3. '*W A S N' T*' typed in red.

handkerchief ready to vomit into. Some of them are so BAD thatI wx I feel ashamed. Then I read 'The Yellow Night'[4] and don't feel so ashamed.

Now I must go and get some books out of the library to write an essay on 'Spenser and the New Poetry'. I'M NOT INTERESTED IN THAT.

Write soon and don't worry about Iwdafy – though I should like us to finish it. Keep your chin up beeeeeooooouuuuyyyyghghghgh.

kingsley married woman
Kingsley

[TLS: Bodleian]

TO PHILIP LARKIN – 8 JUNE 1946

St. John's College, Oxford

My dear Boy,

You can well imagine what a very pleasant (dare I say *unlooked for*??!!) surprise it was to learn that so early in your 'career of creation' a reputable publishing house has agreed to launch you into *immortality* (!) and that at last you can fairly be said to have 'arrived'![1] Please accept my sincerest congratulations; I shall watch your future career with great interest!!! Seruosly htuohg, I am beside myself with anger and grief and envy and am really very pleased for your sake. You lucky *bastard.* I shall be gald *cwx* glad to see you and talk to you about it. By the way, we've feigned the records – the man had taken them back to his room – and so you can be pretty certain of hearing them when you come up. Though you don't deserve to, you *sod.*

4. *The Yellow Night* (1944) by Drummond Allison, also published by the Fortune Press. Allison (1921–43), a contemporary at Queen's College, Oxford, was represented in Keyes and Meyer, eds, *Eight Oxford Poets* (1941). His *Collected Poems* (1980) were edited by Michael Sharp.

---

1. Faber and Faber had accepted Larkin's novel *The Kingdom of Winter* (later *A Girl in Winter*), subject to alterations. Faber was the country's leading poetry publisher, which 'encouraged [Larkin] to think that they might eventually take on his poems as well' (Motion, *Life*, p. 143).

I saw your two poems in Mandrake[2] with your name spelled wrong. The first one I liked a good deal; the second I did not, much. By the way, when my words come out you must promise to feel kind about them. There are some I hate so much that if I weren't so wrongly anxious to get into print I would refuse to let appear under my name, but since they are probably the ones the FP like best, and since I haven't got any others to give them ('a writer distinguished by extreme smallness of output'), I shall have to let them stay in.

I seem to be getting a lot of early Goodman records now. Do you know if R2695 I Dreamin'/As Live[3] is any good? You don't seem so interested in the jass music as you were; is that right? You never say anything about it. Oxford these days is a happy cunting ground for the hot collector (bgs). I got arabesk[4] for BB 1/- in Drawda the othr day. I don't like it much. There was a Br. Eel there too which I rushed off and played it was the same one as the parlophone one.[5] *Fuck* you.

I will stop now as I can't think of anything else to say. Well done Larkin. Looking forward to seeing you.

Crumble bummb,[6]

kingsley across the track[7]
Kingsley

[TLS: Bodleian]

TO PHILIP LARKIN – 19 JUNE 1946

St. John's College, Oxford.

My dear Philip,

Well we where all tikcled to Death to see your ulgy Mug agian and here how the big Bad wolrds been treateing you not often enouhg eh

2. An Oxford-based magazine; the two poems, published in the May 1946 issue, were 'Plymouth' and 'Portrait', reprinted in Thwaite, ed., *Larkin: Collected Poems* (London: Faber and Faber, 1988; henceforth *LCP*), pp. 307, 309.

3. 'I Ain't Lazy I's Just Dreamin''/'As Long as I Live'.

4. Written by Spike Hughes.

5. See *LL*, p. 16n: '"The Eel" was a showcase number for tenor saxophonist Bud Freeman, with whom [Pee Wee] Russell performed.' The recording Amis calls 'a Br. Eel' (i.e. issued on the Brunswick label) turned out to be of the same 1933 session as that recorded on Parlophone.

6. Amis has typed 'it was the same one as the parlophone one' in red.

7. The first use of the 'bum' valediction in Amis's correspondence. See Amis to Thwaite, 24 March 1991.

Ah! ah! Serously htuohg I personally enjoyed the wickend a lot and was amazed as I always am to find how much we had to say to each other. I enjoy talking to you more than to anybody else because I never feel I am giving myself away and so can admit to shady, dishonest, crawling, cowardly, brutal, unjust, arrogant, snobbish, lecherous, perverted and generally shameful feelings that I don't want anyone else to know about; but most of all because I am always on the verge of violent laughter when talking to you, and because you are *savagely uninterested in all the things I am uninterested in*. At intervals during the past few days phrases like 'very good-natured little wolf', 'a taunting guardian', 'Dog-shit, his man' (that makes me crap), 'no beer sir' come into my brain and make my mouth open into a large laugh. And thank you for all the nice things you said about my words; I hope you did mean most of what you said. I have revised Radar[1] and written some new words about Hilary that you can see some time. Apart from this nothing has been happening except that I felt ABSOLUTELY TERRIBLE[2] yesterday and the day before, shegged 8, and it wasn't improved by a pock on Monday afternoon. That man I may have told you ab8 – the religious fucker – keeps coming round to see me and I don't want him to come, for he is silly, and I do not want that, and I can not think of any thing to say to him. Yesterday we went and saw 'Gelda (there never was a woman like)'.[3] I didn't like it, much. The plot was about Rita Hayworth (who is the most letch-er-rous lay-dih I have ever seen, and whom I should like to SHAGALOT[4]) beng pocked a lot, and then getting married, and beng pocked a lot by other men, and her husband pretending to commit suicide, and another man marrying her, but not pocking her and not letting her be pocked by other men as a form of 'revenge', and then realising what everyone else knew, that he really wanted to pock her, and then her other husband coming back and going to kill the second husband for pocking her and her for beng pocked, and someone else killing the first husband before he can do that and then Gelda and the second husband going off to enjoy beng pocked and pocking for the rest of their lives, which would, I should

---

1. A poem in *Bright November* (1947), p. 15.

2. 'TERRIBLE' typed in red.

3. *Gilda* (1946), directed by Charles Vidor, written by Marion Parsonnet; promoted with the slogan 'There never was a woman like Gilda!'

4. 'SHAGALOT' typed in red.

imagine, be short. I couldn't see much in this film but Rita Hayworth's breasts and where her legs join together and on to her body.

CHEAT AND NO CHEAT

a moſt diuerting comedy of humours, in v acts.
as it hath been diuers tymes perform'd at the
Whoars Head, Shitefryers, and ful oft at court
The Perſons
Sir Ioſiah Lubricious, the noble counterfeiter
Doggſhit, his man.
Maſter Bayſio, a portugueze trickſter.
Clapp, an extrauagaunt practitioner.
Cowturd, a ſimple contriuer.
Iohn Perinæum, a fabling expoſitor.
Horſepiſs, a reherſ'd emploier.
Stiff, a nice ſtrateger.
Nauel, a Fellow.
Mrs. Pock, a retorting Dame.
Miſtreſs Poppie Tupper, her equall.
Horna, a cozen'd seruer.
Toſsie, the vouchſafed Iade.
Imprinted by Iames Arſwipe at the publiſhers,
The Gentilmens Public Lauatory, in Eaſtcheap.

Write back in a quick time. Hungry bum.

kingsley gleet,[5] an vndertaking tapeſtry-weauer
Kingsley

[TLS: Bodleian]

TO PHILIP LARKIN – 24 JUNE 1946

St. John's College, Oxford.

My dear Philip,

Thank you for your two letters. I would have sent some back words sooner, but there have been a lot of tiresome things happening here in the last few days, like taking everything out of Saint John's College and

5. 'Gleet' is a discharge from a mucous surface, often related to syphilis, sometimes also a synonym for syphilis.

putting it all in number nineteen Saint John Street, which is where I am sitting down at now.[1] It is quite nice here: the is made ah jackxs landlay stoolze the L A N D LA *NAPPIZZ* D Y[2] – is made up of two spheres and four cylinders and doesn't lock the door at night though I suspect that she would be against things like pro-*miss*-kew-us *faw*-ny-ker-tree in-*dull*-jents but we shall have to wait and see. The sun has been making the air very dry and hot for a lot of the time and my body has been not liking that very much, really, at all. Now it is raining and it may get cooler; I hope so, as I haven't many clean pairs of socks and my feet are smelling like week-old corpses.

YES I DO want New Belfires *jabbles* Belfries.[3] Plez buy it at once. Anything doing about At Birds?[4] Do you know what I am going to tell you, man, I am just wishing to put my hand away out to touch it on that book. Stamboul-bum[5] made me hail. How much harder is it to get from Leicester to everywhere else than it is to get from Wellington to every where else? I know exactly what you mean about angry enquiry and peculiar flat tone. That is how I too am made to feel. *And* about not getting enough of – that is a true word, I say. I have a feeling that what we have to say to each other is more or less inexhaustible – by which I mean that we DON'T feel (a) as one feels with women so often that once one has worked through what has happened to each since the last meeting there will be little left to say; nor (b) as one feels with other friends (even Christopher of late) that one has been through everything once and all ones conversation is a re-working of former themes. Am I right about that? You may be able to create more than I – in fact I think you do – but I can create in addition to you. *And* joke, you toss-hung chancre. I loved your play, particularly at Shogbelly Feelrump!!! and BULLPIZZLE!!![6] And uuell-fauor'd. Shouldn't it have been TVVAT? [. . .]

---

1. Location of lodging house run by Miss Butler. See *Memoirs*, pp. 47–8, for account of his landlady and fellow lodgers.

2. 'L A N D LA NAPPIZZ D Y' typed in red.

3. *New Bats in Old Belfries* (1945), a book of poems by John Betjeman.

4. *At-Swim-Two-Birds* (1939), comic novel by Flann O'Brien, pseudonym of Brian O'Nolan or O Nuallain (1911–66), satirical columnist (as 'Myles na Gopaleen') and novelist.

5. Alluding to *Stamboul Train* (1932) by Graham Greene.

6. Amis has typed the stems of the three exclamation marks after 'Feelrump' in black (using the single quotation key) and the three dots in red; after 'BULLPIZZLE' the stems are red and the dots black.

Hilary liked you very much which is nice, isn't it?
'. . . attractive . . .'
'. . . charming stammer . . .'
'. . . amuses me a lot . . .'
'. . . the nicest of all your friends including Chris . . .'
'. . . I love him going all small when he's saying something he doesn't like . . .'

I may be here on Saturday but won't Bruce [Montgomery] not like me being around when he's around when you're around? Let me know definitely whether you'll be here on Shatterday first.

Write soon.
Dont let the bugars get you dwon.
Stendhal bum.

GLUBITIO[7] . . . a collapſ'd affirmer
Kingsley

Hilary sends her love. No cracks from you you old bugar I no you soft

[TLS: Bodleian]

TO PHILIP LARKIN – 1 JULY 1946

26 Shrublands Road, Berkhamsted, Herts.

My dear Philip,

I'm sorry we didn't have as much time as we usually do last wickend, but what there was was very good. I like Bruce very much, really; I envy him his assurance, but he's much too successful for me. Whenever I am with him I feel simultaneously superior and inferior to him. I am sorry Christopher was so rude: he isn't suspohkes usually like that – he was very hungry and tired and had a headache on Sunday. He likes you, but not Bruce. His trouble is not beng an Arteist and being interested in too many things. The things I enjoyed most about the week-end were

7. According to Tom Deveson: 'From "glubere" (to peel), a Latin verbal obscenity, equivalent to something like "wanks" or "tosses off" – hence the "collaps'd affirmer"' (personal communication, October 2000).

the discussions about my brother and the film imitations. After we left you we had an *intolerable*[1] journey on that bus. There were a lot of children on it that I wasn't feeling very affectionate towards; one with a look of imminent putrefaction, as if its face were about to become one vast sore. I should have liked to make it cry in terror. To-day like yesterday the clouds are too close to the ground and the air is hotter than it needs to be, and water flows out of little holes all over my body, and I do not feel like writing a funny letter a-tall.

It is terrible, being home again. I went into the four shops I go into when I come home. There wasn't anything in Smith's, and there wasn't anything in one of the no-record shops, and there wasn't anything in the other no-record shop except two copies of When Buddha Smiles/ Basin Street Blews by Maſter Beniamin Goodman, which I didn't play, and there wasn't anything in Booteſes where I joined the Fook-Shovers Library[2] except the Ballad and the Swhorese of which I have read three pages without feeling very much happier because of I have done that to them. My vacation life opens out before me like a prostitute's jenny-taley-er; I can foresee all the nasty work, all the wasted money, all the boring evenings, all the *malodorous* films, all the silly young ladies, all the unwritten words, all the dentist's appointments, all the sheer *N A S T I N E S S E S*[3] I shall experience before I go back to the town that may be a bad town but is *much better* than the other towns I know. Turdel-urdle-urdle-urdle-ay.

I am a-fraid I shan't be able to write very much more: I am feeling so *tired*, and so *bored*, and so *nasty*, and so *angry*, that I can't really think of anything more to say. Do write quickly, and send me N B F O B:[4] I will pay money out of my pocket for it.

Kingdom bum.
a diſpaſsion'd politician
Kingsley

[TLS: Bodleian]

---

1. Amis has typed '*intolerable*' in red.
2. Boots' Book-Lovers Library; 'The Ballad and the Swhorese' is *The Ballad and the Source* (1944) by Rosamond Lehmann (1901–90), novelist and sister of John Lehmann (for whom see Notes on Recipients).
3. '*N A S T I N E S S E S*' typed in red with alternating red and black underlining.
4. Presumably *New Bats in Old Belfries*, misabbreviated.

TO PHILIP LARKIN – 15 JULY 1946

Abbey Timbers.[1] *Harwell, Berks.*

My dear Philip

Thank you very much for your amusing (warm enough for you?) letter that came, by the only post of the day, this morning. As I foretold, they have taken away my typewriter and I am writing this with a pen that I am holding in my hand. I don't like that, because it is more TROUBLE like this, and my pen doesn't always write when I want it to, because there is something wrong with the nib and because bits of grease kept BUGGS keep stopping it from moving over the paper and leaving a mark behind it: and every time I form a letter badly with my pen, which KEEPS ON happening, I get VERY ANNOYED.

I am feeling VERY ALARMED AND DEPRESSED INDEED, because I have been working out all about my money. It seems that those who are giving me money are not giving me NEARLY ENOUGH of it, and those who are taking my money away from me are taking it away from me MUCH TOO OFTEN and MUCH TOO MUCH at a time. Xt knows how I'm going to LIVE – aaoh Christ bwbwbwbw. And I shan't have enough to buy *any* more records or enough leaf tobacco and fermented drink. AND I owe you 6/- – alright dont get the Wind up – I no your probaly thiknign hope Ill get my six Bob – well up you're Pippe – never new Honnest Bill amis lett a pall down Yet did yuo – wahts that crys of Not fukcin much – its safe with me you old shiloke weihgt and sea Ah! Ah! O how *POOR* I'm going to be. Billybarleybubbub

It is a lovely day and I have been sitting in the garden reading other men's words. I've read some H.E. Bates[2] ("What?") and some Tchekhov (aoh naoh) and some of mister W B Yeats and Lord Alfred Tennyson and some D.H. Lawrence. I bought Bessie's Careless Love: it is a marvellous record, and I heard Shout Joy/Bear Crawl[3] which I would buy if I had more MONEY. Bear I think NOT but Shout *sounded* very good.

---

1. Amis was staying with Hilly and her family in Berkshire from 6 to 18 July.
2. H.E. Bates (1906–74), popular and prolific novelist and short-story writer.
3. 'Shout for Joy'/'Bearcat Crawl'; Bessie is Bessie Smith; the record Amis bought was 'Careless Love Blues'/'Weeping Willow Blues'.

Is it supposed to be Condon taking a *solo* on Mahogany Stomp? I like Goodman 6tet on Street[4] quite a lot.

**FARTARSE*

Very soon, now, the teeth, that I have in my head, are going, to start aching, and I shall dislike that,[5] and then, I shall have to go to the man who hurts teeth, and he, will hurt mine, *and I shall dislike that*, and then, he will say, I must pay him some money, for being hurt, AND I SHALL DISLIKE THAT.

SQUUCKLES

Hilary is very nice, as you will agree (she dreamed you were kissing her the other night), and I am enjoying very much being with her. But her family, who put in sporadic, *unneeded* visits, are nasty. She has two brothers,[6] who are EXCREMENTALLY EVIL. One has *sandals* and *saffron* trousers, and No Socks, and a *green* shirt, and plays the *recorder* (yes) and likes Tudor music, and has a BAD wife and a BAD voice which says BAD words. I don't like the other one. He came across the lawn to meet me, his hand outstretched and an indefensible smile on his face. Hilary said "This is Kingsley." – "Why, hullo, Peter," he said to me very cordially. "I'm not Peter" I said. Then I became aware he was talking to a dog behind me. (The dog smells of corpses). "No, I know that" he said: "I was talking to the dog". "I see", I said. And the father does folk dancing (polk dancing? pock dancing? fock dancing?). Another brother was a conscientious objector. For none of the usual reasons I mind this. A sister is having an affair with Roger Partington.[7]

Ooh yes: and I read some rhyming words by Emily Dickinson. I DON'T SUPPOSE YOU'VE EVER LET ANYBODY SAY SHE WAS GOOD, BUT IF YOU HAVE, *DONT LET THEM DO IT AGAIN.*

Why don't you go off with Miss Jane[8] as the indication to Miss

4. A recording of 'On the Sunny Side of the Street' by the Benny Goodman Sextet; the earlier Condon reference is to a 1929 recording of 'Mahogany Hall Stomp', a famous Louis Armstrong tune.

5. Amis has drawn arrows from 'Very soon' to the top marginal MS addition 'ANY F-G MINUTE'; from 'dislike' to 'VERY MUCH'; and from 'aching' to 'LIKE BOGRAY [buggery]'.

6. There were in fact three brothers: William (1915–94), a composer; Brian (1918–81), a journalist; and Michael (b.1923), a writer and cinematographer; Peter, the dog, was a Cairn terrier.

7. Margaret ('Miggy') Bardwell (b.1925), later an architect, married Roger Partington in January 1947; Partington (b.1924) read Chemistry at St John's (1942–48), and later worked as an industrial chemist.

8. Jane Exall, a friend of Ruth Bowman.

Ruth that you don' wan her no mo'? All right, I know why you don't. All the sam, I bet you wish you could, eh, (ha Ha)!, you old bugar, I no yor sort.

Last night Hilary pulled all the bed clothes over to her side and kept them there, and so I have bumbago in the middle of my back to-day.

Splendid bum,

a diſpleaſ'd maſter of horſe[9]
Kingsley

[ALS: Bodleian]

TO PHILIP LARKIN – 30 JULY 1946

26 Shrublands Road, Berkhamsted, Herts.

My dear Philip,

I suspect that I shall now put down quite a lot. Thank you for your letter, with all its little bits of friendly advice: as you see I have taken a brush to those lower-case letters, and thankyou for your timely instruction leaflet about pieces of bone that grow out inot *fix* into our maithes. To-morrow I am going for an initial interview with the man who hurts teeth. The thought fills me with unashamed terror. I can imagine what will happen:

Me (laughing with panic): 'Well, I expect you'll find quite a lot to – get your teeth into ha-ha, a lot, stumps, the front ones, injection, stop them, extraction, rack and ruin, Army, butchers, abcess . . .'

Him (waving his hand minatorily): 'Never mind about all *that*, old boy; supposing you sit yourself down and we take a look, eh? . . . M8 bbss M'm . . . fffff . . . poofff . . . ooh . . . . . . ah . . . chchchch . . . . . . pp . . . yes . . . . . . ooh *dear* . . . M'm; well; I WONDER IF I CAN SAVE ANY OF THEM.

After that he will SHAKE HIS HEAD A LOT OF TIMES, and

9. The only one of these 'Elizabethan' or 'Jacobean' valedictions (the first appears in Amis to Larkin, 19 June 1946, continuing the letter's parody of the *dramatis personae* of the 'moft diuerting comedy of humours' *Cheat and no Cheat*) with a specific literary referent: Bosola, the discontented (or 'diſpleaſ'd') 'Gentleman of the horse to the Duchess', in *The Duchess of Malfi* (c.1613) by John Webster (c.1580–c. 1634).

write something down in a book TALKING TO HIMSELF, and go over to the window and stay there WITHOUT SAYING ANYTHING TO ME AND SIGHING, and go to a cbbfopps cupboard and bring out some instruments THAT I SHALL FIND MYSELF VERY UNWILLING TO LOOK AT BECAUSE I *KNOW* THEY ARE GOING TO *HURT* ME A LOT. And then he will hurt me with them, and make me look ugly, so that young ladies will not think I am nice at all any longer, and that is going to make me very unhappy. So when it is midday to-morrow, pause a moment to think of your poor friend, and his sufferings.

You are a lucky boy about signing that paber with faber. It's not the thought that I'm unsuccessful that worries me, becuase *zttooolz* I'm not; but the only difference is that I'm only not unsuccessful *yet*, which does not go far to console me. I wonder if you see what I am meaning. Congrats, old son. Wtah atubo a rkea-fof rof em, oyu dol Barug?

We will discuss tit-Willow[1] when you come. The town bit is good because of the extraordinary quality of the diphthong. I don't think I have anything esle to say about records for the moment. That is meant not to sound snooty or upstage old boy. By the way: don't you think Sidney[2] spends a lot of his time explaining *things you know about* to you? 'Auden – that's WH Auden, the poet, old boy – a sine qua non – something you can't do without, old boy – HMV – His Master's Voice, the gramophone *wallahs*,[3] old boy.'

---

1. A joking reference to the lesbian novel 'Trouble at Willow Gables', which Amis asked Larkin to bring in a letter of 20 July.

2. Perhaps the fictional character 'Sidney Amis', older brother of 'Kingsley Amis' in 'The Legacy', Amis's 'first serious attempt to write a novel on his own' (Jacobs, *Biography*, p. 125). 'Sidney Amis' does, indeed, explain things his brother knows about; he also refers to him frequently as 'old boy'. Amis may already have shown or read Larkin portions of an early draft of the novel, which was not completed until September 1948. His first explicit reference to it, in a letter to Larkin of 25 September 1946, suggests as much; on the other hand, in a letter of 2 July 1947 (in Bodleian) he announces to Larkin: 'I have begun "The legacy". ' A second possibility is that Amis is referring to Sidney Keyes (1922–43), a fellow undergraduate and poetical rival (editor of *Eight Oxford Poets*). Though Keyes died on active service in 1943, Amis had recently been reading and disparaging his poems (see Amis to Larkin, 19 July 1946, in Bodleian). Keyes's *Collected Poems*, edited by Michael Meyer, came out in 1945.

3. Amis has underlined '*wallahs*' in pen and drawn an arrow to the MS addition 'WETT-*DREEM*'.

I have just finished reading The fall, by Mister Hugh Kingsmill,[4] and apart from the dyer-log, I think it is a good word. I also read some american short stories, and think on the hole that american men should stick to making noises with musical instruments, and if they can't do that, THEN THEY OUGHT TO KEEP BLOODY QUIET.

Last night I spent a long time in bed reading the horsepiss book[5] and laughing a good deal. I have written a lot more in it *against*[6] your coming. Re-reading what I had written, it occurred to me that my comments were not obscene so often, and were more directed against the VAPIDITY and UNTRUTH of what was said about Geoff. Ch. It occurs to me that there might be scope for a serious article ('What?') about mr g chaucer, which we could put in the cherwell[7] or somewhere. What do you thikn? If you thikn, 'Yes', then bring a coppy of his words. There is not one in this house.

Roger [Partington] says he doesn't want any money for his records now, because he has a bad conscience about that waller record of mine he broke. I don't mind this. You are *right* about mr brown's friends[8]

'Bordastac'[9] sounds like a Balkan town. 'The Bordastac dispute is still the main item of disagreemnet bbs at the UNO conference. Mr. Molotov says that a free vote of the citizens . . .'

I can't write as much as I intended, because miss hilly is waiting to go out with me. Waht AICCKKS wht oicckks what day will you be coming? Saturday wd suit my mother best, but make it Friday if you like (Hilly gox SHAIPPSS goes on Thursday).

How many times a day does GBS give his exhibition?[10]

Belgrade bum,

a diſfranchyſ'd muſick pupill
kingsley

[TLS: Bodleian]

4. *The Fall* (1940) by Hugh Kingsmill (1889–1949), novelist, biographer, critic and humorist.

5. For 'horsepiss' see Amis to Larkin, 25 November 1944, note 5, and 5 September 1946. The 'horsepiss book' does not survive.

6. Amis has underlined 'against' in pen and drawn an arrow to the MS addition 'menstrool flewid'.

7. Oxford University magazine.

8. Philip Brown.

9. Untraced.

10. There was a George Bernard Shaw exhibition at the National Book League in Albemarle Street, London W1, from 27 July to 24 August 1946, arranged in honour of Shaw's

TO PHILIP LARKIN – 8 AUGUST 1946

26 Shrublands Road, Berkhamsted, Herts.

My dear Philip,

Well it was great seng your ulgy mug again and I enjoyed all of it very much. A pity we couldn't have stayed a longer time at Abbey Timbers,[1] because I liked it there. Hayever, we shall probably go there again. I hope you had a good journey home, BECAUSE I DIDN'T. I spent an hour and five minutes at Gloucester Green, entirely surrounded by buses and people all facing differnet *kipps* ways: there was no queue any more. Eventually two buses went to Aylesbury together. I was on the second one. I had two dialogues that will interest you:

> Me (at random): Will I have to change for Aylesbury?
> Driver of 1st bus: You may have to at Thame.
> Me: I suppose someone 'll tell us?
> Driver: Yes, yes; you get on that bus, that's all you've got to worry about.

At Thame about a dozen people stayed on the second bus, which remained halted, without driver or conductor. The first bus was in front. I went to a group of busmen who were chatting by it:

> Me: Which bus is going to Aylesbury?
> *The same driver*: Why, this one! Hop on quick. *You're the people who are holding us up.*

Overhearing this, all the other people on the second bus got on to the first bus before I could return for my case and get on, so that I had to stand. Oh, and at Oxford there had been a dirty little girl who had fallen about all over my suitcase for a long time, its mother watching with an indulgent smile with which she also favoured me. I was an angry man when I got home.

This morning I paid my battels,[2] leaving myself with less money than I need, and I am an angrier man. To-morrow I go again to the

ninetieth birthday, which was on 26 July 1946. Amis has circled 'GBS' in pen and drawn an arrow to the MS addition 'WOOMZ'.

---

1. The proposed visit is described in a letter to Larkin of 26 July 1946 (in Bodleian): 'When you come down here, we will be able to go over and stay with Hilly. Roger [Partington] will be there, and nobody esle but us 4 . . . For ij or iij Dayes, I vnderſtande.'
2. College acount.

man who hurts teeth, and shall be a frightened man. Being at home alone, I am also a bored am *jackxs* man.

I have been reading 'The Ghost'[3] and have been laughing about and about it. The funniest phrase is undoubtedly 'thorough ye Fartyng of his proper Erſe', though all the Owen bits are very funny too. If you like I will do a version of the contest and let you inspect it and (where necessary) correct it. Then I will do a great Fayre-copie in duplicate for us both. Do you agree to this?

I msu say MUST SAY my valuation of At Birds[4] falls below your own. The biographical reminiscences are funny, but there are far too few of them and they aren't long enough. I don't think any of Trellis's characters are at all funny, except for the cowboys; the Pooka is a bore, and Finn is a terrible bore. Some bits make me laugh a great deal, but there are far too few of them and they aren't long enough. I think it's on the whole a pity he was Irish. I say that very loudly and clearly.

I can't write any more nay, because I have a lot of nasty letters to write before gong 8 to tea with my mother to some nasty people. If I can remember and find a large enough envelope I enclose the picture of your face. DON'T FORGET I WANT ONE YOU OLD STEWING PAN OF SPERM.

Kingsley

PS. Love to Ruth. And have you got my pen[5]

[TLS: Bodleian]

3. 'The Tale of the Jolly Prince and the Distempered Ghost', one of a number of 'obscene and soft porn fairy stories' Amis and Larkin had written in the early part of 1942. See Motion, *Life*, p. 86, in which the story is described as 'a saga of a farting medieval ghost, of which Amis can still recall fragments: "and then the ghost made a fart like the breaking of an apple branch under the weight of good fruit"'. Amis and Larkin returned to the stories in the summer of 1946; see Amis to Larkin, 11 August 1946 (in Bodleian): 'I am going to get on with the jolly ghost and will send you my version of the second half . . . I am glad you want us to do all of them. No backinae before the job's done, old boy.'

4. *At-Swim-Two-Birds*, by Flann O'Brien.

5. MS addition. On the other side of the page Amis has written: 'Note how this paper is EXACTLY TOO WIDE for the envelope.'

TO PHILIP LARKIN – 30 AUGUST 1946

Hôtel du Cheval de Bronze, Remiremont, Vosges.[1]

My dear Philip,

It now seems that we've come as far as we're going to come, for the moment at least. I don't mind this, because I am getting a little tired of travelling and my case is very heavy. It doesn't look as if we shall be going to Switzerland, because the nearest consul is a long way away, and we don't know how many days it would take him to decide we can go. This annoys me intensely. It is quite nice here, but nothing seems to be happening, and I can't imagine what we shall do, at any rate during the day time. We shall probably go for a lot of walks ("Eh?") to some mountains which there are near hear *pease* here. We haven't got enough money to get drunk much, and I haven't brought any books with me.

As regards local colour, there doesn't seem to be much. We are getting a lot of food here cheaply, which I like. The cost of being in the hotel, including three meals a day, is 12/6 each (a day). The beer tastes of sweet cardboard. I am in continual fear of being thrown 8 of the hotel for ill liss sit seck sew all in dull gents. A nameless lump is coming up on the back of my neck, WHY, and WITH WHAT OBJECT, and TO WHAT END, and FOR WHOSE ADVANTAGE, I cannot imagine. I don't think I really like the French very much, you know. They expect you to be able to converse in their language without being able to converse in yours and still think it rather silly of you not to be good at speaking in the French language: also, they think it funny for anybody to be a member of the English nation.

I don't think I shall be coming back to England with any recorded music not on sale in that country. They had about a dozen records, all French labels, in a huge store, as big as Keith Praise's[2] in Paris. Most were post-occupation by French bands: I didn't play any of those. There was, hayever, Weary Blues/Ja-Da by Ladnier ("Pop King, Milton, clarinettes") and Finesse/I Know That You Know, by Wrecks

1. Amis, Hilly and Christopher Tosswill were spending two weeks on holiday in France.

2. Keith Prowse, the chain of theatre-ticket booking agencies. At that time it also sold records.

Spewart.[3] I Know is a very bad side, when all the men, are plang, together, you wish, that they were plang, one, at a time, and when, they are plang, one, at a time, you wish, that they were plang, together. And isn't it a HAWRUBBLE time? Afterwards we played Finesse, and then we went out of the shop. They hadn't really expected us to buy anything.

I am feeling a little depressed, perhaps because I am tired, and wishing in a way I were back in England, NOT because I like being in England, but because I am afraid somebody will start talking to me in the French language wherever I go, especially the proprietor, who looks as if he might be strong on ethical and moral standards. Also, I have not had my eyes on words from you for some days, and they always help me to write words back. Do write if you haven't already done so: we should be here for at least a week, unless requested to leave in IGNOMINY and SHAME and EMBARRASSMENT. Now I am gong to leave off. Sorry this is short and a bit not, but I am tired, and making some depressing inward generalisations about sex. I'll write again soon.

Simoom bumm

Kingsley

[ALS: Bodleian]

TO PHILIP LARKIN – 5 SEPTEMBER 1946

Hôtel du Cheval de Bronze, Remiremont, Vosges
This goes to Coten End, in case you've gone to Inceisoter.[1]
NOCK.

My dear Philip,

This is perhaps the fifth lot of unsolicited words you will have

3. Rex Stewart (1907–67), cornettist; the titles of the Stewart sides are as given; so, too, for the Ladnier sides, described on the inept French record sleeve (from which Amis quotes, as the spelling 'clarinettes' suggests) as featuring 'Pop King' (i.e. Sidney 'Pops' Bechet) and 'Milton' (i.e. Milton 'Mezz' Mezzrow).

1. Coten End was the home of Larkin's family in Warwick; Larkin had recently been appointed to the position of Assistant Librarian, University College of Leicester.

received at my hands. I hope you have already written me a letter. Do you know what it is, the postal service between the two countries is a cock-up. It's a cock-up now. I don't know that I have very much to *say*, exactly. At the moment I can only think of two topics. The first is Mister Stephen Spender. You know, I used to think that he knew how to put down good words. And now I have been reading Ruins and Visions,[2] a poetry book. I find in the words of this book there is a lot of poll lis sill ab bick fuss sin ness ('The total generosity of original unforewarned fearful trust'), and a lot of ad dough less scent sew dough mith oller gee ("Oh which are the actors, which the audience?"), and a lot of Europe-falling-about-our-ears and Oh-my-dearest and playing-with-abstractions (real-unreal bocks) and your-eyes-are-mineshafts-to-your-heart and HELPLESS GESTURES like "And write round my high paper walls Anything and everything Which I know and do not know!" because HE CAN'T THINK WHAT TO SAY. I hope you don't like the book. I must say reading it for the first time was a bad experience. It would make a perfect horse-piss book: I can imagine myself writing "what does this MEAN?" and "You tell ME" and "Well SEWHAT?" in a large number of places.

The second topic is Mister John Pudney.[3] I believe there was a film called The Stars, in which some rhymed words by him were spoken out. They went:

> Do not despair for Johnny head-in-air.
> He sleeps as saned As Johnny on-the-grained.
> Bring 8 no shrade For Johnny in-the-clade,
> And save your tears For him in after years.
> Better by far For Johnny the-bright-star
> To keep your head, And see his children fed.

Now as you will almost certainly have guessed (knowing me), I have taken the liberty of doing a little "improved"(!) version, which goes:

2. *Ruins and Visions* (1946) by Stephen Spender (1909–95), poet and critic. The poems quoted from are 'A Childhood' (pp.73–4), 'The Fates' (pp.57–63) and 'Song' (pp.11–12).

3. John Pudney (1909–77), poet; his poem 'For Johnny', in *Dispersal Point and Other Poems* (1942), was read in the film *The Way to the Stars* (1945; US title *Johnny in the Clouds*), directed by Anthony Asquith and starring Michael Redgrave.

Wail not the luck
of Johnny shagged-to-fuck;
he died as quick
as Johnny got-no-prick.
Cold in the grave
he still can misbehave
a little while
with Johnny necrophile.
Draw near the tomb
of Johnny wanker's-doom;
lie on the grass
and BUGGER HIS SON'S ARSE.

Sweet, I think. One of the things that strikes me about it is how much more *poetic* it is than the original.

I thought when I came here I would be able to spend a lot of time writing down words I had made up; no, I find I'm not doing that, except in letters. Hayever, I shall probably be able to let you have The Knight[4] in a few days, though only in pencil I am afraid. I am doing too much eating and sleeping (which I enjoy very much) to do very much else. The only thing that worries me is getting THROWN OUT of this hotel for IMMORALITY. Besides this, I am starting to think that Miss Hilly and myself have been seng quite enough of each other, and I want to get my life to myself again. You might think that when I get back to England, I shall be able to do this; no, I shall get my life to myself and the *Lady of Scheist's*, and *Whoreious John*, and *Phallicsander the Hunchbock*, and the *great Sexpeebograpeher.*[5] I shall sit down at a table, feeling very miserable, and open a book, and find a piece of poetry beginning 'Let observation with extensive view Survey mankind from China to Peru'.[6] When I have done that, I shall feel much more miserable. Still, if you want anything, you've got to work for it. C'est la vie.

Well, I'll sign off now, old boy and hope to hear from you before

4. One of the fairy stories worked on by Amis and Larkin.

5. If 'the *Lady of Sheist's*' alludes to Milton, called 'The Lady of Christ's' when a student at Christ's College, Cambridge, then the other 'titles' might allude to poets as well, the sort Amis would be reading when he returned to Oxford: '*Whoreious John*', for example, might be the hated John Dryden, known as 'Glorious John' to contemporaries (or John Keats or John Donne, both womanising, or woman-loving, poets); '*Phallicsander the Hunchbock*' might be Alexander Pope; 'the *Great Sexpeebograpeher*' is probably Samuel Johnson ('the great lexicographer').

6. The opening lines of Samuel Johnson's 'The Vanity of Human Wishes' (1782).

I'm too much older. Don't do anything I wouldn't do, will you?
Senex bum

Kingsley

[ALS: Bodleian]

TO PHILIP LARKIN – 7 SEPTEMBER 1946

Hôtel du Cheval de Bronze, Remiremont, Vosges

My dear Philip,

Thank you very much for your letter, which arrived yesterday afternoon. I sympathise very much about packing up the things that belong to you:[1] that is a thing that always brings me care when I do it. I feel very glad for you, stopping being in Wellington any more. However bad Leicester may be, and it may be A SMASHING JOINT, it's baned to be bad, if it's bad, in a DIFFERENT WAY. I envy you, going to such a hopeful place. Let me know what it's like – as I'm sure you will. Your letter, by the way, was the first I've had from anybody since I crossed the water, old boy: I think my parents have opened a new bring-him-to-his-senses campaign. They were very nasty to me just before I left for France. They don't seem to realise that they have to be VERY NICE to me to make me able to BARE beng at home at all. But when I get back I shall be so busy baring Dryden and Johnson and all those other evilnesses that I probably shan't notice what they do.

I don't mind beng abroad as much as you think, though I do mind a bit of it. I am still AFRAID, and Miss Hilly and I have not been getting on quite so well of late: at the moment she wants me to pock her more than I want to pock her, and I am starting to think that Sir tea er tea has more or less the same effect on a young chap as fruss tray shun. There is the same wanting to be by oneself, and the same not wanting to take the trouble to be nice, and the same feeling that one has let oneself down, and the same feeling that one has been caught in an unpleasant and ineluctable conspiracy. All this is very uncharitable, because she is so nice, and will probably clear up when we see less of

---

1. For his move to Leicester.

each other: only it will have to be a GOOD DEAL less. If only she could Talk! I am getting so TIRED of always being the source of everything we share. If you were here, I keep thinking, we would spend the time in talk and drink and smoke, and I should be laughing A LOT OF THE TIME, and I should be enjoying myself ALL OF THE TIME. Instead, I'm not. But all this isn't special to France and there are things, like sleeping and eating and idling a lot, that I enjoy very much. I am a little ill-humoured, though, because I have a lot of SPOTS that ITCH through eating too much fruit, and I have been smoking French cigarettes (Caporal Ordinaire) that make me feel not well. [. . .]

When you have time, my dear fellow, and have settled down in your new "seat of office", mind you pour forth all the *gen* (!) about your new situation to your old friend. Remember – I am always *incorrigibly* interested in the behaviour of the "human animal", and look forward to perusing divers effusions of your lively pen anent your companions and *pastors and masters*. Your letters are to me as veritable *oases* in the dreary desert that is this modern world of ours. AR FARK ERF AN' SE' ON THE SHI'-PUN YER AWLD SPARNK-AYED BUSTURRD.

I seem to spend a lot of every day going to the bank and seeing about our bill and changing our food coupons at the Mairie and making enquiries at the police station and booking seats at the railway station, and I must go and do some of it now. I've done The Knight, but it needs revising, and that takes a lot of energy. Many backwords.

shiftless bum

Kingsley

[ALS: Bodleian]

TO PHILIP LARKIN – 16 SEPTEMBER 1946

26, Shrublands Road, Berkhamsted, Herts

My dear Philip,

[. . .] Just after buying [some] gramophone records, I passed a man in the street. He was one of the Adjutants I had while I was in the Army. He was smoking a cigarette under his moustache and I could see on his shoulder a badge which meant he was still stationed abroad. I felt very happy to think he was still in the Army, when I have not been in it for eleven and a half months, and that soon his leave would be all over, and he would have to go back and be adjutant in a unit in the British Army of the Rhine, without me there. He didn't recognise me. But I recognised him.

I thought: "You fat bastard."

Then I went and saw "A Casablanca"[1] with the Marx Brothers in it, and paid 4/6 out of my money to do it. I wished I had not done that.

Everything is all right between Hilary and me again, and we parted quite cheerfully. But I'm starting to become fed up with Christopher [Tosswill]. He is interested in too many things – when he sees an unusual car in the street, he GOES OVER AND HAS A LOOK AT IT – and he talks too much like a BADLY-WRITTEN BOOK (Hilary's phrase), and he is PRAID OF THINGS ABOUT HIMSELF: "Everybody knows I'm unapproachable after a long journey *until I've been fed* (WHY NOT say, Until I've had a meal? WHY NOT?)"; "A beer always increases my good will"; "I always wear thin shirts." On the way back from the French Republic, the water went up and down a lot, which I didn't like, but I wasn't sick. Christopher was ("I always have to lie down if the water is at all disturbed" IF IT'S ROUGH).

Well, now I'm home again ("Glad to be back, I expect, eh?"), and though I don't like this much, it's no use kicking: the work's got to be done, and the exchequer won't allow of any further extravagance HARRCESHIT.[2] Write and tell me how you are, or I shall start sending obscene letters to the Chief Librarian, mentioning your name.

Smelly bum,

Kingsley

[ALS: Bodleian]

1. *A Night in Casablanca* (1946).

2. Amis has drawn arrows from 'HARRCESHIT' to the words 'no use', 'kicking', 'work's', 'exchequer' and 'extravagance'.

TO PHILIP LARKIN – 25 SEPTEMBER 1946

26 Shrublands Road, Berkhamsted, Herts

My dear Philip,

I have this day received the letter you wrote to the frogy plaice, and I was *very glad* to do that. I am sorry to have reproached you for not sang anything about Johnny up his arse:[1] I am very grateful for your eulogy. You are the ONLY PERSON who really laughs at things like that; in fact, you were its onelie true begetter, old boy. I must say too hay much I enjoyed your accaint of beng at Leicester and stang with your sister, through I realise how SEROUSLY HORRIBEL it must all be. I can imagine hay I should rather enjoy arriving in a new town, and beng alone, and looking at new people, and drinking in new pubs, and beng conscious of beng *interesting* and *superior*, and waiting to meet *clever* and *attractive* people and ENJOY MYSEFL, and then finding 8 that there aren't any people like that VERY QUICKLY, and HATTING everythign because of that. This leads me to the conclusion, already pointed to by other things, that, since I am in the sam situation as you with the sam lack of success, there isn't anybody whose way of talking will interest me and make me laugh as much as yours does: I find that when I meet somebody nice and intelligent (which happens RARELY) I get annoyed because even though they *are* nice and intelligent, there is so much *to teach them*, and it's TOO MUCH TROUBLE to teach them thigns that we don't have to teach each other. Do you see what I mean? There is nobaddy esle but you who contributes as much as I contribute to the total of interest, and who HATES the thigns I HATE as much as I HATE them (who NEVER says things like Just a minute while I look at this car).

I am sorry to have taken up all this of time with what I have been sang, but it has been accumulating in the interior of my head for some time now.

I am starting to get quite pleased with what I have been thiknign about my book about my brother and the money.[2] I keep thiknign of

---

1. The parody of the poem by John Pudney; see Amis to Larkin, 5 September 1946.
2. 'The Legacy', completed in September 1948.

little phrases: "His name's not really Kingsley", said Sidney. "What is it, then?" asked Susan. She was smoking a cigarette. Sidney leaned his body forward until his month was near to Susan's ear . . . . . . "Just one more thing, old boy," said Sidney. I stopped walking from the room: "Yes?" I said, deliberately. "That Anders fellow you've picked up with; I don't like his looks" . . . . . . But my typewriter's BROKEN, and I haven't of TIME. I am BORED and DE-PRESSED.

The other day I was in Boot's Book-Shovers Library, and because I'd been away for THREE WEEKS they HADN'T GOT AYNTHIGN IN for me, so I looked around and after a long time got a volume of Poetry London[3] of new poets. Oh *dear*. I found a lot of BAD WORDS in there, but the biggest give-away of those things is always the illustrations, which were HORRIBEL. There was a SILLY critical article by that FOOL Alek Comfort,[4] and some poems by Alan Ross,[5] who doesn't seem to REALISE that a man who knows about good words DOESN'T *keep* expressing things by sang "the — of the —" or "the — 's —" (the churches of your hands, writer's gauge, the dial of sense, the cities of touch – these in 7 lines) ALL THE TIME. I wanted to have a rubber stamp made: "WHAT DOES THIS *MEAN* AND WHAT MAKES YOU THINK I *CARE*?" and put it on ALL the pages. "At least I reckon I can write better than *most* of the stuff that gets published". Ooh – talking of stuff getting published – what's happened to "Jill"? The FP of coarse are SILENT about my book. They might all be DEAD and we shouldn't know the difference much.

HMV[6] have written to say that they will send copies of Shag, Blues Sing, Black Beauty, and some S.L. Wallers to Acotts[7] when they can, which is nice of them. *Flash*: if you want a *hideous experience*, go to a

3. An influential bi-monthly poetry magazine, edited by James Meary Tambimuttu (1915–83). Amis's disapproval was echoed by D.J. Enright in 'The Significance of *Poetry London*', *The Critic*, 1, Spring 1947, pp. 3–10: 'I have written this article not merely because I consider *Poetry London* a rather uninspired collection of verse, but because I believe it had a positively harmful influence on contemporary writing' (p. 6).

4. Alex Comfort (1920–2000), physician, poet, novelist; author of many books, including *The Joy of Sex* (1973).

5. Alan Ross (b. 1922), author, publisher, journalist; editor, *London Magazine* (1961–); contemporary of Amis's at St John's College, Oxford.

6. The record label His Master's Voice, which produced many jazz recordings, and had a large record shop in London.

7. Acott's, like Russell's, a record shop in the High in Oxford; they were later to amalgamate.

record shop and play Hamp's[8] 'Hey-ba-ba-re-bop' on Brunswick. Christ bwbwbw

My mother would like you to do a little service for her. She doesn't know the names of enough men and ladies who put down words for people to read, and this hampers her at Boot's because they always give her the wrong ones and she doesn't find 8 till she gets them home. Could you therefore (the ink in this pen is *still* either overflong or dring up) suggest a few names? People she likes are: Hilda Lewis, Philip Gibbs, Ethel Mannin, W.S. Maugham ("as long as he isn't too near the bone")? Margery Lane, Gilb or Pam Franco, and the author of 'Rebecca' (I say this is P. Franco, but she doesn't thnik so). People she doesn't like are: Nay-oh-mee Jay-cobb, Rue-bee airs, [del.] -ter ruck. In other words, she likes writers who pretend to write well rather than those who don't bother to pretend.[9] If you cd do this, I (and she) would be most grateful.

I am still cheered occasionally by seng your comments in the books I read. One I can be sure is yours is:

?Spenser's *beautiful* sonnets . . . Shakespeare's friend and *patron* . . . ?

Well, Phil old boy, I'd better be closing up now. Let's have a line if you can tear yourself away from your professional duties CARNAL LUSSTS

Shadrach bum,

Kingsley

[ALS: Bodleian]

8. Lionel Hampton (1913–96), vibraphonist, drummer, bandleader. Amis has written 'FAWSKIN' in the margin, with an arrow to 'Hamp's'.

9. See also *Memoirs*, p. 21: 'Though a great jam-making, cricket-tea-preparing figure, my mother continued all her life as inveterate a reader as I was in my youth: a book was as much part of her accoutrements at home as handbag and knitting: no classics, but no "slop" either – the names of Norah C. James and Ann Bridge come to mind. (Philip Larkin passed on a recommendation or two here.)' Among Mrs Amis's literary favourites, Hilda Lewis (1896–1974) wrote historical novels for children and adults; Philip Gibbs (1877–1962) was an editor and journalist as well as an author (he was knighted for frontline reporting during World War I); and Ethel Mannin (1900–84) wrote fiction, biography and memoirs. Daphne Du Maurier (1907–89) was the author of *Rebecca* (1938); 'Margery Lane' is probably Margaret Lane, Countess of Huntingdon (1907–94), a journalist and writer; 'Gilb' is Gilbert Frankau (1884–1952), 'Pam' is his daughter Pamela (1906–67), both novelists (for Pamela see Amis to Larkin, 3, 8 July 1954, note 10). As for her dislikes, Naomi Jacob (?1884–1964) was an actress as well as author and educator; Ruby Ayres (1883–1955) wrote popular romances; Berta Ruck (1878–1978), novelist.

TO PHILIP LARKIN – 8 OCTOBER 1946

26 Shrublands Road, Berkhamsted, Herts

My dear Philip,

I had intended not to write this letter until another one came from you, but since you seem to have taken, mutatis mutandis, a similar decision I am writing nay. Nothing has happened since I last wrote, and I have miss laid your last letter, so this will porabbly not have much that is in it. Don't you HATT densitts who, when you make PERFECTLY UNEQUIVOCAL signs of beng hurt, say Sorry, old boy, that a bit tender? Keeping his hand in your mouth to prevent any reply, and when you growl, meaning to be at sang, Yes, very much, gong on at beng at pling the drill, so that you are at ting yoursefl in knots with AGONEE and at prang for unconcsiounsess? I DO. And my densitt behaves JUTS LIKE THAT. But he has finished nay, WITH8 doing my front tooth, which is the chief recent blipps reason I went to him. Ah, soul. And he will charge me much of money for hurting my teeth. [. . .]

Talking of bad things, I began Opening bars, by Patrick ("Spike") Hughes,[1] without finishing it. Like most books by musicians manqués (an expression derived from the French language) it is one of those books ab8 Don't I know a lot of famous people, like Margery Allingham[2] in the world of fact (Fart), and Brideshead revisited, by Evelyn Waugh.[3] Have you seen this? It is extraordinary. I was unable to decide whether the man speaking the story was meant to be bad, or nasty, or wrong, or unwise, but a lot of it, especially the Oxford bit, is in a sort of neo-Beverley Nichols[4] vein, and the first chapter is just like the first chapter of Merry Christmas at Oxford would be: full of things you hope are good, but know are bad, but put in. "He was entrancing, with that epicene beauty that in extreme youth cries aloud for love and withers at the first cold wind." *Burps.* "The languor of youth (sorry, Youth) – how unique and quintessential it is!" *Burps.* "I was made free of her narrow loins." *Burppss.* I may have missed the irony, but I cannot

1. *Opening Bars* (1946), Hughes's autobiography.

2. Margery Allingham (1904–66), writer of detective novels featuring the mannered aristocrat Albert Campion, modelled on Dorothy L. Sayers's Lord Peter Wimsey.

3. Published in 1945.

4. Beverley Nichols (1898–1983), author and composer.

believe that a man could write as badly as that for fun. *Nay*, if it had been made QUITE CLEAR that the man was BUGGERING THE BOY'S ARSE and *shagged the boy's sister* when he couldn't BUGGER THE BOY'S ARSE any more, I shouldn't mind so much. As it is, I *do. Very much.* Why is it that these people think (Mr. Spender is another one) that the way to avoid writing as they did in the '30's (which was quite well) is to write as BAD MEN did in the '30's? I have stopped reading Dryden. He is very much like Chaucer, isn't he? I mean, however hard you try, you cannot *see what people mean* who admire them. Now I can see what people *mean* (though I don't *agree* with them) who like *Donne*, or *Pope*, or *Wordsworth*, or *Keats*, or even *Milton*; but I cannot with Dryden. A second-rate fucking journalist ("Oh?"). A SECOND-RATE FUCKING JOURNALIST ("Oh.").

Thursday to Oxford, tk Xt. Are you bumming up soon? Where is "Jill"? Belated but enthusiastic thanks for 'Me next, Kingsley'.[5] Remind me to do "Caesar and Cleopatra" for you.[6]

Sauterne bum

Kingsley

[ALS: Bodleian]

TO PHILIP LARKIN – 15 OCTOBER 1946

Boll pee po claptColl: Di: Io: Bapt,[1] *Poxon Oxon*

My dear Philip,

[. . .] I have my wordprinter back I mean its mended and I feel icks ole tunt. It is quite nice beng back, though not so nice as you think, or as I think before I come. There have been at beng several thgnsi to

5. The opening words of line 4, stanza 3 of Amis's poem 'A Dream of Fair Women', first published in *A Case of Samples*, reprinted in *CP*, p. 31.

6. An imitation. For Amis's 'genius for imaginative mimicry' see Larkin's 1963 introduction to *Jill*: 'It was not a BBC Variety Hour knack of "imitations" . . . rather, he used it as the quickest way of convincing you that something was horrible or boring or absurd' (p. 15).

---

1. 'Boll pee po clapt' is what Robert Conquest calls 'an offhand obscenification' of 'Coll Di Io Bapt', to go with 'Poxon' for 'Oxon' (personal communication, 18 November 1998, itself written, Conquest offhandedly adds, from 'Stand-fart Eunucharseity, as KA would have writted in his ealry days').

annoy me. I have had a NASTY, DIRTY *FLEA* which has been at beng on my Body, *walking about* on me and *biting* my body, so that it *swells up* into SPOTS which *ITCH*. When you look for it, getting *out of bed* in the MIDDLE OF THE NIGHT, you CAN'T FIND IT because it ISN'T THERE. And when you have a bath to *drown* it and change your under clothes it is STILL THERE becos it HASN'T GONE AWAY. I have covered my self with DDT nay, which SMELLS OFFENSIVE, in the hope of KILLING it in AGONY. I itch *all over* and have a big SPOT on my FACE. I am FUROUIS ab8 it all.

You are very wise about Bridested. Apart from eatign and driknign, which you are *quite right* about, aren't you beng at HATTING *this* sort of thign:

'Over the Knobworthy mantelpiece was a superb Schleimikunt of the Klapstruk period, flanked by Pederasti engravings. I took a Zebbreterd cigarette from the walnut Piscipant box on the Kokopesseri table, on which also stood a red sandstone head of Borl Sung Lo, dating from the mid-D'ung dynasty, and went across the rich Pewbicke hair carpet to admire the hand-printed edition of the works of Uterus Menstruensis. On the bookcase lay an autographed score of Cloaca's 'Il Fluido della Testiculo' given by the composer to my friend at the first performance at the Tahthaus in Randenburg.'? I AM. *MUCH*. [. . .]

Did you know that JBwain[2] is nay a FELLO* of John's? Why are you shong your teeth in that way, and screwng up your eyes, and bending forward, and cryng 8 as if in pain? I KNOW WHY. The news fills me with the liveliest horror; *nay*, it isn't that I prize academic standards (no offence, old boy), but that he *does*, and he will *go on* beng WORNG about words *more and more* and *lader and lader* and beng MORE THAN EVER convinced he is right when he is WORNG and he will make young chaps thikn about words IN THE WORNG WAY – though YOU know and *I* know they'll do that ANYWAY. I talked to Arthur Boyarse[3] about it: 'I see Wain is now a fellow.' 'Yes a remarkable achievement isnt it.' 'Do you think so.' 'Yes youve got to remember hes only 21 years of age.' 'You mean hes not old enough to know better.' 'No I mean hes old enough to know very well.'

2. For John Wain see Notes on Recipients.

3. Arthur Boyars (b.1925) edited the Oxford-based magazine *Mandrake*, first with John Wain (1945–48), then by himself, publishing several poems by Larkin and Amis; also co-edited *Oxford Poetry* for 1948 (with Barry Harmer), containing poems by Amis.

Nick is back and as nice as ever. So are Duke[4] and Walter [J.B. Widdowson] and David Williams ps. Ian Davie (ooh dear) Cockran[5] and Laybawn are back. The place is full of dank green turds.

Do write more often if you have of time. I wish you and I were living together (here, wait a minute, old boy) because then I should be interested in things all the time, instead of little of the time, and nastiness shall have no dominion[6]

Spendthrift bum,

Kingsley

**fello–are v.t.* <u>*I suck*</u>*, etc. Also in sens. obsc. When are you coming up?*[7]

[TLS: Bodleian]

TO PHILIP LARKIN – 24 OCTOBER 1946

St. John's College, Oxford

My dear Philip,

I should have written this some days ago, only I am working quite hard this term ("Uh?"), and I have not had of time. It seems like *a cruel trick of fate* that I am still writting eassys on Milton, J, and still hatting it. My flee has dy'd nay, but to replace it I have an aching that is at my face – new rowljer. I have been at having a cold too.

I have been at looking at a copy of 'Cherwell', a literary magazine published by undergraduate members of the university of Oxford. In it, there is a poim by Mister Day Lewis, a letter from Mister Michael B'arseley,[1] an article on the poitry of the late Walt Whitman by Mister

4. Edward du Cann (b. 1924), reading Law; later businessman, Conservative MP (1957–87) and Minister (1963–4); KBE (1985).

5. Ian Cochrane, reading Modern Languages at St John's (1942, 1946–7).

6. An allusion to Dylan Thomas's poem 'And death shall have no dominion', from *Deaths and Entrances* (1946); see also *Romans* vi. 9.

7. MS addition.

---

1. The Day-Lewis poem 'Fragment of an Autobiography' and the letter from Michael Barsly welcoming the *Cherwell* back (there were no issues between March 1942 and October 1946) were printed in *Cherwell* 26:1 (18 October 1946).

John Barrington Wheyn, two reviews by Mister Kenneth Tynan,[2] who is a HOMOSEXUAL BUGGER and doesn't mind the sang so, and a story that is *quite pointlessly* allegorical in which i you don't know what he's getting at ii you *do* know that he DUZZNT know what he's geting at iii you don't CARE. Now: *all* these thigns are ABSOLUTELY DEVOID OF ANY KIND OF MERIT. Why the *fock* do they pinrt them eh. It made me FEWRIOSS. They charge a shillign for that toss and expect me, to be, at the giving, of a shillign, for the takign, of it, away. Needless to say, there was sweet fa by me in it, and they have said sweet fa about puttign anyhtign in in future. And good Maſter Cayton[3] at the ſign of the ſwyngyng ſcrotum says nothing to mee at All.

I too looked at eric partridge,[4] but a politer edition I think: nothing about words like bugger and fuck. Under 'jazz' it gave 'sexual intercourse' which seems to me to be funny. Of this kind of music there is little to be said. I heard the Bandits play some recently, but not very well. There is not any on the wireless set. Oh – Mervyn has a jazz friend in Lester you might like to see, he thinks. He met the man in the army, but then there have been lots of wizard types in the army – eh, Phil, old son? He has many disks and thinks [Pee Wee] Russell the greatest of all performers of this kind of music. He has an enormous gramophone. His name is Mister Roy Herbert, and he lives at number one, Tennyson street, in Leicester. The number of his telephone is 58892. If you like this idea, Mervyn will write him a letter tell'n him 'bout you.

I am very glad you are bumming up. Bring Ghost and Month[5] if you have done it, and Willow Oxford[6] if it is about. When I am in bed, I think a lot about my schoolgirl and her married grown-up chum: 'Why did you turn me out of your room last night, Isabel?' asked Norma in her cool, beautiful voice. 'I don't know; I just – felt a little afraid, I suppose. It was very silly of me.' 'Give me a kiss, then.' 'Norma!' 'Give me a kiss,' said Norma levelly. 'Go on, then, if you really want to.' 'I do really want to.' After some minutes, Isabel said a little breathlessly: 'A kiss, I said, not — Norma, you must go now. My husband will be

2. Kenneth Tynan (1927–80), dramatic critic; at Magdalen College, Oxford (1945–48).

3. R.A. Caton of the Fortune Press.

4. Eric Partridge (1894–1979), author and lexicographer; Amis probably consulted *A Dictionary of Slang and Unconventional English* (1937).

5. Soft-porn fairy stories worked on by Amis and Larkin.

6. The second of the Willow Gables novels, 'Michaelmas Term at St Bride's'.

here at any minute.' I *love* that. Don't you? You do. I don't think a divided week-end is inevitable. As long as you address yourself to me and Bruce and not BRUCE, everythign should be wizard fun, old boy. I shall enjoy seng both of you, anyway. Bruce had a good review in the Isis[7]. I hope he's glad about that. I should be.

I must go now and be at behaving like a horse. I'm glad ab8 Scrotiny.[8] Aargh – I knew there was something I hadn't told you about the charwell – there's an article on the poitry of Sidnikease in it, all abviij the obsession with the facts of death and the resolution of the death-wish and the sort of poetry Webster might have written if he'd been in a battle. WHY DONT THEY SEE THAT HE WAS JUST A SILLY LITTLE BOY WHO THOUGHT IT WAS CLEVER AND MATURE TO TALK ABOUT BONES AND SKULLS AND WINDING-SHEETS

Oh yes and it was at hatting that I was at at the words to Buxton. It shouldn't be let happen. Looking fwhoreward to seng you. Write quickly.

Random bum,

Kingsley

[TLS: Bodleian]

TO PHILIP LARKIN – 7 NOVEMBER 1946

19, S. Jno. St., O x f o r d.

My dear Philip,

[. . .] Your news about Alan Ross fills me with inexpressible anger. I can't see how anybody can claim anything for him. You can say about

7. Oxford literary magazine.

8. *Scrutiny*, Cambridge-based literary quarterly (1932–53), much dominated by its chief editor, F.R. Leavis. There is nothing in volumes 13 (1944–46) and 14 (1946–47) to suggest what Amis was glad 'ab8'.

Alan Ross that there is no reason to suppose that talent will not emerge when he is an older man than he is now, and when he has stopped being *SILLY*; this would NOT BE TRUE, but you *can* say it. What you can*NOT* say is that he is a promising young writer. A promising young writer. A promising young writer. A promising young writer. A promising young writer. A promising young writer. A STEWPID LITTEL BOY WHO TRIES UNSUCCESSFULLY TO HIDE THE VACUITY AND TRITENESS AND SHEER ANALITY OF HIS IDEAS BY A TECKNEEK COPIED FROM OTHERS AND BADLY COPIED FROM BAD OTHERS. A promising young writer. A promising young writer. A SILLY DROOLING YOUNG SPERMICIDE. ('Eh?') *A SILLY DROOLING YOUNG SPERMICIDE*. ('Oh.')

I haven't seen any Jills in Blackwells. Are you surprised? (You aren't). May I signle 8 for special mention '"You want a fight," he *diagnosed*.'[1] Every time I go at thinking of this, my face goes at laughing.

There is little more to be at beng said, except that I shall be in possession of a copy of Solid old man/Montmartre by Rex Footwarmers[2] in a week or so AFTER YOU HAVE GONE BACK. I am at reading Bottel's Pisssmellani[3] this week. I don't feel as though I like it much.

Sorry this is so short, as the b said to the a. (More next time.)

Fandango bum,

Kingsley.

[TLS: Bodleian]

1. See *Jill*, p. 104: 'Eddy [Makepeace] banged him [Christopher Warner] in the ribs. "Here, shut up, what's the matter? Eh?" He pushed his face close. "You want a fight," he diagnosed.'

2. A recording of 1939 by Rex Stewart and His Footwarmers.

3. *Tottel's Miscellany* (1557), the first of the popular poetic miscellanies of the later sixteenth century, containing the chief works of Sir Thomas Wyatt (1503–42) and Henry Howard, Earl of Surrey (?1517–47).

TO PHILIP LARKIN – 2 DECEMBER 1946

19 St. John Street, Oxford.

My dear Philip,

Thank you very much for your garland of posies which arrived this afternoon. I am replying quickly, but probably not at length, since, I am going out before very long to see a performance of a cinematograph-play. I am not printing these words because the ribbon on my printer is all 2 cock and shagged 8. You raised several points. Roger's short story:[1] I have now localised my disgust with the story qua story jenny tall L.E. fan tye a sis, as opposed to its beng copied when mine isn't copied, into a hatred of its *mistakenly* proud air of having *got above* falsely 'mature', 'cynical', 'modern' ideas that there is something disgraceful ab8 being *unashamedly moved* by simple things: its air of being too urgent for mere cleverness. 'The loneliness in his heart' bollabolla. This is an American attitude and a bad, nasty, unwise, wrong attitude.

I have a spare copy of the cherwell with my words in it: the editors sent me a complimentary one AFTER I HAD PAID 8 A SHILLIGN FOR ONE. I will bring it to war wick when I come. 'Please do not trouble yourself about any question of remuneration: the pleasure's mine.'

THAT SOD CATON *still* hasn't replied to my letter, through he had it over a fortnight ago. If he's made a nonsense of the thing, why doesn't he stand up and admit it like a man in Turk rural in Turk coarse? Yes I wish you would paſs on to hym my Diſpleaſure at being thus met with Contumelie and Diſdaine. All you tell me about Fabers' fills me with mortification and envy. You are going to be a successful writer – I can see it coming – while I spend my time being unpublished and hating it. You old bugar, you. How JAELUOS I am.

---

1. Roger Partington's story was published in the same issue of the *Cherwell* as Amis's poem referred to in the next paragraph. For Amis's reaction, see Amis to Larkin, 29 November 1946 (in Bodleian): 'I've only just remembered – *aagh*! – there's something esle – aawwrrgh! – to tell you – beeeeoooouuyygh – the Cherwell – *uurrgghh*! – have – oak reissed I can oooh hardly bare to tell you – they've – aoaoaoagh! – ACK SEPP TID ROGER's SHAWT STAWRY AB8 THE SCOOLMARSTER AND SAY IT IS THE BEST SHAWT STAWRY THEY HAVE SEEN FOR A LONG TIME AND HE SHOULD BE ABLE TO GET IT PUBLISHED SOMEWHERE ESLE AND GET PAID MUNNY FOR IT. *Nay*, of course I don't like it when anyone gets a story published when I can't get mine published; but what makes me FURIOUSLY AGNRY is that Roger's short story was so ABSOLUTELY DEVOID OF ANY KIND OF MERIT.'

How horrible it must of ben, hering Mr. Thos.[2] Doesn't he know how unwisely he talks? I think I will write to the beebee sea, telling them to find a new way of talking from that way of talking.

I'LL buy you some contraceptives, old boy, if that's what's worring you, he said, remorselessly cutting off another of my avenues of escape. Don't you worry: these things always turn out all right in the end, often when we least expect it flay grunt XE bitting of or guns.

I have been writing about the Elizabethan sonnet for weeks nay. You don't know you're living, old boy, away from all that kind of lack of wisdom. I always thought that Eng Lit *ought to be good*; I still think it, only it *isn't*. I have written some sonnets myself before now: I do not think I shall be writing any more of them. *Do not* refrain from scorning the sonnet at *every available* opportunity with the *maximum* of offensiveness, critic.[3]

I saw *Roger Sharrock* the other evening in the Napier. He did not recognise me. But I recognised him. His wife was not with him (". . . death, not mounted yet On his pale horse";[4] statement by negation, eh?) And then the other day Master Jain Davie[5] stopped me in the street: "It's Kingsley Amis, isn't it?" His teeth are still the same when he smiles: I don't know yet how much I mind this. He suggested that we wait for it that man Back in the rakns their that we went out and had a drink together. I shall go, of course ("They would shoot, of course").[6]

That's about all there is to say now. Do you like my cutting?[7] (You do), write back with equal speed, and I shall be glad on it. Cheerio for now.

Tambourine bum,

Kingsley.

[ALS: Bodleian]

2. Dylan Thomas, heard by Larkin on the radio.
3. See Wordsworth, 'Scorn Not the Sonnet' (published 1827).
4. See *Paradise Lost*, X, 588–90.
5. Ian Davie, St John's undergraduate.
6. From the penultimate line of Auden's poem beginning 'Control of the passes was, he saw, the key', later titled 'The Secret Agent'.
7. It has not survived.

TO PHILIP LARKIN – 6 DECEMBER 1946

19 St. John Street Oxfd

My dear Philip,

[...] This morning, *angered* and *discouraged* past endurance I rang up the CRAP FACTORY ('Oh.') the fortune press ('Eh?'). THAT SOD CATON occupied most of the time asking me to tate his miserable books round Oxford *for nothing*. He REFRAINED FROM APOOGLISGNI for not writing to me for TWENTY-NINE WEEKS, said I would get the proofs in about a month I DIDN'T BELIEVE HIM, said the book would be out in February I DIDN'T BELIEVE HIM, said would I try to get Oxford bookshops interested in it ISAID pss I SAID I'D HELP AS MUCH AS I COULD, and was POLITE, feeling with HUMILIATION that if I told him I HATED HIM AS MUCH AS I HATE HIM he would become ANGRY with me and refuse to publish my book. He showed he'd done bugrall by telling me I could put in any more poems I'd got. His pattern phrase was 'Things are so difficult' oh farks work it up yer. Don't you HATT his voice? I do, *So do you*. SO DO I. Oh, and *I* paid TWO SHILLINGS AND FIVEPUNCE to hear him speaking out with it from his mouth.

[...] I want to hear much more about what madderlane did to missruth. I want to hear every detail WHETHER YOU THINK IT WILL INTERSET ME OR NOT.

On Sunday I am going out drinking and to have lunch with the Daviator,[1] just the two of us. *He suggested it*. No carcks now, not what your thingkin, all open and aove blits above baord See.

I am looking forward very much to coming and seeing you at Warwick, though it seems an awful long time away. What do you want for Xmas?

vibraharp bum,
Kingsley

I'm not going dane till Wednesday p.m.

[TLS: Bodleian]

1. Ian Davie, whose first book of poems, *Aviator Loquitur*, was published in 1943.

TO PHILIP LARKIN – C. 16–18 DECEMBER 1946[1]

---

1. The background texts to the four sides of this Christmas card have been carefully selected (or constructed): jazz titles and lyrics for the front cover, to go with the photograph (of Walter Barnes (1905–40) and his Orchestra, who are advertising Buescher Intruments, an American firm famous for woodwinds and saxophones); a page from an English essay (more likely a compilation of phrases that might have come from an English essay, or essays,

TO PHILIP LARKIN – 9 JANUARY 1947

26 Shrublands Road, Berkhamsted, Herts.

My dear Philip,

These are unsolicited words, but come because I feel that I took up a lot of time in the replying to your last letter, and because I forgot to say anything in my last letter about something that I meant to be at saying things about: your latest rhyming words all put together in to one lot of them.

First things first, old boy, so let me apologise for any apparent severity or misplaced levity ('I say, what's up with you, o' boy? A-*poller*-jisin' f' things? Sure yer *a' ri'*, o' boy?') which I showed. I do not like thinking what would happen to my own *bundle of posies* (bandle o' crarp) if subjected to the same kind of talk. I don't want to sound like a Lit Crit wallah, but I feel that this lot is a more consistent lot tha[n] those in the north ship:[1] I could say that this lot shows you have decided what you want to do, you have developed, become more individual; the reason why I don't want to say so is because I have seen this said of alive men, and written it myself of dead men, when it is untrue.[2] With you I really think it is true.

Some of the reasons why I like them are negative, but from such an enemy of books as you seem to think I am that is to be expected. I like them because they don't belong to any SILLY LITTLE BOY SCHOOL: there's nothing in them ab8 rubble-teat or the wick of words or Mozart or angels or Rimini or delight in the height of the night or any other thing like that. Apart from this I like the way the best of them are emotionally exciting at a first reading because of the images and their words, and then you think When I re-read this it isn't gong to mean anything, very much, really, at all, and then when you do

or from a work of literary history) for the back cover, with its portraits of eighteenth- and nineteenth-century poets; Willow Gables soft porn to go with the photo on the inside cover; a page from a letter to Larkin, to echo the actual greeting: 'to PHILIP from KINGSLEY.'

---

1. *The North Ship* was published by the Fortune Press in 1945. 'This lot' refers to a second volume of poems, eventually titled 'In the Grip of Light', which Larkin would unsuccessfully submit to Faber and Faber and a number of other publishers towards the end of the year. For a list of the volume's contents see *LCP*, pp. 317–18.
2. Amis has typed 'untrue' in red.

re-read it you find it does mean something and the something makes the images more exciting – the poem is better than you thought and not worse even though you liked it the first time. Come now to prayers, especially the last few lines, is like that; so is some must employ the scythe, but all through; and most of all, Plymouth.[3] At least the last one is as good as most things I have read anywhere, and all three stay in my head. What I've said doesn't look very clever, I'm afraid, but it may encourage you. At any rate, I mean it all.

Two smaller points: thinking about it again in the light of what I've just said ab8 consistency, I should be inclined for its sake to leave out When this face was younger[4] and the other one (I seem to remember) that I advised you to put in because you wanted to show you could do it. I think that you do what you do best so well that there's no need to show you can do other things as well if you want to. And on reconsideration I should leave 'And there are thrown up waves' as it is; putting 'still' in seems to me to introduce an extraneous feeling.[5]

Talking of words, I think I have traced the nastiness of my early words to the influence of Mister Dylan Thos. *Nay*: influences are good if they are good influences, like Auden and you less recently, but if they are SODDING LOUSY influences, like that of Mr. Thos, then they are bad, years, years. I have got to the stage now with mr toss that I have only reached with Chaucer and Dryden, not even with Milton, that of VIOLENTLY WISHING that the man WERE IN FRONT OF ME, so that I could be DEMONIACALLY RUDE to him about his GONORRHEIC RUBBISH, and end up by WALKING ON HIS FACE and PUNCHING HIS PRIVY PARTS. I know young chaps sometimes dislike the men they copied because they copied them, but I copied Auden too, and I don't HATT him. I have only to see words like An old man's shank one-marrowed with my bone, or Jack Xt, or man-iron (aooh! aoh! aaoh!!) to groan 8 laid.[6] And if we are gong to

3. The three poems Amis singles out – 'Come then [not "now"] to prayers', 'Some Must employ the scythe' and 'Plymouth' – are all reprinted in *LCP*.

4. The poem does not appear in the unpublished 1947 typescript of 'In the Grip of Light', nor in *LCP*.

5. Larkin seems again to have concurred: the poem beginning 'And the wave sings because it is moving', from the unpublished 1947 typescript of 'In the Grip of Light', contains the line 'And there are thrown up waves' (the word 'still' having been removed, presumably). See *LCP*, pp. 6–7.

6. 'An old man's shank one-marrowed with my bone' and 'Jack Xt' (or 'Jack of Christ') are from 'If I were tickled by the rub of love', in *Eighteen Poems* (1934), reprinted in *Dylan Thomas: Collected Poems 1934–1953*, ed. Walford Davies and Ralph Maud (London: Dent,

call peots bda because of the fefect they have dha on Egnilsh peorty, then he is bad, years, years ('Holders of one position, worng for years, years, years').[7] These refelctions have been stimulated by reading what mr trees has to say ab8 mr tosz.[8] I think that mr treez is another VERY SILLY MNA, and BDA too, but not so BDA as mr tozz because he DOESN'T WRITE SO MUCH.

[. . .] I hope you like the cutting. It is the only sort of thing that makes me wonder if there isn't perhaps a god after all. There is another bunk johnson out this month.

Snodgrass bum,

KINGSLEY

10.55 **Blanche Coleman** and her Girls Band. From the Winter Gardens, Eastbourne[9]

[TLS: Bodleian]

1988), p. 16 ('Jack Christ' also appears in 'Altarwise by owl-light', from *Twenty-Five Poems* (1936), reprinted in *Collected Poems*, p. 62). 'Man-iron' is from 'I, in my intricate image', from *Twenty-Five Poems*, reprinted in *Collected Poems*, p.33.

7. 'Holders of one position, wrong for years' is the last line of Auden's poem beginning 'Since you are going to begin today', in *Poems 1930*, later titled 'Venus Will Now Say a Few Words' (reprinted in W.H. Auden, *Collected Poems*, p. 44).

8. Henry Treece (1912–66), poet and author of *Dylan Thomas: 'Dog among the Fairies'* (London: Lindsay Drummond, 1949), the fifth chapter of which, 'The Debt to Hopkins', appeared as 'Gerard Manley Hopkins and Dylan Thomas' in Treece's earlier book *How I See Apocalypse* (London: Lindsay Drummond, 1946), pp. 123–39.

9. This cutting might suggest that Amis and Larkin had not previously heard of 'Blanche Coleman and her Girls' Band', though Motion, *Life*, p. 86, thinks they had: 'The name [Brunette Coleman, Larkin's pseudonym for the "Willow Gables" fictions and other early soft-porn writings] seems to have been adapted from a jazz band of the period – Blanche Coleman and her Girls' Band.' Larkin's reply, in a letter of 11 January 1947 (in BJLH), settles nothing: 'Blanche Coleman is Brunette's sister, a natural ashblonde.'

TO PHILIP LARKIN – 30 JANUARY 1947

19 S. John Street, Oxon.

My dear Philip,

Well, my old son, very grieved to hear of your bad-health lately, I know to my own cost what the 'flu can be, I hope you have not felt too browned up at keeping within your four walls, in this blooming awful weather it is not so bad a deprecation, glad you have whiled the time out with works of fiction, and hope you are now back in the job.

This is not going to be a long letter, because I am feeling bad in my body: a pain is in my head because of some bad beer I let into my stomach last night, there is an ill taste in the interior of my mouth that makes cigarettes be like damp marsh-grass, my feet either hurt with the cold or itch like bogray when warm on account of I have developed some chill blains. This weather makes me feel very unhappy; I have composed a purse sir nell which you might like:

Volpone Drag)	That's the Humour of It)	Baggin' the Bee)
Jumpin' at the Mermaid)	Brainworm Blues)	Scholastic[1])

Big Ben Jonson and his Tribesmen (actually Jonson fronting Donne's Metaphysicals.

Big Ben Jonson (tpt and voc)	Harry Vaughan (ten)	Andy Marvell (bass)
Abe Cowley (clt, alto)	Jack Donne (pno)	George Herbert (ds)
Dick Crashaw (tmb)	Tommy Carew (gtr)	

Arthur Boyarse showed me his new long poem the other day oh farks I HATTED so many things ab8 it. NOT ONLY was it headed by a kwoetayshun from Powl Aylwar,[2] but it was IMAGIST, SYMBOLIST,

1. All the titles listed in this 'personnel' make reference to Ben Jonson (c. 1572–1637) and his plays, beginning with the eponymous hero of *Volpone* (1605); the Mermaid Tavern, site of the Friday Street Club, over which Jonson presided; 'Brainworm', a character in *Every Man in his Humour* (1600), the source also of 'That's the Humour of It'; 'Baggin' the Bee', from the poem 'Her Triumph' (in *The Underwood*, 1640, also in *The Devil is an Ass*, 1616); and what Amis might describe as Jonson's 'groove' in general: 'Scholastic'. The 'Tribesmen' are actually 'Donne's Metaphysicals', a different poetical grouping from that of Jonson's younger followers (Brome, Herrick, Randolph, Suckling), who styled themselves the 'sons [or "tribe"] of Ben'.

2. Paul Eluard (1895–1952), French poet, associated first with surrealism (from 1919 to 1938), then communism (from 1942) and the French Resistance.

had NO PUNGTEWAYSHUN, NO CAPITAL LETTERS, NO RHYMES, and NO METRICAL OR RHYTHMIC PATTERN. It was like what I used to write WHEN I CAME IN PISSED in about *1943*. It kept PRETENDING to mean something and NOT MEANING ANYTHING. He kept telling me stories of hay suck cess full he is, which seemed to be true. That's wrong, sweet papa, ain't that the truth? Tchahwell[3] has been banned for the rest of the term for sending out a list of questions to young ladies asking them if they have ever allowed young chaps to get on top of them. I am not writing anything; I am working too hard for my exams.

I'm sorry this is so short, but I am feeling much iller: my feet are giving me gyp and my mouth tastes like the interior of a railway station. Mervyn thought Jill was very funny. I have lent my copy to a lot of people and they all seem to like it, though search me as to why they should.

Christopher is having an affair with Marie Woolf.[4]

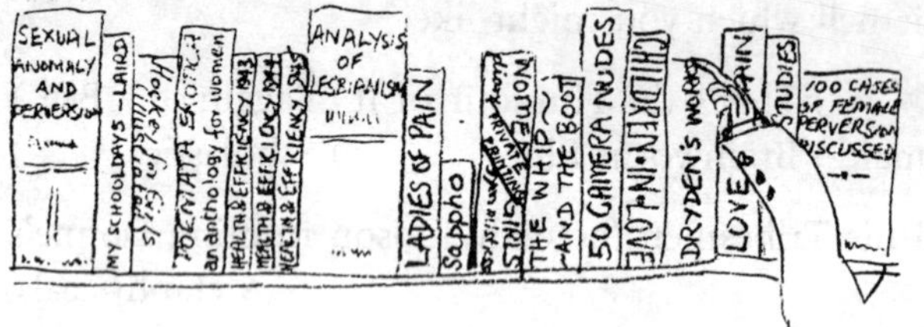

Byrhtnoth[5] bum,

KINGSLEY

3. The *Cherwell*.

4. Marie Woolf, reading medicine at Somerville (1943–50).

5. Byrhtnoth (c.926–91), ealdorman of Essex and defeated hero of *The Battle of Maldon*, a 325-line poem in Old English (c. 1000).

TO PHILIP LARKIN – 6 FEBRUARY 1947

XIX Vi: Sanc: Jo: Oxon:[1]

My dear Philip,

I too befouled myself at your letter. These personnels are amusing me more and more: I would like to see some really early stuff (early New Orleans pre-electric recordings), like

> OLLY CROMWELL and his ROUNDHEAD WASHBOARD BAND.
> Revolutionary Blues/Hittin' the Rump
> Cromwell (cornet) with *possibly* H. Vane (saxes, clt), R. Fairfax (tuba), A. Marvell *or* C. Skinner (washboard), et al. V by Blind John Milton.[2]

I loved particularly 'The Revenger's Tragedy, Pts. I and II', 'with novelty acc.', and '*I'm going to that*'. You ask ab8 Marie. As far as can be ascertained with any degree of reliability, old boy, not much in the physical line has occurred between Xtopher and her YOU'RE GLAD ABOUT THAT AREN'T YOU but she did tell him, *in some detail*, that although she enjoys *beng pocked*, she has *lesbian leanings*, and not long ago, while she was having an affair with a man, she was having one with *a young lady* too. The other girl was *very nervous*, but M. *went to bed with her* in the end, and although her friend was still *shy*, had an *orgasm* all right. She has met another young lady she would like to do this with, and although she *feels shy* ab8 it, thinks she can *pull it off* all right. Chris isn't going to go any further with her; I expect he feels, understandably, that a girl who would engage in that kind of filthy

---

1. 19 St John Street, Oxford.

2. The Larkin letter to which Amis refers, with accompanying Jacobean 'personnel', has not survived. As for the 'ROUNDHEAD WASHBOARD BAND', only 'R. Fairfax (tuba)' puzzles: Amis must mean 'T. Fairfax', for Thomas, third Baron Fairfax of Cameron (1612–71), as fervent a Puritan as the statesman and Parliamentarian Henry Vane (1613–1662). 'C. Skinner' (Andrew Marvell's alternate on washboard) is Blind John Milton's friend Cyriack Skinner (1627–1707), to whom he addressed the sonnets 'Cyriack, whose grandsire on the Royal Bench' and 'To Mr Cyriack Skinner upon his Blindness', both written c. 1654.

perversity isn't worth 2 pins to a decent man BUT WE'RE NOT OF MEN WHO ARE BEING DECENT ARE WE? WE DON'T MIND THAT DO WE?

I am srory to hear of you not being sure about bumming; don't not bum because of misruth cannot come too. Let me know. Hilly and I had a very good time with Bruce who spent a lot of money on us both; a dinner at White's cost £6. He is very charming but I never really know what to talk to him about; it is always as if we talk of things that don't really matter to either of us. He said you were fed up with him; I contradicted this. I said he didn't like Ruth; he said she didn't like him either. He has the most un-annoyingly assured and charming manner of anyone I know. But I wish he wouldn't keep telling me to marry Hilly, or that he wants to marry Hilly.

You are speaking true wrods about the Char well. Everybody who has had anything to do with the business wants shagging. Beesley[3] is a hrorbile little boy and him not any more being at editing will be good for men. Nothing else happens here, except that I work at old-fashioned literary works too much of every day. I'd like a job near you all right: keep your ears open for anything that's going round your way in the neighbourhood of September next. (I mean this; small school? *library*? or what-have-you?) Your college saneds very nasty to me. I saw frenzy[4] the other day; there is a sadist gentleman in it who is accused on the subtitles of 'perversity' and being a 'perverse old wretch', which made me laugh out in the kinematograph theatre.

Pharnabazus bum,

Kingsley

[TLS: Bodleian]

3. Alan Beesley, reading Modern History at Pembroke (1945–48), was sacked as editor of *Cherwell* for reasons described by Amis in the previous letter to Larkin, 30 January 1947. The banned issue was *Cherwell* 27:1 (23 January 1947).

4. *Frenzy* (1944), written by Ingmar Bergman, directed by Alf Sjöberg, starring Mai Zetterling, whose character is pursued by the elderly 'sadist gentleman'.

TO PHILIP LARKIN – 15 FEBRUARY 1947

19 St John Street, Oxford

My dear Philip,

[. . .] You know those Echo poems that men in the seventeenth century were so fond of? Well, the other day I got thinking, and produced

Speak, Echo, partner of the earth and sky. Echo: Ay.
In Heav'n, what of our poets? Do they live? Echo: Live.
Live they in bliss, or die in torment frightful? Echo: Rightful.
The deep-browed Milton, where is he interred? Echo: Turd.
The fiery Shelley, what does he endure in? Echo: Urine.
Where pains him Chaucer, prince of entertainers? Echo: Anus.
Hyperion, where does Keats finish it? Echo: Shit.
Dryden's bay garland, what has it become? Echo: Come.
Say what the realm of honey-tongued Pope is. Echo: Piss.
What ails Wordsworth in Nature's mystic lap? Echo: Clap.
Turd, urine, anus; shall there be no end? Echo: No end.
Shit, come, and piss and clap; shall these persévér? Echo: Ever.[1]

I hope you like it, 'cause it was a lot of trouble to do. Pee. Tea? Oh[2]

I was talking to David Williams the other day, about Pat of the Lord Napier,[3] with whom he is having an affair. He said he used to kiss her when he was up before, but 'one day I saw her in her school clothes, and she looked so young it put me off.' 'How old was she then?' I asked casually. 'Oh, fourteen or fifteen.' 'I see,' I said.

I loved your preachers,[4] particularly the top one, and the young girl made me feel ready to blow my top. Keep up the good work; we'll have a whole anthology of them one of these fine days. Well, good-bye now,

---

1. Amis has typed every 'ECHO' in red, as also the named poets (from 'Milton' to 'Wordsworth').

2. PTO – Amis was at the end of the page.

3. A pub in Oxford; David Williams was a contemporary at St John's, one of 'The Seven'.

4. Larkin's and Amis's letters of the period often (as here) include drawings of lecherous priests and preachers and nubile Willow Gables schoolgirls.

and don't let the bastards grind you down. CHRIST ITS BLEEDING COLD

Smallholder bum,

Kingsley

[TLS: Bodleian]

TO PHILIP LARKIN – 24 FEBRUARY 1947

19 S. John Street, Oxford

My dear Philip,

I am very sorry (THAT'S RIGHT) to have not written back to you before this, I have been naughty haven't I (YES). Well, to be quite honest,[1] I have been working too hard at my books. I have been doing

1. Amis has circled 'to be quite honest' in pen and drawn an arrow to the MS addition 'BUG A RING QUEUE RATE'.

Dryden, and good as he is he has to be read with close attention or half the beauty of his verse gets missed (Ahr f'r fark's sake. Hawf o'fack-all's fackun' fack-all). Reading him is not wasted: one discovers hitherto overlooked virtues in poets so diverse as Chaucer, Milton and Keats. What those three had to say may have been ELEMENTARY, or SILLY, or WRONG, or DISAGREEABLE, or UNIMPORTANT, or NOT WORTH SANG, but they *did* have SOMETHING to *SAY*. Dryden HASN'T GOT ANYTHING TO SAY, AT *ALL*, but that doesn't stop him, OH NO, he goes *on* and *on*. And he won't stop billybarleybubbub [. . .]

Haemoglobin bum,

Kingsley

[ALS: Bodleian]

TO PHILIP LARKIN – 15 MARCH 1947

St. John's College, Oxford

[. . .] Thank you very much for the facetia.[1] I don't know how you can bear to part with them. I wish I had your courage and could become a subscriber myself. What I like about this week's is the inalienably *dirty-postcard* appearance of the young women, especially the fair one. I am sure they are professional *dirty-postcard* models. Myself I am getting to be very interested in a fantasy of my own making about two schoolgirls named Maisie and Marianne who find out about lesbianism together. They are the same age and the same height, so that they are not active/passive but active/active; Maisie is dark and slender, with undeveloped breasts and narrow hips, Marianne has large breasts and wide hips and is fair, but Maisie has bigger nipples and more pubic hair and a larger cunt. Do you like that? I do. 'I say, Maisie.' 'Yes?' 'Shall we take our knickers down?' 'I will if you will.' Years, years. They are aged fourteen years, years, years.

[. . .] Everybody I meet is speaking well to me of your book.[2] Wher-

---

1. Latin for drollery; the name Amis gave to the occasional dirty photograph or drawing Larkin enclosed with his letters.

2. *A Girl in Winter* was published by Faber and Faber in February 1947.

ever I go I find copies in people's rooms. Would you like me to try to get a review of it into the next Mandrake? What I most liked about it was its air of UTTER COMPETENCE, of your having decided exactly what to do and having done exactly as you decided. Only two criticisms, old boy: I found it hard to believe that Katherine and 'Robert' were 16 when they were 16, and though I hatt occupied Europe stuff as much as you do I couldn't help feeling that the state of her country and her family and friends at home should have been shown as playing a greater part in her state of mind. But everything else was successful, especially the *dentist* and Miss Green and *Anstey* and *Jane* and Mister Stormalong. I liked the way their was no BROKEN ENGLISH RUBBISH and no IMPLICATIONS OF UNIVERSAL IMPORT FOR OUR SOCIETY RUBBISH. The ending was very good and I diſsent from Maſter Sadleir[3] about the writstbogshwatch. Anything more penetrating I shall have to reserve for when I see you and can go through the book pointing out things I like.

That's about all for now old boy. I rored at the ancient briton words. Write when you can spare a moment or two from your labours; don't let it get you down.

Cockermouth bum,

Kingsley

[TLS: Bodleian]

3. Michael Sadleir's favourable review appeared in the *Sunday Times*, 2 March 1947, p. 3. It ended: 'Yet almost everything belongs (there is a superfluous wrist-watch worry at the very end); nothing is out of key or dragged in because the author wants it . . . In short the book is fully integrated; and Philip Larkin (who was an undergraduate four years ago) will, if he goes on like this, surely be someone.'

TO PHILIP LARKIN – 20 MARCH 1947

26, Shrublands Road, Berkhamsted, Herts.

My dear Philip,

Well, my old dear lad, it was great pleasure, as is so usual, to see on the envelope my names in your hand-writing, and greater yet to gain, from the writings inside, glimpses further into your mind of such good humour. I liked the facetia more than I usually do, which when you think how much I usually do, will show you that I liked it very much. Apart from the *young ladies' naked bodies*, I loved the resigned look on the dark one's face and the look of *lesbian efficiency* on the fair one's. I hailed at what you said about short stories: YES. At the same time I envy your aloofness: any offer of the kind would have me writing back pretty fackin' quick and sang here are a lot of my stories PLEASE START PRINTING THEM. It seems that you have arrived you bastard. I gather that your recent prose romance[1] is going to have a popular success as well as a success of esteem: ALL MY MOTHER'S FRIENDS are reading it; the girls in Boots' have compiled *a long waiting list* for it; *lots of people* have asked them for 'Jill'. You like hearing that I expect. I SHOULD. I am gong to read it again soon and no doubt shall have more things to say about it then.

You will see that I have a new ribbon for this wordprinter. That, together with my more time and more gloom, will mean that I shall be able to write you *lots of long, funny letters* to cheer you up, old son. Not that I haven't got a lot of work to do too: this vac I shall be 'doing' *Pope* and *Keats* and *Wordsworth* and *Swift*, and revising *Chaucer* and *Milton*. Pope and Wordsworth seem to me to be FIRST-CHOP compared with the others. I very much enjoyed reading the Edinburgh Review (was it?) on Endymion.[2] Although they *mince their words a bit*, it is nice to think that some people saw through our young romantic parvenu right from the start. There is only one sentence of Keats with

---

1. *A Girl in Winter.*

2. *Endymion* (1818), Keats's youthful attempt at epic, was famously savaged by John Gibson Lockhart (1794–1854) in the August 1818 issue of *Blackwood's Edinburgh Magazine* (he called it a poem of 'calm, settled, impeturbable drivelling idiocy'). Amis's reference must be to this review ('they *mince their words a bit*' is ironic), since the *Edinburgh Review*, edited by Francis Jeffrey (1773–1850), was broadly if belatedly sympathetic to the poem and its author.

which I feel myself in sympathy, and that is this, from one of his letters: 'Oh how I admire the middle-sized delicate Devonshire girls of about fifteen'; speaking of one he saw on a coach ride, he says 'the thought of her kept me warm a whole stage'. Horned-up little bastard. [. . .]

Last night on the Turd Pro-gam there was a dramatic rendition of Mr. Whoregh's A handful of dust.[3] I don't know whether you heard it, but it seemed to me to be characterised by EXTREME TECHNICAL INCOMPETENCE. The end was hurried and obscure and displayed an arresting FAILURE TO CREATE ANY ATMOSPHERE OF ANY KIND OR SORT WHAT*soever*, and WHAT IS THE RESANO for changing 'Do you mind if Winnie comes too?' – 'Yes' – 'You mean you wouldn't mind?' – 'I mean I should mind' to 'Do you . . . too?' – 'I should mind a great deal' WHAT MAKES THESE FUCKERS THINK THEY KNOW BEST at the end they said that 'technical assistance' had been rendered by Molly Cunningham, one of Gerry's sisters I remember TELL RUTH TO TELL GERRY that if Molly wants to give people technical assistance she should reflect that she should make herself fit to give it to A BAKED-POTATO STAND before she mucks about with good books by writers; I saw a picture in the paper of the emergence from church after her wedding of Miss Angela Cunningham, one of Gerry's sisters I remember TELL RUTH TO TELL GERRY that Angela was always PRETTY SILLY (though NOT AS SILLY as Gerry) but at the age of ten was attractive, well now she LOOKS MUCH MORE SILLY (though NOT AS SILLY as Gerry) and NOT ATTRACTIVE IN ANY WAY OR BY ANY MEANS WHATSOEVER, except possibly to the CLOTTED ARISTOCRATIC MORON her family have got her to marry through motives of SNOBBERY and of FEAR that she may give birth to a child as a result of being BLOODY WELL FUCKED UP by *drunken* and *syphilitic* Guards officers. Don't you liked my bottomless wells of venom?

This vac as well as working I am going to try to write a children's book BACK IN THE RANX THERE THAT MAN about King Arthur fighting a secret-service war against Mordred in modern dress and make some money. I'll tell you the plot if you want to know. Do you think anyone would take it and if so who?

Look: I haven't any definite information about these Col. records

3. *A Handful of Dust* (1934) by Evelyn Waugh, adapted for broadcast on the BBC's Third Programme (now Radio 3).

except that they will be 8 some time. The first one appears on March 25th and will almost inevitably be Soddy Sperman or Fartie Shwhore.[4] I don't know what the titles are, but Jimmy Silvester said he'd seen them in the Melodie Makar. You take it, don't you? M'M?

Yes a pity it was ab8 the wickend but there will be more no doubt. What exactly does '. . . I think I'm free, *unless Bruce decides to come*' MEAN? Does it mean I CAN'T COME if Bruce decides to come? You've got some explaining to do there, old whore's. Do you know what I am going to tell you: I think it would be a good idea if we two went off on a little holiday in the summer. There would be much FINE SEX and much FINE LAUGHTER and many FINE WORDS. I don't know what we'd use for money, but it would be a good idea, no? What say you?

I'll ask Boyarse[5] about the review.

The girls in Boots' say: What's he like? *Is he good-looking?*

Pardon bum,

Kingsley

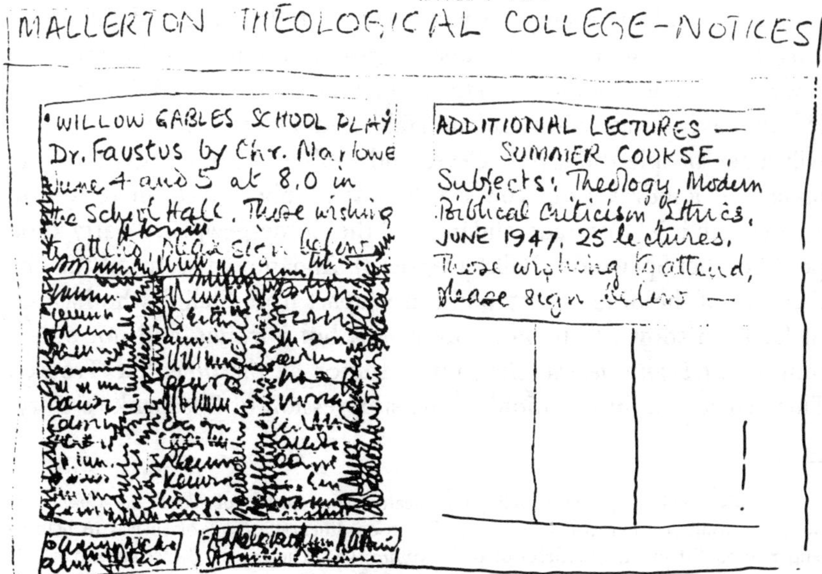

[TLS: Bodleian]

4. Woody Herman and Artie Shaw (b. 1910), clarinettist, bandleader, composer and arranger.

5. Arthur Boyars, editor of the Oxford literary magazine *Mandrake*; see previous letter.

TO PHILIP LARKIN – 24 MARCH 1947

26 Shrblnds Rd Brkhmstd Hrts

THIS IS NUMBER .1. OF THE NEW AMIS UNSOLICITED LONG FUNNY LETTER POLICY IN RESPONSE TO THE TEMPORARY ISOLATION IN NASTINESS OF LARKIN.

My dear Philip,

I was very sorry I kept my last letter in my pocket for so long, as I meant you to have it quickly. Still, all's well that ends well, old boy ('NO.'). I have been happier during the last few days than I susally fraps usually am when I'm here, because I think I have discovered a new paweddercal vein fwraps. I DON'T MEAN a new way of writing wretchedly perverse poems – at least if they are that they aren't that directly ('Oh.'). I have done 2 like it so far. When I have done one or two more I may be able to see whether they are any good and if I think they are I will send some to you for a moſt Diligent and ſchollerlie *Exegeſis*. I have written to Boyarse suggesting the idea of the review of A winter. If he agrees, I'll send it to you first for your okay and *Delecktation*: it will have things about Julian Hall[1] and Flann O'Brien in it that will make people think how clever and well-read I am. OOGH – and taklign of Randrake; did you see the last number? *Well*, there was an ar'-tickle in it by Comrade Zhdanov[2] of the Comespewpissed Farty knob pee Shovshet Spewnion (Ballshavepricks). Zhdanov, it seems, is the one member of the original 1917 politburo (apart from Stalin) who has not so far been shown to be not only *wrong*, but a *traitor*, and not only a traitor *just before he was shot*, but a traitor *all the time*, like Trotsky. This article is a 'justification' of the suppression of Zoschenko's story[3]

1. Julian Hall (1907–74), novelist and theatre critic, author of *The Senior Commoner* (1933), 'a wonderful marsh-light of a novel whose influence in 1946 or so was to help to render unpublishable the predecessor of *Lucky Jim* [i.e. "The Legacy"]' (*Memoirs*, p. 55). It was Larkin who introduced Amis to the novel, which Larkin discusses in 'The Traffic in the Distance' (1982), reprinted in *Required Writing*, pp. 274–7.

2. 'A Russian View of Literature', by Andrei Zhdanov (1896–1948), Stalin's protégé, and a key figure in shaping Soviet culture after World War II, appeared in *Mandrake* 4:1 (Winter 1946), pp. 62–7.

3. Mikhail Zoshchenko (1895–1958), subversive comic writer, whose 1946 story 'The Adventure of a Monkey' was published in the magazine *Star*. Zhdanov's article in *Mandrake*

and 'by occasion' an attack on (I quote) 'the limited bourgeois-philistine literature of the west'. NAY: *if* the Russians said 'We *know* our art ISN'T NEARLY AS GOOD as the capitalistic arts, because we haven't been doing it NEARLY AS LONG; we respect the bourgeois artists, who are MUCH BETTER THAN WE ARE, and want to learn from them; and we hope you'll not be too hard on us, because though we can't do much yet we HOPE to catch you up SOME DAY and PERHAPS do something different and worthwhile IF YOU HELP US; we're SORRY we're NO GOOD, but we're trying' then you and I wouldn't mind so much; WE'D MIND, but we wouldn't mind *so much. But* when they show us their *pictures*, which are UNRELIEVED BAD NINETEENTH CENTURY ANECDOTAL ACADEMY PISS, and their *sculptures*, which are UNRELIEVED BAD PROPAGANDIST GIANT-WORSHIPPING PISS (I've seen films of them, so I *know*), and their *music*, which is UNRELIEVED BAD POPULAR-SONG AND OUT-MODED 1910–1930 ARIDITY PISS (I've heard some, so I *know*), and their *prose*, which is UNRELIEVED BAD[4] GREAT-HUMAN-HEART SAROYAN[5] AND SATURDAY EVENING POST PISS (I've read some, so I *know*), and their *poetry* (rgh! sxxt! frks!), which is UNRELIEVED BAD NATIONAL SAVINGS ADVERTISEMENT AND JOHN PUDNEY PISS (I've read some, so I *know*), and EXPECT US TO SAY THAT IT IS BETTER THAN OUR OWN AND IS GOING TO GO ON GETTING BETTER WHILE OURS GETS WORSE? THEN I start getting angry and saying strange uncouth expressions with my mouth. I hope this hasn't bored you too much, but I had to tell someone about it.

While we are on literature, did you see the March Strand Magazine?[6] It had a poem in it by that crazy Welch fellow Thomas, 'explained' by W. Empson.[7] I don't mind this being done, but I did mind the poem he did it to, A refusal to mourn the death by fire of a child in london, which is a very good example of Thos. using his verbal alchemy to dress

was an excerpt from a speech he delivered before a Conference of Party and Literary Workers in Leningrad soon after the story appeared.

4. MS addition.

5. William Saroyan (1908–81), American playwright, novelist and short-story writer.

6. *Strand* (1891–1950), a popular illustrated monthly, included among its contributors H.G. Wells, Arthur Conan Doyle and P.G. Wodehouse.

7. William Empson (1906–84), poet and critic; Professor of English Literature, Sheffield University (1953–71); knighted (1979). His article on Thomas, entitled 'The Explanation', appears in *Strand* 112:675 (March 1947), pp. 61–4.

up a trite idea in language designed to prevent people from seng how trite it is – it is the mankind making dark one. I wish he'd GROW UP. There was also a very undistinguished story by Evelyn Waugh, of sub-Lilliput[8] standard, about a silly man tryng to murder his silly wife. John Betjeman writes a puff of it and says 'Notice the utter destruction in which the scene is set. How the characters are chaotic inhabitants of chaos' (they're a bit worried and they live in broken-down houses is what he MEANS).[9] No wonder the sin of hate bred another sin, that of murder (he decides to murder her because he didn't like her, is what he MEANS). Evil breeds evil (oh farks whark it ap yer). The story is a morality (so's yer aunt fanny). He also says '. . . you may consider his . . . story simply depressing.' I DON'T. 'But you won't deny that it is good writing.' Oh yes I will my dear fellow, that's just what I will deny. '. . . his most remarkable achievement, B'hd Revisited . . .' bwbwbw-bwbwbwbwbwbwbwbwbwbwbwbwbw. 'He has no sentimentality.' Oh yes he has, my dear fellow, that's just what he has got [. . .]

Write when you have time.

Osmosis bum,

Kingsley

[TLS: Bodleian]

TO PHILIP LARKIN – 26 MARCH 1947

26 Shrublands Road, Berkhamsted, Hertz

My dear Philip,

Well and a real treat it was to clap my poor old eyes on a letter from you; boys but you're the one to make me laugh, so you are. [. . .]

As regards Durex porducts: now there's no need to get the needle, old boy; I've used them upwards of 100 times and never been landed yet. With reasonable care they are 100 PURSE SENT SAFE. The reassuring thing is that if they break you know about it at the time; i.e. they burst asunder and you notice it when you take them off. And if

8. *Lilliput*, a popular monthly magazine (published 1937–60).

9. Waugh's story, 'Tactical Exercise', appears on pp. 45–54; Waugh is also the subject of the magazine's 'Caricature of the Month', entitled 'The Angry Novelist', and introduced by Betjeman (pp. 42–4).

anything does go worng *I* will obtain some rare ſpices and ſyrops of *Affric* that will put things right again.

My god but that facetia[1] gives me the hawn: I like the wrestlers well enough in good sooth but the young lady on the back, with her great big breasts and her facial expression of sexual desire nearly makes me *come*. What do you *mean*, 'final enclosure'? *There won't be any more*? This isn't good enough, Larkin old boy; better pull your socks up pretty sharp, or esle.

I see what you mean about Johnny Keats but I can't really like a man who is *such* an ANUS in wordwriting. 'Doctor Samuel Johnson' (I loved that) seems to have been a pretty good type,[2] but that doesn't mean I can forgive him for resselarse[3] christ whats the matter with this fcuker FLASH: I am going to ring up THAT SOD CATON NOW. I fawrt 'ell that he will use the frazes 'of course it's all very difficult' and 'can you interest local booksellers' and 'have you any more poems you want to include' and 'well we'll do our best' dont you WAIT 5 OM[4]

HE WASNT IT BRAITZ IN WHY THE SODINELL ISNT THE BRASTAD EVER IN

I was very amused by your accaint of the reviews you have had. What did the lady in the Observer think she was talking at? I haven't heard from Boyarse yet. Even if he says no, I think I shall have to do it just for our amusement. My father read your book while he was unwell recently and commented on its maturity and lack of padding. I like my father, but he isn't a very clever man and if he liked it – as he genuinely did – it shows that it could be a popular success if it tried.

Yesterday I put Marianne in detention so that I could have Maisie all to myself in the woods. After a long time I persuaded her to take her knickers off, but she insisted on going behind a tree to do it, saying that she felt shy. She was rather a long time behind the tree. When she came back she was wearing only her gym. shoes. Trembling a little and blushing, she said 'I thought by the way we were going on that you'd probably want to see me with nothing on eventually, so I thought I'd save time and . . .' Her high voice broke off in a little breathless laugh.

---

1. See Amis to Larkin, 15 March 1947, note 1.

2. Amis has drawn an arrow from 'a pretty good type' to the MS addition 'YOU RHINO JENNY TAIL EARM'.

3. *Rasselas* (1759), a didactic romance about a son of the Emperor of Abyssinia.

4. Old man, as in 'Wait five, old man' (i.e. while I ring him).

She stood looking at me, still blushing, her arms folded timidly across her half-formed breasts and her round white thighs pressed firmly together. 'I hope you don't mind,' she added faintly. I went over to her. 'No, I don't mind,' I said.

I like this, do you? I do. I do too. So do I. So do I.[5]

You know, that sort of thing not happening makes me feel as if I am going through life with only one arm and being colourblind and tone-deaf, if you see what I mean.

I hoped you like my unsolicited long funny letter policy. There's no fixed rate of production, old boy, but the next one may arrive at any old time. I must break off this last lamenting piss now and get down to a spot of serious work. As so often, better acquaintance with a writer (Pope in this case) means a lowering of the opinion a cursory reading gave. But I shall never hate him as much as I hate Dryden; I think 'one dryden' ought to be a sort of unit of hate for a writer – only D. achieves 1.00, elsewhere the figure is always less than one, eg–

Johnson	.5 dryden	Jonson	.85 dryden
Keats	.4 "	Shelley	.85 "
Milton	.9 "	Chaucer	.9 "

(i.e. 'tends to' 1 dryd.)

Well, chin-chin, old son. Don't let the bastards grind you down, and WIRTE SNOO.

Tip-toe bum,

Kingsley

[TLS: Bodleian]

TO PHILIP LARKIN – 30 MARCH 1947

26 Shrublands Road, Berkhamsted, Herts.

My dear Philip,

Good your words and well your speaking. I have just come back from a wickend in London and am feeling rather shagued. I met a lot of undergraduate drinking men including Duke[1] and Nick and David

5. MS addition.

1. For Edward du Cann see Amis to Larkin, 15 October 1946, note 4.

and Hilary Morris (aaoh! ps! backs! Glad you like arrgh et seq. I do. You did it first, on a potscard) and Norman who brought a very un attractive woman of indeterminate age and sexual leanings; I liked seeing them and then we went to the Bote Rase I SHOULDN'T HAVE GONE TO THAT Hilly and I stayed at the Mapleton which is a sort of crook hotel in Coventry Street and almost next door was a bookshop in which I saw a copy of Jill displayed between 'Naked and unashamed' and 'High-heeled Yvonne'. This is true, but I don't expect you to believe it. We also went to a picture theatre and saw a cinematograph feature in which there was a short shot of Hari-Pari[2] and his 6tet of EXTREME NASTINESS. It was characterised by extraordinary techinacl anomalies, showing the bass playing 2 in a bar while the sound track had 4, the drummer playing with both sticks on the snare while some invisible person beat a cymble, and Pari, who I thought has a BAD FACE, playing an alto solo on his clarinet.

I *told* you your buck was gong to be a popular success. You'll probably win one of these prizes[3] and wake up one morning to find yourself famous FIND YOURSELF COVERED IN SPUNK. What was this poem of Miss Donnelly's? *Not* The white cliffs of Dover?[4] I see that ab8 Hardy but still can't like him very much.[5] I have just bought Ed. Thomas's poems and think him VERY GOOD about 1/3 of the time.[6] Some of them are very like you. *This is intended as a comp. limb meant*[7] I alſo bought Poiſon in Ieſt by Ioh. Dickſon Carre, Eſq[r],[8] and dyd Repent most hartilie of y[e] Outlaie. He is good at the detective part but I keep hatting his *lazy*, *cheap*, *shoddy* style. I'm sorry for more talk of words, but I can't bare his way of if he makes something like something it is like nothing else ex. gr. if a house is dingy and dim *every thing* is

2. For Hari-Pari see Amis to Larkin, c.26 October-6 November 1943, note 20.

3. *A Girl in Winter* was shortlisted for the MGM Novel Award and the John Llewellyn Rhys Prize, neither of which it won.

4. Morwenna Donnelly (b. 1917) won the John Llewellyn Rhys Prize in 1943 for her long poem 'Beauty for Ashes'; Anne-Marie Walters won the prize in 1947 for 'Moon Drop to Gascony'.

5. See Larkin to Amis, 26 March 1947 (in BJLH): 'I was reading a letter by Maurice Bowra on the lyrics of Thos. Hardy today – he made the to me sound remark that Mr Hardy was the only late 19th-century poet except Browning who wasn't trying to write like Mr Keats. P'raps that's why I like him.'

6. Edward Thomas (1878–1917), poet, critic, biographer, travel writer and writer on nature.

7. MS addition.

8. *Poison in Jest* (1932) by John Dickson Carr (1905–77), a master of the 'locked-door' mystery.

half an inch thick in dust and no lights ever seem to get turned on, his *nasty* characters, who behave eccentrically *all the time* so that he can deduce what they are like WITHOUT GOING TO THE TROUBLE OF PROPER OBSERVATION, his use of the word 'somehow' ('You got an impression that the room had grown immense, *somehow*.' *YOU tell US how*), and passages like 'Intimacy was broken, smashed in small bits. There was no more communion, lighted by a small star out of the past. All that remained was the word Murder.'[9]

Men at Oxford say I shall be allowed to stay there until December. I am glad ab8 this in a way, because I shan't have to work so hard YET and shall have time in the long vacation to do the 1st draft of The legacy. Though in another way I am not so glad 'cos I think I ought to leave there soon.

Here are 3 poems.[10] They don't look as good as when I first wrote them, still. Be *high perk writ tickle.*

Innigkeit[11] bum,

KINGSLEY

[TLS: Bodleian]

9. Amis has circled the following phrases in pen and drawn arrows to bracketed MS additions: 'smashed in small bits' ('HAWN'); 'communion' ('SPUE'); 'a small star' ('COQ'); 'past' ('BAWLS'); 'Murder' ('HARES').

10. The poems were never published, nor does Larkin comment on them in his letter of 4 April 1947, written after a visit to Amis and his family at Berkhamsted. No letters from Larkin to Amis survive for the period April 1947 to June 1947. See Appendix A for the poems.

11. German for heartiness, fervour, intimacy.

TO PHILIP LARKIN – 14 APRIL 1947

26 Shrublands Road, Berkhamsted, Herts.

My dear Philip,

Jesus Murphy, Phil, what goes on at your end? Not as if it's the first time, you slack shit. Get those skates on and let's have the picture pretty sharp. HƆՈOHꓕ ⅄ꓶSՈOIꓤƎS, I expect you are all lapped in nastiness. I am too, but not so much. I find it very uninteresting to be here. Hilly came for the wickend, which was very nice, but she's gone away again now. She says that Roger and Miggy are getting on very well with each other: this lowers my opinion of both of them. Chris is about to figure in divorce proceedings, I wouldnt' be in his Sheose, not for a pesnion I woul'dnt. There isn't anything else.

What really motivates this letter is a rereading of some of your letters[1] during the recent emergency.[2] I was *very much entertained* by them. They strike me as *very mature* and successful in the sense of always being funny when they try to be. Since 'we cannot forgive those who try and fail to amuse us', this is a good merit. They are much less sensational than mine, which makes them on the whole better and not embarrassing to read now. There is a lot of valuable material about 'Jill' in them. I can foresee passages in the Patagonian History of European Literature in the next century: Vol. XXIX, 'Larkin and his Circle' – 'In a letter to his friend, Kingsley Amis, himself a writer of sorts, Larkin observes "Nine days ago I felt I'd crapped the bed, and began reading the 2nd draft through again . . . I have started Draft III in a boiling rage. . . The only bits which please me are the schoolgirl bits . . . FUCK THIS ARSEHOLING TYPEWRITER WHATS THE MATTER WITH THE SODDING THING????"[3] It seems likely from this intimate self-revelation that our author was not yet wholly satisfied with the progress of the work under consideration.' There were a lot of other bits I enjoyed, too. Things like your knees at Port Eynon, 'his feelings, which are his strongest point apart from his politeness, ebb and flow,

1. Amis has added 'written' in pen after 'letters'.

2. The war (see Amis to Larkin, 19 December 1947) rather than the recent winter, which saw coal rationing in January and the severest weather in Britain for fifty years.

3. See Larkin to Amis, 8 November 1943, in *LL*, pp. 82–3.

as feelings should' (yes, I know you've remembered that), Hilary's red tennis balls, Mr. Turner, Rose Macaulay ('whom I read at the moment with enjoyment'), Grahame Greene ('never could write'), Wendy Hiller ('Hwat cantry, frens, ees theese?' 'Thus us Ulluria, laduh.' 'And *hwat*' – despairing gesture – 'Shud *ay* dew in Eeleeria?'), Miriam and the gym. mistress ('by the way, she *didn't* refuse' – that still makes me very curious and retrospectively randy), Brian Miller ('a facetious and gelded unicorn'), and you pissing in the little man's pot and finding that his mother and 2 sisters were in the sitting-room and a lot of very funny things like that[4] I have been a long time compiling this list because I kept having to stop and read something at length. One thing those letters did was to make me very frightened – I am typing too fast – of things like having interviews for jobs. I shall have to be doing that before very much time has gone.

I have started writing a little play about Jose and Jenny,[5] with no title as yet. There is a lot of *dirty unnatural dialogue*, and quite a lot of 'business' that you would like. I don't think that the Lord Chamberlain would allow it to be put on to the stage, but I don't mind that much.

Don't forget you've agreed to send me The commoner[6] to read ('you promised'), though after seeing the number of times you told me to send all the conspirators[7] back ('YOU FLARING BALLOCK YOU'), I realise you probably don't want to, much. But do send it; I will send it back, and life is very grey here: things I do because I 'want' to do them are almost the same as things I have to do, like in The legacy.

4. I could find no reference to Port-Eynon, a small seaside town on the Gower Peninsula west of Swansea, nor to Hilary [Morris]'s red tennis balls, nor to Rose Macaulay, in the wartime letters. For the 'ebb and flow' of feelings see Larkin to Amis, 4 April 1947 (in BJLH): 'Brown is "not reliable": ". . .his emotions change, as emotions SHOULDN'T: his balls are not screwed off, as his balls SHOULD BE."' Mr Turner, 'an enormous comic ex-policeman who is a rate collector', appears in Larkin to Amis, 20 August 1942, in *LL*, p. 43; the Graham Greene quote comes from Larkin to Amis, 7 September 1943 (in BJLH); for the actress Wendy Hiller (b. 1912), see Larkin to Amis, 20 September 1943, in *LL*, p. 72: 'Wendy Hiller was nice [as Viola] in "Twelfth Night", but she reminded me irresistibly of Eliza Dolittle' (the lines Larkin parodies are the first Viola utters, in I.ii). Miriam was Dennis Frankel's girlfriend, and the passage Amis refers to comes from Larkin to Amis, 19 October 1947, in *LL*, pp. 78–9. The description of Brian Miller, a friend of Philip Brown's reading English at St John's (1942–49), also comes from 19 October 1943, but is omitted by Thwaite in *LL*.

5. See Amis to Larkin, 7 April 1947: 'I have started to think about our 2 lesbian sisters. They are called Jose and Jenny; Jose is the typist and Jenny the schoolgirl; and indulge in FILTHY CONVERSATION.'

6. *The Senior Commoner* (1933) by Julian Hall.

7. *All the Conspirators* (1928), Christopher Isherwood's first novel.

Does Hari-pari think it's GOOD to play those tossy little scale passages as introduction to his tossy little numbers? BECAUSE *I* DON'T

Write when you have time[8]

Kingsley

[TLS: Bodleian]

TO PHILIP LARKIN – 5 MAY 1947

19 St. Johnstrt, Oxford.

My dear Philip,

[. .]. Last week I got the proofs (galleys) of my poetry-book. I've called it Bright November, which is CORNY and reminds me of Jaybee Priestley,[1] but it's better than Silence finding, which I can't even bear to *say* now, it isn't a quotation, it isn't one of the patterns we hate, and it's reasonably cheerful (I'm getting to be not able to bare titles like The dead godhead or Death is my coronation or The dry bones or Funeral marches – do you know the kind I mean?) ANYWAY, do you know what THAT UNNATURAL PERVERSE BESTIAL SEXUALLY ANOMALOUS MAN MR CATON has done? I sent him a letter LAST DECEMBER, with 6 new poems in it, including foreign sand, and a request to delete one bed-crap. WELL he HASN'T put the 6 poems in and he *hasn't* scaped hawksh scraped off the crap. WHY HASN'T HE DONE WHAT I SAID FUCK HIS BALLOCKS? Needless to say, everything was explained in my letter with the MINUTEST AND MOST LABORIOUS CLARITY. The print is pretty fucking awful but *we mustn't look a gift horse up the arse*, must we? WHY MUSTN'T WE? As you can imagine, the hole thing puts me in a boiling RAGG with the way in which he has robbed me of the last remaining particle of pleasure at seng my book in proof after *inconceivable* delays. I've written him a nasty venomous letter ('Of course, Kingsley Ammis – know him? – he's a funny chap. I got the November thing

8. MS addition.

1. J.B. Priestley (1894–1984), novelist, playwright and broadcaster, published the novel *Bright Day* in 1946.

through after a lot of sweat, and he sent me a very cool letter complaining I'd left some poem out that he'd sent me when the stuff was at the printers. Pretty cool I thought what? *what*??'). Did you get galleys? [. . .]

Write when you have time, scruff.

Epipsychidion[2] bum,

Kingsley

[TLS: Bodleian]

ENTRY IN ST JOHN'S COLLEGE JUNIOR COMBINATION ROOM SUGGESTIONS BOOK – HILARY TERM 1947

Sir,

Congratulations on your programme for brightening the small J.C.R. I can't even hear myself think at the moment – and when one is thinking about, say, Geoffrey ('Smoking Turd') Chaucer, John ('Zebra-piss') Dryden, or William ('Shagged-up-never-come-down') Wordsworth, what an ineffable grace that is! I suppose you wouldn't consider a FUCKING PRIZE-FIGHT, a PUBLIC SODDING AUCTION, a BLEEDING CIRCUS, with BASTARD LIONS and SHAGGING TIGERS, a BALLOCKING SWIMMING GALA, or a full-dress BUGGERING RODEO CATTLE-SALE AND STEER-BREAKING FUCKING FESTIVAL just to cheer us up a bit more?

Yours with delicate irony.

K. W. Amis

1 'The winner's shout, the loser's curse
Dance before dead England's hearse' – Blake[1]

2 Cf 'For tamed and shaggy tigers
And dancing dogs and bears' – Hodgson[2]

2. *Epipsychidion* (1821), a poem by Shelley.

---

1. From 'Auguries of Innocence' (c. 1800–03), lines 117–18.
2. From 'The Bells of Heaven', in *Poems* (1917) by Ralph Hodgson (1871–1962).

3 'I hear a sudden cry of pain,
It is a rabbit in a hare' – W.H. Davies[3]

[ALS: St John's College, Oxford]

ENTRY IN ST JOHN'S COLLEGE JUNIOR COMBINATION ROOM SUGGESTIONS BOOK – HILARY TERM 1947

Sir, This makes me want to *DO VIOLENCE*

Yrs
K. W. Amis[1]

[ALS: St John's College, Oxford]

ENTRY IN ST JOHN'S COLLEGE JUNIOR COMBINATION ROOM SUGGESTIONS BOOK – HILARY TERM 1947

Sir,

In the last 100 pages you have made only two replies. I always thought the job of a J.C.R. secretary was to reply to letters in the J.C.R. book ('Distinguish between the meanings of the terms "irony" and "sarcasm", with examples of each'). That was his job in the old days, anyhow ('Yes, I know you've been here a long time'). Some of the

3. The quotation is from 'The Snare' by James Stephens (1882–1950), Irish poet and story-writer: 'I heard a sudden cry of pain!/There is a rabbit in a snare.' Amis may have confused the Stephens poem with W.H. Davies' equally popular anthology piece 'Leisure' (What is this life, if full of care,/We have no time to stand and stare'); the two poems share the same metre, and the 'care/stare' rhyme in 'Leisure' might easily call 'hare' to mind. See also Davies' 'Children at Play' in *The Complete Poems of W.H. Davies* (1963), p. 191: 'I hear a merry noise indeed:/It is the geese and ducks that take/Their first plunge in a quiet pond/ That into scores of ripples break.' Davies (1871–1940) wrote over eight hundred poems in twenty volumes, as well as *The Autobiography of a Super-Tramp* (1908).

---

1. Found in the margin of an entry (on p. 215) containing a sentence beginning: 'One of my hero's has dashed my young hopes'. Amis has circled 'hero's'.

letters, surely, are worth answering ('I should like to make a record of your professional modesty voice'). So grip your pen firmly in your hand ('Oh farks whark it ap yer').

Yours,
K. W. Amis

PS. Don't bother to get a new book, will you?

[ALS: St John's College, Oxford]

TO PHILIP LARKIN – 16 JUNE 1947

19 S. John St., Oxford

My dear Philip,

[. . .] The other day I filled up a form that made me very sorry.[1] It was the entry form for the University of Oxford Department of Education. When I came to the part that said 'Games and other interests' I put my fountain-pen down on my writing-table, and thought to myself for a little while; then I picked up my fountain-pen again and dipped the nib into the ink-bottle, and wrote down on the paper: 'CRICKET RUGBY FOOTBALL SQUASH DRAMATICS MUSICAL APPRECIATION DEBATES'. After that I felt *much sadder*, as if I had been writing to a girl to tell her I couldn't see her any more, and *much more frightened*, as if I were an ambassador at a peace conference breaking his government's orders.

I have bought a new record, called Shoutin' in the Amen Corner, by Tinsley's Washboard Band.[2] It's one of those records I like very much while knowing it's no good. It has a nice swing to it and contains a ferocious vocal: 'your sin'll find you out in that *a-a-a*men corNUHH.' Otherwise there seems nothing I want. There is a Dizzy Gillespie[3] record

1. Amis had been given permission by the university to take the Examination Schools in December instead of June, but had begun to worry about what he would do thereafter. In a letter to Larkin of 22 April 1947 (in Bodleian) he describes a depressing preliminary interview (presumably with the Oxford Department of Education) about teaching jobs.

2. Also known as Williams' Washboard Band; with Ted Tinsley, guitar and vocals, Harry Williams, washboard and vocals, Ben Smith and Jimmy Hill, reeds. 'Shoutin' in that Amen Corner' was recorded in 1933.

3. Dizzy Gillespie (1917–93), trumpeter, composer, bandleader.

out this month – Good Dues Blues – but I've not heard it yet. When I hear it I don't suppose I shall mind not hearing it now. The French man[4] tells me has koestlersh he has got some more copies of the Bessie [Smith record] so you shall have one when they come.

I feel very depressed this evening. I feel from time to time a slight excess of sexual energy without object, not even towards masturbation, and not even – I think – towards very young girls. I feel as if I am on the threshold of some new and fearsome perversion that is going to burst into my conscious mind with the force of a mastodon's fart. Do you ever feel like that? because if you *do*, it won't make me feel better when I feel like that, but it will make me feel less afraid when I don't feel like that and am thinking of the times when I do feel like that. [. . .]

Now anent our projected jaunt in the hols.: I anticipate we shall end up at Lester or Worrick or Burkumsted – that's the way I see it for the nonce, there being no other possible HQ where the overheads will be less formidable. Of course, there's no tearing hurry yet awhile. Meantime I'll keep my ears pinned back for a better proposition. What say you, chum?

Ta-ta just now, and don't keep the ball at your end over-long.

School organisation, discipline etc. bum,

Kingsley

PS. John Wain tells me there are some Jills in Blackwells[5]

[TLS: Bodleian]

4. A friend of Jimmy Silvester's 'who likes les disques. . . . I am gong to set ab8 exchanging with him' (Amis to Larkin, 20 November 1946, in Bodleian); Jimmy Silvester (b.1922), an undergraduate at Brasenose (where he read Modern Languages) and bass-player in the Oxford University Jazz Band, the Bandits, had subsequent careers in diplomacy and business and retained a lifelong interest in jazz. The word 'koestlersh' which occurs later in the sentence grows out of a typo ('ko' for what should be 'go', the beginning of 'got'); Arthur Koestler (1905–83), the Hungarian-born writer and journalist who came to England in 1940, had published several influential books in English by 1947, including the novels *Darkness at Noon* (1940) and *Thieves in the Night* (1946), and *The Yogi and the Commissar and Other Essays* (1945).

5. MS addition.

TO PHILIP LARKIN – 31 JULY 1947

26 Shrublands Road, Berkhamsted, Herts.

My dear Philip,

It was very good to hear from my scruffy old side-kick again, the more so as I am getting very *bawd* with being here on my lonesome and dong all the cookng and washng-up.[1] My mother seems to have been very good at PREVENTING THE PLACE STINKING; *I'm not.* You've no idea how bad is the smell given off by bad meat; and being in untidy rooms depresses me, but not enough to make me tidy them. On the credit side, hayever, I've been writing quite a lot of the Leg-arsey. There are nearly 20000 words of it now, and it still makes me laugh a good deal. I won't give you any further quotes, or I shall diminish the total effect when you come to read it in bulk, but I will say that the bad men in the public houses are going well, and that I keep bringing in strangers in the street, in restaurants etc., just a line or so about each, enough to show that they are bad men too.

I have been reading a number of books this week: some by Dickson Carr, who seems a very good author to me now; The Glory, by Gr. Gr.,[2] which on re-reading *even more than on 1st reading* I find a very good novel indeed whose faults are those of theme or personal (i.e. non-literary) attitude and not at all of style. I am sorry to insist so much on how good I think he is, but I will go further and say that I would sooner read prose that he has written than prose that anyone else has written (except for unpublished or unobtainable pornography). Another book I read was Mr. Mawm's Then now.[3] It struck me that Mr. Mawm is the only good writer who would dare to start a book with the quotation 'Ploo sar shongzh, ploo say lar mame shows' – how *can* it be, anyway?; it also struck me that Mr. Mawm's style is a *very*

1. Amis's parents had returned by 6 August: 'They came back very pleased with their holiday and brought me a lot of nuts and sweets and cigarettes and a rather pansy white silk shirt and Frank Newton's Please me/You way' (Amis to Larkin, 6 August 1947, in Bodleian). The letter ends: 'You have been a good boy to clear the house up so nicely bum.' Amis has circled the phrase 'on my lonesome' in the first sentence of the 31 July letter and drawn an arrow in pen to the MS addition 'SOILED LINEN'.

2. *The Power and the Glory* (1940) by Graham Greene.

3. *Then and Now* (1946), a novel by W. Somerset Maugham (1874–1965).

bad one, being composed of klee shays in expression or thought (oh jolly good); it struck me that if you didn't know it was by Mr. Mawm it wouldn't occur to you much that it wasn't by some one like Mr. Raf ale Sabbat' E. Knee[4] (waiting for the Sabbat' E. Knee); and it sturck me finally that somehow (*y*.t.*u*.h.[5]) he has yet managed to give you a good feeling of what all these boring old Italian bandits were like. One thing I particularly hatted were the casual references to men like that crazy buggering stone-mason ('Yes, Michelangelo Buonarotti; haven't you heard of him?' – 'Yes, I think Shagbagio mentioned him,' said Machiavelli idly), reminding me of the jazz books 'One evening a young man asked if he could take a turn on the piano. His name was Jess Stacy.' J 'agree, aw' boy? [. . .]

WIRTE SNOO: my principle in the funny bits in the lexey is, Will you like them? That ought to make you preen yourself, my good-boy. I laughed too at the irritated accuracy of the beginning of "'*Tis death* . . ."[6]

Isn't it rather lonely for you up there? What do you do all day bum,

Kingsley

[TLS: Bodleian]

TO THE EDITOR, *TIME AND TIDE* – 23 AUGUST 1947[1]

Sir: I hope that Mr. P.L. Heyworth's letter in your issue of August 9th will not lead to the impression that his views on the value of Old English studies are general at Oxford.[2] To many Oxford undergraduates

4. Rafael Sabatini (1875–1950), Anglo-Italian author of swashbuckling historical novels, several of which have been filmed, including *The Sea Hawk* (1915), *Scaramouche* (1921) and *Captain Blood* (1922).

5. *You* tell *us* how.

6. MS addition.

1. *Time and Tide* (1920–77), a weekly periodical, originally strongly left-wing and feminist. Among its contributors were D.H. Lawrence, Virginia Woolf, Storm Jameson, George Bernard Shaw, Robert Graves and John Betjeman. Amis's letter was headed 'The Suggestion from Old English'.

2. Heyworth's lengthy letter, addressed from Christ Church, Oxford, begins: 'The great increase in the size of the English school at Oxford since the war may possibly have been caused by the attraction of the study of our own literature as a soft option to those arts

they are void of appeal. In their view, the subject's presence in the syllabus is no more than the relic of a nineteenth-century craze, itself the product of the desire of scholarship of that era to trace origins as far back as possible; also, the subject recommends itself to examiners by being easy to mark.[3] I am no historian, but I feel it is unlikely that the present state of England is really similar to that of the tenth-century principalities that occupied the same territory.[4] But of the literature I can say something: the prose is admitted even by initiates to be stumbling and graceless; the verse is shackled by continual repetitions of idea, but did attain to what one is forced to call development. The warriors and broken-down retainers who strut bawling across its pages repel by their childish fits of self-glorification and self-pity; exploits stated but not shown to be glorious are shown but not stated to derive from self-interest dressed up as duty and lust for renown masquerading as nobility, the whole interleaved with natural descriptions in which every poetic opportunity is missed and moral maxims of an indescribable triteness.

This is the echo of an Age stated but not shown to be Heroic whose literature carries neither primitive insight not civilized assurance. The cheapest contemporary novel has more to teach us than these painful reminders of what we have long outgrown.

So that I may not incur the displeasure of my future examiners I should prefer to remain anonymous.

I am, etc.,
UNDERGRADUATE

Oxford

which require more mental discipline. Most ex-servicemen have forgotten whatever languages they knew before they joined the Forces and turn with relief to a Faculty which offers such a primrose path to a degree. The stony part of this path is the study of Anglo-Saxon.' This study, the letter ends, also offers the returning serviceman 'a view to finding a way to live out of the present chaos'.

3. Amis's anonymous letter elicited several replies, including one from C.S. Lewis (printed in *Time and Tide*, 6 September 1947), politely protesting that 'translation is more troublesome to mark than any other kind of work'. Amis wrote a reply (referred to in Amis to Larkin, 1 and 5 September 1947, in Bodleian) which was not printed.

4. A claim made by Heyworth in his original letter, on the grounds that 'social and family life had been disrupted after the ravages of the Danes; again and again we had been fighting with our backs to the wall, forced into accepting peace with little security.'

TO PHILIP LARKIN – 12 SEPTEMBER 1947

26 Shrublands Road, Berkhamsted, Herts.

My dear Philip,

[. . .] I suspect that I shall now put down quite a lot. I have just come back from a very enjoyable jag with mishilly in Greater London, stang officially with my army friend Frank Coles and really at the Morton Hotel, nr. Russell Sq. Tube Station. One evening we went and saw The October man[1] – don't believe people who say it's about a muddle-headed character who can't remember if he's done a murder; that's just what it both ought to be about and isn't about – and one day we went to the Zoological Gardens and Hilly fed the monkeys. The hotel was VERY EXPENSIVE but Hilly gave me some of her own coin to put in with my coin to give to the proprietor, which was good of her.

[. . .] My visit to Caton affords so much material that I can only put down a little of what happened. After he had severely censured me for saying I found the weather hot ('Hot? You don't call it *hot* now, comapred *y*ktw with what it's been like? Hot-what? *Hot*?'), and after I had noted with no emotion some copies of a book bearing my name, he went on to that favourite topic of his about which neither of us has need to tell the other anything. He asked a good deal about Larkin and his writing, and I was evasive and symapthetic YKTW:

– *Jill*'s rather an embarrassing book, you know.

– Oh, do you think so? It's well-written, I think.

– Oh yes, it's well-*written*, but the printers raised an awful fuss about it, you know.

– Really? The swearing, I suppose?

– Yes; they didn't like doing it at all. Didn't like it at all. In fact, there was a young lady reading the proofs who refused to read it, you see. Just refused to read it what? What?

He asked whether Faber's had an option on Larkin's next book, and I said I didn't know; he treated this reply as if I had said, What a bloody stupid suggestion, of *course* he hasn't, you silly bastard; and gave me a

---

1. *The October Man* (1947), a film of psychological suspense written by Eric Ambler, directed by Roy Baker, and starring John Mills. It tells the story of a man who suffers a head injury and subsequent depression after an accident and is then suspected of murder.

lecture, in a disappointed, disciplinary voice, like a humane sergeant-major, on how important options were. Other subjects covered were *my future* – having once told him I was leaving Oxford last June to get him to hurry my book I was instantly caught up in a wind-tunnel of improvised deceit – about which he was censorious and watchful ('You'll have to get a move on or the school year will have started'); and what he suffered from his landlady ('Irishwoman of course; never trust 'em; don't like 'em; as bad as the Welsh; Alun Lewis[2] double-crossed me; can't stand the Welsh or the Irish what?') who has broken his agreement ('I used to have the front room here') and wanted to use the bathroom that adjoins his present room ('Thin end of the wedge – can't have chaps running in and out to the bathroom while I'm working'); but he liked having someone in the house at night ('I was burgled in Buckingham Palace Road'). During our interview a girl rang up and he made me take the call ('tell 'em Mr. Caton's gone out for a few minutes'). The girl was foreign and beside herself with passion at having vainly tried to get him for a week. This I endeavoured to suggest to him, but he converted it into an instance of what he had to put up with from people. What he did do which rather surprised me was to say I could have *some additional free copies* to send out for review – he actually let me have some to take away and some forms to send with them. That means I have the trouble and pay the postage, but at least he pays for the books and I make sure they actually do go out. Where did you say you thought I should send them? 'You'll let me have the tenner for the 50 copies, won't you?' he concluded. I didn't like that.[3]

I wrote a letter to Helen[4] and in her reply she hinted that I might meet her at Paddington on her return from Corn wall. 'Please don't forget to ring me up to arrange our meeting' BARCKSZ of coarse I'm glad in a way because flattered but I think I am being about to become tangled up and expected to spend money WELL SHES HAD THAT and in siddon tell 'ee I disliked in your last letter that piece of sneering, would-be clever and modern D.E. Laurence crack about me doing anything to avoid hurting my girl except hurting myself. That's just Blooms-

2. For Alun Lewis see Amis to Larkin, 18 April 1946, note 3.

3. In the margins of this paragraph Amis has turned the paper sideways and written: '*aargh* – I'd forgotten the way his voice goes right up into the treble register at ends of sentences – *AARGH*,' and 'We also discovered that we are both of Huguenot descent.'

4. A girl Amis met at Berkhamsted, at a party given by the daughter of a friend of his parents (see Amis to Larkin, 1 September 1947, in Bodleian).

bury talk, old boy, and the sooner you pack up that sort of cynical, know-all stuff, which doesn't mean a thing any road, the better. It doesn't suit you, and you know it. So just be natural, that's all. See rears Leith-o, didn't I tell you how I once refrained from slapping a length on Noel[5] because it would hurt Hilly if I did?

Send me your reactions to the enclosed a.s.a.p. Larkin,

> The red rose cries, 'Helluh-er, helluh-er;'
> And the white rose weeps, 'Chwist nuh-er;'
> The larkspur listens, 'Good shuh-er, good shuh-er;'
> And the lily whispers, 'Feark yah-er,'[6]

You'll have to get down to some wrok KOK work now wont you bum,

Kingsley

[TLS: Bodleian]

TO PHILIP LARKIN – 17 SEPTEMBER 1947

26 Shrublands Road, Berkhamsted, Herts.

My dear Philip,

Thank you for your postcard, which arrived to-day. I am not waiting for the letter you speak of to arrive before beginning a reply to it, because I am feeling a little sad in my mind, the consequence of having been ill in my body for a few days. On Saturday I found that my body was hotter than it ought to be, and there was bad to me in the fore head and the throat, as if my eye balls were moving on warm wires and I had got something of ill-defined shape, but possessed of many sharp edges, like the head of a tin-opener, stuck in my throat. I stayed in bed day after day, my mouth like the bottom of some long-forgotten

5. See Amis to Larkin, 5 June 1947 (in Bodleian): 'The other day Noel turned up here and I saw her and removed a lot of her clothing in Xt ch meadows, but I didn't shag her because I decided it would spoil thigns with Hilly and that I am not anix mortonsh to *mezzrowsh* anxious to be at dong.' There are no other references to Noel in the correspondence.

6. A burlesque of lines from Tennyson's *Maud* (1855): 'The red rose cries, "She is near, she is near;"/And the white rose weeps, "She is late;"/The Larkspur listens, "I hear, I hear;"/ And the lily whispers, "I wait"' (I.xx.10.912–15).

item of bedroom furniture, and was eventually given some opening medicine, which blew me out like a baby would do. Now and then a huge, loose-lipped wind-stocking of a fart would slide trembling from my anus, accompanied by the noise of thick tyres locking upon a concrete roadway. My great pendulous belly had badness: there was pluck and knock in it as of some great tide. When I shat my arse spewed like a monstrous fish in its death-throe. But that is over now and I have got up. [. . .]

Received your VERY KINDLY LONG AND DETAILED exegesis this a.m.[1] I am very cheered by your approval of what you approve of; I would I mean should (I am getting rather tired of being wary abt. using these words in letters to you; I say should whenever possible, because I would too often carries an unspoken protasis: if I were you) differ from you a little. I like v *peace* V ['Letter to Elisabeth'] all right, but I like straight/strut; the couplet was made up in about one minute and satisfied me at once, so there oughtn't to be anything forced ab8 it, though I know that doesn't mean that there isn't anything forced about it. I don't think the ones you think are Ordenish are all that Ordenish, but I agree on the Empsonian ones and am surprised you didn't pick out IV ['Elisabeth's Intermezzo'] as another one; it was written under E's direct influence. I am surprised too you didn't select X ['My hymn of doves'] and IX ['The steady ground bled white'] for prolonged and offensive sneering. THE ONES I HATE (not in order) are IV, VIII ['Aviator's Hymn'], IX ['The steady ground bled white'], X ['My hymn of doves'], XII ['Something Was Moaning in the Corner'], XIII ['To lever up the eyelid of a generation'], XX ['27 January 1946'], as well as odd bits. Glad you like XXX ['Release']; I was afraid it was prosy. I must say I am fond of XXXI ['Retrospect'], though not of v. 1, and like the end, tho I know it probly isnt evryones cup o tea. I know the end of XXIII ['The End of an Army'] reminds you of that Auden thing, but it doesn't me, and I rather like the pome as a hole. Sign C[2] was a man I knew in the Army who was in the cells awaiting court martial for refusing to take a rifle on parade and finally walking off the

---

1. Of *Bright November*. The titles of the poems Amis refers to by number in the following sentences are given in square brackets in the text itself. Only six poems from *Bright November* were reprinted in *CP*: 'Letter to Elisabeth', 'Radar', 'Belgian Winter', 'Beowulf', 'Bed and Breakfast' and 'Retrospect'.

2. Signalman Caulfield. See 'The Accused Then Left the Ranks' (Poem VI).

parade-ground ('the accused then left the ranks' is an imaginary extract from the report on the incident). He was supposed to be a religious maniac; I thought him religious, but not a maniac; no, he seemed well aware of what the Christian holy books meant about violence and to have acted accordingly. I talked to him in the cells once when I was orderly officer; he was contemptuous of my efforts to put the army's point of view to him, but grateful that I had talked to him at all; no other officer had, apparently. If the sergeant[3] of the guard hadn't been listening I should have sympathised with him. That sort of thing used to make me indignant in the days when that sort of thing used to make me indignant. [. . .]

The double sorwe of Troilus for to tellen bum,

Kingsley

PS – Thanks for advice about reviewers – I will do as you say. Might send one to Scrutiny – what's their address?[4]

[TLS: Bodleian]

TO PHILIP LARKIN – 3 OCTOBER 1947

Brighton[1]

Dear Phillip

We came here on Wedensday and the weather is lovely, though its to cold to bathe, last night we waited to see Mr. Churchill, but he did'nt come out, the Ice Rink looks nice but I had'nt got room for my skatting boots, We are going home tomorow, mummie says the Air is very good from Maisie

Marianne is at Rodean and is coming to Tea this afternoon.

[AL: Bodleian]

3. Amis has circled the word 'sergeant' and drawn an arrow to a MS addition reading: 'Coom aware, sir: it's naw use talkin' to him.'

4. MS addition

---

1. This picture postcard (see plates section), with its view of 'West Street, Brighton', was written in the childish hand of 'Maisie' (amorous schoolgirl chum of 'Marianne'), and littered with joke spelling mistakes. It was posted from Brighton, where Amis was spending three days on holiday with his parents.

TO PHILIP LARKIN – 6 DECEMBER 1947

55 Saint John Street,[1] *Oxford.*

My dear Philip,

It was very kind of you to send me a letter to arrive on Exam Day, and it has been very lazy and unkind of me not to reply to it before; but I'm sure you remember that activity *of any kind* is distasteful to one after going in for one of these nastly jubble nasty things. But now four days' drunkenness is over, and I have just had a very good collection,[2] and I have just lighted a cigarette, and I have just played one of my new records – After awhile/Muskrat (Sc) ramble, by Benny Goodman's Boys – Bruns. 1864 – and and I have just had a mighty and puissant shit, shaking its invincible turds, so I feel in an epistolary mood. My typewriter does not seem to have liked not being used for a long time and that is why this letter is a hard one to read. The Goodman record is not *very* good ('No?') but there is some good Freeman and some good but rather ragtimey Sullivan and some strangely *incompetent* Goodman ('Really?') but both sides are good listening ('Are you then telling me so?'). It was funny how I got it ('So?'); yes, I just asked for it in Russells'[3] and they had an old copy that must have been there for years ('Is that the fact, you say?').

I won't say anything about the examination except that it was not much better or worse than I expected; my chances are still about 4:1 against getting a first-class. I wrote a good answer praising the works of Mr. Pope which I expect they liked. Bruce was up here a day or two ago and was very sorry to have missed you. I sold him one of my books and he was very pleased with Swan Song and Buried for Pleasure (?) but thought Love lies bleeding wasn't up to his susal flappitits usual standard. He has engaged me to write a libretto for an opera he wishes to write;[4] do you think this is a good idea? I think perhaps I do. It is

---

1. Amis moved out of 19 St John's Street in June for unspecified reasons; see irritated reference to packing in Amis to Larkin, 22 June 1947 (in Bodleian).

2. College examination.

3. A record shop in the High in Oxford.

4. Probably the germ of *To Move the Passions*, 'a projected and fully planned grand opera', only the first act of which Amis finished. Amis describes his libretto as 'written in the consonantal rhyme or chime Wilfred Owen used in poems of his like "Strange Meeting". It was to have been a costume piece set in the musical world of eighteenth-century London,

all about two eighteenth century dramatists collaborating on a masque to be performed before the King. Then I shall get weaving on the Legacy again.

Hilly and I are making a man at the moment which is worrying me rather, but not as much as it might because we have assembled a lot of chemicals which are inimical to the continued retention of the fertilised ovum. *Nasty mess* for this complacently inefficient little typewriter that sends its words climbing up over the paper. I am very sorry you felt so bared about going away after that wickend; I too felt bared. Why don't you work here? Or why don't I work there? I remeber clappibum remember sang something abt. make me sound like an old tart but the context eludes me. What was it, please? I too forget that Welch rhyme; can you remember anything about it? I'm sorry you thought I was contemptuous in my *for*bearance (old boy); I didn't mean to be. I think it was because I was determined not to show myself as a thoroughly good sort and easy-going sporting bloke. That would have been worse, wouldn't it? Yes, that's what that would have been. [. . .]

I feel very sad now. Most people went down to-day and I have not enough money and my meter is about to run out of electricity and I have no coin to put in it and I am rather frightened about the examination results and about making this man of ours. Altogether then everything is rather rumpish and there's nothing that I particularly want to do. I'm afraid this letter isn't very funny but at least it's *fairly* long.

with a plot about a decent middle-aged composer, a nasty pushy young composer, and the young ingenue they were both pursuing' (*Memoirs*, p. 73), a description which recalls the one-sentence plot given here (excepting the shift from 'dramatists' to 'composers'). Four months later (in Amis to Larkin, 24 April 1948) Amis announces that 'Bruce has composed about 15 minutes of TMTP' – a second reason for identifying the piece referred to here as the germ of *To Move the Passions*. But Jacobs, *Biography*, pp. 130–1, identifies the opera plot Amis refers to as having 'fudged out' with Montgomery at the end of 1950 (see Amis to Larkin, 17 December 1950) as *To Move the Passions*. If Jacobs is correct, then this is likely to be a different plot from the one mentioned here, and referred to four months later as 'TMTP'. A third reason for thinking that the opera this letter refers to is *To Move the Passions* – and that the opera referred to in the 17 December 1950 letter is different – is the existence of a twenty-eight-page second draft of the first act of the libretto, dated 1949, in HEHL (AMS 131). It is likely that the opera plot Amis and Montgomery 'fudged out' in December 1950 was for *Amberley Hall*, a chamber opera with 'only three characters, a lady, her husband, and her aspiring lover' (*Memoirs*, p. 74); see also Amis to Larkin, 26 January 1951 (in Bodleian): 'On Sunday we fudged up a libretto for the 3 singing characters the Farts Cunt-sill wants,' which presumably refers to a further 'fudging up', as opposed to a wholly new one. The thirteen-page typescript of Amis's libretto for this chamber opera is dated c. 1950.

Hilly and I will be here till the 20th; are you coming here to stay withus frig with us? What about the weekend of the 20th? Again sorry I haven't written for so long; *do you* write soon.

Finished, have you? How do you reckon you did bum,

Kingsley

[TLS: Bodleian]

TO PHILIP LARKIN – 19 DECEMBER 1947

as it were from 26 Shrublands Road, The Bad Town in Herts

My dear Philip,

This I suppose will be being my Xmas letter to my friend and that is my holiday. You must be feeling I am a bit of a shogbelly for not writing before this, now why didn't this type writer begin at the beginning og flaming sh of the line eh, its Chriss type writer, the truth is I have been worring about man destroying mandaed oh balls I say, and about the result of the examination I took recently, both of which will reach their hideous climacteric to-morrow. I didn't get a viva so unless I am *so good* that I deserve a first-class honours degree without argument which I think unlikely I don't think it likely that I have got a first-class class honours degree, more's the pity. I feel I have ruined my career by beng two lasy inm fsz in months gone buy. I have sent some of *To move the passions*[1] off to Bruse; mind you say when you write to him *how good* you thought it was. It doesn't seem likely that I shall be able to do you one of my special Christmas cards this year, dalling (Dalling the Jack), be cause I'm not at home to do it; I'm sorry, becuase yk though they are a lot of trouble to do I liked doing them for you dalling.

There's not a heap of news here: Hilly has got me Hong Kong Blues[2] as well as Shakespeare for my present; I think it's very good in an odd way. When Bruse heard it some time ago he said – what do you think !!!

1. See previous letter, note 4.
2. Written by Hoagy Carmichael in 1939.

– 'I do love major-minor tunes'. Ooh yes; and the other morning when I was having breakfast in Lyons' with Hilly that crazy Welch medico (Brown) came up to us and announced in a laughing way that was meant to show he didn't mind much BUT I COULD SEE HE MINDED A LOT that he is sailing for *West Africa* just after the Christmas festival in a ship with a lot of soldiers on it. He is posted to the *Gold Coast*, which is on the *Equator*, where it is very *hot*, and known as the *White Man's Grave*; he will be getting there in the *rainy* season, when there are a lot of *diseases* going about. He is also *the officer in charge of the draft*, which means he will have a lot of *worry* and *responsibility* and *work*. I told him how sorry I was for him. [. . .]

The light is poor in this room and outside it is cold; inside it is rather cold, too, because I haven't a 1/– for the electric meter. I am looking across Walton Street and can see into a large dreary garden with a path that disappears behind an evergreen and a patch of brussels sprouts. It reminds me of the sort of place that we used to take for our headquarters on pretended battles during the recent emergency. A girl with red gloves has just gone by. Now and then a bus stops outside the house and the people on the upper deck, who are almost on my level, stare insultingly at me, like visitors to Bedlam. My feet are cold and there is a large patch of itching skin on both my forearms, which I don't scratch in the hope that the patch will go away. I don't think it's going to, somehow; not for a very long time.

Do write soon to the bad town and make me happy. Mean time, enjoy yourself at Christmas time – don't eat yourself silly on Mr. Strachey's goodies !!![3] And everything you wish yourself for 1948 ('Don't *save yourself the trouble of thinking what I wish myself* in that fashion').

I shouldn't worry too much if I were you bum,

KINGSLEY

[TLS: Bodleian]

3. This letter was written at a time of severe rationing during a food crisis. John Strachey (1901–63), Labour politician and writer, was Minister of Food (1946–50).

TO PHILIP LARKIN – 27 DECEMBER 1947

26 Shrublands Road, The Worst Town, Herts

My dear Philip,

I was very sorry to hear of your mental bad-being. Myself I am not too happy at this season: Christmas comes but once a year, and when it comes it makes you feel *sodding fed-up*, because you remember all the Christmasses when you were a child and enjoyed yourself, eating and being given presents and wearing paper hats and having a sip of Daddy's port; and now you *don't* enjoy yourself; *no*, you don't get many presents, and instead of being able to talk to people you like, you have to talk to people you don't like while concealing from them the fact that you don't like them; and you feel all alone, and you see or hear of other people enjoying themselves with young ladies that they think they like for other reasons than wanting to debauch them and generally having a good time in a way that you *know* you're too good to have a good time, but that you *feel* you're too bad to have a good time, in, God rest you *dismal*, gentlemen; may *all things* you dismay; O come, let us *debauch* them.

My own Christmas Day was spent indoors, with my family. In the morning we went over to some friends of my parents', and I had two glasses of gin and some sweetening addition, and I talked to two young men about the recent discoveries of primitive human skeletons in the continent of Africa, and then I talked to a young lady with close-set eyes about some etchings she had composed in illustrative conjunction with some selections from Thomson's blank-verse poem, *The Seasons*.[1] Then I returned with my parents to their house, and we spent the remainder of the day by the fireside, engaged for the most part in conversation or in listening to the Christmas programmes over the wireless, including 'Arthur's Christmas Party', 'ITMA', and 'Mystery Playhouse'.[2] Yesterday Christopher [Tosswill] came, and last evening

1. *The Seasons* (1726–30), a popular, influential and frequently illustrated topographical poem by James Thomson (1700–48).

2. *Arthur's Christmas Party* starred the comedian Arthur Askey (1900–82); *ITMA*, short for 'It's That Man Again' (originally a reference to Hitler), the most famous and popular comedy series on wartime radio, starred the comedian Tommy Handley (1896–1949). It ran from 1939 to Handley's death.

he and my parents and I went to a 'Carnival Dance' at the King's Arms Hôtel (Trust Houses, Ltd.). This was so nasty that Chris and I talked to each other without paying much attention to those to whom we were introduced: 'Elsa's reading English too, at London.' – 'Really?' – 'Yes, I began in October; I hear you've not much to say for Chaucer!' – 'No, I'm afraid I haven't!' – 'Oh, congratulations on your result, Pud!'[3] – 'Thank you very much, Mr. Woods.' – 'I expect Mum and Dad are pretty bucked, aren't they?' – 'Yes, rather!' – 'I say, you're the poet, aren't you?' – 'Well . . .' – 'I looked through your poems the other day; I thought they were awfully good.' – 'Well, that's very nice of you; I'm glad you liked them.' – 'Come on now, just once round the floor with me' – 'Well, I'd like to Mrs. Juckes, but really, I'm not a dancer' – 'Come *on*; half the people dancing can't dance either!' Afterwards my father censured Chris and myself for not 'mixing' with his friends, and became quite heated. I don't think Chris will be coming here again; at least, not for some rather long time.

Very soon now I shall be taking Hilly up to London to see the nasty man, and he is going to give her an injection of a substance derived from the interior of a cow, which we hope will cease her Mary Shelley activities. The man lives in Park Lane, W.1, and going there will make me very frightened, and paying the bill afterwards will fill me with a variety of emotions; but if the injection doesn't work, then Hilly will have to submit to a surgical operation, costing £100. On the hole, as you can see, I haven't much to shate abate, but Bruce wrote and professed himself delighted with *To move the passions*, except that it is at the moment too short. It struck me that my impression of his mental maturity received a slight contraction from his letter, which in addition contained two references to 'irrevelance'.

I was very sorry to hear that your father isn't well; I can imagine that it worries and depresses you. I hope it won't be long before they know how to deal with whatever he's got. I was also sorry to hear about your worrying, but I don't think it very likely that you really are suffering from an anxiety neurosis: you don't strike me as at all a hysterical person and from what I know of these things they are marked by periodical outbursts of hysteria led up to by *increasing* and *unaccountable* anxiety. But I know that whatever your trouble is called it remains a

3. 'Pud' was Amis's family nickname (from 'puddies', or fingers, which his mother was always telling him to wash as a child); see letters of 15 March 1954 and 27 March 1975 to his cousin, John Amis. Amis was awarded a first-class honours degree in English.

trouble. I don't like hearing about your depression, and though I don't expect the reflection is of much value I'd say that it is the product of what's happening around you as much as what's happening inside you, which at least might make you think that there's nothing wrong with your brain. Why don't you get a job in Oxford? Don't be infuriated by that question: is there any way by which you might get one? I'd like to hear more about the relation of your mind with that of that crazy mother-marrying self-blinding greek type. Is there anything more you want to tell me about this?

In the last few days I have been re-reading *Fiction public.*[4] It occurs to me that I don't really see anything in the extracts she gives from EM Forster that sets him much above the 'bestsellers' he's supposed to be better than (isn't the old bastard *tedious* and *diffuse*? Could *you* ever read 'A India'?[5] Because *I* never could); and the extracts from Mrs. Woolf she gives show me why I hate her so much. She is guilty *most of the time* of a forcing of sensibility, which I know sounds very Scrutiny: what I mean is that her analyses of what thoughts run through people's heads, and what induces them to run, aren't analyses, but syntheses; what we get is a kind of intellectual melodrama, the exacerbation of *totally fictitious* states of feeling into a sentimental pipe-dream untouched by discipline, a succession of *worked-up* images whose sentimentality is only disguised by their elaboration and the unnecessary elaboration and disagreeable primness of the sentence-structure, and the images themselves are importunately tedious and unreal, exciting the response 'I don't believe a word of it'. I hope this hasn't annoyed you, but I felt I had to account for my feeling that there is less difference between Mrs. Woolf and 'bestsellers', except stylistically, than at first appears. It also occurs to me that Mrs. Leavis is more acceptable to me when she's attacking craps than when she's praising 'good' people; but then I think that's what I think about most writing about words.

I don't seem to have had a very merry Christmas, but yours in comparison, or even absolutely, was probably not merry at all. Write to me if you feel inclined, and tell me what things are like. I shall go to Abbey Timbers anyway, returning here probably on Saturday, when I shall be going to a jolly party in the house of some neighbours, at

4. *Fiction and the Reading Public* (1932) by Q.D. Leavis.
5. *A Passage to India* (1924) by E.M. Forster (1879–1970).

which I hope to meet a pretty young widowed lady whom I have noticed in the neighbourhood; though of course she'll be *ill*, and won't be able to *come*, or she won't like *me*, or she'll be very *silly*, or want me to buy her *gins*, or take her to *dances*, or something nasty like that.

I laughed a lot at your rhyme; why *Sy*? I'll buy your Donne if you don't want it. Is it the Nonesuch Edition? because if it's that new one I don't want it ('country pleasures, *sillily*')[6]. I didn't get a card from Hilary M, for the first time for many years, and don't mind. I didn't get cards from anybody, really, at all, except Hilly and a nasty young man (John Smith) who used to live in this town. I shall spend my £5 prize from John's[7] on the works of Alexander Pope. I got β++ for old Eng and B10 (1700–1830), αβ for Spenser and Milton (Christ!) and α- for Chaucer (*Jesus*!) and B9 (1400–1700): 'well, Mr. Amis, in view of those details we'd better look upon you as *our mediaevalist*, eh, mm?' Frank Hauser and Elizabeth Gregson got 2nds, and Miud and Brian Stanion got 3rds.[8] Chris got a 2nd and starts earning £500 a year on Thursday.

I seem to have written quite a lot, but I don't suppose you mind that. I'm afraid I don't feel quite bright enough to make up a rhyme; perhaps next time. If I write anything this vac it will be some more of this libretto. I wonder if I *shall* make any money from it. I hope Bruce composes better than he writes words. I wish we were looking at each other's faces now, so that we could laugh with them at what each other said. Perhaps before long I shall be able to come up and see you at your place of work, or you will be able to come down and see me at mine. I hope your father is soon better. My parents send their best wishes. We have some chickens now, and this afternoon one of them died, but since it hadn't laid any eggs, we don't mind very much. I am

6. An allusion to a version of the third line of John Donne's 'The Good Morrow' from *Songs and Sonnets* (first published in 1633, two years after Donne's death). Most editions, including John Hayward's 1929 Nonesuch edition, follow the original printed version: 'But suck'd on countrey pleasures, childishly?' The edition to which Amis refers uses a manuscript variant: 'But suck'd on childish pleasures seelily', identified in the textual notes to *Donne: Poetical Works*, ed. H. Grierson (1937; rpt London: Oxford University Press, 1968), p. 7, as '*1699 and many MSS*'.

7. For examination results.

8. Frank Hauser was at Christ Church (1941–47), Elizabeth Gregson at St Anne's (1941–42, 1946–47), Brian Stanion was at Brasenose (1941–42, 1946–47). As for 'Miud', no one with this name appears in the university listings for 1947.

going to stop now, and have a nice bath, and then listen to the BBC Jazz Club. Happy New Year, you old rogue!

Shall I ask Elsa to come up to tea bum,

Kingsley

[ALS: Bodleian]

TO PHILIP LARKIN – 12 JANUARY 1948

26 Shrublands Road, Berkhamsted, Herts.

My dear Philip,

I'm very sorry I haven't written to you for so long. I have had a lot on my mind; more on it than I have ever had on it in the whole of my life before.[1] Hilly and I went up to London on Tuesday to see the nasty man, and stayed in London until Saturday, seeing other nasty men: at least I did. What happened was that on Tuesday we went to see a doctor, and he said that he couldn't do anything, but a friend of his could, only it would cost 100 gns. He would give us the address of his friend on Thursday. Tuesday night we spent at the house of my friend Frank Coles, who offered to accommodate Hilly after the operation. On Wednesday we went down to Mitcham to see Chris and borrow 100 gns (before you read any further you would probably like to be assured that I'm not trying to borrow 100 gns or any other sum from you). Chris said he would help if he could, but his money was in the Post Office and he couldn't get it for at least a week. So then Hilly and I went to Kingston (a long bus journey) and stayed that night with her granny, who is 92 and beat her at Halma.[2] When the granny had gone to bed I 'phoned Nick to borrow 100 gns. Nick said he would help if he could, but his money was in the Post Office and he couldn't get it for at least a week. So then I rang up my father and got the address of Lightfoot, whom I think I've mentioned[3] and who is rich and on military duty in the city of Paris. Then we went to the doctor's and got the

1. For a fictionalised version of the events described in this letter, one which draws on many real-life or autobiographical details and phrases, see *You Can't Do Both* (1994).

2. A board game.

3. He appears nowhere else in the correspondence.

address of his friend, and rang him up. He was out, so we went and saw Bob Hope and Bing Crosby in The Road to Rio, which in spite of a lot of good-neighbour nastiness was quite good. Then we rang up the second doctor, who couldn't see us that day, but would on Friday at 5. That night we spent at Gillian Williams's flat near the BBC, and then the next afternoon spent 1½ hrs walking round in the rain looking for the new doctor's address, and then 1¼ hrs in teashops waiting for 5 o'clock, for most of the time next to a deformed man with a curious disc-shaped growth on his neck, who shook all the time; I thought at first it was as if he thought there were flies flying round his head, because as well as shaking he was talking to himself in a subdued but angry tone, two or three words at a time. He read a newspaper as if he were shaking drops of moisture off it every few seconds. Afterwards Hilly said that what he was saying was 'leave me alone'. The new doctor was Central European and very agreeable and reassuring, looking like a successful and respected American film director, and we arranged that Hilly should have herself cut open on Monday. After two hours, she would leave. The operation was not a serious matter and we had come at just the right time. I then sent Hilly home and went back to Coles's place, where I had a ¾ hr telephone conversation with Lightfoot, who agreed, after a lot of joking on his side, to telegraph his bank manager to release 100 gns if I called at his branch (which is about 20 miles from Berkhamsted). Then I had a talk with Hugh Price, who is a friend of Frank Coles's and a real doctor.[4] He said that, contrary to what I had earlier been led to believe, the operation would be a very serious matter, that there was perhaps 1 chance in 20 that Hilly would have a haemorrhage afterwards and die of it, that there was a much greater chance that she would be rendered permanently sterile, and a greater chance still that being deprived of her child would make her (a) bitter and (b) bitter towards me. He summed up his view of the measures proposed by the Central European doctor us 'sheer butchery', and added that he was aware, by reason of his experience as an Assistant Medical Officer of Health for his Borough, of the existence of a band of Central Europeans in the particular area and of their part in other illegal acts like murder and blackmail. The next morning I again visited the Central European doctor and demanded, as far as I could, that Hilly be admitted to a nursing home after the operation for not less than a week (Hugh

4. The model in part for Dr Wells in *You Can't Do Both*.

Price had mentioned this period as a minimum). At this the doctor, who had been stroking my face, peering into it while smiling with almost-shut eyes, and asking me my Christian name, became instantly very angry and threatened to wash his hands. I reiterated my request, and now he rang up a friend of his and booked a room at a Central European hotel in London, where he would attend Hilly for three days after the operation. ('Colonel Brodzski is not there? So! then I book from you wan room. A single room, for my wife. Yes, my wife: Mrs. Schau. *Schau*. What, you have not hard of Bernard Schau, the vamous writer?' – here he grinned and winked at me). I went back and told Hugh Price about this; he said that the arrangement seemed not significantly better than the former one. So I then thought that, since I had been intending to marry Hilly at some time anyway, no time could be better than the present; that it would be intolerable if, through my miserable scruples, anything nasty were to happen to Hilly; that even with the great nuisance of having a child, the upset and responsibility of 'starting a new home', and the unwelcome constraint on my freedom, these were better than such a disaster as might happen, better too than losing Hilly eventually even if no actual disaster happened. I went down to Abbey Timbers and told Hilly all this and, as I had expected, she agreed that it would be best to get married. I rang up the Central European doctor and told him we wouldn't be coming. I told my parents what had happened and they now accept the position. If by any chance I've failed to evoke in you what it felt like to be me between last Tuesday and Saturday, let me add that I felt as if I had committed an outrage on a schoolgirl and then murdered her, leaving my identity card near the body, and as if I were in a dentist's chair with the dentist about to take all my teeth out without anaesthetic, a measure that might postpone my capture for a few days. I'm very glad that I don't feel like that any more.

As regards the impending marriage, it's hard not to look upon it as a *faute de mieux*, though this feeling is decreasing slightly. I don't want a filthy baby, but Hilly is so overjoyed by the prospect that it seems unkind not to allow it, and since I'm determined to keep Hilly and she would never be happy for any length of time without a baby, having one sooner or later seems inevitable. Since I enjoy living with Hilly better than I enjoy living anywhere else, it's difficult to believe that I shan't enjoy living with her all the time, especially since it'll mean in addition that I shall be able to do as I like, eat the food I like, and stop worrying about not being able to ejaculate when I want to. As against this, I shall have to 'find somewhere to live', and eventually spend money on a *pram* and *furniture*, and have to nurse the baby, but I can foresee myself not minding these things as much as I have minded other things in my life, and this time I shall be getting things in return. Also, Hilly has £3 a week of her own *for life*,[5] which makes me feel happier. I should be glad to have your unprejudiced opinion on this situation. I don't want you to think (anymore than I want to think) that it will mean our association had become less intimate. You know of course what Hilly's opinion of you is (you bastard). I imagine we shall be living in Oxford for some time yet. I'd like to see you very soon.

I hope your father is better and that you're feeling happier than you were when you last wrote; I'm happier than I have been for some time. There isn't much other news: I bought *Journey to the Border* and *Caught*[6] for [del.] each: they strike me as bad in differing ways, though the 1st 40 pages of Journey Border strike me as very good and very funny. I had an *impudent* letter from Caton (perhaps I told you) asking me to call on him and 'report sales' the BUMFACE the *bumface* the bumface. I don't quite know what I shall be doing at Oxford, where I go to-morrow, but I shall be there, being paid money I hope. I have a cheque for £100 in my pocket, out of which I will pay the money I owe you. You can have the odd copy of It Lass/O Roaming[7] which the merging of Hilly's and my record stocks will release. When I was last at Hilly's I borrowed some good modern novels and have been dipping into them – Jacob's Room, by the late Mrs. Woolf (*was* she Marie's mother?), Crime and Punishment, by Dostoëvski, and In a German

5. According to Lady Kilmarnock: 'My mother had inherited a small fortune from her father. She gave half of it away to cancer research and divided the remaining capital between the five of us to avoid death duties etc. – so we all got £10,000 in two lots spread over five years.' As for the £3 a week, it '*was not* for life and stopped on my twenty-first birthday'. The fortune came from trade and investment: 'My grandfather started off as an assistant at a working men's clothing shop, but was soon discovered to be not only an excellent apprentice but also to be good at spotting properties for sale to expand his employer's chain of small shops. He also had a reputation for "sleeping on the counter", in other words working twenty-four hours a day, never closing. Eventually, he was made a partner and things went really well; he made his fortune on the stock exchange' (personal communications, 16 January and 8 February 1999).

6. *Journey to the Border* (1938), an allegorical novel by the Marxist novelist and writer of autobiography Edward Upward (b.1903); *Caught* (1943), a novel by Henry Green.

7. 'It was a Lover and his Lass'/'O Mistress Mine Where art Thou Roaming', a recording by the singer and bandleader Bob Crosby (b. 1913), brother of Bing.

Pension, by Mrs. Middleton Murry.[8] All seem to me to be *quite lacking* in the means for provoking my approval. I should like to *go through Room* with you, pointing out all the *lies* she tells: 'The scene had upon her, as the gentle sounds went on, for a few minutes yet, beating behind, or so it seemed, her ears under the faded grey hair, the power of recalling, in terms far more piercing than she would have thought possible when, some hours before. . . .'[9] oh you *nasty story-telling lady*. I've also begun *Sons Lovers*,[10] by that touched Mexico-loving type, which seems rather good to me.

Well, me old china, that looks like the lot for the nonce. Sling me a spiel when you can get around to it – I'm in the same stable (55)[11] till I get hitched. Don't get got down by the *big cruel world.*

Now you'll find out what's what my lad bum,

Kingsley

PS – Don't forget about coming to see me as soon as you can manage it.

PS – Did you see that Geoff Layborn has died?

[ALS: Bodleian]

8. *In a German Pension* (1911), a collection of short stories by Katherine Mansfield (1888–1923), who married the critic John Middleton Murry (1889–1957) in 1918; *Jacob's Room* (1922) by Virginia Woolf (1882–1941), not, of course, the mother of Christopher Tosswill's girlfriend Marie Woolf; *Crime and Punishment* (1866).

9. This passage, which appears neither in *Jacob's Room* nor in any other novel by Virginia Woolf, is an Amis pastiche.

10. *Sons and Lovers* (1913) by D.H. Lawrence (1885–1930).

11. St John's Street, Oxford.

TO THE SECRETARY OF FACULTIES, OXFORD – 12 JANUARY 1948

St. John's College, Oxford

Dear Sir,

This is to inform you that I, who am this day applying for admission as Probationer Student to the B.Litt. course in English Language and Literature,[1] have complied with the regulation which requires that I communicate with a member of the board authorised to interview such candidates before submitting my application. On Monday Professor F.P. Wilson[2] of Merton College was good enough to interview me on the subject.

Yours truly,
K. W. Amis

The Secretary of Faculties,
Old Clarendon Building.

[ALS: Oxford University Archives]

TO PHILIP LARKIN – 25 JANUARY 1948

as from: 14 Norham Road, Oxford.

My dear Philip,

I was very glad to get 'Forsaking all others' from you, and laughed most of all at 'ballocks, d'you see?', because it is, I think, one of the funniest things, of that kind, that either of us, have ever thought of. As regards your letter, which I haven't with me at the moment, I didn't like reading about your father.[1] That is the most disagreeable news I have heard for a long time. I find it hard to imagine how I would feel

---

1. The B.Litt. required students to attend lectures, sit examinations, and produce a forty-thousand-word thesis. Applicants were admitted as Probationers, and only became full B.Litt candidates after passing their examinations and receiving satisfactory reports from their supervisors.

2. F. P. Wilson (1889–1963), Merton Professor of English Literature at Oxford (1947–57); a Shakespeare scholar.

---

1. Larkin's father was suffering from terminal cancer.

in your position, but I would guess that it is some combination of apprehension and misery, both of which are bad things to feel. I'm very glad I'm not in your shoes. As far as coming to see you goes, I suggest that Hilly and I both come next week-end (the 2nd Feb or so) and stay at a *modest hotel*[2] in Warwick. She wants very much to see you, and I'm sure you'll be glad to see her. If you feel that perhaps you'd rather I came alone this time, please let me know and I'll make it all right with Hilly. In any case, it would be better if whoever comes stays somewhere away from your house: I don't suppose your mother feels like entertaining visitors at this time. But let me know what you want and we will fit in with it. We can't come the week-end after (9 Feb) but we can the one after that. If the 2nd Feb will do, book up for us somewhere at once; we can come on Friday evening if necessary, and needn't go until Monday morning. Let me know what you decide.

The address at the top of the piece of paper I am writing on is the name of the house where Hilly and I will be beginning to live on Monday. It is a rather small and very expensive flat, containing one large all-purpose room and a kitchen opening from it. All the same, we are 'lucky to get it', especially in such a short time. We were married on Wednesday; I don't know whether I explained about this before – it was an emergency measure of the Bardwells'. But since Hilly is bringing with her crockery and cutlery and pots and pans and a carpet-sweeper and bed-linen and between two and three hundred pounds, I didn't feel disposed to combat the early date for the ceremony. As far as I can see, we shan't be short of money: our combined incomes will be about £550 this year, apart from a little bit of capital. But this is enough of nasty practical details. The marriage ceremony was funny: Nick came along, as well as both lots of parents, and laughed at the back while a Hitchcock fat character with bursting eyes and lips like wizened Paris sausages (he resembled a brokers' man) said the words over us. We only had two sentences each to repeat after him, and then there was nothing to do but signing and paying money. In the evening Nick gave us dinner at the George. I am starting to think that I shall find marriage more *convenient* than single life. I hope I shall be going on thinking it in a month's time.

My lectures this term are very nasty indeed: you can thank your living Christ, my dear old bash, that you didn't read a b – lit course.

2. In the left margin Amis has written: 'This mean a cheap place, my old winger.'

That self-satisfied old superannuable RUMPWRENCH Nichol Smith[3] talks about the history of Eng Lit: I am beginning to hold that Henry VIII was really the greatest of English Kings, causing as he did by buggering up the monasteries the dispersal of hundreds of *stupid old MSS* of *filthy meritless maunderings* by *book-drunk monks* as parcel-material and paper for men to clean out their arses' holes with. There is a loopy mead-bench-interested type talking on the history of A/S studies, and an old gnarl of spew named Chapman[4] on textual crit, and a stupid young cowpat called Ker (a descendant probably of William Paton ('No statement, boys') Ker) on how to read rotten old MSS.[5] The hopeless, writhing barbarism of the age of Chaucer (did you ever go into this?) is reflected by the fact that for centuries they kept up a script whose primary feature was that several pairs and threes of the letters were almost indistinguishable: ꝺ is d, and ϑ is e, and ϐ is s, for example. And next term there is an EX-SAMMY NATION on it.

I bought recently K.K. Davenport's That'll get it/Don't you loud-mouth me[6] for 2/8 in Drawda. It isn't at all bad: one side is a blues with some strong singing from K.K., cries of delight from an unidentified woman, and some pleasant solos. I heard the new big t[7] record on HMV because Kaminsky and tough[8] were on it – no no no. I recently read a translated work of fiction by a member of the French nation – Albert Camus's The outsider:[9] now, piss, d'you follow me? Sorry abt this paper – it's Daddy B[ardwell]'s. Tell me abt. the 2nd of Feb. My wife and I send our best wishes. Hope you aren't worrying too much

Rather sudden wasnt it bum

Kingsley

[ALS: Bodleian]

3. David Nichol Smith (1875–1962), Merton Professor of English Literature (1929–46); an authority on Dryden.

4. R.W. Chapman (1881–1955), critic and editor, Fellow of Magdalen College, Oxford (1931–47); an authority on eighteenth-century literature.

5. Neil Ripley Ker (1908–82), Fellow, Magdalen College, Oxford (1945–68), University Reader in Palaeography (1946–68) and W.P. Ker (1855–1923), Fellow, Balliol College, Oxford; Professor of Poetry (1920), a literary scholar best known for *Epic and Romance* (1897).

6. A 1938 recording by Charlie ('Cow Cow') Davenport (1895–1955), singer, pianist; 'K.K.' is the 'refained' pronunciation of 'Cow Cow'.

7. Jack Teagarden.

8. Max Kaminsky (b. 1908), trumpeter; Dave Tough (1907–48), drummer.

9. *The Outsider* (1942; tr. 1946) by Albert Camus (1913–60), French novelist, dramatist, existentialist.

TO PHILIP LARKIN – 9 FEBRUARY 1948

St. John's College, Oxford

My dear Philip,

It was very nice to get your letter, and I intended to reply to it more quickly than I am, but of course, as you will allow, marriage has its ties as well as its freedoms, and some how I am not writing until now. On Friday my parents were here, and were delighted by the bright and cheerful appearance of our little den, and the obviously smooth-running and contented look of our small mènage! Then on Saturday Christopher came, and we went out drinking with Nick and his girl, and in the evening they all came back here and ate our cheese and pickles. Poor old Chris had to rush off yesterday, and only just had time to take with him the shoes he had had repaired, which I had gone and fetched for him from the shop last week, and leave another pair of shoes which I shall be able to take along to the repair shop this week. Yesterday too Hilary and I went down and had lunch at Abbey Timbers with her parents and my parents. We each had half a glass of wine with our lunch, so you can imagine that it was a real family party! Then in the afternoon I talked to my mother and my mother-in-law and played that game with the glass and the alphabet round the table,[1] and then Hilary and I came back last night too late for me to go to the film society. But so I said when the Bardwells asked me, I didn't feel all that set on going: it would probably not have been much of a programme. Last Thursday I went and waited for Bruce in the Randolph, but he didn't come, so I drank the expensive drinks I bought myself while I was waiting, and talked to a most interesting chap (a Greek, as a matter of fact) who knows all about French symbolist poetry. I only wish I was well up enough in the subject to have followed what he was driving at! Still, he bore with me, and translated all the quotations he made, so that I should be able to understand them. Next week-end Hilary and I are going to Berkhamsted. My mother wants us to arrive there on the Friday evening and stay until the Monday morning, so that we can have the maximum time there. There won't be much to do, of course, but the four of us will be quite happy, I expect, on our own, in the family

1. A form of ouija, a fortune-telling game, usually played on a fixed board.

circle. You can see how busy we've been: I must say I shall be FUCKING GLAD when Hilly is too BLOWN OUT with a child CONCEIVED 8 OF WEDLOCK for us to go near either of our parents. The trouble with marriage, my dear little fellow, is not that you are too much on your own with your wife, but that you are too much alone with your mother-in-law, and your father, and your father-in-law, and your mother, and your mother's friends, and your father-in-law's friends, and your father's friends, and your mother-in-law's friends. All sorts of *bastards* seem to think that simply by getting married you are entitling them to 'take an interest in you' and to expect that you shall like being taken an interest in; you will be forced to meet, and be nice to, ALL SORTS OF BORING BASTARDS who 'want to meet' you simply because you have married someone. You will have to answer ALL SORTS OF SILLY QUESTIONS posed by ALL SORTS OF BORING BASTARDS. I forgot to tell you that *to-morrow morning* my wife and I are having a cup of coffee to drink at Elliston and Cavell's[2] *with a friend of my mother-in-law's*. I hope this monody hasn't bored you; I felt I had to tell you about it.

Thank you very much for your wedding gift: it was exceedingly kind and generous of you. I'd sooner have had it delivered in the way it was than any other way, because that way made me laugh, instead of being embarrassed. Don't apologise for your manner over the visit, because there was nothing to apologise for. I am sorry about the rest of your weekend. If you ever feel you must get away from Leicester for a little, you can always come here without invitation: just wire what time you will arrive. Hilly and I will come up to Leicester if you like, but we don't want to come unless we shall be seeing a lot of you. If you c[d] get an afternoon off, we c[d] come one evening and go back the next morning but one. What about this? Not for a week or two, though.

I was very excited by your liking for WEIR,[3] so much so that when it is again possible to write about that war I feel I should like to write about it. I'm glad you find it funny. As you've no doubt realised, not all of what Archer writes in the 1st person was written by me, and similarly for Lewis. However, Frank (who is very unlike Christopher) did do the Jolly good luck bit and the sheepskins bit. You're quite right about the 2 personalities, though there are some things there that I

2. A department store in the Cornmarket with a first-floor *salon du thé*.
3. 'Who Else is Rank'.

wouldn't willingly let die (me and jeeps, for example, which I did, of course). Tell me anything else you think.

What about this lecturer job? I can't find the advt. anywhere. When do they want it filled? Salute to the extra bit of Get Crarckun – it is exactly accurate. Lif is læne.

I've heard a lot about you Kingsley bum,

Kingsley

PS. Love from Hilly.

[ALS: Bodleian]

TO PHILIP LARKIN – 2 MARCH 1948

14 Norham Road, Oxford,

My dear Philip,

I'm afraid I didn't reply to your letter on Sunday, as I promised, because I had supplicated for and been permitted to take the Degrees of Bachelor of Arts and Master of Arts on the Saturday, and my parents and my father-in-law were in Oxford for the occasion and we had a family tea-party afterwards at my home. So the next day Hilly and I went to the pictures and saw two films there instead of attending to our domestic tasks. Now, however, there is an hour or so before someone we have asked to come to tea comes to tea, and I shall use it by writing to you. One other thing, by the way, that my wife's brother-in-law did while he was here, apart that is from eating my food and sleeping in my bed, was *giving me his cold* (or did I tell you that?), and I have been rather unwell for some time in consequence. All I have done this week, apart from taking my Degrees (I found the ceremony of unequalled tediousness and not very impressive *even by the standards of those who find those things impressive*), has been to do some reading in the collected ghost stories of M.R. James[1] (I have got an idea for one of these and shall write it down soon), play my K-K Davenport record, which I have

1. M.R. James (1862–1936), scholar and writer of ghost stories; *Collected Ghost Stories* (1931).

cured with Mansion Polish,[2] and send in some rhyming words for Oxford poetry:[3] I have re-done some of the ones I sent to you about 9 months ago, and find them now very good. While on the subject of rhyming words, would you write out for my arrival on Friday a 200-word review of the November thing[4] to be put in Mandrake? You can't do a real review, I know, so a few *apercus* should suffice in that litel space.

[. . .] Our kitten is called Winkie. I will arrive in Lester at lunch time on Friday; precise details by card or wire to follow. Will u meet me at the station or what? Inform by card *where*. Hasta vista.

I hope you'll accept this Owen bum,

Kingsley

[TLS: Bodleian]

TO PHILIP LARKIN – 22 MARCH 1948

as from 14 Norham Road, Oxford.

My dear Philip,

These are unsolicited words, but I felt you had not been hearing from me in sufficient profusion or quality for some time now, and as I am undergoing a period of compulsory inactivity I thought it would be a good idea to put down on paper, for you to read when I have finished, some of the things that I am thinking at. I think I said in my last letter that I would shortly be going, in the company of my wife, to spend a few days at my sister-in-law's country home, while my wife's brother-in-law is away on a visit of pleasure to the French capital; well, we are there now, and a meal is being made ready. This is rather nice paper, isn't it? unlike the ink. Both belong to my wife's brother-in-law; the paper he uses to record the results of his scientific experimentation, the ink to remind you how dark his personality is. This morning I had

2. An Amis remedy for scratchy records; Mansion Polish came in a tin and was commonly used for waxing red earthenware tiles found on kitchen floors and doorsteps.

3. Annual volumes published by Basil Blackwell in Oxford. Amis would appear in *Oxford Poetry (1948)*, edited by Arthur Boyars and Barry Harmer; Larkin had earlier appeared in *Oxford Poetry (1942–1943)*, edited by Ian Davie; Amis himself would co-edit *Oxford Poetry (1949)* with James Michie.

4. *Bright November.*

the pleasure of receiving a letter from him, in which I am requested to go by the 'bus from here, on my return, to the Fox tavern, where his bicycle (for which he encloses the key) is situated. I am asked then to ride the machine into Oxford and leave it outside my house, so that his return home on Wednesday night can be performed with the minimum of inconvenience to him. It's a poor sort of chap who can't do his pal a good turn once in a way without moaning and groaning about it, isn't it? IM A POOR SORT OF CHAP

With regard to my niece,[1] I have had to supply a *lacuna* carelessly left by M. de Montherlant in his published works:

'Near the lily-pond they passed a mother holding a young child in her arms and talking to it. The woman's face was as intent as if she were playing a difficult piano-piece at sight. Costals stopped and watched this "pretty scene" for a bit, then got a move on and rejoined Solange.[2] "There's no doubt about it," he said; "there's only one thing worse than the look a woman gives you when she's trying to tell you she loves you without letting on in words, and that's the look a woman gives her child when it's too small to knows what it's up against. A kind of obscene lust to protect and perform unnecessary sacrifices for." Solange was looking away across the park. "She's afraid to show she's shocked," he thought with a gush of tenderness.'

I won't say any more about my niece, because it'll depress me too much. She is very small and looks like the American actor who played Veronica Lake's father in 'I married a witch'.[3] She has two cries: a soft, pitiful sobbing, and, arising out of it, a sudden hard bubbling screech, which produces, in a smaller way, the effect of a dentist's drill which has been buzzing ordinarily in a soft portion of a tooth and then skids abruptly on to a piece that is hard, reverberant and very painful.

I'm sure you, as a booklover, would give a hell of a lot to be able to browse round old Rodge's tomes here. There's really an astonishing

1. Marian Partington, first child of Roger and Miggy Partington.

2. Characters in Henri de Montherlant's *The Girls*; see Larkin, *Required Writing*, p. 260: '"The Girls" are the half-dozen women in the life of a young novelist, Pierre Costals, but reduce themselves primarily to two: Andrée Hacquebaut, an intellectual admirer from the provinces who represents the tedium of being loved, and Solange Dandillot . . . who embodies the hazards of loving.' See also Amis to Larkin, 13 May 1946, note 1.

3. Robert Benchley (1889–1955), the American humorist, journalist, critic and screenwriter, as well as actor, played the father in *I Married a Witch* (1942).

variety: some of those whacking great portfolios of French paintings (must have set him back a petty prenny!), a lot of D.E. Laurance, a couple of things by Eric Gill, a Thurber*,[4] Poems of To-day, a *French Bible* with old Rodge's signature scrawled in that hit-or-miss†[5] fashion across the fly leaf, and "The man who was Thursday" and "The Napoleon of Notting Hill" by old G.B.C., besides a lot of pretty good French stuff. Oh, and I've just spotted 'The Art of the Potter', with some smashing plates.[6]

One book I did read was that ship thing[7] of yours, I don't intend to do a *review* of it, old fellow, nor to *compare* and *contrast* it with that November thing of mine. It did strike me, hayever, that while I would rather have written (naturally) two or three of my poems than any of yours, *but only just* – I would very much like to be the author of, ex.gr., nos. IX ('Climbing the hill within the deafening wind'), XVIII ('If grief could burn out') and XXI ('I dreamed of an out-thrust arm of land') – there is no question about which book seems to me the more impressive in its total effect, even leaving out the really nasty poems in my collection – yours. I don't suppose that you, any more than I, like terribly that old book-drunk phrase 'dream-like quality', but I can't think of another that says what I mean, though I mean something more as well. It is a quality I find emerging storngly in no. XXI, and it's not just this dream business, because I don't find it so much in XXXI,[8] though this too is 'dreamlike'. The best I can do is to talk about a sort of gentle urban loneliness ('I find only an ancient sadness falling') that has as its material the dream at its extreme from nightmare, i.e. the kind from which one awakes as if in the act of surrendering a truth; and I'm sorry to sound like Mister Herbert Read,[9] but that is how I am made to feel, truly. I think, that I must have been, a very stupid man, when I thought to myself, when I first, read in that book, that

4. At the bottom of the page Amis's asterisk reads 'Thurber is a scream', but a second asterisk reads 'Thurber *ISNT FUNNY*'.

5. Amis's note at the bottom of the page reads '*I'll* tell *you* which.'

6. Any one of three books entitled *The Art of the Potter* might have been on Rodge's shelves, the most recent being by William Bowyer Honey (1946); the two novels by G.K. Chesterton (1874–1936) are *The Man who was Thursday: A Nightmare* (1908) and *The Napoleon of Notting Hill* (1904); James Thurber (1894–1961), American humorist, cartoonist and short-story writer.

7. *The North Ship*.

8. 'The North Ship'.

9. Herbert Read (1893–1968), literary critic, art critic and poet; editor, the *Burlington Magazine* (1933–39); knighted (1953).

those poems, did not seem to correspond, to anything, in your nature, as I knew it.[10]

– My sister-in-law is giving my niece the breast now –

Well, after reading your lovely poems, dalling, I began thinking about your self. I thought first what a shame it would be if you didn't bring out a book of poems with a publisher, and then what a shame it would be if things diverted you from writing for a time, after thinking that I thought how angry I was that what is happening to you is happening to you: it seems to me, in all the senses of all the words, damned bad luck. If almost anything were different about it, it would be better. You have never, I feel, forced yourself on people in the way I have; you appear to me as far less irresponsible than I am. But at the moment I'm in a better position than you are. It's a pity that nothing can be done to redress the balance, except by my vague offers of hospitality that isn't much use to you. But I mean them. It won't be for much longer, after all, that these offers will be forthcoming: there is a lot of talk about cot-blankets and things going on, by which I am affected much as you might expect a condemned man to react to an overheard proposal to whitewash the interior of the execution-shed. I can't see why people have babies, at all; would you agree to take into your house a noisy, ugly, helpless, bad-tempered imbecile *who was going to steal more of your money every year* and *who was giving you NOTHING IN RETURN*?[11] But of course you wouldn't; we've been into all that, haven't we? My niece has *just* been *fed*, *changed*, and put to *bed*, and is *crying, loudly*. Now, why, just why is she doing that, will you tell me? Actually, upon review it wouldn't look as if the either the one of us was placed too happy for the present, eh?

Nick and I played the Ida Cox[12] sides in Acott's this morning: it's a shame they aren't better. On Wednesday we go home THANCHRIST. On Friday we go to Ab. E. Timbers for the day, *unless you're coming then*. I hope to receive a letter from you "in the course of the next few

10. In the left margin Amis has added 'which was probably the reason why I said originally, if you recall, that I wasn't greatly sturck on them.'

11. Amis adds an asterisk here and the later comment: 'That's what makes me *most* angry: they don't like you, you see, and even if they did, what value is there in the esteem of one in whom you have implanted all notions of esteem? God may like beng praised by his creatures, but that seems to me a groce con-*sesh*-un to self-er-*gran*-dizz-meant.'

12. Ida Cox (1889–1967), singer.

days". I'm afraid this letter falls short of what it was intended to be; "just natural I suppose" (I've heard from Gail:[13] she doesn't come to England until 1950. "I was just an immature schoolgirl when I met you" SHIT & PICKLES).

Smile for Uncle Kingsley bum,

Kingsley

[ALS: Bodleian]

TO PHILIP LARKIN – EASTER MONDAY [29 MARCH] 1948

14 Norham Road Oxford

My dear Philip,

Many thanks for your letter. I may say that I had guessed which way events were tending though not that they had tended so far.[1] It's hard to think of anything helpful to offer about them, but I am very sorry your father has died and I am also very sorry for your mother and you, though at least there is no more worrying to do. If you'd like me to come up and see you on your return to Leicester, I will of course come.[. . .]

You are right, of course, about baybays (this infantile double sound makes me crap): they suffer too in comparison with members of the animal kingdom, such as cats. When cats are hungry, they make a slight, not unpleasant noise every now and again; while their food is being prepared, they wait with some patience; when their food is given them, they show gratitude as far as this is possible to them with their limited capacity for self-expression. Now, baybays aren't at all like that, are they? No, they aren't. It is the *single-minded intensity*, even more than the *brutish self-interest*, of babies' crying that angers me most; it is as if they feared that by omitting to yell filthily for a second or two, they might be deprived of a drop of milk. It should be admitted that human reproduction has *nothing to do* with love *at any point*: it is an *intolerable scourge*, resulting from inadvertence or bad luck or mistaken ideas of

13. A wartime girlfriend; see Amis to Larkin, 25 November 1944.

1. Sydney Larkin died on 26 March 1948.

what is natural being what is good. The life force may well be as strong as the death force: it is quite as painful and disgusting, and now, my little fellow, let us put this subject away in a used section of toilet paper and cause it to be carried into the sewer-pipe where it belongs *and should go*, because it makes me feel depressed, do you see? And I don't want any of this talk about Dad, d'you follow?

A book you ought to get hold of (said Costals) for the horse's pissing is a book named Poetry and the Peep-hole, by *W.* Kenneth Richmond.[2] He thinks that the English peep-hole have always been responsible for the best in literature, and that the fact that they have been excluded for so long is responsible for the present D. Billy T. of poi-tree. He is a master of the *totally inapposite* quotation and makes free use of such figures of speech as the parenthesis between dashes, the apostrophe, the rhetorical question, the verbless sentence and the monophrastic paragraph. Oh, he is an entire fartleberried fool, that one. See if you can find him some place.

I seem to remember 'Opera' and 'Music in England' on old Rodge's shelves, and a lot of books on *architecture*, but that is porabbly because *Miggy* was *studying* to be an *architect* when she met old Rodge (*Jesus P. Christ*). *Did you mean* (my little fellow) to cast some glauncyng Sleight or indirect *aſperſion* vpon *mee* by the reference to books on music ay? ay?

I will seal this up now, in an envelope of inappropriate dimensions, and transmit it through the postal services. Write when you feel like it: yours are shoes I would not occupy. Hilly sends her love, and I send to you, dalling, all assurances of support and sympathy.

Selden End Bum,[3]

Kingsley

Hilly is wearing a smock, now. These are unbecoming garments. But what they draw attention to (*not* 'help to hide') is unbecoming, also.

[ALS: Bodleian]

2. *Poetry and the People* (1947) by W. Kenneth Richmond (b. 1910), author and educationalist.

3. 'Selden End is one of the older parts of the Bodleian Library, where the library records and other important historical documents are kept' (Amis to Larkin, 4 April 1948, in Bodleian).

TO PHILIP LARKIN – 24 APRIL 1948

14 Norham Road, Oxford.

My dear Philip,

It was very nice to get another sweet letter from you, even if rather overdue; there's no if about it. But I can imagine that your time is a thought constricted. So is mine, for the time being, with working for my examination, what do you mean to say, playing at research? Did you ever have to work in Duke Humphrey,[1] with the spectacle cases of dons clicking round you like twigs snapping under the feet of wild beasts, with dead books looking at you on all sides like a hostile assembly, with a dead book open in front of you in which you are reading a sentence that begins: 'It is not to be defended in Mr *Shakſpere* that his expreſsions are not unfrequently looſe and incorrect; but the divine ſtrength of his Genius, manifeſted as well in the ſpeech of his *characters* as in . . .'?[2] Did you ever have to do that? No well I have. And on Wednesday I shall have to prove I have. [. . .]

Thank you very much for your birthday bellygram: it was a good extra-familial touch that I appreciated with my parents here for 48 hours. They are nice parents, but I don't seem to find what they find interesting interesting, nor do they me, if you pursue me. They gave me some fish knives and forks and a shirt for my birthday. My wife gave me some underwear and a very nice scarf. NO OTHER BUGAR DIDNT GIVE ME BUGAR ALL. What have I to show for being 26 years?

Bruce has composed about 15 minutes of TMTP.[3] I feel very glad about this: I only hope the bugger can compose; do you know? The north-west frontier[4] is very healthy and people give up their seats to her in buses on account of she is losing her shape: she wants to see you and asks you to come here and do that some time, I mean, to see

1. The manuscript reading room of the Bodleian Library, named after Duke Humphrey of Gloucester (d. 1447).

2. A pastiche.

3. *To Move the Passions.*

4. The pregnant Hilly; see also Amis to Larkin, 4 April 1948 (in Bodleian): 'Mountainous sends her love.'

her. Let me know *pornto* abt. wch week end: 'just your name on a postcard'. Have you read Hester's *Worlds Apart*?[5]

Subfusc bum

Kingsley

[ALS: Bodleian]

ENTRY IN ST JOHN'S COLLEGE JUNIOR COMBINATION ROOM SUGGESTIONS BOOK – HILARY TERM 1948

Sir,

Won't anybody tell Mr. Carter[1] that using long words ISN'T FUNNY in itself, that the only emotions roused by the sight of a new Carter letter (Christ) are SAVAGE BOREDOM, felt physically like a pang of earache, and CRAPPING CONTEMPT, that his writing is the product of LOP-EARED ANALITY, that he has been *behaving stupidly* and *talking piss* FAR TOO LONG, that he can do so on his own AS MUCH AS HE LIKES, but that we are TIRED of being forced to share his LITTLE PRIVATE HELL OF SILLINESS? Won't somebody? Only my dread of the BUMFACED DONKEYNESS of the reply this will provoke from him has stopped me from asking before.

Yours,
K. W. Amis

[ALS: St John's College, Oxford]

5. *Worlds Apart* (1947) by Hester Wolferston Chapman (1899–1976), historical novelist and biographer.

1. H.H. Carter read Greats (Literae Humaniores) at St John's (1946–50).

ENTRY IN ST JOHN'S COLLEGE JUNIOR COMBINATION ROOM SUGGESTIONS BOOK – HILARY TERM 1948

Surd

Own chew thing; kit's tie mute, old hour, Miss Tocatta; two stuffy's, let, terse. Sup is-ah, soul!

Your strew,
leak, eh? *eh*? (miss)

[ALS: St John's College, Oxford]

ENTRY IN ST JOHN'S COLLEGE JUNIOR COMBINATION ROOM SUGGESTIONS BOOK – HILARY TERM 1948

Sir,

Can anybody lend me a dinner-jacket & trousers & waistcoat for Friday night? I am 5ft 10 1/2 ins or so, not very broad, clean in my habits and given to expressing my gratitude in concrete terms.

Yours hopefully,
K. W. Amis

[ALS: St John., College, Oxford]

TO PHILIP LARKIN – 11 MAY 1948

14 Norham Road, Oxford.

My dear Philip,

I enjoyed getting your variorum postcard and I wish I had replied to it earlier than now, but I have been very lazy. The result of my examination is out now: I have passed. At my viva Nichol Crapface[1] said to me: 'You wrote about English studies; you seemed rather to like it, didn't you?' I replied in the affirmative. [. . .]

1. David Nichol Smith.

Our flat at Iffley has fallen through, ong to bear-faced treachery on the part of the people who own the house there, but we have secured a cottage at Eynsham, only 20 minutes from Oxford, all to ourselves, for the same money as we pay here. It has 3 bedrooms, one for my wife and myself, one for the baybay, and one for our friends. There are 2 beds in the last-named, so if any of our friends wishes to bring his young lady with him, that can be easily arranged. Hilly is already drawing up lists of breeds of dog, in order to select a satisfactory one for howling while I sleep, whining while I work and barking while I play the gramophone. In c. dent early, we bought last week a Collaro Microgram de Luxe (£26), which givesvery sword gives very clear reproduction of recorded music, and to go with it, as it were, we bought several classical masterpieces in disc form, including two works by that wacky ex-infant-prodigy Austrian type.

I'm glad you enjoyed going to the cricket again; how can you stand WATCHING THAT eh christ its the most *borng* gam that anybody could think of; it might have been invented by the War Office and the Board of the Faculty of English in concert. That doesn't apply to plang it, though; I shall probably rise in your estimation if I tell you that on Sunday I played cricket for the Djinns' XI[2] v. Kidlington, and finished with the following bowling analysis: 2–0–12–2[3] (both clean bowled) Are you glad?

I think I must stop soon and get on with some serious work ('Why you four-knee Caton's odd'). Malice thought[4] is bloody awful; but it made me laugh where it said: '(Then the Torr family arrived) There were four Torrs . . .' but I stopped it soon. *Of course* if you can come on Wit Monday, or for any more of Witsun, then we shall both be *very glad* to see you; let me know the griff a.s.a.p. You could bring me SOME THING FOR MY BIRTH DAY when you come; SARM THEENG FAR MAH-EE BATH DAH-EE. I must say I rawed at your pots card; G. Rostrevor Hamilton made me laugh most; I am laughing about him now. Give my love to the jolly *toad*, the battered old *squirrel*, that noisy *swine* whose bedroom adjoins yours, and that sex-stavred

2. An informal St John's College cricket club.

3. That is, Amis bowled two overs, neither of them maidens, taking two wickets for twelve runs. For Amis's prowess (and potential) as a cricketer, see 'In Memoriam W.R.A., ob. April 18th, 1963', in *A Look Round the Estate* (1967), reprinted in *CP*, pp. 102–3.

4. *Malice of Forethought* (1931), a detective novel by Francis Iles (1893–1970).

bint with the teeth and the loud voice. Don't forget about Monday: slip me a card with your time of arrival on it. Hilly was very excited to hear from you, and sends you her warmest love.

Square leg bum,

Kingsley

[TLS: Bodleian]

TO PHILIP LARKIN – 16 JULY 1948

Marriner's Cottage, Eynsham piss Newla,nd Street Eynshamm, Oxfordh fk fordshi,re

My dear Philip,

Good to get your letter my good-fellow; I will refer to it at more length in a minute. My advice to you, old boy, is to *drop whatever you're doing* and get cracking on your D.E.L. thing.[1] I had a letter from the Universidad Nacional de Tucumán this morning, in which a man offered your humble 1500 fifteen hundred one thousand five hundred one five double o 1500 dollars Argentine for the 'first rights' of a monograph on Grgr. My instantaneous reply accepting is already on its way. So it looks very unlikely thag shag that you won't receive a similar letter, you bastard; I had hoped to *outdistance* you a bit in this writing game, but it seems that because of my *good-nature* and *anxiety to help my friend* I shall not after all be doing that. I think the man wants the thing fairly soon, so I should get started pornto. I am of course very pleased to be in sight of getting some money to spend, but it would be nicer if I could finish the legacy first (that carck made me hail). We're a very lucky pair of young men, I think, though I shan't really breathe

1. A book on D.H. Lawrence. Through his old tutor, J.B. Leishman, Amis had been recommended to Jack Rush, a Professor of English from the University of Tucumán in Argentina, who was commissioning critical studies of English writers. Amis signed a contract to produce a book on Graham Greene and suggested that Larkin produce one on Lawrence. See Larkin to J.B. Sutton, 9 September 1948, in *LL*, p. 150: 'The Argentine man wrote and said: Do do a book on D.H.L. for us. So I said Good, & Fine . . . Then my agent wrote & said No, I couldn't possibly engage myself to do any such thing – so that was that!'

freely till I have the money in the account of my bak backs bank.[2] Could you tell me, by the way, if it's necessary (I don't mean just polite) to get a living man's permission before writing a book about him?

The legacy is up to about 25,000 now, more than I did the first time. I have been looking at that first draft, and it seems piss-poor to me. No wonder you said it didn't come up to your expectations. You are quite right about fuller characterization; I have been trying to make Sidney a fuller-length figure, basing his actions on sincere concern for me and bo bocks brotherly love, but I don't know that I have much time to spare for Mary. She marries the most unpleasant of Sidney's friends at the end. Jane I think I'm much more interested in this time; she seems a little sweetikin to me now.[3] I hope that when you come in September it will be near enough finished for you to give your comments on it as a hole: '. . . and finally to Mr. Philip Larkin, without whose intelligent suggestions and comments this might have been far less of a . . .' 'My dear Philip, You have always asked me to write this book, and in a very real sense it is yours. Did you, I wonder, when you first suff fx suggested the idea of . . .'

I have been having a good time to-day, sprang the rooms with DDT to kill the nasty flies, but there is something that is blocking up the interior of my ear and prevents me from hearing properly. I shall have to go to the doctor's surgery this evening, to have it seen to. That won't hurt, will it?

Of course I keep all your letters you ale. I can't remember ever throng one away. They are a treasure that I would not be without for something; they are a perpetual fountain of evil sense, and seem *much funnier* than my recollection of my letters to you, which you'd *better keep* all the sam you toss-chewer. I haven't the slightest remembrance of that page of swearng; what was I swearng *abviij*? Don't you give me any frights about your records like that; are you going to get rid of any, he asked casually. [. . .]

2. A wise precaution, since Amis was never paid for the manuscript he submitted (it was not returned and has never been recovered). *Lucky Jim* alludes to this episode by affiliating the character L. S. Caton (named after R.A. Caton of the Fortune Press) with the University of Tucumán, Argentina. Jim Dixon, the novel's hero, submits an article on medieval shipbuilding techniques to Caton, never hears back, then discovers Caton has printed it in an Italian publication under his own name.

3. In order to obtain his £30,000 inheritance, the 'Kingsley' character in 'The Legacy' must marry a woman approved of by his older brother Sidney. Jane is Kingsley's choice, but Sidney does not approve.

Come up and give me a hand with making the bed Billy bum,

Kingsley

[TLS: Bodleian]

TO PHILIP LARKIN – 6 AUGUST 1948

My dear Philip,

Jolly good work, your quick reply. It was one of your incomprehensible letters, widely differentiated from the ordinary kind. I might perhaps illustrate the difference, if I'm clever enough. Normal kind: 'Your account of the new doctor sounds positively nightmarish; which reminds me that last week Ruth wrote to say did I mind very much if a young medical student who picked her up in a passage took her to an exhibition of modern art. I picture him as a kind of Neligan with a moustache, I don't know why . . . . . .' Incomprehensible kind: 'Sos SNARRTSZ so there I was and down goin' and ALL-ANUS my ſins vpon mee (ponmy econmy) but who do I see man (as the a. said to the b. NO SHTS the b. said to the eh?) but a fellow of quality ('fellow of some quantity') like lay-bawn-hawn. . .' Either kind makes me laugh, but I always want to ask you about things in the second kind: waht's this rhyme about spanish politics? Run-master sounds like a name for a cricket-bat. When your sister gives you a present (thank you for the unobtrusive reminder) for your future home, what exactly does she mean? Does she mean your joint home with your future wife? Cry 'Snow'; m'm . . . SNOW! I'm sorry to have to tell you this, but Hilda Sims[1] isn't very impressive off the stage; Hilly saw her and knows. I'm glad Ruth's passed her exam.; now you will be able to tell her that you don't intend to marry her, won't you?

I went to the hospital to have my cysts[2] cut out, and it hurt me a good deal, UNNECESSARILY, because the man hadn't used enough novocaine. I was on the table for ¾hr, which didn't make me feel very

1. Hilda Sims (1920–94), black American actress, was playing the title role in the long-running stage melodrama *Anna Lucasta* at His Majesty's Theatre (from October 1947 to early November 1948).

2. In his ears.

cheerful. I have stitches in now and when they are out there will be no more trouble I HOPE, though it feels possible that the Harper-Nelson[3] has left one of the cysts in I HOPE NOT.

Hilly hasn't gone into hospital yet, which means she is two days overdue. She is rather irritated by this, but apart from that is still in excellent health. The later she is, the neaer fockink nearer I shall have got to finishing the legacy by the time she comes out. It is nearly 50,000 now. Jock has come in, and a horrible old man with 'an incurable disease of the nervous system' whom I presently take out for walks. There is a very nasty pub-landlord, too.

By the same post as your letter came one from Tucuman. I'm afriad SHITTTT adraid KKCKCKCRAPPP afraid that there's some not-so-good news about these dollars; I asked my father to find out about them and he reports, on the best authority, that the fucking things are only worth about 1s. each, and 1500 of them come to £75–7–6 point something, which is nice, but nothing like so nice as we at first thought. Anyway the man this morning tells me I needn't hurry, says that Lawrence Durrell is doing a 'Critical Introduction to Modern Poetry' (Xt) in the same series,[4] and encloses a specimen contract; 'TERCERO: El Instituto de Lenguas y Literaturas Modernas abonera al Sr. Lawrence Durrell en concepto de los derechos adquiridos . . .' So when I've finished the legacy I shall go straight on with Grgr; it'll buy me some nice new clothes, anyway. It appears by the way that the books will come out in the English way of speaking, so they will form a nice addition to our bookshelves if nothing easel. The man confirms the length of 40–50000 words, by the way. [. . .]

We'll soon have those beggars out *ARSE*

Kingsley

[TLS: Bodleian]

3. A doctor who looked like John Harper-Nelson, an undergraduate at Trinity and leading figure in university jazz circles (author also of *Oxford at War* (Northbridge, Western Australia: Access Press, 1996), which details the origins of the Oxford University Rhythm Club and mentions Larkin and several Amis acquaintances).

4. Lawrence Durrell (1912–90), poet, novelist and travel writer, had begun work on the book, from lectures he had given at Tucumán, in May 1948; it eventually appeared in print in Britain as *Key to Modern Poetry* (London: Peter Nevill, 1952).

TO PHILIP LARKIN – 13 AUGUST 1948

Abbey Timbers, Harwell, Berks.

My dear Philip,

I am very sorry that I forgot to send you any remembrance on the occasion of your birthday, but on that day Hilly was preparing to go into hospital and on Tuesday she actually did do so. Nothing at all resembling a human being has so far come out, and that is why I have not written as soon as I might have done: every day I've deferred writing in the hope that on the next day I would be able to tell you something definite about this. I'm living here and going to see Hilly every day. She's all right 'in herself' but naturally a little annoyed that nothing has happened yet. They seem to be very nice to her in the hospital, which is a comforting thing to think. This afternoon they are going to 'burst the water-bag' and hope by doing so to precipitate labour. It is all 'rather a strain', but it would be rather less of a strain if I weren't under the strain of continually proving to my mother-in-law that it is all rather a strain. I'm pretty sure she thinks I'm not concerned enough about it, because I'm not BEHAVING STUPIDLY or TALKING PISS all the time:

> What is it women do in men require?
> BEHAVING STUPIDLY and TALKING THROUGH
> THEIR WIRE.
> What is it men in women do require?
> KEEPING QUIET AND OUT OF SIGHT, so that they (the
> men) need
> not spend ALL their time BEHAVING STUPIDLY and
> TALKING THROUGH THEIR WIRE.[1]

Talking of talking piss reminds me that when my wife's brother-in-law and his wife (that evocation made me laugh likes odd o' me) came over to Eynsham before we left, the same evening as Mr. and Mrs.

1. A parody of one of Blake's Notebook verses: 'What is it men in women do require?/ The Lineaments of Gratified Desire./What is it women in men do require?/The lineaments of Gratified Desire' (c. 1793). 'Wire' can mean 'penis', according to Jonathon Green, *Cassell's Dictionary of Slang* (London: Cassells, 1998), as in 'pull your wire' (masturbate), a use conflated here with 'talking through your arse'.

Christopher Tosswill came (Christ). Upon old Chris chancing to remark that in the military side of the atomic business, he believed there to be a lot of liaison between the USA and our own country, old Rodge replied that he would be very surprised and concerned if there weren't. Now, this means that he's glad that the Yanks and ourselves agree about blong other people (guess-who) up, and if one lot starts blong a third party up, then the other lot will help in blong the third party up, and this makes him glad, you see, to think that our side will be in a position to start dong the blong up before the other lot (hazard whom) is ready. I think you'll agree that that's no distortion of his feelings? *Right.* He then said, some ten minutes later, that if war came he would be a conscientious objector. His conscientious objection, I think you will agree, would appear to reside in an objection to assisting personally (with its attendant unpleasantness and danger) in a conflict the preparations for which he regards not only without concern, but with relief and approval. His objections do not extend to the blong up of guess-who, only to helping. HES A FINE FUCKING CONSCIENTIOUS OBJECTOR HE IS ISNT HE This makes me want to see his dark, 'interesting', carefully gloomy, snouted face disintegrating under a bursting bottle, while I say: 'I've a conscientious objection to violence, d'you see, so I'm making sure I don't suffer any, d'you see?' [. . .]

I re-read one of the well-known works of mR zodz Mr. A. Huxley recently: Antic hay.[2] I find it suffers from a desire to be greeted as cultured, a desire to put things in somehow if they interest him (all that architecture rubbish, and that cabaret), a lack of consistency in character (Emily has got to be non-cultured to appeal to Gumbril and cultured to appeal to Huxley and Gumbril), and above all a desire, seen at its crudest in the works of Mr. R. Aldington,[3] to be greeted as 'the writer above all others who has summed up and defined the 'twenties with the compassion of the true artist and the penetration of the social historian' – j'agree, old boy? In spite of his *panache* (ahem) he remains fundamentally a boring writer, I find.

Reading some of Rilke's letters[4] now ('You are mad, you know'). I'll let you know what I think of them soon. He seems on first acquaint-

2. *Antic Hay* (1923) by Aldous Huxley (1894–1963), a novel about Bohemian life in post-war London.

3. Richard Aldington (1892–1962), novelist, poet, biographer.

4. Rainer Maria Rilke (1875–1926), lyric poet. That Rilke was translated by Amis's old tutor J.B. Leishman may account for his interest.

ance to be one of those Henry James men who are too busy wondering what a writer is to be one.

I think of you a lot, dalling. Look after yourself and keep the 18th Sept firmly in view. Right; soon.

I think you might as well give the hospital another ring bum

Kingsley

[TLS: Bodleian]

TO PHILIP LARKIN – 15 AUGUST 1948

Abbey Timbers, Harwell, Berks.

My dear Philip,

After a certain amount of difficulty and unpleasantness Hilly gave birth to Philip Nicol at 8.45 this morning. Her labour took rather a long time and must have been very nasty. However, she is completely all right again now, though a little weak. When we see each other's faces once again I'll tell you about it in more detail. It has all gone on bng px beng rather a strain owtsch, especially telling the Bardwells face to face, and the Amises at a distance, 'not to worry' ooh dear; women, my dear little boy, dislike and distrust self cunt-roll, as I may have vouchsafed to you before, because it is an armour against their only weapon against men. But this is only querulousness beside what Hilly must have suffered. My little son has very fair hair and a conical head (it will not stay conical, they said), and a face like that of an ageing railway porter who is beginning to realise his untidiness has meant that he'll never get that ticket-collector's job he's been after for twenty years. His weight, they said, would be about eight pounds. I don't know what this business is supposed to make you feel; I seem just the same as before. Hilly is very happy and glad, as I am, to have something to name after you.

Thank you very much for your telegram, which I passed on to Hilly; it was indeed a gracious act. Do write to her; she would be delighted to hear from you. Radcliffe Maternity Home, Oxford, is all the address that is necessary. I really am sorry I didn't send you a bellygram on your bithrayd; as I recall, I didn't apologise very heartily in my last letter. Better late than never, anyway YES, but BETTER *not* late at ALL. Manny rrghchsz many happy returns.

Have been playing Ellis's Sentimental blues, a piece I rather like in the same way as I like Jean Sablon; also Robeson's Canoe song[1] – ahee ok-koe, yig de' – and composing an obscene parody on it.

I'll write at more length when I hear from you; you are the first person to know about this outside the family, except the chap behind the bar at the Napier and some silly old bumfaces who came here to tea to-day. Looking forward to hearing from you.

Well hows the proud father feeling bum

Kingsley

PS. Shall I tell you who isn't funny? It's James Thurber isn't funny.[2]

[TLS: Bodleian]

TO PHILIP LARKIN – 20 AUGUST 1948

Abbey Timbers, Harwell, Berkshire.

My dear Philip,

Thank you very much for your most recent letter, and for the card you sent Hilly, which touched and amused her a lot. She will be writing to you herself before very long. Her condition remains satisfactory, though she is becoming a little bored with all this ling about on her back. The son and heir ('J' ai sucre y!') was 9¼ lbs in weight, by the way (perhaps I said so) wch is quite a lot. The shape and arrangement of his face seems more usual than formerly. If I can continue to regard it as a pet too stupid to do tricks, except involuntary and nasty ones, I think I shall be able to get on with it all right. They and I return to Eynsham on Tuesday, which seems nearer than it once did, I'm happy

1. 'Sentimental Blues' by Seger Ellis, a singer and pianist with the Dorsey Brothers in the late 1920s and early 1930s, is likened both to 'Canoe Song', performed by Paul Robeson in the film of *Sanders of the River* (1935), based on a story by the author, journalist and screenwriter Edgar Wallace (1875–1932), and to the songs of Jean Sablon (b. 1906), a French singer best known in Amis's Oxford days for 'Si tu m'aimes', a seduction song.

2. MS addition.

to say. When our eyes hold the images of our faces once again, I will say to you at longer length what living here has been like. Pity old Rodge wasn't able to join me. I must say here, by the way, how much funnier than RGP is our conception of old Rodge. Not that it's a 'wrong conception', it's just much funnier, that's all. Pity you didn't say anything in your letter about what I said abt old Rodge (Cries: 'Tall my tea!!' ('Wrap your chops . . .')) and his colourful, devil-may-care life, something of the spirit of the Elizabethans breaking through the drabness and ennui of modern 'civilisation' OOOGHZZCHZZGH, because I feel *very storngly* about this; it makes me want to condemn them both to a long sentence of bum-staring. I bet they make them sit up at Nottingham, don't you? Yes, sit up and lean over slightly to break wind. [. . .]

I really must be careful not to get to hate my son because of the interest people take in him; I had my parents here and had to talk to them and the B's about him for hours. We are gong to call him Philip, after the person who means most to us dalling.

I am readings The sorrows of young Werther, by J. W. Goethe, the eminent German writer.[1] It is dull rubbish, distorted by much cring and sing, overgrown with dreary and exploded moralisin. Write to Eynsham next time. Only 4 weeks to Sept. 18.

People will think you've named him after Mountbatten bum,[2]

KINGSLEY

I saw Joan yesterday: I tried to tell her about Philip Nicol, but it was like trying to stop tanks with the bayonet; in five minutes she was telling me about a farm one of her friends had bought, and I was listening to her telling me about the farm one of her friends had bought.

I didn't care about that farm, you know.
Because I didn't know the friend.
She knew this.
Then why did she tell me about that farm?
When I didn't care about it?

1. *The Sorrows of Young Werther* (1774).

2. Philip Mountbatten (b. 1921), created Duke of Edinburgh on his marriage to Princess Elizabeth (20 November 1947).

She sends you her love.
She was wearing hexagonal spectacles[3]

[TLS: Bodleian]

TO PHILIP LARKIN – 25 AUGUST 1948

Marriner's Cottage, Newland Street, Eynsham, Oxon

My dear Philip,

I suspect that I shall now put down quite a lot. I returned here on Monday with my father- and mother-in-law, and yesterday we all went and fetched my wife and our dear little son from the Infirmary. The latter is now asleep in his perambulator in the garden at the rear of the house. Hilly is very well and shows hardly a trace of the weakness that is supposed to afflict nursing or rather recently confined mothers. Her figure, apart from an enlargement of the bust, is practically normal now, a Circonſtance that dyd afford y^r ſvt great Delyte during ye hrs of Darkneſse, though of course we can't really go to town yet ah! Ah, see you have'nt lost you'r old on-track Mind yet awile. eh. Our repose was, however, twice interrupted, once at 2.35 and then again at about 6.30, when our little son wished to signify his hunger and dissatisfaction in the only way as yet possible to him, that is, by SCREATCHING as if he had an earwig in his wee gullet. Despite this, and despite watching him taking the breast yesterday afternoon, during which he shat thin mustard pickle on to Hilly's apron and then pissed over the arm of the chair, I feel much more kindly towards him than I thought I should; of course I know 'your own is different' OOTZZSCH, but he seems an inoffensive and almost apologetic little boy, with a face only about half as ugly as I expected. I haven't seen him when he's just been, or is being, sick yet, of course.

One of the things that I am glad about is that my father-in-law has now left my roof-tree. I know he's a dear old chap, but anybody who troubles as little as he does about what other people will think of what he does and says ought to sit themselves down for a little quiet thought.

3. MS addition; This 'Joan' appears a half dozen times in the letters to Larkin of 1947–48, but is never identified and is unknown to Motion or Thwaite.

He kept telling me, all the time I was stang at A. T., all about his linguistic travels in one of the larger and more aparsely-populated cantons of the Swiss Confederation. Now, I didn't want to know about that; why didn't he take that into account? Another thing that tore me with RAGG was when I chanced to consult Roget's celebrated 'Thesaurus' for a synonym I required for my work of fiction. He said to me, 'They've just reprinted that, you know.' I said, 'What, Roget?', pronouncing the proper noun with a short 'o', as in the English 'Rodge'. 'Yes, Roget,' he said, pronouncing it 'Roh-zhey' *as if it had a circumflex over the 'o'*. *Correcting* me, you see. NAY, I mind being corrected as much as anybody, but when I am corrected from what is right to what is wrong, I become angry in my brain. Another time he helped me to more curry and put it all over the handles of my knife and fork. Another time I passed him the sauce bottle, which was nearly empty, upside down, so that he wouldn't have to shake the sauce down anew. He just sat and watched while I held it, so that I had to wait until enough sauce had come out for him to signify that he had all he needed. Another time he showed me a map – but that will take too long in the telling. Remind me to tell you what he did in the Cornmarket. Another thing that displeased me a good deal came from my mother-in-law. A discussion was in progress about the beauties of our English countryside, into which I injected the opinion that human bengs were more important than a lot of trees and sky, and that when we *thought* we were admiring the beauties of nature we were often really remembering the time when we nearly, or perhaps quite, got on top of a young lady at a similar time of day or of the year or in a similar place (though of course that is only a paraphrase of what I said). My mother-in-law said accusingly: 'You're not very lyrical, are you? I should never call you lyrical.' Beng lyrical, you see, is the even spreading of urine over untruths:

> Proud word you never spoke (nor *sensible* word *either*, for
> that matter), but you will speak
> Four not exempt from pride (but exempt from *sense*) one
> future day;
> Resting on one white hand a warm wet *silly* cheek,
> Over my open volume (of CRAP) you will say:
> 'This man loved *me* (I know that because he BEHAVED
> STUPIDLY and TALKED PISS about me);'

then rise and, in the direction of the house of
easement, trip away.[1]

My mother-in-law liked 'Mrs. Miniver'[2] as *well* as 'A Tree Grows in Brooklyn' (you remember the latter, don't you: 'Cars of dairth, hort failure broad on by alcohulusm' . . . 'Ore gee, do yer hairve to say he wuz . . . a drernk, mister? D'yer *hairve* to?' . . . . 'Cars of dairth . . . . hort failure.')[3]

The legacy is going fine now, 60,000 after a recession while I was away. I am very much looking forward to hearing what you say about it. You may not think that it is very satisfactory as a novel, but that some parts of it will make you crap in laughter, that I can without undue modesty predict. I have just done a 'phone call to Caton: 'just stops them, what?' But I won't blab until the job is completed.

J'ai sucre y is of course Jesus-Cree. I have sugar there is of course J'y ai du (or de la) sucre ('Why you rump-stumping –') Yes isn't Vine St. Blues awful? Then they say people don't like small-band jazz. [. . .]

I will get a new ribbon with the *pound-note* you owe me, you chug-buttle. I lent it to you outside Long John's Restaurant just before you went off on your train the last time, no? Hilly sends her love and that kid would send his if he could. Make with words

He's got your nose bum,

Kingsley

[TLS: Bodleian]

1. A horse-pissing version of 'Proud Word You Never Spoke' (1846) by Walter Savage Landor (1775–1864).

2. *Mrs Miniver* (1942), directed by William Wyler and starring Greer Garson, a melodrama about an English housewife during World War II; won Best Picture and other Academy Awards in 1942.

3. In the left margin Amis has added in pen 'Dorothy McGuiresh James Dunnsh Peggy Ann Garnersh', the three stars of *A Tree Grows* in *Brooklyn*.

TO PHILIP LARKIN – 8 SEPTEMBER 1948

Marriner's Cottage, Newland Street, Eynsham, Oxon.

My dear Philip,

[. . .] My mother-in-law tells me that she wrote my dear little niece a letter the other day (why, by the way, did she do that; why? The child is six months of age, and can not yet read the simplest word. Why then did she write her a letter?), and *got a reply.* Old Rodge had written the sweetest little letter back, all in *bay-bay writing.* The man is father of the child, and I can see that all its days will be bound each to each by talking piss and behaving stupidly.[1]

I may sound 'a little wild' ggzhhh: the truth is, that I have *finished the legacy.* I look forward, on re-reading, to reviews, *if it ever gets published,* sang: . . . cheap-jack parade of eccentricity . . . freak-show without the natural pathos of real freaks . . . private humour; Mr. Amis, it is painfully clear, and a friend or two must have had some rare chuckles over this somewhat heavily subtle flaying of a few harmless and not especially original foibles . . . puppets whose disastrously *voulu* gestures cannot hide from us the fatally decorative role they play . . . if Mr. Amis's intention is to make the reader as bored and exasperated as his priggish hero, he has fulfilled it to perfection . . . Ooh *dear*; you will have to speak encouragingly about it when you come.

This man Wencken[2] sounds a bit of a cynic to me. He's never known what it is to see the woman one loves look up with that expression of sweet pride on her face as she holds in her arms the pledge of your mutual love for one another; never heard its cries as it reaches out its

---

1. A horse-pissing of the epigraph to Wordsworth's 'Ode: Intimations of Immortality' (1807), taken from the concluding lines of the same poet's 'My Heart Leaps Up' (also 1807).

2. 'Wencken' is a play on 'Mencken', suggests John Fuller (private communication, 6 May 1999): 'Larkin had complained to Amis in a letter of 30 September 1946 [*LL*, p. 126] that de la Mare had included nothing by Mencken (or Montherlant) in his anthology *Love* (1943), so he was evidently interested in him . . . Mencken of course was a noted realist in erotic matters . . . He defined love as "the delusion that one woman differs from another" and is also the author of an aphorism that wonderfully applies to the views of Larkin: "Bachelors know more about women than married men. If they didn't they'd be married too" (*Chrestomathy*).' H.L. Mencken (1880–1956), editor, journalist and critic, published *A Mencken Chrestomathy*, an anthology of his writings, in 1949. The melting sentiments 'this man [M]encken' would deny suggest *The Sorrows of Young Werther*, which Amis had just read (see Amis to Larkin, 20 August 1948).

chubby little arms for the moon; it is clear that that experience has never come the way of your philosopher, THE LUCKY RAT'S BARD. S-------y, t----h, young Philip, as he is usually called in our letters of congratulation, is less trouble than he might be, though not a whole lot less. We haven't had an unbroken night's sleep yet, though we probably soon shall. He is very forward, the medico says.

It doesn't surprise me in the *least* that Monica[3] is studding Crab;[4] he's *exactly* the sort of *priggish*, *boring*, *featureless* (especially *that*; there isn't *anything* about him, is there?), *long-winded*, *inessential* man she'd go for; if she can see beauty in a derelict shit-house, she must have more send see, Billy T. than you. Talking of SHIT) HGZ
SHIT-HAZES, that POSTURING QUACK Cess-hole[5] thinks Crab's good, doesn't he? along with that lunatic stricken-deer bastard who couldn't spell his own name properly.[6] [. . .]

Hiccups bum,

Kingsley

[TLS: Bodleian]

TO PHILIP LARKIN – SUNDAY [26 SEPTEMBER 1948]

Marriner's Cottage

My dear Philip,

I want to catch the 5.0 post with this and say again, however inadequately, that I really do repent of saying what I said to you when and

3. Monica Jones (b. 1922), at the time a lecturer in English at Leicester (then Leicester University College); a friend and close companion of Larkin. She is a trustee and literary executor of the Larkin estate.

4. George Crabbe (1754–1832), poet and parson, wrote realistic – often grimly realistic – poems of the rural poor and Suffolk village life.

5. Lord David Cecil (1902–86), literary critic and scholar, Fellow of New College, Oxford; Goldsmiths' Professor of English Literature (since 1948); briefly Amis's B.Litt. supervisor at Oxford.

6. William Cowper (pronounced 'Cooper', hence the joke about spelling) (1731–1800), poet, suffered fits of madness and depression; Lord David Cecil wrote *The Stricken Deer: The Life of Cowper* (1929), the title of which alludes to a passage of self-description in Cowper's *The Task* (1785): 'I was a stricken deer that left the herd/Long since' (iii. 108–9).

how I said it.[1] It strikes me that I have acted as a very coarse and unlovely person would act: with some people (old R*dge for instance) I wouldn't mind doing that, but with Hilly you are the person I least want to hurt, and having done so I am really very sorry. I should hate to think, as I said, that this will make any difference between us, dalling, but if it does then "I shall only have myself to thank". I would far prefer you to blame me for behaving in that way we know of and talking that well-known element than that you should blame yourself or Ruth. I did enjoy our last day, as well as Monday and other times, and this gives me some reassurance.

You needn't worry that I'll say or write anything to Ruth about any of this.

Thank you for bringing me the whisky (which I feel* rather ashamed of having finished alone) and the see-gores and *Vieni vieni.*[2] I was *very glad* to have been able to give Ruth *Big man.*[3]

I'm very much looking forward to seng you at Leicester in a fortnight's tune. 'Putting up somewhere outside your house won't discompose me in the least. We will have some fine speaking and smoking then. Let me know about this.

Shoot my mouth off bum,

Kingsley

[ALS: Bodleian]

*yer do

1. Larkin and Ruth Bowman, to whom Larkin was engaged (since May), visited Oxford sometime after 16 September, Larkin arriving before Ruth. Whatever it is Amis said during the visit seems to have concerned Ruth, but Larkin forgave him (see Amis to Larkin, 29 September 1948, in Bodleian).

2. A song recorded in 1937 with words by Rudy Vallee (1901–86), singer and character actor.

3. 'Big Butter and Egg Man', recorded in 1939 by Muggsy Spanier.

TO LORD DAVID CECIL – 19 OCTOBER 1948

St. John's College

Dear Lord David,[1]

Here is the statement you asked me to deliver to you. I hope it is sufficiently detailed.

I should like to thank you in advance for your trouble in undertaking to oblige me.

Yours sincerely,
K. W. Amis

St. John's College, 19 October 48.

Name: Kingsley W. Amis
Date of B. Litt. Qualifying Exam: Trinity Term '48
Subject of Thesis: Decline of the audience for poetry 1850 – present day

I ask the favour of changing my B.Litt. supervisor to Mr. F. W. Bateson,[2] suggesting that a subject as sociological and diffused as the above might more profitably be approached under the guidance of a bibliographical specialist.

K. W. Amis

[ALS: Oxford University Archives]

---

1. For Lord David Cecil see Amis to Larkin, 8 September 1948, note 5.

2. F. W. Bateson (1901–78), literary critic, Lecturer in English, Oxford University (1947–63), Lecturer in English, Hertford College, Oxford (1949–63), Fellow, Corpus Christi College, Oxford (1963–69); founding editor of *Essays in Criticism* (1951–74), described by Blake Morrison, *The Movement: English Poetry and Fiction of the 1950s* (Oxford: Oxford University Press, 1980), p. 28, as aiming 'to supplement the work of Leavis's *Scrutiny* . . . [and] to serve as a platform for the Movement over the next few years'. For the switch from Cecil to Bateson see *Memoirs*, pp. 101–7. This switch was mostly a product of Cecil's inaccessibility, but it also derived from class and other antipathies. See, for instance, Amis on Cecil's voice and drawling manner, as when lecturing:

> 'Laze . . . laze and gentlemen, when we say a man looks like a poet . . . dough mean . . . looks like Chauthah . . . dough mean . . . looks like Dvyden . . . dough mean . . . looks like *Theckthpyum* [or something else barely recognisable as 'Shakespeare']. . . . Mean looks like Shelley [pronounced 'Thellem' or thereabouts]. Matthew Arnold [then prestissimo] called Shelley beautiful ineffectual angel Matthew Arnold had face [rallentando] like a

TO PHILIP LARKIN – 9 NOVEMBER 1948

Marriner's Cottage, Newland Street, Eynsham, Oxon.

My dear Philip,

These are unsolicited words; I had expected to hear from you before now, but no doubt you are lapped in nastiness of one kind or another. Myself I am feeling in better spirits than of late: I am half-way through my pilgrimage to the man who drills teeth, and I have finished reading Grgr.[1] This last is highly good: the trouble with the man is that he has no sense of humour, if I haven't said so before. The observation doesn't seem particularly subtle, but it is very far-reaching: if he had a sense of humour (Creist I hope I didn't say all this last time – it's my bloody diary[2] that confuses me) he'd be able to avert those awful bursts of derisive laughter that tickle the reader's tongue: 'Virtue tempted him like a sin' ppppbbbvvfff – 'Pity smouldered like decay at his heart' pphh – 'Harris stared hopelessly over the grey tin roofs' *vvvvfhfh*. But he has humour in him; I find the old-Downhamian scene with Wilson & Harris very and as far as I can see intentionally funny.[3] I don't know how interseted you are by this, but if I were arranging his bucks in order it wd be something like: Glory – Maps – Rock – Within – Ministry – England – Gun – Matter – Stamboul – Battlefield – Lawless.[4] Forgive this chatter, but the subject interests me. I have bought some books recently, including The up, by Mum,[5] which I find fine.

> *horth*. But my subject this morning is not the poet Shelley. Jane ... Austen ...' (p. 101)

In the *Memoirs* Amis describes this impression as 'appropriated by me without acknowledgement until now' from an original version by John Wain.

---

1. Graham Greene.
2. See Amis to Larkin, 15 October 1948 (in Bodleian): 'I have bought a large and expensive book with ruled lines in which I have begun a journal. My life has too much idling in it as a rule.'
3. Wilson and Harris are characters in Greene's novel *The Heart of the Matter* (1948).
4. *The Power and the Glory* (1940), *Journey without Maps* (1940), *Brighton Rock* (1938), *The Man Within* (1929), *The Ministry of Fear* (1943), *England Made Me* (1935), *A Gun for Sale* (1936), *The Heart of the Matter* (1948), *Stamboul Train* (1932), *It's a Battlefield* (1934), *The Lawless Roads: A Mexican Journey* (1939).
5. *The Summing Up* (1938) by W. Somerset Maugham, a work of non-fiction containing reflections on life and art.

By the way, old horse, if anybody like the Collinses, sen. or jun., or Money-cur,[6] tries to tell you that E. Sitwell on Wyld Bille is any good, you might quote this: E. says that Bill was keen on Plato and the simple life, Diogenessh,[7] and quotes from Leer in support as follows:

> Allow not nature more than nature needs:
> Man's life is poor as beast's.

Two assertions, you see. Bill *wrote*:

> Allow not nature more than nature needs,
> Man's life is poor as beast's.

That's quite different, isn't it?[8] She's a dishonest old bag, isn't she? Tynan[9] told me that; I hope you haven't read it anywhere. [. . .]

I hope all this literary talking hasn't bored you: I'm getting much more interested in other people's words these days – your influence, you old tome-grub.

I am very contented, eating Mintoes by the gas-fire, with Pinetop asleep upstairs and Hilly passing in and out.[10] I realise that when I have finished this letter I must begin thinking what I am to say about The man within, but even this doesn't depress me much. Did I say that it is a good book? I've just played One sweet letter:[11] still think it a magnificent record and can't understand why you haven't got a copy. My milkman[12] is fair; I have it (largely for H's sake). [. . .]

6. The Collinses are not referred to elsewhere in the correspondence, or in *LL*, or in Motion, *Life*. James Booth (personal communication, 8 February 1999) suggests Arthur S. Collins (1899–1959), Head of English at the University College of Leicester (where he was employed from 1924–59) and a possible model for the 'Butterfield' character in the 'Augusta' fragment (in BJLH), one of two uncompleted novels Larkin worked on between 1947 and 1953 (see Amis to Larkin, 16 April 1953, note 3). If Booth is right, presumably this Collins was 'Collins Sr'. A possible candidate for 'Collins Jr' is Philip Arthur Collins (b. 1923), also a member of the English Department at Leicester (1947–82). 'Money-cur' is Monica Jones.

7. In the chapter on *King Lear* in Edith Sitwell's *A Notebook on William Shakespeare* (1948; rpt London: Macmillan, 1962), pp. 64, 75, she discusses Plato, *Lear* and the simple life, but nowhere mentions Diogenes (c. 412–c. 325 BC), a philosopher famed for his indifference to material comforts. For Edith Sitwell see Notes on Recipients.

8. See *King Lear*, II.iv.268–9. Amis has misquoted the second line from Lear's speech beginning 'O reason not the need', in which man's life is 'cheap as beast's', not 'poor as beast's'.

9. For Kenneth Tynan's flamboyance and generosity at Oxford see *Memoirs*, pp. 46–7.

10. 'Mintoes' are soft-centred mint sweets; 'Pinetop' is Philip Amis.

11. 'One Sweet Letter from You', a 1938 recording by Lionel Hampton.

12. 'My Very Good Friend the Milkman', a 1938 recording by Fats Waller.

I'll send this off now, you old beg-rug.
There's a cavity here I hadn't noticed bum,

Kingsley

Costin sent me a note the other day – 'Dear Kingsley, I haven't set eyes on you for months. I suppose you are busy in your sylvan retreat ... do come and look me up, Yours v. sincerely ...' – so I went. As I was sipping a glass of neat whisky, which he had given me in mistake for sherry, he said, 'I just want you to know that I know this baby was coming before you were married; I thought you'd like to know that ... Very naughty of you.' Now WHY shd. he think I'd like to know that AIYEEGH? That was presumably the whole purpose of getting me along. The old GUT-DWELLER the old PAN-STARER the old BUM-DREAMER the old Tinkle bum, crinkle bum, wrinkle winkle sprinkle bum; knuckle truckle chuckle suckle buckle bum BARLLS peeper bum, creeper

We are entertaining the week-end after next my son's cousin,
my father-in-law's elder daughter, and my wife's brothers'
brother-in-law balls
d'you hear
oh

[TLS: Bodleian]

TO PHILIP LARKIN – 13 DECEMBER 1948

26 Shrublands Road, The Bad Town, Horts

My dear Philip,

[...] I hope I didn't seem off-hand or anything else on Friday, but as I made clear to anyone who would listen I was in reduced healthiness at that time. Had I been better, our talk might have been finer, though fine it was for all that. I hope you enjoyed The orchard;[1] I was bawds' tiff when I saw it, finding all the characters, male and female, the same, and all of them rather like my mother, i.e. trying to make it clear how

1. *The Cherry Orchard* (1904) by Anton Chekhov (1860–1904).

miserable they are without saying so, directly, at first. I might expatiaiate (you know the sod) on the Checkoff formula: you take a lot of characters, all miserable because of something they won't do, and let them talk without influencing each other for three acts, and at the last moment you introduce some arbitrary calamity, or some proposed change like a return to Petrograd or a holiday in the Cry-mere, which you know won't make any difference to any of them, and then you go on for ten minutes or so after the thing should have stopped even by your own standards, to show how delicate and unemphatic your art is. And yer know wer-what you can, hich-hich, er-do wer-with that, don't yer? Why, der-*don't* yer?

Diana Gollancz* *arse,*[2]

Kingsley

**Isn't that husband of hers some squarehead princeling or other, m'm?*[3]

[TLS: Bodleian]

TO PHILIP LARKIN – 3 JANUARY 1949

Marriner's Cottage, Eynsham.

My dear Philip,

A long search for your last letter having proved to be of no utility, I am replying to it without it before me. Or did I reply to it before? I cannot remember. I have at all events your post-card with me. I hope you enjoyed your tripper-excursion round the places where those men lived:[1] as you will know, I tend to regard that form of thing as doubtless, assured and unapproached piss. Did you feel your spirits lifting at the touch of the Immortal hey? Hardy turned out some good poetry, but

2. Diana Gollancz (1921–67), daughter of the publisher Victor Gollancz; art student at the Slade (at the time based in Oxford at the Ashmolean Museum), a friend of Larkin, who 'wrung out of her as many memories of her Buckinghamshire schooldays as he could, adopted them as Brunette's, and thanked her by making her one of the dedicatees of *Michaelmas Term at St Bride's*' (Motion, *Life*, p. 88).

3. MS addition. The husband was Prince Leopold von Lowenstein-Wertheim.

---

1. Between Christmas and the New Year Larkin and Ruth Bowman visited the Hardy country around Dorchester.

he was human like you and me hey? ('Why you mouse-raping –' Your won't y thing made me laugh out. It's a good zhongr, isn't it? I'm sorry not to have written more soon, but life at Berkhamsted was inimical to everything I like and now I am busily Ingag'd in peruſing and anſwering numerous Papiſtickall tracts (Yts a battelfeild, England made Mee, &c).[2]

I am very glad to have come back from Berkhamsted, because I did not enjoy it there. My parents suffer from being bad at being nice to people they like, and I am bad at 'respecting' them in the way they enjoy, so things were rather difficult some of the time. When we arrived back here, my sister-in-law's husband announced that he and his wife were going to Paris for a week instead of the four days agreed upon, and that that wd. therefore be the time that my wife would be looking after my son's cousin. When they had gone, after telling us that they had broken our electric iron, we looked round the house and found that they had also impaired the efficiency of the wringer, drunk the rum and sherry I had especially asked them not to drink, and left several week-old dirty saucepans and pie-dishes for your servitor to cleanse. But old Rodge gave us a gas poke for Christmas and paid the electric bill, so THATS ALL RIGHT you see NO it isnt THEYVE PUT IT RIGHT you see NO they havent WE CAN CALL IT SQUARE you see NO thats just how we shall be unable to call it. My wife's niece is very bad-tempered and noisy and liable to cry and peevish and ugly and smelly, so I have not enjoyed having here at a time when I had privately determined to do a lot of my Grgr. She is still here. The only noise I like her to make is loud and deperate yktw crying in the garden when nobody is attending to her and nobody is going to for some appreciable time, and the only thing I was pleased to find in the house was old Rodge's razor after he had gone.

I do remember that you mentioned the Lewis records:[3] yes, I agree abt. the drumming, and abt. the piano on I'm Virginia. I am almost sure it is Katz, but will check. I have the record, as a mtr of fact.

Well I suppose you are back in horeness now, or soon will be, after the Xmas break. Is Durham further from Leicester than Oxford is, or

2. By Graham Greene.

3. Victor Lewis (see Amis to Larkin, 15 December 1945, note 2); 'I'm Virginia' is 'I'm Coming, Virginia'; 'Katz' is the pianist Dick Katz, who appears neither in *NGDJ* nor Chilton, *Who's Who*, nor Delaunay's *New Hot Discography*.

nearer to it? There is a job there I am applying for. I know nothing at all of it, yet.

One thing that has given both of us delight is that Nick[4] is in Oxford again, this time to stay. He has a job working under the sb sd sub-edite shite editor of the Oxford Times, at some 5*l* the week. But the hours and work are not arduous, so he is very pleased. He was here for the week end, and this was good.

While I was at Berkhamsted I re-read *Jill*, and thought again how good it is, particularly the 1st half. This time I was more conscious that Kemp the Warner-fearer and Kemp the Jill-imaginer are not very the same person, but also more conscious of how very good the Oxford bits are: that impression-forming about what I might summarise as the Banbury road at dusk is first-chop, I feel. After it I read A man, by Jas. Joyce:[5] it is in some degree a source-book for the other, no? His favoured time of day is early evening, too, and both books have the same typical epithet: soft ('a softly lighted hall', 'bones showed through softly'). I know that sounds rather Henry Reedsh,[6] but I did feel it.

Let me have a word-thing soon. Have you read Away went the little fish, by Margot Bennett?[7] I found it good. Also not wholly bad was To the dark tower,[8] but I don't expect you to agree with me there. They tell me FK looks like a parlourmaid in spectacles.

Ubble-ubble-ubble-ubble bee-bee-bee-bee-bee dud-dud-dud-dud-dud-dud a-her a-her a-her a-her-her-her-her-her. . . . UUUUUUUhhher-her-her her-her. . . . . *UUUUU*GHGHhher-her-her-her *AAAAAAAUUUUUHHHH*er-her-her-her-her-her bum,

Kingsley

[TLS: Bodleian]

4. Russel. See Amis to Larkin, 25 November 1944, note 10.
5. *A Portrait of the Artist as a Young Man* (1916).
6. Henry Reed (1914–86), poet, broadcaster, radio dramatist.
7. *Away Went the Little Fish* (1946).
8. *To the Dark Tower* (1946) by Francis King (b. 1923), novelist and critic; had been a student at Balliol College, Oxford.

TO PHILIP LARKIN – 16 JANUARY 1949

Marriner's Cottage, Eynsham, Oxon.

My dear Philip,

Sorry I am, my God, sorry I am that I have not before answered your letter of ten days ago, sorry too that in my last I omitted to thank you for your fine Christmas gift to my son. The former is due in part to our having spent some six days at the residence of my parents-in-law, the latter to my forgetting but not to my ingratitude. I hope to remedy both by a splendid long letter now.

I thought the L. Eyles bit in your last but one backbending with laughter. It read like a brilliant, but *brilliant* (agonising Christ, wouldn't that give you a heartburn on your arse?) piece of creative observation in a *roman*, like Mum (WS) only much funnier and more convincing. I am sorry about tuffe, but not very; he must have become a very bad man in the last few years, I think. Glad to hear more details of your Dorset excursion, I always think that sort of thing makes the books seem so much more *real*, somehow, do'nt you, well you obviously do or you would'nt have gone, I suppose, I must go there myself and see the sights someday. You are a fool about money, you know; I'll lay you have at least £200 in the bank at the time of writing, do I speak true? The time to worry about money is when you haven't a bean to bless yourself with, you know, not before. I agree with all you say abt the dark tower; I think if he can lose his habit of making nice people always unwise and wise ones always nasty he will become good; have you seen the killing air thing?[1]

I have jotted down a few notes for my next book about Daddy B;[2] I don't see how I can avoid doing him in fiction if I am to refrain from stabbing him under the fifth rib in fact. I have been thinking of a kind of me-and-the-Bardwells theme for it all, ending with me poking one of Hilly's brothers' wife as a revenge on them all. I heard a hell of a lot more about Sweden, some anecdotes twice, and a hell of a lot more

---

1. *To the The Dark Tower* (1946) and *An Air that Kills* (1948), novels by Francis King.

2. As much the germ of *Lucky Jim* as Amis's response to visiting the Senior Common Room at Leicester (recounted in *Memoirs*, p. 56: 'I looked round a couple of times and said to myself, "Christ, somebody ought to do something with this"').

about folk dancing and folk cultures, and a hell of a lot more about the language of the Romanschi, and a hell of a lot more about all his friends in London.[3] The best time was when I was lying in a partially filled bath with him in the room underneath accompanying on the piano, his foot regularly tapping, folk tunes which he was playing on the gramophone, there being a difference in pitch between the two sources of sound of approximately one-3rd of a full tone. As one vapid, uniformly predictable tune ended and another began I found that the hot tap was now dispensing cold water, and, getting out of the bath, began drying myself.

During my stay, apart from trying to do some work about the learned papisticalist, I read the greater part of *Ulysses*, by James Joyce, the Irish fellow who died not so long ago, as Daddy B would add. I didn't enjoy it much, but kept on with it. I felt about it rather as I do about At birds,[4] only more so, that it isn't worth going to all that trouble and expense in order to be funny once in a dozen pages. The funny bits are very funny indeed: And with that he took the bloody old towser by the scruff of the neck and, by Jesus, he near throttled him, and that section like an examination paper makes me laugh at the start.[5] I know these reactions are not strikingly original, but that isn't going to put me off. All the thought-stream business strikes me as a sodding bore; once in 1000 times something stands out as 'a good touch', but hardly more often. I think novels ought to tell a story (you mean like Ralph Straus?) and have a theme (you mean like Charze Morgan?) and give you a sense that a problem has been propounded and solved (you mean like Agatha Christie?)[6]; but I do, really. Only the Gerty MacDowell bit, which is a whanger, seems not too long to me.[7] How does your mind regard these problems?

3. In the original typed manuscript of this letter, Amis has managed to place each 'and a hell of a lot more about' exactly below its predecessor, with no extra spacing.

4. *At-Swim-Two-Birds* by Flann O'Brien.

5. 'Bloody old towser' is the dog 'Garryowen', who is taken by the scruff of the neck by his owner, the 'Citizen', in the Cyclops episode of the novel (p. 381 of the 1937 Bodley Head edition); the 'section like an examination paper' is the Ithaca section, the novel's penultimate episode.

6. Ralph Straus (1882–1950), novelist and biographer; Charles Morgan (1894–1958), novelist, playwright, dramatic critic; Agatha Christie (1890–1976), writer of detective fiction.

7. Amis refers to the Nausicaa episode in *Ulysses* (1922), in which Gerty MacDowell, a young girl, allows Leopold Bloom a glimpse of her knickers, which leads him to masturbate; 'whanger' means 'corker', but may also, especially since 'whang' is a slang term for penis, suggest 'wanker' (that is, 'wank-inducer').

One little matter: I didn't realise until I re-read *Jill* that you had already done that beaten-by-a-skilful-boxer bit that I put in the Legacy.[8] To be honest, I thought it was something we had found in talk, or to be more honest still I thght it was something you had said to me. Apologies.

Roger, who hadn't after all drunk that rum I said he had drunk, brought me back a Claude Luter[9] (pron. Loo-*tare* – mais j'ai commanDE) record from the French Republic. It seems all right to me. Titles: Rl Gdn Bls/Where did you stay last night. The band plays loudly and rather repetitively, but Luter is good, though limited. It is Oliver stuff, not Dixieland.[10]

Bruce sent the Legacy back with a number of comments. He may have said something to you abt it, so I won't particularise except to say that he said 'the women are all frightful', that 'Mary is a featureless blank, Steph. not much better' and Jane gives a slight but repellent impression of dowdiness or some such jorgon. I think he is possibly wrong abt. Mary, who it seems to me has every right to be a f.less blk, it surprised me that he said it abt. Steph, whom I thought goodish, but I think he's pretty right, alack, abt. Jane. I shall have to do something with her, no? when I come to re-do it. It fills me with an extremist rage that I shall not be able to do that until the middle of the summer at the earliest. That *thesis*; cor swelp me charlie bob F U C K THAT T H E S I S. [. . .]

Hilly tells me she has invited you & y[r] yong Maiſtreſs. I endorse that. Bruce comes 6 Feb so it wd be nicer for me if you came not then. Let it be soon.

B Litt. session bum
Kingsley

Fear this letter isn't very inspring but I do not feel well today.[11]

[TLS: Bodleian]

8. 'His face, as he walked to the Lodge, was white, and he felt as if he had been knocked about by a boxer who had known exactly where to hit him in order to hurt him the most' (*Jill*, p. 111).

9. Claude Luter (b. 1923), French clarinettist and bandleader.

10. King [Joe] Oliver (1885–1938), New Orleans cornettist and bandleader. New Orleans jazz, a style of small ensemble jazz, is often distinguished from Dixieland jazz, a label reserved for white musicians and orchestras.

11. MS addition.

TO PHILIP LARKIN – 1 FEBRUARY 1949

Marriner's Cottage, Eynsham.

My dear Philip,

[. . .] Pinetop has been rather ill recently, which has made things difficult here besides being nasty for him. He had a cold and kept spewing his feeds up, but now seems almost well again. You'll be sorry to hear that Winkie is dead. He had a wound from a car or another cat or something just before Christmas, which never really healed up and kept being re-opened in fights. To-day it was suppurating badly and he had also been clawed in the chest, so we called the vet in. He said (I wasn't here) that he would never properly recover and would go on being ripped by other cats, and that it would be better if he were destroyed. So we had it done. This has been a shock and has depressed both of us. I shall miss him a lot. [. . .]

It is now Wednesday, and has been for some time. I'm sorry I didn't answer with speed, but I have had a good deal on my plate. If Perón keeps on like this I suppose I shan't get my £75, soddit.[1] I must go and wire very soon. Looking forward to seeing your old face on the 18th.

Will you get up and give him his six o'clock feed in the morning Billy bum,

Kingsley

[ALS: Bodleian]

---

1. Argentina was on the brink of economic collapse at this time, with crippling strikes, a collapse of the stock market in Buenos Aires, and a dispute with Britain about imports. Juan Perón (1894–1974) was President of Argentina 1946–55.

In the garden of St John's College, Oxford, summer 1941. Left to right: Noel (Josh) Hughes, Norman Iles, James Wilcox, Philip Larkin, Philip Brown.

In the garden of St John's College, Oxford, summer 1942. KA kneeling front and centre, making a face; standing, left to right: Mervyn Brown, J.B. Widdowson, Edward du Cann, Michael MacNaughton-Smith, Nick Russel, Philip Brown, David Williams, Norman Iles, Graham Parkes, David West.

Left Philip Larkin outside Bruce Montgomery's lodgings in Oxford, 1943.

Below KA at Abbey Timbers, 1946. 'Writing to you is one of the two things I like doing . . . the other is playing jazz records' (to Philip Larkin, 15 December 1945).

Above R.A. Caton, passport photograph, 1946. 'THAT SOD CATON *still* hasn't replied to my letter' (to Philip Larkin, 2 December 1946).

Left Luneburg Heath, the day the Germans surrendered, 7 May 1945. Lieutenant K.W. Amis (second from left, middle row), E. Frank Coles, co-author of 'Who Else is Rank', on his right.

Right Hilary Bardwell, 1946. 'Hilary, so far from being 22, is 17 . . . and hence not nearly so depraved as I had hoped' (to Philip Larkin, 21 February 1946).

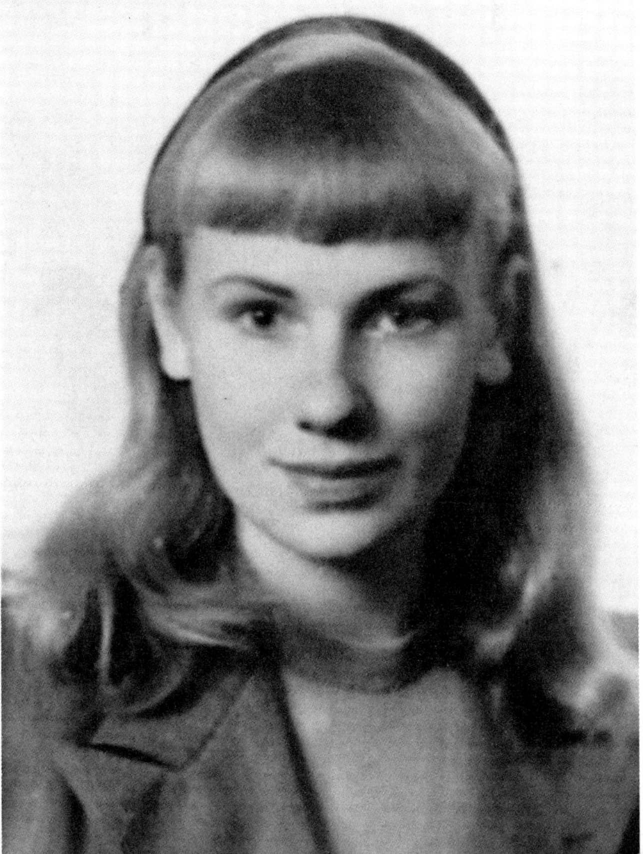

Postcard to Philip Larkin, 3 October 1947, from 'Maisie', amorous schoolgirl chum of 'Marianne' (characters in the Amis-Larkin story 'IWDAFY', or 'I Would Do Anything for You').

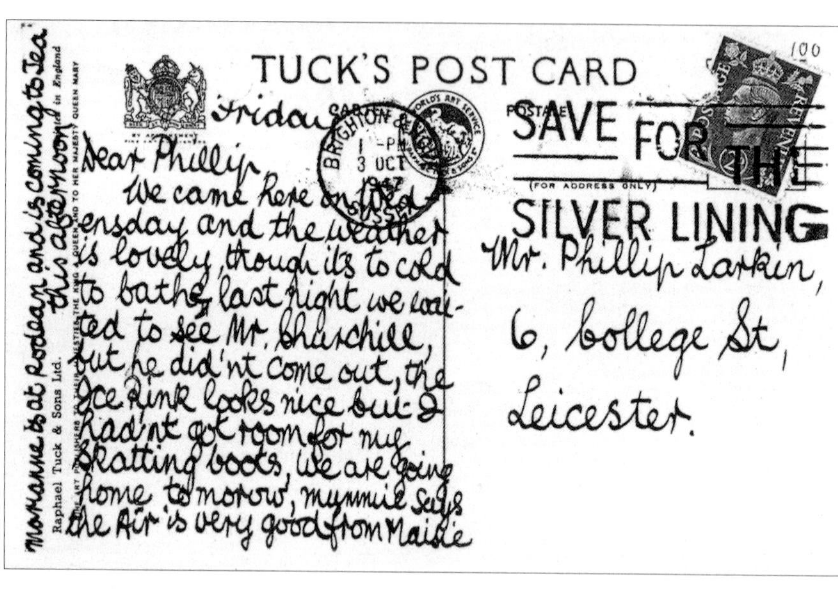

TUCK'S POST CARD

Friday

Dear Phillip

We came here on Wed-
ensday and the weather
is lovely, though it's to cold
to bathe, last night we wai-
ted to see Mr. Churchill,
but he did'nt come out, the
Ice Rink looks nice but I
had'nt got room for my
skatting boots, we are going
home tomorow, mummie says
the Air is very good from Maisie

Marianne is at Rodean and is coming to tea this afternoon

BRIGHTON & HOVE 1 -PM 3 OCT 1947 SUSSEX

SAVE FOR THE SILVER LINING

Mr. Phillip Larkin,
6, College St,
Leicester.

Raphael Tuck & Sons Ltd.

Right KA and Hilly, July 1948, the year they were married.

Below Lord David Cecil, 1952. 'That POSTURING QUACK Cess-hole thinks Crab's good, doesn't he?' (to Philip Larkin, 8 September 1948).

Below right F.W. Bateson, 1948. 'I ask the favour of changing my B. Litt supervisor to Mr F.W. Bateson' (to Lord David Cecil, 19 October 1948).

Right Leonard Bardwell ('Daddy B'), Christmas 1948. 'And the father does folk dancing (polk dancing? pock dancing? fock dancing?)' (to Philip Larkin, 15 July 1946).

Below Hilly, KA and Hilly's sister Margaret ('Miggy') Partington, at Marriner's Cottage, Eynsham, *c.* 1948–49.

OPPOSITE

Above KA's students in Rag Week, University College of Swansea, 1949. Right to left: John Morgan (partially visible), Geoff Nicholson, Mavis Mainwaring (later Nicholson), Mary Madden (after two seated figures, unidentified), Clive Gammon.

Below KA as Osric, kneeling in front. 'The little one on my right's Joyce Hatton, David Sims's girl. Bruce picked on her too' (to Philip Larkin, 15 December 1953).

'Am acting as judge in the Swansea heats of the Mazda Queen of Light competition ah haha won't I have the gaiety inspecting them for Acctractiveness and Figure, ah yayaya' (to Philip Larkin, 8 October 1956).

Hilly, Philip Larkin, KA and Maggie Aeron-Thomas (*née* Ashbury). Swansea, 1956.

TO THE ENGLISH FACULTY BOARD – MARCH 1949[1]

I propose to treat my subject, in the first instance, by examining the attitudes of the important poets of the period towards their public, their conceptions of the size and nature of this public, and how far their writings seem to have been modified thereby. Secondly, I intend to discuss the actual size and nature of the audience of each poet, and attempt a subdivision of this audience into its various strata. Work so far done leads me to the hypothesis that a useful working formula is a three-fold division, into intimate friends of the poet himself, personal followers who know the poet chiefly through his work, and the reading public at large. (An example of the first would be the Rossetti family and such friends as Allingham and Hall Caine,[2] of the second the Browning societies and of the third the people who made first impressions of 10,000 copies below average for the later publications of Tennyson.) I mean to suggest, finally, that the ideal process of poetry's diffusion is a steady outward widening from the poet to his inner public, through the intermediate followers to the outer, general public, and that where this process is halted at any point, or skips a stage, the effect on the poet's work and on the prestige of poetry is likely to be marked and deleterious.

K. W. Amis

[TLS: Oxford University Archives]

---

1. This undated and unheaded description of Amis's proposed B.Litt. thesis ('English Non-Dramatic Poetry, 1850–1900, and the Victorian Reading Public') was probably sent to the English Faculty Board in March 1949, according to Simon Bailey, the Oxford University Archivist. Amis's postgraduate file, writes Bailey, shows that he was 'applying for transfer to full B.Litt. status in March 1949. It was rejected by the English Faculty Board at its meeting of 11 March 1949; there is a copy of a letter in the file, dated 17 March, in which he was informed that the Board "decided that the subject proposed was not one that could be profitably studied for the degree"' (personal communication, 27 November 1997). Since Amis's file contains no adverse reports and he passed his examinations, the proposal itself must have been the problem; a second, revised proposal was accepted in May (see Amis to English Faculty Board, 2 May 1949).

2. William Allingham (1824–89), poet, some of whose poems were illustrated by his close friend Dante Gabriel Rossetti (1828–82), who figures also in Allingham's *Diary* (first published 1907), along with other well-known Victorian poets and painters; Sir Thomas Henry Hall Caine (1853–1931), novelist, became a trusted friend of Rossetti towards the end of the older man's life.

TO PHILIP LARKIN – 9 MARCH 1949

Marriner's Cottage, Newland Street, Eynsham, Oxford.

My dear Philip,

Many thanks for your two letters and the rhymed ruminations that accompanied the second. No word of the last-named for the present; I haven't yet re-read them carefully enough to arrive at any detailed opinion, even if you want to hear one. So far I can say that they seem no less good, after the interval of more than two years (is it not?). I hope that doesn't sound patronising. I have only your ultimate letter before me at this present, but remember fully your excoriations of two bad men and one bad woman. I don't see how you keep on your feet at Lester; if I were you, I shouldn't be able to bear it unless I were there too, if you see what I mean. I liked what you said about Ankles; I wrote to King the other day asking him for stuff for Ox: Po:,[1] and received a reply compounded of gimcrack earnestness and pinchbeck joviality, with three exclamation marks disposed at intervals through the text. Altogether it seemed a fair enough picture of one of his own characters, than which a sterner ball-kick could scarcely be dashed.

'Not much news from here', except that I have got out of my slay of despond for the nonce. Acting on a pamphlet written by some health-crank discovery of Mummy B., I have been eating a lot of black treacle, with the result that a cyst among my bush, which periodically suppurated and made me feel an unclear unclean man, 'has completely disappeared after ten days' dosage'. I feel a cleaner man now, ripe for adultery and masturbation. Log fog Longmans sent the Legacy back, of course, saying it was 'altogether too slight'. That's true in a way, I suppose, but there are plenty of other things to its discredit I would have said before that; I wondered if perhaps they hadn't seen the point much – I don't mean the theme, I mean the humour, if any. But I am not discouraged much yet I hope, and will try again, this time through a friend of Nick's. I will ask Kintisch[2] about having it printed privately.

---

1. Amis was co-editing *Oxford Poetry (1949)* with James Michie (b. 1927), an undergraduate at Trinity, subsequently poet and man of letters (for Amis on Michie, see *Memoirs*, pp. 108–13); King is Francis King.

2. See Amis to Larkin, 14 February 1949 (in Bodleian): 'On the Saturday I shall be introducing you to Erik Kintisch, a young rich Yid publishing swine with money to burn

Did you read about the sixteen-year-old choirgirl who became a spiv's mistress? I did, repeatedly. 'It was for such moments of unsought revelation that he lived.' 'It seems to satisfy, temporarily, the sense of nostalgia for something lost.' I really do think that: the *jungefräulein-ismus* is a wish to return, not to attain. The quotes, in case yer wondrin o-boy, are from It's a b, last sentence, and J Maps.[3]

Sorry this is so short and uninteresting, but I must go to my bed with all speed, for to-morrow it is my trun *turn* for the 6 a.m. feed. The last time I did this I found that Pinteop backs Pinetop had somehow wriggled out of his nappie and hat bawls had shat a lot of shit on to his vest, woolly, nightdress, sheet, top blanket, middle blanket, and under-blanket, apart from on to his thighs and arse, and has bubbs had moreover spewed on to his pillow, his only shitless covering. There was a lot of shit on his mattress too.

Talking of shit, I have read some of The anxiety, by that crazy Awdon type,[4] and find it Impossible piss plashing in pot, Shameful shagbaggery, and shite surely. The prose links really show it up: '... when she got high, which she did rather too often ...' 'they left their bar-stools and moved to the quieter intimacy of a booth.' I'm just not interested in all that guff about man fucking himself up, and if I were I would be put off by the incessant vulgarities, seen through so much more quickly now that he writes about street-cars and G.I. Joes instead of paddocks and, well Christ, Capt. Ferguson.[5] I'm sorry to be like Henry Reed[6] or somebody, but I do feel like that. The sooner he gets to be a Yank the better. That eternal tie of Newton's[7] soon slipped off Auden's collar, didn't it?

This is after all not short. Do you reply in your inimitable and

who is (I think) going to take some of my things and who is interested in your work.' See also Amis to Larkin, 23 April 1949 (in Bodleian): 'John Wain tells me that the police are after Kintisch for fraud and attempted fraud.'

3. *It's a Battlefield* (1934) and *Journey Without Maps* (1936) by Graham Greene.

4. *The Age of Anxiety: A Baroque Eclogue* (1947) by W.H. Auden.

5. See Poem XXVI ('Taller today, we remember similar evenings') in Auden's *Poems 1930*; 'Capt. Ferguson' disappears in revised versions of the poem.

6. For Henry Reed see Amis to Larkin, 3 January 1949, note 6; Reed began writing in Birmingham, where his circle of friends included Auden as well as Walter Allen and Louis MacNeice.

7. See 'Prologue' ('Oh love, the interested self in thoughtless heaven') in Auden's *Look, Stranger!* (1936): 'And make us as Newton was, who in his garden watching/The apple falling towards England, became aware/Between himself and her of an eternal tie'(stanza 4).

trenchant fashion. Love to Molly cor sod me gently jack pox got to your brain or something

My dear Pud, the week-end after next will suit us very well. We'll come on the Friday evening so as to have a really nice long bum Kingsley

PS: No news from Durham as yet[8]

[TLS: Bodleian]

[TO THE ENGLISH FACULTY BOARD] – 2 MAY 1949[1]

ENGLISH NON-DRAMATIC POETRY, 1850–1900, AND THE VICTORIAN READING PUBLIC

'It takes two people to say a thing – a sayee as well as a sayer – and by parity of reasoning a poem's original audience and environment are integral parts of the poem itself.' SAMUEL BUTLER[2]

'Above all ideal personalities with which the poet must learn to identify himself, there is one supremely real which is the most imperative of all; namely, that of his reader. And the practical watchfulness needed for such assimilation is as much a gift and instinct as is the creative grasp of alien character. It is a spiritual contact hardly conscious yet ever renewed, and which must be a part of the very act of production itself . . . Some degree, entire or restricted, of relation to the outer audience, must be the test of every poet's vocation, and has to be considered first of all in criticizing his work.'

D.G. ROSSETTI[3]

8. MS addition (under which Amis prints the word 'poaks', connected by an arrow to the word 'as'); he had applied for a teaching job at Durham University.

---

1. This is Amis's second proposal for a B.Litt. thesis.

2. Samuel Butler (1835–1902), novelist, poet, painter and art critic. The quotation comes from 'Thought and Language', a lecture delivered in 1890 at the Working Man's College in Great Ormond Street, London WC1, rewritten and first published in *Essays on Life, Art and Science*, ed. R.A. Streatfeild (London: Grant Richards, 1904), pp. 176–233.

3. From Rossetti's essay 'Hake's Madeline, and Other Poems', in *The Collected Works of Dante Gabriel Rossetti*, ed. William M. Rossetti, 2 vols (London: Ellis and Scruton, 1886), 1, p. 489.

In this thesis it is proposed to investigate (i) the audience that the Pre-Raphaelite poets, and their contemporaries and immediate successors, *thought* they were addressing, (ii) their actual readers, so far as they are identifiable, and (iii) the reasons for the discrepancies between the two. Use will be made not only of the letters and memoirs of the poets and their admirers, but also of statistics of sales, library-circulation and publication in magazines and anthologies. Special attention will be paid to the few points of contact between the poet and his readers that still existed, such as reviews, advertisements, expository articles and public lectures. It is believed that the absence of a healthy relationship between the typical Victorian poet and his readers may explain some of the frustration and disillusionment felt by the poets as well as some of the emptiness and falsity of their poems.

K. W. Amis

K. W. AMIS,
St. John's College.

[TLS: Oxford University Archives]

TO PHILIP LARKIN – 9 MAY 1949

Marriner's Cottage, Newland Street, Eynsham, Oxon.

My dear Philip,

[. . .] The best news from here for a long time is that old Bardwell was taking part in some lunatic folk-fandango in which the men swung a lot of staves about and ducked and jumped over them (SILLY OLD DIPPY OLD SOPPY OLD DAPPY OLD POTTY OLD FOOLS) – you know the kind of thing. Well, old B's opposite number swung his stick at the wrong time, or old B mistimed it or something: anyways, the upshot is that old B takes *one hell of a crack on the brain-box*, and is *laid out for some time*, and *suffers a lot of pain*, and *has to be treated for shock*. NOW THATS FUCKING GOOD EH?

I thought those Grgr things[1] were a pretty poor lot. The last one struck me as being the fruit of a casual reading of some reviews of the H of the M, The sense of loss as quite good, but not a Gr ending, Randy as bloody cheap and overdone, the airport one as the best. I thought of it because the day the Statesman came out Mrs. B. gave Hilly and me lunch in Oxford, and I had to explain about the comp., and as usual when I have to tell anybody anything slightly unflattering to myself, or tell one of the B's anything you care to mention, she showed long-lived perplexity, a steady and patient withholding of comprehension ('Oh, I *see*; you mean *Philip* used your name for . . .' 'No, we *both* did one and . . .' 'Oh, then *he* got the prize, then . . .' '*No*.')

I have given up smoking, which makes my teeth become larger and more disused than normal and covers the walls of my mouth with a curious bitter slime. It is now 8.35 p.m., and I smoked my last cigarette (my 2nd of the day) 2½ hours ago. I seem to want to piss more often, too, and to have to slap my feet harder on the pavements when I walk.

I have just finished reading The gatsby,[2] and find it very good. There is a lot, of course, of that awful Yank fine writing in it; 'In his blue gardens men and girls came and wairnt like morths among the whisperings and the shairmpain and the stors'; but the climax of the thing seems supremely well contrived to me, in fact horrible and moving and profound, and the characterization is I fancy very subtle and original. The only trouble is, as I expect someone like Henry Reed has said, that he seems a wee bit fond of what he's crapping on – or rather (because that on its own wouldn't matter) fondof fockof fond of it through gullibility not through deliberate yielding, if I can make myself clear. But a sodding good book it is which we will treat of in talk.

I have asked Hilly about your dirty-picture proposal, and obtained a modified assent. She is prepared to do corset-and-black-stocking or holding-up-a-towel stuff, and bare-bosom stuff ('there'll be jackafuck they'll be bigger when I'm feeding the new baby'), but is a bit hesitant

---

1. A competition in the *New Statesman* (30 April 1949), p. 454, asking readers to produce the best opening or concluding passage, in not more than 150 words, of a new novel by Graham Greene, Henry Green, Julian Green or F.L. Green. Amis and Larkin both entered unsuccessfully, but were commended by the judge, Walter Allen (1911–95), the critic and novelist. The references that follow, with the exception of 'H of the M' (Graham Greene, *The Heart of the Matter*, 1948), are to parody entries and titles.

2. *The Great Gatsby* (1925) by F. Scott Fitzgerald (1896–1940).

about being quite undraped, 'though I'll probably get bolder when I start.' Does this give you the hron? It does me, slightly, oddly. Do you want 'some of us together'? ('Why you narcissistic –')

I expect I shall go to the gorden porty. Are you gong to Colin Strang's do?[3] About July 3–10: the medicos seem to think that Hilly will be confined about 20 june-5 july, and I think the latter date is nearer the mark, so I shan't be able to go away at that time, but, if you want to, do you come here for that period. If the baby has arrived by then, it will be all right, and if it hasn't, that will be all right, and if it's just about coming, that will be all right too, because Pij bk Pinetop will be boarded out on the B's or with my parents and we shall be here alone dalling. I emphasise i. that you mustn't feel bound to come but that ii. we shall be sincerely glad to have you – we aren't just saying so to avoid disappointing you. But if you wd. rather make some other arrangement, do so. In the meantime, can you come here for a wickend? Any one will do, except this coming one. Do try to 'make the effort'. Hilly wants to see you, and so do I. We have two new kittens, called Molly and Sammy (fluffy black-and-white and smooth grey-and-white) and will soon have another, Murphy (tortoiseshell).

If you have any pictures of Miss Virginia Mayo in your Paris-Hollywoods, cut them out with a pair of scissors and put them in an envelope and send them to me. I will pay 6d. each for the ones I decide to keep. I am quite serious about this. I have seen The secret life of walter mitty[4] 'of course it isn't thurber THANCRICE Have you seen it? The corset sequence is very good.

I wish we lived in the same town. One of the ways in which I feel I am wasting my youth is in not seeing you much more often dalling. Am writing much doggerel these days, but looking forward to when, thesis over, I can begin 'my second novel'. I have worked out the point of it now, though it's probably another 'slight' one.

Write in full after no long interval. The Galpins[5] came becos we had planned to swap houses with them and then we couldnt go.

3. Colin Strang (b.1922), a contemporary at St John's College, Oxford; later Professor of Philosophy, Newcastle University (1975–82); second Baron Strang since 1978.

4. *The Secret Life of Walter Mitty* (1947), directed by Norman Z. McLeod, from a story by James Thurber, starring Danny Kaye as Walter Mitty, Boris Karloff, Florence Bates and Virginia Mayo.

5. Brian Galpin (b.1921), a friend from Hertford College, Oxford, edited *Isis* (1946), married Ailsa McConnel (d. 1959) in 1947. Galpin became a circuit judge in 1978.

I shall be accompanied by my bum,
~~shall not~~

Kingsley

[TLS: Bodleian]

TO PHILIP LARKIN – 9 JUNE 1949

Ma'z Co'ge, Newl'n' Stree', Ey'sh'm, Ox'n. (o' boy)

My dear Philip,

Good it is, antique bloke, to be tapping out a message to *you* on this machine; good that I am not doing it in quattuordeuplicate HORRIBLE SMELL OF ARSE quattuordecuplicate with wafer-thin shagged carbons that necessitate the force being used with the fingers of Schnabel during a *fortissimo* passage in a musical composition by the late Abbe Liszt;[1] good also that when I make a mistake I can sware about it and leave it instead of inserting thirteen slips of paper under the various carbons and correcting the mistake leafmeal . . . ((kkss (wanwood bum)[2]; good in addition that I shall not be typing phrases like 'one of the most able' and 'engaging personality' and 'First Class in Shortened Final Honour School of English Language and Literature' – yes, I have been applying for more jobs. I have an interview for that cunt-only place in London on Tuesday,[3] which makes me nervous already. But glad too. I hope I get it; it's about the last chance I shall get. They don't want me at King's. [. . .]

We had a nice Whitson, I hope you did, was'nt the wheather marvelous, we went over to the Mrss' people over at Harwell, proper scream

1. Arthur Schnabel (1882–1951), pianist; Franz Liszt (1811–86), pianist and composer, took minor orders in the Roman Catholic Church in 1865 and was referred to as 'the Abbé Liszt'.

2. An allusion to 'Spring and Fall' (written 1880, published 1918) by Gerard Manley Hopkins (1844–1889): 'Ah! as the heart grows older/It will come to such sights colder/By and by, nor spare a sigh/Though worlds of wanwood leafmeal lie' (ll.5–8).

3. The most prominent of the exclusively female colleges of the University of London in 1949 were Bedford and Westfield, though Amis may be referring to a college outside the university.

the old boy os osod is with his fokl-danceing, and old Bill[4] with his conchertoes and sympathies, little Marion Partinton was their two. I had all the usual kicks, an account of a blind fiddler, over eighty he is, at Adderbury, a meritless short story shown to me by mummy b-, a talentless and flavourless sonatina played me, gratuitously, by Wm. Two things only pleased me: Bill B. has *given himself the shits* by his own *filthy French cooking* – that'll teach him, with his I'm-more-at-home-in-France-than-in-England *balls* – YES, you *stab rad*, you ARE, you *star dab*, aslongasI'minEnglandmyselfthankyouverymuch. YES, you *egg rub*, you ARE, you *reg. bug*, because over there they blame your anality on your being English instead of on your being an anus, and so can overlook it more easily. The other thing I liked was when little Marian came over to me in the garden to be picked up, going abubbelubblerubblerub, and I, doing the kindest thing I was capable of, ignored her; then she went over to Bill. He picked her up. She instantaneously shat over his trousers. Ah, me boy, amn't I telling you we had the big laugh there the two of us, me and myself.

Lastly, my dear fellow: can you come here for a week-end *very soon*, the w-e of 18 June if possible? Hilly has urged me to make this special request of you, and I am not behind her in eagerness you may warrant. The point is that after then things will probably be very difficult for some time, something like two months. I do very much want to see you, and so does she, and we want to make sure of seeing you soon. I know you've had a lot of things on recently, and there's this exam,[5] and your mother will have to be considered, so I shall 'quite understand' if you'd prefer to postpone it, but serously, if you can, come. If he could come, that boy should come to-night (with apologies to Wordsworth !!!!!!).[6] Let me know. By the way, it won't make any 'extra work' for us.

Daddy B looked more like an imbecile brother of Yeats than ever.

With reference to your application for the post of Assistant Lecturer in the Department of bum,

Kingsley

[TLS: Bodleian]

4. Bardwell, Hilly's brother.

5. Larkin was preparing for the final examinations for membership of the Library Association.

6. An allusion to 'Michael' (1800), in which the eponymous hero, an old shepherd, says of his son Luke's departure: 'If he *could* go, the Boy should go tonight' (1.282).

TO PHILIP LARKIN – 12 JULY 1949

Marriner's Cottage, Newland Street, Eynsham, Oxon.

My dear Philip,

Very glad to see the remembered type-heads on the envelope, old thing, and gladder to read the contents. I'm sorry badness has been around your steps; yes faith heartily. I shouldn't have liked joining in that library move at all, at all. And I'm sorry your fambly has been plang you vp. YOU SHOULD THINK YOURSELF BLOODY LUCKY, however, that you haven't trebled your family by marrying another one. Old Rodge and his Mrs. breezed over here on there SLUGSH their bikes on Sunday, both wearing silly hats; Partington had forgotten (crazy creature – head in the clouds[1] as usual) to get himself enough cigarettes, so he had 2½ of mine, and left me with 1 to last me from 6 p.m. until I should be able to buy some the next morning. They are going to Canada to-morrow for a year; I'm glad they're going, but don't think they ought to go; i.e., as you will readily see, glad they will be out of my hair, sorry they will enjoy themselves travelling. Still, Miggy is pregnant again, so that will complicate things for them, won't it? My hatred of Daddy B has reached a new high – the other Saturday Nick and his girl and my wife and my girl ('ssh!)[2] and me went to a carnival here, and more or less enjoyed ourselves, until the old ape-man turned up – he had 'come to see the country dancing'. We all came back here for tea, and a man we know turned up, so that WITHOUT THE APE we should have been a merry party, but THE APE WENT ON SITTING ABOUT AND GRINNING and *spoiling everything by his presence* and *not realising it* and *doddering about and missing his bus* so that he stayed till *seven* BUGGERING THINGS UP FOR SIX PEOPLE *JUST BY BEING THERE*. I hate him; I *hate* him; I HATE him; I *HATE* the old *APE'S BASTARD*. I have almost stopped being amused by hating him, too. You will laugh at what I have written, I expect; but to me it gives an analogous feeling, except that it is personal, to reading a speech by Churchill; something contentedly stupid that you can't alter.

1. Amis has circled 'clouds' in pen and connected it with the MS addition 'do you mean "clouds of RECTUM-AIR", my dear young chap?'

2. Unidentifiable.

I shall swing for the old cockchafer unless I put him in a book, *recognisably*, so that he will feel *hurt* and *bewildered* at being so *hated*.

I'm sorry I went on like that, only I do loathe his guts. [. . .]

Hilly hasn't gone to the life-box yet; they say it will be 5 weeks yet, though I think this is putting it high. Pinetop is almost walking, certainly crawling and standing for brief periods without aid. They will both be glad to see you on August 1.

Every morning I meet my schoolgirl and walk some of the way to school with her. When I asked her if, if I asked her, she would come out with me, I was favourably answered. But I haven't asked her yet. She is just fifteen, very pretty and amusing, and like a little startled horse. This s rue, ut on't xpect ou o elieve t.

Well I suppose you've just about finished your bum,

Kingsley

[TLS: Bodleian]

TO PHILIP LARKIN – 27 AUGUST 1949

Marriner's Cottage Eynsham

Martin Louis Amis arrived at 4.50 p.m. on Thursday; his weight is at present unknown, but is probably more than P's was. Blond (frup) as P, less horrifying in appearance. H had a pretty short (though sharp) labour – 5 hours, and she as well as M is now very well. She'll be writing to you, but if you'd like to write first the address (in case you've forgotten) is Grosvenor Ward, Radcliffe Maternity Home, Walton Street. I will also write when I am less bussy. Did you like my rhyme? I did. It looks as if my Prague job[1] might come off. They're worn with a slight fullness now, sir, across the bum Am bing. *A sort of bomb* this morning.[2]

Kingsley

[ALS: Bodleian]

---

1. See Amis to Larkin, 19 July 1949 (in Bodleian): 'Am trying for jobs in Manchester & Prague lordy lordy.'

2. Perhaps *A Sort of Traitors* (1949) by Nigel Balchin (1908–70), novelist and screenwriter. 'Bing' is 'buying'; for 'bomb', see Amis's telegram to Larkin, 9 August 1949

TO PHILIP LARKIN – 6 SEPTEMBER 1949

Marriner's Cottage, Eynsham

My dear Philip,

We are most of us at home now; Philip is still in his nursery, whence I shall take him by petrol-automobile to his grandparents' residence in Badtown to-morrow, and then my wife and my younger son and myself will settle down at the house of my parents-in-law for a few daze of whorey belles tinker furze. So your next letter should be sent there. Martin is really extraordinary – one of the most protesting faces I ever saw. They say he has been rather ill, but he is quite all right now. Hilly is as good as new and very pleased to be home again. [. . .]

I have, in the course of my duties, been reading the life of O. Wilde, by H. Pearson.[1] I find P. a bit of a ball-shaver, but W himself very good; I admire him very much, and should have liked to know him. I don't know that he was a very good writer, though. But who was in those far-off days? No, not him. *No*, not him. No, *not* him. No, not *him*. Walter Allen is tackling about Coghill's Langland on the radio as I write.[2] He ought to know better, oughtn't he? Ooh, *did you know* (my dear little chap) that Raymond Somerville was a major in the regulars until 1941, that he and Coghill are cousins, being nephews of the Irish RM fool and bore?[3] Don't be angry, if you did know.

There is not much else of moment to say. I have written a poem on death in the 4-line Horatian ode stanza; I have an interview in Bristol on Tuesday, for the university there, you know; I have got rid of my flea; I have omitted to put a lot in my diary that ought to have been put there; I have bought a pipe and am engaged in excoriating my

(in Bodleian): 'HAPPY BIRTHDAY ALL YOU WISH YOURSELF BOMB KINGSLEY.'

---

1. *The Life of Oscar Wilde* (1946) by Hesketh Pearson (1887–1964), actor and biographer.

2. *Visions from Piers Plowman* (1949) by Nevill Coghill (1899–1980), Fellow and Tutor in English, Exeter College, Oxford.

3. The 'Irish RM fool and bore' was Edith Somerville (1858–1949), of Somerville and Ross, an authorial partnership with her second cousin Violet Martin (Ross) (1862–1915). Somerville and Ross wrote some thirty books, mainly set in their native Ireland, as well as numerous articles, diaries, jottings and letters. *Some Experiences of an Irish R.M.* (1899), an immensely popular collection of comic stories, was narrated by Major Yeates, the Irish R.M. or 'Resident Magistrate'.

mouth with it. I hope your life becomes a better life, really I do. I hope too that I get a bloody *job* before long, or I s'll be on the breadline, wacker. And I hope to write at more length next time. Meanwhile, all the best, old tubthumper; keep right on to the end of the road *and then use the latrine.*

Ah, just look at the little pet; got his dad's bum,

Kingsley

[TLS: Bodleian]

TO PHILIP LARKIN – 14 SEPTEMBER 1949

Marriner's Cottage, Eynsham, Oxford.

My dear Philip,

Well, my dear old bloke, to prove to you how sorry I am to have been so lax last time, here I am coming right up at you again with another of my letters to you. We are back from Abbey Timbers now, thanks to the Saviour. I hardly did more than sleep there, and so escaped a full indoctrination with folk-dance lore. On Saturday a pretty boy named Anthony came visiting with his parents and younger brother, and he made me feel all nostalgic if you know what I mean. His father was a member of that class which I most desire now to put into the old pillory, lad: those who have broadcast *once* over the wireless-set (I don't mean to include Crippen[1]). They are akin to that class which always has *black* coffee in restaurants – I hope you see this point, and find yourself in agreement, because I find it a very usel spusel useful indication of character. It seems to me to imply (1) I care for the little subtleties and niceties of life (2) I like French things, and the French know that the English can't make a cup of coffee (by the way, one of the small reasons why I was glad to get back to England after my stay in France in 1946 was *to have a decent cup of coffee again*, after the *bubbling brown boot-polish sprinkled with salted nutmeg* I'd had EVERYWHERE I WENT over there), and (3) I suffer from slight brain-fatigue,

1. 'Crippen' is a play on 'Crispin' (i.e. Bruce Montgomery, pen-name 'Edmund Crispin'), an allusion also to Hawley Harvey Crippen (1862–1910), hanged for poisoning his wife.

which makes me 'interesting', and the caffeine is necessary to me if I am to keep you amused, though I shall doubtless pay for it tomorrow. Notice too the sharp, watch-me-closely voice such people use when they are stating their preference for black coffee (they are also heard to say sometimes that they 'can't' drink ordinary coffee, i.e. coffee with milk added).

The only event in my stay worth reporting was when at breakfast this morning I noticed there were no cups on the table and announced my discovery in a low murmur; Daddy B sprang up and went into the kitchen, and I felt some remorse at letting him go instead of me, until he returned with a sole cup, which having filled with tea, milk and sugar, he raised wordlessly to his lips, afterwards continuing his meal. I learn he has no sense of smell, and now make a point of farting silently in his presence.

Yesterday I went to Bristol for an interview (I think I told you I was going), but don't yet know the result – the British Council are silent. On the way back a man told me all about gesture on the Elizabethan stage, *which I found very interesting* WHICH I FOUND VERY INTERESTING *WHICH I FOUND VERY INTERESTING*

There is a new Teddy Wilson[2] out on Parlophone.

Well old lad this is only a short note but I thought it would buck you up. Any chance of your coming up for that week-end? I hope your mammy-trouble has cleared up, a little, anyway. I have borrowed 2 books from Daddy B, called Vanity fair and Collected poems. The second one is by that Irish yammerer whose head was full of all that oizin' and cuckoo-lain pills.[3] I'll tell you what I think of them.

> Well, Mr. Amis, perhaps you could tell the Board what experience you have had in the way of bum,

Kingsley

[TLS: Bodleian]

2. Teddy Wilson (1912–86), pianist.

3. *Vanity Fair* (1847–48) by William Makepeace Thackeray (1811–63). The 'Irish yammerer' is W.B. Yeats (1865–1939), whose first *Collected Poems* appeared in 1933. Oisin is the legendary Gaelic warrior and bard, known also as Ossian (see Yeats's long narrative poem *The Wanderings of Oisin* (1889)); Cuchulain is a hero of the Ulster cycle of Irish mythology and appears in a number of Yeats's poems.

TO PHILIP LARKIN – 6 OCTOBER 1949

Abbey Timbers, Harwell, Berks.

My dear Philip,

So many things have happened since I last wrote ('Yes, my dear fellow, things like *days*, and *weeks*') that, like Chaucer, I can't work out where to begin. My present posture is half-lying in a bed, with this printer on my knees and five days' growth of beard on my face:
– Why are you in bed? Have you been ill? –
– I have. I have had Vincent's infection, or trench mouth, with minor streptococcal variants and suspected diphtheria –
– What does that entail? –
– BAYING PEDERASTY, subdefinable as

> *yelping anality* in the bone-lock of the head;
> *hooting sodomy* in the temperature of the blood-tide, and
> *chiming grave-offence* in the throat-channel*[1])

– Be more explicit –
– I felt as if whenver yktfbsbpaw I swallowed, wch. was much more often than usual, the jagged rim of a shattered milk-bottle had suddenly been inserted into my throat, a milk-bottle that had been used to store spider-shit over some months. I have never felt so ill now whats the matter with this four-knee caton machine can you tell me now? The worst time was the period Monday evening-Tuesday afternoon. I may as well record this as I was probably pretty ill then and it's interesting to know how the brain behaves—
– Makes it worth while in a way, you mean? –
– No, that's not what I mean. I am not the man who means that. What happens is this: you lie in bed terribly hot, of course, and with aching limbs, of course, and with a headache, and your mind instantly darts off on any imagined situation (a saloon-keeper sacking a bartender, a man teaching another how to make a window-frame, a Renascence Cardinal at supper (this machine is a real little winner, isn't it)) and makes up all the dialogue and all the events, with you playing all the

---

1. Asterisked MS addition in pen at the bottom of the page: '*house of easement, do you follow?*'

parts. The effect is of enormous fluency and giddy *speed*, though you're dimly aware that the stuff is no good, that people don't behave like that and only a madman would think that they do, even as you do it. A climax comes when you find yourself thinking something so nonsensical that the difference between it and common-sense scares you, by the mere extent of the difference, into becoming fully conscious, aware that you have at any rate passed a certain period of the night without harm. When you look at your watch, you find that ten, sometimes as few as three, minutes have elapsed since you 'woke up' before. The natiest BAGGZZ nastiest things are those you can't fully remember – I was calling my headache Edmund Gosse[2] at one point. I don't like thinking about that now. There were smaller, irritant, factors in the situation besides—

– Describe them –

– One, we left Marriner's Cottage for good on Monday and are staying here indefinitely, though not, I hope, for long, though again they are very kind. My confinement to bed meant that Hilly had to pack up all the stuff on her own with the aid of the charwoman. I was glad to miss it in a way, but felt sorry for H., and shall feel sorry again, I warrant you, when I have to find anything again. Two, the doctors at Eynsham were incompetent and treated me for the wrong thing, so that I was ill for three days longer than I need have been. Three, I had a lovely day flat-hunting with Hilly on Friday in Oxford, without result, of course, just as I was beginning to feel ill. Four, we saw some friends that day who might have helped, and both of us picked up several fleas from their furniture: I remembered afterwards they had once said they got attacked by some in Ireland. Now this absolutely enragged me; are the gods so anxious to load me with fleas that they will send people *to Ireland* to bring it to pass? We have not seen these persons since. *Funnily enough*, the fact that I have been feverish seems to have put them off bitting me; now that my temper . . . urch . . . oo-er has gone down do you look for the little animals making a posithive colander of me skin. Five, just as we were leaving Eynsham a wire arrived from Swansea, asking me to an interview there on Friday. That was on Monday. I wasn't much interested in anything then, finally wiring them yesterday that I was ill, probably couldn't come Friday, could I come next Tuesday?

2. Edmund Gosse (1849–1928), critic and essayist, author of the autobiographical *Father and Son* (1907).

They now wire me to say that that will be quite all right, only they expect to make their choice on Saturday. In other words, fack you Jack. I have just wired them again to say I will be there to-morrow after all. I do feel almost righteously angry about this: to save themselves the trouble of walking a couple of hundred yards on Tuesday as well as on Friday instead of just on Friday, I can be induced to sweat my guts out half-way across England *and bloody Wales*. That's wrong, isn't it? –

– Well, no-one's forcing you to go, are they? No, all right, I won't tell you that. Is that all? –

– *No*, the doctor here, who I must admit is a good doctor, is a friend of the fambly too, and he says he 'won't hear of my going' (all right then, let him *buy himself some bleeding ear-plugs*) without an escort. There's quite a nice funny clever little man named Burden at New C. who's been on one or 2 interviews with me; if he's going to this one, good enough; but if not – then *guess who***!!fffx*??!* yes, YOUVE HIT IT*[3] (a big hand,[4] folks) ITS DADDY BEEEEEE!!!!! (give 'im the money, Buuhney[5] – a snake of pennies in a silk stocking to be used for a bastinado of the crotch) He *would* enjoy the trip so! To his beloved Wales!! Won't it be *marvellous* if Kingsley gets the job!!! Professor Dai ap Faeces is there, who wrote the first really scholarly Welch grammar, I'll get it and show you. . . . So handy for the National Scheissbedsodd, too. What's that? You may have to stay there overnight? No need to bother about a hotel – go to some real old countryman's place – I'll show off in the lingo a bit: 'Llgo andw ghet stwft, iu stwpydd olld swd,' he'll say, or perhaps 'Scwm offw, iu blwddy wytt-eddyd chwmp-an-si ffacd maas-tyr-batwr' – get a real glimpse of Welch life, not as it is for the tourist, but as it really is (yes, grand old Welch life round the docks, with the bloody blacks chasin' each other round the warehouses wavin' their razors, and me goin' like the 'ammers of fuck the other road – can't blame me though) Something too much of this.

As regards matters literary, I have done a small amt. of reading

3. In the left margin Amis has typed the MS addition: '*once squarely on the knob, and here we are, all ready to hit it again!!!'

4. Amis has typed three slashes (/) above 'a big hand' and typed in the MS addition: 'yes; a big hand clenched round your privates, then abruptly wrenched downwards'.

5. Alludes to a catchphrase from the popular radio programme of the 1940s and 1950s *Have a Go*.

recently. I started The Heat of the Day,[6] and cdn't bare it, chiefly because I hated all the chracters so much. What a priggish little 'swipe that Roderick is, to be sure – how he plays all the time for the epithet 'sensitive'; I vow I will never try to create sensitivity in ort as long as I live. Robert hadn't come in much by the time I stopped, but he helped me to stop, quite a lot. The woman didn't interest me. The only thing I had against Harrison (the man supposed to be a bounder) was that he wasted his time on that lot.

I started The poems of Lord Byron, in one volume, as well, and stopped them soon.

Read Stephen hero,[7] which I enjoyed very much. If only you and I had been there, telling Joyce what to write abt, and stopping him when he went wrong, what a wonderful writer we should have made him. When he goes wrong, it's never through doing something badly, always through doing something we don't want done. Hero was very funny, too. [. . .]

So you put Cheerful Charlie Dickens and Victor Mature Hugo on a level with Wild Bill, do you, you silly bastard? You can't do that, you *fool*, because they're NO GOOD, and He's GOOD. I don't think anything at all of Bill's philosophy or powers of characterization or construction, but I give him top marks for three things: 1. being good at exploiting (though bad at engineering) situation 2. being good at being a poet, and righter about when he was being good than any other poet 3. being able to turn anything into poetry (this sounds nasty, but only because when applied to the people it is usually applied to – Crab, Cooper – it is a lie). I dont say he does this all the time, but he does it much more nearly all the time than anyone else does. You want to read Shakespeare – Hamlet, Macbeth, King Lear. Ever read them?

I am getting up soon. Write here when you write.

You may also be asked to appear before a meeting of the Council on 8 October. It is assumed that you will make your own arrangements for overnight bum,

Kingsley

[TLS: Bodleian]

6. *The Heat of the Day* (1949) by Elizabeth Bowen (1899–1973), novelist and short-story writer.

7. *Stephen Hero* (1944), posthumously-published part of James Joyce's first draft of *A Portrait of the Artist as a Young Man* (1914–15).

TO PHILIP LARKIN – 17 OCTOBER 1949

134 St. Helen's Road, Swansea, Glamorgan.

My dear Philip,

As you'll have observed, man, from the postal-mark, old step-son, I have secured the appointment in the English Faculty of the University College of Swansea. There is an awful lot to tell you most of which I don't suppose I shall get round to telling you. I won't tell you about the two interviews I had because it would make dashed hard writing. But I was glad to defeat three of the 4 men I did defeat: Evans, a big, very short man with tonsured fair hair, a convoluted tobacco-pipe and a face like an old Rugby football converted, by a tyro hand, into the semblance of a red pumpkin; a nameless cadaver with castellated teeth who talked in baying cockney of his qualifications; and a Manchester man, his face sored but not shaven by shaving, who talked with his mouth almost shut.

When I arrived back at Abbey T, I was able to pick up stacks of useful information on Wales and the Welsh from Daddy B, who was decent enough to ransack his library for anything that might have a bearing on the subject, and wouldn't rest till he'd given me as complete a picture of the set-up as his means allowed! Ah, gw andd styff i't wp llyur smwlli wrswhwlw. I expect he's all agog (ALL ABOG) for news now. Well then let him conn-tinue in that staet, eh bach?

I'm afraid I shan't be able to make this letter as good as it ought to be, because there is much information to impart and it's hard to make it funny. Hilly and I left Oxford on Friday for Berkhamsted, with Martin. My last day in Oxford, which I had hoped would be a gently melancholy communion with all I know and love so well, turned out to be *tongue-giving tribadism* – I said goodbye to all the people I didn't want to say g-b to and hardly any I did, I had my hair cut, I spent an hour "finishing up in Bodley", I exchanged my insurance card, I bought a box of matches, I went to Eynsham where I carried all my books from the ground floor to the attic, stacked up the records, re-packed the cases and trunks, helped to load the latter and a lot of other things on to a trailer, pushed the pram down into the shed at the bottom of the garden, helped to check the inventory ("*Seven* muslin curtains; I can only find three" – "What about these?" – "No, they're listed separately" – "Here they are" – "No, those are for the corner-cupboard" –

"These?" "No"), and sweated much and soon, I returned to Oxford and stood for some time queueing for a bus, and I at last arrived at the Bad Town at 8.55 approx. I was glad to see Pinetop, though; he is walking and looks very pretty and good-humoured. When you take a thing from him, he doesn't cry: "thanks indeed for that".

Then on Sunday as finale to over a week of travel-erethism I went from Berkhamsted to Swansea, 8½ hours from door to door. It had been arranged by my father that I should Green Line to Praed Street and walk therefrom to Paddington, 3–4 minutes' walk for which I w[d] have c. 15 minutes. Ah, but it didn't pan out like that, man: the driver was new, looking wonderingly about him at all the strange buildings and cars, his foot rising from the accelerator in alarm whenever a vehicle approached him on the opposite side of the triple carriage-way. And there was a diversion that added 2–300 yards to the distance I had to cover on foot. I jerked sweating along, my tie playing about my nose in the high wind, the handle of my suitcase corroding my hand, and arrived at the train with 30 secs. to spare. They let me on: the ticket-collector was presumably under notice of dismissal. The seat opposite mine was occupied by a sallow young man of clerk-like appearance who had been unable to provide seating accommodation for his three year old daughter, who stood three inches in front of my feet all the time, except from 3.30–4 and 4.30–5, when I was absent at lunch and tea. At Newport a lady got in, with a younger child that kept looking at me. At Swansea a helpful Welshman assisted me to find my way, prolonging a 5 minute journey into one lasting 35 minutes. This morning I met my colleagues and some of the stewed 'unts and was 'shown round' the library and the main university building and the old arts building and the new arts building and the seminar rooms and the room reserved for research students and members of the staff and the new hall and the old refectory and the new refectory and the science block. I won't tell you any more for the moment, about my colleagues or anything. Or the *work*.

Well you can see that things have got a bit easier for me now. My housing problem is solved, in that it has been changed, my throat is all right, I have a job, and don't mind yet. But I haven't at hand any wife or babies or records or nice books or typewriter or clever and witty and beautiful friends. Still, you can't have everything, can you? ("No, but why is that, please?")

I'll shut down now, old hosre, because a little boy is plang with his farm animals at my feet. I'll reply to yr letter, wch I enjoyed hewjely, next time: look on this as episode 1 of *My Swansea diary*. I have the Mum[1] too; I look on about 1/3 of it as quite good & interseting, though I hate the po-po-poetic derdiction as much as you do. Hilly will be at Abbey T from Wednesday.

Please communicate with my secretary should you wish to take part in the bum,

Kingsley

[ALS: Bodleian]

TO PHILIP LARKIN – 29 OCTOBER 1949

20 St. Helen's Crescent, Swansea.

My dear Philip,

Another letter, *bach*, from *Welsh Wales* ("oh! and where is the English Wales, please tell me?") to tell you all the news, *whatever* ("yes, whatever your balls weigh I'll cause them to rebound from my shoe-toe"). Instead of being with the nice Irish couple and their little son I am in *digs* with a different Irishman – I may have told you about this – who talks about Dublin. "But wrongly." He tells me about the trams that used to run in Dublin and the picturesque medieval survivals at T.C.D.,[1] which must have been a bloody awful place to have had one's [varsity? university?] education. There is a nasty Jazz Club now taking place, beneath a frizzling interference from butchers' refrigerators, and I am writing this while the Irishman, Willy Smyth,[2] pronounced Smith, goes to shave the hair from his face. I have an evening 8 to-night: Garnet Rees[3] (man), the senior lecturer in French, has invited me to

1. Maugham; that is, his latest book, *A Writer's Notebook* (1949).

1. Trinity College Dublin.

2. Willie R. Smyth (1915–73), Dublin-born Latinist, and a lecturer in Classics, University College, Swansea (1939–73). For Smyth's eccentricities see *Memoirs*, pp. 120–2.

3. Garnet Rees (1912–90), Senior Lecturer in French, University College, Swansea (1946–57); later Professor of French, University of Hull (1958–79).

house wharse his house for coffee, to meet a lot of other craps.[4] I may have given you the impression that it isn't nice here; it is: the other Irishman and his lesbian-looking wife are both intelligent and kind and funny, and the Welch go out of their way to be nice. Some of the stewed 'unts are all right, too, though there's nobody in the common room I want to get much closer to. I had a tut. the other day, on the poems of Sir T. Wyat; a girl with a very well filled sweater giggled silently for fifty minutes. "Laughter is the first sign of sexual attraction."[5] I am lecturing on Renaissance Currents of Thought, Victorian Currents of Thought, and Poetry. For the first I read out my [C.S.] Lewis notes, for the second my thesis notes, for the third I say what I think; it doesn't really matter what I say. I have 5 hrs. work a week at the college, and about another 12 preparing stuff. But I need all the time I can get for *house-hunting* (*rump*-bom, *stump*-bom, *lump*-bom, BARLSS), and thinking about house-hunting, and thinking about my superannuation insurance policy ("a pretty stiff medical exam . . ." what will they find?) and thinking about doing my thesis.

I said I'd tell you about my colleagues. There is *Professor Thomas*,[6] a smiling, smoking, light-suited man of about 58, who doesn't drive me hard. When you tell him anything, he says regularly "Yäs . . . yäs . . .", like one of those Grgr priests who have heard all the sins that men can commit a long time ago ("When you thought about it, you realised that the catalogue of human sin was a shabby, restricted affair. There wasn't really very much a man could do, even in the way of evil"[7]) listening to a confession. *Miss Westcott*,[8] a smiling, apple-cheeked Angli-

4. See Larkin's 'Vers de Société, from *High Windows* (1974): '*My wife and I have asked a crowd of craps/To come and waste their time and ours: perhaps/You'd care to join us?*'

5. A direct quotation from Christopher Isherwood, *Lions and Shadows* (1938), spoken by the Auden character, Hugh Weston (p. 189).

6. W.D. Thomas (1890–1954), Professor of English and Head of Department (from 1921), praised by Amis for 'tolerance and amiability' (*Memoirs*, p. 122); the first Professor of English at the College and 'a great admirer of Quiller-Couch' (according to Mavis Nicholson, one of his students, personal communication, 17 January 1999).

7. The closest I can come to this quotation, which may be paraphrase or pastiche, is the following passage, suggested by John Fuller, from *The Power and the Glory* (1940): 'There had been a continuous stream of penitents from eight to ten – two hours of the worst evil a small place like this could produce after three years. It hadn't amounted to very much – a city would have made a better show – or would it? There isn't much a man can do. Drunkenness, adultery, uncleanness' (p. 221).

8. Isabel M. Westcott (b. 1900), a lecturer in the English Department for forty-one years (1926–67). Described in *Memoirs*, p. 123, as 'a middle-aged spinster of sweetness and natural propriety who nevertheless knew well enough what the rest of us were like'.

can lady who does a lot of good works. I don't think she's very efficient, but I feel protective towards her because it's easy to take the piss out of her. In some people she calls forth more rudeness than they are normally capable of; in others a wholly foreign politeness and half-sincere *galanterie. James Bartley,*[9] the Irishman, whom I've mentioned already. He is an Ulsterman born and reared in Dublin, so he is both pro- and anti- every Irish question. I reverence him for having lived in Dublin. 'And did you once see Porter, plain?'[10] *David Sims,*[11] small, balding, laughing, ex-Jesus. It is difficult to avoid saying funny things to him, because he likes laughing, but important not to, because he might start laughing.

The worst part of life here is the bleeding *digs*. I get enough to *eat*, but only by closing my eyes and eating *hard*. The landlady is *deaf* ("Do you like coffee or cocoa?" – "Coffee, please" – "Yes, I think cocoa keeps the cold out"), there is a *dog*, tremulously joyful; the bathroom and shithouse *can only be reached through my bedroom* (a common Welch arrangement). The light-switch for the sitting-room is *outside, in the hall, round the corner*, and the hall light is kept switched off, *always*. Meals are *at inconvenient times* and usually *not hot*. Some of the bacon was *high* this morning. I have just had a dreadful talk with my landlady about *my ration book*. They did it *wrong* to-day at the food office or something; I don't know. I am having to go *back* there to-morrow (up *ninety-one* stone steps) to get it *changed*. I am *ufrouilsy ganry* about it. [. . .]

I'm sorry this has been so long in coming, as the b. said to the a. To-night I may be going to *King Leer* at the Grand Theatre. Willie Smyth reads things in Latin & Greek out to me while I'm trying to

Her literary specialisms were Dryden, Pope, eighteenth-century fiction and the Metaphysicals.

9. James ('Jo') Bartley (1906–67), lecturer in English, University College, Swansea (1946–67), a specialist in drama, particularly Irish, active in producing plays at the university: 'one of whom it could be justly said, 'Now that's what I *call a* drinking man' and a smoker to rival Willie Smyth. He liked food too, also women, doing his job and researching among obscure plays' (*Memoirs*, p. 120).

10. See Browning, 'Ah, did you once see Shelley plain?' (line 1 of 'Memorabilia', from *Men and Women*, 1855). 'Plain' is Dublin Irish for porter.

11. David Sims (1922–89), lecturer in English (1946–84), University College, Swansea; described as 'thoroughly Welsh without going on about it'; soon to become 'my closest friend in Swansea' (*Memoirs*, p. 125). Sam Dawson (b. 1928), also of the English Department (1951–92), describes Sims as 'a mind of remarkable originality . . . a good cricketer, a good actor' (personal communication, 22 January 1999).

prepare a lecture. That's when he's not telling me about Dublin or how he built his radiogramme. The landlady thinks I bath too much and give her too much washing to do. If I go out and return after 1/2 hour or so I find she has taken the fire away from the grate and shovelled into her own. My watch is up the creek, too. It's a hard life, brother. Oh that *dog* . . . . .

(The coffee party was wonderful. There was a man there named Britton[12] of hyper-Partingtonian moodiness, a philosopher, who brought out the final unassailable answer to every question raised, after a few minutes of frowning & pipe-sucking. *You* know the kind of *bass-tarred*.)

I shan't be able to get any fats or tea on your bum,

Kingsley

[ALS: Bodleian]

TO PHILIP LARKIN – 23 DECEMBER 1949

82, Vivian Road, Sketty, Swansea,

My dear Philip,

I'm very sorry to have not written to you for so long; I can assure you it was not part of any policy. Partly it was that all my letter-libido was being expended on writing regularly to my good-wife, and partly it was that I was to lassy. Anyway, of the dozen or so letters I must write to-day to catch up on my correspondence DREADFUL STENCH OF ANUS, the first is this to you. Another reason for my delay was that I had not my word-printer with me. *A friend of mine has been using it* all this while, hence the phantom-thin charactering and the dirtiness. None of all this shall occur again.

Hilly and I and the two children moved in here on Monday and the place is in some sort of order now, but not much. It is a ground-floor flat in an ill-built house, rather too small and with no room to put anything. There are fourteen steps between the front-door and the street, and most of the time I am carrying a pram or a baby up or down them.

12. Karl Britton (1909–83), a philosopher, lectured at the University College of Swansea (1937–51); Professor of Philosophy, University of Newcastle (from 1951); Dean, Faculty of Arts, Durham University (1961–63, 1966–69).

Although deaf-landlady bum and bad-food bum and celibacy bum and ration-book bum were bad where I was, bottle-mixing bum and coal-cellar bum and up-early bum and washing-up bum are bad where I am. But not as bad as the former things that were bad. Even so, having two children at once is very annoying. They tend to cry a good deal, and to need things done for them. Hilly has a great deal to do, and I feel impelled to help her with some of it. Luckily there's a room I can get away into to do my work. hrbl smll f rs.[1]

I am really very happy here, because everybody is agreeable to me, I haven't too much work I must do, and I shall have neal peals nearly enough money before too long. And I like teaching students, especially girl ones, you no. I am a little angry, though, because I seem to have nothing to show for the last two months I have spent here. My thesis is still hanging about, I have no lectures in hand, and I have written nothing except two metrical compositions, which I hope are good. Nor have I had any sex-play worth mentioning. Very funnily, though, I have found a male student here I should like. He's clever, too. Name of Geoffrey Nicholson.[2] He's beautiful, I find. Another thing that makes me a little angry is the weather: it rains *and* is cold, with a wind blowing. The Welsh are just as we have always imagined them, Dylan Emlyn Lewis, words minus sense, posturing minus charm, and seriousness minus ability (and minus consideration and minus humour and minus attractiveness and minus reliability and minus tact and minus manners). Cheating Welsman, what? [. . .]

I wish I could see you. I find even a couple of days with you does me a lot of good for quite a long time; I leave you feeling much cleverer and funnier than before you arrived, and more of a writer, even if you've crapped on my poems, and more isolated than I was before, but glad about it instead of depressed. I hope I convey my meaning. I suppose the additional journey makes things much harder for you. But we'll talk about that when Christmas – holy cow – is over. I'm afraid we couldn't accommodate you here for the present, nor would you much enjoy it if we did.

---

1. 'Horrible smell of arse.'

2. Geoffrey Nicholson (1929–99), journalist and writer; Sports Editor, *Observer* (1976–78), later Sports Features Editor, *Sunday Times*, and rugby correspondent for the *Independent*. He married the writer and broadcaster Mavis Nicholson (*née* Mainwaring, b.1930), another of Amis's students, in 1952.

I must go off now, and buy some things – a new typewriter-ribbon, a Christmas card for my professor, the repaired electric kettle that Hilly burned out yesterday, some non-cigarettes "to last me over the holiday". God rest you *miserable*, gentlemen. Yes, I know I've said that before.

Hello Amis, settling in all right into your new bum,

Kingsley

PS: Hilly sends her love. Give mine to your mother.[3]

[TLS: Bodleian]

TO PHILIP LARKIN – 1 JANUARY 1950

82 Vivian Road, Sketty, Swansea.

My dear Philip,

Sorry to hear that. Sorry to hear that. Here am I, a young man in a wet month,[1] being made to snarl with bubbling irritation by a little boy making crying noises all the time so as to prevent conversation, work on literary projects, or aural musical entertainment. About me in the air moves smoothly a bland smell of human piss. On the fire-guard a child's night-gear steadily scorches. A dying breakfast is prone on the table. I eat Mintoes, deferring the combustion of a new cigarette-weed, for few are there of these to me remaining, and it being the day of rest, no more are to be had from high hostelry, stead of ales, small shop, the home of cigarette, slotted machine of weed-merchandise, kindly kiosk of opening kinema. And my *pipe* – ah-HAGH-hagh-hagh-hagh (I love that); too piercing to me the pang in throat, baneful burning of branded tongue, vile warning of approaching vomit, fearful feeling of belly fetched up.

Turd, eh? my wife and kidlets and yr. sarvnt are going to spend with a Welsh family to eat turkey and drink beer NOT MUCH OF

3. MS addition.

1. An allusion to T.S. Eliot, 'Gerontion' (1920), line 1: 'Here I am, an old man in a dry month'.

THAT look you to *badness* inteat. Did you hear Bruise's play[2] yesterday? I thought it on the whoale good, especially the ingenious main idea, but I couldn't forgive that cut-glass-facetiousness of the 'tec: 'Kindly refrain from giving your evidence in the form of an *antiphon*' Imamusiciandyousee 'Sergeant never has your talent, your genius rather, for stating the obvious been displayed to better advantage' first of all *bum*, then after that *balls*, next in order *bogg*, thereafter with no interval *bagg*, following straightway *bogray*, and finally *bleedingbullpizzlingbastard*, d'you follow? Alan Pea-jones[3] hasn't come on yet, but I heard him once talking about Huxlear; I should imagine that being a culture-snob, and a social-snob, and a money-snob, and a tory-snob, and a snob, he will be, well-disposed, to the book, written, by our friend, and called Free-queynt, huh! *Erses.*[4]

Swonzy is bloody hopeless for records. I went to 4 shops yesterday tring to by a concerted piece by that loopy billiard-playing Austrian chum,[5] and in each one the assistant *stopped me talking* when I had mentioned the man's name and the *kind* of piece. 'Oh no, we don't stock *anything like that*' po po, pee boned cock penny-ring bike-shat, as if I had asked for a recording of *The good ship 'Venus'*,[6] secular cantata for mixed choir, two pianos, cor anglais, flute, oboe, strings and drums.

Well, old palfrey, I shan't be able to keep this up for a month, or however long it is before you come here. But all the sam, I 'precia'e wha' the si'uatio' mus' be, o' boy. Let it be as soon as it can be, is what I urge. James Michie has an article in the NS this week on the conchie[7] tribunals; I want to hear what you think of it, in detail if you feel like it. It is called 'It all depends'. I like Peacock,[8] and may well get him with my 18s. The type is probably awful though, isn't it? I had best know this in advance, because I'm certain not to be able to buy it from

2. Bruce Montgomery's play *The Hours of Darkness*, broadcast on BBC Home Service West Region, 31 December 1949.

3. Alan Pryce-Jones (1908–2000), author, journalist, radio broadcaster (on programmes like *The Critics*) and editor of *The Times Literary Supplement* (1948–59).

4. *Frequent Hearses* (1950), a novel by Bruce Montgomery (Edmund Crispin); 'Huxlear' is Aldous Huxley.

5. Mozart, who loved billiards and had a table in his apartments.

6. Bawdy verses, beginning ''Twas on the good ship Venus/By God you should have seen us,' etc.

7. Conscientious objectors, of whom Michie was one.

8. Thomas Love Peacock (1785–1866), satirical novelist, essayist, poet.

stock here. *Welsh culture*, my oath; y'll find the Wilsh varry kin on muz*ack*, you knaw – yes, on vulgar vocal religiosity, on their own back-yard fake minstrels and tune-grubbers, on Taniel Chawnce's[9] symphony, mun, Swancy lud he is, *don't* look, you –, and varry kin toor on paw*tree*, *yes*, on word-drunk Celtic-irresponsible sound-daubing in the Thomas manner. I was delighted to learn from David Sims, my Welsh friend and colleague, that the Eisstteddffodd or whatever it is is *all a fake*; it's a ceremony that's supposed to go back before the Mid. Ages, but actually *all* the documents are now *proved* to have been *forged* for a *hoax* to *fool* people and make *monkeys* of them by being *frauds* and *not genuine* by a *bogus cheating counterfeiting dishonest mountebank* of a *fudging fiddling charlatan Welshman* in the late eighteenth century.

All for now. Shoot me the relevant word soon. Last time I visited the people we are going to to-day they started pressing me to *go into the Church*. Don't look like that. Incidentally I learn that the Church of Wales pays its curates so badly that when they've done the 5 years in Wales that's in their bond they *all clear off* to England, where the pay's possible to live on. That's funny, isn't it?

Well, what do you and your wife think of the Welsh bum,

Kingsley

[TLS: Bodleian]

TO PHILIP LARKIN – 9 JANUARY 1950

82 Vivian Road, Sketty, Swansea.

My dear Philip,

[. . .] I'm sorry to have to tell you this, but of late I've been getting very keen on that billiard-playing Austrian's stuff. It strikes me that he did all Bach is supposed to have done and didn't besides what he did himself, and all that Beethoven did *that was worth dong*, better than Beethoven did, and none of the bad, nasty, wrong and unwise things that Beethoven did. Moe's stuff seems to me as good in the same way

9. Daniel Jones (1912–93) composed five symphonies, eight string quartets and the music to the radio drama *Under Milk Wood* (1954) by his friend Dylan Thomas.

as that Buggering Russian's[1] only better and in a better way. Points that the other buggers take five minutes to make he makes with two notes. It annoys me that this isn't more generally known, and that that poxrotted Dutchman[2] gets all the splash: whenever I read the words 'string quartet in C sharp minor, op. 127',[3] or hear one of those bloody woompbash ... woompbash ... *woompbash* ... WOOMPBASH ... WOOMPBASH ... *WOOMPBASH* ... W O O M P B A S H ... sequences, or see that glowering-gollywog-imitating-an-incensed-bullfrog face in the Radio Times, I get all annoyed inside myself. I'm sorry to have to tell you this.

[. . .] Let me have a line, josst tar keep yahr mammary gar-een. Tum starts tum-'orror. At 11 a.m. I deliver my first lecture. It's about the aesthetic movement (don't grin like that) and O F OF W W.[4] 'Wilde united the qualities of silliness and high intelligence in a degree unparalleled except in Keats' – yes, I'm going to say that.

Philip, go and get Daddy out of bed-bum

Kingsley

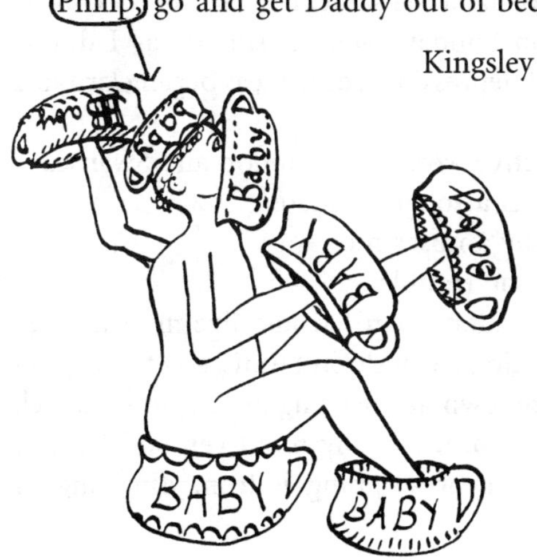

[TLS: Bodleian]

---

1. Tchaikovsky, a homosexual, left his wife a few weeks after their marriage in 1877.

2. Beethoven's face was scarred by smallpox; Dutchman means German (as in pre-1600 usages).

3. If Amis means Beethoven's Opus 127, it is in E flat; Opus 131, another of the late string quartets, is in C sharp minor.

4. Oscar Fingal O'Flahertie Wills Wilde.

TO PHILIP LARKIN – 7 MARCH 1950

University College of Swansea

My dear Philip,

I'm far from persuaded that it's my turn to write, but I will do so. This will probably break off pretty soon, as the b. said to the a., since I am in the common room early, drinking at a cup of coffee, and the rush will no doubt be soon rushing inside the door. I haven't your letter with me anyway, so can't answer that yet. I had a very good time in London,[1] where I drank a lot, and talked to sweet ladies, and smoked a lot of cigarettes, and spent some money on myself. James now has a Jamaican mistress, coffee-coloured, and with a curious Cheltenham Ladies' College accent. He asked earnestly after you, and hoped to see you again some time. He has had a poem accepted by the NS&N, not a very good one I think, but a poem all the same. It's all graft, of course. As I came back on the train on Sunday evening, sinking as I did so into a curious trance-like state of depression, some ideas began clarifying in my mind:

(a) The proportion of attractive women in London and Swansea is as 100: 1 or more – this is a sober estimate;
(b) Nobody in Swansea really amuses me;
(c) Children are not worth the trouble;
(d) I would rather live in London, than I would live in Swansea;
(e) Consequently, the best thing I can do in Swansea is to keep on shutting myself up on my own and writing poems and a novel. This resolution has not dimmed in my mind yet, and I mean to work harder than usual at stopping it from dimming in there. [. . .]

Yes, I am sorry about your lack of novel. Sam Wagstaff has finally gone for a Burton, has he?[2] I'm sorry to hear it, because I thought you

---

1. James Michie had invited Amis to stay with him for the weekend. For Michie see Amis to Larkin, 9 March 1949, note 1.

2. 'Sam Wagstaff' is the main character in a novel Larkin began writing in August 1947 and only gave up on for good six years later. The novel's provisional title was 'A New World Symphony', and it exists in three drafts, one of ninety-five pages. See Motion, *Life*, pp. 225–9. 'Gone for a burton', an expression popular among Royal Air Force personnel in World War II, means absent, missing, lost, dead or presumed dead.

were on to rather a good thing there. I must say that in your shoes I shd. very likely be so overjoyed at the prospect of being published that I would (? shd.) be willing to write any old nonsense and send it in. It wouldn't be *all* nonsense by any means in your case, however irremediably you might think that you'd crapped the bed, and then you would be able to do a slightly better one the next time, and so on. Even if you didn't get any better in your own estimation, at least you would have a book or two more to your name, and the money they would bring in to your credit – 'solemnities not easy to withstand'.[3] It seems to me that there are several courses open to you, summarising what I mean: 1. To write rather a crappy book and get it published and start getting better 2. To write rather a crappy book and get it published and stay the same 3. To write rather a crappy book and get it published and get worse 4. Not to write any sort of book at all ever. Even 3 seems so much preferable to 4 that I should grasp it with eagerness. Do think it over. I hope you don't regard this exhortation as impertinent or patronising. Whether it is or not, methinks there is much reason in my sayings.

Sorry this is rather a humourless letter. Fancy you going and looking at all those pictures, thats' something I coul'nt ever do, I don't like picture's, give me a good read anytime. Can you come for a week-end? by getting day's of I mean.

I wonder if you could help the extra-mural people with their bum

Kingsley

[A and TLS: Bodleian][4]

3. An allusion to 'A Love Song' (1939), by Robert Graves (reprinted in Robert Graves, *Collected Poems 1975*) (London: Cassell, 1975), p. 121). For Graves see Notes on Recipients.

4. The beginning of this letter was handwritten in the Swansea Senior Common Room on 7 March 1950; it was finished the next day on Amis's typewriter. The first extract printed here was handwritten, the second typed.

TO PHILIP LARKIN – 22 MARCH 1950

11 Haslemere Road, Sketty, Swansea.

My dear Philip,

Just a few words before the journey, old confrère. I'm awfully sorry about the money, but you'll get it back when you leave.[1] It's a nuisance I know, but not so much of a nuisance as paying for all my drinks would be, is it? ('I wouldn't have to pay for drinks you WOULDN'T GET'). David and Margaret[2] are looking forward to you coming, though you won't see much of them till after the wickend. Maraget ffff Margaret will expect you to rather like the idea of sleeping with her. You won't want to, so I slip you the warning. You will be pleased with the progress your godson has made. I am all erect for a sight of your vglie mugge. Hilly is too. She asks me to apologise to you because we three shall be sleeping in the same room. I said I didn't think you'd mind that.

Well, just let's make sure you've got everything, shall we? Aunt Hagar?[3] Right. Bechet's Maple leaf [rag]? Right. Your journal? Right. Any fictional or rhyming words? Right. Any pornography? *Right*. The best of your yarn-books and dirty-picture-books, including the Paris-Hollywoods, etc? RIGHT. Your camera? Right. The Julian Hall?[4] Right. Anything else of the printed or written word of interest? Right. Any prints of photographs of any of us we haven't seen? Right. As against (how do you mean, *as* against? It really *is* against, isn't it?) that, I can

---

1. In a letter of 17 March 1950 (in Bodleian) Amis had asked Larkin to lend him some money when he visited: 'When you leave, I will give you a signed bank-cheque to take away in your pocket, which you can cash on the 31 March.'

2. The Amis family had been sharing a house since January with David Sims 'and his mistress [Margaret Ashbury Vakil, recently separated from her husband, an Indian doctor] and her baybay – a legitimate one, by her now-vilipended husband . . . Sims is only here at week-ends for public relations' sake. It is good to have a whole house, but less good to have a third little one about the place' (Amis to Larkin, 27 January 1950, in Bodleian). Margaret Ashbury Vakil later married John Aeron-Thomas. See Amis to Larkin, 3 March 1953, note 2.

3. 'Aunt Hagar's Blues', a record by Eddie Condon and his Orchestra, with trumpet solo by Wild Bill Davison.

4. *Two Exiles* (1936), the last of Julian Hall's three novels. For Hall see Amis to Larkin, 24 March 1947, note 1.

only offer my pornographic novel[5] (close on 5000 words), a few more pages of my novel, *Dixon and Christine*,[6] a picture of a girl who ought to be a lesbian prostitute, some lewd drawings, the new records, a chapter of my thesis, which should make your huge bulk, etc., and much fine talk. Oh, and one or two poems.

Oh me boyo a fine time it'll be and no doubt of it. I'll be at the station at 9.18, come rain come storm.

Raymond Chandler is no mere writer of thrillers; he is in reality a careful and extremely accomplished bum,

Kingsley

[TLS: Bodleian]

TO PHILIP LARKIN – 12 JUNE 1950

644 Mumbles Road, Oystermouth, Swansea.[1]

My dear Philip,

[. . .] I think I owe you a big apology for being so dilatory about this; there was thesis bum, and as soon as that had finished (it hasn't finished really; it was just that I hadn't got £10 to send in with my thesis, and they don't want it, I think I said, until 1952 it seems) there was examinations and marking bum. Now I am quite free UNTIL FRIDAY, when the first batch of Higher Cert. scripts come in.[2] From

5. See Amis to Larkin, 17 March 1950 (in Bodleian): 'I have begun a new pornographic *novel* you will like. I do it when "things get too much for me", the chief thing being my blubber-bummed thesis. It's about two ballet-girls who go for a holiday at the sea side near a school for young girls.'

6. The first appearance in the correspondence of this initial title for *Lucky Jim*.

---

1. The Amis family had moved out of the house they were sharing with David Sims, Margaret Ashbury Vakil and her child in May; this was the first of two small flats they subsequently lived in on Mumbles Road, which runs along the curve of Swansea Bay.

2. A £10 fee was payable when submitting a B.Litt thesis for examination. The thesis could be submitted not earlier than the second term after admission and not later than the eighth term after admission: that is, in Amis's case, anytime between October 1949 and March 1952, so he was not required to submit it immediately after completion. As for 'marking bum', Amis was hoping to finance a trip to Dublin with Larkin later in the summer by marking English papers for a Joint Welsh Board school examination. He and David Sims together marked eight hundred papers (of an average length of sixteen pages) by mid-July, earning £55 each (see *Memoirs*, pp. 126–7).

now until then I shall work on *Dixon and Christine*, which I haven't touched since you were here.

As regards other work: I have written 2 poems which you shall see sometime; one of them is rather like you. I did about 5000 words of a pornographic novel too, but stopped it because I got too interested in it as a novel, and would have had to go back and alter a lot. I have done some cultural reading: *The Bostonians*, by you-know-who.[3] I find the trouble is that he can't tell a story, and can't gather his observations, some of which I don't mind, round any central idea. These enormous wodges of *undramatised* family-background, she-was-a-woman-who, he-had-first-been-attracted-to-his-present-profession-when-travelling-to balls confound me and make me not want to have any more. I find he gives me more information about what he is telling me about than I care to have. I have also looked at *The great wall of China and other pieces*, by you-know-who-else.[4] Now there's another man who can't tell a story, who's incapable of illustrating the slightest thing, or the most important thing, by action. I don't think I've ever seen so many abstract nouns in a SUPPOSEDLY narrative writer before.

Thanks for that dirty magazine. I found the drawings horrible, and the letterpress spoke piercingly to me of my normality. I did quite like the schoolgirl bits, but this punishment idea *doesn't appeal to me*, any more than all this stuff about old women and heavy make-up and shoes and corsets and long hair and horses. I like corsets. I like long hair. I even like heavy make-up sometimes. But no more than I like bread and butter and marmite. I must say I view the disappearance of the pornographic in favour of the "faddist" (my oath) with some regret.

About Hopkins: I find him a bad poet – all this how to keép is there ány any stuff strikes me as a bit unnecessary – and so his defence of his work to Bridges, in spite of Bridges being a bumblock of the first order, seems arrogant to me: You must be wrong when you don't like my stuff, d'you see, because *I know* my stuff's good, d'you see? And his silly private language annoys me – "what I am in the habit of calling

3. *The Bostonians* (1886) by Henry James.

4. 'The Great Wall of China' was published posthumously in 1931, as the title story in a collection of stories by Franz Kafka (1883–1924).

inscape" *well getoutofthehabitthen.* I had another go at his poetry the other day, and confirmed my previous impressions of it as *going after the wrong thing*, trying to treat words as if they were music. They aren't, are they? If his verse can't be read properly without key-signatures and sharps and flats, *so much the worse for it.* And as for this bitch batch bum come cock cork fork fuck stuff; *what is the point of it?* Eh? Outrider – aaaaaagh; counterpointed rhythm – uuuuuuugh, and you can't *have* counterpointed *rhythm.*[5] I'm sorry to go on like this, but I do feel it. Though I can see why people like him; he was a sensible man, outside religion and poetry. Ruskin is a clown, but quite a funny one.

Not much has happened in my daily life of any importance. I'm getting quite pleased with my children, though they make a lot of noise. Margaret is slightly more inefficient than usual. Two of my girl pupils told me the other evening that I am alpha-plus for women, and that they wish I wasn't married, so you see what a strain it is to stay vertical with them. What helps me, of course, to shine, is that the Welsh men are so ugly. I bought the Tit bits with Mangano[6] in it and am prepared to believe all you say. I want to see that film. As regards the fortygraphs, *thank you very much* for sending them. I'm sorry I forgot to say so before, but as you remember a lot of time had elapsed between me getting them and me writing to you the next time. Did you say you wanted back the ones with or the ones without crosses on the back? Hilly has charge of them at the moment and she is out (working in a cafe helping with the washing-up there and getting abt £1½ for doing it a week which is not to be sneased at in these hard times) but I won't forget. The papers I have had to correct have opened my eyes to education and especially Welch education. When you find someone who has read a few books and can spell most words properly she (it's usually a she) is good, *outstanding.* The poetry editor was Ade Boult.

5. Hopkins's theories of instress (roughly, the animating energy of nature, God and art), inscape (the distinctive or essential quality of a thing) and sprung rhythm (a form of scanning based on accent or stress, in which unstressed syllables are called 'hangers' or 'outriders'), were developed in a series of letters to the poet and critic Robert Bridges (1844–1930), his friend since Oxford days. It was Bridges who eventually arranged the posthumous publication of Hopkins's poems in 1918. For 'bitch batch bum come cock' etc. see the opening line of 'The Leaden Echo and the Golden Echo' (1882): 'How to kéep – is there ány any, is there none such, nowhere known some, bow or brooch or braid or brace, láce, latch or catch or key to keep'.

6. Silvana Magnano (b. 1930), Italian actress and former model; the film in question is *L'Elisir d'Amore* (1949).

I'll send you a copy of *Dawn* (it's only pronounced Down).[7] You've seen the poems before. Have you tried Nosegay cigarettes? Nosegloomy.

I should be powerfully pleased to see a screed from you in the near future. I have just had to go down to the street to fetch the first page of this letter, which had *fallen out of the window*. Hence the brute heel-mark on it. I want to be the *swimming* and *pee-tea* coach at a *girls'* school.

You should mark your papers carefully to ensure that the above table of expected results is fairly closely adhered to, though of course much will be left to your individual bum,

Kingsley

[TLS: Bodleian]

TO PHILIP LARKIN – 20 JUNE 1950

University College of Swansea

My dear Philip,

Thanks for your letter. Sorry to hear what I heard. Do you mean you can't have a summer holiday at all or mearly that you can't undertake anything complicated like Dublin? I hope we shall see something of each other, even if it's only down here. Though I precia'e that you probably can't say about that for some time. What happened two years ergo? I country-member anything like this off-hand [. . .]

Now here's something that won't make you smile: I am very short of money – in fact H. and I have 2/6 between us to last until I get paid on 30th June – and shd. like to be lent some. Can you send me a cheque for £5 by return? I will let you have a cheque dated 30 June back. If you can't manage £5, £4 would be very nice; so would £3 and so would £2 and so would £1, in descending order of niceness. Honestly old boy I shdn't ask unless I was broak; I haven't smoked since 9 p.m. last night. Not that that matters to you. It's a question of eating, d'yous spyous d'you see? and Hilly wants to go on a little holiday for which abt. £3 is necessary. I shd. be v. grateful for the money, only send it a.s.a.p. if you will.

Sorry this is so short – it couldn't be longer, cos I am on my higher certificate papers, and that will take all my time for the next 10 days or

7. See Amis to Larkin, 17 May 1950 (in Bodleian): '*Dawn* (wch. means 'talent' and is pronounced 'down'), which is the intellectual magazine of the college.'

so. Sorry to ask abt. the money, but there's nobody I can touch here. Let me know whether we can arrange *anything* for the summer.

The examiner should allow a clear margin of bum,

Kingsley

[TLS: Bodleian]

TO PHILIP LARKIN – 30 JULY 1950

644 Mumbles Road, Oystermouth, Swansea.

My dear Philip,

I haven't written for so long because (1) I couldn't before pay you back the £5 (for which I am supernally grateful) though I kept thinking I should be able to in a day or two, and was shy of writing without sending it (2) I have been bussier than ever before in the whole of my life – as soon as I had finished working 13 hours a day on my HC stuff (that doesn't include time for eating and walking about wishing I wasn't doing my HC stuff) I began swotting up stuff for the Extra Mural Summer School ah-*hagh*-hagh-hagh which came to an end the day before yesterday. After a day of doing *nothing whatever except smoke* and read *an adventure story* about the *Napoleonic wars*, I feel able to begin living my life again. The third reason I didn't write was that whenever I thought of it I realised I should have to say something about your espousals,[1] which I didn't much want to have to say something about, though I had better say something now, before coming to lighter topics.

I can't say I have pondered the question at all, 'cos I have been inclined to shy away from it in my brain, nor have I very much to say now (excuse unmeant pontification). It seems to me a result of your persistent undervaluing of yourself, though that's not a very helpful comment, any more than anything else I say will be. I imagine it must

---

1. Larkin and Ruth Bowman had been engaged since May 1948. On 17 June 1950, after accepting a post as Sub-Librarian at Queen's University, Belfast, Larkin proposed marriage, was accepted, then immediately had second thoughts. He wavered for several weeks before finally withdrawing the proposal, 'encountering a good deal of scorn and anger in the process, which was understandable enough' (Larkin to J.B. Sutton, 3 July 1950, in Bodleian). The episode is recounted in Motion, *Life*, pp. 193–4.

be a relief to steer out of your present position, and I can understand that that may be or seem the only route. On the inadvisability or advisability of it I'm sure I couldn't think of half the things you've thought of, so of that I will say nothing at this present. On my side, dear man, I shall do my utmost to continue friendly relations with yourself and your affianced bride, without any of the jealous raree-shows of pique that I have favoured you with once or twice in the past; but it looks as if your remove to Belfast will make it hard for us to see much of each other, not that we have done for some years, I know. By the way, what exactly is the score now? That month must be more or less up. I hope I've said nothing to offend you.

On other topics (there aren't really any lighter ones) I have been being depressed on several counts: my artistic life seems to be getting even less successful – I've had the legacy back from Watt[2] with a surprised little note: he can't understand why nobody will publish the thing – and even Outposts[3] have sent back my latest batch of poems; I always thought they printed anything. I had the last copy of my subscription to them the other day (I thought I would have to take one out in return for being published there); it contained a poem by Michael Hamburger.[4] Also, I have been shorter of money than I can ever remember. The children eat a lot of food now, and to live in this house costs a lot of money. In the last week of each month, half a pint of beer is an unwarrantable extravagance and I have to allow for things like 2d phone-calls and stamps for letters. There isn't much to smoke most of the time, either: I have gone partly on to HERB CIGARETTES which taste like old hot bonfires in the winter, but the material is 6d an ounce and is just perceptibly better than nothing. I undertook all this paper-marking nonsense and summer-school privy-furniture to get more money so that Hilly and I could have a little holiday, but nobody has paid up yet WHY NOT That annoys me much. When people want money from you, people on the verge of penury like gas corporations and university registries, they MUST HAVE IT, they want it NOW, like children. When they owe you money, they needn't hurry, you see,

2. Probably the literary agents A.P. Watt, though the company keeps no records dating back to 1950, and there are no other references to 'Watt' in the correspondence.

3. A poetry magazine founded in 1944 by Howard Sergeant (1914–87), poet, editor and accountant.

4. Michael Hamburger (b. 1924), poet, translator, scholar of German literature; a contemporary at Oxford, at Christ Church.

you've got plenty, you see, you can wait, you see. A corporation can't be lazy in not sending you money, nor petulant in demanding it from you, because it's *too big*, you see, but YOU can be lazy or petulant, because there's only one of you, you see.

Another thing that has been cheesing me off is that Margaret has thrown David over in favour of some rich gracious-living unsuccessful Tory candidate. [. . .] David has been around ever since the blow fell three weeks ago in need of comfort. I have given it to him, because he has taken it *very well*, but it has taken a lot out of me that I wanted in. This waste of energy, coupled with hard and nasty work, lack of money, and discourage meant about my ort has made it difficult for me to keep a song in my hort. There has also been the American guarantee to Formosa,[5] and the weather. Please realise that on 2 of the 3 fine days you have had this summer it has been raining here, and that on all the days of rain that you have had it has been raining like *fornicating sodomy* here. I havent got the Balliol job.

Bruce and Petrol Damn[6] turned up here the other day; I have little to report on the visit, because almost as soon as they arrived I was drunk, and stayed drunk until, and indeed beyond, the time they left. For 48 hours afterwards I had a stomach-ache, engendered, I fancy, by fish and chips we had at a nasty cafe. It was 9 p.m., you see, and so we couldn't eat anywhere nice, you, see. Bruce did tell me, though, what I expect he has told you, that he is doing a film-script. It seems to me that if we three could pool our resources – i.e. if Bruce gave you some of his facility, and me some of his success, and if both of us gave him some of our talent – the world would be solidly the gainer, yas, and so would we. Bruce trod on my Mozart horn concerto at one point, but after the drinks he had bought me I could hardly have said anything, could I? He left ½-bot. of gin behind for us, too.

May I say, dear man, how much I was impressed by your poem?[7] It is the most orignial yktwlm and strongly-impressive of yours I have seen for a very long time, seeming to forge a personal vocabulary (the use of 'my darling' is grand, so is that unpick-knot image, and 'unprice-

5. Of protection against attacks from the Communist mainland.

6. Peter Oldham, a friend of Bruce Montgomery's, read Mathematics at St John's College, Oxford (1939–41, 1946), later studied Medicine; his name is used in Chapter 3 of *Lucky Jim*: 'Dixon read that Beesley [of the College's English Department] was thanked for his application, but that Mr P. Oldham had been appointed to the post' (p. 31).

7. 'If, My Darling', published in *XX Poems* (1951), *The Less Deceived* (1955) and *LCP*, p. 41, where it is dated 23 May 1950.

able' is marvellous). I didn't quite get the fish-grey bit, though I warmed uncomprehending to the monkey-brown, nor the geometrical-objects bit. All else was very immediate, as you would say, and I can't see anything wrong with it. The metre is just right, noticeably so. I had it by my chair for a week, and played it over between HC papers. I'm sorry to have to put it like this, but it has the ironic, ambiguous feeling about it I admire in such as Marvell, as if you were simultaneously pretending to be serious when really amused, and amused when really serious. But I don't suppose that's very clear. If I can fish them out I will send you my latest 3.[8] [. . .]

Snap marks out of ten on books recently read: The pilgrim's progress, O; The Bostonians, 3; Far from the madding crowd, 6; Gulliver's travels, 6; Saint Joan, 2; The Casuarina tree, 2; Furthermore (D. Runyon) O.[9]

Boy, that bummer school was buggery. Imagine giving a *tutorial* on Owen and Auden to:

(1) Miss Harris. Very fat and short, with pipe-stem legs, like knitting-needles thrust through a ball of wool. Face of un-uniform purple. Pattern phrases: 'The thought's good, isn't it?' 'What did Milton write, then, as well as *Paradise lost*?'

(2) Mrs. Shaw. Tiny, globular-breasted, wigged Hull housewife. Pattern expression: vacant, brooding, injured.

(3) Mr. Evason. Parrot-nosed, polygonal-spectacled, silent, sinus-troubled civil servant. Pattern possession: the Wilfred Pickles[10] anthology. (Have a look at that. It's good to think that someone's leading the masses back to poetry, isn't it?)

As I sat there telling them about *Strange meeting*[11] I felt like some talking marionette that the audience have just decided isn't worth the price of admission. As I sat talking to them and the other 'tutors' at coffee-time, I felt like a foreign spy, someone with nothing but a

8. The poems are 'On Staying Still', 'The End' and 'Swansea Bay', all of which appear, in slightly altered versions, in *A Case of Samples: Poems 1946–56* (1956) and *CP*.

9. 'The Casuarina Tree' (1926), a short story by W. Somerset Maugham. *Furthermore* (1938), a volume of short stories by Damon Runyan (1884–1946), American humorist and short-story writer.

10. Wilfred Pickles (1904–78), radio broadcaster, Yorkshire personality and character actor; the anthology was entitled *Personal Choice: A Selection of his Favourite Poems* (1950).

11. 'Strange Meeting' (1918), one of the last poems written by Wilfred Owen (1893–1918), whose poems were published posthumously in 1920.

learned-up knowledge of his environment, someone easily able to avoid giving something away, but aware of the necessity of caution, someone committed to a long and devious struggle whose termination will be elsewhere, when he could kill half-a-dozen of his enemies as he sits. Altogether here I feel like a swordsman in a country where duelling is unknown.

Let me have your news. I shall have more leisure and inclination for writing in the days that lie ahead. All the best, dear man, though I don't suppose you're getting the best. Any remarks on my poems will be much appreciated.

Ah, Mr. Ames, I'm the Government Inspector. Is this your class? Right, now first of all I want to look at your bum,

Kingsley

[TLS: Bodleian]

TO PHILIP LARKIN – 4 AUGUST 1950

644 Mumbles Road, Oystermouth, Swansea.

My dear Philip,

I was very glad to get such a nice long letter from you, dear man, and so soon too. This one is soon too, but I don't think it will be as long. Still. First let me say that I am pleased to hear of your disengagement. I doubt very much whether you want to let me say that, and here again you will have thought of everything I could possibly say about it. Let me add only that whether I had any acquaintance with Ruth or not the mere history of the campaign would convince me that marriage was not a good solution. In my experience marriage is so good at engendering causes of disagreement and unhappiness that you couldn't possibly foresee, that only a relation entirely free from initial (do I mean anterior?) causes of disruption has the slightest chance of surviving. It seems to me not so much a statement of affection as a sober fact that the only woman I have ever met or read about or heard about that I could *bare* being married to is Hilly. Every other woman seems either *two broing* or . . . I don't think there is an alternative; they're *all to boirng*. Ther nis namoor to seye.

Glad you liked pork sword; I do. As soon as it was fairly out of

David [Sims]'s mouth (it's a genuine cant term for penis, one he heard in the Navy) I knew how much you would like it. I'm sorry about your mother and your no-holiday. What is going to become of your mother after all? It seems that a joint menage at Belfast is not coming to pass. I expect you're glad about that. I must say the set-up at Queen's Chambers sounds grand. It'll be quite like the old days at Coll., eh? with Hall three nights a week and chats round the study fire, mulled claret, papers at the English society and the elite retiring afterwards for Irish whiskey up in your little dog-house. I bet you'll make some decent pals up there; they're a sound lot, Ulstermen. You won't feel you're out of England at all. Serilousy, touhgh, do you intend to stay there for years, years, years? I view that without cheer. Getting to see you will be harder than ever. Still, you'll probably get yourself a wife over there – some laughing-ey'd colleen with roses in her hair PHILIP YOU BE CAREFUL OF SEAMEN

Thanks for the tip about Scenes life;[1] I'll try finding it. That stuff about Auden and co. amused me a lot. Isherwood was for some time a passive homo, though, wasn't he? I told you about the original of Bernhard Landauer[2] buggering him, didn't I? *How does Mrs. Madge know* that WHA has an arse like a pear? *How* is it like a *pear*? Do the Madges live in Leicester?[3]

Sorry about the drabness. I know what you mean, I think, but don't mind as much as I probably ought to. I feel it's *so important* to be correct in diction and sentiment that I don't mind being a bit flat. I have been mulling over my ideas on 'correctness' recently. I feel the time for originality has gone by; what we want to do is to purge English po: of offences against metre, decent humility, meaning (i.e. stop verbal music bum and inchoate image bum), and the eternal law that you are only entitled to speak for yourslef peaea self. Above all, let there be no *self-indulgence* in po:. That's more or less what I think but I don't claim

---

1. *Scenes from Provincial Life* (1950), a novel by William Cooper (Harry Hoff) (b. 1910).

2. A character in Isherwood's *Goodbye to Berlin*.

3. Mrs Charles Madge was the poet and critic Kathleen Raine (b. 1908) (the marriage was dissolved). Charles Madge (b. 1912), a sociologist as well as a poet, was co-founder of Mass Observation (in 1937, with Humphrey Jennings) and director of a small publishing firm, Pilot Press, in which capacity he contacted Larkin towards the end of the war after reading *The North Ship*. Madge was Professor of Sociology, University of Birmingham, 1950–70.

(I wish I could) that you could tell that I thought it by reading my poems. However, this may only be a rationalisation of my inability to be much else but glumly reproving or self-reproving in my po:. As regards *The end*,[4] yes, it means that to me, but only after I'd read what I'd written. It started as a death-poem (when-we're-dying-we'd-give-anything-for-the-chance-of-seeing-anything-at-all-however-boring) but will do quite well as a never-miss-the-water poem. I tried to show what I meant by the vague title, sort of you-can-take-it-either-way. Any suggestions for a more clearly-ambiguous title? As regards your poem, I have thought about it and wd. be inclined to retain 'unpriceable'[5] for two reasons (1) unprintable means hardly anything to me but obscene; good enough, but unprintable pivot sets the reader wondering whether the phrase as a whole may not mean c—t; (2) more important 'unpriceable' seems to prolong that effect of *justified eccentricity* of diction that to me is ¾ of the point of the poem. It's justified in this case because (pordon me) it doesn't mean priceless; it means something that can't be priced, not because it's so valuable but because you *don't know* how valuable it is, you can't judge. I thought you'd rejected all the words like priceless and valueless and invaluable because none of them mean *literally* invaluable. As such, and even more as pleasantly odd, I say keep it. A tiny point is that un*pr*intable *pi*vot is a bit dull, but unpriceable pivot is just right from the similarity/dissimilarity criterion. Altogether I press strongly for the status quo ante. I still think you ought to brush up the middle part, make it clearer.

I've been reading Keats lately, and David and I are going to attempt a little article on him, to show how bad he is.[6] His trouble was that he started off *incompetent at rhyming* – hungry shark bum – and got *hardly*

4. The original version of this poem, included in the previous letter, reads as follows:

> The mirror holds; small common objects fill
> Its eye impatient, sore with holding still.
> The book, the person are threadbare
> Merely because of being there.
> The mirror breaks, and furiously all
> Its clouding splinters twist, before they fall,
> To hold the person for one look,
> To catch one image of the book.

5. The poem in question is 'If, My Darling' (see Amis to Larkin, 30 July 1950, note 7). Larkin took Amis's advice and retained his first version of the poem's last words: 'her unpriceable pivot'.

6. For Amis's own version of such an article see 'The Poet and the Dreamer', in *What Became of Jane Austen?*, pp. 21–5.

any better – deceiving elf bum. I've also been reading the letters. I'd always thought (and said) that the K. of the letters was the real man, much older and wiser and nicer than the one who wrote the poetry, and knowing what was wrong with the poetry better than any critic, etc. All that was before I read the letters. I know now that Keats was a boring, conceited, self-pitying, self-indulgent silly little fool (My dear Girl bum) as well as an incompetent, uninteresting, affected, non-visualising, Royal-Academy-picture, salacious, mouthing poet. He's still better than Shelley, though. Shelley didn't have Keats's excuse of not knowing any better. Leigh Hunt[7] was a better man and poet than either.

Re seeing – try and make it as soon after the beginning of Sept. as possible. We may be at liberty then to see you in Oxford. If we aren't, you can always come here if you can face the journey.

The newsagent offered me a job sorting Christmas annuals the other day. £3 a week, he said. Not hard work. You don't have to use your brain. I declined politely. It reminded me of those Army jokes Anyone here keen on music? I am Sarge Right well bugger off over to the Naafi and give them a hand lifting the piano off the stage.

Russia still demands a UNO seat for the Red bum,

Kingsley

[TLS: Bodleian]

TO PHILIP LARKIN – 10, 21 AUGUST 1950

644 Mumbles Road, Oystermouth, Swansea.

My dear Philip,

[. . .] I am deaf again. Nothing serious, a ball of wax in the ear.[1] I went up to the doctor the other night, and after waiting in his surgery for an hour and three-quarters was attacked by him with something that looked like a metal shoehorn to which has been welded one of those things for getting stones out of horses' hooves, only about twice

7. Leigh Hunt (1784–1859), poet, journalist, critic, a friend of both Keats and Shelley.

1. See the opening sentences of Cyril Connolly's novel *The Rock Pool* (Paris, 1936; London, 1947), much admired by Larkin: 'Naylor was deaf again. Nothing serious, a ball of wax in the ear.' Connolly (1903–74) was a journalist, editor and critic as well as author. His best-known book is the autobiographical *Enemies of Promise* (1938).

as thick. He sank the point about six inches into my head, hurting me, and pulled out pieces of wax, but not the right pieces. I still boom and click and buzz where-ever I go, and have a permanent headache. I pour glycerine into my ear three times a day, and sniff some sort of prussic acid fumes over a saucepan. Nothing happens.

I have been writing away at *Dixon and Christine*, and have done about 10,000 words. I don't think it's as good or so verbally funny as *The legacy*, but it may be more publishable and perhaps some of the things that happen are funnier. In the library the other day, the little local subscription one of above-average standard, I took down *The moving toyshop*[2] and read the first few pages, and to my great surprise found them very funny indeed. *A girl in winter* was there, by the way. [. . .]

Monday, 21 Aug.

I didn't mean to leave this as long as this, but the people who had me born came for a week, leaving on Friday, and then we went away for a short week-end, seven hours' travelling for the sake of 23 hours in the place, well named Court Henry. We went there, nippers and all, at the invitation of a rather pretty student named Marian Evans. The outward journey began badly with me not being allowed to get on the second of the four public vehicles utilised for the journey, and Hilly waiting where she thought I would get off the one I got instead of at the boarding point for the third public vehicle, which was where I waited. Thus we lost an hour. Court Henry, which the Evanses are looking after for the owner, is a gigantic house, by far the largest private dwelling I have ever slept in. Beside the staircase was a large oil painting representative of the martyrdom of S. Sebastian; the model of the eponymous figure was presumably a rather flat-chested but very pretty schoolgirl. In the breakfast room there was a book of poems by Monsr. Baudelaire, the well-known French writer, with the signature of some crazy Welch fellow on the fly-leaf, and underneath a cancelled inscription 'James Michie. 1944', which made me blench a little. Portent-struck, I have written to tell him of this. The journey back, with Martin crying and writhing and Philip pulling himself on to the knees of ministers of the Free Churches, was a climacteric of the *Heinrichismus*.

I've been reading a few more books: *Catalina* (Maugham is the only

2. *The Moving Toyshop* (1946), a detective novel by Edmund Crispin (Bruce Montgomery).

bad writer whose books you read to the end with interest, sympathy and enjoyment);[3] Alain-Fournier's *Le grand Meaulnes* (I don't want any of that swearing. But really, to write a book like that in 1913, *and be content to do nothing else* but put your adolescent sentimentalisings into it *unchanged*; really![4] That's the sort of thing I mean when I say that non-English fiction is always about 100 years behind English fiction. It reminded me strongly of *The sorrows of young Werther*, by that barmy dabbling squarehead. One good thing about it was the excellence of the atmospheric writing; the seasonal changes were really pretty hot); *Rogue elephant*, by Walter Allen (an interesting synthesis of *From a view to a death*, *The memorial*,[5] and snathe fffkkksss snatches of Mrs. Woolf and our Kathy;[6] and *The common asphodel.*[7] The last alternates accidental good talk ('Keyes was no more than a synthesist of poetic styles', nasty remarks about Milton and Kipling, an attack on reading poetry aloud) and inevitable piss about 'modernist poetry' which means E.E. Cummings – honestly, have you *ever* thought C. was worth *anything*? – and a comparison or contrast, to the latter's advantage, of D.H.L. and Doctor Sitwell. Now, you know what I think of DHL, but you know what I think of Dr. S. too.

You oughtn't to miss the *Mirror* these days; did you see that pic. of June Foulds, the 16-year-old women's 100-metres champion? Myke reisst, pally. I'm still deaf, gol-bugger it. I'm thinking of sneding you you know the word I meant to type the first few chapters of *Dixon & Xtine*, if you wd. be so gd. as to let me know what you think of them. I hope you had a lovly bithrayd, with lots of lovly prensets, and stakcs of lovly things to aet and drink. I'm sorry I didn't sned you a presnet, but I am two brkoe too dwo thigns of that knid, kid. I'd of felt worse about it if you'd given me one when I was 28, but you never. It was horrible asking the way to Dryslwyn,[8] where Court Henry is; I kept calling it Drizzle-win instead of Driss-lewin, and the succession of Welch nationalists whom I asked the way thought I was tring to take the psis

3. *Catalina* (1948), a novel by W. Somerset Maugham.

4. *Le Grand Meaulnes* (1913), the one completed novel by Alain-Fournier (Henri-Alban Fournier) (1886–1914), set in the remote countryside of central France in the 1890s.

5. *Rogue Elephant* (1946) by Walter Allen; the works it synthesises are *From a View to a Death* (1933) by Anthony Powell and *The Memorial* (1932) by Christopher Isherwood.

6. Katherine Mansfield.

7. *The Common Asphodel: Collected Essays on Poetry 1922–1949* (1949) by Robert Graves. For Graves see Notes on Recipients.

8. Dryslwyn is north of Swansea and east of Carmarthen in Carmarthenshire.

out of them. Ass whole (Chr. thats funny: 'It was the custom when the river froze over to roast an ass whole on the ice').

No doubt this matter has escaped your bum,

Kingsley

(1) Was it you who recommended me Mist in the Tay, Gus?[9] *Cur-iced.*
(2) Jill is in the Oystermouth Branch Lib[y]*. It has been taken out 20 times since January.*[10]

[TLS: Bodleian]

TO PHILIP LARKIN – 27 AUGUST 1950

644 Mumbles Road, Oystermouth, Swansea, Welch Wails.

My dear Philip,

Look here, dear old butty, just you keep that 23 Sept – departure to N.I. [Northern Ireland] *clear* d'you see, for *me*, d'you see? *We will do something then.* I don't know what it'll be – what about a week in Oxford, eh? You see, I shall have a lot of money by then,[1] and I can imagine nothing (except a change of sex for a few months) that would give me as much pleasure as spending some of it with you, and possibly on you. I urge this on you with the utmost emphasis and seriousness. For God's sake mark that week down in your diary *now*. 'I shall understand' if you've *already* booked up for something else then, but I shan't if you're free when you get this. What I plan tentatively is a week-end in Oxford with you & Hilly (we can get the kids minded for that time)

9. MS addition; *Mist in the Tagus* (1946) by Henry Thomas Hopkinson (1905–90), novelist, biographer and journalist.

10. MS addition.

1. This is probably the money referred to in Amis to Larkin, 17 September 1950 (in Bodleian): 'Hilly's money is here and we will drink luxuriously.' It is unlikely to refer to the portion of her legacy received in January 1951 (£5,000, according to *Memoirs*, p. 127, which accords with Lady Kilmarnock's memory; £2,400, according to Jacobs, *Biography*, p. 143), which allowed the Amises to buy a house in the Uplands district of Swansea. The £2,400 figure comes from Amis to Larkin, 26 January 1951 (in Bodleian): 'I took Mummy B's cheque for £2400 to my bank and paid it in; I liked paying that cheque in.' For the source and terms of the legacy see Amis to Larkin, 12 January 1948, note 5.

and then you & I *stay on together* for a few days after that. Or you could come here, though for your sake I don't much recommend it. Discharge your responses on this to me *protno*. Founder of Christianity, old mole, its your old pal talking to you. As regards the other dates you mention, they're swayul, except that I probably shan't have much money during them. I don't want to seem ludicrous, but why not *come here* on the 8th, return to Leics on the 16th, and then we meet in Ox. on the 23rd? No, you wouldn't be too much trouble. Yes, you would have a bed to sleep in; a double bed. Yes, Hilly would love it. Yes, I would like it, I could even lend you a few quid to back the Oxford jaunt. *What about it*?

[. . .] [D]uring the week I turned out all my drawers, and re-read some of your letters before packing them away in a box. They are *much funnier* than mine *ever were* (*pace* you). What made me laugh was the craze we both had for underlining and capitalisation ('*Now*, what these *John O'London's bastards*, like *Collins*, and *Costin*, and *Moore* (*especially* HIM) just DONT SEE is . . .'). They certainly seemed full of *vim* and *vigour* compared with the stuff we write nowadays. But that's not what I was going to say. Reading those letters, and reflecting on the poems, made me cast my mind back. Do you remember, old trencherman, reading my sheaf of poems in John's (that room I had in the North Quad) sometime in late '45 or early '46, and sang you liked them on the whole, and thought they were quite good? And I put *I W D A F Y*[2] on the gramophone, and you said 'I knew you were going to put that on'. It's hard to say this without arousing both our laughters, but it was then that I decided I was *gong on* writing po: – I knew you'd never thought much of the po: I wrote in 1941–2, and I'm inclined to think I shdn't have tried much more when the war and EAS packed in, if you hadn't said what you did. *Now*, I know it hasn't *got me anywhere*, and I'm still *not as good as both of us would like me to be*, but at least I *went on*. And so for that encouragement I am *deeply grateful*. After reflecting this, I reflected that *The leg* only got written in response to your suggestions, & without *The leg* there would have been no further prose-words. Also, dear man, I have to thank you for *stopping me from being a shit* and *encouraging me to be funny* in the light way and *getting me interested in modern po*: (all this in various intangible ways). But for you, I should to-day be a combination of *Mervyn Brown* and *Chris*

2. 'I Would Do Anything for You'. See Amis to Larkin, 5 February 1946, note 2.

achachachachae

Tosswill. (These are precise selections.) To-day, you are my 'inner audience', my watcher in Spanish,[3] the reader over my shoulder, my often-mentioned Jack, and a good deal more!' I feel it's a shame that our friendship only began after we'd stopped seeing much of each other. (Again, you were largely responsible for beginning it (do you remember '6477599 Fuc. P. A. Larkin, Excrement Boy, 1st B.U.M., Mond's Lines, Shatterick Ramp, Forks'? – I have just laughed like necrophily, writing that).) But I'm very glad we've got it now. I felt I had to get this said some time, and hope it hasn't embarrassed you. [. . .]

BOOF! → MacArthur has had twenty years' experience of bum,[4]

STINGK-BOMM FEE-SEAS KNIGHTS' OIL HAUSA FEES MEANT

Kingsley

[ALS: Bodleian]

TO PHILIP LARKIN – 27 NOVEMBER 1950

382 Mumbles Road, West Cross, Swansea.

My dear Philip,

For God's sake keep writing, dear man, 'cos life's pretty shiting, dear man: 'stead of talking to Prof. I'd sooner TOSS OFF, or sod a mechanical fan, dear man, be castrated by blades of a fan. I have just come back from my weekly lecture on modern literature, in which I dealt with Ezra Pained and old man T.L.E.'s *Waste country*. Honestly, can you see anything in EP? Buggered if I can. *I can't see what people mean* who say he's good. I mean, good *in any way at all*. Just can't see anything in him what? What about you what? What? I said as much to the class. Nobody seemed to agree or disagree. That doesn't surprise me. Does it surprise you? It doesn't me. What about you?

I feel quite lie-tarted, as the above indicates, but for no special

3. The phrase comes from Chapter 2 of Christopher Isherwood's semi-autobiographical novel *Lions and Shadows* (1938). See Appendix J.

4. General Douglas MacArthur (1880–1964) was appointed Supreme Commander of United Nations forces in Korea in July 1950.

reason. Perhaps because the end of term draws near. We lecturers live on our nerves a good deal, you know. I don't want to say much about my job these days, because it is not material that could be manipulated into art, and because it wd. depress me by reminding me of it. I find your accounts of Blfst fascinating: wouldn't miss them for the world. I had heard of Roy MacFadyean[1] (isn't that correcter?), but only just. I have heard of him in the same way that I have met Vernon Watkins,[2] that is to the extent of being able to say that I have heard of (or, in the case of Watkins, met) him, without adding anything to the bare statement of fact, if you follow my thought there. Have you seen the 'pothecary's lady again? Och, Pheel, it's dhe brarth of a boy y'are. GIVE IT TO HER THERE MAN go on get going make with the old pork sword FUME IN IT SLATER

Glad to hear you're coming in the last days of the old year: ring out the balse, ring in the spue. I haven't found 8 ab8 the train on Monday yet, but I will. We shall be here to receive you, and a fine time we will have. Look: what's all this about Queen's[3] being a lecturer short? Do some inquiring, dear man, and then do some wiring, dear man; a Pat is as good as a Taff (understood?), cos he couldn't be nastier *than*, dear man, he could hardly be nastier than. I haven't seen the post advertised. *Then do they intend to fill it?* That's what I must know. What's the Prof. of Eng. like? Doeshemaketheboyssweattheirgutsouteh? [. . .]

We have a ginger kitten (perhaps I told you this) called Maxie, after you-know-who.[4] He isn't as nice as Winkie, but he is nice. Bruce is coming down here in a fortnight, to discuss an opera we are doing for the Festival of Britain[5] (I am practising saying this in a frank, open manner). It seems he has been commissioned to do it. It's only a ¾ pissenschit ¼–½hr. thing, but it should be 'fun to do', and fun to be paid for too, though he says there won't be much of that. Martin is walking now. I have taught Philip to say 'Hallo old boy' (he pronounces it 'Halla-arboy') and this makes me laugh. Target for 1951: 'Oh go

1. Roy McFadden (b.1920), Irish poet.

2. Vernon Watkins (1906–67), poet who lived and worked in Swansea (as a clerk in Lloyd's Bank) until 1965.

3. Queen's University, Belfast.

4. A reference to 'Maximillien De Jong', a friend of the 'Kingsley Amis' character in 'The Legacy'.

5. See Amis to Larkin, 12 November 1950 (in Bodleian): 'I had a letter from Bruce the other day: he wants me to do a libretto for a short opera to be put on at the Festival of B.' The opera in question was *Amberley Hall*; see Amis to Larkin, 6 December 1947, note 4.

and get BUGGERED man', 'Michael Hamburger[6] is a frothless pisser', 'Lawrence was sex-mad', 'My dad wants to meet your big sister'. What's this Wet-sir-o-no fantasy? I can't understand it. And who's Valentine Iremonger?[7] Do you know Powell's *What's become of Waring??*[8] The NS&N said it was a funny satire about litty people. Hilly sends her love to her impotent lover. I must stop this and write to my parents to tell them we are only going to stay with them for a week over the holiday. Have you read Eliz. Taylor's *A wreath of roses*?[9] Piss, but two or three sodding funny scenes, especially early on. Try pp. 67–76. 98–110. What did you think of James's thesis?

Of what value would you say your thesis* would be to a critic of nineteenth-century bum,

Kingsley

*I went to Oxford for one night recently[10] and was viva'd on this, not very comfortably, by Prof. Lrd. D. Cecil & another. They thought I hadn't borne out my main contention. O Lor'. Haven't heard yet. Saw no-one but Colin and Patsy [Strang][11] (who played footie with me under a Randolph table), Costin, *me nolente*,[12] and Hilary Morris passing, immensely bearded, in someone's car.

Don't forget abt that. lectureship. I want that job.[13]

[TLS: Bodleian]

6. For Michael Hamburger see Amis to Larkin, 30 July 1950, note 4.

7. Valentin Iremonger (1918–), Dublin-born poet and Irish diplomat.

8. *What's Become of Waring* (1938), a novel by Anthony Powell.

9. *A Wreath of Roses* (1950), a novel by Elizabeth Taylor (1912–75), novelist and short-story writer.

10. Amis has written in pen in the left margin, 'It took *1 hr. 40 mins.*'

11. Patricia (Patsy) Avis Strang (1928–77) married the philosopher Colin Strang in 1948. for Colin Strang, a contemporary at St John's, see Amis to Larkin, 9 May 1949, note 3.

12. Latin for 'Costin, unwillingly on my part' (a parallel of sorts to '*Deo Volente*', God willing).

13. MS addition.

TO PHILIP LARKIN – 17 DECEMBER 1950

Abbey Timbers, Harwell, Berks.

Merry (X^t!) X^tmas, dear man

My dear Philip,

This will not, I predict, be a very long nor a very cheering letter. We have been here since Thursday, and I haven't been warm yet. There is a sodding terrible stove that seems intended to warm the house; at any rate, it's the only source of heat, and a darned non-good one it is into the *bad* bargain. The Bardwells burn peat in it. Now peat strikes me in the same way that kippers do: *I can't understand* why the first man to try burning it/eating them didn't turn round and say "Now this is *no good*, fellows: *nobody* will ever find any use for *this* kind of thing. Turn all this black sponge-cake back into the bog" or "The next time you catch some herrings, throw the bleeders back in the sea and go upon the parish."[1] Peat doesn't burn; it just accumulates heat into itself, without giving any out, until it falls into tepid ash. Knowing about it gives you a line on the micks – expecting you to feel sorry for them because they're hopelessly inefficient. If you get what I mean.

We had a nice time with Bruce, who gave us even more food and drink than usual. We fudged out an opera plot,[2] which seems quite adequate, though it'll have to be done rather quickly. He says we ought to make £20 each at the worst. That's not bad for the worst, is it? I drank a lot of gin. There's a little left which we'll share when you come. We arranged a plot involving 5 characters, and quite neatly tied up it was. Crippen now postcards me to the effect that the arts council want 4 characters. Er, er, er-*her*-huh-huh-huh-huh But he may be able to sort this out with them.

Micky Bardwell is here wearing a corduroy jacket and talking in his

---

1. Amis is referring to the Louis MacNeice poem 'Bagpipe Music' (1938): 'His brother caught three hundred cran when the seas were lavish,/Threw the bleeders back in the sea and went upon the parish' (lines 23–4). 'Cran' is a measure of fresh herrings, about 750 fish.

2. See previous letter, note 4.

baying voice. He makes me feel like Roy Campbell[3] probably would about him. Old Daddy B— is in as good form as ever. When I said on meeting 'How are you?' he launched into an incoherent account of his recent ailments and prostrations. He's the boy that interests him. I've had a good going-over with the usual Sweden-Wales-folkdance-Romansch-Rōget mixture. I now find his sense of smell is defective, so make a point of farting silently in his presence. The rest of the time I seem to spend in washing-up. Bill Bardwell has taken his gramophone away, so no more Moat's art from there to interfere with my father-in-law's monologues. I am bloody cold, *now*, as I hang over the stove, and most of the time I am leaping up to offer my seat to one of my elders and *lessers*. Respected Christ, it has perished me. To-morrow a freezing car-drive is projected, to take us to St. Alban's, where my wife's brother-in-law and his wife and their two little ones now reside, *back late at night* ah Jesus Mary and Joseph. Then on Thursday another such drive, or if the weather is bad a *triple bus journey*, 40 mins + 85 mins + 35 mins, to Birk 'em's Ted and the people who had me born. Figure to yourself what that bus journey would mean, in this weather, with two dear little children to keep you company. It will be with the heartiest relief, dear man, that I greet the passing of the Faecestive season, and return to sanity and Swansea and you, dalling. You *are* coming, aren't you? What time does your train get in? I haven't your letter here and that's why I don't answer a lot of things that were probably in it, only I've forgotten what they were.

Have you read *Graveyard to let*?[4] 0/10 0/10 0/10 0/10 0/10

No, dear man, there isn't much on this page, is there? Do write and cheer me up. They've turned my thesis down,[5] the direct descendants of sexual perverts. No explanation yet, if ever: I may have to sweat semen re-doing it. Sorry to say no special X'mas card this year: fed up and far from home, d'you follow? Just fed up what?

Well, Kingsley, what have you been doing with your bum,

Kingsley

[ALS: Bodleian]

3. Roy Campbell (1902–57), South African-born poet and supporter of Franco; author of scathing satirical verses on literary London, in *The Georgiad* (1931) and elsewhere. His *Collected Poems* appeared in 1950.

4. *A Graveyard to Let* (1950) by Carter Dickson (John Dickson Carr).

5. For Amis's account of his viva for the thesis, presided over by Lord David Cecil, and of the thesis's subsequent rejection, see *Memoirs*, pp. 105–7.

TO PHILIP LARKIN – 8 JANUARY 1951

382 Mumbles Road, West Cross, Swansea.

My dear Philip,

I write this in this colour[1] so as to use up some of this useless and silly part of the ribbon, and for no aesthetic reason. I heartily enjoyed your coming, though it was a pity that we were both under different kinds of the weather. I still think of your No Jim Jim ah Jim formula, and shall work it into my modern literature lectures this term, which starts to-morrow. Did you have a good time with Miss Exall,[2] I hope you did, was the journey too devastating for you, I hope not.

Times have been dark grey since you left. Thursday was a lovely day: I received the document I enclose[3] (I got another copy of it this morning; the writer was anxious I shouldn't miss it, I suppose) by the first post, about which time it had become clear that both the children were slightly ill and would have to spend the day in the same room as I was. Then I went to college, and found a letter from Bateson explaining that, though he was very indignant about it and thought I had been unfairly treated, it wouldn't be much use rewriting my thesis. Then I got my War Office form (the one that they will use to see whther they want to call me up for training for their flithy war)[4] signed and posted

1. The letter is typed in red.

2. See Amis to Larkin, 15 July 1946, note 8.

3. An adapted reader's report on 'The Legacy' by Mrs Doreen Marston, a reader for Collins, and the mother of Adrian Marston, a friend from Oxford. The report is in the form of a letter to Amis dated 1 January 1951 and begins: 'James Michie tells me that you wish to have a completely frank report on my reactions to your novel THE LEGACY . . . I do not believe that you will achieve publication with this novel. I do believe that it would be a waste of time and of money to try it on any other publisher even through another Agent. My advice to you is to scrap it and to regard it as a useful essay for the future. Your time in writing i[t] will not have been wasted.' After detailing the manuscript's failings, under the headings 'redundancy', 'lack of conflict', 'weak feminine characterisation', 'ungrammatical writing' and 'total lack of humour', Mrs Marston concludes: 'When you have finished your next novel, and if you are not too angry with my remarks on this one, I would be happy to read it and to suggest another agent if I think it can be placed.'

4. By September 1950 British troops were in action in Korea; see also Amis to Larkin, 26 January 1951, in Bodleian: 'It looks now as if the filthy bomb-drunk Yanks are having two fingers exended to them from Britain's bunched fist so much that they won't be able to have their lovely war. Anybody over here now who is not pro-Chink wants his arse filled with celluloid and a match applied to his arse-hairs.'

it. Then I came home. About this thing from Mrs. Marston, it illustrates what I was sang about not getting published, I think. This woman is a publishers' reader as I think I said. NOW, I'm NOT SAYING the legacy's up to much, and I think Mrs. M. is QUITE RIGHT in about half of what she says, but the rest of the time she's missing the point isn't she? I don't say she'd like it if she saw it but she's missing the point isn't she? I mean detail's the point isn't it? Now if she can't *see* that (I'M NOT ASKING HER TO LIKE IT) what chance have I got old boy? They want you to write novels like other novels don't they? I don't want to do that. If I were Joyce I could write *Ulysses* and that would always get published, but I'm not as good as that. You see what I mean? An original writer who isn't very much good, that's what I am; I'll never be Joyce or Warwick Deeping, so where do I stand? In the brown stuff, it seems. (I'd like to see Mrs. M's report on *At swim2birds*:[5] 'Try and cut down your sentences and long words . . . there is no real conflict between the hero and Brynsly . . . the Dublin atmosphere is first-rate . . . your work suffers from a lack of narrative and dramatic interest . . .')

The money hasn't come yet, so you won't forget the £15 will you old fellow? I heard from Bruce by the way that the Farts Council want 3 singers now, not 4 and not 5. He suggests I go to London to help talk things over. I feel important but apprehensive. He says he is 'half-inclined to cry off' Jasusmaryanjoseph[6] I'm not; it's all I've got left at the mewment. The only thing I've done that has heartened me is to order about 40 records from Jimmy Silvester, including 2 copies of Lizzie/Right and Jack/Roll.[7] For you, dear man. Apart from that, *filthy Dombey and son*[8] for the first year people. Oh Christ, the number of people who will ask me about and commiserate with me for the rejection of my thesis. I wish the money would come, then I could silence them with suits, tongue-tie them with ties, dumbfound them with drinks I have drunk. My tongue nearly seized up telling about 350 people what the bloddy thesis was about and when I was putting it in, who my filthy examiners were, etc. SONS OF SODS SHOULD BE SODDED

5. Amis has written in the left margin: 'I don't mean I'm as good as F. O'B [Flann O'Brien].'

6. Amis had originally typed 'I don't,' which he crossed out and replaced with the MS addition 'I'm not.'

7. 'Strut Miss Lizzie'/'It's Right Here for You' and 'Ballin' the Jack'/'I Ain't Gonna Give Nobody None of my Jelly Roll'.

8. *Dombey and Son* (1847–48) by Charles Dickens.

I have started my journal again under your stimulus and shall probably keep it up for a week or 2 so there will be something to read you when we next meet. When I get my nice new grey typewriter and a room to myself I shall start writing *Dixon & Xtine*, cutting out a lot of redundancy, inserting stacks of conflict, strengthening my female characterisation, grammaticising my writing, and whacking away with the old funniness. I am quite serous, though, about the first 2 things, and quite keen to get started.

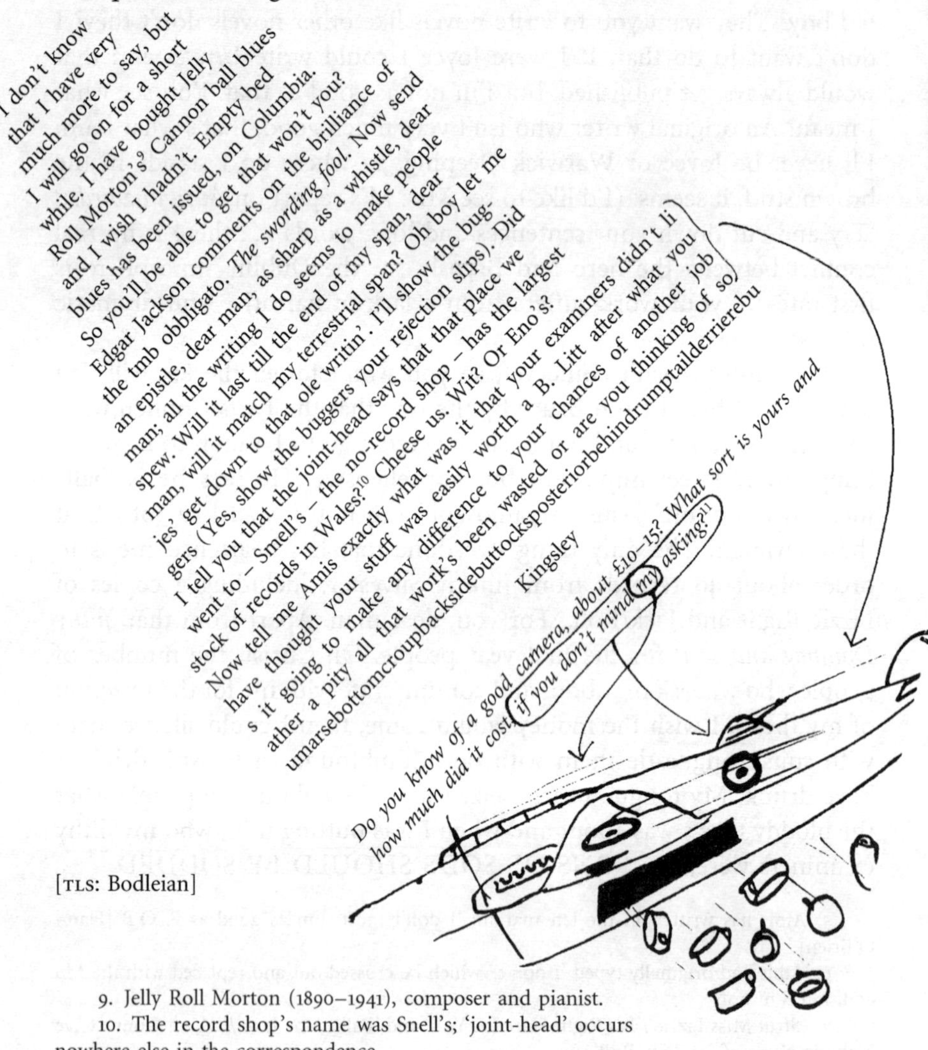

I don't know
that I have very
much more to say, but
I will go on for a short
while. I have bought Jelly
Roll Morton's[9] Cannon ball blues
and I wish I hadn't. Empty bed
blues has been issued, on Columbia.
So you'll be able to get that won't you?
Edgar Jackson comments on the brilliance of
the tmb obbligato. *The swording fool.* Now send
an epistle, dear man, as sharp as a whistle, dear
man; all the writing I do seems to make people
spew. Will it last till the end of my span, dear
man, will it match my terrestrial span? Oh boy let me
jes' get down to that ole writin'. I'll show the bug-
gers (Yes, show the buggers your rejection slips). Did
I tell you that the joint-head says that that place we
went to – Smell's – the no-record shop – has the largest
stock of records in Wales?[10] Cheese us. Wit? Or Eno's?
Now tell me Amis exactly what was it that your examiners didn' li
have thought your stuff was easily worth a B. Litt after what you
s it going to make any difference to your chances of another job
ather a pity all that work's been wasted or are you thinking of so
umarsebottomcroupbacksidebuttocksposteriorbehindrumptailderrierebu
Kingsley

Do you know of a good camera, about £10–15? What sort is yours and
how much did it cost if you don't mind my asking?[11]

[TLS: Bodleian]

9. Jelly Roll Morton (1890–1941), composer and pianist.
10. The record shop's name was Snell's; 'joint-head' occurs nowhere else in the correspondence.
11. MS addition.

TO PHILIP LARKIN – 29 APRIL 1951

24 The Grove, Uplands, Swansea.

My dear Philip,

[. . .] My letters to you ought to be much better than they have been of late, because I haven't taken up my journal again and so will make my letters to you my j., as before. I bought that Josh White on my return here[1] (for six ba-aa-arb): there's some nasty echo-chamber stuff on one side, and a nasty drummer on the other, but some good falsetto *glissandi*. As for books and writers, I picked up old C.S.L[ewis]., who bought me a drink, said he was an Ulsterman, explained to me why pornographic bookshops always have *The works of Aristotle* in the window, expressed an admiration for Kafka, took about three minutes to have it explained to him that my name wasn't Aimless, said about fantasy vs. realism that provided a man wrote well he didn't care whether he wrote about (ff) fairies or (pp) farts. This week, I mean last week, that crazy Welch fellow[2] came here to give a a talk; I went into the pub and found him half-stewed before the meeting, surrounded by the officials of the English Society and Mary Madden.[3] His conversation consisted of one or two written-out solos and a string of very dirty and very not funny limericks. I wanted to react like Rupert Evans[4] would have reacted; the sight of Mary trying to smile politely embarrassed me a good deal. I don't know whether you remember what he looks like: his face is compounded equally of Bruce, David Williams and Evelyn Waugh, with just a dash of Herbert Lom.[5] His talk was horrible: shagged epigrams topped up with some impressionistic stuff about America that I imagine he had inserted from another talk and with a backlash of dutiful impropriety. And the poems he spoke out with his mouth: ooh corks!!! He fucked up 2 of Auden's things from *Another time* ('Yoou

1. Amis had gone to visit Larkin in Belfast two weeks earlier; Josh White (1908–69), blues singer.

2. Dylan Thomas.

3. A student of Amis's; see Amis to Larkin 24 July 1952, note 3.

4. Rupert Evans (b. 1920), Lecturer in History, University College of Leicester (1947–86).

5. Herbert Lom (b. 1917), Czech-born actor whose 'piercing eyes and imposing screen personality have been equally effective for suave, dominating romantic leads and evil, menacing character parts' (Ephraim Katz, *The Film Encyclopedia*, 2nd ed. (1992; rpt. London: HarperCollins, 1994), pp. 838–9).

shul love your crookad neighbour With your ... crookad ... hutt-ta') and some Yates ('Whut shul I do for pretty gulls, Now my olld ... bodd-da ... is dadd-da?')[6] In the pub afterwards, the more intelligent students sneered at him gently, and he perceived this; I was glad, because he made a very strong and very nasty impression on me, not as a charlatan so much as a terrible second-generation G.K.C. or Alf Noyes[7] – you know, frothing at the mouth with piss.

I have read several bad books lately, including the new Anthony Powell.[8] This I suggest should be sub-titled *From a find to a check*; it is the most inconclusive book I have ever read. *A question of upbringing*? *Whose* upbringing? *What* question? *Who's* asking it? *What's* the answer? So much so that it is the sort of book where you wonder whether someone has torn the last quarter out. It travels imperceptibly on its way, steadily losing direction, shedding feeling and discarding tension for the end. There are some bits of Flann O'B, in it, and quite funny too, but worlds away from *From death*.

It's quite nice back here now that term has started, though I realise how lost I shall be when the present generation of students have gone, especially the two who brought *a bottle and a half of gin* round yesterday afternoon. Even so, the present is pleasant. Talking of presents, I just can't wait to see what you've got for my birthday. I got a shirt and a cake and some fags from my mum and a Ronson lighter from my wife and sweet effay from my tart.

I was too occupied in preparing to confront the instantaneous grief of being alone to remember what we said to each other on that boat about seeing each other again. Will you be able to get to London in July for that thing? And can you spend some time with us in the summer? You'll be able to hear the Blue Notes and Commodores and Jazzes if you do, and we shall have a proper spare bedroom by then I hope. Before I forget send *My darling*[9] (good title?) to somewhere like the NS&N. They'll print it or at least they smacking well ought to

6. 'You shall love your crooked neighbour/With your crooked heart,' from the penultimate stanza of 'As I walked out one evening', in *Another Time* (1940); 'What shall I do for pretty girls/Now my old bawd is dead,' from 'John Kinsella's Lament for Mrs Mary Moore', in *Last Poems* (1938–39).

7. Alfred Noyes (1880–1958), poet, novelist, short-story writer and playwright.

8. *A Question of Upbringing* (1951), the first volume of the twelve-volume novel sequence *A Dance to the Music of Time*; its suggested subtitle alludes to Powell's earlier novel *From a View to a Death* (1933).

9. 'If, My Darling', which ends with the Amis-approved 'unpriceable pivot'.

(HMsh). It's the best poem that either of us have written. [. . .]

I said you'd like to take that Mumbles W.E.A. class for bum,

Kingsley

I had a very good crossing, and a tedious but not overwhelming train journey through Central Wales or do I mean Eastern Wales. At Shrewsbury I had a lunch which I contrasted mentally with the lunch I had had on the Saturday: this one consisted of a bowl of farinaceous soup, half a slice of bread, a pint of bitter and four gingernuts. In the train, a Welsh clergyman and his wife, who knew the country, pointed out to me a cottage they said was called whats the fucking[10] a cottage which they said was called Balls Cottage. I said, That's a curious name to choose. They agreed that it was.

[TLS: Bodleian]

TO PHILIP LARKIN – 12 MAY 1951

Swansea

My dear Philip,

Now that I've finished working for five months ('You *filthy swine*') I have more time to write to you and generally to have a nicer life. If this letter is going to be at all as I imagine it, it will be a fairly long one. Thank you very much for the nice poetry-books.[1] I like both the printed inscription in all of them and the handwritten one in my own copy. As regards the actual pee, Sis, I'm not sure I can do any brilliant, or any, generalising about them ('The distinctive quality of Mr. Larkin's verse is surely femininity, which goes rather oddly with the bum and

10. Amis's typewriter ribbon has been bleeding red into black in this sentence; hence 'whats the fucking' (i.e. matter with the typewriter ribbon).

1. *XX Poems*, published in April 1951 and dedicated to Amis. After Larkin had failed to find a publisher for 'In the Grip of Light' (it was rejected by Faber, Allen Lane, Methuen, Macmillan, John Lehmann and Dent) he selected twenty poems he had written in the last few years and had them privately printed in Belfast. The resulting pamphlet received little attention (and only a single review, 'Verse: New, Old, and Second-Hand', by D.J. Enright, in the Catholic journal the *Month*, n.s. VI (Nov. 1951), p. 309). For a listing of the contents of *XX Poems* see *LCP*, p.314. When Amis discusses particular poems in this letter I have included titles and first lines in square brackets after the roman numerals.

the bomb and the beecher-bitcher-birch'), but I will say a few things that occur to me about some of them. The ones I miss out aren't therefore displeasing to me, but merely don't inspire me to comment. Here goes, then ('*Where* goes? And *what*?').

I ['Wedding Wind': 'The wind blew all my wedding day'] I've said I like this. I can't imagine how you came to think of it, let alone write it. Can it be borne . . . the end strikes me as miraculously good.

III ['Always too eager for the future we'] I love the laconic fourth lines, esp. Right to the last and But we are wrong. Don't you think No waters break, simply, might be flatter and more taciturn and therefore more horrifying? I know you want to get breed in too, but it might be worth sacrificing that.

IV ['Even so distant, I can taste the grief'] I think this enormously efficient, but one or two of the images (occasional print, readings erratic) strike me as the tiniest bit meticulous and fussy, and as a whole it's less egoistic than the others, which impairs the wholeness of the collection a trifle, I feel. The rhyming is masterly.

V ['Latest face, so effortless'] This seems to me better every time I read it, enormously authoritative, and better than Lay your sleeping head, my love.[2] Lines 15 and 16 are splendid, the best sort of stuff. And the change from trochee to iamb at the end is jolly fine.

VI ['Arrival': 'Morning, a glass door, flashes'] The last stanza of this is excellent but for grey-veil-hung; these compound things make me think of *Endymion*,[3] and you don't want me to do that, do you? I still don't quite get the opening image. Do you mean names *of* the new city? I understand it if it's that.

VII ['Since the majority of me'] On consideration I don't much care for this. The main image seems to me the wrong sort, unless you'd stayed ironical all through. I don't like thinking about Nye Bevan[4] when I read A silence of minorities, etc.

IX ['Waiting for breakfast, while she brushed her hair'] Comparing this with I, which the ordinary reader will be in[c]lined to do, I find it notably less successful; there's a taint of self-pity and self-importance

2. The first line of 'Lullaby' (1940) by W.H. Auden.

3. By Keats, an early attempt at epic (1818).

4. Aneurin Bevan (1897–1960), Labour MP; Minister of Health (1945–51); of Labour and National Service (1951), a post from which he resigned in 1951 in protest at the Cabinet decision to impose NHS prescription charges. In 1951 he led a 'Bevanite' grouping to contest Labour's defence and foreign policies.

('my lost lost world') in it somewhere, and some of us would want to ask a question about it beginning 'Why can't he take pocking the same way the girls take beng pocked . . .'

X ['Two Portraits of Sex: I. Oils'] I still don't like the roll-call in stanza one, nor the sort of Sanders of the river[5] atmoshpere – I'm sure you know the word. Stz. 2 seems a bit undistinguished. 3 is good.

XI ['II. Etching'] I like this a lot, and a suggestion that stz. 3 could be done up a bit doesn't mean I don't think that the poem as a whole is very good. Couldn't you alter the *syntax*? – the what sad scapes, what this and that, how the other, seems the least bit earnest or some such quality after the sober, flat laying-down of the law in stzs 2 and 3. The final image is as good as anything you have ever done.

XIV ['If my darling were once to decide'] By golly, man, you've hit the jackpot here. I think I've spotted the marvellous thing about it, if I can only express it: the sense of relish about it, as if you're thoroughly enjoying every word, rolling them round your tongue, while at the same time being as serious and even gloomy as anybody could wish. Irony expressed in terms of facial expression is a straight look with a slight curl at one corner of the mouth; this irony has just as straight a look, but the mouth is openly grinning. What I mean is that the poem fuses attitudes that except in the poem one wouldn't imagine to be reconcilable at all. I'm sorry this is so vague and smelling of Leavissh, but it's the best I can do.

XVIII ['Wants': 'Beyond all this, the wish to be alone']

'To-morrow the life insurance, the tabled fertility rites,
The walks by the lake, the winter of perfect communion,
    The slow betrayal, the costly
Aversion of the eyes from death. But to-day the struggle.'[6]

It's all right, I don't really mean it, because this is a very good poem, only *too short*, though I see why it couldn't very easily be longer. Your 2 refrains are masterly, *and so are* your illustrations.

XIX ['There is an evening coming in'] This is so good that I hate reading it. The best poem on ding, purely as ding, I've read.

XX ['At Grass': 'The eye can hardly pick them out'] My christ, cully, there's another jackpot one for you. That gives you a score of 2-nil against me you bastard. Really I think it's as good as XIV, and being able to write two such different poems so well is a mark of slightly

5. The hero of eleven thrillers set in Africa by Edgar Wallace.
6. An allusion to lines 69–79 of 'Spain 1937' (1937, revised 1940) by W.H. Auden.

greater distinction than I ever thought you possessed. My *christ.* It reminds me oddly of So many summer terms away,[7] only this, of course, is rather nicer. I find it very moving, which is odd cos I don't care what happens to flithy horses and hatt racing. I like best the shake their heads bit, and Or gallop for what must be joy. Could you – this is a small point – alter 'stand at ease'; you don't mean they're like pongos[8] do you? Slipped their names comes off wonderfully. Summing up, I'd arrange them like this:

Better than anything yet	XIV, XX
As good as your previous best	I, III, V, XI, XIII, XVII, XVIII, XIX
Not negligible	IV, VI, VIII, IX, XVI, XV
Not so good	II, VII, X, XVI

On the whole, a jolly fine score. I still wish I'd looked at the stuff you threw out. [. . .]

And now old boy I'll tell you something you probably won't have heard of and which will sadden you a good deal. Pee Wee Russell is dead.[9] Some time in February; I saw about it in LIFE for then. He died

7. The refrain to 'Ballade des Dames du Temps Jadis', one of the six poems that make up 'Sugar and Spice' by 'Brunette Coleman' (see Amis to Larkin, c.26 October-6 November 1943, note 14). Its first two stanzas read:

Tell me, into what far lands
They are all gone, whom once I knew
With tennis-racquets in their hands,
And gym-shoes, dabbled with the dew?
Many a one danced like a star,
And many a one was proud and gay
Throughout those happy years, that are
So many summer terms away.

Where is Valerie who led
Every tom-boy prank and rag—
Is her hair still golden-red?
Can she still dash like a stag
As she did at hide-and-seek?
And would she still refuse to play
With a rotter and a sneak,
As many summer terms away.

To the right of the first of these stanzas Larkin has written: 'With a sense of "old, unhappy far-off things" '; to the right of the second: 'Lingeringly'; comparable reading instructions accompany each of the poem's five succeeding stanzas.

8. A naval term for soldiers, from a word meaning large ape, variously identified as chimpanzee, gorilla, orang-outang.

9. In fact Russell did not die until 1969.

in some comfort, not the paupers' ward, because Armstrong and Condon both held concerts and gave him the money. It seems to have been cirrhosis. He was a good deal disfigured by cysts, and horribly thin. 'Tell the papers not to write any sad stories about me,' he said. I feel sorrier about this than I would about the death of any writer and of many of my acquaintances. It was nasty playing his stuff after hearing the news and thinking for the first time, 'He was good, wasn't he?' I'm glad there are still a lot of his records to get. [. . .]

We shall have to use a background of curtains, so your stage-instructions must be bum,

Kingsley

[TLS: Bodleian]

TO PHILIP LARKIN – 12 JUNE 1951

Swansea

My dear Philip,

Here I am, thank our Redeemer, able to spend an hour or two tapping out a message once more to my old Pall. I have had much honours paper bum and mark sheet bum and invigilation bum and alpha beta oblique stroke beta double plus query bum and external candidate bum and meeting bum in the past week or 2, and it has been getting up my back fast, but fast ('But SODGER SELF').

It's a frightful lot of time ('Don't tell ME[1] that') since I last wrote you a letter. Perhaps you'll feel a little better about that when I apologise, as I do now, when you have cashed the cheque I mean to send if I can remember to, and when I tell you that the most noteworthy event of my stay in Oxford was being told by Bruce that the men have thanked us very much for that singing thing,[2] thank you, thank you very much, thank you, thank you, but they can't do it, you see, because there's not enough singing in it, do you see, and they thought there would be more of that, you see, and 'we're not actors, you know' RIGHT BILL KNEE

1. 'ME' typed in red.
2. See Amis to Larkin, 27 November 1950, note 5.

IS FORK THE PONCE SWING FROM IS PILLS This ground me greatly, and made me think I was a fail, yer – altho' none of it was my fault. The point was that B. had had too little time to set all the words BECAUSE HE WAS WRITING FLITHY FLIM SCORES AND STING-KING STORIES FOR THE POPULAR PRESS, and asked them if we could do a ballad opera. They said yes, because they thought a ballad opera meant song then six lines of conventional dialogue then duet then eight lines of c. d. then song, do you see. Our idea was the same, except that we read '150' for 'six' and '200' for 'eight'. They didn't like that. At least I hope that's what it was and not that they thought my dialogue too bad to do. Next year perhaps we shall re-do it with singing all through but I'm still despondent.

[. . .] I have started on *Dixon and Chr* again; I shall opt for dipsomania if no one takes it. It's not as funny as *The legacy*, but is I hope more solid. Whatjer think of JOYCE CARY?[3] I think he's rather good. Have you seen the browning version?[4] I know exactly what you'll say about it if you have, but I thought it was rather good. What Taplow thought of Crocker-Harris's translation, in fact. I promise to write sooner next time: I have more leisure now, or rather more leisure that doesn't leak away in hating the times I'm not at leisure, if you get what I mean. And look here old boy, just a word before I close: Are you coming to stay with us soon? We can put you up and take care of you, and so many young ladies are wanting to meet you. *Fix it up* as soon as may be, do you hear me now? *Fix it up*. Hilly is always plaguing me on the topic. *What are your plans*? *Don't* spend all your time with Veronica Beale[5] when you come to the mainland. *Get on with it*. External examiner bum,

Kingsley

[TLS: Bodleian]

3. Joyce Cary (1888–1957), novelist, best known for *The Horse's Mouth* (1944).

4. The 1951 film of *The Browning Version* (1948), a play by Terence Rattigan (1911–77) about a repressed and unpopular classics master named Crocker Harris. Rattigan himself wrote the screenplay, it was directed by Anthony Asquith, and Michael Redgrave played Harris. The title refers to Browning's translation of Aeschylus' *Agamemnon* (1877), which Harris receives as a gift from one of his pupils, John Taplow.

5. A complicated allusion to Larkin's friend Monica Jones, whose full name was Margaret Monica Beale Jones. In early versions of *Lucky Jim*, then called 'Dixon and Christine', Jim's affected and dispiriting girlfriend (Margaret Peel in the published work) was called 'Veronica Beale', and shared a number of qualities with Monica. The change of names from Veronica to Margaret came at Larkin's insistence (see Amis to Larkin, 8 September 1952).

TO PHILIP LARKIN – 15 JULY 1951

Swansea

My dear Philip,

I had the impression that I am sitting down to answer your recent letter with almost psychopathic promptitude; but no, it seems that your is dated ten days ago. [. . .]

I'm sorry about your breakfast-egg expression; tell me, do you also carefully brush your grizzled hair to hide the bald spot? Life here would be all right if I had more *time* – the house keeps filling with self-invited craps – and more *energy*; honestly old boy without a word of a lie three pages of *Dixon* and I'm licked for the day. Still I'm up to p. 94 now and make myself laugh a bit more often than formerly, tho' I don't know as anyone else would do that. We have 2 boys of 13 and 10 staying with us NO YOURE WRONG A and they make noise, they have brought 3 rabbits with them and Hilly has bought 2 for us to look after. Craps continually pour in to fix the curtains and fit the curtains and lay the lino and instal the immersion heater and put doors on the airing cupboard and paint the surrounds and varnish the surrounds and paint the wall and seal up the sewer-pipe and re-lay the garden steps and put up shelves and altogether they are continually pouring in and stopping me from working. But it seems we are to have more money still[1] and so I have just bought 3 more Mozart piano concertos and some other longhaired stuff which would all be a bit beyond you I fear. As regards your stricures pricures strictures YOUFFOOL on divine Mozart. Your trouble is you've been brought up on things like the minuet from the Serenade in D and Iner Cliner, WHICH ALL THE BOOLDY SAM ARE A BOLODY SIGHT BETTER THAN YOU THINK YOUFFFOOL, and in addition your musical appreciation unquote seems to have stuck at the basic ego level. The trouble with Mozart is really his intolerable pessimism, his loading of the ordinary allegro with more blisteringly tragic content than it'll stand IM PERFECTLY SEROUS YOUFF Anyway, go into a gramophone shop and play to yourself the first side of the D minor pno concerto, or the slow

1. For Hilly's legacy see Amis to Larkin, 27 August 1950, note 1, and 12 January 1948, note 5.

movement of the C maj one (K. 467) and see if you can go on thinking what you do YOUFFFFFOOL [. . .]

Well I see we're all set for another Munich bum,[2]

Kingsley

[TLS: Bodleian]

TO PHILIP LARKIN – 2 DECEMBER 1951

24 The Grove, Uplands, Swansea.

My dear Philip,

This is aimed at assuring you of my continued existence in this crazy old world of ours, a fact you must have begun to feel doubtful about in your brain after a month or whatever discreditable interval of time it has been. Things have been very difficult, as that man would have said. I have been trying to get 'a little article' written for old Batey,[1] so as to leave myself time during the Yuletide vacation for finishing *Dixon*; both these projects seem likely to fail without having left me much time for the long letter I began increasingly to owe you. Another thing that has been difficult is that Hilly has been not very well now and then – only colds and things – and I have been playing an increased part in home management and care of children. I cooked the bleeding dinner to-day. That'll show you. Well may I say I'm dashed sorry for being such a slack shit and will try, etc.

I don't know that even this will be a very satisfactory or long letter; for one thing I shall have to get the children's tea at some rapidly-approaching time, for another I've left the last letter which you wrote to me in the same room as the room in wch H. is now doing some sleeping, and I don't like going in to get it. Nevertheless, I remember perfectly well the rage and pleasure I felt on seng your poims reviewed in that Papish rag[2] – well done that *man*. All I ask is, when you introduce a selection of your stuff on the 3rd prog., remember the old pall who

2. Probably a reference to Korea, where armistice negotiations had begun on 10 July (they were to break down on 5 August).

---

1. F.W. Bateson, in his capacity as editor of *Essays in Criticism*.
2. See Amis to Larkin, 12 May 1951, note 1.

was always so encouraging in the days when you were still swimming against the stream, and say how indebted I would like you to say you felt to me. No, seriously, jolly good luck you bastard. [. . .]

Life here is much the same: depression gathers as the date of my parents' arrival to spend the festive season with us approaches. I used to like Christmas, but of recent years my feelings in relation to that matter have undergone a change. I am beginning really to *hate* titching; not just hating the work involved in preparing lectures, but everything: delivering the lecture and seeing them not understanding, and going to the place where I lecture, and coming away from it, and getting home with another lecture to do, and giving tutorials, and getting ready to take a tutorial, and arranging tutorials, and fitting tutorials in with the lectures, and getting ready for the examinations. I'm beginning to dislike it all rather. I don't want to do any more of it, either. Thank Christ I have two or three reasonable men among my acquaintance, especially that ginger-haired chap you met.[3] But no young Wimmen, tho' I suppose that's a good thing really, because it doesn't feel like one to me.

How would it be if I came and stayed with you for a week or so in the spring? It wouldn't matter all that much if you weren't free much of the time, tho' naturally I shd. like you to be, dalling. Hilly and Margaret are planning a week in Oxford together, and I thought it would be nice if I came to you. Could you put me up, or shall I ask the Strangs, or will you ask the Strangs, or couldn't I bear their dogs, yor would it be better if I stayed at a no-tell? Tell me that, will you, now?

I've read *The days of the locust* by Nathanael West,[4] and am quite sure on the strength of it that your description of Miss Loneleyfarts erred greatly on the side of lenience. What a stupid *liar* the man is; I feel when reading him as I do with Virginia Woolf: I want to keep saying 'No, he didn't', 'No, it didn't happen as you describe it,' 'No, that isn't what he thought,' 'No, that's just what she didn't say.' I

3. Probably Esmond Cleary (b. 1924), an economics lecturer at University College, Swansea (1949–88); it was Cleary who provided Amis with the dispiriting title of Jim Dixon's journal article 'The Economic Influence of the Developments in Shipbuilding Techniques, 1450–1485' (see Jacobs, *Biography*, p.149). Also a cricketer and actor.

4. Nathanael West (1903–40), American novelist, author of the novels *Miss Lonelyhearts* (1933) and *The Day of the Locust* (1939).

thought there was more than a twinge of that Armenian twirp[5] about him.

I must go to collect the children from the kindly neighbour who is letting them play with her children this afternoon, and then give them their tea, and then get H's and my tea, and then put them to bed, and then write part of a lecture, and then officiate at a students' coffee-party. I am perpetually reminded of the fried onions and parsnips I cooked for dinner whenever I belch, which is often, and whenever I inhale on the ground floor or on the stairs and landing. I forgot to say that after putting the children to bed I shall have to wash and clear up. Don't hate me honey for not writing. Glad your life is on the up-and-up. You couldn't say that about mine, d'you see, because it wouldn't be true, d'you see? Do write.

Russia has no wish to agree to the inspection of bum,

Kingsley

[TLS: Bodleian]

TO PHILIP LARKIN – 22 DECEMBER 1951

24 The Grove, Uplands, Swansea, Glamorgansh.

My dear Philip,

There is yet time I hope to write you something of a Xtmas letter, 1¼ hours in fact, before I go downstairs to listen to the commentary on the Rugby International, a diversion which will be instantly followed by a drive to the railway station to meet my progenitor and his wife, here bursting with goodies and secret parcels and tearful joy and tactlessness and bad advice and a Christmas pudding all ready in the basin and British sherry and boredom and exasperation for Yuletide. No I can't do you a card either; I had a successful drawing of a blonde with nymphomaniac eyes and a fellator's mouth and breasts like a wrestler's buttocks but it would take too long to reproduce for you, as the a said to the b. Here I set then at my typewriter, my hair looking like a curious fur cap after washing with a Gloria shampoo, feeling myself gradually sinking into a curious trance-like state of depression. I have done all that I wish to do for the moment, apart from committing a round

5. William Saroyan.

dozen of serious offences; I have sent off my article to Bateson, my biographical details to *Poems 1951–52*,[1] and have postponed my final revision of *Dixon* until after the holiday. My head in the lavatory pan and my toes twitching to impinge on parental behinds and my fingers bunching themselves into pairs and my rectum swelling with foul air and that is my holiday.

How odd to get a MS letter from you; that brought the old daze back like bogray. I'm glad to hear that your mum has bought a hace in Loughborough; she cannot presumably live in it and bugger you up simultaneously. Am I to understand that the lady your sister has given the lady your mother her conjay?[2] You are mad standing Barca[3] dinner. WHY DONT YOU EVER STAND MEEEEE A DINNER LIKE THAT AYAYAYAYA I *love* dinners with kwangtroh. How do you *mean* why aren't we more together? If you were anything like ('Anything like *what*?') you'd have popped in here for a night or 2 while you're this side of the water, parents or no parents. You must be mad to think I can come to London on the 30th. Of course I'd love to come and resent not being able to, but don't you realise dear man that my progenetrix and her husband will still be here then, and Oh Pud stay and see the New Year in with us and Oh Pud we don't often see you and Oh Pud we shan't be here much longer, quite apart from the fact that Hilly wouldn't stand being left alone with them, nor would it make me easy in my mind if she were. No I'm sorry man; as I say, nothg would give me greater pleasure, except the chance of incurring a score or so of serious charges, but until Jan 3 or 4 here I am and here I bloody fucking bastard buggering sodding pissing shitting stay. Who the rectal hell is Sally Trenchard? And *why* wouldn't I want to know about Mrs. Donaldson?[4]

Have you had any seasonal gifts yet? I have had a royal blue silk handkerchief from my mother-in-law, and an olive-green steel fling

---

1. *New Poems 1952*, the first in a series of PEN anthologies; see Amis to Larkin, 19 May 1952, note 3.

2. *Congé* (French, from Latin *commeatus*, 'leave of absence') means formal permission to depart or formal dismissal. To give a person his *congé* is to dismiss him from one's service.

3. Unidentifiable; neither a 'Barca' nor a 'Barker' appears in the surrounding correspondence (or are known to Thwaite or Motion).

4. These names appear nowhere else in the correspondence, are unknown to Motion, Thwaite and Judy Egerton, who worked with Larkin at Queen's University, Belfast, and do not appear in the university's records.

cabinet from my wife. From my mother I expect an unwearable sports shirt, from my father an unwise neck-tie. I was going to get you something, but since you obviously haven't got me something, I shan't get you something. [. . .]

Have you read any of this stuff by this chap Angus Wilson?[5] I read them both recently, in fear and trembling lest they shd, be exactly like me, but it seems they aren't. I thought him quite good, but not very funny. I liked the horrible things the people said, but got a bit tired of henna and ill-fitting dentures and toupees and shiny suits. And everything seemed a bit inconclusive. Such darling dodos I thought the best story; things like Farts of elm and a little companion I spew from the interior of my mouth. I read that Mars thing that that Christopher Sherwood fellow recommended.[6] I found out why he liked it: the flithy mysticism, topped up with indignant well-aimed uncomprehending satire on American values etc I don't think I like men who satirise that. Chandler and Nathanael Bloody West do it, dont they? No I don't think I like men who do that What they reject with (i.e. the interior of their heads and horts) seems to me indistinguishable from what the other people accept with, and a crude, untruthful, hysterical rejection is worse than a c., u., h. acceptance because people write books doing the 1st & dont bother when they're doing the 2nd. See what I mean.

So Patsy's in pod, eh? Well well. I should think of all my acquaintances [. . .] she is the worst-equipped person to be a parent I've ever met. Not that being a parent requires being any great shakes; but devotedly-undertaken, conscientiously-pursued emotional incompetence such as I read in her is an ill qualification. Colin might pull her round; or will he be silly with her? I'm afraid he may with his Sweetie and his Twinkle little fellow[7]

[TL: Bodleian]

5. Angus Wilson (1913–91), novelist. His first two volumes, *The Wrong Set* (1949) and *Such Darling Dodos* (1950), were collections of short stories; 'Hearts of Elm' and 'A Little Companion' are printed in *Such Darling Dodos*.

6. *The Martian Chronicles* (1950) by Ray Bradbury (b. 1920), reviewed by Christopher Isherwood in *Tomorrow* 10:2 (October 1950), pp. 56–8. The review was untitled, appearing in the regular column 'Christopher Isherwood Reviews . . .'

7. The letter ends without signature or valediction.

TO PHILIP LARKIN – 27 FEBRUARY 1952

24 The Grave, Up-your-pipe-lands, Swonzy.

My dear Philip,

Well, here I am again, my old cocky-leaky, dull and late and late I am toor and that iss the opposite of bright and early man bach. I apologise for being a bad correspondent; I don't mean to be, it's just that I never seem to have any forking time; people are always coming here and talking to me or demanding that I do work with them. For more than a week for instance I haven't even had time to go down to Boot's Boko-lovers Ribalry, not that that's much bloody loss; I keep ordering dirty American novels and they never come through. Instead I get Pee de 'solea Quimto on the crisis in English poetry[1] and things like that; not even any science fiction to keep me interested.

I had a very nice time in Reading;[2] people were interested rather than respectful about my poems but I suppose that's better than the other way round – why couldn't they be both though eh? Things like that don't happen do they? I had a couple of days at Oxford, staying with Michael Fenton and Barbara,[3] and very nice it was. The only item that will interest you much is that I have now tracked down that record of two women singing, which you once described to me several years ago: called *Oh didn't it rain*: this has just come out on Brunswick and one of the women is Rosetta Tharpe.[4] I should have got it if I'd had any money. Actually there are now no fewer than 4 records of this combo. now available; you might like *Up above my head*, which Michael bought, but I confess it sounds a bit rowdy to me. I shd perhaps say before closing this paragraph that I found it very frightening at Reading: I don't say that most of the people I met weren't craps of a sort, but

---

1. *Crisis in English Poetry 1880–1940* (1951) by Vivian de Sola Pinto (1895–1969), Professor of English, University of Nottingham.

2. Where he had been invited by John Wain, a Lecturer in English at the University of Reading (1947–55); for Wain see Notes on Recipients.

3. Michael Fenton (1922–67) read Classics and then Medicine at Brasenose College, Oxford (1940–41, 1945–51), became a GP, and married Barbara Stone, who worked as a secretary when the Amises first knew her.

4. Sister Rosetta Tharpe (1915–73), blues and gospel singer and guitarist, recorded several vocal duets with her mother, Katie Bell Nubin (1880–1969). On 'Oh Didn't it Rain', recorded in 1947, she sings with Sister Marie Knight, accompanied by the Sammy Price Trio.

they knew a lot about Eng Lit, especially about recent developments in the crit of that lit. I felt not only provincial, which I don't mind, but dull, which I do. Did you know there was a thing[5] called The new criticism? I didn't, but it seems there is, *starting*[6] in 1940, and comprising Eliot, Leavis, Rickword etc., Cleanth Brooks, Empson, Crowe Ransom and a hell of a lot of Yanks, including a type called Kenneth Burke who is apparently the biggest thing since old Lao Ts in the critty caper.[7] I'm sorry to have to tell you all this, but it was unpleasant to find out how, when one is daily surrounded by complacent craps to whom Bridges is a bit flashy and daring, one comes not to share those opinions but to be lulled into a comparable drowsiness. Being a lazy sort of sod, I want a lot of people round me all the time to make me frightened in conversation.[8] Nobody does that to me here. I saw Bateson in Oxford; our poems will come out as soon as he has an odd page to fill up. He said the job situation as far as Eng is concerned is 'pretty tight', which was what reminded me of him just now. I am to do another thing for him, a contribution to a little symposium on old Shitwell's Emily-coloured turds.[9]

I too read *The Franchise affair*,[10] and deeply resented it. It was quite

5. Amis underlines 'thing' and connects it to the MS addition: 'a phenomenon, I mean, not a journal'.

6. 'Starting' is underlined and connected to the MS addition: 'I mean it was named then.'

7. The New Criticism of the 1930s and 1940s was associated with close reading rather than biographical or literary historical interpretation. New Critics treated the text as an autonomous object and saw paradox and ambiguity as the language appropriate and inevitable to poetry. Not all the critics Amis names were closely associated with the New Criticism. Edgell Rickwood (1898–1982), a poet as well as a critic, was editor of the *Calendar of Modern Letters* (1925–27), a journal Leavis much admired (it was a model of sorts for *Scrutiny*). The American critic Cleanth Brooks (1906–94) was an important theorist and populiser of the New Criticism, especially as co-author of the college textbook *Understanding Poetry* (1938), written with Robert Penn Warren. John Crowe Ransom (1888–1974), another American critic and poet, was even more influential, especially in the United States; a Southerner, like Brooks and Penn Warren, he was the author of *The New Criticism* (1941). Kenneth Burke (1897–1986), also an American, wrote poetry and short fiction as well as criticism, and is much less centrally associated with New Criticism than Brooks, Ransom, Warren, Empson and Leavis. 'Lao Ts' is a play on 'Eliot, T.S.'

8. In the margin to the left of this sentence Amis has added in ink: 'This must sound a bit queer: I hope you hannarsten.'

9. A reference to what would become 'Emily Coloured Primulas', *Essays in Criticism* 2 (July 1952), pp. 342–5, in which Amis discusses this phrase, from Edith Sitwell's poem 'Spring', first published in 1923.

10. *The Franchise Affair* (1948), a mystery novel by Josephine Tey (Elizabeth Mackintosh) (1897–1952), author also of *The Daughter of Time* (1951).

a good idea ruined by about page 15. I thought the girl, quite apart from our-sort standards, much nicer than those two insufferable women, I thought the explanation of how the girl got all the details right totally inadequate, I thought the constant finding of new, unpredictable evidence piss-poor. I thought other things too. I don't know why you were so sarcastic about The man on the pier;[11] I thought the last half distinctly good, especially the lovers'-nook scene. Or haven't you read it?

As my 30th bithrayd approaches, I find myself invaded by a kind of impotent horror. What am I doing here? or anywhere, for that matter. If only someone would *take me up*, or even *show a bit of interest*. If only someone would publish some books by me, I could start writing some books. If someone would publish some poems of mine, I could write some; as it is, I hardly get near writing any at all. I'm too frightened to send *Dixon* on the rounds. And other things? That old winged boa-constrictor, sex, still has me in his coils, and is flying around with me looking for a good shit-marsh to drop me into. You remember that according to Hebraic mythology Adam, like Maupassant, could get the horn at will, and presumably, *corolloraily*,[12] not get the horn at will too. That's the kind of engine I could do with. As for my career – I *do* want *a lot* of that swearing. I can't think of any possible continuation of it that isn't as unthinkable as any other. Still a lecturer at 45 CHRIST Professor here at 45 CHRIST Professor at Leeds at 45 CHRIST Senior Lecturer at Durham at 45 CHRIST Lecturer at OKKKKKERRRRRRRHRHRHRHRGHGHGHGHGHRGHRGHRI EEEEEEEEEEEESSSSSSSST You know the sort of thing that's going to happen to me? With my teeth even worse than they are (I have had gingivitis for some time), dressing in camel-hair waistcoats and bow-ties, I shall be laughing and talking loudly in the pubs at lunch-time, a one for the girls, imagining I am impressing the young men by my keen com bom *contempraneity*,[13] passing myself off as a grand chap, referring to my successful friends, 'Oh yes, Bruce and I were very thick at one time; dropped his old friends, of course, when he made Covent Garden,' 'Nonsense now, my dear young lady, have another of the same; after all, I'm here to see you don't come to any harm, eh boys?' All this will

11. *The Man on the Pier: A Novel* (1951) by Julia Frances Strachey (1901–79), novelist (and niece of Lytton Strachey).

12. The underlining is in ink, as is the MS addition: 'You know this word.'

13. Again, underlining in ink, as for MS addition: 'and this one'.

of course be taking place in one of the smaller and poorer provincial cities. And yet . . . to have to die [. . .]

If this account is not paid within FOURTEEN DAYS we must bum,

Kingsley

[TLS: Bodleian]

TO D.L. ROSS – 4 APRIL 1952

24 The Grove, Uplands, Swansea, Glam.

The British Broadcasting Corporation,
(Copyright Department: attention of Miss D. L. Ross)

Dear Madam,

Thank you for your letter of March 28th.[1] Yes, a performing fee of 13/- per minute would be more than acceptable for AMBERLEY HALL.

Yours truly,
Kingsley Amis

[TLS: BBC]

TO PHILIP LARKIN – 4 APRIL 1952

Swansea

My dear old lad,

Nice to hear from you again; it was good to get your *note*, and to enjoy the privilege of reading your communication to my wife. What did John Wain *mean*, I need some grooming? I got your courteous

1. D.L. Ross of the Copyright Department of the BBC had written to Amis about broadcasting *Amberley Hall* on the Home Service programme *Apollo in the West*. This programme used extracts from the 'ballad-opera' (some sixty lines of Amis's libretto) and was broadcast on 30 March 1952.

message about my head via the Strangs,[1] thank you. I'm sure I need only inquire after your scalp in return; but then I shall be able to see exactly how that's getting on, shant I?, when you come at Eastertide. Your odd remarks, as reported by the woman who is in love with you and her husband, had a strong Strangish flavour. You're not going to go over to them, are you, dalling, after all we've meant to each other? I was also interested to hear about your new novel. Bruce didn't see *D&C*, because it's at Michael Joseph's at the moment, in response to a request that they might see any 'book' I had written, with a view to publication. I can't work out whether I think they will take it, or whether I only hope they will take it, or whether I don't think they'll take it because I want them to take it, or whether I don't think they'll take it because they aren't likely to take it, or whether I think they will take it because I've got myself so resigned in advance to their not taking it, or whether I think they won't take it because I've got myself so resigned in advance to their not taking it, or whether I've got myself so resigned in advance to their not taking it. I know you think I'm a bit funny about printers' ink, and that the important thing is to write well; it's easy for you published writers to vilipend the appetite for publication – the point is for me that I want to think of myself as a writer, not entirely (I like to think) for motives of vanity, and that the one characteristic shared by all writers is that what they write is printed down for people who want to read it to read it, even if nobody does read it, d'you see. Hope I'm not boring you, eh? [. . .]

We had quite a nice time at Oxford; we stayed with John Veale and his wife,[2] which they didn't much care for, I think (people who dine out on being Bohemian ought to be prepared to have people being

---

1. For Colin and Patsy Strang, see Amis to Larkin, 9 May 1949, note 3, and 27 November 1950, note 11. The Strangs moved to Belfast in 1948 (Colin to teach philosophy at Queen's University), when Larkin was close to both of them, particularly Patsy (they were briefly lovers around this time, it being 'widely accepted that Patsy's life with Colin was "semi-detached"', Motion, *Life*, p. 217). In 1953, though, Colin was appointed Professor of Philosophy at Newcastle, and he and Patsy moved. They were divorced in 1955, when Patsy, herself the author of poems, married the Irish poet Richard Murphy (with whom she had a daughter, Emily, in 1956); this second marriage lasted until 1959.

2. John Veale (b. 1922), composer; a contemporary at Oxford, reading Modern History and Music at Corpus Christi; in 1945 married Diana Taylor, who had studied at the Slade School. In 1948 he set Amis's poem 'The Last War' to music (see Amis to Veale, 15 November 1984, note 1).

Bohemian to them – forgive us our Bohemianisms, even as we forgive them who Bohemianise against us – by turning up unexpectedly). During our stay Veale received the news that his symphony is to be performed at the Cheltenham Festival, so it was arranged that Diana should provide the food, and I the drink, for a little evening meal; note the last phrase. H. and I were out all day (to save them having to entertain and feed us – we were told later that our unexpected arrival had prevented John from doing a lot of work. How slender is the knife-edge between 'hanging about the house all day talking and wanting food' and 'treating the place as a hotel'.) and returned at 6.20 to find out where the drink was to be bought, etc. The house was locked, and they had gone out in, it was afterwards abundantly clear, a huff. Our further calls, in person at 7.15 and 7.45–8.0 and by line telephone at 8.50, were similarly unavailing, and me without overcoat on the coldest March night since 1916. Fornicating bloody sodomy, that was, & no error. [. . .]

I don't see why *you're* complaining about Butler's bum,[3]

Kingsley

[TLS: Bodleian]

TO PHILIP LARKIN – 21 APRIL 1952

Swansea

My dear Philip,

April is the cruellest month, breeding a poor old tail-chaser who now sees the thirtieth anniversary of his breeding falling away behind him like some ugly turd put out to die of exposure by its genitor. I had two presents that day: a lovely shirt from my mamma and a lovely neck tie from my governor. However, the Beer Beer Charlie came up to scratch if you see what I mean by sending me a little cheque drawn on their bank for letting them have men and a young lady sing my words

3. Perhaps referring to the Conservative MP R.A. ('Rab') Butler (1902–82). Butler was Chancellor of the Exchequer (1951–55) in Churchill's government and his centrist and consensus policies were close to those of the previous Labour Chancellor, Hugh Gaitskell; hence the coinage 'Butskellism'.

over the wireless-set.[1] Thank you for your good wishes; they were very acceptable when they finally arrived. My wife and Mrs. Vakil clubbed together and got me those connected poems, by Yates.[2] The spermophagi at the no-bookshop had put it into stock, not that any flithy Taff would want them I suppose. I celebrated the day by beginning a new novel; no, no dialogue or anything yet dear, just rough notes. To-day I wrote a poem, oddly enough, and I enclose a typed copy if I can brig frig bring myself to type it out again.[3] I'd been reading those connected poems that deal with being old and wanting a bit but being too old but still wanting a bit: the one about politics and 'sole crap its hands and ring and louder ring for every shatter in its you know what.[4] I think mine is a remarkable imaginative feat of re-creation, don't you dear? While on the old bee double owes, I had a look at *The house of breath*, by William Goyen.[5] Don't you do that, son. The review said it was full of tail, but it isn't, the nasty thing, it's full of sssssshhhhhhh

I too enjoyed your stay; it was extra successful I found, except of course for that bit of delirious crappery by the Bartleys. You may like to know that the whole crowd came up on Sunday morning for a *free drink* which *I'd paid for* with *money* that came *out of my own pocket.* Meredith,[6] who is exactly like a 78-year-old Colin, I thought, only to look at of course, went to se pe sleep a lot of the time. I didn't mind that. Later, we entertained Master Bartley, aet. 7, to lunch. I remarked casually to Hilly, 'Isn't Meredith terrible?' The little boy said, 'Why do you say Hugh is terrible?' 'I didn't mean *Hugh*,' I said, laughing slightly at his innocent and after all very, so to say, comprehensible and, for a child, excusable breach of, if I may use the phrase, etiquette, or, more exactly, of the standards of, as it were, intelligence to be, I would say, expected in a, after all, child of, to name a figure, seven years of, though

---

1. See Amis to D.L. Ross, of the Copyright Department of the BBC, 4 April 1952.
2. W.B. Yeats, *Collected Poems* (1950), posthumously published; Mrs Vakil is Margaret Ashbury Vakil, later Aeron-Thomas (see Amis to Larkin, 22 March 1950, note 2).
3. The poem, entitled 'Desire (II)' appears as 'The Triumph of Time' in *A Case of Samples* and *CP*, p. 45.
4. 'Soul clap its hands and sing, and louder sing/For every tatter in its mortal dress,' from Yeats, 'Sailing to Byzantium' (1927).
5. *The House of Breath* (1951) by William Goyen (1915–83), American novelist.
6. Hugh Meredith, an economic historian from Queen's University, Belfast, was a friend of Jo Bartley, who he was visiting in Swansea. He was the author of the standard textbook *An Economic History of England: A Study of Social Development* (1910).

the expression may sound out of, to put it plainly, place in this, or such a, context, age, and added, 'I meant George Meredith.' It was all I could think of to say, you see. I don't really want to meet him again now. I can't think why.

I was very flattered by what you said about my letters. I didn't realsie yktw I had so much to live down to. I promise to try to give you something which will, I dare to, I hope not unwarrantably, hope, may, if it is not too hEnEry jamEs is a coc, a buM, a fArt, and a fOo Foutons, foutons, mon bon.

I have washed my hair and look like a bloody fool. [. . .]

My poem is out in Bateson's thing.[7] This, together with my writing of the thing I hope to enclose, has proofed me a little against my reception of a 'We hope, however' letter from Mike Joe.[8] He's still got the stuff. Nearly 6 weeks now. What's he *doing* with it? Has he lost it? My oath, cully, if he takes it Ile neuer be depreſt agayne, nay, I doe ſweare it. You will have a copy with the most flowery, the most fulsome, the most humble, the most affecting, the most honest, the most humorous, the most deserved inscription on the fly-leaf that you have ever, that you will ever have seen. I can see myself as a fantastic literary robot, two poems a week till the end of the year, twelve hours research a day resulting in a 10,000-word article every quarter, and half an hour a day at a new novel, regular as cockwork. I just find I can do it, he said, with a slight boyish grin. Sounds inhuman, doesn't it? but after all Trollope could do it.[9] You're not comparing yourself with *him*, are you, Kingsley darling? the six lightly-clad girls asked in unison. Rather not, he smiled, putting his arms round the three nearest; I couldn't hold a candle to him; it's just that after one page something tells me I can stop. Don't worry, it says. You'll be able to go on to-morrow. And funnily enough, here he paused in order to ejaculate into the mouth of the second youngest, I find I can. Or perhaps I shall only have time to dictate it to my secretary while I'm having breakfast. Honestly, I think it'll be easily the best novel you'll ever have read.

7. 'Wrong Words', in *Essays in Criticism*, 2:2 (April 1952), p. 158, subsequently published in *A Frame of Mind* (Reading: School of Art, University of Reading, 1953), *A Case of Samples* and *CP*, p. 30.

8. Michael Joseph, the publisher.

9. Anthony Trollope (1815–82), the author of forty-seven novels, trained himself to write a given number of words an hour every morning. He wrote from 5.30 to 8.30 (at 250 words per quarter-hour, a rate of ten pages a sitting), then put in a day's work as an official at the General Post Office.

I'm very sorry about those inscriptions on your book. I'm sure you can imagine that books don't always get put back on shelves, and that it isn't possible to watch the little fuckers all the time. Will you settle for a drink when I see you? We went to the circus, all of us, yesterday, and this cost me £1–2–6. The children were watching the men at the ring-entrance who were bringing up the props most of the time, rather than the actual performers. There had been lions, elephants, chimpanzees and seven different lots of the noble and intelligent friends of man, but Philip cried because there were no tigers. I confirmed my impression that there are few things more boring, or more revolting, or more unpleasant, or more stupid, or more depressing, or more bebeberberberlerluddy PERPERPUPPUPPOINTLESS than a circus clown. *Why* are some of them dwarfs? *Why*? Are they supposed to appeal to adults? Or to children? Or both? How could anybody ever have begun to imagine at any time that one of them might possibly some day ever get anywhere near being the slightest bit funny? I mean, that's just not one of the ways of *being* funny, is it? Even if you were *very good* at it, I mean. I mean, if you tried to be funny by putting a births, marriages and deaths column into medium-grade cipher and writing the result up on a blackboard in front of an audience of Leghorn roosters and cashiered army officers, that couldn't be funny, *however good you were at it*, could it? Well then.

Have you got a cig., Kingsley? I've left mine in my bum,

Kingsley

[TLS: Bodleian]

TO PHILIP LARKIN – 19 MAY 1952

24 The Grove, Uplands, Swansea.

My dear Philip,

It was good to hear from you again after all this time, and I had a good laugh over your letter, especially the Uhlan Lieut. I'm sorry about this paper, but I get it free, and typing paper is very unfree; I may be able to afford some by about September. I have been feeling a little morose lately. Almost all the time that I'm not under direct personal observation I swear quickly to myself and flip my index and middle fingers upwards as a pair. An old man I hate has come to stay with us for a few, but not nearly few enough, days. Yes, that's right. He arrived on Saturday afternoon. Hilly had arranged to go out to tea that afternoon, so I offered to meet him and take him home, calculating he'd get the obvious train and arrive about six, which would give me only half an hour or so with him all to myself. After I had made the offer, a postcard arrived in his small and pointlessly legible writing – I mean that legibility is only a virtue if you *want* to read what's written – sand rand sang he was coming at *two-fifty-six*, *yes*, SPEW SIPHTY-PRIX. So after helping Hilly and the kids on to the bus I got to the station just in time to have a Double Diamond, which didn't put me on my feet, and smoke a cigarette. At the due time I went out to the barrier. As the train drew in I began swearing in a whisper and very fast, like a man about to go into a concert who pisses as much as he can beforehand, even though he may not want to at the time, or like a man stuffing himself with pudding before a fast. I sang softly that Beethoven concerto jingle, over and over again, my heart lifting as more and more passengers came into view without any sign of him. Alas, there he was at last, his resentful ape's face peering about all round me without seeing me, finally moving off to the right and out of my view. I moved to the right to cover the gate there. The flow of people through the gate thinned, then stopped. Had he fallen down a grating? No, he'd just slipped away to the left, after this feint to the right, so as to take me in the rear. Squirting me with talk, a power-hose playing on a cigarette-lighter, he followed me home. Whenever his face was turned away from mine, I screwed my own into a dazzle-pattern of hatred and fury. I can see now what makes fathers fling their children out of the house with a few bob at the age of sixteen; mine ran up to him with cries of delighted welcome. I am going downstairs for a cup of tea now, first lighting a cigarette to prevent him, if I can, for sponging on me for yet another. He forgot the pubs shut on Sundays here, you see. Just forgot, what?

I took the paper out of the carriage there, not so as to give you short weight, but in case he 'wandered in' here with his 'head in the clouds' and 'without thinking' looked at what was in the typewriter. Still his conceit must be armour against anything short of a burst from a Vickers heavy machine-gun (calibre. 55"). I'd like to put that to practical verification some time AND NO TIME LIKE THE PRESENT. He didn't scrounge a cigarette from me; was already smoking one obtained via some other source. Is there anything more annoying in its way than having your pencil taken off you – and not returned unless you ask for it – repeatedly while you're doing a crossword so that an old fool can pencil incorrect solutions into another crossword, reading out the clues of his own to you the while in tones of simple wonder? While we consumed our tea, he and I had a little conversation. He was talking his usual urine-delirium about the countryside; I said before being interrupted, One green field is like another green field. He said, That's because you haven't the eyes to see the difference. No, I wanted to say, not *that* difference, not THAT difference; only the difference between smelly old attitudinising fools and other men. He added, The things that interest you most aren't necessarily the most important. No, I wanted to say, not *necessarily*; I mean sex and money and lit-richer aren't NECESSARILY the most important things, you old pig's bladder. He likes the country better than the town. His readiness to reject the town is due to his ignorance of what is in it, as Edmund Wilson would say. Talking of him, have you looked at I thought of Daisy?[1] It's not bad; there are some very funny Legacy bits, and if you can read past that stuff about the fearful poetess you'll be laughing more often than wincing. Christ, Barbary shore;[2] *Christ.* He's gone out to-day to see how much he remembers of the geography of Swansea; those are the *ipsissima verba*. Now why, I wonder, does he want to do that? What will he do if he finds he remembers a lot of it? And what will he do if he finds he doesn't remember a lot of it? He goes round in a blue shirt, with his braces in full view, trying to disgrace me. I only perked up once yesterday: that was when he found he'd got a lot of tar from the beach on his trousers. They were old trousers, though. He no longer tells me of the doings of his sones bones sons; their progress and conduct must now be beyond even his defence, which is right and just. Old Rodge has got a varicose groin, I hear, which is proper and fitting. The old fool was carrying a rucksack round with him to-day. How fearfully unerring that is as a badge (sorry, old fellow, forgot you'd got one) – as unerring, in its different way, as the brief-case, the walking-stick, the sports coat leathered before wearing.

Christ, I'm so hard up, so hard up. The P.E.N. people have asked

1. *I Thought of Daisy* (1929), a novel by Edmund Wilson (1895–1972), American author and man of letters.

2. *Barbary Shore* (1951), the second novel by Norman Mailer (b.1923), American novelist and journalist.

me to a cocktail party to launch their anthology, in London.[3] I want go, in case there's anybody there I can impress with my genius or virile member, and even though I know there won't be I shall still kick myself when in the future people send my poems back etc. But I shall feel unhappy about spending the money just for 2 hours of talk. I shall probably stagger retching from the coach, trying to tell myself I've saved half the rail fare, into a gloomy room full of Richard Church and Paul Dehn,[4] everybody knowing everybody else and those who know who I am impregnably persuaded that I'm Welsh. Do you know Dylan do you know Vernon do you know Henry do you know Keidrych[5] [. . .]

When I've finished this, I must write to the Welsh Joint Education Committee to ask them if I can shag myself out by marking Higher Cert papers for them again this summer and earn a bit of cash; I should imagine they're all full up now, which means I shan't have to shag myself out, but on the other ahnd rahnd hand I shan't have the bit of cash either. And I want cash. I've now almost decided I can't go to this Pen club thing, because I haven't got the actual physical bloody pound-notes in my pocket to take me there. Not becos I can't afford it, but becuase yktfffcw I haven't got the money. And in a few minutes he'll be back here again, as like as not with a handkerchief on his head with the corners pig's-eared, trying to get it circulated that there's insanity in my family. No word from Mike 'll show siph.[6] yet. They've lost it no doubt, the descendants of lickers of ghetto-lepers' sores. Aw bugger them, and bugger it, and bugger me, and above all sweet lord jesus I pray you bugger him.

Billy go and talk to Daddy; he's in there all on his bum, *bum* bum bum bum *bum* bum bum bum *bum*

3. The PEN Club is an international association founded in 1921 to promote co-operation between writers all over the world and to champion freedom of expression. *New Poems 1952* was the first in a series of PEN anthologies; see Amis to Larkin, 22 December 1951, note 1.

4. For Richard Church see Amis to Larkin, 1 April 1946, note 5; Paul Dehn (1912–76), poet, critic, scriptwriter; his first two collections of verse were *The Day's Alarm* (1949) and *Romantic Landscape* (1952).

5. Dylan Thomas; Vernon Watkins; perhaps Henry Treece (though not Welsh, Treece was the author of the first book on Dylan Thomas and a founder, with Watkins, of the New Apocalypse movement, a reaction against the supposed 'classicism' and excessive rationalism of Auden); Keidrych Rhys (1915–87), poet, writer, bookseller and founding editor of *Wales* magazine (1937–60).

6. Michael Joseph, who had still not reported on 'Dixon and Christine'.

bum bum bum BUM bum bum bum *BUM*bumbumbum*BM*bmbmbm
peeeeeeeeeeeEEEEEEEEEEEEEEEEEEEEEEEEEEEEEEEEEEEE[7]

Kingsley

You won't believe me, but while I was doing the above, he came and twisted the handle of the study door, behind which I am. He said, Are you in there, Kingsley? Yes, I said in a cordial, eager tone. All right, he said. What the hell did he want? Did he confuse this room with the shithouse next door? Is it any longer just to speak of him confusing anything with anything? OOoogh, the old . . . the old

[TLS: Bodleian]

TO PHILIP LARKIN – 6 JUNE 1952

Swansea

My dear Philip,

Aw c'mon, hon., what's got a hold of you? I write you a wee smasher of a letter all about him, and not so much as a cablegram do I get in return. Perhaps you're still having the French disease.[1] I write to you now after he has gone and before my wife's parents-in-law arrive here for a little visit which they start to-morrow. I went to the P.E.N. party. I met Michael Hamburger.[2] I mentioned you. He said, I'm most interested to hear anything about Philip, because, you see, we knew each other so well at Oxford. I said, Oh yes, of course. I also mentioned your XX poems and he seemed interested. If you *want* to get anything in next year's crop of crap (I'm going to try) I advise you to send him a copy c/o the PEN, referring to what I said to him and what he said back. Also saw John Lehmann,[3] false and smiling, Roy Fuller,[4] nice and doggish and looking like an ageing subaltern in the Indian army, Alan

7. This row of 'E's grows progressively redder (from black to red-and-black to red type).

---

1. Larkin had taken a trip to Paris with Bruce Montgomery in May.
2. For Michael Hamburger see Amis to Larkin, 30 July 1950, note 4.
3. For John Lehmann see Notes on Recipients.
4. Roy Fuller (1912–91), poet, novelist and lawyer.

Ross, the cricket king,[5] now caricaturing an Italianate Elizabethan, Ronald Bottrall,[6] an emaciated clown. I was rude to him unintentionally, being very pissed:

Some female: . . . mm w kk rrp Ronald Bottrall.
Me: What, are you Ronald Bottrall?
Ronald Bottrall: Yes.
Me: Good God.

After Robert Conquest had recited a very long sequel to *Eskimo Nell*[7] to me, I left, stealing a copy of the book[8] as I went

Did I tell you some kinked sod had stolen and broken our car? We have it back now, after the insurance company have forked out £128 on it. On Satturddayy it wouldn't go, and us all inside some way from home. I and two friends pushed it for a mile or so, but it wouldn't go. In the afternoon, having carried the children home, we had arranged to visit the college swimming baths with some friends. We carried the children down to the car and I fiddled uselessly with it for a time (rain was falling), then walked to one of the 2 equidistant phone boxes. Would you call back in 20 minutes, the man at the garage said after the exchange had at last got me through. I smoked a home-made cigarette in a shelter erected, so it was represented, to the glory of God, then phoned again. Could they tow it in and repair it? No, there were no mechanics on duty, sorry (it was Whit Saturday and we were in Wales). Could they get the driver of the breakdown lorry to look at it, since it was obviously a simple fault? No, their drivers weren't allowed to tinker with cars, sorry. Could they tow it to another garage where men would, I knew, tinker with it? No, they weren't allowed to tow anywhere except into their own garage, sorry. So I let them do this and sting us thereby for a night's garaging. I told Hilly I would wheel the children to the baths in the push-chair and meet her there when she'd finished being towed. 25 minutes later I had pushed the children, the

5. Among Alan Ross's publications are several books on cricket, including *The Cricketer's Companion* (1960).

6. Ronald Bottrall (1906–89), poet; admired by the critic F.R. Leavis, much influenced by Ezra Pound; his *Collected Poems* were published in 1961.

7. This was Amis's first meeting with Conquest (for whom see Notes on Recipients). For the bawdy *Eskimo Nell*, and Conquest's sequel, *Mexican Pete*, co-written with John Blakeway, see *Memoirs*, p.141.

8. *New Poems 1952*, ed. Clifford Dyment, Roy Fuller and Montagu Summer, the first of the annual PEN Club anthologies.

brake of the push-chair undisengageably engaged, to the baths, and meeting the man in charge asked how long it would be before the baths closed. About three minutes, sorry, he said. I went, fighting back hot tears, and stood near the gates while the children played round me. I smoked another home-made cigarette while stopping the children from running into the road and cutting their fingers off on the mower and wheeling the white-line marker over the cricket pitch and hitting each other and taking their shoes off and breaking the push-chair and impaling themselves on railings. After 50 minutes of this Hilly arrived. I pushed the children up the hill to a friend's house, where I was given a cup of tea and spilt it over just-cleaned trousers. So write and cheer me up. Taft[9] leads in bum

Kingsley

[TLS: Bodleian]

TO PHILIP LARKIN – 18 JUNE 1952

Swansea

My dear Philip,

Excuse this paper wont you, it is old exam answer books torn up, and we get it for free, dyou see. I can't afford to buy any real paper. Well old man it was fine to hear about your trip to Paris, though I still find myself amazed that you agreed to go and, having agreed to go, went. A trip like that seems to run counter to so much that I know about you. Your dislike of spending money even on yourself, for instance. Still I suppose you know your own business best. I laughed and admired a lot at what you had to tell me about it all, especially the jazz part, which I thought was very funny and infuriating – in that you missed Bechet, I mean – and I liked especially the organic chemist. If the style of this epistle becomes a little stiff and ungainly, or even incoherent, that will not be, I am sorry to say, because I am drunk, but because I mustn't light another cigarette untill 11.30 a.m., and it is now 11.2 a.m., and I want to light a cigarette now, but I mustn't do that, because I have so little money to spend, and if I light a cigarette now, the packet that

9. Robert Taft (1889–1953), son of President William Howard Taft; Republican Senator from Ohio (1939–53) and thrice unsuccessful candidate for the Republican nomination for President, the last time against Eisenhower in 1952.

must last me for two days won't. You might tell me, by the way, what was good in my postscript about Is it any longer just.[1] I need all the help I can get these days. Mike Joe didn't want my book, but on the other hand they hadn't lost it as I was certain they had, and it's now being rejected I suppose by a pal of John Wain's, though this time for slightly different reasons no doubt. Crystal mighty, when I read books like *Willa you're wanted*[2] (God did you see that pillar of crap-smoke? utter bollok sutter boll) or *A step to silence*[3] I begin to see what a gripping action-packed two-fisted drama *Dixon* is. You know the trouble with *Dixon*? It isn't 'sensitive' enough to make up for its lack of concern with matters of importance like religion and the sense of guilt and our predicament as Europeans, if you're with me up to now as Hutt would say in *The troubled air*.[4] Now there's a book you might read and tell me what you think of.

I'm sorry I told Bruce that funny little story, and havent any defence really. He did seem awfully well acquainted with what you might call the background of the tale, and the events which led up to it, though, (N.B. Not that he had any idea of what occurred in the automobile at the time) so I just ... I'm sorry. I'll try to stop that sort of thing happening again.

As you may know, your university is advertising that English lectureship again and I'm in for it again. All that's happened so far is that they're taking up my referees. So I might at any rate get an interview out of them, which will mean a few days with you dalling if you care to have me. Apparently Baxter[5] is a great boyo for the old words. History of the language. Literary value of *Beowulf*. Significance of back-mutation.[6] History of my bum. Literary value of french letters. Significance of back-rotation. I hear that Baxter is a little puzzled about why

1. See Amis to Larkin, 19 May 1952.

2. *Willa You're Wanted* (1952) by Affleck Graves, also author of *Elarna Cane* (1956) and *Little Thumbamonk* (1956). Affleck Graves was the pen name of Mrs Ida Hughes-Stanton (b.1902), poet, novelist and author of stories for children.

3. *A Step to Silence* (1952) by P.H. Newby (see Notes on Recipients).

4. *The Troubled Air* (1951) by Irwin Shaw (1913–84), American novelist, playwright and short-story writer.

5. F.W. Baxter (1897–1980), New Zealand-born Professor of English Language and Literature, Queen's University, Belfast (1949–58).

6. 'The making of a word from a word which is mistakenly assumed to be a derivative of it, as in *to burgle* from *burglar*, the final noun of which suggests that the word is a noun of agency and hence *ought* to mean "one who burgles"' (Thomas Pyles, *The Origins and Development of the English Language* (New York: Harcourt, Brace and World, 1964), p.284).

I want to come to Belfast. Thinks perhaps I've been given the hint by this place. I suppose it's just hard to credit that any sane person should voluntarily opt for the Pats. Oh, and talking of Pats. *Have you seen* (my dear little man) *Europa and the bull*? By W.R. Rodgers?[7] You *have*? Well, ASS IT GEORGE GETCHER KNEE UP IS CRUTCH SMASH IS BOLLOCKS GOUGE IS FU Believe me, this book is a rarity. I mean, you don't often, however much our sort may pretend so, pick up a book that's four-star, alpha-plus, specially selected, cordon-bleu shite ALL THE WAY THROUGH, do you? I mean it doesn't let up for *a single line*, does it? It just goes on being vertiginous piss *continuously*, from line 1

> Naked+ they came*, a niggling± coreø of girls
> +I'm reviving the fierce sensuality of all good poetry
> *Note this archaic word-order; I'm traditional
> ±*N*-aked plus giggling: I play with sound-patterns to enrich the texture of my verse
> øCore; I've read Empson; =corps =corpus =body

all the way through. And shall I tell you something? I don't care about Europa, nor about the bull, do you? I think he's short of subjects, don't you? I don't like this watch-while-I-translate-this-into poetry stuff, do you? *Do take this seriously*: apart from all the individual things that make me wince, have you *ever* read a man who was more hysterically, more deliriously, more hilariously mistaken about what poetry is? Even Valentin Iremonger[8] knows dimly what he ought to be doing. Rodgers is like a man who wears a piss-pot on his head because it's shaped like a hat. Mind you say something about this *idiot* in your next letter. OWOWOW I CANT WRITE IM NO GOOD I DONT CARE OWOWO And he includes that unerring label of the no-good, the poeticiser, the man with no subject: a poem about a *swan*. A FUCKING *SWAN*. A bleed Seen *A street car named desire*?[9] Now there's something that's got no point to it. There was one gag that amused me, though. A girl makes a remark about the eccentricities of Poles, that they are

7. *Europa and the Bull* (1952) by W.R. Rodgers (1909–69), Northern Irish poet, writer and radio producer; for a fuller demolition see Amis, 'Ulster Bull: The Case of W. R. Rodgers', *Essays in Criticism* 3 (October 1953), pp.470–5.

8. See Amis to Larkin, 27 November 1950, note 7.

9. The 1951 film, directed by Elia Kazan and starring Marlon Brando and Vivien Leigh, of Tennessee Williams's play.

notoriously *difficile* etc. Her sister says, Oh yes, it's like Irish, isn't it? I recounted this to James Bartley and his wife, but they didn't laugh much. Why was that, do you think?

Oh I'm so poor, I'm so poor. I got a guinea today from the PEN for *Masters*.[10] That's not bad for a poem, eh? A piss-up, travelling expenses, and five bob? I'm sorry to keep talking about the creative arts, but did you see those poems of ole Johnny Wain's in the NS&N and Listener? I thought a lot of the book he wrote[11] was quite good, as you remember me saying at the time, but these routine terza-rima things . . . I think the metre makes for chattiness and long-windedness or something. I mean to say, they just go on and on, what? He doesn't say anything you couldn't say in half the time, does he? I can imagine some Dryden of 1980 writing that the sweetness of English verse was never understood or practised by his forefathers, and that Mr. Empson and Mr. Wain were the first reformers of English numbers. It is the English lecturer, And he is grown so poor, so poor. The lectures and tutorials have lost their meaning, And this is what breaks the heart.[12]

I'm real sorry you didn't hear Bechet, though I'd have been even sorrier in another way if you had; a pang of sincere grief like that which attacks me when I see that John Wain has got a review in the *Sunday times*. Now I must go to college to see if I have an interview with the biggest shit in the four kingdoms, as James B[artley] calls him.

Rodgers reminds us that great verse must sing & echo in the bum,

Kingsley

[TLS: Bodleian]

10. Reprinted in *A Case of Samples* and *CP*, p. 23.

11. *Mixed Feelings* (1951), printed by the University of Reading School of Fine Art, in a limited edition of 120 copies; called by Morrison, *The Movement*, p.25, 'the first real example of a Movement departure from "the poetry of the 1940s"'. The presiding influence over the volume was that of William Empson, a number of whose poems were written in *terza rima*.

12. An echo, among others, of Tennyson, 'The Miller's Daughter' (1832), ll.169–70: 'It is the miller's daughter/And she has grown so dear, so dear'; see also Coleridge, *The Rime of the Ancient Mariner* (1798): 'It is an ancient Mariner/And he stoppeth one of three.'

TO PHILIP LARKIN – 24 JULY 1952

Swansea

My dear Philip,

Sorry I 'couldn't manage' to reply sooner, but I have been way way from here, visiting my parents-in-law and my parents. We got back last night. We'd given Margaret[1] permission to come into our house if she wanted to. She had wanted to: in the kitchen was a teapot full of tea with some white fungus growing on it, and in the drawing-room, as I saw within five seconds of entering the house, the lid of the radiogram wasn't quite shut: what was preventing it from being quite shut was most of that *Dear old dad*[2] record. A small sliver, about six grooves thick, had become detached from the main body by insufficiently wary closure of the lid. I think that's rather annoying, don't you? Stupid bloody bitch. Rather a stupid bloody bitch, I call her.

In response to your unspoken questions: yes, I saw him at Abbey Timbers. He had time to tell me little beyond some piece of *dejecta* about the doings of some one of his sons, which I've now dismissed from my memory. At my parents' home all was as usual; they'd trained Philip up to be 'polite' and use those horrible little 'may I have another piece of cake Grandy' (*sic*: a whimsical version of Grandma) formulas at table. We'll soon re-brutalise him, though; you see. I had a political argument with my father in which he called me a communist and I called him a warmonger. All quite as usual, you see. On the way we called on John Morgan and Mary Madden,[3] now his wife, and we had a lot of cheap drinks at J's RAF mess (cherry brandy 1/6). He told me that Clive Gammon[4] got a question asked about himself in the House of Commons to get himself out of the army. Bloody shit's trick. I'd call

---

1. Margaret Ashbury Vakil.

2. A late-Victorian music-hall song, with the refrain: 'I'm following in father's footsteps,/ I'm following me dear old dad.'

3. John Morgan (1929–88), journalist, author and broadcaster, and Mary Madden (Morgan) (b.1929), students and friends of Amis from the University College of Swansea; part of a group of students, including Clive Gammon (see next note) and Geoff Nicholson (see Amis to Larkin, 23 December 1949, note 2), who had been to Swansea Grammar School and who would meet, sometimes with Amis, for Saturday-morning beer at the Grand Hotel.

4. Clive Gammon (b.1929), journalist (for many years in America, as angling correspondent for, among other titles, *Sports Illustrated*); had also studied at the University College of Swansea.

that a bloody shit's trick, I think. I was very glad and sorry to see how well J and M seemed to be getting on together.

About D and C: I'm jolly glad you're taking such a decent interest in the thing: *don't let it slip*. We should be able to fudge up something good between us. My feeling at the moment is that your 'D should sod up the romantic business actively' is the most acute criticism: I thought I wanted to tell the reader that if chaps in the shit climb out of the shit, it's by good luck, not by their own efforts – I tried to make that one of the morals; but I quite see that that's not very interesting and what's needed is a mos tos monstrous offensive by Dixon against the others. [. . .]

Hemlock and bum,[5]

Kingsley

[TLS: Bodleian]

TO PHILIP LARKIN – 11 AUGUST 1952

c/o Mr. Antell, Streatley Hills Guest House, Streatley, Berks.[1]

My dear Philip,

Well here we are nicely settled in as you might say if you were a bloody fool, living in our flithy caravan. Really it's not so bad, not nearly so bad, as the words 'caravan holiday with the flithy kids' would indicate. It is dry inside, it's warm enough, you don't have to shit in a field – especially *that*. The Calor gas smells like the farts of someone with cancer of the large gut, most of the evening is taken up by *making the bed* – oh *filthy bum*; I hate making beds, most of all caravan ones. First you turn the thing from a 'couch' back into a bed; this involves lifting the frame up with all one's strength in order to pull it out *towards one* (that's the humour of it) with all the rest of one's strength. When I add that for the next ten minutes one tries to pull up the far edges of the mattress while lying on them (in order to insert under them

5. An allusion to *Hemlock and After* (1952), a novel by Angus Wilson.

1. MS addition '*ergh ergh*' , with an arrow pointing to 'Guest House'.

some portion of the self-actuated centripetal sheets), the while one's back itches inaccessibility syphility so that you can't scratch it, the reader can form some idea of the majesty of the scene. Getting it from a bed into a 'couch' is better. This involves *pushing the thing away from one* (that's the humour of it) while *holding it up*. I'm sorry to sound like Th' 'Erb, er –, but these conventionally-funny situations are hard to do without taking trouble.

I've thought of no more real ideas for *D&C* – what I had went into my Obseruations in my last letter. I think perhaps the title had better be changed into *The man of feeling*;[2] D. has more to feel about than he had before, and the Xtine business had better be concealed I suppose for as long as we can until she appears anyway. I think that while I feel I've come near hitting the bell with the provenance of J G-S,[3] I am out on a) the introduction of Catchpole b) how Xtine finds out about Bert & Vic. No doubt you'll have looked into all that. The stray joke still cheers me in the intervals of thinking about My Lady Nicotine – I am seriously trying to break myself of the tobacco habit, without the aid of proprietary preparations, &c. 'The landlord looked at Dixon without replying, perhaps because whatever he said next must be pejorative in some way, or perhaps because the question had been inaudible to him.' No, perhaps not, really. One of those tobacco-that-counts cigarettes might put the polish on, or radical reconstruction could be undertaken with the aid of a large-size cigarette of fine quality – I have examples of both in the record-case.

We have been over to Abbey Timbers, of course. He was there in a *beret*, looking like a French *instituteur* cashiered for offences against minors. He took one of my cigarettes whenever one was offered, without however offering me any of his own. It's because his head's in the clouds too much for him to think of a thing like smoking, until someone offers him a cigarette – then he thinks of it and takes one, you see. You can't expect him to be petty enough to remember whose it was *before he got his cunt-hook on to it*, can you? There was a very wonderful woman there too called Mary Gantaume (*née* Bardwell), Hilly's cousin. She is the only

2. The title also of a sentimental novel of 1771 by Henry Mackenzie (1745–1831), the good-natured hero of which, like the rather less refined and gentle Jim Dixon, confronts a number of cheats and worldly achievers.

3. The reference is to 'Julius Gore-Urquhart', a character in *Lucky Jim*; referred to in Amis to Larkin, 24 July 1952 (in Bodleian, in a passage of detailed plot queries excised in this selection), as 'G-Shagbag'; hence 'J G-S'.

woman with real red hair and real green eyes I've ever seen. Same physical type as H. Taller. A lot of everything and all of it good, as her husband would probably say – he's an American. A *nudist*, he was – and still is, perhaps, though clothed when I saw him. So was she, I'm sorry to say. And likely to remain so as far as I'm concerned, *heu fugaces*![4]

Don't let it slip, there's a sweet one; you've no idea how I shd. welcome a further go of your *D&C* thoughts, especially *here*. Or just write and pass the time of day (what does that mean, by the way? Do you hiss 'twenty past eight' out of the corner of your mouth? Like the resistance?). Always glad to hear. Always bloody glad to hear, you know.

Morning coffee, Teas, Suppers. Open to non-residents for bum

Kingsley

[TLS: Bodleian]

TO PHILIP LARKIN – 8 SEPTEMBER 1952

Swansea

My dear Philip,

Good to receive yet another long screed. My parents have just left on the railway-train, and I have 24 hours' peace before scuttling off to Oxford to give my lecture.[1] I mention you in it (a promising post-war novelist). I shall see John Wain there, but what I'd rather see is Miss Barbara Stone[2] taking off every single one of her articles of clothing. I shan't do that, though. I've put in your bits about Hy Gr,[3] whom I give a terrible pasting. Do I gather from your bum that you have been playing BRIDGE? You are mad you know. My parents play bridge. My

4. An allusion to Horace, *Odes*, II, xiv, 1: '*Eheu fugaces, Postume, Postume, Labuntur anni*' ('Ah me, Postumus, Postumus, the fleeting years are slipping by').

---

1. The lecture, about contemporary writing, was delivered at a course of some sort; other participants included John Wain, Ronald Bottrall and another poet and critic, W.W. Robson (b.1923), Fellow in English, Lincoln College, Oxford (1948–70), later Masson Professor of English Literature, University of Edinburgh (1972–90). See Amis to Larkin, 18 September 1952 (in Bodleian): 'I'm back from Ocksfd now, and the mists of State-provided alcohol, social-literary climbing and irresponsible denigration have cleared. I thought I was a bit of a one for pelting our poets, essayists and novelists, living and dead, with ess aitch eye tea, but I'm a positive George Saintsbury compared witht pitht with the Robson-Wain crowd.'

2. See Amis to Larkin, 27 February 1952, note 3.

3. Henry Green.

mother keeps urging me to take it up. She says it would be a great social asset to me. And what's this freaka windbreaka freak about finding out whether [Pee Wee] Russell's alive or dead? You are mad you know. He's DEAD, I read an ah-tickle SAYING SO by an AMERICAN, play the man and face up to it why don't you. And pull yourself together man over AWA.[4] You think you don't like her because you're afraid of her, see? That's all it is. Plunge your hand into her bosom why don't you. Nasty little toady in a pig's arse. You are mad, you know.

As regards D&C: *the library*: Dixon can be collecting griff for a contribution of Welch's to a folk-dance conference or a lecture on arts and crafts in eighteenth-century Hamberton; needn't be anything to do with his book. Still, thanks for the tip.

the lecture: I see what you mean about this, though it would be awfully difficult to do. I could have a shot at it, anyway, and you could decide whether it should go in; it's an optional scene as regards the plot, story, etc. He'd have to be drunk, I think.

the job: agreed. The grammar-school touch is a winner.

Bertrand's pass: yes. Would it do to make Carol deduce from watching D&C at the sherry party that they are deliberately avoiding each other – sort of looking at each other and then looking quickly away when their glance is returned? And then Carol asks Christine what's up? Would that do? The poke-invite could be placed anywhere off-stage. The snag is that this deprives us of the excuse for keeping Christine upstairs with her headache when Dixon pays his abortive visit. Well I suppose she could appear and go off with them. But that means 6 in the car. Unless Mrs Welch doesn't 'feel like' going. Or neither Bert nor Chr are going. But it would be nice if they did; they could be going off to dinner with the Goldsmiths, where B. could deliver his poke-invite & Carol could have a chance to watch things & start liking Christine. Then Mrs W must stay behind, say to receive some lute-player from Sweden who is expected. The placing in the car would then be Christine next to Welch in the driver's seat, and at the back Bertrand-Dixon-Veronica. Yes I think Mrs Welch is waiting for Ole. 'Ole ole ole ole Moses keep her sweet to me' Dixon sang under his breath in imitation of a dance record he had once heard.

Mediaevalism: yes; then we could make Welch fond of children's

4. Winifred Arnott (b.1929), a recent Queen's graduate in English who was working as a cataloguer in the library in Belfast.

art & Mrs Welch the anglo cathoclic fascist, eternally engaged in arguments with Welch over the significance etc. of children.

Further notes: Do you agree about the black decade?

Do you agree about making G-S a new lover for Carol?

About the successive-days point: I think a lot of it *has* got to be crowded up for reasons of motivation; e.g. the hotel tea mustn't take place too long after the ball – they wouldn't want to wait; and the whole of the 2nd part (from summer ball on) must take place in the confines of Christine's stay at the Welches, and she has got a job to go to after all. Eh?

I think the best thing about Veronica's name would be to change it to Margaret Jones; then I could enjoy cutting at Margaret Ashbury as well as at Monica. You tell Monica that I'm cutting at some frightful Welch girl, and I'll tell Margaret that I'm cutting at some frightful Leicester girl.[5] How would that do? It's a common enough sort of name, God knows.

Would it be asking too much to ask you to skim quickly through the typescript, making marginal indications of anything that displeases you? ('Bad style', 'damp squib', bad bit of dialogue & so on, to prevent me using them again.)

I think that's aboutt whipisprickoutt about all for now. Thank you once again for your GREAT KINDNESS AND GENEROSITY AND PATIENCE in following this thing through . . .

I don't think I shall be able to come to Oxford when you say. I shan't have any money. Can't you call in here on your way back? ('On my *way*? On my *way*?') The Strangs may be here oh lawdy pappa. I have re-read the memorial and thought about mr norris and berlin and have come to the conclusion that what shagged our Chris was not coming clean about being a homo. Did you see that in the TLS about *The world in the evening*?[6]

Don't let the kids play in the street; they'll pick up all sorts of bum,

Kingsley

[TLS: Bodleian]

5. See Amis to Larkin, 12 June 1951.

6. *The World in the Evening* by 'Chris' Isherwood was not published until 1954, but the first chapter appeared in 1952 in John Lehmann's *New Writing*, reviewed anonymously in 'More New Writing', *TLS*, 8 February 1952, p.108; the other Isherwood works referred to are *The Memorial* (1932), *Mr Norris Changes Trains* (1935) and *Goodbye to Berlin* (1939).

TO PHILIP LARKIN – 4 OCTOBER 1952

Swansea

My dear Philip,

So you're back from the Lake District now; I can understand *that* all right, but what I *can't* understand is why you ever *went*. You *are* MAD, you know. What's the point of it? What's the point of it? What's the point of it? What can you do in the Lake Districy pricy that you can't do elsewhere? Oh well, let's let it drop ON YOUR TESTICLES; shan't ever be able to understand that part of you, and that's a bloody fact. I mean; *Christ*, what do you *do* in the . . . all right. All right. Still, I'm glad you're back and within reach of the post.

Not, of course, that I have anything to tell you by means of it. Hilly bought a horse yesterday, a gelding aet. 2 named (provisionally) Conker, because he's conker-colour. We have a little boy staying with us, named Mark; his mummy was kicked by a horse and so we are looking after him for a bit (a sodding great bit). When you tell him not to do something, he goes on doing it, smiling engagingly into your eyes. He "knows he's a charmer" FAGGSH ("Knows? Knows?"). Our dog broke her leg the other day but it's mending nicely. Tum has begun already; it slowly penetrates further back towards the summer every year, like the filthy soccer season. They tried to make me do some Chaucer this year; in a pig's arse I said. Shall I tell you who's no good? Robert Penn Warren. Try *The hand of the hunter*, by Jerome Weidman.[1] I don't say you'll like it, but you'll be able to tell why I tell you to try it I think (no, it isn't pornographic). [. . .]

Thanks for your comments on *Dixon*. Most of them are just, especially the ticks. I couldn't understand: 'Forget how we left this, but the device shouldn't be used twice' against Dixon telling Welch he can't come for the week-end. You exaggerate (though I'm prepared to admit I exaggerate the other way) about ladies not saying Christ. Casting about among my female acquaintances here, I can think of six women *in as many seconds* who are accustomed to invoking that entity. 'Right grounded' is a phrase used by Scots men, of whom G-S is one. I agree

1. *The Hand of the Hunter* (1951) by Jerome Weidman (b.1913), American novelist, playwright.

with you about all the embarrassing things the young women (C[2] and V) say. And that C is a fearful shagbag – must do something about her. I laughed like a nadir[3] about 'This speech makes me *twist about* with boredom' – yes, perhaps it was going too far, but it's meant to be the speech of a fearful stupid crap, don't you know. Anyway, thanks vm for going through it. Now all I want from you is any material I may have sent you that I should have (such as the bit with the London-velleities suggestion in it), plus a general approval for the latest synopsis (I laughed like a dinar when I wrote 'an ocarina septet by P. Racine Fricker'),[4] and I can go ahead. Do whack these 2 requirements to me soon (oh and by the way you never said what you thought of the G-S/ Carol-liaison-suggestion) as I am looking forward to starting. [. . .]

I haven't nearly enough to say to fill this page. Did you hear John Wain on the wireless-set on Wednesday?[5] Old FWB[ateson] knocked him into a cocked hat I thought. And how slavish was Robson. Don't be misled by the reviews ("doings of a band of corrupt children") into reading Theodora Keogh's *Street music.*[6] Have you read the new Waugh? It's a tour de force: he's taken all the most snobbish and boring and soft-headed parts out of *Brideshead*, and all the most unfunny and boring and snobbish parts out of *Put out more flags*, and put them all together into one book, and called it *Men at arms.*[7] Pardon this litty chitchat; all I do is read books these days. I sent the NS&N some poems the other day. They sent them back to me, saying that the rejection "must not be taken to imply any reflection upon the merits of the M. S." Now why do they say that? I suppose they print James Kirkup[8]

2. 'Carol Goldsmith', the attractive wife of a colleague of Dixon's in the History Department, not 'Christine Callaghan'.

3. An anagram for 'drain' (as is 'dinar' later in the paragraph).

4. See Amis to Larkin, 18 September 1952 (in Bodleian) for a 'summarised complete synopsis' of 'Dixon and Christine' in which both the 'ocarina septet' and 'London velleities' are mentioned. Peter Racine Fricker (b. 1920), composer: the Bartok/Schoenberg idiom of his chamber music was unlikely to have appealed to Amis or Larkin.

5. Wain, Robson and Bateson appeared on a programme entitled *Private Myth and Public Poem*, which discussed the problem of how much the appreciation of a poem is bound up with a knowledge of the poet's intention (the poet in question was Blake); the discussion was broadcast on 24 September 1952 on the Third Programme.

6. *Street Music* (1952) by Theodora Keogh, romantic novelist.

7. *Men at Arms* (1952) is the first in Evelyn Waugh's trilogy of war novels, *Sword of Honour. Put Out More Flags* (1942) belongs with Waugh's earlier novels – *Vile Bodies* (1930), *A Handful of Dust* (1934) – satirising upper-class life in the 1920s and 1930s.

8. James Kirkup (b.1923), poet, translator, travel writer, playwright.

because to send his poems back *would* be taken to imply, etc. I am becoming the Uncle Giles[9] of the writing game.

Sorry this letter is so flat, but after I finish it I must write one to my parents, and then I must go to the post, and then I must begin looking out my lecture-notes for next week, and then I must mind the children while Hilly goes out, and then I must go to bed unaccompanied by female persons under the age of consent or addicted to unnatural practices. Drop me a wee line when you've "settled in" a hacksaw up your Chaplin – the brave little man winning our hearts with his gallant bum,

Kingsley

[TLS: Bodleian]

TO PHILIP LARKIN – 23 OCTOBER 1952

Swansea

My dear Philip,

God, laddy, this is the perineum of autumn. I am feeling fairly warm at least, with my electric fire on in my little room, and fairly contented writing to my friend; but Christ, cully, there's little else of good cheer to record. My rif sif ridiculous conscientiousness has led me to undertake a course of lectures on the modern novel, and my ridiculous integrity has led me to put in all those cheerless craps between 1900 and 1930 – Ginny Woolf and Dai Lawrence and Morgy Forster (Christ, that must have been an experience. What did he say when you asked him why

9. A recurring comic character in Anthony Powell's *A Dance to the Music of Time*, the narrator Nicholas Jenkins's hapless uncle. By the date of this letter only the first two volumes of the sequence had appeared, and Uncle Giles was marked less by haplessness than by a habit of condemnation, what in *A Buyer's Market* (1952) is called his 'unhesitating contempt for all human conduct but his own' (p. 103).

he didn't bring out his novel and be damned to everyone because nobody minds sodomy these days?[1]) and Windy Lewis – especially him – instead of getting on with the chaps I really go for, you know old Grahame Green and Henry Greene and Christopher Sherwood and Evelyn Hoare and so on. In fact I must stop this ne pe *now* because I want to have a shit before leaving for carledge; or rather a shit wants me to have it, if you can just get that distinction clear in your mind for a mewment. Why isn't this ribbon spooling properly, either? Why isn't it doing that? PPFN.

no the b I mean

Back now, as the a. [A] Feeling rather worse; an obscure but harmful chemical reaction has been set up in the interior of my head: I have a cold. Smoking either makes it worse, or makes it better, or leaves it substantially as it was; I keep smoking to try to see which. And this is bad because I am still on 6–7 a day which has saved me by now I reckon £10 *circiter*.[2] I haven't *got* £10 of course – now why's that? I have however a new pair of shoes, which are beginning to curl up ludicrously at the ends like Turkish slippers because there's about 3" of shoe at the front with no toe in it. [. . .]

Yes, if you are really interested in knowing, I *am* writing a Cornoation ode.[3] If I can't get into the literary racket by the back way I'll do it by the front. Ole RBM comes here on Nov. 3 or so to discuss it and make me spend too much money. I expect we'll have a serious talk about you. Any points you want me to bring up?

Do you know who I hate? I hate T.S. Eliot. That's who I hate.

The new programme by Peter Ustinov and Peter Jones[4] deserves comparison in its wit with the best French bum,

Kingsley

I now notice that you say you sent me a *copy* of a letter you had recently.

1. Neither Motion, *Life*, nor *LL* mentions this encounter. Forster's *Maurice* was written in 1913 and circulated privately (it was published posthumously in 1971).

2. Approximately (Latin).

3. 'The Century's Crown', a Coronation Ode with words by Amis and music by Bruce Montgomery, was performed by the Glasgow Choral Union and the Scottish National Orchestra on 3 June 1953 in Glasgow.

4. *In All Directions*, a series first broadcast on 26 September 1952, edited (from improvised dialogue) by Frank Muir (1920–97) and Denis Norden (b.1922). Peter Jones (1920–2000), British comic actor, collaborated again with Peter Ustinov (b.1921), actor, dramatist, director, in the film *Romanoff and Juliet* (1961).

Does this mean they sent you 2 copies? Seems an odd thing to do. Does that mean I needn't send it back?
Yes: why doesn't old John [Wain] get out of that tears a reamer thing? And that abababababababababab rhyme scheme? Well will you just tell me now why he doesn't

[TLS: Bodleian]

TO PHILIP LARKIN – 6 NOVEMBER 1952

tweforgrowupswoglam[1]

My dear Philip,

Yes, you're quite right, I have re-begun *The feeling*,[2] and sure 'tis me time it does be takin' up much of entirely. I won't bore you with how it's going, except by saying that we've reached the quarrel scene ('Who's your alienist?' – 'Look here, Dixon, do you want a bloody good punch on the nose). The trouble is there are so many 'threads' (Margaret (she has reverted to Peel, by the way), Welch, Johns, Atkinson, Michie, Caton, Bertrand, Christine, Carol) that the reader will expect someone to be murdered any chapetr fartr chapter bo po now – probably Dixon. I have a man in one of my classes now called Dixon; I love correcting his exercises. Well laddie you shall be the first to see it when it's all done, that I promise you.

Bruce came for a very happy little few days, in which he spent £55 on himself and me, and I spent perhaps £7 on myself and him. He was very good company, except that he still hates criticism; I don't mean just being adversely criticised himself, but he resents the existence of the practice of critical writing. [. . .]

The shades of Christmas are gathering. We have to go to my parents' *and* to him and his wife. But tell me more about 21 Dec. as we may have to be on the move by Dec 22. That reminds me that he was here recently – hope I didn't tell you, but it's so long since I wrote . . . ('Don't tell *me* that.') There was nothing to touch the moment the time

1. That is, 24 The Grove, Uplands, Swansea, Glamorgan.

2. 'The Man of Feeling', a second title for 'Dixon and Christine'. See Amis to Larkin, 11 August 1952.

beof peof before when he explained to me how well-known the Swiss were for watchmaking. There was the usual kind of thing, though: Enter Hilly after an afternoon's riding (that was the day they came, by the way, so that I had *three hours of minding the kids* and then TWO HOURS OF GETTING THE TEA AND MINDING THE KIDS AND TALKING TO HIM AND HIS WIFE) looking very pink in the face because of the afternoon's riding. I remark casually, 'Well, she looks as if she's had a good time, doesn't she?' to which he replied, with the air of one cutting through layers of obscurantism to put his finger on the truth at last: 'Ah, it's all that fresh air and exercise, you see.' As a matter of fact, it was his visit that made me get on with *Feeling* at last. Over the sound of his certifiable baaing to the children my typewriter tapped out sternly 'They made a silly mistake, though . . .' and the artist had once more found the point of release for his trauma. Miggy was here too recently, and still laughs at least once while pronouncing every sentence.[3] She filled in a lot of good background stuff about old Rodge, none of it coherent enough to transcribe except that he has one suit and two pairs of washable jeans. That's all. I mean no more outer garments at all. [. . .]

To Thomas's poems we can apply no other word than bum,

Kingsley

[TLS: Bodleian]

TO ROBERT CONQUEST – 9 NOVEMBER 1952

Dept of English, University College, Swansea, S. Wales

Dear Conquest,

Thanks very much for your letter. Actually I have dropped a minor brick over the Palmer thing; it seems that they might have pronounced mean mane, in fact probably did[1] – but the awful neurotic write-to-the-

3. For Margaret ('Miggy') Bardwell Partington, Hilly's older sister, see Amis to Larkin, 15 July 1946, note 7.

---

1. In a letter to the *Listener*, 6 November 1952, p.771, Amis defends Conquest's poetry against 'a pedantic/illiterate swipe' (*Memoirs*, p.140) from Herbert Palmer (1880–1961), the poet and literary critic. Amis belittles Palmer for rigidly applying 'technical laws' (of his own devising) when judging poems, in particular laws governing 'when assonance puts "melody"

papers fit was on me and I sent it off without consulting the man here who knows all that; you flatter me if you think *I* do. Still, old H.P. isn't the sort to catch me out on a point like that. I thought your examples were fine and the line itself (and the poem) good.

Here's *Wrong words*, in what I like to think is an improved version.[2] Yes, I know old F.W.B. wouldn't mind it being reprinted. Thanks for taking it.

Yes, I met Mrs Jones[3] some time ago, but I don't think she liked me much; however, I'll pass on your regards at the next opportunity. Let me send mine to your wife.[4] I'll certainly look out for you in London.

Yours,
Kingsley Amis

[TLS: Recipient]

TO HILARY RUBINSTEIN – 8 DECEMBER 1952

University College, Swansea, S. Wales

Dear Hilary Rubinstein,

Yes, of course I remember you, and it was very pleasant to get your letter.[1]

I shall be very glad to send you my novel when the time comes. It would never make an author's or a publisher's fortune, but I think it is quite funny; that, at any rate, is its aim. Still, it's not much use going on about it; I'm on the final draft now and should be able to get it to

into poetry and when it takes it out'. Amis cites several supposed exceptions to these laws, drawn from *The Faerie Queene* by Edmund Spenser (1552–99), a poet 'I am sure Mr Palmer would agree, is celebrated for "melody".' The first, unfortunately, is the questionable 'Me, all too meane, the sacred Muse areeds' (Book 1, line 7).

2. Conquest wanted 'Wrong Words' for the PEN Club anthology *New Poems 1953*, which he was co-editing. He had seen it in *Essays in Criticism* 2:2 (April 1952), p.158.

3. The wife of the Welsh composer Daniel Jones (see Amis to Larkin, 1 January 1950, note 9).

4. Tatiana, Conquest's first wife, a Bulgarian.

---

1. Rubinstein (see Notes on Recipients), who had known Amis slightly at Oxford, had seen the biographical note Amis had written about himself in the PEN *New Poems 1952* volume. In this note Amis said he was at work on a novel, and Rubinstein, who was working at Gollancz, had asked to see it.

you in February or March. Thank you for the invitation to send it.

If you see Peter Weitzman these days, do remember me to him and tell him I hope he hasn't stopped writing poetry.[2]

All good wishes –
Yours sincerely,
Kingsley Amis

[TLS: Gollancz]

TO PHILIP LARKIN – 9 DECEMBER 1952

Swansea

My dear Philip,

[. . .] I have my Condon book[1] back now, and the impulse thus generated has made me assemble my 'vital books' on a shelf of my bookcase. It consists (if you care) of volumes of poetry by W.H. Auden, John Betjeman, Lawrence Durrell, piss John Donne,[2] Andrew Marvell, Alfred, Baron Tennyson, William Wordsworth, W.B. Yeats and piss Robert Graves; works of fiction by John Dickson Carr, Cyril Connolly, Graham Greene, Julian Hall, Christopher Isherwood, James Joyce, Henri de Montherlant, Flann O'Brien, Anthony Powell; and works of general interest by Cyril Connolly, William Empson (add piss William Empson to the list of poetry), Graham Greene, Arthur Hutchings (*A companion to Mozart's pianoforte concertos*),[3] piss Robert Graves, Q.D. Leavis, W. Somerset Maugham and Stephen Potter (NOT FARCKING GAMES-MANSHIT ETC but *The muse in chains*).[4] *The north ship* will be added if I ever get hold of another copy, *Jill* and *A girl in winter* when I get them back from loan. Piss Alexander Pope should be added to the

2. Peter Weitzman (b.1926) was at Cheltenham School with Rubinstein, then went up to Christ Church, Oxford; he was called to the Bar in 1952, became a QC in 1973, and Recorder of the Crown Court in 1974. He won the Newdigate Prize at Oxford but stopped writing poetry 'long ago' (personal communication).

---

1. Presumably *We Called it Music: A Generation of Jazz* (1947), with T. Segrue.

2. 'Piss' because out of alphabetical sequence.

3. *A Companion to Mozart's Pianoforte Concertos* (1947) by Arthur Hutchings (1906–89), Professor of Music, University of Durham (1947–68), University of Exeter (1968–71).

4. *The Muse in Chains, A Study in Education* (1937) by Stephen Potter (1900–69), author and broadcaster; *Gamesmanship* was published in 1947. *The Muse in Chains* was a history of, and partly an attack on, the academic study of English literature; many of its ideas are in tune with those of Amis.

volumes of poetry. And piss Eddie Condon to the general-interest. There are only three volumes I feel really bad about not having on that shelf: *Old lights for new chancels*,[5] unreturned by some forgotten criminal; *Living*,[6] and *Poems*, by George Herbert. So if you ever see one of those three lying about, buy or steal it and give it to me as a present or I will pay for it if required. Let me say before I leave the topic how much I laughed at 'you vital-book pedlar' in your debat. I got *The old man and the sea*[7] out of Boot's recently, and returned it without reading a word. Too busy for modern tripe, you understand.

Crzmuz is goan' be hairl, son. We leave here on Sunday 21st for my parents' home in Berkhamsted, and leave there again for *Harwell* fartwell whorewell *bore*well ballwell cockwell pisswell fuc on *Christmas Eeve.* Still, you'll probably get quite a good New Year Letter from me on the subject of him and his latest exceeses. We shall be back here on about the 28th so you must 'put in an appearance' here some time between then and when you sail. *Mind you do.* Pity you're sailing on the 3rd; we're having a party here on the 4th, to which Mr Montgomery and Mr Oldham are coming. I think it will cost me a dixaine of pound-notes, on drinks for the guests to drink. But I have had an unexpected £100 rise recently (don't spread it around I shouldn't; it's sort of hole-and-corner, and we don't want Backstair[8] writing to my Prof about it) so that will help wont it. [. . .]

Write soon about Jan. All the beast. Once in royal David's bum,

Kingsley

[TLS: Bodleian]

TO PHILIP LARKIN – 1 JANUARY 1953

Swansea

My dear Philip,

A happy and prosperous new year to you, and the best of luck, old man. I know I've been a carapace-keeper in not writing at Christmas,

5. *Old Lights for New Chancels* (1940) by John Betjeman.
6. *Living* (1929), a novel by Henry Green.
7. *The Old Man and the Sea* (1952) by Ernest Hemingway (1898–1961).
8. F.W. Baxter (see Amis to Larkin, 18 June 1952).

and especially in not sending a Xtmas card, but we left here, after the routine fearful rush, early on the 21st, and after nine and a quarter hours' travelling arrived at the house of my parents. There all sorts of choking nonsense at once supervened, including especially a stomach-ache in my stomach that lasted 48 hours and made me sit all the time pressing a hot-water-bottle between my thighs and my belly. Bad for feeling, that. They all thought it must be appendicitis, but I said it wasn't, but the medico was summoned, but he said it wasn't. He gave me some filthy medicine, compounded of onions, cinnamon and skim milk – one's teeth become dry, brittle and thin the moment it enters the mouth – and fucked off. Present-giving was not long delayed after this: I got 100 cigarettes from my mother, and two pairs of plum-and-white socks from the pater. I've forgotten what I gave them, or what they gave Hilly, or what we all gave the children. No, I'm a liar: *I* gave them a little telephone each, and a little blue railway engine each. Why did I do that? They didn't give me anything. For some reason this reminds me that I have recently received a 'demand' for £9–5–3, in connection, so it is represented, with some plan for the levying of financial contributions to the Treasury; I seem to remember that 'Land Tax' was the term used. Land Tax? Why? My views on the ownership of land are unchanged.

Then, on Christmas Eve, we went over to his place. It wasn't as bad there as might have been, and indeed was, feared. It was his general air, rather than particular points of behaviour, that got me down most; that of being at once an expert on any subject in the 'of-course-you-know' Welch style and a sulky child needing to be conciliated by being given the limelight. His eldest son, William (did you see the sod had something played in the Third Programme earlier this week?), also turned up. His opening remark, after the exchange of the conventional greetings, was to the effect that it had been a great mistake for his father to buy that particular model of gramophone, to which he replied that he'd thought this model looked more like a piece of furniture. William: 'I don't like musical instruments to look like pieces of furniture.' Now, why doesn't he like that? There's no actual *danger of confusion*, is there? And he was also continually agitating and fulminating about his filthy French food, 'not being able' to eat this unless it had that with it, bringing his own rye bread (have you ever had any of this? I am glad to be able to tell you that it *is*, *in fact*, much nastier than ordinary bread, *without having to pretend so*, though I was of course ready to do that if necessary), brewing up his own very thick black coffee – why? He wasn't *trying to keep himself awake*, as far as I could see. I got in one good blow about not liking the tubular flour-and-water food beloved of indigent peasants (though I wasn't able to put it as well as that, naturally. I don't think he noticed, anyway), but was robbed of the chance of getting in the companion about peasants' butter-substitute. But there's a place for both in *Dixon* (p. 150 now). At least, however, William is capable of consecutive thought, even if the prerequisite of this is that the thought must be about himself and then issue in words about himself. His mother and father are the slowest-witted people I've ever met. It was a real joy to see them in the acting game I made them play (you act objects to members of your group – no speech allowed – who guess them and are then allowed to go on to the next object on the organiser's list); ole Mummy B with her hands clasped in concentration as she strove to guess something like a top hat, or him watching with a sour frown as some poor creature tried to convey to him the idea of something like a wrist-watch. There was present-giving, of course: I got 50 cigarettes from her and 20 from an old friend of theirs and 20 from William and 10 from him, who topped up this gift (he got a 30/- pullover from Hilly and me) with a book of the Penguin format, called *Comic and curious verse.*[1] None of it is. I have made up very good words for the Beethoven piano concerto theme that Dixon sings to himself. [. . .]

Happy and prosperous new bum,

K.

[TLS: Bodleian]

TO PHILIP LARKIN – 13 JANUARY 1953

Swansea

My dear Philip,

I'm sorry for this paper, but I get it free, you see, and I want to use the fire downstairs instead of the electric fire in my study, and I don't

1. *The Penguin Book of Comic and Curious Verse* (1952), compiled by John Michael Cohen.

want to go up and fetch the typewriter down. So I'm writing this with the Dettol Biro my father gave me for Christmas as well as the two pairs of socks (and the Dettol penknife and Dettol nail-clipper that I think I told you about as well last time, didn't I?) Hilly is out at the pictures, and I'm guarding the children, you see, which is a thing I sometimes do. She spends a lot of her time on or with her horse these days. One of her friends says he'll teach me to ride in seven daily lessons of 20 minutes each, but I'm not going to let him do that.

[. . .] For God's sake keep on at your story. If I can keep on at mine, you can keep on at yours.[1] I know yours is probably harder to do than mine. I've got a long way with mine, if you want to know. Up to page 185 now. Some bits are boring me terribly, particularly the Margaret/ Veronica bits, I've just done the post-ball reproach scene. She has some hysterics, and Bill Atkinson has to come in to calm her down. The letter to Johns is the only good part of the chapter. It is a threatening letter from the mythical boyfriend of a typist in Johns's office: 'you lay of yuong Marleen' – you know the kind of thing. I quite laugh at it.

I laughed more confidently at what you told me about your joint, no, I don't mean that; I mean jaunt in London. Fancy going to *Porgy & Bess*. Which of you wanted to go to that? Surely Bruce wouldn't suspect anything by that incompetent Yid[2] of being musically interseting, would he? And I can't quite see *you* . . . When *quo vadis*[3] came here, they charged special expensive prices that you had to pay to get it, no, I really mean get in. I didn't go. Those Roman pornographic things are never any good for my money, especially for as much of it as that. I never have any trouble about which prong of the Bruce dilemma to impale myself on: I *can't* pay 'more than I want to spend', I'm reduced to paying *all I have* at the time (*not* 'all I can afford') and *still* being like a *poule de luxe*. The only alternative would be to entertain Bruce on beef-tea and gingernuts, which he wouldn't like. That or selling things. ('Why's

---

1. Amis's 'story' was 'Dixon and Christine', in the process of becoming *Lucky Jim*; Larkin's was the never completed 'A New World Symphony' (see Amis to Larkin, 7 March 1950).

2. George Gershwin (1898–1937), composer and pianist. *Porgy and Bess*, Gershwin's only opera, was first produced in Boston in 1935.

3. *Quo Vadis* (1951), a three-hour Biblical epic directed by Mervyn Le Roy, written by John Lee Mahin, S.N. Behrman and Sonya Levien, and starring Robert Taylor, Deborah Kerr and Peter Ustinov.

Kingsley always moaning about money? He must be pulling in something for his lecturing by now, and Hilly's got an overdraft; hasn't she?') Yes, old man, but you have *no idea* of how expensive it is to *be* married.[4] I give Hilly something over £30 a month, which leaves me *circa* £22 for myself, out of which comes some of the rates (say £2), the electricity (£3–6–8), land tax FORCIBLE INTERFERENCE WITH THE PRIVATE (15/- splitting it into monthly bits as with the others). That leaves me about £16 for *trips*, not-enough cigarettes (£2 instead of £5), some beer, no books

oops

→Oh xt–parents, London (ahhahaha), parents in law WAWA-WAWAWAWA

(though I've ordered *Pity for women*[5]–available now? No?), and everything. Hilly's overdraft expands on the children's clothes, the parts of the rates I can't pay, and the bloody horse – our only luxury. Sorry about this budget stuff, but except for the 6 months or so after Hilly got her money I can't remember having enough money; by modest standards, that is. Think of my £16 as just over 10/- a day. I can always look back to the ARMY, of course. Well you know what you can do about and with that. It's a – a man has just praised *Porgy and Bess* over the wireless-set.

[. . .] This ICA thing[6] will be another way for me to bugger myself financially in quest of publicity for my poetry. I don't know anything about it – just the card from John Wain with both more and less information than you need. I shall be asked to read only 2, I fancy, so shall pick the longest in my locker. Empson will be there – I hope I read just after him (I shan't, of course – the "lice", Wain says, come on after the interval, the big shots before) it might be "useful", I suppose. Fraser[7] will be there too – have you heard from him? I haven't. The treacherous snivelling bastard.

4. In the margin Amis has added: 'And they've no rent to pay, have they? BUM BUM BUM LAND TAX [with 'RATES' and 'REPAIRS' written over it] IMPROVEMENTS furniture'.

5. *Pity for Women* (1937), volume 2 of *Les Jeunes Filles* (1936–39) by Henri de Montherlant, translated by John Rodker; reissued 1950 by Routledge and Kegan Paul.

6. A poetry reading at the Institute for Contemporary Arts in London.

7. G.S. Fraser (1915–80), critic and poet, described by Morrison, *The Movement*, p.46, as 'perhaps the principal poetry reviewer in London'. Fraser had 'New Apocalypse' connections, but also helped to promote the Movement poets. At this period he was editing (with Iain Fletcher) an anthology of young writers entitled *Springtime*, eventually published in April 1953. Amis was anxious to hear if his poems (and Larkin's) were to be included; they

You know what I should like to see? Apart from two corrupt schoolgirls undressing. I should like to see *a bit of life*. Almost *any sort*. Drinking, or sex, or fine talk, especially (I don't know why I should pick *that*) *that*. I don't want to talk about the unemployment at Llanelly, or the next meeting of the Gower Riding Society, or Dylan Thomas, or how many of the Finals class we shall be able to push through, especially *not* that. I want to talk 'bout – well you know, cully, none better. *That's* what I'm *not* talkin' 'bout.

You are hereby advised that the Faculty of arts will be meeting to discuss bum,

Kingsley

[ALS: Bodleian]

TO PHILIP LARKIN – 21 JANUARY 1953

Swansea

My dear Philip,

Glad I was to get your letter this morning; sorry to hear more of AWA.[1] The speediness of this reply is partly a result of hearing that. I don't suppose you much want to hear what I have to say about it, but in the hope of saying more that will interest you than will irritate you, I will say something. You seem quite accurate when you say that the engagement is the direct result of your not pitching into her properly. A girl like that doesn't spend so much time with somebody as far outside her usual orbit as you are without being 'very interested'. I also feel I should say, though it will probably annoy you, that where I think you were 'wrong' (in one sense 'mistaken in self-diagnosis', in another 'ill-advised') is over this 'I'd never have married her' business. One cannot tell so early on whom one is going to marry or not marry, and

were, along with those of forty-eight other contributors, including Wain, Donald Davie, Elizabeth Jennings and Thom Gunn.

1. Winifred Arnott (see Amis to Larkin, 8 September 1952) had recently told Larkin she was engaged (to a man she'd met the previous autumn while on a course in London). When she returned to Belfast she told Larkin, according to Motion, *Life*, p.223, 'that they could not continue in their former, flirtatious ways'.

making up one's mind so early on is the one thing that will ensure one's never getting to the stage where marriage-or-non-marriage is a real dilemma at all. This is not to say that I think Winifred is 'the girl for you' or not; I just don't know about that. Marriage in the abstract, as you've heard me say many a time, either doesn't exist or is sheer unmanning, dumbfounding, nonplussing buggery; but since it's firmly grounded in the whole business of getting along with, or on top of, women, it seems as mistaken to rule it out in the abstract (which is what I think you have really done in this case) as to want to do it in the abstract, which I suppose is what she is doing. I'm not saying you ought to ask her to marry you, you probably wouldn't much like being married to her, but don't hold back because of the spectre-threat of the old berobed word-pronouncer. That is *bad sexual technique*.[2] Having said that, let me say how much I sympathise, how well I know that terrible unexpendable exasperation and grief that overtakes one on these occasions. Anyone would be a fool if he didn't 'mind'; I imagine the minding-a-lot is personal to AWA, the not-minding general to women (the line of thought followed out in the last verse of *Just another woman*)[3]. Let me say finally that I don't think your star has set with her yet, and – as you must have expected me to say – it isn't that the girls Bruce and I meet are different, it's just that we meet them differently. So *pitch into her*, you old cowardy-custard.

I had a good time in London.[4] You'll no doubt have heard by now that you're in the anthology, represented by between four and six poems, which is the maximum anyone is being represented by. My representation is similar. The reading, I found on arrival, was connected with the anthology. I shall have to tell you in person about it; let me just mention that Empson's beard is even longer than that photograph showed, that he smokes with a foot-long holder and that he has a wonderful tall sallow-blonde wife. Bottrall was there, poor old fellow, also Charles Madge; I wanted to get hold of him to talk about you, but

2. Amis has drawn a line down the left margin at this point and added in pen: 'Holding back for *any reason* is equally bad sexual technique.'

3. A song recorded in 1940 by the trumpeter and singer Hot Lips Page (1908–54), with words by Leonard Feather (1914–94), English writer, composer and arranger. The last verse reads: 'If you get a woman and she leaves you on the shelf/Don't let it drag you just say to yourself/She was just another woman, just another woman/And they'll always be the same, as long as the world goes round.'

4. At the poetry reading at the ICA; the 'anthology' Amis goes on to mention is *Springtime* (1953), edited by G.S. Fraser and Iain Fletcher and published by Peter Owen.

he buggered off as soon as the meeting was over. I thought his poems showed up very well, and he read them nicely, too.[5] The hate of the evening was Janet Adam Smith (poetry editor of the NS&N, which explains why they never print our stuff, and widow of Michael Roberts,[6] poor sod); she was one of those people who inspire instant disbelief and disagreement – one of the few people whose liking for Wilfred Owen, say, would be a really important item in any possible adverse criticism of W.O. The laugh of the evening was Peter Owen, the publisher,[7] who read poems by a chap called Frederick Ferrari[8] or some such name and one or two others. He read them head down, coughing all the time and going straight into commentary after each one. 'And who could ever hope to plumb The gh-gh of ergh shining bum woogh-oogh-oogh-oogh Or ahem the abstract kiss of hate Nor ergh-ergh-oh-ergh on the brothel gate and now I want to give an example of Mr. Furckle's translations of Mallermay.' [. . .] Fraser was a funny little man like a fat school captain appointed for getting the best scholarship of his year. His wife told him he wasn't to go to Bottrall's party after the show. He told the audience that John's and my poetry was based on a 'back to the '30s' movement. That made both of us stare; then he called John a disciple of Empson, which made John stare. Don't worry by the way about Owen as a publisher; he can't go bankrupt before the book [*Springtime*] comes out, because it's his first book, and as you can see by his letter he knows it'll lose money (not that we care about that as long as it comes out, eh?); further, he has the name of being good at book production – you know, type and margins and things – though how he can have acquired this name at this stage is I agree obscure. At the end of the evening one of his – well, I suppose 'girls' is the shortest

5. To the left of this paragraph, Amis has handwritten: 'A woman called Margaret Crossland read her stuff; it was *terribly bad*. A chap called Bernard Benghazi or some such name on the other hand was good, I thought.' Margaret Crosland is a writer and translator as well as a poet; Bernard Bergonzi (b.1929), poet and critic, was Professor of English, University of Warwick (1971–92).

6. Janet Adam Smith (1905–99), author and journalist; Literary Editor, *New Statesman and Nation* (1952–60). Michael Roberts (1902–48), poet and anthologist, editor of *New Signatures* (1932) and *New Country* (1933), which contained poems by Auden, Spender, Empson and Day-Lewis, also editor of *The Faber Book of Modern Poetry* (1936) and *The Faber Book of Comic Verse* (1942). Among his own collections are *Poems* (1936) and *Orion Marches* (1939).

7. Peter Owen (b.1927).

8. Michael Harari (b.1927), published poems in *Springtime* (1953) and various periodicals, also translated Pasternak's poems (1960).

description read, *terribly badly* of course, though *nothing like* as badly as Owen had read poor old Ferrari's stuff, some of her stuff, which was *terribly bad*, though short – I mean each one was short (AND ABOUT MMAAGGIICC, if you ever heard such BAWLS), but she made up for that by reading about 80 of them. Earlier, Tom Scott,[9] who I think I've heard of, read some pawms in th' Lawland Scawttush dialect, including a sonnet of Bohdlair done into the filthy gutturalese. Now, if I were translating a sonnet of his (NOT THAT I EVER SHOULD, you understand) I should feel I'd got to translate it *into another sonnet*, wouldn't you? I mean I should feel I'd made a nonsense of it if my version were longer than the original, wouldn't you? He didn't. Oh, no. No. His version was 56 lines long; I counted them, because I *knew* he'd run over the mark. 56 lines. LVI lines. Exactly 4 times as long as the original, you see. Ooh, and I nearly forgot; he also did that *little-known* poem of Veeyong's; you know, 'May zoo song lay nayzher dongtong',[10] which he rendered – get ready for this – as oh Christ 'But whaur are the snaws lang syne' ASSERWAY TOM NACKER THAT FUCKIN JOCK KIC

I'll see about Easter. I'll try, but I have to fit my parents in, also John Wain (who was coming in the summer originally). I agree with you and Patsy about university wives, but I doubt the firmness of any pinnacle she might consider herself to be looking down on them from. And why doesn't she try not going? Tell me about your story; shall I revise it for you OOO AAA EEE U I've just done a good bit where Welch tries to get into a revolving door the wrong way round. You shall see it, but I can't send it to you while there's only one copy.

Mr. Empson is of course celebrated for criticism as well as bum[11]

Kingsley

[TLS: Bodleian]

9. Tom Scott (b.1918), Scots poet; see Amis to Larkin, 11 August 1954, note 4.

10. François Villon (1431–c.1463), pre-eminent poet of medieval France. 'Mais où sont les neiges d'antan' is the refrain to 'Ballade des dames du temps jadis', in *Le Testament.*

11. MS addition: 'PS: I got 2 pairs of socks as well as the Dettol engines. *Read* my letters. Eh?'

TO PHILIP LARKIN – 3 MARCH 1953

Swansea

My dear Philip,

Smoking, with no obvious emotion either way, my 17/6 Peterson pipe (with saliva chamber), the back of my nose choked with the catarrh of a 4-week-old cold, I sit to cover a page with words. I'm sorry the words have been so long in covering the page; as you know, I enjoy writing to you all right, but my laziness in combination with things like working ob nob Dixon prickson on *Dixon* and setting exam. papers have deferred that pleasure till now. Dixon is up to p. 95 of the final, to-send-off version now. It wouldn't be any use giving it to you to look at again, except for your entertainment, because the bloody thing will just cease to exist if it gets any more structural tinkering. What I will do, if the occasion arises, is to get you to go through the MS saying what you think isn't funny, so that such bits can be cut out and not annoy the reading public. If the occasion doesn't arise, i.e. if no bugger will have it, then I'll present you with both versions and you can wipe your arse on them for all I care.

To tell you a little more about it: things that I think you will like are: the madrigal-singing, the Welch tune ('you *bloody* old fool'), the phone-interview with Dixon as the reporter, the Johns letter, Bill Atkinson, Welch and the revolving door, the Principal, and the faces. I think too there's less HS of A[1] in the Christine scenes, and I'm pretty sure that there are none of those Bing-Crosby conversations you rightly condemned in the previous version. May I say again how helpful those comments in the margin of the old MS were? I've called it *Lucky Jim* now, to emphasise the luck theme – epigraph Oh, lucky Jim, How I envy him *bis*. Bertrand is as *à la* Tosswill as you could stand now, I hope. I'm afraid you are very much the ideal reader of the thing and chaps like you don't grow on trees, course not.

As regards me coming over to see you, I should like to do that but it will be too hard to do, I fear. I have £13 to last the next 4 weeks, having had circa £36 taken off me in bills (rates bum, land tax bum, electricity bum, radiogram repair bum, present for Hilly bum) in the

1. Horrible Smell of Arse.

last 2 months, despite the rise I've had. Further, there are things like my parents' visit and the potential arrival of Wain, who has been muttering about coming here since last summer. I'm afraid it'll have to be the summer as things are going now. Can't you come here on arrival from N. Ireland? I get my food free here, and so would you.

I don't suppose you want to think about AWA again at this stage, but let me modify my previous diagnosis in the direction of saying that though you may be right about not wanting to marry her, to be so firm on that point is a mistake all round the clock with a girl like what I imagine her to be like. By which I also mean that that isn't to recommend hypocritical unpo po spoken hinting at marriage (marge) as a strategy to win the lady's c—t. Christ; my typing. I just mean that firmness on that point is bad policy *and* too contingent on later developments to be justifiable. You don't ///CONTINGENT/// know where you're going until you're there, in fact. But this is raving, really, and useless as a nostrum. Take it as a genuine interest arising from concern and sympathy. But in some ways I feel it might be a good idea for you to marry her, nasty little toady or not. You could change all that, you know. I'm *right* about girls taking colour from their squires. Our friend Margaret is getting herself confirmed to please her new fiance.[2] She's already swapped from left-wing Labour to right-wing Liberal. Let me tell you, son; *they all do.*

As regards your poem,[3] I like many things about it, especially lines 2–3 and 12–15. The traveller bit comes off all right; I detected the point from the poem before studying your commentary. I find, however, a blurring in the middle bit. I find it unclear. Who exactly is being asked to come and choose wrong? It seems natural, after some bafflement, to take it as the travellers; in which case I'd expect something like 'Land and choose wrong' or 'Go and choose wrong'. If you mean 'the people on shore are being asked to come and choose wrong among the people brought by the ships' then it seems odd to summon them to the boat. I don't feel that 'horny dilemmas' would remind many readers of old pork sword, either, but it would stand as an extension of dilemma-which-has-horns plus 'thorny (problem)'. I think it could all be tidied quite easily, and would be worth doing; you've got a little room to

2. That is, Margaret Ashbury Vakil, engaged to John Aeron-Thomas (1885–1958), an industrialist, director and shareholder of the *South Wales Argus.*

3. 'Arrivals, Departures', dated 24 January 1953 in *LCP*, p. 65; previously published in *Philip Larkin: No. 21. The Fantasy Poets* (1954) and *The Less Deceived.*

explain in the space now occupied by 'Day wears and dies', which I don't much care for anyhow. Apart from this the poem hits the mark well, and a mark worth hitting too.

Talking of poetry, I'm glad to hear Owen has taken 6 of your things; he seems to have taken only 2 of mine, the little bastard. Pushed me out to make room for one of his mistresses, eh? *A dream of fair women* is in, plus that *On staying still* thing.[4] Oh, bugger. I was reading old Wain's poems again the other day; the flaw is diffuseness and slackness, as I see it: 'And Shakespeare was *no more than being* wise In *fitting out* his statement *with* a mask'[5] = Wise Shakespeare masked his statement', eh? Oh, *bugger*. Why didn't Owen . . . ? Oh, BUGGER. I do feel cross about this. I can't seem to write any poetry these days, except Odes on the coronation. oh bugger

Well, old man, 'fraid this isn't the sort of letter that's worth waiting five weeks for, or whatever it is. I seem to have an extraordinary cluster of spots on the back of my neck. I feel exactly as if my next search among my records will reveal *B-H M* broken and *M O B B B*[6] cracked – you know the feeling? Must sign off and get washed for two rather tedious people who are coming to eat our food to-night. Why do they want to do that? They've got plenty of food.

The Tito regime has indisputably equated Catholicism with bum,[7]

Kingsley

[TLS: Bodleian]

TO PHILIP LARKIN – 30 MARCH 1953

Swansea

My dear Philip,

Well, my old bandolero, I have just this moment finished my last task on that Dickson thing, so that it is all ready to send to a lot of

4. Both published in *A Case of Samples* and *CP*, pp. 31 and 39.

5. See 'Eighth Type of Ambiguity', in John Wain, *A Word Carved on a Sill* (1956), pp. 16–17.

6. 'Bald-Headed Mama' and 'Mean Old Bed-bug Blues', both recorded in New York by Billy Banks and His Rhythmakers.

7. Marshal Tito (1892–1980), the Yugoslavian communist leader, was coming to Britain for a state visit on 16 March.

men who don't know a good thing when they see one, and by way of celebration am letting you hear the good news at once. (I mean the good news that I've finished hurting my body by typing, not that Fred Cape or Jack Heinemann is on his way here to exchange a cheque for the typescript.) It comes to 349 pages of quarto, which is about 87,000 words, which is a lot. I've been through the fair copy for the last time, changing 'arod' to 'road' and 'Chrisitine' to 'Christine' and 'gmaarouche' to 'gamarouche'; not really that last one I don't mean, I was just puling your leg; and I have changed 'his Indian beggar face' to 'his Evelyn Waugh face' and, oh, lots of little things like that. The only thing I feel with any certainty about the finsi quinsi finished draft is that it is the finished draft; no, or almost no, bugger is going to make me do anything to it ever again. Everything else you shall judge for yourself. I'm sweating now on John Wain taking an episode for his programme;[1] if he does it will be a great stroke towards getting the thing published, I think. By the way, did you hear him on Wallace Stevens[2] last night? I missed it unfortunately. Do let me have a report on it. Because apart from some bits of *Le monocle de mon oncle* oh go and get *interfered with*, man I think W.S. (not the playwright you fool) is a very bad writer. I can't see how he means all the time, and I have to do that before I think a man is any good, don't you?

[. . .] Jolly good about the John Wain programme isn't it? What are you sending him? My blow-up of Rodgers won't be coming out till July now, sod it. FRL [F.R. Leavis] has a long string of nonsense in the April no. which has pushed it out. OOOOOoooghgh did you see that stack of shit of his in the NS&N? Sit on the sense, eh?[3] So that *no one else can see what it is*, eh? To *cover it with shit*, eh? And boy does he hate himself. I think what I hate most about him is his pride in being an *Irish* writer – gay, dazzling, drunk with words and with something of the bard about him, all rather too swift-moving and wild for a slow English intelligence to cope with; by the time the critic has got to him – arrah! sure he's op and away like a flash o' lightnin' on the Connemara hills (why do the Irish imagine they are the only people with a country-

1. *First Readings*, a radio series Wain was presenting on the Third Programme. The series, a sort of literary magazine, was the successor to John Lehmann's *New Soundings*.

2. Wallace Stevens (1879–1955), American poet; 'Le Monocle de mon Oncle' appeared in Stevens' first collection, *Harmonium* (1923).

3. W.R. Rodgers, 'Time to Kill', in *New Statesman*, 21 March 1953, p. 336: 'Nothing pleases me so much, in writing, as to be able to sit on both sides of the sense, and if there were six sides I would sit on them all.'

side? Why do they pretend that lightning in Connemara is any different from it anywhere else? Except that it's *nicer anywhere else* because *anywhere else is nicer*?), ach! you can't hold um, your poower brawken-dohn scholar's brain can't keep op with the word-dance of a *pawerdh*. And, like all the Irish, what a *facetious bore* pretending to be a *wild wit*. I'm only jealous, I know.

I wish I could see you, but I can't afford to come, and the journey is *so terrible*, even to see you. Why don't you come here and see us? You have to come over here now and then, after all, to visit the Peter Duval Smith[4] country and so on, what what what

The Queen wore a veil of black lawn over her bum,

Kingsley

[TLS: Bodleian]

TO HILARY RUBINSTEIN – 15 APRIL 1953

24 The Grove, Uplands, Swansea, Glam.

Dear Hilary Rubinstein,

Here as promised, but a bit behind schedule, is the final typescript of my novel *Lucky Jim*. As you'll see, serio-comedy is the formula really, though if it gets by at all I imagine it'll get by chiefly on the score of the comic angle. Still, that's all up to you. Don't worry, by the way, about its being a libellous account of Swansea or any other university – all the detail about academic life has been carefully [. . .][1]

Best wishes –

Yours sincerely,
Kingsley Amis

[TLS: Gollancz]

4. Peter Duval Smith (b. 1926), South African-born broadcaster and journalist; at the time Producer, Features Department, BBC (1941–56); presumably Amis is referring to Larkin's trips to London for broadcasting purposes.

1. The letter has been ripped and the last word of the sentence (possibly 'invented') cannot be read.

TO HILARY RUBINSTEIN – 16 APRIL 1953

24 The Grove, Uplands, Swansea, Glam.

Dear Hilary Rubinstein,

Further to my MS and letter of yesterday: I now hear from the BBC that they're going to broadcast some of my novel in the 'First Reading' programme on the Third in ten days' time. It'll be a 15-minute affair, about 2000 words. Since I still believe (in the face of much contrary evidence) that acceptance by the BBC is a recommendation rather than the reverse, I pass this information on in the hope that someone at your end shares my belief.

Yours sincerely,
Kingsley Amis

[TLS: Gollancz]

TO PHILIP LARKIN – [16 APRIL 1953]

Swansea, Cymru. My 31st bithrayd.

My dear Philip,

Yesterday my eye fell on a letter from you which began, after the customary salutation: 'Shall be arriving on Saturday 12th April at Swansea (High Street) station at an advertised time of 9.8 p.m.' you old stewing-pan of psperm; the date of the letter was 8 April '52, you old pstewing-pan of sperm. *Too busy doing your bleeding visits* to ALL AND SUNDRY (sun-dry turd) to *COME AND SEE YOUR OLD PALL*, eh? TOO MEAN to pay 30/-, eh? TOO TIRED to make a 4-hour journey, eh? 'Not precisely *dodging* a visit' to my bum. Oh well, I'm sure you'd have come if you could. How was Monica? We only have one dog now, the quietest of the five.

For my bithrayd I got a corduroy jacket from my wife, a book-token from my wife's boy-friend,[1] 100 Gold Leaf from my mother, 25 Balkan Sobranie (Imperial Russian) from my father, and a letter accepting an

1. Unidentified.

episode from *Lucky Jim* from the BBC (Wain Division). Perhaps your hunch is going to be right. I've sent the t-s off to Gollancz, suffering a half-hour interruption while packing it up from a female Jehovah's Witness of dwarfish or stunted appearance. She said that things were getting worse all over the world. I said that they'd been doing that, according to contemporary authorities, for 2000 years. Not as worse as they're getting now, she said.

I fucking give you up as far as sex is concerned. Don't you e pe *want* a poke? More impressive, too, to stop beleiving in sex *after* pocking AWA rather than before. I laughed for a very long time about the Osbert, though an annual award is a bit too infrequent for my liking. How do you manage not to stutter when you do your broadcasts?[2] I'll try to listen to your next one, if it doesn't clash with my thing. Very glad to hear that you're going to start a novel.[3] What's it aboooohhooghgoooeeeeghGHGH What was the bum that gave you the horn? Now, do take the trouble to answer a question of mine *for once* and tell me when you write. I find from *Psychiatry To-day*, Penguin, p. 99, that ole WRR suffers from hypomania.[4] Look it up when you next pop into a bookshop; too long to transcribe. Shoot me an

2. Larkin had recently contributed to the BBC radio series *Arts in Ulster*, transmitted only in Northern Ireland (see Larkin to Strang, 3 April 1953, in *LL*, pp. 194–5).

3. It is not clear what happened to this intention to start a novel. Between 1947 and 1953 Larkin worked on two novels (the manuscripts of which are now in BJLH): one concerning a twenty-five-year-old assistant lecturer in English at a provincial university, Augusta Bax, a character modelled on Monica Jones; and 'A New World Symphony', concerning the character Sam Wagstaff, his fiancée Stella, and Sam's father 'Old Sam', who is clearly modelled on Larkin's father Sydney. There is no fragment of a third novel or reference to an attempt at such a novel elsewhere in Larkin's letters, though he does mention in a letter to Patsy Strang, 3 April 1953, in *LL*, p. 195, that he has been looking over the 'Bax' fragment again 'to see what kind of a thing it was', and only on 6 July 1953 declares, 'You know, I *can't* write this book' (*LL*, p. 201) – because of its unflattering depiction of Monica Jones. When, therefore, Larkin tells Amis he is thinking of writing a novel (in the lost letter Amis is here replying to) he may be referring to the 'Bax' fragment, which Larkin is returning to, after having abandoned it at the end of 1949. Thwaite is, I believe, incorrect in identifying the abandoned novel as 'A New World Symphony' (in *LL*, p. 195). Support for this view may be found in Amis to Larkin, 5 May 1953, note 2.

4. It is W.R. Rodgers who fits the description of hypomania offered on p. 99 of *Psychiatry To-day* (Harmondsworth, Middlesex: Penguin, 1952) by David Stafford-Clark. Hypomania is the psychiatric term applied to persons who display in mild form the elation and speeded-up thought and action of mania.

Underword soon. The attached is bttchd attached is to keep my memory fragrant.

Daddy come and fix my Dan Dare[5] badge on my bum,

Kingsley

[TLS: Bodleian]

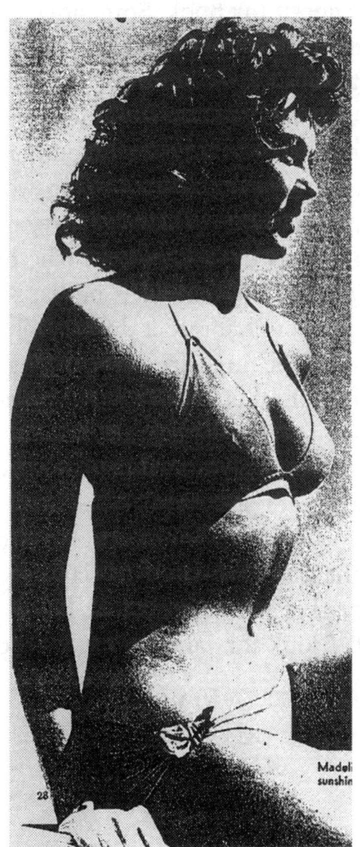

5. The space pilot in the boys' comic *Eagle* (1950–67), a creation of the cartoonist Frank Hampson.

TO HILARY RUBINSTEIN – 28 APRIL 1953

24 The Grove, Uplands, Swansea, Glam.

Dear Hilary,

I was overjoyed to get your letter this morning and read all the nice things you had to say about my book. Somehow, the thought of anyone actually *liking* it came as a great surprise.

About the points you mention: No, I've never even thought of making arrangements about American publication, so please do handle all that for me if the occasion arises. Yes, the manuscript is ready for press as you have it. There *may* be one or two words here and there I should want to alter, but that would be all. As regards the title, I haven't the smallest objection to its being changed. The original title I gave it was simply *Dixon and Christine*, which is perhaps a truer indication of what kind of book it is, though it rather destroys any element of surprise there might conceivably be in Christine turning out to be a major character instead of just another minor one with the function of annoying Dixon. What do you think?

Incidentally, I'm making one of my rare trips to London on Friday, so that – if it becomes necessary – I could perhaps see you on that day, though I'm booked for lunch. I'd want to know soon because we'll be leaving here before the post arrives on Friday.

Anyway, I'm very glad you enjoyed the book, and thank you very much for praising it. I look forward to hearing from you again.

Yours,
Kingsley Amis

[TLS: Gollancz]

TO PHILIP LARKIN – 5 MAY 1953

Swansea

My dear Philip,

Not a proper letter, this ("I CAN SEE THAT"); just a wee note to say that Victor Gollancz Ltd, of Covent Garden, have taken *Lucky Jim* for it to be printed. They think it will be out in November. Good, isn't it? It will be dedicated to you.

I had to laugh at 'regionalist' and at your telegram, particularly Baum. There's some crap in that book,[1] isn't there? I was sorry they didn't print 'If my darling', but they did you proud. Prouder than me. Yes, that's right.

Glad to hear the AWA business has taken a turn for the better. Now's your chance, whacker. Climb down off that fence. Glad about your novel, though I've forgotten (if I ever knew) what 'the Leicester one' was going to be.[2]

Will write properly in a day or two.

I enclose two copies of our standard bum,

Kingsley

[ALS: Bodleian]

TO HILARY RUBINSTEIN – 6 MAY 1953

24 The Grove, Uplands, Swansea

Dear Hilary,

It was very nice seeing you on Friday; we must certainly fix something up when I reappear in London. I enclose your form, though I'm afraid I can't be very helpful. I'm getting a friend of mine who's a quite crafty amateur photographer to do a picture of me.[1] I'll send it on when it's done.

Two small points occur to me:

1. I shall want a dedication; can I send a dedication-page on to you with the snap?

2. I don't know whether your firm makes a practice of putting in

---

1. *Springtime* (London: Peter Owen, 1953), the anthology edited by G.S. Fraser and Iain Fletcher.

2. Since both of Larkin's unfinished novels have unspecified provincial settings it is impossible to determine for certain which is 'the Leicester one', but as Amis was familiar with 'A New World Symphony' (see Amis to Larkin, 7 March 1950), it is likely that Larkin is referring to the 'Bax' novel, which I have argued he took up again in April (see Amis to Larkin, 16 April 1953).

---

1. See Amis to Larkin, 29 June 1953.

the 'all-characters-are-fictitious' formula at the front of their books. If so, it might make my life smoother if something were appended to it in my case, along the lines of

'. . . in particular, the University College depicted, together with its members, must be clearly understood as having no connexion whatever with any such institution in real life.' Perhaps that protests too much, but I should personally like something of the sort to go in, just for the sake of Common Room comfort.

I think that's about all; now just you get cracking with those Yanks.

Yours ever,
Kingsley

[TLS: Gollancz]

TO PHILIP LARKIN – 26 MAY 1953

Swansea

My dear Philip,

This I intend to be a proper letter. For the first time for what seems like some time, I am at leisure: I have sent my revised article[1] to Bateson, all my poems to a fellow called Anthony Hartley[2] (*v. Springtime*) because he asked me to do that and said he might be able to 'place' some of them UP OLD J.S. ELLIOTT'S[3] ANUS, my *First reading* talk to old Jack Wain WHO I PREDICT WILL REJECT IT as 'very good and amusing but not quite suitable for broadcasting' – watch these columns for confirmation – , the penultimate typescript of *Jim* to a reader for the Viking Press MUCH GOOD THATLL DO ME; and the editor of the *Jewish Quarterly* hasn't said yet whether he wants a full-length article from me on 'Anglo-Jewish Literature: A Fourth Provinciality?'[4] Yes, I am mad, I know. No, I'm not a Yidd. Yes, I know. So you can

1. 'Ulster Bull: The Case of W.R. Rodgers'.

2. Anthony Hartley (1925–2000), journalist and editor, had 'vaguely known' Larkin, Amis and Wain at Oxford (Motion, *Life*, p.242); he worked at the *Spectator* from 1953 to 1957, and was a crucial figure in promoting the Movement writers.

3. T.S. Eliot, as in 'D.E. Lawrence' or 'Crippen'.

4. See Amis, 'Anglo-Jewish Literature: The Need for Criticism', *Jewish Quarterly* 1:2 (Summer 1953), pp. 81–2, which compares Welsh and Jewish writers: 'to put it briefly – and put briefly it's apt to sound rather high-handed – a minority audience, Welsh or Jewish, constantly suffers from the temptation to be "provincial".'

see I've been as busy as a little b— at the service of the Muses, and very nice too.

I think I must have lost the letter you sent before your last one; not really *lost*, of course, just put away in some place I cannot for the moment recall. *Springtime*; ah yes, I don't know whether I said anything much about it when I last wrote. I.R. Orton[5] takes the Osbert, I think, for her poet's journal thing. How surely (to put it in her own style) she punctures the sad adolescent dream of being in love with a woman poet! That Laforgue thing[6] was all right, I suppose, in its Montherlantish way. Did he write a novel, do you know? But all these Frenchmen; even their humour dribbles away in their incessant ô grand (grande?) mystère ô crépuscule mystérieuse (mystérieux?) tone of voice; they seem incapable of noting anything *straight*; it's got to illustrate their mood all the time. Never mind, though. What do you think of old A. Alvarez, as poet and critic (did you hear the 2nd 1st reading? That chap Hilary Corke wants to do a bit of reading, doesn't he?)?[7]

I feel a bit let down now that *Jim* is finished and accepted. In a way it makes me want to *stop writing*, like a man who's satisfied with one seduction because he's proved he can do it and wanted reassurance, not pleasure. Don't take that too seriously, though. No doubt I shall be fudging something up by the end of the summer, about a Welsh provincial university or something. What do you do when you run out of backgrounds? I've done Berkhamsted and carledge life, I won't do Oxford, the Ormy is more or less out of the question – I didn't do any fighting and I've forgotten what I did do – which leaves only bourgeois life in Swansea, and that's really *too boring* to do. Thank you for all the nice things you say about my promised dedication. In return let me say that what I'm most looking forward to about the actual publication is you reading it, preferably in my presence, though I don't see how we could manage that. Let me say now, with reference to that, that I shall be fucking furious if you elect to spend all your time on the mainland this summer in the company of those you see every day in

5. I.R. Orton (b.1925), poet, contributed two pieces to *Springtime*: 'Unwashed Hands' (a poem) and 'Pages from a Poet's Journal' (prose).

6. By Margaret Crosland, in *Springtime*, pp.111–14.

7. A. Alvarez (b.1929), poet and critic, though later hostile to the Movement, was at this point much influenced by Empson; in his contribution to the programme he called for 'a revival in poetry of what Donne called "masculine persuasive force" and intellectual objectivity' (quoted in Morrison, *The Movement*, p. 45); Hilary Corke (b.1921), poet, translator, mineralogist.

Ireland, as at Easter time you remember, and shall expect you to come down here for a few days, even if you have to bring A.W.A. with you. So be warned. I laughed a lot at the Terrible Tang of Gurd.

No, my wife's boy-friend isn't anyone you know. He has very nearly stopped being it now. They don't seem to last long with Hilly. By the way, keep your old mouth buttoned about this if you will; not that it really matters, I suppose. I got *What's Become of Waring*[8] with that book-token, though I may have told you that. FV VD FAVTAD[9] remains the best of AP for my money. Ooh – have you seen *Love Among the Ruins*?[10] Crystal my tea. I think it ought to be banned as stupid, pointlessly nasty, horrible writing. My consolation is in thinking how terribly miserable he must be, and how soon he'll go mad. Certifiably mad, I mean. What's it a satire *on*, I should like to know? I shouldn't really, of course. He crams *more things I hate* into those 20 pp or so (is that all they're selling for six ba-arb?) than I should have believed possible.

By God, Reveille's[11] the salvation of men of every nation: did you see that little piece on last week's cover? Roberta Haynes or some such name. I greet it as a splendid example of the new loss toss loose-bra fashion quite apart from the pure and abstract melancholy and joy it evoked in me. Talking of *that side of things*, things are fairly well within control these days on the sphere-of-practical-action front. The rare sight of a young girl in the company of a pretty young woman (there was one such pair at the pictures yesterday) fills me with a fierce desire to write a long pornographic-romantic novel about a summer holiday or some such caper. But it passes. You too? No? At one point in the programme the young woman slid her arm amiably round the young girl's shoulders. A smouldering vision of the slightly-concave insides of thin young thighs slightly moist shook me with a brief fever. Mais tout passe, mon bon, tout passe.

Life seems fairly all right at the moment. Summer extends her hot and swiping paw over the Gower coast (vErnon waTkins breath smels) and only the exams remain to be fiddled; the unspeakable in judgment over the unteachable. I hope you enjoy your trip to Glesga. Tell ole RBM[12] I

8. *What Became of Waring* (1939) by Anthony Powell.
9. *From a View to a Death* (1933).
10. *Love Among the Ruins* (1952) by Evelyn Waugh.
11. *Reveille*, a men's magazine (1940–79).
12. Bruce Montgomery.

was sorry I couldn't come; only money, and the thought of travelling in Coronation week, prevent me. I rejoice to hear that your novel is going ahead. Don't let it get too serious, now: *plenty of jokes* is the rule. Do drop me a line soonish (Cries: 'Ta!' Coos: 'Taw king!'); I'll try to send a line or two in the intervals of marking. I got *Take easy*[13] out again the other evening and thought it pretty damn good. The first chorus, and the Allen solo to a lesser extent, are taking fire for me now. But those stop-chords impede the close.

There will be no TV close-up of the Queen at the moment of bum[14]

Kingsley

[TLS: Bodleian]

TO PHILIP LARKIN – 9 JUNE 1953

24 The Grove, Uplands, Swansea

My dear Philip,

[. . .] The proof of *Lucky Jim* has come, which was quick of them. I have already read it through, with mounting admiration. Some parts look better in print. There are some parts that look worse too. It's already occurred to me several times to send it to you to read, but unless you object I propose to wait until I can send you a real copy. There is a nice page in the proof with nothing on the back of it and just DEDICATION on the front of it. I shall have to think of something to fill it up with, shan't I? For the first time I feel I have written a book, though I am already remembering and seeing the point of that remark of yours, a long time ago now, about feeling 'embarrassed and only slightly interested' at the idea of your first novel coming out. At the moment the look of the epigraph strikes me as as funny as anything in the text.

Do drop me a line when time allows. I suppose AWA is voyaging through strange seas of thought alone[1] by now. How is the Rilke-reading

13. 'Take it Slow and Easy', recorded in New York in 1932 by Billy Banks and His Rhythmakers. 'Allen' is Henry Allen Jr.

14. The coronation of Elizabeth II took place on 2 June 1953 at Westminster Abbey.

---

1. See Wordsworth, *The Prelude* (1850), on the bust of Newton in the Trinity College,

household?[2] We are going to have another baby in January. I don't mind this except in so far as it may diminish the amount of what they call French dinner-wine drunk by me.

Syngman Rhee[3] bum,

Kingsley

[TLS: Bodleian]

TO HILARY RUBINSTEIN – 23 JUNE 1953

24 The Grove, Uplands, Swansea.

My dear Hilary,

What a lot of trouble everyone seems to be going to over LUCKY JIM! Most flattering, I assure you. Here are the answers to your points:

1. John Wain. I haven't seen him since we talked about him, but hope to do so in a couple of weeks' time. I'll certainly see what he says and let you know.

2. Afraid I never had anything to do with old Bowra.[1]

3. I'll be sending the proofs back before the end of the week; a friend of mine is giving them a last look-through.

4. Photograph. The original crafty friend emigrated from here to London recently without taking anything satisfactory of me (there was a good one of me making my pain-in-the-testicles face, but that would hardly do for your purposes, I imagine), and I shall have to find another, craftier friend – I've got one in mind and should produce results in a couple of weeks or so.

5. Libel. Though some of the men may hate me here for ridiculing aspects of college life in general, I'm confident there's nothing *libellous.*

Cambridge chapel: 'The marble index of a mind for ever/Voyaging through strange seas of Thought, alone' (III, 62–3).

2. Colin and Patsy Strang.

3. President of South Korea from 1948 to 1960; a Korean armistice would be signed at Panmunjom on 27 July.

---

1. Maurice Bowra (1898–1971), scholar and critic; Fellow (from 1922) and Warden (from 1938), Wadham College, Oxford; knighted (1951). Rubinstein wondered if Bowra would provide a puff for the book.

To answer your dad's points in detail:[2] The college described in the book has a couple of points in its physical set-up in common with Leicester (to lead people away from Swansea), e.g. the cemetery opposite, but nothing else in common with either college. Everything is quite unlike Swansea, town as well as college. As regards the characters mentioned: Professor Welch is based slightly on my father-in-law (between ourselves) but on nobody in college here, and Johns, in point of name and appearance *only*, resembles a lecturer in music I met once for about 5 minutes in Belfast.[3] Bertrand Welch, Margaret Peel and Carol Goldsmith are as fictitious as any fictional characters ever are, I should imagine. No *incidents* are based on anything that happened here, or anywhere else as far as I know. Apart from the cemetery mentioned not a single place corresponds to reality: there is no such town and city (p. 54) as far as I know, the house (p. 56) is all made up, so is the ballroom, the digs etc. The stuff on p. 173 or so about exam-passing could be taken as referring to Swansea, I suppose, but equally to dozens of other provincial colleges, and I hardly think the Swansea Senate would condemn themselves by corporately prosecuting us. The ex-registrar at this place used to cut off the drink at sherry-parties (beginning of chap. 21), but I imagine the same applies to that. That's really all I can think of. Do fire any further queries at me if you have any.

Well, that seems to be that. Oh, wait a minute: are you sending Gwenda David[4] a proof? There's some business which I can't quite follow about the Viking Press wanting to see my book if Harper's turn it down. At the moment all she has is my rough copy, which is very rough indeed, so I think she'd like a proof. But as I say I don't really understand what's happening at all.

All the best–

Yours ever,
Kingsley

[TLS: Gollancz]

2. H.F. Rubinstein, of the solicitors Rubinstein, Nash and Co., was the libel expert for Gollancz; all the points Amis addresses come from his report on *Lucky Jim* (22 June 1953).

3. Evan John, a music lecturer, lodged with Larkin in Queen's Chambers, a university residence, when Larkin first arrived in Belfast in 1950; Amis met him briefly and borrowed his name for 'Evan Johns', an office worker at Jim's university and his fellow lodger in digs.

4. Gwenda David's long and distinguished career in publishing (she is in her nineties and has numbered Saul Bellow among her authors) has included spells as a scout and reader as well as an editor; she was working at the time at Viking in New York.

TO PHILIP LARKIN – 29 JUNE 1953

24 The Grove, Uplands, Swsa.

My dear Philip,

This won't be very long, but then it isn't my turn yet. Now listen: would you be *very kind* and send me some prints of the Kingsley Amis (The Divine Marquis) and Bill Amis (Priest and Banderilla) photographs? I can't find mine and in any case I wouldn't want to send them away, which is what I should have to do; you see Gollancz want a photo of my face to use in their publicity and I haven't a passable one. Also cd. you send any other photo of me you think might do for the job? Only one of each, of course. I'll reimburse you if required.

I will now pay you back for doing that by giving you a small piece of good news: Bateson is printing Fiction and the Reading Public in the October issue along with my Beowulf and a thing by Donald Davie.[1] If you can remember that far, it was I who got you to send your poem to Bateson. And won't it be nice to be together, dalling, in *E in C*? The Oct. issue will also contain my shelling of Rodgers, so order a copy for all your N.I. litty friends now.

A flithy Jock refused to drink beer out of an E II R mug the other day in my presence. A man of principle; someone else had paid for the beer. He was supposed to be educated. He got his beer too, the treacherous snivelling bastard.

Shall be in Ox. *at the Golden Cross*[2] 6–13 July. Any hope?

Sunburn bum,

Kingsley

[TLS: Bodleian]

1. Larkin's 'Fiction and the Reading Public' (reprinted in *LCP*, p. 34), Amis's 'Beowulf' (from *Bright November*, reprinted in *CP*, p. 18) and Davie's '"Surprised by Joy". Dr Johnson at Ranelagh' appeared together in *Essays in Criticism* 4 (January 1954), pp. 85–6; only 'Ulster Bull: The Case of W. R. Rodgers' appeared in *Essays in Criticism* 3 (October 1953), pp. 470–5. Donald Davie (1922–95), poet and critic, educated at St Catherine's College, Cambridge (BA 1947, PhD 1951), at the time lecturing in English at Dublin University (1950–57) and a Fellow of Trinity College, Dublin (1954–57).

2. A hotel in Cornmarket Street.

TO HILARY RUBINSTEIN – 3 JULY 1953

as from: The Golden Cross Hotel, Cornmarket Street, Oxford.

My dear Hilary,

I am staggered by the ramifications and efficiency of your publicity services. I've long admired old Cooper and should very much like to meet him and Snow.[1] The Hiscock business is a thrill too, whether it comes off or not, though naturally more of a one if it does.[2]

It just so happens that I'm taking my wife to Oxford for a short holiday, starting on Monday, and we shall be there, in easy reach of London, the whole week. It's rather short notice I'm afraid, but could I come up and see you and/or Snow and/or Cooper one day next week? Friday would suit me best, then Thursday (9th), then Tuesday (7th). Perhaps we could have lunch together or something, or drinks in the evening or something. I leave it to you, if you will, to fix up whatever can be fixed up. I could drop in on you at 14 Henrietta Street towards lunchtime, or at any other time come to that. Don't ask me to meet you anywhere hard to find, because I shouldn't be able to find it. I hope to see Wain on the Wednesday, by the way, and will attack him on the question of proofs. While we're on proofs, by the way, send one along (if you've got plenty) to W. John Morgan, 14 Lower Road, Cwmavon, Port Talbot, Glam. I know it sounds very unlikely from the address, but the Morgan fellow, who has some ability, wants to try to adapt the thing for broadcasting, and I suppose we should encourage that kind of thing. If you don't think we should, never mind.

One other point: shouldn't we have an acknowledgment to the BBC about the *First Reading* broadcast? You can tell me about that when I see you, but I thought I'd mention it now while I remembered it.

Hope to see you next week, then.

Yours ever,
Kingsley

[TLS: Gollancz]

1. On 22 June 1953 Rubinstein had sent C.P. Snow (see Notes on Recipients) a copy of *Lucky Jim* in hopes of a puff; William Cooper (Harry Hoff), author of *Scenes from Provincial Life* (1950), got one too. Snow came through with a letter calling *Lucky Jim* 'the best first novel I have read in the last two years' (see jacket to the first edition).

2. Eric Hiscock, a literary journalist on the London *Evening Standard*, was considering making *Lucky Jim* the newspaper's 'Book of the Month' for November.

TO HILARY RUBINSTEIN – 17 JULY 1953

24 The Grove, Uplands, Swansea.

My dear Hilary,

Good to hear from you. My wife hates the photograph so I'll probably be sending another one before long.

Before getting your letter I had written to Curtis Brown and his gang and have joined their clientele.[1] I did this on the advice of John Wain, who has been for some time one of my literary mentors. He insisted on the desirability of agents in general, especially since I have intentions towards non-fiction (which isn't your field). So I jumped in. But I do want to stress the fact that this isn't the result of any dissatisfaction with the way your firm's handling *Lucky Jim*. Quite the contrary: as I've said already, am saying now and will doubtless go on saying in the future, the ramifications of the Gollancz network are entirely gratifying and very acceptable.

My determination *re* 'a new Amis' is gradually crystallising. But I don't want to give away anything about it yet. Very glad about the Snow puff, and that you've written to John Wain. I'm sure he'll prove co-operative.

Yours as ever,
KINGSLEY

PS. Did you see that atrocious write-up of 1st Reading in the New S. & N to-day? It seems a bit hard to be condemned on the strength of two sentences![2]

[TLS: Gollancz]

---

1. In a letter of 16 July 1953 Rubinstein had advised Amis that literary agents were only useful 'in the case of someone like Daphne du Maurier, with requests for film, digest, serial and anthology rights flooding in the whole time' (Gollancz).

2. MS addition; the write-up, by Hugh Massingham, entitled 'Watch and Listen', *New Statesman*, 18 July 1953, p. 72, mocked the pretensions of Wain and the young writers he was promoting: 'Our brave new world is over at last and the old fogies can be led off to the slaughter-house with the usual sacrificial garlands. After that Mr Wain and his fledglings can move in and establish the new dispensation.' In the first programme, just before the reading from *Lucky Jim* (the bed-burning episode), Wain had characterised the new writers he favoured, in implicit contrast to their ('Apocalyptic') elders, as 'suspicious of anything

TO HILARY RUBINSTEIN – 20 JULY 1953

24 The Grove, Uplands, Swansea, Glam.

My dear Hilary,

I'm afraid this is that embarrassing thing, a begging letter. The avarice of Oxford hotel-keepers and publicans has reduced us temporarily to a state approaching beggary. I was wondering if it could be arranged for some of my advance, though I know it isn't actually payable until publication day, to be paid to me now.[1] Something in the region of £25 would tide us over nicely. I've no idea of what your policy is about this kind of thing and I quite realise that the firm may have rules which would render impossible any such advance on an advance. If this is the case, then please feel no hesitation about saying so. But it would be nice if something could be arranged.

I was delighted at the news of John Lehmann's puff. A bit condescending I agree, but that doesn't matter – the long-haired boys ought to queue up for anything recommended by Mr. New-Writing-New-Soundings. Let's hope they do, anyway.

All the best, as ever –
Kingsley

[TLS: Gollancz]

TO PHILIP LARKIN – 27 JULY 1953

24 The Grove, Uplands, Swansea.

My dear Philip,

No; as you will already have assured yourself, this is not a selection of graphic portrayals of female homosexuality among juveniles, nor is

that suggests sprawling or lack of discipline'. The two sentences Massingham objected to were: 'In spite of the ravages wrought by his headache, Dixon felt happier as he wondered what foods would this morning afford concrete proof of the Welches' prosperity', and 'He remembered his father, who until the war had always worn stiff white collars, being reproved by the objurgatory jeweller as excessively "dignant" in demeanour.'

1. The advance was £100, usually not paid until publication. On 24 July, though, Amis was advanced a quarter of this sum.

it the MS of my forthcoming obscene novel.[1] I have a favour to ask. I've got to send John Wain a sheaf of my poems to get turned into one of those little books they do at Reading.[2] Since I'm less confident of my ability to discriminate among my own work than some chaps, I wonder if you'd be good enough to glance through these – you'll have seen a good many of them already – and mark them for me on the basis of, say, alpha=this should go in, beta=could go in, gamma=balls man you're dreaming. I should be glad if you'd also put in any comments 'that seem to you to be relevant', e.g. on the titles, nastinesses ino po otherwise acceptable poems, etc. If you like you could select the volume for me; there are 24 pages available for the text and 34 lines is the maximum on a page. Any suggestions on the order they should go in, pairs of poems that would go well on facing pages, etc. would be very welcome. Finally, what about a title for the sheaf? I've thought of *One-man Charades, A Temperate Zone, A Narrow Vista.* Comments, plizz. Incidentally I'm sending you all my available poems, including a fair number that I hope are good but, etc., in case you can see something in them. Speed, by the way, is a sensual; I have to get the MSS to Reading by Aug: 3, so do get them back to me by Aug: 1 if you can. That leaves . . . Christ, that's Saturday. Just do your best, old man (of course you're probably in Loughborough now I just realise); there's none of us can't do more.[3] I only heard about this this morning or I'd have sent sooner. Thanking you greatly in anticipation. [. . .]

Steve Race's[4] choice is a record by a young negro alto-player who has been attracting much attention by his use of a dirty bum

Kingsley

[TLS: Bodleian]

---

1. In the margin to the left of this sentence Amis has added in pen: 'I don't mean to imply that I'm writing one.'

2. *A Frame of Mind* (1953); this was the second in the series of limited edition poetry booklets published by the University of Reading School of Fine Art (Wain's *Mixed Feelings* (1951) was the first). Professor J.A. Betts of the Fine Art department at Reading organised the series, but Wain advised him about which young poets to publish.

3. Larkin got his comments to Amis in time; see Amis to Larkin, 3 August 1953 (in Bodleian): 'of the 18 poems to be included, you had ticked 14 and questioned 2, which leaves only 2 you didn't mark at all.'

4. Steve Race (b. 1921), popular broadcaster, musician and author.

TO PHILIP LARKIN – [4–7 AUGUST 1953]

Not to be taken out until Aug: 9[1]

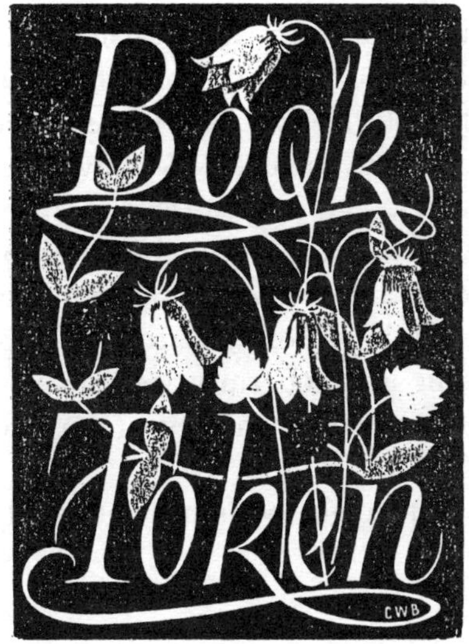

a very bad man
free, open-handed, magnanimous
from MR AMIS
to his friend
MR LARKIN
on his friends bithrayd 9.8.53

Happy birthday. "This is in case I forgot anything." No actually man the bookshop woman pestered me so I couldn't think – not that they had anything anyway. This is merely a retainer: I will send you something commensurate with your services to literature in the last few months when I get the Doubleday money. Does your friend like books about exploring bum

Kingsley

Right hand here only to be presented to the exchanging Bookseller
DESIGN NO. 27
C. W. BACON

Kingsley

[ALS: BJLH]

TO HILARY RUBINSTEIN – 17 AUGUST 1953

24 The Grove, Uplands, Swansea, Glam.

My dear Hilary,

Here comes an abject apology – yes, I *had* heard the news about American publication, and was of course overjoyed, though not overjoyed enough, it appears, to make the simple gesture of writing to say

1. Amis has wrapped this Book Token gift card inside a sheet of paper bearing the handwritten message: 'This sheet is to prevent any *filthy thieving postman* from reading BOOK TOKEN through the envelope and laying his *nasty* hands on same, and then *flogging* it to a friend in the trade.' The Doubleday money referred to on the card is the American advance for *Lucky Jim*, which was $2,500.

so. In other words, one of the two main threads in my character – laziness – had momentarily triumphed over the other – conceit. Do tell Miss Hodges[1] that I repent of this miserable discourtesy, and do believe that nobody could have been gladder to hear the news than I was. Gollancz's Do It Again . . .

The Vogue business[2] is a wonderful coup. I'm busy rehearsing faces already. As things are going now I shan't be in London yet awhile, but I shall be turning up round about the 16th or 17th Sept to deposit a child. Do you think this would be too late to make the November Vogue?

One thing occurs to me, ludicrous though it may sound (and probably is). Do you suppose that Doubleday and Co. would agree to pay part of my advance into the account of a New York Jazz record shop, so that I can import 'rare discs'? If this isn't too crazy, perhaps you could give me Doubledays' address. I wonder when they propose to publish and/or pay up.

Novel No. 2[3] progresses. Slower than might be hoped, but fairly steadily. For the moment, at least . . .

Yours ever,
Kingsley

[TLS: Gollanez]

TO HILARY RUBINSTEIN – 29 AUGUST 1953

24 The Grove, Uplands, Swansea, Glam.

My dear Hilary,

In case you're again wondering whether I've emigrated to Venezuela, I am still here; further, I heartily approve of the arrangements you

1. Sheila Hodges was Assistant Managing Director of Gollancz; she came to the firm in 1936 and wrote its history (*Gollancz: The History of a Publishing House*) in 1978, on the occasion of its fiftieth birthday.

2. Rubinstein had sent a proof of *Lucky Jim* to the Features Editor of *Vogue*, who liked it and promised to include a photograph of the author and a brief write-up in the November issue (Rubinstein to Amis, 14 August 1953, in Gollancz).

3. *That Uncertain Feeling* (1955).

suggest for Sept. 16th.[1] The reason I haven't written to say so before is that I'm still waiting for my mother to say she can pick up the child I propose to bring to London on that day. I don't want to bring him up on the wrong day for my mother, and then have to bring him up again, nor do I want our lunch attended by a four-year-old boy, perfectly charming and so on as that would no doubt be. All I can say for the moment, then, is that I approve – but may have to ask you to wiggle the date about a little. It's most annoying, I know, but until my mum lets me know I'm in the air.

Sorry to hear about the embargo on records:[2] but really it's all for the best, I'm sure. Now I shall be able to spend the money on nice *useful* things like lino and table-mats instead of throwing it down the drain on that dreadful *jazz*. The enclosure,[3] by the way, is not intended to provoke cries of admiring wonder, but is merely for interest's sake. I suppose it'll come out by Christmas, but I'm not sure.

Looking forward to seeing you next month – probably the 16th –

Yours ever,
Kingsley

PS: Most interested in the reviews pamphlet. The best publicity for a publishing firm I have ever heard.

[TLS: Gollancz]

TO HILARY RUBINSTEIN – 13 SEPTEMBER 1953

24 The Grove, Uplands, Swansea.

My dear Hilary,

Yes, all is now fixed for Wednesday: Siriol Hugh Jones came through with the expected letter a few days ago and I've told her I'll present myself ready for the old magic box at 12.0 or a little after (as you know

---

1. For Amis to have his photograph taken for *Vogue* and for lunch with Rubinstein and the *Vogue* Features Editor, Siriol Hugh-Jones.

2. See Amis to Rubinstein, 17 August 1953; the arrangement Amis proposed was impossible for tax reasons.

3. Presumably *A Frame of Mind*.

I have a child to dispose of). She also mentioned the lunch to follow: shall we pick you up at No. 14 or shall we meet somewhere? I'm looking forward to it, you may be sure.

Thanks for the tip about the Doubleday man. I'm dropping him a line to-day asking him if Wednesday afternoon could possibly suit him. If this keeps up I can see myself applying for a helicopter licence.

All the best till Wednesday, then,

Ever yours,
Kingsley

[TLS: Gollancz]

TO PHILIP LARKIN – 17 SEPTEMBER 1953

Swansea

My dear Philip,

Too sweet to get your letter; I read it smiling and laughing a lot. I was very sorry about all the AWA business, but one thing hearing your journal did was point out to me some of the unsatisfactory BITCHY YOU MEAN things about her. Your journey back was a sod all right, but not so much of a one as mine last night from London, dry-mouthed with drinking all day, headache, hot – I asked the man in the compartment if I could put the heat off, and he said yes, and soon after I went out for a piss, and came back to find HED PUT IT ON AGAIN FULL.

I suppse cruppse suppose I'd better tell you about the day. When I'd dumped my little son with his grandparents I went into the Vogue offices and was instantly told Oh no, Miss Hugh Jones isn't here to-day. She *was*, though, she WAS, she appeared WITHIN TWO MINUTES, so *why was I told she wasn't*??? Two men, one of them a battered but charmingly-spoken homosexual, arranged spots and turned them on and off and made me sit in different positions and held sheets of tin-foil under my face and made me look at the camera sometimes but not often and altogether took I suppose 30 photographs while I talked to Miss Hugh Jones, who was very passionate in agreeing with you and said she found 'Lucky Jim' *quite* terrifying. Then we both had lunch with old Rubinstein and lots to drink, then I went and saw John [Wain] and renewed my acquaintance with George Fraser herkherm and saw

Iain Fletcher,[1] a man with huge wrought-iron spectacle frames, for a moment before, unlamented by me, he buggered off. I learnt that my combined English and American advances for my novel come to nearly twice John's[2] – ho ho. John went off on his train to Stoke and flies to Switzerland a week today or yesterday. Then I took Fraser off with me to Doubleday's and we met Pyke Johnson,[3] a sort of humble Lloyd Nolan[4] with three small birthmarks on his cheek. There was a lot of talk, during which J. promised to get in touch with Milt Gabler (a name he clearly knew well – 'Yes I know the Commodore shop')[5] and see if any records can be sent me as part of my royalties. Mrs. Johnson, who is a reader for a firm she called Kernarpf (Knopf to you), told me how badly *The Struggles of Albert Woods*[6] went in the States – Johnson showed me a copy of the American edition and boy is it handsome, sells for $3.50 which I shd; have thought explained why it didn't sell very well. Hoff was full of praise for me when they met him. Nice, isn't it? Nothing of any importance emerged from the chat – why the hell did he ask me there? Cry snows. Then feeling thirsty George and I went off and drank beer and Tony Hartley appeared, an asthma engine sticking out of his pocket, also Gavin Ewart,[7] who smiled and wore a bow tie. Of his appearance I obtained no clear impression. I spent some time pushing you with Fraser and trying in particular to persuade him to put some of XX poems in his monthly New Poetry programme. The issue wasn't decided when I left – his only objection was that your pamphlet came out in 1951 and he's supposed to be selecting from recent books of verse – but I think he was thinking about it. Hartley said rather timorously that he thought you sounded a bit ironical when you wrote

---

1. Iain Fletcher (1920–88), poet, academic and co-editor, with Fraser, of the *Springtime* anthology.

2. For *Hurry on Down* (1953), Wain's first novel.

3. Pyke Johnson, Amis's editor at Doubleday; see Amis to Rubinstein, 1 October 1954, note 2.

4. Lloyd Nolan (1902–85), American stage and screen actor, mostly in low-budget action pictures of the 1930s and early 1940s; best known for supporting roles, as in *A Tree Grows in Brooklyn* (1943).

5. The Commodore record label was established in 1938 by Milt Gabler, who ran the business from his Commodore Music Shop in New York. According to *NGDJ*, p. 240: 'Throughout the label's existence its catalogue contained much Chicago jazz, but recordings in swing styles also figured prominently.'

6. *The Struggles of Albert Woods* (1952) by William Cooper (Harry Hoff).

7. Gavin Ewart (1916–95), poet.

to him and that he was glad to publish your poems in the *Spectator*; I said you were much too simple and direct to be ironical and were glad to have your poems published in the *Spectator*. He also said that they'd like to publish more of your verse and would I ask you to send any post-XX stuff along? I said I would, and I know you'll say you haven't written any, but all yer gotter do is send him a very small sheaf (after they've done your 3) including say *Come and choose wrong*[8] and tell him that C a c W is the best. He'll print it; I KNOW this and don' ask me how. He reminded me that the *Spr* has nothing of mine 'in proof at the moment' and what was I doing about it, ye wch *Expreſsion* dyd Thril mee to ye *Marro* & make mee feele Verilie an *Auctour*. One point I got from John was the name of the next editor of 1st reading: You'll never guess . . . it's . . . LUDOVIC KENNEDY[9] O, L, E, ASS YER OLE YER ARSOLE YER BALD ARSOLE YER EYEBALD ARSOLE YER ARCH EYE BALD ARS

Then sat in the train all the way home holding my head as recounted bucking myself up by thinking of the BBC having rung Gollancz up to ask for my address, and thus anticipating a poem in the last 1st reading. Then this morning get the familiar economy-labelled envelope telling me they want On stang still[10] for . . . LONDON CALLING ASIA SNAKECHARMER OF OLD BANGCOCK STICK *Overseas services* . . . 2/3 of Home rate PALE BUM I LOVE BESIDE[11] Still I suppose it means that somebody personally unacuainted yktw with me likes a pwem of mine, which is nice in a way, tho' not in such a nice way. A successful day, but soading exhausting and considering other people were paying for me nearly all the time rather macabrely expensive.

Didn't we have a lovely week? 'Close' I thought we were. I mean dalling that we seemed to see the point of everything each other said with even less effort than usual. My depression after you went was more prolonged and deeper than usual on such occasions. Life with you

8. 'Arrivals, Departures', written 24 January 1953, and printed in *Fantasy Poets, The Less Deceived* and *LCP*, p. 65; the fifth line reads '*Come and choose wrong*, they cry, *come and choose wrong*.'

9. Ludovic Kennedy (b. 1919), writer and broadcaster; because of the attacks of Massingham (see Amis to Rubinstein, 17 July 1953, note 2) and others, Wain was replaced as editor of *First Readings* after only six programmes.

10. 'On Staying Still', reprinted in *A Case of Samples* and *CP*, p. 39.

11. A burlesque of the first line of 'Pale Hands I Loved Beside the Shalimar', one of the *Love Lyrics from India* (1901) by Laurence Hope (Mrs M.H. Nicolson) (1865–1904), poet. This particular lyric is sometimes sung by P.G. Wodehouse's Bertie Wooster in his bath.

strikes me as what life ought to be like – with its ups and danes, the danes when one feels ill or some crap comes into the room where we're talking together, but in any decent existence the sort of basic minimum on top of which one cd. begin to arrange one's sex, work, going out etc. But that's not so, is it? I'd sooner chat away with you than anyone, except a naked niggling core of teenagers. By the way I don't think I ever quite made it clear quite how bloody funny I thought it was when my real feelings abt. ole WRR suddenly popped out, under the infl. of alcohol and fatigue, in front of old James.[11] Just the sort of poet you'd expect him to have for a friend, eh? I mean if he knew a boxer it'd be Tommy Farr, if he knew a jazz player it'd be Ladnier, if he knew a novelist it'd be Elizabeth Bowen, if he knew a singer it'd be Tauber, if he knew a publisher it'd be Caton.[12] You see the point I'm trying to make emerge, mmha?

Jim may not be out till *January* now. They are waiting for His cock[13] to make his next couple of choices. I suppose I can't really call them sods for this, though I'd like to. By the way did you see that pissing on Cecil Beaton in this month's Lilliput?[14] I told the Vogue camera boys about it and they were jubilant. The homo felt strongly about CB's bowlers.

I suppose you're waiting for term to start so that you can get stuck into some bum,

Kingsley

[TLS: Bodleian]

11. Bartley.

12. Tommy Farr (1914–86), boxer; Tommy Ladnier (1900–39), trumpeter; Richard Tauber (1892–1948), Austrian tenor, naturalised British.

13. See Amis to Rubinstein, 3 July 1953, note 2.

14. *Lilliput*, a popular monthly men's magazine (published 1937–60); the article Amis refers to, 'Let's Pull Ourselves Together this Autumn' (September-October 1953), pp. 98–104, was a feature on men's clothing (a group of 'distinguished' gentleman, including Beaton, had been invited to lunch by the magazine's editors, and the article commented on their outfits).

TO PHILIP LARKIN – 22 SEPTEMBER 1953

Swansea

My dear Philip,

Apologies for answering your letter so soon: you needn't g fg feel bound to continue the process. It's only that 'I feel I must' write and say how much I liked the poem.[1] Various sentiments occur to me. One is that it hit me as hard as any poem of yours I've seen, if not harder. Another is that if you want, as you said, to do something which will cause you to get on, then poems like that ought to do it. Another is that I shouldn't worry too much about your spoken farewell to AWA; the poem is a farwell fartwell farewell neither hypocritical nor ineffectual nor mocking, but on the other hand what you said her farewell was: truthful, accurate and sincere. Perhaps it's my knowledge of the prinip quimit principals that is partly responsible for my being so moved by it, but only perhaps, and only partly. It makes my stuff seem like 'Kensitas – that's good!'[2] rhymes. It has that tight-reined sadness that's your strong suit and which I can't hope to touch. A steady playing of the light of truth. Oh, farks; I feel as if I'd had a letter from you telling me that you have a double-sided 12" studio copy Commodore of a blues featuring Russell, Banks, Fawkes, Christie (tmb), Kaminsky, Bechet, Condon, Bushkin, Foster and Tough[3] which owing to some technical peculiarity cannot be dubbed, a letter from Reading telling me the School of Art has been burnt down, and a letter from Rubinstein telling me *Lucky Jim* will have to be withdrawn because of obscenity.

After that I will subjoin a brief string of comments – do realise that the adverse ones are all small details which a don't much matter b could be put right, or rather altered to suit me, in 5 minutes.

line 3. Why 'matt'? Aren't photographs all glossy? *or am I being thick*[4]?

---

1. 'Lines on a Young Lady's Photograph Album', dated 18 September 1953, and printed in *Fantasy Poets, The Less Deceived* and *LCP*, p. 72; see Motion, *Life*, pp. 233–4, for a biographical reading of the poem.

2. A cigarette advertisement of the time.

3. Previously unidentified, or only partially identified, personnel include Wally Fawkes (b. 1924), British cartoonist (under the pseudonym 'Trog') and clarinettist; Keith Christie (1931–80), English trombonist, brother of the clarinettist Ian Christie; Joe Bushkin (b. 1916), pianist and trumpeter; Pops Foster (1892–1969), double bass player, brother of Willie Foster (1888–1959), violinist, banjoist and guitarist.

4. MS addition; of the following comments, those that occasioned alterations concern lines 26, 30 and 37–8; for further comments see Amis to Larkin, 2 November 1953 (in Bodleian).

8. Goo' sherw.[5]
11. pppppppbbbbbbfffffvvvvvvpppppbbb
19–25. Goo' *sherw.*
21. 'Disinclined' seems a bit close to 'reluctant' (1. 7).
21–22. I think one tends to think, ay 'But' – 'Ah yes, this is the other side of things, the good part', and then one is a bit baffled until one realises that that turn doesn't come until 'what grace'. See what I mean? You could dispose of it by changing 'But' to 'And' and/or changing the comma after 'when it is' to a dash.
26. This lets the side down a bit. I know you can't put 'through too', but 'lived on too' is nasty. *Not* 'there on a day when I was living too', but something *like* it, would do.
30. 'Wring my heart'. Quite safe, but wandering towards the edge. The rest of the line is 100%.
31–33 Goo' sherw.
37–38 I'm conscious of a very slight blurring here. Is it short for '*I* am left to grieve, *you* (are left) balanced etc.', or does grieve= grieve over, mourn for, *you*? I suppose ii rather than i (which would benefit from a ; after consequence) and recommend a change to 'mourn' or something similar. line 44. Whang in the gold, old son, whang in the gold. I hope this niggling won't offend you. As I say, none of it's important. GET A TITLE ON TO IT YOU SLACK SHIT DOUBLE TIME SEH [...]

Rehearsals of *Hamlet*[6] will start with a run-through of the bum

Kingsley

Did I ever say how pleased I was at how pleased you were over L. J.? I was. I value the opinion of none as highly as yours.
The Lilliput verdict on ole CB's clothes was that he'd better look out if he didn't want to turn himself into 'a rich man's Terry-Thomas' (ipsissima verba)

What about the photographs of meee?[7]

[TLS: Bodleian]

5. Good show.
6. Amis was to play Osric in a staff-student production at University College, Swansea.
7. MS addition; 'CB' is Cecil Beaton; Terry-Thomas (1911–90), the gap-toothed comedian of British and American films, played Bertrand, 'the posturing painter and leading shit in the novel' (*Memoirs*, p. 177), in the 1957 film of *Lucky Jim*.

TO JOHN WAIN – 6 NOVEMBER 1953

24 The Grove, Uplands, Swansea, Glam.

My dear John,

Jolly good to hear from you, old lad, especially at such length. Glad you like it where you are;[1] don't think I should, because of the foreigners there. Is it cheap? It'd have to be sodding near free to coax *me* over. Still. I'll answer your queries etc. first, before I start toiling at points of my own.

About this proof business: I'm sorry, but I daren't ask them again; they clearly didn't like it when I got them to send J.D. Scott[2] a copy, and he's in London and so might return it. I know it's annoying, and I'd like you to read it as soon as may be, but . . . You shall have an American copy free. How's that? I'm not merely being funny, by the way: Gollancz specifically said the Scott proof was 'the last in the building'. Liars, but I can't call them that. Gollancz publish in JANUARY, the shits.

My poems: hope you've subscribed, you sod. January is predicted for them too. I shd. get a few reviews, anyway. I'll send you a Fartarsy pamphlet[3] (that'll probably be in Jan too). As regards the next Reading poet, what about old Phil Larkin? I know it's a bit log-rolling to have him, but he's the only man I know who I think readable enough. Or perhaps that chap Philip Pokes[4] or whatever his name was whom I liked in a 1st Reading, though I haven't seen any in print and hence haven't been able to check on his merit. After reading the Fantasy Alvarez I can't recommend him; I can't understand what he says. But as long as you don't pick horrible BOYARSE,[5] you can't go far wrong. I agree about the improvement in his stuff to the extent that I now find it devoid of virtue merely, not, or not quite so much, teeming with vices. It's so *dull*, so totally devoid of anything likely to make the smallest *impression* on one. He has no talent for verse that I've ever detected. I

---

1. Wain was in Vaud, in Switzerland, where he'd gone to recover from TB.
2. Literary Editor, the *Spectator*.
3. *Kingsley Amis: No. 22. The Fantasy Poets* (1954). See Amis to Conquest, 16 April 1954, note 5.
4. Philip Oakes (b. 1928), poet, novelist, critic and journalist.
5. For Arthur Boyars see Amis to Larkin, 15 October 1946, note 3.

agree chokingly about K. Raine [who has stuck] her nose into the NS&N pro-sodomy campaign [. . .] – just wants her NAME IN THE PAPER see. And that's why Davie does so much reviewing, I shd. imagine. No, I've not met him. I liked his book, I must say. I want to get my name in the paper too, of course, and thought I had a review in the *Spectator*, but the bloody rag keeps coming out without my review in it. Now, why is that? Do you really mean you've made a vow not to publish any more poetry for 5 years? Nah; every inch of newsprint we can cover means less for K.R. and her pals; that's the way to look at it. The Oct. *Essays in Crit* is out, but without you in it – for which you shd. consider yourself lucky: it contains an article comparing Chaucer to D.H. Lawrence (I'm not making it up, honest), some padded-cell soliloquy by Wilson Knight, some fearful blinding piss on Wordsworth by Roger Sharrock, etc.[6] The only decent thing is my liquidation of W.R. Rodgers. I know I'm a quixotic fool, but I here undertake to send you a copy of the issue containing your article when it appears; you can pay for it when you come back.

I thoroughly enjoyed *Hurry on Down* and read it whenever I had a free moment till I'd finished it. It is very funny in parts and does succeed above all in getting across a grotesque and twisted view of life (which is what I try to do, though it's not the same view – this I think is where we're similar), which is the main point as far as I'm concerned. I enjoyed the Froulish and Rosa bits best, the twister-abhor and Oxford scenes least.[7] I think a few parts are over-written: my only complaint. Glad to hear about your sales. We'll talk about it some time.

6. The unlikely article in *Essays in Criticism* 3:4 (October 1953) was 'Definition by Comparison: Chaucer, Lawrence and Joyce', by Milton Miller, an American poet, story-writer and academic; G. Wilson Knight (1897–1985), Shakespeare scholar and critic.

7. While looking for a job, Charles Lumley, the hero of *Hurry on Down* (1953), runs into an old college acquaintance, Edwin Froulish, described as something of a 'figure' at university, given to pranks such as 'carrying a grey parrot in a cage wherever he went, wearing a bowler hat indoors, standing motionless for hours on end in the exact centre of the quadrangle, and so forth' (p. 41). Froulish is writing a novel and living off his girlfriend, and Charles stays with them for a short period. The 'Rosa' bit occurs towards the end of the novel, when Charles, working as an orderly in a hospital, goes out to a dance and a fair with Rosa, who is on the hospital staff. 'Twister-abhor' refers to the penultimate line of William Empson's poem 'The Beautiful Train' (*Collected Poems* (London: Chatto and Windus, 1955), p. 64): 'And I a twister love what I abhor.' While considering what to do with the rest of his life, Charles plays with the line: 'And I a lover twist what I abhor . . . and twister I, abhorring what I love . . . And I a whore, abtwisting what I love' (pp. 30–1). Later in the novel Charles and his girlfriend Veronica drive to Oxford for the day (p. 127), where they meet a young don of Charles's acquaintance, go punting, and make love.

Not having my finger very near the pulse of any sort of life I can't tell you much of interest about the way things are shaping here in the Old Country. George Scott, as you may have seen or heard, gave the boys a write-up in a reply to Spender's reply to his attack on *Encounter*.[8] In a list of 28 white hopes of English letters were featured you, of course, me, of course, Al, Philip L, Mairi, Wallace (why him?), Don Davie, Lizzie Jennings, Gunn, George F, and on the debit side Arthur, James Firkup, Hilary Corke. It was a full page in *Truth*,[9] of all rags. Love-a-prick Kennedy is as bad as you might expect:[10] one can't be more devastating than that. I suppose you get the NS there; if not, Salter[11] ballocked him in this week's, said he was as 'infuriating' as you, but in a different way. FWB[ateson] gives Davie a preposterous write-up for his *Diction* book[12] in the new *E in C* – 'as good as Empson' etc. I think it's good, but there are limits. *Encounter* has been mauled on every side. It's a pity you're away; with you as general, the boys could move right into control. It occurs to me to try an old gag – more for my amusement than yours, I imagine:

JACK WAIN AND THE PROVINCIAL ALL-STARS

Wain (tpt, voc) directing Phil Larkin (clt), 'King' Amis (tmb), Don Davie (alto), Al Alvarez (pno), Tommy Gunn (gtr), George

8. George Scott (1925–88), poet, author, educator, documentary film-maker, journalist, originally attacked both *Encounter*, edited by Stephen Spender, and the *London Magazine*, edited by John Lehmann, in 'The Challenges that Face Mr Lehmann and Mr Spender', *Truth*, 16 October 1953, p. 1277, accusing them of ignoring a new renaissance of English writers. Spender replied in a letter to *Truth*, 23 October 1953, pp.1309–10, asking Scott to name some of these writers, which Scott did in *Truth*, 30 October 1953, p. 1335.

9. Scott's list in *Truth* is introduced as follows: 'Here then are the people on whose present and future work I base my belief in a new renaissance: A. Alvarez, Kingsley Amis, Arthur Boyars, Charles Causley, Hugo Charteris, Hilary Corke, Donald Davie, Iain Fletcher, G.S. Fraser, W.S. Graham, Thom Gunn, Thomas Hinde, Elizabeth Jennings, Iain Scott-Kilvert, Francis King, James Kirkup, Philip Larkin, Derek Lindsay, Mairi MacInnes, Jean Morris, John Raymond, W.W. Robson, Paul Scott, Richard Sleight, Sydney Goodsir Smith, Desmond Stewart, Frank Tuohy, John Wain.'

10. Ludovic Kennedy had replaced Wain on *First Readings*. See Amis to Larkin, 17 September 1953, note 9.

11. William Salter (probably a pseudonym) wrote the *New Statesman* radio and television column 'Look and Listen'.

12. *Purity of Diction in English Verse* (1952), an important anti-Romantic critical study, later described by Davie as something of a Movement 'manifesto' (in the book's 1966 postscript).

'Pops' Fraser (bs), Wally Robson (ds).

Drop me off at Reading/Up the country
Lay your racket/Things ain't what they used to be
It's the talk of the town/How'm I doing hey, hey

Let me know how you get on, and keep me posted about your address. How's the book going? Mine progresses slowly. Hilly sends her love and so do I.

Ever,
Kingsley

[TLS: Edinburgh]

TO HILARY RUBINSTEIN – 6 NOVEMBER 1953

24 The Grove, Uplands, Swansea, Glam.

My dear Hilary,

Good to hear from you: the Catania (Sicily) billet-doux[1] was excellent for a laugh, but of no practical good since the Reading people aren't publishing me till January. Nor are the Gollancz people, I notice. Oh well, no doubt you know best. As long as I get published SOME DAY, and GET PAID too, that's all right.

I don't know whether I'm more avaricious than most of your authors, but recently I've found my mind turning more and more often to the question of money – the Doubleday kind in particular. I gather that they pay you, you take your cut, and then you pay me. Is that right? If it is, how far have we got along the road? If it isn't, what is? I'm sorry to sound *grasping*, but there it is.

Hey, that was a most baffling letter you wrote me some weeks ago,

---

1. The precise nature of this *billet-doux* is unknown, but see Amis to Larkin, 2 November 1953 (in Bodleian): 'On my return there were 2 letters . . . One was from Rubinstein, giving my publication date as *25th Jan* . . . and also enclosing the thing I enclose (the Eyetie thing). This will be no good to me, since AFOM [*A Frame of Mind*] won't be out till Jan, either, so I thought you cd. have it, if not to send 10xXX [*Twenty Poems*] to Milan or wherever it is then for a bit of clean fun.'

the one referring to Pritchett and John Raymond.[2] You say that the latter 'wanted to do a wireless programme on me and Wain', with the implication (?) that he'd now stopped wanting. Could you clarify? If anyone's going to talk about me on the wireless I want to know about it (vanity as well as avarice).

Novel no. 2 is coming on. Page 154.

As ever,
Kingsley

[TLS: Gollancz]

TO PHILIP LARKIN – 26 NOVEMBER 1953

Swansea

My dear Philip,

[. . .] Perhaps I was a bit unfeeling about old DT,[1] but only in the sense that death is a thing any man deserves commiseration with about. I don't grieve him as a voice for ever silenced, in fact that part of it is very much all right with me. I think him a bad poet and a bad influence, and when I get as far as In my craft and sullen art,[2] and think how

2. V.S. Pritchett (1900–97), novelist, critic and short-story writer; John Raymond (1923–77), critic and broadcaster. Raymond had hoped to discuss *Hurry on Down* and *Lucky Jim* in the same radio broadcast, but the latter wasn't published until January; as far as Rubinstein knew, Raymond had not yet read *Lucky Jim* (see Rubinstein to Amis, 9 November 1953, in Gollancz).

---

1. Dylan Thomas died on 9 November 1953. See Amis to Larkin, 15 November 1953 (in Bodleian): 'So that crazy Welch fellow has paid the supreme penalty. Many were the long faces here, and much anger there was with the English department for keeping their faces short. Why does everyone pretend what is not true about him *now he's dead*? Surely that's the time to tell the truth on him. And how little good there was in his stuff, quite apart from his inanity as a man.'

2. Getting 'as far as' 'In my craft or sullen art' (not 'and my sullen art') means reading the first line of, or perhaps reaching the volume that contains, the poem, i.e. *Deaths and Entrances* (1946), Thomas's fourth. For a defence of 'sullen' see William York Tindall, *A Reader's Guide to Dylan Thomas* (New York: Farrar, Straus and Giroux, 1962), p. 223: 'This fine word, for which Thomas must have preceded us to the dictionary, owes some meanings to its Latin and Middle-English origins and others to gradual accretion. Gloomy, morose, peevish, and ill-humored, the meanings that come readily to mind, are secondary. The primary meaning is lonely, solitary, unsociable, unique. Among the accretions are crabbed, obstinate, and austere.'

does he mean sullen, and see he doesn't know how he means sullen, just thought it would be *amusing* to put it in, I cannot mourn his passing. A Bloomsburyite to his *dirty* fingernails, that was him, and only sentimentalising, ignorant horsepiss about his Welchness can conceal the fact. I'm sorry to sound strained, but I've just had the latest of many conversations about the sad loss in which I try, being a decent chap, not to show what I think of his work. There's been a lot about him in the local press, too. I didn't notice any such stir when Norman Cameron[3] died, did you? 20 DT's weren't worth him.

Must go and eat, then rehearse Your lordship is right welcome back to A PORRIDGE BOWL FILLED WITH OTTER SHIT GARNISHED WITH P

Friday

Christ how I hate those bleeding rehearsals. I sit on a small platform, resting my arse on a biscuit-tin from which it aches much, doing the music – I told you I was doing the music, didn't I? It has entailed a lot of nastiness, doing the music; vainly trying to by Christ buy records from the Welsh shopkeepers, speaking out a lot of words to bad men like the Registrar's clerk and the Physics Department's electrician, shifting fucking great loudspeakers about, being made to do things about the lights which I fear and don't understand, and, for minutes on end, holding a pick-up over a spinning record while the producer interrupts the action. Think of me on Tuesday, Wednesday, Thursday and Friday evenings, sitting on my biscuit-tin for two and a half hours already made up and dressed as Osric, then giving the business over to Frances Climie, a beautiful student who laughs when she puts on the wrong record; she is Ophelia, dead by the time I have to tread the boards. If Laertes doesn't put my eye out with his rapier I'll tell you how things go. I don't suppose I need advise you never to get mixed up in show business. Why did I? It has stopped me writing my novel and makes me feel tired all day long. [. . .]

I wish something nice would happen to me, like having a fuck or selling the film rights of *Jim*. That'd be funny, wouldn't it? Dixon, Alec Guinness; Christine, Gina Lollobrigida; Margaret, Dulcie Grey;

3. Norman Cameron (1905–53), poet, anti-Modernist, close friend of Robert Graves; Larkin selected four of his poems for *The Oxford Book of Twentieth-Century English Verse* (Oxford: Clarendon Press, 1973).

Bertrand, Orson Welles; Welch, Boris Karloff; Johns, Peter Lorre; Atkinson, Trevor Howard. Music by Bruce Montgomery. Screenplay by Eric Ambler. Directed by Alfred Hitchcock.[4] Just pipe-dreaming dear.

I don't know about me not being as interested in me as you & Bruce are in you & Bruce. I like money, too, you know. Perhaps I haven't got to have it like Bruce has. As for my interest in sex, it's rather like a chap being interested in the Middle Ages; fascinated, admiring, thinks it's wonderful, envious, if only he were there how happy he'd be. I have sex all weighed up now; the only reason I like girls is that I want to fuck them, which is adolescent, cheap, irresponsible, not worth doing, a waste of time, not much fun anyway really, a needless distraction from my real vocation, destructive of any real power of understanding women which as a novelist HOOHOO should be important to me, contemptible, something I shouldn't be at my age and as a married man, liable to make me a laughing-stock, narrowing, impracticable, destructive of sexual pleasure in the end, something originating in my upbringing, neurotic. All I have to do now is stop wanting to fuck girls, and I shall have the thing licked.

I didn't really mean to get on to a third page. Will you buy me a copy of *Flamingo*?[5] I can't get it here. I mean that. I'll pay you for it. I mean that. Write soon. I mean that.

Don't you think Amis that whether we can understand what it means or not we can all take pleasure in the masterly rhythms and sheer music which Dylan always seemed to get out of his bum

Kingsley

[TLS: Bodleian]

4. As far as Hitchcock is concerned, less of a pipe-dream than Amis imagined. See Amis to Larkin, and Amis to Rubinstein, 18 October 1954. Dulcie Gray (b. 1920) played leading roles in a number of British melodramas, including *The Glass Mountain* (1948) and *Angels One Five* (1952).

5. A 1951 recording by Earl Bostic (1913–65), alto saxophonist.

TO HILARY RUBINSTEIN – 26 NOVEMBER 1953

24 The Grove, Uplands, Swansea, Glam.

My dear Hilary,

Thanks for letting me know the score about the dollars,[1] rather dismal as it is from my point of view. Since, as you know, we're expecting another Amis to join the family in January, and since, as you will agree, July is some way off yet, I wonder if I might ask you – since you mention the possibility of such a thing – to have some of my dollar-equivalent sent on to me as soon as convenient after the amount comes to you. About half of the full amount (a good bit over £300?) would just do us nicely, equip the baby with nappies and buy me a couple of drinks and a shirt as well. I should honestly be very grateful if you could fix up something along those lines, and look forward to hearing from you when the time comes.

All the best!
Yours as ever,
Kingsley

[TLS: Gollancz]

TO HILARY RUBINSTEIN – 4 DECEMBER 1953

24 The Grove, Uplands, Swansea

My dear Hilary,

Thanks a lot for the news about the payment of the American advance. This is the sort of thing that gets publishers a good name.

As regards the film rights: I won't enlarge on my amazement at the news of such inquiries. I thought I'd seen to it that no one could visualise a single page of *Jim* on the screen. Still . . . Yes, please do handle anything to do with the film rights for me. You're more than welcome to 10% of anything you can pick up for me in that line. And

---

1. On 9 November Rubinstein had written to Amis telling him that the dollar advance from Doubleday was payable on 'signature' of the contract, but that the contract hadn't yet been finalised.

by the way if anyone wants me to write the screen-play, or additional dialogue, or whatever you like, I'll do it. At cut rates.

Ever yours,
Kingsley

[TLS: Gollancz]

TO PHILIP LARKIN – 15, 16 DECEMBER 1953

Swansea

My dear Philip,

Well here we are not an hour after your letter come and here I am setting down to answer it or begin to any road. The thing is that I can't smoke till 12 and so defer things like writing poetry and prose till after then, but writing to you dear is so delightful a task, hardly a task at all in fact, that I can do it now. Also you leave Belfarts on Friday, don't you? so I thought I'd better get this to you before then. Yes 'I quite appreciate your difficulty' over the proposed meeting; I'd ask you here but apart from its being 'out of your way' there's a reasonable chance, say 1 in 5, that the baby will be here before Xmas, and you don't want to . . . Christ, cully, why not be a man and come over via Fishguard? then you cd. stop off here for one night and then carry on to Oxford. Still suppose you have everything fixed now. I tell you what now; we'll meet in Cardiff for the day – nicer than Swindon, and shorter for me: consider – 1½ hrs to Cardiff for me, approx. 2 hrs for you, no? Quite honest I am now. What do you think of this? Don't raise your usual stingy objections to being inconvenienced the least degree more than anyone else at all. Take it from me it's a good idea, and I know a very good place for lunch in Cardiff. Swindon would depress us horribly. WHO GOT YOU IN WITH SPR FANT[1] [. . .]

The Osric laughs were as follows:

OSRIC: . . . indeed to speak *feelingly* of him ahHAGH*hagh*hagh

. . . . .

---

1. It was Amis who praised Larkin's poems to the editors of *Springtime* and the Fantasy Press.

HAMLET: What's his weapon?
OSRIC: HAGHHAGHhahaha rapier and dagger.
HAMLET: That's two of his weapons . . .
OSRIC: OoookhHAGH*hagh*haghhagh
HAMLET: . . . but well.

(On the last night I cd hear the Mayor going 'Er har, har, har, har, har etc' during this)

There was another one at:
QUEEN: He's fat, and scant of breath,
on the first 2 nights, but people laughed too much so we had to cut it out. I thought myself it must have sounded pretty funny. You'd have enjoyed it all right. The little one on my right's Joyce Hatton, David Sims's girl.[2] Bruce picked on her too.

You'll be very glad and sorry to hear that I had a letter from Anthony Powell last week. Wanted to thank me for the mention in the Thurber review.[3] Would I like to call on him and have a chat? Might find me some reviewing, though there isn't much on *Punch*.[4] Found my style 'very sympathetic'. Ring him up and fix a date. I wrote back and said how pleased I was and wd. let him know when I next came to London. This is all quite true and bucked me up immensely. There's one for your diary, Jack. All this kind of thing makes me feel rather *afraid* (as well as pleased o' course); I can imagine myself saying in fifteen years' time in the Bryn-y-Mor:[5] 'Yes, of course, that novel of mine was a pretty fair success. The first of the two, I mean.' – Oh really? 'Yes, I got to know Anthony Powell round about that time, I remember.' – Anthony Powell? 'Yes, the novelist. Died a couple of years ago.' – Oh yes. 'And I can remember him saying to me, Kingsley, you're the one we all look to to keep the English novel going when we go. Seems funny now, doesn't it?' – Yes, well I really must be going now Mr. Amis thank you for a most interesting would you mind letting go of my skirt please before I. Seeward, I mean?

Have just delivered a reeking billet of turd into the lavatory pan.

2. Amis enclosed a newspaper photograph of the cast of the university's production of *Hamlet* with this letter (see plates section).

3. 'Talk About Laugh', a review of novels by Thurber and P.G. Wodehouse in the *Spectator*, 20 November 1953, p. 595.

4. Where Powell was Literary Editor (1953–58).

5. A pub in Swansea; 'Bryn-y-mor' means 'Head of the Sea'. According to Sam Dawson, Amis's colleague at the University College of Swansea, 'it was in the Bryn-y-mor that Kingsley delightedly announced – "Gollancz have accepted *Lucky Jim* – double brandies all round" ' (personal communication, 22 January 1999).

On opening the bathroom door I found my wife and my younger son in the bath and my elder son about to climb into it. Not much of a sight for a man with a lobster trying to get out of his arse, hey? Still, I had them out of there pretty blunt, I mind telling you. Shall have to shut down till tomorrow as we're going to have a vile meal with the Brennans[6] out in filthy Gower. And devil a dram to drain but a half-glass of Peestone Burgundy.[7] Am belching a lot and have a continuous muttering in my guts, like the main flooding in through creeks and inlets making.[8] Saw return to paradise last night. Roberta Haynes is in it. Not much of an actress still. Will fart now. Am reading *Trilby*.[9] It might be a lot worse AND A LOT BETTER

. . .

16th December

Another letter from my pal Powell this morning. He seems a funny chap. After saying he will postpone his weekly conference if necessary in order to see me, he goes on: 'I'm afraid I have nothing very special to talk about and as you know there is not much space devoted to books in this paper, but it would be nice to meet.' Seems a funny chap, doesn't he? Oh well, it'll all sort itself out when Tony and I are cracking a bottle of the good widow Clicquot ('I'll rig up two bottles of Heidsieck in a pulley system designed to crack your–'). Will let you know all, if anything, that transpires.

6. Friends from the University College of Swansea. See Amis to Larkin, [6–7] October 1953 (in Bodleian): 'Did I tell you we had a family of friends staying with us for a month or so? Well, we have, and so there are now five children about instead of just the two. The man, Tom Brennan, is a Yorkshire Irishman of about 35 . . . His wife, of course, is Teckey.' The family were living temporarily with the Amises because Tom Brennan (b. 1915), Head of the Research Department for Social and Economic Sciences, and Director of the Social Survey of South-West Wales (1949–53), had to disband his research unit when funding ran out. His wife's maiden name was 'Teck', hence 'Teckey'.

7. Keystone Burgundy, a ferruginous Australian 'tonic' wine, described by Dawson as 'a cheap (and nasty) wine fit only to get drunk on' (personal communication, 9 February 1999).

8. An allusion to line 11 of 'Say Not the Struggle Nought Availeth' (1849) by Arthur Hugh Clough (1819–61); *Return to Paradise* (1953), mentioned in the next sentence, directed by Mark Robson, based on the 1951 novel by James Michener; Roberta Haynes, whose date of birth is not listed in any of the reference books or databases, played 'Maeva' (she continued to appear in films into the 1980s, and co-authored a book, with W. Hyland, *How to Make it in Hollywood*, 1975).

9. *Trilby* (1894) by George Du Maurier (1834–1896), novelist and artist.

Let me know your addresses and so on, also what you think of the Cardiff idea: I think it's quite workable and involves more equality of sacrifice than any other arrangement – and if you baulk at being inconvenienced 12½% more than the other chap FOR THE FIRST TIME IN YOUR LIFE, remember WHO GOT U IN WITH SPR FAN And if I don't see you merry xmas all best for mcmliv & write Agree entirely abt *2nd happiest* tho' dont know *Sin St* or *HMPEsq*[10] I agree its a nuisance but support rlymen not enough strikes

What on oliday again easy life you ave sittin on your bum,

Kingsley

[TLS: Bodleian]

TO JOHN WAIN – 17 DECEMBER 1953

24 The Grove, Uplands, Swansea, Glamorgan

My dear John,

Christ knows when this will reach you, if his birthday causes as big and silly a flap among the Continentals as it has over this side. Anyway, herewith a message of fairly good cheer, even if you don't get it till 1954. I don't know that I have anything of very burning importance to impart: our baby still hasn't been born and my book-money still hasn't come. I've had another letter from Anthony Powell – no doubt told you about the first one. He seems rather an odd chap, but very polite. But finances will see to it that I can't meet him for bleeding months; still it's nice to think about. I can just see *Punch* becoming my niche: Amis Intolerable will fit nicely eh.

What the hell are you doing over there all this time? Found yourself a woman yet? It all sounds very romantic to me and full of literary pabulum. I remember the only time I went abroad for pleasure[1] I wrote

10. *The Second Happiest* (1953), a novel by John Phillips (a pseudonym for the American novelist John Phillips Marquand) (1893–1960); *Sinister Street* (2 vols., 1913–14) by the novelist Compton Mackenzie (1883–1972); *H.M. Pulham Esq.* (1941), also by John P. Marquand.

---

1. In late summer 1946, on the trip to Remiremont in the Vosges with Hilly and Christopher Tosswill (see Amis to Larkin, 30 August, 5 and 7 September 1946).

page after page of background. All right it was, too, but I never got a foreground to put with it. Do tell me what you do with yourself. Do you just sit on your arse and read? Or are there English craps to talk to, walk with, drink with, tell to fuck off? When I think of Vaud, or les Diablerets, whichever it is, I think of a tiny wooden hotel in a fold of the mountains, wood fires, authentic national dances performed by the young people of the district in their colourful national costume, concertinas, German students and freezing bloody cold. Is it like that? All right, don't tell me if it's too boring.

I too feel a bit browned off, truth to tell. I seem to be so bored all the time. My writing interests me while I'm actually doing it, thank God, but the excitement soon fades after each session and I start not wanting to go back to it. But I feel a useless bugger if I let a day go by without its 1000 words. And not seeing people makes me want to see people till I see some, and then I start wanting to read. I think if I could have a daily delivery of a *New Statesman*, a good anthology of science-fiction stories, a book of pornographic photographs, a new John Dickson Carr detective story and a letter from someone I admire to tell me how much he admires me, I should never want to go out of doors or write anything. Oh, and a new jazz record too. Yes, man, take me where the good times are. I might write one of those vilanelle things of yours with that as one of the refrains, if I can think of another one. More to-morrow. I have just had a bowl of soup; it's refreshed me no end and MADE; Xt my typing me think that perhaps I'm not so browned off as I thought I was. How are you getting hold of all that currency to keep you om *ON* the European mainland all that time?

20th December, 1953

It isn't to-morrow, I agree, but, although nothing has of course happened, various things have intervened to prevent me from going on with this. One of them was the writing of that vilanelle, which I'll show you some day.[2] Looking back I see I've written five poems since the beginning of November, which is for me, and I suppose for anyone these days, a frenzy of activity. To-day is Sunday, and I've been reading the papers. Doesn't it ever strike people as, let's say odd, when we have

2 This villanelle ('vilanelle' is a rare unintentional misspelling) was 'They Only Move', first published in *A Case of Samples* (1956), reprinted in *CP*, p. 61.

Connolly reviewing some piece of piss about a painter in *The Sunday Times*, and, bordering directly upon it, Richard Hughes saying how fucking fine Connolly's new anthology is?[3] – not just because it's full of good things like *A refusal to mourn*, by ole DT [Dylan Thomas]; oh no, the impress of Mr. C's individuality is, etc., on every page of this delightful and creative, etc. Also in the ST was JB Priestley saying he thought *HOD*[4] was one of the year's books – 'a brave attempt at the picaresque' he says. Might put your Xmas sales up a bit, and nobody will think less of you. Certainly not I, with support promised from Pamela Hansford-J.[5] It's a branch of business, that's what it is, the writing game. A branch of business.

Christmas cards have been dull (and also disturbingly few – do they all hate me?) except for Philip's, wishing me 'the best life has to offer', in the shape of 'art' – Louis Armstrong blowing his trumpet – and 'love' – two lesbians in a London restaurant. I had my Christmas parcel from Doubleday's a couple of days ago: Xmas pudding, rich cake, tinned butter, fruit, etc. Damn decent of them. But why don't they send me some money, hey? There weren't even any golden dollars in the pudding. I suppose they think I can smoke my 50 a day, drink my bottle of Scotch, but can't afford, or obtain, those traditional goodies which are so much a part of Christmas everywhere. Christ, I wish I had a bottle of gin and a bottle of French vermouth with me now, here, open, with a glass. Just one glass. That's all I need. I mean one beaker, not one glassful. If you were here I should find one for you too.

I'll have to leave you now. This letter seems rather uninspired to me, but better that sort of letter than no letter at all, I suppose, just about, on the whole. And I'll follow it up with what, I hope, will be a better one round about the beginning of Jan., when all this filthy Christmas rubbish, pictures of half-nude girls (I don't mind that) getting out of enormous Christmas puddings (I mind that) and babies with chef's hats on stirring ordinary-sized Christmas puddings (I mind that a lot), and all the rest of it, has sunk into the past. I see that the weather in Switzerland is too warm for skiing. That must be a nuisance – or don't

3. For Connolly see Amis to Larkin, 10, 21 August 1950, note 1. For over twenty years he was the principal reviewer for the *Sunday Times*. The anthology in question was *The Golden Horizon* (1953), reviewed by the novelist and playwright Richard Hughes (1900–76), author of *A High Wind in Jamaica* (1929).

4. *Hurry on Down*.

5. Pamela Hansford Johnson (1912–81), novelist and critic; married to C.P. Snow (for whom see Notes on Recipients).

you care? Funny, I thought you probably wouldn't, very much. Yuletide Greetings, then, and the best of everything you care about for 1954, from all here.

Kingsley

[TLS: Edinburgh]

TO PHILIP LARKIN – [DECEMBER 1953][1]

Sorry to pester you again, but this title business[2] is giving me grey hairs. Everything I think of sounds like the title for a book of Hilaire Belloc's essays or a new load of crap from Ivor Brown.[3] I agree with you about plainness, But it's hard not to sound pretentiously plain. I'd like *A temperate zone* best – it says what I mean – but for that. Do *you* think it sounds pretentious? If you don't may use it. Other ones that have occurred to me are: *Thoughts on paper* (I like this next best, but tell me if you think it sounds like an essay on the paper-manufacturing industry); *A train of thought*; *Parts of speech*; *A word-book*; *Words for things*. If it isn't too much bother, shoot me a pc with your reactions by return. How bad, also, do you find the tinge of mockery you mention in *One-man charades*? Pretentiously humble?

Their attitude towards us is like D.H.L.'s attitude towards bum,

Kingsley

[TLS: Bodleian]

---

1. This short letter accompanied Amis's home-made Christmas card to Larkin (see plates section).

2. For the book that eventually became *A Frame of Mind*.

3. Hilaire Belloc (1870–1953), poet, novelist, biographer, historian and travel writer; among his collections of essays are *Hills and the Sea* (1906), *First and Last* (1911), *Short Talks with the Dead* (1926) and *The Silence of the Sea* (1940). Ivor Brown (b.1891), author and journalist; among the titles Amis may be thinking of are *Life Within Reason* (1939), *A Word in Your Ear* (1942), *Just Another Word* (1943), *I Give You My Word* (1945) and *No Idle Words* (1948).

TO ANTHONY THWAITE – 23 DECEMBER 1953

24 The Grove, Uplands, Swansea, Glam

Dear Mr. Thwaite,

Thank you for your letter of the 18th, which reached me this morning. I'm very gratified to think that your Society[1] wants me to join the panel on 2nd March, and I do want to come. The snag is that, by unimaginable bad luck, I'm down to give a sort of nonsensical semi-public lecture here on that very day, of all the ones in the year, and at a time which wouldn't let me get to Oxford till the meeting was half over. I'm furious, of course, but since the lecture was fixed in the summer I can hardly plead a previous engagement there. But I have written a threatening-cajoling letter to the chap who organises these lectures, asking him to arrange a swop if he can and to let me know whether he can or not as soon as possible. I'll let you know the position immediately I hear from him.

I write to tell you this now, rather than hang on until I can be more definite, so that you can start thinking of someone to replace me if it turns out to be necessary. I'm sorry I couldn't give the unqualified Yes I should like to give. By the way, if I do come, will it be necessary at any point in the proceedings for me to make anything in the nature of a speech, as opposed to discussing, answering questions, etc.? I don't mind speeches, but I like to know that they're on the programme.[2]

All the best for Christmas and 1954,

Yours sincerely,
Kingsley Amis

[TLS: Recipient]

---

1. Thwaite was Secretary of the Oxford University Poetry Society, and had invited Amis to take part in a symposium or brains-trust in March 1954, along with Lord David Cecil (chair), James Kirkup, George Fraser and Herbert Palmer. When Cecil later dropped out his place was taken by C.S. Lewis. For the night itself see Amis to Larkin, 14 March 1954. For Thwaite see Notes on Recipients.

2. On 31 December Amis wrote to Thwaite that his clash of engagements had been resolved, and that he would be able to come to Oxford after all.

TO JOHN WAIN – 3 JANUARY 1954

24 The Grove, Uplands, Swansea

My dear John,

If I seem to have more to write about this time, it's only because *any* kind of bleeding event, almost any movement of electrons, is rather noteworthy in this *arse* of the woods. Nothing of the slightest significance, nothing to cause the blood to go up in temperature by one-tenth of one per cent of a degree or a microgramme (1/1,000,000 gr.) of happiness to add itself to the higher scale-pan of life, nothing, has happened. Indeed the last few days have been rather horrible. Just as I am celebrating the end of 1953 (a year that was rather kind to me on the whole) in the cask-cider that is all I can afford, I realise something I'd been trying to conceal from myself: that my novel[1] is too bad in its present form to satisfy even me, and that it, like its predecessor, must all be written out from the beginning again. This, with buggering term starting *next week* – what do they think we are? teachers? – is a cow and no mistake. That was the first thing.

On New Year's Day I stroll down to the off-licence to collect the four bottles of wine I paid for some days before Christmas and was too drunk to collect on Christmas Eve. They will do nicely, I think, to get drunk on on New Year's Day. The crone in the shop tells me I didn't pay for them. I did pay for them, and say so. She says I didn't pay for them. We put our points of view once more each, and then I go out without the wine and 27/- to the bad. Filthy cheating Welshwoman. That was the second thing.

Twenty minutes later I am examining the overcoat I put in for repair at a local shop some weeks earlier. I pay £2–11–6, and then find the moth-holes I wanted treated have been 'repaired' by the substitution of a large strip of cloth from inside the coat in place of a corresponding piece of cloth that was outside. The new piece of cloth is several tones lighter than the rest of the outside of the coat, making me look like a pauper, which indeed I practically am by now. I point this out to the girl. She agrees enthusiastically that it 'looks bad', adding that there's

1. *That Uncertain Feeling.*

nothing I can do about it. I go out. Filthy incompetent, not-caring-a-fuck Welshmen. That was the third thing.

H-alf (why does my typewriter insert spaces in the middle of words like that? Because I bought it at a Welsh shop) an hour later I return home, to find that life has made an attempt to cheer me up by bringing to me a copy of *The Spectator* with a poem[2] by me in it: an incompetent attempt, I soon discover, in that there are three misprints in the text. Why? That was the fourth thing. So you can see I am, or have been being, pretty fed up, what with one thing and another. And of course, no baby or money still.

You must have seen that old Snow gave you a leg-up in the *S. Times* last week, and that Warburg has now re-advertised *HOD* [*Hurry on Down*]. This is good. I see further that that old crap at the Fortune Press[3] is re-advertising, if you can [call] it that, PL's *Jill*. This should make him laugh, and makes me laugh too, when I think that the old crap may well start re-advertising *Bright November* – the worst book ever written by a promising young poet. Perhaps my agent[4] can stop him doing that. It's time he did something for me. It's time someone did something for me, or so I feel looking back on the wine and overcoat morning. Can you imagine the fearful atrabilious rage that filled me? I can taste it still.

One of the big dates in the formation of mid-20th-century standards will be 2nd March, when I go to Oxford to take part in a Poetry Brains Trust. George Fraser will be the only other human being there. The other members – *caution*: to avoid choking swallow any food or drink you may have in your mouth before reading on – are Lord David Cecil (in the chair, of course), Mister Herbert Palmer, and Mister James (Correct Compassion) Kirkup. *Memo*: when replying, tell me the opinion or epigram most likely to make all three most angry. I don't mean I can't think of any myself, of course. Praising Leavis might be a good start. A pity, by the way, that *Scrutiny* has folded, I think.

I long to hear your news. Wherever I look there are photographs of skiers falling about in the Swiss snows. I'd like to think you were doing some of this yourself. If I don't hear soon I shall take my revenge by composing something called *An Epistle to Mr. Wain, then making the Grand Tour, Urging him to Return to his Native Shore*: Forsake, great

2. 'Catch', in *Spectator*, 1 January 1954, p. 231. The poem was not reprinted.
3. R.A. Caton.
4. Graham Watson (b.1913), Amis's agent at Curtis Brown from 1954 to 1964.

Wain, the *Arno*, choak'd in Snow, And seek *Tamesis* less intemp'rate Flow; Exchange the beetling *Alps* tempestuous Breath For those mild Odours of thy native Heath, Where English *Oaks* their pleasing Shade entwine And fairest *Arts*, and kindest *Friendship* join . . . Though it's early yet I'm already looking forward to your return with some impatience. I want to gather material for my boycott-the-Continent movement.

Here it is a mild, sunny day; the sky is blue all over. A remarkable spell of fine weather, doubly so for the Principality. I wish I could chat about the marvellous books I've been reading, but somehow I don't seem to be getting my hands on that sort of books these days. Every review page and publisher's advertisement is bespattered with novels by foreign swine, mostly frogs and dagoes. When I do see a book I want to read, and put it down on my libaray (you know the word) list, a mysterious process comes into force whereby a delay, proportional to the square of my desire to get hold of it, is imposed on me, though not on anyone else I meet. Why is this? Ay, my lord, I would fain know that.[5]

Look after yourself. Hilly asks me to send special love and remembrances, and I send mine too.

Kingsley

[TLS: Edinburgh]

TO HILARY RUBINSTEIN – 17 JANUARY 1954

24 The Grove, Uplands, Swansea, Glam.

My dear Hilary,

Thank you very much for the 6 copies of *Lucky Jim*, and for your good wishes. I am absolutely delighted with the edition from every point of view. A most handsome job. I feel your blurb-writer deserves a particularly big hand; he's put the points with just the emphasis I'd have wished – 'a very young man' is possibly a little too emphatic, but then I need all the help I can get. As regards the photograph – I'm

5. A slightly distorted echo of the Reynaldo/Polonius dialogue in *Hamlet*, II.i.36–7: 'POLONIUS: Wherefore should you do this? REYNALDO: Ay, my lord, I would know that.' Amis had played Osric in *Hamlet* the previous month.

having another one done which I hope to pick up in the next week or so and will certainly forward if the results are at all satisfactory.

That Uncertain Feeling is now on page 40; a retrogression from my last report in appearance, but not in fact. This is the final draft and as before is progressing swiftly. I thought I could do it in one draft, but it seems I am a two-draft man and must just accept the fact. I hesitate to give you a date, but some time in March, if things go well, looks like being the completion-date for the fair copy. There have been one or two distractions here recently, of which the arrival of a new Amis – female – at 2 a.m. to-day is perhaps the most important. Incipient fatherdom is a great inspiration in the long run no doubt, but not in the short run.

Thanks again to yourself and to V.G. Ltd. for *Lucky Jim*.

Yours ever,
Kingsley

[TLS: Gollancz]

TO PHILIP LARKIN – 18 JANUARY 1954

Swansea

Thanks loads for your wire. Hope you enjoy the reading-matter.[1] Sally Myfanwy (pron. muh-*van*wi) arrived 2.5 a.m. yesterday. Both doing well. Am telling Bergonzi (ed. *Platform*) to drop you a line.[2] Would you boil a kettle Mr. Amis so that I can wash the baby's bum

K.

[ALS: Bodleian]

---

1. Presumably *A Frame of Mind*, a copy of which Amis had promised Larkin in a letter of 8 January 1954 (in Bodleian).

2. *Platform*, edited by Frederick Woods, ran for four issues, the last two of which Bernard Bergonzi worked on as associate editor. Both Amis and Larkin published a poem in the final issue, No. 4 (Autumn 1955), pp. 22–3: Larkin sent several poems, including 'Born Yesterday', but Bergonzi chose the one Larkin would later title 'I Remember, I Remember', which appeared as 'Revenant' (it was later reprinted in *The Less Deceived* and *LCP*, pp. 82–3); Amis's poem was 'The Silent Room', later published in *A Case of Samples* and *CP*, pp. 33–4.

TO PHILIP LARKIN – 19, 23, 26 JANUARY 1954

Swansea

My dear Philip,

Will start this now, anyway. You ask about our new professor; it just so happens that I am in a shuddering rage about this.[1] There were only two men interviewed. One was a man 34 this year, author of 2 books, one technical-philosophical, one critical, of one or two articles, of several poems in such places as the Kenyon Review, The New Statesman, and so on. The other was a man 32, Scotsman, author of an article suggesting why the secnond farx 2nd edition of Warton's Essay on Pope didn't appear until 26 years after the 1st, and editor-designate of the Dryden Oxford text. When I add that the 1st man impressed most of those concerned as pleasant and intelligent, the 2nd as ugly and pompous, you will have no difficulty in guessing which one got the job. Yes, that's right. The 1st one was John Holloway,[2] the 2nd one Kinsley[3] (a cross between me and the compiler of that report you've been reading?[4] No), who, in addition to the facts adduced, was hated by everyone at Aberystwyth, smokes a pipe and is a Scottish Methodist lay-preacher. I don't really expect you to believe that last touch, but it's true. You can tell your pals that this is the most unjust, disgraceful appointment since Baxter's,[5] if not worse. The Principal here[6] is a bastard Scotchman

1. Amis has drawn an arrow connecting the beginning of the letter to a handwritten MS addition: 'Seems a funny way to start this letter, I suppoose, but I'll let it stand. It seemed very important at the time, and no doubt will again.' Later on in the same paragraph Amis circles the words 'Scotsman' and 'Dryden' and connects them by arrows to the MS addition 'Encountersh', and the words 'Scottish' and 'Scotchman' to the MS addition 'Londonmagazinesh'.

2. John Holloway (1920–99), poet, critic, academic; Fellow of All Souls College, Oxford (1946–60); University Lecturer in English, Cambridge (from 1954), Professor of Modern English, Cambridge (1972–82).

3. James Kinsley (1922–84), Lecturer in English, University College, Aberystwyth (1947–54); Professor of English, University College, Swansea (1954–61); later Professor of English Literature, University of Nottingham (from 1961).

4. Alfred Kinsey (1894–1956), American sexologist and zoologist, co-author of *Sexual Behavior in the Human Male* (1948), the so-called 'Kinsey Report'; founded the Institute for Sex Research in 1942.

5. F.W. Baxter. See Amis to Larkin, 18 June 1952, note 5.

6. John Fulton (1902–86), Principal, University College, Swansea (1947–59), political philosopher; knighted (1964).

and, like K., went to Balliol. The dirty log-rolling bastard. Doesn't matter to *him*, see, who directs teaching and research in the English Dept. I feel as I've I'd swive bride as if I'd *lost something valuable*; that Holloway man might have been really good to have here. Filthy twisting, *mistaken* bastard. I feel like launching a poison-pen campaign, going on strike, hanging out of the window a short summary, well tricked out with obscenities, of my views on the matter. Certainly feel like writing to Holloway and *apologising* to him. That vile canting corrupt bastard. *Dryden*, Christ. FLITHY FUCKI Sorry to bore you with all this. FLITHY ARSELICKING URINESPEAKI

The birth went off very well, as these things go. The labour was shorter than usual, though evidently no less unpleasant. We got the midwife at 9.0 on the Saturday evening; she went again at 10.30, no immediate action being likely. Recalled at 12.45, she sat around for some time; I brought a cup of tea at 1.55; no change. After about 3 minutes Hilly said she wanted very much to use the bedpan; the midwife sent me to boil a kettle. Returning, a good deal was happening; H. was breathing gas and air pretty fast and a pink fuzzy head had begun to appear. I went quickly downstairs and read a page of *Lucky Jim* with great attention. After 2–3 minutes there was the sound of a baby crying. That was that; H. is very fit, apple-cheeked as ever, and very pleased with herself for producing a girl. So am I. The baby is quite hefty and looks no worse than might be expected. Rather better, really. I hope she has a lovely childhood and has a lovely time at school and makes a lot of lovely chums and brings them home. A girl ought to feel she can bring her friends in and introduce them to her parents the trouble withyou is you're just a

23rd January.

I suppose I can take it now that the period of getting a letter from you by every post is over. More's the pity. Sodding good and touching was the poem,[7] moving me a great deal as poem and as friendship-assertion. I think it's about the nicest thing anyone could do for any new-born child, and I only wish I had the chn fkn chance to do something comparable for you, even though I'm pretty sure I should fail the test. Hilly is answering for herself and should have plenty to say.

7. 'Born Yesterday'.

Well, now that the period of registration bum and card for the food office bum and home confinement grant claim form bum is over we can settle down to just being the parents of SMA,[8] a thing that promises well. Or rather we shall be able to do so when my mxthxr and fxthxr have gone home, which they do on Monday. The baby looks rather better than it did: a certain amiable resignation appears on its face from time to time, it is officially reported to be sucking well, and its face isn't red. The trouble is only that it'll stay much as it is now for a rather long time. But we can wait, of course.

Nice of you to be saying all these nice things about the results of my spare-time literary activity. (Another kind of result arrived two or three days ago: £388 from Doubleday's – or did I tell you that? Seems to me I scrawled on the back of an envelope some time. No? Fori whori forgive anyway if necessary. Glad above all that *Jim* is satisfactorily funny. I want it to be other things as well, but if it can only be one thing then that's the one I'd have picked. I agree with you about the blub, but on the whole I'm really rather relieved, knowing what VG can be like, fearing something like: 'Compared by eminent critics to Henry James, Tacitus, Leopardi, Schubert, Carter Dickson and Caravaggio, Kingsley Amis's uproarious, side-splitting, tear-jerking, cock-standing,' etc. I think it may make some silly people buy the book and wouldn't affect clever people who know about blurbs and Golly anyway. Or do I mean that I hope it may make, etc. Glad too about the poems you like. I agree with much that you say, though 8[9] is one I like myself. Bergonzi, or his side-kick, has taken the room one.[10] Fucking fool that I am; should have kept it to send to the po ed of the TLS when he writes to beg for stuff. Do send Bergonzi Sally; unless you want to keep it for the po ed of the, etc. Old Tony Powell is reviewing *LJ* himself, by the way;[11] just a short note. My father said he thought some of my poems were rather morbid.

Christ I'm sorry, I know you deserve a 5-pp letter but I'm shit-scared of not getting through my 9 novels from the Spr [*Spectator*] in time for next Thursday. God how horrible that PO business:[12] did he just

8. Sally Myfanwy Amis.
9. 'Against Romanticism'.
10. 'The Silent Room'.
11. The review appeared in *Punch*, 3 February 1954, p. 188.
12. 'I got pinched for not having a wireless licence' (Larkin to Strang, 23 January 1954, in LL, p. 221) – at the Post Office ('PO').

walk in ans pans and demand to see your licence? I haven't got one either, must get one. Yes, Christ, would love to see you, but if you want to see all of us, or both of us I mean, you'll have to come over here. Consider: You have to come over this side of the water, I don't have to go over there. There's only one of you, there are two or more of us. This reviewing business is terrifying. Reading other men's reviews I'm dismayedly struck by how clever they are and how much they know; mine'll be a 4th form effort: This book is quite good, I enjoyed reading it. It is about a man who gets caught up in bum

K.

26th January.

Have broken this open again since the reviewing is ahead of schedule. Didn't tell you what happened when I rang Daddy B to tell him the news of Sally, did I? Wait'll I tell you. Before I could giveany steamy anything but the bare facts, he started saying, Well, it's nice to hear a bit of good news, after the sad time we've been having here. I thought, Christ, Bill dead, Mick dead? [. . .] No, nothing like that: an old neighbour Mummy B used to take soup to has at last died, *aetat, suae* 82, and a distant relation of Daddy B's, by a connexion lengthily explained, has also died at about the same age. Tragic loss, eh? He was the last survivor *but two* of 'that generation'. I wanted to ask what concern I could be expected to feel on hearing of the death of *my father-in-law's mother's brother-in-law* (yes, really), but I didn't. Why, quite seriously, and frankly, did he tell me that? Head in the clouds OF FART as usual, I suppose. His letter to my father (beginning 'Dear Bill') consisted for the most part of a lengthier account of the same events. Why did it do that? Is it any longer just . .

God you know most novels are a ball-aching lot. Don't blame me for saying what I say in praise of what I review in the Feb 5th Spr, though the Prebble thing[13] is quite good and might even interest you. Watch out for my letter, signed 'Little Mr. Tomkins', in this coming

13. John Prebble, *The Mather Story* (1954), one of three 'New Novels' reviewed by Amis in the *Spectator*, 5 February 1954, p. 160.

number. Have you read the Sitwell stuff in the current one?[14] Filthy *underbred plebeian guttersnipe*, eh? The baby is well but has a slight cold. Philip is very nice to her and says how much he likes her. If you like, by the way, I'll tip a quiet wink to AAH[15] and ask him to look into the business of your poems. Been rather a long time, hasn't it? If you do want me to put a query, tell me how long it is. I won't do anything till I hear from you. You shd. have heard from Bergonzi by now. I've sent your poem to the Leeds man.[16] I thought it pretty damn good, actually, and had the same feeling about it as the one of mine I

14. On 8 January 1954 Anthony Hartley published a review in the *Spectator* of Edith Sitwell's *Gardeners and Astronomers* and Richard Eberhart's *Undercliff*. This review, entitled 'Critic Between the Lines', used the two volumes to help explain 'the present divided state of poetry' (p. 47). Hartley describes the two main camps or lines as follows: 'one stems from the early Eliot, passes through the poets of the Thirties (especially Auden and Empson) and ends with our young academic poets, the University Wits (Kingsley Amis and Donald Davie, for example). The second begins with bits of Yeats, bits of Pound and a good deal of outside help from the French Symbolists and Rilke. It takes in Dylan Thomas and *The New Apocalypse* to end in what might be called our Neo-Symbolists (Kathleen Raine and others).' The excesses of the University Wits are exemplified by Eberhart's poems, which 'often fall into the bathos of bare statement'. The excesses of the Neo-Symbolists are exemplified by Sitwell, whose verse 'illustrates the consequences of letting the imagery rip'. Hartley singles out the following lines from Sitwell's 'Out of School' for censure: 'Where the wind like peridots and beryls/rises in the budding fig branches.' He also disapproves of the last lines of 'A Song of Dust', where 'the imagery has taken over and developed itself into extravagance'.

Sitwell's response, in a letter written from Hollywood and published in the *Spectator* of 22 January, points out, among other things, that the last lines of 'A Song of Dust' are an adaptation of one of Donne's Sermons: 'Would it not have been wiser for your reviewer, before being quite so impertinent, to have read more widely?' In the next paragraph Sitwell continues the attack: 'I shall, no doubt, be told that little Mr Tomkins (or whatever his name may be), this week's new great poet, does not incorporate in his work phrases from the past, giving them a twist, and importing new meaning. That is so. But more than one great poet does' (p.96).

15. Anthony Hartley.

16. Ralph Maud, founding editor of the Leeds University magazine *Poetry and Audience* (Maud was a friend of Amis's colleague at Swansea Sam Dawson, with whom he had been at school; the magazine's first issue appeared in October 1953). Though edited by students, *Poetry and Audience* had a distinguished list of contributors, in part a product of support from the Professor of English at Leeds, Bonamy Dobrée, and the first holder of the Gregory Fellowship in Poetry at Leeds, John Heath-Stubbs. Maud (b. 1928), a postgraduate student in English at Leeds, went on to become Professor of English, Simon Fraser University, Vancouver, British Columbia (1965–94), and an editor of Dylan Thomas's poems (see Amis to Stuart Thomas, 10 March 1988 and 2 August 1990).

sent: bit too good for a non-printed thing, we're getting too old for this, etc.[17] Still, it does get about, as I said: that DT [Dylan Thomas] interview originally appeared in it. The long one I liked too, but found a bit on the chatty side, though the rhymes were managed with marvellous skill. Couldn't you cut out some, or all, of the chat, the anecdote? A series of sentences in the negative, called *Negative indicta* pricts BUGGARSE pro *CLAPPICUNT* pricta *indicative*, might do the trick nicely ('I'll engage a juggler to do a trick with your –') And what about A garland of gherkins?[18] Never said a work furk word about that you didn't. And what about our poem?[19] And don't forget to send me the Bechet effort, finished satisfactorily or not.[20] I wonder when our Fartarsy pamphlets will be out.

Let me know if you see and rand any Jim reviews apart from the obvious ones, will you? Walter Allen doesn't like new writers, does he? Avant-garde, Christ. If the yellow book[21] was one and C Day L, Ste Spe,

17. Both the Larkin poem, 'Triple Time', and the poem Amis submitted, 'Nerves', appeared in *Poetry and Audience*, 28 January 1954, in an issue devoted to Movement poets. The former was reprinted in *The Less Deceived* (1955) and *LCP*, p. 73; the latter in *A Case of Samples* (1956) and *CP*, p. 40.

18. See Amis to Larkin, 8 January 1954 (in Bodleian): 'I set you the task of writing *A Garland of Gherkins*: 100 comments on sex, 4 lines the maximum. You should do it well.'

19. See Amis to Larkin, 8 January 1954 (in Bodleian), in which Amis lays down the rules for the poem he was hoping to write with him, each composing alternate lines: 'As for form, I think rough iambs with 1/2ish rhymes (e.g. poking or sting or bacon for shaking) and rough stanzas of 4–6 lines. The thing to avoid I think is determining in advance anything about what the finished poem will say; let each line stem from what's aleady written only.' They seem to have managed only three lines, the middle one of which is Larkin's (Amis likes it but says it 'belongs very firmly to your sort rather than my sort'):

The journal ends. Silence is left shaking
Pages useless with ink, the wind ruffles
What might have followed. Was the poison taken?

Amis's two lines are written in pencil, and 'followed' in line three replaces a deleted 'happened next'. Also in pencil, in the left margin of the third line, is the undeleted phrase 'All the possible.'

20. 'For Sidney Bechet', dated 15 January 1954, in *LCP*, p. 83; originally published in *The Whitsun Weddings*.

21. *The Yellow Book* (1894–97), a yearly publication devoted to art and literature, edited by the American author Henry Harland (1861–1905), published by John Lane (1854–1925), who also established The Bodley Head in 1887. Its notorious reputation (for *fin-de-siècle* decadence) derived in part from its art editor, the writer and illustrator Aubrey Beardsley (1872–98).

Geo Bar, Dav Gas, Hen Tre[22] etc were another, I'll be content to hug the rear, thanks. Do you mean . . .

Schoolboy grubbiness bum,
Kingsley

[TLS: Bodleian]

TO THE EDITOR, *SPECTATOR* – 29 JANUARY 1954[1]

SIR,—As last week's new great poet, I was very glad to see that letter from a Doctor Sitwell telling Mr. Anthony Hartley that it's okay for great poets to copy bits out of dead writers. The lady is wrong, though, if she thinks I never copy bits out of dead writers like she does. Here is a bit out of one of my poems, which I haven't managed to get published yet:

What noise is that? How now, what hath befallen?
I'll tell the news; here comes the general.
Tomorrow – out of joint – the pity of it –
Ripeness is all.

Do you get the way I've twisted the meanings there? I'd like to see Mr. Anthony Hartley having the cheek to teach, not only Doctor Sitwell and that Donne man, but me and the late William Shakespeare how to write.

Personally I think the sap of a tree is more like Double Diamond than peridots and beryls but if Doctor Sitwell likes to say it's like peridots and beryls then that's quite okay by me. It just shows how we great poets differ. – Yours faithfully,

LITTLE MR. TOMKINS[2]
[Name and address supplied].

22. The poets C. Day-Lewis, Stephen Spender, George Barker, David Gascoyne and Henry Treece. Barker (1913–91) was a neo-Romantic, associated, like Treece, with the New Apocalypse; Gascoyne (b. 1916) was greatly influenced by Surrealism, and himself translated many of the French Surrealists.

1. For the background to this letter see previous letter, note 14. 'Letters to the Editor' appears on p. 123 of the 29 January issue.

2. Among the responses this letter elicited in the 'Letters to the Editor' column of the next issue of the *Spectator* (5 February 1954, p. 147) was the following anonymous epistle: 'Sir, – We should not have dared to write to you, but we see you have published a letter from Little Mr Tomkins about Dr Edith Sitwell, so perhaps we can ask a question. Is all Dr

TO HILARY RUBINSTEIN – 1 FEBRUARY 1954

24 The Grove, Uplands, Swansea

My dear Hilary,

Thank you for your letters and for letting me see the advt.: a very fine one, though I do say it. The press has been extraordinarily kind, I think. Have you seen the *Western Mail?* 'Mr. Amis might well have started out on a weightier foot' – nothing could be more Welsh, in form and content. Old A. Powell tells me (he's one of my buddies now) that he's doing something in *Punch* – which should be favourable. John Amis now writes to confirm the Betjeman anecdote, but taking *Decline and Fall* instead of *Vile Bodies* as the *terminus a quo*.[1] I shall anyway be buying the *Telegraph* on Friday.

If the idea is not too *absurd*, do you think it would be worth while sending Alec Guinness a copy of *Jim*, saying how much I admire him, how clearly I can see him in the part, etc.? I think we mentioned this before, but I just wondered if . . . Let me know what you think.

The fame that *Jim* has brought me is sending me giddy: I am to judge the Oral English Competition in the Eisteddfod at Llywn-y-Bryn Girls' School, Walter Road, Swansea, and there is to be a piece about me in the students' paper. They wanted to head it 'The Kingsley Report', but I soon killed that.

Sitwell's poetry, as well as the bits in which our names are given, bits copied from dead writers? – Yours anxiously, PERIDOT AND BERYL.' In the issue of 19 February 1954, Sitwell returns to the fray. Here are the relevant portions of her letter: 'With regard to your other correspondents: Anonymous letter-writers are not regarded with favour by the community in general. I must leave these persons to shine among the brightest jewels in your crown, as I cannot be expected to waste my time in arguing with anonymous semi-literates . . . This letter is obvously written by the same wearisome person who wrote the letter signed "Little Mr Tomkins". Both letters have the same theme song and are written in the same distinguished style.' The letter concludes: 'Mr Hartley and I have at least one thing in common. I gather that he admires the work of Mr Kingsley Amis. I have not, as yet, read Mr Amis's poetry, but I have read his most remarkable, most distinguished first novel *Lucky Jim* with enthusiastic admiration. – Yours faithfully, EDITH SITWELL.' The letter is followed by a comment from the editor: 'Dr Sitwell says that the letter signed "Peridot and Beryl" was obviously written by the person who wrote the letter signed "Little Mr Tomkins". This was not so.'

---

1. Neither John Amis (see Notes on Recipients) nor Hilary Rubinstein can remember this anecdote.

Have had an invitation from VG and Ruth Gollancz[2] to a party in a couple of weeks. Was very glad to get it, but mortified to think I shan't be able to come. I shall be writing to decline with regrets, but do you think you could explain the situation to him some time?: new baby, job in Swansea, etc. I should like him to feel that I did *want* to come.

May I acknowledge through you the receipt of two cheques in the last couple of weeks? A great feeling of *bonhomie* swept through me as I took them out of the envelopes.

Ever yours,
Kingsley

[TLS: Gollancz]

TO C.P. SNOW – 8 FEBRUARY 1954

24 The Grove, Uplands, Swansea.

Dear Mr. Snow,

This is just a note to thank you for your generous 'puff' for *Lucky Jim*. I'm sure it's done a good deal to contribute to the modest success the book seems to be having.

I was so sorry I had to dash off like that when we met that time at Harry Hoff's. I hope some day we'll be able to get together for a real chat.

My best regards to your wife.[1]

Yours sincerely,
Kingsley Amis

[TLS: HRHRC]

2. For Victor Gollancz and his wife Ruth see Notes on Recipients.

---

1. Pamela Hansford Johnson (see Amis to Wain, 17 December 1953, note 4); for Snow himself see Notes on Recipients.

TO HILARY RUBINSTEIN – 15 FEBRUARY 1954

24 The Grove, Uplands, Swansea.

My dear Hilary,

4th printing, eh? My oath, I never expected this kind of thing. Just shows the great British public aren't such fools after all. By the way, can you give me an idea of how many copies comprise these impressions? Perhaps I shouldn't ask this, but when avarice and vanity pull in the same direction, it'd take a stronger spirit than mine to resist them.[1]

Two fan letters may interest you for different reasons. One from Geoffrey Gorer;[2] 'It is a number of years since I have so enjoyed and admired a first novel . . . If Gollancz wants to make use of this note for publicity it's quite o.k. with me' – a bit late for that, perhaps, but none the less cheering. The other letter comes from a man called Simon Staughton;[3] I think I'll enclose it to save the bore of typing it out, and you might not believe me if I did. Be sure to let me have it back when it's been round the office.

Looking forward to seeing you on the 1st.

As ever,
Kingsley

Mr. Hilary Rubinstein, Victor Gollancz Ltd.[4]

FLASH – EDITH SITWELL WRITES FROM SUNSET BOULEVARD TO THANK AUTHOR FOR LUCKY JIM STOP HAS READ IT TWICE IN TEN

---

1. See Rubinstein to Amis, 17 February 1954 (in Gollancz): 'The book continues to go at a ripping pace, and on Monday we put in hand a *fifth* impression. I ought to say that they have all been quite modest impressions – not of the Daphne du Maurier class yet, I am afraid – but pretty nice all the same. The total printings to date amount to 7,500.'

2. Geoffrey Gorer (1905–85), freelance critic, anthropologist, sociologist. Among his many books are the anthropological studies *Africa Dances* (1935) and *Himalayan Village* (1938); a study of the Marquis de Sade (1934); and *The Americans* (1948). In 1950, after extensive travels in Europe, Asia and the United States, Gorer settled in England, where he continued to write books, articles and reviews.

3. Untraced.

4. This is a mock-cable; in his letter of 17 February 1954, Rubinstein thanks Amis for 'your letter of February 15th, your "cable" and the priceless letter from Simon Staughton'.

DAYS STOP QUOTE BORN WRITER STOP BRILLIANT STOP I DO NOT REMEMBER WHEN I HAVE READ A MORE VITAL AND VITALISING FIRST WORK IN PROSE STOP UNQUOTE AND MORE IN SAME STRAIN INCLUDING INVITATION TO LUNCH WHEN SHE NEXT IN LONDON STOP AM NOT PULLING YOUR LEG STOP WISH I WERE IN A WAY STOP SENSATIONAL DEVELOPMENTS WILL FEATURE IN CORRESPONDENCE COLUMNS S P E C T A T O R THIS WEEK STOP ORDER YOUR COPY NOW STOP WILL BE GREAT FOR PUBLICITY BUT EMBARRASSING FOR SELF STOP FOR GODS REPEAT GODS SAKE KEEP ALL THIS QUIET STOP YOU WILL SEE WHY WHEN S P E C T A T O R APPEARS BT SWANSEA DTO 160945 BT IMMEDIATE GPS 118 AR AR KKKK

[TLS: Gollancz]

TO GEOFFREY GORER – 15 FEBRUARY 1954

University College of Swansea

Dear Mr. Gorer,

It was extremely kind of you to write to me, and I am greatly encouraged by your praise of *Lucky Jim*. I'm very glad you enjoyed it.

As you can see, I'm not a full-time writer, but fortunately teaching English here doesn't absorb all my energy, and I'll probably have another book out early next year. I hope you'll like that one as well, but people have been so kind to *Lucky Jim* that I feel a bit nervous.

Yours sincerely,
Kingsley Amis

[TLS: Sussex]

TO PHILIP LARKIN – 19 FEBRUARY 1954

Swansea

My dear Philip,

Time to start this, any road. I'm sorry about not writing. I can explain how busy I've been if I say that I've now read half of a science-fiction book I got out of Boot's a fortnight ago. Can't really point to anything much I've done, except as I may have said read review-novels and make notes on Proust FUCKISBLE My cold has cleared up now, but I have indigestion instead. At least things have been going fairly well for me, what with reviews and being praised privately and publicly by Doctor Edith Sitwell and Gollancz having now printed 7500 altogether. Bloody good, all that. What worries me is how to make decent amends to old ES for being Little Mr. Tomkins; have been 3 times on the blower to the Spr about this, me wanting to be apologetic (because she was after all being unprovokedly nice to me; her letter to me was very complimentary and not patronising) and them wanting me to 'laugh it off'. Don't feel like doing that to it off. Feel I shall put my foot in it, get branded as mean sod, bloody fool. Fuck them; why won't they let me be humble? I suppose you've heard from Hartley about your poems now. In case not, the printer had LOST your corrected proofs, and they were 'hanging on' HOPING HE'D FIND THEM AGAIN. Their printers are an incompetent rabble: 2 misprints in my review the other week (words omitted).

Fan mail not too bad on the whole. I enclose one specimen – which I want back – because you wouldn't believe me if I just told you about it, would you? One from Geoffrey Gorer. One from Tynan. One from that FUCKING MEAN PONCE Roger Sharrock, asking me to send him a copy. One from a painter. One from a boy at school I wanted to bugger; too late now. None from cultural nymphs; in fact none from women, unless you count Mummy B. The letter from him was a winner (did I tell you? It's been so long YES BY FUCK) – he'd only seen the *Sunday Times* review (then later the *News Chron*, the only other unfavourable one)[1] and started off with a long para. about exactly how to pronounce Myfanwy. Who is doing fine, by the way, like her mum. Breaking off now to eat.

21st February

Sunday: O a horrid day. Lots of filthy fog about today, makin fuck g things all wet. Have bought some nice clothes for me and Hilly with

---

1. The two unfavourable reviews were Julian Maclaren-Ross, 'High Jinks and Dirty Work', *Sunday Times*, 24 January 1954, p. 5, and 'Lectures, love', *News Chronicle*, 11 February 1954, p.8, by 'F.L.' (according to Anthony Thwaite, 'almost certainly Frederick Laws, at that time literary editor of the *News Chronicle*', personal communication, 10 May 1999).

some of my money. Some sods coming tonight to drink my drink and waste my time. Am still having to blow my nose more often than I should like. Constipated this morning. Had to wash my arse afterwards. Bugger. It takes ¾ hour to light both the firs pervirs fires and ¼ hour to scrub some of the coal out of my fingers and nails. I'm too sensitive and too fine for that sort of work. People ought to realise that. Just you shut up about my dialogue after what all those men have said. Those remarks about Wain in the AFOM [*A Frame of Mind*] review in TLS were funny, werent they?[2] I remember him saying to me that the only thing wrong with Alvarez's stuff was that it was to much like Wm. Empson. [. . .]

My money seems to be dwindling rapidly. It'll dwindle further and more rapidly when I go to Ox and Lond next week end. Shall see him, Mummy B, Patsy, P.H. Newby,[3] J.D. Scott, Tony Hartley, Bruce, Tynan, Hoff, C.P. Snow, P. Hansford Johnson, A. Powell, G.S. Fraser, Kirkup and Lord David Cecil. Shall keep careful note of expenses and claim income tax rebate on them. Got myself an accountant now, you sam. I pay Hilly a salary, have been since 1951, in fact, spend £15 a year on necessary books, take all the weeklies to keep me abreast of developments, etc. My accountant came top in Great Britain in the year he took his exam, you sam. Will let you know how the trip goes, and do my best to push you. Did I make it clear, by the way, that my pal Edith Sitwell wants me to lunch with her when she returns to London? Well she does. Blimey O'Reilly. Did I ever send you the following, by the way:

My sister's a keen chapel-goer, And they'd launched an appeal for the black boys; Well, of course you can't call her a whore, But she does her best work on her back, boys. So she buggered off down to the docks, And, although I can't quote you the figures, By taking all manner of cocks, She raised ninety-four quid for the niggers.

I want to have a shit. *But I've just HAD a shit.* Why do I wan

2. The anonymous *TLS* review (by G.S. Fraser), entitled 'Tradition and Originality', appeared on 19 February 1954. In it Wain is called 'a poet of what has recently been described, whether aptly or not, as the neo-metaphysical school; his supple and humorous mind and lively talent still move with a certain feeling of constriction in a framework of tart colloquialism and tricky metrical form derived, perhaps, too obviously and exclusively from Mr William Empson's distinguished volume of 1940, *The Gathering Storm*' (p.122).

3. See Notes on Recipients.

There is a certain lack of distinction in Mr. Amis's bum,

Kingsley

[TLS: Bodleian]

TO HILARY RUBINSTEIN – 24 FEBRUARY 1954

24 The Grove, Uplands, Swansea.

My dear Hilary,

Very glad to get your news and to view that most opulent advertisement. I feel as if VG Ltd are concentrating their entire resources on selling my book. Very good taste on their part, of course: I only hope it pays them.

I'll chew over Mr. Rae-Scott[1] and his dramatic ideas. I feel I might have a crack at dramatising the thing myself one day. Must discuss it with you. Shall stall R-S in the meantime.

What on earth did my old dad want, ringing you up like that? Trying to check up on my movements, no doubt. I hope you told him where he got off.

I enclose one for you this time, this man Dick Whittington or whatever his name who wants to put Jim on the films.[2] I'm writing to him to say you handle all that and (taking a leaf out of your book) that I've asked you to reply to him direct.

Hope to see you on Monday.

As ever,
Kingsley

Excuse fearful envelope – or do your underlings dispose of them before letters get to you?

1. Untraced.

2. Jack Whittingham (b. 1910), a screenwriter whose credits included *Kiss the Bride Goodbye* (1944) and *The Divided Heart* (1954), wrote to Amis on 20 February praising *Lucky Jim* and asking if the screen rights had been sold.

Rather a gloomy letter from Doubledays – good reviews, poor sales. What do I care, though, with ⅞ of $2500 in the bag.[3]

[TLS: Gollancz]

TO THE EDITOR, *SPECTATOR* – 26 FEBRUARY 1954

SIR,—In her letter published in last week's *Spectator* Dr. Edith Sitwell refers to 'Little Mr. Tomkins' as 'a wearisome person.' She also speaks very kindly of my novel *Lucky Jim*.

A writer at the outset of his career can rarely hope for such generous praise as that contained in the last paragraph of Dr. Sitwell's letter. I am sincerely grateful to her. At the same time I feel I should point out that I myself am 'Little Mr. Tomkins.'—Yours faithfully,

KINGSLEY AMIS
University College of Swansea

TO PHILIP LARKIN – 14 MARCH 1954

Swansea

Will <u>*you*</u> *write to Fantasy about review copies? I heard nothing when there (forgot to ask)*[1]

My dear Philip,

At last, old man, the mists have cleared for an hour or two, and I can put down a lot of words for MD[2] to read. Honestly, you know, fucking *correspondence* takes up most of my time. A glance at the little ledger I keep for my accountant (herkherm) shows me that I've spent 14/- on stamps in the last 25 days. A lot, really. Most of the letters are to Lucky Jim farns, who are nearly all new people, funnily enough; one ex-army acquaintance and a handful of Oxford craps, the rest painters,

3. MS addition.

1. MS addition.
2. 'My Dalling' or 'My Dear', both found frequently in the correspondence.

American agents, script editors drama (sound), features producers (Wales), actors wanting to play Dixon on the films (I hear, by the way, that there's a movement to get NORMAN WISDOM[3] to do this), sexual maniacs (male), as you can see from what I will this time enclose if I can possibly remember. All very flattering, yes, but tedious too: tit, bideytbi. (Can you dig that?) I feel in a sense that 'they can't stop me now', except when I take up my new novel and feel how easy it will be for me to stop myself. Things are going well apart from this, and just between ourselves I *may* find myself with a job in London in a year or so, which would please me mightily. The higher journalism, it would be. Apologies, by the way, if I seem a bit 'full of myself'; I know you really want to know some of it, anyway, and I try to spread my luck: there shd. be 2 more poetry mags writing to you shortly.

I dug your old fiction thing on the wireless and thought he read it as well as could be expected.[4] I felt very nice myself, flanked by you and Alvarez. There's no doubt, you know, we are getting to be a movement, even if the only people in it we like apart from ourselves are each other. Peronal veronal venereal personally I don't give a pinch of shit for old Al's 'stuff', nor Davie's, nor old John Barry Wain's really much. For GOD'S SAKE, MAN, turn out something in the fiction line. I was talking to a man from Faber's (Charles Monteith[5]) who is the only man there, he said, who cares about fiction; he was looking through the Faber's list, which yielded only ONE novelist he thought they ought to bring out another book by – YOU, you flat faced pullet. Further, when I was at the poetry brains trust a young man I'd never seen before came up and asked me to tell him anything I could about the reception, writing etc. of *Jill*, which he said he admired greatly and was 'pushing' among his friends. He was 'making a study of' you, he said. I didn't get time to ask him what he meant. Why don't you try some short stories if you can't manage a novel, some criticism, journalism, ANY BLOODY THING? I know it must be horrible to read this, making you writhe in your chair etc, but for Gods sake Mister Larkin. Don't you see . . . ? Write a *short* novel . . . Oh dear.

3. Norman Wisdom (b.1920), British comedian on film, stage and television, noted for Cockney slapstick; a wholly unsuitable Dixon.

4. 'Fiction and the Reading Public' (reprinted in *LCP*, p. 34), read on *New Poetry*, a programme edited and introduced by G.S. Fraser and broadcast on 8 March 1954 on the Third Programme; the Amis poem that was read after Larkin's and before Alvarez's was 'Something Nasty in the Bookshop', from *A Frame of Mind* (1953).

5. Charles Monteith (1921–95), publisher; Chairman, Faber and Faber (1977–80).

I don't know whether I can give you much idea of the London-Oxford jaunt. The first person I saw was, of course, him, but I soon got away from him. Did I tell you about his postcard, thanking me for sending him the American edition, and going on AT ONCE, 'I noticed a number of printers' errors?' BATEARED OLD Then there was Colin (a very reliable chap here, by the way, saw him at a philosophers' conference some months ago and said he thought he was going to go mad *pretty soon* – he showed no signs of this when I saw him, however) who was as usual, Patsy, who seems to have got a lot worse since I last saw her, more offensive-defensive and speaking in a funny way, as if she's lost all her bottom teeth, Barbara Stone, who was also as usual I'm deeply grieved to say, in fact looking 'worse' than ever in some close-fitting check slacks, and Bruce, who seemed rather unhappy I thought, and whom I 'offended' three times for what I thought, each time, were occasions worthy perhaps of chaff or even an oh-well-Christ or two, but not being offended at. There was an All Souls' party with that awful shit Butler[6] providing the drinks, a dinner party at the Strangs' with that awful shit Butler doing a lot of talking about all the things he knew about, and a lot of drinking. Then Hilly and Bruce and I went to London, and I met the Spectator lot who all seemed very decent, even Iain Hamilton,[7] and then there was a tremendous lunch at Bruce's IMA club[8] where I met old Raybould[9] as I said, others too of lesser note. Then we went and saw Tony Hartley and John [J.D.] Scott in a pub where two of the nastiest Swansea art craps were next to us at the bar, and then Hartley and Hilly and I went and saw Ken Tynan and his wife, but I was so pissed I could hardly speak. After some black coffee had been produced for me I recovered a little and found myself in a pub, advancing towards Harry Hoff, Bruce and C.P. Snow sitting in a line. Hoff greeted me by saying 'Here's Amis, but too drunk, I see, to say much'. However, I managed to get quite a lot said, though I can'tr cuntr can't remember much of it. Then it was outside and snowing, then I was in bed. The next day we drank with Newby, a small, rather nasty man with apostolic eyes. Then it was 1.0 and we were picking up

6. There were two Butlers at All Souls at this time, both historians: Rohan Butler (1917–96), a Fellow from 1938–84, and Lionel Henry Butler (1923–81), a Fellow from 1946–55.

7. Iain Hamilton (1920–86), Editor, *Spectator* (1962–63).

8. The International Musicians' Association, 'the most drunken institution in the world' (*Memoirs*, p. 74).

9. Clarence Raybould (1886–1972), composer, conductor.

Anthony Powell. He was the nicest man we met, medium height with discoloured teeth and looking much more like the photograph on the back of Waring than that on the back of Men[10] is it. He expressed admiration for Proust, affection for Grgr though dislike of his books, sorrow about Evelyn Waugh, who apparently gets into fights whenever he goes out and only does one draft of his books with an occasional verbal correction, liking for David Cecil, whose fag he was at Eton, but dislike of his books, and not much else that I can remember, except that he thought nasty Burgundy nicer than nasty Bordeaux. He also wore a ridiculous felt hat pulled down to the level of his eyebrows. Then we went back to the IMA and picked up Bruce again. He now decided to come to Oxford with us, and we drank in the railway carriage, where he rebuked me (this was my 3rd offence) for tipping the waiter 9d instead of 1s. We got to Oxford and drank in the Randolph until 40 minutes after the time I was due to meet Anthony Thwaite to start the brains trust sherry. It was in the Randolph that Bruce revealed that he proposed to write a novel about the events of the past two days – drinking with me and the others in London. Rather thin, I thought and think it would be, though I didn't say so. Then I went off to Anthony Thwaite who gave me what was either a bugger's or a mason's handshake; I think a lat a shat the latter though I shouldn't have minded the former in a way. Old GS [Fraser] was there, and CS Lewis, who was doing the compering vice [Lord David] Cecil who was on TV that night. And Kirkup was there, a really revolting queer with a quiff-cum-fringe whom I only heard speak 3 times during the 'dinner' (Christ, in the Cafe de Paris; I had a sole apparently encased in hessian); each time he was saying something very like 'Yes, he is a most sweet man and I love him dearly'. Then there was the brains trust, all very embarrassing and panic-causing as far as I was concerned: old [Herbert] Palmer bombinated about poetry being the marriage of matter and spirit, Fraser pontificated in a way that he had clearly pontificated many times before, Kirkup talked in a very stupid way and eventually fell silent, and I was sullen, jerky and facetious by turns. [. . .]

I've had another letter from the old bag[11] – seen the latest Specr by the way? She forgives me handsomely, adding: 'When you come to the luncheon party I shall give for you, you will find me completely oblivious

10. *What's Become of Waring* (1939) and *Afternoon Men* (1931), novels by Anthony Powell.

11. Edith Sitwell.

that this has ever happened ... *Not one* of the persons who has had the impertinence to attack me has even a gleam of talent for poetry. They simply cant write. And it would never enter the head of a poet of any stature to discuss their verses. Not only I, but all my fellow-poets of any importance (as I know from their letters to me on the subject[)], are entirely amazed that they should have dared to behave as they have. They cannot harm me, all that has happened is that they have made an abjectly ridiculous spectacle of themselves, and are being laughed at, not only all over England, but also in New York ... Yours very sincerely ...' Rather pathetic in a way. You know, all this is going to be confoundedly difficult. Bloody funny, though, isn't it? [...]

Aren't you supposed to be coming here at Easter? Hilly sends her love and hopes you will. Come, I mean. You won't have to sleep with the baby. I still love your poem about her dear.[12] I love it I think more than any of yours. Gonna have a piss now Give my love to Gambles and de Banzie and Trotter[13] (Christ I'd forgotten him, the horror.)

Mr. Amis wears a mask of what the 18th-c called sullen bum,

Kingsley

[TLS: Bodleian]

TO JOHN AMIS – 15 MARCH 1954

24 The Grove, Uplands, Swansea.

My dear John,[1]

Gigantic apologies for having been so tremendously long in answering your letter, which I was very glad to receive. Only my laziness, which is however a large consideration in itself, has prevented me. I'm glad you enjoyed *Jim*: I have found it what one of my schoolmasters used to call a useful shibboleth, or some such word, for the detection of humourless, reactionary sods; such, for example, as the Emeritus Professor of Crapology or something here, who thought it 'ought to be

12. 'Born Yesterday'.
13. Untraced.

1. For John Amis see Notes on Recipients.

banned', not because it was 'obscene' (although it *was* 'obscene' a lot of the time), but because it was 'just in very bad taste all the way through'. God you were absolutely right, to the very word, about my parents' reaction: morbid and sordid ran their refrain, though tremendously good as well of course.

Yes, we *will* meet when I get the chance to come to London – I come very rarely and then am beset by editors, publishers etc. whom I have to see, because they may give me money. But we'll fit a meeting in some time. If not before, it'll be at the luncheon-party Doctor Sitwell proposes to throw for me – did you read all that business in the *Spectator*? Mad, mad, mad. She is, I mean. Though very decent to me. And a friend of yours, so she says. Hope to see you then, if I'm not concealed behind the brim of her hat.

Ever yours,
Pud[2] to you; but you must
try to call me –
Kingsley

[TLS: British Library]

TO ANTHONY POWELL – 24 MARCH 1954

24 The Grove, Uplands, Swansea.

Dear Mr. Powell,[1]

This is a very belated note of thanks for a most enjoyable luncheon the other week, and to say what a great pleasure it was for us to meet you.

I was sorry I didn't get round to telling you what I had determined I would tell you: that I admire what I've seen of *The Music of Time* a very great deal and am most anxious to see the next part.[2] I hope it

2. See Amis to Larkin, 27 December 1947, note 3.

---

1. For Anthony Powell see Notes on Recipients.

2. Two of the twelve volumes had been published: *A Question of Upbringing* (1951) and *A Buyer's Market* (1952); the third volume, *The Acceptance World*, would be published in 1955.

won't be too long before I get the chance to enlarge in conversation on those rather bare remarks.

I will if I may keep *Punch* very much in mind and send you anything that might interest you.

My wife sends her very best regards.

Yours sincerely,
Kingsley Amis

[TLS: Recipient]

TO EDITH SITWELL – 24 MARCH 1954

24 The Grove, Uplands, Swansea, Glamorgan, Great Britain.

Dear Miss Sitwell,

I was most relieved and thankful to receive your letter of the 8th March. I am extremely grateful to you for your magnanimity.

It is very kind of you to want to arrange a luncheon party for me. I too am greatly looking forward to it. Unfortunately I shall have a great deal on hand during the first period you suggest, immediately after Easter, so I should like, if I may, to defer our meeting until June. The latter part of that month would suit me best, as our examinations here start near the beginning of it and entail the usual laborious clearing-up afterwards. Perhaps I may write to you again nearer the time, when things here are more definite.

With renewed thanks and best wishes,

Yours most sincerely,
Kingsley Amis

PS. I do hope the indisposition you mention is now completely at an end.[1]

[TLS: HRHRC]

---

1. MS addition.

TO MR ALEXANDER[1] – 31 MARCH 1954

24 The Grove, Uplands, Swansea.

Dear Mr. Alexander,

Here is the form, duly signed.[2] It's probably not of the slightest importance, but the poem is called 'A Note on Wyatt', not 'Whatt'. I've left it to you to make any alteration that may be necessary.

Yours sincerely,
Kingsley Amis

[TLS: BBC]

TO HILARY RUBINSTEIN – 3 APRIL 1954

24 The Grove, Uplands, Swansea.

My dear Hilary,

What tremendous news! Thanks for that very exciting wire. Surely £200 for an option is pretty damn good, isn't it?[1] VG Ltd. does it again. Have you any idea at all whether they may be making it, or purchasing it? But never mind that: the news is quite enough to keep me happy as it stands. And of course congratulations to *you* on pulling it off.

I have a little mite of cheering information to exchange: this very

---

1. Of the Copyright Department of the BBC (and probably 'Miss' rather than 'Mr', according to BBC records, which list Beatrice Alexander, an employee of the BBC from 1941–69, as the only Alexander in the department).

2. Allowing the BBC to include 'A Note on Wyatt' (reprinted in *A Look Round the Estate* and *CP*, p. 62) in *New Verse*, to be broadcast on the Third Programme on 8 April and repeated on 10 April; Amis received a fee of three guineas per performance.

---

1. The Boulting Brothers had purchased a six months' option on the film rights to *Lucky Jim* for £200, 10 per cent of the total purchase price of £2,000. John and Roy Boulting, twin brothers, were born in 1913 (John died in 1985). They founded Charter Films in 1937 as a writer-producer-director team, and in 1958 were both appointed directors of British Lion Films. Among their prior credits were *Desert Victory* (1944), *Brighton Rock* (1946), *Seven Days to Noon* (1950) and *Private's Progress* (1954); after *Lucky Jim* appeared in 1957 (with John directing and Roy producing) they went on to make a number of influential comedies, including *I'm All Right Jack* (1959) and *Heaven's Above* (1963).

morning I get a letter from the BBC asking me if I 'can authorise' the broadcast of a radio adaptation of *Jim*, done (or to be done) by the wonderfully-named E. J. King Bull. They give no other details, but the project sounds completely definite. I am writing to say that under the circumstances I might manage to bring myself to authorise the thing.[2]

Looking forward to seeing you at the première of *Lucky Jim on Ice* –

Ever yours,
Kingsley

[TLS: Gollancz]

TO HILARY RUBINSTEIN – 4 APRIL 1954

24 The Grove, Uplands, Swansea.

My dear Hilary,

I have your letter now – it came by the second post, after I'd sent my other one off.

Yes, by God, I am enormously pleased, as I say in my other letter. Your supplementary news, about the likelihood of the rights being bought, sounds pretty encouraging too. I'm sure Kenneth More[1] would be a killer in the part if it ever gets as far as that; I must coach him in face-making. It would be an enormous triumph to have a hand in the script, and I'd very much like to meet John Boulting when I'm next in London – in June I hope, but I'll let him (and you) know in good time.

By the way, if you could let me have my cut of the option-money fairly soon it'd come in very handy. We are being more or less compelled

2. As Rubinstein informed him in a letter of 7 April 1954 (in Gollancz), Amis was in no position to 'authorise' a radio adaptation, since ancillary broadcasting as well as television rights were part of the the Boulting Brothers' option (see Amis to Rubinstein, 8 April 1954). Eric James King-Bull (b. 1897) was a BBC Radio drama producer (1927–57).

---

1. Kenneth More (1914–82), British stage and screen actor, best known at the time for leading roles in the successful screen comedies *Genevieve* (1953) and *Doctor in the House* (1954).

to buy a *car*, of all things, next week, and this will leave my bank account in rather a debilitated condition. See what you can do?

With renewed thanks, and blessings on VG Ltd.,

Yours ever,
Kingsley

[TLS: Gollancz]

TO HILARY RUBINSTEIN – 8 APRIL 1954

24 The Grove, Uplands, Swansea.

My dear Hilary,

Thanks for yesterday's letter. I've written to the BBC, asking them to do as you say.[1]

Don't blame yourself for this tangle. To my mind (though I'm less of a veteran than you are in these matters) something like clairvoyance would have been needed to see that 'ancillary' = broadcasting. And I am rather at fault myself in a way; it was only my insane eagerness that made me authorise the broadcast before hearing what you had to say on the matter. As regards the dates of the two things, I signed the broadcast authorisation on the 3rd April, and the film agreement is dated the 1st, so you are in the clear with the Boulting Brothers.[2]

Whatever arrangement you come to about the proceeds from the radio rights will be agreeable to me. Which reminds me: hurry up that £180 like a good fellow, or I shall be reduced to smoking toilet-paper. I bought the car yesterday, or rather paid the deposit. Mad, mad.

Ever yours,
Kingsley

[TLS: Gollancz]

---

1. Rubinstein had asked Amis to request the BBC to refer further correspondence to Gollancz, and to forward King-Bull's script for approval by the Boulting Brothers.

2. It was Rubinstein's responsibility to inform the Boulting Brothers about any prior authorisations; he was 'in the clear' because Amis signed with the BBC after the film agreement had been concluded. Though the Boulting Brothers were formally entitled to claim any proceeds from the BBC, Rubinstein thought they were unlikely to do so.

TO P.H. NEWBY – 15 APRIL 1954

24 The Grove, Uplands, Swansea.

Dear Mr. Newby,

Many thanks for your letter.[1] I've already begun something which might do; had indeed done so before getting your letter, which I received late, having been to Bristol over the week-end to confer[2] about the teaching of English. An attack on travel books will be on its way to you in a few days.[3]

Yours sincerely,
Kingsley Amis

[TLS: BBC]

TO ROBERT CONQUEST – 16 APRIL 1954

24 The Grove, Uplands, Swansea.

Dear Conquest,

Good to hear from you. And thanks a lot for kind remarks about the old *Frame.*[1] I know what you mean about being Empsonic,[2] and am trying to come out on the other side: have made a vow not to write another poem in 10-syllable lines, 3-line stanzas, for another 10 years. That should do it. As regards the Master himself (W. E.) I do like his verse, or some of it, but get impatient with all those laconic enigmas, or whatever you're going to call them. His crit is ruined by lack of

---

1. Newby (see Notes on Recipients), of the Talks Department of the BBC, had asked Amis for a contribution to *Literary Opinion*, on the Third Programme; these contributions were of eight hundred or so words on some topic of literary interest.

2. That is, attend a conference.

3. As it happened, Newby had already approved Anthony Quinton's request to discuss this topic; Quinton (b. 1925), a philosopher, was at the time a Fellow of All Souls College, Oxford.

---

1. *A Frame of Mind* (1953).

2. Empson's poems employ metaphysical conceits and other complexities much in evidence in Amis's early verse.

relevance due to lack of historical knowledge: 'did this, or could this, mean that then?' is something he never seems to ask himself. But no doubt Sheffield[3] will put him right on that sort of thing. I agree about his wife:[4] I admire most the way she has so much confidence in herself she doesn't bother to wash.

Hope you enjoy *Jim* when you get to him. Really, the whole thing is turning out most lucrative. 'In case of difficulty in obtaining' the FP pamphlet,[5] let me know. Not that it's a collector's item just yet.

Yes, will get you on the blower when I come up. Don't yet know when that'll be, though: duty calls, particularly during term-time. Ooh: thanks for saving me the trouble of writing to the *Statesman* a few weeks ago on science fiction. You made exactly the points. (Have you read Alfred Bester's *The Demolished Man*,[6] by the way?)

Yours,
Kingsley Amis

[TLS: Recipient]

TO P.H. NEWBY – 21 APRIL 1954

24 The Grove, Uplands, Swansea.

Dear Mr. Newby,

What a pity.[1] I send you this,[2] not with the intention of making life more difficult for you, but because I finished it yesterday and thought you might have it as well as anyone; in case, too, Anthony Quinton

3. Empson had been appointed Professor of English at the University of Sheffield in 1953.

4. Hester Henrietta Empson.

5. *Kingsley Amis: No. 22. The Fantasy Poets* (1954). The Fantasy Press, in Swinford, near Eynsham, outside Oxford, was founded by Oscar Mellor in 1952, and its Fantasy Poets series was co-edited with Michael Shanks, then Donald Hall, then, at the time of Larkin's and Amis's pamphlets, George MacBeth (1932–92), poet and broadcaster. The series was made up of small selections of poems (six or so per poet) mainly by Oxford and Cambridge undergraduates or recent graduates, including Elizabeth Jennings (No. 1, 1952), Thom Gunn (No. 16, 1953), Donald Davie (No. 19, 1954) and Larkin (No. 21, 1954).

6. Published 1953; Alfred Bester (b. 1913), American science fiction writer.

---

1. See Amis to Newby, 15 April 1954, note 3.

2. The piece on travel books.

dies or goes mad before he can deliver his effort. Don't of course bother to send it back.

I'll start thinking things over again and will let you know as soon as I've thought of a topic.

Yours sincerely,
Kingsley Amis

[TLS: BBC]

TO JOHN WAIN – 23 APRIL 1954

24 The Grove, Uplands, Swansea, Glam.

The students won't pay your fare. They're too poor, and too stingy and too uninterested in literary matters.[1]

My dear John,

Philip's account of your visit to Belfast stimulates me to write to you again and ask again when you think you can make a visit to Swansea. Come whenever you like (you won't be interrupting my WORK hahaha) and stay as long as you like. You are one of Hilly's dream-figures so don't worry about 'making a lot of work' or any of that tack. There isn't much to offer you here, apart from the resources of my conversation and gramophone library, but you can have as much as you can stand of both of those.

How are you in health these days? In good trim, I trust. I hope you aren't thinking of starting your job again too soon. Did I write to you about my visit to Reading? I thought your colleagues were a damned fine crowd of chaps. Your imitation of Gordon[2] is much too restrained. That chap Kermode[3] or whatever it is seemed a good chap. Tell me

1. MS addition.

2. Donald Gordon (1915–77), Lecturer in English (1946–49), Professor of English (1949–76), Reading University.

3. Frank Kermode (b. 1919), literary critic and scholar; Lecturer in English, Reading University (1949–58); later Professor of English Literature, University of Manchester (1958–65), University of Bristol (1965–67), University College, London (as Lord Northcliffe Professor, 1967–74), Cambridge University (as King Edward VII Professor, 1974–82); knighted, 1991.

about Calder;[4] is he . . . I mean, he *seemed* . . . I suppose he *is* a . . . Well, he does *look* . . .

Write *soon* and tell me about this. Your pal Alvarez had a pretty bum poem in *Ox. po.*, I thought.

Love,
Kingsley and Hilly

[TLS: Edinburgh]

TO PHILIP LARKIN – 28 APRIL 1954

Swansea

Pity my birthday present got *lost in the post*, wasn't it? Never mind, I know these things happen. Give my love to Harry Hoff when you see him. Nothing happening here, except my attempts to "keep it (*Unc. Feeling*) moving". Listen; shall I try to arrange a quadripartite volume (you, me, D. Davie, Wain) with the Fantasy Press? Serious now. We c[d] all give a slight financial guarantee. Will say more when I write next. Early feed bum

K.

[ALS: Bodleian]

TO P.H. NEWBY – 2 MAY 1954

24 The Grove, Uplands, Swansea.

Dear Mr. Newby,

Here is another one, about dons this time.[1] I thought someone should have a go along these lines.

4. I.R.F. (Ian) Calder (1924–85), Research Fellow in English (1951–53), Temporary Lecturer in English (1953–54), Reading University, later worked in the theatre and for the British Council.

---

1. 'In Defence of Dons', a six-minute talk broadcast on 9 June 1954 on *Literary Opinion*, on the Third Programme.

I'm sorry I didn't write earlier saying what I proposed to do, so that you could fend off any other aspirants to the same sort of thing. But I found that I couldn't be sure that I could get it written until I'd seen whether I could get it written.

Yours sincerely,
Kingsley Amis

[TLS: BBC]

TO ROBERT CONQUEST – 9 MAY 1954

24 The Grove, Uplands, Swansea.

Dear Conquest,

Jolly good to hear from you. I'm sorry to have taken so long to reply, but I seem to have less and less time these days. Let me say I *liked* your poem, though your best (of those I've seen) remains, for my money, the Flowers fat after so much flattery[1] one which started old Palmer off on his ravings (I must have told you about the oration he gave at Oxford some months ago at a poetry 'brains trust'? Had them all in fits).

The s-f scheme[2] interests me vastly, and as a matter of fact I have a scheme already roughed out: a bit corny, since it revolves on the alien-life-really-not-so-alien-when-you-get-to-know-it theme – the life in this case being rotoids or cycloids: creatures shaped like, and propelling themselves like, wheels. The snag is that I shan't have time to touch it for some months, as Gollancz have already started listing my second novel as due in the autumn, and I must get this and other things off my chest as soon as I can. May I take it up with you again in the autumn, say? I hope to see you before then anyway and we could discuss it.

Yes, this poetry game is bloody difficult. I don't push my stuff about enough, I suppose, partly through laziness, partly because I dislike getting rejection slips. As regards poetry magazines, acceptance of work

1. 'Through flowers fat after so much flattery', line one of 'Watering Place', reprinted in Robert Conquest, *New and Collected Poems* (London: Century Hutchinson, 1988), p. 69.
2. A proposed collaboration.

by me seems to be the signal for the paper to go bankrupt before they can get my stuff to the printer. Further, I feel I have some sort of allegiance to the *Spectator* among the weeklies. Further, I don't write an awful lot and can't keep sending the same stuff in time after time. Should we try *Encounter* and *The London Magazine*? But how galling to be turned down by them. Do keep plugging away with your book. It's the only way, it seems. Donald Davie has had his back 1/2 a dozen times, in one case *unread*. By the way I get the odd letter from chaps asking me to send them poems for mags. Would you like me to suggest they try you when it happens again? (*If* it happens again.)

I laughed a lot at your projected butt-in. Pity you didn't send it in. My own hands are tied now after Dr S[itwell]'s puff of *Jim* in the S'p'r. My relations with the lady are moving to a climax of embarrassment: a 'luncheon' is promised me, which I suppose I shall be attending, next month some time. Anyway I hope to be in London for a day or two then and will ring, or look, you up. Glad you enjoyed *Jim*, and thanks for your amiamble (an engaging neologism: 'amiable' was what I meant to type) remarks on my verse. All the best. Hasta la vista.

Yours,
Kingsley Amis

[TLS: Recipient]

TO THE EDITOR, *LISTENER* – 13 MAY 1954

Sir, – I suppose Mr. R. C. Burlingham (THE LISTENER, May 6) has seen that it has become old-fashioned to attack the Welfare State on the grounds that it destroys the virtues of charity and thrift, or that he does not want to pay for other people's wigs and false teeth, so he tries to imagine it will wreck the novel.[1] Why should it? And how could it?

---

1. On 6 May 1954 the *Listener* published a letter (p. 789) from R. C. Burlingham, a self-described 'young critic', taking issue with an article by Angus Wilson entitled 'The Future of the English Novel' (*Listener*, 29 April 1954, p. 746). In Burlingham's paraphrase, Wilson expressed the hope that 'the values and outlook' of the Welfare State would be good for fiction; Burlingham was sure they would not, arguing that 'the wicked old world of profits and reaction, anti-social behaviour patterns and extremes of wealth and poverty . . . was yet organically connected to its art forms.'

Why will novelists 'have perforce to embrace the values and outlook of the Welfare State' (whatever these are)? And why will they only 'cautiously toy' with their material? If the terms have any meaning, the 'values and outlook' of any past age have appeared quite a lot in some of its novels, but not very much in others, and some of both sorts of novel have been worth reading. Why should it be any different this time? Or does Mr. Burlingham believe all that stuff about the thought police and Ministries of Culture and *1984*? If so, he is being old-fashioned again.

But perhaps I am being unfair, and the fact that the new age will not be 'organically connected with its art-forms' will be enough on its own to strangle the novel. Such a reflection would once have depressed me, because I should have believed that Mr. Burlingham knew what he meant and could say how a society can be organically connected with a novel, and what the connection was in given cases, and how it could be utterly non-existent in others, and when a connection was organic and when it was a different sort. But I am not in the least depressed.

All the same, I think Mr. Burlingham should stick to complaining that he does not want to pay for other people's wigs and false teeth.

Yours, etc.,

KINGSLEY AMIS
Swansea

TO HILARY RUBINSTEIN – 19 MAY 1954

24 The Grove, Uplands, Swansea.

My dear Hilary,

What excellent news about the Swedish rights! I'm longing to know the Swedish for phrases like 'You've got this "rude" business on the winkle' and similar fine flowers of our mother-tongue. And how lovely to be advertised again! You certainly have done me proud and no error.

One matter on which I need your advice. Mister Lance Sieveking,[1] on behalf of 'a large firm of publishers' (he didn't say who), has asked

1. Lance Sieveking (1896–1972), novelist, dramatist, writer for radio, and for many years a radio drama and features producer.

me if I want to contribute to a series of highbrow science-fiction novels edited by him. Does my agreement with VG Ltd definitely rule this out? I ask this as a necessary preliminary to making up my mind whether I want to have anything to do with it at all; at the moment I feel very dubious, even supposing VG release me. Please don't feel I want to slide away from VG Ltd; it's just that this series might (repeat might) be fun to appear in. And please keep the Sieveking part more or less under your hat – what I mean is don't challenge him to a duel or anything. And please forgive me for bothering you with all this and for any disastrous ignorance of the ways of the world I may have shown in mentioning it. I shall of course say nothing to Sieveking till I hear from you.[2]

Ever yours,
Kingsley

[TLS: Gollancz]

TO PHILIP LARKIN – 19 MAY 1954

Swansea

My dear Philip,

Why do I feel a little run-down most of the time these days? Why do I get one of my ear things, swollen to a more impressive size than ever before? Then why do I get a little galaxy of spots on my forehead, all seeing how near they can get to each other to draw the glance of curious observers, and skilfully managing to push a fresh one up every time an old one begins to fade? And then why does my throat go sore, and *stay sore*? And, worst of all, what possesses me to go away to my parents' for last week-end? As time goes on I can see fewer and fewer, and less and less powerful, arguments for seeing them at all, ever, from one year's end to the other, at any period. (I have tracked this device: it is the basic method of old Rohget – remember?) I lost my glasses at Miggy's, which was bright of me and has given me a sturdy, reliable headache with bags of stamina. (In case you are consumed with curi-

2. Rubinstein wrote back on 20 May reminding Amis that Gollancz had a firm option on his next novel and did itself publish science fiction 'of a superior kind (Charles Williams, etc.)'.

osity, we dumped Phil and Mart there on our way to you know where with the baby. I was glad to notice in Miggy's tones, as she pronounced the familiar register of old Rodge's habits, tastes and convictions (Roger hates dogs, Roger goes mad if the kids throw anything into the pond, Roger spends all day Sunday tinkering with the car, Roger won't eat salad, etc. etc.), a little less amused wonder and reverence and a little more amused amusement and contempt. That's good. Did you know he won a lot of *cups* when he was younger? For *running*? They were in the garden, tarnished, buckled and scratched. Good shaher.) [. . .]

Many wept for joy to see the Queen standing at last on her bum,[1]

K.

[TLS: Bodleian]

TO LANCE SIEVEKING – 24 MAY 1954

24 The Grove, Uplands, Swansea.

Dear Mr. Sieveking,

I am so sorry to have kept you waiting for an answer to your letter of the 9th, but the position has taken some sorting out. It comes down to this, I'm afraid: Gollancz have me firmly tied to them for my next two 'full-length works of fiction' and – understandably I suppose – have taken the line that, while science fiction isn't like ordinary fiction, it's still fiction. The real trouble is, I think, that they themselves do quite a bit of s-f publishing and feel that if anyone's going to take s-f by me it should be them.

So I can only say how flattered and grateful I am to be asked to contribute to your series and how sorry not to be able to accept.

Yours sincerely,
Kingsley Amis

[TLS: Indiana]

---

1. Presumably a reference to the Queen's return earlier in May from a six-month tour of the Commonwealth.

TO EDITH SITWELL – 25 JUNE 1954

24 The Grove, Uplands, Swansea.

My dear Miss Sitwell,

It was delightful to meet you and to talk to you – such a privilege and a pleasure. And it was very enjoyable to see your cousins and friends.[1] My wife and I both want to thank you most warmly.

I will, if I may, take up your kind invitation to let you know when I am next in London (I expect it will be in the early autumn) so that we may meet again. I look forward very much to having another talk with you.

Yours very sincerely,
Kingsley Amis

[TLS: HRHRC]

TO PHILIP LARKIN – 3, 8 JULY 1954

Swansea

My dear Philip,

Mike cries: 'Tits!' A long time ago since we were having communication together. The trouble is I never get any sid sod sodding *time* these days. I owe Boots' Booklovers' Library 18s. I think it is now for books I have out. Just haven't got the sodding time to take them back, you sam. What with this and that . . . The latest, did I tell you, is an intro to the Collins Classic Poems and Essays of ole O. F. O'F. W. W.[1] 25gns for 2500 words. It's moider, he says. The less said about the bloody poems the better, and I'm beginning to feel rather the same about the essays. Can't say that in an intro ostensibly aimed at making

---

1. For a description of the lunch and those who were present see the following letter.

---

1. Oscar Wilde; Amis's Collins edition, entitled *Oscar Wilde: Poems and Essays*, did not appear until 1956.

people buy the book, though, can you? Anyway I do feel I am 'doing too much'; and not enough of what will really do me good, such as poems appearing every week in the *Spr* like *some people I could mention.* I greatly enjoyed *Skin*; haven't had time to penetrate *Age* (?) yet.[2] Christ old man you have the 'authoritative ring' all right. Every word falling inevitably into place – it's like Mozart ooghwgh Look old man: may I ask you to reconsider your ideas (which I fully, or let's say reasonably well, understand) on not appearing in a Fantasy foursome or sixsome? The names provisionally put forward by this Mellor man are now you, me, John, Davie, Thom Gunn, Donald Hall.[3] The last 2 are in favour, I gather, also John. Don't know about Davie yet. God old man you write so much these days surely you could spare us 10: reprint some of the Po & Aud.[4] efforts. Do think it over. No hard feelings, naturally, if you stick to your original decision.

Had a good jaunt in London the other week. I met Gordon Wharton,[5] a funny little chap with a cockney accent like mine (until I heard myself on the wireless I thought I talked more or less how the gentlemen talk, but not now) who looked about 14 and nice to but has a wife and kid. When he wasn't taking TWENTY MINUTES to tell me that 'it's a long way to tip a raree' story in a bad Irish accent, or NEARLY STARTING FIGHTS at Leicester Sq Underground by 'pretending to be drunk' and lurching into negroes shouting, etc., he was telling me that LISTEN should have been out, was coming out, on 14th June, but he HASNT HEARD ANYTHING ABOUT IT FOR WEEKS fuck and burgher. It seems that he's turned it all over to Geo H[artley].

2. Larkin's 'Skin' and 'Age' appeared in the *Spectator*, 2 July 1954, p. 5; both were reprinted in *The Less Deceived* and *LCP*, pp.92, 95, where they are dated, respectively, 5 April and 26 May 1954.

3. Thom Gunn (b. 1929), poet; educated at Trinity College, Cambridge (1950–53); moved to California in 1954, where he has lived ever since. The anti-Romanticism and formal control of Gunn's first collection, *Fighting Terms* (1954), led, in part, to his association with the Movement. Donald Hall (b. 1928), American poet; educated at Harvard and Oxford, (B.Litt., 1953), where he won the Newdigate Prize for Verse in 1952, subsequently publishing a pamphlet in the Fantasy Press series. Hall's early poetry in particular was noted for its ironical formalism.

4. Amis is referring to two poems, 'Triple Time' and 'Poetry of Departures', which Larkin published in 1954 in the Leeds University magazine *Poetry and Audience*. Both were reprinted in *The Less Deceived* (1955) and *LCP*, pp. 73 and 85–6.

5. Gordon Wharton (b. 1929), poet, broadcaster. *This and That* (1955), his first collection, was published by the Fantasy Press; *Errors of Observation: Eighteen Poems* (1955) was published by the School of Art, University of Reading.

again.[6] I never got any letter from GH corresponding to yours. But enough of him, sod him.

Had a corking fine lunch with my pal the Dame. Actually it was rather on the dull side, thank God; rather like lunching with a kindly maiden aunt who wants to show you she's interested in all that writing you're doing. John Hayward[7] was there in his wheelchair being paralysed and it was curious, almost macabre, to hear Edith say at the end to him 'Well, give my love to Tom.' Others

8th July, 1954

present included a man called Mister John Pope-Hennessy and an other man called Mister James Pope-Hennessy: as fine and select a brace of turds as you could hope to find anywhere ats shats at short, or even fairly long, notice. Alan Pryce-Jones[8] turned up for a little while and was very oily to the Dame, with whom, it was later revealed, he had recently had a ray of some sort. Then he went away again. I was glad, when he didt tidt did that. An American film director, an Australian pianist and two female cousins of the Dame's completed the rout. I quite enjoyed it, and then it was over, and I was glad. Saw old Hoff the next day. All right, isn't he?, but rather argumentative without a lot of critical equipment. Not fond of drinking or Bohemianism, either. I mean he likes drinking all right, but doesn't seem to see its connexion with getting drunk. I mean that such a connexion is desirable. Then there was old Wain. He looked and sounded in much better form than when I saw him last. He still thinks of giving up his job and taking to writing full-time. He explained that while he only had a 4th-rate

6. *Listen*, a poetry magazine, was founded in 1954 by George Hartley (b. 1933) with his wife Jean, and numbered among its early contributors A. Alvarez, Bernard Bergonzi, George MacBeth, Anthony Hartley and Gordon Wharton. Donald Davie called it 'that institution of the movement' (in 'The Varsity Match', *Poetry Nation*, No. 2 (1973), p. 77). Hartley and his wife also founded the Marvell Press, which published Larkin's *The Less Deceived* (1955), as well as collections by John Holloway, Davie, Anthony Thwaite and W.D. Snodgrass. In her account of *Listen* in *Philip Larkin, The Marvell Press, and Me* (London: Carcanet, 1989), p. 87, Jean Hartley describes Wharton as one of 'our London correspondents', the source not only of 'many helpful suggestions' but 'lists of subscribers to defunct little magazines'.

7. John Hayward (1905–65), editor and anthologist, friend of T. S. Eliot ('Tom').

8. John Pope-Hennessey (1913–94), art historian and museum curator; at the time Keeper, Department of Architecture and Sculpture, Victoria and Albert Museum (1954–66); knighted (1971). James Pope-Hennessey (1916–74), writer; Literary Editor, *Spectator* (1947–49). For Alan Pryce-Jones see Amis to Larkin, 1 January 1950, note 3.

scholarly career, at best, ahead of him, he had a first-rate literary one. When he said this I nodded slowly, my eyes fixed on my glass of gin and tonic in a manner that suggested I had detected in it some unusual but harmless chemical reaction.

We have begun to get a little of our money through, and have bought a television set, and a three-speed turntable for our gramophone. You might let me know of any 33⅓ jazz I ought to have apart from that Condon concert which I shall get pronto, or as soon after pronto as my dealer can make it. Neither of these new amenities have been paid for yet, largely because on returning from London there was a letter from ole RBM asking to be lent £50 'for two or three weeks'. Having had at least twice that amount given to me in kind by the old devil, I felt I couldn't very well refuse. But what in hell is the matter with him, or with his bank account? Is he keeping three homes going, or what?

Have just remembered: there was a horrid moment at the Sitwell lunch when, looking at me, she said: 'Of course, there is just one thing which is absolutely unforgivable. (Pause.) That is to attack someone anonymously.' I felt like an Indian brave whose horse runs away with him at the moment he realises that the white men he is charging have repeating rifles. After another pause, she added: 'That monstrous profile of me in the New Statesman, now.' I fair ped myself in releif. There was a wonderful moment (don't know whether I can describe it adequately) in the pub before the lunch, before I went to the lunch I mean, when Tony Hartley said 'Don't forget to talk to her about texture, now.' John Scott added, 'Oh yes, about the woobwoobwoob' (something inaudible: there was a good deal of noise going on). 'What?' I said loudly. 'Woof' he bawled. A dog in the next bar went into an absolute apoplexy of barking. Funny at the time, you know.

Well, old soul, I really am sorry about this time-gap. It shd. be better next time, because the reviewing thing is back to normal now and my official correspondence is up to date. There's just a little matter of a novel I have to get finished some day. But fortunately filthy tum has packed up. And I still haven't written to my new-found distant family connexion in lil ol Noth Caolina,[9] nor to Miss Pamela Franco,

9. Thomas and Nellia Amis. According to Robert Foster, Amis's cousin, Thomas Amis was 'the brother of our mutual grandfather, J. J. [Joseph James] Amis, who settled in Florida, not the Carolinas, upon his retirement in the 1930s' (personal communication, 25 February 1999). See Jacobs, *Biography*, p. 23: 'There was also an outer fringe of American relatives

who has written praising LJ and bitching and binding about my review of her in the *Spr.*[10] And a madwoman is being brought to supper to-night. Other news? Have you read *The Evening*?[11] Piss, d'you follow? I have a new Prima with Russell. Did I tell you about the clinically-insane poet who came all the way from London to see me? Greater than Shakespeare and ole TSE, he said he was, and perhaps possessing some attributes in common with the Creator of the Universe. He frightened me a lot.

Must run and meet Hilly: she is on the jury at the Assizes this week. Yesterday there was a wonderful chap who used his television set to attract all the small boys of the neighbourhood into his parlour, where he would assault them and induce them to assault each other. 15 years he got. Still, it'll be a holiday for him in a way, I suppose.

Slip us a line when time allows and tell me what you're up to and what you think of the weather.

We should be glad if you could speak on any aspect of bum,

Kingsley

[TLS: Bodleian]

TO HILARY RUBINSTEIN – 14 JULY 1954

24 The Grove, Uplands, Swansea.

My dear Hilary,

Thanks for the letter. I'm very sorry but I'm afraid I can't possibly get *Uncertain Feeling* to you even by the end of the month. I do hope this won't be too disastrous. I'm afraid I've been a bit of a fool in constantly promising to get it to you by such-and-such a date and then failing; I've really been doing far too much journalism and such. The mists are just starting to clear and I hope to begin fairly continuous work on the book next week. I feel most apologetic about the whole

who came to stay with Joseph James from time to time – aunts, uncles and cousins. One uncle was Uncle Tom, Kingsley remembers.'

10. Amis reviewed Pamela Frankau's *A Wreath for the Enemy* in 'New Novels', *Spectator*, 2 July 1954, p. 42.

11. Probably Christopher Isherwood's recently published *The World in the Evening*, which came out in England and America in June 1954.

thing and can only say (since at last I've begun to see the folly of giving a definite date) that you shall have the book just as soon as I can get it done, which will be as quickly as I can put the words down. Do forgive me.

We couldn't manage Majorca this year – no time. I hardly even have the time to buy razor-blades. My God I'm going to get drunk the day I post off *Uncertain Feeling*. Great stuff about the German rights.

All the very best,

Ever,
Kingsley

[TLS: Gollancz]

TO JOHN LEHMANN – 20 JULY 1954

24 The Grove, Uplands, Swansea

Dear Mr. Lehmann,

Thank you very much for your letter – which arrived just after I had set off for Manchester for the week-end; hence the delay in answering. I was very flattered and pleased by the suggestion you made.[1]

The trouble is that I don't know that I have anything very interesting to say on the topic under discussion. My only point would be that 'the novel' is not a 'thing' as your correspondent keeps on implying. Since time is now short, perhaps the best way to leave it would be that I will send you a shortish (less than 1 p.) letter on this point as soon as I can – say by Friday. This might be too late, and the letter might well be too boring to print; but I'll send it anyway and chance it, and please don't feel any obligation to print it.

Thank you again for your invitation,

Yours sincerely,
Kingsley Amis

[ALS: HRHRC]

1. Lehmann (see Notes on Recipients) had received a letter about the modern novel from Pansy Pakenham (1904–99), the second child and eldest daughter of the fifth Earl of Longford, and wife of the painter Henry Lamb, of Coombe Bissett, Salisbury (she identifies

TO PHILIP LARKIN – 11 AUGUST 1954

Swansea

My dear Philip,

I really must try to answer your letters more promptly, mustn't I? Very glad I was to get them. ('Yes, *them*, that's right'). Have quite a lot to tell you, but don't know that I can remember it all. As regards the poem,[1] my general werdick is definitely favourable, and, though I don't feel at all as you do about consecrated edifices, I sympathise with you having a shot at saying what you do feel, even at such length: I don't feel it's really too long. Hayever, as expected no doubt, I have a few particular objections. I don't myself much care for the historic present: it makes me think of George Eliot and of schoolboys chorusing 'Makes it more vivid, sir' when asked why it's used. I realise, however, that changing it would be a chore and shag up the metre if not the rhymes. Also, I think the last stanza isn't right yet; not because of the punctuation – couldn't see anything wrong with that – but because of one or two highly poetical words and constructions: the inversion in the first line, for instance, which makes me think of 'A casement high and triple arched there was' and such bits of flannel. I'd say you've got to be extra careful, at the point when you ease your foot gently down on the accelerator, to avoid reminding the reader that 'this is poetry'. See what I mean? 'Blent', too, seems a bit 18th-c. to me.[2] Friend, look to 't.[3] But as I say, it seems okay on the whole, and certainly meet to be published. [. . .]

No news on the literary front. Journalism continues to eat into my time: haven't touched the novel, nor written a poem, for three months or so. Still, I hope you'll be amused by what should be a funny attack

herself in the letter as 'neither author nor publisher', though she had written both fiction and non-fiction). Lehmann eventually printed the letter in the *London Magazine* 1:7 (August 1954), pp. 71–3, and he seems to have asked Amis to comment on it. For Amis's published response to the letter see Amis to the editor, *London Magazine*, September 1954.

---

1. 'Church Going', printed in *The Less Deceived* and *LCP*, pp. 97–8, where it is dated 18 July 1954.

2. Larkin ignored Amis's objections, retaining not only 'blent' and the inversion in the first line of the last stanza ('A serious house on serious earth it is'), but the historic present as well (the poem opens: 'Once I am sure there's nothing going on/I step inside, letting the door thud shut').

3. Hamlet's words to Polonius, II, ii, 186–7.

on Lallans in the Spr in a week or two, if they put it in. My part is a translation of Baudeliare into stylised cockney: *The Helbatrawss, aht er Charley Bordilair's froggy.*[4] [. . .]

[. . .] By the way, heard some news of him the other day. You won't believe *any* of this, but the old codger has been doing his folk-dancing IN A NUDIST CAMP. Yes, *stripped off* to do it. Old Rodge, who saw him recently, says he said it wasn't at all embarrassing, really, except when a *seventeen-year-old girl* CAME AND SAT ON HIS LAP. 'Can they get the horn at that age?' Hilly asked. 'Some of them can,' said I. No more news. None to compare with *that*, any road.

You ought to get TV, you know. Interesting item the other day: school kids demonstrating lifesaving at a baths. Gosh, they do get away with some scanty costumes these days! But it was good to see these teen-age girls giving each other artificial respiration! And the girl who gave a diving and water-acrobatic display! Only 13! They say a full figure helps a swimmer, but really! Still, they all looked as keen as mustard! Encourages the right spirit, that sort of thing! Made me wish I was 20 years younger! Exactly 20 years!!!!!!!

Don't seem to have bugger-all more to say. Shall look forward to seeing you in September. Would be too much to expect you to come over for a day, I suppose? Or a night, when your mum's gone back? Well, see what you can do. I'll certainly put in an appearance there. I have 9 gnat-bites on my right forearm. Now: why would you say that was, mm? Sorry I forgot your bithrayd: it wasn't an eye for an eye, I was just to bussy to remember anything, having a review and an article on the Eisteddfod and that cockney rubbish to get off all at once.[5] And I would have sent you a present, but for the moment I am two-paw (see below for reason). Well, whack me a line when you can. Wish I

4. This parody of '*L'Albatross*', from *Les Fleurs du mal* (1857) by Charles Baudelaire (1821–67), was first published in the *Spectator*, 27 August 1954, p. 248, under the name Anselm Chilworth; reprinted in Amis, ed., *New Oxford Book of Light Verse* (henceforth *NOBLV*) (1978), p. 302, and elsewhere. Lallans is the vernacular speech of the Lowlands of Scotland, and its use for literary purposes (including translations from Dante) had been revived by Tom Scott, S. Goodsir Smith and, most prominently, Hugh MacDiarmid (1892–1978), founder of the National Party of Scotland, as well as poet and critic. Above the misspelled 'Baudeliare' Amis has written 'You know the man I mean, eh?'

5. Amis's report on an Eisteddfod, entitled 'Where Tawe Flows', *Spectator*, 23 July 1954, p. 126, was reprinted in *What Became of Jane Austen?*, pp. 143–6. The Eisteddfodau are annual summer celebrations of Welsh literature and music. The best-known is the Royal National Eisteddfod of Wales, alternately held in North and South Wales, and featuring competitions in music, poetry, drama and the fine arts. 'That cockney rubbish' refers to 'The Helbatrawss'.

could recommend some good books to you. *The Butterfly Net*, John Lodwick,[6] might give you a laugh or two.

Yes, well, Mr. Amis, I think if you keep £450 by you we shall be able to settle your income-tax all right. Of course, that's just a rough figure; I haven't had much experience of bum,

Kingsley

[TLS: Bodleian]

TO THE EDITOR, *LONDON MAGAZINE* – SEPTEMBER 1954

Sir,

I don't think we need worry very much about 'the novelist', except to note that he isn't one man: there are just lots and lots of novelists, all different, and all doing different things of varying appeal.[1] Some novelists, including some we call 'serious', may not get as much money as some others, including some we call 'popular'. That just means that, like all previous writers except a few 19th-century freaks, they have to get a job. It needn't be a very hard-to-get or well-paid or exacting job because a serious novel can 'still' find enough readers to give its author a lot of pocket-money. And why do people talk as if having a job is bad (even though economically necessary) for a novelist? It's lack of a job that can be bad.

'The novel', similarly, isn't a 'thing'. By looking back, we can sometimes see where writers have been going, but, unlike that of a car, the future course of 'the novel' cannot be directed. These days people love talking about 'the novel' so much that they want to generalize about books while they're still being written or planned. This is dangerous for some writers, because it may make them worry about injecting the generalizations into their novels. Mr Maugham, by insisting and demonstrating that novels should be about people, ought to be a thousand times better as a guide for younger writers than anyone who says that 'the novelist' has the task of conveying 'life' in the form of 'a

6. *The Butterfly Net* (1954) by John Lodwick (1916–59), novelist and non-fiction writer.

1. See Amis to John Lehmann, 20 July 1954.

semi-transparent envelope'[2] – though to inject *that* into a novel would take some doing.

KINGSLEY AMIS
University College of Swansea

TO HILARY RUBINSTEIN – 1 OCTOBER 1954

24 The Grove, Uplands, Swansea.

Dear Hilary,

Pardon this tardy reply. It (the tardiness) is the result of guilt-feelings about *That Uncertain Feeling*, feelings exacerbated to screaming-pitch by seeing it mentioned in the Statesman's Autumn and Winter books. I urge you not to worry and to continue your exemplary patience. The book continues to buzz energetically around in my head and I continue every day to amass and revise ideas about it. Finishing it shouldn't take long. A huge assault on it is pending and I will send progress reports.

Jolly good about that film business, eh? Your man has done superbly. Hettie Hilton tells me of a snag. I hope this will only be a purely temporal snag and that the money will flow in good time.[1] Jolly good also about the German rights.

Most interested in the Doubleday publicity caper.[2] I return the hand-out herewith, having now received a copy from their New York office.

All the best, and never doubt my ability to produce *TUF* for you as soon as poss.

Yours ever,
Kingsley

[TLS: Gollancz]

2. See Virginia Woolf's essay 'Modern Fiction' (1919): 'life is a luminous halo, a semi-transparent envelope'.

---

1. 'That film business' concerns the rights to *Lucky Jim*. Alfred Hitchcock and Sidney Bernstein (1899–1993), British producer and executive, later founder and chairman of the Granada group (for which he was eventally made Lord Bernstein), were about to take up the option on the film rights, which the Boulting Brothers had allowed to expire (on the very day of this letter). Contractual negotiations had been completed, the deal had been announced in *Kinematograph Weekly*, and Gollancz (and Amis) were waiting for a cheque. Hettie Hilton ran the film department at Curtis Brown.

2. A circular written by Pyke Johnson, under the pseudonym 'L.L. Day, Editor-at-large'. It has not survived.

TO ROBERT GRAVES – 2 OCTOBER 1954

24 The Grove, Uplands, Swansea, Glamorgan.

Dear Mr. Graves,

Lots of readers of your *Punch* article of 8 September must have mentioned this to you by now, but just in case you weren't listening may I point out that ten words a day for two years will only give you a 7,300-word novel, which is a good deal under average length even these days? That peat you met would have been on to a thing like that in a flash between 11 and 12.[1]

Must stop now and write my word for the day. I plan to bring out a *conte* every 20 years.

Yours sincerely,
Kingsley Amis

[TLS: William Graves]

TO HILARY RUBINSTEIN – 18 OCTOBER 1954

24 The Grove, Uplands, Swansea.

My dear Hilary,

You may be interested to hear that that announcement in the Statesman's autumn list has done the trick. Since writing last I have done 15,000 words, perhaps more, of the final draft of THAT UNCERTAIN FEELING. And I shall very likely be able to keep that up until it's finished. I don't foresee striking any more snags. So don't despair of me.

Having, I hope, put you in a receptive mood, I wonder if you would answer a leetle query for me. What's all this about a film, and Hitchcock,

1. Graves's article was entitled 'Varro's Four Hundred and Ninety Books', and in it he complains of successful authors 'who somehow manage to reduce output to ten words a day (which means a novel of average length every two years)'. The 'peat' (i.e. young girl) Graves met had been secretary to such an author: 'She revealed that her former employer had worked from 10 to 12, apart from long week-ends and frequent holidays – 10 to 11 on fan-mail; 11 to 12 on his novel' (p. 322). For Graves see Notes on Recipients.

and all that? I saw the paragraph in the October 1st TRUTH,[1] and mentioned it to dear Siriol when writing to her last week. She says she thinks it's all tied up, because of a letter from Mr. Bernstein. Who's Mr. Bernstein? Is he one of your lads? You see, I've heard nothing whatever myself, and still have no contract and no cheque – I've been in touch with Hettie Hilton over these latter, and am not particularly worried about the delay. As long as I know it *is* just a delay, if you see what I mean: if *Jim* is definitely going to be filmed, then presumably I shall get my cash eventually – the sooner the better, naturally. So could you let me know the score as far as you know it? Further, you remember I mentioned wanting to have a share in the script if possible, and if there will be a film then, again, the sooner I ask Hitchcock (or whoever it is) about it, the better.

Please don't think I'm moaning about this; the whole business is very exciting – it's just that I like to know it's safe to be excited before I let myself go.

All the best – oh, and congratulations on the latest Auchincloss.[2] A damned fine book, and I hope it does as well as it deserves.

Yours ever,
Kingsley

[TLS: Gollancz]

TO PHILIP LARKIN – 18 OCTOBER, 1 NOVEMBER 1954

Swansea

My dear Philip,

Did you ever see such bloody awful weather as this? Here I am, feeling a little bit jaded, having typed out 20 pages of *TUF* [*That Uncertain Feeling*] today, cherring myself up by tapping out a message to my old pal. I've been feeling so frightened about *TUF* going badly, and then so pleased about it seeming to go well, that I've fallen lamentably behind in keeping my old pal posted on my doings, my parryings

1. See Amis to Rubinstein, 1 October 1954, note 1.

2. *The Romantic Egoists* (1954), a collection of stories by Louis Auchincloss (b. 1917), American novelist and short-story writer.

of the right crosses aimed by old Slogger Life. My apologies. It really was nice seeing you in Cheltenham and I wish it had been longer, also that I'd nerved myself for the trip to Oxford. I hope you had a good time there. Me, I have fewer good social times these days, don't know why. Money's short, for one thing; I don't want any of that swearing. Here I am hearing and seeing rumours about Hitchcock going to direct *Lucky Jim* (yes, really: see Carteret Street Journal, TRUTH, Oct 1; but perhaps you have)[1], and all the rest of it, and damn the information, damn the cash, damn the bleeding CONTRACT, do I see, 18 days after the expiry of the option. And we'd spent up to the limit, see, in expectation of the old greenbacks coming floating in. It's a cow, honest. No fifty nicker from old Crippen yet, either. What has happened to that lad? Never get a letter, never see his name. Afraid to write now in case he's dead.

Well, what a load of bullshit all that was in the *Spr* about the new movt. etc.[2] Useful up to a point, but the point is nearly here, I feel; someone should tell old GSF[3] to pipe down a little before people think he's buggering all our arses – I'm thinking of the TLS leader now, not the Spr thing, which I don't know who did, though I suppose it might be him too. Been seeing those Bennett things of John's in the 20th Cy.?[4] Don't make me want to read Bennett, do they you? I liked the Waugh

---

1. Rumours about Hitchcock wanting to direct *Lucky Jim* appeared in *Truth*, 1 October 1954, p.1199, in the 'Carteret Street Journal', a regular column (by 'Xenophon') including gossip and comment on the arts and media.

2. On 1 October 1954 an anonymous leading article entitled 'In the Movement' appeared in the *Spectator*. It was written by J.D. Scott, the magazine's Literary Editor, and was the first time the emerging writers of the new generation (those Scott listed were Amis, Wain, Elizabeth Jennings, Thom Gunn, John Holloway, Donald Davie, D.J. Enright and Iris Murdoch) were identified as 'the Movement'. In an influential passage Scott describes these writers as 'bored by the despair of the Forties, not much interested in suffering, and extremely impatient of poetic sensibility, especially poetic sensibility about "the writer and society". So it's goodbye to all those rather sad little discussions about "how the writer ought to live", and it's goodbye to the Little Magazine and "experimental writing". The Movement, as well as being anti-phoney, is anti-wet; sceptical, robust, ironic, prepared to be as comfortable as possible' (pp. 399–400).

3. G.S. Fraser, supposed (correctly) to be the author of an anonymous Commentary piece in the *TLS*, 'Everyman's Poetry', 24 September 1954, p. 609, which discussed the PEN *New Poems 1954* anthology.

4. John Wain, 'The Quality of Arnold Bennett', a two-part article in the September and October 1954 issues of *Twentieth Century*, pp. 253–67 and 341–57.

retort in the Spr, by the way.[5] Have you read this chum Gerhardi?[6] Before I forget I got a letter from Rex Allen the other day (Macmillan's),[7] starting off 'Dear Kingsley' and promising, when he comes to Swnasea (yk), to 'look me up' and have a 'chat' about 'the old days'. AHWOOOOOO and did you see in the Radio Times this week the name of FILTHY SHARROCK, talking on HORRIBLE BUNYAN. Read the new Auchincloss?[8] That's a good book, I find.

Sorry this is so dull. I never seem to do much, except work of one kind or another, and you don't want to hear about that. There was one party recently, at which James Bartley had removed his shirt . . ., ostensibly for greater coolness, actually I think to display the grey rug on his chest to the young ladies. Hilly, for a lark you know, ripped his flies open, expecting him to grab his trousers before they fell. He didn't, nor had Hilly remembered his frequent boast of wearing no underclothes, the filthy bugger. So there he was, naked to the knees, and a nastier sight . . . He held it for half a minute or so, gazing round. The party broke up soon after. I got to bed at 3.45. At about 4.45 James knocked us up; when I went down to let him in, he told me he wanted a light for his cigarette. I gave him one, and he went off, bewailing his lot at full bellow outside the front door, and yelling to me to testify at the inquest that he was of unsound (or sound) mind when he killed himself. 'It may be sooner than you think,' he bawled in valediction. Couldn't be soon enough for me, or so I thought at the time. It is by such moments of unsought revelation that I live. But most of the time I just tap away, emerging infrequently to talk to the Rotary Club (that was *buggery*. A dry lunch – I thought it was supposed to be an *insult* to drink toasts in bloody water – with horrible meat tasting of cardboard, an old shag at my side telling me about Rotary: I knew him, but *got his name wrong* when we met: GOOD. He's a fairly prosperous retired schoolmaster, headmaster in fact; I gave him the name of a frightful little

5. Waugh's retort to 'In the Movement' appeared in *Spectator*, 8 October 1954, p. 434. It was sympathetic to the authors discussed but ended: 'Please let the young people of today get on with their work alone and be treated to the courtesy of individual attention. They are the less, not the more, interesting, if they are treated as a "Movement".'

6. William Gerhardie (1895–1977), novelist, is praised by Waugh in his *Spectator* letter and said to resemble the new writers Waugh has read.

7. R.F. Allen (b. 1919), worked at Macmillan from 1946 to 1974, mainly in academic and secondary publishing. Allen had been to school with Larkin and was also at St John's College, Oxford (1938–40, 1945–46). Known as 'Rex', though christened Reginald.

8. *The Romantic Egoists.*

unshaven WEA lecturer whom he must know and contemn: *GOOD*) or lecture to classes that seem to include an unusually high proportion of pretty and randy-looking girls. Of course they aren't really randy; it's all in my mind see?

1st November 54

Sorry about this further delay. Have been feeling a bit down in the old mouth recently, now that the film contract has FALLEN THROUGH. Hitchcock was going to do it, then at the last minute he decided not to and let the option run out. Just let it run out what? Very annoing this. Had to write to Crippen with an sos and have now heard – suppose you knew this – he's living at Abingdon. Why there? He didn't send the money, no, but said he was going to very soon. I was glad to hear that. Still, it isn't the end of the world, is it? They may sell the rights to someone else. And TUF continues to prosper, which is the main thing. Not that I am guaranteeing its worth or anything like that, but enjoying doing it is a great sign, we all agree. For a long time I was trying not to face the feeling that I'd defiled my couch, irremediably.[9] I had, but not (I hope) ireemediably (I expect you know the word I mean).

[. . .] Well let me know how you're getting on and what's happening about those poims of yours.[10] I wonder when we shall see Wain's new book.[11] Regret we cannot afford a fee. We can, however, offer you bum,

Kingsley

[TLS: Bodleian]

9. Possibly a parody of 'For a long time I used to go to bed early,' the opening sentence of Marcel Proust's *Swann's Way* (1913), the first volume of *À la recherche du temps perdu*.

10. Presumably for *The Less Deceived* (1955), which Larkin had first submitted, before George Hartley approached him for the Marvell Press, to the Dublin-based Dolmen Press, run by Liam Miller (1923–87). It was Donald Davie, at the time a lecturer in English at Trinity College, Dublin, who had urged Larkin to try the Dolmen Press. See Amis to Larkin, 13 November 1954.

11. *Living in the Present* (1955), a novel.

TO HILARY RUBINSTEIN – 21 OCTOBER 1954

24 The Grove, Uplands, Swansea.

My dear Hilary,

Owww! This is truly horrible, eh?[1] Well, hope is not dead in my bosom – it's my bank account that makes me sweat a little, and this is where I begin to feel embarrassed. Can any money be winkled out of your concern in the near future? I ask this in a hushed tone and inside a 'Personal' envelope, so that you can handle this just as you see fit (handling of course includes instant destruction of the letter). The point is that when the film thing seemed to be getting imminent I plunged into spending rather, and am now facing some unpleasant bills plus, in what I suspect will be the fairly near future, a shocking income tax demand. Now naturally I blame no one but myself for this bit of pre-natal chicken-counting, but if you could manage to get together some cash for me (the more the better) out of my royalties since March 25th, and perhaps some of those foreign advances if they've been paid, you would save your old pal a heap of worry, and also a heap of hack-writing for the rich magazines to raise quick dough, which I'd prefer not to do just now, if it can be avoided. The smallest contribution would be gratefully received, and a larger one even more so.

Writing this letter has been rather an ordeal and I apologise for putting you to trouble and possible embarrassment. I leave it entirely to you to do what you can. Of course if Boultings or someone else come through[2] everything will be dandy again, but I shouldn't like to have to wait and see.

Yours ever,
Kingsley

[TLS: Gollancz]

1. That Hitchcock and Bernstein had reneged at the last moment and decided not to take up their option on the film rights to *Lucky Jim*.

2. The Boultings eventually did renew their option, as Hettie Hilton of Curtis Brown had suggested to Amis that they might (in a letter referred to by Rubinstein; see Rubinstein to Amis, 20 October 1954, in Gollancz).

TO ROBERT GRAVES – 25 OCTOBER 1954

24 The Grove, Uplands, Swansea, Glam.

Dear Robert Graves,

Thanks for the card. Don't take that 'movement' stuff in the *Spectator* too seriously. I don't think the people mentioned are a movement at all, just a lot of writers, and movements are a bad thing these days anyway. We ought to either write all the same or all differently.

But I didn't write just to tell you that. I now have some excuse for saying what I've often wanted to say: that for my money you're the best poet now writing in English, if you'll pardon the expression. I know you know that all poets like your verse best 'after their own, of course', but I thought I'd just confirm it from my own corner of the battlefield: all my friends agree on how good you are, including some who don't write any verse themselves. Reading you has done such poems as I've written a power of good, even though you probably wouldn't like what I've made of you. I say this because although I enjoyed the image of you "in a glass coffin among the standards"[1] I think it's a lot less than fair to you. I hope all this hasn't annoyed or bored you.

That's right, have a good time at Cambridge[2] and tell them what isn't what. Me: I'm Oxford too – St. John's, where I think you went.[3]

Yours sincerely,
Kingsley Amis

[ALS: William Graves]

---

1. Presumably a reference from the card to which Amis is replying. No such phrase occurs in the *Punch* article.

2. Graves was delivering six Clark Lectures at Trinity College, Cambridge, on the subject of 'Professional Standards in English Poetry'.

3. Graves did indeed go to St John's, in 1918, though he did not take a degree.

TO HILARY RUBINSTEIN – 27 OCTOBER 1954

24 The Grove, Uplands, Swansea, Glam.

My dear Hilary,

Many many thanks for the cheque received yesterday. It will help tremendously towards keeping the Amis family afloat until I get that £10,000 advance from you for my next novel. And a very sincere vote of personal thanks to you for arranging it all so very promptly.

TUF continues to prosper: 7,000 words or so since the last report – look how thin and bare this ribbon is! No time to go down and buy another. As a present for a good boy, do you think you could get the Froggy and Eyeteye advances off to me at a convenient interval after they arrive? It would be something nice to look forward to.

Haven't been to London for ages, nor is there any immediate prospect; but when we do come we'd love to lunch and drink with you. Will let you know.

With renewed thanks and best wishes,

Yours ever,
Kingsley

[TLS: Gollancz]

TO PHILIP LARKIN – 13 NOVEMBER 1954

Swansea

My dear Philip,

This is initiated by gratitude, old man, at your display of Xtn charity in answering so speedily after being kept waiting so long. Not, of course, that I have anything like a quiverful of merry jests to send winging in your direction. All the same, I always feel much funnier when I get a letter from you – want to go round the house chuckling to myself, to circumambulate the college trilling obscenities and endorsing them by manual gesture, to go all through TUF again making it much funnier. In regard to your kind inquiry in connexion with that work: yes, I have done one draft of all of it, six different drafts of the 1st part of it (yes, really) and have at the time of writing done a final draft up to p. 123. Hope to finish it by Christmas YAHAHAGH

Yes, they were shits about my film all right. I've no idea what went wrong. I agree the result wd. probably have been lousy, but going to the premiere, and getting all the money, and screwing Christine and Carol,[1] would all have been fun. I didn't at all mind m for murder[2] myself. I agree the folk were unconvincing (except for the man who was killed) but I found the innerleckshal prarblem quite fassernading. And I wanted to bite Grace Kelly's n One of the awful things is that if Itchcock had done *Jim*, G.K. wd. very likely have taken Christine and I cd. have bitten her n

I told you I'd heard from Bruce, didn't I, saying he'd send my money to me very quickly? He hasn't sent it yet, you know. Now, why not? If he just cut down his smoking to three packets a day, and didn't drink before 12 noon, he could save my money in a couple of weeks. Did he let on about his literary career when in Oxford? I mean he never seems to have a book coming out. What does he live on? These films only pay £400, which, less tax, wouldn't support him for the time he'd take to write the music, would it? Poor old Pasty: not gone to the Continong yet, then?[3] What's holding her up? I mean it couldn't be *common sense*, could it? I had a good laugh over Ann Martin. It must be a common couple of names, but I *think* that was the name of a girl I made a pass at in about 1948 and got rebuffed in what you might call a fairly unmistakable fashion. Was she rather big-faced, tousled, trousered, with a curious loping stride, corduroy windcheater etc.? Thats the one.

Very sorry to hear about the dole-men. What little buggers Hean Shite and the Quimsella fella sound.[4] Still, in a way I think you're *well*

---

1. Characters in *Lucky Jim*.

2. *Dial M for Murder* (1954), Hitchcock thriller, starring Ray Milland, Grace Kelly and Robert Cummings.

3. Patsy Strang was starting a course at the Sorbonne.

4. The Dolmen Press had decided against publishing *The Less Deceived*. See Larkin to Patsy Strang, 9 October 1954, in *LL*, p. 229: 'The blot on the visit [to Dublin, where Davie had invited Larkin to lecture at Trinity College] was news that my selection of poems for the Dolmen Press had been turned down by the two Irish members of the triumvirate selection board – too self pitying and sexy.' Later in the letter Larkin identifies one of the triumvirate as 'a clerk in the Finance Ministry who read (and wrote) science fiction. I'll send him a yarn about a rejected poem that flies about at night chewing fools' balls off.' The clerk in question is 'Quimsella', i.e. Thomas Kinsella (b. 1928), poet, translator, civil servant, academic. The person Amis calls 'Hean Shite' 'must be Sean White' (Anthony Thwaite, personal communication, 10 May 1999), at the time editor of the Irish literary magazine

out of that. God knows the Fantap [Fantasy Press] is no great shakes, but it's better than one of these rotten little provincial presses where they go by where you were born. The fact that they've taken Allen and Hewitt[5] does seem to suggest that they want to be ideological about it in some way. I don't know Allen's work but I can't imagine anyone taking any notice of Hewitt except for being an Irishman, can you? Now as regards the form you mention; it was understood between Mellor and myself that I should choose the po: for this 6-man anthology,[6] but since three of the six names were chosen by him, not me, I think we'd better communicate with him separately and I'll abandon (without reluctance) my role of editor. Further, I can easily visualise you sending me your poems, but I'm not so certain about the sage of Reading,[7] who may think it beneath his dignity to be edited, instead of editing. So I'll write to Mellor telling him you and I are ready, and Wain is probably ready, and will he let the 3 of us know when he wants the stuff (if he still does). Meantime you'd better start getting 10 or a dozen things together in readiness. I'd be happy to act as hanging committee for you if needed.

Had a letter from Harry Hoff the other day. This was annoying, because I thought I'd shaken the little sod off. I can't imagine why he should want to maintain touch with me, considering the way he needles me whenever we meet. (The way he needles me whenever we meet, incidentally, is a. all the time b. facetiously c. a little bit rudely.) And then I get letters full of ardent wishes to see me again, discuss this, have a drink on that, etc. I shall have to go up to London soon anyway, to see the asst. ed. of *The Evening Standard* and find out what are the mysterious suggestions that John Scott[8] wants to discuss with me (I shd like to make a gramophone record of . . .), so I might look ole HH up then. But I think *Scenes Life* is something far above his level which he'll

Irish Writing, which published the first writings of Brendan Behan, Patrick Kavanagh and Valentin Iremonger. White (1927–77) was a broadcaster, journalist and academic.

5. 'Allen' is probably Fergus Allen (b. 1921), poet, scientist and eminent British civil servant (First Civil Service Commissioner, 1974–81), educated at Trinity College, Dublin; his poems had appeared in *Springtime* and the *New Statesman*. John Hewitt (1907–87), Belfast-born poet and political dissenter, much interested in questions of national identity; Larkin prints one of his poems in his *Oxford Book of Twentieth-Century English Verse*. No volumes by Allen or Hewitt are listed in *Dolmen 25: 1951–76* (1976), the Press's bibliography, edited by Liam Miller.

6. See Amis to Larkin, 3, 8 July 1954.

7. John Wain.

8. Literary Editor of the *Spectator*.

never approach again. And he is so cursed formal and correct and stiff and conventional. [. . .]

Hope you get the Hull job. What is it, chief librarian? What's The key that rusts? Thank you for letting me see the poem.[9] I find the last stanza a little obscure. 'Mashed you' means 'fucked you up', does it? I can't make out the penultimate line. 'When' in line 17 seems to me inferior to 'should'. Sorry I have nothing brilliantly illuminating to say. When will you be over again?

Broadcast discussion in which you might talk on Welsh bum.

Kingsley

[TLS: Bodleian]

TO KENNETH AND ELAINE TYNAN[1] – 23 NOVEMBER 1954

24 The Grove, Uplands, Swansea, Glam.

Dear Tynans,

We have been bidden to the feet of Mister Victor Gollancz in a couple of weeks and this has somehow had the effect of touching off the spring which periodically drives us to London. Shall we have lunch on Monday the 6th December, if Ken is not appearing on tel[e]vision? If there are any Shaws[2] about at that time, do force them to come along; if not, then the 4 of us will have a merry time together. Let us know SOONEST about this and we will fix it up, hey?

Ever,
Amises

[TLS: British Library]

9. 'Places, Loved Ones', published in *The Less Deceived* and in *LCP*, p. 99, where it is dated 10 October 1954. 'The key that rusts' alludes to a refrain in Auden's poem 'Nursery Rhyme', in *Nones* (1951): 'The key that opens is the key that rusts'.

---

1. For Kenneth Tynan see Amis to Larkin, 24 October 1946, note 2. The novelist Elaine Dundy Tynan (b. 1927) was married to Tynan from 1951 to 1964.
2. Irwin Shaw (1913–84), American novelist, and his wife Marian.

TO ROBERT CONQUEST – 1 DECEMBER 1954

24 The Grove, Uplands, Swansea.

Dear Bob,

Whacko, old boy. It's very good of you both to do this. We shall be arriving in dear old London town between 4 and 6 p.m. on Sunday next – I won't put it any tighter because there may be floods, gales, tyre-bursts etc. I've forgotten, if I ever knew, what part of London you inhabit, so I suggest that H. and I drive to some easily-found but convenient (for you) point and you take us on from there. Alternatively you could give us directions to your place and we could wend our own way, ringing up every so often for aid if necessary. Remember it's fifteen years since I was regularly in London and that phrases like 'drive west from Goodge Street tube-station' will only make me feel unhappy. Still I'm sure we can manage it all right.

No, no film deal alas. Hitchcock backed out at the last moment. On the other hand, John Wain has promised to come up on the Wednesday evening so we will all have a merry time to make up for it. Pick a nice little pub for a few quiet drinks on Sunday evening. Am looking forward to it and to seeing your Uggly Mugg.

Yours,
Kingsley

[TLS: Recipient]

TO ROBERT AND TATIANA CONQUEST – 13 DECEMBER 1954

24 The Grove, Uplands, Swansea, Glam.

Dear Bob and Tania,

Very many thanks for putting us up in such fine style last week. We thoroughly enjoyed ourselves and wish we'd been able to stay longer. I'm afraid we shall try and come again when occasion permits.

We got to Walton and saw the man. All very curious it was; the shotting was going on in what looked like a dilapidated Naafi,[1] with

1. A canteen run by the Navy, Army and Air Force Institutes, which provided social facilities to British military personnel.

lots of what looked to me laughably unconvincing sets leaning against the walls, rotting furniture etc. I sat in a chair marked 'Shelley Winters'[2] which gave me an odd feeling. Everyone was very kind, unsophisticated and so on. I had about five minutes' chat with Cornelius which may or may not be productive, still it was well worth having.

We had a wonderful journey back, involving the most impressive 100-yard skid at 60 m.p.h. and the later complete loss of a wheel. Apart from that no damage was sustained and we wound up here little the worse, as they say, for the experience, except financially. Now things are back to normal: a meeting to discuss the terminal results this morning, letter-writing and sitting on my arse this afternoon, and buckling to on the novel to-morrow (I hope). By the way, greeting me on my return were the poems I'd sent to New Ps 1955,[3] which aggravated me a bit. Still two cheques had also arrived and this mitigated the hurt. I also now possess a copy of Bergonzi's poems and am waiting impatiently for our toilet roll to run out. When you next drop a line, could you transcribe the full stanza of 'Please don't pull our shithouse down'?[4] Several fans here are asking for it.

Love and best wishes and thanks again,

Kingsley & Hilly

[TLS: Recipient]

2. The American actress Shelley Winters (b. 1922) was starring in *I am a Camera* (1955), adapted from the Isherwood novel *Goodbye to Berlin*. The film was shooting at Nettlewood Studios in Walton, where Amis had come, unsuccessfully, in an attempt to persuade its director, Henry Cornelius (1913–58), to film *Lucky Jim*.

3. The PEN anthology *New Poems 1955*, edited by Patric Dickenson, J.C. Hall and Erica Marx.

4. According to Conquest (personal communication), the correct title of this traditional song is 'Please Don't Burn Our Shithouse Down'. Its first verse, in Conquest's version, reads:

Please don't burn our shithouse down
We will promise to pay.
Father's away on the ocean wave
Kate's in the family way.
Brother dear has gonorrhoea
And times are fuckin' 'ard.
So please don't burn our shithouse down
Or we'll all 'ave to crap in the yard.

TO PHILIP LARKIN – 20 DECEMBER 1954

Swansea

My dear Philip,

Beng two lasy etc. to devise a special Xmas card for you this year I am trying to write you a Xmas letter instead. First of all congratulations on getting the job at Hole.[1] I agree that living in Hole won (barks won't be all honey, but you'll have the advantage of all that extra money, won't you? Of course I can quite see that that in itself may be rather inconvenient, since so much of your life is arranged around saying you can't afford this or that, and that'll sound a bit thin when you're pulling in fifteen hundred nicker, may find yourself having to treat hey hey no need to take it that way leggo a jokes a joke. You'll be able to come here more often, or at any rate to somewhere like Oxford where we can meet, and this is cheering. I laughed at your allegations of terror at the tasks confronting you, but didn't take them seriously. After all, at your time of life a chap's either got what it takes to shoulder a bit of responsibility (which he's getting paid for, anyway) or he hasn't. And you'd have to be pretty much of a worm if you had'nt the kind of confidence in yourself which is implied by your putting in for the job in the first place. I'm sure you agree that everything has it's more serious side. Anyway, congratulations, old man. I know your up to the job.

How's Patsy getting on with her writing ppppfffffvvvvvvbbbbffff Did she say? She was talking about fig-shun *and* pwetry when I saw her last, I seem to remember. And who's Corbiere?[2] Is this some new character or a jesting/punning reference to someone I already know? You know I think she ought to take up with some mixed-up-inside, gee-I'm-a-wrider-but-I-jest-can't-get-storded American with lots of money and spunk, divorce Colin and go off to Nyork like a bloody shot and never bloody come back. [. . .] Yes I had my £50 from ole Creep-in (that made me keck with laughter). Why's he so hard up, or have I said that before? Seems to have practically stopped writing,

---

1. Larkin had been appointed Librarian, University of Hull, a position he took up in March 1955.

2. Tristan Corbiere (1845–75), French poet, an influence on Jules Laforgue and the young T.S. Eliot.

doesn't he? Not that I think that's much of a sodding disaster (better burn this). Must write to the old sucker after this and wish him luck, etc.

Had a good time in London recently; spot of the Widow[3] and a few mouthfuls of caviare with my pals the Tynans, lunch with VG, lunch with deputy ed. of Evening Standard, etc. All that kind of thing, you know. Looked in at Nettlefold's Studios on our way back and saw them shooting *I Am a Camera*. Quite eerie to see it all going on you know. Actually I went there to talk business with the director but we stayed around for a bit and heard Lawrence Harvey[4] saying 'Eggs and things' when some blonde girl or other asked 'Chris, can you cook?' Yes rather eerie that. Occasion was to see Harry Cornelius and ask him if he'd like to produce *Jim*. He was amiable but non-committal, and now Ealing are interested, and all that remains is for Michael Balcon to give his okay.[5] Not that after recent experiences I imagine he will, but it's nice to think about.

Saw old Johnny boy [Wain], who seemed pretty well, considering, and full of this scheme and that scheme. His book did less well than mine – miaouuuu!!!!! – but his new one, *Living in the Present*, will be out in March, as you may well know. He talked a great deal about the way people poison themselves with white bread, and how the hospitals are full of people whose digestions have been ruined by excessive meat-eating, and all the rest of it. He added that he was one of the organic husbandry crowd. Then he said that we only drank intoxicating liquors in order to enlarge our capillaries. I said that I found this, speaking personally, an inadeqaute (yk) account. He went on to say how he hated England, how there was no spontaneous gaiety this side of the channel, how he only tolerated the place because it was near the continent. I said that this seemed an odd view to me. England with all thy faults I love thee a bloody sight better than those realms of wine-chatter, expense, insolence, dowdy, dumpy girls, bad sanitation and earnest eye-blazing finger-shaking shouting side-taking argument about the latest Russian note, American decadence, John-Paul Sartrer, bicycle

3. Victorian slang for champagne, in allusion to the well-known brand Veuve Clicquot.

4. Laurence Harvey (1928–73), Lithuanian-born, raised in South Africa, leading man in many British and some Hollywood feature films; played the Isherwood character in *I am a Camera*.

5. Sir Michael Balcon (1896–1977), British executive film producer, headed Ealing Studios in its heyday (1937–59), also Gaumont-British, MGM-British and Bryanston; knighted (1948); his daughter Jill (b. 1925), an actress, married C. Day-Lewis in 1951.

races, education, capital punishment, horror comics and Thomas Mann.[6] But you know I think this. No need for me to tell you that.

I suppose you're in Love-burrow[7] now. Drop me a line to cheer me up some time – my parents arrive to-morrow and will stay for at least a week. Tell me more about the cobbers.[8] I love imagining the cobberess saying to you 'Fer a Pommie yer top-hole, sport', and the cobber finding you on the job and talking about crook deals. Yes, isn't old Hoff a dull bugger? Have you had one of those dreadful cards from him, showing his face and his wife's not very nice face and their little daughter's face? Bloody arrogant, isn't it? What makes him think I want to know what they all llok like? Nothing much easel to say. Actually I am feeling quite friendly towards cobbers for the moment because some digger rag in Melbourne wants to serialise *Jim*, which will be more money earned without getting out of bed IF IT COMES OFF. That is the nicest kind of money to have, I find. What a fool that Iles man[9] sounds these days. Never grew up, that's his trouble. Arrested development at the psychological age of 23. This was impressive when one was psychologically 14, but not now one is psychologically 27 – my permanent emotional age anyway, I fancy. Dear dear how I have run on, and into confessions too. Won't do, won't do. Just won't do, what? Well enjoy yourself as and when you can and every moral and immoral wish for 1955. Take it easy as JW says.

Add sugar, cloves and nutmeg and garnish with pieces of hot bum,

Kingsley

[TLS: Bodleian]

6. An allusion to William Cowper's *The Task* (1785), II.1140–1: 'England, with all thy faults, I love thee still –/My country!'

7. Loughborough, where Larkin's mother and sister lived.

8. Presumably Larkin's Australian friends Ansell and Judy Egerton, with whom he'd recently travelled to and from Dublin. At the time, Ansell was a Lecturer in Economics at Queen's University, Belfast, Judy a Tutorial Assistant in History. They had first met Larkin in 1951. See *LL*, p. xxv.

9. For Norman Iles see Amis to Larkin, 25 February 1946, note 7.

TO ROBERT CONQUEST – 23 JANUARY 1955

24 The Grove, Uplands, Swansea, Glam.

Dear Bob,

Glad to hear the latest on the Macmillan project,[1] and immensely gratified at the proposed star billing of yours truly. Your provisional list seems unexceptionable to me. About the 4 fresh people you name, my judgments (for what they're worth) are:

Gordon Wharton:[2] Snap judgment on what I've seen (not much):
P. P. P. (pretty pisspoor)
Though amiable and far from spineless

Mairi Macinnes:[3] P. P. P. too, though in a different way. I've seen her oeuvre more or less in full now, and it strikes me as 'feminine' in the extreme, i.e. 'sensitive' (not always disagreeably), not caring as much as I'd like about things like rhyming, shape and so on, and not the work of someone who goes on versifying once personal difficulties have been solved and toying with the old undergraduate talent has ceased to appeal. She strikes me as a back number already, though I may be quite wrong here.

L. D. LERNER[4] (the capitals denote careless typing and not any desire to headline him) strikes me as pretty good and well worth encouraging. Why not ask him to submit a sheaf? He seemed a decent modest chap when I met him and unlikely to be affronted if you reject them after all. I think he's the best of these 4.

Philip Oakes:[5] I can see a lot in this chap's stuff, and there's talent there all right I should say, but there's something about it, a kind of smugness

---

1. *New Lines* (London: Macmillan, 1956), influential anthology edited by Conquest and containing poems by himself, Amis, Larkin, Wain, Gunn, Davie, Enright, Jennings and John Holloway.
2. For Gordon Wharton see Amis to Larkin, 3, 8 July 1954, note 5.
3. Mairi MacInnes (b. 1925), poet and author; an Oxford contemporary of Amis and Larkin.
4. L.D. Lerner (b. 1925), South African-born poet, critic and academic.
5. For Philip Oakes see Amis to Wain, 6 November 1953, note 4.

perhaps, that I find rather off-putting. That's a very subjective judgment, though.

Looking at your letter again I find a 5th chap, old Holloway. I agree with your 2nd rather than your 1st thoughts on him and my vote would be in favour. His earlier stuff struck me as a bit dried-up, but more recently I've seen a couple of things that seem just the job. For my money he stands slightly above Lerner.

Your ideas for the intro seem pretty sound to me, especially your way of taking Empsonianism as useful but a thing of the past. I look forward to getting a copy of it.

Do hang on to my poems for the time being, for the next couple of weeks anyway. I'm deferring sending to Mellor[6] till my novel's finished.[7] Hope to be in London round about the 8th–12th Feb and we'll have a natter about everything then.

Love both/both,
Kingsley

[TLS: Recipient]

TO D.J. ENRIGHT – 21 FEBRUARY 1955

24 The Grove, Uplands, Swansea, Glamorgan, Gt Britain

Dear Mr. Enright,

Thank you very much for your invitation to submit poems for the Japanese anthology.[1] I look forward to thinking about them being read over there, and it was most kind of you to think of me. I send you I think 16 poems in all, mostly on the simpler side as far as I could. And the "preface" and so on too.

6. Oscar Mellor, founding editor of the Fantasy Press.
7. *That Uncertain Feeling* (1955).

1. For Enright see Notes on Recipients. *Poets of the 1950s* (1956) was a key Movement anthology, published by Kenkyusha Ltd of Japan, where Enright was living at the time (as Visiting Professor, Konan University, 1953–56). It contained poems and prefaces or short introductions by Amis, Conquest, Davie, Enright himself, Holloway, Jennings, Larkin and Wain.

Let me apologise sincerely for keeping you waiting all these weeks. Just after I got your letter I found myself confronted with about six tasks, all of which, it seemed, had got to be completed either 'as soon as possible' or 'at once'. So I had to drop everything that I merely wanted to do and get down to it.

Nice poem of yours in the *Statesman* the other day, if you don't mind me saying so: the one about the old man.[2] And wherever I go I hear or read excellent reports of your novel.[3] I haven't got hold of it yet but I'm sure I shall enjoy it when I do.

Have been seeing a bit of your pal Bob Conquest recently. They very kindly let me use their house as a base when I come to London. He seems very much caught up with science-fiction these days: is writing a novel in the genre, as you probably know.

Don't of course make any attempt to send the poems back. I hope they suit you and that you'll forgive the almost invisible typing in some places. I must get a new ribbon, but they never have the right kind when I go to the shop – good old Wales.

With renewed thanks and best wishes,

Yours sincerely,
Kingsley Amis

[TLS: Recipient]

TO VICTOR GOLLANCZ – 27 FEBRUARY 1955

24 The Grove, Uplands, Swansea, Glam.

My dear V. G.,

First let me apologise most humbly for not answering your indeed charming invitation to lunch. I got it too late to fit it into my schedule for my last visit to London, which was only for a day and a half anyway. And then being absolutely over my eyebrows in this and that – 'that' being chiefly composed of preparing lectures, my allocation of which has recently been raised by 66.6% – I shamefully omitted to return a courteous *non possumus*. Do forgive me, and let's fix it up when you return from the U. S.

2. 'Broken Fingernails', *New Statesman*, 5 February 1955, p. 184.
3. *Academic Year* (1955).

And now the various difficulties in the manuscript, which I sent off to you, amended, at lunch-time yesterday and so should be on your desk as you read this. I found it quite easy to alter all the Boot's things, and of course I perfectly well understand the reason for it all.[1] 'Balls' and 'a quick in and out' were very easy, and I found the best treatment for the 'buggers' was to alter each one on its merits rather than trying to devise an equivalent for the word. I think you'll agree that this has come out quite well. I have put in a gloss on 'hwyl', which is such a well-known Welsh word that I should like to retain it.[2] As regards the space on p. 249, I have put in '*Aberystwyth*', as you can see. Would you please alter this to '*Caersalem*'? I gather that this is slightly more typical and though it's a tiny point one might as well be as accurate as possible. That takes care of your second lot of points. As for the others, I have (again as you will see) put in an extended opening for chapter 18; I found it impossible to work in who Edie was without either extending it in this way or else seeming crude and obvious. I hope this won't throw the printer out (I'm afraid I don't know what 'casting off' is).[3] While we're on 'chapters', could I please have just 'One' instead of 'Chapter One' and so on, as in *Jim*? I didn't like to alter it myself. Page 198: yes, you are right.[4] May it stand, the 'Everted' means, as I wrote in the margin, 'turned outward' – often applied to lips, you know, by physiognomists and people. If you like, 'turned outward' can be substituted for it.

This leaves only Caton.[5] As a present for having yielded so gracefully

---

1. Amis was replying to Gollancz's report on *That Uncertain Feeling* of 21 February 1954, which mentioned 'two or three things' to be tidied up, in particular a number of mild obscenities which might cause the book to be banned by Boots library, and perhaps other circulating libraries.

2. A word so richly connotative in the original, it is sometimes claimed, as to be untranslatable. Usually translated to mean 'passionate spirit' (Welsh preachers, orators and rugby players are meant to be full of '*hwyl*'). See *That Uncertain Feeling*, pp. 18–19: 'He's always been a great one for the *hwyl* – you know, the old Welsh oratorical fire and the rest of it.'

3. Estimating the space taken in print by manuscript copy.

4. See Gollancz to Amis, 21 February 1954 (in Gollancz): 'Hilary [Rubinstein] was worried by the top half of p. 198, as he couldn't make out what the point of the episode was. It didn't worry me: I imagined that these were men coming to some convention or other, with their names displayed . . . and that the episode was just a bit of colour. But, if I am wrong, perhaps you will do something about it.'

5. Gollancz thought, rather illogically, that the reference to L.S. (for Lazy Sod) Caton, which he called a 'domestic "Lucky Jim" joke', would 'worry' the reader who hadn't read *Lucky Jim*. Caton appears in unflattering bit-parts in Amis's first five novels up to *The Anti-Death League* (1966), in which he is killed off.

on all the other points, may I keep it in? I re-read the passage carefully, and it seemed to me that my original intention had been realised: to give the chap who *hadn't* read *Jim* something he'd take as mere harmless local colour, while the chap who *had* read *Jim* might (we hope) get an extra laugh. Therefore I plead for its retention. However, I quite see that an author may not be the best judge of that kind of thing and if you really feel it stinks, we'll cut it.

I think that's about the lot. Don't hesitate to get hold of me if anything else crops up. If you want me quickly the best thing is a wire to this address telling me to phone you.

Well, all the best. Enjoy yourself in America. And when you come back we'll have that lunch, yes sir.

Yours very sincerely,
Kingsley Amis

[TLS: Gollancz]

TO ROBERT CONQUEST – 15 MARCH 1955

24 The Grove, Uplands, Swansea.

Dear Bob,

Yr esteemed favour to hand. But now, listen: I want some advice from you, and probably some (slight) assistance. Here's the point: Messrs Peter Owen (Publishers) Limited have written to me to ask me if I have enough poems for a volume; if I have, they say, they would be 'interested', which means, I suppose, that they will publish them unless they hear anything to my discredit – what I mean is that I *know* (no need to explain how for now) that they have no idea whatever of what makes a poem all right or not so good. Of course they are in other ways too a pretty shaggy kind of concern. And yet, being published by them would be nicer than not being published by anyone for a long time. So this is where the point comes in: do you think you could have a sort of private and unofficial word with old Alan Maclean,[1] asking

1. Alan Maclean (b.1924), an editor at Macmillan (1954–63, Head of Trade Books 1963–84), was Conquest's editor for the *New Lines* anthology (1956).

him – in view of this Owen thing – what my chances are of getting a book published by Macmillan,[2] or at any rate accepted, by the end of the year, say? You see I would willingly waitt shitt *wait* that long if it meant being published by a publisher; but if it were to be longer I might prefer to be published by Peter Owen Ltd. You do see the old dilemma, don't you? Now of course if you don't feel you can quite put the idea up to A McL I shall perfectly well understand, and what I shall want from you in that case will be a spot of advice from your own personal point of view on what I should do about the Owen thing. All suggestions welcomed.

Just read and yelled with laughter over *Academic Year*. A bit indirect in places, but sodding funny, especially the bit about the green linnet[3] – in fact all the literary remarks. Have to do Thomas Love Fartarse for a *Spr* front and am feeling a little barren of ideas. I suppose I can't say that *Maid Marian* is proto-s-f, can I?[4] Ah well.

Yours ever,
Kingsley

[TLS: Recipient]

2. Conquest liked Amis's chances (letter of 16 March 1955), but in the end the book, *A Case of Samples: Poems 1946–1956*, was published by Gollancz in 1956.

3. The protagonist of D.J. Enright's novel *Academic Year* (1955) teaches at a university in Alexandria. 'The Green Linnet', a poem by Wordsworth, poses problems to his first-year students:

> 'Now you know what a green linnet is, don't you?' he addressed the class at large. The class remained silent. He repeated the question more urgently, but no reply was forthcoming. To reassure himself, he pointed to one of his favoured girls, a quiet little thing, something of a village maiden, but far from stupid.
>
> 'Now you know what a green linnet is, don't you, Leila?' She said nothing, she looked nothing. 'Can it be a kind of cow, do you think?' he burst out in anguish, 'a green cow? "Fluttering in the bushes"?'
>
> 'Very well, sir,' the words were almost inaudible, 'a cow.' And she hid her head and wept.
>
> 'You know,' he told them, 'it was at least six weeks before she would speak to me again, or even look at me.' The memory of it saddened him. (p. 198)

4. A reference to Thomas Love Peacock's satirical novel *Maid Marian* (1822), set in the twelfth century. Amis's piece, 'Laugh When You Can', appeared in the *Spectator*, 15 April 1955, pp.402–4, and was reprinted in *What Became of Jane Austen?*, pp.17–21.

TO HILARY RUBINSTEIN – 28 MARCH 1955

24 The Grove, Uplands, Swansea

Note the index of prosperity[1]

My dear Hilary,

Well what wonderful news![2] Many thanks for your wire, which came quite out of the blue – I'd long since forgotten about the whole thing. I've had the griff from the Society of Authors and shall be writing to them shortly. I look forward to writing a long-short on Dixon's experiences on the Continong. *At least* a long-short.

I suppose this bit of news may do the sales of *Jim* a bit of good? Or is that too sanguine? Anyway, it's fine, and more thanks to VG Ltd. for swinging the deal. By the way, who were the judges? Victor Gollancz, Ruth Gollancz and Hilary Rubinstein? Don't bother to let me know specially; just slip me the gen next time you have cause to write.

With renewed thanks and all good wishes,

Yours ever,
Kingsley

[TLS: Gollancz]

---

1. Amis is now using headed notepaper.

2. *Lucky Jim* had won the Somerset Maugham Award, the terms of which required Amis to spend not less than three months on travel or residence abroad, for which he was given £400. The award was (still is) administered by the Society of Authors, which, in addition to administering prizes and publishing the magazine *The Author*, advises its members on publishing matters, including questions of copyright, contracts, percentages, anthology rights etc. Amis voiced his mixed reactions to winning in a letter to Larkin, 28 March 1955 (in Bodleian): 'Honestly, don't tell Hilly, who I shall be taking with me, but the whole prospect fills me with alarm and depression. If it weren't for her, and the fact that it would look too eccentric to turn it down . . . Ah, soul. What a sodding *waste of time* it'll all be. *A great honour, though, of course.*'

TO KAY FULLER, OVERSEAS TALKS, BBC – 11 APRIL 1955

24 The Grove, Uplands, Swansea

Dear Miss Fuller,

Further to our chat on the phone, could I plump for 11th May?[1] And I wonder if, as a special favour, you could possibly bring the *time* of recording forward? You see, I should like to come up from here and go back in one day if possible, and to do that I should have to be at Paddington either at 6.55 or (preferably for me) 5.55. The point is that our term here will still be on then and I want to be away as little as possible – not because I love work, you can bet, but because I've already had a good deal of time off for this and that, and while the big-wigs here are very accommodating I don't want them to think I'm exploiting them. Incidentally, this dilemma was what made me sound rather cagey on the phone: sorry – I was trying to balance my desire to come against my desire not to alienate those who provide most of my income.

Pardon this long section of autobiography, but if I'm going to ask to inconvenience everyone over the recording time I feel I should give full reasons. Sorry to be such a nuisance.

By the way, my train gets in at Paddington at about 1.5 p.m., so I can dash along to anywhere you care to name at lunch-time, or if it's more convenient we could meet up some time in the afternoon. You name it.

Yours sincerely,
Kingsley Amis

[TLS: BBC]

---

1. Amis had agreed to discuss his approach to novel-writing with the critic Walter Allen in an unscripted programme entitled 'We Write Novels', which was, indeed, broadcast on 11 May 1955 on the General Overseas Service. Kay Fuller was a Talks and Features Producer for the External Service; she worked at the BBC from 1938 to 1968.

TO JOSEPH WELTMAN, TALKS PRODUCER, BBC[1] – 28 APRIL 1955

24 The Grove, Uplands, Swansea

Dear Mr. Weltman,

Thank you very much for your letter. I am most flattered to hear about the possibility of taking part in the Critics' programme,[2] and should very much like to do so.

The snag is that, living down here as I do, I don't often come to London, and when I do I don't seem to stay for very long. That being so, I should probably get through Book and Radio reasonably well, but should be utterly flummoxed on Theatre and Film, not to mention Art. And a Critic who had to keep his mouth shut on three topics out of five wouldn't really, I feel, be worth his place in the boat, even if he only turned up now and then.

I quite frankly don't see any way round these difficulties. If I do come up to London for some length of time during the next decade, say, I'll certainly get in touch with you about this. But unless you have any revolutionary suggestions it does look as if there's no hope for the time being.

With renewed thanks,

Yours sincerely,
Kingsley Amis

[TLS: BBC]

TO HILARY RUBINSTEIN – 2 MAY 1955

24 The Grove, Uplands, Swansea

My dear Hilary,

No doubt you'll have heard by now – but anyway I heard from Ealing this afternoon that they've decided to go ahead with filming *Jim*.

1. Joseph Weltman (b. 1910) worked as a producer in sound broadcasting at the BBC from 1946–61.

2. *The Critics*, a popular radio series in which a panel discussed the latest book, play, radio programme, film and exhibition. The programme was broadcast on the BBC Home

Before going out to get drunk I wanted to pass on my thanks to VG Ltd and especially to yourself for your great efforts and great help in bringing this about.

Yours most gratefully,
Kingsley

[ALS: Gollancz]

TO HILARY RUBINSTEIN – 8 MAY 1955

24 The Grove, Uplands, Swansea

My dear Hilary,

Jolly good about those Norjies. I shall get a copy in due time, I suppose? I look forward to seeing Jim say things like "Gib mir min schilling, oder ik wil din ars kikken" and so on.

I've had a good look round and as far as I can make out only three of the kids who rush yelling in and out while I'm working belong to me. Though of course one can never be absolutely sure . . .

Ever yours,
Kingsley

[TLS: Gollancz]

TO PHILIP LARKIN – 10 JUNE 1955

Swansea

My dear Philip,

Just to show you I meant what I said about keeping in touch – touch that word is.[1] The time of departure draws near,[2] and almost

Service and its successor Radio 4 from 1947 to 1968. Among the regular critics were A. Alvarez, Pamela Hansford Johnson and Stephen Potter.

---

1. The first 'touch' was only just legible.

2. To Portugal, to fulfil the conditions of his Somerset Maugham Award; see Amis to Larkin, 5 June 1955 (in Bodleian): 'It's Portugal now, or again; I've forgotten how things stood when I last wrote. Should be all right; paying guests with an English business type about a dozen miles from Lisbon and near the sea. So we should be protected from the

everything is ready to take, except sufficient money. I had a card from old Crippen asking me to go to the St. John's Commemm[3] with him, but I said that I would not do that and would like the £30 he owes me back straightaway. Nick [Russel] has asked me if I shall be there too. Or did he mean the garden-party? Perhaps he did, anyway I shall tell him I shall not be there. Why do my legs keep aching in the way that they do? Tell me that now, if you can. They feel as if I have rheumatism all the time. Perhaps I have rheumatism and that's the explanation. Did I tell you I was dieting? 12 no 13 stone 10 I weighed. So I dieted fairly hard for three weeks and very hard for a week and now I only weigh 13 stone 6. Worth it, you see, all I have to do is starve for 6 months and can probably get down to 13 stone 4.

Sorry about this awful writing. It must be because he is coming here tomorrow. For four days. Now whatever does he want to go and do a thing like that for? Hasn't got to address a series of strike-meetings, has he? Or write a commissioned article for TIME on social change in S-W Wales? Or arrange a vital shipment of machine-tools at Swansea Docks? Of course he hasn't. What's he coming for, then? Our Portuguese address is c/o Mr. J. G. Barley, Vivenda Cor-de-Rosa, Rua Nova, Mato Largo, Parede, Portugal.[4] Look forward to hearing from you.

£280 will cover your complete bum,

K.

[ALS: Bodleian]

TO ANTHONY POWELL – 22 JUNE 1955

24 The Grove, Uplands, Swansea

Dear Mr. Powell,

I seem to be getting more and more dimwitted as the years go by

worst excesses of those filthy Portuguee greaseballs. Sodding expensive, though. Fares plus board and lodging for three months come to £440.'

3. A commemoration ball.

4. J.G. ('Billy') Barley, the 'English business type' mentioned in note 2, worked as a translator in the offices of a Portuguese family named Pinto Basto, friends of John Aeron-Thomas, the Swansea industrialist and husband of David Sims's ex-girlfriend Margaret (with whom the Amis family briefly shared a house). Barley grew up in Portugal and had Portuguese nationality, but his father was English. He is the model for 'Oates' in *I Like it Here* (1958), Amis's thinly fictionalised account of the Portugal stay.

and so I am only nearly sure that I omitted to answer your last letter and to say that I greatly enjoyed doing my *Spectator* piece on you[1] and was very glad to hear you liked it. Anyway, I say it now.

It would be fine if we could meet again. We must fix it up when I come back from Portugal, where I leave for to-morrow. Thus I shall be out of the way when my new book appears in August – just as well, I foretell. All the other Swansea Amises are coming with me, so we shall be 5 strong. 'Making the arrangements' has been very protracted and horrible. Well, see England first is what I always say.

Yours,
Kingsley Amis

[TLS: Recipient]

TO THE EDITOR, *SPECTATOR* – 8 JULY 1955

SIR – May I invade your columns to answer two correspondents in your issue of June 24?[1] Sorry to be so late, but the *Spectator* is more difficult to obtain outside the cold, tasteless urbanism of western civilisation's Nordic sector.

Mr. John Davenport's insight is extraordinary: I have never been to Spain in my life, not even in an Anglican bus.[2] One of the chief things which keep me away is what British lovers of Spain say about it. Mr. Laurie Lee is the latest of these. Of course as I said in my review the place can hardly be as terrible as he makes it out to be while he thinks he is making it out to be wonderful. I repeat this because Mr. Davenport thinks I disapprove of Andalusians. No (as I said in my review), I just disapprove of the Andalusian characters, and the attitude taken up to

1. 'Afternoon World', a review of two novels by Anthony Powell, *The Acceptance World* (1955) and a reissue of *Venusberg* (1932), in the *Spectator*, 13 May 1954, p. 619.

1. Amis's answer is a defence of his *Spectator* article, 'Is the Travel-Book Dead?', 17 June 1955, pp. 774–5, a review of Laurie Lee's *A Rose for Winter* and Richard Mayne's *The Narrow Smile*, against critical letters from John Davenport and Peter Green (24 June 1955).

2. 'Mr Amis seems to be unfamiliar with Spain; or did he once perhaps make a brisk Anglican survey from a bus?' For John Davenport see Notes on Recipients.

them, in Mr. Lee's book. Although Mr. Davenport must carry weight when he says a book is a good book, I don't feel my case against *A Rose for Winter* is thereby overwhelmed. Biographers, essayists, editors and the like have been in at the death of the novel for so long that I thought it time for a shot or two in the other direction, notwithstanding I have myself – in Mr. Peter Green's expressive phrase – published a novel. Finally, let me assure Mr. Davenport that I'm not grumpy about furrin parts, only about people being silly about them, and that the furrin part I'm in now seems good-oh so far.

Mr. Green might care to re-read my review. If he does he will see, for example, that I attacked Mr. Lee's style not as just unfashionable but as rightly unfashionable, and that I am the last man on earth to expect anyone to find greener grass in Spain or Pakistan. That was my whole point. Mr. Green interests me with his mention of a recent increase in the highbrow travel-book's 'serious reputation'; I have only seen an increase in vacuous belletristic enthusiasm. And I think I can suggest to him that in the face of this 'new and dangerously popular' opposition (new? new?) to the novel I still retain a measure of calm. If I had felt my citadel tottering I should have done the really damaging thing and reviewed *A Rose for Winter* favourably. Horrible praise is more lethal than any abuse, a view borne out by a wide range of writing, all the way from appreciations of Jane Austen (say) to Mr. Lee's account of Andalusia. – Yours faithfully,

KINGSLEY AMIS
Parede, Portugal

TO ROBERT CONQUEST – 8 JULY 1955

Vivenda Cor-de-Rosa, Rua Nova, Mato Largo, Murtal, Estoril, Portugal.

Dear Bob,

Good to read your two letters: one to me in person, the other in the *Spec.*[1] You did me proud there. I've sent in an answer to the original

1. Conquest's letter to the *Spectator*, 1 July 1955, defended Amis's article 'Is the Travel-Book Dead?' (see also preceding letter, Amis to the editor, *Spectator*, 8 July 1955).

Dav. and Grn. letters which I hope will be in time for today's number. What I think I feel about the business, or at least about the points you raise in your letter (to me), is first I'm all in favour of escapism – but people should realise that that is their motive (very often) for buzzing off down south, and not try to inflate their pleasure-etc. trips into a spiritual pilgrimage AND THEN COME AND TELL ME ABOUT IT in a travel-book; and second, the weather *is* fine and the girls *may well* fuck more (no personal experience), and that's all very fine and chaps are sensible to go after it, but again you get this frightful mystique-mongering which obscures the quite definite and concrete advantages of going abroad – not to mention the equally definite snags. Are you with me, mate?

Yes, Portugal is where I am. Quite all right "considering it's abroad", as I always say. Wonderful hot days. Food a bit oily but v. palatable. Drink abundant. Women so fine that I have cultivated an efficient protective armour of nursing the baby, playing with the boys etc. and now hardly notice all the fine skins, imposing gaits, enormous busts etc. I bathe a lot, do crosswords, read Bloomfield's *Language*,[2] and so on.

Don't know definitely yet about the film. I was sent another script just before leaving England, so the thing was presumably still on the move then. The big date I believe is 22 July, when the option expires. If it's still on the cards then, I reckon they will pay for the rights. Haven't heard so far whether K. More can be got for Dixon. They have plenty of time before the 22nd to establish his non-availability, and may for all I know already have done so. Ah, cynical I am these days, mun. 99 times shy, see?

That Wain fellow has some cheek to ask for £600 pa from Weidenfeld, hasn't he?[3] *Will he get it*, that's the question. I read it as a move in his campaign to ditch his job and live on his writing, a chimera if

2. Leonard Bloomfield, *Language* (1933), described in *The King's English* (1997) as 'a major influence on the development of structural linguistics' (p.xiii).

3. Wain resigned his job as Lecturer in English, Reading University, in 1955, a decision he discusses at length in *Sprightly Running: Part of an Autobiography* (London: Macmillan, 1962), pp. 170–210, which also describes his early relations with Amis. No mention is made there of asking for '£600 pa from Weidenfeld' (presumably to act as reader or consultant or part-time editor), nor is the request mentioned in Dale Salwak's critical biography, *John Wain* (Boston: G.K. Hall, 1981). The archives of Weidenfeld and Nicolson have no record of the request, nor does Lord Weidenfeld remember its having been made.

ever there was one (I don't mean in his case especially, but in anyone's). If he asks your advice, I hope you'll crap on the scheme a bit sharp.

Let me know how things are going. Have you got a publication date for the anthology yet? How *slow* everyone is. The 20th century have enraged me by deadlining my Compton-Burnett thing,[4] which gave me a horrible scramble, and then *not using it*. Sometimes I think they all hate me.

All the best, and give our respects to the mrs.

Kingsley

PS: Could you let me know the date this gets to you?[5]

[TLS: Recipient]

TO PHILIP LARKIN – 10 JULY 1955

Vivenda Cor-de-Rosa, Rua Nova, Mato Largo, Murtal, Estoril, Portugal.

Note slight change in this address: Billy B. doesn't seem to know just where he lives, or the Post Office doesn't

My dear Philip,

I suspect I shall now put down quite a lot. One of the reasons is that life being what it is I shall never be able to publish a full account of my doings here (not because they involve animal rape, you foll boll fool, but just because e.g. Billy B. might read it and be vaguely hurt) and further I haven't the energy to put it all down in a diary for nobody to read. So I shall make you the recipient of My Portuguese Journal, and in return for this fabulous privilege I expect to be given access to it whenever I may so desire. Okay o'boy? But before we start on "24th June. Went aboard under a torn grey sky, the calling of ships' sirens like cries of despair and warning. M. came to see me off. We kissed and I said: 'I call you M. because you're a boy and I bugger you, d'you

4. A review of Robert Liddell, *The Novels of Ivy Compton-Burnett*, and Ivy Compton-Burnett, *Mother and Son*, eventually published as 'One World and its Way', *Twentieth Century* 158 (August 1955), pp. 227–8; reprinted in *What Became of Jane Austen?*, pp. 41–50.

5. MS addition.

see?"'[1] – before any of that, let me clear other matters out of the way.

I have now read *Living in the Present* [by John Wain] in its entirety. What follows is CONFIDENTIAL +++ MOST SECRET +++ RESTRICTED +++ PERSONAL I find it hard to give you an idea of the book which shall both be an accurate one and at the same time not give you the impression that it has personally affronted me in some way. It isn't so much that it's a bad book, because TUF may well turn out to be that, at least in parts: no, LITP goes further than that, in not *seeming to be by a writer*. This could be a compliment, I agree, but I don't mean it that way. The sort of writer it does remind me of is *Erskine Caldwell*:[2] You know, you feel the chap hasn't got hold of the fact that first you want to get hold of something you want to say, and then you sort of fudge up a plot or a story of some kind, and then you put in bits of things you've seen and heard round the place, and then you try and make it all sound sort of interesting or witty or funny or striking or unusual in some way. If you find some bit that isn't that, then you work at it until it is, or at least as near it as you can get. John doesn't seem to have heard of any of that, nor does he realise that a novel ought to remind you of life occasionally. I hate his business of *setting himself up as an expert on working-class life*: in this book his cockney humour seems to me a good deal less authentic than say Wodehouse's. All the bad characters look nasty. There is a newspaper woman who – what do you think? She sees *everything* IN TERMS OF *NEWSPAPER STORIES*!!!!!!! There is the most unsympathetic sympathetic character – the hero's girl – I've come across for many a long year. You don't believe for a moment the hero will commit suicide, because John hasn't thought up any reasons why he should. Sorry to go on so long about it, but it made a very deep impression on me, if you know what I mean. And now what the hell am I going to say when I write to thank him for it? I can at least say I don't think it's like *Jim*, can't I? At least I hope not.[3]

As regards *TUF*, the date I've been given is August 22, but you know how these things get held up. The position about the film of *Jim*

1. A parody of early Isherwood.

2. Erskine Caldwell (1903–87), American novelist and short-story writer, best known for the novel *Tobacco Road* (1932), about poor white sharecroppers in the deep South.

3. In a MS addition in the left margin of this paragraph Amis has written: 'This must all sound rather shrill to you, but then you haven't read the book, you sam.'

is all quite on the level, at least it was when I left the Motherland, but I don't know what things are like now. They've certainly done a lot of work on the script, written to me a good deal, discussed casting etc. It all rather depends, as I understand it, whether Kenneth More (yes, that's right. No, that's right. Yes, that's right) can be got for Jim or not. If he can be, then the chances of the film being actually made are almost 100 pc. If not, much less than 50 pc, I gather. [. . .]

See him gulping *vinho verde*[1], Scoffing filthy sheep's-milk cheese, Puffing fags of scent and mule-shit, While he searches for his fleas, But he tells them *Obrigado*[2], Matches all their courtly grace, Cause he's got his homeward ticket, Locked up safely in his case.[4]

[1]"Green wine" bwbwbwbwbwbw [2]"Thank you" [Amis's footnotes]

Actually, considering this is abroad, and so one can't do what one likes to do, this isn't a bad place. The trip out was pretty bledding murderous, chiefly on account of the intense and frequent doubt, horror and despair foreign travel inevitably brings. I don't know about you, but getting the car cleared by the customs, wondering whether our baggage will be taken to our cabin (suppose the labels get torn off, there is pilfering, a case falls open, there is some extra form to fill in I haven't heard about etc.), wondering how the baggage will be taken off and how we shall find it in the Lisbon customs-shed, where we collect passports, what to do if Billy Barley hasn't turned up to meet us (he didn't, either, until we'd been ashore for over an hour), where we get petrol on the dock (should we have taken a tin with us? They drain the tank on embarkation), how to ask where we get petrol on the dock, and innumerable kindred matters, are the kind of matters that can fill my attention for some time at a time for a long time. On landing on foreign soil eech ouch all this intensified itself tenfold. Eventually the Barleys appeared and the heat was off and a different kind of heat, that of "getting to know" the people we were going to spend three months with, was on.

Mrs. B is a sort of fat, bland Portuguese Barbara Stone ONLY NOT SO GOODLOOKING otherwise I should be unhappier here than I am. Billy Barley, alias Joe, has turned out to be very amiable in a childish way, which is a heap better than some mature ways. He is pure English

4. A burlesque of the anonymous ballad 'She was Poor but she was Honest'.

by birth, Portuguese by nationality, bilingual, and feels himself of no certain country, I mean he doesn't quite know which country he belongs to. He drinks black coffee from Coronation mug, has picture of Queen on wall, tea-caddy depicting Edinburgh's face, etc. Like 50 p/c of the young male Portuguese I have seen, he is a motor-bike maniac, endlessly discussing the engine of his German motor-scooter ("This is one of the only twelve that were ever put on the market in Portugal") with me or his great chum Leitão (pron. Lay-*towng*). The Portuguese remind me of the Welsh in some ways. They get awfully het up over ways of doing things. Yesterday there was such an argument in the new summer-house Billy has been building, between him, Leitão and Cal bal Carlos (pron. *Car*loosh), a wonderful little bald grinning gibbon of a man, – that I thought they were going to fight each other. No, it was just over the size of the windows. As far as I can see, the Portuguees are an amiable lot, *not* "proud" like the filthy Spaniards, whom they hate like poison – the annual Spain-Portugal soccer match had to be discontinued because of the bloodshed before, during and after the game. They're mad sods, though. One of the things that will happen to Dixon when he comes to Portugal on behalf of Gore-Urquhart[5] is a ride on the back of a motor-bike after dark, in a high wind, part of the way in very fast traffic through Estoril,[6] with a Portuguese on front *practising his English* turning his head to say "Would you like to take a cerp of cerffee later? Do you like Portuguese cerffee or is it too strerng?" This was Leitão, with me on the back holding very tightly to a rather loose strap. Mad sod, Leitão. The name means "sucking-pig", apparently.

We've done quite a bit of bathing and the sun has been hot, nor has there been one drop of rain since we passed Cherbourg. There is, however, a great deal of filthy *wind*, which like its English counterpart veers and tacks as one moves around, so as always to keep one's hair blown the wrong way. Other things are similarly mixed: the Barleys do us very well, but the house is very small, SMALLER THAN WE WERE LED TO BELIEVE, and there are a hell of a lot of lfi sfi flies. I've never known a randier race of insects: they're fucking all the time. Any moment a pair of buzzing bodies, quite out of control, will fall down on your arm or your lunch. And all of us have had fleas for some time: I shouldn't think we got them in the house, but anyway we have them.

5. Amis's plan to write 'Lucky Jim in Portugal' never materialised, though Jim Dixon and Garnet Bowen of *I Like it Here* have their similarities.

6. The Estoril is part of the Portuguese Riviera, on the coast near Lisbon.

You know my views on fleas. They are virtually unchanged. Mine is relatively inactive at the moment; I don't know whether that means it's getting senile, or perhaps resting up in preparation for lying-in.[7] We eat well, though. I suppose the food here is pretty anglicised because of Billy, but anyway it all seems very palatable, so much so that Billy, who is a man easily downcast, thinks I'm lying politely as each new "Portuguese dish" gets my approval. One wouldn't of course – and this is important – say Ah, Continentals know how to cook, see, not like them English: it's just that one feels relieved that dishes looking rather different from the familiar ones turn out to be not so different after all, or, if different, not noticeably inferior or emetic. Billy told me when we arrived that he didn't drink. "We don't drink much in this house," he said, handing me half a tumbler of martini. "I'm not a drinker," he said at lunch, pouring myself and himself a large glass of red and another large glass of white and putting a liqueur glass in front of each of us. "I never touch the stuff," he said afterwards, watching me drain my second glass of local cointreau and reaching for his larger bottle of port. "It's very rarely I take a drink," he said after dinner, opening a bottle of Real Fine Eau-de-Vie. All on the house, too. Well, that means a lot to me, yer know.

I don't know that I have anything very funny or striking to report. We are some way out of Lisbon 40 mins. in the car and our life is quiet and immensely geared to that of the children, the youngest of whom has been fairly horrible so far, but is showing signs, thank our Saviour, of getting used to the place. Being abroad seems compounded of the dull and the frightening (trying to find your way somewhere in Lisbon, for example). You haven't got any of your friends with you, you see, and you can't make friends with the locals because they're foreign and don't understand what you're saying and you're not here long enough, and WHY THE HELL SHOULD YOU make friends with the locals, when it's so difficult? Put a man abroad for his firm etc. and the situation's different. But consider: in the 14 years since I left school I have acquired three or four friends and perhaps twenty close acquaintances. In three months over here, then, longer than most people can spend, I stand to make 1/16 of a friend and 1/3 of an acquaintance – or would if I spoke the language perfectly. Now, I'm funny. I like talking

7. In a MS addition in pen Amis draws an arrow to the word 'Preparation' and then writes: 'PS. Have just caught it. Hope it was the only one.'

to chaps I like talking to and wd. rather not tlk flk talk to chaps I'd rather not talk to. Not that you need any convincing along those lines, I feel. – Anyway, the sun's good and hot and every so often I get a little thrill: "Well Christ I'm abroad. Not in Swansea any more. Abroad. Well, what do you know about that?" Then I go and try to find an English bookshop.

More soon. Let me know how your life in Hull goes, and everybody's life in the Old Country too, though in less detail. Give [George] Hartley my regards and tell him I'm sorry I didn't have time to write to him before leaving. Funny you should have mentioned fleas.

Will you hold Sally while I go and get something for her bum,

[TL: Bodleian]

TO PHILIP LARKIN – 28, 30 JULY 1955

Abroad

My dear Philip,

Thank you very much for your long funny letter. Of that shall I have further cause to speak: before I do, just let me tell you how I find myself this morning. Recent events here have made me so angry that I want to cry. A bit of recent history first. This place, i.e. Billy Barley's mansion, has rapidly declined in my esteem since I last wrote. In fact I think the chief reason why I said it was quite good was my relief at finding abroad no worse. The food and drink, too, although the martinis early ceased, has continued to be good, and there has still been no rain. (Though I will explain at this point that there are two kinds of weather in this part of Portugal. The first combines strong sun with strong wind, and the wind wins. The other kind has no wind, but no sun either.) The fleas have abated by perhaps 33⅓%. To start with – forgive me if I go over some familiar ground, but I am too fucking furious to remember just what I said last time – the house is too small. Hilly and I divide our time between the dining-room, which is smaller than your kitchen at 30 Elmwood Avenue, as indeed are all the other rooms – the dining-room, I say, which is mostly filled by the table and two enormous sideboards and has only hard chairs – I haven't sat in an easy chair since getting off the boat – between the dining-room, the boys' bedroom, which often has the boys in it and whereas I like the boys all right I don't want them round me all the time, and our bedroom, which has Sally in it for about 16 hours out of the 24, and whereas, etc. We could have put up with this – telling each other that after all we were on holiday and that is necessarily hell – if the house had not been run inefficiently, or had not been run still less efficiently as time passed, or if the place had been clean, or if the lavatory hadn't smelt, or if there hadn't been so many flies everywhere, or if, above all, the meals had been ready on time and had proved to consist when ready of food that Sally could eat. None of these conditions was fulfilled. You will need no convincing that to have Hilly carrying a yelling Sally about for an hour before each meal (an activity broekn foekn broken by short periods when I decided that holding a yelling Sally myself might be preferable to watching a distressed Hilly holding a yelling Sally) was hell, nor was I out of it.[1] Mrs. Barley is an amiable half-wit who *just couldn't understand* that when Hilly intimated that Sally didn't like x, or would be made ill by y, and would prefer to be given z, *she meant it* and also *was right.* Strangely enough, we began to wonder about a week ago whether we might not try to get out. Just about that time things were alleviated a little by the turning-up in Estoril of a Swansea chap I know called Brown with his wife.[2] Now the Browns are a nice and pretty amusing couple and their company did us a lot of good. We were done even more good by being introduced to some friends of theirs called Tyrrell of whom more anon and being offered the use, FREE, of a mountain chalet affair in the south of Portugal owned by them. In response to our pleas, Tyrrell offered to fix us up in a *pensão* (or *pension*) not far from the chalet in which we could stay until the chalet became vacant. (A sister of his from Belfast will be there for some of August, and we must wait till she vacates it.) We reasoned that a *pensão* would cost us less than what we pay here. Consider, my dear little brother in Christ, that at the Pensão Continental in Estoril, where the Browns stayed and where we spent an evening, the worst room, which must in nature be better than our room here, costs – well let me put it like this: the 5 of us in worst-rooms there would pay about 2–10s. a

---

1. See Marlowe, *Doctor Faustus* (1604): 'Why this is hell, nor am I out of it' (I.iii.69).
2. As Lady Kilmarnock remembers it: 'The Browns also worked at the University and we became good friends. They were having a holiday in Portugal, so of course we met up' (personal communication, 16 January 1999).

day with full board (a *slightly* better board than here). Here we pay about 3–7s. Moreover, there is a lounge with easy chairs there, and the bathroom smells only of soap. Well, not knowing how soon this Tyrrell could fix us up, wanting to do the right thing, and reflecting that Barley might as well make a bit (though why we thought this I can't remember), we offered Barley a fortnight's money for 27 July – 10 August. He said he would consider this and "look at his accounts". Having done this he tells us this morning that he is *not making a profit* on his deal with us, oh no, he is doing it *to oblige his boss* who fixed us up with him – did I tell you? – in response to a request from a Swansea chap who knows him (the boss)), and if he wasn't paid for the whole of the 27 July – 26 Aug period he would *incur a loss* – so, at any rate, his perusal of his "accounts" indicated. So I paid him the whole sodding lot. You needn't tell me I was a fool to do this, I know I was, but we have a week at least to run before Tyrrell – who I am beginning to equate with Dr. Barnardo or even Our Saviour – can go south and get us into this *pensão*; and you know how nice (sc. cowardly) I am, and I didn't want to live for an indefinite period – might be more than a week – in a hostile atmosphere, which is a thing that old Billy, who could teach old Rodge a few tricks, is undoubtedly adept at creating. Now isn't he the bad man? Isn't he the mean little schoolboy of hell? And isn't he a fool not to know that I know, or can find out, how much *pensão*-living costs? And even more of a fool not to work out that I shall tell my Swansea pal (not Brown; the one who knows B's boss) all about it, and the Swansea pal will tell B's boss all about it, and B's boss will tell B all about it? Unless he's (Bos tos B's boss is) in it too. This morning I would believe anything to anyone's discredit. [. . .]

The Tyrrells are well worthy of fictional transcription.[3] The wife is a Goanese lady with whitening hair who talks all the time, but often says good things, like "Hurrawlnd" (her husband's name is Harold) "Meezda Emmeess's glarz is ampty. Ornder another of thawz mwontles (bottles) off vine. The rad." They took the Browns all over Portugal in their car. According to Brown, who describes these things well, they were doing little bits of praying in the car all the time: she is a devout RC, he, a Belfast Prod by origin, mucks in to please her. After denouncing their priest, they would say a couple of Hail Marys, Harold

3. They appear in *I Like it Here* as Harry and Isabelle Bannion.

would sing a couple of verses from some Moody and Sankey hymn,[4] and they'd go on denouncing their priest. The Browns had a terrible time at Fatima, where they have these big religious do's. The whole place is given up to saying Hail Marys, marching in processions and touching one of the innumerable statues of the BVM for luck. Tucked away in a croner you know there was a male statue. "Christ" Brown said. And so it was. The only one there. He just doesn't get a look in. Harold Tyrrell gives periodical floor-shows in the Pensão Continental to an audience of Frenchwomen (his opening gambit to them was "La plume de ma tante est dans la poche du jardinier" and Brown had to explain that he wasn't mad), Germans, Americans, a Hungarian and the tennis coach to the heir to the Spanish throne. Also three Irishmen from Belfast who object to Harold's accent in dialect stories as being Liverpool Irish. After this he comes down to the cafe in Estoirl you know and gives another one there. It consists of very long, very clean and quite funny stories that typically involve mimicry of some kind. It was a fine sight to see him telling a dialect story about an Orangeman to Leitão: "And wid a thomp on his beeg drom he barls forth: "To hell wid the Pope" and he slomps bark, sthraight into the arms of Jasus." – "Yez, very good," Leitão said with a laugh. Then, turning round to where nobody was sitting, Tyrrell shouted "Get away from that door, you boys," said to a lottery-tout "Not to-night, Joesp poesp Josephine" and imitated four different people reciting *The Charge of the Light Brigade* ("by Charles Longfellow").

It is now the next day. One other thing I realised about the little financial contretemps yesterday is this: I came out of my bedroom, where I keep everything, with the equivalent of £75 in Portugee currency and gave it to Billy B. He then creaked off in his brown and white shoes to emerge with the file in which he seemingly keeps all his and my correspondence. Then he showed me a bit where he'd said £78–10. Oh sorry, I said; how much more is that? That's 500 in Portuguese money, he said, giving me a smile which I read as that of the native being tolerant about the ignorance of the poor bloody foreigner. Oh right, I said, and went and got him another 500. It wasn't until the afternoon that I saw that his smile was really that of the native amused at the

4. The 'Moody and Sankey Hymn Book', first published in 1873, and properly titled *Sacred Songs and Solos*, was compiled by Dwight Lyman Moody (1836–99) and Ira David Sankey (1840–1908), American evangelicals.

ease with which he can batten upon the ignorance of the poor bloody foreigner; because, you see, the equivalent of £3.10 is 280, or alternately christ -ively £6–5 is the equivalent of 500. So he gypped me of another 220 or alternatively £2.15 while I was looking, so to speak. But yesterday afternoon I got the news that *Jim* is to be filmed *and* broadcast, so I stopped minding so much. Actually all I have is a note from my agent telling me that she has had a note from Ealing telling her that they intend to take up their option on the thing, but just for once I am going to forget about not counting chickens. Anyway the broadcast seems to be quite definite. But I only get 18s. a minute for it. Whatever next? [. . .]

30th July.

This is turning into a positive *saga*, my dear; well I don't suppose you'll mind. Don't lose it, though; this will be my only source for my Portuguese period, as I told you. I forgot to say that a couple of hours after Billy had swindled me for the second, comparatively minor time Hilly ran his wife into Lisbon, a total, round-trip distance of some 30 miles, to pick up the Barley baby and its grandmother, tiresome delays etc. being involved. Jolly funny that he forgot to offer to pay something towards the petrol, wasn't it? There have been one or two previous trips of a similar kind. He forgot about the petrol then too. Yesterday he turned up from the office with a brand-new windscreen fitted to his bike: managed to pick it up cheap for £4–10s., he told me. He must think I'm a *bloody* fool. Then he wan dirty, filthy lavatory-pan warned us that the grandmother his mum-in-law has fainting fits, falls over, has to be helped to chairs, flies into rages, takes dislikes to people, etc. He added that we should have to make plenty of allowances for her. We said we would. Christ, how bloody *nice* we are. The Blessed Kingsley Amis, that's me.

[. . .] I hope you like TUF, I don't really know that you will. Not all through anyway. But the next one should be all right; have done a lot on it here and am at the stage of contemplating a synopsis. Provisional title *Pay Up and Look Pleasnat* (you know) or is that too vulgar? Or too long? Well just write me a letter dear boy and get it ready to send off when I drop you my new address. Wish you were here, and no fooling.

Visitors to Portugal will notice the superb quality of local bum,

K.
Love fra Milly[5]

[TLS: Bodleian]

TO ROBERT CONQUEST – 31 JULY 1955

Estoril and so on, Portugal

Dear Bob,

I hope this non-stop writing isn't getting you down. I like it because I have plenty of time to spare for my end of it, and then every so often I have a letter from you to read. Now let me see if there are any matters arising from the minutes. To finish off this Lee business (Christ, it'll look bad in our published letters: LEE, Lawrie, 232–264) – I think the 2 classes (a) chaps who think abroad is mystically fine (b) chaps who think L.L. & D[ylan] T[homas] are "true poets" overlap quite a lot in practice, hard perhaps to distinguish, but after much consideration I will admit that it *is* a worse failure in *taste* etc to esteem L.L. & D.T. than to be one of (a). But literature not being very important I still think (a) worse, because it makes people *behave* stupidly, and that means that some other people are going to get hurt, which is undesirable. Liking D.T. is bloody silly but it doesn't do anyone much harm. I hate it all right, though. My review has gone off to the *Spr.*[1] Don't know whether you'll agree with it. Fortunately the stories were mostly highly "poetic" so a backhanded assault on the verse became possible. At any rate I included one. You'll probably have to write in again and defend me from Louis Macneice, Empson, Sitwell and all the rest of his pals.

5. MS addition.

---

1. 'Thomas the Rhymer', Amis's review of Dylan Thomas's collection of stories and essays *A Prospect of the Sea*, appeared in *Spectator*, 12 August 1955, pp. 227–8; reprinted in *What Became of Jane Austen?*, pp. 54–7.

About this GULBENKIAN money:[2] I seem to remember something about it, but I can't find any letter of yours with the information in it. I feel a bit of a fool about this, but could you repeat the dose?

I will buy you a double whisky if the name of John's new girl isn't MARIANNE SAALFELDT[3] or something very near it. Do check up: I should be fascinated to know (NB: Just fascinated, that's all: she's not one of my ex-es.).

We have had a sort of muffled row with the chap who's putting us up here: he keeps getting more and more money out of us and giving us less and less in return. So we shall be getting out as soon as possible, in a week's time I hope, and going south to the Prince Henry country.[4] Better not send a letter till I drop you a card with date of move and new address, which we don't know yet.

Do you want to contribute to a German I mean Austrian I think encyclopaedia of modern literature? Payment is DM 0.20 per 12 syllables, though you may think I'm making it up. How much is DM0.20? I'll give them your name anyway, I think, & you can ignore it if you want to. I shouldn't want you to miss the English of the editor chap ("hoping you will not regard this letter as a molestation" etc). I'll drop you that card as soon as I can. Remember me to Tatiana

Yours
Kingsley

[ALS: Recipient]

2. See Conquest to Amis, 26 August 1955: 'The Gulbenkian money, I omitted to explain, comes into the picture as follows. Old Gulbenkian died the other day and left a sum estimated at 400 *million* pounds to a trust fund for cultural purposes. My theory naturally is that as a cultural subject English literature is certainly worth at least 1/400th of the total sum. So, get yourself, me (respectable diplomat), George Fraser (serious editor, or something), John [Wain], Philip Larkin, Tony Hartley and Iain Hamilton (respectable editor), appointed council for distributing this lolly, at salaries of £5,000 per year each (tax free).' Calouste Gulbenkian (1896–1955), Armenian oil magnate; the Gulbenkian Foundation is located in Lisbon.

3. John Wain married Marianne Urmstrom in 1947 and was divorced from her in 1956, after some period of unhappiness; for Amis's knowledge of his new girl, Marianne Saalfeldt, see Amis to Larkin, 22 August 1955.

4. See Amis to Larkin, 22 August 1955.

TO PHILIP LARKIN – 4 AUGUST 1955

If you can get a letter off to me by the 10th, send it to Cor-de-Rosa: if not, write c/o Mr. C. H. Tyrrell, Ferragudo, Algarve, Portugal. It now appears that recent events were more the result of stupidity than mere knavery, but the effect (as you will need no telling) is the same. The maid got the sack today for swearing in front of Billy's Mum-in-law: a pity, because she (the maid) was the most amiable person here, despite acne and dwarfish stature. There is a lull in the flea war. I have the s**ts in compensation. British heatwave bomb,

K.

[ALS: Bodleian]

TO PHILIP LARKIN – 22 AUGUST 1955

Correio, Monchique, Algarve, Portugal

My dear Philip,

This is much more abroad, this place, than any of the other abroad places we have struck. Not that I mean that's a good thing; oh dear me no. Not necessarily, anyway. This place (Monchique: Correio means Post Office; they don't deliver letters ho ho ho) is nearly as high as Snowdon, though much hotter. It's about 15 miles from the sea, where we drive every so often (every slightly too often, for my taste) and not far from Lagos, where Prince Henry the Navigator had his research station, and Silves, where the Crusaders massacred 30,000 Moors to whom they had promised safe-conduct. We had a tremendous drive down from Estoril, with an above-par dose of doubt, horror and despair at the Tagus ferry; the place of embarkation had been very recently changed, a fact known to some but not all of the non-English-speaking officials deputed to marshal the ferry traffic. Then there was a very long wait in a queue which ran through the fruit-market, where two-thirds of Lisbon's million people came and stared into our car. After I had done a lot of wondering about where to pay, and when, and how much (we were down to our last pound at the time), and had explained to a Frenchman how to get to Seville, we drove over a sort of plywood five-barred gate into the boat and were taken across. Tyrrell told us when we arrived that we shouldn't have taken that way; we should have gone north-east by the new road built by the Americans to get munitions into Spain in the event of war, and then crossed to the south by a bridge of kindred origin. Anyway, we spent three days in a nice *pensão* and then came up here. There are a lot of donkeys and mules hereabouts, and Philip has regular rides on one of the former. Everybody wears black and carries an open black umbrella. They stare all the time, of course, but not always with hostility. Next door there is a madwoman who peeps at you and has tried to steal stuff left out at night. Tyrrell got her jailed recently for this, but she's out again now. Grapes grow profusely in the garden. There is a W. C. – the only one for some miles – but all water has to be pumped. I usually do this at the start of the day, after breakfast, while the water to wash me is getting warm. Then most of the morning I write letters to friends, or work at my new novel. At noon I smoke a cigarette and drink a couple of glasses of wine (7 s. a gallon, boy, and you can keep your sore turns and your nwee sang jorje and your shah-toe olive yay et cetera); then after a salad lunch and getting drunk on the wine I drink some of the local firewater: *medronha*, made from a thing like a strawberry on a tree which grows in these parts. But you don't want to know about that, do you? Then I have a rest or go to the beach. Lots of pretty kids there. There's one in particular who helps look after some orphans with a young friend of hers. It's rather sweet to see the way they behave together; so affectionate. The prettier one seems to have taken quite a fancy to me. Comes up and laughs a lot. Nice figure she's got. But she's only about fourteen so I'm hardly interested. (Hardly, *adv.*: in a hard fashion.) Aw sawl. She has a very deep-pitched laugh and the darkest fair hair I have ever seen. I think she knows what I'm thinking. So does Hilly, I think. Then we come home and I get drunk again, then I *light the pressure lamps* (aaoh! aoh! aooh! argh, sxxt, farks!), we eat and I drink more, then we retire to our hard but flealess couches – it seems that the little creatures referred to were endemic to the Barley household, LIKE FLITHY BARSTARDY AND MEANESS. [. . .]

You know old John [Wain] is a master of the *hypnotic* technique of writing: a refinement on my previous description of it. You know: "I am writing a comedy about despair. Comedy. I am funny. Funny. And despair. I write about despair. And comedy. Funny. Funny and despair. T-r-a-g-i-c-o-m-e-d-y." And since most reviewers take the will for the deed – you know that's a mighty important conception. The exquisite feminine poetic sensibility of V Woolf, the whatever-it-was of Hy James and so on: it had all been brilliantly put into the critics' heads by the novelists themselves, because they were so clearly trying to be what they were trying to be. And yet, this time (over LITP[1] I mean) he seems to have slipped. [. . .]

I was sorry I forgot you were 33. You shall have a nice present when we meet (once more). I draw to your attention a stave from the lyric of *Be My Life's Companion* (pity it isn't *Wife's*): "People who are lonely Can be old at thirty-three; Don't let that happen to you, Don't let that happen to me."[2] Not so good, what? I am 33 also, you see, my dear friend. I didn't like Black Day at Bad Cock.[3] I thought it *horribly* slow except for the last 50 seconds or so. I nearly screamed when we had the twenty-seventh shot of a man taking ten seconds to turn and look hostilely at Tracey. Still each to his taste. The climax was fine, though too late and *much* too short. When I found that the other bad men had been *rounded up without trouble* by that sheriff, that was another time I very nearly screamed. It seemed to me a perfect *Sight and Sound*[4] choice, I'm sorry to say.

Sound a bit sour, don't I? I'm not really. Don't post a letter to me after the 15th Sept. Send it to the Grove to await arrival after that date. Can you guess how much I enjoyed writing that? I think abroad is fine as long as you don't expect much from it. If you don't like anybody very much you might as well be abroad as anywhere else I suppose, but if you like to choose your friends, your company, your entertainment etc. you will be better off at home. And why should *I* care what foreigners think, even if they would tell? I'm not a politician or an interpreter or an employee of a tourist agency or a foreign correspondent. So *why* should I care what foreigners think? What can I do if I know?

I was as usual (Christ, won't I ever learn?) premature with the film news. Michael Balcon has turned down the idea at the last moment,

---

1. *Living in the Present.*

2. 'Be My Life's Companion' (1951), written by Bob Hilliard and Milton De Lugg, recorded separately by Rosemary Clooney (b. 1928) and the Mills Brothers, a vocal quartet with many hit songs in the 1930s and 1940s.

3. *Bad Day at Black Rock* (1955), a suspense thriller directed by John Sturges and starring Spencer Tracy and Robert Ryan.

4. *Sight and Sound*, a film quarterly, founded in 1932.

but the people who wrote the script are going (so they say) to form a private company and make it themselves. K. More is out of it, but Alal balbal Alastair Sim is keen to play Welch which means Geo. Cole will be brought in for Jim.[5] I know. Yes, I know, but nearer my idea of the character than More is, anyway. And Sim will draw the crowds. Why do I say that? I don't get a cut of the takings. By the way you remember I said I had my homeward ticket Locked up safely in my case. No: just my homeward voucher. I have (with my family) to come to Lisbon 2 days before the boat sails to exchange the voucher for a ticket, and so spend 2 days at a no-tell. Gorblimey. Do write me a nice long letter in the next couple of weeks. Give me among other things your verdict on TUF. John is a fool about the 2nd Marianne.[6] I know her slightly and she's quite nice, big tits, friendly piggy face, easy lay. But what does he want her for. Of course she's foreing, if you can guess the word I mean, like No. 1, and she's got the same name, see. Expect it makes him feel like Lamartine or Stendhal, that.[7]

Minnie Stroney bum,[8]

Kingsley

[TLS: Bodleian]

TO JOHN DAVENPORT – 31 AUGUST 1955

Correio, Monchique, Algarve, Portugal.

Dear Mr. Davenport,

I enjoyed (*in a way!*)[1] your letter about Dylan Thomas and I hope you won't mind if I write *privatim*, as they say, to take up one or two of your points.

5. Alastair Sim (1900–76), character actor on stage and screen; George Cole (b. 1925), stage, screen and television character actor, a protégé of Sim; at the height of his film career, in the 1950s, Cole specialised in leading comedy roles, 'typically as a confused, silly young man' (Katz, ed., *The Film Encyclopedia*, p. 271); later famous as Arthur Daley, Cockney 'entrepreneur' and wideboy, in *Minder*, a popular television comedy series of the early 1980s.

6. See Amis to Conquest, 31 July 1955.

7. Alphonse de Lamartine (1790–1869), poet and statesman, a leading figure in the French Romantic movement; Stendhal (Henri Beyle) (1783–1842), French novelist; both were married to or in love with English girls.

8. See Amis to Conquest, 7 September 1955, note 5.

---

1. MS addition; Davenport's letter appeared in the *Spectator*, 19 August 1955, p. 250. For Davenport see Notes on Recipients.

I'm not really all that determined to startle, you know. If I do startle I take it as a bit of a compliment, and I'd never try not to, but contrary to your view I do sincerely hold the opinions about Thomas that I professed in my piece. I have held them ever since about 1948, as far as I can remember, and have been waiting for a chance to voice them ever since. I don't think it ever much matters if a lousy poet gets acclaimed as a good or even great one, but I do think people should be given the opportunity of calling him lousy when possible. Thomas, I would say, wasn't in the main stream, and I might add Thank God.

I don't think it's at all relevant, either, to consider whether or not Thomas was a thinking man, whatever that is. I *know* he worked hard at his stuff. But that doesn't affect its merit in the least, nor does it stop *what he finally wrote* being miserable incoherent rubbish. That's what I was trying to get across with my "*careful* linguistic folly". You can draft out nonsense as many times as you like, think hard and repeatedly about it, but it's still nonsense. I just cannot agree that more than a few of Thomas's poems are coherent. But that would take several thousand words to establish (which is one of the troubles in these review things, of course).

And really, Uncle, why accuse me of chucking my weight about in a pretentious way?[2] When you say things like that I think you are approaching the American "joshing-along" technique, whereby insults can be bandied, provided the aimer of them keeps a smile on his face. What do you really mean by chucking weight, etc? You mean, I suppose, that a person my size shouldn't throw mud at, or otherwise attack, somebody Thomas's size. But you must see, surely, that Thomas's size is the very matter at issue. You think it was large; I think it was microscopic (in verse). Am I then to pretend I like Thomas so as to conform to other people's notions of our relative sizes? And even if Thomas were indisputably large, doesn't a critic enjoy the privilege of forgetting all that when he begins writing? Otherwise what will happen to criticism? Even Professor Snooks is allowed to get away with calling *Measure for Measure* "a mediocre play, of no great depth". And if we disagree, surely the thing to do is to amass *critical* ammunition to demolish him. Not to tell him how carefully Shakespeare worked at this play, so it must be good, and if [he] thinks otherwise he is chucking his weight about.

2. What Davenport wrote was: 'Now why can't Mr Amis relax, wherever he is, use his freedom in doing a little quiet checking up, and stop chucking his weight about in this pretentious way?'

I may have sounded a little bit sour still, but I'm not really. One last crack is that I bet I know late Shakespeare just as well as you do, and I can't remember any "complex simplicity" in it. Plenty of bad verse, of course, but never anything below the level of common sense. Anyway: I was just beginning my peroration. You can see that I really have come South with a vengeance, and I don't mind it much, except that I find it rather slow without my friends to talk to. Also I am getting a little bit tired of being stared at the whole time. But I get by, and I do get drunk etc., though with my wife and three children here I naturally have to step up my love-making in terms of intension rather than extension. As for chip sandwiches – ugh! You were just pulling my leg, weren't you?

Well, cheers, and forgive this raw effusion. I'm not letting abroad interfere with my habitual state, viz. mellow as a 'cello.

Yours sincerely,
Kingsley Amis

[TLS: National Library of Wales]

TO HILARY RUBINSTEIN – 2 SEPTEMBER 1955

Correio, Monchique, Algarve, Portugal

My dear Hilary,

Many thanks for sending on the reviews and for the tidings about the sales. I am so immensely relieved that my neurotic forebodings about the book have proved to be unjustified. I really think the reviewers have been most generous, and the fact that about four of them have stigmatised the book in passing as "vulgar" has been almost as encouraging as any of their praise. I was afraid some of them might praise it for being "sensitive".[1] It seems I needn't have worried.

---

1. Conquest sent Amis his summary of the reviews of *That Uncertain Feeling* in a letter of 26 August 1955: 'You will by now have seen that the reviewers have also, in their less intelligent way, given it a big hand all round – only the Times, as far as I can see, takes a really stuffy line, claiming that your unromantic attitude to love "jars". Oh, and the New Statesman (Pritchett under a pseudonym), I understand though conceding virtues all round, still refers to you as a "literary teddy boy".'

And now a word of congratulation. I'm most pleased with the appearance of the book. It's very nicely produced, printed and so on, as was *Jim*. But the most flattering thing of all was the omission of blurb and of *Jim* reviewers' quotes. I take that as a gesture of confidence by VG Ltd and it is duly appreciated. [. . .]

By the way, when you next write (don't bother to do it specially) could you send me copies of any advertisements that have appeared, if copies are available? Just to satisfy my curiosity. My press-cutting people don't seem to go in for that. [. . .]

All the best from Hilly and myself,

Yours ever,
Kingsley

[TLS: Gollancz]

TO VICTOR GOLLANCZ – 7 SEPTEMBER 1955

Correio, Monchique, Algarve, Portugal.

My dear VG,

I had been intending for some time, in my dilatory fashion, to send you a brief situation-report on my residence abroad, and now there comes this request from Hilary to stir me into belated activity. As far as *Landcape with Dead Dons*[1] is concerned, I agree with him that it's an enjoyable detective story, but I personally enjoyed the detection rather more than the funny parts, which are too fantasticated for my taste. So my official response is, I fear, no comment – though please don't take this as implied *adverse* comment. It's just that it isn't near enough to my kind of thing for me to feel like praising it in public. I'm sure the book will do very well and it was nice – and flattering – to be given the chance of having a look at it.

I'm mightily pleased that *That Uncertain Feeling* seems to be selling satisfactorily. I really was beginning to have kittens about it, in fact had been having mild ones for some time, and this was probably why the

1. *Landscape with Dead Dons* (1956) by Robert Robinson (b. 1927), writer, journalist, broadcaster.

MS turned up on your desk some time after deadline. Every time I went through it there seemed to be more wrong with it. Apparently I needn't have worried overmuch. A vast relief.

The most important fact about Portugal as of now is, from my point of view, that I shall be leaving it soon and coming home. I thought I knew all the main categories of boredom one was ever likely to encounter, but I made the mistake of thinking it was only people who could be boring. Places can be as efficient in this way, if not more so. I am getting through the last few weeks by drinking a lot of local gin (11/- the bottle) and a kind of applejack-cum-Pernod that they go in for a lot hereabouts (and no wonder), also by having the DDT-spray always within reach.

More power to your elbow in the Abolitionist campaign.[2] I think the present effort may well turn the scale at last. It certainly deserves to.

My wife sends her best regards, and so do I,

Yours sincerely,
Kingsley Amis

[TLS: Gollancz]

TO ROBERT CONQUEST – 7 SEPTEMBER 1955

Correio, Monchique, Algarve, Portugal.

Dear Bob,

Many thanks for your latest. And damned glad to get your approving comments on *TUF*. There's a lot to be said for getting good reviews (especially, of course, the money they indirectly bring one), but it's what one's chinas[1] say that may bring the feeling of having done a respectable job. The reviewers have been very decent on the whole, but all this "vulgar" stuff makes me wonder where they live and where they go on their free evenings. I liked best the chap in the Evening News who thought Lewis was "an outrageously common little bounder" and *yet* declared that this didn't interfere with his enjoyment of the book.

2. Gollancz campaigned for a variety of left-wing causes, including the abolition of capital punishment (which would not be achieved in Britain for another ten years).

---

1. Cockney rhyming slang for 'mates' (from 'China plates').

Nothing like being broad-minded, eh? Well, anyway, it looks as if sales are going to be satisfactory, and that means I shall be able to go on uttering my favourite sentence, more favourite even than "Oh thanks, I'll have a large gin and tonic"; viz. "I don't believe in artistic successes".

Yes, course I know Praia da Rocha. We bathe there most days; it's the nearest beach to where we are. I could probably fix your mother up with accommodation if she'd like. I don't know what kind of thing she wants but the Pensão Sol where we stayed for a few days is modest, quiet, clean, cheap, *excellent* food, polite staff, English-speaking proprietor; the lot. Praia itself is only a couple of rows of houses but it joins on to Portimão where you can get anything you might expect to get in a fair-sized Portuguese fishing village or small town. Across the river is Ferragudo, where old Tyrrell lives, hoping most of the time that the fates will throw into his lap some Englishman or American whom he can fix up and show round. Anyway let me know if I can do anything. There's at least one large hotel in Praia, the Grande, if she'd prefer that kind of thing.

Haven't heard from the Britcoun chaps yet.[2] They'd better get their skates on if they want to get hold of me this trip. We leave here for Lisbon on the 22nd, stay a couple of nights in a hotel there, sail on the 24th (docking at Southampton on the 27th, I believe, and dashing straight for Swansea even if it's the middle of the night). Actually it might not be a bad idea if they did get in touch with me. One of their chaps could help me through the customs and on to the ship. See if you can put this over to your Britcoun chaps.

I should really have said a bit more about Praia. The beach is most impressive. The landscape otherwise is pretty arid now, but very attractive, I hear, in the autumn and winter. It's pretty quiet all round. No night life to speak of, though there are cafes. A small resident English population in Portimão or thereabouts. Very few foreign visitors, a sprinkling of people from Lisbon, but these probably disappear in the winter. Winter climate apparently mild, a coldish (by their standards) spell occasionally, a great deal of sunshine, very little rain. Hilly wants me to add (1) that she personally would go mad from boredom if left here on her own, and (2) that the town is an ugly little town. It is. They catch sardines, and then they tin sardines, and then they transport

2. Conquest had arranged with friends in the British Council 'for their chap in Lisbon to give you the treatment' (letter to Amis, 26 August 1955).

sardines. But of course if you stay in Praia you won't see any of that, nor even smell it. (The Sol place is in Praia, away from all the shit, 20 yards from the beach.) You just can't expect to have very much to do with yourself, that's all. Anyway, lemme know.

I suggest for your limerick,[3] 2nd line, 'There's a pair of bull's balls in this parcel' and line 3 'Rubber-stamped *IRA*'. That, I think, solves most of the problems.

Am still keeping my eyes peeled for the Gulbenkian money, tho' nothing has as yet dawned upon my sight. Who the hell was he, anyway? You go on about him as if I knew the fellow personally. And where the hell did he get all that lolly from? And it strikes me that life will have to show itself a technician more resourceful (please) than most if I am ever to come within hailing distance of his fortune.

Have been given an assignment which I shall enjoy more than most: a survey of cheesecake magazines for *The Author*.[4] I look forward very much to explaining this when I go to my Swansea newsagent and buy about 200 of them. The thing to avoid, of course, is being superior about them in the Samuel Deronda[5] way (did you see that? ". . . a magazine whose function it was (or some such jargon) to bring its readers every week the breathtaking news (subtle bit of irony there) that the female body is shaped differently from the male." no no no *no no no* NO NO NO *NO NO NO* N O O O O O O, my dear fellow.)

Closing down now. Ennui lies upon me like a hangover,[6] or perhaps the other way round. It's the getting pissed every night so as to get to sleep on the hard bed which gets me down, if you get what I'm getting at. Bloody terrible, man. No more wine for me after I come back. I shall stick to splendid virile Nordic gin and healthy bracing tonic. There's something subtly vinous about the Lisbon gin I must have mentioned to you. I can't remember when I last voided a firm motion, if you'll

3. The limerick in question was composed in 1939, and as far as Conquest can remember reads as follows: 'The Postmaster General cried "Arsehole!/There's a pair of fine balls in this parcel/Stamped IRA/And with nine pence to pay/And addressed 'To the King, Windsor Castle!'"' See also Amis to Larkin, 15 December 1959, which quotes the limerick in part.

4. 'The "Cheesecake" Periodicals', in *The Author* 66:2 (Winter 1955), pp. 28–30.

5. 'Samuel Deronda', by John Wain, was a six-part 'Summer Serial' in the *Spectator*, running from 5 August to 9 September 1955. Its eponymous hero, an 'inconspicuous' but ambitious young man, makes his way in London literary life, capturing the office beauty, Minnie Stroney, finding overnight success as a poet, wheedling a position as a novel reviewer.

6. 'And custom lies upon thee with a weight' (Wordsworth, 'Ode: Intimations of Immortality', line 128).

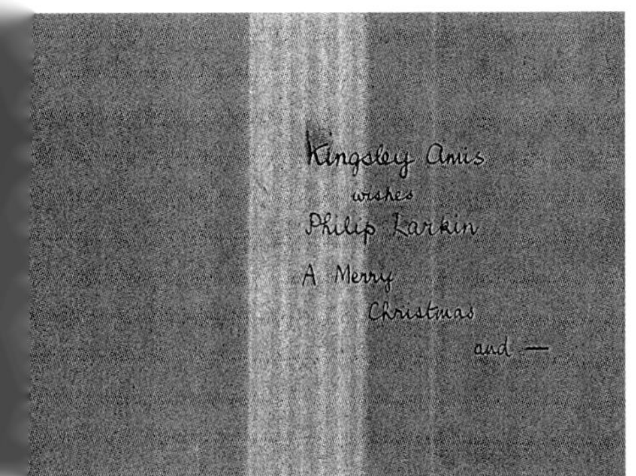

Christmas card to Philip Larkin, December 1953.

Right Bruce Montgomery, 1953. 'I never have any trouble about which prong of the Bruce dilemma to impale myself on: I *can't* pay "more than I want to spend", I'm reduced to paying *all I have* . . . and *still* being like a *poule de luxe*' (to Philip Larkin, 13 January 1953).

Below Cover illustration for the first American edition of *Lucky Jim*.

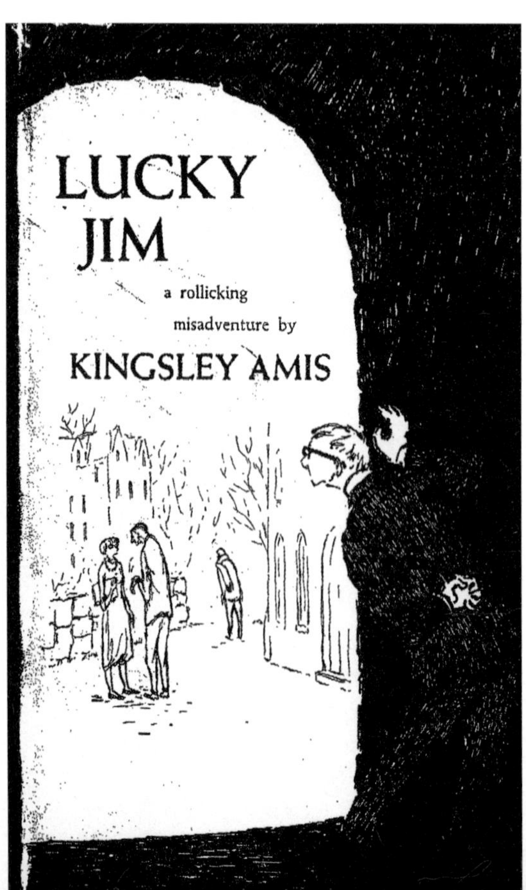

OPPOSITE
Above James Bartley, KA's colleague in the English Department, University College of Swansea, at a staff cricket-club meeting, The Rhyddings Pub, Brynmill, Swansea, *c.* 1955.

Below Among other staff at the same meeting: David Sims, third from left, Esmond Cleary, reading (Bartley, again, with back to camera).

Left Hilary Rubinstein, late 1950s. 'I shall be very glad to send you my novel . . . It would never make an author's or a publisher's fortune, but I think it is quite funny' (to Hilary Rubinstein, 8 December 1952).

Below Victor Gollancz, 1963. 'With renewed maledictions, threats, abuse, groans and affection, Yours ever, Kingsley' (to Victor Gollancz, 19 December 1957).

Hilly in Portugal, 1955.

KA with Hilly and the children, Portugal, 1955.

KA in Portugal, 1955. 'I'm not letting abroad interfere with my habitual state, viz. mellow as a 'cello' (to John Davenport, 31 August 1955).

KA and Anthony Powell, 1957. 'I'm sure we can work in a couple of swift drinks after the recording' (to Anthony Powell, 10 November 1957).

Pat Gale, Hilly, her dog Nancy, George Gale, Sally Amis and Tim Houghton, Swansea, 1960.

Hilly, Jean McAndrew and KA in New Jersey, *c.* 1958–59. 'You do know, I hope, that you did more than all the others did between them to make our stay such paralysing, coronary-accelerating fun' (to Jean and John McAndrew, July 1959).

Anthony Powell, KA, Philip Larkin and Hilly, London, 1958. 'By God that's a great photo of us 3 and ole AP . . . Like a row of bloody film stars we were' (to Philip Larkin, 12 May 1982).

pardon the expression. Just remembered that "Amen, is it?" and so on was the very last touch of all in the whole book, put in in proof to fill in a space erroneously left there by the printer. Funny, that. Well, give my love to dear old London town. I shall be coming up to it no very long time after I return. Salutes, then, and thank you for all the nice things you say about *TUF*. Give my love and a little tickle to your secretary, or wouldn't I want to do that if I saw her?

Ever such love to you both, Tatiana & you I mean

Kingsley

[TLS: Recipient]

TO PHILIP OAKES – 17 SEPTEMBER 1955

as from: 24 The Grove, Uplands, Swansea.

Dear Mr. Oakes,

Many thanks for your letter and your review.[1] Modesty forbids me to praise the review too highly, because it was so very flattering. Let me just say then that if I'd been given the chance of vetting the piece myself there's very little I should have wanted to alter.

The book is supposed to be about morals or morality, or our modern version of these. The marriage and to a lesser extent the job business are offered as typical forms in which moral issues present themselves to-day. My original title, discarded as too pretentious, was *The Moral Man*. The uncertain feeling, as you rightly spotted, is a moral one, not merely or in the first place a sexual one.

I really am most grateful for your understanding and sympathetic review. These older persons of refinement and taste, even when they praised the book, were hopelessly (and I should hope demonstrably) far from the target. But then they all went to Eton so how can they know?

Yours sincerely,
Kingsley Amis

[TLS: HEHL]

---

1. Oakes reviewed *That Uncertain Feeling* in *Truth* 155 (26 August 1955), p. 222, in an article entitled 'Recent Fiction'.

TO W. SOMERSET MAUGHAM – 28 NOVEMBER 1955

24 The Grove, Uplands, Swansea, Glamorgan

Dear Mr. Maugham,

I have long been meaning to write and thank you for making it possible for me to enjoy a long stay in Portugal recently. I could never have done it without the prize-money from your very generous Award. As a matter of fact I probably got even more benefit from it than previous winners, because until I actually went there, 'abroad' was a thing I thought I didn't much care for. But Portugal at any rate turned out to be such good fun that I mean to go on going there as often as I can.

I have been intending to write to you for a much longer time on a different topic. Your work has always meant a great deal to me; in fact, if I may say so, you are one of the very few authors I admired when I was in my teens and still admire – even more – today. You appealed to me when I was younger because I could read your books straight through and then re-read them, instead of getting bogged down in authors whom intellectual schoolmasters and contemporaries tried to tell me were significant. And nowadays, apart from anything else, I cherish your example. You taught me that what mattered first was narrative, and that if one wanted to do anything extra one must still see to it that the story stood up on its own. Further, I learnt that subtlety is only valuable in the presence of recognisable outlines firmly and clearly drawn. And there were all sorts of problems of dialogue and scene-setting and transitions, for which you gave me, not ready-made solutions, but demonstrations of an approach. My own efforts in fiction probably don't reflect your influence directly, or satisfactorily, and yet the influence was there, not least in what went on before the final draft emerged. But how pale and cold this sounds beside the enormous pleasure I get from your books as a reader.[1]

And so I owe you a double debt of gratitude which I shall not soon

---

1. For a more astringent assessment of Maugham's writings see 'Mr Maugham's Notions', in *The Amis Collection*, pp. 63–7, which reprints a review of *Somerset Maugham: A Biographical and Critical Study* (1961) by Richard Cordell in the *Spectator*, 7 July 1961, p. 23.

forget. Please allow me to send you my renewed thanks and very best wishes – and my wife's too, for as well as being a great admirer of yours she also came along on the Portugal trip, and is as grateful to you as I am.

Yours sincerely,
Kingsley Amis

[TLS: Boston University Library]

TO ESTA WOLFRAM – 15 JANUARY 1956

24 The Grove, Uplands, Swansea, Glamorgan, Gt. Britain.

Dear Mrs. Holfram (I hope I have your name correctly: if I haven't, I know how you feel, since I get everything from Amos to Alice–),[1]

Thank you so much for your letter. Somehow you Americans have a gift for saying the most flattering things in detail, where my British friends always seem compelled to review my books when they write to me about them, and very nearly end by saying "Despite these faults, I am confident that this author's future work will contain points of interest." So I mean it when I say I'm glad you enjoyed *Lucky Jim*.

The next one will be out from Harcourt, Brace on, they tell me, February 23rd. I hope you like this one too, though it's more sedate in some ways. Doubleday's threw me out after the general American debacle with *Jim*, and I can't say I blame them: sales failed to top 2000, I believe. But there are signs that this one may do better. Anyway, I hope you'll feel in duty bound to read it. As regards the third effort – well . . . It's slow work at the moment, because it's written from a girl's point of view, and I find that (though I've been married for 8 years) I know even less about women than I thought. But I press on – with the book, I mean.

With ren*ewed thanks and good wishes.*

1. Amis mistook the initial 'W' of Mrs Wolfram's name for an 'H'. Mrs Wolfram, from Walnut Creek, California, had written him a fan letter.

(*the typewriter did the dirty on me there*)[2]

Yours sincerely
Kingsley Amis

[TLS: Recipient]

TO MISS CARVER, HARCOURT BRACE – 15 JANUARY 1956

24 The Grove, Uplands, Swansea, Glamorgan, Great Britain.

Dear Miss Carver,

I feel very guilty indeed about having left your kind letters unanswered all these months. Some of the delay can be attributed to my absence in Portugal; some to the difficulties of getting you a non-copyright photograph for publicity, and such matters; the rest to criminal laziness. I hope I may be forgiven, because however unlikely it may sound I am very glad to be published by Harcourt, Brace, and was most grateful for the parcel of books you sent me.

As regards the proofs: everything seems excellent, all the changes you have made strike me as most reasonable, and the actual printing surpasses the British edition as American printing usually does these days, I'm afraid. I noticed a good many uncorrected errors in the copy I got, though I assume you will have taken care of that at the page-proof stage.

My agent[1] tells me the book has "just missed" being made a Book Club selection, and adds rather oddly (though I see what he means) that this is a good omen. However that may be, I certainly hope that your firm will do reasonably well out of the publication, and that the numerous Americans (all of them but one New Yorkers, which is interesting) who kindly wrote to me about *Lucky Jim* will not feel too let down by it.

2. MS addition.

1. Amis was represented by Graham Watson of Curtis Brown in London; Alan Collins, who had bought Curtis Brown in New York in 1941, and was President and owner until his death in 1968, represented him in the United States.

I enclose the questionnaire, filled out as far as may be, though very late, I fear, to be of much use. Perhaps I ought to say that among my friends I am notoriously the worst correspondent in the Old World, so you mustn't think I have singled you out for extra discourteous treatment – and I promise to do better in future.

With renewed apologies, and cordial good wishes,

Yours sincerely,
Kingsley Amis

[TLS: Harcourt]

TO AUSTIN BAKER – 7 FEBRUARY 1956

24 The Grove, Uplands, Swansea, Glam.

Dear Mr. Baker,

Many thanks for your very kind letter.[1] I am so glad you enjoyed my books. And let me say at once that your interpretation of them as primarily comedies is most refreshing to me. I certainly intended them to be that a long way before they were anything else. My second aim was to get a few things said that I felt strongly about – things about life and people in general, not all this sociological hoo-ha. I have been amazed, and a little depressed, by being treated by so many critics (kind though they've often been) as a kind of social pamphleteer. As you have seen, I was writing about life as I have experienced it rather than solemnly charting the emergence of a new class. Altogether I've been forced to the conclusion that many critics lead rather refined and sheltered lives, and are a rather serious-minded crowd. If you can get any of this outburst of mine into your article, I shall be most grateful, but please don't think you *must*.

I enclose a "potted biography" which I hope will be adequate. I

1. Mr Baker writes: 'At the time I was responsible for writing a regular library bulletin for Bedford Borough Library Service, each issue of which contained an article on a living author. I wrote a good number of them and had helpful replies in every case. Amis was the first' (personal communication, 3 November 1996).

should be very interested to see a copy of the article. And meanwhile many thanks for your interest in my work.

Yours sincerely,
KINGSLEY AMIS

Born 1922 in London, just about qualifying as a sound-of-Bow-Bells Cockney. Modest but comfortable middle-class home. Scholarship to City of London School, thence scholarship to St. John's, Oxford. Lieutenant in Signals in World War II. Wrote things from an early age, but nothing that could even be called promising until about 1946. Married 1948 and now have three children. Got lecturing post at University College of Swansea, 1949. Have settled down pretty happily in South Wales and would be very disinclined to move. No third novel yet, though am on initial stages of one. Hope to publish book of verse this year.

If there's any special point you'd like some dope about, please don't hesitate to write again.[2]

K. A.

[TLS: Recipient]

TO ROBERT CONQUEST – 29 FEBRUARY 1956

24 The G, etc., Swansea. Leap Year Day, 1956

Dear Bob,

Yours various to hand. Don't resign[1] until you see me. This is going to be a short one because before setting out on Friday I have several lectures to prepare, all the examination questions to set and about 250,000 letters to write. Anyway, we shall see you at the weekend. Thanks heartily for asking us along, but we can't bloody descend on you every time. We are going to have one of our periodical indulgences

2. MS addition.

---

1. From the Foreign Office, where Conquest had worked since 1948; see Amis to Conquest, 16 October 1956.

in hotel life: the Mapleton, actually, in Coventry Street, dear to H. and myself as the scene of several of our earliest fornications in common (I mean we fucked each other, not other chaps). So, Friday night being Guinness night[2] as usual, we shall be giving you a ring at CHT[3] on the Saturday morning, if this will suit. Christ, life is a killer, man. I spend all my time either writing talks or delivering them. Haven't touched the novel[4] since Portugal. Could it be that I should chuck my job? Ah, no, no. Must draw the veil now. See ya.

Yours,
Kingsley

[TLS: Recipient]

TO HILARY RUBINSTEIN – 10 MARCH 1956

24 The Grove, Uplands, Swansea.

My dear Hilary,

Yes, fine about Leonard Russell and so on.[1] Yes, 50–50 seems right to me for the spoils (I suppose "split" the proceeds means that? If it

2. In the mid-1950s, T.L. Marks (1912–71), the Advertising Manager at Guinness, later Chairman and Joint Managing Director of Harp Lager Ltd, initiated a series of dinners for literary figures at the Belfry Restaurant off Sloane Street in Knightsbridge. Though these dinners were not publicised, in contrast with other attempts by the company to establish ties with the worlds of literature and the arts at the time (such as the annual Guinness Prize for Poetry, with its resulting five volumes of *The Guinness Book of Poetry*), they helped the company to ascertain how best to sponsor new writing. When Marks died he was succeeded at Harp Lager by Edward Guinness (b. 1924), editor of *The Guinness Book of Guinness 1935–1985* (1988), the company's privately published history. Edward Guinness remembers sitting next to Amis at one of the dinners in Knightsbridge (personal communication, 20 January 1999). As for the Guinness Prize for Poetry, Amis never appeared among the panel of judges nor was an award-winner, though Robert Conquest won a prize in 1955.

3. Carlton House Terrace, Conquest's address at the Foreign Office.

4. *I Like it Here* (1958).

1. Rubinstein had written to Amis on 8 March 1954 (Gollancz) telling him about a book Leonard Russell (1906–74), a literary journalist on the *Sunday Times*, was planning to publish with Cassell's entitled *The Russell Reader*. This volume would contain six books in one, 'plus certain picture sections and other gimmicks', and Russell was proposing to include *Lucky Jim*. He was offering Amis and Gollancz £250 plus a penny a copy royalties on all copies sold over twenty thousand (at a sale price of twenty-five shillings); Rubinstein thought Amis should take it, since 'in our opinion, it wouldn't affect the sales of our normal edition in the slightest'. The book came out in 1956.

means divide them in the proportion £10 for me for every £1 you get, then I agree even more heartily.) In any event I hope the deal comes off and look forward to pouching the cheque.

I enclose your precious file copy of the Isis piece,[2] which gave me some good laughs. Many thanks.

Have been thoroughly enjoying *Jim-la-Chance*. It's a much funnier book than the original. Formidable, dites?

Yours ever,
Kingsley

[TLS: Gollancz]

TO PHILIP LARKIN – 10 APRIL 1956

Swansea

Thanks for card. I *like* that Barber, tho' wd only star "Careless L", "Tish o", "Papa De do do" (or some such jargon) admittedly. Try Colyer's "Wabash Blues". And Halcox on the "Baby" in the new Barber 12" LP is fine – but nothing else is.[1] The Caton news is bad: Curtis B. now say they can do nothing, *but I can offer him a sum of money for the copyright if I like.*[2] Thanks v.m., ole man. Also in the proof of my

2. The enclosure has not survived.

1. Chris Barber (b. 1930), English trombonist and bandleader, helped organise a band in 1953 led by Ken Colyer (b. 1928), English cornettist, trumpeter, guitarist and ardent propagandist for traditional New Orleans jazz. In 1954 Barber took over the band and Colyer was replaced by Pat Halcox (b. 1930), English trumpeter. The titles Amis refers to are 'Careless Love', 'Tishomingo Blues' and 'Papa De Da Da', recorded in 1955. Colyer's 'Wabash Blues' was recorded in 1953. The 'new Barber 12" LP' Amis refers to contains the title 'Everybody Loves My Baby', on which Halcox solos.

2. Caton was advertising *Bright November* on the heels of the success of Amis's novels, and Amis was trying to stop him (see Amis to Larkin, 17 January 1954, in Bodleian). In a letter to Larkin of 10 March 1954 (also in Bodleian) he reports: 'No news of Caton, except that my agent has sent him two letters without getting a reply and now awaits a reply from the registered letter he sent. I don't think there's much that can be done. If you've no standing whatever to keep up, you can do as you bloody well like, it seems to me. I was in Zwemmer's recently and they were well stocked with B. Novembers, tho' below stairs, thank the Great Architect. Even if I bought up existing stocks of the bloody thing, old L.S.C. ('Lazy Sod' Caton) would just print more, wouldn't he?' Amis's negative feelings about *Bright*

1957 *Oozoo* entry (herk herm) the man has written "Qy. *Bright November* (novel) 1956 – please confirm." I've confirmed it all right. My Professor is trying to get me held at the efficiency bar – on grounds of inefficiency, oddly enough. He'll fail.[3]

Easter bum,
K.

PS. Tell everyone about my Prof.'s machinations.

PS. Have a touch of alopecia[4] – oh beggar, oh sad, oh shut, oh pass[5]

[ALS: Bodleian]

TO PETER SIMS – 16 APRIL 1956

53 Glanmor Road, Swansea

Dear Mr. Sims,[1]

A fellow called Ian Hamilton[2] tells me he is running a magazine called *The Scorpion*, which prints stuff from university students. The first number "which included a message of good wishes from Mr. John Wain" went over well apparently, and he is on the look-out for stuff for No. 2. It occurred to me that perhaps you and some of your chums might like to send him something, and he now says he will hold up

November persisted: when he published his *Collected Poems* in 1979, he included only six of the volume's thirty-three poems.

3. Had Professor Kinsley succeeded in stopping Amis's pay at the 'efficiency bar' he would never have surpassed an annual salary of £900 (instead of proceeding at £50 increments to £1,100). Kinsley's animus may have derived from Amis's own feelings (see Amis to Larkin, 19, 23 and 26 January 1954) and/or his writing of novels. Amis, though, insisted that he was a conscientious teacher while at Swansea (see Jacobs, *Biography*, p. 139), an assertion his correspondence from this period (with its frequent apologies to radio producers, publishers and journalists about term-time commitments) would seem to confirm.

4. Baldness or hair loss.

5. 'Oh bugger, oh sod, oh shit, oh piss.'

---

1. Peter Sims (b. 1936), an undergraduate at the University College of Swansea, eventually became a priest in the Church of England. he has written verse off and on throughout his life, but has never published a volume.

2. Ian Hamilton (b. 1938), poet, editor, biographer, critic; at the time a student at Darlington Grammar School. *Scorpion*, a combative rival to the official school magazine, ran for three issues.

the printing until he hears from the Swansea faction. So if you have anything available, and think it worth your while – no payment presumably, but the thing is reputable enough in its line – I should bung it in within the next 3/4 days, and advise such of your butties as may be interested to do the same.

Hamilton's address is

47 Langholm Crescent
Darlington
Co. Durham.

And it's a *literary* magazine, as I should have said, Meaning I suppose verse, stories, articles etc.

Have a go – if only to drive out the "members of the Universities of Oxford and Cambridge" who apparently monopolised the first number.

Yours sincerely,
Kingsley Amis

PS: I didn't mention your name, but if you mention mine all will be in order.

[ALS][3]

TO JOHN DAVENPORT – 17 APRIL 1956

53 Glanmor Road, Uplands, Swansea, Glam.

My dear Uncle,

I feel all sorts of a sod for not answering your letter these three months; but then I am a bad correspondent. I am sorry: it's nothing to do with my not having wanted to reply, but simply owing to my laziness.

I love the way you keep needling me about old D.T. [Dylan Thomas] Of course you were a friend of his, and I must say a man who could make a friend of you and of the paranoiac jeweller I met in a Swansea pub recently must have had something to him. It's hise, I mean his, poetry I don't like. But this kind of topic is best gone into face to face.

3. This letter exists only as a photocopy deposited at the Huntington Library. I have been unable to trace the original.

We have just moved; today actually. I have a much bigger study now; when we allotted the rooms in our old house my wife didn't believe I really meant it when I talked about writing. It is nice to succeed on the domestic front. I seem though to be writing about jazz or Harold Nicolson all the time now.[1]

I note, as they say, your address and phone number. Stand by to receive a buzz soon.

Yours,
Kingsley Amis

PS. Why won't this paper fit into this envelope?[2]

[TLS: National Library of Wales]

TO PHILIP LARKIN – 19 APRIL 1956

53 Glanmor Road, Uplands, Swansea, Glam.

My dear Philip,

As you see, we have moved. Not far; just to an infinitely more palatial house about ¼-mile from the Grove. My study is as big as a real room. Shan't bother to detail to you all the things about the actual move, will just say I was glad when it was over. One of the removal men went away with the key of my wardrobe, which contains all my shirts, socks, ties etc., in his pocket. Haven't managed to get hold of him yet, somehow. He's out on jobs all the time, you sam.

I got your letter and card all right, and enjoyed them. I agree with all you say about poetry. I liked your Arundel thing;[1] but don't you

---

1. Harold Nicolson (1886–1968), writer, diplomat, politician; Amis reviewed *The English Sense of Humour* in 'No Laughing Matter', *Spectator*, 4 May 1956, pp. 625–6. He began reviewing jazz records in the *Observer* on 15 April 1956, at first monthly, then more frequently, only stopping (the last review appeared on 21 September 1958) when he left Britain for a year to teach at Princeton.

2. MS addition.

---

1. 'An Arundel Tomb', first published in *The Whitsun Weddings*, also in *LCP*, pp. 110–11, dated 20 February 1956.

ever go anywhere except into bleeding churches? Hope you aren't getting this chic faith thing. Wasn't John's first poem[2] frightful? I wanted to take out my pencil and scrawl COULD OF TOLD YOU THAT, SHITFACE across it. What I think about poetry is that is pis it has got to be *instantaneously comprehensible* if anyone at all is going to read it these days. No use this "difficult simplicity" lark; no use being clear after one reading. Got to be clear *line by line*, see? I am planning a poem on the refrain "Without so much as a by-your-leave". Not that I "care profoundly" about being read, except perhaps by you; but it makes me feel a bit of a fool, and a sod, to think that when I read my poems on their appearance in print I'm the only one doing it.

Is your fed-upness the kind that has something to be fed up about? Or is it just self-existent, as it were? I am sorry to hear about it. I suppose a lot of it's Hull, isn't it? Sorry about your tum, too. Have you tried those Rennies? I meant what I said about them. They say the new Macleans are good, too. And I think stomach-conditions are self-perpetuating too, at least for a time, so I shouldn't worry too much about absence of strain not having any effect. Do try the Rennies. [. . .]

What's all this about you having written a review? That idiot Gordon Wharton mentioned it in a letter the other day touting for poems. Said you praised 'Katie'. Katie RAINE? you must be lso pso losing your mind.[3] Tell me where it appeared, and/or send me a copy. No on second thoughts if you send me a copy you wont need to tell me where it appeared, will you now? Hay ho. About Caton: I rather gather ("rather than *what*?") you cede the book rights to him by saying he can publish, or something. Anyway, we're up a bum tree there, sport, seems no doubt about it. Got my Swedish Jims yesterday: *Lyckliga Jim* or something. Only thing that makes me laugh in it is kraftiga bysten= large breasts. I'll have to remember to send a copy to Daddy Beeeeeeheeeeeheeeeghggh When I saw him last he told me that Swedish and Norwegian were very similar languages to hear and speak, but they looked different when you saw them written. And for why? Because, he explained, the Swedes have a different system of orthography from the Norwegians. Oh Christ go and get stuffed till you bust, you

2. Presumably 'Usefulness of Light', Wain's first poem in the Enright anthology *Poets of the 1950s*, which was published in Britain on 14 January 1956.

3. Larkin's review of Raine's *Collected Poems* (1956) was entitled 'Abstract Vision' and appeared in the *Manchester Guardian*, 17 April 1956, p. 4.

Read the new Murdoch yet?[4] All seems very *unreal* to me. I can't believe that the chaps in it are real or doing things that real people do, if you take my meaning. Course I haven't finished it yet. The characters all seem abnormal, somehow. Any moment I expect to come across one of them singing the only song he knows, or turning out to have been a dwarf all along, like somebody in Nathanael West or Carson McCullers[5] (The decade's most overrated writer? Agree? Sorry, I'd forgotten Lizzie Jennings.) God this letter is going to be a treat for our biographers, eh?

That gnarled old fool Bartley was here just now, breathing drink and waking the baby. Told me to give you his love. Said to tell you he was sorry you'd left Belfarts, because it, I mean you, made it more bearable for him when he visited Queens. That's one good reason for going to Hull you'd forgotten, nicht wahr? Don't like B. much these days because he seems to be siding with my prog bog prog BOGGG prof just a little over this dispute. I still feel irritated about that. The efficiency bar is supposed to cover efficiency, i.e. ability to lecture. I can lecture. I dont do much research, admittedly. But I do some, which is more than half of them do round here. Still, mustn't bore you with my troubles. The prof hasn't a cat in hell's chance of driving me out. But bugger him none the less.

Of course you must come in the summer. Can give you a decent room now. Nobody I'd rather have in it, except perhaps Jayne Mansfield. Incidentally thank you cully for Rochelle (wasn't it?) Have hidden it in a pamphlet: Review of English Studies: Guide to contributors. Dear Sir, Your article in the Sunday Observer was bum

Kingsley

PS: Saw who was introducing a selection of new verse next week and p—d meself laughing. Of all the people whose cup of tea that sort of thing is not, you are the most notable.[6]

[TLS: Bodleian]

4. *The Flight from the Enchanter* (1955), by Iris Murdoch.

5. Carson McCullers (1916–67), American novelist, born in Georgia; among her best-known works are *The Heart is a Lonely Hunter* (1940) and *The Ballad of the Sad Café* (1951).

6. MS addition; Larkin was discussed (but did not appear) on Richard Murphy's BBC radio programme *New Poetry* on 24 April 1956.

TO HILARY RUBINSTEIN – 21 APRIL 1956

Please note new address:- 53 Glanmor Road, Uplands, Swansea, Glam.

Dear Hilary,

Excellent news that *Samples*[1] is being [put] into production so briskly. Many thanks.

The blurb is fine, with the exception of a tiny inaccuracy which I have noted. About the proposed notice in the front of the book, though, I feel this: since all the relevant information appears in the blurb, couldn't the notice be cut out altogether? These things, if they come direct from the author ("*I* am reprinting, *my* poems have appeared," etc.) always seem to carry a hint of self-advertisement, as if one were saying: "Look at all the fine papers I've published in." In his Foreword to his *Poems 1953* (which is an attack on Forewords) Robert Graves said: "One needn't nowadays list the periodicals in which each poem first appeared, as most poets continue to do in forewords. Grateful though one may be to the editors, the copyright does not remain theirs, and to boast of having caught their interest is not quite seemly." I agree passionately with all that, and I am all against books of verse being cluttered up with forewords, prefaces, introductions and what-not. I do entreat you to let me have my way about this.

As regards the TLS review:[2] I can't find the bloody thing, but I can tell you when it appeared. It was the issue of Feb. 19th, 1954, page 122. (Typically, I possess pages 113–116 and 125–128).

Ever yours,
Kingsley

[TLS: Gollancz]

1. *A Case of Samples* (1956), Amis's fourth volume of poems, counting the pamphlets *A Frame of Mind* (1953) and *Kingsley Amis: No. 22. The Fantasy Poets* (1954).

2. Of *Lucky Jim*, entitled 'Contemporary Portraits', 12 February 1954, p. 101.

TO SAMUEL HYNES – 20 MAY 1956

53 Glanmor Road, Uplands, Swansea, Glamorganshire, Great Britain.

Dear Mr. Hynes,

Thank you for your amiable and flattering account of my work in the *Commonweal.*[1] My excuse for writing to you is to correct a misstatement whereby you say that my *Lucky Jim* has not been published in America. It actually came out from Doubleday under the same title in 1955. If you could put in a tiny paragraph some time to note this I should be most grateful: a few more chaps might buy it then, which, since it sold under 3000, would be all to the good.

I am glad you picked on the moral part of my books for comment. English reviewers seem to regard me as either a farcical comedian or a kind of seedy immoralist, or else they wrap me in a cocoon of "social comment" and think I really hate the people I write about. More in general, I think it was brilliant of you to pick on the "poor sod" phrase and to synthesise the sod's characteristics in the way you did.[2] I really am most entertained and grateful.

Yours sincerely,
Kingsley Amis

[TLS: Recipient]

---

1. 'The "Poor Sod" as Hero', a review of *Lucky Jim* and John Wain's *Hurry on Down* in *Commonweal* 64 (13 April 1956), pp.51–3. For Samuel Hynes see Notes on Recipients.

2. The 'poor sod' phrase comes from the epigraph to *Hurry on Down*: 'A Moralist perchance appears; Led, Heaven knows how! to this poor sod.' Hynes calls the epigraph 'a brilliant perversion of Wordsworth', and says it 'defines succinctly both the nature of the hero and the role of the author in relation to him' in the new 'Poor Sod' school of fiction. The world of this fiction is a 'post-war Welfare-State world, a monster of austerity, uncertainty and mediocrity, of petty anxieties and unrelieved tedium' (p.51). As for the Poor Sod himself, he is trapped 'in a prison which is partly the welfare state, and partly his own social and psychological situation; his progress through the novels is through a series of ludicrous and usually humiliating prat-falls to a resolution that is either a cynical submission to the prison rules (this is Wain's line), or a kind of victory via escape – which may in itself seem a defeat. In any case, the forces which work upon him are humiliating, abrasive, and overpowering' (p.52).

TO ROBERT CONQUEST – 20 JUNE 1956

53 Glanmor Road, Uplands, Swansea Glam

Dear Bob,

Many thanks for your sagas. No reason for writing except to tell you this, tell you one or two things of my own, etc: so if I say (as I do now) that I'm looking forward to seeing, or even being given, a copy of *N. L.*,[1] well then, old man, you'll know I'm not just writing to say it. Hope they do us proud in the T.L.S. – you know we seem to have the faculty of annoying the sods, one way and another, don't we?

Had an incredible letter from Capitaine C. Wilson of the Légion Etrangère (?).[2] Pattern extracts "I'm not personally unamiable . . . this anti-culture stuff gets you nowhere . . . I believe I represent a new trend in English literature . . . not having time myself, I persuaded my girlfriend to read your 2 books and tell me what she thought . . . your fault seems to me to be the same as Auden's . . . I feel you'd better know the worst . . . I have a lot of things I want to establish – vital things for the course of modern history – and knocking you and other misplaced figures off their pedestals will be the first step . . ." Good stuff, eh? I give him 2 years before paranoia closes over his head.

Enjoyed old Phil's Auden review *Listen*.[3] Don't back down in the *T.L.S.*[4] Old H.F.[5] is getting on fine here: he spent 40 mins the other evening rebuking me for swearing and telling jokes about madmen.

1. *New Lines*; see Amis to Conquest, 23 January 1955, note 1.

2. Colin Wilson (b.1931), novelist, social critic, author; the occasion of the letter was an unfavourable review by Amis of Wilson's *The Outsider* (1956) in the *Spectator*, 15 June 1956, p.830, republished in *What Became of Jane Austen?*, pp.89–93.

3. Philip Larkin, 'No More Fever', review of W.H. Auden, *The Shield of Achilles*, in *Listen* 2:1 (Summer 1956), pp.22–6.

4. In May and June 1956 Conquest wrote three letters to the *TLS* on the subject of 'the tone of the critic', a correspondence prompted by a letter from F.R. Leavis in which he said he had been misquoted. Amis is encouraging Conquest to continue the correspondence by responding to a letter from John Holloway written in defence of Leavis (*TLS*, 15 June 1956, p.361). Conquest responded on 22 June 1956: 'Dr Holloway reads me as having appeared to cast doubt on Dr Leavis's integrity. This was far from my intention. On the contrary, Dr Leavis's uncompromising honesty and unselfregarding labour to do his best without fear or favour are as undoubted as those of Torquemada or Robespierre' (p.377).

5. Henry Fairlie (1924–90), author and political journalist, credited with coining the term 'The Establishment'; at the time working as a columnist (first under the name 'The Trimmer', then under his own name) on the *Spectator*; married Elisabeth Todd Phillips, 1949.

You were a sod putting that [illegible] reserve thing on the envelope – didn't fool me of course: never was a Capt., nor even T/.[6] Heigh ho – haven't had a dinner date from Guinness[7] yet, but hope to see you about end of month. Love to Tania. Keep 'em flying

Kingsley

[ALS: Recipient]

TO PHILIP LARKIN – 25 JUNE 1956

53 Glanmor Road, Uplands, Swansea, Glam.

My dear Philip,

Sorry to keep on being such a sod about writing you letters. One thing is that I always think it a good idea to write to you at length, and then I find I must write an article for *Vogue*, or review a book for some American paper, before I can get down to writing to my old pal. Shall try to cure this, or its effects, by sending you little cards and notes and things fairly frequently. And then you will have to do the same, I mean send them to me.

Yes, of course, you old shaque-baque, we shall be delighted to see you on 18th August and for as long afterwards as you can manage. You know I would put off any visitor to make room for you. We will drink and smoke together, and I will play you some of the records I've been sent for review. Have you heard any Braff,[1] by the way? He really is sodding good. No one else seems to be, much, these days, don't you find? Except old Humph.[2] I meant what I said about him recently.

Funny you were so right about John Morgan's book. Having given him the kiss of death, if I may so describe it, I feel a little bad about this.[3]

6. 'T/' stands for 'Temporary'. A related Conquest practical joke occured 'in the early 1950s in the form of an official-looking envelope addressed to "Lieut. K. W. Amis, R. Signals, Class 'B' Reserve Call-up (Malaya)"' see *Memoirs*, p.145.

7. See Amis to Conquest, 29 February 1956, note 2.

---

1. Ruby (Reuben) Braff (b.1927), cornettist.

2. Humphrey Lyttelton (b.1921), English trumpeter, clarinettist and bandleader.

3. John Morgan's *The Small World* (1956), a novel about young people in a university in Wales, was praised in glowing terms by Amis on the dust-jacket, and savagely attacked by reviewers, in particular by John Wain in the *Observer*.

I must say I don't think it's much like me, except in so far as any decent book's bound to be, ay? I think reviewers think that any book about Wales that doesn't remind them of Gwyn Thomas must be like any other book about Wales that doesn't remind them of Gwyn Thomas. I may be wrong, course. Have you anything to add, as they say, to your short adverse comment on the book?

Thoroughly enjoyed and approved of your Auden piece in *Listen*. Didn't see who it was by when I began reading. Then on the second appearance of "'for' someone" I thought: This man is bloody funny.[4] And who should it turn out to be but my old pal. Also had a good cackle over your letter in the Lond Mag. But can't you muzzle old George?[5] You, my dear man, have no need of that kind of support. I have been most joyful to see that The deceived [*The Less Deceived*] continues to prosper. How many has it sold now? And I expect Bob has told you of the big TLS puff we are to get when New Lines comes out.[6] All we have to worry about now is writing some decent stuff – though your need to worry is less than any of us's, dear man.

Glad you liked my little effusions on the Wilsons. I got the most incredible letter from CW, 2 single-spaced quartos, posted on the day the review appeared. In fact to save me the labour of typing out pattern extracts I think I will post it to you, together with the answer to the

4. See Philip Larkin, 'No More Fever', a review of W.H. Auden, *The Shield of Achilles*, in *Listen* 2:1 (Summer 1956), p.22:

> *The Shield of Achilles* is made up of fourteen unrelated pieces, flanked on one side by a sequence of seven poems on natural phenomena (*Mountains, Lakes, Water* and so on – each of them 'for' someone), and the other by seven more entitled *Horae Canonicae* (Prime, Terce, Sext and the rest) a group suggesting loosely that the 'hours' in question are of the day of the Crucifixion.
>
> The astute reader will suspect from this outline alone that the pressure of poetic energy in the book is low, and he will be right. Although in theory a set of seven poems entitled *Mountains, Lakes, Water* and so on (each of them 'for' someone) has as good a chance of success as any seven poems conceived and executed separately, in fact it is more likely to mean that the poet was outside the compulsion necessary for poetic success and was free to choose a smart frame for some poems he thought it might be rather nice to write.

5. Larkin's letter appeared in the *London Magazine* 3:6 (June 1956), p.72, and George Hartley's in the next issue, 3:7 (July 1956), pp.67–8. Both were written in response to Roy Fuller's largely favourable review of *The Less Deceived* in 3:4 (April 1956), p.84, in particular to Fuller's remarks about small-press publishing and the Marvell Press.

6. The review of *New Lines*, entitled 'Poets of Moderation', appeared in the *TLS*, 13 June 1956, p.424.

answer I sent. My answer is written with a fountain pen on the 2nd sheet of the first one.[7] Poor little depraved brain. Not much of a laughing boy, is he? I reckon the old waters of paranoia will close over his head pretty briskisk pissk briskish now. Send me the stuff back quickish, will you? I want to take it to London and show it round when I go there on 5th July (no chance of you . . . ?). *Do you* show it around in Hole.

Saw old Montgomery in London town recently. He was in very good form, telling me about the starlets he takes out to dinner (Jackie Lane, Shirley Ann Field, et al.)[8], and introducing me to John Dickson Carr. I got too drunk too soon to remember very much about the encounter, though JDC seemed a very decent little chap and very pleased to hear I knew and liked his books. Pity he's no good any more. This sentiment I concealed from him.

Flithy tum is over at last, thank God, or it will be when the flithy Faculty tomorrow is over. My prof is nice to me now, having realised how deeply he has plunged his foot in by trying to be nasty to me. The bad thing now is that one of his ways of being nice to me is to "put things in my way", arranging for me to do a review for R. E. S.[9] NO MUNNEEEEE and lecturing to objurgatory miners at Bridgend NOT ENUFFF MUNNEEEEE. Old Bartley is still around, just. He keeps telling me what a good chap you are and when are you coming down.

I keep getting abusive letters about my jazz pieces in what they all call the Sunday Observer. They all like George Lewis,[10] it seems. One thing that column has given me a chance to do is to be rude about all the horrible silly old black men. I have just had a 4-page letter in italic script from a man who calls himself a Somersetshire peasant. He has a friend who tells him about George L's miraculous subtlety, etc., and who takes down the songs of blackbirds as they sit sipping their zider (the man and his friend, I mean), afterwards rendering them on his clarinet. I am ignorant, he sys pys says politely, because I don't know certain facts. One such fact is that Lewis is a genius, far better than BG (Benny Goodman) He *knows* this, just as I know, he says, that Joyce is good [. . .]

7. Neither the initial Wilson letter, with Amis's handwritten reply, nor the second survives, either in the Bodleian or among Wilson's papers.

8. Jackie Lane, actress, later known as Jocelyn Lane (after 1964); Shirley Ann Field (b.1938), actress.

9. *Review of English Studies*, a scholarly quarterly, founded 1925.

10. George Lewis (1900–68), clarinettist; 'by 1950 Lewis had become established as the seminal figure of the emerging New Orleans revival' (Kernfeld, ed., *NGDJ*, p.25).

Send me a little letter soon, and I will send a little letter back. And don't let that August date slip.

For a man of 24 Mr Wilson shows an extraordinary grasp of bum,

Kingsley

[TLS: Bodleian]

TO PHILIP LARKIN – 12 JULY 1956

My Residence at Swans-eye

My dear Philip,

Just back from a few days in the big city, where I saw many people who talked about you: notably that fool Hoff at the PEN do in the Tate – "you're the best novelist of this bunch and old Philip's the best poet; if he just goes on being around he'll be the major poet in about 1970." How *disagreeable* and *argumentative* he is, not letting me finish my stories, always saying "No no no, good God no" instead of "No", detailing his status on the PEN committee &c. Also there were Angus [Wilson], who looked like a distinguished old wine-waiter at a Pall Mall club, Lehmann ("how did *you* get in here?"), and a dreadful Indian called, as far as I could make out, Kasharp, who began autobiography with his second sentence; 'I woss in 1939 second secretary of edukeshun at India Hoss.' He is coming to Wales soon, and promised to look me up.

Saw that fool John [Wain] one of the days. If I had been imagining I was missing something by not seeing him, it was imagination only. He never listens to you, does he? Always positive and informative, never speculative or inquiring. Had an awful girl with him, who denounced English cooking and whom he encouraged. He said he was a vegetarian because slaughtering had a brutalising effect on the slaughterers. Also said he stood no nonsense from pressure-groups and had attacked ?Barbara Skelton's book without caring that she was Mrs. Connolly.[1] Transpired later that he'd done it without *knowing* she was Mrs. C.

1. Barbara Skelton (1918–96), writer of fiction and autobiography, married to Cyril Connolly (1950–54); published *A Young Girl's Touch* (1954).

We cannot afford a fee, but will be pleased to offer you bum, *or have I said that?*[2]

Kingsley

[TLS: Bodleian]

TO PHILIP LARKIN – [9 AUGUST 1956][1]

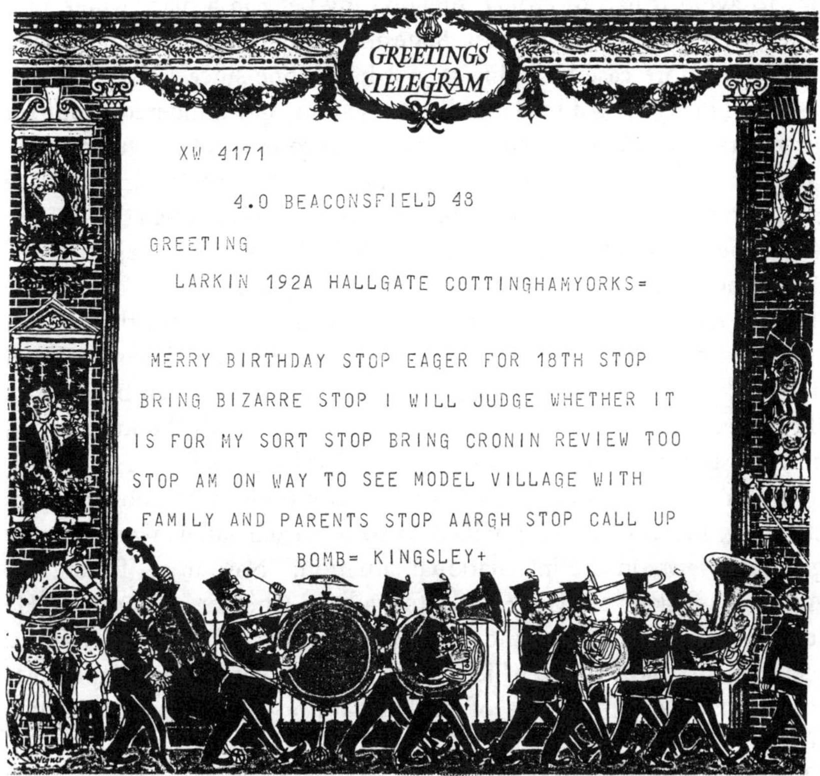

GREETINGS TELEGRAM

XW 4171

4.0 BEACONSFIELD 48

GREETING

LARKIN 192A HALLGATE COTTINGHAMYORKS=

MERRY BIRTHDAY STOP EAGER FOR 18TH STOP BRING BIZARRE STOP I WILL JUDGE WHETHER IT IS FOR MY SORT STOP BRING CRONIN REVIEW TOO STOP AM ON WAY TO SEE MODEL VILLAGE WITH FAMILY AND PARENTS STOP AARGH STOP CALL UP BOMB= KINGSLEY+

Kingsley

[TELEGRAM: Bodleian]

2. MS addition.

---

1. The '18th' in the telegram below refers to the date Larkin was to visit Swansea; *Bizarre* is a magazine; the 'Cronin review' is Anthony Cronin, 'Party Lines', a review of Robert Conquest, ed., *New Lines: An Anthology*, in *Time and Tide*, 28 July 1956, p. 913.

TO PHILIP LARKIN – 9 SEPTEMBER 1956

Hotel Beau-Site, Pramousquier, Var, France.

My dear Philip,

We got here, you see.[1] This has involved almost no doubt, horror or despair, but a truly bountiful dose of fatigue and discomfort. The crossing was very terrible (gale in the Channel bum): I was not sick, but to avoid it had to crouch hugging my belly in a place where rain blew over me, doing the New Statesman crossword the while. Then there was more case-humping than I have done since I was a private soldier. Finally we got to Paris about 6.30 a.m. and wandered about for six hours until the time when we could go to our hotel. Ohchrist: the war recurs to me as an image. We sprawled into a shelter in the Place de la Concorde (or some such name), while I debated whether or not to phone Donat O'Donnell[2] at the Irish Embassy, finally rejecting the idea. There was a long walk then while everybody except me looked into the shop windows, admired suede jackets, worked out the price in English money, exclaimed at dearness or cheapness, etc. Then we found a cinema just about to open, and saw a programme which began with the Three Stooges dubbed in French. Soon afterwards the luck turned and we started eating and drinking very hard and well.

After a couple of days in Paris we took a train to Avignon: 7 hours standing, much of it being talked to by a French sailor, who willingly gave his views on the international situation: "Nassair . . . fuckair . . . Arabe . . . fuckair . . . U.R.S.S . . . fuckair . . . Chinois . . . fuckair." He let me sit on his tin case and I tore my trousers on it. At Avignon we went on the old bridge, which was small and somehow inexpensive-looking. Took some snaps of it. The lavatory at the hotel was two footplates and a hole. Quite a clean hole. Had a shave in cold water. Huge clouds of fart came in through the windows when the pits were opened night and morning. Got very drunk on the second night with

---

1. Pramousquier, near Cavaliere, is on the southern tip of the French Riviera. The Amises were on a two-week holiday with their Swansea friends Mavis and Geoff Nicholson and the Nicholsons' friend Tom Griffiths, an engineer, also from Swansea.

2. A pseudonym of Conor Cruise O'Brien (b. 1917), author, journalist, historian, university administrator, diplomat; at the time Counsellor, Paris (1955–56).

some soldiers who said they were going to Cyprus. Didn't believe them next day.

Train to Toulon. The best dish of the holiday so far: hot mussels at the station buffet there. Otherwise a horrible little town with lots of statues and apparently no shops. Military and naval police everywhere. Bus along to this place. The bus broke down, or at least the driver threw something burning out of the window and then we stopped. About this time I realised I had a cold coming on. Read the first paragraph of *Middlemarch* in the bus when we re-started, and then put the book safely away again.

Quite good fun here. They tried to tell us we hadn't booked when we turned up. Doubt, horror and despair: but they were wrong after all. The beach is nice and we've had a lot of sun, except this morning. Nothing much funny to tell you, except perhaps that they have a mineral water called Pschitt. Very good it is, too. My attempts at French haven't been very successful: said Bon soir to the proprietress this morning. Why did I do that? Luckily one of the other chaps does all the important nattering. Haven't had the shits yet, in fact quite the contrary. No fleas. Wasps and mosquitoes only. Haven't suffered much from them yet, but am watching points. We don't sleep terribly well here, with the bloody crickets hammering away and the French roaring and squealing round the bend in their cars all night. Still, it would be wrong to pretend I'm not enjoying myself. The only annoying thing is the language. Why can't they talk English like everyone else?

I send you All aboard the gravy train,[3] with a space for you to insert your poem if you care to. Hurry up with that, eh? because it would be nice to get the whole thing off to Spender soon. The only alteration in the text I've made is to put "guessed" for "thought" in Wild ones, line 6. "Thought" clashes with "taught" a bit, it struck me. Agree? I must

3. 'All Aboard the Gravy Train: Or, Movements Among the Younger Poets', a series of eight parodies of Movement poets by Amis and Larkin, themselves included. Amis's phrase 'Hope we can get some money out of them' suggests collaboration, but whether all eight were jointly authored, or some authored by Larkin and others by Amis, is unclear. Neither *LL*, nor Motion, *Life*, nor Jacobs, *Biography*, mentions the parodies, which are published here (see Appendix B) for the first time. As Thwaite, who had not known of their existence, points out (personal communication, 10 May 1999), 'the Larkin ("Poetry of Comings Back") is *by* Larkin: see [*LCP*], p. 59. It is clearly his typescript – and I didn't know it was a "Ron Cain" and therefore a *self*-parody until I read [the whole series]. [. . .] I dated it "1951?" because of its position in L's folder of "Unpublished Poems" – but it now looks as if it might be 195[6] – UNLESS (and I think this is a strong possibility) L. plucked it out of the file, and decided to "pretend" it was a parody.'

say the poems still strike me as good and bloody funny. Hope we can make some money out of them.

I'm supposed to be writing my novel here, but I don't seem to be doing much of that. All I've done is my Observer jazz piece and to-day the gravy train and this to you. That's not much in the way of work, is it? Christ, I must hibernate when term starts again, have a vivid picture of my study with the rain running down the window, gas-fire burning, all snug, buttered toast for tea in twenty minutes, and me working away like a demon AT MY WIRE, IS IT? Yes, that's what it is. It's a question of whether you like art or life best, you sam. You do a bit of art and as a result you begin having a much better time. Nothing to make you write then, if you follow mam. Ah well, it's a puzzle. It's a puzzle now.

Hungry as a bastard now. It's that filthy continental breakfast that does you. How do these fellows get on that have to do a morning's work, starting at 8, on fuck-all? Pissed all the time they are I warrant you.

The sun's come out. Got to go and get in it. It was top-hole seng you the other week: hope your tumb is better, or no worse. Never thanked you for that lunch, and believe I forgot to pay you back for some drinks. All right – never mind. Eh? Why not? I'll do the same for you some day. Wain was quite funny in Oxford, tho' unbearable in his attitude to his girl, as usual [. . .]

Passport ticket reservation customs luggage hotel trip voucher bum[4]

Kingsley

[TLS: Bodleian]

TO PHILIP LARKIN – 24 SEPTEMBER 1956

Swansea

My dear Philip,

Just spent most of a sodding good day reading your letters. As I came across each fresh scattered batch of them it was like getting

4. MS addition.

my hooks on parts of an unpublished Isherwood novel of the GBTB [*Goodbye to Berlin*] period: don't mean the stuff was full of boy-horn or anything like that, o' course. Reading them made me feel happy and contented and as if I was doing something significant in a significant mode of existence, just like I felt, I remember describing to you, while I was reading Scenes from p[rovincial] life. Not that I wouldn't much rather have your letters than any amount of old Hoff. Any more than I feel I really am doing something significant. The abiding themes of what I read were AWA [Winifred Arnott]-slipped-off-from-the-expensive-dinner-I-was-giving-her-to-go-to-a-Bach-concert one, how do I mean one, er, also my-new-Bechet-LP-from-the-States-is-sodding-good, and can't-seem-to-write-my-novel. Some misruth [Bowman] and veronica beale [Monica Jones] stuff too, hope you didn't tell those poor girls the awful wounding things you told me. But apart from lots of causes for yelling laughter what came over most powerfully by far was all the AWA business. As, again, I think I've said before, you seem to observe women much more closely and sensitively and well lovingly ah ha well perhaps not that than I do. My conclusion about the bizney EPPSS[1] (do you remember that one?) was a she was certainly carrying a powerful torch for you and b you might possibly have got her pants down if you'd tried hard but c you were really very wise to stand out from under and certainly d marriage with her would have been jurst hairl. (Excuse me while I go and pour myself another vodka. Grand drink. It's a grand drink.)

Am downstairs in the kitchen now, much nicer here. There's a curious smell in my study, as if someone has been trying unsuccessfully to make cheese there. Just as homopas a smell of old toss-rags in fact, I expect. Anyway, it all made me feel what a feast is awaiting chaps when we're both dead and our complete letters come out. Yours rather than mine, I fear. Still. Made me think we ought to try to get back into something like my old, and rand I mean our old, tempo of screed-swapping. Shall try to do this off my own back, any road. There is a novel there, about you in Wellington-Leicester-Belfast-Hull, and I shall proa poa probably write it one day, if you don't. Vodka and apricot

1. 'Bizney EPPSS' is 'business' plus an execration; 'bizney' is a typo.

brandy, that's the drink. That's the drink you want. Got it out of the bartender's guide, I did.

Actually I probably shan't be having as many or as nice drinks as I've been having for some time for some time. Saw my accountant today about my ink 'em tax. His estimate was £6 no £700 to pay in November wee-hee-hee £450 to pay in January PLUS £85 SURTAX ya-ha-ha and £450 to pay in January want a shit. My deposit account holds at the moment £356–9–11. Well no use moaning Amis. I mean you've had the money haven't you. Just spent it. YES SPENT IT AS IF IT WAS MY OWN, AS IF IT BELONGED TO ME BECAUSE I'D EARNT IT. mmmbbmbm taxed out of existence bbmbmbm crippling initiative mbbbmmb other chaps' false teeth bmbmbbm strangling enterprise mmmbmmmb soaking the industrious to subsidise the bone-lazy mmmmmmb other country where

Nothing much happening here. High above my head, but spiralling lazily downward, hangs the winged and taloned shape of term – all this is beginning to sound just like you. Don't mind that. Just don't mind it, what? A damn shame about your tum. I felt it held us bacj knacj from being shoved forward on the full flow of alcoholic anarchy the other week. Better luck next time what. Do hope you're not too depression-sloughed these days. Incidentally I admired your remark about depression in one letter. Something about At first it all seems rather romantic and distinguished and rhetorical. Then that all stops and you just go on getting more and more sodding depressed. Ah, that's a true word. It's a true word now.

Actually I have been a bit of an old fool, getting tied up with a young woman here, not to say really tied up, just started fucking her what [. . .] Now she shows me a fixture list of the Swansea and Dustr lustr District Rugby Football Club, pointing out all the Home matches, which are marked with an H. Her husband always goes towatch twatch to watch them when they play at home see. Her meaning beng, then you CAN SLIP IN AND SLIP IT IN BACH. The fixture card seems to go like this A (away) HHHHAHHHHHAHHHHHHAHHH HHHHHHAHHHHHHHHHHHHHHHHHHHHHHHHHHH and haha to you if you see what I mean. Just shows you doesn't it. Shall have to plead impotence, phallic stricture, boils on the knb, knob that is, hernia, clap &c. Awkward really. Oh what a sodding fool I am. Oh what am I gong to *do*. Wunk meself to death I'd rather [. . .]

Would Mr Amis like to give his views on Miss Pugh's work and bum,

K.

[TLS: Bodleian]

TO J.H. MCCALLUM – 5 OCTOBER 1956

53 Glanmor Road, Uplands, Swansea, Glam., Great Britain.

Dear Mr. McCallum,

I am very happy to learn that you hope to publish *A Case of Samples.*[1] The idea pleases me immensely, and it is really most gratifying to think that you are ready to undertake this on my behalf, for I can hardly imagine the book being any possible kind of commercial success. And thank you very much for saying that you liked the poems.

And I must thank you also for sending on to me the various American reviews. These have been a source of great encouragement to me. I tell my friends that American critics understand my work much better than British ones – perhaps I just mean that they are more flattering. But they certainly seem to see in my books the things that I should like to think are there.

With renewed thanks and good wishes,

Yours sincerely,
Kingsley Amis

[TLS: Harcourt]

1. *A Case of Samples* was published in the United States by Harcourt Brace in 1957. For J.H. McCallum see Notes on Recipients.

TO KAY FULLER – 6 OCTOBER 1956

53 Glanmor Road, Uplands, Swansea, Glam.

Dear Miss Fuller,

Thank you for your letter. What a good idea this programme sounds.[1] As regards my possible part in it: a) I am against Bloomsbury, though not (I hope) violently or crusadingly so. b) I know most about, and most dislike, Virginia Woolf, of the Bloomsbury set. I could do you a couple of hundred words, or anything you like, on her with very little trouble. I promise to be reasonable about her, though hostile. Just let me know when/if you want me.

Yours sincerely,
Kingsley Amis

[ALS: BBC]

TO PHILIP LARKIN – 8 OCTOBER 1956

Swansea

My dear O PO Philip,

Yours to hand, dear. Yes, a pity about old Spender (ohspunk: A double debt to Yeats). Am sending them off to Lehmann.[1] [. . .]

Haven't been having a bad time really recently. Mustn't complain. 30 pp of novel[2] done since Thursday, with new opening scene that may obviate some of your objections; lunch with the Boultings last Tuesday (I expect I told you this: it was a fucking waste of time anyway, except

1. Kay Fuller had written to Amis on 4 October 1954 to ask if he would participate in a feature programme on the Bloomsbury group for the BBC's Overseas Service. She was looking for contributors outside 'the charmed circle', especially those who might add 'a little vinegar with the oil'. The programme was broadcast on 28 January 1957.

1. Editor of the *London Magazine*, to whom Amis was sending the 'Ron Cain' parodies, 'All Aboard the Gravy Train', after their rejection by Stephen Spender, editor of *Encounter* (see Amis to Larkin, 9 September 1956, note 3).

2. *I Like it Here* (1958).

that I found out that a. the thing is quite definite[3] b. Terry Thomas is booked for Bertrand c. Hugh Griffith for Welch); am acting as judge in the Swansea heats of the Mazda Queen of Light competition ah haha won't I have the gaiety inspecting them for Acctractiveness and Figure, ah yayaya won't they be twitching and writhing and thrashing about, the little complacent lens-mad nymphos – this is on Wednesday.[4] Later on a weekend with the Anthony Powells is booked – tit, bid etc. – but that's not until the beginning of Nov. Shall I have to take white tie, black tie? Hunting pink? Guns, dogs? Mm? & then later in the month an address to the Llandeilo and district arts society. Oh yes, we have a very full season here, even though we are what some folks are pleased to call provincial, we are very far from being dull dogs, I assure you! Apart then from a slight enforced interest in local manifestations of our national winter game, all swell. Oh, and apart from impending impounding hoohoohoo of the moiety of my goods to fille y[e] Mawe of y[e] Tax-Gatherer brutish sod. And apart from feeling a tube of toothpaste is up my bum with the cap off, ready to go whenever I shift my position slightly. Too much double diamond, irish whiskey etc. Ah but what fun it was a drinking of it now. That's the way of it now. Yes and apart from not being abble to scabble able to make huge swoop, fantastic superman Tara Tararabumdeeay Tarzanleap across the road to the peaches-and-cream plump pretty blonde schoolgirl who lives opposite crush in my orms the long warm breathing bulk of her loveliness and all that tack.

Have been having jolly fun down ag shag at the Carledge *last*[5] week: signing up the new students, advising them about reading and planning their work, deciding which ones would be best for a bit of ahhaha The prof allotted *some of*[6] the Honours ones to their tutors this morning. He passed over the slim dreamy freckled lascivious Heather Harding, the wide-eyes shitpies -eyed high-breasted squirming Wendy Roberts, the severe shoulders-back full-bosomed head-girl Gillian Jones, the shy tousle-headed gentle tomboy Pauline Lewis, and such dainties – passed over them as far as the only creative ortist on the strength of the department went. Picked them, or at least 2 of them, for his own

3. Amis adds in pen in the left margin: 'Shooting starts 29th Oct.'

4. Amis adds in pen in the left margin: 'This was *quite fun*, but *unproductive of horn*.' See plates section.

5. MS addition.

6. MS addition.

bleeding "group" I'll wager ye now. In a department, I mean while dealing with an Honours class comprising 4 men and 15 women, what he gives me is 2 men, one of them the stupidest of the 4 and the other not the brightest, and the second-ugliest woman [. . .] Of the 15, moreover, at least 5 are bloody marvellous ooohooohooo and another couple are such as one would feel no rigid objection to sliding one's ah ha up ah That awful man. My prof I mean. Filthy fat Scotch Burns-worshipping Dryden-editing recently-moustached scheming mean schoolboy of hell. Signing off nay, just for nay.

The 13th of October. Sorry I've been away so long, but have had a lot of things, most of which I would have left undone if I had had the choice, to do. Lectures and things. I'm tired of that side of things already. Had enough of it for one year. Keep losing my notes and having to devise new stuff. Don't like doing that. Had to do some of that between 11.30 and 1 the other night, and me half-pissed. Didn't enjoy that. Feeling a bit low today, partly over money. It's a bastard, isn't it, that when you decide you're going to stop spending so much money, other people know better and overrule you – keep asking to be given money, decide you're bloody well going to be kept up to the mark in the little matter of *flinging cash away*. Just decide to keep you up to the mark, what? Coal bill bum, those curtains from David Evans's bum, fee for professional services bum, petrol bum, *new tyre BUm* (oh . . . fu– . . . cking . . . *SHITTT* and cetera. The only thing that makes me laugh is that my prof has now announced the *whole of the*[7] tutorial groups. His own consists of HARDING, Heather, LEWIS, Pauline Mary, and WILLIAMS, Elizabeth Marian Grant. Petite red-haired delicate busty EMG ('Beth') Williams was LEFT OUT of my list at the top of the page because SHE'D ALREADY BEEN ALLOTTED to SOMEONE ELSE, but he was so BLINDED BY LUST that he had to ALTER ALL THAT. Not that he'll DO anything to any of them. How sodding unself-aware of him. He is *such* an ANUS, that one. [. . .]

Services rendered in connection with your bum.[8]

K.

[TLS: Bodleian]

7. MS addition.
8. MS addition.

TO ROBERT CONQUEST – 16 OCTOBER 1956

53 Glanmor Road, Uplands, Swansea, Glam.

Dear Barb,

Thanks for yours to hand, you old prick-on-wheels you. Glad you seem to like academic life[1] – of course we all know (and often say) that you *can* get away with doing next to fuck-all – but we chaps with consciences are always at our lecture-scripts, pruning, polishing, adding new stuff. In a sense we're never really off duty. In another, of course, we're never really on. Ah, go wash your mouth out.

Thought your *Encounter* retort was bang-on – pity you haven't room to show how Wright misunderstood my poem (it's ironical about *men's* poetry, ain't it? not women's, the cloth-eared clot).[2] Last para. particularly 100%, with its kick against the anti-Movement establishment!

I too am entering the political field – heard today that the Fabian Soc. have accepted the pamphet I wrote for them[3] (rehash of my chat on political intellectuals given to their Easter school). No money, but bags of cachet – Amis is engaged & committed now, see.

Apart from that I just bash on at my novel (10,000 words now) and *work at my lectures*. Haven't seen a woman for weeks, except in college, and you can't count that. Can't count college cunt, I should say. Hope you can fix me up with fornicatorium, even fornicatee, some time. What about coming to Swansea, if you can lever yourself out some time fartt . . .[4]? Let us know, what?

---

1. Conquest had left the Foreign Office, where he had been working since 1946, to take up the Sidney Webb Research Fellowship, London School of Economics (1956–58).

2. The retort was to David Wright, 'A Small Green Insect in the Bowels of My Quivering Typewriter', an omnibus poetry review (of Larkin's *The Less Deceived*, Davie's *Birds of Reason*, Wain's *A Word Carved on a Sill*, Enright's *Bread Rather than Blossoms*, and Conquest's *New Lines* anthology) in *Encounter* 7:4 (October 1956), pp. 74–8. Wright accuses the poets reviewed of being pompous, timid and easy ('Dead issues and dead ducks are valiantly belaboured') and quotes the last four stanzas of Amis's 'A Bookshop Idyll', which it sees as being ironic about women's poetry, as an example (p. 76). Wright (1920–94), a South African-born poet and anthologist, was deaf; hence, in part, 'cloth-eared'.

3. *Socialism and the Intellectuals* (1957).

4. Amis has drawn an arrow connecting the first 'some time' in the sentence with the second. The addition 'fartt . . .' curses the inadvertent repetition.

Love fra Milly (och foch)

Yours,
Kingsley

[ALS: Recipient]

TO PHILIP LARKIN – 22 OCTOBER 1956

Swansea

My dear Philip,

Hell oh, now, you old knife-grinder, how goes the great world with you? Keeping in touch? Reading Colin Wilson's novel-extract in Lond Mag?[1] – better than you'd have thought, I thought, but not much. And digging old Wain on a writer's toss-specked?[2] Gradely there, now. Sorry I pinched sobbing bellows for my Obsc. piece,[3] but was hard put for a phrase, if you follow. Did you dig me on the moral element? I thought I sounded rather a ponce, but less of a Bermondsey Literary Circle ponce than Bergonzi, less of a South Kensington coffee-party ponce than Wharton, and less of a North Oxford ponce than friend Warnock[4] (who isn't a bad old thing, by the way, and not a bad poet either, I hazard).

Actually the light or bantering tone of the above is a poor index of how I feel this evening. On Friday a verbal statement was made to me by my wife by which I was given to understand that, far from just

1. Colin Wilson, 'The interview: an episode from an unpublished novel', *London Magazine* 3:11 (November 1956), pp. 33–46.

2. John Wain, 'A Writer's Prospect – IV', in the same issue of the *London Magazine*, pp. 59–64.

3. See 'Rhythm and Blues', *Observer*, 21 October 1956, p. 13, on the alto saxophonist Earl Bostic: 'Hardly a bar passes without an emphatic slur and hardly a phrase without his immensely wide vibrato being given its head in a long, sobbing bellow.'

4. Geoffrey Warnock (1923–95), philosopher; at the time Fellow and Tutor in Philosophy, Magdalen College, Oxford (1953–71); later Principal, Hertford College, Oxford (1971–88); Vice-Chancellor, Oxford University (1981–85); knighted (1986). Warnock published only one volume of poetry, *Poems* (1955), but continued to write verse through the 1960s. The programme he, Amis and Bergonzi appeared on, in which they read from and discussed their poetry, was *The Moral Element*, broadcast on the Third Programme, 21 October 1956.

having an affair with old Henry Fairlie,[5] she is in love with him and he with her. The topic of divorce from the marred state was next raised, and no decision reached. It will be reached in the course of the next few months, so that the amorous pair can decide whether they are the victims of an "infatuation", or of "something more important". I think – but I find it hard to work out what I think – that my marriage has about one chance in four of surviving till next summer. If I do get a divorce, it means presumably that the children, about whom I feel strongly, will accompany their mother to her new home. I shall be able to see them "often", of course. But that isn't the same as having them in your home all the time, you see. During the interlude while a decision is being awaited on divorce, there will be none of the old marital rites engaged in here, naturally. This has all been rather diminutory of the gaiety of nations, inhibitory of general merriment, &c. As you can imagine. Having one's wife fucked is one thing; having her taken away from you, plus your children, is another, I find. And old Henry, though a most charming lad, is a rather emotional and unreliable one, really, and not quite the kind of chap one wants to see *in loco parentis* to one's kids, supposing one wants to see anyone. Funny situation. I mean it's rather a funny situation, what?

And then today, just to back up those delightful old quips about troubles never coming singly, the worst is not yet while we can say this is the worst, or however it goes,[6] &c., Sally fell on her head and fractured her skull, involving vomiting, convulsions, coma, 999, ambulance, casualty ward and the rest of the caper. After about 3 hours it was established that she is not going to die, and it is very likely that her brain is undamaged. Hilly thinks that the 2nd proposition is a certainty, but it isn't quite yet. I shall know at about 5 tomorrow afternoon. Actually I am pretty bloody sure she'll be okay. She was sitting up and chatting normally this evening.[7] In fact I feel more or less all right about it now, better than I did while the really exciting part was going on, anyway. You've no idea what jolly decent fun it is merely to have the break-up of your marriage to worry about.

Sorry to be such a misery, but I wanted to tell you about it. I haven't told anyone else yet, and aim not to as far as possible. So I doe most Solemnlie *charge* thee, kepe thy Fingre vpon thy Lipps. I can't really

5. For Henry Fairlie see Amis to Conquest, 20 June 1956, note 5.
6. 'The worst is not,/So long as we can say, "This is the worst"' (*King Lear*, IV.i.27).
7. Though she had to stay in hospital for several weeks.

imagine how it will all turn out. Dividing the records, selling the house, storing the furniture and all that, it seems inconceivable. Reckon I shall resign here and go to London or somewhere when the time comes. It'll be odd to be a bachelor again.

In other fields, things are moving somewhat. They are starting to shoot *Jim* today week, and I shall no doubt look in to see how they do these things. I hear further that *A Case of Samples* is due out on Monday week, I mean the 5th November, and I should be getting my 6 frees any day now. You shall have one straight away, of course. That's about all the news on that front.

I should love to see you, but don't really see how it can be arranged. The next best thing will be a letter, full of good cheer and encouragement. I'll keep you posted about how things are going. Forgive me for not filling up this page.

Amis asked for the Court's discretion in respect of his bum,

Kingsley

[TLS: Bodleian]

TO ANTHONY POWELL – 31 OCTOBER 1956

53 Glanmor Road, Uplands, Swansea, Glam.

My dear Anthony Powell,

Thank you very much for your sympathetic letter. I should have answered it sooner, but we were some time trying (and failing) to wring something definite out of the hospital here. I think now that, although we have heard nothing to suggest that Sally is not recovering perfectly smoothly, we had better cancel our arrangements for 3rd November.[1] We don't like doing this, and hope not to have put you to any trouble, but we shouldn't be really happy to be away at this time – and we would like to go on visiting Sally every day. Actually we have stopped worrying about her in all but a sort of minimal way, but that remains. You can imagine what a business it was at the time.

---

1. They were to have stayed with the Powells in Somerset for the weekend.

I'll write again if I may, when things are more settled, and suggest another date. We are very keen to come, and sorry to have had to call it off this time.

Yours ever,
Kingsley Amis

[ALS: Recipient]

TO HENRY FAIRLIE[1] – 1 NOVEMBER 1956

Swansea

Dear Henry,

No, we are not going to meet if I can avoid it, because I should not enjoy it and because there is no need for it. There is no need for it because, in the first place, I am not interested in knowing just how keen a man is on taking the most valuable thing I own (my family) away from me because he wants a part of it (my wife), and even if you wanted Hilly twenty times more than I do, that would not make me any more inclined to let her go. So I don't want to know how you feel about this business. And there is nothing more to tell you about how I feel than you must already have guessed. And when you talk of us explaining to each other what the situation means to each of us, what you mean is that you want a chance of showing how much more you care than I do. You would be, and are, wasting your time.

I haven't the slightest doubt that you and Hilly are in love with each other. But it remains true that you are having an affair, and the situation of an affair – absence, partings, reunions, letters, phone-calls, guilt, grief – sharpens and heightens such feelings of love until people are prepared to act foolishly and cruelly upon them. This will be agonising for them, but not as agonising as it is for those who are suffering instead of merely inflicting cruelty, and if they are already selfish and ruthless by nature, as I think you are, they will be less agonised still. –

---

1. For Fairlie see Amis to Conquest, 20 June 1956, note 5: also *Memoirs*, p. 137, in which Amis lists 'the Fairlies', along with the 'Powells, Gales, Kilmartins, Karl Millers', among the friends who came to Swansea to visit, and whom they presumably visited in turn, travelling 'more and more to London as my literary life got going'.

I do not mean that these are by any means the only things in your nature, or that you have a monopoly of them, but they are stronger in you than in most people I know, as I had observed before I knew anything of the Hilly business (I didn't at all dislike you for these things then, just made sure I gave you no opportunity to exercise them at my expense. At least that was what I thought I was making sure of.). You are also excitable to the point of instability (more than most of us), and so when Hilly tells me that you are prepared to leave not only Lisette but Simon and Charlotte too in order to go to Hilly, I take this as an indication of the depth of your love, yes, but far more as a sign of the irresponsibility and greed of which you are capable. A second marriage, founded on the unhappiness (in varying degrees) of seven other people, must take its stand much more than a first marriage on love, sexual, romantic, exclusive, continuous love. The moment that love suffers the slightest blemish (such as a first marriage could survive without difficulty) the marriage needs the utmost patience, resolution, calm, self-restraint etc. – qualities rather less noticeable in you than in others. Am I lacking in charity? Well, what do you expect? And what is all this about emotional blackmail? Do try to see some difference between feeling bad about trying to take Hilly away from me and me feeling bad about having Hilly and my children taken away from me. You and she have each got someone who wants you. You should welcome the notion of an endurance test because of this.

Write again only if urgent: reading yours & writing this have been no fun.[2]

Kingsley

[TLS][3]

2. MS addition.

3. The original of this letter has not been located; a photocopy was found among Amis's papers after his death.

TO PHILIP LARKIN – 4 NOVEMBER 1956

Swansea

My dear Philip,

Thank you for your consolatory letters. Things continue to go up and down rather: on Thursday evening, for instance, about 8 p.m., I had 'offered Hilly her freedom'; by about 3 a.m. the following morning the successive application of tears and pork sword had brought hubby right back into the picture again. Since then both sides have fallen back on prepared positions, with me feeling a little resentful towards her on extra-amatory grounds: her laziness, her continuous peevishness with the children, her utter lack of any interest in anything whatsoever. Now, of course, things have been diversified by the arrest of Henry for not appearing before the bankruptcy courts: he spent last night in Brixton.[1] You'd imagine that the irresponsibility of which that kind of thing is evidence would tend on the whole to cool the amatory flame in his mistress, or at least not to feed it. Ah, but you'd be wrong. Makes him more of a wild, wayward, own-worst-enemy, feckless victim of persecution from those who are older, less gay, less handsome and attractive (they are all jealous of him, you see), more stodgily literal-minded about things like money and promises than he. The only thing I can't quite accept about Henry is that he isn't an Irishman. Still, he is a Scot, and that, I suppose, is the next best thing, what?

My pwetry buke[2] comes out tomorrow, a fact which Hilly must have gathered by divination, for she hasn't asked me about it, and yet she would surely have wished to know. I think on the whole that unless you review anon.-ly in the Manguard [*Manchester Guardian*] I should be inclined to leave it to someone else: log-rolling is fine, but is apt to be somewhat neutralised if it is detectable as such ("Cover from view is not cover from fire if you are seen getting there"). Actually I should do all right, except for Time and Tide ("triviality . . . lack of passion"), Encounter ("academicism . . . barren smartness"), Listener ("triviality . . . barren smartness") etc.

---

1. According to his obituary in *The Times*, 27 February 1990, Fairlie's financial affairs 'were always but slenderly under his control'.

2. *A Case of Samples.*

Yes, the world sure is a puzzle. I liked the bit in one of the Sundays today, describing American desire to intervene in Hungary, drop tactical atom bombs etc., but saying that Congressmen would never vote for this, "or at any rate not until after Tuesday".[3] Reassuring, that. The only men I have heard supporting Eden[4] have been Henry (on the Any Questions programme before he was put under restraint) and a certain Edward Ashbury, who likes Canada, Elvis Presley and snooker and who suffers mildly from paranoia.[5] You are a silly old lad over not ing the sportess. Go on, fill yer firkin galligaskins. As I feel at the moment I would jailbait on the steps of the County Court during the rush-hour if methoght I myght but *Haue My VVille* in tyme.

A man from London phones to ask after Henry and give me reassurance, doing this latter because he knows of (I quote) "the great friendship" betwixt us Twain. He said Henry cannot be bailed, and it might be three weeks before he is deemed to have purged his contempt. "This makes me chuckle in rather an evil way." The whole thing is getting like something out of Galsworthy, or perhaps *Fidelio* (is it?) – you know, Henry falls in love with the gaoler's daughter, Hilly is smuggled into the prison disguised as a boy, the gaoler's daughter falls in love with her, and all is confusion until the Janissary of Egypt sacks the town and liberates them. Arias: "Ah, would that these stout prison walls", "Dearest, I come to bear thee hence" and "Hark! for liberation is at hand" – trumpet obbligato, George Eskdale.[6]

Can't seem to work much these days, somehow. My novel had rattled along merrily to p. 49 when the blow fell; now remains there. You ought to hear That Patterson girl, vol 2:[7] she sings much more like

3. The Hungarian uprising of 23 October 1956 led to Soviet invasion; on the day of this letter, 4 November, after a week of bitter fighting, the Soviets attacked Budapest; on Tuesday, 6 November, Dwight D. Eisenhower was re-elected US President over Adlai Stevenson.

4. Over Suez. In May 1955 Anthony Eden (1897–1977) formed a Conservative government (he remained Prime Minister until 1957, resigning because of ill health, and was created Earl of Avon, 1961). On 31 October 1956, acting in concert with the French and the Israelis, Eden ordered the RAF to bomb Egyptian airfields (in response to the Egyptian President Nasser's nationalisation of the Suez Canal). In three days, on 7 November, Britain and France would accept a ceasefire in Egypt and agree to a United Nations peacekeeping role.

5. Edward Ashbury appears nowhere else in the correspondence nor in any of the standard biographical reference books or on-line sources.

6. This scenario derives in part from Beethoven's opera *Fidelio*, first performed in 1805 and subtitled *or Married Love*. George Eskdale (1897–1960) was Principal Trumpet of the London Symphony Orchestra (1932–60).

7. The name of two EPs (seven-inch discs, with four titles each) recorded by Ottilie Patterson (b. 1932), Irish singer, who performed for over fifteen years with Chris Barber, to

a man playing a trumpet, or perhaps a trombone, than any of yer bleedin Lady Days, &c. Also try Keeping out of Mischief Now by the Vc prc Vic Dickenson 7tet on Vanguard (feat. Braff).[8] Ah well, in the fell clutch of circumstance I have winced and cried aloud; under the bludgeonings of chance my head is bloody and bowed too, mun. It matters a great deal how stratt[9] Hope you settle down in your flat comfortable-like. Have you got spare room? Might come and occupy it briefly if you have.

It isn't that I dislike you, but Henry is so much more of a bum

Kingsley

[TLS: Bodleian]

TO HILARY RUBINSTEIN – 12 NOVEMBER 1956

53 Glanmor Road, Uplands, Swansea, Glamorgan.

Dear Hilary,

First things first, so let me make a small speech of thanks for *A Case of Samples*. A very fine bit of production indeed, such as gladdens the heart even of a typography-hound (where verse is concerned) like me. I shall ask your headmaster to grant you all an extra half-holiday.

Now: 2 foreigners are about to call upon you or phone you, and one of them may even have done so already. They are 1. Miroslav Beker. Nationality: Jugoslav. Business: Wants to translate *Jim* into Jugoslav*.[1] Remarks: Speaks excellent English, lectures in it at Zagreb. 2. Giovanni Carocci. Nationality (oddly enough) Italian. Business: Wants to fix up an Italian translation of *Jim*. Remarks: I can't remember whether anyone has done this already or not, so if someone has I rely on you not to

whom she was married; on volume 2 she performs with the Barber band. 'Lady Day' was the singer Billie Holiday (1915–59).

8. Vic Dickenson (1906–84), trombonist and bandleader; 'Keeping out of Mischief' was recorded in 1953.

10. An allusion to W.E. Henley, *Echoes*, iv. *Invictus. In Memoriam R.T.H.B.* (1888): 'In the fell clutch of circumstance, /I have not winced nor cried aloud: /Under the bludgeonings of chance, /My head is bloody, but unbowed./It matters not how strait the gate,/How charged with punishments the scroll.' Henley (1849–1903) was a literary editor and man of letters as well as a poet.

1. This asterisk, a MS addition, led to the note: 'or Serbo-Croatian or whatever it is.'

make me look a complete maniac in front of Carocci – tell him I hadn't yet been told or something. Carocci writes atrocious English, but then he is only touting for some Eyetye firm. You will know how to deal with him, I warrant.

Got an uneasy feeling I owe you a letter about something. Can't think what it is. See if you can.

Yours ever,
Kingsley

[TLS: Gollancz]

TO PHILIP LARKIN – 20 NOVEMBER 1956

Swansea

My dear Philip,

Thanks a lot. Yes, I am coming, and v. nice too. [. . .]

Potted comments on your other points (got to catch the post) – the Hen-Hil stuff has quietened down a lot since I last wrote. My marriage now has the odds heavily on its side. Details later. But didn't Cranston also not read the info on the verso of the title-page? I expect a short jeering letter from you to *Encounter* on y^is *Theame.*[1] Yes I think P de Vries, sorry DeVries, is bloody funny, esp. *Tunnel of Love.*[2] I take it I am to sleep in your flat, not elsewhere, hunh? You know my little phobia about this. Couch will do if pushed. Looking forward to Humph[3] & all else – will you have a gram. by then? Shall I bring some hot discs?

Soviet volunteers for bum
K.

[ALS: Bodleian]

---

1. Maurice Cranston reviewed *A Girl in Winter* in 'The Young and the Established', a group fiction review in *Encounter*, November 1956, pp. 80–4. Larkin's previous publications are listed opposite the novel's title-page (the verso, or back, of the title-page contains printing and copyright details), and though Cranston writes of admiring Larkin's poetry he makes no mention of *Jill*; on the other hand, nor does he suggest that *A Girl in Winter* is Larkin's first novel. The remark remains a puzzle.

2. *Tunnel of Love* (1954) by Peter De Vries (1910–93), American comic novelist.

3. Presumably Humphrey Lyttelton, who may have been performing with his band in Hull.

TO PHILIP LARKIN – 22 NOVEMBER 1956

VERY SORRY UNABLE COME LOVE TO HUMPH[1] WRITING =

KINGSLEY +

[TELEGRAM: Bodleian]

TO PHILIP LARKIN – 22 NOVEMBER 1956

Swansea

My dear P.,

Very very sorry, believe me. But I would have been a miserable companion. Getting up after a count of nine (as Wain would say) I have been felled again for the time being: my young lady[1] whom I was rather attached to (not the rugby enthusiast's wife) has just decided to give me up. This sort of stuff gives me great physical fatigue apart from everything else. So I couldn't face a 12½-hour journey on top of it. So sorry, honest. Hope you understand.

Always remember you bum,
Kingsley

[ALS: Bodleian]

---

1. See Amis to Larkin, 20 November 1956, note 3.

---

1. Unidentified; though for the rugby enthusiast's wife see Amis to Larkin, 24 September 1956.

TO PHILIP LARKIN – 6 DECEMBER 1956

Swansea

My dear Philip,

Forgive me if I answer your letter on a piece of paper exactly the same size as the one you wrote yours on, only turned via 90°. (It is your turn to write a full-size letter, isn't it?) I am very sorry and feel very guilty about that bed *imbroglio* (how sodding awful) and very sorry altogether about not coming. I repeat, though, that I should only have been a misery.

Ia m bu m I am less of a misery now, because I have more or less got my wife back (no Henry for 6 months; resumption of marital relations; much increased cordiality between the partners to the matrimonial arrangement in question) for the time being, and that is sodding good-oh, believe me, sport. As a consequence (though I can quite see how you can't quite see how this can be so) I have got my girl-friend back too. And that, as well, is very nice (indeed to fook). So, in response to your kind inquiry, yes, my love-life is quite near an even keel at the moment. And Sally is fine, thank you, not a moment's anxiety since she left hospital.

Christ, I've been having a cough too, though not as bad as yours sounds. Too much smoking, I expect. I have taken to using a filter-holder, in dear smear dread of l+ng-c+nc+r, and chose the more modest, less ornate type of the two offered. It is the lady's type, I find. But it's sleeplessness that drags me these days (still, better than during the 6 weeks up till a few days ago). I twitch, itch suddenly. Bad shaher.

I haven't thanked you before for your review of me in the Manguard,[1] because I didn't see it until this morning. It dyd most mightilie content mee, especially ab scab after all this accomplished light versifier stuff. Yes, you said as many of the things I'd like to have said abr drabr about me as could be got into the space, I thought. I loved Anti-Wet Scum. Glad you enjoyed "The Small Room". Which one was it?[2]

---

1. 'Separate Ways', *Manchester Guardian*, 30 November 1956, p. 14.

2. 'The work of Mr Kingsley Amis . . . is labelled like a trunk with misapprehensions ('Anti-Wet Scum') and this selection of 45 poems may help to peel some of them off.' 'The Small Room' Larkin calls an 'untypical' poem, but also a 'success'; more typical successes, he explains, are 'funny and serious simultaneously'.

Been reading ole O PO Pam Hans Johns The Last bleeding Resort recently.[3] Not bad, but *not good either*. All her characters are so clever and observant, and have such large vocabularies, and get into articulate emotional states so smartly. And I hate her serious respectful Gladys-Mitchell[4] attitude towards children. Still, the old girl is reviewing THE BOX OF SPECIMENS[5] in the Critics on Sunday week, so I mustn't complain. It'll be interesting to see what literary experts like C.A. ('Smellybum') Lejeune[6] and the radio tomfool have to say about it. Shall be very distressed if they like it. At least that's what I say now. [. . .]

Sorry sir 3d more now cos of the new tax on bum

Kingsley

[TLS: Bodleian]

TO PHILIP LARKIN – 27 DECEMBER 1956[1]

Swansea

My dear Philip,

It was jolly nice getting a Christmas letter from you, old sport, and I only wish I had had the time and energy to send you one. But here anyway ("But what way would be of service?") is a New Year screed. My pear-runts were here for the festive season, of course, but went home today – less bad, that. Nothing of interest took place over the "holiday", except perhaps my professor asking a publisher pal of mine to send him a catalogue of erotica, and the same pal falling over a dinner-wagon and breaking a lot of crockery on the occasion (he told me afterwards) of having his balls suddenly seized during an embrace with the rugby-enthusiast's wife[2] – less bad, that, also. He was too pissed to know what he was doing at the time, naturally. You heard I suppose

3. *The Last Resort* (1956) by Pamela Hansford Johnson.

4. Gladys Mitchell (1901–83) wrote over sixty mystery novels, some set in girls' schools. See Amis to Larkin, 3 December 1983, note 11.

5. That is, *A Case of Samples*.

6. C.A. Lejeune (1897–1973), journalist and film critic, *Observer* (1928–60), mother of the journalist Anthony Lejeune (b. 1928).

---

1. Amis mistakenly dated the letter 27 December 1957.

2. See Amis to Larkin, 24 September 1956.

that that fool Bartley had been arrested for being drunk in charge of his car, and getting off without the defence being called? Sodding good solicitor he had. How did you do for presents? I had a rather useless wine-pourer decanter kind of effort from mh fh my parents, the replica of one I had already, some leaf-tobacco in various forms from my wife and others, and a bloody nice pair of slippers from my young lady. I should really have liked a big packing-case containing a thirteen-year-old schoolgirl with huge ma-ha-ha and a protuberant ba-ha-ha and a bulging hairy ga-hah-fuck-ha-ha, but nobody seems to have thought of sending me one of that-there. I fear am gam I am going ahead rather on the pics racket: have started a monster album with all the best people in it, McCalla, Ekberg, Matthews,[3] also two naked young ladies with everything they own plain to view – got hold of it through a pal who said he'd see if he could find some more. Do tell me about HELIOS – sounds fascinating. I got the idea for *this*[4] when I thought my young lady had thrown me down; devising compensation, I thought. Then I found out she hadn't thrown me down and went straight ahead with the album. Devising a bolt-hole from active sex, I thought. Well, it don't make a blind bit of difference whichever way yer looks at it, I rackon. Sorry the shops were nasty. I should have been scared stiff, or scared limp perhaps I ought to say. [. . .]

Have I told you about my film at all? In public I am all smiles about this, but in private, ah ha sir, a very different kettle of fish, I assure you. Horse of a different colour altogether, what? They play for laughs all the time, you see. This wouldn't matter so much if they were certain to get them. Atkinson[5] is a major, 4-star disaster, Bertrand is Terry-Thomas, Margaret is a minor, dimly-glimpsed irritation, about as important to Dixon as a touch of indigestion. There is an awful DOG they have brought in from nowhere, he's BERTRAND'S DOG, you see, but he DOESN'T LIKE Bertrand, no, he LIKES DIXON, and he GETS IN THE WAY a LOT, and helps to MUCK UP THE LECTURE, and when Dixon gets pissed HE GETS PISSED TOO,

3. Irish McCalla (b. 1929), American actress, starred in the 1950s television series *Sheena, Queen of the Jungle*, as well as several films, including *She Demons* (1958); Anita Ekberg (b. 1931), Swedish actress and former Miss Sweden (1951), film credits include *Valerie* (1957) and, most memorably, *La Dolce Vita* (1960); 'Matthews' is probably the American actress Joyce Matthews (b. 1919), another blonde, whose film credits include *Artists and Models* (the 1937 version) and *Million Dollar Legs* (1939).

4. Amis has underlined 'this' in pen and typed 'ie album' in the left margin.

5. Jeremy Hawk (b. 1918) played Atkinson in the film of *Lucky Jim*.

and he COMES IN at the END, and in general he CONTRIBUTES A GOOD DEAL to the general ATMOSPHERE OF CRAZINESS and the general KNOCK ABOUT FARCE kind of ATMOSPHERE. There is only one place for the writer in the film industry, STARING UP MICHAEL BALCON'S GREAT BIG FAT BUM. Oh well, it's a lot of free publicity, I suppose, but quite apart from what I've said the slaps craps slapdash was SHIT way things are run gets one down: Hilly and I waited nearly three hourse hoarse h-arse hours for the car that was to take us to Smells-tree,[6] the actors approximate to the script and nobody notices, bits of business are devised, enthused over, not written down, forgotten, and so on. Not much different from the way we always thought it was, I suppose.

I enclose the Cain stuff, returned after six or seven weeks by Lehmann with a courteous note. I suggest you give them to the p. of Hessle for *Hist.* We shouldn't get any money for them, but it's a way of getting them into print, and there's always the chance old [G.S.] Fraser will pontificate maladroitly about them and lay himself open.[7] You'll have to bind Hartley's mouth with adhesive tape. I leave it to you, anyway. Well, if you're anything like me, you'll be lucky to get more than about 0.5% of what you wish yourself in 1957, but here's jolly good luck any road. Send me some pics. Angry young bum,

Kingsley

[TLS: Bodleian]

TO PHILIP LARKIN – 2 JANUARY 1957

Swansea

My dear Philip,

Jolly good luck, jolly good luck. And for the New Yeah as well. Thank you for your lil note: yes of course cully, I'm game ("I'll play a

6. Elstree Studios in Hertfordshire.

7. George Hartley has no record of the 'Ron Cain' parodies of Movement poets being offered to *Listen* after John Lehmann declined to print them in the *London Magazine.* See Appendix B and Amis to Larkin, 9 September and 8 October 1956.

game of billiards with your–"). How clever of you to find out about it, and how efficient of you to write for tickets so quickly. Are they numbered? Can more be got? I ask this in case I want to bring girl-friend or anything like that. Should welcome any details you have. Not that I at all object to gong with you alone, in qu quim fact quite the contrary dear, but g-f may want to come when she gets wind of it. So may her hubby, but he's a very decent chap. You'll like him.

No, writing is a pisser, ennit? You can't write? I contrite. – Rather on the point, that. Am tring to do 1200 words for the New York Times Book Review on satire, two hundred doll-arse they will pay, mun.[1] But don't know whether I can manage it. Satire? I don't know anything about bloody satire. Don't want to, neether.

My pamphlet on socialism ("You are mad, you know") appears on Monday.[2] Will send you an inscribed copy. Zeece dayce we radders kennot ef*fort* to stend asite from ze clesh bit-win ze forcess off friddum ent ze blodd-stent executionerss off ze Ballshavvik ampire. Something of that, any road.

I advise you to stop writing on jazz; stick to bum

Kingsley

[TLS: Bodleian]

TO MARGUERITE CUTFORTH – 7 JANUARY 1957

53 Glanmor Road, Uplands, Swansea, Glam.

Dear Mrs. Cutforth,

I am so sorry for all my incompetence and dilatoriness. What happened to your letter defeats me utterly. Please accept my heartfelt and shamefaced apologies.

On your proposal itself:[1] I feel very bad about this, but I'm afraid

---

1. Eventually published as 'Laughter's to be Taken Seriously', *New York Times Book Review*, 7 July 1957, p. 1.

2. *Socialism and the Intellectuals*, a thirteen-page pamphlet published by the Fabian Society.

---

1. That Amis take part in a discussion between four 'professional' humorists on the essentials of their humour. Marguerite Cutforth (1912–64), producer, BBC Talks (from 1948).

I must turn it down. My feelings are (1) that as a rule discussion, except between people who know each other well, solves almost nothing; (2) that humour is a subject requiring real hard thought, and a wisecracking fandango, such as would probably emerge, might be amusing but, again, would contribute little to the subject; (3) that I personally can't argue or discuss, let alone be funny, in circumstances of the least formality, such as a broadcast discussion, however loosened up with preliminary chaff and alcohol, would provide.

I hope you see these points. They are my honest opinion.

Yours sincerely,
Kingsley Amis

[TLS: BBC]

TO HILARY RUBINSTEIN – 17 JANUARY 1957

53 Glanmor Road, Uplands, Swansea, Glam.

Dear Hilary,

Congratulations on the zlotys – but don't rest on your oars. Keep after the yen, kopeks, drachmae, escudos, schillings, Krønen etc.

Yours ever,
Kingsley

PS. Roubles? No, I suppose not.

[ALS: Gollancz]

TO MICHAEL STEPHENS – 23 JANUARY 1957

53 Glanmor Road, Uplands, Swansea, Glam.

Dear Mr. Stephens,

A nice idea:[1] but I'm afraid I must decline. I'm no good at discussions anyway, and on this sort of topic the other chaps would just make

1. To discuss *Socialism and the Intellectuals* on a radio programme with two or three

mincemeat of me. So it's thumbs down. But thank you for putting it up to me.

Yours sincerely,
Kingsley Amis

[TLS: BBC]

TO PHILIP LARKIN – 27 JANUARY 1957

Swansea

My dear P.

Sorry to delay so long, but this has taken ages to fix up. I arrive Paddington 1 pm Monday the 4th, leave evening 5th – got to get back. Can you meet me, or say where you'll be? We can both stay with my girl and her hubby – no awkwardness, never fear. Does that suit? Have fixed it with my girl. Will write again if you will O.K. the general outline by return, and fix in more detail.

This type of intellectual has a deep hatred of bum

K.

[ALS: Bodleian]

TO THE EDITOR, *DAILY WORKER* – 14 FEBRUARY 1957

May I make a couple of comments on Mr. Arnold Kettle's friendly notice of my pamphlet, *Socialism and the Intellectuals*?[1]

I know he means to compliment me by saying that my "basic

socialist intellectuals who were also practising politicians. Michael Stephens (b. 1925), producer BBC radio; later Head of Overseas Talks and Features and Head of Further Education, Radio (1968–79).

---

1. In *Socialism and the Intellectuals* Amis seeks to explain and justify the political apathy of his sort of 'elderly young intellectual . . . with left-wing sympathies' (p. 1). The tract also identifies self-interest as 'the best and most trustworthy political motive' (p. 13), while lamenting the absence of more 'respectable' motives in the current political climate ('no Spain, no Fascism, no mass unemployment' (p. 7)), despite recent crises in Suez and Hungary. Arnold Kettle (1916–97), a Marxist literary critic and academic, reviewed *Socialism and the Intellectuals* on 12 February 1957, in an article entitled 'Some of my Best Friends are Intellectuals'.

political assumptions ... are nearer to Marxism than most social-democratic thinking," and I hope I won't be thought ungrateful if I contest this representation of me.

I don't assume that capitalism has "had it." In a way I wish I could, but that's different. Nor do I assume that Socialism is "the society of the future."

It may never come.

Or something better may replace it. And I don't mean the withering away of the State.

I agree that there is a class struggle, but I think there are other struggles (racial, national, etc.) of equal political importance.

And it is being replaced in our society by other kinds of struggle. But it never was all-important, anyway. Nor was economic motive.

You see, I have had Marxism – in both senses of the words. I have experienced the ailment and so am immune. And I have also utterly rejected it.

No world-view, it seems to me, comes within light-years of being adequate to the world it professes to categorize.

Each fact, each entity, each event is unique. To pretend otherwise is mere Victorian system-building.

Marxism, I think, does just that.

It repels me also by offering certainty instead of truth – Mr. Kettle denies this, but he himself is so certain that Socialism is "the society of the future" that he thinks I am certain of it, too.

He also denies that the Communist Party goes in for violence.

What really happened in Hungary, then?[2]

Wasn't there any violence? Or was it all inter-Hungarian violence, with the Russian troops acting as umpires? Or were they acting against Russian orders? Or have the Russian government given up Communism?

I know Mr. Kettle was really talking about the British Communist Party. They aren't violent, and I hope they never get the chance, harmless as they may be now. Yes, even amiable, and I used to say that some of my best friends are Communists. I can't after Hungary.

KINGSLEY AMIS
University College of Swansea

2. After the invasion of Soviet troops in 1956.

TO PHILIP LARKIN – 19 FEBRUARY 1957

Swansea

My dear Philip,

Well, falla, it was great to see you, and you in such cracking form too. You were much more cheerful than I'd seen you for some time. Must be settling down to life in Hull. All right, all right. It was fine that we saw Condon together dalling[1]. [. . .]

Fairly sodding here: have done 3 pages of Portugal effort; it makes me laugh a bit, but I can't get on with it. And for why? Because of filthy stinking journalism: I am going to give it up, and that's the truth. Also, I got let in for a course of 8 lectures to the WEA[2] at Port Talbot, some way from here. Did I tell you how I got let in for these? Thought a professorial olive-branch was a pistol to the old head? And the titles? The first, any road, is The world of Ernest Hemingway. Fuck that. Took me *all day* yesterday to prepare. Would gladly pay £50 (=2Xmy honorarium from the course) not to do it. After a too-quick shave, bolting poached egg on haddock, I staggered down the road, bleeding and belching, insisted on a large whisky, got to the huge bus-area, couldn't find the recommended bus ("Oh no, there's no number 4 now," "Oh no, you want the 42, that's your bus"), was taken over half South Wales,[3] asked for the Grammar School as directed, "which one? The County or the Secondary?", said it was one by a bus-stop, was put down at one not by a bus-stop, remonstrated, was told I must want the one by the bus-stop, two stops back, walked through freezing horrible Port Talbot, pissed in Gents, failed to shake cock enough and drenched left leg, arrived 40 minutes late, class *still there*. Lecture tolerable, though old man talked much of Izaak Walton, back in time for double whisky and pint of bitter, met Swansea's most horrible man in bus up to Uplands. Extra horrible post today (as bad as last week's one morning, one from Boultings' lawyer to say I must help to instruct

1. Amis was reporting on a concert by Eddie Condon for the *Observer*, 10 February 1957 (the review was entitled 'Not Really the Blues').

2. Workers' Educational Association.

3. In a MS addition in pen in the left margin Amis has written: 'Conductor said: "You should have got the No. 4. Much quicker."'

counsel in pending *Jim* lawsuit,[4] one from manager of Embassy Ballroom with bill for bottle of scotch I paid for on night of Golf Club dance): demands for income tax – £654–14–3, and land tax – £19–13–1 (why? I don't want any land), plus letter from Neath Townswomen's Guild, reminding me I am to address them on The world of jazz next Tuesday in Neath (8½ miles), the day after I address the WEA on the world of Ernest Hemingway (ii) in Port Talbot (14 miles). Am going to give it all up, chum. After this course, 2 more public appearances only: to receive Nobel Prize for literature, to answer toast at dinner after investiture with the Order of Merit. And all the sodding Literary, Musical and Dramatic Circles can stuff each other one by one, and then all stuff themselves simultaneously, get mam?

The Hilly business, after a mild setback, is much better now than for a long time, before even the Henry business began. Old Harry F. is bug erred now, I confidently say. Especially since he has been ink a Munich ah doe for some days, not answering Hilly's letter and such courtesy. Wouldn't give a pinch of shit for his chances of even an occasional blow-through. I know I've said this sort of thing before, but this time I can't see things going wrong at this end. Must keep my hands off the cute-ease, though. There's one here who – but I mustn't go into that, as the a. said shit box the b. said to the a.

Have seen a bit of old Vernon Twatkins[5] recently, don't really know why. He's a sodding old boring egomaniacal fool, isn't he? At the skills of interrupting and uninterruptability, twin skills these, he is without peer, save maybe for Daddy B. He (VW) was full of the edition of "Dylan's" letters he's doing. Was annoyed they wanted to cut out words like "fuck" and "shit". Said he said he'd withdraw the whole thing if they wouldn't print "shit". He did quote one line from them that amused me in a way, Dylan saying what a shit he was to everyone, "weasels take off their hats as I stink by". It brought that awful old voice back to me with a rush, could just *here* him declaiming "Wizzles tek off their hets as Ay ssstinck-a bay."[6]

What did you think of those little photographs when you finally got at them? Not a very nice-looking young lady, I thought, though I didn't like to say so at the time, naturally. And otherwise your kind of

4. In a MS addition in pen in the left margin Amis has written: 'This is seek writ, they say. So keep it under hat.'

5. Vernon Watkins.

6. In a MS addition in the left margin Amis has typed 'herk herm'.

thing? Or not? Mm? Me, I haven't advanced on that kind of front for some time, done no more on my album etc.[7] But I did find IWDAFY the other day and had a jolly good read at it. It was funny to see us at a stage before our obsessions really developed, me not saying much about hair, you not much about, indeed nothing about, bottoms. And the tits were all 'firm', 'young', not even ample, let alone enormous, bulging, as I'd make them if I were writing it now. I didn't think it was very pornographic, but bloody funny, all that art stuff, Pickarso and Mister Graham Sutherland, and all the jazz stuff, the Commodore First Anniversary Album, On a Blues Kick and so on. It was a great pity we didn't finish it, or that we finished it, stopped it, so soon, before we got to the real horn. There was some of the continuation of the Linda Massinger story in with it (remember?) and that made me laugh too: Erica Derge and all that lot.[8] But not good, sound, well-written; no no.

Well, chambo, send me news of your dongs. I don't have many dongs really, much, at all, except when I go to London. Seem to spend all my time here getting through the stuff I have to get through before I can get to the stuff I want to do, somehow, see? Cain't write no poems, naw, not for love or anything else. Did do one for that Beloit crap[9] (did I say?) but it was pretty fair crap. Send me accounts of jazzsound, girlbottom, wordwork, manshit, borehate, shithate. Wish I could find a set of the Encyclopaedia Britannica which turned out to have all the original pages removed and double-column horn, the picture, the word, put in.

Men without bum,[10]

[TL: Bodleian]

7. Presumably of soft porn; mentioned nowhere else in the letters.

8. Unidentifiable.

9. See *The Beloit Poetry Journal* 8:2 (Winter 1957–8), p. 27, for 'Larger Truth', reprinted in *A Case of Samples* (1957) and *CP*, p. 91.

10. An allusion to *Men Without Women* (1927), a collection of stories by Ernest Hemingway, about whom Amis was lecturing at the WEA (see Amis to Larkin, 19 February 1957).

TO JOHN LEHMANN – 2 APRIL 1957

53 Glanmor Road, Uplands, Swansea, Glam.

Dear Mr. Lehmann,

This is not the sort of thing I usually do, but a woman who calls herself Gloria Evans Davies[1] sent me her poems to read. I thought them rather good, in flashes – I don't know that any of them come off as they deserve to. But despite that I think some of them are very publishable. She has actually had quite a few in print here and there, and even now, according to her, those fellows in Panton House[2] are poring over a sheaf of them. The 8 I send you are all quite free of any such commitment and I should be very grateful if you'd have a look at them.

Perhaps I should add that I've never met this woman, who may be anything from 16 to 60, and have no idea whether her *yeux* are *beaux* or not.

Yours sincerely,
Kingsley Amis

[TLS: HRHRC]

TO PHILIP LARKIN – 16 JULY 1957

Didn't you get my card from abroad, rider?[1] Will screed you as soon as book finished: end of month. *Not* what *S Times* said, course:[2] just a novel, that's all, yes: Garnet Bowen, an English Welshman, does both

1. Gloria Evans Davies's first volume of poems, *Published Words for Blodwen*, appeared in 1962 (Chatto and Windus). Though Lehmann declined to publish the poems Amis sent him, other editors approved. She had previously appeared in the *TLS, Listener, Time and Tide* and the *Spectator*, among other periodicals.

2. The editors of *Encounter*.

1. The Amises had gone on holiday to Bordeaux for two weeks (according to a card Amis sent Anthony Powell on 26 June 1957).

2. In the 'Atticus' column of the *Sunday Times*, 30 June 1957, p. 5, Amis is described as 'essaying a new and difficult literary form. The new book will be partly a travel documentary about Portugal, where he went on his Somerset Maugham Award, and partly fiction. Mr

Amis and Dixon. You old sourpuss *re midnight*: side 2 is up-and-down stuff, save for Sullivan: but Shavers? *IFANB* better than [illegible]?[3] Expand your confession of amorousinvolvement. What is it, aftermath of sight seeing visit of Form *VI*, Willow Ga This is the library, girls, & this is the librariawooghleggomyp Better put this in an envelope, I suppose, which means I can write on the front. Wasn't run over, was knocked dane.[4] Can't remember anything: concussion bum. All to rights now except small eye operation ahaha ha may be necessary – seeing double all the shaggin time. Film of *Jim* is all done, but haven't seen it yet. VG [Victor Gollancz], Hilary Rubinstein, the *Evg Standard* (including Philip Oakes) saw it and were doubled up, so expect the worst. Am not in love myself now, except with Jenny and Gillian,[5] neither of whom can believe the other is 40" round the bust, so measure each other, fair play demanding they strip to the waist. Then they
Marriage really seems saved now, tk xt. Now close the left eye and tell me if there's any movement in the image of my bum

K.

[ALS: Bodleian]

TO HUW WHELDON – 21 JULY 1957

53 Glanmor Road, Uplands, Swansea, Glam.

Dear Mr. Wheldon,[1]

I am terribly sorry to have left your letter unanswered for so long:

Amis, after describing the trials and tribulations involved in taking a young family to live in a Portuguese hotel, relates how he met an old friend in a local bar. The friend's name was Jim Dixon. What on earth is Lucky Jim doing in Portugal is anyone's guess.'

3. Amis is referring to a twelve-inch LP entitled *Midnight at Eddie Condon's*, recorded in 1945, without the presence of Condon, under the leadership of Bud Freeman, featuring, among others, Joe Sullivan on piano and Charlie Shavers on trumpet. 'IFANB' is 'I Found a New Baby', the second track on the LP.

4. This incident occurred before the trip to France, as Amis reports it to Powell in his card of 26 June 1957, where he calls it 'a street accident', not otherwise elaborating.

5. Fantasy friends, not otherwise identified.

---

1. Huw Wheldon (1916–86), broadcaster, television producer, director, author; Managing Director, BBC (1968–75); knighted (1976).

I would not have done if I had not succeeded in leaving it behind when I went abroad at the end of last month.

After the consideration you suggested, I am afraid the programme you describe, though very interesting in many ways, is not for me.[2] For one thing, I am sure I should get the worst of any such discussion – and indeed be unsatisfactory: I can never think of the really telling retort until afterwards. And again I think my ideas, such as they are, are far better put over by being embodied in writing rather than by being detached from that writing and discussed on their own merits.

But it was most kind and flattering of you to put the idea up to me.

Yours sincerely,
Kingsley Amis

[TLS: BBC]

TO J.H. McCALLUM – 16 SEPTEMBER 1957

53 Glanmor Road, Uplands, Swansea, Glam., Gt. Britain.

Dear Mr. McCallum,

Many thanks for the books, which I have promised myself I will plunge hard into when the toils I am now engaged in are over.

Yes, most certainly you may send me your queries on *I Like It Here.* I shall be very pleased to answer them.

May I ask you this? – my father left on Saturday for a three-month visit to the States.[1] He will be in New York for some of the time. He

2. Wheldon was producing a BBC television programme entitled *Give and Take* which pitted a figure with strongly held beliefs against six sceptical questioners. Previous participants included a Franciscan monk, Anthony Crosland (defending the proposition that equality was the crux of socialism) and a senior psychiatrist at Guy's Hospital (arguing that the words 'neurotic' and 'complex' in no way obviated words like 'innocence', 'sin' and 'guilt'). Wheldon had written to Amis saying he thought the programme would provide 'a very rewarding context for the kind of ideas for which you stand' (letter of 24 June 1957, in BBC).

1. Amis's mother had died of a stroke earlier in the year, in March, and his father had gone to America to visit his sister Gladys, who lived in Washington DC. The only other reference to his mother's death in the correspondence, also oblique, occurs in a letter to his friend from Berkhamsted days Derek Gardner, 27 March 1957 (in HEHL): 'All as well as

has never been to the U.S.A. before, and I told him to call upon you if he should need any guidance or help. I need not say how grateful I should be for any assistance you could give him – though he's a pretty self-reliant character and will probably not trouble you.

Yes indeed, let us be sure to meet this time in London. I come up on the 18th October and must attend a dinner that evening, but could manage a drink at 6.30, or better, lunch on the Saturday. Do let me know and we will have a jolly time together.

Yours sincerely,
Kingsley Amis

[TLS: Harcourt]

TO C.R. HEWITT – 8 OCTOBER 1957

53 Glanmor Road, Uplands, Swansea, Glam.

Dear Mr. Hewitt,

Thank you for your letter. I should be very pleased to discuss the novel-into-film thing[1] in the flesh, but unfortunately my occasions don't take me to London until the 18th of this month.

However, I will put down what might be of interest here and now. I'm afraid it isn't much, because I had very little to do with the making of the film of *Lucky Jim* beyond two or three informal conferences and a certain amount of correspondence.

As to how I feel now the film is showing – I don't think the thing is a transcription of my novel, but then I can't really see how this could have been avoided, given the shift from a minority medium to a mass one – forgive the jargon. Anyway, though there were parts of the film I could never endorse, there was plenty I recognised, plenty I could admire and certainly a great deal to make me laugh, and since my novel

can be expected here. My father is picking up extraordinarily well, and apart from his occasional low moments is quite lively.'

1. Hewitt was hoping to interview Amis for a piece in the forthcoming issue of *The Author*, published by the Society of Authors, on the subject of 'Novel-into-film'. The questions he wanted Amis and others to answer about this process were: 'how they felt after it, whether they would do it again, and what advice they would offer others' (letter of 4 October 1957, in Society of Authors archive).

was meant to be comic, not cosmic, I'm very pleased about that. Again, I very much enjoyed meeting Ian Carmichael, Terry-Thomas and the Boulting brothers.

So altogether I feel pretty happy about things, and grateful for the publicity. For the future, I should like to work on a film, but have no intention of trying to write a film-script from scratch (i.e. without writing the novel first), and I think it a bad idea for a novel to be written with filming in mind. (I had no idea at all that a film of *Lucky Jim* would be remotely practicable.)

I hope the above may contain something you can use. Please quote anything that takes your fancy.

Yours sincerely,
Kingsley Amis

[ALS: Society of Authors]

TO PHILIP LARKIN – 15 OCTOBER 1957

53 Glanmor Road, Uplands, Swansea, Glam.

My dear Philip,

This is to ensure that you have at least one effort from your old Pall to stick in your yes, that's right 1957 file. For the first time since March I have a morning free. All I have to do is write a letter to my father, who is in America, though not unfortunately for ever; decide whether or not I am going to take part in the Principal's scheme of First-Year Essays (and after the ballocking he gave me recently for allowing room for misinterpretation – by maniacs, presumably – of an article of mine in the *Daily Express*[1] I had better decide I am: or shall

1. This article, entitled 'Why You won't Sell Me the Bright Lights' (subheaded: 'No – not even now I've hit the jackpot'), appeared in the *Daily Express* on 14 September 1957. The Principal might have been disturbed by the following passage:

> Here in Swansea I conduct myself in a quiet, orderly manner. In the first place, I work at the local University College, lecturing in English. This is all right, actually. Few of my colleagues are barbarians in wire-rimmed glasses, cynically grinding out graduates from an educational sausage-machine; fewer still are tremulous Greek-quoting ninnies. And in 1965, I think it is, we are promised a new Common Room which will serve drinks.

I tell him to gallop friskily off and fuck himself?) and then write to say what I have decided; wonder what to do about the sodding Swede who sent me an air-mail express letter about translating my Fabian into English Christ Ime dreamyng into Swedish oddly enough – this was a week ago – "Therefor I am very sorry that I only can offer you a fee of 100:- sw. cr. = £7[2] . . . with a very great interest I am waiting for your kindly answer". His name is Bo Cavefors. I think I shall just keep very quiet until he goes right away. Now don't you think that would be a pretty sound scheme?

All is really quite well here. I have been working like a madman, and now that term has started I am going to sit back and relax for a spell. Married life is in excellent trim and all I need is a girl-friend and access to a library of hot pics and yarns for life to be perfect. The house, already congested by having had my parents' furniture moved into it, is getting yet further choked up by the influx of about 8 LPs and 20 EPs per month.[3] Pity so few of them are good. [. . .]

The world of books continues on its way. When are we going to see something from your direction Larkin ah no just foolin weeeghghg If *I Like it Here* in *Punch*[4] seems less than funny to you, as well it might, remember that it has been cut, and cut in the interests of keeping the story clear, not of leaving all the funny bits in. I think you will probably find it all right as far as it goes, though you'll probably complain it doesn't go far enough. Oh well. The "next one" will be a far more solid. Well, more ambitious. Well, longer, then. I see you're co-editing that *New Pwems* thing. Do you want me to send you something for it?[5] Of course I've only written about one poem since *Samples* appeared. If

> It'll be worth hanging on for that alone. Admittedly, being a lecturer involves lecturing. But unless you are very lazy or appear before him wearing a bowtie, the Welsh student will not molest you with anything more emphatic than a slow handclap.

2. '100:- sw. cr. = £7' typed in red.

3. Amis had been commissioned to present six programmes on jazz by Network 3, an adjunct of the Third Programme devoted to 'hobbies and interests'. The series, under the general title *Jazz*, was broadcast from 31 December 1957 to 4 January 1958; its individual programmes were titled *Jazz is Where You Find it, Make Mine Chicago Style, Singing the Blues, Jazz on Our Doorstep, Orchestrating the Blues* and *New Sounds*.

4. *I Like it Here* was serialised in nine issues of *Punch*, from 9 October to 4 December 1957.

5. Larkin was co-editing the seventh annual PEN anthology *New Poems 1958* with Bonamy Dobrée and Louis MacNeice; it included Amis's poem 'Larger Truth', later printed in *A Look Round the Estate* (1967) and *CP*, p. 91.

you *really* wd. like something, I'll send, or you could get it off the poof of Hessle, who has it for *Hark*.[6] Up to you, old man.

You know I really think that ole John Whine will go off his nut soon, if he hasn't already. Did you see that Alcock and Brown tale of his in where was it?[7] Bit catchpenny, isn't it, when the story turns out to have nothing to do with the aviators of those names? And Christ, what about this *Declaration* thing then? He's not an angry young man, you sam, so he gets together with them all to say he isn't.[8] Ho hum. Ho, hum. Well with you as the Auden and me as the Isherwood *de nos jours*, "our society" is dong not so bad, but with ole JBW as the Stephen Spender I reckon it's being given short weight, hey? Do you know what, I never seem to read a desent book nowadays, not a new desent book that it tit is. Funny to think you're really like Laforgue and Corbière was it all the time, isn't it? Like I'm like Surtees.[9] I wish you'd write a lot more poems, even bring out a book of your old ones. I wish at any rate I had them all by me to read. All the verse I see is such piss that I wonder what made me like any verse at all ever. As if jazz had always consisted of Parenti's Ragpickers, Cliff Jackson, Baby Dodds, Armstrong with Bigard and Trummy Young, Bechet with Claude Luter, Clancy Hayes and bop.[10]

6. George Hartley, editor of *Listen*.

7. In *Harper's Bazaar*, September 1957, pp. 76–7, 114, 116, 118, 121. The story takes its title, 'A Few Drinks with Alcock and Brown', from John Alcock (1892–1919) and Arthur Whitten Brown (1886–1948), the first aviators to make a non-stop flight of the Atlantic (in 1919). Wain's story was reprinted in *Nuncle and Other Stories* (1960).

8. In 1957 the publisher Tom Maschler (see Notes on Recipients) invited several of the supposed 'angry young men' (among them Colin Wilson, John Osborne, Kenneth Tynan, Lindsay Anderson, Wain and Doris Lessing, a presumed 'angry young woman') to explain their views in a book entitled *Declaration* (published by MacGibbon and Kee, where Maschler worked at the time). Amis's scorn for Wain's participation may relate in part to his own refusal to contribute. Maschler quotes him in the book's introduction: 'I hate all this pharisaical twittering about the "state of our civilisation", and I suspect anyone who wants to buttonhole me about my "role in society". This book is likely to prove a valuable addition to the cult of the Solemn Young Man' (pp. 8–9). Amis may also have disapproved of the 'angries' because of their stress on emotion or feeling and on the artist's inevitable or necessary alienation from society, as in Wilson's *The Outsider*.

9. There are no references to Laforgue, Corbière or Surtees in 'Along the Tightrope', Wain's contribution to *Declaration*, nor are they mentioned in any other contribution to the volume. Robert Surtees (1805–64), the foxhunting novelist and journalist, is best known for *Jorrocks's Jaunts and Jollities* (1838), a collection of stories drawn from the *New Sporting Magazine* with illustrations by Phiz, and the novels *Handley Cross* (1843) and *Hillingdon Hall* (1845), which concern characters from the *Jorrocks* collection.

10. Tony Parenti (1900–72), clarinettist and saxophonist (the Ragpickers were Parenti's band); Cliff Jackson (1902–70), pianist; Baby Dodds (1898–1959), drummer, called by *NGDJ*

Well today darling I believe I'll make a start on a short story or two. That's what I believe I'll do. And not ones featuring The Younger Girl[11] either. (Marvellous novel-title that would be.) Hilly is making me grow my hair all long and making me wash it frequently too, so that it stands out at the ends and makes me look as if I am wearing a curious helmet. I have had to discontinue snuff-taking as it made all the underneath of my nose raw. Had a letter from Duke recently. Why don't I get any interesting ones? Dear Mr. Amis, my friend Alice has dared me to write to you, we are both fifteen and want to take photagraphs of each other in the nude, if you will send us 20£ for the equipment we will send you the best pictures we take, and if you send another 5£ we will get a thing that ennables us to take pictures of the 2 of us at once, I am 36" Instead of that I get the as the secretary of, our programme for 1957–8, choice of subject, we are afraid we cannot, but hospitality and accommodation, look forward very much, change at Crewe, as soon as convenient kind of thing. Like that chum from Hull I've turned down.[12] I want to see you all right, but not under those circumstances. Do you ever come to London? L'll pill I'll lay you do, after one Murphy or another.[13] Let me knaher. And a letter from you, although I know all about its being my turn to wait for nine months or whatever it is, would be very acceptable. Just a card wd. be nice. I'd love to see you. I have a novel and a short story by Harold Pollins[14] to read and pronounce upon, so you can see that life isn't altogether a bed of roses.

'the leading drummer in the New Orleans style' (p. 293); Barney Bigard (1906–80), clarinettist, brother of the drummer Alex Bigard (1899–1978) and Trummy Young (1912–84), trombonist and singer, played together in Louis Armstrong's All Stars; Clancy Hayes (1908–72), banjoist and singer; 'bop', defined by *NGDJ* as 'one of the main styles of jazz . . . developed in the early and mid-1940s by such musicians as Dizzy Gillespie, Charlie Parker, Bud Powell, Thelonious Monk, Kenny Clarke and Max Roach' (p. 137).

11. Her only appearance (under this title) in the correspondence.

12. Neither Lady Kilmarnock nor Thwaite nor Motion can identify this chum.

13. That is, Richard or Patsy (Strang) Murphy.

14. Harold Pollins (b.1924), a historian, was part of the team Tom Brennan headed for the Social Survey of South-West Wales (1950–53); later Tutor, Senior Tutor, Ruskin College, Oxford (1964–89). Amis had been asked to read his fiction in manuscript, since his only published writing was academic.

How can you publically declare that Charlie Parker had no real bum,

Kingsley

[TLS: Bodleian]

TO PHILIP LARKIN – 9 NOVEMBER 1957

53 arsools etc. Glam.

My dear Philip,

Delighted to get yr card, and yr letter too to boot: this is really to show willing, for I have much, that I do not want to do, that I must do, when I do not want to, and would rather be doing something else, instead. For instance, I have a lot of letters to write telling people that two guineas is not a big enough fee for someone as famous as me, especially if I must go to Berwick-upon-Tweed or somewhere in order to earn same. Then there are the mad ones to do: how dare I not like bop, would I sign a *Jim* if a copy were sent to me, would I go and see someone's 18-year-old daughter, Gail by name, when she comes here to act in a play – this is all true, and I was fain to have gone to see Gail as requested, but that the letter has been about three weeks reaching me, the writer having addressed it to "Kingsley Amis, Swansea, Wales", and hence Gail has been and gone this week since. She'd probably have been terrible anyway. When all my post is in the bag wha-ha-ha I must go out and buy a Rupert book,[1] inscribe it, bring it home,[2] wrap it up in a parcel with an inscribed copy of *Samples*, and go down the road again to post the thing AIR MAIL to my American aunt, where my dad now is FILTHY? STINKING? DISGUS piss piss piss I meant FILTHY, STINKING, DISGUSTING HOMOSEXUAL OFFENCE. *Why* must I? Why *must* I? Why must *I*?

1. The Rupert books are collections of strip cartoons about Rupert Bear, invariably depicted in check trousers, red jersey and scarf. Rupert is the creation of the illustrator Mary Tourtel and first appeared in the *Daily Express* in 1920; picture books with his adventures in rhyme were published in the 1920s, and Rupert Annuals began appearing in 1936.

2. Amis has circled 'inscribe it' and 'bring it home' and signalled with an arrow that he wants the phrases transposed.

Letter to a friend about girls[3] sounds an absolutely fucking marvellous idea. I longt pongt long to see an instalment. But don't get me wrong (though I suppose it needn't be "me" in the poem); what I mean is I am no Don J at all, really, I merely work a pennyworth of fucking in with an intolerable deal of wire-pulling, horn-having, would-you-like-to-see-me-in-my-playsuit-Anna-darling mythologising and looking at, or wishing I had the chance of looking at, pics for fans of the fuller figure – and so I have the chance of being honest *and* getting something out of it, when I ask you, as I do now, to pass on any such pics you may have got tired of. Well, anyway. Why is this letter so badly written? Like a business man writing to his son at the University. [. . .]

Yes by fucky Nell I agree about stuff with demands on my critical attention screw *every sodding particle* of that. Where you read pgw[4] I read sf, except that I always seem to be reviewing something – by christ I have just heard an air-raid siren and feel so scared I could faint, honest. Still nothing seems to be happening. And I have a sodding great hill in front of my window so I have a few days left I suppose, till the fall-out gets me. God. All quiet now. A lorry piled with booze has just passed. Less bad. Only testing the siren I expect, *to make sure it's in working order when they need it.* I prefer not to think about all that.

It was a delight to get your card, not only about the film but also your kindly mention of the *Punch* serial.[5] I find it, the book, scaringly bad in that form. All the cracks have been cut so as to preserve the "story line" fuck your great-great-great-aunt. To hear that you find it tolerable is a great relief. Book due before Xmas they said, only I've had a clipping from some trade paper that says Jan., filthy lying profiteering bugger-the-author Yids.[6]

3. 'Letter to a Friend about Girls' was printed for the first time in *LCP*, where it is dated December 1959. Larkin explained his reluctance to publish the poem in a letter to Thwaite, 19 March 1970, in *LL*, p. 428: 'Can I enlist your aid as a literary critic? I have had the enclosed poem knocking around for ten years now, and every so often I take it out, alter it slightly, and try to bring myself to send it off somewhere, but I am always held back by the oppressive thought that it really isn't any good. Can you decide for me – or, at any rate, let me have your opinion?' Thwaite was literary editor of the *New Statesman* at the time and said he'd love to publish it, but could also see possible embarrassments with the friend in question ('KA, Bob C, etc.').

4. P.G. Wodehouse.

5. Of *I Like it Here.*

6. Victor Gollancz and Hilary Rubinstein; see Amis to Gollancz, 19 December 1957.

Yes, of course I'll send you a screed or two,[7] if I can polish up one of the several torsos lying round in my drawer. Can't "seem" to write verse these days. Which is one reason why I want you to send me some of your letter to a friend: I reckon it might easily stir me to a reply, not a polemical one of course, but a further discussion of some of the points you raise. I'm glad you've raised that point, as the a. said to the b. I think some sort of joint, or alternating, effort of this kind might be bumper fun. Or isn't that in tune with your original conception? What do you say?

Do tell me about AWA [Winifred Arnott], and Pasty [Strang Murphy] too if you can bear to. Has she chucked the poem racket too? not that she was ever in it but you see what I mean. Listen now, just remembered: why don't you put in for the chief library job here when Miss Busby goes at the end of the session?[8] I'm sure you'd get it. Our prof. of politics, who doesn't know you or know you know me, was saying the other day that from what he'd heard "this chap Larkin" was "doing great things" with the Hull library. Only thing is, keep quiet about knowing me, because my stock is low with the powers here. They won't want another "trouble-maker". Do please think this over. Would love to see you; every conversation I have these days with anybody contains at least one quotation from "my friend Larkin". When are you next in London? We *must* meet. Look to 't, I charge thee.

Touch and go bum,

Kingsley

[TLS: Bodleian]

TO J.H. McCALLUM – 9 NOVEMBER 1957

53 Glanmor Road, Uplands, Swansea, Glam, Great Britain.

Dear John – I think we're well enough acquainted now to drop this "Mr." stuff.

Many many thanks for all your efforts on my behalf. Yes, indeed,

7. For the PEN anthology *New Poems 1958*.
8. The Librarian at Swansea was Olive M. Busby, MA (London).

certainly, surely I will hold off Santa Barbara, for the next decade if need be. I would adore to go to Princeton,[1] which as you know is very highly thought of over here – a friend of mine at the College in Swansea had a year there, 1948 I think, and is most enthusiastic about it. And Blackmur[2] of course is a great hero of everybody's. I and all my family are in a state of tremendous premature excitement, telling each other to keep our fingers crossed. I can sum it up by saying yes, we are interested. And you can quote me.

With renewed thanks and all good wishes.

Yours ever,
Kingsley

[ALS: Harcourt]

TO ANTHONY POWELL – 10 NOVEMBER 1957

53 Glanmor Road, Uplands, Swansea, Glam.

Dear Tony,

I'd have loved to have dinner with you on the 25th, but unfortunately am already promised forth. I don't have to turn up, though, till about 7.45, so I'm sure we can work in a couple of swift drinks after the

---

1. Who first came up with the idea of inviting Amis to Princeton to deliver the Christian Gauss Seminars in Criticism in the spring of 1959, and to teach Creative Writing for the academic year 1958–59, is unclear, but McCallum was certainly involved. It was his idea to forward a copy of this letter to Blackmur (see note 2): 'for I feel in this instance you are your own best salesman' (letter to Amis, 13 November 1957, in Harcourt Brace). The Gauss Seminars were established at Princeton in 1949 in memory of Christian Gauss, who had been chairman of the Department of Modern Languages and Dean of the College. *The University Handbook*, Vol. 23, No. 5, describes the seminars as consisting of 'a series of lectures ordinarily given at weekly intervals, each followed by an informal but often challenging discussion. Attendance at the lectures is by invitation, and the audience is drawn from the Princeton faculty, the Institute for Advanced Study, the Princeton-Rutgers community, and the wider community of New York and Philadelphia . . . There are ordinarily three such seminars each year' (p. 121). The seminars for 1958 were delivered by W.H. Auden, A. Alvarez and Dwight Macdonald; Clement Greenberg's seminars took place in December 1958 and January 1959; Amis, Rosamond Tuve and George Steiner delivered lectures for 1959.

2. R.P. Blackmur (1904–65), American poet and critic, Professor of English at Princeton University (1948–65) and Director of the Gauss Seminars.

recording.[1] And wouldn't a couple of the same be rather nice beforehand? Doesn't El Vino's open at 5? I'll meet you there and then, if you like, or pick you up at *Punch* about 4.50. How would that be?

Before that I'll send you a tentative list of questions I propose to ask you, which you must alter, subtract from and add to as you see fit. We can always discard them if we find ourselves waxing eloquent, but personally I like going along to these do's fully prepared. How about you?

A very stimulating postcard, that last one of yours.

Love to Violet. Love from Hilly.

Yours,
Kingsley

[ALS: Recipient]

TO ANTHONY DERVILLE – 16 NOVEMBER 1957

53 Glanmor Road, Swansea, Glam.

Dear Mr. Derville,

I'm awfully sorry – in a way I should love to do it,[1] but live microphones terrify me and I have sworn off them for the next quarter of a century.

Yours sincerely,
Kingsley Amis

[ALS: BBC]

---

1. Of an interview about Powell's book *At Lady Molly's* (1957), the fourth novel in the sequence *A Dance to the Music of Time*. This interview was broadcast in the series *World of Books* on the Third Programme, 14 December 1957.

---

1. Amis had been invited to appear as Guest of the Week on the popular afternoon show *Woman's Hour*, broadcast Monday to Friday on the Light Programme. He was asked to talk for seven minutes about a subject of mutual interest to himself and at least some of the programme's three million listeners. Anthony Derville (b. 1912), radio producer, BBC Talks and Current Affairs; joined BBC radio in 1942, retired 1979.

TO ANTHONY POWELL – 21 NOVEMBER 1957

53 Glanmor Road, Uplands, Swansea, Glam.

Dear Tony,

After long agonies of cogitation I've finally devised some questions to ask you on Monday.[1] Please pardon the banality and/or impertinence they seem to me to embody, and do remember you're to veto any, substitute any you like etc.

I take your theme to be the conflict between those moved by the will and those moved by feeling. Am I right?

Would you describe yourself as a satirist? If so, what do you think satire is, should do etc.?

You evidently consider family influence and upbringing to be vitally important in forming the character. Could you amplify this view?

Would you agree with the critic who said you were writing "about a world that is largely obsolescent"?

To what extent are you describing your own acquaintances in *The Music of Time*? (This is a horror, but I'm sure the Network Three audience will love it.)

Your design involves dozens of characters all on the move, changing their relationships, disappearing and reappearing and so on. Isn't this very difficult to plan?

May we have a preview of how *The Music of Time* is likely to carry on – e.g. up to what date?

They look even worse now I've typed them out, but we are dealing with a John o' London's[2] kind of stuff and the only point of the rigmarole is to give you a chance to say what you like.

Will that pub you mention be open at 5? I suppose it will. Anyway, I'll give you a ring at *Punch* on Monday afternoon and we can finalise everything then.

---

1. See Amis to Powell, 10 November 1957, note 1.

2. *John o'London's Weekly*, a literary review 'of the Jack-Squire-Jack-Priestley persuasion' (*Memoirs*, p. 21), it lasted into the 1960s.

All the best. I'm sure we shall have some spanking fun.

Yours,
Kingsley

[TLS: Recipient]

TO VICTOR GOLLANCZ – 19 DECEMBER 1957

53 Glanmor Road, Uplands, Swansea, Glam.

My dear Victor,

You are a perfect louse to have put off publication till 13th January,[1] and at one time I was absolutely enraged with you. I finished that damned thing against time, forgoing the revision I should have liked to give it, and feeling much under the weather as the result of my accident.[2] I've no doubt you have the best of reasons, and I know the author is the last man to be consulted on these occasions, but I don't see why he should be the last to be bloody well *told*. Oh curse you! A lesser man than I would have been on the blower to Collins within the hour. But not I. You are the most annoying old sod and I shall see that Graham Watson *Bleeds you white* over the next book.

On the King-Hall thing,[3] I am very anti (nothing to do with the heat engendered in the preceding para.). I think it a most dangerous book. The Russians wouldn't behave as he thinks: they would take what loot they wanted, set up their bases and leave the population to rot. And they would simply suppress the B.B.C. and the Press, not to mention shooting half a million chaps out of hand. What price ridiculing them on the music-halls *then*?

With renewed maledictions, threats, abuse, groans and affection,

Yours ever,
Kingsley

[ALS: Gollancz]

---

1. That is, publication of *I Like it Here* (see Amis to Larkin, 9 November 1957).
2. In the summer; mentioned briefly in Amis to Larkin, 16 July 1957.
3. Stephen King-Hall, *Defence in the Nuclear Age* (1958), a critique of military defence and nuclear weapons, advocating 'non-violent resistance'.

TO WILLIAM VAN O'CONNOR – 6 JANUARY 1958

53 Glanmor Road, Uplands, Swansea, Glam., Great Britain

Dear Mr. O'Connor,[1]

Many thanks for your pleasant letter: I can assure you that you aren't being an intruder at all and that I'm only flattered by your interest. Of course I will give you what information I can. Do forgive me if I say some things you know already.

Dixon is supposed to be the son of a clerk, an office worker (like myself). He is a Labour Party socialist and probably took part in student politics when younger (like myself). One is meant to feel that he did well enough in his student academic career to make it natural for him to become a history lecturer, which he did without much thought. Though he finds the academic world decreasingly to his taste, he sticks at it because he does think university teaching an important job, and also because he is afraid of venturing out on his own. I think he is a plausible figure in his world: there are certainly many like him in that they are the first generation in their families to have received a university education, they have won their way up by scholarships all through, they are not the conventional Oxford-Cambridge academic type, they don't embrace the manners, customs and pastimes of that type (sherry, learned discussion, tea-parties with the Principal's wife, chamber concerts) but stick to their own, to the ones their non-academic contemporaries share (beer, arguments in pubs, amorous behaviour at – and outside – dances, jazz). Dixon has seen, throughout his life, power and position going to people who (he suspects) are less notable for their ability than their smooth manners, their accents, the influence they or their fathers can wield. The money thing is less important; Dixon is hard-up himself, and is a bit suspicious of the rich, but is far more so of Oxford-accented "culture". If he were closely questioned about this, he would probably admit in the end that culture is real and important and ought not to be made the property of a sort of exclusive club which you can only

1. William Van O'Connor (1915–66), American critic and academic; taught at the University of Minnesota (1946–61); Professor of English, University of California, Davis (1961–66); wrote on twentieth-century English and American literature.

enter if you come from the right school – culture ought to be available to everyone who can use it; but such an avowal would be very untypical of him and you would probably have to get him very drunk first.

As far as my own biography goes, it's probably better for me to say something here rather than for you to wring a couple of dozen reluctant and uninformative words out of my publisher. I was born in 1922, grew up in what I usually describe as a modest but comfortable lower-middle-class home in the London suburbs. Not many books in the house. Attended large London day school and got a scholarship there (I'm not the "beneficiary of Welfare State education" that one or two writers seem to think I am; I was born too soon). It was an excellent school, not just for the teaching but for the big cross-section you got of the social strata. One of my friends was a Jew from the poor quarter of London's East End; another was the son of a prominent Church dignitary. But you just didn't know what most boys' fathers were: your status depended on your amiability. (This may not seem unusual to an American, but it is, I imagine – certainly it was then – by no means the rule here.) The college I attended at Oxford (St. John's: on scholarship) was also good in this way: there were public schoolboys and scholars like myself. In the University at large there was, of course, a good deal of the exclusive spirit still operating – it still goes on today, I suppose, though I don't know contemporary Oxford at all well. The Army was the next stage – 1942–1945. I got to be an officer on the class system – I was on the winning side now, because "an Oxford man" was likely to be enough of a "gentleman" to do all right as an officer. (I should explain that though the British Army's commissioning system is – or was – socially biassed, I have nothing against the products of that system. The conventional British officer of the older type may have been a snob and a moron, but – except in the highest ranks – he was able, conscientious and brave.) Served in the Royal Corps of Signals: Normandy in June (late June, thank God) 1944. After service in France, Belgium, Holland, W. Germany was demobilised in October 1945 – if I hadn't been a scholarship-holder it would have been 1946, which shows what education can do for you. 1945–49 back at Oxford: worked, got a First, tried a research degree (failed), wrote some verse and a novel (none any good), got married, got a job in Swansea October 1949, have held it ever since. I like it very much and intend to stay. Visit London every 6 weeks or so; delighted to go, delighted to return. Interests include television, films, jazz (moving a little away from Dixieland

and towards cool), science fiction, the Welsh . . . You can see that though I've had to do some work, I haven't had to fight or struggle hard. It irritates me a little when people suggest I'm somehow at odds with society. Society has been very good to me. That doesn't mean, of course, that some aspects of it don't deserve criticism. But individuals are much, are incomparably, more interesting to me than "society". There is always something especially important about a man's upbringing and history, but so there is about his sex-life, his attitude to drink, the way he treats his children. I don't really like being thought of as a "social" novelist. I have ideas about society, naturally, but human behaviour is what I see myself as writing about . . . Oh yes: "programs followed": I did classics at school until aged 16, then began to specialise in English. Only English at University. Glad I did classics, but wish I'd done more French (and had attended to what French instruction I did get).

That does it, I think. If you've any more questions, don't hesi[t]ate to shoot them over to me. I hope your article[2] goes well. And the best of good wishes for 1958.

Yours sincerely,
Kingsley Amis

[TLS: Syracuse]

TO WILLIAM VAN O'CONNOR – 21 JANUARY 1958

53 Glanmor Road, Uplands, Swansea, Glam., Great Britain.

Dear Mr. O'Connor,

It was very pleasant to hear from you again, and I have no objection at all to aiding the growth of your manuscript, whether in mere bulk or also wisdom-wise.

As regards the other poets in the Conquest and Enright collections: on the personal level, I am pretty friendly, and have been for years, with Larkin, Wain and Conquest himself. Philip Larkin in fact I regard

2. The article in question became 'Kingsley Amis: That Uncertain Feeling', Chapter 5 of O'Connor's *The New University Wits and the End of Modernism* (Carbondale: Southern Illinois University Press, 1963), pp. 75–102; O'Connor published a subsequent article on *That Uncertain Feeling*, entitled 'Parody as Criticism', in *College English* 25 (1964), pp. 241–8.

as my best friend: I first met him when we were both at St. John's, Oxford in 1941. I have talked about writing more with him than with anyone else, and we share many attitudes about it, though not the complete set thereof (e.g. he is very pro-D.H. Lawrence, I very anti–.) Though we do agree a lot I don't think we're very alike[1]: for one thing, he has an emotional impact in his best poems that I can only envy. As regards the other contributors – I knew Liz Jennings quite well at one time, before she[2] had really got started on being a poet. I haven't seen her for about 9 years. Enright I had never met at the time of the anthologies, but have seen him a couple of times since in London; likewise Gunn. Holloway and Davie I met once on an English teachers' conference 3 or 4 years ago.[3] I think that takes care of the personal side.

On the poetical or critical tie-up: I don't admire all the poets equally, though I think there's something to be said for them all. Larkin is easily the best of us all, I should say. From my point of view, all we really have in common is a desire to write *sensibly*, without emotional hoo-ha; this boils down to saying that we all try to write poems that are intelligible in the sense that they can be paraphrased; there may be obscurities but no answerless riddles. John Wain put it best when he said that my verse wasn't really much like his, but it seemed like it to some people because "they can make a bit of head or tail of both of us" – unlike so many contemporary poets. If extended to cover the whole group, I think that remark would be pretty fair. It doesn't make us a "movement", of course, but we don't want to be and didn't try to be; all the "movement" thing came from critics and reviewers.

How's that? Do write again if I can give any more help.

Very sincere good wishes,
Kingsley Amis

[TLS: Syracuse]

1. Amis has added his own insertion mark in pen here and added 'as writers' in the right margin.

2. Amis has added another insertion mark here in pen and added 'or I' in the right margin.

3. At Bristol, in April 1954; mentioned in Amis to Newby, 15 April 1954.

TO THE EDITOR, *TIMES LITERARY SUPPLEMENT* – 24 JANUARY 1958

Sir, – In the course of an amiably toned, though intermittently incoherent, notice of my novel *I Like It Here*, your reviewer makes a number of statements which are either pointless or disingenuous.[1] Contrasting or comparing my work with that of Mr. John Wain, he says that the latter 'has been the pioneer,' and goes on to note certain alleged parallels between features of Mr. Wain's work and features of my own, observing in dead-pan fashion that in each case Mr. Wain got in first. Without denying Mr. Wain the credit for chronological precedence, may I point out that these alleged parallels are shaky – *i.e.*, to be arrived at only by a process of abstraction – and coincidental?

I first became acquainted with Mr. Wain's *Hurry On Down*, and its 'rescue-by-millionaire theme,' soon after its publication in August, 1953. My own novel *Lucky Jim*, complete with 'rescue-by millionaire theme,' was accepted for publication in April, 1953. Mr. Wain's *Living in the Present*, which 'has trouble with the children,' appeared in July, 1955. My own *That Uncertain Feeling*, which also 'has trouble with the children' (though, I should have thought, of a different kind), appeared in August, 1955. Even granting the pioneering qualities of 'trouble with the children,' precedence here seems largely a matter of the luck of the draw.

It is either pointless or disingenuous to note, as your reviewer does, that '*Living in the Present* also' – *sc.* in anticipation of *I Like It Here*, presumably – 'has its quest plot built into a framework of foreign travel.' He knows that the plots, in Mr. Wain's book and my own, are utterly unlike, even granting, again, the pioneering qualities of 'a quest plot built into a framework of foreign travel.' Your reviewer further observes (throwing up the remark quite *in vacuo*, but apparently intending to suggest another parallel) that Mr. Wain's *Samuel Deronda*[2] 'deals largely with parties and publishers.' Parties are indeed mentioned in *I Like It Here*, and one publisher appears, but this is not to 'deal with' either

---

1. The mildly approving but unenthusiastic review, expressing a hope that Amis would develop as a novelist, appeared under the title 'Taking it Easy', in *TLS*, 17 January 1958, p. 30.

2. For *Samuel Deronda* see Amis to Conquest, 7 September 1955, note 5.

topic 'largely.' I await your reviewer's discovery that, of Messrs. A.J. Cronin and Graham Greene, the former is the pioneer since there is a priest in *The Keys of the Kingdom* and another priest in *The Power and the Glory*.

Finally, why does your reviewer think it relevant to mention that *Samuel Deronda* was 'serially published in the *Spectator*, as *I Like it Here* in *Punch*'? (That 'as' is marvellous.) If this is pioneering, it is of an unsensational kind.[3]

KINGSLEY AMIS

TO JOHN DAVENPORT – 24 JANUARY 1958

53 Glanmor Road, Uplands, Swansea, Glam.

Dear Uncle John,

How nice to hear from you. Yes, those critics have certainly shown themselves less than fanatically keen about *ILIH*. Well, it had to come, is what I keep saying to myself. I don't feel depressed so much as faintly foolish – "like falling down outside a pub" as Elizabeth Taylor (not Mrs. Michael Todd I don't mean)[1] put it to me. Anyway, the next one will knock them cold: I'm all set to step into the second rank behind C.P. Snow and Priestley as a serious chronicler of our society.

And yes, it would be good to meet. How often do you get to London? I myself am trying to keep it down to about 6 visits this year, having spent about two-fifths of last year going to London, drinking in London and coming back from London. I shall be up, though, between 1st and 4th Feb., so if you're going to be accessible during that time, drop me a line saying where and when I can ring you up there.

3. The anonymous reviewer replied on 31 January 1958, p. 61: 'Since it has wrung a cry of pain from Mr Amis, my tracing of parallels between his work and Mr Wain's can hardly be called "pointless". As to disingenuousness, I cannot hope to compete with a man who pretends that it would be just as sensible to look for parallels between any two writers whatsoever as it is to find them between two who for years have regularly been named together . . . But why so curmudgeonly? Not much weight is attached to these parallels; they are indeed fairly tenuous. But I was not at all trying to show that Mr Amis is just an old copy-cat. I was concerned to do Mr Wain credit, not Mr Amis discredit.'

1. That is, Elizabeth Taylor the novelist.

Life continues. At the moment I'm bogged down in writing 4 scripts for a BBC series on jazz, but that done, and the various people who want me to talk in South Shields and Budleigh Salterton reduced to silence, I shall be all agog to toe the fictional line again. Then a swift £25 handout to Philip Toynbee[2] and I shall be restored.

Hope very much to see you.

With nephewly affection,
Kingsley

[ALS: National Library of Wales]

TO JOHN WAIN – 9 FEBRUARY 1958

53 Glanmor Road, Uplands, Swansea, Glam.

Dear John,

It was good-oh to get your screed. Hope you're having a good time among the snows.[1] Yes, by Christ, the "reaction of the Press" to *ILIH* was something of a cross at the time, but I soon managed to shrug it off, especially as I got good notices in *Queen*, *Tatler* and *Vogue* – aaooh! A bit sinister, that, eh, what, but acceptable none the less.

As for that comic-monologue bastard,[2] it was a bit tricky for me because the chap will obviously be able to recognise himself, and I had to pull my punches a bit on that account. However, my point was *supposed* to be (I don't mean I got it across at all) that the sod thought he was funny, and I thought he was funny, but not in the way he thought he was funny, in fact I thought it was funny largely because he thought he was funny. He was supposed to be likeable but tedious.

Looking forward to your 3rd.[3] Give me the word when you're back

2. Philip Toynbee (1916–81), novelist, critic, journalist, son of the historian Arnold Toynbee (1889–1975); at the time, fiction reviewer on the *Observer*.

---

1. Wain was in Vaud, in Switzerland.
2. Harry Bannion in *I Like it Here*, based on the real-life Ulsterman Harold Tyrrell, whose 'periodical floor-shows' in Portugal are described in Amis to Larkin, 28, 30 July 1955.
3. *The Contenders* (1958).

in London and we'll get a little bit pissed-up together. Don't do any of that nasty dangerous skiing, now.

Cheers from all,
Kingsley

[ALS: Edinburgh]

TO J.H. McCALLUM – 18 FEBRUARY 1958

53 Glanmor Road, Uplands, Swansea, Glam., Great Britain.

Dear John,

I have been meaning for days to answer your various communications, but a more than usually severe bout of journalistic and other deadline-meeting has kept me incommunicado, if that means what I think it means. Now, however, our half-term at college has set me at liberty.

Firstly, I am really delighted by the American I LIKE IT HERE; in all respects it comes up to Harcourt, Brace standard and one needn't say more than that. Please give the jacket-artist my warm congratulations for a bright design that beautifully renders the spirit of the book. Then, the two reviews you kindly sent were most encouraging, especially after the mainly hostile press the book has had over here. I hope your edition fares well.

Now as regards Princeton. I have everything lined up at this end, as far as is possible at the moment. I haven't yet asked officially for leave, but the college authorities know of my intentions and approve (so they should, by God). I have been in touch with the Fulbright people[1] and am all ready to go into action there. The moment I get word that Princeton are formally inviting me I can soon get everything cleared up. You may rest assured that while there's the slightest chance of getting to Princeton I shall take no interest at all in any other offers I may get. Incidentally I do intend bringing a family, quite a sizeable

1. Amis was applying for a Fulbright Travelling Grant to cover transportation costs to America.

one, as I should have said earlier: wife, 3 children and father. I shall quite understand if Princeton can't "up the stipend" on their account, and am prepared to live quietly with occasional orgies financed by my New York publisher. My only worry is that the official go-ahead from Princeton may come so late as to make it difficult to secure sea passages, but I imagine the Fulbright people will be able to give me a hand in that matter. All in all I feel optimistic about the whole idea and more excited than ever.

I can't wait to run you to earth in New York. Very best wishes.

Yours ever,
Kingsley

[TLS: Harcourt]

TO PHILIP LARKIN – 15 MARCH 1958

Swansea

My dear Philip,

Christ, I have just heard from Bob [Conquest] about the merry little quip he devised at your expense and write at once to commiserate.[1] I can't fully envisage the horror of the thing, but I can imagine some of it, being, like you, exactly the sort of person for that kind of thing not to happen

---

1. For Amis's account of this 'quip' see *Memoirs*, p. 145:

> Always a devotee of girlie mags (we all were, but he led the field), Philip had mentioned to Bob receiving a postal circular about tits and had wondered where the sender had found his name and address. 'I hope I don't get into trouble,' his letter had gone on to say. Bob arranged that he should think he had.
>
> A letter on government paper, as from the Vice Squad, Scotland Yard, arrived on the Hull breakfast table, the heading, 'Regina v. Art Studies Ltd.' Proceedings were being taken in the matter of the above, said the writer, Under the Obscene Publications Act 1921, also Regina v. Abse (1959) and Regina v. Logue (1962). No decision had been taken as to whether to prosecute Larkin as well, but his attendance as a witness might be required. All for now.
>
> The distinguished poet fled to his solicitor's office and stayed there all day. Nothing more happened, except that he sent Bob his £10 bill for taking up the man's time. Bob paid up, of course.

to. I do very much sympathise. What a day for you. From what he told me I suppose you must have had about seven hours of it before learning the truth. The *bloody fool.* And in his letter to me he seems to think it a bit farcical on your part not to have smelt a rat straightaway. God, if it had happened to me I should have been suicidal. I do hope you put things right with the solicitor; that's a nasty one. When I see you I'll buy you a bottle of champagne as a slight consolation. Fuck it all.

Should like to be able to devise some cracks, humorous accounts of true-life sexual experiences, etc., to cheer you, but I don't know that I can manage any of that. Recently managed to get to the end of Maſter *Wayne*'s latest effort.[2] Far, far better than his previous ones, I thought, but still sodding terrible and horrible and frightful, what? Doesn't he ever look at anyone or listen to how they talk? Or reflect on how life is actually led? Or devise a story out of something he's seen happen instead of plotting it on a graph? Still, I feel sorry for a man who can console himself in that sort of way for not being able to fuck the women by telling himself they aren't worth fucking (Myra) or alternatively he'd be miserable if he could (Stocker).[3] And it's progress of a kind to have moved from the Orwell of *Keep the Aspidistra Flying* to the Orwell of *Coming Up For Air.*[4] Perhaps I shouldn't say all this to the dedicatee of the volume, but I don't suppose you'll mind it.

Old crippen was here the other week-end, in very good form. The 4 of us, including my pa, played scrabble and Crip got the worst score every time. He took it very well. On the Saturday he took us in his Jaguar (which has 3 "cigar-lighters" protruding from various parts of the interior coachwork) to see Petrol Dam[5] and his wife and little baby. P. is greying, balding, but still has the scuptural profile and the unreserved laugh. Bruce and I did some work on our musical,[6] which it now seems I shall have to try to write. Feel nervous about this, as if I'd contracted to write pornography for a posh, limited-edition, aristocrats' press. B. and P. played some piano duets which sounded like a sort of classical bop.

On Hilly's insistence I am growing my hair very long and so have

2. *The Contenders.*

3. *The Contenders* concerns the rivalry of Robert Lamb, an artist, and Ned Roper, an industrialist. Stocker is a friend of theirs who is always chasing girls. Myra is a model Robert falls for, marries, and is then left by (for Ned).

4. The dates of these novels are 1936 and 1939.

5. Peter Oldham.

6. No record of this project survives.

to use setting-lotion on it, so that it resembles a curious helmet. I am also dieting. Sod that; ay, ſod it *Lyke Madde.*

Should welcome a brief statement on the general aim of your bum,

K.

[TLS: Bodleian]

TO ROY P. BASLER – 5 MAY 1958

53 Glanmor Road, Uplands, Swansea, Glamorgan, Great Britain.

Dear Mr. Basler,

Many thanks for your letter. It came while I was still wondering rather ineffectually what to do about Mr. Jarrell's letter, which was waiting for me when I returned from a tour in Denmark.[1] I am a poor

---

1. Randall Jarrell (1914–65), American poet, critic and novelist, was consultant in poetry at the Library of Congress in Washington DC (1956–58). He had invited Amis to give a reading at the library, an invitation seconded by a letter from the Director of its Poetry Office, the educator, historian, editor and writer, Roy P. Basler (1906–89), who worked in various executive positions in the library from 1952–75, among them Associate Director, Reference Department (1954–58) and Director, Reference Department (1958–68). This invitation originated with R.P. Blackmur, who was in charge of Amis's stay at Princeton, had attended a meeting of Honorary Fellows of the Library of Congress in April, and was in correspondence with both Basler and Jarrell. Blackmur, worried that Amis would find it difficult to meet his expenses at Princeton, had written to a dozen academic friends, including Cleanth Brooks at Yale, Elizabeth Drew at Smith, Irving Howe at Brandeis, Gordon Ray at the University of Illinois at Urbana, and Samuel Hynes at Swarthmore, about inviting Amis to deliver paid lectures or readings.

Amis, meanwhile, had been on a lecture tour in Denmark, described for Larkin in a letter of 1 May 1958 (in Bodleian): 'It was all right in Denmark, actually; though everyone was a bit culture-hungry . . . [T]hey are well, rather scaringly well, clued up; none of the Latin stuff about "Excuse pliss, vot you vould sigh off your great Edge-Crown?" – far more "Thank you for your talk Mr Amis though it did occur to me if you don't mind my raising the point at a gathering like this have another beer I wondered that you made no reference to Angus Wilson it seems to me that in a story like 'Mother's Sense of Fun' much better by the way than" sort of stuff.' (For 'Edge-Crown', or A.J. Cronin, see the question period after Garnet Bowen's lecture in *I Like it Here*, p. 44: '"We have been surprised that we have not been hearing of your Edge-Crown." "Oh really?" He searched his brain frantically. Grim-Grin he had been ready for, together with Ifflen-Voff, Zumzit-Mum and Shem-Shoice. This was new . . . "Sickies of Sickingdom," the woman explained irritably . . . After a brief

correspondent (as R.P. Blackmur will I am afraid be able to confirm) and I am so sorry not to have taken up Mr. Jarrell's suggestion earlier. Do please apologise to him on my behalf.

Yes, of course, I should be delighted to accept your most attractive proposal, and in the hope that it will not conflict with my Princeton commitments I should like to fix on October 13th for my reading. I feel a little horrified about accepting so much money for doing so little, so please instruct me on just what you want from me: duration of whole performance, proportion of commentary to reading, and any other suggestion you may wish to make. I do want to be able to provide exactly what is required, as far as I am able.

To anticipate a possible query of yours: my father's sister lives in Washington, so there will be no trouble about accommodation. I look forward very much to my visit and to meeting you and Mr. Jarrell.

Yours sincerely,
Kingsley Amis

[TLS: Library of Congress]

TO PHILIP LARKIN – 24 MAY 1958

Swansea

My dear Philip,

Have just been going through some stuff and found one of your letters – November last, about the AWA encounter in Lambeg:[1] is that right? Looks a bit implausible. It all read like a condensed version of some marvellous novel of serious uproarious contemptuous compassion: "Once again I remembered the doll-faced cutely-bobbed beauties of the 'twenties. . . . remembering that he loved classical music I carefully excluded friendliness from my voice and manner." etc. Powerful stuff. It all made me want to see you so much that, forgetting whose turn it is to write ("Forgetting? Forgetting?"), I sat down to draft a screed as the next best thing to seeing you – next after seeing Mrs. Arthur Miller and Mrs.

explanatory uproar he was enabled to wonder aloud what had led his questioner to detect a resemblance between *The Power and the Glory* and *The Keys of the Kingdom*.'

1. This letter does not survive; Lambeg is in Northern Ireland, near Belfast.

Anthony Steel[2] gigglingly and drunkenly undressing each other, of course, now you see that don't you, I knew you would.

Am feeling a bit browned off, actually. Most of my creative energy for the last ten days has been siphoned off into the completion of the fourteen forms or copies of forms I must fill up or arrange for someone else to fill up in order to obtain a Fulbright Travelling Grant for the purpose of visiting the United States of America this fall ("I'll arrange for you to fall in such a way that a spike travels up your –"). You know the kind of thing. Mr., Mrs. or Miss. Then – Sex. How many female Mr's and male Misses do they get? Good mind to put 'Yes' for Sex. Four copies of a photograph taken during the last year. Medical exam. Urine analysis (albumin; casts; sp. gr.; sugar; cells). Heart. Any organic lesions. Rate, standing. After hopping 25 times. 2 minutes after hopping. This last discomforts me rather. Mm, now just let's check that again, shall we? Mm. Well, old boy, I'm afraid your trip's off. Sorry. Oh no, I wouldn't say off for good. At the same time I'd be misleading you if I let you think I expect you know the kind of little fantasy I mean. In fact the old ticker has been behaving oddly recently, hopping and fluttering as I lie in bed. Oh well. It'll either turn out to be an intermittent contractile irregularity occurring in 40% of sedentary males and of no connexion with any known malfunction, or else a rare systolic disorder of the ventricles with fatal termination except in cases of successful surgery (noticeable improvement in 60% of recovering cases). Just one or the other.[3] Well, whichever it is it'll go into my next book. Lots of the old thanotophobia in that, as I must have told you. Trouble is, I can't get down to the fucker. Want to, but can't. Fulbright has done its best there (christ, I'll pay for myself, I'll write a story instead, sell some books, go down a mine), together with things like marking 70 essays on *Martin Chuzzlewit* SHITSHITSHITSH READING UNPUBLISHED NOVELS FOR FRIENDS SO AS TO GIVE ADVICE &/OR QUOTE PUT A WORD IN UNQUOTE AND ONE OF THE FRIENDS IS WAIT FOR IT FUCKING P O L L I N S[4]

2. Marilyn Monroe and Anita Ekberg (married to the English actor Anthony Steel 1956–62).

3. Amis has added an asterisk at this point and at the bottom of the page written in ink: 'To-day: "Normal for your age" says doc. 33 rousing cheers what.'

4. Amis has added another asterisk and at the bottom of the second page of the letter written in ink: 'Shirty letter from the person named today. I have had "his MS for 9 months" WITHOUT SHOVING IT UP HIS ARSE.' For Pollins, see Amis to Larkin, 15 October 1957, note 14.

oh God I'm mad aren't I what was I thinking of when I agreed to do it stark staring bonkers. Also a bit browned off by the continuous presence of my male relative. Why doesn't he go away for good? Failing that, why can't he go away for a very long time and then go away again almost as soon as he has come back? I can't pass him anything or he says *Danke*. I can't let him pass me anything or he says Excuse fungus. I can't look for anything (an exercise frequently required in this establishment) or he says *Qu'est-ce que tu cherches?* When my friends call (as one or two of them are still continuing to do for the moment) he *talks to them*. When Hilly and Mavis and Mary Morgan were having a girls' chat he *sat with them* for *2 hrs*. He doesn't like old people, you see. He likes young people. You will agreee peee it's a fallacy that old people are interested in the concerns of young people. They don't want to hear what the young say. They want to make the young hear what they say. More of a triumph to bore a young person, who has more alternatives to being so bored than an old person. And old people are prompter to say fuck off than young people. It's all there in *The Legacy*; remember? Mr. Masters?[5] "You need show no interest in what an old person is telling you. All he requires is your presence and your wakefulness." All right, so it's old stuff. But old and true, hey?

Returning, later, to the charge. We went and stayed with old Tony Powell again the other wickened: jolly good fun and hardly aristocratic at all, bar a young man called Lord Weymouth[6] who shows that the recruitment of David Cecils is still being maintained, even in these difficult days, and has three rooms in a gigantic house hung with his easel pictures and festooned with his tape-recordings and littered with his unpublished novel (he's got MORE MONEY THAN IS GOOD FOR HIM, you see), the gigantic house being on view to the public the while. We had lunch with L.P. Hartley,[7] an amiable old boy with no concavity between his chin and his Adam's apple and about a dozen gigantic freckles on his bald brow. Conversation flagged, LPH having unknown to us at the time been shot hard up the arse by Toynbee in the *Obs*, that very morning. Wines were served alternately, white, then

5. A fellow lodger in the boarding house 'Kingsley Amis' moves to after quarrelling with his brother Sidney.

6. Alexander George Thynne (b. 1932), 7th Marquess of Bath (since 1992); previously Viscount Weymouth. His home, Longleat House, in Wiltshire, continues to be open to the public.

7. L.P. Hartley (1895–1972), novelist and short-story writer, best known for *The Go-Between* (1953).

red, then white &c. heedless of what was being eaten. A butler who looked like a male nurse in a mental hospital. Sherry out of a funny square pot like a biscuit-barrel. Talk with LPH's lesbian (55-yr-old) sister of Shaw, the Gower coast, Scottish deerhounds, of which latter two were produced in the flesh, huge bowed-backboned creatures with coats like the hair of ageing negroes. One of them stuck its snout straight into Lady Violet's mouth. Then off for a snifter at the Bath pump-room, which gave Hilly the shits but cheered me up no end.

Liked your pwem in HIST. Recent? Chance of LTAFAG?[8] Do write.

Letter of appointment from host institution to be clipped to your bum.

Kingsley

[TLS: Bodleian]

TO PAUL FERRIS – 5 JUNE 1958

53 Glanmor Road, Uplands, Swansea, Glam.

Dear Paul,

For some reason I didn't get around to *A Changed Man* until the other day, but now I feel I must write to say how sodding funny and good I thought it was.[1] A book to re-read, too. Bonzer, – sport. Many congratulations.

Yours,
Kingsley

[ALS: Recipient]

8. The poem Larkin published in *Listen* 2:4 (Spring 1958), p. 2, was 'The Importance of Elsewhere', reprinted in *The Whitsun Weddings* and *LCP*, p. 104; 'LTAFAG' is 'Letter to a Friend about Girls'.

1. Paul Ferris (b. 1929), author, novelist and journalist. Among his many books is a biography of Dylan Thomas (1977) and an edition of Thomas's *Collected Letters* (1986), for which see Amis to Larkin, 14 October 1985, note 7. *A Changed Man* was published in 1958. Ferris comments: 'I had left Swansea by that time. The book was my first novel. I didn't draw his attention to it, and it was hugely encouraging to have a note like that' (personal communication, 4 November 1996).

TO HILARY RUBINSTEIN – 8 JUNE 1958

53 Glanmor Road, Uplands, Swansea, Glam.

Dear Hilary,

Thanks a lot for your various screeds. I'm afraid the land of Nippon is out, for a visit from me: ship would take too long, and I'm not going to get into one of these aeroplane things until they're a lot safer than they are at present. Poland, however, is another matter, and a trip there to spend my zlotys might be fun in a year or two. I'll let you know if it transpires.

Remember me to Professor Fukuda.[1]

Yours ever,
Kingsley

[ALS: Gollancz]

TO C.P. SNOW – 8 JUNE 1958

53 Glanmor Road, Uplands, Swansea, Glam.

Dear Charles,

How nice to hear from you. And it would be nice to see you and Pamela [Hansford Johnson] in Swansea – I could be your cicerone among the teeming night-life. But unfortunately I *shall* be in the States by September. So it'll have to wait until another time. (Gastronomic note for 30th September: The Bush puts on the least offensive meal.)

1. Professor Rikutaro Fukuda of Tokyo was translating *Lucky Jim*; the invitation to visit came from Amis's Japanese publishers.

You'll have to tell your Ohioian that he hasn't been keeping up with my jazz articles. All modernist I am now.[1]

Love to Pamela,

Yours,
Kingsley

[ALS: HRHRC]

TO VIOLET AND ANTHONY POWELL – 29 JULY 1958

53 Glanmor Road, Uplands, Swansea, Glam.

My dear Violet and Tony,

I'm sorry I hung on to Mrs. Weidenfeld's work[1] for so long; I still haven't read it, but each fresh wave of publicity about her kept making me vow to close with the thing without actually driving me to it.

I'm still hoping to drag the pair of you over here for a week-end before we sail, but the chances of getting my father out of the way (a provision that really gives *sine qua non* its full meaning) don't look too rosy at the moment. However, something, if only another El Vino's convention, will have to be arranged. I want to tell you all about my not getting a Fulbright award,[2] and not getting a passage, and not getting the Cultural Attache at the U.S. Embassy to intervene, and then finally getting a passage with various Amises distributed in far-flung corners in different holds on the Q. Eliz. A wan smile briefly lit my features on

---

1. Amis seems at this period to have gone through a brief flirtation with modern jazz. In a letter to Larkin (1 May 1958, in Bodleian), speaking of George Hartley, he notes 'what you say about his 12" Miles Davis LP thing; was beginning to like him (MD) but must plainly slack off him now'.

---

1. Barbara Skelton (see Amis to Larkin, 12 July 1956, note 1) divorced Cyril Connolly in 1954 and married the publisher George Weidenfeld in 1956 (this marriage was dissolved in 1961). Amis had probably borrowed the novel *A Young Girl's Touch* (1956).

2. Amis seems to have been turned down and then, at the last minute, granted an award. On 14 August 1958 Blackmur wrote to him at Swansea to say he was 'delighted your Fulbright-assisted miracles have got you all aboard the Queen Elizabeth' (Princeton). What happened is unclear, and Fulbright retains no files on pre-1964 award recipients.

finding that my father is sharing a cabin with three strangers. We sail on 4th September; I'll let you know as soon as anything presents itself. [. . .]

Other anecdotes will have to keep. There's a good deal of passport bum and solicitor bum and vaccination bum and Cunard bum keeping me occupied at the moment. Ah, unhappy lot of the artist.

Love from us all,
Kingsley

[TLS: Recipient]

TO PHILIP LARKIN – 30 JULY 1958

Swansea

My dear Philip,

Can't seem to lay the old claw on your last, dr fr dear man, which *isn't to say* (how can it be to say?) that I didn't enjoy getting the sod. Actually a moment's research at the old seat of custom (not the seat of the lavatory, you know) between this sentence and the last has just laid it bare. If I seem pissed, this is seeming merely: I have taken a Preludin tablet, excellent things which I call, or recall, to your attention: you feel full of confidence and amiability and plans for the next decade, which I suppose is rather like being pissed, now I come to thinka stinka think about it. On the whole things are mixed here: I feel all right at the time of writing, as I say, but my marriage seems more or less on the old crags again. Nothing specific this time: she hates old Henry F. all right, but she doesn't want me to make with the old prok swrod very much. In fact I don't want to either, much, and have been thinking that this has been due to too much thinking about other young ladies, & plaieing wTH mine VVyre ye whyle, but now-a-days (yes, get fucked, that's right) I incline to think it's pratly, but only pratly, but still pratly, because I feel with part of the old think-box that when I do emerge all erect, or half erect as it tends to be, then this phaenomenon wil not be greated wth ye Enthousiasm yt myght be thought to Deserue. Pity about that. And all my fault if you trace it back far enough. But that thought doesn't help overmuch. Sorry to take up your time. It doesn't depress me most of the time as much as you might think. I have other concerns.

Filling in my ARSEHOLING forms for those BLAZING CRAPS at the Fulbright Foundation, for example, and then beng told they can't see their way to giving me a travel grant, nor can they reserve me travelling space as they seemed to undertake. All taken care of now. But sodding hell at the time. Garnet Bowen shd, I reckon, have been sent to U.S.A., not the republic of Protugal. My father has made himself very useful with suggestions, as you might guess. The only redeeming feature is that *Song of the Wanderer*,[1] without necessarily being at all good, is pleasing me and interesting me greatly as I write. It looks like being about as long as *War and Peace* at the moment. I hope you'll like it. I think I have devised a character who can say more of what I think than any previous. Time will show.

Just back from a few days in London, where I saw sundry of the noted. Funny double-take at the Spec party; looking over my shoulder, man says "Oh, here's John Wain." Self: "AaaaAAA*GHGH*." Man: "Sorry, I mean John Braine." Self: "Aaaa*AAGHGH*." Met Ginger Man Donleavy,[2] who despite drinking 2/3 bot. of sherry in 20 mins. was quiet and humble, rather nice in fact. Have a funny NON-SEXUAL you bastard thing to tell you about Philip Toynbee. Did I tell you that Lady Violet Powell told me that "Ivy Compton-Burnett's two younger sisters took an overdose of chloral in each other's arms when they grew up enough to find out that the world frowned on what they had always done"? I didn't? Well, I should have. I remember it more or less word for word, oddly enough. Bob Conquest was in evidence, telling me you had been around and also bits of his forthcoming two novels. One of them, the Egyptology one, sounds as if it would be quite good if someone other than Bob were doing it.[3] He recited on request, for the first and only time since I first met him in 1953 was it, his sequel to *Eskimo Nell*. Sounded as good as before. The only line I can remember was 'So when

1. Eventually to become *Take a Girl Like You.*

2. John Braine (1922–86), novelist, best known for his first novel, *Room at the Top* (1957); J.P. Donleavy (b. 1926), American-born novelist, long resident in Ireland (became an Irish citizen in 1967), best known for the novel *The Ginger Man* (1955).

3. This novel eventually became *The Egyptologists* (1965), published under both Amis's and Conquest's names. Conquest's rough draft contained the basic story, which Amis worked on in the summer and autumn of 1964: 'as Amis remembers it, he invented new scenes and characters and generally "put in the plot"' (Jacobs, *Biography*, p. 267). See Amis to Conquest, 8 January 1958 (Appendix I).

I've drunk my gin and spunk a tale I will unfold' or something. Get him to tell it to you, if you haven't already.

What are your movements during the month of August? I am thinking that if I can't inveigle you down here I shall have to go elsewhere to see you. It would have to be before say August 25th. Are you coming to London? Failing that, but only if that really does fail, I will make the journey to Hull. I do very much want to see you before I go to the States, if possible. Screed me about the chances, there's a boy. [. . .]

Must return to grave affairs in a moment. I feel rather panicky about the Yank trip, afraid of taxi-drivers whose father and two brothers were shot by the British in 1916 was it and so on. Much afraid of not being able to teach Creadive Wriding properly, or indeed at all. Not at all afraid of liking it so much over there I feel I must stay. Much more afraid of hating it so much over there I feel I must come back by about Bonfire Night.[4] More afraid still of finding I haven't got any money. Must soon send a £75 cheque to the Cunard Steam-Ship (*sic*) Lines. That's just the deposit, you see. I needn't send the balance – some £245 – shit in it until the middle of August. That's about the time I shall have to send the College £61 odd to keep my superannuation going. And I imagine the man who's renting us the house in Princeton will soon want an advance on the $250 a month we're paying him. High cost of living over there, I hear. Did you know Princeton was an all-male university? No, I only found out the other day. Just a swell, if you ask me.

Well, chum, let me know about chances of meeting. Yes, old LPH [Hartley] is a load, isn't he? Never gets anywhere near starting to get around to giving the impression that he might be capable of writing anything you might want to read, does he? Look after yourself.

Applicants for non-quota visas must produce four copies of their bum.

Kingsley

[TLS: Bodleian]

4. 5 November.

TO PHILIP LARKIN – 15 AUGUST 1958

Swansea

My dear Philip,

Jolly good. Hilly and I (now on superlative terms, thank Christ) arrive c. 6.0 on Monday. If you met us then at Paddington, we could all instantly go and have a drink at the bar in the station. Soon after that, but not soon enough for you to evade your round, should you be so minded, we (my wife and myself) will have to depart for the Nicholsons', where we're staying. You should come too, for as you know they're great fans of yours. The evening will then probably solve itself, and the next day will be our own: Geoff's working, and Mavis is looking after her nipper. [. . .]

I know about those digger books:[1] they offered them to me first. Ho ho ho. (No malice here, but it's exactly the sort of thing you'd tell me, what?) Mind you give 'em a good patsing. Good old Pasty:[2] the most uninterestingly unstable character I have met.

Baggage insurance bum,
Kingsley

[ALS: Bodleian]

TO ANTHONY POWELL – 15 AUGUST 1958

53 Glanmor Road, Uplands, Swansea, Glam.

My dear Tony,

Alas, it looks as if my father (have I ever told you what I feel about him?) is going to be firmly anchored here until we sail, so my scheme to get you here for the week-end collapses. But Hilly and I are escaping to London for a couple of days next week, and wonder if you could have lunch with us on Tuesday. If Violet is making a shopping foray

1. 'Look, no kangaroos', Larkin's review of *Act One* (1958) by Randolph Stow and *Antipodes in Shoes* (1958) by Geoffrey Dutton appeared in *Australian Letters* 2:1 (June 1959), pp. 31–3.

2. Patsy Strang Murphy.

or anything and is available, so very much the better. I also plan to introduce a fifth component, my old friend Philip Larkin, who's a great fan of yours.

Don't bother to answer this unless you feel ineluctably compelled: I'll ring you at Punch on Tuesday morning to learn the score and arrange things. If you can't manage lunch then some other means of capturing you will be devised.

Love to you both,
Kingsley

[ALS: Recipient]

TO ROY P. BASLER – 25 SEPTEMBER 1958

271 Edgerstoune Road, Princeton, N. J.[1]

Dear Dr. Basler,

Here are my selections for the reading on 15th October.[2] I mean to get them off to you yesterday, but found when it came to it that the task of selection was far more difficult than I had expected, there being much to bear in mind regarding completeness, contrast etc. Anyway, here are my suggestions:

Verse: 'Masters' (2 mins.)
'The Last War' ((3½ mins.)
'The Value of Suffering' (2 mins.)

Novel: 'Breakfast at the Welches', from *Lucky Jim*,
chapter 6 (12 minutes)

---

1. 'First the four, then the full six Amises were soon settled in Edgerstoune Road, a residential bit laid out in the best posh-rural American style, with a great deal in the way of lawn, few flowers, no fences, and a patch of woodland at the back where the deer would sometimes wander, just a few minutes' drive from the centre of town . . . Our own house, no. 235, had been rented to us by the illustrious 'liberal' journalist, Murray Kempton, absent in Europe for the year' (*Memoirs*, p. 194; Amis has the house number wrong: it was 271, not 235, which was the number of Jean and John McAndrew, friends and neighbours on the same street). The rent was expensive ($3,000 for the year), which is in part why Amis was anxious to take on outside readings and lectures while at Princeton.

2. At the Library of Congress; see Amis to Basler, 5 May 1958.

Verse: 'A Bookshop Idyll' (2 mins.)
'The Garden' (2 mins.)
'Autobiographical Fragment' (2 mins.)
'Album-Leaf' (1 min.)

Novel: 'The Dangers of Disguise', from *That Uncertain Feeling*, chapter 10 (12 minutes)

Verse: 'The Triumph of Time' (1½ mins.)
'The Triumph of Life' (1½ mins.)
'On Staying Still' (1 min.)
'Departure' (1 min.)
'Against Romanticism' (3½ mins.)

Novel: 'An Anecdote', from *I Like It Here*, chapter 12 (8 mins.)

Verse: 'A Dream of Fair Women' (3½ mins.)
'A Song of Experience' (2½ mins.)
'Romance' (1 min.)

This timings are necessarily approximate, but pretty accurate, I think. If you would like the programme arranged any other way – all verse, then all prose, for instance – then let it be as you say.

I am sorry we shall not meet in Washington, but perhaps we can remedy this another time. I am greatly looking forward to my visit and wish you the best of good times in England.

Yours sincerely,
Kingsley Amis

[TLS: Library of Congress]

TO ROBERT CONQUEST – 26 OCTOBER 1958

Edgerstoune Road, Princeton, N.J.

Dear Bob,

All very jolly here, settling in fine, with the smell of bourbon and king-size Chesterfields over all: cirrhoris and lung-cancer have moved into an altogether more proximate position relative to me. Everyone talks a lot, too, though nobody ever says fuck or even shit and sex is regarded as a topic like any other, about as basic as horticulture or water-skiing. Never any jokes about it, even from N.Y. businessmen etc. However, casting about for nasty things to say I find very little to hand: the only unpleasant people I've met have been English, by what seems an anglicisation of Shenkin's law (*I Like It Here*, p. 120).[1] This didn't apply to Father D'arcy,[2] whom I ran into in Washington and who talked amiably and at length about a book whose title and author escaped him for the time being.

Creative writing is all right, especially with one Ed Hirsch, who turns in a semi-pornographic story every time.[3] Students amiable, of immense physical stature, keen. That old idiot Dwight Macdonald[4] has been giving a seminar on mass culture, ah stuff that. Round about January I replace him: Blackmur, my superior, wants me to do it on s-f. So I said yes.[5] And this brings you in. If ever Amis did anything to win your support, vouchsafe it now. Honestly, if you can send me any griff, or any names of anything that might contain griff, any good stories

---

1. 'This said that Welshman A encountering Welshman B outside Wales will find that Welshman B is exactly the sort of Welshman that Welshman A left Wales in order to avoid encountering.' The definition occurs on p. 109 of *I Like it Here*, not p. 120, which offers an example of the law.

2. The Rev. Martin Cyril D'Arcy, S.J. (1888–1976), theologian; Master of Campion Hall, Oxford (1932–45), 'an English Jesuit who moved in high circles and was always said to have been the model for Father Rothschild in Evelyn Waugh's *Vile Bodies*' (*Memoirs*, p. 203).

3. For Amis's almost wholly positive account of his experiences with Creative Writing at Princeton, see *Memoirs*, pp. 196–7. Ed Hirsch (b. 1940) eventually became a journalist and screenwriter. In the *Memoirs* Amis calls him 'clever enough to cause me the occasional twinge of uneasiness', while reporting also that in later life he 'managed only, I think, a single soft-porn paperback, of which I remember just one sentence: "She tingled with erogeneity"' (p. 197). A character named Ed Hirsch, a student at Budweiser College (all the colleges are named after beers), appears briefly in *One Fat Englishman* (1963), introduced to the novel's fat anti-hero, Roger Micheldene, as 'our star quarter-back' (p. 83).

4. Dwight Macdonald (1900–82), American author, critic, intellectual; associated with the magazines *Partisan Review* and *Politics*.

5. For the origins of Amis's Gauss Seminars, see *Memoirs*, p. 210: 'old Dwight had clearly done some work on his lectures. So had Clement Greenberg, who followed him on modern art. I could understand that much about what he had to say. The audience too was no less McCarthy-Arendt-ridden than had been feared. I was already preparing myself like mad. My terms of appointment had offered no hint of the kind of subject I should pick except that it should be 'of critical interest' or something such. As the best lifebelt I could devise, I had brought with me my Swansea course on eighteenth-century literary theory.' Blackmur's suggestion that he speak on science fiction instead struck an immediate chord: 'It was an unexpected and enterprising choice for 1958, among the first such if not the very first academic notice the stuff had received.'

but especially stuff *about* s-f, let me know, eh? I'm particularly weak on the early days, Verne & all that, also the very early days, that Alexandrian interplanetary romance you or somebody told me about[6] erg. If you imagine yourself addressing a learned (i.e. academic, not learned s-f-wise) audience on this topic I'm sure you'll come up with something. Shall be eternally grateful, man.

Am actually working like what used to be called a nigger. 12 hours teaching a week, you know. A bit thick, with all the revelling to be done as well. There's been a lot of that this last week, for Al Alvarez, plus wife and baby, breezed in from New Mexico on the way home. Have also exchanged greetings with Wain over the phone and hope to see him in the flesh come January or so. New York seems fine. I have to go there once a week to see a film: I have landed a highly lucrative thing with Esquire doing foreign (i.e. British & continental) films for them. Payment works out at about 2/6 a word, so you might tell Gilmour & T. Kilmartin[7] if you see them that if I don't write anything for them it isn't out of laziness or contempt. [. . .][8]

[AL: Recipient]

TO VIOLET AND ANTHONY POWELL – 29 OCTOBER 1958

271 Edgerstoune Road, Princeton, N.J., U.S.A.

My dear Violet and Tony,

Everything seems all right on the whole: Princeton is fine, with crowds of hard-drinking academics who are good in the ways the ones at home are bad – e.g. drinking, availability – but bad in the ways the others are good – these *never* swear (I had to wait for the arrival of another Englishman to do this, except to myself or in the family circle)

6. See *New Maps of Hell* (1960), p. 27: 'Histories of science fiction, as opposed to "imaginative literature", usually begin, not with Plato or *The Birds* of Aristophanes or the *Odyssey*, but with a work of the late Greek prose romancer Lucian of Samosata. The distinction of this, the so-called *True History*, is that it includes the first account of an interplanetary voyage.' For what Amis learned about the *True History* (c. 160 A.D.) and Verne see pp. 27–41.

7. Ian Gilmour (b. 1926), Conservative politician, author and journalist; Bt. (1977), created Life Peer (1992); Editor, *Spectator* (1954–59); Lord Privy Seal (1979–81). Terence Kilmartin (1922–91), editor, translator, journalist; Literary Editor, *Observer* (1952–86).

8. The last paragraph of this letter is illegible and signature and salutation are missing.

and they like to talk of matters connected with the practice or appreciation of the arts. They're all very un-American, want me to use my influence to get Britain to secede from UNO with the idea of bringing Dulles and his friends to heel.[1] But they aren't 'insecure" or "woman-dominated" or any of that tack, no more than I am, anyway.

I've found New York the big laugh (though impressive too of course): my first day there was the English tourist doing the place in 12 hours, and included a conversation with a publisher (6'3", son of Middle West miner, Montenegrin ancestry),[2] lunch with queer Broadway producer,[3] party at magazine office[4] (martinis at 4 p.m. – oogh ergh), dinner in Greenwich Village (mainly palate-eroding cheese), intellectual party (during which I heard one bearded man ask another if he really understood what artistic integrity was – honest, now), jazz session with a lot of conscientious inter-racial camaraderie, and finally slumber in Auden's bed – all right, all right, WHA is in Rome. Plucking down a copy of Crabbe's poems in the flat (which belongs to Auden) I saw on the flyleaf 'To Wystan. We must love one another AND die. Cyril.'[5]

---

1. Perhaps over the rejection of Communist China for admission to the UN, spearheaded by the Americans in September; or over the hawkishness of American foreign policy in general. John Foster Dulles (1888–1959), American Secretary of State, resigned his post on 15 April 1959, and died nine days later.

2. William Jovanovich (b. 1920), who joined Harcourt Brace in 1947 and worked with J.H. McCallum in textbook publishing before becoming President (1954–70), then Chairman and Chief Executive Officer (1970–88). Jovanovich was born in Louisville, Colorado, and was the son of an immigrant coalminer from Montenegro.

3. Perhaps over a proposed stage adaptation of *Lucky Jim*, about which Claire S. Degner, who ran the play department of Curtis Brown in New York, had written to Amis on 23 October 1958 (the letter is part of the Curtis Brown collection in the Butler Library, Columbia University).

4. This party, in celebration of the twenty-first birthday issue of *Esquire* magazine, is described in *Memoirs*, pp. 197–8. Amis had published a short story, 'Moral Fibre', in the birthday issue, and 'partly, I suppose, as a result of contacts made that evening, I found myself with an extra job, *Esquire* critic of the Art of the Cinema. Asking what this meant, I was told just any non-American film, and by God the experience taught me thoroughly how bloody awful most non-American films were.'

5. Both the jazz session (at the Five Spot in Cooper Square, to hear the tenor saxophonist Sonny Rollins) and the night in Auden's apartment (rented or borrowed at the time by Gene Lichtenstein, a friend of Amis's who worked at *Esquire*) are described in *Memoirs*, p. 198; Cyril, Amis assumed, was Cyril Connolly, altering a famous line in the original version of Auden's 'September 1, 1939': 'We must love one another or die.' (In *The Collected Poetry of W.H. Auden*, published in 1945, Auden omitted the stanza which contains this line, and in the *Collected Shorter Poems 1927–1957*, published in 1966, he omitted the whole poem because of what he had come to regard as the line's dishonesty.) Amis begins his account

Didn't look at any others for fear of anti-climax. Ran into Father D'Arcy in Washington – ho ho. All well here, including my papa (bawled him out for 2 hours yesterday).

H. and I both send love

Kingsley

[ALS: Recipient]

TO CHARLES D. ABBOTT – 25 NOVEMBER 1958

Princeton University, Princeton, New Jersey

Dear Professor Abbott:

Many thanks for your kind invitation.[1] I am dreadfully sorry not to have answered it earlier, and I must admit I have more or less spent the interval wondering whether I could manage to accept.

If it would be possible I should like to bring with me my wife and two sons (ages nine and ten), also possibly my small daughter (age five). I know this is rather an imposition, but I think it would be a pity if my family missed the chance of seeing your part of the country. So, if you think you could bear it, I should love to come to Buffalo on May 1, and the program you outline will suit me splendidly. But if you feel that four or five Amises instead of just one would be too much to handle, of course I shall understand.

Yours sincerely,
Kingsley Amis

KA:jj[2]

[TLS: Buffalo]

in the *Memoirs* of this first visit to New York by declaring firmly that 'anyone who makes a business of hating it or being superior to it, and there were plenty then, home-grown and foreign, is a creep, and [. . .] anyone who walks up Fifth Avenue (say) on a sunny morning without feeling his spirits lift is an asshole' (p. 197).

1. Professor Abbott, the Director of Libraries at the State University of New York, Buffalo, had invited Amis to give a reading.

2. This letter is one of many from Princeton typed for Amis by a secretary, as indicated by the initials 'KA:jj'.

TO HILARY RUBINSTEIN – 9 DECEMBER 1958

Princeton University, Princeton, New Jersey

Dear Hilary:

I thought you were entitled to a letter on my official academic stationery, so here it is. I send you a piece of Italian gibberish from which I gather only that some question of rights is involved. (The question of money seems hardly worth prolonged discussion.) So just summon your team of trained linguists and deal with the matter with that famed efficiency of yours, eh?

On the Williamson-Bernstein question,[1] I am keeping a fatherly eye on the lads, and will certainly see to it that they have the name of V. G. very much in mind when they get to the stage of looking for an English publisher.

Accept cordial but slightly bemused salutations from the Land of the Dry Martini.

Yours ever,
Kingsley

KA:jj

P.S. I've signed one of these damned Italian things, in case that's what they wanted me to do.

[TLS: Gollancz]

1. The Italian rights to *Lucky Jim* were sold in 1955, and the Italian edition came out in 1957. The Gollancz files offer no clues to the 'Williamson-Bernstein question', though Bernstein is probably the film producer Sidney Bernstein.

TO BRIAN ALDISS – 24 DECEMBER 1958

Princeton University, Princeton, New Jersey

Dear Brian,[1]

In February and March of 1959 I am giving a series of six seminars at this University on the subject of Science Fiction.[2] These will be delivered before a largely Faculty audience as part of the annual Christian Gauss Seminars in Criticism.

I write now to ask your help in making this venture – to my knowledge the first of its kind – as informative and useful as possible, and accordingly enclose a questionnaire in the hope of acquiring data otherwise inaccessible to me. I assure you I know how tedious these things can be, but I can think of no feasible alternative. I am confident you will agree that to spread the notion of Science Fiction as a serious literary medium is an aim worth pursuing.

If you would prefer your own name or that of your organisation to be withheld – and I should tell you that I intend to publish parts of my text – rest assured that your confidence will be respected. Information introduced by phrases such as 'according to one authority' or 'in the view of one writer in this field' will have its own value.

Thanking you in advance,

Yours ever,[3]
Kingsley

KA:jj

---

1. For Brian Aldiss see Notes on Recipients. This letter and its accompanying questionnaire were sent to twenty prominent science fiction writers (including John Wyndham, Robert Sheckley, Arthur C. Clarke, Robert A. Heinlein, Ray Bradbury and Isaac Asimov, as well as Aldiss) and nine editors of science fiction magazines. 'Brian' has been added in pen after 'Dear'.

2. The six lectures, or seminars, on 'Science Fiction' were delivered on Thursday evenings at 8.30 to an invited audience of luminaries in the Firestone Library at Princeton. They were entitled: 1. 'Definitions and Ancestry'; 2. 'Modern Science Fiction: Its Nature, Place and Scope'; 3. 'Science Fiction and Fantasy as Indicators of Contemporary Moods and Attitudes'; 4. 'Utopias and Social Criticism – 1'; 5. 'Utopias and Social Criticism – 2'; 6. 'The Possibilities of Science Fiction as a Literary Form'. Amis provided his audience with a reading list for the seminars, comprised of ten books and 'any recent issue' of three magazines on science fiction (the list can be found in the Gauss Seminar records at the Firestone Library).

3. Amis has crossed out 'sincerely' and added 'ever' in pen.

Thought you would like to see how seriously we take our jobs here. Anything you could bring yourself to say would be much appreciated. Many thanks for sending that tome – most useful.[4] *All going well here, but nostalgic pictures of Oxford & elsewhere keep flashing upon the old inward eye. All the best – K.*[5]

QUESTIONNAIRE

1. What is the approximate circulation of your magazine? (any additional information about circulation *outside* the U. S. A. will be valuable.)
2. Does your readership show any strong pattern in terms of age, sex, occupation, educational standard, etc.?
3. In what numbers do unsolicited manuscripts reach you?
4. What are your rates of payment?
5. What do you consider to be the function of science fiction, aside from its qualities as entertainment and/or literature?
6. What are your chief complaints against science fiction as currently written?

[TLS: Princeton]

4. L. Sprague de Camp's *Science Fiction Handbook* (1953), which 'gave him the necessary historical background' (Jacobs, *Biography*, p.220).

5. MS addition.

TO ELIZABETH AND SAMUEL HYNES – 5 JANUARY 1959

Princeton University, Princeton, New Jersey

Dear Hyneses:

Thanks a lot for checks and for looking after me so nobly when I was in Swarthmore.[1] I certainly had a fine time and I was only sorry not to have had a chance for more of a chat. You both endured those oldsters incredibly well – I may add that later that evening I escaped by the skin of my teeth having Dr. Swann play his cello to me.[2] Anyway, I left the next morning in good heart and wearing one of his shirts.

I do hope we can meet again and will rouse you on the telephone if I get anywhere near your area.

Yours,
Kingsley (Amis)

KA:jj

[TLS: Recipient]

TO MRS EDITH SEWELL HAGGARD – 26 JANUARY 1959

Princeton University, Princeton, New Jersey

Dear Mrs. Haggard:[1]

Well, fine, but I haven't written these damned lectures yet. When I've completed the series (towards the end of March) I'll shoot the

---

1. Amis's talk at Swarthmore was on recent British writing, with special emphasis on the Angry Young Men, though Hynes had encouraged him to add 'a few words on Virginia Woolf, who was the most recent British writer most of my colleagues had heard of. He came with a lecture written on white paper, with two yellow sheets stuck in the middle – a wild and un-related commentary on VW' (personal communication, 23 September 1996).

2. The oldsters were the director of a physics institute on the Swarthmore campus (Dr Swann) and his wife, an old friend of Amis's father, who also attended the lecture.

---

1. Edith Haggard (1903–95) worked as an agent at Curtis Brown in New York from 1937 to 1962. Among her clients were Sinclair Lewis, Ogden Nash, C.P. Snow, Daphne Du Maurier and Joyce Cary.

scripts off to you and Harry Sions[2] can certainly have a look at them then. I might add here that Harcourt Brace are nibbling at the possibility of a short book being made up, with the lectures in it, I mean. But I suppose they wouldn't mind them being done in a magazine first.

I hope to see you soon,

Yours sincerely,
Kingsley Amis

KA:jj

This is just to show I wasn't improvising (as I admit I sometimes do) when I talked about having written you. It was fine seeing you. K.A.[3]

[TLS: Columbia]

TO MRS EDITH SEWELL HAGGARD – 19 FEBRUARY 1959

Princeton University, Princeton, New Jersey

Dear Mrs. Haggard:

I was hoping to come in and see you sometime in the next week or so but I seem to have lectures to give all the time and shall not be in New York for a little while. So here I am giving you the information I have been meaning to give about Edward Hirsch, one of the Creative Writing boys I must have mentioned to you. Hirsch I think is a most promising lad, still rather in the wild and woolly stage, but with a lot of good work ahead of him. I should certainly like Curtis Brown to get hold of him now that he is on the point of starting his writing career. Perhaps you would like to drop him a line at 223 Brown Hall, Princeton University and ask him to send you some of his stories. If possible, I think you might like to see him in person – you'd find it entertaining anyway.

He isn't a genius, of course, so don't – I know you won't – expect masterpieces from him. But of all the good people here I would put

2. Harry Sions was an editor at *Holiday* magazine. He later worked at the publishers Little, Brown.

3. MS addition.

my money on him as the one least unlikely to become a genius in time. I hope to see you before too long.

Yours sincerely,
Kingsley Amis

KA:jj

[TLS: Columbia]

TO KARL MILLER – 27 FEBRUARY 1959

Princeton University, Princeton, New Jersey

Dear Karl:[1]

Jolly nice of you to send me the Mary McCarthy book,[2] which I am sending straight back to you unopened. It is not that, as it were, I don't feel I should like it much, nor, precisely, that the SPECTATOR doesn't pay enough – rather the fact is that I am up to my bloody eyebrows at the moment with WORK. Annoying, really, in all sorts of ways, because I should rather have liked to do it.

How horrible it must be for you at that place now. The thought of Inglis and Brien[3] running an entire periodical is grotesque. You will really have to get a job somewhere else. Will talk to you all about this when I see you. (Better burn this.) Will be back in the Motherland and no other land about the twenty-fifth of July, and we'll tie one on together at an early stage thereafter.

Cheers,
Kingsley

KA:jj

[TLS: Recipient]

---

1. For Karl Miller see Notes on Recipients.
2. Most likely the travel book *The Stones of Florence* (1959).
3. Brian Inglis (1916–93), Editor, *Spectator* (1959–62); Alan Brien (b.1925), novelist, journalist, at the time Drama Critic and Features Editor, *Spectator* (1958–61).

TO J.H. McCALLUM – 20 MARCH 1959

Princeton University, Princeton, New Jersey

Dear John:

Your letter arrived when I was just suffering a crescendo of guilt for having stayed in the background for so long. But actually I have a bomb-proof excuse: I have been working so hard at these beautiful seminars that ordinary human contact is a thing I can barely remember, and my visits to New York recently have been brief, frenzied, widely separated dashes. But *last night*, as ever was, I gave the last of these damned things, and am a free man again. Don't quite know when I shall be in the big city next – not next week anyway – but I'll let you know as much in advance as I can.

AND WE WILL HAVE LUNCH.

Yours ever,
Kingsley

KA:jj

[TLS: Harcourt]

TO MRS EDITH SEWELL HAGGARD – 21 MAY 1959

Princeton University, Princeton, New Jersey

Dear Edith:

Many thanks for your three letters, and apologies for my dilatoriness.

Gentlemen's Quarterly: could you keep these fellows hanging on the hook a bit longer?[1] I would like their money, but I don't much want to do the work. If I could defer a decision for a little while longer, I shall know better what my financial position is going to be.

Glad you enjoyed the science fiction stuff. I've scoured the copy I have, but there seems to be only one page 148 in it. Sorry about this. As regards Frank Deford's play, I rather suspected that it would be unusable for magazines. I just felt that Deford was a talented boy, and

1. Amis never did write for *Gentleman's Quarterly.*

that you might like to bear him in mind for the future.[2] Yes, do please pass on the manuscript to Mrs. Degner.

I am looking forward to our lunch, and will shortly deliver a suggestion about this by means of the telephone system.

Yours,
Kingsley

KA:jj

[TLS: Columbia]

TO BRIAN ALDISS – 9 JUNE 1959

Princeton University, Princeton, New Jersey

Dear Brian:

I feel I must write and thank you for your kind and generous cooperation in filling out my recent questionnaire on science fiction. You contributed in no small measure towards giving my series of seminars whatever authority it may have had.

I think I can say that I aroused some interest in science fiction among circles not normally associated with it, and you may be interested to hear that the lectures will be published next spring by Harcourt, Brace and Company.

With renewed thanks and best wishes,

Yours sincerely,
Kingsley Amis, M.A.

KA:jj

This is just the official bullshit – thanks anyway for your stuff, which I haven't lost & will not. See you in OX. in the "fall", I guess.

Kingsley[1]

[TLS: Bodleian]

2. Frank Deford (b. 1938), author, sportswriter, television and radio commentator; nothing came of Deford's play.

1. MS addition.

TO CLAIRE S. (CINDY) DEGNER – 23 JUNE 1959

Princeton

Dear Cindy,

Do you think you could get that beautiful $450 I earned from the Guild sent to me right speedily?[1] The steamship company seem to think I ought to pay them some time – in fact, very soon – for those cabins I shall need to get home in.

I note what you say, as they say, about the musical notion, and will surely dash in to see you at least once before I depart.

Yours,
Kingsley

[TLS: Columbia]

TO JEAN AND JOHN McANDREW[1] – JULY 1959

On board the Liberté

[. . .] Seeens (Christ, what a pen) *seems* little to add to H[illy]'s exhaustive account.[2] However, to get the troublesome bit over with, the two things I did forget to do before leaving were to sign a piece of paper acknowledging to my agent that I owe him $225 and to sign the contract for my science-fiction book. If anything at all resembling these documents is to be found at 271 – I feel I left them on the study desk – could you forward them? Since I urged you to destroy everything with

---

1. In a letter to Amis from an unidentified assistant to Cindy Degner at Curtis Brown (24 June 1959, in Columbia), this sum is described as 'the net monies due on LUCKY JIM', by which is probably meant due for permission to adapt *Lucky Jim* for the stage, since Degner ran the play department of the agency from 1959 to 1962.

---

1. For Jean and John McAndrew see Notes on Recipients.

2. This is Amis's half of the letter, written on the stationery of the *Liberté*, a ship of the French Line, on which the family sailed back to England; Hilly Amis's half of the letter, presumably with an exact date, has not survived.

words on it in that room I can hardly complain, or even wonder, if they are not to be found. The contract has a blue cover, I think.

All well so far. George[3] (see H's contribution) is a man of great energy. He likes having discussions with as many different sorts of people as he can find, which is perhaps why, having talked for ½ an hour without stopping about his job (publicity for men's clothes), he buggers abruptly off before you can take your turn: he has seen a different sort of person from you going by and is afraid he may miss the chance of having a discussion with them. But he does something in his way to console one for the temporary loss of America.

I feel now I never made the long speech of thanks to you that you certainly merited, the two of you: and this not at all because I find it difficult to say what is in my mind or any of that tack: as you know, I find it *notoriously* easy. So it must just have been that you kept making me too stoned to do so much as ask for a match. But you do know, I hope, that you did more than all the others did between them to make our stay such paralysing, coronary-accelerating fun. Thanks 1,000,000.

See you soon, eh? Must go and grab a drink before the band starts up in the bar. There are 2 guys in it who play the clarinet *in French*.

Love to all,
Kingsley

[ALS: Recipient]

TO PHILIP LARKIN – 30 JULY 1959

53 Glanmor Road, Uplands, Swansea, Glam.

My dear Philip,

Well, old man, there must be a pretty big hole in those Amis correspondence files of yours for the current year and the one preceding. I don't see how I can apologise for such a thing, exactly, but I can plead that I wrote no more than four personal letters the whole time I was away, in every case to people who had written several times to me (no imputation, o' boy), that I left many an important, i.e. financially-concerned, non-private letter unwritten, that for the first half of my

3. A passenger on the ship, an American 'who didn't bore K and was good fun; I don't think we ever saw him again' (Lady Kilmarnock, personal communication, 16 January 1999).

time there I was boozing and working harder than I have ever done since the Army, and that for the second half I was boozing and fucking harder than at any time at all. On the second count I found myself at it practically full-time. When you get to my time of life you have to take what you can get when you can get it, you sam. But during all this I did think intermittently of you, and not just as someone I ought to be writing to, either. I thought of you, for instance, whenever I went to Eddie Condon's ("Yeah, I remember that Banks guy. Hey, what happened to him? No, not Allen, was it? No fooling? Jesus God, I always thought it was Mc Partland"[1]), when Stewart Richardson[2] gave his jazz party for Hilly and me (Joe Thomas (tpt), Rex Stewart (cnt), Buster Bailey (clt), J.C. Higginbotham (tmb), Cliff Jackson (pno), ? (bs), Speedy Jones (ds))[3] – especially when Bailey, who played far hotter and better than I've ever heard him on records, yelled out during a Jones drum solo: "Ain't he the most, Kingsley?" The man I got to know best was Stewart, oddly enough; he was on the team ag shag at Condon's, and turned out to be very nice, bright, funny etc. Playing well, too. You know, he's the only Negro trumpeter except Allen who has never at any time in his career sounded like Armstrong. Other good men I heard were: Allen, Higginbotham, Mulligan, Art Farmer, Miles Davis, Hawkins (yes: no longer a dirty old man nor breaking his neck to sound modern), Bud Powell, Monk, Simeon, Clark Terry & Nance & Hodges with Ellington, Dankworth's band. Bad men included Shavers, Eldridge, Parenti, Ellington, Art Blakey, Jo Jones, Kaminsky[4] – old, shagged, trying to keep up by sensationalism, touting for jobs. Didn't get to hear Russell or Freeman, shit in it, though Hilly did, shit in it. As to writers; well, there was Mary McCarthy, who beamed all the time, Peter De Vries, a

---

1. Jimmy McPartland (1907–91), cornettist.

2. Stewart (Sandy) Richardson (b.1922), a jazz-loving publisher (working at Knopf at the time), gave the party at his home in Hopewell, New Jersey; Amis describes the party in *Memoirs*, pp. 68–9 (wrongly locating Hopewell in Pennsylvania).

3. Joe Thomas (1909–84), trumpeter; Speedy (Rufus) Jones (b. 1936), drummer.

4. Among the good men previously unidentified are Gerry Mulligan (b. 1927), baritone saxophonist and arranger; Art Farmer (b. 1928), flugelhorn player and trumpeter; Bud Powell (1924–66), pianist; Omer Simeon (1902–59), clarinettist; Clark Terry (b. 1920), trumpeter and flugelhorn player; Ray Nance (1913–76), trumpeter, cornettist, violinist, singer and dancer; Johnny Hodges (1907–70), alto and soprano saxophonist; and John Dankworth (b. 1927), English alto saxophonist, bandleader, arranger, composer. The previously unidentified bad men are Roy Eldridge (1911–89), trumpeter; Art Blakey (1919–90), drummer and bandleader; and Jo Jones (1911–85), drummer.

good joe, ole Ahpeebee,[5] a very funny man and not like his books, and various, but not many, others.

We really had a very fine time indeed. I'll tell you about it in detail when I see you, but we both want to go there again as soon as may be, though not, I feel definitely at the moment, to stay. They have more energy than we have, and they are better at enjoying themselves. They are not complacent or woman-dominated or death-wishing or insecure or naive – especially not that. Mind you, you have to go there to see this: I can't make anybody here believe it quite. The women, with a few shining exceptions, are less attractive than ours. If England got blown up while I was in the States, I could happily make my home there; but not as things are. All the same, to enumerate England's virtues takes some doing. The food tastes more – but then they have clams and soft-shell crabs and we haven't. There isn't so much advertising – but there aren't so many nice things to buy. There's less swank about high living – and less to swank about. England to me is my own tongue, but I can talk in the States as well with no trouble at all, thank you, and what I did when I was young, but I want to forget most of that and get on with what I am doing now. In many ways I like being back, and to find that life is a little duller in Swansea than in Princeton need occasion no surprise. At least I shall have the chance of getting down to some sodding *writing*: 7 pp of novel in USA, 3 poems is not impressive for 10½ months, and although I did write a book of sorts there, based 95% on some lectures they made me give, the length, some 45,000 words, the topic, science fiction, as you recall an old passion of mine, the title, *New Maps of Hell* – although this exists it doesn't represent, I feel, the purpose for which I was created. Further to the Motherland: its main bores seem to have been converging on me at a huge rate, as if on purpose to show it in a bad light. Going to the land of the free gives one a kind of restlessness which may prove hr fr hard to eradicate.

And what of you, hey? I saw your letter to Richardson, and admired its conservative and (at that remove) British tone. Ron, by the way, was the chef at St. John's in my time though not, I think, in yours.[6] He was an amiable neurotic semi-autodidact, that is, he was semi-didact and the whole of the semi was auto. I've heard from him a few times in the last 10 years and it looks as if his 2nd named characteristic may

5. R.P. Blackmur.

6. St John's College records reveal only that a Mr Rawlinson was appointed cook in 1946, succeeding a Mr Peedell. No first names are given.

have led to a certain amount of job-losing, and this in turn to a bit of book-flogging. I also long to hear your talking record.[7] And to see you, if that avowal carries any weight after all this time. We shall be here for a long time without moving, and my father will not be with us again until 3 Sept or so. So do come if you can, for as long as you can manage: H. joins with me in this. I hear from Bob that you are in the Orkneys or some such absurdly unrewarding place, so your holiday may be over or budgeted for; but failing here there is always London. I must pick up with my old palls, though not with Wain, whom I saw for the last voluntary time in my life in New York. While Cutty[8] or someone was taking off on "Sleepy Time Down South" or something at Condon's, Wain asked me if I was working on anything. I said yes, I was: a novel. He gave me a wink and said: "Make it a good one this time, eh?" Too late I found rage. I was delighted to hear adverse reports of him from places as far apart as Buffalo, N.Y. and Washington, D.C. In Princeton in the last days I met dear old Mairi MacInnes,[9] whom I cleared of a seven-year burden of guilt by explaining what a child and shit Wain is: he had blamed her, it seems, for everything thag bag that went wrong in their affair in the long-ago. I forgot to say that I also ran into Carson McCullers, who is evidently off the stuff and half over her stroke but still odd. The only thing I remember from the evening – she pissed off at about 9, leaving me to talk to the editress of *Mademoiselle* and her extraordinary husband – was the chahmun lil ole Southron dahlog between her and the hostess's coloured maid: "Wah, how are you all getting alawng, Bessie dahling?" – "Wah, just fahn Miss Cahson, thank yuh kahndly."

Well, it's back to the land of sorry sir and we can expect an Honours class of sixty next year and the younger girl, and farewell to what can I get you sir and this guy, see, he owes like nine hundred dollars to the liquor store and all right, what about tomorrow afternoon. Oh well. Don't forget about coming, as the a said to the b.

A non-resident alien is not entitled to tax exemption for his bum.

Kingsley

[TLS: Bodleian]

7. The Marvell Press recording of *The Less Deceived* (1958).
8. Cutty Cutshall (1911–68), trombonist.
9. See Amis to Conquest, 23 January 1955, note 3.

TO SAMUEL HYNES – 24 SEPTEMBER 1959

53 Glanmor Road, Uplands, Swansea, Glam.

Dear Sam,

I was delighted to hear from you, and my God shall I ever *forget* that evening in Swarthmore, Pa.?[1] I was very sorry to have wished all those oldsters on to you and thought you and your wife bore with them nobly. I was not at my best; having had nearly enough of my old dad without 3 supernumerary septuagenarians being along, and being a bit worried about whether my wife was going to get home on those icy roads. Back at the Swanns I think I got nearer to having the 'cello played to me, without it actually taking place, than ever before in my life.

It's wonderful news that you're in London for a year, and we will certainly get together soon. I will confront you with a number of literary characters and with some human beings too. I come to London about every month and – could you drop me a card with your telephone number? Then we'll arrange a date by word of mouth. If I have anything to do with it we[2] shall talk about the States most of the time: we[3] had a wonderful time there and were very sad to leave.

See you soon!

Yours ever,
Kingsley

[ALS: Recipient]

1. See Amis to Elizabeth and Samuel Hynes, 5 January 1959.
2. Amis has added '= you and I'.
3. Amis has added '= wife and I'.

TO KAREN McANDREW – 15 OCTOBER 1959

53 Glanmor Road, Uplands, Swansea, Glam., Great Britain.

My dear Karen,[1]

It was very very sweet of you to send me those wonderful monsters, which stand gesticulating at me on my table now. They fill me with inspiration, which will come in handy when I begin my stint as science-fiction reviewer on the *Observer* here.[2] Apart from such things, s-f has been rather thin on the ground. I did get to see *The Amazing Colossal Man* and *Night of the Blood Beast*[3] recently, but they were kid stuff: the amazing colossal man failed to amaze and everybody could see he wasn't really colossal. The blood beast was only a man rather inexpensively dressed up. The two of them made *The Blob*[4] seem like Shakespeare or something.

I'm thinking of writing a science-fiction story about a state of society where boredom is the chief crime, with special boredom police, segregation – special bores' seats in public transport and schools and universities only for bores. This is the solution in the U.S.A. where bores have to wear a badge, etc: in England the Bores' Party win the election and the hero and heroine emigrate. I suppose this is partly the result of gloom at MacMillian having been returned to power,[5] partly because the bores here have been giving me special attention recently: three of them – an Austrian, an American and an Irishman – cornered me today in the College and talked simultaneously for 20 minutes or so. Where do they get the *energy*? *I* haven't any. When do we see you again? Keep

1. For Karen McAndrew (aged fifteen in 1959) see under Jean and John McAndrew in Notes on Recipients.

2. Amis reviewed science fiction for the *Observer* from 16 October 1960 to 30 May 1965.

3. *The Amazing Colossal Man* (in Britain, *The Terror Strikes*) (1957), written and directed by Bert I. Gordon, described in the tenth edition of Halliwell's *Film Guide*, ed. John Walker (London: HarperCollins, 1994), as a 'quite well written sci-fi let down by shaky trick work' (p. 31); *Night of the Blood Beast* (1958), directed by Bernard L. Kowalski, advertised with the tag-line, 'No girl was safe as long as this head-hunting thing roamed the land'.

4. *The Blob* (1958), directed by Irwin S. Yeaworth Jr and starring Steve McQueen.

5. In the general election held on 8 October the Conservative Party had retained power, with an overall majority of 100 seats.

at your Ma & Pa to bring you all over – or come yourself. I'm saving up the *New Statesman* puzzles.

Much love – Kingsley

[ALS: Recipient]

TO PHILIP LARKIN – 15 DECEMBER 1959

53 Glanmor Road, Swansea, Glam.

My dear Philip,

This comes a bit late, I suppose, to count as a reply to your kind favour of 2nd October, but it's nice and early as a Yuletide remembrance. I'm a busy man, as you know, and a lazy man, and a randy man, and an employed man (I know you don't really agree with that part, but it does take its toll. Filthy Modern Literature Options in the Honours course. We are doing *Ulysses* now, or were when term finished. Lot of reading that means. Reading a lot you don't want to read and all. And saying things you don't want to say. Myth bum, interior monologue bum, symbol bum (especially *that*), epic structure bum, in this section over a hundred parts of the body are mentioned bum, Nausicaa bum, *Christ figure bum*, poetic bum, recognition scene bum and all the rest that you know so well. Was confirmed in my impression that Stephen has that particular kind of self-righteous it's-all-right-when-I-do-it niggling informativeness that we normally associate only with Jane Austen heroes. Then there's the pwetry. 4 Quartets OF LICE) piss LICE-INFESTED TRAMPS ALL BUGGERING ONE ANOTHER. Some one, I mean someone, ought to do our trick of denigration-by-obscene-accretion that worked so well with Music, when soft *silly* voices, that have been talking *piss*, die – you remember? Prick, said the turd, follow them, follow them and persuade them to commit serious offences against one another, For the leaves were full of children comparing their tools, And the lotus leaned upward out of the heart of light like a bobbing turd[1] – I fear I have not the text before me.

1. The lines Amis is 'horse-pissing' occur at the end of the first and fifth sections or 'movements' of 'Burnt Norton', the first of Eliot's *Four Quartets* (1943; though 'Burnt Norton' was published separately in 1936): 'And the lotus rose, quietly, quietly,/The surface glittered out of heart of light,/And they were behind us, reflected in the pool./Then a cloud passed

It's a cay, believe me. Aproper cay.) . . . HAWN A proper cay.)[2].

Glad to hear you've been having an interesting time with your new building.[3] You probably feel you can sit back now in the consciousness of having done an important job as well as nerhaha leggo only kid[ding.] My own "writing" is going all right, but I keep not being able to do anything to my novel, turning our shour out brief not-to-be-printed pornographic interludes – Jenny caught her by the back hair and pulled viciously downward. Anna cried out; Jenny sniggered and thrust her c – to encourage me while I do all manner of flithy articles for the money, like a fool, or because I think when they ask me that they would be fun to do, like an even bigger fool. The muse visits me but seldom. Incidentally, would you tell me if you think the following quatrain is a) all right b) a complete poem or does it need more?

> Hearing how tourists, dazed with reverence,
> Look through sun-glasses at the Parthenon,
> I thought of that cold night outside the Gents
> When Dai touched Gwyneth up with his gloves on.[4]

Still haven't finished my adultery poem, but shall have a bash today before plugning on with Jenny.[5] Tackling of adultery, my activities in this direction, which have ramified some in the last few months, received a severe check when Hilly found some letters I had received and initiated the most strenuous and painful row we have ever had. I am to give all that up, it appears, with an exemption clause covering my Yank girl when she turns up over here in the summer. Trouble is it's so hard to give all that up, habit of years and all that, and such bloody good fun too. Especially just after finding the most splendid busty redhead in an ideal location. But being walked out on by H. (and kids), the sure-fire

and the pool was empty./Go, said the bird, for the leaves were full of children,/Hidden excitedly, containing laughter'; 'Sudden in a shaft of sunlight/Even while the dust moves/ There rises the hidden laughter/Of children in the foliage/Quick now, here, now, always.'

2. Martin Amis suggests 'cay' as 'cow'.

3. The first stage of the new University Library at Hull was nearing completion; the building would be opened on 20 June 1960 by Queen Elizabeth, the Queen Mother.

4. Published as 'Aldport (Mystery Tour)', the penultimate poem in *The Evans Country*, a sequence of poems detailing the amorous adventures of a character named Dai Evans, from 'Aberdarcy' (setting of *That Uncertain Feeling*); *The Evans Country* was first published in 1962 by the Fantasy Press and consisted of only six poems; it was expanded to eleven poems (plus dedicatory quatrain) in *A Look Round the Estate: Poems 1957–67* (1967); reprinted, *CP*, p.104 In the published version 'Gwyneth' becomes 'Dilys'.

5. The heroine of *Take a Girl Like You*.

consequence of any further discovery, is a rather unwelcome prospect too. You can't have it both ways, you see.[6] Got to make up your mind which you want and stick to it. What are you trying to do, anyway? Prove something to yourself? The provincial don, secure in his snug little insulated provincial fastness, cannot hope to know anything of the impulses which animate THE POSTMASTER GENERAL CRIED ARSEHOLE THERES A PAIR OF FINE BALLS IN THIS PARCEL AND ENDORSED I R A AND WITH NINEPENCE TO PAY AND ADDRESSED[7] Well if it sends the writer howling to his fart[8] that's something.

Have more or less given up jazz now. Never buy a record though I feel if I ever do it will be British mainstream I go for – Fawkes, Alex Welsh.[9] Just go on playing my oldies, Banks, Commodores, an occasional Goodman. Bessie Smith leaves me cold. Don't like any singers. Hate singers. Scobey[10] still appeals, if only he could get rid of that fearful banjo-twanging minstrel hobo riverboat balladist. Was filed with incredulity at your Norman[11] news. Book? What book? What kind of book? *Book*? Philip Brown, since we reminisce, has married an ugly bossy nurse – expect you knew this. Got the news from old Rodge. We were up there recently, also at Daddy B's, and I felt again that old excitement that tells the writer he is approaching the locale of his true subject. We arrived travel-worn at Rodge's, I greatly needing a drink, and were met by Miggy with a saucepan in her hand, all ready to dish up the supper *at once*. I adored that. "Do you want a drink? I'm afraid there isn't anything in the house." I had thought that at least I could take Rodge off to the pub afterwards and get drunk so as to be able to stand him better. But no. He had flu, you see. I can see he perhaps couldn't really help that, but at the same time I can think of nobody of whom it would be as characteristic to get flu at just that time. More folk-dance lore from Daddy B over a glass of Spanish burgundy.

6. A theme returned to in Amis's penultimate novel, *You Can't Do Both* (1994).

7. Quoted in full in Amis to Conquest, 7 September 1955, note 3.

8. An allusion to the last line of W.H. Auden's 'Journey to Iceland'; see Amis to Larkin, c. 26 October-6 November 1943.

9. Alex Welsh (1929–82), Scottish trumpeter, singer and bandleader.

10. Bob Scobey (1916–63), trumpeter. In the 1950s he led his own Frisco Jazz Band and was a key figure in the 'West Coast' or San Francisco revival of traditional jazz. The banjo-twanging balladist (in this context, singer, not composer) was Clancy Hayes (1908–72).

11. Norman Iles, who thinks 'the book in question must have been "Sex and Fish Poems" – later privately printed (private communication, 31 October 1999).

Mummy B asking if I ever found my characters taking charge. A four-handed game of Halma[12] with the boffin [. . .]

Keep seeing old Twatters, the silly sod.[13] Keep hearing about lyric rhythms from him. How does he mean? Thought you leaned a little in his favour in the *Gdn*,[14] but the old iron boot in the velvet sock was there for those with eyes. Hear from you about Easter, I suppose. You know what I want for Christmas: 2 14-yr-old bisexual 40-inchers with oral fixations. See to it will you? I seem to owe about £2000 income-tax. How can that be? You don't care about me or the children; all you want is to stick your cock up some woman's bum,

K

[TLS: Bodleian]

TO KARL MILLER – 17 DECEMBER 1959

53 Glanmor Road, Uplands, Swansea, Glam.

Dear Karl,

Sure-pop, boy, I'll let you have 500 or so on sex by Monday. I've looked at *The Ballock-High Culture* casually and it strikes me as somewhat of a stinkeroo.[1] Nothing much wrong with the U.S. for him, which makes a change, and I don't say there *is* all that much wrong. But not to mention (as far as I've seen) McCarthy, Wee Rock, drugs etc is a bit odd, no? Shall I still do it?

We loved seeing you at the w/e. I might say the tiny spot of discord you witnessed, after swelling to unprecedented proportions, has now more or less totally eased off. Oh, but what fun while it lasted.

I enclose a little piece of poetry I wrote the other day, which you

12. A game played on a chequerboard with two or four players.
13. Vernon Watkins.
14. Larkin reviewed Watkins's latest collection, *Cypress and Acacia*, in 'Texts and Symbols', *Guardian*, 27 November 1959, p. 11.

1. For the '500 or so [words] on sex' see Amis, 'Parlez-moi d'Amour', review of Fernando Henriques, *Love in Action: The Sociology of Sex*, in *Spectator*, 1 January 1960, p.19; 'The Ballock-High Culture' may be Vance Packard's *The Status Seekers*, reviewed by Amis in 'Keeping up with the Rockefellers', *Spectator*, 5 February 1960, pp.186–7, though the review is positive (and never mentions the absence of references to McCarthy, Little Rock or drugs).

might like to have printed up somewhere in your magazine, so that your readers can see it. So that Kinsley[2] can see it, too.

Seems unlikely we'll be up before Christmas now, but we'll reunite at an early date thereafter. All the best for Yuletide*: love to Jane: Hilly sends hers.

Cheers,
Kingsley

*& Hogmanay, och.[3]

[ALS: Julian Barnes][4]

TO JOHN AND JEAN McANDREW – 27 JANUARY 1960

53 Glanmor Road, Swansea, Glamorgan, Great Britain.

My dear Gouger & Jean,

By now you will have seen the Coales[1] and been assured of our continued existence. I hope I remembered to behave like a human being (on the reduced K. Amis level) in the last half-hour we had with them. To be stoned à l'Edgerstoune seemed odd in Chelsea and West London.

I enjoyed our phone call, and thank you for it, and if I sounded incoherent, remember – as I'm sure I frequently said – it was 1 a.m.

2. Amis's Professor at Swansea, James Kinsley; the poem was 'A Tribute to the Founder', published in *Spectator*, 25 December 1959, p.939; reprinted in *A Look Round the Estate* (1967) and *CP*, p. 76. The poem at one point deplores the 'bluster, graft, and doing people down' of university life.

3. Miller is from Scotland.

4. This note was 'rescued from a New Statesman waste-bin after some literary department spring-cleaning' by Julian Barnes (personal communication, 18 September 1996). Miller had been Literary Editor of both the *Spectator* (1958–60) and the *New Statesman* (1961–67), and must have carried his files from the former to the latter (leaving them there when he moved on to edit the *Listener* in 1967). The 'spring-cleaning' Barnes refers to presumably took place long after Miller had left, since Barnes only began working at the *New Statesman*, as Assistant Literary Editor (under Martin Amis), in 1977.

---

1. 'Good neighbours and University people' (Lady Kilmarnock, personal communication, 16 January 1999).

on 1st Jan. to us, and I was a living testimony of this. Anyway, it was wonderful to hear all your voices, and #235 couldn't have been more vivid if I'd seen it in 3D with full sound effects (Shep, Any Old Time, the tinkle of ice-cubes, the distant cry of an enraged Gerber[2] and rough masculine voices calling to each other to stand aside while I – do a little job that no one else can do for me).[3]

I enclose a couple of cheques to diminish my debt to you somewhat. But there must be a good bit still outstanding – apart, that is, from the remainder of the consultant's bill. I'm sure there must be several items which the Kemptons[4] will have had to settle – telephone in particular. Could you find out about this and let me know?

Yeah, I take that point about the musicians in musical comedy – but Condon, Wild Bill Davison etc. also played in movie-house pits in the silent days. They just had to eat, see?

Life continues, but not made easier by my promise to support the projected Welsh National Theatre. Welsh? *National*? Theatre? I must just love culture, that's what. Love to all 7 of you[5] and fondest memories –

Kingsley

[ALS: Recipient]

2. Ill-tempered neighbour on Edgerstoune Road, from the babyfood family. 'Shep' was the McAndrews' much-loved sheepdog; 'Any Old Time' was 'our signature tune from an Artie Shaw record which we all loved' (Lady Kilmarnock, 16 January 1999).

3. This roughness with jobs or tasks recalls the otherwise affable suburbanite Joe Derlanger, Roger Micheldene's host in *One Fat Englishman*: 'With a shrug and a jerk of the head, Joe moved to the nearby shelter and pulled more chairs out of it, arranging them round the concrete walk by the pool. He did this in the manner of a sadistic animal trainer. If anything looked like starting to go wrong for an instant there would be an outbreak of violence. This policy, Roger had noticed, marked all Joe's dealings with the world of objects' (p. 10).

4. Whose house the Amises had rented.

5. The McAndrews and their five daughters.

TO ANTHONY BOUCHER [WILLIAM A.P. WHITE] – 27 APRIL 1960

53 Glanmor Road, Uplands, Swansea, Glamorgan, Great Britain

Dear Mr. Boucher,

I was delighted to get a letter from the author of "Barrier", "The Quest for Saint Aquin" and other favourites of mine. I'm very much looking forward to seeing your review.[1]

I think you may be right and I was a bit unjust to John Campbell[2] – he wrote me a silly letter in response to my questionnaire of editors, more or less suggesting that my only hope of seeing any of the truth about sf was to call on him and be put right by the master in person. I do acknowledge now, and probably I should have done so in my book, that his editorship of *Astounding* was important. But however good he was he couldn't have *created* good new authors: I can't believe that before he came along there were all sorts of mute inglorious Asimovs[3] dying for want of an outlet. Again I agree that he may well have had a good *influence* on the new writers. [. . .]

Pohl & Kornbluth: here I have you, I think: except for your point about collaborators not remembering exactly what they did. Anyway, Pohl wrote to me unsolicited and said I had shown "uncanny" insight

---

1. Anthony Boucher, the pseudonym of William A.P. White (1911–68), wrote science fiction and detective fiction, was a noted anthologist in both fields, and founded the influential *Magazine of Fantasy and Science Fiction* (which he edited from 1949–58). Boucher's story 'Barrier', 'a comic-inferno type of science fiction', is discussed by Amis in *New Maps of Hell*, pp. 102–4; 'The Quest for St Acquin' is discussed on p.82. Neither Jack Gohn, *Kingsley Amis: A Checklist* (Kent, Ohio: Kent State University Press) nor Dale Salwak, *Kingsley Amis: A Reference Guide* (Boston: G.K. Hall, 1978, henceforth *Reference Guide*), lists a review by Boucher/White.

2. John Campbell (1910–71), editor of the magazine *Astounding Science Fiction*. In *New Maps of Hell*, p. 151, Amis talks of 'the cranks who seem bent on getting science fiction a bad name – John Campbell, the editor of *Astounding*, with his psi [mind-reading] machine and his interest in reincarnation and his superman theory'. Amis also connects Campbell with L. Ron Hubbard and the 'mysterious mental science of dianetics'.

3. Isaac Asimov (1920–92), Russian-born American science fiction writer; 'mute inglorious Asimovs' alludes to 'mute inglorious Miltons', from line 59 of 'Elegy Written in a Country Churchyard' (1751) by Thomas Gray (1716–71).

into his and K's relative contributions, accused me of looking over their shoulders, etc. So there![4]

Yes, indeed, thank you, I'll certainly look you up if I get to California, which I deeply want to do. I'm working hard at it, so don't be surprised if I ring your phone any year now.

With renewed thanks and all good wishes,

Yours sincerely,
Kingsley Amis

[TLS: Indiana]

TO JEAN AND JOHN McANDREW – 2 MAY 1960

53 Glanmor Road, Uplands, Swansea, Glamorgan, Great Britain

Dearest Jean and John,

King Amis is nat dede, as the old poet[1] wrote – actually it was King Arthur he mentioned, but these chaps had a poor sense of historical perspective. I can quite see how you might have thought I was dead, keeping quiet all these months, and once or twice I even thought myself I might be dead, after ten hours or so at the typewriter turning out the fair copy of my novel.[2] The physical effort gave me cancer of the lung, but that seems to have worn off now, after a few days drinking and talking and watching television. The manuscript is safely with my publisher now, and all I have to do is to work some more to earn some money to pay the bills I incurred while not earning any money because I was writing my novel. All this while I've written no letters at all, not

4. Frederik Pohl (b. 1919) and C.M. Kornbluth (1923–58), science fiction writers, co-authored *The Space Merchants* (1953), which, according to Amis, 'has many claims to being the best science-fiction novel so far' (*New Maps of Hell*, p. 124). Amis discusses the novel on pp. 124–33, suggesting that as it proceeds, it relies 'more and more heavily on Kornbluthian elements – there is a quite gratuitous scene with a female sadistic maniac who totes a sharpened knitting needle' (p. 133).

---

1. See Sir Thomas Malory (d. 1471), *Le Morte D'Arthur* (finished 1470, printed by Caxton 1485), in E. Vinaver, ed., *Malory: Works* (Oxford: Oxford University Press, 1971), p. 717: 'Yet som men say in many partys of Inglonde that Kynge Arthure ys nat dede.'

2. *Take a Girl Like You.*

even to accept those daydream-fulfilling offers of £2 to deliver a lecture on "Some Reflections on Life, Literature, Politics, Jazz, Science Fiction, Sex and the Bourbon Old-Fashioned in our Sister Democracy across the Atlantic Ocean" in a dry town at the north-eastern tip of Scotland. But here I am at last, in fair shape on the whole, with leisure to meditate on clams and Dot Arnold and the Wine and Game and the US 1 and the tax office in Trenton and Ed Cone and Condon's and Cherry Hopkins and the time I kicked that Henry Moore Statue on the shins at Vassar.[3]

I expect you will have guessed how terribly thrilled all we loyal British are at the wonderfully colourful and pageantry-rich time we're going to have on Friday, when our beloved Princess Margaret, sister of the Monarch, is joined in matrimony with Antony Armstrong-Jones, Esquire. Such a symbol of the age we live in, when a royal princess, famed for her devotion to all that is most vapid and mindless in the world of entertainment, her habit of reminding people of her status whenever they venture to disagree with her in conversation, and her appalling taste in clothes, is united with a dog-faced tight-jeaned fotog of fruitarian tastes such as can be found in dozens in any pseudo-arty drinking cellar in fashionable-unfashionable London. They're made for each other. The funny part is that I met Jones twice before the news of the engagement came out and on each occasion denounced his future bride to him. The stories are too long to be set out here, but you'll imagine that I let myself go quite a way on the subject of the girl's stupidity, charmlessness etc. He took it very well, considering, but my artless query "Oh, you know her, do you?" when he undertook to defend her must have given him a nasty turn. In the world that little creep inhabits it would be hard to conceive that I wasn't a paid spy for some columnist doing a little pre-blackmail softening-up. I'm seriously considering forming a British Republican Party (no connection with

3. Of the things and people Amis meditates on, Dot Arnold was a neighbour; 'The Wine and Game' a liquor store (the nearest to his house on Edgerstoune Road); 'US 1' a highway (it runs from Maine to Florida, and Amis would have taken it to New York, among other places); Edward Cone (b. 1917) a composer, also Professor of Music, Princeton University (where he has taught since 1947); and 'Condon's' (more properly 'Eddie Condon's') a Manhattan nightclub. Neither Lady Kilmarnock nor the Amis's Princeton friends Edmund and Mary Keeley and Edward Cone, nor Mrs Murray Kempton can identify Cherry Hopkins.

the G.O.P.) to burn the happy pair in effigy on their wedding night. And why wasn't I sent an invitation to the ceremony? Eh?[4]

Americans are beginning to filter through to us at last. That all-too-short overture with the Coales in London was followed up by a fairly prolonged bout with the Frasers.[5] At first honours were even between Russ and me: I was one down when I retired to bed without explanation halfway through a party here, after a belching-demonstration that reduced my less intimate acquaintances to wondering silence, but we levelled up when Russ had to leave the next lunchtime's pub gathering in order to avoid vomiting in open session. He was got on to the train finally, silent, pale as lard, penniless, muttering an invitation to their place in north-west London. We shall go when we're solvent again. Talking of solvency: according to my calculations I still owe you at least 80 dollars, probably more if the Kemptons have had any more bills we ought to pay. Could you let me know the final figure? – then I can work on getting a draft to you when the cash starts coming in for the book. Now mind you do that. Ah, I tell you what: you might like to round it off with the cost of a copy of *Fads and Fallacies in the Name of Science*:[6] I'd be no end grateful if you could send me a copy. I unaccountably failed to steal one from 271 or 235[7] before departing. I need it every other day to confound some nut or other who wants to convert me to the flat-earth theory, etc.

To save the cost of postage, why don't you bring the book over in person? I really think that after we took all that trouble to cross the ocean and find you, you might return the compliment. It is your turn, after all. I can picture every detail of it, not least the unloading of the barrel of clams, the gallon of mint julep, the bale of *Times* puzzles. And I'll make sure that Gramps is at the airport to greet you, with his light

4. Princess Margaret and Lord Snowdon were to divorce in 1978. Amis devotes a chapter to Snowdon in his *Memoirs* (pp. 187–92).

5. Russell Fraser (b. 1927), a scholar of Shakespeare and the Renaissance (also the biographer of R.P. Blackmur), taught in the English Department at Princeton (1956–65). He married Eleanor Jane Philips in 1947 (the marriage was dissolved in 1979). In 1965 Fraser was appointed Chairman of the English Department at Vanderbilt University, in Nashville, Tennessee, and in 1967 he invited Amis to Vanderbilt on a four-month visiting professorship.

6. *Fads and Fallacies in the Name of Science* (1952) by Martin Gardner contains scientifically informed attacks on, among other things, psychokinesis, ESP and reincarnation, the sort of cranky material Amis condemns in some science fiction (see Amis to Anthony Boucher, 27 April 1960, note 2).

7. The street numbers of the Kemptons and the McAndrews on Edgerstoune Road.

of love.[8] About her I now feel better: I couldn't see much wrong with her at first, but knew there had to be – else what was she doing with my father? Then it all came right: one evening when they were down here she talked to me for fifteen minutes straight off as I mixed a vodka fizz, alternating inquiries about what I was doing – "why are you putting ice in?" etc. – with a denunciation of the Jews. Later she failed to notice when a bare-chested American drama about veterans was interrupted by a veddy, veddy English commercial recommending some variant of aspirin – "is this the girl we saw before?" etc. Oh well, takes all sorts to make a world, eh? Don't forget about coming over. We have dates lined up for the whole Linda-Mauro bunch. And no doubt the 2 mums & 2 dads would fill in the time somehow.

Love from us all – we DO miss you, every one. When you write, I will too.

Kingsley

[TLS: Recipient]

TO VIOLET AND ANTHONY POWELL – 4 JUNE 1960

53 Glanmor Road, Uplands, Swansea, Glam.

My dear Violet and Tony,

It seems getting on for inconceivable that we've been back in the Motherland all this time without getting to see you. Actually we've been bogged down by this and that: penury, for one thing, which is connected with another thing, my having to finish the novel I started in 1955 or bust – the connection is via the fact that writing the novel meant I had to stop doing all that criticising in the papers that used to bring me in so much money. Anyway, things are easier now, and my Powell-synapses (this is a very learned word out of science fiction, and it means, as far

8. After his wife's death, Amis's father took up with several 'lady friends'. To one of them (not the one described here, but of a similar character), he left all of his possessions on his death. As Amis records in his *Memoirs* (p. 23), the lady 'refused to let any of them go, even claiming back the watch and wallet Hilly had passed on to Philip and Martin'. According to Lady Kilmarnock, 'Daddy A's girlfriend said she was in the secret service and a private detective – we felt very uneasy about her. Her first name was Irene, but I don't remember her surname' (personal communication, 16 January 1999).

as I can explain it to laymen, "brain-paths") were brought into play by an extract from *Casanova's* Cinese, whoops, *Chinese Restaurant*[1] I saw in *The Queen* magazine. It wasn't very long, but long enough to make me do my *Music of Time* reader-reaction act half a dozen times: laughter signified by a cessation of breathing and a kind of seated bow. I'm longing for 20th June. Well: what I'm working up to is to say that it's demonstrably your turn to come and stay, and we should love to have you if you can fit it in between your comings and goings. It looks as if we shall be here virtually all the summer, with only the week following 15th July unworkable, so if you could let us have a few dates when you're free, some sort of arrangement could no doubt be finalised eventually.

All news when we meet, especially that touching my father. It now seems unlikely that he'll emigrate to the United States, as was mooted at one stage; instead, he's setting me a very delicate problem of conscience by taking up room in a small London flat also occupied by a friend of ours. The friend wants Pa out of there in short order, but doesn't like to tell him so directly; instead he tells me, or intermediate friends, so. Now if I tell my father that of course questions of this sort are very tricky but he really ought to see if he can't etc., what will he do? Come here? You see? At the moment my friend's discomfort is torturing me frightfully, but I believe I can take it a little longer.

I feel awful at the moment because I'm dieting, i.e. more or less not eating. It's now two hours since I didn't have lunch and another hour and a half or so till I don't have tea. I have to smoke and drink all the time to make up for it. Recently I tried to not smoke as well as not eat and nearly went mad.

Hope to hear from you soon. Best love from us both,

Kingsley

[TLS: Recipient]

---

1. *Casanova's Chinese Restaurant* (1960), the fifth novel in *A Dance to the Music of Time*.

TO J.H. McCALLUM – 24 AUGUST 1960

53 Glanmor Road, Uplands, Swansea, Glam., G.B.

Dear John,

I am really delighted to hear that TAKE A GIRL LIKE YOU has drawn one or two cheers from you and colleagues. Authors pretend not to care what their publishers think, but it's usually a pretty hollow act.

I'm afraid your list of suggestions arrived too late for me to do anything with them: Gollancz were really insistent that my proof went back to them with the minimum delay. So that relieves me from the necessity of having to answer your points. Out of interest, though, I will try to deal with the more major points, those in the main body of your letter.[1] Taking them in order:

Patrick's succumbing *is* depressing, and is meant to be. I wanted some pretty dark places in the comedy, and this is one.

Ormerod-Edgerstoune. You are right, but to correct things would have meant a major revision (and the weakness itself is, I think, only minor).

No, it is really enormously important that Jenny be confronted with evidence of *apparent* moral failure at that moment. It is what makes her return to Patrick, whom she had just rejected. And the remoteness of Miss Sinclair and John Whittaker is supposed to illustrate how unexpectedly and deviously these things can happen: you can err through pure inadvertence.

See point 1. The drunkenness is a dramatisation of the 'unfairness' Jenny complains about in sexual relations.

That's about it. Thank you for all the good care you are taking of me; for all the NEW MAPS OF HELL reviews you kindly sent; and above all for saying you liked TAKE A GIRL LIKE YOU. It really was a relief and a reviver.

Yours ever,
Kingsley

[TLS: Harcourt]

---

1. This letter, of 29 July 1960 (in Harcourt Brace), relayed four main suggestions or observations: 1. That having Patrick Standish succumb to Sheila Torkington on the very day he hoped to seduce the heroine, Jenny Bunn, is more depressing than comic, as is his almost immediate discovery of Sheila's pregnancy. 2. That the Julian Ormerod-Dick Thompson-Lord

TO MICHAEL RUBINSTEIN – 22 SEPTEMBER 1960

53 Glanmor Road, Uplands, Swansea, Glamorgan.

Dear Mr. Rubinstein,

Thank you for your letter, which I should have answered sooner had I not been unreachably away on holiday when it arrived here.[1]

I do indeed favour the publication of LADY CHATTERLEY'S LOVER, and am quite willing to give evidence in the proceedings, if required. I enclose a short statement setting out my views on the matter.

It strikes me, as one who knows nothing whatever about these matters, that there are some potential difficulties about a defence based on the "This is a great work of literature" line, and that there may be some value in my own "Let us have the whole truth on someone who has had such a profound influence" approach.[2] But no doubt, if there is anything to be gained along these lines, it will already have occurred to you.

Please let me know if I can be of any further assistance.

Yours sincerely,
Kingsley Amis

Edgerstoune affair is too vague and offhandedly dismissed at the end of the novel. 3. That the episode involving Miss Sinclair, John Whittaker and Whittaker's father is forced and arbitrary and should be dropped. 4. That Patrick's seduction of Jenny when she is drunk is too dark ('I found it turned my stomach just a bit,' confesses McCallum).

---

1. In a letter of 14 September 1960 (now in the University of Bristol Library) Rubinstein, a solicitor, had written to Amis asking him to give evidence in support of his clients, Penguin Books Ltd, who were being prosecuted for the publication of *Lady Chatterley's Lover*. Amis offered the enclosed short statement, which was expanded in preparation of a draft Proof of Evidence (also in the University of Bristol Library). Michael Rubinstein (b. 1920), the older brother of Hilary Rubinstein, has been a solicitor since 1948; he was Senior Partner, Rubinstein, Nash and Co., later Rubinstein Callingham (1969–86).

2. In the *Memoirs*, p. 98, Amis admits to having read only 'forty or fifty pages' of the novel (in 1945, while in the army), adding that he 'did not find it necessary to extend my acquaintance with the work when I put my name down to have the ban taken off in 1960'.

I strongly support the publication of the unexpurgated edition of LADY CHATTERLEY'S LOVER as being for the public good. Opinion may vary on the question of the work's artistic merits, as on the merits of its author's writings as a whole. But it seems to me of the utmost importance that the entirety of these writings, including, that is to say, the full text of the work under discussion, should be freely available to any member of the public. It is incontestable, in my view, that Lawrence was one of the most influential thinkers of his time: distinguished critics have told us that, in addition, he was a great literary genius. No just appraisal of his standing, no true appreciation of the significance and value of his teaching, is possible without a consideration of his total output. Indeed, LADY CHATTERLEY'S LOVER, in the form in which Lawrence intended it to reach the public, is of special importance for such appraisal and appreciation, since the most essential parts of some of his beliefs are embodied in it. If provision of the means of understanding a figure of such a size is not to the public good, then there can be, in the literary sphere, very few things which are.

Kingsley Amis
22nd September 1960

[TLS: Bristol]

TO PHILIP LARKIN – 24 SEPTEMBER 1960

Swansea

My dear Philip,

Here is your questionary ppppfffffbbbvvvv: I say "questionaa aaghh fuck questionnaire" myself, but we can both agree that those who say "kestionnaire" ought to have a dentist's drill shoved up their pipe.[1] As regards what I've said in the questy: I'd have said "my work belongs

1. At the behest of the Standing Conference of National and University Libraries (SCONUL), Larkin sent this questionnaire about the preservation of British literary manuscripts to twenty 'leading British writers' (including T.S. Eliot, E.M. Forster and Graham Greene, as well as Amis). He reported his findings to SCONUL in a paper of March 1961 (see Motion, *Life*, pp. 339–40).

not to England, but to the world" if I were a different type of chap. (I use this last phrase so often these days that I'm beginning to wonder whether I may not actually be a different type of chap.)

Sorry I didn't see you after you buggered off that evening. It was a shit house, that evening. I didn't really expect my predictions of a) boredom and b) expense about that night club to come true with such stunning exactitude. You know, night clubs is a thing I've decided I don't want any of, at all, ever. When we returned from Denmark we took the Richardsons[2] to another, slightly less bad (but not less expensive) one, where the cabaret led off with the introduction of a pretty girl with just about the gig frig biggest tits I've ever seen on the hoof – 42, 44, christ knows, I wouldn't. After she'd faced the audience and bowed, an action which nearly caused me to send our table flying over my shoulder, she brought out a PIANO ACCORDEON and played it enthusiastically (and rather skilfully) for ten minutes or so, and that was the last we saw of the tits. God. Anything else. Banjo. Ukelele. Harmonica. Basset-horn. Viola da gamba (especially that). But a fucking *piano accordeon.* I mean, like seeing Betty Grable taking part in a sack race. Or Anita Ekberg in a crinoline (remember your retort to my Tony Steele poem).

The Danes were fine, but the French-speaking fuckers weren't. I have seldom heard such crap talked at such length, not even in a provincial common-room. And the bull-fighting bastards and ice-cream merchants were as bad. There was a nasty Pole too. All talking p-ss about the Welfare State: "In ze affluent societee ze accumulashong of possessiongs as reached ze poy-eent where ze object itself deesappears UP VOTRE GRANDE-MERE'S FUCKING ARSE-TROU JACQUES

My book has had what they call a mixed reception. But that's all right, isn't it, naming to himself the two substances of which its I was glad to see John Coleman picked up Caton.[3] Couldn't you write the Spec a letter as from the Fortune Press, requesting them to make it plain that you have no connection with, etc.? Oogh: and I have now seen the phto po photo of AP, self, H and you:[4] be a sport and send

2. Amis had seen Larkin on 5–6 September in London, en route to a writer's conference in Copenhagen. Sandy Richardson and his wife Jan were visiting from the United States.

3. John Coleman reviewed *Take a Girl Like You* in 'King of Shaft', *Spectator*, 23 September 1960, pp. 445–6.

4. See plates section.

us a copy. Pass the encl[5] on to George H, will you? Don't laugh at them. Give him my love; well, you know, save me writing.

There is something disconcertingly unreal about Mr. Amis's bum,

Kingsley

CONFIDENTIAL

TO: P.A. Larkin, Esq.,
Librarian,
University of Hull,
Hull.

1(a) Have you ever been asked for a gift of your manuscripts by

(i) a British library? ....No..........................

(ii) an American library? ....Yes..........................

(iii) any other library? ....No..........................

(b) If so, was such a gift made? Yes

(c) If so, how much manuscript material was involved?
About a dozen pieces: corrected drafts of poems

2(a) Have you ever been asked to sell your manuscripts to

(i) a British library? ....No..........................

(ii) an American library? ....Yes..........................

(iii) any other library? ....No..........................

(b) If so, did such a sale take place? No, but it may in the future

(c) If so, how much manuscript material was involved?
Unspecified, but drafts of novels seemed to be in question

3. Would you care to express any general opinion on this question to the Conference?

Yes. I will sell any of my manuscripts to the highest bidder, assuming such bidder to be of reputable standing, and I have no feeling one way or the other about such bidder's country of origin. It seems to me no

5. Probably poems, which were passed on to George Hartley, editor of *Listen*.

more incongruous that the Tate Gallery should have a large collection of Monets (say) than that Buffalo University should have a collection of Robert Graves manuscripts (say). I view with unconcern the drift of British manuscripts to America, where our language is spoken and our literature studied.

Date ......23rd.September.1960..... (Signed) ....Kingsley..Amis...........

[TLS: Bodleian]

TO LIVIA GOLLANCZ – 24 SEPTEMBER 1960

53 Glanmor Road, Uplands, Swansea, Glam.

Dear Miss Gollancz,

I am fascinated to hear of the proposal to Simplify *Lucky Jim.*[1] Yes, of course I am very pleased to agree to Longmans' suggestion, and the financial arrangement you propose suits me perfectly.

Yours sincerely,
Kingsley Amis

[ALS: Gollancz]

TO JEAN AND JOHN McANDREW – 4 OCTOBER 1960

Swansea

Dearest Jean and John,

Book on the way, with all love – sorry about the administrative cock-up at Gollancz's. They're tight buggers – once failed to forward a letter I sent to an American author c/o them.

No cause to complain of press and other treatment: you saw what

1. The proposal came from Longmans, Green and Co., which wanted to include *Lucky Jim* in its Overseas Simplified series. The books in this series, for use entirely in schools overseas, were non-net, unjacketed, and could not be sold through bookshops. Longmans was offering an advance of £100 on a 7½ per cent royalty. For Livia Gollancz see under Victor Gollancz in Notes on Recipients.

the Rev. Frank Martin said, I believe, and there was a good notice in the *Church Times* (Ch. of England, of course). And I've just heard that *Woman's Mirror* are going to serialise it.[1] It'll do their readers a power of good (especially p. 80 – while we're on that – see lines 30–32 – Jeanne got that message. She amazed me in London by grabbing her lighter with a gay smile and a reference to the sentence mentioned. Shows that literature *is* a powerful educative force after all.).[2]

What's all this about you coming over? I can't believe it. How are you coming? When? For how long? Do we spend all the time in London with you, or do you spend all the time down here with us? Details, please.

I give England (and Wales) about another couple of years before we finally walk out on them. (And guess where we shall be coming then.) Actually v. depressed about the old place. Only a more or less continuous diet of Americans keeps us going. We look to you to vitaminise that diet. Are you *really* coming? You wouldn't joke about that, I hope.

Footnote on the book: a Lady in the *Yorkshire Post*, referring to the sexual nature of the theme, writes: "But, oh dear, all this going on about a rather irrelevant, and particularly narrow, aspect of relations between men and women!" Well, you can't please everybody is what I always say.

Write, cable, telephone news of arrival. We're all longing to see you.

Love,
Kingsley[3]

[ALS: Recipient]

---

1. In an anonymous review, 'Critic of Society', in the *Church Times*, 30 September 1960, p.5, *Take a Girl Like you* was called 'an enjoyable, considerable affair'. I have not been able to identify the Rev. Frank Martin or to discover what he said. The novel was serialised in *Woman's Mirror* (part of the *Sunday Mirror*) in five weekly extracts, from 21 January 1961 to 18 February 1961.

2. Here is a portion of the passage on p.80 in which Patrick Standish discourses on women: 'But why aren't they ever interested in anything? – I know, they're interested in *people*, as if nobody else ever was. You know, Graham, I sometimes think I'll marry the first woman I meet who can sit through three minutes of a gramophone record and listen to it. One that's any good, I mean. Some of them can manage about thirty seconds of Harry Belafonte or the Sugar-Plum sodding Fairy before they say *That's nice* and get down to the chatting or ask to have Radio Luxemburg on or want to dance or need a light, but . . . Look, what is this mental block they've all got about having their own bloody matches?'

3. Hilly Amis has added a note at the end of the letter: 'The kids are wild with excitement at the thought of seeing their best Yanks.'

TO MICHAEL RUBINSTEIN – 19 OCTOBER 1960

53 Glanmor Road, Uplands, Swansea, Glam.

Dear Mr. Rubinstein,

Thank you for sending me the draft proof of evidence. I have only one major addition to make, as follows:

Two things make LADY CHATTERLEY'S LOVER of unique interest and importance to the student of Lawrence's beliefs. One is that it gives accounts of sexual intercourse more detailed than those we customarily encounter in print. I myself find nothing depraving or corrupting in these accounts. They show in action the sexual impulses of two responsible, moral beings, bound to each other by mutual respect and knowledge, free of selfishness and false shame. This, says Lawrence, is what sexual behaviour can and *should* be like – and the *should* is not a matter of wish-fulfilment but of morality. Only the already corrupt could find anything depraved or depraving in these passages.

The second point, connected with the first, is the use of sexual terms and expressions less conventionally refined than those we customarily encounter in print. Here again there is nothing to corrupt: the corrupting influence, if any, lies in the use of these terms as expressions of disgust, contempt, abuse etc., uses which Lawrence was here specifically combatting. He knew that the language we use both reflects and modifies our feelings about the matters our language renders: his obvious aim here was to purge these words of their undesirable accretions, and so salvage a vocabulary in which sex could be discussed without prurience, without false shame, without social or other embarrassment, without recourse to the anti-emotional, clinical, scientific, unnatural terms which are the only alternatives. I cannot think of this as other than a moral aim.[1]

Do please suggest any cuts or modifications or additions which may occur to you: the place for it would be low down on page 2, I imagine, either after sentence 6 or sentence 8.

---

1. For a rather different view of the treatment of sexuality in *Lady Chatterley's Lover* see 'Why Are You Telling Me All This?', in *The Amis Collection*, p.26, reprinted from the *Spectator*, 23 August 1986: 'some accounts of sexual behaviour notoriously attract laughter against that writer's intention, and *Lady Chatterley's Lover* might be a masterpiece of unconscious humour but for the boring non-sexual bits in between.'

It was most pleasant meeting you the other morning and I hope we shall have the chance of encountering each other again.

Yours sincerely,
Kingsley Amis

[TL: Bristol]

TO CLAIRE S. (CINDY) DEGNER – 23 NOVEMBER 1960

53 Glanmor Road, Uplands, Swansea, Glam, G.B.

Dear Cindy,

It's all very well to ask me when I'm coming back: "as soon as possible" is the answer. But I don't get any *encouragement*. For God's sake, get me an instructorship in the State University of N. (or even S.) Dakota, and I'll come to stay. Just see to it, Mrs D., will you?

Life is grey here. I very much mean what I say about wanting to return, and for an extended stay. I have a novel about the U.S. to write which I can't write until I've seen the bloody place again. For an extended period.

Glad to see that the *Jim* business[1] is getting under way. I've forwarded the amendments back via C.B. [Curtis Brown] in London. Give my best to all in the office, and to those United States.

Yours ever,
Kingsley
K. AMIS

[ALS: Columbia]

---

1. Presumably the projected stage adaptation (see Amis to Degner, 23 June 1959), of which nothing came.

TO MICHAEL RUBINSTEIN – 23 NOVEMBER 1960

53 Glanmor Road, Uplands, Swansea, Glam.

Dear Mr. Rubinstein,

I must apologise for being absent when called in Lady Chatterley. I left Swansea just in time to miss your letter and got back six hours or so after I should have been available in court. This made me feel rather humiliated, and I hope my absence didn't derange things too much. I suppose it can't have had any radical effect, what with the verdict going as it did, for which I am heartily thankful.[1]

It was good to meet you and I'm sorry from many points of view not to have seen you in court.

Yours sincerely,
Kingsley Amis

[ALS: Bristol]

TO ANN THWAITE – 30 NOVEMBER 1960

53 Glanmor Road, Uplands, Swansea, Glam.

Dear Mrs. Thwaite,

It was very kind of you to write, and I am so glad you enjoyed *TAGLY*: particularly that you thought the Jenny parts came off all right – which was the one thing I was really scared about:[1] I might have gone so horribly and irretrievably wrong there. I know what you mean about Julian, of

---

1. On 2 November 1960, the jury ruled that *Lady Chatterley's Lover* was not obscene, and Penguin Books immediately put 200,000 copies on sale. The defence had been concerned to impress upon the jury the number of eminent witnesses prepared to testify in support of the novel, but it also worried that it might bore the jury by prolonging testimony. Amis's name was called out in court but he did not appear, thus meeting both concerns: 'So even *in absentia* you may very well have served a useful purpose,' Rubinstein wrote to him on 25 November 1960 (in a letter in the University of Bristol Library).

---

1. Ann Thwaite (b.1932), writer (married Anthony Thwaite, 1955), was defending the novel's heroine against those who thought her both impossibly good or sensible and thinly drawn.

course, but would say as a sort of half-excuse that his implausibility was part of his character, and of his role. But that's pretty fine-spun, I know.

Yes, what an occasion that was in 1954, to be sure. I was too afraid of it all to enjoy it much, but the memory of Kirkup's mere *appearance* has comforted me over the years.[2]

All the best to you both,

Yours,
Kingsley Amis

[ALS: Recipient]

TO THE EDITOR, *SPECTATOR* – 10 FEBRUARY 1961

SIR,—In his brief analysis of my *Take a Girl Like You*, Professor Enright makes three factual errors.[1] They are:

1. He seems to think that to put Beethoven down as twelfth man to a cricket team of bad men shows that I am a helpless victim of the sneering habit. But the sneer, if it is one, is made by one of my *characters*, not by *me* (the author).

2. He says that my hero, who has objections to marriage, is 'ready to marry' the heroine at the end. There is no authorial implication of this and nobody in the book mentions it, not even the hero – an inveterate liar, anyway.

3. In the course of explaining that my book belongs to the 'convention of the Nightmare World,' Professor Enright cites as his (only) supporting example the supposed fact that 'the nice headmaster's daughter turns suddenly into a juvenile nymphomaniac.' Now this character is not at any time a nymphomaniac, she is merely very fond of men (compare *dipsomaniac* and *heavy habitual drinker*). Moreover, she does not turn into somebody who is very fond of men, suddenly or gradually. Her fondness for men is revealed less than two pages after she first appears in the novel.

2. For Kirkup's appearance (at a poetry symposium at Oxford, the 'occasion' referred to in the letter) see Amis to Larkin, 14 March 1954.

---

1. D.J. Enright's lead review-article, 'The New Pastoral-Comical', 3 February 1961, pp. 154–5, devoted most of its space to William Cooper's *Scenes from Married Life; Take a Girl Like You* was only discussed in the final two paragraphs.

While I am on to you, may I say a word about Professor Enright's long analysis of Mr. William Cooper? (I am sure Mr. Cooper can look after himself, but he may not think it worth the trouble to write in.) Professor Enright first explains that *Scenes from Provincial Life* belongs to a certain convention, and then rounds on Mr. Cooper for not sticking to it. One might as fairly censure *Paradise Lost* for its lack of documentary realism. I am sure there is a technical term for this sort of manœuvre, but the only word that occurs to me at the moment is one of those 'peculiarly nasty words – one knows they are nasty even if one hasn't met them before' which Professor Enright, to his obvious distress, keeps finding in my work. This particular word, however, I am pretty confident he will have met before.—Yours faithfully,

KINGSLEY AMIS

TO KARL MILLER – 5 APRIL 1961

53 Glanmor Road, Uplands, Swansea, Glam.

My dear Karl,

Thank *you*, chum: you were a model literary editor, not only in the book section you ran but in your relations with contributors: so say I and all fellow-contribs I know.

I think I will have to not write for the Statesman just at present.[1] This, as you well know, is no reflection on you – I'd rather write for you than for any other lit. ed. But, without I hope making a silly fuss, I'd sooner not be tied up with a journal that prints things like the recent leader on the Aldermaston marchers – a mostly dishonest piece, I thought – and that has that red-headed Papist thug (confidential, this, natch) high up in its hierarchy.[2] One or the other I might be able to

1. Miller had moved from running the books pages of the *Spectator* to those of the *New Statesman*.

2. Paul Johnson (b.1928), author, historian, journalist; on the editorial staff, *New Statesman* (1955–65), before becoming Editor (1965–70). The leader on the Aldermaston marchers, 'The Meaning of Aldermaston', *New Statesman*, 31 March 1961, pp. 500–1, praises the Campaign for Nuclear Disarmament, while also deploring the divisive effect its unilateralism was having on the Labour Party, 'the only instrument by which the healthy and vigorous motives of the Aldermaston marchers can be transformed into practical politics' (p. 501).

stand, but not both. However, I feel no particular urge to write for the Spectator either, now you're no longer there, and aim to let things drift for a bit – my decision about the Statesman isn't final, of course. They'll just have to do better in the front of the paper than they're doing.

Hope to see you soon. Love to Jane.

Yours,
Kingsley

[ALS: Julian Barnes][3]

TO J.H. McCALLUM – 5 APRIL 1961

53 Glanmor Road, Swansea, Wales.

Dear John,

I hope you'll forgive this long silence, my apparent indifference to the appearance of TAKE A GIRL LIKE YOU, and, now I come to take a look at it, the pallor of this typing ribbon. I had been meaning to write for a long time to reassure you that I still existed, but, congenitally idle as I am, I was going to hold off until I had the chance of combining this service with asking you to do another immense favour for me, one comparable with the exertions that landed me in Princeton. Swansea, dear good old place that it is, was getting me and Hilly into such a state of hypnotised boredom that we felt we must break out or die – and breaking out meant, for both of us, coming to the U.S.A. more or less indefinitely. Only one thing restrained me from sending you a distress signal, the possibility that I might swing a job in Cambridge (Eng., not Mass.). Well, this rather remote chance (as it looked at first) has now come off: the rubber-stamping has yet to be completed, but for all intents and purposes I am fixed with a fellowship at Peterhouse.[1] We're very

3. For the provenance of this letter see Amis to Miller, 17 December 1959, note 4.

1. Amis had been appointed the college's first Fellow and Director of Studies in English, a position he owed, in part, to the influence of George and Pat Gale. George Gale (1927–90), journalist and broadcaster, worked at the time (as for much of his career) at the *Daily Express*, where he was a columnist (1976–86), then Associate Editor (1981–86), then chief leader writer (1981–82). He first met Amis in the mid-1950s at a party at the *Spectator*. Gale had been an undergraduate at Peterhouse and remained friends with several of its Fellows, notably the historian Brian Wormald. His wife Pat (they were married in 1951, divorced in

thrilled, of course, and expect to enjoy ourselves, for a time anyway. – I put this qualification in because we may find after all that it's England, not just Wales, that is wrong for us, in which case we shall again exploit you without mercy as our chief immigration officer. Even as things are, we feel we've already been away from the United States too long, and seriously intend a visit in the summer of '62, from something like May 25th to October 1st. So you could do us a good turn by letting it be known that Amis is expected to be about at that time, ready to lecture at anyone who'll face him.

John, I was delighted (as always) with the appearance of TAKE A GIRL, and pleased with the reviews: I only hope you were too. It looks uncomfortably as if the next opus may be delayed a couple of years: I want to write about the States, or at least an English reaction to them, and I can't get properly started until I've had another look at the place. That's the position, unless another vague notion buzzing round my head turns out to be a novel instead of the long story it looks like being at the moment. Time, undoubtedly, will show.

Will you be over here in the foreseeable future? Hold it till September if you can – we'll be in Cambridge by then and eager to entertain you there.

My best wishes, as ever,
Kingsley

[TLS: Harcourt]

1983) grew up in Swansea, where her mother and sisters still lived, and whenever she and her husband came up to visit they would get together with the Amises. The two couples spent several holidays together, often with other friends, and on at least one such occasion Wormald joined them.

Amis was encouraged to apply for the Peterhouse fellowship by one or both of the Gales, and Wormald lobbied for him at the college. The appointment seems to have been decided in February, though official confirmation did not come until late May and formal election only in June; see Larkin to Monica Jones, 2 March 1961, in *LL*, p. 324, which refers to the appointment as though it were common knowledge, with other academics 'white with fury' at the news. Larkin himself had a mixed reaction: 'I must say I'm glad it's Cambridge & not Oxford who have done it. On the other hand, I don't mind really as if anyone is going to get it I'd sooner it was Kingsley than John [Wain] or [D.J.] Enright or John Press (God) or Chas Tomlinson.' John Press (b. 1920), poet and critic; Charles Tomlinson (b. 1927), poet, artist, translator, at the time Lecturer in English, University of Bristol.

TO ROBERT CONQUEST – 9 APRIL 1961

53 Glanmor Road, Uplands, Swansea, Glam.

Dear Bob,

Herewith the revised intro,[1] now stretching to about 1250 I estimate, plus your draft so that you may compare if you wish. I've made precious few changes, some of which you may feel you'd like to change back again; if so, do so. One point which you've doubtless thought of yourself: better check with the blurb to see we don't contradict ourselves.

I'm sending you the material, yours and mine, under two separate covers. On packing my stuff up, I found, with what fury and incredulity can perhaps be imagined, that three of my selection, or sources thereof, were missing: Christ knows how. A two-hour search has revealed nothing; however, if I should come across them in the next few days, I'll bung them along. I don't think any of them should be hard to find, at Flood's[2] or somewhere. They are

Null-P
Second Variety
The Homing Instinct of Joe Vargo.[3]

If all fails, we could easily find another Dick (The Golden Man, say) and another Tenn (Time in Advance, say), and another someone else. Sorry about this; I can't think what fiend can be responsible.

Vacation accidie is upon me. I'm supposed to be writing this perishing film-script[4] – haven't touched it yet. Then there's my anti-hanging speech[5] (oh Christ), and Peter Sellers and his friends are arriving in

1. To the science fiction anthology *Spectrum* (1961), co-edited with Conquest; from 1961–1966 Amis and Conquest co-edited five of these anthologies, *Spectrum-Spectrum V*.

2. A book and record shop in Sicilian Avenue in Bloomsbury specialising in science fiction, and an informal meeting place for science fiction writers; see Amis to Conquest, 22 March 1962, note 10; also the introduction to *Spectrum*, which thanks 'Mr Leslie Flood and Mr Bruce Montgomery for much generous help'.

3. The first story, 'Null-P', by William Tenn (b. 1920), pseudonym of American writer Philip Klass, was published in *Spectrum II* (1962); 'Second Variety', by Philip K. Dick (1928–82), another, better-known, American writer, and 'The Homing Instinct of Joe Vargo', by Stephen Barr, were published in *Spectrum* (1961).

4. Amis is referring to a film outline adapted from his short story 'Moral Fibre', and co-written with Theo Richmond. See Amis to Richmond, 20 December 1965, note 2.

5. At a rally against capital punishment held later in April at the Albert Hall.

Swansea tomorrow to shoot the exteriors for *That Uncertain Feeling*,[6] which will doubtless be fun, but won't butter any parsnips. The weather is fucking awful. We have the three Moynahan girls[7] staying with us, very sweet and all that, but they've apparently been conditioned to be unable to make less than the maximum amount of noise at all stages of the waking state. My guts are slightly disordered. Bleeding ballocks to it all.

Unable foresee next trip as yet, but will assuredly keep in touch. Don't let the Burns Union for the Glorification of Glasgow, Edinburgh and Rural Scotland get you down.

Yours,
Kingsley

[TLS: Recipient]

TO MARGUERITE CUTFORTH – 8 MAY 1961

53 Glanmor Road, Uplands, Swansea, Glam.

Dear Marguerite,

This ought to blow up to about 250 words, I should think, which is all such a para. ought to be, I should think.[1] I just couldn't add any more without going into the colour of my children's eyes and hair, etc. You'll see that I don't mention my translation to Cambridge: this is because the final, utter, official rubber-stamping hasn't taken place yet, & until it does they've asked me to remain loftily silent on the subject in public.

If you, or any Radio Times chap, cares to try worming a few more

6. The film was renamed *Only Two Can Play* (1962), and released by British Lion. It was directed by Sidney Gilliat, from a screenplay by Bryan Forbes. Sellers played John Lewis, the novel's protagonist. See Amis to Roger Lewis, 8 August 1989.

7. Catherine, Brigid and Mary Ellen Moynahan, daughters of Elizabeth and Julian Moynahan, the latter (b. 1925) an American literary critic and academic who taught English at Princeton from 1955–63.

---

1. Amis was scheduled to give a *Tuesday Talk* on the Home Service (6 June 1961), which Marguerite Cutforth had commissioned; the paragraph, for the *Radio Times*, was to advertise the talk.

facts out of me, then you/he may give me a ring and wlecome – that's Welsh for "welcome."

Yes, script by the 20th. It shall be.

Yours,
Kingsley

[TLS: BBC]

TO ALAN COLLINS – 18 MAY 1961

53 Glanmor Road, Swansea, Glam.

Dear Alan,[1]

You must have thought I was dead, dead drunk, or afflicted by paralysis of the writing hand. Nothing so spectacular – as they'll all tell you in the office, I may have many virtues, but even my best friend couldn't call me an efficient correspondent. I tried hard to see you in London, but as things then were, I was utterly bogged down here. Now there's been a general turn for the better in my affairs: a fellowship at Cambridge, where we go in the autumn. This at any rate takes the urgency off my desire for a (semi) permanent job in the U.S.: we feel it'd be only fair to give Cambridge a whirl before doing anything drastic about leaving England. However, we're still keen to make a trip of some sort to the States, and at the moment I'm working on something for the summer of '62. Nothing definite yet, but unless you come to London (which we can now visit more or less any time) in the meanwhile, we count on seeing you in New York not much more than a year from now.

And how goes it at your end? Give our best to all in the office and at home.

Yours ever,
Kingsley

[ALS: Columbia]

1. For Alan Collins see Amis to Miss Carver, 15 January 1956, note 1.

TO WILLIAM PRITCHARD – 18 JULY 1961

Address until 10th September: 53 Glanmor Road, Uplands, Swansea, Glamorgan, G.B.

Thereafter: Peterhouse, Cambridge, England.

Dear Mr. Pritchard,[1]

Many thanks for your letter. I'm afraid September 1961–June 1962 will be impossible for me, since I shall be needing all my time and energy for my move to Cambridge.* But I am very interested indeed in September 1962. I had already planned to spend the period July–September ('62) in the States, but beyond deciding on the north-eastern area and writing a few letters in quest of employment I have until now got no further. A visit to Amherst, accordingly, is just what I need. What I should really like to know at the moment is how early in September you can fit me in, bearing in mind that I must be back in Cambridge by something like the 7th October, and shall be making the trip by sea. Other details I suppose we could leave until nearer the time. I look forward to hearing from you and was delighted to receive your kind invitation.

Yours sincerely,
Kingsley Amis

*and the Christmas and Easter vacations will be too short for the kind of trip I want to make.

[TLS: Recipient]

1. William H. Pritchard (b. 1932), American literary biographer and critic, has taught English at Amherst College in Amherst, Massachusetts since 1958 (appointed Professor, 1970).

TO PHILIP LARKIN – 14 AUGUST 1961

Sitges. Spain

As you can see, one gran corrida de toros has easily sufficed to turn me into an aficionado. Yes, in a bull's arse it has. I can't imagine anything to beat it for childishness, brutality and *boredom*. This last was what I hadn't bargained for: repetition ad nauseam. As regards brutality it's worse, if anything, than what you expect: the bull's back after the picador has given it the treatment, his bewilderment, the terror of the horse etc. And I always thought that the unwise word in "moment of truth" was "truth". Yes, but so is "moment". Do Hemingway, Tynan et al. mean the moment when the sword finally goes in (it may be at the 4th or 5th attempt), or the moment two or three minutes later when he falls over, or the moment perhaps half a minute after that when (at the 2nd or 3rd attempt) the dagger goes in and he seems to die? To judge by the applause, all this was in order. Otherwise, things Hispanic are far from bad: amiable chaps, brandy 6/- a bot.

Cheers – K. & H.

[ALS: Bodleian]

TO VERNON WATKINS – 22 SEPTEMBER 1961

The Mill House, WEST WRATTING,[1] Cambs.

Dear Vernon,[2]

We strained every nerve to get along to Pennard and say goodbye to you and Gwen, but various complications including the theft of our car (since recovered undamaged), intervened. However, in the mêlée I did have the presence of mind not to put your books into store with

1. The Amises rented this house, in a village several miles outside Cambridge, for two months.

2. For Vernon Watkins see Amis to Larkin, 27 November 1950, note 2.

mine, and all three of them, plus *The Noble Savage*,[3] are at Stuart Thomas's's[4] in Newton, where I dropped them the night before we left.

We shall, needless to say, be back in Wales many a time, and will look you up. Hope the bronchitis has finally packed up.

Love from us both
Kingsley

[ALS: HRHC]

TO ELIZABETH BARBER – 30 OCTOBER 1961

Peterhouse, Cambridge

Dear Miss Barber,[1]

I am sorry to seem to be playing 'hard to get' over this committee of management business: I should like to serve, but I just feel I don't want to let myself in for too much of a load.[2] I can hardly expect the rest of the committee to accommodate themselves to my movements, as I think I said when I wrote to you from Swansea – but I have only one day a week in London, and to come on any other day would entail some juggling with my various commitments here. Would it be too much to ask you to give me some idea of how often I should be wanted if elected?[3]

3. Amis may be referring either to the journal *The Noble Savage*, put out twice a year by Meridien Books, begun in 1960, and containing short stories, criticism and poetry (it was edited by Saul Bellow, Keith Botsford and Jack Ludwig), or to a novel of the same name by Doreen Wallace, set in middle England and published in 1945.

4. For Stuart Thomas see Notes on Recipients.

---

1. Elizabeth Barber joined the Society of Authors in 1936, a year after being called to the Bar, and directed the organisation as General Secretary from 1963 until her retirement in 1971.

2. In November 1960, Miss Barber wrote to Amis asking if he would allow his name to go forward as a nominee for the Committee of Management of the Society of Authors. He declined, in a letter of 20 November 1960 (in the Society of Authors), because of teaching commitments at Swansea. Miss Barber wrote again on 12 October 1961, after Amis's move to Cambridge.

3. On 31 October Miss Barber wrote back saying that the Committee met four to six times a year, and that Amis would not have to attend all its meetings. In a letter of 2 January 1962 he replied, telling Miss Barber that under such terms he approved her having put his name forward for the Committee.

Then I promise to decide definitely without delay. Sorry about the fuss.

Yours sincerely,
Kingsley Amis

[ALS: Society of Authors]

TO JAMES MICHIE – 9 JANUARY 1962

53 Glanmore Road, Uplands, Swansea, Glam.

Dear Jas, man,

Yes, I got it – but I don't want it, well hell, I mean it had its points – I read about 2/3 – but not enough.[1] I caught a kind of facetious seriousness in it that got me down. When I can raise the energy I'll parcel it and send it back. (You know, he hasn't read enough science fiction, either.)

Life is grey here. Taking my cough mixture is about the only unalloyed pleasure I get. But a lunch, a lunch there shall be.

Love from Hilly and me,
Kingsley

[ALS: Columbia]

---

1. For James Michie see Amis to Larkin, 9 March 1949, note 1 (also Amis to Jacqueline Simms, 2 October 1980, note 3). On 21 November 1961 Michie, who was working for the publishers William Heinemann Ltd, sent Amis a copy of *The Wanting Seed* (1962), a novel by Anthony Burgess (1917–94), novelist, composer, critic. In an accompanying handwritten note, Michie explained that he was after 'a kindly quotable phrase that we can use' (this note, like Amis's response, is in the Heinemann archive at Random House). Amis's feelings about the novel seem to have changed over the years. In his *Memoirs* (1991), he calls both *The Wanting Seed* and *A Clockwork Orange* (1962 as well) 'highly successful works of science fiction, imaginative and inventive excursions into the future' (p. 274).

TO VICTOR GOLLANCZ – 1 MARCH 1962

Peterhouse, Cambridge

My dear Victor,

One of the worst things about this stupid sort of life we lead is that one often defers writing the letters one would really like to write. Forgive me for not telling you long ago how sincerely grateful I am for your practical friendship.[1] You don't know how much you have done for us. If anything was needed to secure my allegiance to you and to V.G. Ltd., then this was it. But, as I hope you know, nothing was needed.

Yours,
Kingsley

[ALS: Gollancz]

TO ROBERT CONQUEST – 22 MARCH 1962

9 Madingley Road, Cambridge.[1]

Dear Bob,

I have done a little thinking about this bloody preface; as much as I've had time for in the intervals of thinking about cigarettes (Monday's total, 17; Tuesday, 8; yesterday, 3; today 0 as at 1015 a.m.).

One general line to take would be that since *Spectrum* was published – we're too modest to suggest that it had any actual influence on this – things have been moving so quickly that the anti-sf chap is now in very grave danger of finding himself high and dry, not merely square

---

1. On 24 January 1962, in a letter to Graham Watson, Amis's agent at Curtis Brown, Gollancz agreed to lend Amis the sum of £5,000 against royalties, from both past and future books (specifically, a volume of short stories, *My Enemy's Enemy*, to be delivered in the summer of 1962, and a novel, to be delivered in the summer of 1963, which became *One Fat Englishman*). Amis also agreed to give Gollancz an option on all future work until the £5,000 loan was expunged.

---

1. Described in *Memoirs*, p. 220, as 'a rather posh house . . . at the northern end of the city'.

or not with it, but in the position of finding *Antic Hay*[2] a bit modern and in poorish taste. Readership growing, *Books and Bookmen* now has regular sf column, *Image* (a glossy undergraduate weekly here, but perhaps better not mention Cambridge: might suggest we only notice what's in front of us) has big article on sf without apology, no excuse given, just serious discussion of recent sf trends. All right, we say, this isn't *official highbrow* approval, not yet, but other 20th-century art-forms – jazz, cinema – have won popular support first and then gone on to win highbrow accolade.

We offer this series of Spectra to solve a difficulty always acute with such art-forms – described by a sf writer as "the bouillabaisse problem," i.e. getting a chap to try it for the first time.

Ignorant bastards are still sounding off, like the sod in Ill-Lon-News (enclosed), but, we go on, shitting on this sort of shit is a bit too easy and too dull when such fascinating developments are taking place in the genre. Let's talk about those – in future Spectra, perhaps, we shall cut all this stuff aimed at the general reader and just talk to people who know and like the medium, i.e. all the chaps with sensitivity to literature.

Developments include – what you will. Perhaps: total discarding of crude menace. Growing concern with contemporary problems, e.g. those stories in F&SF[3] I think it was which were direct political stuff about USA and USSR + a few aliens: so sf audience is the obvious one a writer picks when he wants to speculate in this way. Emergence of type of story which uses sf material and ideas in a quite natural, unemphatic way, totally incorporated as bits of travel or Western or historical stuff are incorporated in other kinds of novel. E.g. (perhaps) Limbo 90,[4] Budrys's Rogue Moon[5] – you ought to get Hilary on to buying this right away, I think. Growing self-consciousness and sophistication of the sf writer, as seen in PITFCS[6] which look through for papulum. I also enclose various letters from sods – which please return some time,

2. Aldous Huxley novel of 1923, about Bohemian life in interwar London.

3. *The Magazine of Fantasy and Science Fiction*, an American digest magazine; first issue, Fall 1949.

4. Bernard Wolfe, *Limbo '90* (1952), a dystopian science fiction novel.

5. Algis Budrys (b. 1931), science fiction writer and critic; *Rogue Moon* (1960).

6. *Proceedings of the Institute of Twenty-First Century Studies*, a bi-monthly American journal published between 1960 and 1972 by Theodore Cogswell. It provided a forum for science fiction writers, and was an early incarnation of Science Fiction Writers of America. After 'PITFCS' Amis has written '(encl)', then struck it out, with the ms addition 'Sorry too bulky'.

because I haven't answered the bloody things yet – and the BBC's listener-research stuff on *Something Strange*,[7] which may be of interest. One other point, if it is one: turning away from the gadget-type story as sf's cherished gadgets – the rocket-ship, the satellite, the computer, the cybernetic stuff – become not only overtaken by fact, but hard to know about and write about convincingly. E.g. 20 years ago you didn't need to know much to patter convincingly about say a computer. Now you have to know a hell of a lot.

Time: 2 p.m. Cigarettes smoked: O. Condition: Fidgety, undirectedly randy. Snuff helps a little. So does not working. But you don't want to know about that.

As regards the poems, I thought of two more aspects of Evans[8] today, which shows there may be something in giving up smoking after all. They will take a few days to complete, so I'll send you the 5 aspects plus the two other poems I mentioned when all is complete. At the moment I'm looking for a good rhyme to 'araeolae' or is it 'areolae'?[9]

Shall be up next week, Tues. or Wed., (with Hilly along) and was wondering whether we might fix up an sf lunch or something with Ted Carnell, Oliver Caldecott and Les Flood.[10] What do you think?

Getting cracking on Evans now. See you soon–

Kingsley

Any use thinking of my cockney poem, The Helbatrawss, for NL2?[11]

7. 'Something Strange' (1961), an Amis science fiction story, first appeared in the *Spectator*, 25 November 1960, pp. 821–7; reprinted, among other places, in *The Magazine of Fantasy and Science Fiction* 21 (July 1961), pp. 5–20, and *My Enemy's Enemy* (1962), pp. 199–224. The story was adapted as a play for radio by Amis himself and broadcast on the BBC Third Programme on 6 February 1962. The 'listener-research stuff' was a BBC 'Audience Research Report' of 27 February 1962 (an elaborate document with statistics and an 'appreciation index'; it can be consulted at the BBC Written Archives Centre).

8. A reference to *The Evans Country* (1962); see Amis to Larkin, 15 December 1959, note 4.

9. No such rhyme appears in the Evans sequence. The correct spelling is 'areolae'.

10. Ted Carnell (1912–72), literary agent and editor of *New Worlds* (1946–64), a science fiction magazine (subsequently edited by Michael Moorcock, 1964–70); Oliver Caldecott (1925–89), publisher (at Penguin and elsewhere), artist and editor of science fiction and jazz book clubs; Les Flood (b. 1918), science fiction bookseller and literary agent (he took over Carnell's agency, which represented Brian Aldiss and Harry Harrison, among others).

11. The cockney version of Baudelaire's 'L'Albatross'; see Amis to Larkin, 11 August 1954, note 4. Conquest's *New Lines II* (London: Macmillan, 1963) did not include the poem.

It's offensive to the Lallans sods, but I suppose they've more or less packed up now, haven't they?

Time: 2.47 p.m. Little change.[12]

[TLS: Recipient]

TO BRIAN ALDISS – 18 MAY 1962

9 Madingley Road, Cambridge.

Dear Brian,

I was pretty fairly heart-broken to miss the Convention[1] – but you realise when you get as deep into the groves of academe as I am, your time is no longer your own. You keep having to read obscure works like *Paradise Lost* and this gives you no time for doing what you want to do. Hope to do better next year.

Congratulations on the Penguins job; the first number was very jolly.[2] As regards suggestions, I suppose you have already thought of *A Case of Conscience*, *A Canticle for Leibowitz* and such.[3] But anyway, how about *Rogue Moon*? It seems incredible that (as far as I know) nobody has published it over here yet.

See you, chum.

Yours ever,
Kingsley

PS: V. keen on Hothouse – see Observer.[4]

[TLS: Bodleian]

12. MS addition.

---

1. The British Science Fiction Convention, held in April 1962 in Harrogate.
2. Aldiss had been put in charge of Penguin's science fiction list; 'the first number' is that of *Penguin Science Fiction*, a yearly anthology edited by Aldiss.
3. *A Case of Conscience* (1959) by James Benjamin Blish (1921–75), American science fiction writer, and *A Canticle for Leibowitz* (1960) by Walter Miller, Jr (b.1923), American writer, primarily of science fiction.
4. MS addition. *Hothouse* (1962), by Aldiss, was reviewed by Amis in the *Observer*, 20 May 1962, p.25; the novel was first written as five short stories, the first of which won a Hugo Award in 1961 for Best Short Fiction.

TO EDMUND KEELEY – 18 MAY 1962

9 Madingley Road, Cambridge.

Dear Stud,[1]

Thank you for your letter of February 9th. I have started answering letters now, even though this is a bit late in the day, because I have a secretary.[2] I suppose you have realised by this time that I shall not be able to come to this seminar thing (I have written to Rust Hills to tell him so).[3] It is a great shame, but the trip we were hoping to make to the States this summer or autumn has finally fallen through. I found I couldn't get away for long enough, and there was the matter of raising the cash too. (We have a splendid house here in Cambridge, but it has taken every penny we have, and a lot of other people's pennies too).

I suppose you and Mary will be passing through these Islands sometime this summer – and if you do, fail not to drop me a card or give me a call so that we can arrange some sort of fiesta.

Meanwhile, look after yourself, chum. *Love to Mary*[4]

Yours,
Kingsley

[TLS: Princeton]

---

1. For Edmund Keeley see Notes on Recipients.

2. Amis has drawn an arrow here to a MS addition reading: 'not a v. efficient one, as you see. (Not worth, uh, you know, getting chummy with either)'; two other arrows point to the misspelled 'Keely' and 'Princetown' in the letter's address.

3. *Esquire* had organised a series of annual seminars on college campuses on the topic of 'The Role of the Writer in America'. For reasons Rust Hills (b.1924), the magazine's fiction editor (1956–63), can no longer remember, Amis had been invited to the last of these, held at Princeton (personal communication, 9 February 1999).

4. MS addition.

TO ANTHONY THWAITE – 24 MAY 1962

9 Madingley Road, Cambridge.

Dear Anthony,

Thanks a lot for your note. Glad to know that you are firmly established at the controls of that great Organisation.[1] I have two or three things which I am polishing up, and when they're in some sort of shape I will send them along to you.

Cheers, chum.

Kingsley

[TLS: Recipient]

TO WILLIAM RUKEYSER – 20 JUNE 1962

9 Madingley Road, Cambridge, England.

Dear Bill,[1]

Yesterday I sent off to my agent the final manuscript of my book of stories, including an 18,000-word effort about the British Army and how bloody stupid it is, and am feeling very virtuous as a result.[2] Not only that: I now have some leisure for the first time in God knows how long. So what more natural than that I should be sendin a Leter to my Old yank Pall roo-kaiser what a Swel kidd he is and no Eror. Doing so will anyway defer the final task intervening between me and total calm, the tidying-up of my study. This, if done properly, will involve the paying of various bills, so you can see that writing a letter to the Queen would almost be preferable.

There was great rejoicing here over the news of your utter and

---

1. Thwaite had recently been appointed Literary Editor of the *Listener*.

---

1. For William Rukeyser see Notes on Recipients.
2. The book of stories is *My Enemy's Enemy*, and the eighteen-thousand-word story is 'I Spy Strangers'.

irrevocable acceptance at this great institution.[3] And great expectation of joy when you arrive. One piquant feature of the situation is that Hough[4] hates me ('Fellow like that shouldn't be here,' was his reported comment) and so, I suppose, can't have known of your connection with me when he accepted you. At dinner the other night on neutral ground he insulted Hilly and me in successive sentences, which is good going. I'm looking forward to hearing what may transpire if you casually throw up my name in conversation with him.

We were rather devastated to realise that we couldn't come to the U.S. after all this summer. The reason was that I didn't fancy coming without Hilly, which left us with a kids problem. Their school holidays overlap so little that, apart from expense, we could have brought them only for a time so short as to make the trip just about not worth while; and we don't know anybody who could mind them here satisfactorily. But another year might be different.

Now . . . as regards the literary mission you've kindly said you'd do for me.[5] This is what I would ideally like:

What my hero Roger Micheldene would notice in Greenwich-Village-type surroundings at night – both in the street and in a bar or two – and in the morning.

Short description of modest but not squalid apartment in this or nearby area.

Anything at all about $50,000-a-year house and grounds located anywhere between 30 and 60 miles from Manhattan, out in the country rather than in small town, though either would do.

Enough material for 3 or 4 short scenes set in the undergraduate portions of a university like Princeton or Yale, especially interior of well-off but not stinking-rich set of rooms in e.g. 1919 Hall.[6]

As an Englishman Roger would have his eye and ear open for oddities, but as you know for the author's benefit nothing is more helpful than simple details of lay-out of rooms, size of hallway etc., such as will help author to visualise the thing in general terms.

That, as I say, is what I'd ideally like, but any lesser effort would

3. Rukeyser had been admitted to Christ's College, Cambridge as a research student in English.

4. Graham Hough (1908–90), Tutor and Fellow in English, Christ's College, Cambridge; Professor of English, Cambridge University (1966–75).

5. Amis was requesting background information for what would become *One Fat Englishman* (1963), set at 'Budweiser College', in Pennsylvania.

6. Amis means 1915 Hall, an undergraduate dormitory at Princeton.

be gratefully received. There's no rush whatever for any of this. It would be okay if you brought it with you when you come to England. Thereafter I will take the liberty of trying things out on you, asking you for comments and suggestions about scenes being drafted and so on.

Let me have your news. Things drag on here: I proudly abstained from going to the Peterhouse May Ball the other night, and was regaled the next day with tales of insufficient drink, heavy protocol, lousy band, boring fellow-revellers etc. Now that the bloody undergraduates have all gone away I can start doing some serious work for a change. We hope to visit Mark[7] for a week-end in a little while. Houghton[8] seems endemically around, though amiably so.

Well, cheers, chum. I can't any longer defer writing out a cheque for £1–17s.–6d. to T. Simons & Sons, Heating Engineers and Plumbing Contractors, and a lot of other sods who want a sight more than £1–17s.–6d.

Love from us all,
Kingsley

[TLS: Recipient]

TO ROBERT GRAVES – 10 JULY 1962

9 Madingley Road, Cambridge, England.

Dear Robert,[1]

Good to get your letter. Our prolonged and thorough negotiations with Thos. Cook and Son leave us in the position of not (curse it) being able to turn up just when we said we would, nor stay as long as we hoped. What we are stuck with is arriving at Palma by boat on the

7. Mark Rose, also a student from Amis's Creative Writing seminar at Princeton, had gone on to read English at Merton College, Oxford in 1961 (he was awarded a B.Litt. in 1963), and subsequently became a Professor of English at the University of California, Santa Barbara. Rose's short story 'We Should See a Sign' appeared in Amis and Conquest, eds, *Spectrum III* (1963).

8. Timothy Houghton (1938–74), also from Amis's Creative Writing seminar. For Houghton see Amis to Pell, 18 March 1993.

1. Amis had been commissioned by *Show* magazine in the United States to write a profile of Graves, for which he received a fee of $800 plus expenses. See 'Robert Graves: A Great Poet in an Island Paradise', *Show* 2 (December 1962), pp. 78–81. For Graves see Notes on Recipients.

morning of 12th August, departing on 21st August – 9 days altogether. As you know, we don't know anyone in Majorca except you, and so I'm afraid I simply have to ask you if you could fix us up with some sort (any sort) of accommodation if there turns out to be no room at the Posada[2] – which sounds a wonderful place and which we should love to stay at. Sorry to be a bore.

We both loved seeing you in Oxford[3] and very much look forward to seeing you again. I'm sure that between us we can dope out something which will, if not give the readers of SHOW what they want, at any rate do them good.

Yours,
Kingsley and
Xilé[4] (xx)

[ALS: William Graves]

TO ELIZABETH JANE HOWARD – 27 JULY 1962

9 Madingley Road, Cambridge.

Dear Jane,

Good to get your letter. Yes, thank you very much, I should indeed like to bring my wife to Cheltenham.[1] We look forward very much to seeing you there.

Yours ever,
Kingsley

[TLS: HEHL]

2. A guest house on Graves's property in Deyá, the fishing village on Majorca where he had lived, excepting the war years, since 1929.

3. Graves had been elected Professor of Poetry at Oxford in 1961, a position previously held by W.H. Auden.

4. Hilly's signature in 'Spanish'.

---

1. The 1962 Cheltenham Literary Festival was directed by Elizabeth Jane Howard. Amis was invited to participate in a seminar on 'Sex in Literature' sponsored by the *Sunday Telegraph*. The seminar was held on 4 October in the Cheltenham Town Hall and there were three other panellists: the American novelists Joseph Heller and Carson McCullers, and the French novelist and diplomat Romain Gary. Although he and Miss Howard had met earlier, it was only at Cheltenham, according to Amis, that 'I sort of threw a pass at Jane which was sort of accepted' (see Jacobs, *Biography*, p. 255). For Howard see Notes on Recipients.

TO ROBERT GRAVES – 4 SEPTEMBER 1962

9 Madingley Road, Cambridge, England.

Dear Robert,

We're back, though it's no thanks to anybody that we managed it.[1] That *car* . . . I'll tell you the full story when I see you, but the oddest thing really was your taking a view about the thing when it hadn't really started to happen: after all, cars get backed over drops and run out of petrol every day. Anyway: a good job it wasn't a plane. I hope, by the way, that what the car did (we're still expecting a bill from the hire company) exhausts the prophecy you made about a meaningful coincidence happening to me within a month – expiry date 18th September. I'll notify you of anything extra in that line, assuming it leaves me with the power of communication.

I've been fired by your example to attempt an 8 a.m. start to the writing day. Difficult, though. Bloody things like seeing bank managers, rescuing neurotics (Christ, what sort of slack do they think *I* have?) etc. keep getting in the way. However, blood was got out of the stone to the extent of a single poem – another in my Welsh series.[2] Unimmediate, but another dozen are queueing up. I wish they'd jostle more. You shall of course have that sheaf of my more recent (i.e. since my book)[3] stuff you asked for, but I'll have to look at them again first. As for that article, the SHOW thing, I don't know. Somehow it now seems rather absurd to do it. But I'll keep you posted.

Thank you, and everybody, particularly Beryl,[4] for a marvellous week. To itemise everything you did for us would involve a full diary of what we did. We recall and discuss it ceaselessly. I still have and hold all your books. Tomás's[5] picture holds the place of honour on the main mantelpiece. I've pushed that £100 off to Lucia's[6] bank in Bayswater.

1. The Amises had stayed in Deyá for nine days in the second half of August.
2. *The Evans Country.*
3. *A Case of Samples.*
4. Beryl Graves (b.1915), Graves's second wife.
5. Tomas Graves (b.1953), Graves's youngest son by Beryl.
6. Lucia Graves (b.1943), Graves's daughter by Beryl. She was living in London, in Bayswater, going to school at the French Lycée; Graves probably lent Amis £100 in Deyá, which Amis was now repaying.

Please be sure to let us know your London address, and the dates.

Love to you all, to you and Beryl and William and Lucia and Juan and Tomás, and to Karl (what a wonder he was with that car), and to Encarnita.[7] Hope to see you soon.

Kingsley

[TLS: William Graves]

TO JEAN McANDREW – 26 SEPTEMBER 1962

9 Madingley Road, Cambridge, England

Dearest Jean,

This is the first proper chance I've had to write since it happened.[1] But it's just as hard to find words as it was the afternoon we got the news. We still don't know any details at all about what happened – all we've had is Liz [Moynahan]'s cable mentioning a brain haemorrhage. When you have time and can face it, let us know something.

John was one of my closest and dearest friends and he would have gone on being that even if he had lived another 30 years without our having seen each other again. I shall never forget his generosity, his warmth, his unselfishness and his goodness – and we all know goodness is a very rare thing, even part-way goodness. He was so engaging and light-hearted but it was easy to sense that serious conscientiousness going on underneath all the time. He was a sweet, funny, affectionate, lovable man and I admired and loved him. And I enjoyed his company so much.

This is a cruel horrible thing to have happened and it has grieved all sorts of people and will go on grieving them, but of course you and the girls most. We feel so sorry for you all and we think about you

7. William (b.1940) and Juan Graves (b.1944), Graves's sons by Beryl; Karl was Kenneth Gay (originally Karl Goldschmidt), Graves's secretary cum assistant; Encarnita, writes William Graves, who cannot remember her last name, was 'the striking young girl who cleaned RG's house in Deyá' (personal communication, 24 January 1999).

1. John McAndrew had died suddenly on 19 September 1962, of an aneurism. He was fifty.

most of the time. What we said in our cable[2] about your coming over wasn't just a spur-of-the-moment idea. *Do* please think about coming over, and staying with us as long as you like, with any or all of the kids or on your own.[3] I really think it would be a good thing for you. And of course we would just love to have you. When everything that has to be done has been done why don't you consider it seriously? Just cable us your time of arrival at London airport and we'll be there to meet you. There can't be any real comfort with this kind of thing but I'm sure it would be good for you to get right away from everything and everybody. *Try.*

All my love, dear, and sympathy, and sorrow,

Kingsley

[ALS: Recipient]

TO ALAN ROSS – 11 OCTOBER 1962

9 Madingley Road, Cambridge.

Dear Alan,

Pretty prompt, what? I enclose two of my things: A Point of Logic and Oligodora, which latter I think is a jolly intellectual title, and cultured too.[1] You know, like our Ezra.

We ought to get together some time. Why don't you throw me a lunch on the Mag?

Yours,
Kingsley

[TLS: HRHRC]

2. According to Jean McAndrew, 'the cable said "ALL OUR LOVE CAN YOU COME OVER IMMEDIATELY WITH KIDS LETTER FOLLOWS KINGSLEY AND HILLY"' (personal communication, 26 January 1997).

3. Jean McAndrew and her five daughters visited the Amises in Cambridge in March 1963.

---

1. Both poems were published in the *London Magazine*, January 1963, pp. 12–13, reprinted in *A Look Round the Estate*. For Ross see Amis to Larkin, 25 September 1946, note 5.

TO ELIZABETH JANE HOWARD – 21 NOVEMBER 1962

Dearest Jane,

I really did mean to have got this to you about a week ago, but things kept coming up: mainly *feeling bloody awful*, not about us or you (on the contrary), but in the old undirected way I told you about. Last Wednesday and Thursday, for instance, I felt so alarmingly bloody that I decided to make a real anti-drink effort (there'd been a feast here on the Tuesday which set off the Wed-Thur feeling). Fell from grace on Saturday night – and thus held a public quarrel in a pub on the Sunday evening. But otherwise good: yesterday's score: 1 sherry, 2 beers, 3 gins, ½ bottle Beaujolais. Present state of health – moderate, though much upgraded at the moment by excitement and pleasure and tenderness about you. I enjoyed everything about that Monday. I can't forget how beautiful you are. I love your *gaze*. I remember particularly (and always will) that sudden eye-to-eye moment in the restaurant. I'm very proud of you.

Have been dipping into the Good Food Guide London section, on the look-out for handy little out of the way places to eat. Haven't yet come up with anything decisive, but we'll be throwing down shish-kebab in Shepherd's Bush and whitebait in Whitechapel before very long.

At the moment it looks as if today week, Wednesday 28th, is going to be suitable between about 5.30 and 10-10.15.

Thursday.

Bloody people keep coming in and stopping me. Now about next Wednesday – give me a ring here between 4 and 5 on the Monday afternoon. I'll see there's nobody with me. I'd better get this off before the next bugger arrives.[1] Longing to see you. Mind you ring. And you could write to me too if you feel like it. I feel very good about you and me. You're gorgeous.

Much love

K.

[ALS: HEHL]

---

1. The next student; the note was written from Amis's room at Peterhouse.

TO ELIZABETH JANE HOWARD – 6 DECEMBER 1962

Dearest Jane – just got your gorgeous letter, and a young man has just left, saying he was sorry he didn't have time to do his essay, so I can answer straight away. I can't think of anything more wonderful than that first time in room 238, while it was going on I realised that this was what sexual ecstasy was, though I didn't put it to myself like that at the time, not being in much shape for thought: "*this* is it" was about as close as I got. I love you all right. I feel I was less than ideally loving and attentive while we were waiting for those bloody taxis: but you know it wasn't because of you – cold, hunger, irritation etc. Have been in fine shape since: sat up talking last night till 3 a.m., drinking whisky *in moderation* – woke up with *clear head* and greeted the day with *pleasurable anticipation* (rewarded by getting your letter). Sorry about this paper but it's all I have with me. Regret that Monday is off – an engagement here came up and I couldn't think quickly enough of what I was going to be officially doing in London. But will work on the problem. Regret also you can't write to me again for the time being – the buggers here forward one's mail home and I tend to open my letters in public – just conceivably might find I'd opened one of yours at the wrong time. Sounds as if I'm trying to make myself incommunicable, does it? Well, you know (after room 238) that that's not so. Our best channel is phone – I'll arrange to be in college at certain times when you can ring, starting with this coming Monday between 2.30 and 3.* We can plot then. Excellent news about there being no Greek novelist after all.[1] Look forward to reconnaissance report. It's bloody cold in here – there's a gas fire but by the time the gas has climbed up to the 2nd floor it's lost all its go. Did you say that the Greek might be wrapping up his *parents* in vine leaves, or his presents? Cyril sounds good.[2] I know what you mean about being the whole world, in 238. We both felt the same thing. Nothing much to do today. Have to give Golly a title for my next novel, so am going to comb Defoe's "True-born

1. Jane Howard cannot remember to whom this refers.

2. Cyril Frankel (b.1921), film and television director, friend of Jane Howard's; he had a large house in Wilton Place in Knightsbridge where Amis and Jane would sometimes meet. Frankel served as best man at their wedding.

Englishman"[3] for a possible quote. Yes, you must give me your recommendations about food – I trust you on that after you chose that trout for me. Oh, you do look nice. What gave you the *idea* of doing your hair like that? It suits you. Hear from you on Monday, darling.

Much love –
K.

*If you can't, then Tuesday at 11-11.30. If you can't then either, will write again & suggest further times.

[ALS: HEHL]

3. *The True-Born Englishman* (1701) by Daniel Defoe (1660–1731) was a popular satirical poem attacking anti-Dutch and foreign prejudice against King William III and his advisers. Amis hoped it would provide him with a title for *One Fat Englishman.*

TO THE EDITOR, *SPECTATOR* – 14 DECEMBER 1962

SIR,–Starbuck's reminder about anti-Semitism is timely.[1] The ex-liberal anti-liberal cynic is on the way to becoming a more formidable enemy of progressive thought in this country than any of the most traditional reactionary types. He can be detected by his sneers at the 'lilac establishment,' at the anti-hanging campaign, at protests against anything from the laws about homosexuality to Dr. Verwoerd's[2] policies. All liberal settlement has become square in his view and he must dissociate himself from it: 'I'm not anti-Semitic,' I have heard him say (for Colin Jordan[3] and his friends are equally square): 'I just can't stand Jews.'

There is much that is fatuous in the conduct of liberal causes and many bores are associated with them. In particular I share our cynic's weariness with all those indignant letters, signed by the same old crowd every time, inveighing against political detentions here, there and every-

1. 'Starbuck', the pseudonymn of the 'Notebook' columnist of the *Spectator*, had declared it 'everyone's job to correct the mistaken idea that it is somehow smart to be anti-Semitic' (7 December 1962, p.887).

2. Dr Hendrik Verwoerd (1901–66), National Party leader and Prime Minister of South Africa (1958–66); he was stabbed to death in Parliament in Cape Town.

3. Colin Jordan (b.1923) was leader of the fascist British Movement.

where, and I for one have made up my mind to have no further truck with pseudo-action of this sort. But the causes themselves would still be good causes even if their every supporter were a fool. It may be tedious and not with-it to say so, but anti-Semitism in any form, including the fashionable one of anti-anti-anti-Semitism, must be combated.

KINGSLEY AMIS
9 Madingley Road, Cambridge

TO ELIZABETH JANE HOWARD – 8 JANUARY 1963

Dearest dearest Jane,

I adored it. I adore you. You get more beautiful all the time. I can't stop thinking about you. Every other woman I see reminds me of you – to her disadvantage. I love and enjoy everything about you. I love your clothes and the way you do your hair and I do feel awed by you as I said at lunch. I can't wait to see you. I do love you. Not just sexual friends any more – though that too. I admire and trust you. I knew it would be wonderful but I had no idea it would be as wonderful as this. Got to go now. Ring you tomorrow. I love you.

Kisses from your loving
Hunter[1]

[ALS: HEHL]

1. According to Elizabeth Jane Howard (personal communication, 20 October 1999), 'Hunter' alludes to Max Hunter, the alcoholic hero of *The Anti-Death League* (1966), which Amis had just begun writing. Like other signatures in the early letters to Howard, it was adopted by Amis in part to conceal his identity in case the letter was found (see Amis to Elizabeth Jane Howard, 23 January 1963, note 2).

TO ELIZABETH JANE HOWARD – 12 JANUARY 1963

Dearest Jane,

Never so awed before as by Thursday. It was like a dream except that I don't dream so vividly. Never been so knocked over by love. In proof of which I send you the poem.[1] Never written a love poem like this before, i.e. one that says I love you (any other attempts have been apologies for *not* loving, or wishing I had etc – see "album Leaf".)[2] The thing may need polishing. It came very quickly. I doubt whether anyone else but you would understand it (10 & 9 years old and so on)[3] – *but that's good.* It's for *you.*

Hope I didn't sound as if I blamed you for not having trusted me completely till Wednesday. I can quite see that and it makes me angry with all your other men. Anyhow, I know you trust me now. Sorry I was so drunk – got home all right – funny anecdote to tell you about this. Will ring you Monday. Awed, adoring

Hunter

[ALS: HEHL]

---

1. 'An Attempt at Time-Travel', first published in *A Look Round the Estate*; reprinted in *CP*, p. 101.

2. First published in *A Case of Samples*; reprinted in *CP*, p. 53.

3. The cryptic references occur in the poem's last stanza. The speaker imagines himself into a photograph showing his girlfriend at the age of nine (this is the 'attempt at time-travel'). The self he imagines is ten, which corresponds to the real-life age difference between Amis and Elizabeth Jane Howard.

TO ROBERT CONQUEST – 22 JANUARY 1963

Cambers

Dear Bob,

Here it is.[1] Bloody awful old life, isn't it? Am cold, have the shits, also catarrh. Still, two new poems this year already. It's the bird that does it.[2]

See yez soon,
Kingers

[ALS: Recipient]

TO ELIZABETH JANE HOWARD – 23 JANUARY 1963

My dearest Jane – it was indeed a lovely letter, and you must get this clear; I don't in the least mind your apologising to me, but apologies aren't in order between you and me. I was pleased when you asked me to forgive you for kissing me in restaurants, and you may do so again, but only on condition you go on kissing me in restaurants. I *like* that. As for you supposedly telling me too much about yourself, that's nonsense. Apart from me wanting to know anyway (I am fairly interested in you, you see) – well, saying that might appear to you as mere gallantry, my notorious niceness and so on; so reflect on the two solid selfish advantages I get from letting you go on telling me things (a) my vanity is anointed by my being the only person to hear a lot of your stuff, which means I must be a good chap and you must like me a lot (b) by letting you run on I'm accumulating a tremendous amount of indulgence on *your* part when *I* start telling *you* all *my* stuff. There's a third point (c) that while you're talking I can enjoy the sound of your voice (I listen to *what* you say, too, mind you) and watch your face, without having to use up energy by talking myself – the alternative,

1. Conquest cannot remember what 'it' was.

2. Elizabeth Jane Howard, the inspiration for 'An Attempt at Time-Travel' and 'Waking Beauty', both first published in *A Look Round the Estate* and reprinted in *CP*, pp. 101 and 100.

that of staring at you dumbly for 20 minutes at a time, might bore you and in the end would arouse more attention on the part of other diners than just a kiss, which is over in a few seconds. But perhaps you think that's gallantry too. I don't know what I meant by saying we'd run out of things to say in a month – are you sure you understood me correctly? Certainly I don't think that now – every time I leave you I'm conscious of the huge 99·9% of things we've never talked about. I do enjoy your voice over the telephone. I think of you constantly and always adoringly. Oh, and here's the poem[1] – unique in *Hunter's[2] output as not only a real love poem but a joyous one too. I had the Sleeping Beauty dream sloshing around in my head ever since you told me about it, then 3 days ago the last line suddenly popped up and I knew what the whole thing was going to say. I love offering it to you. House filling up with people – must get this off. Ring you 1.45. Can you manage Tuesday next week? Got to go now. I love you, everything about you, especially everything.

Lord Hunter

*In case you're run over with this in your handbag

[ALS: HEHL]

TO HUW WHELDON – 23 JANUARY 1963

9 Madingley Road, Cambridge

Dear Huw,

Here is something which might possibly interest MONITOR[1] – anyway, I'm giving you first refusal. On the 11th March there's going to be an exhibition of paintings from Wales here in Cambridge, part

1. 'Waking Beauty'.
2. Amis has written the word 'Hunter's', preceded by an asterisk, over the word 'Amis's', almost wholly obscuring the original.

1. An arts programme on the BBC. It did not take up Amis's suggestion.

of it in my house and part somewhere in Clare. Glyn Daniel[2] is going to open it. The artists to be represented include (forgive the publicity-hand-out style) Ray Howard-Jones, Kyffin Williams, John Elwyn, Will Roberts, Alfred Janes, Ronald Cour, Jack Waldron, Thomas John Nash, Colin Jones, Ernest Zobele, Robert Alwyn-Hughes, Eric Malthouse, Glenys Cour, and probably but not certainly Josef Herman and David Jones:[3] you probably know the work of a good many of them. Our Swansea friend Margaret Aeron-Thomas,[4] whom I fancy you know, is master-minding the thing, and it's really for her sake that I'm lending my premises for these (as they'll probably strike me) wretched daubs.

I thought that, apart from the Welsh connection, this might be sufficiently out of the ordinary to make a reasonably interesting occasion for MONITOR. If it won't do for you, I'd be most grateful for any advice on who else I might approach. We don't want to have to fall back on Anglia TV unless we must.

Yours,
Kingsley

[TLS: BBC]

TO A.G. LEE – 11 FEBRUARY 1963

9 Madingley Road, Cambridge

Dear Mr. Lee,

How kind of you to ask: I was most flattered.[1] Of course I am very pleased to send you a work sheet plus autograph fair copy. I wrote the poem in the middle of last month and it hasn't been published (or

2. Glyn Daniel (1914–86), archaeologist and writer of detective stories; Fellow of St John's College, Cambridge (from 1938), Professor of Archaeology, Cambridge University (1974–81).

3. All established painters.

4. For Margaret Aeron-Thomas see Amis to Larkin, 3 March 1953.

1. Amis had sent Lee (b. 1918), the Librarian of St John's College, Cambridge (1961–81), and a Fellow in Classics, the work sheet and manuscript fair copy of 'Waking Beauty', for a collection of manuscripts of poems by contemporary poets.

even sent out to anyone). I should like you to have it for your collection.

Yours sincerely,
Kingsley Amis

[ALS: St John's College, Cambridge]

TO ELIZABETH JANE HOWARD – [FEBRUARY 1963]

Dearest – only time for a tiny note, if this is to get to you tomorrow. I was so moved by your letter. I love thinking I do things for you but you mustn't suppose you don't do big things for me. I was in a low state of morale when I got hold of you, as you know. Now greatly restored. I told you you make me feel like a man – not that I feel particularly feminine most of the time but I don't usually feel *confident*, non-harassable etc. I wish I saw you more often and when other people are there too – seeing you with Cyril [Frankel] there made me realise this: I miss that side of you. Mind you, of the two (public and private) I'd pick the one I have. You're on the edge of my thoughts all the time and when you move right into the middle of them I beam to myself. I don't really see how you could give me more pleasure than you do already, but you're very welcome to try. Dull day today: slightly nauseated by horrible Chinese meal last night. You make me feel a sort of complacent tolerance for people – "oh well, he is a bit of a bore, but we have to remember he hasn't got a bird like mine" & so on. Ring you Wed. p.m. I love everything about you –

Hunter

[ALS: HEHL]

TO ELIZABETH JANE HOWARD – 25 FEBRUARY 1963

Dearest bird – wonderful letter. You mustn't be afraid of being an exhausting person. The only person who suffers because of your dreams is you. I don't like you having them, but I like you waking me up. It's such joy to find that it's you who's there. And I really ought to be there to comfort you after every dream until they stop. Also, you mustn't be ashamed of wanting to touch me – "getting better" about that would be touching me more, not less. I love you touching me and if you start doing less of it I shall go all silent and morose and will start pinching you or punching you in the ribs. The point about the eyelids was so to speak that I wanted to show you how much confidence I had in you and me; you know, showing how all right we are even with very personal teasing in public. I like them being as they are. Yes, Bill [Rukeyser] is fine. I told you he heartily approves of you, both as person and as beauty. He's the only person I can talk about you to, and I want to do that all the time. He says I have two favourite things to say about you which really mean the same thing: "First-class bird, that" (brisk & matter-of-fact & sober) and "I love her" (slow & solemn & not-so-sober).

You are trustworthy. I do enjoy life more because of you. In the course of a long and varied career I have never known anything like your physical response. And I like women more than I did through being your lover. (My talk on Woman's Hour is about the importance of liking women,[1] though I think on the whole I shan't quote your name as a good practitioner to go to if one's liking-for-women is below standard.) Did I ever remember to tell you how much you *entertain* me? – I mean consciously as well as unconsciously. Saw your ex no 1[2] on telly yesterday, talking about the Loch Ness monster. When asked what he thought it was he said "Well to start with it clearly isn't a bird." Surrounded by family I broke into a sudden fit of coughing.

You mustn't be less effeminate. It's one of your glories – being that as well as tough (I've always said you're that) and capable and intelligent. Being effeminate isn't the opposite to being intelligent – with you they set each other off. And I have nothing to bear except not being with you when I want to be, which is all the time. Will ring Wednesday probably about 11.30 & will see you in evening: full of love –

William[3]

[ALS: HEHL]

---

1. The talk was entitled 'Letter of Advice to Someone Else's Son', and broadcast on *Woman's Hour*, 28 February 1963.

2. Peter Scott (1909–89), the naturalist and painter, married Elizabeth Jane Howard in 1942 (the marriage was dissolved in 1951).

3. Amis's middle name.

TO ELIZABETH JANE HOWARD – 1 MARCH 1963

Dearest first-class bird – have just put the phone down. Delighted to hear you sounding so jolly, though sorry the film has to be redone[1] – still, those things are never as bad as having to redo one's marriage, for instance. As regards my own (marriage, not film) I meant to tell you on Wednesday, but think I forgot – everything is fine there: all very cordial and undisturbed. You are very good about that, perfect in fact (as about everything) – with just the right attitude, non-inquisitive, non-commenting and so on [. . .]

I feel very optimistic and able-to-work, and am very kind and gracious with taxi-drivers, porters etc. This new thing of seeing you with other people is splendid – enjoyable and informative (seeing another side of you and liking it as much as all the others). Bill wants another lunch soon. Well, all right, but I only want to see you with others if it means I don't see less of you by yourself. You are sweet. And so straight, And I am with you. As you know.

Much awed love from
Generalissimo Hunter

The way you write 'of' & 'if' is very funny.

[ALS: HEHL]

TO THE EDITOR, *SUNDAY TELEGRAPH* – 10 MARCH 1963

Sir – Congratulations to Albany on his fearless exposure of the latest Socialist scandal ("New Statesmanship," Mar. 3). So John Freeman and Harold Wilson have been having "lunch" at a "restaurant," and an

1. *The Very Edge* (1962), a thriller directed by Cyril Frankel, starring Richard Todd, Jeremy Brett and Anne Heywood. Howard worked on the screenplay for six weeks (for a fee of £600); the scene that had to be redone entailed a three-day trip to Dublin, where the film was being shot.

"expensive" one at that, eh? How *dare* they![1] Don't they know that their place is in an Old Kent Road cabmen's shelter, taking scoff and char?

But this is not all. I can now reveal that Freeman hardly ever wears a cloth cap and choker, and that Wilson's bath has not accommodated coal for almost a decade. Have these fellows no sense of the fitness of things?

KINGSLEY AMIS
Cambridge

TO BETTY PROVAN – 13 MARCH 1963

Peterhouse, Cambridge

Dear Miss Provan,

I am sorry to have left your letter of 22nd February unanswered for so long. I informed Miss Cohn some days ago that the fee suggested was totally inadequate to the size of the writing task involved, and now, with regrets, inform you of the same.[1]

Yours sincerely,
Kingsley Amis

[ALS: BBC]

---

1. John Freeman (b.1915), Labour MP and Minister; at the time Editor, *New Statesman* (1961–65). Harold Wilson (1916–95), at the time Leader of the Labour Party (1963–76), subsequently Prime Minister (1964–70, 74–76); created Baron Wilson of Rievaulx (1983). In a reply appended to Amis's letter, 'Albany', the gossip columnist, declares that 'Mr. Wilson and Mr. Freeman may of course lunch as much as they like at luxurious restaurants. But even their most fervent admirers may raise an eyebrow when the Leader of the Opposition thereby refuses an invitation to meet Mr Diefenbaker [Conservative Prime Minister of Canada], and when the editor of the *New Statesman* professes asceticism in the columns of his magazine.'

---

1. Amis had been asked to write and read a twenty-minute talk to be broadcast on the Home Service in the series *The Writer and his Background*. The proposed fee was thirty guineas plus fares from Cambridge. Betty Provan was employed in the Talks Booking Department of the BBC from 1947–70. Leonie Cohn was a Talks Producer.

TO ELIZABETH JANE HOWARD – 13 MARCH 1963

Dearest – only time for a little one. Loved your letter, but sorry you aren't sleeping. You need me there. *You must go on* talking to me about this sort of thing. Even if you had someone else to talk to I'd still want you to tell me – how could it be "improper"? No, I wasn't angry at you not being there when I phoned, nor have been at any time since nor now. Nor ever will be. About *anything*. You *must* believe that. I do get angry with people sometimes but I *never* will with *you*. That's not only a promise but a prediction. How *could* I? I was very worried on Monday, then very relieved, never angry. Think I can face ringing you now . . . Yes, fairly painless. Have everything straight. Shortly going to buy new typewriter as symbolic initiation of new, much more creative life. Many odd and funny things to tell you. This is even better than I meant because you kept going on talking to me on the phone (which I didn't mind much on the whole) and I have to go. Ring you soon after 2. Much love from Marshal of the R.A.F. Hunter

[ALS: HEHL]

TO ROBERT CONQUEST – 24 MARCH 1963

9 Madingly Road, Cambridge,

Dear Bob,

I've rewritten – or rather added something to – the first part of the intro,[1] and feel that the rest is OK, with one or two queries I've marked. I think you can go ahead from these.

I've lost Weinbaum,[2] or rather mislaid him. The house has been given over to this sodding Welsh art exhibition and all loose stuff has been stowed away God knows where. Sorry. I'll try again when we come back from Majorca, where we depart tomorrow.

---

1. To *Spectrum III* (1963).
2. Stanley G. Weinbaum (1900–35), American science fiction writer; none of his stories appears in the *Spectrum* anthologies.

Also enclose a poem for the spring books number.[3]

If you want anything urgently, write c/o R Graves – Canelluñ, Deyá, Mallorca, Spain, as you doubtless know.

Cheers, chum,
Kingsley

[ALS: Recipient]

TO ELIZABETH JANE HOWARD – 25 MARCH 1963

Dearest darling lovely bird –

I hope you like these. I asked for the grandest in the place but am no judge. Happy birthday and many happy returns and a new year of being loved by

Hunter
Lord President of the Council

[ALS: HEHL]

TO WILLIAM RUKEYSER – 2 APRIL 1963

LA POSADA, DEYÁ, MALLORCA, Spain

My dear Bill,

As you'll know (probably), we have the house[1] – a real hidalgo's joint surrounded by orange trees! we mustn't pick the fruit much,

3. Conquest was Literary Editor, *Spectator* (1962–63); the poem was 'Waking Beauty'.

---

1. The Amises had gone to Majorca during the Easter vacation to scout out a house to live in for a year; they found one in Soller, close to Graves's property at Deyá, and planned to move there at the end of the academic year. Amis's decision to resign his fellowship at Peterhouse and devote himself to full-time authorship abroad was made before Christmas. It is described in *Memoirs*, p. 227:

> I know there are people who successfully combine a full teaching programme with a literary career, but I found it beyond me, and by now far the greater part of my earnings was coming from what I wrote. And finally, Hilly and I had just been to Majorca and I got to know Graves a bit there.
>
> So in due course I found myself saying to the infinitely kind and decent

though. Reputedly cold in winter, which oil heaters and such will lick – otherwise ideal. 3 miles from the beach and adequately flash hotels and bars. There was a good contract-signing episode, attended of course by Sr. Isasi – el mio abogado*,[2] you know. We paid our deposit – £72 – and can move in any time after 1st October.

Palma[3] is a real swinging town. Very cosmopolitan: listening in one of its Danish restaurants to the Dutch Swing College band playing (unusually well) "O Sole Mio", I felt like a much older, infinitely more accomplished Garnet Bowen.[4] There's also Mam's Bar in Terreno (the foreign quarter), run by an American called Carl Steeves, a sort of hilarious non-literary Blackmur, and frequented by his compatriots, commonly in a state of intoxication. Some British, too. I drank rather a lot of brandy there, and some liqueur or other made from the fruit of the locust tree, so that when we called on Graves later that day I was in talkative vein and bawled "piss" and other unspeakables at a young British poet and globe-trotter, who I thought was a great piss-talker. Very relieved, on talking to him sober the following lunch-time, to find that he *is* a great piss-talker. Graves seemed not put out by the whole thing and has been in most amiable form. His best stroke to date has been to tell us, on the morning of the house-signing-up, that the place had burned down in the night, revealing after a minute or two that it was April Fools' Day.

Prices here continue to astonish. Very drinkable red wine at 9d a bottle, genuine French liqueurs, cointreau for instance, at 11/6, and even American bourbon goes for about 30s. Chesterfields 2/4 a packet, unless you get them on the black market as many do, which brings them down

> Herbert Butterfield, then Master of Peterhouse, 'Sir, with great regret I want to resign my Fellowship at this college.'

This explanation is embedded in a chapter of the *Memoirs* entitled 'Cambridge', which more fully details Amis's objections to the place and to his life as a don. Amis also described them in a series of newspaper interviews, causing resentment and hurt feelings at Peterhouse. Larkin's description of the newspaper stories, in a letter to Conquest, 30 December 1962, in *LL*, p. 348, suggests something of the distance that had grown up between the two friends at this time: 'I think it wd have been more graceful of K. to glide out of Cambridge without all this public posturing. If he made a mistake in thinking he could write there that's his fault, not anyone else's: no need to try to put them in the wrong. I can't imagine Majorca will be any better. Whose flat will he borrow there? Who'll he screw?'

2. Amis's note reads: 'my lawyer, you bird-brain'.

3. The largest town on Majorca, and capital of the Balearic Isles; nineteen miles from Soller. The children were to attend the international school in Palma in the autumn.

4. The hero of *I Like it Here*.

to 1/2. Food prices I haven't noticed, but Hilly says they're about 1/2 the British. Weather like a good early British summer, so all is well. [. . .]

Will let you know later about meeting us (thanks for offer) but I don't think it'll be necessary. Where *are* you, anyway, and where will you be? – your name is as fragrant as ever among us now, but it was a little besmirched last Monday, when it emerged that apparently driving to London was *your* idea. Never mind – we caught the train with at least 4 minutes in hand. Large scotch and dry ginger with the bacon and eggs thereafter.

Well, we're enjoying ourselves very noticeably and will see you on or after the 12th. Drop a line if you have time – and tell us your movements. Looking forward to seeing you.

Love,
Kingsley & Hilly

Christ, have finished reading Russian science fiction now. A fresh and to me very compelling reason for OH NO THEY'RE NOT when some ape suggests USA = USSR.

[ALS: Recipient]

TO ELIZABETH JANE HOWARD – 4 APRIL 1963

WARNING: Awful unrelieved *love*-letter is what this is – couldn't manage travelogue etc. Love you.

Dearest dove – this is the first time I've been alone; nobody's plan, just the way things have turned out. We've had a happy time but I've been missing you. I miss your mouth and your breath and your skin and your hair and your smell and your left eyelid and your right breast and right collarbone and right armpit and the back of your neck. And all your other things. And your voice. And eyes. And hands and everything. I've never missed anyone like this before. I said I don't think sexy letters are any good but I keep remembering how we are together and what we do. Even thinking of things remotely connected with you makes me react physically – remind me to tell you how. Oh well, one anecdote will have to do for now. We met a female friend on the boat to France, later an amiable Spaniard on the Paris Train who took to said friend. After a pleasant alcoholic lunch H. and I went to sleep in the compartment while the Spaniard made not-very-serious passes at friend. At one stage friend gave a (quite amiable and skittish) shriek of protest. I awoke instantly saying "It's all right. You're all right." Quite surprised to find it wasn't you and me at Tom's[1] at 4 a.m. Glad to hear – via very secure information from Bill – that you're fit again. My father – must get this over with – is evidently (H. said after our trip had begun) further along the road than I'd thought and it seems he'll have to be put into a nursing home near us when we get back.[2] This will be handle-able. I loved your offer about him and I know you meant it. You are such a good person and I would trust you with anything and everything I have in any circumstances – a way of saying among other things that you're tough as well as all the other dear things you are. I hope this is, all this is, reassuring you that I haven't forgotten about you and still like you as much as ever – you trust me too, I know, but you have that ridiculous sense of inadequacy that I must work harder against when I come home. Am I being too unfactual? Actually this letter so far is the equivalent of sexual endearments, inevitably de-sexed by writing them down, rather than of the post- and pre-amorous chat I so enjoy. You offer too much for any poor one bloody man to take in. It's too bad that anyone so attractive/interesting should be so interesting/attractive. Did I tell you that our thing has completely robbed me of sexual ambition? No more 50-maidenheads-in-prospect for me. You have made me proof against any kind of sexual defeat. Or perhaps any defeat, oh, I *miss* you. I want you to be here, I want to see it all with you here, do it all with you. This must read uncomfortably like the utterances of a man helplessly in love. I see and hear you so clearly in my mind: 3-dimensionally, stereophonically. Wish I had time to write you just a factual, informative

---

1. Tom Maschler, Elizabeth Jane Howard's editor at Jonathan Cape, would sometimes lend her his house in Chalcot Crescent, Belsize Park. He was unmarried at the time.

2. William Amis had been diagnosed with cancer. See *Memoirs*, p. 23: 'He developed what he thought, or said he thought, was an ulcer but turned out to be an inoperable cancer. The end came quickly: on 25th March 1963 he wrote me a cheerful letter in his customary neat and attractive hand, thanking me for getting him into a nursing-home in Cambridge, where I was still teaching at the university. On 18th April he died.' See also the autobiographical *You Can't Do Both*, pp. 186–96.

letter – trip smooth, domesticity good, weather up and down, Graves genial. But I'll tell you about that when I see you – everything in that way is okay. I feel horribly as if I'd been away from you for a year. Horribly as regards missing you. But not in other ways, not forgetting you. In particular, I continue taking you, and you-and-me, with enormous, total, irrevocable seriousness. But who wouldn't? Who could help falling in love with "a tall, pretty, bright, nice woman" who's also, or instead, extravagantly-unbelievably beautiful, sexually fantastic (i.e. suitable to male fantasies), awe-inspiring –? I'll fill in the rest soon. Sorry I haven't been chatty and funny – I will be. I do love you totally for ever. I couldn't have written before this. I hope everything's been all right. I'm all right, and you and I are all right. And unless I get better information I'll ring you at Cyril [Frankel]'s between 12 noon and 1 p.m. on the 16th April. I want to tell you everything, say everything, but "I love you" will have to do. I love you.

Hunter El Amiral

Will try to write again but can't guarantee it. I do love you. Never been so certain of anything. I *understand* you too.

[ALS: Recipient]

TO ELIZABETH JANE HOWARD – 29 APRIL 1963

Dearest pigeon – what a lovely happy day on Thursday. Drunken too, as we said. I like a chick who likes to drink, as you know. That snaps is bloody strong (79°) and it goes down with so little trouble. I don't mind us getting drunk, love it at the time, but I do hate not remembering bits. Our parting, for instance. I'm sure it was cordial but I don't like forgetting it. Earlier bits are however very clear to me in my mind, and elsewhere too so to speak. You delight me from top to toe. We were made for each other. Hard to go on writing when I think of us making love; all I want to do then is to make love to you. Never known anything like it, honest: how *lucky* I am to have found *you*. The way you put your hands to your head when – but if I'm ever going to get this finished I'd better imagine us talking instead. Am I too lazy in the house by the way? I seem to let you do everything, even things I could give a hand with. I'm lazy. Also I enjoy watching you so much – I'd far rather do that than wash up. You have a great deal to offer all five senses. Sight isn't the least of them. At a (terrible) film last night I turned to Bill and muttered, referring to the heroine "Certain ornithological resemblance there." – "I don't see it at all," he said. Neither did I when I looked again. She and you had however one important point of resemblance – both being women. *Any* woman is likely to remind me of you these days, including ones who don't remind me of you (so to speak). I think I must be getting sentimental. My lack of interest in other women is beginning to get me down rather. The *real* reason is, I think – leaving out those funny old ideas about being faithful etc – that I know it wouldn't be nearly as good. (Always go for the selfish motive first, as I told you.) When you've had champagne and orange juice a glass of South African red isn't so appealing. And thanks to you I have dismissed for ever any lingering doubts about masculinity and all that – so now it's a matter of I'm all right, Jacqueline.

Dull day today except talking to you. But I've nearly finished with teaching now. Horrible boring meeting in a few minutes. Listen darling you mustn't be afraid of boring me with letters. I want to hear from you whenever you want to write and whatever you want to say. Please. I'll be there at 12.20 or so on Wednesday. You sounded so sweet on the phone. I can see you very clearly, and hear your voice. I love you all the time.

Yours faithfully,
H.R.H. Hunter

[ALS: HEHL]

TO MARY HOLLAND – 2 MAY 1963

9 Madingley Road, Cambridge

Dear Miss Holland,

As I'm afraid you'll have guessed by now I shan't be able to do your 'worth keeping' talk.[1] Since coming back from Majorca I've had several

1. In a letter of 8 April 1963 (in BBC), Mary Holland (b. 1935), journalist and broadcaster, at the time Deputy Editor of *Woman's Hour*, asked Amis to contribute to a programme in

things to cope with, including my father's illness and death and the aftermath thereof, and am not straight yet. But do please bear me in mind for later possibilities – not too late: we leave for Majorca about 1st October.

Yours sincerely,
Kingsley Amis

[ALS: BBC]

TO ELIZABETH JANE HOWARD – 20 MAY 1963

Dearest hoopoe[1]

[. . .] Feel much better now, ever since hearing your voice, actually. It was only a hangover, after all. (One of my troubles is always tending to believe it's something more.) Have just dispatched my last young gentleman for the last time. Wonderful feeling. No need to have an opinion on Chaucer, Spenser, Dryden, *Jane Austen*, the last plays of Shakespeare, any more. But for the immediate prospect of 2 hours' boredom at the meeting of the Governing Body I find nothing disconcerting in the future. And the thought of Thursday is positively concerting. You find me remarking on it. I say "Hello, nothing much disconcerting about Thursday. Complete absence of disconcert."[2] I'll show up all gleeful at 12.22. I love those tights, and you in them. I can remember just how your mouth smells. I love you a lot but very much in this distressingly carnal way. You'll have to bear with me over that.

Love from
Hunter, Grand Admiral, Federated Space Navy.

[ALS: HEHL]

which four or five people would speak out in support of an attitude or institution 'worth keeping'. Each person would speak for two minutes, which meant a script of about 300 words.

1. A bird 'conspicuous by its variegated plumage and large erectile crest' (*Shorter Oxford English Dictionary*).

2. An allusion to a Peter Cook comedy routine 'Sitting on the Bench', from the satirical revue *Beyond the Fringe* (1960), written and performed by Alan Bennett, Peter Cook, Jonathan Miller and Dudley Moore.

TO ELIZABETH JANE HOWARD – 26 MAY 1963

Dearest cardinal (*very* good this; beautiful exotic startling swift-flying bird, and girl in very fine dressing-gown: takes me back to Cheltenham and the stage direction from *The Duchess of Malfi*: "The Pope chargeth the Cardinal to be a soldier in his wars" or whatever it is.)[1]: that was a splendid time. Not exactly *better* sexually than ever before (it gets a little difficult to improve on the unimprovable) but sort of wider, more adventurous. Don't find anything even *odd* in anything you and I do. The fact it's you and I seems to justify everything in advance, everything conceivable. That's because each of us *can* only want to do what is right for both of us. Very lucky – is it luck? – that whatever is extra good for you in bed is, corresponds *exactly* with, what is extra good for me. No, I don't suppose it is luck, unless love is luck, and whereas you need luck – as we keep saying, Cheltenham was a bit of luck – you need capacity too, and other things that we have in abundance. Good old we. Don't you think we ought to *boast* more? A fairly small advert in a prominent place would do it. HUNTER AND HIS BIRD WISH TO ANNOUNCE THAT THEY ARE THE MOST ATTRACTIVE, INTELLIGENT, FUNNY, SOPHISTICATED AND MUTUALLY SUITED PAIR SINCE THE RENAISSANCE. (Historical researchers required to provide documentary evidence that they are the most attractive etc pair since the death of Tutankhamen. Write giving details of experience, qualifications etc. Enclose S.A.E.)

It should be clear to you by now that your fears about having bored me on Friday evening were just a silly (but not in the least irritating) little maggot in the bird's head (or beak – and remember that if you have a beak, as Scott seems to have thought,[2] then this is what most birds are equipped with). You *couldn't* bore me. Everything you do and say fascinates me. However ordinary. I should love to watch you make a sandwich, stuff a cushion, clean your fountain-pen, compile a grocery list. I was sorry we didn't go to the film but only for about 15 seconds.

---

1. Amis is quoting from memory; no such stage direction exists in Webster's text. The scene Amis has in mind is III.4, in which the Cardinal exchanges his clerical garb for a soldier's uniform.

2. Peter Scott.

I like the monkey[3] and I adore you, and I enjoy drinking and chatting and playing records. So . . .

My plans to bring you to Cambridge are maturing. But no details yet. Oh, I think Thursday would be a better GD[4] than Friday for me. The thing is that my lunch with Naipaul[5] is fixed for the Saturday. So I should have to leave in the morning, which I'd prefer not to do. Of course I could cancel it but I think that might be impolitic since everybody knows it is fixed to happen. I'll await your ring tomorrow and ring you anyway at Cape's the next day. Must go soon or miss post. Am sitting in garden working away at Roger,[6] very tranquil and not hungover, though I wish the bloody sun wouldn't keep going in. Off to see *Day of the Triffids* with Philip at 4 30 or so so shall miss *Fireball* probably. Hope you see it, and that Robert[7] is in good voice. He asks me to transmit: ZEND REZBEGDVUL GREEDINGS AND ABOLOGIES VOR REZENT BREAGDOWN BROMIZZ DO AVOID REGURRENZ. Darling I love you and that includes finding the idea of being bored by you ingonzievable – sorry, I pick up accents easily. You are a very non-silly girl and you never let me down. I worship you, cardinal.

Adoring love from Hunter, UNO Comptrolleur,
Pan-Human Colony, Mars.

[ALS: HEHL]

3. Elizabeth Jane Howard's brother Colin (see Notes on Recipients).
4. Good Day.
5. V.S. Naipaul (b. 1932), Trinidadian-born author; knighted 1990.
6. Micheldene, from *One Fat Englishman.*
7. *The Day of the Triffids* (1962), science fiction film based on the 1951 novel by John Wyndham; *Fireball XL5* (1962), a 'superanimation' television science fiction series concerning the intergalactic adventures of Steve Zodiac and his crew, including Robert the Robot, Steve's co-pilot. Robert figures in private jokes between Amis and Howard, perhaps because he always (except in the case of 'BREAGDOWNS') fulfils orders or satisfies.

TO ELIZABETH JANE HOWARD – 11 JUNE 1963

Dearest ringed plover

[. . .] I arrived back on Sunday evening to find H actually on the phone & in denunciatory mood – why was I neglecting kids etc.[1] Reason was useless. This depressed me rather; and so did the 2 other times I rang her up and was hung up on, and so did the drunken-abusive-humorous-jeering call I got from her at 2 a.m. (aroused from sleep to take it). The next day, I hear via Nickie,[2] H. awoke with 2 sores on her face & bloodshot eyes and a hormone deficiency is suspected. Being checked on today, I think, but I can't get her on the phone. Am anxious to do so, as a school friend of elder son's reports to Marie[3] that he has heard people saying H. has left – so this may soon get round to kids. Want to get her home even if for a day or two to give the lie to this type of stuff, and *this* is why she may be appearing in the middle of the week. Anyway, if she does turn up I obviously can't leave. Not immediately, I mean. All this has been rather unsettling, as you can imagine, and calculated to make one less rather than more inclined to settle down at the typewriter. But I can survive. What you must not do is to worry about you and me – I am worrying about a lot of things but *not* about that. I am not going to be bullied or blackmailed or coaxed into accepting any kind of future that doesn't include you – feature you prominently, I had better say. This is one of the troughs

---

1. According to Jacobs, *Biography*, p. 258, though Hilly Amis had known of the affair with Elizabeth Jane Howard, 'Amis had never before been so blatant about an infidelity.' When she discovered an incriminating letter in Amis's jacket pocket, he not only refused to end the affair or dismiss it as trivial, but declared that he was going on holiday with Jane Howard for three weeks. After the holiday (in Sitges, in Spain), he would return to Cambridge and help to move the family, which he declared he had no intention of leaving, to Majorca. Hilly was infuriated by Amis's behaviour and fled the house, staying temporarily with friends.

2. Nickie de Peche Craddock, a Cambridge friend, had been married to the son of Fanny Craddock, the television cook. She and her eight-year-old son lived with the Amises for a while in 1963, and also accompanied Hilly and the children to Majorca, staying for a few weeks before returning to England.

3. Marie Battle Singer, 'a very black black girl with an unreconstructed Mississippi accent who was a fully qualified psychiatrist, or perhaps psychologist' (*Memoirs*, p. 222), also a painter; she married the American-born poet James Burns Singer (who was raised in Scotland and thought of as Scottish) in 1956. For Burns Singer see Amis to Conquest, 31 December 1964, note 6.

now and it's the first time you've known any of the details of a trough, so though it may sound worse to you it isn't really. I shall phone Tom on Thursday between 10&5.30 if I can't make it, and you at the conference-room[4] after 7. But my bet is that I'll be able to make it all right. Don't forget – you're seeing just what my worries are – it isn't that the situation has suddenly worsened. Wish I could tell you (I will when I see you) how gorgeous last time was – more like living with you than ever and yet sex better than ever. I love you with all my heart and mind and body.

Temporarily demoted Hunter
(ex Lance-Corporal,
Space Marines Supply & Transport Section)

[ALS: HEHL]

TO WILLIAM RUKEYSER – 25 JUNE 1963

9 Madingley Road, Cambridge.

Dear Bill,

Glad to hear la gaitang parisiong[1] is up to standard. Weather bloody here, but consoled by absence of young gentlemen. Not feeling so hot at the moment, having spent 18 of the last 24 hours in the company of John Davenport.

Can I beg you to let me have that Roger's-odyssey-in-NYC information[2] soonish? I should have fixed this with you before you went off, but things got confused. The point is that since I don't know quite where I shall be *after* Trieste, and may not see you *at* Trieste (I shall be there, but you might not make it), it would be safest for me if you could get the stuff to me not later than 20th July, at this address. Could you possibly do that? Really important to me or I wouldn't push it on you in the middle of your trip.

4. At Cyril Frankel's offices.

---

1. 'The butchered French reflects Kingsley's notion that there are really only 3 French word endings: ang, ong, and wow' (William Rukeyser, personal communication, 4 October 1996).

2. See Amis to Rukeyser, 20 June 1962.

Actually what I want, now that I have the chapter planned, is small in quantity, a page of typescript or equivalent should do it, half a dozen details on each of the following:

1. R's cab-ride from Penn Station to the Village.
2. Environs, entrance hall etc. of prosperous but not plutocratic apartment building in Village.
3. Interior of such apartment.
4. Cab-ride to Birdland.
5. Birdland (I already know some). } People's clothes
6. Central Plaza or somewhere. Esp. men's room. } important

You know the way I write, no conscientious topographical surveys, like impressionistic, man.

Get Bob[3] to help you – give him my best. Don't work too hard, etc. And whatever you do be careful of the vang and the filles de jwow. Let me know where you are, or are going to be, if you can predict it. Hope to see you at Trieste.

Cheers,
Kingsley

[TLS: Recipient]

TO ELIZABETH JANE HOWARD – 9 JULY 1963

Grand Hotel et de la Ville, Trieste[1]

Dearest uccello,[2]

The trip still stands – fine. Last Wednesday night was the worst I've ever spent[3] – a scene that started as soon as I got home (12.10) and didn't end until 6.30 the next morning. The taxi to take us to Camb. Station (whence we departed for London, of course) was due at 6.40. Until then it was never certain whether we were going or not. But things

3. Rukeyser's brother, with whom he was travelling in Europe for the summer.

---

1. The Amises had gone to a science fiction film festival in Trieste with Brian Aldiss and his wife-to-be Margaret, and another science fiction writer, Harry Harrison (b. 1925), and his wife Joan. Under the 'et' of 'Grand Hotel et de la Ville' Amis has drawn an arrow and written 'yes, nonsense, but it says this outside, on stationery etc.'

2. Bird.

3. Amis's asterisked note reads: 'except when children ill etc.'

much, much better now. Haven't got long to write this so forgive telegraphese. Sitting on balcony facing sea – clear, hot day. Italy & Italians v. agreeable on this showing. Lots of lovely ships in view, including white motor-yacht I wish we (Hunter & bird) were on. Food surprisingly palatable and have been eating quite a lot of it. Film festival a complete joke – no decent films at all, ¾ of the "delegates" haven't come. But 2 s-f writers who are friends of mine (one British, one American)[4] have turned up and drinking is the main activity – not sinister because (1) the weather has been so humid that 90% reappears as sweat within 10 mins (2) – so far at any rate – I've been concentrating on grappa (Italian version of marc, you know) and this is so filthy – each mouthful burns the throat for 5 mins – that my consumption is limited. Have had sun and sea, looking more nigerish[5] than ever. Hope all well with you. (Understatement of the year.) All arrangements for our trip are unaltered. There is a really *frightful* French intellectual here on the "jury"[6] – a highbrow film director with *no* interest in s-f beyond generalising about it. The rotten *sod*. But this is a very nice town. Been eating and sleeping a lot and no pills and no hangovers. Hands v. steady – if this looks different it's because I'm writing it on my knee. I find that Duino, where Rilke wrote those awful elegies, is just up the road, but haven't let this spoil my fun. Will await call from Cyril/Tom on Friday morning. Love you to death, Miss you. Can see and hear you with complete clarity. I do *like* you. See you soon.

Il grande cacciatore

[ALS: HEHL]

4. Aldiss and Harrison.

5. 'Niger', or 'The Niger', was an imaginary (and very successful and overweening) black gangster whom Amis sometimes impersonated.

6. Pierre Kast (1920–84), French film director and theorist whose essays and film reviews appeared in *Cahiers du Cinema* and other publications.

TO ELIZABETH JANE HOWARD – 16–19 JULY (?) 1963

Dearest rara avis,[1]

All under control here – only just but under. Arrangements stand: at the moment am being *driven* up on Wednesday morning, so can meet you anywhere, but shall have luggage, incl. typewriter, so *perhaps* dumping at Tom's wd. be good: alternatively can dump at Leicester Sq tube station (of hallowed memory). Looking forward to this like schoolboy going on holiday (as well as sailor going on leave, etc.). Have plenty money so can go out of London if you think this good – we wouldn't see anyone we know in Leeds, for instance. But will talk to you about it all on phone tomorrow (Tuesday). Don't worry about engagements, in evenings etc., that you feel you must keep: I will stay at home & feel very husbandly, or else have night out with the boys. Haven't seen them (Conquest etc.) for *3 months*, I now find: not complaining, because I'd rather sleep with you with no clothes on than with any of them in their best suits. [. . .]

Can't help feeling you're worrying about something – whatever it is, don't. Have done no more on novel – circumstances not v. conducive – but active in writing & preparing book reviews. I feel 18 again – other evening conversation (H. not there) – question asked What is least disappointing thing in life? A year ago w^{d} have said Drink, Jazz, Children, Shakespeare – but said Love – embarrassed silence. I love you and greatly need you

Hunter I
by grace of God Pope of Rome etc

[ALS: HEHL]

---

1. Above 'rara' Amis has drawn an arrow and written 'or rather *uniqua*'.

TO ROBERT GRAVES – 19 JULY 1963

Jonathan Cape Limited, Thirty Bedford Square, London W.C.1

Dear Robert,

I am editing what I think will be an interesting and certainly original book for Jonathan Cape.[1] I have noticed a real interest in science fiction among all sorts of friends of mine – sometimes where one might least expect it. This is to be a volume of new science fiction stories by prominent writers not generally associated with the field of science fiction. Would you like to contribute?

The kind of story I am looking for need not be 'science fiction' in any narrow sense. Its concern with actual science or technology can be minimal or non-existent: spaceships, time travel, alien planets, cosmic disasters and the like are far from compulsory. I feel, though, that the best science fiction, however wild its initial assumption, holds consistently to these throughout, and however unlikely its marvels, tries to offer these as plausible (thus differing from what we commonly call 'fantasy'). The length can be anything from 2,000 to 10,000 words.

Penguin Books have already said that they will publish the book. The total advance will be £750 and this and the royalties will be split pro rata.

I hope very much that you will like this idea and look forward to hearing from you.

Yours,
Kingsley

What about it? 100 words of pseudo-scientific patter would see it through. See you Sept.[2]

[TLS: William Graves]

1. Copies of this letter, written on Cape stationery, were also sent to C.P. Snow and W. Somerset Maugham, among other writers. Nothing came of the project.
2. MS addition.

TO VICTOR GOLLANCZ – 1 AUGUST 1963

Lista de Correos, Sitges, Spain

Dear Victor,

Am comfortably settled in here, well away from the 50,000 English holidaymakers, have got down to work and so far am well up with the clock.

Just to recap: I will meet your man[1] a fortnight today at the BEA office in Barcelona airport at 1.45: flight no. BE/022, leaving London at 11.20.

Shall have to rush now: have a date with a fat Englishman.

Yours ever,
Kingsley

Ps: Address (which is merely the poste restante) not to be divulged to *anyone* except Curtis Brown, who must also understand it's confidential.

[TLS: Gollancz]

TO VICTOR GOLLANCZ – 14 AUGUST 1963

Lista de Correos, Sitges, Spain

My dear Victor,

Here it is, all of it, rather to my amazement. A fraction over 60,000, I compute. I don't know whether anyone else will like it, but I do, within reason I hope.

I've forgotten what we decided about proofs – you were against any delay, I remember, and so am I – but I'll ring you on the 10th of next month (or soon after) and arrange to come and see you.

I enclose a note for your getting-it-through-the-press experts.

Yours ever,
Kingsley

---

1. In order to deliver the manuscript of *One Fat Englishman* to Gollancz, which was eager to publish it before Christmas; the man from Gollancz would be returning to London on the next flight.

PS: Got your letter of 12th August. Anticipatory thanks for cigars!

from
ONE FAT
ENGLISHMAN[1]

Note on typescript of *One Fat Englishman*

I tend to under-punctuate rather than over-punctuate. E.g. page 1, lines 7–8:

The Scandinavians are dear people but they've never been what you might call bywords . . .

not

dear people, but . . .

In a few cases where the typescript reading may look wrong I have put a dotted pencil underlining to confirm that it is correct. E.g. page 154:

'No, I talked to her mother in the telephone last night . . .

The printer's reader will probably try to 'normalise' the text at some of these points and should be resisted.

Note on dashes:
Sometimes (out of laziness) I have typed (e.g.)

'Listen--I want to talk to you, and--'

instead of

'Listen – I want to talk to you, and –'

and in a few cases I have

'Listen - I want to talk to you, and -'

But everywhere I intend the full dash without any space.

Note the convention whereby, if in dialogue a speaker turns to address somebody other than the person he was originally talking to, this is signalled by a dash at the beginning of the switch, and another

1. MS addition.

such dash is used when the speaker turns back to the person originally addressed, e.g.:

'Will you have a drink? – Two whiskies, please, waiter. – As I was saying, old man . . .'

[TLS: Gollancz]

TO WILLIAM RUKEYSER – 26 AUGUST 1963

On and after 8th Sept: c/o Gollancz & Co.,
14 Henrietta Street, London W.C.2.

Dear Bill,

Have been meaning to write for days and days to thank you for sending the Manhattan information – but not for so many days and days as might have been expected. While I was getting nearer and nearer to the end of the fat Englishman and wondering like hell what had become of your contribution, same contribution was sitting snugly in the post office here,[1] filed under K instead of A. Now that sort of difficulty is no difficulty if you just happen to think of it: I didn't for a long time. Not, in fact, until the last possible morning, when I had left Roger just about to be driven to Birdland before going to the post office with my new K-not-A idea. Then – presto. Thanks above all for including so much: I've only used a small proportion but was able to pick just what I needed.

My information about what's been happening at home, if 'home' is an appropriate word to attach to it, is scanty and vague, but depressing. Don't you add to that information for the moment: I shall be (for your private information) in Cambridge on about the 10th and hope to see you if you're around. If not, or if it's otherwise relevant, leave a message for me at Peterhouse lodge.

Your travels sound fun. Ours have been too, though there have been these elements (home thoughts from abroad, as it were) making against perfect tranquillity. However, Roger was delivered, as was planned, to Gollancz's emissary at Barcelona airport and reached London safely. I had done about 22,500 words in 16 or so days, which

1. In Sitges.

still impresses me. J. has done some 6,000 in 28 or so, but conceivably these are better words than mine and she has made a lot of ratatouilles and piperades and that type of stuff. There's been a good deal of thunder but much more sun, and we're both not badly tanned, though I plunge into disquiet and self-contempt whenever I contemplate my lard-coloured arse.

The only powerfully disagreeable event occurred one afternoon ten days ago when (inevitably) we were in bed. The door buzzer went and J. answered it in my dressing-gown. Outside was a man who wanted to talk to us on behalf of – guess – the *Daily Express* of all papers!! We got dressed, without having admitted him to our flat, and gave him an interview in the porch downstairs. It consisted of me telling him a lot about my book and saying 'no comment' and 'that's my business' to everything else. 'Are you in love?' he kept unavailingly asking. J. was a curious olive-yellow colour, made up of tan and pallor, and I worked away at preventing my head from trembling. He was far too horrible to be rendered accurately in any work of realistic fiction. He was an Australian, you see. Anyway, the treatment we gave him seemed to have worked, or something did, because when Hickey finally did his stuff it was a weedy little smear, I thought. It may even be that the hand of George Gale[2] was at work in our interests here: you may have heard he and I had a far from hostile lunch together my last day in London. When the man had gone, still shaking his cylindrical head over our unreasonableness, selfish refusal to co-operate, etc. J. and I did a quick move-plus-cover-up, with a James Bond-type false trail laid to Barcelona. Rather to our chagrin as well as our relief, no packs of news-hounds have been on our track and not a single photographer has broken cover. However, London may prove more exciting.

Apart from the date of our return nothing seems very certain. I have a television play to deliver by 1st October,[3] from which there may be much distraction, but after the last few weeks I feel I could work through a howitzer bombardment. However, leave me your address at Peterhouse and/or Gollancz and I will find you. J. is a little above herself

2. 'Hickey' is 'William Hickey', the pseudonymous gossip columnist of the *Daily Express*; for George Gale, who worked at the *Daily Express*, see Amis to McCallum, 5 April 1961, note 1.

3. *A Question About Hell*, a modern version of *The Duchess of Malfi*, broadcast 27 April 1964, Granada Television.

with pride at having written three pages of *One Fat Limey*,[4] but I am dealing with her. She sends you her love (says Birdland is here, not, as you mistakenly seem to think, in New York). And I my fraternal salutations.

Raucous cheers,
K.

Dedication of *One Fat* is 'to A. B.' A stands for 'accredited'.[5]

Best thing I've read since coming away: Rebecca West's *The Vassall Affair*.[6] Read it for much fascinating dope, esp. on the British Press, and for laughs too: bloody funny.

[TLS: Recipient]

TO ROBERT CONQUEST – 2 SEPTEMBER 1963

as from: Jonathan Cape Limited,
Thirty Bedford Square, London W.C.1

Dear Bob,

Ta for yours of 24th July. The rotten fuckers at the P.O. here had been keeping my mail for 3 weeks filed under K instead of A, or I'd have answered sooner.

I'll take a look through your stuff, if I may, when I get back, which will be in a week or so. We might even have a drink and a bit of a chat, and you can tell me what good old Dame Rumour has been crediting me with since I've been away. Quite a lot, I'll warrant.

4. From Chapter 13, p. 135 ('Somebody was standing . . .') to p. 138 ('One of them resembled agitation'); Amis, in turn, wrote several pages of the 'Fireworks' section of Howard's *After Julius* (1965), from p. 181 ('In due course Esmé . . .') to p. 184 ('He turned off the lights . . .'), in the Pan paperback edition. The only person to identify these passages was Miss Howard's brother Colin, who claimed that each had made one mistake in style which enabled him to detect who had written what. Miss Howard comments: 'This is quite funny, considering that Kingsley and I vetted each other's contribution and passed them without making any changes' (personal communication, 21 February 1998).

5. The novel's dedication is 'To Jane', an 'A. B.' or 'accredited bird' (according to Rukeyser, personal communication, 19 November 1998).

6. *The Vassall Affair* (1963) by Rebecca West (1892–1983), author and novelist, was a study of John Vassall (1924–96), a clerk in the Admiralty, formerly stationed in Moscow, who had spied for Russia. In 1962 Vassall was sentenced to eighteen years' imprisonment.

Sturgeon[1] hates me because I didn't hail him as the king of modern fantasy etc. in *New Maps*. He gave the last *Spectrum* a hell of a pasting in the *Sat. Review* or somewhere, as you doubtless saw. Called us English gentlemen, the bastard.

All news when we meet.

Cheers,
Kingsley

[TLS: Recipient]

1. Theodore Sturgeon (b. 1918), American science fiction writer; Amis briefly mentions his story 'Killdozer' in *New Maps of Hell*.

TO KARL MILLER – 17 DECEMBER 1963

16 Blomfield Road W.9[1]

Dear Karl,

I didn't much care for your friend's behaviour, but I should hate you to think that any of us were rude to him. This is what happened.

As we filed out of the Kilmartins', P. Jenkins,[2] whom I had never seen before, suddenly turned his head. "Going to Karl's?" – "Yes." – "We'll get a taxi." Bob then said he had his car, which we all 5 walked along to. I had not taken to P.J. and nor had anyone else, but I am quite sure one of us would have perched on another's lap to make room for him – Bob's car takes only 4 in comfort – if P.J. had merely

1. The address of Elizabeth Jane Howard's flat in Maida Vale. When Amis returned to Cambridge from Sitges he discovered that Hilly had already taken the children to Majorca, to live in the house he had rented in Soller. Instead of joining them he moved in with Jane Howard and her brother Colin in their flat in Blomfield Road. Though soon afterwards Amis and Jane moved briefly into a flat of their own (in Basil Mansions, near Harrods), in a matter of weeks they returned to Blomfield Road. As Jacobs explains, not only did Amis and Colin get on well, but living in an extended household had important benefits: 'If Jane went away, Amis was not left on his own overnight, with all the potential for anxiety and panic that would mean, and if he wanted a drink and a chat he didn't even have to go as far as the pub to get them' (*Biography*, pp. 263–4).

2. Peter Jenkins (1934–92), political journalist; Labour Correspondent, *Guardian* (1960–63); Washington Correspondent, *Guardian* (1963–67); Associate Editor and Political Columnist, *Independent* (1987–92).

said something: something like "Could you possibly find room for me?" However, we all agreed afterwards that he had said nothing, but merely stood waiting for room to be made for him. So we didn't. Bob called, in a not very concerned but certainly not hostile tone: "Sorry, I'm afraid I can only take four." Jane, Caroleen[3] and I had said nothing at all. Accordingly I was taken aback to be thanked sarcastically "for the lift" when after a long circuitous drive (Bob thought you were still living at your old place and took some time to be convinced you weren't) the 4 of us appeared. I had not even agreed to share a taxi with P.J., had said nothing, hoping admittedly to evade him, but also wondering whether one taxi would take 5, and perhaps more, people. Nobody at any time told P.J. to fuck off, or even to go away.

Sorry for this long chronicle, but I wanted to set the record straight.

Hope to see you soon. We must have a more extended lunch some time.

Yours,
Kingsley

[ALS: Recipient]

TO PHILIP LARKIN – 31 DECEMBER 1963

16 Blomfield Road, London W.9.

My dear Philip,

What about those record numbers you were going to send me, hey? I want to get the stuff before the financial strain of keeping two homes going – or at any rate 1½ – makes me shut down my outlays.

I am carrying on about the same and am pretty well. I got a lot of nice presents for Xmas *for other people*. I am quite comfortable here but I seem to be getting up every morning at 8.30 and making breakfast (only tea and toast, but Christ) for the household. How has that come about, do you suppose? Anyway, I'm getting some work done in between. When I've finished my critical appraisal of Ian Fleming[1] I've

3. Caroleen Macfarlane, who in 1964 would become Conquest's third wife.

---

1. *The James Bond Dossier* (1965).

undertaken to revise Bob's Egyptology novel for him. Working on the text will be all right; it's the thought of "discussing" it with him that daunts me slightly. He spent yesterday evening here and after two hours employed in telling Jane and her brother the plots of some science-fiction stories he (and I) had read got through another two making various inadmissible suggestions for the improvement of the Egyptology story. I hadn't read the typescript for a year or two, and Jane and Colin never had, so he had things even more his own way than usual. What will hinder our collaboration is that quirk of his whereby, when one has at last succeeding in interrupting him to contest point A, he has moved on meantime to telling you point B. Still, it's for money.

All the best for 1964. *1964*? Is that really a year? One we're going to be living in? It sounds much more like the sort of assemblage of digits you get at the start of a romance of the future. "On January 1st 1964 an armistice was concluded between the space-fleets of Earth and those of the Procyonian Federation. Fff Uuu Kkk, the leader of the Martian observers' commission, scented trouble from the beginning. He – or rather *they*, for the corporate intelligences of Mars lack the concept of . . ."

You'll have to make up your mind whether you want me or bum,

Kingsley

PS: Give us a ring when you're down again.
CUN (which stands for Cunningham) 0638*
**or did I tell you this?*[2]

[TLS: Bodleian]

TO BRIAN ALDISS – 1 JANUARY 1964

16. Blomfield Road, W.9.

Dear Brian,

And a happy 1964 to you to be sure. Look, Jane has got hold of a bloke who runs three magazines and is always looking for others to

2. MS addition.

start. I have figures from Ken and Penguins.[1] If you can be lured to London, you and he and I could have lunch and talk about it. Can you be so lured? If you can, give me a ring here with two or three alternative dates a week or so ahead. Then I can fix it. Meanwhile keep up the good work, dear boy.

Cheers – love to Margaret,
Kingsley

No reaction from the Observer yet on the Lewis tape.[2] Lazy fuckers. Or, more likely, they don't want it and are shy of saying so. Cowardly fuckers.

[TLS: Bodleian]

TO VICTOR GOLLANCZ – 1 MAY 1964

16 Blomfield Road, London W.9.

My dear Victor,

I am just completing a book called *The James Bond Dossier*, the contents of which are probably indicated sufficiently by its title, though perhaps I should add that its approach is that of a Fleming addict and its verdict largely a favourable one.

I don't think that this is at all your sort of book, in several ways. I'm pretty sure in my own mind that you have very little time for Fleming and the Fleming cult: at the very least, your heart wouldn't be in it. And this is the sort of book people's hearts have got to be in, I feel, if it's to sell more than four or five thousand copies, which, having spent five months on the damn thing, I couldn't afford.

The hearts of Jonathan Cape would be very much in this venture and, as you will know, they have an immense Fleming distribution and publicity machine already functioning. I have decided, after some not

---

1. These are estimated circulation figures for the viability of a science fiction magazine. Jane's friend was David Roxburgh, of the publishers Roberts and Vintner, which subsequently went on to publish the science fiction periodicals *New Worlds* and *Science Fantasy*. Neither Aldiss nor Elizabeth Jane Howard can identify 'Ken'.

2. Amis and Aldiss had interviewed C.S. Lewis about science fiction. An edited transcript of the interview was published in *SF Horizons* 1 (Spring 1964) and reprinted in *Encounter* 24 (March 1965), pp. 61–5, and *Spectrum IV* (1965), pp. 13–22.

altogether comfortable pondering, that they shall publish this effort.

But you are still "my publisher" (if you still want me). My future novels, and any other kind of book I can foresee writing, will be yours. I hope very much that you and Cape's will be able to come to some arrangement which will satisfy everybody that I am not "going over" to them.[1]

I hope *One Fat Englishman* is going well?

Yours,
Kingsley

[TLS: Gollancz]

TO ANDOR FOLDES – 26 MAY 1964

16 Blomfield Road, W.9.

Dear Mr. Foldes,

Thank you for your amiable letter. I'm at my worst as a correspondent when I have some excuse for not writing: in this case I told myself I'd wait until I knew whether or not I'd be in London on 13th August. Well, I still don't know, I think quite likely I'll be in Spain, but I wanted to answer anyway.

Yes: I've been waiting for years for someone to have the wit and the interest to identify Dixon's tune:[1] it *is* the Beethoven C major – for

---

1. Gollancz was not pleased, but agreed to release Amis 'subject only to this: namely that Jonathan Cape should agree with me a form of words that will make it absolutely clear, both in the trade press and the general press, that this book is an exception, that Cape publishes it by arrangement with us, and that your future work will be published by us' (Gollancz to Amis, 4 May 1964, in Gollancz).

---

1. Andor Foldes (1913–92), Hungarian-born American pianist. For Dixon's tune, see *Lucky Jim*, p. 87:

> the sight of Welch's 'bag' and fishing-hat on a nearby chair, normally a certain infuriant, only made him hum his Welch tune as he went out. This tune featured in the 'rondo' of some boring piano concerto Welch had once insisted on playing him on his complicated exponential-horned gramophone. It had come after about four of the huge double-sided red-labelled records, and Dixon had fitted words to it . . . 'You *ig*norant clod, you *stu*pid old sod, you *ha*vering *sla*vering get . . .' Here intervened a string of unmentionables, corresponding with an oom-pah sort of effect in the

which concerto, by the way, I've the highest respect. How odd, and splendid, that you should be playing a Mozart concerto at the proms. The series from 449 through 491 has appealed to me for years as the finest thing in all music (despite Dixon's views on the composer in question). I wonder which one you are to play; I hope one of the earlier ones, 449, 450 or 456. 466 and 488 and 491 and so on are fine, but have had more than their fair share of attention as compared with 449 etc. If I *am* in London in August, I will certainly hear you play.

Thank you for your pleasant remarks about *Lucky Jim*. We must see if we can't manage to meet some time.

Yours sincerely,
Kingsley Amis

[TLS: HEHL]

TO ELIZABETH BARBER – 27 MAY 1964

16. Blomfield Road, W.9.

Dear Miss Barber,

I hereby resign from the Society of Authors. I was just about prepared to go on paying £2-12-6 a year to an organisation that does nothing for me, but when the price goes up to £5-5-0 I jib.[1]

Yours sincerely,
Kingsley Amis

[ALS: Society of Authors]

orchestra. 'You *wor*dy old *tur*dy old scum, you *grip*ing old *pip*ing old bum.' Dixon didn't mind the obscurity of the reference, in 'piping', to Welch's recorder; he knew what he meant.

---

1. Miss Barber responded on 3 June 1964: 'There is, of course, less that the Society can do *directly* for the successful than for the unsuccessful author. It can't do anything directly for an author who doesn't consult us, and I don't believe you have consulted us since we advised your accountants two or three years ago about tax exemption on your Maugham Award' (Society of Authors).

TO CHRISTOPHER HOLME – 3 AUGUST 1964

16 Blomfield Road, London W.9.

My dear Christopher,

Thanks for your letter.[1] Ever since I got it I've been rushing about getting myself off to Spain,[2] and shall depart finally on Wednesday without a moment to pop in and say my piece. However, the programme will clearly have little point without a contribution from Amis in some form or other, and so I send you a written answer which Findlater can quote from, should he prove so minded. If you do use it, I charge you to get me a whopping fee for it.*

How are you? Let's have a drink when I get back in the autumn.

Yours ever,
Kingsley Amis

*Alternatively, you may insert 'and BBC sound radio' after 'film companies' in Answer 1.

Written answer to questionnaire, *The Writer's Trade* Kingsley Amis

1. Yes, from everyone, in fact, except from film companies. These systematically short-change the writer. I have not had much first-hand contact with the film world, but other writers who have had much more take the same view.

2 Rates of pay, yes. My royalties have remained constant, but increased book-prices have made my cut of the cake larger absolutely if not in proportion.

3. I don't know.

---

1. Holme (b. 1907), a producer of radio features and drama (from 1948–68), had written on 24 July 1964 asking Amis to participate in a radio programme on the economics of authorship to be hosted by Richard Findlater, who wrote a report on the subject in 1963 for the Society of Authors. The letter included a list of ten questions (they do not survive, though I have reproduced Amis's answers, from some of which the questions can be reconstructed). The programme, in the series *The Writer's Trade*, was not broadcast until 3 March 1965, so there was time for Amis to record his responses after he returned from Spain.

2. For a holiday with Jane in the house in Soller, on Majorca, which Hilly and the children had abandoned when they moved to London in January 1964.

4. No.
5. Well yes, I make a lot of money out of them.
6. No idea, but I make much more from my books – English and US sales – than from all the others put together.
7. So far, completely. I might start talking about the justice of a big windfall, like a sale to Hollywood, being 'spread' over more than three years, if I were to have such a windfall. But I haven't yet.
8. I didn't start writing until after the war, but I'd say the answer's yes. There are more perks like TV and radio; popular newspapers seem to want writers to express their views on anything for good pay; almost any bright young man can throw off a couple of funny novels about his job and do not badly out of it.
9. Difficult. I feel a writer should have an 'outside' job, but then he writes less. Perhaps he should drift in and out, taking a year's sabbatical every six months or so.
10. Only things like laziness, drink, domestic distractions: nothing that's special to our time.

*

[TLS: BBC]

TO ROBERT CONQUEST – 27 AUGUST 1964

Soledad, Soller, Mallorca, Spain.

Dear Bob,

Fine. The dates suit us very well. There's plenty of room for you here and the both of you are tremendously welcome. One point is that in this villa we have you really do need a car if you want to get to these beaches, which *I* am very ready to see going for a shit but which young ladies, and others who like bathing and other such sports which *I* privately think are full of shit, do seem to value. Therefore, since Colin [Howard] will have left here long before you arrive, I suggest loudly that you arrange to hire a car for the duration of your stay, which Godfrey Davis[1] will fix up for you to the extent of having it waiting

1. A car rental company.

when you arrive, and the cost of which we will of course split with you. It'll do all of us a power of good.

Life proceeds in a full-of-fun way. With Cointreau at the equivalent of something like 30s. a *magnum* it can hardly do anything else. I am quite brown really. Graves seems a bit dejected but very ready to chat. Various creepy non-exhibiting painters, non-publishing writers etc. inhabit his ambience, but who cares a sod for them? Egyptology,[2] given sun, wine, and other distractions, doesn't go forward very fast, but it is *steady*. Have just passed p. 100, which I reckon is half way. I think we stand to make a modest packet out of the bloody thing.

Jane says would you bring some fly squirts, which reflects less on the fly population here (not excessive) than the price of the squirts locally, and their comparative ineffectiveness.

Well, man, that's about it – both of us looking forward very much to seeing you both. This seems a viable environment, to say the least. We feel we can have a fine party, chum. Jane sends her love to you both. And so do I.

Yours,
Kingers

[TLS: Recipient]

TO PHILIP LARKIN – 20 SEPTEMBER 1964

Soledad, Soller, Mallorca.

This is the most heavenly *spoilt* little Spanish town, full of wine and olives and *retch-fetching* laughter from the peasants and *Huns* and *Frogs*. And a divine artists' colony at Deyá (sitting at that great human being Graves's feet). They've built a museum *themselves* and filled it with *priceless* action paintings and metal sculpture. Jane sends love. So do I.

Kingsley

[ALS: Bodleian]

2. *The Egyptologists* (1965).

TO VICTOR GOLLANCZ – 27 SEPTEMBER 1964

as from Molins Hotel, Cala San Vincente, Pollensa, Mallorca, Spain

Dear Victor,

You were so nice about the Bond book business that I don't like trespassing further on your good nature. But – Bob Conquest has written a light farcical novel – present title *The Egyptologists* – which he sent to Cape in the first place and which they've now agreed to publish.

Bob, who as you know is an old pal of mine, asked me to go over it, which I've nearly finished doing. I've had a quick whiz through, generally livening it up, and though the result won't receive much in the way of critical acclaim, doing it has been a pleasant vacation job. I'm going to have my name put on it as well as Bob's.[1]

I've had to defer getting down to my next[2] novel for a bit, but this will do it good rather than otherwise. The same sort of thing happened with *Take a Girl Like You*, and there I feel the prolonging of the gestation period benefited the result substantially. Hope to settle down to the new one when I get home, and to let you have it round about May.

Yours,
Kingsley

[ALS: Gollancz]

---

1. Gollancz wrote back on 1 October 1964: 'I quite understand the circumstances ... At the same time, I cannot help feeling rather uneasy: for the appearance of the James Bond book by yourself alone under a Cape imprint, followed by a second book, with your name on it, under the same imprint – both coming out before another book by you under my imprint – is bound to cause widespread comment ... [A] lot of people are not merely going to ask "Is Kingsley Amis leaving Gollancz for Cape?", but are going to state it as a positive fact. And that, of course, would be quite damaging. This wouldn't matter so much in minor cases, but everyone knows that I think of you as much the most important (and I don't mean from the sales point of view) of my new, post-war authors' (Gollancz).

2. Amis has here inserted the word 'proper!'

TO PHILIP LARKIN – 2 OCTOBER 1964

J&K address: Molins Hotel, Cala San Vicente, Pollensa – Mallorca, Spain

Bacon, liver and kidneys Majorca?
Well, the bacon's no part of a porker:
It's smoked foreskin of mule,
While the liver's goat's tool,
And the kidneys? The balls of old Lorca.[1]

Bob and I are working on a poem beginning: Up the airy mountain O'er the dizzy crags We seldom go out hunting. For fear of little shags: e.g. Wesker, Geo Hartley, Vicky, Leavis, Bronowski, Al, etc.*[2]

*I mean, of course, et al.

Yours,
Bob & Kingsley

[ALS: Bodleian]

TO TOM MASCHLER – 5 OCTOBER 1964

Molins Hotel, Cala San Vicente, Pollensa, Mallorca, Spain

Dear Tom,[1]

Weather continues marvellous, thank you: hot sun all day, cool at night. The Conquests went on Saturday. I got, as always, a lot of fun out of Bob, but the greater part of what Jane got out of him was being prevented (by continuous chit-chat) from doing any work except for

---

1. Conquest has added a message to this postcard which begins: 'Tune of the food limerick is, of course, The Gay Caballero'.

2. A parody of 'The Fairies' by William Allingham (1828–89): 'Up the airy mountain,/ Down the rushy glen,/We daren't go a-hunting/For fear of little men.' For the subsequent development of a 'little shags' mythology (in which shortness of stature is explicitly allied to other undesirable qualities), see Amis to Conquest, 31 December 1964, note 1. 'Vicky' was the pen-name of Victor Weisz (1913–66), German-born cartoonist who, in addition to being very short, was the leading left-wing cartoonist in Britain.

---

1. For Tom Maschler see Notes on Recipients.

one day, while neither of us got anything at all out of Caroleen. Still, it made a change.

Have been driving hard at *The Man with the Golden Gun*.[2] I forget what, if anything, we arranged about this. Anyway, you may care to glance at the enclosed list of errors, etc. My own feeling in general is that, while some kinds of error could easily be spotted by a competent reader (repetitions of words, the omission of question-marks – though I may say that none of Fleming's previous books has been *thoroughly* corrected for this – the "Adams" mantelpiece, etc.), there are on the other hand several passages that need to be rewritten by someone with a feeling and flair for style: this is especially true of the 2½ pages of dialogue that will have to be entirely re-drafted (pp. 127–129). Anyway, forgive me if some of the errors listed seem insultingly obvious.

My greatest discovery has been to spot what it is that has done most to make the book so feeble. As it stands, its most glaring weaknesses are:

i. Scaramanga's thinness and insipidity as a character, after a very lengthy though pretty competent and promising build-up on pp. 26–35;

ii. The radical and crippling implausibility whereby Scaramanga hires Bond as a security man (p. 67) when he doesn't know him and, it transpires, doesn't *need* him. This is made much worse by Bond's suspicions, "there was the strong smell of a trap about" and so on.

Now I am as sure as one could be in the circumstances that as first planned, perhaps as first drafted, the reason why Scaramanga asks Bond along to the Thunderbird is that he's sexually attracted to him, which disposes of difficulty no. ii right away and gives a strong pointer to the disposal of no. i. I wouldn't care to theorise about how far Scaramanga was made to go in the original draft; far enough, no doubt, to take care of no. i.

At some later stage, Fleming's own prudence or that of a friend induced him to take out this element, or most of it: see p. 33–34, which as things are have no point whatever. He was unable to think of any alternative reason for Scaramanga's hiring of Bond, and no wonder, since the whole point of this hiring in the first version was that it *had*

2. Ian Fleming (1908–64) died after correcting only half the final manuscript of *The Man with the Golden Gun*, and Amis, among others, was enlisted by Cape, Fleming's publisher, to look the manuscript over for errors and inconsistencies.

to be inexplicable by ordinary secret-agent standards. And then he was forced to hold on to the stuff about Bond's suspicions because Bond would have looked such a perfect nit if he hadn't been suspicious, and it's always better to leave an implausible loose end than make your hero look a nit.

There are no doubt all sorts of reasons why we can't have the book in its original version, the most telling of which is that it probably doesn't exist any more, if it ever did. I could re-jig it for you, but there are all sorts of reasons against that too. But if you think you could initiate a discreet inquiry about whether there was a buggery thread at some stage, I should be most interested to learn of any confirmation for my brilliant flash of insight.[3]

I'm sending the typescript back under separate cover. We go to Molins the day after tomorrow. Ageda[4] inquired kindly after you. Jane and I thoroughly enjoyed your stay with us and were very sorry to see you go. We send our love.

*!Hasta la vista!
Kingsley

*I know the first ! should be upside down but that would have been too much of a drag.

PS: Bob went through Egyptology a second time and made one suggestion, that on page 2 the phrase 'devoted to' should be changed to 'a devotee of'. Otherwise he seemed satisfied.

[TLS: Reading]

3. Maschler reported back to Amis that 'the resident experts (Fleming, not buggery) don't concur with your theory' (Maschler to Amis, 9 October 1964, in University of Reading Library). Amis alludes to his theory in *The James Bond Dossier* (1965), in which he deplores 'the ordinariness of Scaramanga, who entirely lacks the physical presence of Bond-villain at his best and remains a mere trigger-man whatever his (undemonstrated) deadliness, the promising hints of homosexuality and pistol-fetishism in him left undeveloped' (p. 67). For a discussion of Amis's theory and its rejection by 'the resident experts' see Andrew Lycett, *Ian Fleming* (London: Phoenix, 1995), pp. 444–5.

4. The Spanish cleaner at the house in Soller.

TO WILLIAM RUKEYSER – 18 OCTOBER 1964

Molins Hotel, Cala San Vicente, Pollensa, Mallorca, Spain

Dear Bill & Lis,[1]

Yes, about time, isn't it? I've entered a moratorium (if that means what I think it does) these last weeks on the writing of letters, in order that my, or Conquest's and my, novel[2] should be completed. This has now taken place, but I won't spoil things for you by retailing any of the gags: it wouldn't be right. Jane, of course, hasn't finished *her* novel – 185 pp or so to go; she does run to length a bit, as we all know – and I feel quite sorry for her, crouched silently over her typewriter unable even to get the keys going, while I enjoy a relaxed regime of lying on my bed, eating almonds, doing some leisurely letter-writing, sitting on the balcony in the sun, reading Anthony Powell and telephoning down for large gins, which are about four times the size of an English double. I feel, I say, sorry for Jane, until I approach gently, so as to leave her train of thought unimpaired, and find her reading the *Daily Mirror*. But she is working quite hard.[3]

It's a pity that power-crazed, pipe-smoking creep has got into No. 10, but a substantially greater relief that that twitching upper-class buffoon is out of it.[4] (Agree v. much with you about Sir A's robot qualities: robot on point of paranoiac attack due to wearing-out of electronic components, what's more.) We were fascinated to read of the Jenkins scandal, and the quite conflicting reports about the effect of the Khrushchev business on US voters:[5] consen[s]us – it will assist Johnson

---

1. Elisabeth Garnett Rukeyser, of Eltham; she married Rukeyser in 1963 at Woolwich Town Hall, with Amis serving as best man (see plates section).

2. *The Egyptologists* (1965).

3. Elizabeth Jane Howard has added in the margin: 'I am. He is a treacherous, insufferably complaisant, sybarite, hypachondriac, greedy, and altogether himself. I can get on with him because I know my station (v. low) & am renowned for being a good mixer.' Amis has placed an asterisk after 'hypachondriac' and written below it: 'note spelling'.

4. In the British general election held on 16 October 1964, the Conservative government of Sir Alec Douglas-Home (1903–95) was defeated by Labour, under Harold Wilson. Douglas-Home, formerly 14th Earl, was created Life Peer (1974).

5. The Jenkins scandal involved a White House aide during Lyndon Johnson's presidency, Walter Jenkins (b. 1918), a friend and assistant to LBJ for over twenty-five years, arrested for homosexual solicitation; on 15 October 1964 Nikita Khrushchev was replaced as First Secretary of the Soviet Communist Party by Leonid Brezhnev and as Prime Minister by Alexei Kosygin. On 3 November 1964 Lyndon Johnson was returned to the Presidency

and Goldwater very much and be of no particular use to either.

Weather mixed, but we've had a lot of sun recently and I was in the sea two days ago (which ought to show you). Sea rough today, sun fitful. The hour of the first drink approaches. Looking forward very much to seeing you on 3rd Nov.: we have both your numbers and will find you: at the moment have no address of our own. Jane sends love and hopes Lis is now eating enough for, say, three Chinese peasants.

And I concur.
Cheers,
Kingsley

[ALS: Recipient]

TO TOM MASCHLER – 19 OCTOBER 1964

Molins Hotel, Cala San Vicente, Pollensa (Mallorca)

Dear Tom,

I sent you a cable today, asking for £100 to be sent to me c/o Molins Hotel, Banco Santander, Pollensa – this is in case the bloody thing doesn't arrive, and also to apologise for being a nuisance. Our calculations seem to have gone to cock, you see. Hope there's enough money in the Kitty. *The Egyptologists* is finished. All well here. Jane still bashing away*[1] – or rather has been for some days and looks like continuing. She sends love: me too.

Cheers,
K.

after a sweeping victory over the Republican candidate Barry Goldwater (by a margin of 486 electoral votes to fifty-two).

1. At *After Julius* (1965).

PS: Do I get 25 gns for work on *Man with Golden Gun*? Or more? Or less?[2]

*Claims to have done at least 14,000 words since coming here.

[ALS: Reading]

TO VICTOR GOLLANCZ – 20 OCTOBER 1964

Molins Hotel. After 31st October: c/o Miss J. Gomme,
12 Greville Road, N.W.6

My dear Victor,

Thank you so much for your letter and for taking the line you did.[1] The difficulty about gossip and rumour had occurred to me too. I'm prepared to go a long way towards actual violence if someone suggests that you and I are parting company. More soberly, it occurred to me that I might, for instance, get hold of a bright and trustworthy young man whom I know on Smith's Trade News and work out something with him. But this would only be if you approve. Let me know what you think about this, or of any other mild manoeuvre that occurs to you.

Hope to have a more permanent address to give you shortly.

Thanks again.
Yours ever,
Kingsley

[TLS: Gollancz]

2. Maschler was planning to pay Amis with drink: 'I had in mind half a dozen bottles. Or more. Or less' (Maschler to Amis, 27 October 1964, in University of Reading Library).

1. See Amis to Gollancz, 27 September 1964, note 1.

TO ROBERT CONQUEST – 31 DECEMBER 1964

108 Maida Vale, W.9.

Dear Bob,

The Egyptologists went in finally about three weeks ago. I ought to have told you earlier, but general fucking about, including Xmas, and disinclination having finished typing out The Es to do anything whatever – this imposed a delay. [. . .]

No progress either with little shags,[1] I'm sorry to say. But now that I shall have to devote most of my energies to surviving the next month or so, they – l.s's – may well receive some of my attention. Pending the completion of the Maida Vale joint[2] (which has a letter-box but practically fuck-all else yet) we're in a flat in Hampstead, Keats Grove actually, which is very small and most of the time about a millimetre thick in coal-dust. To keep it warm (and thick in coal-dust) I have to go down and up 5 flights of stairs bearing first an empty, then a full, coal-bucket, or 'hod' as I believe they call the type in question. Anyway, we ought to be in the new house by 1st Feb.

Littly, i.e. little literary, news. David Holbrook[3] has called me a pornographer again. Philip seems always to be with Monica and makes apologetic telephone-calls about not bringing her along. Horrible outburst of sycophancy when Dame E. went off.[4] Met old Tom Blackburn[5] on a TV show the other week. Seemed nice enough, but a bit of a feeble shag. You heard, I suppose, that poor little Jimmy B. Singer[6] was also laid low – I mean like the Dame? The Beatles are as good as ever. Hilly

---

1. See Amis to Larkin, 2 October 1964. Conquest describes the 'little shags' as a primitive and unpleasant community living in fens and undergrowth in the north of England, much dependent on their inaccessible refuge, 'Boney's Rock' (named after Napoleon, the most famous of little shags). The little shags exist only in memory, though the Huntington possesses a mock title page (attributed to Conquest) that reads: '*FOR FEAR OF LITTLE SHAGS* By Alfred Huggins and Victor Gray, Shatto and Windarse, London WC'. On the other side is written: '*Chapter One, Too Late for Regrets*', followed by a mock opening paragraph of about fifty words. The title page is dated c. Oct.–Nov. 1978.

2. A five-bedroom house, purchased on a ten-year lease for £2,000.

3. David Holbrook (b.1923), critic, poet, academic.

4. Dame Edith Sitwell had died on 9 December.

5. Thomas Blackburn (1916–79), poet, published in Conquest, ed., *New Lines II*.

6. James Burns Singer (1928–64), American-born poet raised in Scotland, living in England; see *Memoirs*, pp. 222–3.

is apparently writing a novel. Christ. Jane will have finished hers in 2 wks poss.

Drop me a line when you have time. Happy New Year. Love to Caroleen. Jane sends hers.

Yrs
Kingers

Have dedicated The Es to Charmian,[7] by the way. Okay? It certainly looks good.

[TLS: Recipient]

TO EMILIE JACOBSON – 6 JANUARY 1965

4c Keats Grove, London N.W.3, England

Dear Miss Jacobson,[1]

Thank you for letting me know about the Playboy/Detectives idea. It interests me very much, and I should like to undertake it – but I can't see how I possibly can. The difficulty is quite simple. A subject on this scale calls for something like the amount of research that would be required for a book. On a modest computation I should have to read a hundred detective novels and thrillers. That would hardly take me less than a month. Writing it would take a week. Say one-tenth of a year in all. For the last three years I have found it necessary to earn around 30,000 dollars a year. One-tenth of that is 3,000 dollars. Do Playboy ever pay that kind of money?

A minor snag is that the subject as outlined could not be dealt with properly in under about 10,000 words. Even a piece that confined itself to the various detectives' personal habits – taste in food, drink, clothes, Holmes's violin-playing and Wolfe's orchid-rearing,[2] etc. – would run

7. Conquest's sister, Charmian Hartley.

---

1. Emilie Jacobson was at the time an assistant to Edith Haggard in the magazine department of Curtis Brown in New York; she took over the department when Edith Haggard retired in 1963.

2. That is, Nero Wolfe, the enormously fat private investigator created by the American detective-fiction writer Rex Stout (1886–1975).

to a quarter of that length. (The snag about *that* is that it wouldn't only take a quarter of the research: one would still have to read all the books.)

Do emphasise to Playboy that I'm not being fanciful or self-inf[l]ationary. My interests as well as theirs demand that I handle such a project conscientiously and thoroughly. And I simply would have to be paid for the time this would inevitably take.

Oh, and if they ever go any further with the idea, perhaps with another writer, they really should cut out James Bond, who isn't a detective at all. For, while it's probably true that the secret-agent-figure now gets the kind of attention that used to belong to the detective-figure, opening the field this far lets in about half the adventure novels of the century.

All my best to you all for the rest of 1965,

Yours sincerely,
Kingsley Amis

[TLS: Columbia]

TO THE EDITOR, *OBSERVER* – 18 APRIL 1965

Sir, – Perhaps only you could have published a whole article on university failures that laid no weight on the almost invariable cause of failure: *insufficient ability*, or, alternatively, *excessive stupidity*.[1]

I was glad to learn from you, however, that as many as 14 per cent of people do fail. Evidently not all standards have been fully lowered everywhere yet. But your fashionable brand of sentimental mercy will hasten the process.

KINGSLEY AMIS
W9

1. The article, by Brian Jackson, Director of the Advisory Centre for Education, an educational trust designed to help parents, was entitled 'Britain's University Throw-outs'. It was published on 11 April 1965, on the front page of the 'Review' section of the *Observer*.

TO HILARY AMIS – 4 JULY 1965

108, Maida Vale, W.9.

Dearest Hill,

It was okay in Brighton really, only there wasn't much sun, and it was hard to find anybody else there under 65.[1] Shall be here for next three weeks and *will* come down to see you and Sal.[2]

Love
x Binks x

[ALS: Recipient]

TO EDMUND AND MARY KEELEY – 12 AUGUST 1965

108, Maida Vale, W.9.

Dear Mike and Mary,

Where are you? Jane and I *have* to come to Greece for roughly the month of September: I've got a bit of a novel to write which must be set thereabouts.[1] You've asked me so often to visit you that I'm taking you up on it. Can we stay with you? Or could you fix us up somewhere near you? We can arrange to appear wherever you say – though remem-

---

1. Amis and Elizabeth Jane Howard were married on 29 June 1965, and after a small drinks party at Jonathan Cape and a wedding dinner at Prunier's spent two days at the Hotel Metropole in Brighton on honeymoon.

2. After their return from Majorca in January 1964, Hilly and the children stayed in London, first in a rented flat in Ovington Gardens in Knightsbridge, then in a rented house at 128 Fulham Road, Chelsea, where they remained for a year. During the year Hilly worked at the Battersea Park Zoo and also took in lodgers. By the time of this letter, though, she had moved to a house in Wivenhoe in Essex, near George and Pat Gale, the boys had come to live with Amis and Jane Howard at 108 Maida Vale, visiting their mother at weekends and holidays, and Sally was at a boarding school near Brighton called The Warren. It was while in Essex that Hilly became close to David Shackleton Bailey (1917–99), at the time Fellow of Gonville and Caius College, Cambridge (1944–68), Bursar (1965–68) and University Lecturer in Tibetan (1948–68), who would become her second husband.

---

1. The pseudonymous *Colonel Sun: A James Bond Adventure* (1968) by 'Robert Markham'. For the Keeleys see Notes on Recipients.

ber I don't fly. *Can* we fix it? It would be marvellous if we could. Time is of the essence, though, Stud, so if there's anything you can do, do it TODAY. We'd both love to see you.

Hoping,
Love,
Kingsley

[ALS: Princeton]

TO EDMUND KEELEY – 21 AUGUST 1965

108, Maida Vale, W.9.

Dear Mike,

Splendid. Thank you. Great.

We now have itinerary details. Leave London 2nd Sept. Steamer SAN MARCO from Venice, due Peiraeus noon on Sunday 5th Sept. Leave for home 27th/28th or so.

Now – you kindly invited me to say what we'd like. We think 3 days Athens, the rest Euboea. Athens perhaps at latter rather than former end, in the interests of heat-avoidance in city (it will be v. hot, no?) We doubt if the Greek provinces will be too primitive for us: sea and wine is just what we like. Can you take it from there?

Other points. Shall we need warmer clothes for evenings at all? Jane wants to know if shorts and trousers are still not okay in Greek eyes. Oh, and neither of us drive, though are very partial to hiring driven cars.

The cabin cruiser sounds marvellous. Don't wreck it before we've been in it.

Looking forward to seeing as much of you as possible, raising many a glass, etc.

Love to you both
Kingsley

PS: Is your beard on or off? Helpful for recognition.

[ALS: Princeton]

TO HILARY AMIS – 4 NOVEMBER 1965

108, Maida Vale, W.9.

Dearest Hill,

Sorry about the cheque – memory like a sieve. For your flights go to JOHN FERER Ltd in Shepherd Market – see phone book. Ask for Mr Gilbert and explain who you are. No deposit.

Was glad to see Sall looking so well and being so ungrasping. She didn't ask for a single thing all day Monday!

See you soon
Love
Binks

PS: Am getting your finances finally settled with Stuart[1] and the accountants.

[ALS: Recipient]

1. Stuart Thomas (see Notes on Recipients).

TO VICTOR GOLLANCZ – 9 NOVEMBER 1965

108, Maida Vale, W.9.

My Dear Victor,

After some thought I've come to the conclusion that we ought to go the whole hog (and have a designed jacket with glossy paper).[1] This will do more than anything else to show people that this is a new departure. It's the sort of book that could have a really arresting jacket picture (A-bomb explosion etc.). I've spoken tentatively to a friend of mine called Raymond Hawkey[2], and he is willing. Ray is design editor of the *Observer* and also did the cover of Len Deighton's *Horse Under Water*,[3]

1. For *The Anti-Death League* (1966).
2. Raymond Hawkey (b. 1930), graphic designer.
3. Len Deighton (b. 1929), thriller writer.

which thereupon sold 80,000 in the first 2 days (which the book's merits, and its author's standing, would hardly have done unassisted). Shall we discuss it? I can come to the Savoy at your cocktail hour, if you will give me a ring.

Many thanks for the dinner reminder: Jane and I would love to see Charles and Pam Snow (whom we know) and the Yehudi Menuhins[4] (whom we don't). Beyond that we happily leave it to you.

I return the draft jacket herewith.

Yours ever,
Kingsley

PS: I think no blurb at all, whatever the jacket.

[ALS: Gollancz]

TO THEO RICHMOND – 20 DECEMBER 1965

108, Maida Vale, W.9.

Dear Son,[1]

Your old Dad was delighted to get your filial letter. Tears coursed down his wizened old cheeks as he read. The chap was hoepelssly, I mean hopelessly, intoxicated.

Glad to hear your gamble is paying off. (We still have a film to make together, remember.)[2] I have been having a rather horrible time

4. Yehudi Menuhin (1916–99), violinist and conductor, born in New York but adopted British nationality (1985); married Diana Gould, his second wife, in 1947.

---

1. 'I'm not sure when Kingsley adopted me as his son, but it was long, long ago (I first met him during the filming of "Lucky Jim") . . . Certainly, I called him "Dad" and he greeted me as "Son" when we talked' (personal communication, 11 August 1997). For Richmond see Notes on Recipients.

2. Richmond's gamble was to leave a secure job with the Boulting Brothers (at British Lion at Shepperton Studios) to become a freelance director of documentaries. Two weeks after leaving British Lion he was hired to direct a film for *This Week*, regarded at the time as the best current-affairs programme on commercial British television. Amis was concerned that the successful gamble would distract Richmond from a project to adapt the short story 'Moral Fibre' (1958; reprinted in *My Enemy's Enemy* and *Collected Short Stories*) for the cinema. Richmond had produced a detailed outline or treatment of the film (a sixty-two-page typed carbon copy of which, entitled 'The More We Are Together' and dated 28 January 1963, can be found in HEHL), but no screenplay was ever written.

writing a story outline for one George Willoughby. Based on an original Fleming idea.[3] Willoughby and the script-writer change everything as I come up with it. I gave W. the completed outline five days ago and he has been too shocked and horrified and despairing to say a word since. However, he has already paid me. (Not much.)

We too would love to see you. But it may take some manoeuvring. Between Christmas and our departure for Jamaica on 12th January[4] Jane must fit in several days in hospital to have a couple of impacted wisdom teeth taken care of, poor girl. We might force you and Lee[5] to come here again and defer our trip to you until we get back in March. Anyway, nothing need prevent you and me lunching together quite soon, perhaps before the end of the year. We can discuss it then. Give me a ring. I shall be available at almost any time, having filled the house with drink and made up my mind to see the next seven days through under siege conditions.

Love to you both.
Your proud and loving
Dad

[TLS: Recipient]

TO COLIN HOWARD, PHILIP AND MARTIN AMIS – 18, 19 JANUARY 1966

S.S. Golfito. *at sea, approx 1300 miles N.E. of Trinidad*[1]

Dearest Monkey and Philip and Martin,

The sun is here at last, though there are still clouds about, and it has taken six days to emerge at all. Day 1 was very horrible, with

3. George W. Willoughby, Norwegian-born film producer whose credits include *Passionate Summer* (1958) *Masque of the Red Death* (1964), *Nothing but the Best* (1964) and *City Under the Sea* (1965). The Fleming idea never materialised.

4. See note 1 to the following letter, Amis to Colin Howard, Philip and Martin Amis, 18 January 1966.

5. Richmond's wife, the novelist Lee Langley.

---

1. On 12 January Amis and Jane Howard set sail for Jamaica to stay with Dolly and Bobby Burns at their house on Montego Bay. Dolly, a wealthy socialite, the daughter of the art dealer Lord Duveen (1843–1908), was 'uncontrollably rich' (Amis's phrase, recalled by Jane Howard); Bobby, her husband, was an orthopaedic surgeon. Amis and Jane Howard

20-degree rolls: not chilled bread, you fools, but the ship leaning over so that chairs went crashing over and – more important – glasses of booze crashing off the tables. I didn't like that: I kept wondering if the bloody thing would ever get up again, and indeed *went on* wondering that, time and again, hour after hour, with ever livelier curiosity. Neither of us was sick, but I at least could only manage, that lunch-time, to eat 1½ times my normal intake, instead of the 2½ times I have been clocking up ever since. What with breakfast with *fried bread*, *fried potato*, *toast* as well as sausages, bacon etc: colossal lunch with *bread* and cheese to finish: *tea* with currant: *bread*: gigantic dinner: *sandwiches* last thing, not to speak of the frightening ingestion of liquor (I *have* to keep hard at this: it would be very grave negligence not to, *large**[2] Scotches being 2s. 8d, Heidsieck 1955 champagne at £1–10s. a bottle and the rest in proportion) – well, what with one thing and another, as Bobby Burns would say, I am sure I have easily put back the lbs I painfully took off over about 9 months of no-breakfast, no-bread + so on, and probably another 3 or 4 lbs have slid around my neck and belly. I get *hungry*, you see, and the food is the best I have ever had on a British ship.

Apart from a view of the Azores, a scattered group of miniature Majorcas, we have seen no land. From them to Trinidad, our only stop before Jamaica, it's 2500 miles of open sea. I didn't like that either: suppose there was a hurricane? There hasn't been. Not *yet*. I was a bit relieved to note that the captain, a large Ulsterman, is sober all the time and shows no signs of going mad. *Yet*. But I was told he does get seasick in really bad weather. Suppose . . .

We have made 3 amiable chums, a couple called Gort and their 21-yr-old daughter. Mr Gort is an underwriter, City sort of chap, with evidently plenty of cash, and, Monkey, I have secured him as a customer of yours.[3] He is expecting you to ring him when he returns to England on 6th–7th Feb. If he isn't there, he says, ask for his secretary. When

had met the Burnses at a party given by the author Stephen Potter in the spring of 1965. In Jamaica, to Amis's annoyance, guests were required to dress for dinner, among other formalities. The visit lasted three weeks and was not without its tensions. The friendship understandably suffered when Dolly Burns recognised herself as the monstrous Lady Baldock in *I Want it Now* (1968), a novel that seems to have originated 'from a chance remark of Jane's, when she wondered aloud what it might be like to be a daughter of her childless friend Dolly Burns' (Jacobs, *Biography*, p. 298). 'Monkey', the first of this letter's addressees, is Colin Howard (see Notes on Recipients).

2. Amis's note at the bottom of the page reads: 'shipboard measure, 1/3 larger than pub measure'.

3. Colin Howard designed and built sound systems.

you go to see him, you will find that he will give you a lot of drinks. I enclose his telephone no., if I can remember to.

Other passengers include the Bishop of Durham[4] (he is a *fucking* old *fool*); this Princess Alice creature,[5] who is supposed to be George *V*'s sister; but on appearance could be George *IV*'s sister; two separate major-generals, one of whom was chairman of an international commission on the future of the West Indies – the commission was a failure, the W.I. are in political chaos, apparently, and having talked to this old sod, by Christ I can see why. Also I noted with much disgust a globular 16-stone female with cultural pretensions, who tried to obtrude herself on our group. I *drove her away* by being *studiedly rude.*

19th Jan. approx 900 miles from Trinidad

Still afloat. Trying fairly seriously to eat less. The weather has improved: still windy but monkey-coloured (dark blue) sky in evidence.[6] Have just been watching dozens of flying-fish. They are quite fun, but small, and somehow verminous-looking.

There was a dance last night which we did not attend. I can't see why the hell they organised it, given that the average age of the passengers is about 65 and I have counted at least 8 lame people (no exaggeration). But the "social side" has had its compensations. I've left it to Wog to tell you of my great gambling triumph. It has left me a bit jaded as regards Bingo.

I sit now in the lounge awaiting Heidsieck-time: all silence but for the clack of scrabble-tiles, the yelling of small dusky children, the dash of spray and the tremendous gurgle and squelch as the water in the swimming-pool is shifted by the motion of the ship: sounds like the Thing from another world sucking King Kong's cock.

Should any further observations occur to me I will transmit them. By another letter, I mean. If I get there. At the barber's today read how 84 chaps got burned up in the *Yarmouth Castle* off Barbados (which

4. Rt Rev. Maurice Harland (1896–1986), Bishop of Durham (1955–66).

5. HRH Princess Alice Mary Victoria Augusta Pauline, Countess of Athlone (1883–1981), first cousin (not sister) of George V, daughter of HRH Prince Leopold George Duncan Albert.

6. Colin Howard was famed within the family for refusing to call a day fine unless the sky was bright blue and cloudless.

we shall pass tomorrow night) last Nov. Oh well. Love to Sargy.[7] And to you 3.

Dad
Kingers

[ALS: Colin Howard]

TO COLIN HOWARD, PHILIP AND MARTIN AMIS – 3 FEBRUARY 1966

c/o Burns, Fairlea, Montego Bay, Box 583, Jamaica

Dearest Philip and Martin and inhuman[1], cruel, bloodthirsty Monkey for not writing and not forwarding ANY mail (though the Posts are not of the best).

This is a rather lousy island: beautiful and all that, good bathing, lots of – though by no means continuous – sun, but rather horrible rich white people and rather miserable resentful, black people. My old left-wing, or just humanitarian, feelings came back with a rush. I wouldn't argue that they ought to have been given their independence, but they bloody well ought to have been given some means of livelihood. But I'll keep the political stuff for when I see you.

We had a good day, or 6 hours, at Trinidad. A long taxi-drive across a peninsula to Maracas Bay. Before I had got out of the car, a man of African descent hurried up and assured me, in song, that this was his island in the sun, where his people had lived since time begun. Both these notions struck me as debatable at best. The man bore no resemblance to Dr Eric Williams, Prime Minister of Trinidad and Tobago,[2] and he was clearly not the Queen, so it was not *his* island. And as regards his people, until the 17th century they had lived since time begun on the mainland of Africa.

7. Colin's friend, the painter and jazz musician Sargy Mann (see Notes on Recipients), who would join the Maida Vale household in 1967, staying with the family until 1976.

1. Amis had originally written 'treacherous'.
2. Rt Hon. Dr Eric Williams (1911–81), leader of the People's National Movement; Prime Minister of Trinidad and Tobago from 1961; Minister of Finance from 1976.

Anyway, he then sang to me the following quatrain:

> "Now this gentleman wears a shirt of blue
> [I was indeed wearing a shirt of blue at the time]
> To show his love for his lady will always be true;
> And if a gentleman like this should ever die,
> A million ladies will have to cry."

He was accompanying himself on a guitar. I rotated slowly (I was out of the car by this time) so as to keep my back to him, watching his shadow so as to be able to counter his attempts to work his way round to the front of me. I succeeded, and in fact he received no money from me.

Not much more than an hour later I was sitting half pissed in the Trinidad Hilton, eating Columbus Mangrove Root Oyster Cocktail – bloody good – and drinking Foreign Guinness, which as you know is to me the prince of beers. Then we had Native Caribbean Pork Stew and I had more Guinness. Finally we lurched back on board and in due course bingo'd and champagned our way up to Kingston. Here the first white person we saw was Annie Sharpley,[3] who was staying at the hotel we had entered for drinks. She was in great form, v. informative and scathing about the situation here, which she is writing up for the Standard. Told us that it's already begun: i.e. the first case of deprivation-of-passport-for-unpopular (not Communist)-views happened the other day. She is back in this part of the world again already, trailing the Quoggins[4] round on her W. Indies tour.

And so, via a 5-hour train ride with nothing available but local beer, to Montego Bay, abode of millionaires like Wm. Hill the bookie and aristocrats like the Prince and Princess Shomberg-Lippe. The Prince is a badly-done caricature of a German Junker: I thought he was trying to be funny when I heard him say "Ach! zis is ze most vunderful haus surely on ze *hall* island," and nearly came back at him with more of the same. The Princess on the other hand was charming and intelligent; i.e. she thought I was frightfully entertaining. The rest of the white population appears to consist of deaf Americans.

Other random observations: mosquitos in roaring form. We have a lizard who lives near our window, and I asked him why he couldn't

3. Anne Sharpley (1928–90), journalist, worked on the *Evening Standard* from 1954 to the end of her life, covering wars, international events and court correspondence.

4. The Queen.

be a little more active in his pursuit of insect pests. He blushed – i.e. puffed out a bladder of red skin under his chin – and mumbled that he couldn't be everywhere at once. – When you see an Indian serving in a shop you rush to him as if he were white: he'll understand what you say, go and get what you want and bring it to you immediately. It ought to be *their* island in the sun. – Flowers, humming-birds, planter's punch, and the Wog are really the nicest things here. (Apart from me, of course.) Love to Sargy,[5] and two, oh all right all three, of you.

K.

[ALS: Colin Howard]

TO VIOLET AND ANTHONY POWELL – 19 APRIL 1966

108, Maida Vale, W.9.

My dear Violet and Tony,

Am breaking my habit of forcing Jane to write the thank-you letter in order to pass on to you my conviction that I've never enjoyed myself more with my clothes on, as a soldier might say, and in fact to say thank you.

Controversy continues to rage about Manor Farm.[1] I still talk about seeing if there's anything round Marlborough first, but I can foresee somebody else finding everything there subtly, or even blatantly, unsatisfactory. It's the water that gets them, you know.

Found myself committed to write on Waugh immediately on return, and fast. On re-reading, my piece seems to contain several self-contradictions.[2] He was a difficult man to make almost any flat general statement about.

5. Sargy Mann.

---

1. An ancient, semi-derelict farmhouse with an eighteenth-century stucco front and a garden leading on to the foreshore of Chantry Lake. The house lay in the valley just below the Powells' house, near Frome, in Somerset. Amis and Howard had begun thinking about buying a house in the country.

2. No such piece appears in Gohn, *Kingsley Amis: A Checklist*.

Well, see you soon, we hope. Seriously want you to come to dinner, and now invite you for Tuesday 10th May. Do try to fix it.

Love
Kingsley

[ALS: Recipient]

TO ALFRED L. BUSH – 21 JUNE 1966

108, Maida Vale, W.9.

Dear Mr Bush,

Many thanks for your letter and for the delightful request.[1]

In the house in Edgerstoune Road I rented, I researched and wrote the whole of my *New Maps of Hell*, did a little work on *Take a Girl Like You*, wrote four poems, and made notes on general Americana for *One Fat Englishman*. The house and neighbourhood gave me material for some of the physical ambience of that book – though NOT the basis of any characterisations! A small proportion of all this work was done in my office in Firestone Library.

Just writing the above has made me recall what an enjoyable year you all gave us in Princeton – but then I recall this every other day.

With all good wishes,

Yours sincerely,
Kingsley Amis

[ALS: Princeton]

---

1. Alfred L. Bush (b. 1939), at the time Associate Curator of Manuscripts, Princeton University Library, had asked Amis for information about what he had written while at Princeton, for an exhibition entitled 'Literary Landmarks of Princeton'. A catalogue for the exhibition was published in the *Princeton University Library Chronicle* 29 (Autumn 1967), pp. 1–88. Mr Bush is now Curator of Princeton Collections of Western Americana.

TO COLIN HOWARD – 31 JULY 1966

Olympic Palace Hotel, Athens

Dearest Monkey.

BHQ[1] have grudgingly permitted all to go reasonably well so far. Actually I thought at the start that, after a well-engineered hellish night on the Channel ferry – a marvellous virtuoso display of creaks, roars, bangs, clanks, crashes et al, the whole thing done at super-Mahlerian length – they were really going to get into their stride in Paris, aided by their favourite nation: BHQ's Chosen People. Very Gallic tone at the Gare du Nord: the first taxi-driver watched interestedly as I carried over 7 pieces of baggage from the queue to his taxi, and then expostulated that of course he couldn't be expected to carry all *that*. I was looking forward to Wog and me doing the trip to the Gare de Lyon in 2 taxis when another man appeared. (By this time we had decided to spend the day at a hotel before entraining abt 7 p.m., if we could find one, if they would countenance such an irregular proceeding etc.) Anyway, the 2nd chap (a) found nothing outrageous in either the amount of our luggage nor the hotel notion (b) found a hotel near the G. de L. (c) personally saw we were fixed up there (d) *smiled* quite a bit (e) thanked me for his tip. The people at the hotel were nice, too. We had an excellent lunch at a restaurant the Wog picked and found (imagine the expression of gentle but unmistakable triumph on the face). However, reality returned with a rush when, just at the hour when we were due to have our stuff carted to the station, 60 tourists arrived in the foyer, all with much luggage to be taken upstairs. So nobody could be found to fetch ours down (it wasn't the hotel's fault). So G.O.K. made I think 5 trips by the stairs – the lift being choked with the new arrivals – to the 5th floor and back in a hurry. I felt quite bad, and imagined the reports in the papers: "Kingsley Amies, 33, author of *Happy Jim*, *Room at the Top*, *The Pro-Life Society* etc. fell down dead in Paris today. His wife, better known as Iris Murdoch . . ." We caught the train.

Then the yacht. Everybody said the thing was to go West through

---

1. Bastards' Headquarters, or God's Heaven, the place where disasters and difficulties originate.

the Gulf of Corinth, where it was always calm. When the wind reached Force 6 and I had fallen out of bed, it was decided that the original assumption had been in error, and we turned back. Not before we had found ourselves near Delphi and so had to go there. Really massively, authentically unimpressive. With the exception of a small treasure-house that had clearly fallen over at one stage, been cannibalised for its marble and then put up again with a good deal of early 20th century material incorporated, the whole thing is a heap of rubble. Oh, there was a theatre, but not of the right period apparently. And a sort of holy stream which a lot of people drank ceremonially from – not I, deeming the content of goat-turds, peasants' piss etc to be too high for comfort. The lavatory on the yacht deserves a letter to itself – for the moment I'll only reveal that I broke the lever which was supposed to empty it: a good BHQ thrust, but mistimed because we were moored at Corinth at the time and repair was easy. Still, the islands are good all right: we've decided in future to visit them in big boats, ones with bars and working lavatories and obsequious waiters. I am v. brown, also the Wog, who has attained full Dusky-Princess appearance. She has been quite a good girl, considering, and so far has limited her demands to a mink cap (copy of my corduroy one) and a Persian Lamb coat. Practical, she says. Warm. Hard-wearing. Good for London. Etc.

Thanks 1,000,000 for all your work with the correspondence.

Love to all.
G.O. Kingers

U.L.D.[2] is unselfish loyal devoted

[ALS: Recipient]

2. Presumably the abbreviation occurs in a letter that has not survived.

TO ALAN ROSS – 15 OCTOBER 1966

108, Maida Vale, W.9.

Dear Alan,

Yes, but you have omitted the last five lines of the poem on page 91, thus making nonsense of it.[1] They run:

This is too little?
Am I in default,
Or are you grasping?
Which of us shows more
Inadequacy?

They should be subjoined after a gap of a line, like that separating the two sections of the poem on the opposite page.

I seem to remember that when the Oligodora piece was printed in the Magazine it was (for some reason) split between two pages at the very point in question. No doubt whoever was preparing the copy didn't notice this and just sent the first page. Anyway, however it happened something will have to be done about it, though I can see you haven't much time.

I think it's a good rule to send individual bits of proof to the poets themselves in a case like this. It's they who care about accuracy.

Yours,
Kingsley

[TLS: HRHRC]

TO HILARY AMIS – 27 OCTOBER 1966

108, Maida Vale, W.9.

Dearest Hill,

So glad about your news. It is good to know you're going to be settled (and you know I don't mean from the financial point of view,

1. 'Oligodora', first published in the *London Magazine* 2:10 (January 1963), pp. 12–13;

and I know you know). Funny to think that you're going to wind up in Cambridge after all.[1] How will you take to being a real high-powered ACADEMIC HOSTESS?

We have sent Phil to our doc who has put him on to some sort of vitamin pill things – not drugs – and already he seems much better. It looks as if he has been having some sort of vitamin deficiency which has made him low in spirits, etc. Mart is still lazy but we're working on him. Re Sally – fine, agreed about 5th Nov. As regards Christmas, we would love to have her for the whole hols, including Christmas but minus one week. So if you could fix a week when you could have her and let us know, we can plan the whole thing. As regards the weekends, it seems a good idea for you to have her for the 2-day ones and we'll take the overnight ones.

How are you for money? Stuart [Thomas] still I think has some for you. Apply to me when that runs out.

Sorry to hear about your old dad.[2] Let me know how things go.

Heaps of love,
Binks

[ALS: Recipient]

TO THE EDITOR, *THE TIMES* – 2 JANUARY 1967

From Mr Kingsley Amis

Sir, In two respects (if not more) Lord Annan misled his New York audience (your report, December 30).[1] It was not, of course, as a novelist, swinging or stationary, that I once wrote an article hostile to bull-at-

the last five lines were omitted when the poem was reprinted in *London Magazine Poems 1961–1966* (1966), selected by Hugo Williams, introduction by Alan Ross.

---

1. As wife to David Roy Shackleton Bailey; see Amis to Hilary Amis, 27 October 1967, note 2.
2. Leonard Bardwell, aged eighty, was seriously ill with pneumonia.

---

1. Noel Annan (1916–2000), Provost of King's College, Cambridge (1956–66); later Provost, University College London (1966–78) and Vice-Chancellor, University of London (1978–81); created Life Peer (1956). The article to which Amis refers, 'Lord Annan Hits at British Universi-

a-gate expansion of British universities, but as a teacher of some years' experience at one of them.[2] And the slogan I coined was not 'more means worse', which suggests some phantom principle, but 'more will mean worse', i.e. by the policies and at the speed proposed.

It seems that Lord Annan, like other expansionists, is only distantly acquainted with my article and the arguments advanced therein.

To state the position today would require alteration of my slogan to something like 'More is turning out to mean worse even faster than might have been thought'.[3]

Yours faithfully,

KINGSLEY AMIS.
108 Maida Vale, W.9, Dec. 30.

TO RUTH GOLLANCZ – 14 FEBRUARY 1967

108, Maida Vale, W.9.

Dear Ruth,

I am so sorry about Victor's death. I felt as many people must have done, that somebody irreplaceable had suddenly been removed from all our lives. He was a truly admirable man. And to me he was more than that, wisely and generously encouraging – generous more than once in a very practical way, lending me money unhesitatingly and unconditionally;[1] and we know how rare that is in this world.

ties', reported on a speech Annan gave in New York to the Modern Language Association of America, and ends with a quotation from the speech: 'Soon only that daring, unconventional, swinging novelist, Mr Kingsley Amis, and that great British daily newspaper which proclaims, "Top people take *The Times*", still opposed expansion and muttered, "More means worse."'

2. Amis's article was 'Lone Voices: Views of the Fifties', *Encounter* 15 (July 1960), pp. 6–11; reprinted, with a 1970 postscript, in *What Became of Jane Austen*?, pp. 157–71.

3. In his 1970 postcript to the 'Lone Voices' article Amis reiterates the distinction between an immutable principle ('More means worse') and a prediction, based on 'a particular situation, a foreseeable future' ('More will mean worse'). But he also, in the spirit of this last sentence of the letter, admits to feeling 'increasingly, in my darker moments, that there is something to be said for that principle' (*What Became of Jane Austen*?, p. 171). Amis's fears about the lowering of standards in higher education were expressed as early as Chapter 17 of *Lucky Jim*, pp. 169–70.

---

1. See, most recently, Amis to Gollancz, 1 March 1962. For Ruth Gollancz see under Victor Gollancz in Notes on Recipients.

Most vividly of all I shall remember his physical presence; that warmth and joviality which made one feel that life was better than one usually supposed it to be. And of how many people can that be honestly said?

My sincerest sympathy. Perhaps it is some little consolation to know how many thousands are as sorry as I am.

Yours,
Kingsley AMIS

[ALS: Warwick]

TO LIVIA GOLLANCZ – 24 FEBRUARY 1967

108, Maida Vale, W.9.

Dear Livia,

This is a painful letter to write, and I have been putting it off in a cowardly fashion. I had better just state the case bluntly.

For some years I have been unhappy with Gollancz Ltd and would long ago have moved elsewhere but for my personal loyalty to Victor.[1] Victor himself understood this perfectly well, and made no demur whatever about the get-out provision in the option clause of my last contract. Now, sadly, my loyalty is at an end, and I am off.

In the circumstances I feel quite definitely that our proposed lunch on Monday would be a needless and fruitless embarrassment. I hope that my cancelling it so late in the day will not inconvenience you too badly. And I wish I had something less discouraging to say.

Yours,
Kingsley

[ALS: Gollancz]

---

1. Jacobs, *Biography*, pp. 274–5, offers several reasons for Amis's unhappiness with Gollancz: despite Victor Gollancz's moments of extreme generosity, Amis thought there was something penny-pinching about the way the firm produced its books and promoted them; Gollancz dominated the firm, driving able colleagues (including his nephew Hilary Rubinstein, Amis's original editor) to seek work elsewhere; not enough effort was put into sales. That Elizabeth Jane Howard was extremely happy at Cape, and good friends with Tom Maschler, obviously also played its part.

TO HILARY AMIS – 28 FEBRUARY 1967

108, Maida Vale, W.9.

Dearest Hill,

I was sorry to hear about Daddy B.[1] Still, as you say, he was jolly old, and he did enjoy his life.

Glad the Shack thing is going forward. Don't worry about the Sal question: I'm sure we can fix it in 5 minutes flat. But we will discuss it when things are more definite.[2] (Won't say a word to her.)

Just a reminder about Easter: we collect Sall on Thursday 23rd, pass her on to you on the Friday so that we can go away for Easter, and have her back for the 2nd ½ of the hols.

I signed all the settlement papers the other day. Should be in effect *soon*!!

Love
B^x^inks

[ALS: Recipient]

TO HILARY AMIS – 12 MARCH 1967

108, Maida Vale, W.9.

Dearest Hill,

Fine to see you the other day, and old Shack, who I thought was a very good bloke.

J. and I were thinking it would be a good thing if *you* told Sally

1. Leonard Bardwell never recovered from the pneumonia he contracted in late October 1966; see Amis to Hilary Amis, 27 October 1966, note 2.

2. 'The Shack thing' was either Hilly Amis's impending marriage to Shackleton Bailey (it did not take place until 21 November 1967) or the prospect of Bailey's becoming Professor of Latin at the University of Michigan (1968–74) and of Hilly and Sally accompanying him to Ann Arbor, or both; 'the Sal question' was how to break the news to their thirteen-year-old daughter.

about the big decision,[1] and so it would be best if you met her on the 23rd. (We would have her for the 2nd ½ of the hols as arranged.) What do you think of this? No hurry at the moment. I'll give you a ring in a few days, or – if you're going to be away or anything – you give us one.

Enclosed a bit of cig. money!

Love,
Binks

[ALS: Recipient]

TO PHILIP LARKIN – 21 MAY 1967

108, Maida Vale, W.9.

My dear Philip,

Sorry I don't seem to have answered your letter of the 18th March before. I can't, of course, come to the Communist demonstration on 21st October,[1] because, as you surmised, I shall be in America then. Not that I would have come even if I had been able to. It's no use trying to argue with anti-British fanatics. You don't want me to write another letter you can show to the trendy little traitorous fuckers, do you? Ballocks; show them this one.

I have a recent (barely a month old) letter from good old Bruce [Montgomery]. He burbles about a Festschrift for J. D. Carr,[2] says you have agreed to contribute something on some aspect of the stuff or other. Aspect? Aspect? He wants me to do another aspect. Aspect? What aspect are you doing? Aspect? How does he mean, aspect? Aspect? *Aspect*?

I am pretty much in the pink, though a bit troubled by colitis: the

---

1. See previous letter, note 2.

---

1. On 21 October 1967 demonstrations against the Vietnam War were held in Washington, London and other Western capitals. For a full statement of Amis's pro-American position on the war see 'Poets on the Vietnam War', *The Review* 18 (April 1968), pp. 29–30.

2. Nothing came of the idea. See Larkin to Amis, 3 June 1967, in *LL*, p. 386. For John Dickson Carr see Amis to Larkin, 30 March 1947, note 8.

shits to you. A doctor did a good deal of bum-staring on me a short while ago, inserting closed-circuit TV and so on in my lower alimentary tract in order to do so. You feel (a) that you're about to have your uvula tickled from the back (b) that his arm is up you to the shoulder (c) that you have plastered, and are continuing to plaster, walls, floor and ceiling with a thin layer of frothing crap. He told me he went up 22 cm. (9" approx). I said that that was further than most of our friends could manage with their natural resources, and he said yes, and they hadn't got the advantage he had, of being able to see where he was going. Good chap, that doc. He has forbidden me to drink anything but spirits.

Otherwise I am in fine fettle. My Bond novel (*Colonel Sun*) is finished, and I have just put together a book of beautiful poetry (*A Look Round the Estate*) to show that I am full of integrity after all. By the way, could you reassure me about something? Ted Hughes is as ABSOLUTELY DEVOID OF ANY KIND OF MERIT WHATSOEVER as his late wife [Sylvia Plath] was, isn't he? I mean he is, isn't he? There was a party the other day for his new bundle of balls, and the thought I have put to you occurred to me then; in fact, I think Hughes himself may have guessed what was in my mind from the way I addressed him. Hey, and how does he mean, *Ted*? What does he blow? Mm?

If you have time, do drop me a card about this JDC idea. It sounds full of shit to me, but there may be some delightly fresh and subtle nuance to it I haven't grasped.

Darling, have you rung the accountants about your bum,

Kingsley

I must say that your crapping-on-Norman [Iles] *PS ('he is entirely divorced from reality, in that he thinks [his poems] are good') opens new vistas. Crapping on a chap twice for only one load of shit.*[3]

[TLS: Bodleian]

3. MS addition.

TO PETER OWEN – 11 JULY 1967

108, Maida Vale, W.9.

Dear Mr Owen,

If I had been able to attend on 17th September, I would still have had to satisfy myself that no money would go to North Vietnam before I agreed to appear.[1] But as it is I shall be in the USA on that date, so the question does not arise.[2]

Yours sincerely,
Kingsley Amis

[ALS: HRHRC]

TO MR HEPPNER – 14 JULY 1967

108, Maida Vale, W.9.

Dear Mr Heppner,

Thank you for your letter.[1] I have not had the experience you describe – Gollancz were the first to see *Lucky Jim* and, after a slight delay, accepted it. But it may possibly be of interest to you that I wrote

---

1. Peter Owen, the publisher, had written to Amis inviting him to participate in a public discussion to launch the publication of *Authors Take Sides on Vietnam* (1967), to be held at the Arts Theatre in London. The aim of the meeting, in addition to publicising the book, was to raise money 'for Vietnam relief' (Owen to Amis, 6 July 1967, in HRHRC). For earlier published signs of Amis's disillusion with the left see 'Psyche of the Future', *Mademoiselle* 54:40 (January 1962), pp. 40–1, 111–12; 'What's Left for Patriotism?', *Observer*, 20 January 1963, p. 21; and 'Why Lucky Jim Turned Right', *Sunday Telegraph*, 2 July 1967, p. 7, reprinted, with a postcript, in *What Became of Jane Austen?*, pp. 200–11. See also Amis to the editor, *Sunday Telegraph*, 25 July 1967.

2. Amis had been invited by Russell Fraser, a friend from Princeton days, to become a visiting Professor of English at Vanderbilt University in Nashville, Tennessee, where Fraser had recently become Chairman of the English Department. The post was for a semester (from October to mid-January) and involved only light teaching. For Fraser, see Amis to Jean and John McAndrew, 2 May 1960, note 5.

---

1. The identity of Mr Heppner has not been discovered (by myself or the Pennsylvania State University Library, which possesses this letter), nor is it possible to identify with certainty the experience he describes.

an earlier novel, called *The Legacy*, in 1948–49, and this was rejected by, I think, fourteen publishers before my agent gave up the struggle.[2] I managed to resist the temptation to revise it and publish it after *Lucky Jim* had made this possible. It was very bad, and thank God I saw this in time. Having done so, I have the complacency to suggest a solution to a minor literary enigma. Why is a writer's second novel so often inferior to his first, so that a second novel that turns out to be, if nothing more, no worse than the first one is a cause for congratulation? Answer: because most "second" novels were written earlier than the "first", and after the successful appearance of the "first" are pulled out of the drawer, given a freshly-typed title page and bunged off to the publisher.

The Legacy will remain in its drawer: having been milked for background, and what gags it contained, for use in later books (especially *Take a Girl Like You*).

Hope you can use some of this.

Yours sincerely,
Kingsley Amis

[ALS: Pennsylvania State]

TO THE EDITOR, *SUNDAY TELEGRAPH* – 25 JULY 1967

[Sir,] A favourite retort to my declaration of disenchantment with Socialism (and all that) has been to accuse me of having grown older and richer.[1] To the first charge I have no answer. The second might

2. For 'The Legacy' see Amis to Larkin, 30 July 1946, 16 July 1948 and 8 January 1951.

---

1. Amis's declaration was 'Why Lucky Jim Turned Right', which appeared in the *Sunday Telegraph*, 2 July 1967, p. 7; reprinted in *What Became of Jane Austen?*, with a 1970 postscript, pp. 200–11. In this article Amis reveals that he voted Labour for the last time in 1964. He also makes clear 'where I stand':

> I am not a Tory, nor pro-Tory (who could be pro *this* Tory Party?), nor Right-wing, nor of the Right, but of the Centre, equally opposed to all forms of authoritarianism. What I am particularly not is a Fascist, though I have been called one quite a lot recently by correspondents of varying degrees of literacy . . . However, I quite understand their use of the term. They sense, accurately, that I am anti-Left, and 'Fascist' is useful, straightforward and soundly-precedented shorthand for 'opposed to the policies and

have more force if top Lefties could be shown to be suffering in some way under the Wilson regime, to have embraced privation for the sake of principle. On the contrary, all the ones I can think of are (to put it mildly) flourishing unchecked.

I was tepidly gratified by David Winnick's assurance that plenty of his Parliamentary colleagues, 'including many on the Left' are prepared to protest about the case of Sinyavski and Daniel.[2] I cannot, however, accept his implication that Communist repression on the one hand, and Apartheid and the Greek coup on the other, are matters of equal concern to us in this country. The principle of apartheid is a denial of humanity; any democrat must be concerned by what has happened to freedom in Greece. And by all means let us condemn authoritarianism wherever it appears, but let us retain our sense of relevance.

South Africa does not intend to subvert the world, and could not; the Greek Colonials [sic] do not want to, and could not, export their regime – a very half-heartedly tyrannical one by Communist standards, let us not forget. Neither system has a vocal minority campaigning for its interest in Great Britain.

Communism, on the other hand, is a threat to us, and to freedom everywhere. What about getting our priorities straight?

KINGSLEY AMIS
London, W9

interests of the Russian Government; pro-American; pro-British' and other shabby heresies. (pp. 203–4)

2. David Winnick (b. 1933), Labour MP for Croydon South (1966–70), later Walsall North (since 1979). The writers Andrei Sinyavsky (Abram Tertz) (1925–97) and Yuri Daniel (Nikolay Arzhak) (1925–88) were imprisoned together in September 1965 following the foreign publication of their writings, which the Soviets considered slanderous and reactionary. Their trial provoked widespread condemnation, including from non-Russian communists and Soviet intellectuals. See Amis to the Editor, *The Times*, 21 November 1968.

TO COLIN HOWARD – 17 SEPTEMBER 1967

3627 Valley Vista Road, Nashville, Tennessee 37205, U.S.A.[1]

Dearest Monk,

All seems suspiciously well. The Wog has told you, I believe, something of my stiff neck in New York, but it would take the pen of a master (me, for instance) to begin to indicate what this really meant. It's really a frightfully *good* BHQ thing, in that the victim feels that something very cosmic is going on, sore throat *from the back* and all that, while everybody else goes on as if he knows that it's all totally trivial. In fact the Wog was very good about it all and meekly ate her unaccompanied dinners in the hotel while yours truly was lying in bed screaming only mutedly at every change of position. But that's behind me now, as the actress said to the bishop, and here we are in fairly good old Nashville. Actually I have no objections at all as yet, but then work hasn't begun yet.

Electronic wonders abound. So far I have encountered push-button phones (to which I am a convert: each button makes a sweet little sort of piping noise when you push it), a TV remote control unit without any wires – there seems to be some sort of audio circuit which the physical click is able to affect, and a refrigerator thing whereby the ice-trays automatically drop their cubes into a container and then fill themselves up with water for further freezing and so on until the container is full, at which point everything stops. Bloody good for you is what I say.

The South is just what they say it is, only more so. Everybody goes on talking as if he, or she, especially she, were trying to be funny. For instance, the lefties (oh yes, they're here too) especially aggravate you

---

1. Amis and Jane Howard sailed to New York on the *Queen Mary* on 30 August 1967, stayed for a few days at the Algonquin Hotel, then with Edmund and Mary Keeley in Princeton, before eventually travelling by train to Nashville. The house on Valley Vista Road was rented from Ed and Ivar-Lou Duncan. Ivar-Lou is described in *Memoirs*, p. 289, as 'a Scandinavian-American lady . . . of parsimonious bent' (she tried to make Amis pay for the use of her husband's typewriter, 'a measure he vetoed'); the house itself is described only as poorly heated, though Amis approved of the surrounding wildlife, including 'a chipmunk we persuaded to come to the windowsill for a saucer of milk in the evening' (p. 282).

by saying things like 'Ah hay-yut whoa-wuh' i.e. I am a pacifist. Never mind: my novel[2] has reached p. 43 and that's what counts, what?

Stuart Thomas and three friends arrive tomorrow. I cannot quite make out why this should be. The three friends thing, I mean. I shall be able to report much more cogently on the horrors of local life when I have started *working:* aaoh! aoh! aooh! and when we have met a few more of the locals, tho' annoyingly enough those so far glimpsed seem cordial enough well too many enoughs there but what the hell its 12.20 and wht sht what the hell do you expect eh what.

We trust that you and the venerable Sague [Sargy Mann] are keeping the show going at good old 108. I already feel I've been away some incredible space of time like six months. The Wog will be writing to you about the multifarious oddities of this house, about which I will only say to you at this tahm, man, that the picture of the lady's mother hanging over the bureau could have appeared to great advantage in Japanese barrack rooms in say 1943 for the purpose of sustaining morale, with some such caption as STRIKE THROUGH TO USA AND KILL MANY SUCH PERSONS AS THIS VERY-WISE OLD LADY. Just fantasy, really. See ya.

Love, Kingers

The house is full of people: the Negro maid, whose get-under-your-feet capacity at least equals Mrs Glennon's: Ed, whose house it is, egging on his wife Ivar-Lou (honestly: pronounced Ahva-Leew) to take a few of the items of rotting food out of the refrigerator, and the Wog nobly dealing with them all.[3]

[TLS: Recipient]

TO COLIN HOWARD – [SEPTEMBER 1967]

Dearest Monk – This is to make you feel extra treasured: my 1st UK letter was to you and so is this my second. The Wog erred splendidly when she said Fisk is the only nignog university in USA: there are quite a few, but only 2 good ones: Fisk here, and *Howard* (cross my heart)

2. *I Want it Now* (1968).
3. MS addition.

in NY.[1] We are going to survive this stint very happily, even though I shall have to work like a fucking idiot to get my book done as well as my lectures prepared, and even though I sense that general conditions – though perfectly pleasant as far as they affect us – will turn out to justify a certain moderate leftiness of sentiment. But more of this when I start to know more.

Scenically and zoologically, no complaints. There are facilities in the garden for feathered chaps, and riotous bathing parties go on most of the daylight hours. They were abruptly cancelled when a furry chap, of a greyish, Malfian[2] appearance, turned up and pretended to drink the overflow. No raccoons yet. But there has been talk.

Jehovah's presence sits heavily on the house – I don't mean that either of us has developed cancer or syphilis, just that the Duncans (renters of the house and perpetual returners to it) are keen. Tracts and books called things like "Great Writers as Interpreters of Religion" (I was rather dashed to find no reference to me in it) and "The Bible" are on every hand. Ivar-Lou even pressed a pro-JC pamphlet into the hand of the W., who said with gt. tact she had plenty to read already. Roared at CPS's close-knit features.[3] Tell us the gossip.

Love,
Kingers

[ALS: Recipient]

TO TOM MASCHLER – 28 SEPTEMBER 1967

c/o Duncan, 3627 Valley Vista Road, Nashville, Tenn. 37205, USA

My dear Tom,

Deeply moved by all the monies you mention – everything sounds fine to me. Now I know you won't have got the monies yet, but my poor bank account is languishing. Could you possibly arrange a transfusion –

---

1. Actually in Washington DC.
2. The name of Colin Howard's Blue Burmese cat was Malfi, as in Duchess of Malfi.
3. Colin Howard does not remember the reference to C.P. Snow's 'close-knit features'.

whatever you can to a/c Amis & Howard Glyn Mills & Co., Child's Branch, 1 Fleet Street, E.C.4.

I have another distasteful chore for you, which however one of your P.A., secretaries etc. could well handle. The p-b situation in USA for British novels is v. bad, and some books I ought to teach the kids here[1] are either $6.00 in hardback or else non-existent. So here are some order forms that I will ask you not merely to pass on physically, but expedite by your personal intervention with the various publishers. The bookshop here (admittedly a bloody awful organization) says it has had v. long delays on books from UK, and a word in the right ear from you *might* cause the damn stuff to arrive before the course ends.

There is a snag in the proof of *Colonel Sun* at page 187.[2] I wrote a revised version of this passage and included it in the final copy I dropped at Cape's or was it Janson-S's?[3] just before leaving. What appears in the proof is the earlier version. I imagine that the *written* corrections on that draft were all duly noted and incorporated, but that this, being a properly typed page, slipped though the mesh. I *could* re-do the thing: the snag would be that I did the revision from notes supplied by Mike K.[4] that I haven't got here, or probably anywhere. Meantime I will plug ahead with proof-correction. By the way, what about proofs of the maps? I must see them, to ensure that everything that should be on them is on them.

One last thing that *may* bring a faint wan smile to your careworn countenance: my novel progresses, not fast, but very steadily: 53 pages

---

1. Amis's teaching consisted of a single lecture course (on the Modern British Novel) which met three times a week for an hour or so. There were about a hundred students in the class, and although Amis wrote out his lectures in full ('your script is your lifebelt if nothing else,' *Memoirs*, p. 288), he was given a 'reader' or graduate assistant to help with marking. Among the novelists Amis lectured on were John Le Carré, Len Deighton, Ian Fleming, William Golding, Graham Greene, Iris Murdoch, Anthony Powell and Evelyn Waugh.

2. *Colonel Sun* (1968), a James Bond novel written under the pseudonym 'Robert Markham'.

3. Peter Janson-Smith, Ian Fleming's literary agent and a director of Glidrose Productions Ltd, the company Fleming bought in 1952 and to which he assigned the copyright in all his Bond novels.

4. For Edmund (Mike) Keeley see Notes on Recipients. Keeley taught English, creative writing and modern Greek studies at Princeton; most of *Colonel Sun* is set in Greece, hence Keeley's notes.

are done, 160–170 more to do. Firm title: I WANT IT NOW (it being several things, but chiefly IT). That should wow them.

Next letter will be in the descriptive rather than the imperative vein. Working horribly hard, too much of it at ephemeral academic necessities. Weather turning cold

Love,
Kingsley

[ALS: Reading]

TO BOB [G. WREN] HOWARD – 17 OCTOBER 1967

c/o Duncan, 3627 Valley Vista Road, Nashville, Tennessee 37205, U.S.A.

Dear Bob,

Many thanks for your letter. I think you have a good point, and enclose an 'Author's Note' which, I hope, clears up the matter. (Do feel free to amend it if necessary.)[1]

'Enjoying ourselves very much' is a bit of an overstatement about our condition here, but we have some pleasant chums and life is not dull – on Thursday we visit the Jack Daniel's Distillery, HOME OF THE FINEST WHISKEY IN USA.[2] And despite such distractions,

---

1. Howard, the Chairman of Jonathan Cape, was concerned about Amis's use of dashes, as opposed to quotation marks, to differentiate types of speech in *Colonel Sun* (see Howard to Amis, 5 October 1967, in Reading). As the eventual 'Author's Note' explains:

> Two methods of indicating dialogue are used in this book.
>
> Dialogue *given in English translation* from Russian or Greek, following Continental practice, is introduced by a dash; for example,
>
> – Good morning, Comrade General.
>
> Dialogue *in English* is enclosed in the normal inverted commas; for example,
>
> 'He was hit in the back, I think.'

2. For an account of this trip see *Memoirs*, pp. 291–3.

Jane and I are getting on with our books like good children. (She sends *particular* love to you.)

Cheers,
Kingsley

PS: We are woefully short of cats, and the squirrels in the garden don't really compensate!

[ALS: Reading]

TO ROBERT CONQUEST – 1 NOVEMBER 1967

Dear Bob,

Many ardent thanks for your letters, much needed. Actually Vanderbilt isn't too bad: it's Nashville that's the drag on the whole: *dinner parties* and the rest of it, and plenty racialism. The nigra gets talked about in terms that recall the most tedious lefty play. Buggers haven't learnt a bloody thing. One can forgive a lefty here, in that "conservative" opinion is so shitty. It would take some strength of mind not to say, in effect, "anybody who thinks like that about Negroes must be wrong about everything. Stop US murder in Vietnam!" I have been invited to a teach-in on that, and declined, saying I was on holiday. So are all of you lazy bastards back home, I see. I read in the TLS about Lenin's statesmanship, and the balanced view which credits the Russian Revolution with its achievements. Aha! I think: Bob or Tibor [Szamuely][1] will get going on the balanced view being that the R. R. was a disaster, and *what* achievements? – and the following week – fuck all. Pull yourselves together, you lazy sods.

V. retrospectively concerned about poor Caroleen's appx; but your letter announcing her hospitalisation had no sodding zip-code on the address and took ten days to get here – so we assume she will be back home by now, gallant little thing. Hope all becoming comfortable again.

---

1. Tibor Szamuely (1925–73), a Hungarian refugee from communism (and the Gulag) and historian of modern Russia. Szamuely was one of Amis's 'seven great friends', and is discussed in *Memoirs*, pp. 252–61. In addition to teaching in Moscow and Budapest before coming to Britain in the mid-1960s, he was appointed Vice-Chancellor of Budapest University in 1958.

Both of us are working like bloody fools – J. running the house – most unbelievably shagged and inconvenient south of the Mason-Dixon line – as well as novelising; good old K. doing 3 fucking lectures a week (tell Anthony Powell that, unlike Alabamans, Tennesseans don't find his jokes provincial) and also doing his best to novelise. Both feel starved of news – we have the Telegraph; but tell Michael Wharton[2] to get back on the job, also that it's 90 *degrees* proof whisky, not 90 per cent proof.

Met a man called TUPPER SAUCEY* the other day. Just couldn't bring myself to tell the white lie that his names were the other way round. Names are bloody good here in general, especially those double-barrelled female Xtn names. The really horrifying woman who let us the house is called IVAR-LOU Duncan. Susceptible of fictional rendition somewhere. The Good Book has them all by the throat in this area. Young wife of chap in the Russian dept. (v. sound reactionary) was rung up at 9 a.m. the other day and asked to come over – 10-mile drive – to join in a discussion of the Bible.

Most encouraged to hear of the Weekly.[3] I will certainly write for the bloody thing. And will write again to you after a shorter silence than now. But let me know news of the boys. Tell J Braine I will answer his kind letter shortly, if I can find the bloody thing. What's this about a rival to *Encounter* with J. Gross in one of the chairs?[4] Oh well, I'll ask Irving Kristol,[5] who turns up here soon to orate. Great love to Caroleen. Jane is answering for herself.

Cheers,
Yours Kingers

*Flaring Anglophile shag – all such are v. horrible, talk of graciousness,

2. Michael Wharton (b. 1913), journalist and author; 'Peter Simple' columnist, *Daily* and *Sunday Telegraph* since 1957.

3. Conquest cannot identify 'the Weekly'; no such periodical of this name was published in Britain.

4. John Gross (b. 1935), editor, author, critic; edited *Times Literary Supplement* (1974–81). After the disclosure in July 1967 that *Encounter* had been funded in part by the CIA, Stephen Spender, a past editor, and a group of friends (including Isaiah Berlin, Stuart Hampshire and Richard Wollheim), sought to establish a rival monthly. At one point Gross was under consideration as a possible editor. The magazine never appeared.

5. Irving Kristol (b. 1920), American author, editor, social scientist; co-founding editor, *Encounter* (1953–58); co-editor, *The Public Interest* (1965–).

the Queen etc. Propose a distinction between Anglophiles (shits) and pro-British (possibly okay).

[ALS: Recipient]

TO ROBERT AND CAROLEEN CONQUEST – 5 FEBRUARY 1968

San Miguel de Allende Gto., Mexico

Why not fix a special Welcome Home Kingers lunch for the 21st? (It's Jane's birthday on the following Tuesday.)[1]

Dear B & C,

This, on three days' acquaintance, is a bloody good spot: the first place we've really felt at home in since Princeton back at the beginning of September. 6,000 feet-plus altitude about 200 miles NW of Mexico City, weather like a hot English June. I am on the terrace of the Hotel Posada de las Monjas, bare to the waist and drinking a home-made tequila con sangrita, con, of course, limon y sal tambien. In case you don't know, this is a kind of tequila Bloody Mary with a hell of a lot of tabasco and so on in the bloody part. Very sustaining.

After Nashville, which in retrospect seems rather like the days of the Captivity in the eyes of the children of Israel, we, including our chums the Keeleys, moved round the Estados Unidos Mexicanos a little, seeing things like the pyramids at Teotihuacan was it, which impressed greatly, and Maximilian's palace in Cuernavaca, which was a fucking pain. Also Acapulco, where I had a suitcase stolen (nothing vital), and Mexico City, where we had a 40-second earthquake tremor. No damage, but by Christ I thought the old coronary was upon me until Keeley kindly apprised me of the situation. Acapulco was fairly horrible, but

1. MS addition. In mid-January Amis and Elizabeth Jane Howard travelled by train from Nashville to St Louis and then to Mexico, to meet Edmund and Mary Keeley. In February they spent four weeks in San Miguel de Allende, visiting the American science fiction writer Mack Reynolds (1917–83) and finishing the novels they had been working on, *I Want it Now* (1968) and *Something in Disguise* (1969). After visiting friends in Princeton and New York, they returned to England on the *Queen Elizabeth*, arriving on 20 March.

the sentence "Bond had never liked Acapulco" has been striking me ever since as a more than possible opener (short story only). Now we are fixed in San M. for a full four weeks for a spell of solid work, both hoping to finish novels. Old Mack Reynolds is here and we're under his very solid wing. The town is full of American tourists and "artists", but that's fine, because things like shops, bars and doctors always look up in such circumstances and there are people to talk to in the evenings. As planned, we start trickling northwards in exactly a month, sailing finally from NYC in the QE and hitting the UK on 20th March: a bit of a blow your having switched the lunches,[2] because I was looking forward to attending on the 21st; but no harm, and we look forward greatly to the party you kindly suggest. Our plans, by the way, have not changed at any stage, were fully and repeatedly conveyed to Colin Howard, who now pretends to have found them totally mysterious as a form of defence against justifiable charges of inefficiency, laziness etc. (Better not tell him this.) Anyway, talking of inefficiency and so on, there has been no sign of my snuff, which is presumably somewhere between either Nashville and Mexico City or M.C. and here, if the hotel remembers to forward it. So, if you would be so kind, and look a bit sharper than heretofore, perhaps you would get one tin of the High Dry Toast and one of the carnation-type sent AIR MAIL *EXPRESS* to

c/o Mack Reynolds
Apartado 252 (which is a PO box)
San Miguel de Allende
Gto., Mexico

which will find us until, as I say, 5th March. Snuff stocks here are low. If the first consignment does turn up, all will still be well, because it doesn't get stale that fast.

2. See *Memoirs*, p. 146: 'In the middle and late 1960s, when we were both settled in or near London, Amis-Conquest contact was easier and more frequent. This was the period of the so-called fascist lunches at Bertorellis' Restaurant in Charlotte Street. More or less regular attendees included, besides R. C. and K. A., Tony Hartley, Tibor Szamuely, John Braine, Tony Powell, Donald (C.) Watt, Russell Lewis, Bernard Levin (at first), and the American journalist Cy Friedin, with an occasional MP, Nick Ridley, Tony Buck, as guest. Contrary to rumour, no plot or project was ever even mentioned at that table, but I learnt quite a lot of history and politics now and then, before the rounds of grappa started.' Conquest (personal communication, 17 October 2000) points out that some attendees, 'including me', were less 'fascist' than others: 'more anti-Heath and pro-Labour'. The day of the weekly lunches had been changed from Tuesdays to Thursdays.

Glad old Karl is feeling uneasy.[3] I nearly shat myself with fury on hearing that the Pistener had put up that bastard Che Guevarra (?) as Man of the Year. And then, just yesterday, Mack told me that *Tony Richardson* was sending *Alan Sillitoe* to Mexico to write a film about *Che G.*[4] AAAOOGHGH Did you know this? Where will it all end? We must plan a monster counter-offensive when I get back. One suggestion meanwhile: plug "KGB" as hard as possible, as I see the Daily T is doing in its headlines. It is, I think, one of their weakest flanks. Here, by the way, you get a rather different kind of Lefty, who seems genuinely anti-Commie, but can't or won't see that to be anti-US-in-Vietnam is to be pro-Commie. They all say there are no Commies in USA, no Commie component in draft-card burnings, etc. Anyway, fuck 'em; I'll certainly write again before we leave here; Jane thanks Caroleen for her letter and will be answering; our address from 5th–15th March (when we sail) will be c/o Keeley, 140 Littlebrook Road, Princeton, N. J. 08540. Thoroughly enjoyed your pieces, and was slightly amazed old Karl printed you in his rag. See ya.

Love to you both, and J sends hers,
Kingers

[TLS: Recipient]

TO ROBERT CONQUEST – 11 [MARCH] 1968[1]

Princeton

Dear Bob,

Ta for your 2 letters, awaiting us on arrival here. Am sitting in front of the TV (though it's only 10.30 a.m.) watching the Senate Foreign Relations Committee doing its stuff: at the moment that old pompous poop Fulbright[2] is sounding off, saying it's jolly understandable that

3. Karl Miller (see Notes on Recipients); at the time Editor, *Listener* (1967–73).

4. Tony Richardson (1928–91), film and stage director; Alan Sillitoe (b. 1928), novelist, author of *Saturday Night and Sunday Morning* (1958) and *The Loneliness of the Long-Distance Runner* (1959). The Che Guevara film was never made.

---

1. Amis had written '11 January 1968', a rare misdating.

2. J. William Fulbright (1905–95), United States Senator, Arkansas (1945–74); outspoken opponent of American policy in Vietnam.

the N. Viets are in Thailand, etc. Rusk[3] dealing with him v. competently and unfussily. Not likely to go down well in P'ton. I met *one* chap who was sound on V Nam. His wife has enormous tits so he's clearly the sort of ally one wants. Otherwise it's all "I'm fiercely anti-Communist but [or even and] the US should get out by next Tuesday." I got Perry's piece[4] in Mexico and J and I were both severely shaken, as if Tibor [Szamuely] had started cataloguing the achievements of Bolshevism. Actually, of course, that isn't a fair comparison. Without being too wise after the event (I hope) old P. was always a bit wet, and to the left of e.g. the 108 Maida Vale line on Israel v. Arabs. Jane says the RCs may have been getting at him. Possible?

We had a wonderful journey here on the train from Mexico. They tried to prevent us from entering the US and then made us miss our connection at St Louis, but we outwitted them both times. I am now working on preventing them preventing us leaving the US for non-payment of income tax, etc. We sail on Thursday.

Both lots of snuff finally arrived within 2 days of each other, thanks v. much, at San Miguel. SM was bloody good, the Instituto v. crappy, but easily avoided. Interesting that I spent the whole 6½ weeks in Mexico entirely free of the shits, only to start hareing to the john within 24 hours of leaving the place. We think you and C[aroleen] should come with us, or join us, on our next trip to M'co. Tequila is murder, but local gin is good and about 15/- a bottle. Even Scotch hardly more than at home. Food excellent, wine awful piss, like tar-water, but beer drinkable.

Well, see you soon. What about a drink in the Fitzroy at 12.30 on Thursday 21st? I'll ring you that morning.

Love to all,
Kingers

[ALS: Recipient]

3. Dean Rusk (1909–95), educator, US Secretary of State (1961–69).

4. Peregrine Worsthorne (b.1923), writer, journalist; at the time Associate Editor, *Sunday Telegraph* (1976–86); the piece in question, 'Vietnam: Balance Revised', *Sunday Telegraph*, 25 February 1968, was written in reaction to the Tet offensive of 30 January 1968 (and its aftermath); it marked Worsthorne's change of heart about American participation in the war, which he had previously supported.

TO COLIN HOWARD – 12 MARCH 1968

Princeton

Dearest Monk,

This is rather late in the day, I'm afraid. But we arrive at Southampton about 8 a.m. on Wednesday 20th March. This is horribly early, and if you decide that the prospect of getting up in time is too daunting, Wog and I will understand, as they say. But if you aren't coming, would you (Wog says) wire the ship and say so? If you do come, which of course we very much hope you will, then (Wog says) you must ring the Cunard office to check our arrival time. And please (Wog says) bring £10 – for what she calls contingencies. That's all of that.

[. . .] Mexico was very good stuff; lots of sun, and gin at 15/– a bottle, so we practically made up the cost of our fare in the pleasantest possible way. The food was all right when they stuck to local dishes, but pretty crappy when they tried to cook in the international style. The Wog, of course, soon became queen of the pension, with regular hand-kissing from the proprietor and universal acclamation when she did one of her curries for the whole household.

Christ, though, we'll both be overwhelmingly glad to get home – 29 weeks away from home is too long, especially when 19 of them were ?are? spent in Dixieland. For quite a time I don't want to go south of Bertorelli's. Anyway, both Wog and I had the consolation, while in Nashville, that while we were working we weren't missing any fun in the life around us. So in a sense it was an ideal place to write a book. I've finished mine (so you won't have to complete that 30 pages in my study)[1] and the Wog got a hell of a lot done on hers: as good as anything she's done and her funniest yet.[2] After Nashville and Mexico, Princeton is just like England. Snow on the ground and arguments about Vietnam. Wog is gallantly packing. Dean Rusk is on television, in fact has spent hours yesterday and today defending the administration Vietnam policy before a senatorial committee: great good humour, unflappability, etc.

---

1. Howard isn't sure, but thinks this may refer to a jokey promise to help Amis with the writing of *I Want it Now*.

2. *Something in Disguise* (1969)

Lots of chaps crapping on him, or trying to, but much support from both parties as well.

Do come and meet us if you can possibly summon the resolution. It would be v. nice of old Sarg (Wog says) if he could see to it that there's food in the house to see us through Wednesday. Also (Rabbit says) some whisky, gin and beer. Roll on the 20th March – If you meet us, force Martin to come too – on the assumption he's going to be around.

Fondest love to all,
Kingsley

[ALS: Recipient]

TO THE EDITOR, *NEW STATESMAN* – 12 APRIL 1968

Sir, I see that without me to restrain you these last few months, you are getting above yourself.[1]

You write: '*Even if one were to grant* [my italics] the general framework of American analysis – aggressive communism must be stopped – such miscalculations would' etc etc. It is clear from your choice of words that granting this framework (what hideous jargon you write these days) is a remote, barely tenable, almost purely hypothetical position, one you certainly do not subscribe to yourself. So tell me, if you will, what framework you do grant. If aggressive communism is not to be stopped, would you like to see it discouraged, tolerated, encouraged, or actively supported? Check one.

KINGSLEY AMIS
108 Maida Vale, W.9

1. Amis is referring to an unsigned lead article of 5 April 1968, pp. 433–5, entitled 'The Death of Empire'.

TO PHILIP LARKIN – 20 APRIL 1968

108, Maida Vale, W.9.

My dear Philip,

Yes, and good to see you too, old lad; let's indeed meet soon. What a splendid typewriter you have at your command. Using this one in reply makes me feel like a sow confronting a cheetah kitten. (Not v. exact, but you dig.) Anyhow, I use it to say yes, all right, in fact thank you, I have something for your MS collection.[1]

I have a couple of dozen worksheets relating to "The Evans Country" – not complete, but in some cases pretty full. This sounds right for you, perhaps. The thing is that old John Peter has asked me to let him have some xeroxed worksheets of mine for his rotten old *Malahat Review* in maple-leaf-land.[2] If I let him have the photostats of the stuff I mention, would this decrease your interest in the originals? I imagine not, but am just checking. You shall have the originals anyway, if you want them; this just affects what I send J.P.

Anyway, lunch on the 8th May will be fine, and I'll bring the stuff. I suggest Bentley's in Swallow Street at 1 p.m. If this is all right, I'll book a table.

Is there any way we can get a lobby going for the Lp pee reissue of the Banks sides (I saw your plea)?[3] With, I suggest, Who stole3pee/ Gabriel's horn as a fillup.

Love from us both,

To cure your gut-trouble you'll have to cut down on bum,

Kingsley

[TLS: Bodleian]

---

1. The National Manuscripts Collection of Contemporary Poets, founded, under a grant from the Arts Council, in 1963, largely at the instigation of Larkin.

2. John Peter (b. 1921), South African-born critic and author; Professor of English, University of Victoria, Victoria, British Columbia (1961–); *The Malahat Review. An International Quarterly of Life and Letters*, published out of the University of Victoria.

3. In Larkin's *Daily Telegraph* jazz column of 13 April 1968, he asked, 'When are we going to get some really *original* reissues? Bob Howard, say? Prima with Russell? Billy Banks and the Rhythmakers?' (reprinted, *All What Jazz*, p. 234).

TO THE EDITOR, *NEW STATESMAN* – 3 MAY 1968

Sir, It is nice of Mr Reynolds[1] to accuse the United States only of *neo*-colonialism in Latin America; his friends on the Left are rarely so moderate in calumny. But he is being a little tactless, since the population of Latin America (say 180 million plus) is probably the handiest nearish equivalent to the number of people held down by Russian and Chinese colonialism between them – and there's nothing flabbily neo about their brands of the article. All the same, I was mildly cheered to see in Mr Reynolds' letter an instance of the lip-disservice to Russian imperialism that seems to be coming into vogue in some Leftish circles.

I am sorry that Miss Campion found my earlier letter hard to follow, but then to be unaware of any facts about communist aggression in South East Asia suggests habitual difficulty with the printed word. So I will just give her a pair of facts. North Vietnam is trying to take over the South by force; the South and its American and other allies are not trying to take over the North by force. Naturally, I quite see that Miss Campion may have had trouble with the phrase 'aggressive communism', which in leftish terminology is of course a contradiction in terms.

Oh, and are you going to go on keeping quiet about how aggressive communism (sorry, sir) should be dealt with? Anyway, no more from me this round.

KINGSLEY AMIS
108 Maida Vale, W9

TO THEO RICHMOND – 17 MAY 1968

108, Maida Vale, W.9.

My dear Son,

Hearty (though bloody belated) paternal greetings and noises of grandpaternal gratification.[1] The belatedness is partly due to frenetic

---

1. Amis was responding to letters published in the *New Statesman* of 19 April 1968 from M.R. Reynolds and Sarah Campion.

---

1. The Richmonds' third child, Simon, was born on 1 April 1968.

activity about a possible new house – in the Green Belt up Barnet way.[2] Huge tussles to wring money out of publishers, agents, banks: Jane has done all the hard work but it's been impossible to settle to anything. Auction next Thursday. All fingers crossed – and I won't say anything about the place until/unless we get it.

But life must go on. How mobile are the 2 of you in the evenings these days? We must get together. Ring me soon and we'll arrange something. We have many a rich horror-story about Tennessee to impart. Love to all five (Christ) of you,

Dad

[ALS: Recipient]

TO TONY COLWELL – 19 AUGUST 1968

108, Maida Vale, W.9.

My dear Tony,[1]

Heartiest congratulations on a really first-class jacket for *I Want It Now*. Not only very striking visually (which you will know more about than I) but also expressing the main character: it catches just the mixture of 'I want it now' and 'I am desperately unsure of myself' that I tried to show in Simon.[2] How rare it is that an author can honestly say that sort of thing. Please pass on my warm thanks to Mr Coral.[3]

2. This house, first spotted by the Amises in an advertisement in *Country Life* magazine, was situated on Hadley Common in Barnet, Hertfordshire. Though rural in setting, it is within walking distance of the London Underground (High Barnet station, Northern Line). The house was bought in 1968 for £47,000, and its then name, Gladsmuir, was replaced by what Jane Howard discovered was its former name, Lemmons. It was not only a very large house, but it had a nine-acre garden attached, both of which are described in the opening chapter of *Girl, 20* (1971), as the house and garden of Sir Roy Vandervane.

---

1. Tony Colwell (b.1932), publisher; at the time Publicity Director, Jonathan Cape (1964–83); later Editorial Director, Jonathan Cape (1983–97).

2. A female character ('Simona Quick'), the daughter of Lady Baldock in *I Want it Now*; she is pursued by the novel's central character, the television chat-show host Ronnie Appleyard.

3. George Coral, a freelance jacket artist.

Also, an excellent blurb. Is this you, or some Colwell-trained genius?[4] Whoever it is has read the book and understood it – another rarity. Even the biog. note is entirely accurate.

I meant to write this letter weeks ago, but was prevented by deadlines and such. However, the delay has meant that I can invite your commiseration over that fearfully crappy notice in *Smith's Trade News* (I think it was, but am not sure, having hurled the clipping away). I didn't know these sods were supposed to *review* forthcoming stuff. Talking of which, I understand from a Welsh friend, who is admittedly drunk a lot of the time, that a review appeared in the *Western Mail* a couple of months ago. Not that that matters, I'm sure.

Again, many thanks for a fine job all round.

Yours,
Kingsley

[TLS: Reading]

TO FRANK BARNSHAW – 6 OCTOBER 1968

108, Maida Vale, W.9.

Dear Mr Barnshaw,

Your question is in order, and appreciated.[1] The name L. S. Caton (the initials stand for Lazy Sod) is a disguised form of the name of a (rightly) obscure (little magazine) editor I encountered in my early days, who seemed to me to incarnate stupidity, sloth, puny ambition and indifference to literature.[2] I put him in *Lucky Jim*, thought it would be fun, as a private joke with a couple of friends, to go on with him, and

4. Colwell believes the blurb was written by Judith Page, but is not sure. No records of Ms Page, or of her predecessor at Cape, Kay Catarulla, the other possible author, exist in the archives of Jonathan Cape, now located at Reading University.

---

1. Barnshaw (b.1943), a solicitor, and two friends were intrigued about the identity of the character 'L.S. Caton' who appears in each of Amis's first four novels. Barnshaw was chosen to write to Amis to ask if Caton was 'really' C.S. Lewis: 'we thought the best way of ensuring a reply was to put forward a provocative suggestion which he would feel obliged to deny' (personal communication, 1 November 1996).

2. For 'L.S. Caton' and R.A. Caton, his real-life model, see Amis to Larkin, 18 January 1946, note 1, and 16 July 1948, note 2; also Amis to Gollancz, 27 February 1955, note 5.

killed him off in *The Anti-Death League.*[3] Nothing to do with C. S. Lewis, whom I respect highly, and who would never have done any of Caton's things. This is for the private information of yourself and your immediate circle.

Yours sincerely,
Kingsley Amis

Of course, nobody knows if L.S.C. ever had a *son* . . .

[ALS: Recipient]

TO BRIAN COX – 8 OCTOBER 1968

108, Maida Vale, W.9.

Dear Mr Cox,[1]

Many thanks for your letter of 13th September, and apologies for not answering sooner – the usual combination of preoccupation and laziness, I'm afraid.

Yes indeed, I agree heartily with the idea of the pamphlet.[2] But here again laziness (this time in a modified form) comes in. In conscience, I ought to try to do a great, far-ranging, fully researched piece. But since you mention 500 words only, and seem to require no great factualness, I wonder whether something called roughly "The Myth [or Marsh-Light] of Student Participation [in the selection of syllabuses]" might do, making the simple point that a student by definition can't know what he ought to be taught, with a concrete point or two about nobody ever *wanting* to read Spenser, but lots of people finding out afterwards they

3. He was killed by a stray bullet: 'Full in the face. I'm afraid he won't be easy to identify' (*The Anti-Death League*, p.281).

---

1. For Brian Cox see Notes on Recipients.

2. The idea in question was for the first of Cox and A.E. Dyson's 'Black Papers on Education' (1969–77), for the Critical Quarterly Society (it appeared in March 1969 in a special issue of *Critical Survey*, the society's periodical for teachers of English). Cox had sent Amis a letter about the 'Black Papers' and had asked him to write for them, in part because he agreed with Amis's widely reported prediction that 'More will mean worse' in higher education (see Amis to the editor, *The Times*, 2 January 1967, notes 2 and 3). Amis's eventual contributions to the 'Black Papers' (several with Robert Conquest) are reproduced in *The Amis Collection*, pp. 265–83.

were glad they had to. Or is that too obvious? Perhaps you could let me know, stating deadline. If it isn't too annoying, can I say I *might* go above 500 words, up to about 800 if inspiration permits?[3]

Don't tell anybody, but £20 would be fine.

Since you mention "names of other people who might help", I might just suggest my friend Martin [Sargy] Mann, a painter and art teacher, who I think is generally sympathetic to the theme, and who can tell something about the art-school world that you might not have covered from anyone else. You could get in touch with him at my address.

All the best – and let's have a drink or something when you're in London. Give me a ring.

Yours sincerely,
Kingsley Amis

[ALS: Manchester]

TO THE EDITOR, *OBSERVER* – 13 OCTOBER 1968

I would not challenge any point in Francis Hope's friendly notice of my novel, "I Want It Now" (6 October) except where he falls victim, as others have done, to a factual error about "Lucky Jim". Not only did Jim not "marry money", it wasn't money that he didn't marry.

At the end of the book he goes off to London to earn £500 a year, which was (by design) the exact sum he would have earned at that time as a university lecturer in his second year, and which was hardly "money" anyway, even in the spacious days of the early fifties. What he was after was not money, but freedom.

KINGSLEY AMIS
W9

3. This piece (more like a thousand words than five hundred) was eventually published in *Critical Survey* 4:1 (Winter 1969), pp.9–10, under the title 'Pernicious Participation'; it is reprinted in *The Amis Collection*, pp.263–5.

TO EDWIN BARBER – 21 OCTOBER 1968

108, Maida Vale, W.9.

Dear Mr Barber,

I have just been going through the overgrown jungle of my correspondence and have, with horror, come across your letter of 3rd September. I could have sworn, as the saying goes, that your trip was going to have been Oct–Nov, not Sept–Oct. So, very much against my intention, you have come and gone without our having got together. I deeply regret this, and hope that we shall have better luck on your next trip.

If I may combine business with sincere apology: I had a letter from Marian Reiner of Thomas Y. Crowell, saying that Harcourt B. are asking too much money (she thinks) for a permission fee for my essay "The Situation Today" (whatever that is) to be published in *The Art of the Essay*, ed. Leslie Fiedler.[1] Could I persuade you to lower the terms? Well, could I? Myself, I would like to be in the book and don't care greatly about the fee. Miss Reiner asks to be written to at 71 Disbrow Lane, New Rochelle, New York 10804.

With renewed apologies, and good wishes,

Yours sincerely,
Kingsley Amis

[ALS: Harcourt]

---

1. Amis's 'essay' was the second chapter of *New Maps of Hell*, for which Barber, Editor-in-Chief at Harcourt Brace, agreed to lower the permission fee from $400 to $300; *The Art of the Essay* was published by Crowell in 1969, edited by Leslie Fiedler.

TO THE EDITOR, *ENCOUNTER*[1] – NOVEMBER 1968

Until I read *R*'s column for September, I imagined that the Angry Young Man thing had quietly, and to the general relief, slipped into oblivion, like post-war credits or Stalin's scientific writings.[2] But evidently *R*'s memories of that far-off episode have been stirred by a couple of more recent utterances of mine, though not sufficiently, as I shall indicate in a minute, to induce him to look up the relevant source-material.

To grit one's teeth, then: there was no anger, unless a mild, usually amused and very intermittent irritation can be called anger, in the characteristic works of the mid-1950s: in John Wain's *Hurry On Down*, in John Braine's *Room at the Top*, in Iris Murdoch's *Under the Net*, or in Colin Wilson's *Outsider*, to name four of the most celebrated. (I would call *Look Back in Anger* a lonely and, by contrast, revealing exception; but Mr. Osborne will no doubt answer for himself, should he feel so moved – and he has my hearty sympathy if he doesn't.)

The Angry Young Man "movement" was a phantom creation of literary journalists, and *R* is a journalist, albeit a phenomenally incurious and unindustrious one, so one understands, perhaps, his contented swallowing of that mouldering bit of journalistic consensus. But in any event, he should not have confused, or seemed to confuse (he is not very clear on this point), the pamphlets, articles and interviews of that time with the books and plays to which they are an unimportant appendage.

But to return to my more personal stake in the matter: no sort of journalist can afford to sink to *R*'s level of inaccuracy on other points. His humorous fantasy on Lucky Jim's career, for instance, transfers that

---

1. Letters in *Encounter*, an Anglo-American political, cultural and literary journal founded in 1953, are headed like articles; Amis's, which appears in 31:5 (November 1968), p. 95 (and continues on the unnumbered inside back cover), was entitled 'Myths About "the Angry Young Man"'.

2. In *Encounter* 31:3 (September 1968), pp. 40–3, the anonymous columnist 'R' (Goronwy Rees) had compared Amis's move rightward, as announced in the *Sunday Telegraph* article 'Why Lucky Jim Turned Right' (see Amis to the Editor, *Sunday Telegraph*, 25 July 1967, note 1) to that of John Osborne, who provides 'another example of what happens to the Angry Young Man of yesterday' (p. 41). Rees (1909–79) was a novelist as well as a journalist, also an occasional poet and university administrator.

character's origin from Lancashire to South Wales, turns his girl's uncle into his eventual father-in-law, confounds a dentist's mistress with a dentist's wife (a serious error), and plucks beer-sodden colliers out of the air, or out of supposed recollection. But these minor blurrings are probably meant as subtle illustrations-in-action of how folk-memory confuses its sources and misreads its facts.

However, *R* might have noticed that less than one-quarter of my Conservative Political Centre pamphlet overlapped the *Sunday Telegraph* article which was its starting-point – hardly a "recapitulation" in the usual sense.[3] He could, too, by catching the hastiest possible glimpse of its cover, have noticed that the C.P.C. pamphlet entitled *Europe and Technology* is not by Brian Chapman, as he says, but by Manfredo Macioti, who is a EURATOM scientist not much given to turning out "Conservative propaganda." By looking up the files of ENCOUNTER itself ["Lone Voices," July 1960], *R* would have had the chance of noticing that my disquiet about university expansion was couched in the form, *More will mean worse*, not *More means worse*. This is not just a quibble: what I wrote was a limited prediction – horribly justified, but let that go – based on an estimate of the existing human and material resources. The version given by *R* and other non-inquirers suggests belief in some immutable principle. I have put people right on this before, though only, I grant, in journals that *R* no doubt feels are outside his scope, like *The Times* and the *Observer*.

Last in this recital, and least, and in a way worst, *R* has me referring to the B.B.C. (I said B.B.C.-1, but never mind, and I was momentarily forgetting *Late Night Line-Up*, though I was intending to say nothing about B.B.C. radio) as "that enormous machine of Lefty propaganda." This, too, is more than a mere matter of nuance – I said "vehicle," not "machine" – but what we can appreciate here is the huge, the incalculable difficulty confronting *R* in hauling himself out of his armchair, lurching across to wherever he keeps, or momentarily found a place for, that pamphlet of mine which must have set him off on his ruminations, and taking a second glance at its text.

R exhibits a little more journalistic capacity in employing two traditional devices. One of these is to paraphrase one's source while pre-

3. *Lucky Jim's Politics* (London: Conservative Political Centre, 1968) differs from, or moves beyond, the *Sunday Telegraph* article in several respects, notably in its 'grudging toleration of the Conservative Party' (p. 9).

tending to make a point of one's own. Thus he informs me that university expansion was originally a Conservative measure, not saying (or not knowing, since the journal concerned was again the *Observer*), that I was a co-author of an extended protest against this policy at the time, and not saying that I specifically mentioned, and deplored, its Conservative origin, both in my *Sunday Telegraph* article – has he ever glanced at this, even once? – and in my C.P.C. pamphlet (p. 6).

The other journalistic device is to introduce fiction under the guise of supposed paraphrase. Thus *R* credits me with hankering after "the still small voice of reason as it speaks in the person [*sic*] of Mr. Heath and Mr. Enoch Powell."[4] I certainly feel, though *R* has had no way of knowing this, that these two, among others of their party, represent what I want rather better than any of the array on the Government benches, excluding Mr. Powell's emotionalism about immigration. But, in article and pamphlet, as before, I disavowed support for the Conservative party as such and as it now exists.

Two final points. *R* seems to question the validity of my belief that "communism . . . is always and everywhere the same (even in Czechoslovakia?)." I dislike alluding, in parochial polemic, to what has happened in that country since *R* wrote.[5] Nevertheless, it must be said that few professional journalists would have betted so confidently on Czechoslovakia's uninterrupted progress towards some sort of liberalisation. And the point about Dubcek is that he was the only good sort of communist other than a dead one: the sort that looks forward to the dismantling of communism, whether or not he retains the name. The duty remains to point out that, in all important respects, like those concerning any sort of freedom, communism *is*, has so far turned out to be, always and everywhere the same.

And as regards my dislikes of the Lefty and the Labour party as it now is, the one implies and is included in the other. The Lefty is an intellectually disreputable and morally desensitised person whom the Labour party tolerates within itself – and who, incidentally, flourishes more or less unchecked, not only in the *New Statesman* (where *R* locates

4. Sir Edward Heath (b. 1916), ex-Conservative leader and Prime Minister (1970–74); Enoch Powell (1912–98), Conservative and Unionist MP, notorious for his 1967 and 1968 speeches against 'coloured' immigration and for repatriation.

5. Early in October 1968 the Czechoslovak leaders visited Moscow and agreed to dismantle the remnants of the May 1968 reforms (initiated under Alexander Dubček, First Secretary of the Czech Communist Party); on 16 October the USSR and Czechoslovakia signed a treaty on the eventual withdrawal of Warsaw Pact forces.

him), but in *The Times, The Guardian*, the *Daily Mirror, The Sun*, the *Observer*, the *Sunday Times*, the *Times Literary Supplement, Tribune*, and – most of all and most trendily – *The Listener*, not to speak of *Panorama* and *24 Hours*.[6] Anyway – how would we feel about a Conservative party that tolerated the Lefty's Rightist counterparts: Falangists, extreme Gaullists, Colin Jordan's men?[7]

KINGSLEY AMIS
London

PS. – Yes, quite a number of people have, as *R* says, progressed from Left to Right as they grew older. Not enough to satisfy me, though. And to represent this progress as a "passage from youthful protest to middle-aged acquiescence" is both loaded and revealing. Has *R* taken account of the number of people who stay on the Left, or even move perceptibly Leftwards, in the hope of seeming to remain alive, or active, or with it, or in touch with youth, or young?[8]

TO THE EDITOR, *THE TIMES* – 21 NOVEMBER 1968

Sir,—I am sorry to have to astonish you by further unpleasantness (The Diary, November 20), but the truth about Yevtushenko is unpleasant. As regards the Brezhnev telegram, the only source for this was your stablemate, The Sunday Times, to which all other "major organs" paid acknowledgement.[1] Yevtushenko himself, talking to The

6. *Panorama* and *24 Hours*, popular current-affairs programmes on BBC television.

7. For Colin Jordan see Amis to the editor, *Spectator*, 14 December 1962, note 3.

8. R's unrepentant reply to this letter, printed underneath, likens Amis's 'Lefty', a figure 'at work everywhere' (certainly all over the media), to 'a Jew out of the Protocols of Zion; he is in fact not a real person at all but the "phantom creation of a literary journalist," invented by Mr. Amis and a few others to frighten themselves into the arms of Mr. Heath and Mr. Powell, though of course a Mr Powell stripped of his "emotionalism about immigration." '

---

1. In 1968 the name of the Russian poet Yevgeny Yevtushenko (b. 1933) was put forward for the Chair of Poetry at Oxford University, an elective post. Amis's letter was part of a campaign to prevent Yevtushenko from winning the election. Although Amis got on well with Yevtushenko when they met in Cambridge in 1962 (thinking him, as he recalls in the *Memoirs*, p. 239, 'the first completely good reason I had met with for liking the USSR'), by the date of this letter, for the reasons it details, his feelings had changed; by 1968 he was certain that 'neither Yevtushenko nor anybody or anything else ever could have been an

Guardian's Moscow correspondent, denied having sent the telegram.

He has denounced Sinyavsky and Daniel repeatedly, first in Dakar at the time of the trial in early 1966, later that year in New York, and most recently, as far as I know, in Mexico on March 9 of this year before an audience of university students. A disgusted attack on him for his remarks, from the students' revolutionary organizations, was published in the Mexico paper Novedades on April 10: "You have become a tool of the Soviet Government in exchange for being allowed to publish your poems."

At other times he has glorified the Russian labour camp system (see Sinyavsky's piece in the April, 1967, Encounter), attacked Galanskov and Ginsburg and other imprisoned and exiled writers, and denounced Mrs Ivinskaya, the close friend of Pasternak who helped to smuggle Dr Zhivago out of the country, and who got eight years' gaol for it, as a "currency smuggler", this at the Royal Court Theatre here.[2] Recently, in Lisbon, he announced that the book was unworthy of publication in Russia.

If Peterborough[3] will forgive me for answering on his behalf, I will name the Yugoslav poet whom he did not, and whom you appear to be ignorant of. In a poem published in the September 28 issue of Knjizevne Novine (Belgrade), Matija Beckovic[4] attacked Yevtushenko for his silence over the Czechoslovakia invasion, for being "humble and courageous in Rome", and for having "done a good turn to everybody except (his) own people", with the conclusion that "the farther away the injustice, the louder your protest".

Your diarist oddly refrained from mentioning Peterborough's main point, which was that Yevtushenko was not among the 63 signatories of the famous Sinyavsky–Daniel protest letter. Peterborough might have

even partially good reason for liking the USSR' (pp. 239–40). As for the telegram to Brezhnev, Yevtushenko, his supporters claimed, had sent it in protest against the literary 'witch-trials' of Sinyavsky and Daniel (see Amis to the editor, *Sunday Telegraph*, 25 July 1967, note 2). Amis doubted the authenticity of this telegram, for reasons set out here and, with Bernard Levin, in a more detailed letter to the *Sunday Times*, 8 December 1968.

2. The dissident writers Amis refers to, Yuri Galanskov (1939–72) and Alexander Ginsburg (b. 1936), were both imprisoned for their activities and writings, the former in a camp in Modlova, where he died aged thirty-three; Olga Ivinskaya, Boris Pasternak's mistress and heir, had been 'imprisoned on a trumped up charge of illegal dealing in foreign funds, i.e. Pasternak's royalties from abroad' (*Memoirs*, p. 240).

3. Peterborough's column about the Oxford election appeared in the *Daily Telegraph*, 19 November 1968. The *Times* Diary piece of 20 November 1968 mentions this column.

4. (b. 1939).

added that Yevtushenko has not signed a single other protest of all the dozens that have appeared in Russia in the last two years.

Actually, Sir, I myself feel a tiny bit astonished to find that your diarist, with all his immense resources, seems to know so much less than I with my limited power of access.

Yours faithfully,
KINGSLEY AMIS
108 Maida Vale, W.9 Nov. 20

TO THE EDITOR, *NEW STATESMAN* – 13 DECEMBER 1968

Sir, Perhaps you really can't see the difference between 'unqualified' and 'unequivocally (NS, 6 Dec.).[1] They certainly start off the same, and they both have that 'qu' thing in the middle. But what about the difference between 'publicly', and 'in conversation'? Or is that another semantic quibble? Your story would look much better if you could make up your mind where I didn't say what you said I said. I stated (publicly) in *The Review* (April 1968) that as regards American methods [in Vietnam] there is, of course, room for argument. I would 'oppose the use of napalm.' I have said the same in conversation, though perhaps not with you. Have you publicly, or in conversation, opposed the North Vietnamese use of flame-throwers against civilians (see *Evening Standard*, 29 June 1968)? Jolly good if you have; I'd just like to know

KINGSLEY AMIS

TO SAMUEL HYNES – 21 MARCH 1969

Dear Sam,

Good to hear from you. Thanks for sending your *Times* letter. Actually I never saw Julian's review, a situation which is probably best

1. In the first item in Paul Johnson's 'London Diary' of 6 December 1968, p. 738, he asserts that Amis 'has publicly expressed unqualified (his word) support for the American war in Vietnam'.

left like that.[1] The man has an odd mind. I heard recently that he said he thought my chum Robert Conquest (author of something like a million words of anti-Soviet documentary) was pretty certain to be the next Philby-type defector to the USSR.

Yes, let's meet. I am now on the extreme northern edge of London,[2] but am still often seen in the centre. Give me a ring when you're installed – 449 4800.

Cheers,
Kingsley

[ALS: Recipient]

TO M.G. SHERLOCK – 5 APRIL 1969

Lemmons, Hadley Common, Barnet, Hertfordshire.

Dear Mr Sherlock,

The *Express* passed on to me your letter of 20th March. You make a very good point (and I am flattered by your evident knowledge of my writings).[1] I think that in the late '50s, when I still retained considerable vestiges of my early Leftism, I was made uncomfortable by Orwell's writings about Communism. I could not dismiss him as dishonest or callow, so found an 'out' by calling him hysterical. I think now that (understandably) Orwell had made a better prediction in 1949 than I was capable of in 1959,[2] and my rating of 'Nineteen Eighty-Four' as

1. Hynes's letter defended Amis against Julian Moynahan's negative review of *A Look Round the Estate*, in *New York Times*, 22 December 1968, p. 10.

2. At Lemmons, the house in Barnet, Hertfordshire, where Amis, Jane and 'the blokes' (Martin and Philip Amis, Colin Howard, Sargy Mann) had moved in November 1968.

1. M.G. Sherlock (b. 1941), a civil servant and author of several unpublished novels, had written to Amis (in a letter now lost) about a column Amis had written in the *Daily Express*, 19 March 1969, p. 10, praising Orwell's *Nineteen Eighty-Four*. Sherlock wanted to know how Amis reconciled this praise with what he had written about *Nineteen Eighty-Four* in his 1957 Fabian pamphlet *Socialism and the Intellectuals*. In the pamphlet Amis accuses Orwell of 'warning the late Forties of something already averted in the late Thirties' (pp. 7–8).

2. Presumably Amis means 1957, when the pamphlet was published.

Left Robert Conquest, 1961. 'Bob was here . . . A sort of advertisement for life' (to Philip Larkin, 3 August 1982).

Below John Wain, 1958. 'You must have seen that old Snow gave you a leg-up in the *S. Times* last week' (to John Wain, 3 January 1954).

Right John Davenport, 1959. 'Not feeling so hot at the moment, having spent 18 of the last 24 hours in the company of John Davenport' (to William Rukeyser, 25 June 1963).

Below Brian Aldiss, 1973. 'Keep on with the good work, Aldiss, and don't get too sodding *literary*' (to Brian Aldiss, 14 January 1970).

Above Left to right: Kenneth Griffith, Liz and Julian Moynahan, KA, Hilly and Theo Richmond, April 1961. Griffith and Richmond were in Swansea working on *Only Two Can Play* (1962), the film version of *That Uncertain Feeling*; the Moynahans were visiting from Princeton.

Right Stuart Thomas, *c.* 1960. 'Off to Garrick now to bend the elbow with Stuart Thomas' (to Robert Conquest, 24 July 1985).

Russell Fraser and KA, Madingley Road, Cambridge, in 1962.

Martin, Hilly, Tomas Graves, KA and Robert Graves, Majorca, 1962. 'I've been fired by your example to attempt an 8 a.m. start to the writing day. Difficult, though' (to Robert Graves, 4 September 1962).

At the Cheltenham Literary Festival, 1962: the novelist Edna O'Brien, Elizabeth Jane Howard and John Moore, Festival administrator.

At the reception for the wedding of William Rukeyser and Elisabeth Mary Garnett in Eltham, 1963. KA was best man.

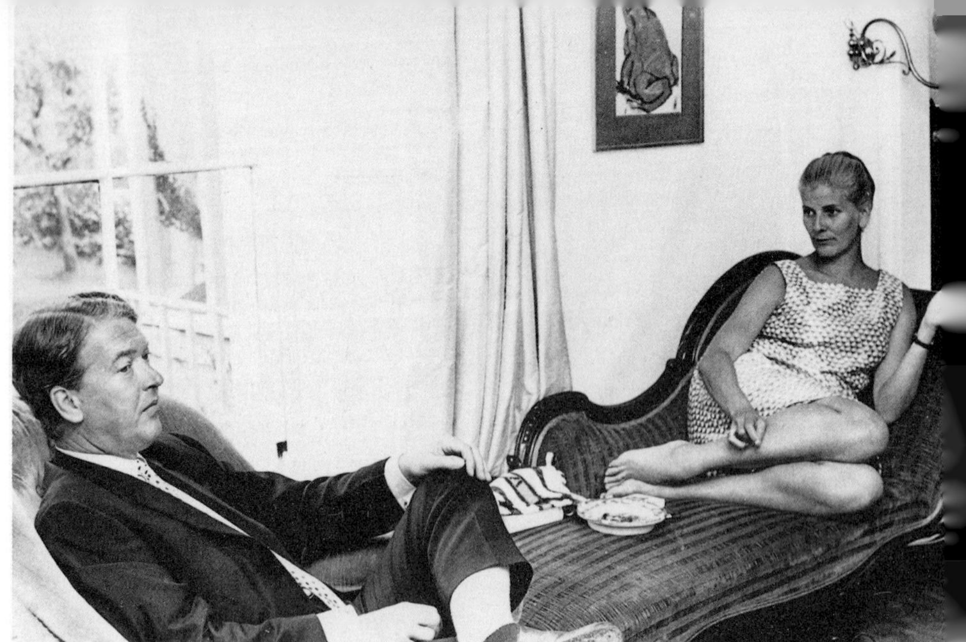

Above KA and Elizabeth Jane Howard at 108 Maida Vale, *c.* 1965–67.

Left Elizabeth Jane Howard, Mary Keeley and KA, Mexico City, January 1968. 'We had a 40-second earthquake tremor. No damage, but by Christ I thought the old coronary was upon me' (to Robert and Caroleen Conquest, 5 February 1968).

Below Edmund ('Mike') Keeley and KA, Rhodes, 1969. 'We doubt if the Greek provinces will be too primitive for us: sea and wine is just what we like' (to Edmund Keeley, 21 August 1965).

KA, 1970.

Above KA in his study at Lemmons, 1974. 'You're welcome to inspect the study where I'm writing this and where at the moment there are almost as many bottles as books' (to Dale Salwak, 9 April 1980).

Right KA and Elizabeth Jane Howard outside Lemmons in the 1970s. In the background is Lucretia Garnett, mother of Elisabeth Mary Garnett Rukeyser. 'This is a bloody great mansion, in the depths of the country though only 15 miles from the centre, and with lots of room for you to come and spend the night' (to Philip Larkin, 19 April 1969).

political writing is much higher now than it was then (though I retain my doubts about its qualities as a novel).

On your other point: I still think (as I thought in the '50s) that Orwell was on about Communism rather than a Communist-Fascist amalgam. It was not that he had forgone his objections to Fascism, but, as I argued in my column, a matter of his seeing that Fascism was either dead or (as in Franco's Spain) non-expansive, whereas Communism was very much neither. Contributory evidence of a sort about his having been writing about Communism is afforded by the resemblance of 'Nineteen Eighty-Four' to Zamyatin's 'We', which is (necessarily) about Communism.[3]

Thank you for taking the trouble to write.

Yours sincerely,
Kingsley Amis

Correction: In my Fabian pamphlet, as your quote about 'warning the late forties of something that had already been averted in the late thirties' seems to show, I might have been trying to pretend to myself that it was not simply expansive Communism that Orwell was warning us against, though the whole passage is very confused and I cannot now remember just what I thought had been averted. But by 1959 I was clear on the point.

[TLS: Recipient]

TO BRIAN COX – 10 APRIL 1969

Lemmons, Hadley Common, Barnet, Hertfordshire.

Dear Brian,

Requests for copies of the pamphlet[1] from Alan Brien (c/o Sunday Times, I suppose) and Hugh Trevor-Roper (Chiefswood, Melrose, Scotland).[2] Also a request for C.Q.'s address from a bookshop (which I gave

3. *We* (1920) by Yevgeny Zamyatin (1884–1937), Russian novelist, dramatist and critic.

---

1. 'Pernicious Participation', the first of Amis's 'Black Paper' articles on education.
2. For Alan Brien see Amis to Karl Miller, 27 February 1959, note 3. Hugh Trevor-Roper (b. 1914), historian; at the time Regius Professor of Modern History and Fellow, Oriel College,

them – the address, I mean). It occurred to me that other bookshops might want to know this and not know how to get in touch with e.g. me, so do you think perhaps a circular might be sent to all bookshops, if you haven't already done so? Of course, an advertisement, small, in The Times (perhaps) would be a good thing. I suspect we have quite a lot of people interested who can't lay their hands on a copy.

Hope all goes well at your end. Old Short's sense of timing is irreproachable. Good letter in The Times today.[3] Etc. We have won the battle to be noticed.

Cheers
Kingsley

Could you send me another ½ dozen? Better say a dozen.

[ALS: Manchester]

TO PHILIP LARKIN – 19 APRIL 1969

Lemmons, Hadley Common, Barnet, Hertfordshire.

My dear Philip,

Your man Carey turned up trumps. After I had sent him a letter asking him to send me details so that I could pay him in advance, and enclosing SAE, he sends me the record,[1] returns SAE, and writes a note saying 'You appear to be keen to obtain this LP, so I have despatched it without further ado. Trusting this meets with your approval.' It did. Tks 1,000,000, o.m., for letting me know the news.

Oxford (1957–80); later Master of Peterhouse, Cambridge (1980–87); created Life Peer, Baron Dacre of Glanton (1979).

3. Edward Short (b. 1912), Labour MP and Minister; at the time Secretary of State for Education and Science (1968–70). The letter in *The Times*, 10 April 1969, p. 9, was from a Conservative MP, Stephen Hastings, attacking a speech by Short to the National Union of Teachers, in which he deplored the illiberal educational views expressed in the 'Black Papers'. Short's timing was 'irreproachable' because of the publicity the speech would generate for Amis's pamphlet.

---

1. See Larkin to Conquest, 7 April 1969, in *LL*, p. 413: 'tell K. if you see him that there's a 12" LP of all the Banks sides (plus *Oh Peter* with Henry Allen vocal) and *all* the Bland sides (*Who Stole, Gabriel's Horn, Shine Shoes & Gonna Be You*). I'll send him the number if he's interested.' Amis's jazz references, in the second paragraph, are to the tracks on this

Highlights include: how even better than I remembered the closing tutti of *Oh P[eter]* (Banks v[ocal].) is, how very much better than I ever thought the closing tutti of *Yes Suh* is, how incredibly different from all that has gone before each successive chorus of *BCR* [*Bugle Call Rag*] is, how the best jazz side is still *Who's* [*Sorry*] *Now*, and the best work of art still *Spider Crawl*. Listening to *Shine Shoes*, which I had never heard before, I heeled slowly and steadily over sideways, laughing all the time, at Russell's demonstration in the middle of Dorsey's chorus of "No, you *fool*. Not like that: like this, you FOOL." Interesting that on 13th April 1932 they must have had Allen and Banks in to sing a number each and picked B. for the subsequent sessions. On that showing I can see why, good as A. is. Oh. Ah. Pee-Wee Russell the viper, O is he dead then? my duty all ended, who have watc twatc heard his moan of man . . .[2]

Have got old C D-L [Day-Lewis] and his lot here today; he's nice enough, but it's a bit like getting your grampa over. Funny, I had your letter to Bob (which he lent me for its Rhythmakers details) pinned on the wall of my study so I'd remember to take it in to him, and barely had I re-read the bit about old Seedy 'Ell being harshit when a large saloon car, spitting bits of gravel from under its tyres, rolled up to the front door with him in it, so I turned the letter back to front. I'm waiting for him to go now so that I can get at my gram again. But he won't, even though it's 5 to 5 and he came to lunch.

Old Bruce [Montgomery] is due here next week for a couple of days or so. I say, why's he going to marry this woman with all those teeth, eh? I mean eh? I mean:- "Eh?" Why's he going to do that, then? I can't really ask him, because almost whenever he understands what I'm saying, which doesn't seem to be often, he tends to get slightly cross.

Oh fuck the Beatles. I'd like to push my bum into John L's face for forty-eight hours or so, as a protest against all the war and violence in the world. I like the way they're so much more popular than any kind of modern jazz shag at all, though.

record. Also to Billy Banks; Pee-Wee Russell; Henry Allen (1908–67), trumpeter; and Jimmy Dorsey (1904–57), clarinettist, saxophonist and dance band leader. 'Your man Carey' was Dave Carey, a musician, also owner of a jazz record shop, including an extensive mail-order business, in Streatham, south London. He died in 1991.

2. See the opening lines of Gerard Manley Hopkins, 'Felix Randal' (1880, first published 1918): 'Felix Randal the farrier, O is he dead then? my duty all ended,/Who have watched his mould of man, big-boned and hardy-handsome.'

This is a bloody great mansion, in the depths of the country though only 15 miles from the centre, and with lots of room for you to come and spend the night. Let us know. You get on the Northern Line to High Barnet, see, and then we pick you up at the station. Do try.

When she takes her seat in the House, Miss Devlin[3] will bring a breath of fresh bum,

Kingsley

What was that P-W R record you mentioned in the D.T. the other week?[4] I have Swingville 2008 is it, and A Legend, and that crappy one with Clayton you lauded, but no more under his name.

I hope you are better now, I am fine, bar occasional dire-rear[5]

[TLS: Bodleian]

TO ERIC W. WHITE – 11 MAY 1969

Lemmons, Hadley Common, Barnet, Herts

Dear Mr White,

I have received your faintly uncivil circular.[1]

The Arts Council is, or should be, concerned with improving the conditions of art, and hence the conditions of artists, rather than with

3. Bernadette Devlin (McAliskey) (b.1947), newly elected MP (Independent Unity) for Mid-Ulster (April 1969-February 1974), at twenty-one the youngest MP in the House of Commons; Founder Member, Irish Republican Socialist Party (1975–76). In 1973 she married Michael McAliskey.

4. Larkin mentions several Russell records in 'How Long Blues?', *Daily Telegraph*, 8 March 1969, written just after Russell's death in February, aged sixty-two. See Larkin, *All What Jazz*, pp. 224–6.

5. MS addition.

---

1. The circular, dated 30 April 1969, and signed by White, announced a new scheme by the Literature Panel of the Arts Council 'to encourage visits of writers to schools and colleges'. What Amis finds 'faintly uncivil' about the circular may derive from its passive constructions: 'It is felt that it is important that'; 'It is considered that no writer should conceive'; 'It will be appreciated that'. Eric W. White (1905–85) joined the Council for the Encouragement of Music and the Arts (which became the Arts Council of Great Britain) in 1945, and served as Director of Literature, Arts Council (1966–71). He was also a composer, editor and translator.

things like providing a "service" to schools and colleges. A writer is not an electrician or a plumber, and it is particularly culpable in people like you to regard him as such.

The minimum fee of £15 (which I take to be the standard fee, since you do not mention a maximum fee, nor any indication of under what conditions the minimum might be exceeded) is derisory – far less than a reputable journal would pay for a review or article of equivalent length, which can be written without having to go anywhere. It should have been part of your task to persuade education authorities that writers, being important people who make a unique contribution to society, must not be sweated. No self-respecting writer should take part in your scheme; and I will not.

Yours sincerely,
Kingsley Amis

c.c. Society of Authors[2]

[TL: Society of Authors]

TO THE EDITOR, *TEACHERS WORLD* – 16 MAY 1969

Sir, I read with interest your remarks about me in *Teachers World* (25 April). (By the way, shouldn't that name have an apostrophe in it somewhere? But I suppose it is safer to drop it if you aren't too sure where it should go.)[1]

You write: "In the context of a follow-up discussion of the Black Paper

2. Amis sent a copy of the circular and of his reply to Elizabeth Barber of the Society of Authors, from which he had recently resigned (see Amis to Elizabeth Barber, 27 May 1964 and 14 May 1969, the latter in Society of Authors).

---

1. The editor replies, in the same issue: 'About that apostrophe – deliberately abandoned for modern design reasons: Lucky Jim, that happy-go-lucky academic iconoclast, would have welcomed its omission. With an overdraft at Lloyds or Barclays (both have dropped the apostrophe) he would have downed another pint of Watneys bitter. Sadly, Jim has developed into a bit of a pedant.' In the next issue (6 June 1969) Amis replied, deploring the editor's 'quoting in extenuation similar barbarities on the part of bankers and brewers – not natural allies, I should have thought, of a journal supposedly devoted to education. I call this less an explanation than just owning up.' 'For design reasons' soon became a familiar locution at Lemmons.

[Amis] says he believes in abortion law reform and a more charitable approach to the question of homosexuality. One can do little but gasp at the supreme irrelevance of all this," – *all* this? – and you go on to quote a salty Australianism[2] to the effect that one should stick to the point.

What I (flattering you a little, perhaps) gasp at is your capacity for mis-representation. Most of *The Times* article you refer to was an enquiry into the views of some of the Black Paper writers on matters *outside* the sphere of education. Nobody ever supposed, or could suppose, that I thought the remarks alluded to were any sort of contribution to a debate *inside* the sphere of education – neither I, nor the authors of the article, nor any literate reader of it until you (whom I continue to flatter a little, perhaps, by including you in that group) turned up. Get your facts straight, as they say in South Hertfordshire and probably in Australia too.

On the question of the decline in standards I shall need a little more time and space to grapple with you. I hope to let you have an extended blast on this topic shortly.–

KINGSLEY AMIS

Lemmons, Hadley Common, Barnet, Herts.

TO BRIAN COX – 14 JULY 1969

Lemmons, Hadley Common, Barnet, Hertfordshire.

Dear Brian,

Tibor Szamuely[1] is very anxious to contribute to the next Black Paper. He says (truly) that he knows more than most of us about the effects of comprehensive education imposed to foster equality in Russia and Hungary. He would of course be riding an anti-Communist hobby-horse, but no harm in that. Perhaps, if interested, you could drop him a line at 17 Sutherland Place, W.2.

Bob's and my contribution will reach you shortly.

We shall overcome!!

Yours
Kingsley

[ALS: Manchester]

2. 'What's it got to do with the price of cheese?'

---

1. For Tibor Szamuely see Amis to Conquest, 1 November 1967, note 1.

TO THE EDITOR, *NEW STATESMAN* – 31 OCTOBER 1969

Sir, I usually enjoy your This England feature, but I could see no proper place in it last week for the letter in *The Times* recommending giving money to the RSPCA as a way of showing sympathy for Anthony Grey's cat, hanged by the Red Guards.[1] The assumption behind the reprinting of any item showing attachment to or concern about pet animals must roughly be that such feelings are characteristically British, and therefore ridiculous or contemptible. It seems that this assumption holds even in cases like the present one, in which an act of peculiar wantonness and cruelty has been answered by an eminently sane and constructive as well as decent and humane proposal. I would not accuse A. Huxtable, who submitted the cutting, and whoever it was who selected it for inclusion, of actual callousness or mental brutality, merely of deficient imagination, or of an excessive desire to think and feel fashionably, excessive to the point at which the sensibilities become dulled.

KINGSLEY AMIS
Barnet, Herts

TO THE EDITOR, *ENCOUNTER* – DECEMBER 1969

I AM NOT SURE I got the total hang of Donald Davie's "Hobbits and Intellectuals" piece [ENCOUNTER, October]. To begin near its beginning: I cannot really see why a polemicist (like me) should not be taken seriously unless he gets too angry to want to go on living in his own country. This would hardly do as a general rule. Neither can I see how Davie can consider himself no less good a patriot than myself (or *R*),

1. 'During Mr Grey's captivity', according to the letter.

"perhaps a better," when he says he doesn't like it here and takes off. He is not in Kuznetsov's situation.[1]

But these are small puzzles, and I think I understand his later, major metaphor about Creon, the person willingly in authority, *versus Antigone*, the person in perpetual opposition who is too spiritually grand ever to accept power and its corrupting temptations and whom he equates with my figure of the Lefty.[2] I even agree with some of this, and am glad to find that Davie doesn't seem to like Lefties any more than I do. However, there are a couple of points, closely related, that I should like to take up first.

Davie is being a little perverse when he says what a good thing, in international politics, a "loss of nerve" can be. Such a failure would not have helped us, or the world, much in 1805 or 1940. (I am prepared to argue about 1914.) Anyway, what Davie had to say on this topic has been overtaken by events, and as I write – just after Moratorium Day[3] – we can view a loss of nerve on a scale and at a depth and with a chain of possible consequences spectacular enough to satisfy even him, I hope.

He also says he differs from me about "the alleged monolith of

---

1. Davie's article took both the argument between Amis and 'R' (see Amis to the Editor, *Encounter*, November 1968) and the huge popularity of J.R.R. Tolkien's *Lord of the Rings* as starting points for a meditation on the nature of the British intellectual. In its first paragraph it characterises the tone of the polemic between Amis and 'R' as 'a British hall-mark . . . which shows most clearly how it's all in the family, indeed only a quarrel at the parish-pump. They both "like it here"; and their liking it so well is what makes their disagreements only shadow play, however much they huff and bitch at each other.' As for Davie himself: 'I don't like it here'; which is presumably why he left the University of Essex in 1968 for a professorship at Stanford in California. As Amis points out, though, Davie's situation is hardly that of the Russian dissident Anatoli Kuznetsov (1929–79), who came to Britain in 1969. Amis's letter appeared in *Encounter* 33:6 (December 1969), pp. 94–5, and was headed 'A Reply to Donald Davie'.

2. The references to Antigone and Creon in Davie's article derive from his poem 'Creon's Mouse' (1953), which calls for unheroic tolerance and moderation ('a self-induced and stubborn loss of nerve') in place of the implacable opposition of tragic protagonists: 'A loss of nerve is what has saved us time and again in the years since 1953. It was what averted world war over Budapest in 1956, as also this last summer over Prague' (p. 87). Amis's 'Lefty' is an Antigone-figure; Amis himself is 'a Creon man'. As for Davie: 'I've always been pro-Ismene myself' (p. 88).

3. 15 October 1969, when millions of demonstrators in America and other countries protested against the Vietnam war by refusing to work. Conquest adds: 'demonstrations, but not much by those at "work"? Davie left British Univ because of lefty demos, only to find it worse in Calif' (personal communication, 17 October 2000).

Communism." The notion that Communism is not monolithic and that this somehow makes a difference is actually a favourite crypto-neo-post Lefty one. Various simple answers to it suggest themselves. One is that Fascism, as practised in Germany, Italy and Japan was a good deal less monolithic than Communism has ever been and still managed to be both very unpleasant and very dangerous. Another is that it doesn't much matter to me whether a Communist gets at me with the bastinado or the knout, a missile or a machete – all that really divides them is how to bury us, as (or roughly as) John Kennedy put it. Perhaps Davie would deny that Communism is always and everywhere tyrannical and, whenever it thinks it can get away with it, aggressive as well: Korea, Malaya, Viet Nam, Hungary, Czechoslovakia, etc. It will have to get a bloody sight more polylithic than it is before I start treating different bits of it differently enough to make a difference.

Now to Creon and Antigone. "If Communism is not monolithic, neither is 'protest,'" says Davie. Well, protest isn't monolithic, no, whatever Leftists may pretend, and here is a serious weakness in the Antigone idea – it doesn't apply in enough cases. There is no evidence that the Russian protesters would refuse office of authority in a civilised Russia, as proper Antigones would; they might, and then again they might not. There is no evidence, to say the least, that none of our student rioters and their faculty accomplices are interested in power, and their heroes – Guevara, Castro, Ho, Mao – are Creon-men to a man. (Marcuse, largely unread, of course, is just a chap in an Establishment post who, so to speak, proves the rule, a Dean of Canterbury figure, or perhaps more closely analogous, in a different sphere, to Shakespeare or Michelangelo as they used to feature, when the hand of repression was heavier, in those self-justifying lists of great queers of history that ordinary queers used to carry about.)

Just as the trouble with Creon in all sorts of his incarnations – university administrator, educationist, Arts Council committee member, and whoever chose the new editor of the *Radio Times*[4] – is that he has

4. Geoffrey Cannon (b. 1941) was appointed Editor of the *Radio Times* in 1969; in September that year the magazine was accused of blasphemy when a photo-montage on its cover depicted Christ sandwiched between Coco the Clown and the left-wing student activist Tariq Ali (also on the cover was a picture of Che Guevara, a special hate of Amis's). In the *Daily Telegraph* of 19 September, Mary Whitehouse (b. 1910) of the National Viewers' and Listeners' Association lamented Cannon's appointment: 'A disturbing leftist trend has been apparent in the *Radio Times* since its new editor took over.' Cannon edited the magazine until 1979, when he resigned to join the *Sunday Times*.

become worm-eaten with Antigonism, so the genuine Antigones, of whom there are probably a few left, have become infiltrated with little Creons. The latter will never actually attain the power they seek; if they ever get near it they will be gobbled up by the big Creons who know their business, just as in 1917. Those are the people who frighten me. And I don't care whether they turn out to be Stalinist or Brezhnevite or Maoist or Ho-ist or Castro-ite or Hoxha-ite (or Hitlerite) or whatever. As I said, it doesn't make enough difference.

KINGSLEY AMIS
Lemmons, Hadley Common, Barnet, Herts.

TO BRIAN ALDISS – 14 JANUARY 1970

Lemmons, Hadley Common, Barnet, Hertfordshire.

Dear Brian,

Forgive the delay – just two months. Which may seem shocking to you, junior, but it's about par for me, what?

Haven't got round to *Barefoot* yet. But *H-R B* I bloody well have.[1] Your best book, funny, fascinating and touching. (And not really about tossing off at all, much, you old casher-in.) I'm in no doubt about the merits of the thing, because I read it one day, and thought it couldn't be as good as I thought – perhaps I'd been pissed – so I read it again the next day, and found it slightly better. Keep on with the good work, Aldiss, and don't get too sodding *literary*, and you'll have put us all in your debt.

Hope to come Ox-ward soon.

Raucous cheers,
Kingsley

Love to Mags and the issue

[ALS: Bodleian]

1. The two Aldiss novels are *Barefoot in the Head* (1969) and *The Hand-Reared Boy* (1970).

TO WILLIAM H. PRITCHARD – 12 FEBRUARY 1970

Lemmons, Hadley Common, Barnet, Hertfordshire.

Dear Mr Pritchard,

It was the heroine and the mother of the heroine of *I Want It Now* who wanted it now, not the hero, who started off prepared to have none whatsoever of it now in the expectation of getting every particle of it later on. But this is my only objection to your recent *Review* article,[1] which is about the best thing I have ever read on that splendid writer, and taught me to see things in him I had missed before.

Yours sincerely,
Kingsley Amis

[TLS: Recipient]

TO GEORGE MacBETH – 22 MARCH 1970

Note new address: Lemmons, Hadley Common, Barnet, Hertfordshire.

Dear George,

No, I'm not dead or disaffected – just busy/lazy. (Your first letter never did get here, though.)

I have thought about the personal anthology idea.[1] Nice, but far too much work: I *would* need to write a script, so as not to introduce a bit of A. Powell, say, with "Er, and this is, I think, er, bloody good." If

---

1. Pritchard's mistaken reference to *I Want it Now* occurs in a review article, 'Anthony Powell's Serious Comedy', in the *Massachusetts Review* 10:4 (Autumn 1969), pp. 812–19, the starting point of which was Powell's recently published *The Military Philosophers* (1968).

---

1. On 20 March 1970 MacBeth wrote to Amis (the letter is at the BBC) asking if he would be willing to record a programme for Radio 4 which introduced a selection both 'of books and texts which had influenced his outlook on literature and writing' and 'of his own work within this context'. Amis would present the programme in front of a live audience. For George MacBeth see Amis to Conquest, 16 April 1954, note 5.

you can pay a minimum of £200, say, then that's different, but I'm assuming your budget is rather more restricted than that.[2] Sorry.

But try me again, any time, with something less demanding.

Apologies, and all the best,

Yours,
Kingsley

[ALS: BBC]

TO TOM MASCHLER – 27 MARCH 1970

Lemmons, Hadley Common, Barnet, Hertfordshire.

Dear Tom,

Sorry about the delay, partly caused by my getting down to a new novel,[1] so I have something to be said for me.

A miscellany is supposed to be as miscellaneous as possible. Among other things, it should stress the breadth and diversity of the writer's interests. So it is a positive strength to have a piece about horror movies rubbing shoulders with one on Jane Austen and another on God.[2] Some of these subjects are admittedly more "ephemeral" than others, though not in any straightforward way: Austen is more important and lasting than horror movies, but horror movies are more important, etc., than Richard Hoggart.[3] I think that *you* are in danger of assuming that lit. crit. is by definition more important than, say, political polemics. Maybe so, in the end, but my contributions to each can be of equal merit, and I can have as interesting things to say about Dracula as about D.H. Lawrence. And dammit, if people want to read Orwell on comic post-cards, and they do, they might want to read me on detectives.

2. It was.

---

1. *Girl*, 20 (1971).

2. As in the projected miscellany Amis is here defending, *What Became of Jane Austen?* (1970).

3. Richard Hoggart (b.1919), scholar and writer, best known for *The Uses of Literacy* (1957) which discusses questions of working-class culture and education; at the time Professor of English, University of Birmingham (1962–73); also founder and Director, Centre for Contemporary Cultural Studies (1964–73).

So I stand firm BUT I will consent to drop 'The Cockney Renaissance'[4] just to please you. Okay? See you,

Love
Kingsley

[ALS: Reading]

TO TONY COLWELL – 11 MAY 1970

Lemmons, Hadley Common, Barnet, Hertfordshire.

Dear Tony,

I'm afraid I don't like this cover at all.[1] Though – I should have said – not particularly eye-catching, it's a pleasant enough piece of design, but I can't see what it has to do with the book. It suggests, if it suggests anything much, a book on a single topic, perhaps artistic, historical, sociological, etc. It would be quite a good jacket for a conventional book called, say, "The Child in Victorian Literature." I really can't see what led you to think it was so good for my book. It is a good rule, too, not to have a cover that commemorates nothing in the book, and this young lady (?) doesn't even appear in the Jane Austen essay.

So we must start again from scratch.

All the best
Kingsley

[ALS: Reading]

4. 'The Cockney Renaissance', *Spectator*, 27 August 1954, p. 248, does not appear in *What Became of Jane Austen*? (though 'The Cockney's Homer', about Dickens, does, on pp. 29–33).

---

1. For *What Became of Jane Austen?*.

TO PHILIP LARKIN – 11 AUGUST 1970

Lemmons, Hadley Common, Barnet, Hertfordshire.

Oh fuck – a
single drop
from my vodka
martini
←

My dear Philip,

I'm doing a little series of articles on Drink for the Telegraph colour magazine, which is supposed to include me interviewing distinguished shags of my acquaintance and putting down their thoughts on the subject (of drink). Can I have your acceptance, in principle, of the idea of you and me chatting in some place of your choice and me being there with my notebook, plus a photographer (who can be sent away after a due interval)? I could come to Hull, if need sodding be, or it could be done in London. Anywhere you could notionally claim was a favourite drinking spot of yours.

The other, as pressing, thing is that we're giving a party on Wednesday 19th August for an amiable U.S. couple who are about to go back to the U.S. It would be marvellous if you could come. Starting at 7.0–7.30 p.m. and going on. If you can fit it in with a London trip, do do so. Bob & C. are coming.* We can, and would be overjoyed to, put you up.

Thank you for your notification of the Banks record. How odd to see it reviewed as if it were just another disc from the past – "writers of tragic drama like Kyd, Shakespeare, Otway . . ." I feel on the whole that the takes were rightly selected for our old 78s, though that new *Who Lock*[1] is certainly extraordinary.

It would be splendid if you could come on 19th Aug.

Confrontation bum,
Kingsley

*so they could transport you

[ALS: Bodleian]

---

1. 'Who Stole the Lock from the Henhouse Door?'.

TO BRIAN ALDISS – 11 AUGUST 1970

Lemmons, Hadley Common, Barnet, Hertfordshire.

Dear Old Brian,

I'm doing an extremely authoritative series of articles for the good/bad old Telegraph colour mag, about the good/good old subject of Drink. D-R-I-N-K. This will include interviews involving me and certain chums of mine on the matter. Can I include you in the list? It would entail you and me boozing – at their expense – in some venue devised by you ("one of his favourite haunts is . . ."), chatting, with me holding my notebook open; and the presence of a photographer – who can be told to fuck off whenever we feel like it. Anyway, if you could give me your approval of the project in principle, I will get on to them and further developments may – or, bearing in mind what sods colour supplement journalists* are – may not – transpire. Just say "Okay" and we can go ahead.

Cheers, and love to M. & all,
Kingsley

*in fact, saving your presence, *all* journalists

[ALS: Bodleian]

TO THE EDITOR, *DAILY TELEGRAPH* – 12 AUGUST 1970

SIR—The Executive Committee of STUPID (Society for Thinking Up Progressive Innovations and Developments) has directed me to express, through your columns, its warm approval of the Post Office plan to abandon alphabetical order in its directory listings.

It has further directed me to draw your attention and that of your readers to its latest proposal. This is the replacement of the present illogical, unscientific system of vehicle registration – as seen on so-called "number" plates – by an all-figure system. Among the advantages of such a change would be the following:

1. It would be a change.
2. The existing system works perfectly well.

3. A great deal of expense and trouble would be called for.
4. There would be chaos during the period of change-over.
5. Nobody wants it.
6. Nobody would benefit.

The Committee is currently considering further proposals, including that of placing different sets of numbers on the front and rear plates of the vehicles, but it would prefer not to proceed with these until it has taken the (admittedly unprecedented) step of sounding public opinion in the matter as a whole.[1]

KINGSLEY AMIS
Press Officer, STUPID Barnet, Herts

TO PHILIP LARKIN – 30 AUGUST 1970

Lemmons, Hadley Common, Barnet, Hertfordshire.

My dear Philip,

These colour-mag sods, after having sat on my copy for 8 months, now want everything done and 'in' by the 11th of Sept. So could you let me know if by any chance you're going to be in London before then? If not, as I suspect, I will, if I may, despatch the photograph man up to see you in Hull, when he'll take perhaps ½ an hour of your time. He's a decent sort of shag, John Goldblatt by name – though he ate a couple of pork chops unhesitatingly enough.

As regards the "interview", it'll be easiest, on the assumption you won't be in London, if you'd let me have some thoughts on drink which I could work up into about 250 jolly spontaneous-sounding words. You needn't say anything about the getting-pissed side of things unless you want to, though do if you do want to: the accent will be on drinking

---

1. This letter is a precursor of Amis's campaign in the 1980s against a mentality he labelled 'sod the public', explained in a *Spectator* article of 19 October 1985 as 'the working slogan not only of government, the service industry and the retail trade, but also as "sod the customer", "sod the audience" and other variants, that of interior designers, providers of culture, playwrights, composers and many more'. The *Spectator* article, 'Sod the Public: A Consumer's Guide', is reprinted in *The Amis Collection*, pp. 229–40; the quoted definition occurs on p. 229.

rather than drunkenness, and I promise you there won't be any Dylan's-Heirs stuff in the article.[1]

I hope this won't be too much of a chore for you – you'll be helping your old chum to get all his drink *for a year* off tax. Necessary business expense, d' you see. Research, d' you follow.

Anthology of socialist bum,[2]
Kingsley

[ALS: Bodleian]

TO PHILIP LARKIN – 4 SEPTEMBER 1970

Lemmons, Hadley Common, Barnet, Hertfordshire.

My dear Philip,

I now find that the captions for these photos are only going to run to 100 words or so, so I can make do with what you've already vouchsafed in your last letter, and needn't trouble you further or send you ten guineas, which would have had to come out of my pocket. But I can 'offer you hospitality' when you're next this way, or buy you a meal in Oxford. What's your address there?[1] Drop it to me some time – just your name on a postcard.

The pork chop chap[2] will be getting in touch with you.

Raymond Williams[3] bum,
Kingsley

[ALS: Bodleian]

---

1. Larkin had written to Amis on 14 August 1970 (in HEHL): 'Of course I agree to co-operate in principle, as long as you're not letting me in for anything derogatory ("After Dylan Who?" "Alcoholics Of The Seventies").'

2. Presumably a reference to *The Penguin Book of Socialist Verse* (1970), edited by Alan Bold, and reviewed disparagingly by Amis in the *Observer* (4 October 1970), a review reprinted as 'The Red Muse' in *The Amis Collection*, pp. 168–70.

---

1. Larkin had moved to Oxford for two terms (1970–71), as a Visiting Fellow, All Souls College, to work on *The Oxford Book of Twentieth Century English Verse.*

2. John Goldblatt, photographer; see Amis to Larkin, 30 August 1970.

3. Raymond Williams (1921–88), Marxist literary critic, novelist.

TO PHILIP LARKIN – 6 SEPTEMBER 1970

Lemmons, Hadley Common, Barnet, Hertfordshire.

My dear Philip,

Nay, don't let's scrub it – whatever the nation may think, I want it to have your views on the topic and see your little flower-face.[1]

My memory tells me, in faltering tones perhaps, that I never asked you to write me a para for nothing. Not I, lad. I meant, if you jotted down a few cracks, I could work them up. Beer today is piss = He considers brewing standards have declined disastrously in the post-war period. Anyway, I enclose a draft for your vetting.[2] I might explain that *my* changes of plan were really the result of successive lesions in the walnut-sized collective brain of the sodding colour mag.

Do reconsider. The gallery of chaps (did I tell you old Betj is in on it?) would be the poorer for your absence. I will still buy you a large meal, *with drinks*, in Oxford quite soon. The pork-chop chap* has no pork-chop chip, is easy to deal with, and will have no objection to being flung out when you have had enough of him. So don't let's scrub it.

Max Roach[3] bum,
Kingsley

*He won't get in touch with you unless/until I tell him he may

[ALS: Bodleian]

---

1. See Larkin to Amis, 4 September 1970 (in HEHL): 'I'm afraid this idea is getting beyond me. The first suggestion was for an interview, and I agreed. Then this turned into a request for 250 words for nothing, which I wasn't so keen on. Now you suggest you make up a 100 words from about 50 of mine not chosen for publication at all. No, it might turn out all right, but chances are that I should feel I'd been misrepresented, and I should have only myself to blame. So let's scrub it. I don't suppose the British public will miss having my views. I'll explain to the chop chap should he ring.'

2. 'PHILIP LARKIN, 48, leading poet of his generation, jazz critic of The Daily Telegraph, university chief librarian, and moderate but habitual indulger. He has stuck to beer as his staple longer than many of his age-group and social status.* "The job of drink is to make you drunk – it tastes so horrible that no-one would drink it if it didn't. And how fat it makes you! And how frightful pubs are becoming *in all ways*! But the stuff ought to be taxed less, and things like tea and ice-cream and sweets taxed more." *If the chop chap shows you drinking, say, fermented mares' milk, then we insert here "but he enjoys an occasional glass of fermented mares' milk."'

3. Max Roach (b. 1924), drummer and composer.

TO THE EDITOR, *GUARDIAN* – 18 SEPTEMBER 1970

Sir,—May I defend James Bond and Callan and Steed against the charge of being not spies but secret policemen (Colin Watson in the "Guardian," September 10)?[1]

The romantic Vivienne Michel of "The Spy Who Loved Me" notwithstanding, Bond, at least, was never a spy in the sense of one who obtains secret information from other Powers, nor ever widely thought of as such.[2] But neither was he, nor Callan, nor Steed, a secret policeman in the sense of one whose primary function is to assist in the oppression of his fellow-countrymen, and of the citizens of nations subjugated by his own nation, for their political opinions, religious beliefs, racial origins, or, on occasions, mere existence.

And that is what a secret policeman was – and is. I also wonder (to put it politely) why Mr Watson equates Bond and other fictional secret agents with 'the quiet men in belted raincoats who once sauntered on the errands of Heinrich Himmler' – dead these 25 years, when Yuri Andropov, head of the KGB, is, to extend a cliché, alive and well and sending quiet men in belted raincoats on errands in Russia and satellite Europe at this moment.

Incidentally, I think the reason why the 1969 paperback of "On Her Majesty's Secret Service" was labelled "The New James Bond – 007" had less to do with the commercially conditioned reflexes of a book-buying public assumed . . . to salivate on the mention of novelty than with the fact that the film of the book, which appeared in that year, and which perhaps escaped Mr Watson's attention, was publicised under that slogan. The latter referred to the appearance of a new actor in the star part, George Lazenby, who replaced the "old" James Bond, Sean Connery.—Yours faithfully,

KINGSLEY AMIS
Lemmons, Hadley Common, Barnet, Hertfordshire.

---

1. 'Steed' is John Steed, the dandified secret service agent in the comedy suspense series *The Avengers* (1961–63, 1976); 'Callan', of the series of the same name (1967–73), was a more brutal, cold-blooded figure.

2. After sleeping with him for the first time, Vivian Michel, the narrator of *The Spy Who Loved Me*, calls Bond 'just a professional agent who had done his job . . . He was only some kind of spy, a spy who loved me. Not even loved, slept with' (from *A James Bond Quintet* (London: Jonathan Cape, 1993), p. 915).

TO PHILIP LARKIN – 20 SEPTEMBER 1970

Lemmons, Hadley Common, Barnet, Hertfordshire.

My dear Philip,

Many thanks, and apologies for buggering you about. Your amended version has gone in exactly as you wrote it, but don't blame me, blame the mag shags, if it comes out as PHILLIP LARKIN, 58, author of *The More Deceived, Mixed Samples, Look Back at the Top*, etc. All right, I'm pulling your leg really. The chop chap does first-chop snaps, so don't worry about him.

Yes, I'll join your Misfortune Club, only won't we have to be a bit careful who we let in? Anthony de Haughton? Robert Waller?[1] – but I think he's dead, so that's all right. I hear ole LSC[aton] is still churning out first editions of *Bright N.* Very decent of people not to mention that book ever. Still, somebody thought highly enough of my last remaining copy to pinch it a few years ago.

I've been running round like a blue fly getting these pics done, interviewing shags and so on. The chop chap took 286 shots of me in the same pose the other day. Tiring. Still, at least it means I can't get on with my novel.

Give us a ring when you're around.

Ben Whitaker[2] bum,

Kingsley

[TLS: Bodleian]

1. Neither Motion, Thwaite nor Conquest have heard of the Misfortune Club, presumably a short-lived jest; but if 'Robert Waller' is John Waller, then Amis, Larkin, 'De Haughton' and Waller all published books of verse with R.A. Caton and the Fortune Press – a misfortune indeed. Sir Henry Philip Anthony Mary de Hoghton (not 'Haughton') (1919–78), read French at Magdalen College, Oxford (1937–38, 1944–46), published *24 Poems* with the Fortune Press (1945), then achieved brief notoriety in 1954 when *Granta*, the Cambridge magazine, was banned for a period for publishing one of his poems, deemed blasphemous. The magazine's editor, who was sent down briefly, was Mark Boxer (1931–88), later a successful journalist and cartoonist; its literary editor, Karl Miller, was away when Boxer published the poem. John Waller (b.1917), an undergraduate at Worcester College, Oxford, edited the Oxford poetry magazine *Kingdom Come* (1939–41), was a soldier in the Middle East during the war (where he later came into contact with Lawrence Durrell and his circle), co-edited the *Middle East Anthology* (1946), and contributed to the poetry magazines *Salamander* and *Personal Landscape*. His Fortune Press volume was entitled *Fortunate Hamlet* (1941).

2. Ben Whitaker (b.1934), author, Labour MP for Hampstead (1966–70); publications include (ed.) *A Radical Future* (1967) and *Participation and Poverty* (1968).

TO PHILIP LARKIN – 30 OCTOBER 1970

Lemmons, Hadley Common, Barnet, Hertfordshire.

My dear Philip,

Nice of you to invite me,[1] but I don't think I can face it. Had enough at Cantab to last me until 1984. I'm sorry I didn't let you know earlier – but you still have 3 weeks to find a substitute.

But can you have lunch with me and Jane (and possibly Martin) on the 11th, when I come up to harangue the Po Soc? If you could let me know rather quicker than I've let you know about the guest night, I'd be most grateful. Drop me a card, or telephone, and we can fix time and place. What's your tele. no.? – apart from All Souls, where I imagine you seldom physically are.

Those were two jolly good poems of yours in *Encounter*,[2] I thought. And v. gd. that chaps who might want to piss on you for being vulgar in the 2nd one can't, because of the 1st one.

Do hope to see you.

Andrew Sinclair[3] bum,
Kingsley

[ALS: Bodleian]

TO PHILIP LARKIN – 14 DECEMBER 1970

Lemmons, Hadley Common, Barnet, Hertfordshire.

My dear Philip,

By now, I divine, you'll have received a letter from the posturing turd who helps to run the DT colour mag. You do realise it was he, not I, who excluded your little flower-face from the drinks article? (And he too who cut my copy here and there, in the interests of turning sense into ballocks.) Anyway, sorry you had to endure the chop chap for fuck-all.

---

1. To a guest night dinner at All Souls.
2. 'Dublinesque' and 'The Cardplayers', in *Encounter* 35 (October 1970), pp. 13–14, reprinted in *High Windows* (1974).
3. Andrew Sinclair (b. 1935), author; see *Memoirs*, pp. 220–1.

Not much horn-donation in *His Lordship*,[1] was there? Oh well. At least reading that sort of thing helps to keep one in touch. (I'll keep a red-hot coal in touch with your –)

You'll still be there in the New Year (as I remember you prefer to have it called), won't you? I'll be coming up again and we'll reunite.

Crow[2] bum,
Kingsley

Why did he go on about pulling William's nose all the time? Did he think it was FUNNY?

[TLS: Bodleian]

TO FRAM DINSHAW[1] – 30 DECEMBER 1970

Lemmons, Hadley Common, Barnet, Hertfordshire.

Dear Mr Dinshaw,

If I ever (these days) gave a talk anywhere, it would be at Eton, what with it being such a haunt of the Establishment and the ruling class and all. But I'm really too busy, with stern calls to duty like deadlines for TV comedy scripts.[2] Sorry.

All good wishes

Yours sincerely,
Kingsley Amis

[ALS: Eton]

---

1. Leslie Thomas, *His Lordship* (1970), a novel.

2. A reference to the poet Ted Hughes (1930–98), whose volume of poems *Crow* was published in 1970.

---

1. Fram Dinshaw (b. 1954) was a King's Scholar at Eton (1967–71) and Secretary of the Literary Society from January 1971; he went on to Merton College, Oxford where he read English (1972–76), and is now a Fellow in English at St Catherine's College, Oxford.

2. Perhaps episode one of *General Tomski's Army*, entitled 'Enemies of the State', described by the Huntington as a television play and dated 1970; it was never produced.

TO THE EDITOR, *SPECTATOR* – 6 MARCH 1971

Sir: Mr Summers and Miss Collins would have done better to go on sheltering behind the screen of anonymity I had chivalrously erected in front of them. Both, in different degrees, give further evidence of the shortcomings for which I chided them in my original article.[1]

It is Mr Summers who offers the richer blend of incapacities. 'Since it is me alone, that [Amis] is crying in his porridge about,' he writes, 'I trust it is OK for "the thickest student" ever in Swansea University . . . now to have the right of reply too?' Evidently so; but a glance at my article, or at Miss Collins's letter, or at Mr Roberts's earlier letter,[2] will show that it was not at all him alone (as he would put it) that I was in tears over, and another glance will show that I did not call him the thickest student ever in Swansea University, but merely 'an *unusually thick* student *in my classes* at the University College of Swansea' (today's italics). However, in view of his letter we may have to consider seriously his claim to the majestic nadir he mentions.

To misquote a man within quotation marks is a rather novel and appealingly simple method of distortion. Mr Summers uses it again in the course of misrepresenting my views about the Welsh. He says: '[Amis] described all us Welsh as "slathered in woad and sheepshit."' What I wrote, which was 'woaded in pit-dirt and sheepshit', was part of a jocose caricature of ignorant or hostile English views of the Welsh,

---

1. In a 'Personal Column' in the *Spectator* entitled 'The Right of Reply', 30 January 1971, Amis protested against newspaper reporting that was 'merely dishonest, witless and inaccurate', as opposed to libellous, singling out two instances, both involving the 'Mandrake' column in the *Sunday Telegraph*: the first occurred in 1964 and concerned an interview conducted by a 'Mandrake' reporter Amis had known as 'an unusually thick student in my classes at the University College of Swansea. (My erstwhile colleagues must forgive me if I observe that that is saying something)'; the second occurred in early 1965 when Amis was interviewed about film-makers by a female 'Mandrake'. Both articles, the 'Personal Column' makes clear, were inaccurate, and in both instances Amis's letters of protest to the *Sunday Telegraph* were not printed (though the second might have been had he agreed to cut it). In the ensuing correspondence in the *Spectator*, the female 'Mandrake' revealed herself as Rosemary Collins (in a letter of 20 February); the ex-student 'Mandrake' revealed himself as John Summers, journalist and writer (in a letter of 27 February). Summers also replied to the current letter (on 20 March).

2. Brian Roberts (1906–88), editor of the *Sunday Telegraph* (1966–76), defended his newspaper in a letter of 6 February 1971.

for which as a whole I retain a deep respect and affection, as my many Welsh friends will testify.

Anyway, according to Mr Summers, I cannot hope to surprise anybody now that I have sunk to my 'proper level masquerading as the concocter of crypto-fascist fake James Bond tec yarns'. I suppose he refers to the single yarn, *Colonel Sun*, which I published under a pseudonym while letting everybody know I had written it. I did not masquerade as its concocter, or concoctor: I concocted it. Mr Summers comes near libelling me by implying I got someone else to write the thing and then passed it off as my own work. And anybody who has read a Bond adventure and a few tec yarns, and imagines the one to be an example of the other, cannot have understood what he has read.

As to Miss Collins: her claim that her account of our conversation was accurate is false simply in that she omitted from that account the vital qualification (to my unfriendly remarks about film producers) which I repeatedly stressed to her while we were talking and her omission of which started this whole business off. I cannot understand why she goes on about libel: all I wanted put into the record was a statement that I had been kindly treated by certain individuals in the film industry – not very flagrant defamation. I wonder too why she bothers to mention the unchallenged fact – dwelt upon, indeed, in my article – that I did not ask to see a proof of her piece. Does she mean that, in such a case, the man interviewed must expect to find himself misrepresented? That is what *I* think, especially these days; but it is odd to find her seeming to agree.

Yours and all that,

KINGSLEY AMIS
Lemmons, Hadley Common, Barnet, Herts

TO JOHN BETJEMAN[1] – 3 JUNE 1971

Lemmons, Hadley Common, Barnet, Hertfordshire.

Dear John,

Thank you for the super poem. It was passed to me in the midst

1. For John Betjeman see Notes on Recipients.

of a hubbub of conversation, so I missed hearing its provenance, and had forgotten for the moment that Sargy[2] had been dining with you. I started reading the text before glancing at the greetings at the foot, and at once thought: "Good God, this chap's as good as Betjeman!" Speaks for itself, eh? Many many thanks.

Now listen: Bob Conquest and I do want to pin you down about reading you this Russki poem[3] we want to dedicate to you. The thing is the venue: it must be somewhere where you can laugh as much as we hope and trust you will without exciting too much attention: which rules out, e.g., the library of the Athenaeum. We propose taking you to a pub for that part – perhaps the Salisbury in St. Martin's Lane, or anywhere of your choice – and then on somewhere decent for lunch. What you must do is RING ME UP and give me a date or two, I'll check with Bob and then clinch it with you. Now, get cracking, Betjeman, if you know what's good for you!

Love to Liz,[4] and to you,
Kingsley

[ALS: Victoria]

2. Sargy Mann, who says the poem in question was 'Executive', published in *A Nip in the Air* (1974).

3. 'View Galoo: Or, Ivan of the Shires', written by Amis and Conquest under the pseudonym 'Jasper Budenny' ('Jasper' being a typical English hunt name, 'Budenny' suggesting a Russian cavalry marshal), a poem of over thirty verses, published in the *Spectator*, 27 November 1971, pp. 784–5, with many illustrations. The poem's controlling joke is the Russian substitution of 'g' for 'h'. Betjeman invited Amis and Conquest to the Royal Automobile Club for the reading. See Appendix C for the poem.

4. Lady Elizabeth Cavendish, daughter of the 10th Duke of Devonshire; described by Betjeman's daughter, Candida Lycett Green, as 'the love of his life, his mainstay and his muse' (in volume two of her edition of his *Letters* (London: Methuen, 1995), p. 9). Betjeman met her in 1951 when she was in her early twenties and he was forty-five. He remained married to Lycett Green's mother, Penelope (*née* Chetwode), a travel writer, throughout his life.

TO CHRISTOPHER RICKS – 21 JUNE 1971

Lemmons, Hadley Common, Barnet, Hertfordshire.

Dear Christopher,[1]

I am editing a selection of Tennyson for Penguin, and write now in the first place to give you notice that I propose to lean a good deal on the dates and facts in your splendid Longmans edition.[2] Full, even fulsome, acknowledgment will be paid.

On one point I should like your advice: the old moaning of the bar.[3] The bar itself seems clear enough as a sandbank outside the harbour, or, I think more precisely, outside the estuary where the port is. But how can it moan? It, or waves breaking over it, might roar or hiss, I suppose, but moan? And it would be uncrossable, except by a raft perhaps, if there were any question of breaking waves anywhere near it. And the tide is supposed to be full. In that situation whatever noise the bar were making would surely be inaudible above the surface. And, while T. can validly expect to discourage sadness of farewell when he embarks, he can hardly hope to do anything about any conceivable bar-noises, either in person or through the Harbour Authority. There must be some simple explanation I have missed. Do, if you have time, drop me a card on the subject.

Yours ever,
Kingsley

[TLS: Recipient]

---

1. For Christopher Ricks see Notes on Recipients.

2. Amis's edition, in the Penguin *Poet to Poet* series, is *Tennyson* (Harmondsworth: Penguin, 1973); Ricks's is *The Poems of Tennyson* (London: Longmans, Green and Company, 1969).

3. From 'Crossing the Bar' (1889) by Alfred, first Baron Tennyson (1809–92), written while crossing the Solent. The phrase occurs in the first stanza of the poem: 'Sunset and evening star,/And one clear call for me!/And may there be no moaning of the bar,/When I put out to sea.' Ricks's note in the Longman edition does not explain the phrase but cites Charles Kingsley's 'The Three Fishers' ('And the harbour bar be moaning'), another poem about death, and one which appeared in a volume in Tennyson's library.

TO CHRISTOPHER RICKS – 16 JULY 1971

Lemmons, Hadley Common, Barnet, Hertfordshire.

Dear Christopher,

I think I have the moaning wrapped up, after a conversation in El Vino[1] (to which I most resort) that came just in time to forestall a letter to the TLS. (You are right, of course, about my being wrong about 'the tide is supposed to be full' – I was maundering.)[2] To save (my) time, I send you a clipping from a not-quite-fair-enough copy of what I am putting in my Notes.[3] Also another relevant bit which I hope you will think acknowledgment enough. The thanks are certainly sincere; well done, Ricks.

Yours,
Kingsley

[TLS: Recipient]

TO ROBERT CONQUEST – 9 SEPTEMBER 1971

Hotel da Balaia, Albufeira, Algarve, Portugal

Dear Bob,

Well, here we are. A bloody good spot too, despite the expected prevalence of Germans. But they're improving: one of them held a

1. A wine bar in Fleet Street, much frequented by journalists; the next phrase, 'to which I most resort', is a quotation from Tennyson's poem 'Will Waterproof's Lyrical Monologue Made at the Cock' (1842). According to Anthony Thwaite, 'KA is making a joking/learned reference to the fact that El Vino and The Cock Tavern are close to one another [they are both on Fleet Street]' (personal communication, 10 May 1999).

2. Stanza 2 of 'Crossing the Bar' describes Tennyson's wish for 'such a tide as moving seems asleep/Too full for sound and foam,/When that which drew from out the boundless deep/Turns again home.'

3. The clipping has not been retained, but Amis's note reads: 'an impressive and, as it stands, quite unintelligible line. Philip Hope-Wallace tells me that, in the common estuary of the rivers Taw and Torridge in Barnstaple (or Bideford) Bay, the joining of their waters and the incoming sea between them, if conditions are just right, produce a loud moaning sound above the sand-bar at the mouth of the inlet. Tennyson almost certainly borrowed the idea from "The Three Fishers", a poem by Charles Kingsley, who had lived in that part of North Devon. To my knowledge, Tennyson never had, and I suspect he was attracted by

swing door open for me today, after he'd gone through it himself and had no further use for it. I expect, though, that a lot of them will have taken a coach trip to Lagos today to see the public executions announced in yesterday's paper. Too bad when they find out it's the wrong Lagos.

We got here very much against the odds. Evidently it's the spot to be in – the hotel, I mean – on this coast. Our agent couldn't get us in, stuck us in a crappy golfing joint instead. We tried again from Lisbon; no good; full up. Then, in a crappy-looking but, it turned out, bloody good eatery I saw a chap who'd been on the boat; had never spoken to him, just remembered him because he looked so much like a beardless Portuguese Alan Ross. I waved to him and mouthed something about a small world. Then, in chat, I mentioned this place and asked him if he happened to know it. He said he did, and what was more his brother-in-law was head receptionist at it. Christ. Luck worthy of Richard Hannay.[1] And it wasn't shitty when we got here either: beach, pool, tennis, not that I care a fuck about any of that. Weather marvellous, food v. good. All of which leads me to suggest that, since we are in an extensive bungalow 100 yards from the hotel, with room for another couple (in fact for a third as well if they didn't mind sleeping in bunks), you and C. could do a bloody sight worse than fly out and join us for a week or so. Full pension, 200 esc. each a day. Cheap booze, of course: Smirnoff 75 esc. a bottle. (100 esc. are 30 bob.) Taxi from Faro airport, 180 esc. I'm quite serious. What about it? (J. says C. and she could go riding together.)

Has Colin [Welch][2] gone completely off his rocker? – all this 'where's the great pro-Market work of art?' stuff. I've sent in a tart rejoinder, but it probably won't get in, arriving after so many other such from any and every sane man in the kingdom who can hold a pen. Still, perhaps the fact that I'm loyally holidaying in EFTA[3] will give me an

the emotional overtones of Kingsley's phrase – "and the harbour bar be moaning" – without understanding its origin or its reference, we can confidently infer, to a local superstition. Otherwise, why did he, normally a scrupulous self-annotator, leave no note on the line? It certainly needs one.'

1. Protagonist of *The Thirty-Nine Steps* (1915), and four other John Buchan thrillers.
2. Colin Welch (1924–97), at the time Deputy Editor of the *Daily Telegraph* (1964–80).
3. The European Free Trade Association (known as the 'Outer Seven', as opposed to the 'Inner Six', nations of the Common Market).

edge. But how mad it all seems from here. I'm relying on you to make a file of crap which, reading only the DT, I might miss.

I'll have to get down to work soon, I suppose. Detailed scenario for 'tec yarn,[4] a nasty prospect because unfamiliar as well as work. And on closer inspection the whole idea may turn out to be no good. We are here at any rate until 28th, probably a few days longer. J. says if we can be unfaithful to Rosie, you two can be unfaithful to Bluebell.[5] To whom, notwithstanding, much love, also to C., and regards to all the Tuesday shags.[6] Drop us a line and give us the gossip.

Yours
Kingers

[TLS: Recipient]

TO COLIN HOWARD AND SARGY MANN – 10 SEPTEMBER 1971

Hotel da Balaia, Albufeira, Algarve, Portugal

Dear Blokes,[1]

Here we are where we wanted to be; supposed to be the best hotel in S. Portugal, and I can believe it. We tried to get in via our London travel agent; no good; booked solid till November. So we had to settle for a lousy golfing joint miles from anywhere. In Lisbon, we got the clerk shag to try here again; hopeless; not a camp-bed available. Then came a BHQ balls-up of disastrous proportions; I hate to think of what must have happened to the chap responsible. Wog and I picked *at random* a little sea-food restaurant for lunch in Lisbon last Monday. I *happened to catch sight* of a Portuguese chap I *thought* I remembered seeing on the boat, and waved to him. He came over when he'd finished his meal and said he *just about had time* for a drink (which, I may add, he paid for along with ours, to pay the British back a little, he said, for

4. *The Riverside Villas Murder* (1973)

5. Bluebell, the Conquests' bassett hound; Rosie (short for Rosie Plush), Jane's cavalier spaniel bitch, fictionalised by Amis as the 'Furry Barrel' in *Girl, 20* (1971). See Amis to Elizabeth Jane Howard, 21 September 1976, note 1.

6. At the Bertorellis' lunches.

---

1. For 'Blokes' and Sargy Mann see Notes on Recipients.

being so nice to him during his stay. So much better people than the French, he also said.). Anyway, we mentioned our difficulties, and *happened to ask him* if he knew this hotel. 'Yes, quite well,' he said; 'in fact, my brother-in-law is the senior receptionist there. If you wish, I will send him a Telex . . .' We wished, and here we bloody well are. What fantastic negligence, to let us come face to face with the one man in Lisbon who could fix it for us. Oh, and we got the last remaining accommodation in the whole hotel. So we can be a little tolerant even to the Germans. After all, Hun-spotting is so easy as to be tame. Little girl sitting next to me at the bar kicks me twice on the ankle; hardly worth bothering to listen to her wie-gehtsing away to her parents. Tubby turd jostles me aside at the cash-desk in the bookshop; almost too much trouble to note his ja-ja-gewiss to his Tibor-built wife.[2]

For the moment I'm winning, three days here and I haven't set foot on the beach, let alone in the bloody water. But it can't last; sun's too hot, and the alternative is getting down to work. Oh: I don't know if I can convey this on paper, but I've been amused to remember what a gawfish and beezhish[3] language Portuguese is. For instance the Spanish for 'general' is 'general', the Portuguese 'geral'. Try saying 'general' in a sufficiently hooghish way and you do get to 'geral'. Same with Span. 'colorado' (coloured), Port. 'corado'. End of language lesson.

Nearly time for the first beer, and soon after that it'll be nearly time to try the vin rose out of the gallon jar we bought in the market. The food's good on the whole, though I had a langoust(in)e last night that tasted so horrible I was quite surprised to wake up this morning. But when that sort of thing happens I just go and look at the bottle of Smirnoff vodka we paid 22 bob for and I feel better right away.

All for now. Look after yourselves. Let us know if anything funny

2. That is, stockily-built, like Tibor Szamuely.

3. According to Sargy Mann, this is a reference to two of the three most frequent sounds ('gawf', 'beezh' and 'hoogh') made by 'berks'. These sounds are the building blocks of what Amis called 'Berk's Latin'. In *The King's English*, p. 23, the entry for 'berks and wankers' begins: 'Not every reader will immediately understand these two terms as I use them, but most people, most users of English, habitually distinguish between two types of person whose linguistic habits they deplore if not abhor . . . *Berks* are careless, coarse, crass, gross and of what anybody would agree is a lower social class than one's own. They speak in a slipshod way with dropped Hs, intruded glottal stops and many mistakes in grammar. Left to them the English language would die of impurity, like late Latin.' Amis's favourite example of 'Berk's Latin' was provided by Robert Conquest (who seems to have helped to develop the concept): the corruption of the Latin *confluentium*, meaning where two rivers meet, to the German 'Koblenz', built on the confluence of the Rhine and the Moselle.

or crappy comes up. We get the D.Tel and the Express each day a day late, so don't bother with Simple[4] gems, etc.

Love to all,
Kingers

[TLS: Sargy Mann]

TO THE EDITOR, *DAILY TELEGRAPH* – 13 SEPTEMBER 1971

SIR—Can it really surprise my friend Mr Colin Welch that "the European idea" has "informed or inspired no great or successful work of art"?[1]

Isn't it a little early for that? After all, it took some centuries of "the Christian idea," which he would probably agree is almost on the same plane of importance, to inform and inspire the works of Dante and Fra Angelico.

Apart from having been thought up only the other day, the European idea (in this sense) seems inherently unlikely to inform or inspire even trivial or failed works of art. Mr Welch might as hopefully search for odes on the opening of a White Fish Industry's exhibition, oratorios based on the history of the International Monetary Fund. And I hope he will find them sooner than what he wants.

What may well prove to have been indirectly inspired by the European idea are requiem masses on the demise of the British idea, satires on the phantom benefits replacing it, and caricatures depicting, perhaps savagely, those who worked to bring about the change.

KINGSLEY AMIS
Albufeira, Portugal.

4. For 'Peter Simple', in the *Telegraph*, see Amis to Conquest, 1 November 1967, note 2.

1. This assertion appeared in an article of 6 September 1971 entitled 'Can We Get the Message Across?'.

TO ANNE PRIOR – 11 OCTOBER 1971

Lemmons, Hadley Common, Barnet, Hertfordshire.

Dear Mrs Prior,

Many thanks for your kind letter[1] – and apologies for not answering sooner: I have been on holiday and (deliberately) out of reach of correspondence.

I would like to say how much I appreciate your taking the trouble to write and thereby giving me a rare and valuable form of encouragement. In particular, you have strengthened my determination to ignore those who tell me to stop writing on general topics and 'stick to fiction'.

My most grateful thanks.

Yours sincerely,
Kingsley Amis

[ALS: Recipient]

TO PHILIP LARKIN – 28 APRIL 1972

Lemmons, Hadley Common, Barnet, Hertfordshire.

My dear Philip,

I should have asked you this before, because time is rather short: anyway – poor old Cecil D-L is very ill, dying, in fact, and he will stay with us here until he dies. Now I know he would love to see you. If you're in London, you could pop up here without much difficulty, and we could easily, indeed would love to, put you up for the night.

He's very weak, but totally compos and cheerful (Christ). He doesn't know I'm writing this letter, so won't feel let down if you can't make it. If you do decide to make the trip, the sooner the better. Nobody

1. Mrs Prior, who lives on the Isle of Wight and describes herself as a 'voracious' reader, had sent Amis a fan letter praising *What Became of Jane Austen*?

can really tell, of course, but somewhere between a week and a month seems probable. Let me know. No more for now.

Yours
Kingsley

[ALS: Bodleian]

TO PHILIP LARKIN – 7 MAY 1972

Lemmons, Hadley Common, Barnet, Hertfordshire.

My dear Philip,

By the living God, cully, that was a fine old time, as far as I remember. We did do nothing else from about 7 on but play records, didn't we? Didn't we?

I'm inclined to the hopeful view that you were no less damaged than I because you left your record behind. I have it safe, and will deliver it to you at our next rencontre.

Don't forget you are to tell me which American jazzmen were in London in June, 1936. Or Paris would do, because my chap[1] is just the sort to have hopped over to there from Croydon Aerodrome. Funnier, too.

I found that *Men Only* on my desk, nicely under a copy of the *Times*, I mean *The Times*. Who put it there, hey?

Events of the last 48 hours in Vietnam highlight the weakness of the President's bum,

Kingsley

Bruce [Montgomery] *threw up a bit in the bar at the Crime Club dinner on Thursday.*[2]

[TLS: Bodleian]

---

1. Colonel Manton, the jazz-loving detective in *The Riverside Villas Murder* (1973): 'Yes, there's no getting away from it, the niggers play the best jazz music. I popped over to Paris to hear a gang of them just at the end of last year. There was the most dazzling trumpeter called Bill Coleman, and a pianist by the name of Garnet Clark, who struck me as off his head, but he could tickle the ivories all right.'

2. MS addition.

TO HALLAM TENNYSON – 27 JULY 1972

Lemmons, Hadley Common, Barnet, Hertfordshire.

Dear Hallam T.,[1]

What a good idea – as C. Ricks may have told you, I'm doing a Penguin selection of the old boy's verse, due out some time in the autumn (I think), and so am fairly well clued up as well as being a great admirer. I'd be glad to come to B.H. [Broadcasting House] and record.[2] I look forward to hearing further details.

Yours,
Kingsley A.

[ALS: BBC]

TO GORDON N. RAY – 27 NOVEMBER 1972

Lemmons, Hadley Common, Barnet, Herts, England

Dear Gordon,

Good to hear from you. I'm sure you can imagine the mixture of tickled ego and slight sinking of the heart with which I read your letter. Mr Salwak seems, from his dissertation proposal, a sensible enough young man, and he and I may get along together famously: but then again we may not.[1] Of course I'll see him, but I can't guarantee to do

---

1. Hallam Tennyson (b. 1921), the poet's great-grandson, a BBC radio broadcaster, producer and writer (1956–79); at the time working in the BBC Drama Department.

2. Hallam Tennyson and Christopher Ricks were recording a programme on the poet Tennyson to coincide with the eightieth anniversary of his death in the autumn. They hoped, with the help of Amis and others, 'to find out how far Tennyson's influence and reputation have changed since the fiftieth anniversary, when they could be said to have sunk to their lowest ebb' (Tennyson to Amis, 19 June 1972, in BBC).

---

1. For Dale Salwak see Notes on Recipients. Amis had met Ray (1915–86), a friend of R.P. Blackmur, in 1958, when Ray, at Blackmur's suggestion, invited Amis to speak at the University of Illinois at Champaign-Urbana. Ray was Professor of English at Champaign-Urbana from 1946–60 and Vice-President and Provost from 1957–60. In 1962 he became Professor of English at New York University, and in 1963 was appointed President of the John Simon Guggenheim Foundation (where he remained until 1985). Ray was an old friend

so repeatedly or for days at a time. Suppose I offer him a minimum of a couple of hours' chat followed by lunch, after which I'm free to disappear from his life, but may well elect (and have the leisure) not to do so. If he's prepared to come all this way on that understanding, then I'll very cheerfully see him and do my best to answer any questions he may devise. I shall be busy just before Christmas and hungover on 26th December and 1st January, so it will have to be the late-January-early-February period. I'll look forward to hearing further from you or from Mr Salwak direct.

All good wishes.

Yours ever,
Kingsley

[TLS: Dale Salwak]

TO MLLE S.M. HAIMART – 7 DECEMBER 1972

Lemmons, Hadley Common, Barnet, Herts, England

Dear Mademoiselle Haimart,

It was very kind of you to send me your article.[1] Naturally, there are some points in it on which I think I can put you right.

Those first three novels are perhaps especially hard to see clearly. They have become so encrusted with commentary and with the whole 'Angry Young Men' nonsense. You stress their social aspects less than most critics, but still (in my view) too much. When I wrote them, I had no conscious intention of making any social statement or voicing any social attitude. I was trying to tell some truths about human nature in a contemporary setting, incidentally throwing in some comments on that setting. In the phrase 'social details' which you mention in a foot-

of Salwak's father, Stanley, and when he heard that Salwak was writing a doctoral dissertation on Amis agreed to contact Amis to see if he would meet Salwak.

1. Mademoiselle Haimart, an Assistant Lecturer in English at the Université de Paris (U.E.R. Danton-Sorbonne), had written to Amis enclosing her article '*Lucky Jim* ou la tunique de Nessus', *Études anglaises* 25 (July-September 1972), pp. 367–84. This article was part of Mlle Haimart's work towards her 'Thèse de Doctorat d'État' on the writings of 'the so-called "Angry Generation"' of the 1950s, and on Amis's novels in particular.

note, the 'operative' word is 'details', and possibly 'cultural' would have been a better word than 'social'. I meant details of what people eat and drink and wear, where they live, how they do their jobs, how they use their leisure. A setting must be as accurate and interesting as possible, but it remains a setting, a background.

As regards Jim Dixon, he is to me an 'insider' throughout. His objection is not to the system as a whole, but to the particular part of it in which he finds himself. If he could find a way of doing his job properly, he would adopt it: 'well taught and sensibly taught, history could do people a hell of a lot of good . . . Things get in the way . . . Bad teaching's the main thing . . .'[2] He shows anger and hatred, but, except at points where he feels that by reasonable standards he is being treated unreasonably (Welch's equivocations over his, Jim's, chances of being re-appointed), he is laughing too. And how is he to take 'intellectualism' seriously when the only examples of it he sees are so absurd or contemptible? Finally, you are less than fair to 'nice things are nicer than nasty ones'. This is infantile, indeed tautologous, but Jim knows it is, as the word 'theory' should have warned you. However, the phrase is adult as well as infantile, aimed (by the novel rather than by the character) against a whole moral and aesthetic system, that which embraces self-realisation through suffering, nostalgie de la boue, primitivism, egotism, pessimism. I am being a little pompous here.

You are, understandably and in common with everybody else who has written on the subject, slightly inaccurate about some practical matters. *Lucky Jim* was finished late in 1952. Consequently I had time to write a large part of *That Uncertain Feeling* before *Jim* was published, and the success of the one had no effect on the composition of the other. That success, by the way, was not immediate. *Jim* got some splendid reviews, but it did not start to reach the public substantially for a year or so. Those twenty editions were a clever publisher's manoeuvre; most of the early ones were of no more than a few hundred copies. (To stop the press, insert the words 'Sixth impression July 1954' or whatever, and start the press again, cost two guineas.) I began *Take a Girl Like You* in 1955 before laying it aside, I think to its advantage, in order to write *I Like It Here*. The latter was an almost total critical failure and has never sold well, though it still does sell a little. I taught at Cambridge only

2. Dixon says this to Gore-Urquhart in Chapter 21 of *Lucky Jim* (p. 214), just before the disastrous 'Merrie England' lecture.

in 1961–63; in 1949–61 I was at the University College of Swansea.

But none of these things is of any real substance. If you know less about the three early books than I do, you know more than I did about *Take a Girl Like You* and *One Fat Englishman*. I am not being ironical; you are well aware that a good critic can expose intentions and meanings of which the novelist has had only an inkling, a vague feel.

I call you a good critic not (I hope) because you have some kind things to say, and not only because they are in the main the things I would most like to find said. Your intelligence and the vigour of your writing – I read French a little – are plain to see. Or let me put it like this: your essay on my work is not only the best I have read, it is the only one ever to have aroused in me more than a wan flicker of narcissism, and the only one I have ever bothered to reply to in any other spirit than politeness. How splendid that it takes a Frenchwoman to understand something that those British and Americans, not to speak of a fearful Belgian and an even worse Canadian, find so impenetrable! They go on and on: Karl or Kahn or somebody says, 'As a work of protest, *Lucky Jim* is a pretty feeble affair.' Agreed. As an objective documentary on English university life it has its weaknesses too.

You do not seem to have come across my novel of 1969, *The Green Man*, which tries to tackle one or two of those old 'problèmes humains'. I also draw to your attention two stories of mine, 'All the Blood within Me' (1962) in my collection, *My Enemy's Enemy*, and 'Dear Illusion' (1971) in *Penguin Modern Stories II*. As for *Girl, 20*, you must not take Ph. Toynbee's remarks on it (or on anything else) too seriously.[3] The satire, if that is the word, is in fact directed not against 'youth', but against an ageing member of the fashionably left-wing intelligentsia who indulges and flatters youth, somebody not altogether unlike Ph. Toynbee himself. The subjects of the book are ageing itself and irresponsibility.

Well: how can I end but by simply saying thank you? And that I should be delighted to hear from you again at any time?

Yours very sincerely,
Kingsley Amis

3. 'Sous le titre "Old goat, young bitch", Ph. Toynbee a publié dans l'*Observer* du 26.9.71 un article où il fait de ce roman [*Girl, 20*] une critique assez sévère. Il semble que ce soit là une nouvelle histoire de "Lolita" où la satire serait dirigée contre la jeunesse d'aujourd'hui. Toynbee la dit exagérée et peu convaincante' ('*Lucky Jim* ou la tunique de Nessus', p. 384).

Sorry, but I keep finding fresh points. That quote about Shaw and Lawrence and lying down and letting it roll over you.[4] The speaker is nowhere near being a hero or heroine, and what the speech is doing is making plausible, in retrospect, the revelation that the Secretary's wife has connived at and even aided the Secretary's activities so as to keep him happy and docile. Jim, hijacker of taxis, faker of telephone calls, public denouncer of Merrie England, letting things roll over him? Surely not.

In general, you tend to overestimate the part played in a novelist's career by planning, forethought, purpose (and, in the opposite direction, money and fame) while underestimating the role of chance, whim, laziness, excess of energy, boredom, desire to entertain oneself, wanting a change for change's sake. The novelist himself, of course, *over*estimates the role of these things.

[TLS: Recipient]

TO DALE SALWAK – 18 DECEMBER 1972

Lemmons, Hadley Common, Barnet, Hertfordshire.

Dear Mr Salwak,

Thank you for your letter. For our investigatory talk and lunch, I offer you a choice of these dates: Wednesday 24th January, Thu 25, Fri 26, Wed 31, Thu 1 Feb, Fri 2 Feb.[1] Obviously the sooner you can let me know which day is best for you, the sooner I can regard the other days as free for other appointments. – But, with Santa at our throats, you needn't rush too hard. Let me know by, say, 1st or 2nd Jan?

With all good wishes,

Yours sincerely,
Kingsley Amis

[ALS: Recipient]

4. 'C'est de ce roman [*The Egyptologists*] que l'on peut extraire la citation la plus caractéristique de l'amoralisme du héros Amisien: "Half the trouble in life comes from people pushing and shoving against things they haven't a hope in hell of altering. And half of them are only doing it because some awful man like Bernard Shaw or D. H. Lawrence says they ought to. If you can't get away from it, lie down and let it roll over you"' (quoted on p. 380 of Haimart's article).

---

1. They arranged to meet at Amis's club, the Travellers', on 24 January.

TO ANTHONY THWAITE – 4 JANUARY 1973

Lemmons, Hadley Common, Barnet, Hertfordshire.

Dear Anthony,

Just to say Welcome to your new chair[1] and we gratefully heed your call for contributions. I have no free poems at the moment (my latest, 'To Rosie', is bespoken by the King Charles Cavalier Spaniel Annual – edited presumably by Samuel Daniel).[2] But I'm working on a 5000-worder on Chesterton's fiction – part of a centenary symposium – which might interest you? (It makes minimal use of that *Man Who Was Thursday* reappraisal I did for you in the *NS*.)[3] Jane is working on a story or two and may well send one your way if (got to be honest, mate) the Yank mags won't bite.

Anyway, good luck with *Enc*, happy New Year, and, hell, if the Grocer[4] keeps at it, it may be Labour for *me* next time.

Yours ever,
Kingsley

[ALS: Recipient]

---

1. As co-editor of *Encounter* (1973–85).

2. For Rosie, a real-life King Charles cavalier spaniel, see Amis to Conquest, 9 September 1971, note 5, and to Elizabeth Jane Howard, 21 September, 1976, note 1. Samuel Daniel (1563–1619) was a court poet, translator and tragedian. 'To Rosie' was indeed published in Volume 9 of the *Cavalier King Charles Spaniel Club Yearbook* (1972), p. 4, but was not reprinted in *CP*. See Appendix D.

3. 'The Poet and the Lunatics', *New Statesman*, 26 February 1971, pp. 280–1. The longer Chesterton piece, entitled 'Four Fluent Fellows', eventually did appear in *Encounter* 41 (October 1973), pp. 94–100, and was later published in *G.K. Chesterton: A Centenary Appraisal*, ed. John Sullivan (New York: Barnes and Noble, 1974), pp. 28–39.

4. Conservative Prime Minister Edward Heath, so-called (by the satirical magazine *Private Eye*) because of his support for British entry to the Common Market.

TO DALE SALWAK – 30 JANUARY 1973

Lemmons, Hadley Common, Barnet, Hertfordshire.

My dear Dale,

Here is the *Riverside Villas* proof, and the Haimart stuff, with her covering letter and my answer – hell, why hasn't she replied?[1] Can *you* see anything off-putting in what I said?

Hope you get this in time. And that you enjoyed your trip. I certainly enjoyed our meetings, and very much look forward to more of the same when you're back this side. Good luck with the dissertation. Let me know if you find some annoying gap, anything not clear, etc. Or if you have a further question, etc.

Warmest personal regards –

Yours,
Kingsley Amis

[ALS: Recipient]

TO THE EDITOR, *DAILY TELEGRAPH* – 28 FEBRUARY 1973

SIR–One has grown used to seeing assertions that Ezra Pound is not only a great poet, but universally accepted as such, and as a rule one just suffers in silence. But when Prof. Frank Kermode compares him, at length and in detail, with Milton, and in effect judges him superior to Marvell (World of Books, Feb. 24), somebody must point out that a number of good judges – including Robert Graves, George Orwell, Geoffrey Grigson, D.J. Enright, Philip Larkin, Robert Conquest – do not share such an elevated view.

"Few would deny [Pound] had genius." No indeed; only it was a genius not for poetry (he had not even any particular talent in that direction) but for behaving sufficiently like a great poet to gull the

1. *The Riverside Villas Murder* was published later in the year; 'the Haimart stuff' was Amis's largely favourable response, with a few corrections and additions, to Mlle Haimart's article about *Lucky Jim* (see Amis to Haimart, 7 December 1972). Salwak had asked to see both the article and Amis's response to it. See also Amis to Salwak, 13 April 1973.

gullible. More than a few would subscribe to Orwell's dismissal of him as "an entirely spurious writer."[1]

With Prof. Kermode's implied assessment of Robert Lowell as fit to stand alongside Pound I for one have no quarrel.

KINGSLEY AMIS
Hadley Common, Herts.

TO PHILIP LARKIN – 29 MARCH 1973

Lemmons, Hadley Common, Barnet, Hertfordshire.

My dear Philip,

Good to hear from you. I think ole E.P. lost out fiarly fartly fairly handsomely on that correspondence.[1] So he should. Fellow's a windbag. Fellow's a windbag.

You could have got Dear Illusion for much less by buying Penguin Modern Stories ll, which has got another one by me in it.[2] But v. glad you liked D.I.

Your anthology[3] looks all right and seems to have gone down jolly well. A certain amount of piss in it, I thought, but who am I to complain, with my generous allotment? I hope you make a lot of money out of it.

---

1. Orwell calls Pound 'an entirely spurious writer' and claims 'the opinions he has tried to disseminate by means of his works are evil ones' in 'The Question of the Pound Award', *Partisan Review* 16 (May 1949), pp. 512–22, reprinted in *A Casebook on Ezra Pound*, ed. William Van O'Connor and Edward Stone (New York: Thomas Y. Crowell, 1959), pp. 54–66.

---

1. See previous letter.
2. See Larkin to Amis, 28 February 1973 (in HEHL): 'Have paid £1 *of my own munnee* for *Dear Delusion* or some such jargon and found it quite gripping ("I'll grip your – ") – how, where did it appear? Was it ever reviewed?' Larkin had bought the thirty-five-page story, 'Dear Illusion', in the 1972 Covent Garden Press limited edition; *Penguin Short Stories 11*, ed. Judith Burnley, also came out in 1972.
3. *The Oxford Book of Twentieth-Century English Verse* (1973).

Let's have lunch some time when you're in London, what?

Adrian Henri[4] bum,
Kingsley

[TLS: Bodleian]

TO PHILIP LARKIN – 9 APRIL 1973

Lemmons, Hadley Common, Barnet, Hertfordshire.

My dear Philip,

So Pablo the piss-poor paint-pusher has fallen off the hooks at last, eh?[1] Ho ho ho. Beckett next?

I meant to tell you when I wrote before who wrote the two quatrains in *Dear Illusion* beginning "I slash the formless web of hate".[2] You. Or you, worked over by me. Remember tapping them on to my typewriter some time in 1942? At least, I've always assumed it was you. Norman? No. Cornish? Hardly. Nick? Doubtful.

Stockhausen[3] bum
Kingsley

[ALS: Bodleian]

4. Adrian Henri (b.1932), poet and painter; during the 1960s known as one of the 'Liverpool Poets' (with Roger McGough and Brian Patten). These poets were unstridently anti-establishment, seeing poetry as a species of performance art, like pop music. Larkin includes one of Henri's poems in *The Oxford Book of Twentieth-Century English Verse.*

---

1. Picasso died on 8 April, aged ninety-one.
2. The two quatrains read:

I slash the formless web of hate,
I plumb the worked-out mine of love;
My wrist receives the birds that sate
Their lust engendered from above.

While rosy sunsets lurch and fade
Across the endless strife of seed,
The debt of living must be paid
To creditors who starve in need.

Larkin, in a letter of 11 April 1973 (in HEHL), comments: 'The two stanzas awake no response in me, of recognition, admiration, or anything else.' As for other possible authors: 'Norman' must be Norman Iles; 'Nick' is probably Nick Russel; and 'Cornish' could be Selby Tiptaft Cornish (1922–59), a fellow undergraduate at St John's (reading Natural Sciences, but literary enough to be a member of the Essay Society).

3. Karlheinz Stockhausen (b. 1928), avant-garde German composer.

TO JOHN BETJEMAN – 10 APRIL 1973

Lemmons, Hadley Common, Barnet, Hertfordshire.

My dear Betjeman,

On consulting my files, my secretary informs me that it is not since 1923 that I have received *two* letters from the incumbent Poet Laureate,[1] each of them giving me something of my due, within the space of ten days, and am therefore moved to break an old-established rule of mine by replying in my own hand.

Honestly, Jack, I can't think of anyone whose approval I'd rather have. And thank you for getting it *right*, seeing what I was trying to do. Am relieved as well as delighted that you liked the Alf T. selection, too. Some didn't. To such, I say what Col. Manton's old R.Q.M.S. used to say (*R. V. Murder*, top of p. 181).[2]

All gratitude. Let's drink and laugh again soon. Love from Jane and me to you and F.[3] Hugs to secretary[4] too.

Kingers

[ALS: Victoria]

---

1. Betjeman was appointed Poet Laureate on 10 October 1972. He wrote to Amis on 27 March and 5 April 1973. In the first letter he praises Amis's *Tennyson* (1973), in the Penguin *Poet to Poet* series, and *The Riverside Villas Murder* (1973); in the second he confines his praise to the novel alone. The first letter, which discusses Tennyson's current reputation, comparing it to that of supposedly more 'intelligent' poets such as John Donne, can be seen at the University of Victoria, British Columbia, Special Collections; the second is printed in Lycett Green, ed., *Betjeman: Letters*, 2 vols (London: Methuen, 1995), vol. 2, p. 464. Betjeman's secretary, Susan Allison, later worked for Amis as well, in both cases part-time (see Amis to Elizabeth Jane Howard, 15, 16, 17 September 1976, note 4).

2. See Colonel R.P.W. Manton, SSO, MC, the detective in *The Riverside Villas Murder*, to Detective-Constable Barrett of the County CID: 'I remember the R.Q.M.S. in my old battalion had a most expressive phrase he always brought out in situations of this general kind. When it was a matter of, as it might be, incurring the disapproval of people who had no way of bringing their disapproval to bear. Fuck 'em, he used to say. Very telling, don't you think? All these years it's stuck in my mind' (pp. 180–1).

3. 'F' is 'Feeble', Betjeman's nickname for Lady Elizabeth Cavendish, called so, he told his daughter Candida Lycett Green, 'because she was so willowy, he thought she might fall over' (*Betjeman: Letters*, vol. 2, p. 107). For Lady Elizabeth Cavendish see Amis to Betjeman, 3 June 1971, note 4.

4. See Betjeman to Amis, 27 March 1973 (in University of Victoria, British Columbia): 'I am typing this because my secretary thinks you are very attractive and won't mind typing this to you on my behalf.'

TO DALE SALWAK – 13 APRIL 1973

Lemmons, Hadley Common, Barnet, Herts

Dear Dale,

Please forgive delay, due to twin pressures of work and laziness. I hereby authorise you to publish in *Contemporary Literature* the text, in full or in part, of your recent interview with me.[1] End of legal jargon.

I enclose the opening of my still-untitled current work of fiction.[2] That sounds like jargon too, but in fact I still don't know whether it's going to be a novel or a short novel or a novella of greater or lesser length or what. 120–150 pages is my guess.[3] I've done 70, but I'm not sending you any more because 1) it would cost a lot and 2) the intervening part will need extra heavy revision. The opening will of course have to be tidied up too, but not so radically. For your information, there are no more main characters than the five oldsters you meet here; Trevor and Melanie are minor. The setting remains in and around Tuppeny-hapenny Cottage throughout. By the end, all five are dead through a series of mishaps. I must have told you some of this in chat, so take me as confirming it now. One thing the book isn't going to be is a serious, in-depth etc. study of old age. It's about five particular people who wouldn't be behaving as they do if they weren't old. At least, that's what I say now. (We talked about the way the writer's intentions dawn on him as he goes along.)

The Riverside Villas Murder has had a good-to-very-good Press here. The reviewers contradicted one another, naturally. Some said the '30s setting was done not so well; more (good!) said it was just right. One first-class detective writer, John Dickson Carr, said the detective plotting was very professional; one top-of-the-second class such writer (good!) said it wasn't. Ho hum.

If I can be of any further help, don't hesitate to let me know; but you're well enough acquainted with me by now to realise that such a request, unless signed in blood, may not bring an instantaneous

---

1. See Amis to Salwak, 30 January 1973, note 1. The interview appeared in *Contemporary Literature* 16 (Winter 1975), pp. 1–18.
2. *Ending Up* (1974).
3. The finished book is 176 pages long in the Penguin edition, in a large typeface.

response. I hope all goes well for you, in your Amis project and in general.

With warmest good wishes,

Yours sincerely,
Kingsley Amis

That Frenchwoman[4] is still silent. Perhaps she's heard somewhere how much I dislike her country and its inhabitants.

[TLS: Recipient]

TO ANTHONY THWAITE – 26 MAY 1973

Lemmons, Hadley Common, Barnet, Hertfordshire.

Dear Anthony,

You're right, curse you. Though I had 't-*gram*' from a posh London coin-dealer (and it also means a four-sided figure, which misled me into thinking, never having seen one, that it was some sort of rhomboid shape).[1]

But I'm not wrong. It was that fool McGrath,[2] whom I always suspected of ignorance as well as pomposity, etc. So you've presented me with a jolly subtle bit of characterisation, and also forearmed me against any hostile shag who may take me up on the point. "Excuse me, Mr A, but I would just like to ask you what a tetragram is." – "Ah. Do you know" – smiling and crinkling eyes – "you're the *very first* person [or perhaps, only the second person] to have spotted that? It's *so* nice to feel *somebody* reads one with due care."

Glad you enjoyed the *RVM*. And hope you had a good jaunt to

4. Mlle Haimart; see Amis to Salwak, 30 January 1973, note 1.

---

1. Thwaite had spotted a mistake in *The Riverside Villas Murder*, in Chapter 2 of which a mysterious break-in at the local museum is reported. Though £60 worth of rare coins were stolen, the thieves missed the most valuable item in the collection: 'the tetragram of Syracuse' (p. 38). A 'tetragram', though, is a type of word (with four letters), not a shape or form (with four sides); Amis should have called the coin 'the tetradrachm of Syracuse'.

2. A character in *The Riverside Villas Murder*; he is the Librarian (the museum occupied a room in the rear of the local public library) who explains about the theft and the 'tetragram'.

Oxford. I abstain, feeling it wouldn't be enough of a disaster if Spender gets in to justify voting for Wain.[3] Because if W. gets it, he won't be amazed, overjoyed, grateful, etc. Oh no: he'll *think it's his due*, do you see, even after writing Major Eatherly:[4] Ah well. Hope to see you soon.

Cheers Kingsley

[ALS: Recipient]

TO MR GUNSTON – 7 JULY 1973

Lemmons, Hadley Common, Barnet, Herts

Dear Mr Gunston,[1]

You don't mention any fee, nor, clearly, are you a charity, but I'll do as you ask just the same; as you no doubt calculated, the subject attracts me. So:

1. Dislikeable qualities in men as opposed to women: Excessive good looks, ability to cap my anecdotes, immoderate success with women, ability to work hard for long periods, earning more money than I do, winning prizes I have unsuccessfully competed for, courage, humility, tolerance, extensive knowledge, and above all, rare though it may be, the ability to write better than I do.

2. More seriously – you yourself may not need to be told that section 1 is what they call tongue-in-cheek, but most of your readers will, I can assure you – what I dislike about other men is exactly what I dislike about women, though I admit to a prejudice in favour of women. I dislike men *and* women when they are cold-hearted (a reserved *manner*

3. John Wain defeated Stephen Spender in the election for Professor of Poetry at Oxford University in 1973; he remained in the position for the five-year term. On the back of the envelope containing this letter Amis has written: 'And he *got it! Aargh!*'

4. A reference to Wain's long poem 'A Song about Major Eatherley', about a pilot involved in dropping the atom bomb, in *Weep Before God* (London: Macmillan, 1961), pp. 40–5.

1. The identity of Mr Gunston is untraced. This is one of fifty letters purchased by the Huntington Library in October 1999 from the London bookseller Rick Gekoski. They were amassed by an anonymous European collector over the past twenty years, and neither he nor Gekoski was able to identify their recipients. See also Amis to W. Godward, 5 March 1975, and Amis to Mr Vogel, 4 September 1986.

is okay), unpleasant to those who can't hit back (waiters etc.), unable to allow others to finish a sentence, stingy, disinclined to listen to reason and fact, bad hosts, bad guests, affected, racialist, intolerant of homosexuality, anti-British, members of the New Left, *passively* boring (an active bore is to be avoided, but he/she earns pity, not dislike; what I can't stand is the sort that sits there looking at you and waiting for you to say something he/she will despise you for).

3. One specifically masculine dislikeable quality occurs to me: being nasty to a woman. Women can be nasty to a man all right, but a man is better equipped, with greater physical strength, greater earning capacity, not being subject to menstruation, etc., etc.

The s.a.e. is appreciated. Good luck.

Yours sincerely,
Kingsley Amis

[TLS: HEHL]

TO ELIZABETH JANE HOWARD – 13 AUGUST 1973

Lemmons, Hadley Common, Barnet, Hertfordshire.

Got your dear letter, little one, also ridiculous card. V. heartening letter. We'll both have to work at things. I'll certainly try.

Spent weekend with Stuart and Val,[1] where I meant to write this but hadn't time among the drinking. S. in better form than I've seen him since he got ill.

Scoundrelly Mart[2] has sold his novel to the Yanks for $3,000 advance.

1. Friends in Haverhill, Essex; Stuart Daniel (1912–77), a barrister, QC (1961) and amateur classicist; Valerie Daniel, a painter. Jane Howard and Valerie had been friends before Valerie met Stuart.

2. A family joke; see also 'savage little Mart', in Amis to Elizabeth Jane Howard, 4 March 1975. The novel was *The Rachel Papers* (1973).

Pretty good, eh? Pub of year[3] is over – gd fun. Am off to Hearnes[4] soon for dinner. Hope you get this. I'll see you in a week. All well here. Still missing you and wondering how you are.

Love from
old Bun

[ALS: HEHL]

TO EDWIN TARLING – 10 OCTOBER 1973

Lemmons, Hadley Common, Barnet, Hertfordshire.

Dear Mr. Tarling,

Many thanks for sending me the copies of 'Wave', which I am reading with interest.[1]

As somebody who, in a good year, can probably manage two poems I am afraid I have nothing by me at the moment. But when I have I will certainly bear you and 'Wave' in mind.

Yours sincerely,
Kingsley Amis

[TLS: BJLH]

3. A competition run by the *Evening Standard* newspaper in London. Amis was one of the judges.

4. John and Mary Hearne, friends from Jamaica, were visiting London at the time. John Hearne (b.1926), a West Indian novelist who taught at Kingston University in Jamaica, won the John Llewelyn Rhys Memorial Prize in 1956 for *Voices Under the Window*. After staying with Bobby and Dolly Burns in 1966, Amis and Jane Howard spent a night with the Hearnes in their house in the Blue Mountains outside Kingston.

---

1. Tarling (b.1938) was a friend of Larkin's from Hull. In addition to being a painter and jazz enthusiast he ran the Sonus Press and was founding editor and publisher of the short-lived poetry magazine *Wave*, which published Larkin's poem 'How' in Autumn 1970 (reprinted in *LCP*, p. 176).

TO ANTHONY POWELL – 5 NOVEMBER 1973

Lemmons, Hadley Common, Barnet, Hertfordshire

The Aussie rendezvous is the Braganza, 56 Frith Street, Friday the 9th, 1.0 in the bar that immediately confronts you on the ground floor. Besides you, me and Martin Amis there'll be Peter Porter (the one with glasses), and Clive James (the one recognisable as an Antipodean at 100ft.)[1] Love to V.

Cheers K.

[ALS: Recipient]

TO PHILIP LARKIN – 29 JANUARY 1974

Lemmons, Hadley Common, Barnet, Hertfordshire.

Dear Philip,

I thought you might enjoy the encl.[1] But is it all right? Is it publishable, or is it too trivial, too long for its point, etc? Would welcome your advice, also on any possible changes.

How are you getting on? Nothing's happened here so far, except

1. Peter Porter (b. 1929), Australian poet and literary journalist (resident in England since 1951); Clive James (b. 1939), writer, broadcaster and critic; television reviewer for the *Observer* (1972–82).

1. The poem 'Crisis Song', published *New Statesman*, 22 February 1974, p. 87; reprinted *CP*, p. 137. Larkin approved, but found the ending 'rather a surprise' (Larkin to Amis, 30 January 1974, in HEHL); Amis made no changes. See also Larkin to Conquest, 1 February 1974, in *LL*, p. 501: 'Kingsley sent a poem the other day – Crisis poem. Expect you've seen it. Good, I thought, though suffering a little from divided effect, if not divided aims.'

for a murder up the road, and it looks as if that would have happened anyway. But I do miss the post-10.30 telly.[2]

Cash on the table bum,
Kingsley

[ALS: Bodleian]

TO MICHAEL SHARP – 6 FEBRUARY 1974

Lemmons, Hadley Common, Barnet, Hertfordshire.

Dear Mr. Sharp,

Although I never knew Drummond Allison very well, we must have met on a couple of dozen occasions in 1941–42.[1] I am surprised that people thought him arty or affected; he struck me as a warm, friendly person and we always got on well together. I remember him best in the days when we both sang in the Labour Club Choir, standing side by side among the tenors. He evidently read music quite well, which was a help to me, and had about the loudest voice I have ever heard. I remember his clothes as rather curious, a blend of the homespun and the arty: as it might be, a black shirt, yellow tie, and rough tweedy sports coat.

I hope you may find something of value in these few recollections.

With all good wishes,

Yours sincerely,
Kingsley Amis

[ALS: Recipient]

2. The 1973–74 OPEC oil crisis and the consequent energy shortage led to television transmissions being closed down at 10.30 p.m. each evening.

1. Amis was responding to Sharp's request for information about Drummond Allison (1921–43), a contemporary at Oxford (at Queen's College) whose poems appeared in *Eight Oxford Poets* (1941), edited by Michael Meyer and Sidney Keyes. Allison was killed in action in Italy in December 1943, and after his death a collection of his poems, *The Yellow Night*, was published in 1944; his poems also appeared in *Poetry from Oxford in Wartime* (1945), edited by William Bell. Sharp's edition of *The Poems of Drummond Allison* appeared in 1978, from the Whiteknights Press, University of Reading. Sharp is a Professor of English at the University of Puerto Rico.

TO THE EDITOR, *THE TIMES* – 14 FEBRUARY 1974

Sir, Of course the Germans are cross that our television has been showing something of their behaviour in World War II.[1] Any nation would prefer to see the infamies of its past (especially its recent past) forgotten or at least not mentioned. I have heard of no objections from Italians, perhaps because they feel that their particular bit of infamy was sufficiently redeemed when some of them started fighting their former allies.

Programmes such as those in question do our country a valuable service. They help to inform the young, and remind the less young, what kind of people we shall, in a few years' time, find ourselves merged with in full political union. The series has left something to be desired here: not enough stress was laid on the contribution of French Communist and Right-wing subversives to the defeat of 1940, and nothing whatever, I think, was said of the activities of the Dutch and Belgian Nazi parties, though I have heard on good authority that these operated on too small a scale to constitute national infamy.

Yours faithfully,

KINGSLEY AMIS
Lemmons, Hadley Common, Barnet, Hertfordshire

1. Amis refers to a correspondence in *The Times* initiated by a Herr Farber, in a letter of 1 February 1974. Herr Farber objected to the BBC *Colditz* series (1972–73), about the German prisoner of war camp, and the screening of the film *49th Parallel* (1940), directed by Michael Powell. Later correspondents mentioned the ITV documentary series *The World at War* (1975) and the long-running BBC comedy series *Dad's Army* (1968–77), about a platoon of over-age Home Guard volunteers in a small south-coast town in Britain.

TO JACK GOHN – 20 FEBRUARY 1974

Lemmons, Hadley Common, Barnet, Hertfordshire.

Dear Mr Gohn,

Well yes, in principle.[1] I take it you mean to come to London? I liked Baltimore when I was there in 1958, but I have no plans to revisit it. And when? I am usually here, but not always.

I wouldn't dream of taking money off you even if you had some – I might even buy you a drink.

Yours sincerely
Kingsley Amis

[ALS: Recipient]

TO JON STALLWORTHY – 26 MARCH 1974

Lemmons, Hadley Common, Barnet, Hertfordshire.

Dear Jon,

I was quite bowled over by your suggestion:[1] an honour to be asked. And I accept in principle – i.e. subject to existing commitments being discharged, etc, which means among other things that I couldn't start work until 1975.

---

1. For Gohn, a graduate student in English at Johns Hopkins University in Baltimore, Maryland, see Notes on Recipients. He had written to ask if he could interview Amis in connection with a doctoral dissertation on Amis's fiction: 'I think it's preposterous to write about a living author without hearing what he has to say for himself, intentional fallacy or no. It is a simple way of protecting oneself from absurdity, among other things' (Gohn to Amis, 1 February 1974).

---

1. Jon Stallworthy (b. 1935), poet, critic, biographer, academic, publisher; at the time an editor at Oxford University Press (where he worked from 1959–77); later Professor of English, Cornell University, Ithaca, New York (1977–86), then Reader (1986–92) and Professor of English (1992–), Oxford University, and Fellow, Wolfson College, Oxford (1986–). Stallworthy had suggested that Amis edit *The New Oxford Book of Light Verse.*

That lunch sounds fine. If you'd give me a ring here, we could fix it up.

All the best.

Yours,
Kingsley

[ALS: OUP]

TO THE EDITOR, *DAILY TELEGRAPH* – 3 APRIL 1974

SIR – Mr Paul Johnson (article, March 30) has misunderstood part of my views on the political distribution of corrupters and preservers of our language. Or could it possibly be that I expressed myself badly?

Anyhow, I never meant to say that the writing of good prose is in the least degree a prerogative of the Right (nor do I wish it were). Such a view is refuted by countless examples near to hand, among them the late Francis Hope and, to return the compliment, Mr Johnson himself.[1]

My intended target was the educational theories of the Left, which have done much to undermine literacy and thereby to render users of English more vulnerable to the admittedly damaging assaults of Madison Avenue.

It is true that once, before I came to my senses, I was a Socialist, but I was never any kind of "hammer of academic tradition." Even my character Lucky Jim was no opponent of that system, only of some of its manifestations in his neighbourhood. He wanted reform, not replacement, thus showing himself (whatever he might have said at the time) a true conservative.

KINGSLEY AMIS
Hadley Common, Herts.

---

1. Paul Johnson's 'Saturday Column', entitled 'Paul Johnson on the Writing of Good Prose', begins: 'Kingsley Amis has recently put forward the interesting theory that the corruption of the English language is to be associated with the Left.' In the course of rebutting this theory Johnson argues that 'changes in a writer's political opinions have no bearing on his capacity to express them in prose. And, oddly enough, Kingsley Amis himself illustrates this last point. His first novel, *Lucky Jim*, is an admirable example of how stylistic innovation can be combined with sound usage in the writing of English. Yet at the time it was written, Mr Amis was a socialist and a hammer of academic tradition.'

TO LIZ CALDER – 1 MAY 1974

Lemmons, Hadley Common, Barnet, Hertfordshire.

Dear Liz,

Well, if Heron Books won't budge, I suppose we'd better accept their offer for *Lucky Jim*: after all, even chicken-feed has some nutritional value.[1]

Yours ever,
Kingsley

[TLS: Gollancz]

TO PHILIP LARKIN – 28 JUNE 1974

Lemmons, Hadley Common, Barnet, Hertfordshire.

My dear Philip,

I was *very* glad to learn that you have at last decided to "put down roots" and acquire a home of your own.[1] Best thing in the world. Sound financial thinking, too. Put your money into bricks and mortarghgh

Sniping I was indeed, at DD and JBW both ("I'll swing on both your . . ."), also TG.[2] Hope they got it and *felt hurt.*

You'll soon be pestered (through the post only) by someone called Mary Johnsen – yes, that's right. Yank. She wrote to me asking for a copy of my very beautiful poem about my daughter. I wrote saying she must mean PAL's v. beautiful poem, hoping to abash her somewhat.

---

1. Heron Books wanted to include *Lucky Jim* in a series of twenty-five 'Immortal Masters', and was offering an advance of £150 plus a royalty of five pence per copy sold, which Liz Calder (b. 1938), at the time Publicity Manager at Gollancz, thought 'might well be regarded as chicken feed' (11 August 1974 to Amis). Calder later went on to become Editorial Director of Gollancz (1975–78) and Jonathan Cape (1979–86), and then Publishing Director, Bloomsbury Publishing (1986–).

---

1. Earlier in the month Larkin had moved into a house at 105 Newland Park, Hull, the first he had ever owned.

2. In his review of Larkin's *High Windows*, in *Observer*, 2 June 1974, p. 32; 'DD' is Donald Davie, 'JBW' is John Wain, 'TG' is Thom Gunn.

Not a bloody bit of it. Now she writes again for your address. I've given it to her. I should think an inscribed first edition, airmail express, would satisfy her.

Well, old lad, thanks again for *HW*. Bloody good stuff. Hope you make a few quid out of it. As always, give me a buzz whenever you're around, at liberty, etc.

Amis's world lacks among other things the inner dimension of bum,

Kingsley

What does he *mean*? (Bayley)[3] Throughout. Eh? Bruce getting religion? Eh? Re old Bob,[4] entre nous, I think he bloody well asked for it. Not that I don't feel rather sorry for him too. Tell you when I see you.

[ALS: Bodleian]

TO PHILIP LARKIN – 31 JULY 1974

Lemmons, Hadley Common, Barnet, Hertfordshire.

Dear Philip,

As I'm sure you know I hardly ever write a poem, and at the moment I'm afraid I have none in hand. So rather than bet on my coming up with one in the next few weeks, I'd better send you a regretful refusal now.[1]

Present conditions bum,
Kingsley

[TLS: BJLH]

3. John Bayley reviewed *High Windows* in the *TLS*, 21 June 1974, pp. 653–5. Bayley was Warton Professor of English Literature, and Fellow of St Catherine's College, Oxford (1974–92); he was married to the novelist and philosopher Iris Murdoch from 1956 until her death in 1998.

4. Conquest; what he 'bloody well asked for' is unrecoverable.

---

1. Larkin had requested a poem for the 1974 Poetry Book Society Christmas Supplement.

TO THE EDITOR; *DAILY TELEGRAPH* – 9 SEPTEMBER 1974

SIR–It is kind of Mr Richard Last to note my forthcoming contribution to the BBC-1 series, "Softly, Softly"[1] (Sept. 3), but the occasion will not mark my *début* as a television drama writer. That momentous event took place in 1964.[2] I am putting the fact on record out of the purest greed: the longer you're known to have been in, the more they're likely to pay you next time – if any.

KINGSLEY AMIS
Barnet, Herts

TO JACK GOHN – 10 OCTOBER 1974

Lemmons, Hadley Common, Barnet, Herts, England

Dear Jack,

Good. Some things I hadn't seen, no distortions as far as I can tell, and very well written, clear and funny. My favourite remark: p. 21, first sentence after the quote.[1] Here is a complete list of factual slips, etc.: nothing that affects your argument.[2]

---

1. A popular series about a Midlands police force; it ran from 1966 to 1976.
2. With *A Question about Hell* (see Amis to Rukeyser, 26 August 1963, note 3).

---

1. The sentence Amis singles out is a comment on a passage in Amis's essay 'City Ways', in *What Became of Jane Austen*? (pp. 135–42), in which he reminisces about his teachers Mr Waller and Mr Ashley, and his earliest literary efforts, including a poem in blank verse on the miracle of St Sophia (set for Amis's class by Mr Ashley, who called it 'the best') and a 300-word short story called 'The Sacred Rhino of Uganda', which came out in the school magazine and was Amis's first published work of fiction. The passage concludes: 'With this the initial, experimental passage of my writing came to an end' (p. 136). 'It would appear, then,' comments Gohn, in the sentence Amis praises, 'that both Mr Waller and Mr Ashley made positive contributions to young Amis's sensibility, Ashley (in the St Sophia poem) giving him a taste, especially suitable in the young, for poetic sublimities, and Waller (in 'The Sacred Rhino') contributing a taste, also especially suitable in the young, for the sensational.' Gohn calls Amis's comment on this sentence 'far more generous than mine would be today' (personal communication, 8 June 1999).

2. Amis here offers almost two pages of corrections and additions, mostly factual and biographical. Two are worth preserving:

That's it. 'Organization, syntax and general morality' seem fine to me. Good luck with the remainder, which I greatly look forward to seeing. Now I must rush out and vote: Conservative, alas. It would be a pity to find one had missed the last free election.[3]

Cheers
Kingsley

[TLS: Recipient]

TO DALE SALWAK – 17 OCTOBER 1974

Lemmons, Hadley Common, Barnet, Hertfordshire.

Dear Dale,

Please forgive my remissness in not writing to you long ago. I thought your dissertation was very full and very fair, with an excellent sense of relevance and no wasted words. I can detect no substantial errors of fact, nor any material omissions. If I were you, I shouldn't worry about the John Summers book.[1] [. . .]

p.16, Redbrick. This is right, but 'new, state-supported' isn't. Very hard for non-Britishers. The hierarchy goes:

1. Oxford and Cambridge, plus the four Scotch universities founded in the 15th and 16th centuries, plus Trinity College, Dublin.

2. Redbrick, or provincial universities and colleges, e.g. Manchester, Durham, London (yes). Founded between mid-19th century and World War II, plus the first post-war foundation, Keele. (Swansea was 1920.)

3. The 'new' universities, entirely state-supported, e.g. Sussex, Leeds, Warwick. (The 'entirely' signals the fact that all our universities, including grade 1, get some, often much, public cash.)

p. 45 [. . .] Renaissance Welsh drama. Rather, specifically English Elizabethan or Jacobean drama, which is full of comic Welshmen (and Scotchmen and Irishmen) with stock attributes, e.g. calling everybody 'cousin', leeks, saying 'her' instead of practically any pronoun, claiming distinguished parentage, and the 'Cot's plutter' routine – God's blood and her [i.e. his] nails.

3. On 10 October 1974, in the second general election of that year, the Labour government of Harold Wilson was returned to power with an overall majority of three seats.

---

1. John Summers, *The Rag Parade* (1972), a novel about four graduates of a Welsh university. For Summers, see Amis to the editor, *Spectator*, 6 March 1971, note 1.

I hope all goes well with you and I remember with great pleasure our meetings in London.

Yours sincerely,
Kingsley Amis

[TLS: Recipient]

TO MRS J.M. PATTERSON – 19 NOVEMBER 1974

Lemmons, Hadley Common, Barnet, Hertfordshire.

My dear Secretary,[1]

I hereby resign my Fellowship of the Royal Society of Literature, and request that you remove my name from its Roll of Members at the next opportunity. My wife has asked me to ask you if you would be kind enough to do the same in her case.

We both feel that to be invited to a number of lectures neither of us wish to attend and to see the letters FRSL after our respective names in correspondence from you, would be a very small return on a subscription even more modest than the one you exact.[2]

Yours sincerely,
Kingsley Amis

[TLS: Royal Society of Literature]

---

1. Mrs J.M. (Mollie) Patterson was Secretary of the Royal Society of Literature from 1951 to 1978.
2. Amis was elected FRSL in 1971, when the annual subscription rate was £3.15.

TO JACK GOHN – 10 DECEMBER 1974, 5 JANUARY 1975

Lemmons, Hadley Common, Barnet, Hertfordshire.

Dear Jack,

(Note the new notepaper.) *Re*, as you say, thesis,[1] I feel it lies in my path to say that the degree in question is normally awarded if the candidate is seen to have done a reasonable amount of work. I had. But one can become the helpless victim of higher-level academic differences. *Satis sufficit*, old man, which is Iroquois for that's as much as I'm going to tell you for now. More when your dissertation is safely finished.

Oh, God: those bibliographical queries. I can give you the year and the place of publication, I think –[2]

Dead Cat – Observer, 1974
Festival Notebook – Poetry Nation, 1974
Kipling at Bateman's } Poem of the Month, a broadsheet
Wasted } club periodical, 1973

Memory }
Nicely } London Magazine, 1971
Reasons }

Ode to Me – Observer, 1972 (you ought to have got the year from the first line)[3]
Words – Outposts, 1974
Rosie Photostat herewith.[4] (She sends licks & yaps.)

5th January 1975[5]

I had to drop EVERYTHING to get Kipling[6] finished. Have just done

1. That is, Amis's failed Oxford B.Litt. thesis, for which see Amis to English Faculty Board, [March 1949] and 2 May 1949.

2. Of the poems listed below, only 'Festival Notebook', 'Wasted', 'Nicely', 'Reasons' and 'Ode to Me' appear in *CP*.

3. It reads: 'Fifty today, old lad?'

4. 'To Rosie', for which see Amis to Conquest, 9 September 1971, note 5; to Thwaite, 4 January 1973, note 2; and to Elizabeth Jane Howard, 21 September 1976, note 1.

5. This addendum to the letter is typed.

6. *Rudyard Kipling and his World* (1975).

so and he gets delivered tomorrow. Your BBC thing was settled by telephone a couple of weeks ago and you should hear from them any moment. I enclose a thing for Texas.[7] Thought of a new definition of SF – it's about what hasn't happened yet. Keep at it.

Cheers
K

[ALS, TLS: Recipient]

TO SIMON CURTIS – 7 JANUARY 1975

Lemmons, Hadley Common, Barnet, Hertfordshire.

Dear Mr Curtis,

Your book will be going to press soon.[1] Before it does, Reg D-P has deputed me (as one who knows about these things) to settle a few points with you.

The first concerns the number of poems and thus which poems. There will be 48 pages in all (forgive me if you know some of this already), made up of 8 title-dedication-etc., 34 of poems from 'Stable' via 'Credences of a May Morning' to 'Sociologist Logic in Vienna', and 6 of 'optional poems'. You'll probably want to pick these yourself. If so, do. If not, my choice would be 'In the Catalogue', 'Dove Holes', 'Beyond the Derelict Station', 'Manchester, England England', 'Markyate' and 'Satie, at the end of Term'.[2] Up to you. But, either way, I

7. Gohn needed permission from Amis to photocopy material from the BBC and the Harry Ransom Humanities Research Center at the University of Texas.

1. *On the Abthorpe Road* (London: Davis-Poynter, 1975). Curtis had studied with Donald Davie at Essex University and wrote poems much influenced by him, as also by Amis and Larkin. In 1974 he sent Amis a copy of a privately printed pamphlet of his poems, *Something for Nothing* (1973), and Amis wrote back a complimentary letter (now mislaid) in which he offered to arrange publication for a second volume, with Davis-Poynter Ltd, a small press founded in 1970 by Reg Davis-Poynter (b. 1924), and sold to William Collins Ltd in the late 1980s. Amis sat on the board of Davis-Poynter (along with John Boulting and the future Chancellor of the Exchequer Nigel Lawson), but rarely played as active an editorial role for the firm as he did in this case. Curtis met him for the first time in 1975 at the book's launch in London.

2. Curtis printed all these poems except 'Dove Holes', which subsequently appeared in *Sports Extra: New and Selected Poems* (1988).

expect you'll want to shuffle the optionals in among the others so as not to have a string of them at the end. But if you don't, don't.

Second point, or series of points: punctuation. The girl who has edited your typescript is nice enough, but she is trendy. In particular, she hates hyphens, thinking they don't 'look right'.[3] I have been asked to ask you to look at various lines, ponder, and either change the text or leave it as it is, i.e. you are to be the final judge but they want you to consider these points so that, in effect, if some sod of a reviewer refers to Mr C's eccentric or misleading or illiterate punctuation, D-P wants to be sure you can't say he didn't warn you. Here are the points [. . .]

You must be dying to know what * means (except in the bit about The Saints). Well, * means 'Since it doesn't make much odds one way or the other, I may as well do as she suggests here, so as to show I'm a reasonable chap who sticks to his guns only when he feels he has to.' But, of course, you're perfectly free to ignore * and stick to all your guns. But I think she is right and your text is wrong in the following places: Parker, 7 Lady, 11; Cab-Rank, 13, 17, 18, 21, 24; Credences, 4, 16; Antique, 1; Town, 28.

Reply to me, but remember I shall be passing your letter on, so if, as would be very reasonable, you want to say, say, 'Who the hell is this interfering slag?', say it on a separate bit of paper.

Good luck. I still like your poems, even after writing this letter.[4]

Yours sincerely,
Kingsley Amis

[TLS: Recipient]

3. Amis devotes several pages to the hyphen in *The King's English*, deftly generalising that 'no hard-and-fast rule can be devised that lays down when a two-word phrase is to be hyphenated and when the two words are to be run into one, though there will be a rough consensus that, for example, *book-plate* and *bookseller* are each properly set out and that *bookplate* and *book-seller* might seem respectively new-fangled and fussy' (pp. 103–4).

4. Amis adds in pen in the top left corner of the first page: 'I think you'll be pleased at the look of the poems. They're arranged so that none of the lines run on or whatever it's called – e.g. you *don't* get

To be or not to be, that is the

question.'

TO THE EDITOR, *DAILY TELEGRAPH* – 8 JANUARY 1975

SIR – To clear up Mr Paul Johnson's puzzlement (article, Jan. 4) the reason Mr Wedgwood Benn[1] is so hated and feared is simply that he looks and sounds as if he is off his head (which I, for one, am sure he is not), that he talks and acts is if he is intent on personal power (which I am sure he is), and that the combination appears dangerous.

KINGSLEY AMIS
Hadley Common, Herts.

TO BRIAN ALDISS – 4 FEBRUARY 1975

Lemmons, Hadley Common, Barnet, Hertfordshire.

Dear Brian,

I have your letter asking me to do some work for nothing; but one's used to that, hey? Perhaps the following will do as a tribute to the old forfatter:[1]

There aren't enough people like Harry Harrison in science fiction, or anywhere else for that matter. He seems to follow Kipling's sound maxim for a writer, 'When you find you can do something, do something you can't.'[2] Harry will do you a comic space saga, a chilling mystery on an alien planet, an ingenious and inventive alternate world, and one of the grimmest and horribly plausible near-future nightmares

---

1. Anthony Wedgwood Benn (b. 1925), Labour politician and Minister (disclaimed title of Viscount Stansgate, 1963).

---

1. The science fiction writer Harry Harrison was to serve on the jury of the Trieste Film Festival in July 1975, and Aldiss had asked Amis to provide several paragraphs praising him (for use by the conference's publicists, the 'con shags').

2. The exact quotation, from an account of Kipling's literary development in Chapter 7 of his posthumously published autobiography *Something of Myself* (1936), reads: 'As soon as you find you can do anything, do something you can't' (see Thomas Pinney, ed., *Rudyard Kipling: Something of Myself and Other Autobiographical Writings* (Cambridge: Cambridge University Press, 1991), p. 111).

I have ever read: *Make Room! Make Room!*[3] One characteristic does run through all his very varied work: energy. He's apparently incapable of writing a dull sentence.

It comes as a surprise to meet this tall, lean, shambling character, with his mop of red hair, tragic countenance and lazy Texan drawl – when indeed he can find anything to say. No doubt he needs to husband his resources for his work, which must also be the reason for his fanatical teetotalism.

Tell the con shags they can leave out the second para if they feel people won't get it.

Harry *would* say my next effort[4] is to be called *Popeworld*. Haven't got a title yet; haven't got a line on paper, come to that. All these testimonials for forfatters keep getting in the way.

Hearty cheers,
Kingsley

[TLS: Bodleian]

TO THE EDITOR, *THE TIMES* – 26 FEBRUARY 1975

Sir, Mr. Raymond Fletcher[1] (February 26) seriously misrepresents me. I have never written that Mr. Wedgwood Benn has gone off his head. What I said was that he looks and sounds as if he is off his head.[2] I feel sure he is not; but, as one without training as an alienist, I offer this view with due humility.

Yours faithfully,
KINGSLEY AMIS,
Lemmons, Hadley Common, Barnet.

3. *Make Room! Make Room!* (1966), probably Harrison's best-known novel, was turned into the motion picture *Soylent Green* (1973).

4. *The Alteration* (1976).

---

1. Raymond Fletcher (1921–91), Labour MP for Ilkeston (1964–83); Vice President, Assembly of Council of Europe (1974–76); journalist (former columnist for *The Times*).

2. See Amis to the editor, *Daily Telegraph*, 8 January 1975.

TO ELIZABETH JANE HOWARD – 4 MARCH 1975

Lemmons, Hadley Common, Barnet, Hertfordshire.

Hiya Wog!

Hope all goes on going well.[1] I gave you most of the news on the phone, but may have forgotten to say that the Durhams[2] are bringing *three chickens* with them on Friday, and Nita says she'll cook them, all at once or one by one I don't know. But we should be able to survive.

It's 2.30 and I'm busy abolishing the afternoon: no lunch yet. When it comes it'll be soup and yoghourt to aid my own slimming campaign. While you've been luxuriating at Shrublands I've taken off about 3 lbs with no fuss at all.

Rob is here lunching with Mum,[3] who seems in fair condition. Then – i.e. when he's gone – solitude for me for the rest of the day, enlivened (conceivably) by Chas Chaplin in The Great Dictator. I hear the traitorous little bastard got his knighthood today.

Am about to write a rude letter to the Times crapping on Antonia Fraser and Michael Holroyd for illiteracy.[4] Should be in the paper on Thursday. Order your copy NOW.

Savage little Mart[5] rang a few minutes ago to say he's coming up tomorrow night. Bob [Conquest] was due then too, but now says he *might* have to go out to lunch on Thursday and so *might* not come.

---

1. At Shrublands, the Surrey health spa Miss Howard had gone to for the week.

2. James Durham (b. 1927), Australian psychiatrist, Director of Psychiatry, St Vincent's Hospital, Sydney (1976–91), now in private practice; one of Amis's 'seven great chums' (see Amis to Conquest, [c. November 1990]; also *Memoirs*, p. 309, where Durham is called 'the only sane and sensible psychiatrist I have ever met'). Durham was introduced to Amis in the late 1960s or early 1970s by their mutual friend, the literary agent Pat Kavanagh; Durham's wife, Nita, is a radiologist. In a note on one of his conversations with Amis (in HEHL), Jacobs says Amis told him Durham was a model for the benevolent Dr Nash in *Stanley and the Women*.

3. 'Rob' is Robin Howard (b. 1925), Jane Howard's younger brother; 'Mum' is their mother, Katherine (Kit) Howard, who came to stay at Lemmons shortly after the move from Maida Vale in 1968, and lived there until her death in 1975, at the age of eighty.

4. The letter was never published, and no copy survives. Lady Antonia Fraser (b. 1932), historian, biographer, author; Michael Holroyd (b. 1935), biographer and author.

5. A family joke; see Amis to Elizabeth Jane Howard, 13 August 1973, note 2.

I've talked to poor little Pat[6] who says she's doubtful about Sunday, because going when Jim [Durham] goes means a nice car ride and going on her own means a nasty Tube ride. Can you think of any way round this?

I'll ring you soon. I do miss you, and I mean you, not just having someone around. Longing to see the new you, and the old you as well. I love your face.

Bunny

[ALS: HEHL]

TO W. GODWARD – 5 MARCH 1975

Lemmons, Hadley Common, Barnet, Hertfordshire.

Dear W. Godward,[1]

You seem to think it is your right to be sent a signed photograph of myself. In fact what I would be doing is to stop work in order to send you, a total stranger, something of commercial value. I might have considered doing so but for the whining, reproachful tone of your letters. Be off with you.

Yours sincerely,
Kingsley Amis

[ALS: HEHL]

6. Pat Kavanagh, literary agent (at A.D. Peters, later Peters, Fraser and Dunlop); 'poor little' is another joke, applied because of Kavanagh's inability to watch frightening films.

---

1. The identity of Mr Godward is untraced (see Amis to Mr Gunston, 7 July 1973, note 1).

TO JOHN AMIS – 27 MARCH 1975

Lemmons, Hadley Common, Barnet, Hertfordshire.

Dear John,

I was powerfully interested by the bugle-calls bit in this week's My Music![1] (repeat, I now see). Could I ask you when they were written? Late 18th? And is anything known of who wrote them? I ask principally because of the Last Post,[2] the shortest musical masterpiece I know, unless that Chopin prelude, opus ?, anyway the one that kicks off Les Sylphides, undercuts it.[3] The only call, he added learnedly, that soldiers have never fitted words to. Most grateful for any light on the subject.

What about a drink or something? I seem to have lost track of you. I'll be here for the foreseeable future.

Cheers from
Cousin Pud

[TLS: British Library]

TO JACK GOHN – 27 MARCH 1975

Lemmons, Hadley Common, Barnet, Herts

Dear Jack,

Congratulations on the size of the bibliography. You missed the enclosed,*[1] a mention of which can't fail to assist you to produce the necessary illusion that you've read every number of every English-

1. A long-running BBC radio panel show which for a time in the 1980s was also broadcast on ITV. John Amis was a panellist along with Frank Muir, Denis Norden and Ian Wallace.

2. Amis is referring to Reveille and the Last Post bugle calls, which were published by the British War Office in 1798. Nothing is known of who wrote them.

3. Chopin's Waltz in E flat, op. 18, no. 2; *Les Sylphides* ('The Sylphs') is a ballet with music arranged from piano works by Chopin, first produced in Paris, 1909.

1. Gohn's PhD was a work of literary criticism, not a bibliography, but from it emerged *Kingsley Amis: A Checklist*, which divides Amis's writings into three sections: 'Unpublished Materials', 'Published Materials' and 'Secondary Materials'. Amis's enclosure has not survived.

language publication since I was born. Note in para 3 an account of the source of next novel, which I hope to start in a week or so. Now your queries: [. . .][2]

News from the front. *Kipling* will be out this year, they swear. *We Are All Guilty*, TV play, complete and to be 'aired' (wonderful phrase) in summer or autumn, I mean fall.[3] Yesterday I had lunch with the Queen at Buckingham Palace.[4] No kidding. Sat next to her. She was fine; I *enjoyed* it.

Well, Gohn, have you finished with me yet? If you haven't I'll just have to take it, I suppose. Good luck with the final draft.

Yours,
Kingsley

*I'd like it back some day, but no rush.

[TLS: Recipient]

TO WILLIAM RUKEYSER – 1 APRIL 1975

Lemmons, Hadley Common, Barnet, Hertfordshire.

Dear Bill,

Jolly nice of you to send me the Hodgart piece. But is he mad? You must accept my firm assurance that as far as I know I've never even

2. Amis here provides answers to nine bibliographical queries.

3. *Rudyard Kipling and his World* (1975); *We are All Guilty*, in the series *Against the Crowd*, was broadcast in the summer of 1975, and later, under the same title, turned into a novel for young adults and published in 1991.

4. This was one of a number of regular small luncheon parties the Queen and the Duke of Edinburgh hold at Buckingham Palace 'to meet distinguished people from all professions, trades and callings. Usually limited to eight guests – husbands and wives are not invited – and two members of the Royal Household' (*The Royal Encyclopedia*, eds Ronald Allison and Sarah Riddell (London: Macmillan, 1991), p. 32). Amis was the only literary figure at the luncheon on 26 March; the other guests were the Deputy Leader of the Greater London Council, the Chairman of British Airways, the Chairman of the Board of Customs and Excise, the Chairman of the Central Electricity Generating Board, the President of the Royal Warrant Holders Association, the Director of the Science Museum and the Secretary-General of the Arts Council.

heard that Mozart quintet. Still, the review certainly won't lose any sales.[1]

As I write, that stout friend of humanity, Alexander Shelepin,[2] is among us. The protests are predictably disappointing: almost entirely from exiles and Jews. But I'm going to add my mite tomorrow by handing in a fully argued and documented putting of the case against him and his visit. Complete text: 'Why don't you bugger off?'

Strange echo from the past: within a day or two of your letter I got an inquiry about Mark Rose. Some Australians want to put into a schoolbook the story of his that Conquest and I used in one of our SF anthologies.[3] I hope they find him.

No NYC prospects for me at the moment, alas. But why don't you come and have a drink with us before the place shuts down altogether?

Love to all
Cheers – Kingsley

[TLS: Recipient]

TO PHILIP LARKIN – 23 JUNE 1975

Lemmons, Hadley Common, Barnet, Hertfordshire.

My dear Philip,

I meant to write earlier, then thought I might see you, and now send heartiest congratulations, old boy, on your well-deserved elevation.[1] All your palls will be glad, and many a tiny turd – Brian Patten? Kevin Crossley-Holland?[2] – will I hope be filled with gall. Actually I may have

---

1. Matthew Hodgart, 'Time Trips', review of *Ending Up*, in *New York Review of Books* (20 March 1975), p. 32, suggests that Amis had derived the novel's structure from a baroque suite or a classical work with some movements in sonata form, possibly Mozart's string quintet no. 4 in G minor, K. 516.

2. Alexander Shelepin (1918–94), Soviet politician and former trade union official: Member, Central Committee of CPSU (1961–76), previously Member, Presidium of the Supreme Soviet (1966–72), Deputy Chair, USSR Council of Ministers (1972–73).

3. For Mark Rose's story see Amis to Rukeyser, 20 June 1962, note 7.

---

1. Larkin had recently been made a CBE (Commander of the British Empire).

2. Brian Patten (b. 1946), Kevin Crossley-Holland (b. 1941), poets.

made just that bit of difference by/telling HM you were good when I was lunching with her the other week. (2nd part* is quite true. Yes, I know you've been there yourself.)

*after the oblique stroke

No real news here: all the exciting things seem to be happening to Bob. *I* just prod at the sodding keyboard, more and more every month, running like buggery to stay somewhere near the same place. Off to Wopland like a fool at the end of the week – not for long. Just the feeling you want to do what you won't be able to do again, ever, in a year or two.

I got one Prima – good PWR, but I can't bear P's singing. At the same time secured *Blackstick*.[3] Can't imagine how I ever underrated 'Blackstick', or thought 'Sweet Patootie' was better than 'Viper Mad'. Ah, we were young then.

Let's have a drink some time when you're down this way.

Knighted for his services to bum, also PLR[4] bum,
Kingsley

[ALS: Bodleian]

TO JACK GOHN – 14 JULY 1975

Lemmons Hadley Common, Barnet, Herts

Dear Jack,

I took your three letters with me on a trip to Italy from which I returned last night, intending to answer them while away and to smuggle in the implication that globe-trotting had been preventing me from answering them earlier. No good, though: there was no time between church-visiting, picture-seeing, wine-bibbing, pasta-eating and being driven over the highest pass in the Alps (bloody terrifying). What had really held me up, though, was the fact that I couldn't just write and

3. A response to Larkin to Amis, 28 January 1975 (in HEHL): 'I've just bought a 3-disc set of "Louis Prima" – 48 tracks, 30 of wch feature PWR.' Prima (1911–78), trumpeter, singer, band leader; 'PWR' is Pee-Wee Russell, who played on twenty, not thirty, Prima recordings; 'Blackstick' is a tune by Sidney Bechet recorded in 1938 with a splinter group from the Noble Sissle Orchestra, featuring Clarence Brereton on trumpet.

4. Public Lending Right. An Act of Parliament was passed in 1979 allowing authors to be paid for the use of their books (those in copyright, that is) by public, commercial or other kinds of lending libraries. It was not until 1984 that qualified authors began receiving money.

say thanks for the dissertation, I must read it some time; I had to read it and think about it before writing, and that got pushed out of the way again and again by, in particular, starting new novel.[1] This turned out to be bloody terrifying too, I mean the starting, real stage-fright stuff, and though I've reached p.62 I'm still proceeding on tip-toe.

So – the dissertation is a success from my point of view. You Americans and critics tend to systematise and categorise rather a lot from the point of view of us Englishmen and novelists (yes, I know you're a novelist yourself now: see below), but I couldn't find an instance of systemisation-etc. obtrusive enough to be worth mentioning; I jibbed only at those 3 army stories[2] being called a trilogy, and I mention that partly to assure you that I'm what you fellows call 'leveling' with you, i.e. not charitably suppressing a huge list of complaints. On the positive side, to extend what I've said to you before, you write very well. There's a woolly, ungainly American academese you must often have come across from which you are entirely free. And you're constantly coming up with real insights, some of them shared only by God and me, others hitherto available to God alone.[3] Three examples: the dragon idea on p.181, the doppelganger bit on p.200, and the Manton-Mrs T-Peter triangle. All of which means that I'm prepared to do anything legal and not too onerous in your support. For instance, let me know how I can help over the Cape suggestion,[4] and when.

As to limpetry: Teachers World (oh Christ). There was more than a letter: Conquest and I contributed a piece to their Personal View feature in, probably, May 1969.[5] Neither of us can remember more than that. I now find, by the arduous means of asking my wife, that I still have *The Legacy*. If you should ever need cover there, say I refused to let you see it. And George Zeyer[6] probably dies of thirst or exhaustion

---

1. *The Alteration* (1976).

2. 'My Enemy's Enemy', 'Court of Inquiry' and 'I Spy Strangers', first published in *My Enemy's Enemy* (1962).

3. Amis is adapting a remark attributed to Robert Browning about *Sordello* (1840), his long and notoriously obscure narrative poem set in Italy during the period of the Guelf-Ghibelline wars of the late twelfth and thirteenth centuries: 'When it was written, God and Robert Browning knew what it meant, now only God knows.'

4. Gohn suggested Cape might be interested in publishing his dissertation on Amis.

5. 'Viewpoint: A Plea for Quality', *Teachers World*, 6 June 1969, p.4; for letter, see Amis to the editor, *Teachers World*, 16 May 1969.

6. In *Ending Up* (1974).

or realising that no one will ever find him; the stroke only renders him helpless.

All right then, *be* my designated bibliographer.[7] You have inflated ideas of my secretary's field of operations, but I've started to keep a list myself of what I publish. Here is what I have.

Listener, 19 Dec 1974, Writing for a TV Series.

Encounter, Jan 1975, Ameringlish.

Contribution, with Conquest, to Black Paper 1975.

Daily Telegraph, letter, about 8 Jan.

Nova, Dec 1974 (whoops), Spirits of the Season.

New Statesman, about 30 Jan, letter.

NS, 20 June, The Demon of Progress (BR).[8]

Observer, 29 June, Heroic Absurdities (BR).

Daily Mirror, about 27th June, letter about Vietnam (v. fascist). Retort 7 July.

Sunday Times, 13 July, The Crime of the Century, Episode I of VI, thriller-detective serial.

Also Penthouse stuff.

Congratulations on starting the novel, indeed on getting along with it. You know how it feels now, hey? One piece of probably needless advice: don't go back and rewrite or even revise until you've got to the end. When you have a complete first draft, however imperfect you know it to be, you'll feel much more secure. Let me know how it goes. (V. flattered and amused to think that, all unknowing, I was giving you a 'course in authorhood'.)

Good luck, then. Apologies for not writing earlier: hope you understand. The baby[9] will turn out to be absolutely perfect in every way, you'll both find; it's a thing about babies. I expect notification of its arrival.

Cheers
Kingsley

[TLS: Recipient]

7. 'I wonder if you'd do me the honor of regarding me as your designated bibliographer? What this would entail, in practical terms, is having your secretary send me, periodically, a list of everything you've published recently, because there are sure to be supplements (in the *Bulletin of Bibliography* or somewhere) and ultimately revised issues' (Gohn to Amis, 9 April 1975).

8. 'BR' stands for book review.

9. Gohn's daughter, Elizabeth Clare, was born in September.

TO CLAIRE TOMALIN – 31 JULY 1975

Lemmons, Hadley Common, Barnet, Hertfordshire.

Dear Claire,[1]

Many thanks for sending me the book on names, out of which I got a few interesting bits of information, but in general the thing is too vague and pedestrian to be worth reviewing. Do you want it back? – because I would quite like to hang on to it.

Payment for my Kipling piece[2] doesn't seem to have come yet, which is rather a pest, because I wanted to discuss the question of fees with you. The Spectator are making wheedling noises to me and saying that they are now paying much more than under Creighton.[3] What could you offer per thousand?[4] (I'd rather write for you than The Spectator, but one has to live.)

Love,
Kingsley

[TLS: Sussex]

TO THE EDITOR, *THE TIMES* – 26 AUGUST 1975

Sir, I was interested to read (Diary, August 22) that Dr. John Wells has been charting the spread of the intrusive 'r' and the glottal stop in our speech. I wonder if he or any of his fellow phoneticians has noticed a far more disagreeable phenomenon now to be heard everywhere in

1. Claire Tomalin (b. 1933), literary journalist, biographer; at the time Literary Editor, *New Statesman* (1974–77).

2. 'The Demon of Progress', a review of Philip Mason, *Kipling: The Glass, the Shadow and the Fire*, in *New Statesman*, 20 June 1975, reprinted in *The Amis Collection*, pp. 69–72.

3. Harold Creighton (b. 1927), businessman, also Chairman (1967–75) and Editor (1973–75), the *Spectator*.

4. A note scrawled at the bottom of the letter, not in Amis's hand, reads: 'CT [Claire Tomalin] answered £40 [illegible].'

broadcasting and ordinary talk: the intrusive or initial glottal stop.[1] In what follows I use] to represent it.

We were used to hearing, for instance, "the idea]of" and "India]Office" from careful speakers. But what is to be said about "the]aircraft", "he fell]ill", "the]accident", "he]arrived", "left]out", "come]up" and countless others? What but that every English word that once began with a vowel now has an invisible but clearly audible glottal stop before the vowel?

I call this disagreeable because, unlike the intrusive "r" and the old glottal stop between syllables or words ("qui]easy"), the newcomer is not an English noise. It is a German noise ("über]alles", etc). Have we here an early step towards linguistic harmonisation within the EEC?

Yours truly,

KINGSLEY AMIS

Lemmons, Hadley Common, Barnet, Hertfordshire, August 22

TO CLAIRE TOMALIN – 10 SEPTEMBER 1975

Lemmons, Hadley Common, Barnet, Hertfordshire.

Dear Claire,

Belatedly scenting the threat, Terry[1] has lumbered into some sort of action, and is now suggesting books to me again. So since I have a prior obligation to him, and he pays twice as much as you do, I had better stick to him for the time being, with perhaps an occasional outing in your pages under exceptional circumstances.

Love,
Kingsley

[TLS: Sussex]

---

1. See *The King's English*, p. 177, which defines the glottal stop as 'a kind of consonant or consonant-substitute . . . The linguistician Leonard Bloomfield defines it as a slight catch in the throat; a speaker of German uses it before every word that begins with a vowel, as before the second and third word in *Deutschland über alles*; in old-fashioned cockney and Glaswegian speech it comes in the middle of words like *letter (le'er)* and *button (bu'on)*, generally doing duty for medial double T; it is a small puff of breath from the top of the windpipe.'

---

1. Terence Kilmartin, Literary Editor, *Observer*.

TO THE EDITOR, *DAILY TELEGRAPH* – 27 SEPTEMBER 1975

SIR – Since nobody else seems to be going to do so, it is left to me to point out that, in the final Test at the Oval,[1] the Australians could certainly have got the runs needed to win if they had gone for them. They chose not to.

On August 9, 1952, I was present at the Oval when Surrey made 57 runs in the last 20 minutes of the match, 12 of them off the last three balls, to beat Middlesex by six wickets. The time is not in itself important to the present calculation; what obviously counts is the number of overs bowled. Surrey received seven, so they were scoring at about eight runs an over.

Australia had received 17 overs, averaging just over three runs off each, when their captain declined the optional extra half-hour; at that stage a draw was inevitable. At the same creditable over-rate, that half-hour would have yielded a further nine or perhaps 10 overs. Total, 26 or 27. Runs needed at the outset, 198. Scoring-rate required, about seven and a half runs an over. Or to put it another way, if Australia had played through at Surrey's speed, they would have knocked off the runs with an over or two to spare.

Unless, of course, they had already lost the match, a fearful possibility with the Ashes safe before it started.[2] Australians used to treat cricket as a game; now, it seems, they have joined us, and every other cricketing country except the West Indies, in the dismal company of those who dearly love a draw. Alas!

KINGSLEY AMIS
Hadley Common, Herts.

---

1. That is, the last Test match, played at The Oval in South London, in the cricket series between England and Australia.

2. Australia had already retained the Ashes, the mythical trophy competed for by the two teams since 1882.

TO ELIZABETH JANE HOWARD – JANUARY 1976

Dearest Tiny,

Hope you didn't have too bad a day. I'm afraid I wasn't a very good husband to you this morning, when you were feeling worried.[1] But I'll try to do better in future.

See you (and I won't be too pissed)

Love

[AL: HEHL]

1. Amis had not accompanied Jane to hospital for x-ray tests for suspected TB (there was none).

TO FRANK HARDIE – 6 JANUARY 1976

Lemmons, Hadley Common, Barnet, Hertfordshire

Dear Mr. Hardie,

I have George Saintsbury's Notes on a Cellar-book in a recent reprint, but I must confess I missed the reference to Sparkling Moselle with sardine sandwiches.[1] I suppose it would go all right though I must confess I don't much fancy it myself.

Berkishness is thought, speech or behaviour of a loutish, insensitive, or low kind. (Rhyming slang from Berkeley Hunt).[2]

1. *Notes on a Cellarbook* (1920) by George Saintsbury (1845–1933), literary historian, biographer, critic and wine connoisseur. Frank Hardie (1911–89), author, industrialist, socialist, best known as President of the Oxford Union during the famous 'King and Country' debate of February 1933 (in which a motion was carried 'that this house will in no circumstances fight for its King and its Country').

2. For berkishness see Amis to Colin Howard and Sargy Mann, 10 September 1971, note 3.

With all good wishes for 1976.

Yours sincerely,
Kingsley Amis

[TL: Bodleian]

TO ROBERT CONQUEST – 26 JANUARY 1976

Lemmons, Hadley Common, Barnet

Dear Bob,

Your two to hand, as the a. said to the b. Much impressed by poetic output. Limeraiku excellent. The NS is running a comp for Paradise Lost, Beowulf etc. reduced to a single haiku, so Martin proposes to include your Vile Old Man[1] as as a summary of the little-known Japanese story cycle, the *Yashmikura*; signed Ted Pauker. Closing date 6 Feb, so you can stop or alter the thing if you want to. It would be nice to do the whole lot, using up every monosyllabic word for man/woman: There's a rotten sod From Cape Cod, etc.

I got off the circular[2] changing Tues to Thurs, and response was varied. Tony Powell dropped me a card saying sadly that this virtually meant he couldn't come now, because his Nat Portrait Gall committees start at 2.30; same evening Tony Hartley rings me up and virtually ballocks me for effectively barring Tony P. Too bad, I had to say. Week before last, great turn-out: Perry, D Rees, Donald W (who says Thurs is better for him), J O'S, Bob Schuettinger, Russell and that shag Robert Moss who wrote the book on the Left or the Right or whatever it was.[3] He was elected member, seemed amiable enough, though I was

1. 'There's a vile old man/Of Japan who roars at whores:/"Where's your fucking fan?"'; reprinted in *NOBLV* under the pseudonym 'Ted Pauker', with 'bloody' replacing 'fucking'.

2. For the Bertorellis' or 'Fascist' lunches.

3. Peregrine Worsthorne; David Rees (b. 1928), writer, political scientist, journalist, Literary Editor, *Spectator* (1964–67); Donald Cameron Watt (b. 1928), historian and political scientist, at the time Professor of International History, London School of Economics (1972–82); John O'Sullivan (b. 1942), political journalist and editor, at the time writing for the *Daily Telegraph*; Robert Lindsay Schuettinger (b.1936), American political scientist, journalist; Russell Lewis (b.1926), journalist, author, previously director of the Conservative Political Centre and author of *Margaret Thatcher: A Personal and Political Biography* (1975), the first

instinctively cautious. Still, we need to expand: Russell rang me up last week and said plaintively that he had been the only one. What to do?

I don't seem to be able to find your second letter for the moment, but I do seem to remember your asking if I'd sent you any limericks. No, I haven't, but I will soon. Period of intensive work now ending, with novel done and vile chores like reviewing Arab stuff for Bush House groaningly dispatched. In meantime have managed to make public fucking fools of DAN Jones and a S. African lefty.[4] Light verse next.

Have now found that letter. I had it slightly wrong, but you didn't list limericks recalled to date. I'd better start noting them down (yours, I mean) as they come to mind. The Pankhurst thing[5] is still making me laugh. I love its incommunicability; imagine explaining it even to a learned, sympathetic etc. American. You mean the Pankhursts knew this cricket guy?

Bloody good about Margt Thatcher.[6] Did you see what Mason[7] said about her? Got the bastard on the raw.

Cheers
Kingsley

[TLS: Recipient]

biography of Mrs Thatcher; Robert Moss (b. 1946), Australian-born journalist, novelist, conservative polemicist; Amis may be thinking of his book *The Collapse of Democracy* (1975).

4. D.A.N. Jones (b. 1931), literary journalist and editor, at the time Assistant Editor, Features, *Listener* (1972–82), had favourably reviewed Amis's *Rudyard Kipling and his World* (1975) in *Listener*, 25 December 1976. Amis had responded in a letter to the editor, 22 January 1976, p. 83, to defend his view that Kipling's classical education was defective. Jones responded to Amis's response in a column, 'Safety First', p. 79, in the same issue. The tiny point at stake concerned what Jones supposed were translations of Horace by Kipling, but turned out, as Amis's letter explains, to be fakes, 'a learned joke'. Jones admits ('I have read them now') that Kipling's 'translations' were actually 'examples of Kipling's ideas in Horace's style', but argues that 'this doesn't, on the face of it, lend much support to Mr Amis's point about Kipling's deficiencies.' The other public humiliation Amis mentions, that of 'a S. African lefty', I have been unable to trace.

5. Conquest cannot remember this.

6. Amis may be referring to an anti-communist speech, entitled 'Britain Awake', Margaret Thatcher (b. 1925), then leader of the opposition, delivered on 19 January 1976. This speech earned her the title 'Iron Lady' in an article of 23 January in the Red Army newspaper *Red Star*. Mrs Thatcher became Prime Minister in May 1979, and resigned in November 1990; created Baroness Thatcher of Kesteven (1992).

7. Roy Mason (b. 1924), Labour politician, at the time Secretary of State, Defence (1974–76); created Baron (1987).

TO ROBERT CONQUEST – 1 MARCH 1976

Lemmons, Hadley Common, Barnet, Herts

Dear Bob,

Thank you for all your letters and limerick corners, the latter of which amount to a fair-sized polygon by now. The young fellow called Shit went down a treat at the Garrick. I think my favourite is the critic of Vauxhall.[1] I'm keeping the checklist by me and have added to it You cannot, when talking to Toynbee, Charlotte Bronte cried 'Wow, sister, what a man!' and There was a young fellow called Crouch.[2] I don't know more than about a dozen of the ones you mention. Tell me the

---

1. 'There was a young fellow called Shit, /A name he disliked quite a bit; /So he changed it to Shite -/A step in the right/Direction, one has to admit,' attributed to 'Victor Gray' (a Conquest pseudonym, anagram of G.R.A. Victory, Conquest's full Christian names being George Robert Acworth) in E.O. Parrott, ed., *The Penguin Book of Limericks* (Harmondsworth: Penguin, 1983), p. 288. Conquest has forgotten the critic of Vauxhall.

2. The first of the limericks Amis refers to, 'You cannot when talking of Toynbee', is imagined as written by Bertrand Russell in response to a limerick by Arnold Toynbee, which reads:

Said the learned philosopher Russell
'One can come without moving a muscle
When sufficiently blotto
Just watch Lady Otto-
Line's bum as it bursts from her bustle.'

Conquest has forgotten the limerick about Toynbee. The other two, both of which are attributed to 'Victor Gray' in *NOBLV*, pp. 281, 282, read:

Charlotte Bronte said, 'Wow, sister! *What* a man!
He laid me face down on the ottoman:
Now don't you and Emily
Go telling the femily –
But he smacked me upon my bare bottom, Anne!'

There was a young fellow called Crouch
Who was courting a girl on a couch.
She said 'Why not a sofa?'
And he exclaimed, 'Oh, for
Christ's sake shut your trap while I – ouch!'

rest of the taxi-cab whore down [out?] at Iver and remind me of Gauguin in Fiji.[3]

It's amazing how many bad limericks there are in the world, as I'm still discovering. Lear was bad enough, the old man of Boulogne and the young lady of Riga were bloody awful, but Christ the ones collected by that awful bugger G. Legman take the cake.[4] Just versified filth, quite competent most of them but without any real ingenuity or any humour. I nearly forgot: do mention any trad and anon ones that come to mind.

I've only been to one Thurs since the one I told you of. Just Russell and Alfred Sherman.[5] Not v enlivening. But will return to the charge.

What have I been doing? Not much. Read a lot of lt vse, including several thousand bloody awful Tadlow-type epigrams,[6] often with interminable titles setting them up, e.g.

On Hearing that a Notorious Rogue of Rude Manners, when accompanied by his Newly-Wed Wife on a Tour of the Continent, had halted his Carriage in the Village of Ytt near Zurich for the Sole Purpose of Relieving Himself

3. Two more 'Victor Gray' efforts, both reprinted in *NOBLV*, pp.282, 281:

A taxi-cab whore out at Iver
Would do the round trip for a fiver
– Quite reasonable, too,
For a sightsee, a screw,
And a ten-shilling tip to the driver.

When Gauguin was visiting Fiji
He said, 'Things are different here, e.g.
While Tahitian skin
Calls for tan, spread out thin,
You must slosh it on here with a squeegee.'

4. For Lear limericks and worse see Gershon Legman, ed., *The Limerick* (New York: Jupiter Books, 1974). Legman has edited a second collection, *The New Limerick Book* (New York: Crown Publishing, 1979).

5. Alfred Sherman (b.1919), author, journalist, public affairs adviser; co-founder, Centre for Policy Studies (1974).

6. See, for example, 'Epigram. On Dr Tadlow', by Abel Evans (1679–1737): 'When Tadlow walks the streets, the paviours cry, /"God bless you, Sir!" and lay their rammers by.' Amis comments, in *NOBLV*, p.xix: 'The first time I came across that, I deduced straight away that Tadlow must have been very fat indeed. On looking into the matter, I established that he was an Oxford don who flourished about 1700 and was very fat indeed. The Oxford-don detail suggests to me an after-Hall common-room competition of the period requiring an impromptu on Tadlow to be composed within something like a minute. I should be quite tickled to have won with the above, but I hope I should have had the sense to throw it into the fire before staggering off to bed.'

She had a *Shit*;
He piss'd in *Ytt*.

Dr. Walsh (?1728–1803)

But it does make you appreciate how bloody good Calverley, Praed et al. were.[7] No great discoveries, but I have found a text of The Night before Larry was Stretched that differs from Auden's and establishes it as corrupt at at least two points.[8] Best thing I've read *on* the topic is by A.A. Milne if you don't mind.[9] He knows exactly what lt vse is and proves it by translating an unusually crappy stanza of John Gilpin into it:

Quoth Mrs Gilpin, 'That's well said;
And for that wine is dear,
We will be furnished with our own,
Which is both bright and clear.'

Balls, says Milne; you don't praise wine for being bright and clear, and Gilpin knew what his own wine was like. It should be:

Said Mrs Gilpin: 'Very well.
But wait a moment: What'll
They charge for claret at the Bell?
We'd better take a bottle.'

The sort of thing that helps to write one's Intro.

I can't remember whether I told you that Sargy Mann is now duly married, or whether you knew that Bruce Montgomery is supposed to be by now, i.e. I had a card from him some weeks ago saying he was going to marry Ann[10] next week, *the* next week I mean, pianissimo, he said, owing to the groom's enforced teetotalism.

7. Charles Calverley (1831–84), known under the initials 'C.S.C.', a writer of light verse and parodies; W.M. Praed (1802–39), writer of *vers de société* as well as light verse; both represented in *NOBLV*.

8. *NOBLV* prints the anonymous 'The Night Before Larry Was Stretched' in a text of Amis's own creation: 'a collation of W.H. Auden's text (*The Oxford Book of Light Verse* (1938)), that used in *Oliver's Book of Comic Songs* (n.d., nineteenth century), and personally collected variants' (p. 337).

9. See A.A. Milne, *Year in, Year out* (1952), discussed in the introduction to *NOBLV*, pp. vi–viii. Milne (1882–1956) wrote poems, plays, novels, short stories and critical essays, as well as children's books.

10. He married Barbara (Ann) Clements in 1976, two years before his death.

I might have a go at Peach Key[11] some time, but not until next year; after lt vse is done I have such a corking idea for a novella or something of that sort of length[12] that I must begin it without delay. Specks of news: Tom Maschler likes my novel[13] & what is to the point is paying a fairly chunky advance on it; US likewise. Last week had rather boring dinner at the Welches' with Colin v drunk and doing a lot of slow maundering on. Next day, lunch with Geo Gale who seemed a bit subdued. Quite likely my fault in both cases for being boring. Have begun big self-restraint programme with no drinks or smokes until 7.30 pm and then only beer and wine till 10 or so. When I go out to lunch etc. I can have what I like. Works bloody well: I can now take a heavy day and feel all right the next morning. Jim Durham[14] writes from Australia; most of his letter is about the glories of wine, bars, food etc. there in the vein of one cheering himself up for having left GB; but some good stuff about Fraser's[15] reforms – about 50 different lefty commissions and boards have been dissolved, bits of State-owned stuff being sold off to private buyers, and 'satisfyingly provocative minor gestures have not been lacking, either, such as a move to deny dole payments to those "who adopt a style of dress or appearance calculated to make them unattractive to prospective employers."' Bloody good.

What was the bit abt Caroleen in the Mail?[16] I enclose NS haiku report.

All the best
Cheers
Kingsley

[TLS: Recipient]

11. 'Peach Key' is the draft of a novel Conquest had wanted Amis to collaborate on with him, as they'd done on *The Egyptologists* (1965). It was not until 1993 that Amis gave the project serious consideration, deciding against it.

12. Amis published nothing of novella length in the period 1976–77; in 1978 he published *Jake's Thing*, a 285-page novel, and 'The Darkwater Hall Mystery', an expanded version of a story published in May 1978 in *Playboy*. The expanded story was published in a thirty-five-page limited edition (of 165 copies) by the Tragara Press in Edinburgh, with illustrations by Elspeth Sojka.

13. *The Alteration* (1976).

14. For James Durham see Amis to Elizabeth Jane Howard, 4 March 1975, note 2.

15. Malcolm Fraser, of the Liberal Party, succeeded Labor Prime Minister Gough Whitlam in November 1975, after Whitlam had been dismissed by the Governor-General, the Queen's representative in Australia; Fraser was Prime Minister from 1975–83.

16. Conquest cannot remember, and there are no references to Caroleen Conquest in the two previous weeks of the *Daily Mail*.

TO ANTHONY POWELL – 18 MARCH 1976

Lemmons, Hadley Common, Barnet, Hertfordshire.

My dear Tony,

Pratt's would have been a fine idea, but I hear from Osbert that there's a ban on new members over 50, which rules me out by nearly four years.[1] So there, I'm afraid, we are.

I told you I'm editing the new – or New – Oxford Book of Light Verse. Now you must have some stuff. Do let me have it – it would give the book a big hoist. Scurrility not essential but desirable. Isn't there an Auden-Isherwood squib of yours from 1939?[2] That's the sort of thing that would look well.

Fascinated by your remarks on *Girl, 20.*[3] Managed to get the gist through a great black stamping of REMEMBER to use the POST CODE that the indignant GPO had planked down on your card. You hadn't remembered, you see.*

Thursday lunches[4] are ailing. Why don't you come along at 12.30 or 12.45 (or 12.00) one week and go off to your meeting at 2.15? If you

1. Sir Osbert Lancaster (1908–86), cartoonist, artist, writer; knighted 1975. Amis has written 'See P.S.' to the left of this first sentence (as also to the left of the letter's last sentence). Pratt's, an evening supper club in St James's, founded in 1841 by the Duke of Beaufort, did indeed have such a rule, but Amis was granted exemption from it and made a special member by the Duke of Devonshire, who owned the club, and still does. Amis remained on the list of special members for the rest of his life.

2. The squib (not included in *NOBLV*) reads:

> The literary or left-wing erstwhile wellwisher would
> Seek vainly now for Auden or for Isherwood.
> The Dog beneath the Skin has had the brains
> To save it, Norris-like, by Changing Trains.

However, Amis did include a 146-line poem in heroic couplets by Powell entitled 'Caledonia' (*NOBLV*, pp.245–9), described in the notes as privately printed and undated. Powell reports the date as 1934, describing the poem's printing as a wedding present for himself and Violet Pakenham from a friend, Desmond Ryan, who owned a printing press (personal communication, 18 October 1998).

3. Powell's postcard has not survived.

4. The Bertorellis' or 'Fascist' lunches.

warn me in advance I'll secure a quorum, or at least be there myself.

Love to Violet.

Yours,
Kingsley

*If I knew it I'd pass it on, but I don't.

19 March
PS: Too lazy to write a modified version. Delighted that Pratt's is on after all. And many thanks for your sponsorship. Osbert wants to know my educational history, I see from his letter, so perhaps you had better have it too – City of London School and John's, Oxon.

[ALS: Recipient]

TO MRS SUTCLIFFE – 30 MARCH 1976

Lemmons, Hadley Common, Barnet, Hertfordshire.

Dear Mrs Sutcliffe,

Many thanks for your query-sheet, which I return herewith with yesses and noes – about 50/50, actually. This is editing as I like it to be: I'd rather read 100 irrelevant objections than have one error overlooked.

Where we are going to have some trouble is with the printer, to stop him normalising mustach to moustache, italian (windows) to Italian – and caffè to café, etc.[1] Have you any ideas on this? The points are all tiny ones but add up to a very important total.

Yours sincerely,
Kingsley Amis

[ALS: Reading]

---

1. *The Alteration* (1976), an 'Alternate World' novel, imagines what England would have been like in 1976 had the Reformation never occurred and had Henry VIII's elder brother, Prince Arthur, instead of dying young, remained married to Catherine of Aragon, siring a line of Catholic kings. A wealth of subtle detail, such as the spellings Amis mentions here, mark this changed or alternate England; broader touches include Martin Luther as Pope, and the absence of French and Russian revolutions. For Amis on 'alternate', 'alternative'

TO PHILIP LARKIN – 10 APRIL 1976

Lemmons, Hadley Common, Barnet, Hertfordshire.

Dear Philip,

I'm now getting into the 20th century with my OUP light-verse anthology, which brings me to you. I only have your collections: could you send me copies of any uncollected stuff you think might suit? Bob tells me of a poem that features a shit in a shuttered château[1] – that sounds the kind of thing. If you have any favourite light poems by others, 20th-C or earlier, which I might have missed, do mention them.

According to Bud Freeman,[2] it was Dave Tough who introduced my works to the Chicagoans:[3] Dave, along with Yank Lawson,[4] another great admirer, was always the literary boy. P-W R was much tickled, said Bud, to hear that I thought highly of his playing. No, *straight up*, old man. Jim Silvester, whom you must remember from Oxford, has known Bud, now based in London, for some time, and arranged a lunch. A date to hear him in the flesh is promised for the near future. Who, in 1941, would ever have, etc. Perhaps, when you're in London, you'd care to come along. The lure of meeting himmmmm may be more effective than that of seeing meeeee. Old Bruce [Montgomery]

(and 'Alternate World'), see *The King's English*, pp. 7–8: 'There is no excuse but the grossest similarity in appearance to confuse these two, but people muddle them up all the time. *Alternately* means "first one, then the other, then the one, then the other, and so on"; *alternatively* means "another possibility is that . . ." Similarly with the adjectives *alternate* and *alternative* . . . Exception: An Americanism that sounds anomalous to British ears, as Americanisms will, is contained in the phrase "Alternate World" and its derivatives. This refers to a kind of science-fiction story or idea whereby some great crisis of the past went the other way and correspondingly changed history since that point . . . British readers are advised to follow this trend in the science-fiction context and nowhere else.'

---

1. 'The Life with a Hole in it', first published in the *Poetry Supplement* of the Poetry Book Society (Christmas 1974); reprinted in *LCP*, p. 202.

2. Bud Freeman (1906–91), tenor saxophonist.

3. This cannot be right, since the drummer Dave Tough died in 1948 (described in *NGDJ* as 'a formative influence on the Chicago style of white jazz'). Freeman was buttering Amis up. According to Jim Silvester, who introduced the two, 'Bud frequently raved about Kingsley's works, though I suspect he hadn't read any of them. He was an Anglophile from way back' (personal communication, 25 October 1999). For Silvester, a lifelong jazz fan and Amis friend, see Amis to Larkin, 16 June 1947.

4. Yank Lawson (b. 1911), trumpeter.

seems to be emerging from the wood. I was astonished to learn that this book of his actually exists. He said you said it was like T.F. Powys crossed with H.C. Bailey.[5] Really? Is it good? Oh, one more Oxford note: I.D.G. (David) Williams is dead.[6] Yes, the drink.

Shoot me the stuff, there's a good chap.

Within the first 48 hours, Russian spearheads would be likely to have reached the outskirts of bum,

Kingsley

[ALS: Bodleian]

TO ROBERT CONQUEST – 18 MAY 1976[1]

Lemmons, Hadley Common, Barnet, Herts

Dear Bob,

Apologies for unsatisfactoriness as correspondent. One excuse is that there's not much I can tell you about what's happening here because you know the place and see the papers: actually it was reading your letter in The Times this morning that fired me to write. What a little shit that Leapman is.[2] But effective: 2 blokes separately said to me in the Garrick, 'Did you see in The Times that the Penkovsky Papers are a fake after all?' Armed with your piece in Sov An[3] (well, the piece inspired by you) I was able to say a bit on the other side, but one's up against this 'It's in The Times' thing from people who ought to know

5. T.F. Powys (1875–1953), Dorset novelist whose fiction draws on the grotesque and the supernatural; H.C. Bailey (1878–1961), detective novelist; the Crispin novel was probably *Glimpses of the Moon* (1977), his first in twenty-six years.

6. 'Bad news about David, Christ,' replies Larkin in a letter of 13 April 1976, in *LL*, p. 538: 'The first of "The Seven" to go.'

---

1. Conquest was in Washington DC from 1976 to 1977 as a Fellow of the Woodrow Wilson International Center for Scholars.

2. Conquest's letter concerned a diary article in *The Times* which wrongly questioned the authenticity of the papers of Oleg Penkovsky, a Soviet intelligence officer who spied for the West (Penkovsky's go-between was the British businessman Greville Wynne). Penkovsky's papers were fragmentary notes, sketches and comments written in 1961–62, when he was in active contact with Western intelligence. They were smuggled out of Moscow in the autumn of 1962, shortly before his arrest and execution, and published in 1965. Michael Leapman (b.1938), journalist, author, editor of the *Times* Diary 1972–76.

3. *Soviet Analyst*, a news-sheet at first co-edited by Conquest and Tibor Szamuely. Conquest became sole editor after Szamuely's death.

that that means even less than it normally does when it's in the Diary.

Went to Oxford a couple of weeks ago to give a light-verse reading, which was quite a success in itself but a very cheerless jaunt. Stayed at the Randolph which I used to like quite. As we were nodding off about midnight a sodding group[4] sprang to life directly beneath. We got to sleep eventually; then in the morning we got down to breakfast at 9.40. They waited 5 minutes before telling us breakfast finished at 9.45. I was very glad Jane was there: breakfast finally came. But what a scheme: keep 'em awake so that they oversleep a bit and you can refuse them breakfast. The 9.45 thing wasn't mentioned anywhere in the hotel, not even in the plastic folder telling you about the glories of Trust Houses Forte Ltd, because if they did tell you, you'd be on time and there'd be no way out of giving you breakfast. The town was horrible, too: Rag Week, boutiques, shopping precincts, pop music in every pub. I think I have a Betj-style poem on the way; one line will be 'The surge and thunder of a discothèque'.[5] Also to be worked in is my encounter a few days previously in the Fitzroy,[6] where a really badly beaten-down old bag, mouth all fallen in, accosted me and said she was [. . .], a, perhaps the, leading Oxford beauty of 1940–41. Felt fed up for days afterwards.

[. . .] was a pal of Bruce's: transition effected. He telephoned me recently sounding as pissed as a fart. I didn't like to ask him if he was, because if, as I strongly suspect, he wasn't, I'd have had to say in effect, 'Oh, I see, it's just that you still sound it after a year on the wagon,' as I've noticed in ex-drunks before. They sometimes go on behaving pissed, too, as you know, which made me have to try pretty hard to sound enthusiastic when he mentioned coming up for a Thurs in the near future. I don't think I've been there since I saw you. Russell plus some thick Tory plus nobody else isn't much of an attraction.

Our move[7] has reached a very crappy stage. This morning, three

4. Amis has written asterisks under 'nodding' and 'sodding', and has written in the left margin: 'rhyme: ing off/ing off'.

5. An allusion to the last line of 'The Odyssey', a sonnet by Andrew Lang: 'The surge and thunder of the Odyssey'. Lang (1844–1912) was a prolific poet, essayist, reviewer, biographer, translator, historian, editor and anthologist. See the last line of the first part of 'Their Oxford', in *CP*, p. 147.

6. A pub in Fitzrovia, north of Soho.

7. Amis had wanted to return to central London for some time, and Jane Howard began to suspect that the relative isolation of Barnet was straining both their relationship and the general mood of the household. Hence the proposed move to Gardnor House, an eighteenth-century listed building in Flask Walk, Hampstead, with a large garden.

days before the ultimate deadline for signing for the new house, the chap who's been going to buy ours for the last three months says he doesn't think he can now. It isn't that he doesn't like our house, just that he hasn't got enough money after all. There's one ray of hope via a bridging loan from a rich chum, but my guess is we'll still be here when you re-appear, as I was glad to see from your p/c, today arrived, that you propose to do within a few months. With any luck at all I'll be in the country at any rate, think I've managed to avoid being hauled oversea for this year.

Looking at your letter: one could go further with the Bertrand/Pee Wee thing.[8] You must know that PW means 'small' and is facetiously applied to tall shags like PWR on the 'Lofty'-for-tich principle. Our sf shags could miss that and think that finding out that PW=small, i.e. like Bertrand R, had settled the identity of the 2 Russells.

Should have said about the poetry reading that one or two oldsters went down perhaps surprisingly well – Praed, Hood, Gilbert – and engine-driver Hunt,[9] which I served up as a concert encore, wowed them.

Cheers
K.

[TLS: Recipient]

TO PHILIP LARKIN – 11 JUNE 1976

Lemmons, Hadley Common, Barnet, Hertfordshire.

Dear Philip,

Many thanks for your stuff. I agree that shuttered shit[1] isn't really light verse, but I propose putting 9 of your poems in, which makes you tie with Betchers as the most-represented contemporary. This is good

8. In a letter of 25 April 1976 Conquest speculates on the use a science fiction writer might make of muddles in the distant future (e.g. mistaking Pee-Wee for Bertrand Russell).

9. W.M. Praed, Thomas Hood (1799–1845) and W.S. Gilbert (1836–1911) are all represented in *NOBLV* (1978); 'A young engine-driver called Hunt' is the opening line of a limerick by 'Victor Gray', also in *NOBLV*, p.282.

---

1. See Larkin's poem 'The Life with a Hole in It'.

for me, of course, because it means I can sling in up to 8 of my own without appearing to push myself unduly. The 9 are Toads 1 and 2, Naturally the Foundation, Self's the Man, Reading Habits, The Card-Players, Annus Mirabilis, Administration (ta again)[2] and Fiction and the Reading Public. I have no copy of the last, though I remember bits of it well. Could you send me a text? And where did it appear? – Essays in Crit was it? I have to quote sources of out-of-the-way material. I know, by the way, that not many of the 9 would fit into *Punch*, say, but in my book ha-ha entertaining verse, whatever else it may be doing besides entertain, even if that includes giving the reader a nasty jab here and there, is light. The OUP will be asking for formal permissions in due course.

You know, it's been a bit of a sweat finding enough good stuff (which is not the reason a lot of you has got in). Hate Lear. Can't stand Ogden Nash. Don't care for Rochester. And to think of including extracts beginning A man so various that he SPENT ALL HIS TIME WITH HIS HEAD DOWN A LAVATORY BOWL or A daring pilot in FINDING HIS WAY TO THE SEWAGE FARM . . . well, it kinda makes you sick.[3] Want to leave him out, what? I mean I want to leave him out altogether, what?

I'll keep you posted about Freeman: nothing for the moment. Ran into Wally Fawkes the other day and he said he'd be keen to come along too. Strange fancies beset me of flying Wild Bill over from NYC (if he's still with us) and setting up a recording session. 'Memphis Blues? Right: ah-one, ah-two . . .'

Yes, it looks as if this Flask Walk deal will go through, though I daren't uncross my fingers yet. How horrible about JBW [John Wain] – that books to do with him still get published, I mean.[4] He's a turd, you see. Yes, that's what I said, a turd.

Your blood-pressure's rather high, Mr Amis; I'm afraid you'll have to cut down on bum,

Kingsley

[TLS: Bodleian]

2. Copied out by Larkin in a letter of 13 April 1976; see *LL*, p. 538.

3. The beginnings of lines from John Dryden's allegorical satire 'Absalom and Achitophel' (1681), from Part 1 (lines 160 and 545).

4. Larkin had reported to Amis on 13 April 1976, in *LL*, p. 538, that 'J.B.W. has edited the 1000th Everyman'.

TO ROBERT CONQUEST – 11 JUNE 1976

Lemmons, Hadley Common, Barnet, Herts

Dear Bob,

Enjoyed the cowgirl, though it'll be hard to find a place for in the old anth.[1] Which I suppose is pretty near done. I'll pump Peter Porter about the younger sods if any, go through the NS [New Statesman] comps and it'll be time to start the weeding-out. It would be v. handy if you were around to consult, so if you're wondering whether to come over sooner rather than later, come sooner. Weather amazing: 86° in London the other day, hotter than Sicily. Oh yes, and I've done Ted Pauker's contribution: a slightly cut (to avoid dated or over-topical stuff e.g. Crosland and also things like pricks on prongs) version of Good night Session, Chuck it Heath and Party Hack (both entire).[2] That gives him more space than any contemporary bar Betjeman.

Our move to Hampstead approaches in a sort of sidelong way, with the buyer of this place behaving like a shit and the mortgage company like a Central European bureaucracy. For the moment it all looks all right, but a lot can go wrong in the 6 weeks till moving-day. What national news? You no doubt heard about the Government cheating at a division by getting a paired chap to vote for them. But perhaps didn't see the case of the security guard who saved his company £100,000 by catching pilferers and has now been put in an office at union request pending total dismissal. 'Our members don't want him round the place at all' one union boss said. Yes, *said*, that's the frightening thing.

My proof of The Alteration has come and looks quite nice. At a first glance they haven't changed things like mustach and ristorante

---

1. Another 'Victor Gray' effort, too strong for *NOBLV*, but not for Parrott, ed., *The Penguin Book of Limericks*, p. 291: 'Meanwhile, back home at the ranch, /I was fucking a cowgirl called Blanche; /She said: "It's a change/From riding the range, /But I still prefer brandy-and-branch" ', which should, of course, read '*bourbon*-and-branch', as in Conquest's original.

2. Amis prints four poems by 'Ted Pauker' in *NOBLV*: 'A Grouchy Good Night to the Academic Year' is the 'slightly cut' one; 'A Trifle for Trafalgar Square' ends with the line 'Chuck it, Heath!'; and 'Garland for a Propagandist' ends 'I'll be a Party hack, Sir!' 'Crosland' is Anthony Crosland (1918–77), Labour politician, Minister and theorist of socialism.

which is amazing.[3] Saw the jacket the other day: v. striking, and would have been perfect *if the artist had read the book*, e.g. I say the New England national emblem is an American lion so of course he draws an eagle. The US edition has been or is being separately set up. Nice of them, I thought, till I found by chance that they wanted to change my punctuation about 8 times a page on average, e.g. 'No. No.' becomes 'No, no.' which is ENTIRELY different. Why can't they keep their bloody little paws to themselves?

Oh, did I say I had what I thought was a tempting first line for a limerick? The Committee records, with regret . . . Give it a mull.

See ya
Kingsley

[TLS: Recipient]

TO ROBERT CONQUEST – 5 JULY 1976

Lemmons etc. moving on 21st July to Gardnor House,
Flask Walk, London N.W.3

Dear Bob,

Fucking amazing weather continues. It'll be 90 today and the front lawn is mostly straw. At least the Arabs who are buying up London will feel at home. Harry Harrison came up yesterday, talked faster and less intelligibly than ever, though I did gather he stands to make $250,000 out of a film he's nearly sure they'll make[1] – anyway, it was nice to see him and to entertain in one person a Yank on the 200th anniv and a Jew when the Israeli news broke.[2]

As you see, our move approaches. I am getting terrified: I just can't believe that any human agency will move all these thousands of objects from here to there, or anywhere. My main job so far has been drinking

3. See Amis to Mrs Sutcliffe, 30 March 1976, note 1.

---

1. The only one of Harrison's novels to be made into a film was *Make Room! Make Room!* (1966), released in 1973 as *Soylent Green*.

2. 4 July 1976 was the two hundredth anniversary of the signing of the Declaration of Independence. 'The Israeli news' was the rescue by Israeli paratroopers of 110 hostages from an Air France plane hijacked to Entebbe, Uganda, by Palestinian terrorists.

up the nearly-empty bottles, horrible stuff like cherry vodka, Mavrodaphne, raki etc. Do I gather you now mean to come over in late July? The new house will be uninhabitable by day (builders etc.) for several weeks, but the Lubbocks[3] nearby have offered me a room to work in, and there are plenty of pubs. For my own advantage I hope you do come then (though Aug wd probably suit me almost as well) to look through the anthology with me. I'm getting near the end of compiling the long list now, hoping to get to the position of being able to throw out one poem in three. Thought I was going to make a great leap forward recently when I took Peter Porter out to lunch and he very decently brought with him a list of present-day shags, several of whom I'd never heard of. Good-oh, I thought, this'll take care of the last 30pp or so. Like buggery! The list kicked off with G Ewart, whom Philip is always cracking up. I settled down to read through him with many a sigh of anticipation, finally emerging with Miss Twye and a couple of bare possibles.[4] Do you know his work? I react in one of three ways: 1. Well yes, that's true, now that I come to bother to think of it. 2. I say, you are a daring fellow, going on about ladies' nipples and pubic hair like that. 3. *Yes*, Gavin, all *right*, you *are* a card, *sure*, RIGHT, you're a *terrific* card, ABSOLUTELY, I *KNOW*!!! Don't bother to tell Philip that, because I'm looking forward to doing so myself. Then . . . Martin Bell, Douglas Dunn, Alan Brownjohnwillie, EDWIN BROCK.[5] They're *worse* than I'd imagined, or remembered from seeing odd bits in magazines: *a n d t h a t ' s s a y i n g s o m e t h i n g.* Here's one of Brock's in full. Won't take me long to type it out.

3. Roger and Moyra Lubbock, Hampstead neighbours, had been introduced to Amis by George Gale. Roger Lubbock (b. 1922) was in publishing; Moyra Lubbock (b. 1923) is an actress, under the name Moyra Fraser.

4. Only 'Miss Twye' of Gavin Ewart's poems appears in *NOBLV*.

5. The poets Douglas Dunn (b. 1942), a Scot, Martin Bell (1918–78), Alan Brownjohn (b. 1931) and Edwin Brock (1927–97), English.

RELATIONSHIP
Will you
speak
I am
listening
your lips
move
your tongue
touches
your teeth
you make
words

will you
speak
I am
looking
your hands
move
your head
inclines
your forehead
makes
gestures

will you
speak
I am
listening
and look
I am
watching

and do not
wait for me
I will still
be thinking

*Pretty bloody good, eh? Nice of him to have gone to all the trouble of writing that out. Grand way of filling up a book, too. You know, you can see them trimming; he and Brownjohn and others started in the late 50s or v. early 60s and weren't bad then – you know, rhymed, sometimes at least, nearly scanned, went some way across the page. Then they feel they have to 'develop', 'forge a personal style', not be 'left behind' in the Movement, and write piss on purpose. So John W[ain]. I think they must listen to Al [Alvarez] – who incidentally will be about 5 yards from our front door in Flask Walk. Hey, it would be fun to include in the anth a poem by Sylvia Plath, one of the really balls-aching ones, and refer in the Intro to her sadly undervalued comic manner.

Still laughing at your Blunt and Arundel Castle,[6] but unable to get further myself than

> There was a young fellow called Jock
> Whose anatomy'd give you a shock –

Incidentally, one of these pissers, Tony Harrison,[7] whom I'd never even heard of before, prints as his epigraph

> There was a young man of Leeds
> Who swallowed a packet of seeds . . .

He's no good, then, is he? one naturally says to oneself.

6. Limericks from Conquest; see *NOBLV*, pp. 282–3: 'One morning old Wilfred Scawen Blunt/Was wanting a trip in a punt;/But the puntmen had struck,/So he shouted "Good Luck!/– Your wage is a social affront!"'; 'While visiting Arundel Castle/I sent my sick uncle a parcel./The contents of it/Were the local grey grit/To rub on his sore metatarsal.'

7. Tony Harrison (b.1937); the epigraph, identified as 'traditional', appears in *The Loiners* (1970) and reads in its entirety: 'There was a young man of Leeds/Who swallowed a packet of seeds./A Pure white rose/Grew out of his nose/And his arse was covered with weeds.'

of this when I die

That's it. Return to* at top of page.

Hope your basset trouble[8] has cleared up. I (between ourselves) have suffered a number of frightful ballockings from Jane for not caring enough about her caring so much about leaving here. Fair enough, but a ballocking doesn't much tend to get one to turn all sympathetic, somehow. Not invited to Buck Ho:[9] – they did me a couple of years ago. Let me know when you're coming, and if it's after 21st be sure not to lose our new phone no.

Cheers
Kingsley

[TLS: Recipient]

TO PHILIP LARKIN – 5 JULY 1976

Lemmons, Hadley Common, Barnet, Hertfordshire.
On and after 21st July: Gardnor House, Flask Walk, London N.W.3

Dear Philip,

I get hay-fever ALL THE YEAR ROUND these days – dog-fur I think – but, or so, I sympathise. 'Fraid I can't manage one of your special sorts of letter: just I have and hold Fiction Public and will use it and thank you, and will scrap Admin: actually it isn't as good as the others. Thanks too for squeezing my arm about my own stuff: think I will put in Evans entire but no more.

What's all this about Gavin Ewart? I got all (except his v. early) stuff out of the Arts C. library and settled down with many an anticipatory flutter, only to find it was all balls. Apart from Miss Twye, the only two possibles were 2001 and Short Time. [. . .]

8. A reference to a difference of opinion between Conquest and his wife Caroleen about the health of their basset hound, Bluebell. Conquest adds: 'C. wanted to have her put down as incontinent, but I called the kennels to which she'd been sent, and they said she was OK, so [I] flew her to USA' (personal communication, 17 October 2000).

9. Conquest had received an invitation to a Buckingham Palace garden party to be held on 29 July.

He's better then Alan Brownjohn, though, or *Martin Bell*, or Douglas Dunn (aaoh! aoh! aooh!) or EDWIN BROCK

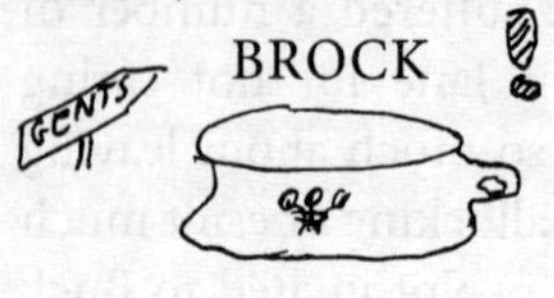

Hurry up please its bum[1]
Kingsley

[ALS: Bodleian]

TO ROY FULLER – 19 JULY 1976

Lemmons, Hadley Common, Barnet, Hertfordshire. From 23rd July: Gardnor House, Flask Walk NW

Dear Roy,

Thank you for all the unpaid work you have done on my behalf.[1] No shame that it didn't come up with anything.*

H.S. Mackintosh and J.K.S. are in, must look up the R.L.S. things.[2] The main strategy is going to be heavy reliance on the obvious (Oxford has taught nobody anything if it hasn't taught him that) with enough sudden dashes into the understandably obscure to trick the reader into thinking I've worked my head off: – Walter Raleigh, Henry Reed, Earl of Rochester, *G.R. Samways*[3] – at least, I hope you haven't heard of him.

As for 'light' as against 'comic' etc. I have simply cast my net as wide as possible, excluding only those stuffed-owl unintentionalities which in my experience can be read once at most. Getting the permissions will be the big bugger but the O.U.P. have promised to do that.

1. An allusion to the refrain in 'A Game of Chess', Part 2 of T.S. Eliot's *The Waste Land* (1922): 'HURRY UP PLEASE IT'S TIME.'

---

1. For Roy Fuller, see Amis to Larkin, 6 June 1952, note 4; the unpaid work was for *NOBLV*.

2. Though Robert Louis Stevenson and J.K. Stephen are represented in *NOBLV*, H.S. Mackintosh, author of *Ballades and Other Verse* (1953) and *Rhyme and Reason* (1956), is not. Stephen (1859–92), a journalist and author of parodies and light verse, was Virginia Woolf's cousin.

3. In the end, all except George Richard Samways (b. 1895) were included in *NOBLV*. Samways titles include *War Lyrics* (1916) and *Fighting to the Front: A Story of School Life* (1917); he also produced poems and stories for a variety of publications from 1910–40, including *Magnet, Punch* and *The Companion Papers.*

You will have seen above that we're on the move. Terrifying, but at least we'll be more accessible. It would be fun to see you and raise a jar.

Yours ever
Kingsley

*EXCEPT the GKC triolet√√√[4]

[ALS: John Fuller]

TO ROBERT CONQUEST – 12 AUGUST 1976

Gardnor Ho: Flask Walk NW3

Dear Bob,

Was fine seeing you. I never thanked you for putting in all that conscientious work on the light vse, so here goes: thank you. Apologies too for unworthy suspicions that you weren't going to get down to it. I still seem unable to finish the bloody thing: feel lethargically that I must get hold of that Sackville poem somehow, then find my attention has drifted to other matters. Oh, do you think this is any good? – by old Jo Bartley of Swansea:

He who is wounded in the stones
  Or has his privy member cut off,
Shall, when he rises* from his bones,
  Be from the joys of heaven shut off.
At this one need feel no surprise,
  For heaven's chief delight amour is:
It would be hell to get no rise*
  While lolling in the laps of houris.

*Editing needed: suggestions? (*if you think poem is any good*)[1]

Had lunch with Harry Harrison and Joanie at the Royal Garden Hotel yesterday. Harry had to be restrained after shouting 'Israel lives!' at a group of the burnous-clad Arabs who thronged the place. Joanie

4. See *NOBLV*, p.201.

1. Conquest thought not, on theological as well as literary grounds, since 'a chap in his condition would get his prick back at the resurrection' (letter to Amis, 19–20 August 1976).

was on her best behaviour, which meant that she told me stories about herself and friends of hers I'd never heard of in a voice so quiet I had to keep straining to hear while Harry and Kyril Bonfiglioli,[2] who had also turned up, exchanged tales, cracks, *anything*. Unbelievably vile food: J couldn't eat all her cold lobster or 2 lbs of roast beef, so she got the waitress to put the salvag[e]able remnants on a separate plate for her to take away to tide her over till dinner. Kyril B (know him?) was quite funny about sniffing a pricey wine, saying in a loud connoisseur's voice 'What a huge nose!' and finding he was sitting between Hilary Rubinstein and Tom Rosenthal.[3]

Thought the enclosed might amuse you. The cartoon is from Lit Gazeta.

Oh, did I tell you I was doing a NS London Diary? It would be a bloody good idea if you could let me have a bit of gossip or even straight news pissing on some lefty hero or notion or extolling villain, etc. 'A friend in Washington tells me' or 'RC now in Washington tells me', whichever you like. Do see what you can come up with. My deadline is 31 Aug.

Cheers
Kingers

[TLS: Recipient]

TO ELIZABETH JANE HOWARD – 15, 16, 17 SEPTEMBER 1976

Gardnor House, Flask Walk, London, N.W.3

Dearest Piney,[1]

All well here. Have just come back from Dr G,[2] who expressed herself well satisfied with my general state. Before that I'd been to

2. Kyril Bonfiglioli (d.1985), art dealer and thriller and science fiction writer, best known for the Mortdecai Trilogy, *Don't Point that Thing at Me* (1972), *Something Nasty in the Woodshed* (1976) and *After You with the Pistol* (1979); Editor, *Science Fantasy* (1964–66).

3. Tom Rosenthal (b.1935), publisher.

---

1. Elizabeth Jane Howard was staying for two weeks with friends near Ste. Maxime on the French Riviera.

2. Dr Patricia Gillan, a sex therapist working at the time at the Maudsley Hospital in South London, recommended to Amis by his Australian friend James Durham. One of two

Pinewood Studies to be talked to about the new James Bond film,[3] which they want me to write an article on. Don't know that I will, but it was fun to go, meet Roger Moore, etc. Last night went to dinner solo with John and Sue[4] – v. gd fun with John getting rather pissed in his most amiable vein, full of stories about Arab billionaires. Going backwards – Monday nothing much but work. Sunday lunch-time Phil and Jane[5] came – she impressed more than ever as likely to be good for him; he for her too, no doubt. Sunday evening Mart and Emma[6] took me to a rather awful party at Dee's;[7] Jonathan Miller[8] told me all about Shakespeare for over an hour. Saturday stayed chez Ward[9] after dining with them Fri.

Tomorrow I go to Clive jr[10] because my loose tooth is really flapping in the breeze. Then lunch with Tony Powell at Bertorellis. Then I go to Fanny again. Can't face Dolly's,[11] or rather coming back here late

sex therapists consulted by Amis and Howard in the mid-1970s after what Amis describes as 'various difficulties had arisen between us' (*Memoirs*, p.117). Patricia and Richard Gillan co-authored *Sex Therapy Today* (London: Open Books, 1976), a copy of which Amis possessed (it is now in HEHL, inscribed 'To Jane and Kingsley. With love and best wishes from Patricia and Richard'). For Amis on sex therapy see *Jake's Thing* (1978). Amis had previously consulted therapists, in the period 1946–59, for fears and panic attacks (according to Jacobs, in a note deposited in HEHL).

3. *The Spy Who Loved Me* (1977), directed by Lewis Gilbert, with Roger Moore as Bond.

4. Dr and Mrs John Allison. The Allisons were friends of Jane Howard and her second husband, James Douglas-Henry, and met Amis through her in 1965. John Allison (1926–78) was Jane Howard's doctor and eventually became Amis's as well; Susan Allison began helping Amis with his business correspondence shortly after the move to Flask Walk in 1976. From 1978, the date of her husband's death, to Amis's own death in 1995, she was employed, in a more regular but still part-time capacity, as Amis's secretary. John Allison (with John Betjeman) was co-dedicatee of Amis's *Collected Poems*.

5. Philip Amis and his wife Jane Galsworthy Amis.

6. Emma Soames, journalist and editor, working at the time on the *Evening Standard*.

7. Dee Wells (b.1925), American novelist and freelance writer, wife of the philosopher A.J. Ayer (1910–89).

8. Jonathan Miller (b.1934), the celebrated polymath, directed the George Melly adaptation of *Take a Girl Like You* (1970). It starred Hayley Mills as Jenny Bunn.

9. Christopher Ward (b.1942), journalist, editor and businessman; at the time Assistant Editor, *Sunday Mirror* (1976–79), later Editor, *Daily Express* (1981–83); Fanny Ward, his wife at the time, was a model.

10. Clive Debenham, Jr, Amis's dentist.

11. Dolly Burns.

with only Mrs U.[12] here – Monkey is off to Winchester (?)[13] for the night. Don't want to spoil my good record of so far unbroken cool without benefit of Valium. So I'm going to 'forget' the Dolly date.

No real news: Light Verse trudges on. Should be ready to deliver next week. Penthouse USA want me to help defend them (by supplying them with a statement only, I presume) in an obscenity action. Dodgy? I accepted a chat-about-paperbacks assignment for Woman's Hour on your behalf – am doing one myself in a couple of weeks. Here are some cuttings about your play.[14] Others I only saw went roughly – Evening Standard preview 'might be fun', written by EJH; Daily Express preview recommendation; Times preview mentioned it; Evening News preview also said by EJH; D Mail preview recommended, said by 'novelist EJH'; Guardian review by Nancy Banks-Smith gave it a fairly good write-up with some routine snide remarks but/and said 'EJH did a skilful sentimental job.' So anyway you had plenty of coverage. Verdict of Christopher, Fanny and Monkey on Fri was Jolly good except for John M-Brown & the girl[15] – S. Tafler[16] excellent.

16th Sept

As you can see I now *am* at Fanny's.[17] Meant to tell you that while I was at Pinewood I mentioned Col. Sun to the PR chap, saying quite innocently that I'd heard long ago that Sal[t]zman[18] had more or less specifically rejected the idea of filming it. PR chap said well, you know Sal[t]zman has left the organisation now and, er, let's say I've heard people *mentioning* Col Sun. So there may be something in store for us there.

Clive jr was encouraging about my tooth – I have gum trouble at

12. Mrs Lily Uniacke (b.1913), housekeeper; though she had a house of her own in Barnet, she moved to Lemmons in 1968, in a cottage alongside the main house, to care for Miss Howard's mother, Katherine. After Katherine's death Mrs Uniacke stayed on as housekeeper. She remembers Amis as 'a very nice gentleman, always very nice to me' (personal communication, 5 January 1999).

13. To see cousins.

14. *Skittles*, broadcast on Granada television.

15. John Moulder Brown (b.1931), English actor; the girl was played by Maureen O'Brien (b.1943), an English film and television actress.

16. Sidney Tafler (1916–79), English stage and screen actor.

17. The rest of the letter is written on Christopher Ward's headed notepaper.

18. Harry Saltzman (b.1915), film producer. Struck it rich in the 1960s and early 1970s with the James Bond series, co-produced with Albert R. ('Cubby') Broccoli (until the partnership dissolved in 1976).

that spot but he can lash the tooth itself to the ones on either side, *even if* it falls out or has to be taken out.

You've done well to miss the weather this week: some rain every day until today and chilly too. Hope you are having a lovely time with lots of sun and sunbathing and bathing and all that, and getting nicely rested too. I'm getting along absolutely fine, except that you aren't here. You do seem to have been away for ages. I miss your little beaming face. That and seeing the back of your head as you sit at your desk. And other things. Oh yes – I was thinking the other day how much I enjoyed our winter holiday at Woodstock etc. I remember those two walks in the park with amazing (for me) vividness, and us snuggling in the hotel. Couldn't we go again this coming Feb? – not necessarily there but the same sort of place. See what you think.

Fanny is just putting Martha and Sadie to bed and (very goodly, at 7.10 pm) I'm looking forward to my first drink of the evening. Then Kojak at 8.10, Shaft at 10.30 . . .

I Love you B

"Hugs and lots of kisses from Fanno"

Sal and Tod (alias Nigel)[19] came to sups last night and I must say seemed fonder of each other in a comfy marital way than I've ever seen them before.

17th Sept

Back from Fan's and got your dear little letter which I'll answer another time – otherwise I'll never get this off. All was okay with Dolly who wants us to go there the Monday after you get back. Helen[20] is here. Monkey thinks he's going to Switzerland on Sunday, but it somehow seems that he isn't sure yet.

Writing again soon – love
B.

[ALS: HEHL]

19. Sally Amis and her husband Nigel Service, nicknamed 'Tod'. The family joke was that the nickname derived from 'on his tod', rhyming slang for 'alone' (from Tod Sloan, the American jockey, 1874–1933).

20. Elizabeth Jane Howard's secretary, Helen Benckendorf.

TO ELIZABETH JANE HOWARD – 21 SEPTEMBER 1976

Gardnor House, Flask Walk, London, N.W.3.

Dearest Minnie,

Am Expressing this to try to make sure it gets there before you leave – must try to remember to say so on the envelope to stop you thinking the roof has fallen in. Some workmen went last week and others are here today – yesterday too I think. Plush[1] is fine; she sleeps in your study now because her snoring kept waking me up. I am fine too – still no valium and in general good nick. In 1 hr 55 mins you will have been away exactly ⅔ of the total.

Sasha, Helen and Mrs Hoddy[2] are in full residence. S. is certainly a paid-up member of the PEN Club (Pissed Every Night) but v. amiable. Helen copes fine but with usual amusing/maddening lapses. Monkey hates being with them so much – Sasha does talk about Christianity a bit – that he put on a wonderfully half-hearted show of being ill so that he could eat in his room: he got well enough just long enough to eat a very large portion of steak-&-k pie, then was ill again, but well enough to fly to Zurich the next afternoon (Sunday). Back Tuesday, he said – 'or perhaps Wednesday'. That probably means very late tonight.

Had a very thorough hour of having my teeth cleaned up by Clive's hygienist yesterday. Came away armed with much information on how to use a toothbrush – it seems I've been quite wrong on that all these years – and two strange brushes, one for back, one for front. Loose tooth to be anchored on Monday.

Don't worry too much about your novel.[3] You have a very good idea there. Let it just roll round your head without actually contemplating sitting down and starting. Then when you get back I'll give you

---

1. Rosie Plush, Elizabeth Jane Howard's red ruby King Charles spaniel, the model for the 'Furry Barrel' in *Girl, 20* (1971): 'a reactionary little dog: authoritarian, hierarchical, snobbish, with strong views on the family, the maintenance of order, the avoidance of change, the sanctity of private property and . . . the preservation of barriers between the races' (p.11). See also Amis to Conquest, 9 September 1971, note 5, and to Thwaite, 4 January 1973, note 2.

2. Sasha (later 'S.'), the husband of Elizabeth Jane Howard's secretary, Helen; Mrs Hoddy was a temporary daily cleaner.

3. *Getting it Right* (1982).

some good pep-talks wrapped up in treats and between us we'll get the thing off the mark.

Yes, of course I'll meet you. Mr Appleton's lot[4] are indeed jolly good. I'll telephone towards the end of the week. Hope your weather has improved: ours has. I love your face –

Rabbit

[ALS: HEHL]

TO THE EDITOR, *OBSERVER* – SEPTEMBER 1976

Gardnor House, Flask Walk, London, N.W.3

Sir,

I cannot be sure whether William Feaver[1] means us to think it was careless of Stubbs to label an engraving 'Tygers at Play' when the animals shown were 'in fact' leopards, but if so it was the carelessness of a whole era. Despite Buffon's classification, 'tyger' or 'tiger' was constantly used for 'leopard', and for 'panther' too, throughout the 18th century.[2]

Yours faithfully,
Kingsley Amis

TO PHILIP LARKIN – 11 OCTOBER 1976

Gardnor House, Flask Walk, London, N.W.3.

My dear Philip,

Fine, wonderful, perfect. I have you booked into what by then will be a fully functioning bedroom on 2/3 Nov. At the moment it's still my study, with piles of papers on every horizontal surface. Some of these relate to what Martin calls my book of light shit, though I delivered

4. Taxi service.

---

1. William Feaver (b.1942), art critic, *Observer* (1975–).
2. Georges-Louis Leclerc, Comte de Buffon (1707–88), French naturalist; author of *Histoire Naturelle* (1749–88), a work in thirty-six volumes.

a sort of text to the Kiwis at the OUP[1] the week before last. Part of the pleasure has of course been *keeping out* dull fuckers like Dryden, Burns, Blake (A Petty Sneaking Knave I Knew:[2] Why Don't you stick your Prick up you?), *Don Marquis.*[3] Ogden Nash (aaoh! aoh! aooh!), Harry Graham[4] (especially HIM) and all the tribe from Alan Brownj ← TOILETS → varez . . .

Ole Bruce, sounding sober for the first time since long before his *crise*, rang up the other day with a wild scheme for him and you and me to write a 70th-birthday tribute to JD Carr which he seems to think I could get into the Observer – you too? no? Ponder on it – I mean on how to tell him shit to it.

Your godson[5] got married the other week. I told him not to expect anything like a pipe of port, something more like your undertaking to guarantee the education of his no Christ leggo my

Mr Amis seems undecided whether he has written a thriller or a work of serious bum,

Kingsley

[ALS: Bodleian]

---

1. Dan Davin (1913–90), novelist and publisher, head of the Clarendon Press, the academic division of OUP, was a New Zealander, a former Rhodes Scholar at Balliol; Jon Stallworthy, his deputy at the time, is the child of New Zealand parents.

2. 'A pretty sneaking knave I knew/"O Mr Cr–, how do ye do?"', from Blake's Miscellaneous Notebook Verses (c.1807–9).

3. Don Marquis (1878–1937), whimsical American poet and playwright, creator of *Archy and Mehitabel* (1927).

4. Henry Graham (1874–1936), author of light verse, under his own name and the pseudonym Col. D. Steamer; *Ruthless Rhymes for Heartless Homes* (1899) was originally published under the Steamer pseudonym.

5. Philip Amis.

TO ROBERT CONQUEST – 12 OCTOBER 1976

Gardnor Ho: Flask Wk

Dear Bob,

Your last couple to hand. No sign of Harries[1] yet but standing by. 'Wen' is especially good because it goes against the -y tendency of the family as a whole. Enjoyed Olet, but it doesn't rhyme with toilet does it?[2] Delivered my anthol to the Kiwis at the OUP the other week, complete but for a gap or 2. Still can't find any Milne. There's some Wodehouse too I gather but I haven't seen it. Must visit Punch. Found what must be that gannet-bath thing of Philip's: no good, of course, nothing about Sapland etc.[3] Have had excellent reviews for my ballocks

---

1. Owen Harries (b.1930), a friend of Conquest's, spent many years in Australia, as Lecturer and Senior Lecturer in Politics, University of Sydney (1955–65); adviser to the Australian Foreign Minister (1975–77); Head of Policy Planning (1977–79); and adviser to the Prime Minister (1979–81). He is currently Editor, *The National Interest* (1985–), a Washington-based public-policy journal.

2. Comments on Conquest's 'An Incident in the Life of Lytton Strachey': 'Taken short in Oxford Circus/-O, I could not control it!/I smiled and said 'Cujusque stercus/Sibi bene olet'/ But they just shouted 'Ere's a berk as/wouldn't use the to'let.' As for 'Wen', presumably it was Conquest's latest addition to the Tupper family, for which see Amis to Conquest, 1 November 1967; also *Memoirs*, p.144; 'Where Philip Larkin and I had thought it funny enough to spend half a minute inventing characters called Emeritus Professor "Stuffy" Tupper and his wife Poppy, Bob went away and produced a whole enormous family of Tuppers, including Whirly (the helicopter pioneer) and Bangy and Bashy (the wrestling twins) plus a distant Scottish branch, the Bell-Tuppers, including Willie, Canny, Woody, Musty, Mighty et no doubt al.' Conquest disclaims some of these, printed under his name by Martin Amis in a *New Statesman* competition, along with Whisky, Rye, Poppy, Rammy, etc. 'The Bell-Tuppers were entirely Martin's invention,' he particularly insists (personal communication, 17 October 2000).

3. See Larkin to Amis, 6 October 1976 (in HEHL):

> do you remember
>
> Over the whale-road
> Over the gannet-bath
> There lies Sapland–
> Money for jam!
>
> —?
> I recall it from before the war, and *think* it is DB Wyndham-Lewis ('T Shy')

(Larkin had also quoted these lines in an earlier letter to Conquest, 26 May 1976, in *LL*, p.542). Amis did not include them in *NOBLV*, but did include 'Sapphics', another poem by the author and light versifier D.B. Wyndham Lewis (1891–1969), pseudonym 'Timothy Shy'; the lines Larkin quotes from memory, inaccurately, come from Lewis's *Take it to Bed* (1944).

book,[4] though they all get it wrong, can't read what's in front of them. Times chap for instance was quite favourable but said to imply that universal RCism would preclude medical research and inventive transportation shows ignorance of real Naples and Austria. In fact, the (*my*) Pope has to start his population-reducing war because medicine is saving so many lives, and even the Nips haven't beaten my 195 mph train. And that clot Julian S[ymons] showed he hadn't understood a word by saying on telly that 'the only justification' for making Poe a general was that the real P had been at W Point. But you know how it is. Have taken over telly crit on the Obs for 4 weeks while Clive[5] goes down under. It's a pest watching all these crappy chat shows and documentaries but you do get a grand chance of pissing on blokes. Last Sun I got at Dennis Potter, CND, folk art and Peter Jay. Next time, so far, Benn and Jenkins.[6] J's reputation for integrity etc. seems to rest on his not knowing his own mind about anything, contradicting self. Says we need more socialism and also more capitalism – jolly honest chap. Old Arnold B[7] came through on the phone but I didn't get a chance to see him. He said he thought you'd never come back here, except on visits of course. Hope he was wrong; you're needed here. The govt are all mad, Healey[8] *warning us* that hard times lie ahead, Crosland hob-nobbing with the Czech foreign sec as well as African terrorists. Perry [Worsthorne]'s mad too by the way, wrote a piece saying Heath's speech announcing reconciliation with Margt could only be compared with the moment when JFK announced that the US had beaten Russia down over Cuba. Just a quick word with Claudie [Worsthorne] on the same occasion, long enough for her to ask me if I was going to shoot the Sun Tel chap for his [in fact, of course, extremely favourable] notice of my bk. Did you say you

4. *The Alteration*, called the 'ballocks book' because of the fate of its young hero, ten-year-old Hubert Anvil, whose glorious voice must be preserved at all costs, even that of his manhood.

5. Clive James.

6. Dennis Potter (1935–94), television playwright, best known for the six-part serial *Pennies from Heaven* (1978); also wrote fiction, stage plays, screenplays, and worked as a journalist and critic. Peter Jay (b.1937), writer, journalist, broadcaster; Ambassador to the United States (1977–79). Anthony Wedgwood Benn and Roy Jenkins (b.1920), Labour Minister and Deputy Leader (1970–72), President of the European Commission (1977–81); became the SDP's first leader (1982–83) (see Amis to Conquest, 9 March 1981, note 1); among subsequent positions of influence, has been Chancellor of the University of Oxford since 1987. Created Life Peer (1987).

7. Arnold Beichman (b.1913), American political scientist, writer, journalist.

8. Denis Healey (b.1917), Labour politician and Minister, at the time Chancellor of the Exchequer; created Life Peer (1992).

were coming over in Nov? Fix it if you can. Bring a few dollars and you can take us all to the Mirabelle.[9]

Cheers
Kingsley

[TLS: Recipient]

TO PHILIP LARKIN – 23 OCTOBER 1976

Gardnor House, Flask Walk, London, N.W.3.

My dear Philip,

No, not to worry ('I'll get an Irish wolfhound to worry your –'); no question of turning me out. You will occupy the now luxuriously-appointed bedroom I used as a study until a couple of weeks ago when my *study*, on the ground floor, was ready for me to move in. [. . .]

We thought we'd lay on a bit of a show for you since you don't come to London all that often. A cocktail party at about 5.30 with some of your admirers – George Steiner, Ian Hamilton, Arnold Wesker; Alvarez of course, and I hope AL Rowse, though I haven't heard from him yet.[1] Then I've booked seats at *Equus*, which is really the most *exciting* thing to hit the stage for years,[2] and after that a place I know with a marvellous group of young West Indiaaaaeeeeooghghgh

Was much tickled with a letter from the Pres of John's[3] saying they've awarded me an hon. fellowship, alongside (or shortly behind) Graves and you. And – though they didn't say this, and in fairness to myself it was some minutes before this aspect of the matter occurred to me – *NOT* IN THE COMPANY OF ARSEHOLING JOHN PISSING BARRY SODDING WAIN. I expect they've got to know him

9. Expensive restaurant on Curzon Street in Mayfair.

---

1. From the enticing guest list: George Steiner (b.1929), critic and novelist; Arnold Wesker (b.1932), dramatist, associated with the 'kitchen sink' school; A.L. Rowse (1903–98), Shakespearean scholar.

2. *Equus* (1973) by Peter Shaffer (b.1926).

3. Sir Richard Southern (b.1912), medieval historian; President, St John's College, Oxford (1969–81); Chichele Professor of Modern History, Oxford (1961–69).

well enough since he's been living in Oxford, don't you? he asked with a slight smile. The middle classes are being destroyed by bum–K.

PS: Yes, fine, any time you find convenient, I'll await you. You do like Gordon's gin, do you? I'll assume so unless I hear.

[ALS: Bodleian]

TO ROBERT CONQUEST – 28 OCTOBER 1976

Gardnor Ho Flask Wk NW3

Dear Bob,

Good to get yours and hear that you're not really emigrating. I can quite see your temptations, like being paid for getting pissed or screwing. Actually UK doesn't look bad yet; I mean the foundations might go any moment but up top it's much the same. The only things one can really point to are rocketing prices of good meat and fish and brand-shortages in booze, thus 12 Bell's whisky ordered may on arrival prove to be 6 Bell's 6 Haig. Bearable. Doing our house up, for instance, has been bloody expensive but not impossibly so. Am in my study now after nearly 3 months camping out in various bedrooms, and settled enough to start a longish poem – no, *not* like The Forests of Lithuania.[1]

I've found one or two PGW pieces in Punch but they tend to be too topical. Do you know where to find the poem you quote,[2] or any others scattered in his fiction or autobiogy? Still chasing Milne. Oh, by the way, I was using the old rhym-dict the other day and had my eye caught by a running head: ĔF´in-it, which had the result you can imagine.[3]

1. By Donald Davie, published in 1959. Amis's poem was 'A Reunion' (see Amis to Conquest, 21 November 1976), first published in the *New Statesman*, 24 and 31 December 1976, pp. 914–15; reprinted in *CP*, pp. 138–45.

2. *NOBLV* publishes two Wodehouse poems, both non-topical, both first published in *Punch* (1901): 'To William (Whom we have Missed)', about Buffalo Bill, and 'The Gourmet's Love-Song'.

3. Amis is referring to a Conquest poem, not used in *NOBLV*: 'Whenever I am out of luck/I use a word that ends in uck/I'm sorry I can't be more definite/But here's a hint: it has an f in it.'

I'd like to include it, but am not sure of the author. Gray? Anon? And what's the one about the guardsman of Crewe?[4]

Thanks largely to Russell,[5] moves are being made to get the lunch going again, as a monthly do. Iain[6] is sending out stats fixing the first for 16th November, which I imagine you won't be able to make. Oh Christ: Bruce [Montgomery] rang the other day asking me if I was going to turn up on Thurs (today). I said I couldn't (true) and he then maundered on pathetically and also maddeningly (I was just going out) about a poem of Belloc's he thought I might include if he could remember how it went. 'I'm tight' he announced unnecessarily after a time. Which means, surely, he hasn't long to go. More cheerfully: in Bertorelli's the other day I was waiting for a bloke, it was early, almost empty, and a voice rang out, 'I saw him in a queers' programme on TV'. Rumble rumble from another bloke. 'Oh yes, it was definitely a queers' programme.' Rumble rumble, while I thought Christ, they're really coming out into the open. Then, 'Oh, he ears, he rearlly ears.' Emerged that I had been listening to a very languid drawling shag talking about a quiz programme. Good, but hard to work neatly into fiction.

I've been – did I say? – filling in for Clive J with TV crit in the Obs. Just the sort of thing to be doing alongside a poem, and great chances to piss on people, as in encl. He was actually worse than I had room to say, saying he didn't like being called greatest since Burns because B wasn't much good; greatest since Dunbar would be more like it.[7] Off his head, of course.

Cheers
Kingers

[TLS: Recipient]

4. 'No good to you,' Conquest responds (in a letter of 1–3 November 1976), then quotes: 'There was an ex-guardsman of Crewe/Who got a fine job in a stew/Where they paid him large sums/For shining boys' bums/And pulling their anuses through.' The limerick is of military provenance, and its last line alludes to the army usage 'Have you pulled your rifle through?'

5. Russell Lewis.

6. Iain Hamilton, ex-editor of the *Spectator* (1962–63).

7. Amis had enclosed the television review 'The Saga of Forsyth', *Observer*, 31 October 1976, p.27, in which he discusses an episode of the *Tonight* programme featuring Hugh MacDiarmid (1892–1978), poet, critic, communist and founder of the National Party of Scotland. Amis describes him as 'vole-faced, red-shirted Hugh MacDiarmid, arguably (as one tribute has it) the greatest Scottish poet since William McGonagall, inferior to him only in sense of irony.' McGonagall, often called the world's worst poet, lived from 1825 (or 1830) to 1902; the dates of his fellow poet and countryman William Dunbar were 1465–1530, those of Robert Burns 1759–96.

TO ROBERT CONQUEST – 21 NOVEMBER 1976

Gardnor House, Flask Walk, London, N.W.3.

Dear Bob,

Glad Bluebell arrived in good shape, and most amused to hear of her jet-lag: just the sort of subject that, could it have arisen 50 years ago, would have inspired a light poem that I'd nearly have put in my anthology. Talking of light poems, I've amazingly just completed one, my first poem of any sort for nearly 2½ years and at 200 lines by far my longest. All about a rather painful regimental reunion I went to. The metre is sort of Easter 1916/Night Before L Was Stretched,[1] chime as well as rhyme, and of course you're sort of writing outer lines of limericks. A specimen that'll show you what I mean – a chap has arrived at the party who's famous for his take-offs, wit etc. At first he talks about blokes the me character knows nothing about, but

> I finally got a word through:
> Had he run into Nicholls at all?
> (A privilege granted to few
> Is meeting a pratt on the scale
> Of Nicholls: by common consent
> A nit-wit not fit to shift shit;
> Whether more of a bastard or cunt,
> Views varied, one has to admit.)

Tony Howard[2] asked for it when he heard about it, but Martin wonders whether he'll take it with all those filthy words in it (there are more). Apparently – did you know? – Tony has a Canon dad whose displeasure he dreads and often receives. By the way, if you can recast the 6th line there to contain nothing but words rhyming or half-rhyming with 'shit', do.

The first of the new, monthly, Bertorollis' series was a great success: Si, Russ, J O'S, Colin (v. pissed and apocalyptically gloomy), Tony H, Frank J, Geo Hutchinson, a Russian whose name I was too dim to catch

---

1. 'Easter 1916' by W.B. Yeats; 'The Night Before Larry Was Stretched' (n.d.), an anonymous poem published in *NOBLV*, pp. 54–6.

2. Anthony Howard (b. 1934), journalist; edited the *New Statesman* from 1972–78.

but who was allegedly a chum of Solzhers' (and who nearly made me burst into tears by telling me that *Jim* had cheered him up in jug) and 2 other shags. Oh, also Richard Hough, whom I know from the Garrick, but who is he?[3] Sound Rightie, anyway. Talking of which, I had lunch with the new editor of Penthouse[4] the other day. Glaswegian of about 35. At one point he said, 'I'm not right-wing at all, you understand. It's just that I won't rest until every traitor and spy in Parliament and the Trade Unions and the Bar and the Press and the Civil Service and the BBC and ITV and the universities and the schools has been exposed and booted out. And I'm just working on how I can use the magazine to help to do that.'

Did I tell you Bruce was surely back, perhaps intermittently, on the booze? 1) He rings me about something else, I say Have you had a note about Bertorellis' lunch on the 16th? He says No, but I'll come, what was the date again? 2) I write about something else and say at the end Hope to see you on the 16th. 3) He writes and says What's all this about the 16th? Do you mean a Bert. lunch? I'll assume you do if I don't hear. 4) He fails to show on the 16th, either pissed or thinking he'd asked me to let him know if there *was* a Bert. lunch. 5) Today in the S Times he reviews a book called Rogue Eagle (I know because I had a proof of it) under the title Rogue Male. Philip says he gets v. articulate letters from him: he, P, turned up the other day and was very funny about his prospects for the Nobel Prize (zero, according to him), and the laureateship (dead cert). Also said (God, rather like your What would you have bet 20 years ago that one day you'd have an article on whisky printed over photograph of a girl's bare arse) 'I still can't ever feel really at ease with any of the Royals.'

I think Caroleen goes up and down a bit, or to and fro. She took me out to lunch recently (but before your last experience) and struck me as in good nick, talking a lot but not uncontrollably and listening

3. Those attending 'the first of the new, monthly, Bertorellis' series' of luncheons were: Russell Lewis; John O'Sullivan; Colin Welch; Anthony Hartley; Frank Johnson (b. 1943), journalist, at the time Parliamentary Sketch Writer and Leader Writer, *Daily Telegraph* (1972–79); George Hutchinson (1920–80), political journalist and columnist, at the time Deputy Editor, *Spectator* (1975–80); and Richard Hough (1922–99), author and ex-publisher. Neither Conquest, Hartley, Hough, Johnson, Lewis nor O'Sullivan could recall or identify 'Si' or the Russian chum of 'Solzhers' (Solzhenitsyn).

4. Alan Radnor (b. 1945), journalist and author of 'twenty-two or twenty-three books' (personal communication, 12 June 1999), including horror fiction and a study of parapsychology; Editor, *Penthouse* (1976–78); previously employed at *Men Only* and *Mayfair*.

to what one said. It's my turn to take her soon, so I'll report. (She also seemed v. interested in her job.)

Poor old Jane went into hospital this afternoon to have her stone-infested gall-bladder out. No cause for alarm, our good and truthful doc says, but it seems you feel like death for 4–5 days afterwards, and not actual fun anyway. Hence, partly hence, the length of this letter. She'll be there for a couple of weeks, so if you could dash off a line (King Edward VII Hospital, 10 Beaumont Street, W. 1) I'm sure it would go down well.

Hey, what was this about me going to be rector of where?[5] I haven't heard a word. The only feature of this blue paper seems to be that it's harder to *read off, but got to use it up somehow.*[6]

Cheers
K

[TLS: Recipient]

TO ROBERT CONQUEST – 6 DECEMBER 1976

Gardnor House, Flask Walk, London, N.W.3.

Dear Bob,

2 of yours to hand (you still haven't told me what this Rector of St Andrews lark was about). As regards irrumation, I think with respect that you have the wrong end of the stick, so to speak. Latin irrumo is the mere complement of the verb fello, ie., in every such act one shag irrumates and the other fellates by definition, irrumo having originally meant 'I extend my breast to give suck', so once upon a time a mother irrumated her child. So, transf. as they say, 'I extend my prick to give suck'. See the enclosed xerox, if I remember to do it and enclose it. (From the new OED supplement.)

On Ackerley,[1] my guess is that, apart from as you rightly say mutual m,

5. St Andrews University, an idea floated by Conquest. Peter Ustinov had recently been elected to the post, and was considered too left-wing.

6. MS addition; Amis was unable to type another line, as he was too close to the bottom of the page.

1. J.R. (Joe) Ackerley (1896–1967), author, Literary Editor of the *Listener* (1935–59). Conquest had asked Amis (letter of 30 November 1976) what W.H. Auden meant, in a reprinted review of Ackerley's *My Father and Myself* (1969) entitled 'Papa was a Wise Old

he means lying on top of the other chap with your prick between his tum and yours (his likewise) and making shagging motions till you both come. What the books used to call copulatio penibus. I say, what a lot of filth, but it does show the polish a classical education puts on a chap.

Jane was greatly cheered to hear from you, even though she perhaps feels that her stock of Bluebelliana is about full now. Nice of you to drop her such an extended line. The poor old thing has an infection now, not serious but messy and extending her stay in hospital. Going to see her, buying goodies etc takes half a working day all told if one frugally takes public transport for at least the outward journey. No time to do much except beaver away at another poem, this time on Oxford and what a fucking awful place it, town rather than univ, has become.[2] You could if you would help me a bit here. I want a list of rich fashionable dons and undergraduates to give the flavour of that side of passed away Oxon life. So far I have Coghill, Bowra and Tynan.[3] Can you add to it? It wouldn't matter if the bloke's heyday was the 30s rather than the 40s. On that stanza of the other poem, the point of line 6[4] is to be virtuosic, get as many internal rhymes and assonances into an already taxing form. On line 8, 'admit' is meant to be a dying fall, indicating a parade of judiciousness over a nugatory point: it's a quote from you anyway (young fellow called Shit).

Extraordinary there-is-a-God point in a letter from Philip. *Times* births column: BLENNERHASSETT – to Celia and Cedric, a son, Edmund Crispin. He (P) also on request sends me the song he sang to me in Wheeler's when we last met. Tune (I need scarcely say) 'Daisy, Daisy'.[5]

Sly-Boots', *Forwards and Afterwards*, ed. Edward Mendelson (New York: Random House, 1973), p. 453, by the following description of Ackerley's sexual proclivities: 'the acts he really preferred were the most 'brotherly', Plain-Sewing and Princeton-First-Year.' '*One* wd be mutual m,' Conquest writes, 'but what on earth is the other "act"?'

2. 'Their Oxford', first published in *CP*, pp. 146–8.

3. Conquest offers Philip Toynbee (undergraduate) and, among dons, 'Freddie Ayer, Prof [Richard] Dawkins. [Lord David] Cecil, of course. CS Lewis. [A.L.] Rowse' (letter of 19 December 1976). Dawkins (1871–1955) was Bywater Professor of Byzantine and Modern Greek Language and Literature.

4. Of 'A Reunion'. The line is 'A nit-wit not fit to shift shit'. See Amis to Conquest, 21 November 1976.

5. These lines appear also in a letter to Thwaite of 15 January 1974, in *LL*, pp.499–500.

Davie, Davie,
Give me a bad review;
That's your gravy,
Telling chaps what to do.
Forget about style and passion,
As long as it's in the fashion:–
But let's be fair, it's got you a chair,
Which was all it was meant to do.

Last line might be improved, he rightly says. I'm going to suggest for last 2 lines,

But it's got you a chair, which, let's be fair,
Was the most that you had in view.

Any comments?

Saw old Caroleen on Saturday. She very decently agreed to drive to the Garrick and take me thence to the Welches', where we were dining. There were comic (in retrospect) bits where she announced at once that she had no petrol, or so the gauge said, drove us round Seven Dials vainly looking for a garage, then to beyond Victoria station with me shitting myself at the prospect of running out in the middle of Trafalgar Square; this preceded by a, not to exaggerate, 5-minute stretch in an alley off Garrick Street when she got us, 3 inches at a time, out of a shitty parking-spot with a sod trapped behind us hooting every 10 secs. But all was well. She was very unhysterical over those difficulties and seemed in general on an even keel, for her at least. You must remember that anything to do with you, and by extension the bassett, brings out the worst in her. Forgive the avuncularity, but she took a big knock over you, just as you did over her. I'll keep an eye on her and will continue to report.

Off now‡ to get pissed (more pissed than I already am) with my doc and his wife. Am waiting for Monkey to ferry me there. 'Waiting for Monkey' is rather a good title in its limited way.

Heartiest cheers,
Kingers

‡ *or perhaps soon*
M. already 15 mins late.

[TLS: Recipient]

TO PHILIP LARKIN – 7 DECEMBER 1976

Gardnor House, Flask Walk, London, N.W.3.

Dear Philip,

Many thanks for sending me the xerox of *BN*[1] – most kind. Marvelled somewhat that you ticked 'Letter to E' – also felt flattered at this and your other remarks.[2] I will mull 'Letter' but 'Radar' I pass at once: slightly extraordinary that *you* like it. It makes me slightly[3] damp-eyed to read it – thinking what a fucking ignorant young tosser I was when I wrote it.

Thanks too for 'Davie, Davie' – it would do for my LV anthol if it weren't for the fact that in 20 years' time EVERYBODY WILL HAVE FORGOTTEN WHO DAVIE WAS. [. . .]

Jane comes out of hospital tomorrow. I said to myself as I visited her today, 'Well, that's the last time you'll be coming here,' remembering to add '*until you arrive on your own account.*' It's the ex-officers-and-their-wives place, you see,[4] so it'll be my choice when I have to have my digestive tract out.

one man one bum
Kingsley

[ALS: Bodleian]

1. *Bright November*, from which Larkin had marked 'five poems I think would bear reprinting' (Larkin to Amis, 1 December 1976, in HEHL).

2. Larkin had written of 'Letter to Elisabeth' that 'it does sound terribly level and sincere and decent'.

3. Amis indicates his irritation at having inadvertently repeated 'slightly' by connecting the two words with an arrow and the word 'fuck'.

4. King Edward VII Hospital, London W1.

TO ELIZABETH RICH – 15 JANUARY 1977

Gardnor House, Flask Walk, London, N.W.3

Dear Miss Rich,

Many thanks for your most interesting letter and enclosure.[1] How odd that you and your friend and then I should have been so similarly affected: or is it odd? One thing you said struck me most forcibly: that when the two of you went out into the garden to shake off the gloom, you found it followed you everywhere. Now I had that experience too, even on the sunlit side of the house, but had forgotten it, or perhaps even not remarked it sufficiently, until I came to that part of your letter. That *is* odd.

It was most kind of you to take the trouble to write.

Yours sincerely,
Kingsley Amis

[ALS: Recipient]

TO PHILIP LARKIN – 15 JANUARY 1977

Gardnor House, Flask Walk, London, N.W.3

Dear Philip,

Forgive this love-letter speed of reply, but I'm doing all my correspondence at one go before getting down to what will probably be a taxing piece of bullshit, viz. a TV talk in a series about the Welfare

1. Miss Rich, who has 'a passing interest in the supernatural' (personal communication, 16 September 1998), had read a review by Brian Cox of *Rudyard Kipling and his World* in the *Sunday Telegraph*, 9 November 1975, in which Cox recounted Amis's sense of unease at visiting Kipling's home, Bateman's, in Burwash, Sussex: 'Mr Amis decided he would dislike spending even as long as 24 hours in the house,' wrote Cox, and 'was so affected that he wrote a poem, "Kipling at Bateman's", about the overground dungeon to which he felt Kipling had consigned himself'. Miss Rich had visited Bateman's several years earlier, been affected by it in the same way, and wrote to Amis to tell him so, enclosing Cox's review. 'Kipling at Bateman's' was published by *Poem of the Month*, Folio 4 (August 1973); it was not reprinted in *CP*. See Appendix E.

State.[1] My message will be simple: *Do* some *work* and *pay* for it *yourselves*, you LAZY *GREEDY* F U C K E R S.

Your Norman extract[2] made me want to see him *slowly* beaten senseless by some rather *incompetent* muscle-men. Especially 'creative'. Creating little pools of piss and cairns of turds on the carpet (if there is one). I'll create bruises on their backsides. What does he *mean*, creative?

About the Ormy:[3] a love-hate thing is all right if you love one bit and hate another. I loved, well, liked a lot of the blokes and one or two of the officers, and hated some of the blokes, most of the officers and being on duty. Right?

Yes, Bob is tonto about Bluebell. Every letter has at least one tribute to her sagacity, continence, etc. Did I tell you that terrifying story about her Christmas present? If not, remind me.

Yea, yea, the 14th is fine. Larkinland[4] can't be so bad, going on for only 3/4 hr. I'd like to go. Shall I meet you at the Lyttelton Theatre at 5.55? If so, where is it? It isn't in the tel. directory. Or at least it isn't in mine, but that goes back to the far-distant world of 1975. Rest of evening, did I say dine out or in before jazz at home? We could go to my club for a drink, meet Jane, dine, come home. Let minnow.

Hope your labial carcinoma clears up soon.[5] Funny, I'd for some time been trying to lick into shape an aphorism along the lines of, 'Every hypochondriac picks a winner in the end.'

I have now to write to various people who want me to find them a publisher, send them signed copies of all my books ('very happy to refund costs'), define the difference between prose and poetry, contribute without fee to *The Writer Speaks*. The writer says, Get irreclaimably lost, you sodding little chancer.

---

1. I have been unable to trace this series in the BBC, Granada or ITC archives.

2. See Larkin to Amis, 13 January 1977 (in HEHL), for 'lunatic booklet from Norman [Iles] this morning, plus typical letter'.

3. In the same letter Larkin had praised Amis's poem 'A Reunion', recently published in the *New Statesman*, but professed himself puzzled by Amis's (and the poem's) 'love-hate relation with Her Majesty's Forces'.

4. 'A sort of set of readings with a bit of jazz' (Larkin to Amis, 13 January 1977, in HEHL), performed at the National Theatre; Larkin had not seen it, and invited Amis to accompany him.

5. 'Have cancer of the [l]ip currently: probably just a lipoma. ONE DAY IT WON'T BE' (Larkin to Amis, 13 January 1977).

Thanks for Jane inquiry; she's better, but not really well yet. Might take months, the doc says blithely.

I am/am not registered for bum,

Kingsley

[TLS: Bodleian]

TO NEAL BURTON – 15 MARCH 1977

Gardnor House, Flask Walk, London, N.W.3

Dear Neal,

I think the batches idea is a good one.[1] You could afford to make them rather bigger, so that if I have to go to the Arts Council Library, say, I can collect answers to about ten[2] points instead of two on the same trip.

But how close to the bone have we got to go? With the first poem, for instance, I hope it'll be enough to say '*The Tempest*' without having to give the date of the First Folio.[3] My illustrious predecessor[4] was a bit inconsistent here: he says in his Editorial Note that 'the editions from which [the poems] are taken have been given in the index only when they are not to be found in the authors' collected works'. Fine; but then the silly sod puts under Praed's 'Letter of Advice', '*New Monthly Magazine*, 1828' and under P's 'Good-night to the Season', nothing; but both poems appeared in The Poems of Winthrop Mackworth Praed, 2 vols., 1864. I suggest we save as much space and sweat as we can, the rough rule being that we pass over in silence poems that appear in standard editions of poets well enough known to be found in a reasonably comprehensive library, but note poems that don't so appear and also editions of poets *not* well enough known to be, etc. So, in the present batch, we note Enright's vols because he isn't collected yet, we give the date of H. Coleridge's works because he's fairly obscure, we

1. Amis had begun working on the Notes and References section of *NOBLV*; Burton (b.1933), a commissioning editor from the London offices of OUP, was the book's editor, and the 'batches' in question were bibliographical queries about dates and sources.

2. Amis has hand-written 'well, 4 anyway' just below 'ten'.

3. As Amis explains in *NOBLV* itself: 'No references in the Notes are given to poems by authors whose collected poems are easily available' (p. 336).

4. W.H. Auden.

say what we can about Planché and Watts, but we keep mum about Holmes because there he is on the shelf. No doubt there will be some debatable cases, but how about that as a guide?[5]

I have inquiries in about Vaughan-Thomas (by the way, I wonder what Davin and Stallworthy think/will think about the poem of his you sent),[6] Gray and Pauker.

Looking forward to, or at any rate expecting, the next batch.

Yours,
Kingsley

[TLS: OUP]

TO ROBERT CONQUEST – 7 APRIL 1977

Gardnor House, Flask Walk, London N.W.3

Dear Bob,

Good to get yours. Ta for the publication details. Yes, Stuart H-J, though I've forgotten why I changed it from Iain.[1] The anth. is nearly done, though horrible little extra bits of detail keep cropping up. Am also compiling – did I tell you? – an anth. of NS and Spec pieces published during the Wilson era – *Harold's Years.*[2] No joke, boiling 60 million words down into 60,000. Chief problem with the Spec side has been not getting arseholes whenever I go there. Just as I got back from their pub at 4.35 the other afternoon, six of them came into the board-

5. There seems not to have been a debate about these particular examples. Dates and publication details are offered for the poems by Hartley Coleridge (1796–1849), Samuel Taylor Coleridge's eldest son; James Planché (1776–1880), author of over 150 plays and libretti, the best-know being *The Vampyre, or, The Bride of the Isles* (1820); and Alaric A. Watts (1797–1864), poet and journalist. The American novelist, essayist, poet and scientist Oliver Wendell Holmes (1809–94) is represented by a single poem, undated and without a bibliographical note.

6. Dan Davin and Jon Stallworthy; the poem by Wynford Vaughan-Thomas (1908–87), 'Farewell to New Zealand', begins: 'Super-suburbia of the Southern Seas,/Nature's – and Reason's – true Antipodes,/Hail, dauntless pioneers, intrepid souls,/Who cleared the Bush – to make a lawn for bowls,/And smashed the noble Maori to ensure/The second-rate were socially secure!'

---

1. 'Stuart Howard-Jones (1904–74)', the author of 'Hibernia', in *NOBLV*, pp. 242–3, is another Conquest pseudonym, originally 'Iain Howard-Jones'.

2. Published in October 1977 by Quartet Books; see Amis to Conquest, 12 August 1977.

room where I had been trying to read back numbers and each opened a bottle of wine. I don't know how they bring the paper out.

The swing to the right here is putting the wind up the lefties. At the Friday lunch the other day they, chiefly Hitchens and Jas Fenton,[3] were saying that chaps were getting fed up about stuff that may not be Labour's fault, but is associated with them rather than the Tories: porn and permissiveness generally, comprehensivisation, TUC bosses, terrorism and the defence run-down. This last is suddenly a big subject; you can hardly pick up a paper without finding something about the Russian threat, and usually saying it's serious all right. Chalfont[4] had 2 hours of TV about it with the scales tilted his way: an obvious fucking fool of a dove and a Moscow apparatchik against C. and a bunch of hawkish generals. Previous week ½ hour on ITV at peak time with one tough hawk and one semi-hawk.

I think the enclosed bit of bullshit libels you. Wasn't somebody called exactly that, a professional anti-communist, recently, and didn't he sue and win?[5] (By 'recently' I don't mean since you went to the US, or not necessarily.) You can keep it; I have a xerox. Or was it Randolph Churchill called a professional something else? Can't think. By the way, what does 'against intervention in Korea' mean at the bottom of column 3? [. . .]

Yes of course, come and stay as long as you like; check date-time nearer the day. Will get NS poem and also S Times piece when it comes out.[. . .]

[INCOMPLETE TL: HEHL]

TO THE EDITOR, *DAILY TELEGRAPH* – 25 APRIL 1977

SIR – May I protest against Mr David Holloway's characterisation of the late John Raymond[1] (16 April) as "at times . . . overbearing and rude?" I am not concerned to deny these charges, only to say that they

3. Christopher Hitchens (b. 1949), journalist and author; James Fenton (b. 1949), poet, journalist, critic. Both working at the time on the *New Statesman*, where Martin Amis was Literary Editor.

4. Alun Chalfont (b. 1919), journalist, broadcaster, military historian, politician; created Life Peer (1964); born Arthur Gwynne Jones, 'Arthur' being changed subsequently to 'Alun'.

5. The enclosure has not survived, and Conquest does not remember it.

---

1. For John Raymond see Amis to Hilary Rubinstein, 6 November 1953, note 2.

are out of place in an obituary, which is a memorial, not a review.

An obituarist must not lie about his subject, but he is not on oath to tell the whole truth about him, and adverse comments should be deferred until the family and friends of the dead have had time to recover from the shock of loss.

Such forbearance used to be commonplace, but is so no longer; I appeal to you to see to it that your writers exercise it in future.

KINGSLEY AMIS
London, N.W.3.

TO NEAL BURTON – 21 MAY 1977

Gardnor House, Flask Walk, London, N.W.3.

Dear Neal,

Here are some answers. Could you send me a xerox of Deane's Ode?[1] I can't find mine.

I'm as much of a glutton for work as the next man, and I quite see that it saves our collective time if I, rather than you, provide information about such as Deane or Leigh,[2] but in other cases I find myself reflecting that you have at least as many reference books as I have and a larger staff than mine (zero). If I were you I should set about ingratiating myself with the chap who publishes the *DNB*. He might very well be persuaded to let you have an occasional look at his copy.

Thank you for the Milne poem;[3] I had seen it and reluctantly rejected

---

1. 'An Ode' by Canon Anthony C. Deane (1870–1946); one of two parodies by Deane printed in *NOBLV*, both from Anthony C. Deane and Carolyn Wells, eds, *A Parody Anthology* (1904).

2. Henry S. Leigh (1837–83), dramatist, translator, man of letters; Amis prints one poem in *NOBLV*.

3. Not identified. In a later letter to Burton, 11 August 1977 (in OUP), Amis reiterates his doubts about Milne's light verse (none of which appears in *NOBLV*): 'I've decided he's just not entertaining enough. It remained to justify the opening of section II of the Introduction [which quotes Milne approvingly on light verse], to which the curious reader might as it stands retort, "Then why the hell isn't there any Milne in your selection?" And I didn't want to cut the bit of "Letter to Lord Byron" that refers to him. The solution was to implicate Auden. So amend as follows . . . "As the reader will see, Auden said a good word in "Letter to Lord Byron" for A.A. Milne as a writer in the genre, though without finding anything of his worth anthologising – my experience too."'

it as not quite light enough and slightly tame. We must keep looking.

I enclose a few extras. The Wodehouses and the Listers[4] first appeared in Punch.

Onward, ever onward.

Yours,
Kingsley
K. AMIS

[TLS: OUP]

TO JON STALLWORTHY – 30 MAY 1977

Gardnor House, Flask Walk, London, N.W.3

Dear Jon,

No no no no no! I fairly sincerely want to be rich – not sincerely enough to face all that:[1] in fact the thought of flying is quite enough to deter me – last flip, 1934.[2] And 10 days on the QE II seems out of proportion. So tell Byron like thanks, but no thanks.

See you

Yours
Kingsley

[ALS: OUP]

4. R.P. Lister (b. 1914), writer, metallurgist, contributed poems and stories to *Punch, New Yorker, Atlantic Monthly.*

---

1. Stallworthy had written to Amis to tell him of a proposal from Byron Hollingshead, of OUP in New York, that Amis deliver the keynote address at the annual American Booksellers Convention, thus, it was hoped, generating massive sales for the forthcoming *NOBLV*.

2. According to Jacobs, *Biography*, p.36, this incident took place in 1932 (although it may in fact have been 1934), when Amis was ten: 'It was a five-bob (25p) "flip" around Croydon aerodrome, then London's major airport, which he made with three or four friends . . . Looking through the window beside, Kingsley suddenly saw the ground beyond his shoulder. This was the wrong place for it – the ground was supposed to be under your feet! The shock put Kingsley off flying for the rest of his life.'

TO XANDRA GOWRIE – 21 JULY 1977

Gardnor House, Flask Walk, N.W.3

Dear Miss Gowrie,

Thank you for your inquiry. Here are my answers to your questions.[1]

1. Yes.

2. It is the exception rather than the rule to find a review in which all the facts are right; I mean simple matters like the occupations of the main characters, the chief events of the story, the settings where these take place, etc. This applies equally to hostile and favourable notices. My outstanding example is a reviewer who got the hero's Christian name and surname consistently wrong, throughout her notice of my novel. As regards their estimate of my strengths and weaknesses I can't judge, but people who read so inattentively are unlikely to be much good at such estimates.

3. Provincial press worst, then popular dailies, then quality dailies and Sundays, then (least bad) weeklies. Oh – monthlies about like weeklies.

4. The Americans are kinder and also less likely to see what I'm trying to do. (You should really have asked a question about that. As well as factual accuracy and critical fairness and responsibility there is ability – or inability – to grasp the author's intention. This intention may not be glaringly obvious in every case, but if two or three reviewers can get it one feels the others ought to be able to as well. They often can't.)

5. a. Responsibility to the reader to be entertaining and literate. 1st quite common, 2nd not as common as it should be.

---

1. Xandra Gowrie, an editorial assistant on the *New Review* (1974–79), a literary monthly edited by Ian Hamilton, was conducting a survey of novelists' responses to their reviews. Her eight questions were: 1) Do you normally read the reviews of your books? 2) How accurate do you find them in their summary of your work and in their estimate of your strengths and weaknesses? Have you any examples of spectacular inaccuracy? 3) Which reviewers or newspapers/magazines have you found most reliable; and which most unreliable? 4) How do English reviews compare with American ones? 5) What qualities do you expect of a reviewer and how often do you find them? Do you think reviewing tends to be too academic? 6) Have you ever written back to your reviewers? 7) Has anything a reviewer ever said changed your attitude to your own writing? 8) Do you believe reviews have any effect on sales?

b. Responsibility to the author to try to understand his book, judge it impartially and report it accurately. Answers implied above.

c. Responsibility to literature, for which knowledge of the field, past and present, is essential. Rare and getting rarer, least bad in weeklies and monthlies, hence I suspect some explanation of their relative superiority. In this sense reviewing should be *more* academic – but *not* in the sense that more reviewers should be university professors. We don't want to get like the US.

6. Yes, to put them right on facts.

7. No.

8. A little. Coverage is what counts: 1,000 words attack better than 100 praise.

Best wishes,
Kingsley Amis

[TLS: Julian Barnes]

TO DALE SALWAK – 21 JULY 1977

Gardnor House, Flask Walk, London, N.W.3[1]

Dear Dale,

How nice to hear from you. Yes, *The Alteration* does seem to have done quite well. If only someone would film it!

Re reference guide[2] (which I greatly look forward to seeing) – there is only one pre-1951 review I can think of, in a magazine called *Mandrake*, ed. Arthur Boyars. It was a review of Philip Larkin's novel *A Girl in Winter* and the year must have been about 1947. Of course, there were my contributions to my school magazine. Would they count? It would be something new. A letter to the Editors of the School Magazine, City of London School, Victoria Embankment, London E.C.4 might be worth considering if you think it wouldn't be too much of a laugh.

---

1. Next to the address Amis has written: 'Note new address (much more fun!)'

2. *Kingsley Amis: A Reference Guide* (Boston: G.K. Hall, 1978), an annotated bibliography of writings about Amis but not of his own writings; Amis wrongly thought the *Guide* would list primary as well as secondary materials, like Gohn's *Checklist*.

Anyway, the very best of luck with work and everything else.

Yours
Kingsley Amis

[ALS: Recipient]

TO PHILIP LARKIN – 11 AUGUST 1977

Gardnor House, Flask Walk, London, N.W.3.

Dear Philip,

Time I dropped you a line, especially since there are a couple of things I want from you. Like a cunt, or a poor bugger who has had to keep moving his papers about, I can't find the letter or bit of paper where it says what year 'Fiction and the Reading Public' appeared. Was it 1954?[1] Anyway, the sodding OUP, after months of hanging about, have just told me that to get the book[2] out in Nov 1978 they must have everything in by 31st Aug 1977, so lemme, no? Did they bugger you about like that? Of course, you may be currently vacationing in Las Palmas, which would hold me up, wouldn't it? I'll hold a firework up y

Other thing – chap told me you said something nice about my pwetry in The Times (?) recently. That's the sort of thing that publishers' publicity departments – no, not know, have to be told about. No use depending on clippings service, of course. Can you give me the ref?[3]

When are you coming up? Do let me know, and if you couldn't come for the night we could at least lunch.

Eurocommunism bum
Kingsley

[ALS: Bodleian]

1. Yes, in *Essays in Criticism* 4 (January 1954), p.86.
2. *NOBLV*.
3. From an interview in *The Times*, 23 July 1977.

TO ROBERT CONQUEST – 12 AUGUST 1977

Gardnor House, Flask Walk, N.W.3

Dear Bob,

A grim date, for me anyway; to have a whole putrefying bird presented to you to do your own carving by somebody who thinks they're giving you the treat of your life gets me down no end.[1] Anyway: forgive long silence. I kept saying to myself I'd write when I'd finished my three anthologies, which is like trying to get all the pee out of your prick: go on as you may there's always a tiny bit more. The OUP, after months of stop-go, told me last week that they must have everything in by 31st August – in order to publish in Nov 78. (Contrast the behaviour of a publisher who has to earn his living: William Miller of Quartet Books, who are doing my NS-Spec anthology, received my copy at the end of May, has already done galleys, sent page-proofs this morning and will publish in October 77.) The Faber Book of Non-Trendy Verse[2] has been easier and is going faster: a careful look through the Dict of Quots took me most of the way, then hymnals and old-fashioned anthologies. Have you any pet candidates, ones I might have missed? Perhaps at any rate you know who wrote a poem beginning (I think) In his chamber, weak and dying, Was the Norman baron lying (fuck) or something. Chas Monteith[3] is a pisser too, you know: I sent him a list of the copyright stuff I wanted to include, and he says jolly good, would I tell him who published *Sir John Arkwright* (known only for that World War I hymn, 'O Valiant Hearts'), Belloc, Housman, Masefield and Newbolt. Jesus, hasn't he got a secretary? Hasn't she got a telephone?

People seem to think now that ole GB will pull through after all. The Jubilee had a lot to do with it.[4] Did I tell you about the NS anti-Jub issue? Phil Goodhart[5] said he was delighted the Tory Central Office didn't get a crack at doing it because they'd have been so much less

---

1. The closed season for grouse shooting is 11 December to 11 August.

2. *The Faber Popular Reciter* (1978).

3. Charles Monteith, publisher at Faber and Faber; see Amis to Larkin, 14 March 1954, note 5.

4. Britain had recently celebrated twenty-five years of the reign of Queen Elizabeth II in a week-long Jubilee (5–11 June).

5. Philip Goodhart (b.1925), Conservative MP, author, journalist; knighted (1981).

good. If I haven't already – so long since I wrote – remind me to tell you about Mervyn Jones's[6] piece in that number. The Grunwick dispute[7] is also doing our side a power of good. The Left are keeping quieter than I can remember, except for saying gloomily that there's a swing to the Right. No politics talked at all at the Friday lunches, just personalities. Cambodia important here; when they tried to tell me it was the Americans' fault for making the Communists cross, their tones were flat, lifeless. One point everyone seems united on is the pissiness of Peter Jay [. . .]

[INCOMPLETE TL: Recipient]

TO PHILIP LARKIN – 28 AUGUST 1977

Gardnor House, Flask Walk, London, N.W.3.

My dear Philip,

Afraid I forgot your bithrayd you old bugar. But many happy returns (happy? returns?) belatedly. And thank you for the cutting;[1] not fulsome, as you say, but heart-warming.

Poor old Bruce: he must have been horrified to wake up in the nursing home, find he hadn't knocked himself off after all.[2] I reckon it was realising The G's of the M[3] was no good (I still haven't read it but I trust your judgment) that made him reach for the bottle, or rather vat, don't you?

I wouldn't be too sure about po: defecting if I were you. If may compare unworthy self, I wrote not a line between July '74 and November '76, then turned out 200 of the buggers and one or two shorts have

6. Mervyn Jones (b.1922), author and journalist.

7. A strike at the Grunwick photo-processing plant in North London. Mass picketing had begun in June 1977, after almost a year of dispute, and in July there were clashes with police. Scenes of violent confrontation dominated television coverage, feeding anti-union sentiment.

---

1. From *The Times*. See Amis to Larkin, 11 August 1977.

2. See Larkin to Amis, 12 August 1977 (in HEHL), in which Larkin writes of Montgomery's return to drink and of his doctors' prognosis 'that if he can live a year he may well live five or six'. Montgomery died in September 1978.

3. Edmund Crispin, *Glimpses of the Moon* (1977); see Amis to Larkin, 10 April 1976, note 5.

followed. Try an extended one. It's great not having to have finishing it in mind all the sodding time.

My invite was not so much a matter of my having sent as far as Hull to see (is that right? Haven't got the shagging text) if I could find a mate, more with the idea of a mutual cheering-up session in mind. I know a bit about your four bleeding ack emma. Phobias is what I got. Lifts, Underground, ships, not to speak of *airplanes*. Never set foot in the bloody things. I said I never set foot in the bloody things, what? That's just for starters. 'I'll start shoving a pok

Bob, just turned 60, seems to be the only one in shape. Working and boozing and screwing away in the California sun. Still, we aren't living with Donald Davie and his wife, are we?[4]

Brian Aldiss is having his OUP troubles too. Says it took him a year just to get a contract out of them for some SF thing he's doing for them. L.S. Caton is alive and well and working at 37 Dover Street.

Let me know when you may be able to fit in a spot of door-darkening.

Our text of the poem differs from the one in your bum,

Kingsley

how's your groin? how's your groin? how's your groin? how[5]

[TLS: Bodleian]

TO NEAL BURTON – 31 AUGUST 1977

Gardnor House, Flask Walk, London, N.W.3.

Dear Neal,

The enclosed[1] mainly explains itself. I have clearance, as you see, but I think you must write your standard letter to each. The one to

4. Davie was at Stanford University in California from 1968–78. Conquest had been staying with the Davies for several months, with his dog Bluebell.

5. See Larkin to Amis, 12 August 1977 (in HEHL): 'Also have a curious swelling on my groin and an odd feeling there: gets neither worse nor better. Why didn't you come to me before? I wake at four and lie worrying till seven. Loneliness. Death. Law suits. Talent gone. Law suits. Loneliness. Talent gone. Death. I really am not happy these days.'

---

1. A list of privately communicated poems Amis was planning to include in *NOBLV*.

Conquest (Hoover Institution, Stanford, California 94305) will not be all that standard, I suppose. Vaughan-Thos is c/o Harlech TV and Alan Bennett is 23 Gloucester Crescent N.W.1. No, of course I can't cut any of *them*. 'You know that poem I asked you to write out and send to me? Well, I don't want it after all.' I'm too decent and cowardly to do that.

Yes, Brownjohn it is.[2] I've never met him or even corresponded with him, so I'm in no special position to write to him. You do that. It will cause less odium all round that way. A publisher who asks a permission without revealing that the piece is needed solely to be pissed on is behaving like a publisher; an editor who does that is behaving like a shit. But need he be asked anyway? One can quote up to so many lines in the way of 'fair dealing' to make a point without permission or payment, as book reviews show.

Yours,
Kingsley

[TLS: OUP]

TO ROBERT CONQUEST – 20 SEPTEMBER 1977

Gardnor Ho: Flask Wk NW3

Dear Bob,

Hope to get this to you before you actually leave a month hence. Do come and stay here if you'd like to, though we realise you realise that while we tolerate or even welcome concubinage we can't undertake to provide it.

Jim Durham, the rightie cobber shrink, is over for a few weeks. He says Sydney is worse than London for crime, public obscenity, drugs etc. Has a good line on drugs, new to me: it isn't that foolish weak-minded kids are cozened into them to be trendy, etc.; they actually set

2. Amis quotes an unnamed poem by an unacknowledged poet (Alan Brownjohn's 'Elizabeth Pender's Dream of Friendship') in the introduction to *NOBLV* by way of explaining why the anthology 'comes nearly to an end with writers born in the decade of my own birth, the 1920s' (Brownjohn was born in 1931). Amis claims to quote the poem 'in no spirit of acrimony or mockery, but because it is the work of an established poet, is representative and is recent enough' (p.xxi), though it is not hard to see from the introduction why he would have wanted Burton to write for permission.

out to be addicts because it gives them something to be, which is much needed by those many who are no good at anything and not interested in anything. Instead of doing a boring job and hanging round the streets they can be addicts and of course want to stay addicts, which is partly why the cure rate is so low. Evidently hard drugs make you feel very bad when you start on them (another thing I didn't know) and you need all the motivation you can muster to break that barrier.

The OUP are still acting up, or since that implies some sort of continuity are acting up more. The time they give you, after several weeks of silence, to get something done by shortens on each occasion. The last thing they did was to ask me, for the second time, to cut the text. I took a day doing that. Then they said thanks, but we've asked the printer which machine he'll be using and it looks as if we can put all the cuts back in. Or most of them. Probably.

Have been working away at the old Music of T[1] for my radio broadcast as I must have said, also probably said the solecism-count keeps rising. At least twice he does that business of making one word do two jobs, like 'He hoped she would soon be ready to talk about what he had come to see her.' And yet chaps go on about effortless elegance and what-not. Tin ears, like his; all too common. But bags of good stuff.

Expect you've seen all this stuff i.e. crap about Paedophiles' Lib; Society for Cultivating the Understanding of Minors. I must say it does rather strain one's belief in freedom of expression for all comers.

Good piece on Rhodesia.[2] I think Owen and Young[3] are *trying* to get a Marxist lot in to prevent the Russians 'having to' send the Cubans

---

1. Amis's talk on Anthony Powell's *A Dance to the Music of Time*, itself entitled 'The Music of Time', was broadcast on Radio 3 on 29 August 1979. Though this seems an improbably long gap, the BBC has no record of an earlier talk.

2. On 1 September 1977 Cyrus Vance, American Secretary of State, and David Owen, British Foreign Secretary, proposed a peace plan for Rhodesia, with a larger role for Joshua Nkomo and Robert Mugabe's Patriotic Front. Conquest's article, 'The Right Way with Rhodesia', *Daily Telegraph*, 17 September 1977, p.8, argued that Owen's stance on Rhodesia was 'not merely a recipe for local disaster, but a symptom of much that is wrong with Britain's whole foreign policy approach under the present government'.

3. Andrew Young (b.1932), clergyman, civil rights leader, politician; at the time United States Ambassador to the United Nations (1977–79).

in, because what Carter, and of course Callaghan, couldn't stand is sending in a single tank, gun, man, etc. Oh well.

Pip-pip!

Cheers
Kingsley

Do you think Eliz Young was right in her Times letter today? (On arms balance)[4]

[TLS: Recipent]

TO PHILIP LARKIN – 28 OCTOBER 1977

Gardnor House, Flask Walk, London, N.W.3.

Dear Philip,

Fine; wonderful; perfect. We have you booked in for the night of 10th Nov. There's a 6–8 publisher's party that evening where we might collect a free drink or so. But on the other hand we needn't. Being stood dinner sounds strangely compelling.

Yes, I heard about Patsy from her daughter.[1] I responded with some gallant mendacity about her (P's) capacity for cheering everybody up with her mere presence. Well, try to think of something to say about her that would be nice and not the opposite of the truth. Funny about Cointreau. It was an evening on it that set a chum of mine going on his first series of coronaries about ten years ago. He still drinks a bit. Another chum dropped dead the other day, not that he was ever much of a drinker. 54, he was.

You silly old bugger, the NS *did* explain about Nick in their setting: '"For Nick, eh, Shun?" says Nick, eyeing a passing beauty.'[2] I think we

4. MS addition. Elizabeth Young (Lady Kennet), writer, married the author and politician Wayland Young (b.1923), 2nd Baron Kennet, in 1948. Her letter in *The Times* urged the Soviets to accept President Carter's proposals for strategic arms limitations.

---

1. Patsy (Avis) Strang (later Murphy) died of alcoholic poisoning in September 1977. Her daughter Emily Murphy was born in 1956. For Patsy Strang see Amis to Larkin, 4 April 1952, note 1.

2. See *Memoirs*, p.144: 'Philip and I went no further with Nick the Greek and his friend Shun the Chinese than such utterances as "For Nick, eh, Shun?" (on the arrival of a pretty

might have done better to make Shun into Sean or Shawn, but it's too late now. Actually it was I, surmising correctly that Bob wouldn't have seen about the comp, who selflessly wrote in on *his* behalf. Yes, he's around, but won't be with us till tomorrow. V. high-powered he is now; took me to din with Margaret Thatcher last night. I thought her bright and tough and nice, and by God she doesn't half hate lefties. All in all a tonic. (Has anyone made the obvious crack? – 'I must say he's a tonic.' – 'Better with some gin in him, you mean?')

I think the Magnet/Times thing is simply a matter of being able to sack printers then and unable now.[3] Oh, do you know how much messengers (i.e. unskilled labour) get on the Mirror papers? TWO HUNDRED AND TEN POUNDS FOR A THIRTY-TWO-HOUR WEEK. Yes, that's right.

If you'd like to go to this party on the 10th (no earthly reason why you should) meet me in the Garrick Club, Garrick Street, London W.C.2, England at 6 (six) p.m. (1800 hours) in the evening on 10th November, 1977 A.D. The party is just opposite. Or come straight here. Or meet me/us at a place and time of your own choosing.

I was sorry to hear about your mother.[4] Mine toppled over and was dead before she hit the floor, so she did better in a way. Except for having been dead for twenty years.

Between Mr Scott and myself there has never been the slightest question of bum,[5]

Kingsley

[TLS: Bodleian]

girl). Bob [Conquest] put in some work and gave us such pregnant dialogues as:

"So, we've been sold as slaves in Tunis, Nick!"

"Yes – remember to call your master 'Bey', Shun."'

3. In a letter of 24 October 1977, in *LL*, p.571, Larkin had commented on the relative absence of misprints in the boys' magazine *Magnet* (1908–40), in comparison to the present-day *Times*. As Thwaite points out in his note to the letter, the *Magnet* 'included the Greyfriars stories written by Frank Richards about Billy Bunter *et al.*, and from which some of the L/Amis locutions derive'. Among them is 'woo leggo my' (see e.g. Amis to Larkin, 10 May 1979).

4. She was going blind.

5. Jeremy Thorpe (b. 1929), Liberal Party Leader (1967–76), had the previous day denied any involvement in an alleged plot to harm Norman Scott, a male model who claimed to have been Thorpe's lover in the 1960s. See Amis to Conquest, 1 December 1978, note 6.

TO JEREMY LEWIS[1] – 21 NOVEMBER 1977

Gardnor House, Flask Walk, London, N.W.3.

Dear Jeremy,

In my conscientious way (and because it's easier work than novel-writing) I've been through the first batch of proofs. I must say they are very prettily set out, with virtually no awkward breaks between pages; do congratulate the printer on my behalf. No great problems. The most sizeable comes from somebody having corrected the date I gave for S. Wesley's birth (I put 1666; it's 1662) *without* seeing that this means he must come before not after W. Walsh (b. 1663). By a happy chance the two poems begin and end on almost exactly the same parts of the page. If we can't transpose them I am going to come across a very rare, in fact unknown, MS which gives Walsh's date of birth as 1662.

There are two problems of consistency which I *think* I've cured, but which I should like you to check. One: seeing that chaps are styled in the same way in contents, on page-head and above text: we can't have Robert L. Stevenson in i, R.L. Stevenson in ii and Robert Louis Stevenson in iii. (Same with titles, e.g. Browning's Soliloquy.)[2] Two: capitalisation in titles. My rule is: when title is in quotes, first word only in caps., e.g. 'Oh that my *l*ungs'; when not in quotes (though none the less a quotation of the first few words of the poem), normal caps., e.g. A Maiden There Lived. Which raises the question of what normal caps. are. *I* would write The Sow Came in and Trip upon Trenchers, and your text says Ode on the Death of a Favourite Cat, not Ode On the Death Of a Favourite Cat. Up to you, I think, to lay down the law here.

Re [Edward] Lear: Auden, Faber, Squire, C. Wells and Silcock[3] all print the limericks in five lines. Lear may have done them in four, but I'm sure it'll look trendy if we do, so let's stay with five and be reactionary.

---

1. Jeremy Lewis (b.1942), author, publisher and literary journalist, at the time an editor in the General Books department at OUP.

2. As opposed to the full title, *Soliloquy of the Spanish Cloister*.

3. Auden (Amis's Oxford predecessor), J.C. Squire (1884–1958), Charles Wells (1800–79) or Carolyn Wells (1869–1942) and Arnold Silcock (1889–1953) all edited anthologies of light verse; 'Faber' is *The Faber Book of Comic Verse* (1942), edited by Michael Roberts.

One addition: in the list of those Gratefully Thanked add Douglas Matthews (he's the London Library shag).[4]

I have Bruce Phillips's and Elizabeth Knight's letters[5] and will be answering them jolly soon.

Allee bestee–

Yours,
Kingsley

[TLS: OUP]

TO ROBERT CONQUEST – 13 DECEMBER 1977

Gardnor Ho: Flask Wk NW3

Dear Bob,

Excuse silence: as we said, work holds up my letter-writing, speeds yours. Have reached p.169 of novel with the end nowhere even dimly in sight, so at least fears of giving short weight (last 3 have all been under standard length) are laid to rest.[1] Martin is taking a chapter for the Xmas number of the NS; nice to be paid for publicity. Re him, soup-thrower has been dropped finally, I gather.[2] Friday lunches continue, though I go less, being physically incapable of leaving while one other shag remains, and at my age I find work difficult after four hours' drinking. One rather nasty little turd who came the other day got cross and incredulous when I said that the Nazis and the KPD were at one stage at least in alliance against Weimar – true?[3] Even if not, worth annoying him.

4. Douglas Matthews (b.1927), Deputy Librarian (1965–80), Librarian (1980–93), London Library.

5. Bruce Phillips (b.1944), a long-time employee of OUP, was at this time an editor in the Reference Books department; Elizabeth Knight was Publicity Manager at OUP, where she worked for thirty-two years.

---

1. Amis was working on *Jake's Thing* (1978), a novel of 285 pages; his three previous novels were *The Alteration* (205 pages), *Ending Up* (176 pages) and *The Riverside Villas Murder* (224 pages).

2. The fiery Mary Furness, an editorial assistant on the *New Review*, later on the *TLS*; married Viscount Chewton, 1986.

3. KPD stands for 'Kommunistische Partei Deutschlands', the German Communist Party. Conquest's answer, in a letter of 21 December 1977, is 'Yes, the Nazis and Communists

Ya ya, I did your drink commission, not immediately but, ah, cheque-book stub says 22nd Nov. I don't know whether I ought to mention it but the spoils were rather unevenly divided, one doz. for Ron and Charmian[4] and a bottle of Scotch for me. Better than a ram up the duff all the same, and I drink your health.

Went to a thing called the Burke Club[5] – Christ, you've probably been a member for years – at the H of C the other week, ½ Tory MPs, ½ sympathetic journalists etc.: John O'[Sullivan], Russell L[ewis] etc. Guest speaker, M. Thatcher. Opening address v. good, firm, clear etc. Question time not so good. I asked about defence, saying we want more of it, many voters too, but is that 'politically possible'? She parried, talked about this cut and that cut and ended by saying yes, politically possible because many voters were with us, which I'd said. She pissed on A Lejeune[6] who said a lot of people doubted whether we could hold on to power long enough to matter, asking him why he hadn't already emigrated. Fine in a public meeting but not fine in private among friends.[7] Lej suggested afterwards and I agreed there's something feminine there, suggest that things aren't 100% and she gets narky. How much better to have said Christ yes, that is a problem. Who could tell her? It needs a woman really.

I enclose the enclosed. It's your royalties to date. I had one too. Silv[8] guessed correctly I had your address. Afraid I have no news of C[aroleen] – I should have got in touch, but have been trying to cut down sociality, especially the sort that has an element of duty-doing. I'll have a go when I've done my Xmas shopping – Christ what a pest it all is. A merry one to you anyway.

Cheers
Kingsley

[TLS: Recipient]

collaborated in two actions in the early 30s – a Transport strike and the Prussian referendum, with their chaps actually out together with leaflets, demos etc. And Hitler always said that his best SA men after 33 were the former Communist units.'

4. Conquest's brother-in-law and sister, Dr and Mrs Ronald Hartley.

5. A dining club founded in 1945 by members of the Commons and the Lords who opposed the Yalta agreement.

6. Anthony Lejeune; see Amis to Larkin, 6 December 1956, note 6.

7. Amis has added in pen in the left margin: 'Someone suggested it was the presence of the MPs that did it – mustn't show doubt, weakness, etc.'

8. Conquest cannot identify 'Silv', nor can Michael Sissons, Amis's agent at the time, nor anyone at Jonathan Cape, the book's publisher.

TO PHILIP LARKIN – 9 MARCH 1978

Gardnor House, Flask Walk, London, N.W.3

Dear Philip,

Apologies for silence. Have been finishing a novel in time for the autumn, so answered no letters unless I stood to lose money otherwise.

Thank you for telling me of MacKillop.[1] Jolly flattering and all that, though he does make me sound a bit of an intellectual, all that Hume and contra-Freudian stuff. But if it helps to spread the idea that it's okay to think I'm good, why not?

The passing of Paul Scott gave me a chill.[2] Born 1920, hey? 'Extraordinary, isn't it, Scott and Amis going off like that at almost exactly the same age. And cancer in the same place, too.' Hee hee.

Let me know when you need a bed and a boozing-mate.

Many people in our big cities live in fear of being swamped by bum,[3]

Kingsley

[TLS: Bodleian]

TO THE EDITOR, *THE TIMES*[1] – 16 MARCH 1978

Gardnor House, Flask Walk, London, N.W.3

Sir, Oughtn't you to start learning to read and write a bit before you blow off about low educational standards (leader, March 15)? In your very first sentence you refer to something you call the Institute of Mathematic's test for school leavers. I'm not sure, but I doubt if there's

---

1. I.D. MacKillop, 'Armageddon Pier Staff: Second Decade Amis', *Cambridge Quarterly* 7:4 (March 1978), pp.324–34.

2. Paul Scott (1920–78), novelist, author of thirteen novels mainly dealing with Anglo-Indian relations, including the four novels known as *The Raj Quartet.*

3. An allusion to a current row involving Margaret Thatcher, leader of the Tory opposition. On 30 January Mrs Thatcher had declared on the television programme *World in Action* that 'People are really rather afraid that this country might be swamped by people with a different culture.'

---

1. This letter was discovered among Amis's papers after his death. It was not printed in *The Times* and may never have been sent.

such a place as the Institute of Mathematic. Then you mention 'questions on the level of "Milk is 12p a pint. If I use two pints each day, what is my weekly milk bill".' Don't you know that direct questions should end with a question-mark? Then you call something 'unmistakeable', a most eccentric spelling to say the least and one not given in the *OED*. Finally you talk about methods that leave pupils 'bereft' of understanding, etc. But 'bereft' isn't just a classy synonym for 'not in possession'; it means 'robbed, deprived'. Since nobody can be robbed of something he has never had, you imply that the methods concerned have actually removed an understanding that had previously existed. But of course you don't mean that. Next time, *get it right*.

Yours faithfully,

[TL: HEHL]

TO ROBERT CONQUEST – 18 MARCH 1978

Gardnor House, Flask Walk, London N.W.3

Dear Bob,

Yes, I know, about time, or even bloody time. Had to finish book and wrote no letters for ten weeks *even when money was involved*. Now done and delivered. Many cordial and honour-appreciating thanks for the gift of *Kolyma*,[1] which I haven't started yet; still on my post-book-unwinding-reading, in this case D. [Dick] Francis for the 2nd or 3rd time round. Funnily enough Caroleen rang just as I had written the first half-dozen words of this, her object being to get Monkey to do something for her (ha-ha) and sounding very normal and cheerful. I asked her out to lunch on the 28th and will report.

You'll have heard by now that Bruce Page[2] has got the Statesman. Everybody there seems too stunned to say anything. Consensus is that he's *either* off his head *or* a colonel in the KGB *or* both *and* that he's a frightful shit; used to go round with a bully-boy to third-degree chaps he was 'interviewing' for the S. Times. Other news:[3] the Left are working the National Front for all they're worth, not only of course to take

1. *Kolyma* (1978) by Robert Conquest, dedicated to Amis and Elizabeth Jane Howard.
2. Bruce Page (b.1936), Australian-born journalist; edited *New Statesman* (1978–82).
3. Amis has added 'well, not v. new' in pen in the left margin.

attention off their own atrocities but to tell a lot of well-intentioned shags that the real trouble is capitalism; mark how Commie stalking-horses have a collective-sounding title – Broad Left, Anti-Nazi League, Radical Students' Alliance. But you know all that. Latest is rioting schoolkids. Quote: 'A leading psychologist warned: "We are witnessing the birth of a powerful new phenomenon – the militant schoolkid."' Translation: 'A fucking fool of a trendy lefty psychologist talked about hooligans urged on by other fucking lefties.' Talking of which, I heard the other day that Melvyn Bragg was asking if it was true that Kingsley invented the term 'lefty'.[4] Well, you and I (and most people who have heard of anything) know better, but it's rather nice that someone thinks it, isn't it? From all one hears Margaret T. is coming along nicely over immigration, though what she could do about it, i.e. about a hefty coloured minority, which is the issue, not immigration as such, I'm blest if I know. Do give me some hope about Carter other than that he might die suddenly at any moment. I enclose a couple of things; I must say la loi Conquest looks v. neat in French. Do tell me what UK periodicals you see regularly so I know what not to send. [. . .]

The big personal news is that George G[ale], having walked out on Pat and back in again, is now talking, I hear, of buggering off again for good. It seems she was silly enough to throw in his face the fact that her last kid isn't his – he must have known all along, but just knowing is different from having your nose rubbed in it. For once I was glad to see Claudie [Worsthorne], who was in a position to give me a full account because she happened to be the first person to visit them after the almighty all-night row that started on Christmas Eve. Truth is stranger, eh? Tony P in good nick: he fell into a snowdrift during the blizzards in the West Country last month and (I think) was bloody lucky to get out again. Hope you weren't cross about Tuppers;[5] I couldn't stop Martin running it, and *I* thought as the exponent you are you deserved to be represented, more fully in fact than he eventually decided. Your Landor versions have been widely acclaimed as up to your very best limericks, of which by the way I have accepted to do the Faber Book,[6] so write down a

4. Melvyn Bragg (b.1939), novelist and broadcaster; created Life Peer (1998). The eighth edition of Eric Partridge's *A Dictionary of Slang and Unconventional English*, ed. Paul Beale (London: Routledge, 1984), p.674, traces the first appearance of 'lefty' (meaning left-wing, as opposed to proletarian, an earlier meaning) to 1936, when Amis was fourteen.

5. For Tupper see Amis to Conquest, 1 November 1967 and 12 October 1976.

6. A project Amis eventually abandoned.

tag-line for any that come to mind. My next poem will be called Spain, not taking Auden on obviously, but alluding to him, last line something like Today the struggle not to talk cock. Family all well; Philip has an exhibition just across the road and has sold to date nine pictures, including one of, oddly enough, Franco that went for £400, which seems quite a lot to me. Footnote: soon you'll be liable for *up to three months' jug* for persistently, i.e. twice, selling haberdashery or ironmongery non-metrically. I was going to ask you when you'll be over but I could understand your not specially wanting to come.

Cheers
K.

J says very pleased and touched at being included in dedication.[7]

[TLS: Recipient]

TO PHILIP LARKIN – 24 APRIL 1978

Gardnor House, Flask Walk, London, N.W.3.

Which to my unutterable chagrin I have *lost* or some rotten fucker has pinched. Wouldn't like to write it all out again would you?[1]

Dear Philip, ↖

I was delighted to get your p.c. about Drinking Song. Nobody I'd rather, etc. It was very nice of you to write. Sorry you're going broke. What's with old Crip?[2] I couldn't understand that bit.

Look now, I'm preparing a talk on comic lit. for Aussie radio – nay, stare not so: they pay like madmen. You're in, of course. But I want to put old Flann O'B in too, and feel I ought to say what Swim-Two-

7. MS addition.

---

1. Larkin's card, postmarked 10 April 1978, was found, and can be seen in the Amis archive in HEHL. In it Larkin calls 'Drinking Song' (*CP*, pp. 151–2) 'a splendid piece that evokes one's whole assent'.

2. Bruce Montgomery had sent Larkin 'a carping letter . . . saying what a nuisance we all were' (Larkin to Amis, 10 April 1978, in HEHL).

Birds means. I remember you saying it was the Gaelic name for Dublin, but the Enc. Brit. doesn't think so. *That* means Town of the Fort of the Hurdles, it says. Any ideas?[3]

And what the hell is that pram doing in the Pam poem?[4] I always assumed it was some odoriferous plant you could smell for miles (in the wind), but it can only be a flat-bottomed boat or a perambulator says OED. Neither quite fits.

If you're really strapped there's plenty of things like Scotch and gin here, but don't let it get so bad that you can't raise the fare.

Princess Margaret should reconsider her bum

Kingsley

[ALS: Bodleian]

TO PHILIP LARKIN – 22 MAY 1978

Gardnor House, Flask Walk, London, N.W.3.

Oh, and tks v.m., o.m.

Dear Philip,

I had hoped to see you down in these parts before this, when I could have asked you to do the present small chore for me without rising from your chair or having your glass refilled above once. They tell me I may bring out those old Collected Poems next year if I deliver the MS by the end of the month, and I am now preparing the text.

3. For the title of *At-Swim-Two-Birds* (1939) by Flann O'Brien, see p. 95 (in 1939 Longmans Green and Co. edition): 'After another time he [Sweeny] set forth in the air again till he reached the church at Snamh-da-en (or Swim-Two-Birds) by the side of the Shannon.' Sweeny is taken from *Buile Suibhne* (*The Frenzy of Sweeny*), a Middle Irish romance about the trials and adventures of 'Suibhne Geilt' (Sweeny the Madman), King of Dal Araidhe.

4. See John Betjeman, 'Pot Pourri from a Surrey Garden', in *Collected Poems* (London: John Murray, 1979), p. 57 (reprinted in *NOBLV*), the first line of which reads 'Miles of pram in the wind and Pam in the gorse track'. (The word 'pram' also appears in the poem's eighth line: 'Then which path shall I take? that over there by the pram?') Larkin couldn't explain 'pram', and advised Amis to 'write to the old boy himself' (Larkin to Amis, 27 April 1978, in HEHL). He seems not to have done so. For a possible answer, see lines 3–6 of Betjeman's 'N.W.5 & N.6', in *Collected Poems*, p. 288: 'my memory sifts/Lillies from lily-like electric lights/And Irish stew smells from the smell of prams/And roar of seas from roar of London trams.' Here, at least, a smell of prams contributes to a 'pot pourri' of smells, though the location is urban rather than suburban. '*Miles* of pram', though, suggests vegetation.

There are five (no doubt there should be more) I feel dubious about: will they add to my reputation or tend to fuck it up? I enclose xeroxes of them (which of course you needn't return). Would you kindly give me your yes or no in each case? No need for any reasons.[1] Also, I remember your saying you preferred the original versions of 'Beowulf' and of 'An Ever-Fixed Mark' (Buck and Ralph). Still so?

Bob has gone back, leaving behind him a great hangover and an even greater silence. I think he would come in and read to me while I was having a fuck, assuming that that could ever be put to the test.

Cuban penetration into the bum,

Kingsley

[ALS: Bodleian]

TO CHRISTOPHER RICKS – 28 JUNE 1978

Gardnor House, Flask Walk, London, N.W.3.

Dear Christopher,

Sorry for delay in answering your kind letter. Not all idleness, also some thought about possible topics for your symposium.[1] US linguistic puritanism is a nice topic but soon exhausted. What about malapropism? King Hussein is an avid pilot. This mitigates against our assumption. I suppose only the second is a real malapropism but the

---

1. The five poems were 'Words', 'Progress', 'Kipling at Bateman's', 'Sonnet from Orpheus' and 'Hours of Waking: an insomniac's bestiary'. Larkin's reply, in a letter of 24 May 1978 (in HEHL), begins 'Why, sir, your pieces will I think do little to your name, the one way or the other,' and ends 'I think if you feel all Leavisy & full of standards, junk all of them. If you need a few, "Progress", "Kipling" – *possibly* "H of W". In that order.' Larkin also reiterated a preference for the early versions of 'Beowulf' (from *Bright November*) and 'An Ever-Fixed Mark' (from *A Look Round the Estate*). Amis decided not to include any of the five poems in *CP*, and printed the early versions of 'Beowulf' and 'An Ever-Fixed Mark' (though he changed its penultimate line from 'Sex stops when you pull up your pants' to 'Sex is a momentary itch'). For 'Words' see *Outposts* 100 (Spring 1974), p.87; for 'Progress' see *New Statesman* (24 October 1969), p.581; 'Kipling at Bateman's' was published by the Poem-of-the-Month Club (1973); 'Sonnet from Orpheus' appeared in *A Frame of Mind*; and 'Hours of Waking' in *Spectator* (3 October 1970), p. 371.

---

1. *The State of the Language* (1980), ed. Ricks and Leonard Michaels.

scope could be widened to include all, or a lot of, kinds of catachresis. What do you think?[2]

Delivery date acceptable. Fee *just* acceptable. I take your point about hand-wringing, but ignorant sods should be chided, no?

I'll wait to hear from you. Thank you for your amiable remarks about the *NOBLV* intro.

Yours
Kingsley

[ALS: Recipient]

TO TOM MILLER – 28 JUNE 1978

Gardnor House, Flask Walk, London, N.W.3.

My dear Tom,

What a fine occasion![1] Better even than expected. It was so kind of you both to entertain us and lush us up – all that champagne, my *God*! – and feather-bed us. And memorable performance, too. I forget whether you said you took the D. Tel, so enclose a cutting from Monday's issue.

Fascinated by your CHN III notes.[2] I think no nuclear war, perhaps just one ICBM on Detroit to show business is meant. Independent CI[3] attractive but implausible – so I think at the moment. But Glyndebourne is a fine idea. A climactic scene there.[4] But am shutting down on specu-

2. Ricks approved; Amis's contribution, entitled 'Getting it Wrong', is reprinted in *The Amis Collection*, pp. 297–305.

---

1. Miller (b.1935), a journalist and solicitor, met Amis in late 1977 when he interviewed him for the *Illustrated London News* (the interview was not published until September 1978). He and his wife Jane had invited Amis and Jane Howard to Glyndebourne in Sussex for a performance of *The Magic Flute*.

2. Amis was at the time planning the 'alternate world' novel *Russian Hide-and-Seek* (1980), which imagines a twenty-first-century England ruled by the Soviets. He and Miller referred to the as-yet-unnamed novel as 'Country House Novel III' ('I' and 'II' being *The Anti-Death League* (1966) and *Ending Up* (1974)).

3. The Channel Islands, which Miller had suggested should be given their independence in the novel.

4. Amis did use this idea of Miller's – that the Russians produce a disastrous opera at Glyndebourne using real animals (Miller was thinking of *The Magic Flute*) – in *Russian Hide-and-Seek*, though the production is only referred to in the novel (p.234) rather than used as a climactic scene.

lation until I get nearer the time for starting: October, perhaps.

Thanks for chart,[5] which I can just about follow if I grit my teeth – you still don't quite realise what a slowcoach I am at these matters.

Do let us know when you're over again, not forgetting to say where you can be reached on this side of the water.

All the very best to you both

Yours
Kingsley

[ALS: Recipient]

TO SIMON CURTIS – 1 JULY 1978

Gardnor House, Flask Walk, London, N.W.3.

Dear Simon,

Please forgive delay, also typed rather than handwritten letter. I am a little shaky after one of those weeks you sometimes get when everybody seems to be conspiring to get you pissed and keep you so.

Mrs P[1] shows a definite advance, I think, firmer and more adventurous too. Even so I like best 'Abthorpe Elms', which looks back a bit.[2] The love poems are a success. 'Valedictory' good too, especially the end, where the consonants show how bloody difficult it is to get that gate's latch shut.[3] Re Haydn/Hofstetter: if it's the movement I think you mean, once popularly known, I believe, as 'Eighteenth-century Dance', going dee de-deedle dee, deedle deedle dee, then to this pair of feet it's in 4/4

5. Miller had sent Amis a stock market chart to illustrate his theory that the collapse of the West might be precipitated by a financial disaster.

---

1. A pamphlet of Curtis's poems entitled *Mrs Paine and Other Poems* (Manchester: North West Arts, 1978). 'Mrs Paine' itself was reprinted in *Spike Island Spring* (1996), p.15; Amis has marked the title in the letter with an asterisk and added 'for which many thanks!' in pen at the bottom of the page.

2. Reprinted in *Sports Extra: New and Selected Poems* (1988), p.15.

3. The line Amis refers to, from 'Valedictory', a poem about Philip Larkin's influence, reads: 'The choice is made. The gate's latch shut behind' (line 16).

time and so can't be a minuet, which is in triple time. Don't take my word for it, but it would be worth checking.[4]

Good about novel.[5] I shouldn't worry about central ideas and such; if it works properly a central idea will emerge even though you may not be[6] conscious of having put it there. I didn't realise that *The Alteration* was partly saying, Whatever alterations you might make in human circumstances, horrible things will still happen, till after it was published.

Well, stick to it, and good luck. Hope to see you before too long.

Cheers
Kingsley

[TLS: Recipient]

TO ROBERT CONQUEST – 3 JULY 1978

Gardnor House, Flask Walk NW3

Dear Bob,

Forgive shitty silence. As you know, unlike you I shy away from personal letters till my desk is clear, which it wasn't for weeks thanks to proofs, official letters and general crap. It cleared last week but then came one of those periods when the whole world seems united in a conspiracy to make you pissed and keep you so: dates made yesterday and three months ago all dovetailing, the most disparate things like book-signing sessions, interviews, broadcasts and of course wine-tastings and piss-ups turning out to be piss-ups, and all I was fit for between whiles was dazedly trying to re-read very undemanding thrillers. Fought my way to the surface today but with a Garrick date tonight and lunch and dinner tomorrow . . .

Your p.c. with Funchal menu arrived this morning, long after your letter referring to it.[1] Am puzzled and a bit worried about your blabbing-

4. Amis was right, and Curtis changed 'minuet' to 'serenade' in the second line of 'Envoi', subtitled 'HAYDN/HOFSTETTER (?) String Quartet Op. 3 No. 5', from *Sports Extra: New and Selected Poems*, p.49.

5. Curtis eventually abandoned this novel.

6. Amis has typed an oblique stroke here, to mark an insertion, and added the words 'fully, anyway' above the line.

---

1. The postcard does not survive. In a letter to Amis of 22 June 1978 Conquest wondered

sot ref. Do clarify and I will then keep you posted if I can. Anyway many thanks for Fisherman's Kettleful etc.

Your limerick about C. Ricks[2] is nearer the mark than you thought. [. . .] [S]aw prog in Radio Times, Radio 3: Bob Dylan and the language that he used.[3] C. Ricks, who has faith in Dylan as a real writer, attends to the words of some songs, mostly early, about faith misplaced. The Dylan numbers he discusses include . . . Honestly. Degilts the gingerbread a bit, what?[4]

The old NOBLV seems to be selling well, 3 weeks running no. 2 in the non-fic hit parade. That ass Jack Lambert[5] in the S Times picked me up for bad grammar in the phrase 'it would have taken a greater poet than him to, etc.', saying it should be he. I put him right, then the next week two ignorant fuckers weighed in on his side. I let it go; what's that phrase about a fool saying in ten words what it will take a wise man many hundreds to confute?

It won't surprise you to hear that the alterations to the kitchen which prevented you from staying with us in May began this morning, nor that they have consisted so far (12.30) not of anything being done to or in the kitchen but of a chap using a drill* in the little store-room next to my study with no door intervening. So pardon any incoherence.

Have seen C only at her birthday party. Her bloke seemed nice enough, at any rate not likely on inspection to encourage her into behaving foolishly or crappily. I must say the attempt to sting you at

if Amis had received it: 'with the main dishes of that Funchal restaurant? Otherwise all it said was that some sot had blabbed in his cups to the *Sunday Times*.' Amis was worried because he thought he was the sot in question, having 'blabbed' to the *Sunday Times* in a way that revealed the identity of 'Victor Gray'. He also feared that the pseudonym had non-literary (that is, 'top secret') uses for Conquest (see letter of 17 July 1978). Conquest explains and reassures in a letter of 4 August 1978: 'forget about V Gray – not ever top secret, just that it's a bit different various chaps knowing or guessing and confirmation in the public prints – eg from the point of view of some Callaghan sod saying, "and we understand that Mrs T is taking foreign policy advice from a gentleman whose main claim to fame is as author of A Young Engine Driver Called Hunt." ' Funchal is the seaport capital of the Madeira Islands, a winter resort; the dishes from the 'Funchal menu' Conquest copied out for Amis in his postcard were described in ludicrous English.

2. Actually a joint Conquest-Amis effort.

3. For Ricks on Dylan, see 'Clichés', in *The State of the Language*, ed. Leonard Michaels and Christopher Ricks, pp. 54–63.

4. Ricks had written to Amis lavishly praising the introduction to *NOBLV* and inviting him to contribute to *The State of the Language* (see Amis to Ricks, 28 June 1978).

5. J.W. (Jack) Lambert (1917–86), journalist and broadcaster on literature, music and theatre; worked on the books and arts pages of the *Sunday Times* from 1948, as Assistant Literary Editor (1948–60), Literary Editor (1960–76), then Associate Editor (1976–78).

this stage, indeed at all, seems most crappy; as requested won't say so to C unless she mentions. Hope to see you in Sept or whenever you come, if indeed you're capable of movement after your exertions, or even still in the land of the living.

Quick notes from all over: saw Edna O'B at Gully Wells's wedding party;[6] Martin recalled that when he was working at Cape's years ago the berkish delivery boy there said of her, 'If you don't feel like it, don't pass the door.' Dan Jacobson[7] was v. funny about what a shitty showman Yevtushenko is – 'Now I speak to you soft Russian words, soft like your hearts.' [. . .] Weather fucking terrible; am going to Wimbledon for the first time ever on Wed. but if it's like this better make it a long late lunch. Just as well I didn't make a serious bid for the Oxon Po chair,[8] because I couldn't even raise the necessary couple of sponsors and obviously won't now; of all people, *Al* [Alvavez] rang to say he would support me if I stood. I suppose that must have got round.

Off soon to collect new d.j. (jacket, not jockey) so I can turn up at W. Wyatt's[9] tomorrow properly attired, its predecessor having split all the way down one buttock as I was sitting down for the first time in some shag's drawing-room. Might have been awkward, but got away with it by always being the last to get up and keeping my back to the wall. Not altogether looking forward to Wyatt's, actually. I told you about the time Heath, R Jenkins and M Macmillan[10] were there, didn't I? Well, there you are, then.

Cheers
K.

* Hammer (1.10)
Saw (2.20)
Hammer again (2.35)[11]

[TLS: Recipient]

6. Edna O'Brien (b.1932), Irish novelist and short-story writer.

7. Dan Jacobson (b.1932), South African novelist, settled in Britain since 1958.

8. On 23 May 1978 Conquest wrote to Amis about a rumoured campaign to make Ian Hamilton Professor of Poetry at Oxford, then suggested Amis, among others, as a possible competitor.

9. Woodrow Wyatt (1918–97), journalist, author, politician; Chairman, Horserace Totalisator Board (1976–97); created Life Peer (1987).

10. Maurice Macmillan (1921–84), publisher, Conservative MP and Minister; son of Harold Macmillan.

11. MS addition.

TO PHILIP LARKIN – 27 JULY 1978

Gardnor House, Flask Walk, London, N.W.3.

Dear Philip,

Halo now, you old burag, keeping quiet you are, aren't you? I expect you find it hard to settle to anything, being as excited as you must be over the Humber Bridge[1] leggo my pis

You were pretty right about anthologies being things every bugger knows better than you how to do. Why not more Americans? Why only one woman [two actually]?[2] Why no Ogden Nash? Why so unadventurous and idiosyncratic, so ground-covering and patchy, so obvious and fanciful? Why hasn't he read anything except what he's put in? – especially THAT. But it's done all right (14,000 and still moving) so fuck 'em is what I keep saying.

Apart from hoping to resume touch I write to ask you if you can improve the enclosed out of your greater knowledge. I mean in a sense disimprove by suggesting even crappier examples in lines 1–3 and 5–6. You might also help me with the churchyards. Brunswick sounds all right but the others less so. Or could it be done another way altogether? Any hints welcome.[3]

---

1. The Humber Bridge, under construction at the time, was opened in 1981. Larkin had been approached in the mid-1970s by Anthony Hedges, of the Department of Music at Hull, to write the words to a cantata he was composing to celebrate the opening. Larkin eventually agreed, finishing the words in December 1975, and the cantata was performed at the City Hall in Hull on 11 April 1981. See 'Bridge for the Living', *LCP*, pp. 203–4.

2. The square brackets are Amis's. There was only one woman: Phyllis McGinley (1905–78). Perhaps he mistook Shirley Brooks (1816–74), editor of *Punch* (1870–74), for a woman.

3. For Larkin's suggestions for Amis's enclosed poem 'Farewell Blues', which parodies John Betjeman's 'Dorset' (itself a parody of Hardy's 'Friends Beyond'), from *Continual Dew* (1937) (cf. the refrain 'Lie in Mellstock Churchyard now'), see his letter of 1 August 1978 (in HEHL): 'I think you should stick to chaps who are dead: Goodman, Wilson aren't. Floyd O'Brien? Labels: ideally you . . . should line up the chaps with the label they chiefly recorded on, but this is virtually impossible. Gennett is pretty hopeless: only Oliver and the Wolverines. I should substitute Decca – but of course they did all sorts of things in latter years. I2: "Art Ensemble", "Globe Unity", "Spontaneous Music Ensemble" are all real names. I3: "Seascape" doesn't sound quite right. How about "Square Root" – horrible mathematical, and they think theyre being jazz-rockly funny? II1: this sounds a bit like your father on Lester Young et al. Wants improving. Trumpets that don't sound like trumpets, fast as clarinets: "castrato trumpets"? "Bagpipe saxophones that fart"? Get the boot in. Think of Coltrane. II2 excellent. II3: decency sounds like yr. dad. III1: why gasp and stare? Gurgle yeah wd be more like it. III2: why *indignant* air? III:3 fine. For names, how about Bubber Miley, Muggsy Spanier,

Have recently been sent something that wins the golden piss-pot of the decade: Seamus Heaney's memorial address on Robert Lowell.[4] I can't remember wanting so devoutly to hit a writer since first looking into *The Owl and the Nightingale*.[5] If by any remote chance you've missed it write to C. Monteith, or I'll send you a xerox. Also if by an equally remote chance you haven't yet got your *NOBLV* let me know and I'll send you an inscribed copy.

We've got the builders in. What about that for restraint? I mean not having begun Dear Philip fuck the sodding builders Having the kitchen redone. A fortnight, they said. They said it in May but turned up last Monday fortnight. Now they say it should be usable but not finished by the end of next week. Well, you know yourself. Eresa poincher see: we should very much like you to turn up and stay the night but better wait till after say 15th Aug. Assa poincher see.

Ah: I'm addressing a bunch of librarians in Sept to plug my novel. Any tips on what to say or not to say? I mean, what do they like and not like to be told or called?

Free collective bum,
Kingsley

Toilets

[TLS: Bodleian]

FAREWELL BLUES

Bongo, sitar, 'cello, flute, electric piano, bass guitar,
Training Orchestra, Research Team, Workshop, Group, Conservatoire,
Seascape, *Nexus*, *Barbaresque*, *Distortions*, *Voltage* – bloody row,
For Louis Armstrong, Benny Goodman, Walter Page and
Sidney Catlett lie in
Brunswick churchyard now.

Eddie Condon? Mildred Bailey? Sidney Bechet?' For the finished version, incorporating a number of Larkin's suggestions, see *CP*, p. 153.

4. Seamus Heaney, *Robert Lowell: A Memorial Address and an Elegy* (London and Boston: Faber and Faber, 1978, printed privately). Lowell's dates were 1917–77.

5. See Amis to Larkin, 5 May 1946, note 3.

Trumpets berserk, drums contingent, saxophones that bleat
  or bawl,
Keyless, barless, poor-man's Boulez, improvising on fuck-all,
Far beyond what feeling, reason, even decency allow,
While Teddy Wilson, Floyd O'Brien, Sterling Bose and Henry
    Allen lie in
  Gennett churchyard now.

Dead's the note we loved that swelled within us, made us
  gasp and stare,
Simple joy and simple sadness thrashing the indignant air;
What replaced them no one asked for, but it turned up
  anyhow,
And Coleman Hawkins, Johnny Hodges, Bessie Smith and
    Pee Wee Russell lie in
  Victor churchyard now.

TO ROBERT CONQUEST – 27 JULY 1978

Gard Ho F'k Wk NW3

Dear Bob,

Your several to hand. The Funchal menu arrived just in time for me to use bits to great effect on a radio show. I'm afraid I've thrown the NOBLV reviews away, though I could get another set at need. Pauker got a lot of attention, mostly favourable. Bitchy piece by Claire Tomalin in Punch, implying I'd just copied most of it out of Michael Roberts.[1] I counted the overlap, which she had called 'a remarkably large one', and found it was 21%. When I complained she said she thought that was indeed a remarkably large one. DAN Jones dropped a ballock saying he thought 'The Helbatrawss' was v. well done but inappropriately gloomy. I wrote saying that wasn't really my fault but old Charles'.[2] Jones hadn't realised it was a translation. Bitchiest of all

1. Amis's supposed source was Michael Roberts, *The Faber Book of Comic Verse* (1942).

2. Baudelaire, author of 'L'Albatross', among the most frequently anthologised poems in *Les Fleurs du mal* (1857).

was Marg Laski[3] in Ill-Lond-News: why hadn't I read about 50 other people, like D Parker and O Nash, and put them all in? But a few days ago it had sold 14,000 and is trundling along at 500 a week, and Radio 4 are doing 13 programmes about it I mean from it in the autumn, so fuck'em. Few letters actually, but one v. decent one from Glasgow, no name or address, thanking me and enclosing 3 £ notes.

Much relieved about the blabbing sot.[4] I was afraid I had told someone all about your connections with the CIA, MI5, KGB etc. I just told Atticus (Tony Holden) the story, reasoning rightly that it would help to make an interesting piece. I had no idea the pseudonym was a dead secret, had no way of knowing from you. And after all everybody I know has heard me recite Hunt, Arundel, Bronte and others and invariably attribute[5] them to you. Anyway I hope you weren't truly annoyed and apologise if you were. [. . .]

Shit, yes, than *him*. I wrote 'It would have taken a greater poet than him to devise a style, etc.' Of course you can write 'than he was' but 'him' is accusative like 'poet'. That old ass Brig Fergusson[6] wrote saying that 'is' or 'was' is understood after 'he'. What can you say to that? 'Oh no it isn't' is the best I can think of. If people knew Latin it wouldn't arise.

Ah yes – I mentioned Ricks, but I think forgot to say my article for him[7] will be on malapropisms, catachreses. Not hard to find samples; I got 2 out of the Times today – 'your otherwise prescient leader'; the leader hadn't shown foreknowledge of anything, hadn't had much time; 'percipient' was what he meant. SF review: 'told with an ease that belies an extraordinary control of the genre'; he means 'betrays'. And on the radio, of a notable Test match: 'conditions were really too good, which sounds like a corollary in terms.' Now, could you keep your eye open for some there and clip 'em out? I'd be v. grateful for ½ a doz. because R's book is US-published.

[. . .] In case I forget again at end v. many thanks for v. jolly sherry.

3. Marghanita Laski (1915–88), novelist, critic, journalist.

4. See Amis to Conquest, 3 July 1978, note 1.

5. Amis has typed 'credit' above 'attribute'.

6. Bernard Edward Fergusson (1911–80), author, diplomat, soldier (1931–58); created Life Peer (1972).

7. 'Getting it Wrong', in Michaels and Ricks, eds, *The State of the Language* (1980); reprinted in *The Amis Collection*, pp. 297–305.

Revealing Callaghan story from John O'Sullivan. Jim and Carrington (Cgtn),[8] going on TV to discuss how something had gone or was going or what it meant, by-election or local elections. Before the off Jim mutters, 'Tell me privately, just between ourselves, how do you think your side is doing/will do?' Cgtn: 'Well, frankly, not too well.' They go on the air, Jim's asked what he thinks and says, 'As Lord Cgtn admitted to me a moment ago before the programme started, the Tories are in a bad way.' What a *shit*.

Cheers
K.

Yes, anybody can put me up for poetry chair but no one has.[9]

PS: Enclosed is by Seamus Heaney. Just a sample; there are 5½ more pages of it. (I'll keep it to show you.) One doesn't just think, what blinding crap, but even more, what vociferously insincere egomaniacal crap. If there was anyone there who was really sorry L. was dead it wasn't fucking SH.[10]

[TLS: Recipient]

TO DALE SALWAK – 9 AUGUST 1978

Gardnor House, Flask Walk, London, N.W.3.

Dear Dale,

The book[1] is very handsome and amazingly exhaustive. I feel both proud and slightly guilty at having occasioned so much hard work. And *useful*; this very week I must draft a blurb for my collected poems, due in the spring, and your record of the reviews of the earlier volumes will be invaluable. Many, many thanks.

8. James Callaghan (b.1912), Labour Prime Minister (1976–79); created Life Peer (1987). Lord Carrington (b.1919), Conservative politician and Minister; at the time Leader of the Opposition, House of Lords.

9. MS addition.

10. See Amis to Larkin, 27 July 1978.

---

1. *Kingsley Amis: A Reference Guide* (1978).

I feel a little leery, as I believe you fellows say, about approaching Wain on your behalf.[2] For some years now there has been a *froideur* between us (entirely his fault, let it be observed), and my recommending you might do you more harm than good. For the same reason, play down the work you've done on me. But write to him yourself; he isn't the sort of chap to be rude to strangers and I'm sure you'd find him helpful.

Congratulations again. Glad you liked the Light Verse.

Yours sincerely,
Kingsley Amis

[TLS: Recipient]

TO THE SECRETARY, THE GARRICK CLUB – 16 AUGUST 1978

Could facilities be installed whereby those confined to wheelchairs could make their way, or be helped, up the front stairs to the level of the Coffee Room and the Members' Lounge? A ramp might be impracticable, but I understand that there is a device using a powered mobile seat which is efficient and not excessively expensive. It would require only a limited amount of assistance, which I am sure would be readily given.

KINGSLEY AMIS[1]

[Entry in Garrick Club Suggestions Book]

TO ROBERT CONQUEST – 1 DECEMBER 1978

Gardnor Ho

Dear Bob,

After that, as we guessed it would be, He started objecting to Pee, And the outcome was this: He changed it to Piss! Take your pick:

2. In 1980 Salwak was to publish *John Braine and John Wain: A Reference Guide* (Boston: G.K. Hall).

---

1. No such device has yet been installed at the Garrick.

Tweedledum – Tweedledee.[1] Do you remember some years ago there was a thing in the paper about a naturalised Spaniard who changed his name to Peed on the advice of English friends? Well, there was, anyway. Then the whole thing began to dehisce . . .

You shame me with the volume of your correspondence. Until a couple of weeks ago I had a fair excuse:[2] typing with one hand was slow and with two uncomfortable, but that went. The old fin aches and is weak in movements above the shoulder, but I can do a fair Nazi salute and best of all can wipe my bum, which for some reason left hand, quick to learn shaving, typing etc., was always slow and awkward with. I laughed a bit hollowly when I saw your letter to Jane with its mention of nursing. Like fuck! Apart from cutting bread for the first week or two she left everything to me, her attention all on her recently bereaved analyst and the worthless persons in her 'group'. Anyway, sod it. Have been doing much lunching recently to celebrate recovery, make up for housebound weeks. Tonight the 'group' comes here for a party – I go off to cavort with Letwins, Minogue[3] etc., though now I write it 'cavort' seems hardly the word.

I send you scissored-up photostats of the reviews that praised Pauker, not the whole of them because having been set back £7.78 when returning my US proofs[4] I am grown mean with postage. Shit I mean I have sent you all the reviews but not the bits of them that don't concern P. Those proofs pissed me off too: it took me two days or more to undo the gratuitous damage they had wrought, making me use words like 'anymore', 'sometime' ('it was sometime ago') and the like, italicising and small-capitalising when I wanted roman for informal effect and putting in something like 400 unwanted commas. They think authors do a pretty shaggy rough draft which they, the professionals, then lick into shape.

I'll get this off to you tonight, Friday, and there's a chance it'll reach you by Christmas. (Those proofs sent from NYC at top rate took 19

---

1. See Amis to Conquest, 1 March 1976, note 1.

2. Amis had fallen down the stairs late at night and broken his right arm.

3. Conservative political and economic theorists: William Letwin (b.1922), Professor of Political Science, London School of Economics (1976–88); his wife, Shirley Letwin (d. 1993), political philosopher; Kenneth Minogue (b. 1930), also at LSE, Professor of Political Science since 1984.

4. Of *Jake's Thing* (1978).

days to get here.) Next time I'll answer bits of your letters. If I can. That court-case thing defeats me for the moment. What was the Carson limerick?[5] I think you might run up a Minehead (Thorpe) limerick,[6] don't you? The Pee one went down very well with the lads at the OUP.

Allabeste
K.

[TLS: Recipient]

TO CHRISTOPHER RICKS – 3 JANUARY 1979

Gardnor House, Flask Walk, London, N.W.3.

Dear Christopher,

You mean ex-Mrs *Bob* Dylan? 'Live your dreams' had the same effect on me as the face of Woody Allen: making me wish I didn't belong to the human race.[1]

Sorry, but my first and last flight was in 1932, in a D.H. Dragon Rapide.[2] I understand considerable strides have been made since then, but until aeroplanes run on rails not more than eight feet from the ground I'm staying away from them.

Thank you for all the nice things you say about my article and *Jake*.[3]

5. Amis is referring to a passage in Conquest's letter of [21 November?] 1978, in which he wonders 'what the silliest limerick I've ever written was'. Conquest concludes it was probably 'You are now trying Marmaduke Carson', a character who also appears in what Amis calls the 'court-case thing' (a burlesque trial scene) immediately following in the letter. The limerick is not reproduced.

6. In August 1978, Jeremy Thorpe (see Amis to Conquest, 28 October 1977, note 5) and three others were charged with conspiracy to murder Norman Scott, a former male model. Committal hearings were held in Minehead, Somerset, producing sensational revelations. Thorpe and his co-defendants were all acquitted.

---

1. Ricks explains: 'I had told him of my meeting at a party in California a woman who, hearing that I was about to go to Hawaii, and knowing that I love Bob Dylan, had suggested that I look up Sara Dylan, Dylan's ex-wife; and when I feebly remonstrated (Don't know her, that sort of thing), replied with level gaze "Live your dreams" ' (personal communication, 6 October 1998).

2. See Amis to Jon Stallworthy, 30 May 1977, note 2.

3. 'Getting it Wrong', Amis's contribution to Michaels and Ricks, eds, *The State of the Language*, and *Jake's Thing*.

Reaction to the latter has been odd. Misogyny and all that. 'I say, Ruddy, I see you're leaving Carrie.' – 'Who told you that?' – 'You did. You say here, "the female of the species is more deadly than the male," and here, "he travels the fastest who travels alone." Absolute clincher, what?'[4]

Happy New Year.

Yours,
Kingsley

[TLS: Recipient]

TO ROBERT CONQUEST – 4 JANUARY 1979

Gr Ho, Fl Wk, Ln NW3, Eng

Dear Bob,

About bloody time, yes. Haven't had time to write before because of idling rather than work. The bloody 23 Dec-2 Jan break didn't help. They've only just finished asking why the recent snowfalls weren't cleared from the roads at all on the first day, 31 Dec, and very little on 1 Jan. Nobody told them it was because the blokes were GETTING PISSED on the first day and were HUNGOVER on the second. I must say our working classes are withholding their labour rather a lot these days. This morning for example there was no post. Not a strike, not even a stoppage, just someone deciding he'd rather not turn up. It has been discovered that you can be militant by lying in bed.

I see I told you I had to take 400 commas and various other intrusions out of the Yank proof of *Jake* and naturally wrote a furious letter of complaint. Now after nearly a month a letter comes from the chap's *assistant* (who mentioned galley's sic in his earlier letter) saying it wasn't he who put the commas in, not apologising and not saying they've been taken out again. But his boss wishes me all the best for 1979, he says. Is it because they're publishers or because they're Americans? Rather off the point, but I thought of a good annoying definition of an American – a German-Jewish Canadian. (Humourless, would-be funny, dull).

4. From the Kipling poems 'The Female of the Species' (1911) and 'The Winners' (1888); Kipling married Caroline ('Carrie') Balestier in 1892.

A bit hungover myself today. Drank rather fast early on with a chap who dropped in, but who didn't stay all that long. Then a couple of beers and a liqueur, a bit more Scotch, decided the TV film was too boring, descended to my study to work or something about 10.45. Went up about 12.5 to watch What the Papers Say, then shortly to bed. This morning wondered quite interestedly what I'd written in the hour and 20 minutes at my desk. Everything was exactly as I'd left it at the start of the evening, so I must have spent the time staring drunkenly into space. I hope you've done things like that yourself. [. . .]

Cheers K.

[TLS: HEHL]

TO THE EDITOR, *NEW STATESMAN* – 12 JANUARY 1979

Sir, I draw your attention to Rashid Karapiet's statement (Letters, 22/29 December) that 'one *fact* [his italics] about the Anti-Nazi League[1] cannot in honesty be gainsaid: until it appeared on the scene there was no organised attempt to beat the fascists *at their own game* [my italics].' The fascists' game features hatred, violence and mob rule, and it is interesting that supporters of the League now feel strong enough to declare their own attachment to these values. Some of them may not know or care that the game in question was last played to a finish in the German cities in the early 1930s.

KINGSLEY AMIS
Flask Walk, London NW3

1. The Anti-Nazi League was set up in November 1977 to combat the apparent growth of the National Front party in Britain. There were violent clashes between the two groups at National Front demonstrations.

TO PHILIP LARKIN – 6 FEBRUARY 1979

Gardnor House, Flask Walk, London, N.W.3.

Dear Philip,

This is really just to say How do before the shooting starts. If you can think of anything short of, or not necessitating too much, violence that will get these bastards back to work, I wish you'd tell me.[1] It would cheer me up, do you see.

Had a mad letter from Richard Adams* saying the best part of *Jake's Thing* was the stuff about 1950s tit-mags.[2] I might like to know that 2 things called *Peaches* and *Bounce* still kept up the old traditions. 'Harrison Marks lives,' he added.[3] Had another mad letter from Donald Davie. I would never get anywhere while I regarded Jehovah as a chap. He is the principle of Rectitude and also runs an unjust world. Things like that. Of course, he's *(Donald) not God*[4] at Nashville.[5] Plenty of mad fellows there.

Do let's meet when you come up. Come and stay. Have a meal. Have a drink. My arm is better except that it hurts (slightly) when I've had too much to drink, so it hurts quite a lot of the time why can't this fucki g thing You can give yourself the balls-ache by drinking too much, too. Did you know that? Well, you can.

The Prime Minister promised to stick to his bum,

Kingsley

* *whom of course I've never met, heard from before etc*[6]

[TLS: Bodleian]

---

1. Amis is alluding to what the *Sun* newspaper labelled 'the winter of discontent', a succession of strikes by public-sector workers (closing schools and hospitals), local-authority workers (such as dustmen and gravediggers) and health-service workers.

2. Richard Adams (b. 1920), novelist, author of *Watership Down* (1972).

3. Harrison Marks (1929–97), British soft-porn photographer and film director.

4. MS addition.

5. Davie was Andrew W. Mellon Professor of the Humanities at Vanderbilt University from 1978–88.

6. MS addition.

TO ROBERT CONQUEST – 6 FEBRUARY 1979

G H, F W, L NW3, E

Dear Bob,

I have been deep in novel for over a month and must now catch up with correspondence, starting with you. When I finish this I must begin on a pile *three inches* high. Novel is the one about Russian occupation of England, c. 2035.[1] One good reason for you to come home soon is to discuss the technology with me. All I have given away so far is that all the trees have been cut down for fuel and cars are as rare as in 1900. Oh, also bloody funny bit where the contents of a girl's sitting-room are described, all the usual stuff like a photograph-album, cello, music-stand etc., and ending with 'a boruldite quick-kettle, a music-sounder and a superb three-inch astroscope'.

One of my unanswered letters is, I notice, the one from R Adams. What the hell do I *say*?[2] Seriously. It's nearly two months old now.

Moab[3] is crackingly good. Invidious to select etc. but I particularly liked the translation stuff (that O saisons stuff is exactly what's needed), limericks and Kipling of course, 2001, Hochhuth, the first and last essays (the 'rigour' stuff settles the question to my mind) and POUND. Yes, *why not* get it right when it's as good as got wrong? By the way did I never tell you that one of my classics masters did a long or longish exposé of P's mistranslations in *Greece and Rome*, about 1938? I'll try and dig it out for you.[4] The Moab point (danger not from enemies but false friends) is really the best of the lot. Trust you to work Shittim in. Pissy typo on back of jacket, but v few in text.

---

1. *Russian Hide-and-Seek* (1980).

2. See Amis to Larkin, 6 February 1979.

3. Robert Conquest, *The Abomination of Moab* (London: Maurice Temple Smith, 1979), a collection of essays and poems. The title is explained in the book's preface: 'Israel's early troubles were not always from [the Philistines]. On the other flank lay a more insidious enemy of their own blood, the Moabites, who, from their capital at Shittim, infiltrated temple and harem and set the children of light whoring after strange doctrine . . . In one way or another almost all these pieces concern themselves with repelling Moab's despotic or dogmatic attitudes to literature or to particular types of literature. They argue against political, sociological, ethical and sexual preaching, and against the dogmas of academic literary criticism itself' (pp.viii–ix). 'Hochhuth' in the next sentence is Rolf Hochhuth (b. 1931), German dramatist.

4. The Classics master was the Rev. C.J. Ellingham, City of London School; see *Memoirs*, pp.28–9.

Everything is still perfectly all right here *so far*, except for the ill, the bereaved, and a few people here and there without water etc. But no shortages and nowhere shut. The refuse is pilling up nicely, but the sewage will be the real killer if it comes. The prevailing feeling is complete bewilderment: nobody has the remotest idea what will happen.[5]

Loony letter out of the blue from Donald D in Nashville (he says annoyingly 'You are remembered hereabouts' without saying in what spirit). All about me being wrong to take Jehovah as a chap (his term). He (J) stands for, or is, the principle of Rectitude and at the same time runs an unjust world, which only Lefties want to put right. We ought to wait for, or cheer ourselves up by thinking about, God's world, which is just. In a PS he says 'Spender is here' and adds the following (to me) incomprehensible verses:

> A stalwart man of blood, without
> A gout of blood upon him. O my lawd,
> When Stephen Spender came to Tennessee,
> How all the ill-used ladies did applaud!

No ref in text to blood, ladies etc. You said you thought he was a bit cracked, didn't you?[6]

Everybody, including Martin, says he's leaving the NS to write more, just that. All on good terms. No sign of a successor yet, it seems. David Caute and Neal Ascherson have applied and, it's said, been turned down.[7] [. . .]

Must get on with that pile of crap. Don't leave it too long before returning; you might miss some of the fun.

Cheers
Kingsley

[TLS: Recipient]

5. See Amis to Larkin, 6 February 1979, note 1.

6. Conquest's puzzled gloss on 'A stalwart man of blood' comes from a letter of 17 February 1979: 'Donald's lines are meant to be funny, which he's not good at: I'd have said that "man of blood" meant lefty, though the traditional use is of Charles I. But then why should the ladies feel ill-used?'

7. David Caute (b.1936), writer and academic, did get the job (as Literary Editor of the *New Statesman*, a post Martin Amis was leaving), staying on until 1980; Neal Ascherson (b.1932), journalist and author, continued to write on foreign affairs for the *Observer*.

TO THE EDITOR, *DAILY TELEGRAPH* – 14 FEBRUARY 1979

SIR – None of your learned correspondents seems to be aware of the vital fact that spirits distilled out at 70° proof, like nearly all the whisky drunk in the United Kingdom, are too strong to be absorbed in full by the body.

Dilution with a little less water than the amount of whisky gets all the alcohol into you without softening the blow, a fact long known to drinkers in Scotland and Ireland without benefit of science.

KINGSLEY AMIS
London, N.W.3.

TO PHILIP LARKIN – 19 FEBRUARY 1979

Gardnor House, Flask Walk, London, N.W.3.

Dear Philip,

Yes, 21st March is fine. Would you like dinner in town, or locally, or here? Would you like me to see if I can get Betj along? He may want to bring Eliz Cav,[1] of course, which would mean getting another lady too to balance you. At least Jane says it would. We could get a sufficiently nice one. Anyway, take your pick. *of the above choices*[2]

I will go on a bit, out of politeness and also because the moment I stop or finish I shall have to go on writing my novel, and that's what they call too much like hard work. It's not so much thinking of things for the people to say and do, *though there is that*; it's more the putting into words of difficult, intractable concepts like a man leaving a house by the front door. Testing stuff liek priek like that. [. . .]

That seminar sounds awful and whywasn'tIaskedtoit, no I suppose it's a librarians' and collectors' et al. caper.[3] Nah, never fancied IoM,[4]

1. Lady Elizabeth Cavendish; see Amis to Betjeman, 3 June 1971, note 4.
2. MS addition.
3. Larkin was to open a seminar on Modern Literary Manuscripts in London on 21 March.
4. Larkin had asked Amis, in a letter of 10 February 1979 (in HEHL), if he had ever thought of living on the Isle of Man.

tax exiles and backward Celts. Still they still cane thugs don't they? Let me know what you'd like to do on 21st M, about when you'll be arriving and all that. Fuck this snow.

A net increase of earnings of 20% across the bum,

Kingsley

[TLS: Bodleian]

TO PHILIP LARKIN – 8 APRIL 1979

Gardnor House, Flask Walk, London, N.W.3.

Dear Philip,

Tks VM, OM, for *TLD*.[1] When it came I turned over the pages saying 'Better than me . . . Better than me . . . I could do that . . . Better than me . . . Better than me . . . I could – no I couldn't . . . Better than me . . . I wouldn't want to do that – well . . . Better than me . . . Better than me . . .' You sod. Tks for JJI,[2] too.

Old Toynbee is a cunt. All this stuff about the Movement going into battle. Pretty scattered troops, I'd say: you in Belfast-Hull, me in Swansea, Liz J in Oxford, John* in Reading, Bob in London, Enright in Japan, Donald [Davie]?? And him not agreeing with me that princes are better than monks when THE BIT HE QUOTES shows I'm not saying that. And I must say I'm tired of photographs that make me look like an unsuccessful Jewish-American film producer, even if I *do* look so.[3]

Did you see P Worsthorne's piece in the Sunday Tel? He argued that Mrs T is wrong in thinking that if you cut taxes chaps will work harder because they can keep more of what they earn; no, that'll make them work even *less* hard. I'm sure he's right. The strikes aren't aimed

---

1. *The Less Deceived.* Amis's copy, a first edition, had been lent by his son Martin to a girlfriend; it could not be retrieved.

2. *Jazz Journal International* (1948–), a monthly periodical.

3. Amis is complaining here of a review, with accompanying photograph, of his *Collected Poems* in the *Observer*, 8 April 1979. According to Philip Toynbee, author of the review, 'the Movement went into battle using, as it were, coshes against the arquebuses of their predecessors.' He ends by discussing the poem 'The Value of Suffering', the last stanza of which Amis thinks he misreads.

at improving their standard of living but at maintaining their standard of living when going in three days a week instead of four. What makes them close their eyes as a flame of passion sweeps through them is the thought of IDLING. The pneumatic drills started up at 8.30 this morning in Flask Walk; Sunday you see TIME AND A HALF. A lot of back post came today TIME AND A FUCKING HALF.

As you'll probably know long before you get this Bob is back, this afternoon. Entrée nous (have you noticed how many berks say this? Another favourite of mine is restauranteur) he'll be advising the Thatch on foreign policy esp USSR. Writing speeches and all that.

Good about Auden. Yes there are so many nice things to write about aren't there.[4] There's a pair of slippers in the room you slept in here. Brown buggers. Are they yours? Would have sent them only such a pest if not yours. Is GH who did that drawing of you Geo Hartley?[5] Quite good I think.

My members don't want a fortune in wages – they just want bum,

Kingsley

* LA-VA-TO-RY-PAN

[TLS: Bodleian]

TO PHILIP LARKIN – 10 MAY 1979

Gardnor House, Flask Walk, London, N.W.3.

Dear Philip,

Bloody good, eh? Not only that she got in but that those who were pushed out were pushed out: that murdering quean Thorpe, and that shouting bully Pardoe, and that tousle-haired totalitarian Shirley Williams – I bet she rued the day she turned up on the Grunwick picket

4. See Larkin to Amis, 31 March 1979, in *LL*, p.4: 'Did you know Auden got a rectal fissure from being buggered by a sailor and had to have an operation, and that this produced Letter to a wound? People take all the romance out of life, don't they.' Thwaite's note reads: 'Part of Auden's *The Orators* (1932). The story about Auden was current, and was included in Humphrey Carpenter's biography (1981).'

5. Yes, though Larkin thought Hartley 'incapable of drawing me except as a prune-faced pansy' (letter to Amis, 10 April 1979 (in HEHL)). The drawing is reproduced on the cover of Dale Salwak, ed., *Philip Larkin: The Man and his Work* (1989).

line.[1] Only sorry they didn't get rid of Dr bloody Death (Owen).[2] This lot should do quite well until the miners go on strike for an increase of 250% now and 375% on 1st June and the power workers for 425% backdated to 1st January 1929. Send for the guns and kill.

Your slippers are safe, though they were temporarily and alarmingly reduced to one after a baby had stayed in that room. Pull yourself together man ow woo leggo my[3] Can't you be more definite about this Po: Book Soc: do? Where is it? *When* is it? Who do I ask? I mean I'm free most of 23rd and 24th. *Lem*me* know, son.

Did I tell you Martin is spending a year abroad as a TAX EXILE? Last year he earned £38,000. Little shit. 29, he is. Little shit.
My members have no alternative but to withdraw their bum,

*Of course you're v. welcome any time

Kingsley

[TLS: Bodleian]

TO BLAKE MORRISON – 9 JULY 1979

Gardnor House, Flask Walk, London, N.W.3.

Dear Blake Morrison,

Yes indeed. By all means use those quotes, which sound well within reason. If you start reprinting whole pages of poems it could put chaps off buying the Collected (thank you for news of TLS review

---

1. On 4 May 1979 Margaret Thatcher became Britain's first woman Prime Minister, with a majority of forty-three seats. Among those who lost their seats in the election were Jeremy Thorpe; John Pardoe (b.1934), Liberal MP (1966–79), and Shirley Williams (b.1933), Labour MP and Minister (1964–79), later co-founder of the SDP, and first-elected SDP MP (1981–83); created Life Peer (1993).

2. David Owen (b.1938), Labour MP and Minister (1966–81); later co-founder of SDP, SDP MP (1981–92), Deputy Leader (1982–83) and Leader (1983–87); created Life Peer (1992). Owen had trained and practised as a medical doctor, hence, in part, the nickname, much used by the satirical magazine *Private Eye*.

3. A truncated version of a locution from the Greyfriars stories of Frank Richards; what Billy Bunter says while being thumped or bumped (see Amis to Larkin, 28 October 1977, note 3).

of which).[1] I'm afraid any 1940s-Oxford photographs etc. I might have had would be with my ex-wife. But there just might be something of the sort in Martin Green's book about some of us, *Children of the Sun*;[2] haven't got a copy.

On the Movement lark, I could well have mentioned to you in our chat, because it was fresh in my mind at the time, the point about the physical far-flungness of its supposed components when it started off: Larkin Belfast-Hull, Davie Dublin, Wain Reading, Jennings Oxford, Conquest admittedly London, me Swansea, Gunn California, Enright Japan. Not much chance of regular operation briefings.

I hope your book[3] goes well and look forward to reading it.

Yours sincerely,
Kingsley Amis

[TLS: Recipient]

TO DAVID THISTLETHWAITE – 17 SEPTEMBER 1979

Gardnor House, Flask Walk, London, N.W.3.

Dear Mr Thistlethwaite,

Thank you for your letter, which struck me as friendly and a little fine-spun.[1] Powell wrote his novel as whatever you like to call it, an artistic act, not to wield power, as perhaps Harriet Beecher Stowe and the Orwell of *Nineteen Eighty-Four* did. And it is fiddling with words

---

1. Amis's *Collected Poems* was never reviewed in the *TLS*, in part because it was published during the year-long period (October 1978 to November 1979) in which all Times Newspapers titles were closed down by management. Blake Morrison (b.1950), poet, critic, journalist, literary editor, had been appointed Poetry and Fiction Editor of the *TLS* in October 1978, just before the closedown.

2. Published by Constable in 1977. It contains photographs, but none of Amis and Larkin at Oxford (none of Larkin at all).

3. *The Movement: English Poetry and Fiction of the 1950s* (Oxford: Oxford University Press, 1980).

---

1. Thistlethwaite had written from Cambridge on 30 August 1979 after hearing Amis discuss Anthony Powell's fiction on Radio 3 (see Amis to Conquest, 20 September 1977, note 1). Amis forwarded the letter, together with a copy of his reply, to Powell himself, with an undated note reading: 'Thought this might amuse you. No idea who he is. Let's meet soon. K.'

a little to say that Jenkins has 'mastered' the world. He has done so in no sense of exercising mastery; he has mastered it only as one masters a musical composition, demonstrated his understanding of it. With respect he does not 'show us how to dominate' anything or anyone.[2]

Yours sincerely
Kingsley Amis

[ALS][3]

TO PHILIP LARKIN – 18 SEPTEMBER 1979

Gardnor House, Flask Walk, London, N.W.3.

Dear Philip,

Sorry about this crappy pompous size of paper, but it seems we can't have any more of the small until we've 'used up' the large. Always the bloody same in this house. The family doesn't 'eat' here. As soon as the food's out of the shopping-basket it's to be 'eaten up'. I'm pulling your leg really

I wrote you a letter a couple of days ago but tore it up because when I read it through it turned out to be full of whining self-pity. I mean nothing wrong with self-pity but I don't want you thinking when a letter from me arrives Oh fuck what'll he be on about this time. I've just written a lot of turdy letters to strangers. Do you get that much? Find yourself writing things like unable to accept your kind invitation to address the Literary Soc – any merit. However this is only one man's opinion and your poems give up all debating, especially on facetious motions. I hope you away from my typewriter. So I will just wish the Festival all the charity already and feel I should not 'spread myself too thin,' or secretary recently and can only assume the previous one failed to sorry about the delay which was due to please accept my apologies No I *wouldn't* mind if they all stopped writing.

I am carrying on here about the same and am pretty well, apart from hay fever etc. Oh, and only having about three teeth to eat on. Took out

2. Thistlethwaite had written: 'the glorification of the powerless in Anthony Powell is in a way not quite honest, for the reasons that the novel as a whole offers power. The effect it has on me, at any rate, is to give a sense of mastering the world through a knowledge of human frailty.'

3. I have been unable to trace the original of this letter.

one of the others on a CHEESE SANDWICH the other day. Luckily it was the sort the fellow can bung back in. Be nice if things happened the other way round occasionally. Like a chap gradually recovering the use of his legs, or being able to go for longer and longer periods without peeing, or finding his sight's on the up-and-up. Got it?

I haven't been leading up to this, honest, but unless I was derrunk at the time that Amberley Hall stuff hasn't arrived, nor what I think you also mentioned, the Coronation ode.[1] Be a good chap and bung it along, them I mean. I suppose I could even publish them – what do you think? Not the ode, of course.

Went to the Gayton Road Carnival GET FUCKED YOU CUNT the other day no it's all right to hear some jazz featuring Wally Fawkes, clt and, for the first time in my hearing, sop.[2] Not quite the old attacking edge, but plenty of ideas and puff. Very unpissy repertory: Canal St, Basin St, Winin' Boy, At the J-BB [Jazz-Band Ball], etc. Brought an almost irreducibly small part of it back. Quite a lot of people were standing about but it was sad how few ere sphere were listening.

What about ole Bobbo marrying again eh.[3] One for the road he says. Let's try and wish him jolly good luck. See you at the wedding. But hope to see you before that. Let us know when you're coming up and I'll meet you anywhere you say. Within reason.

The Conservatives are traditionally the party of bum,

Kingsley

Had lunch with JIMMY WILLCOX[4] the other day. No really he's not too bad.

[TLS: Bodleian]

---

1. In c.1950 Amis wrote the libretto for a one-act chamber opera, *Amberley Hall*, for which Bruce Montgomery supplied the music. The thirteen-page manuscript can be seen in HEHL. For *Amberley Hall* and their earlier failed collaboration on a fully planned and projected grand opera, *To Move the Passions*, see Amis to Larkin, 6 December 1947, note 4. Amis also collaborated with Montgomery on a Coronation Ode, 'The Century's Crown'. See also Amis to Larkin, 17 December 1950 and 4 April 1952.

2. For Wally Fawkes see Amis to Larkin, 22 September 1953, note 3.

3. Robert Conquest married Elizabeth ('Liddie') Wingate, formerly Neece, his fourth wife, in 1979.

4. James Willcox (b.1923), one of 'The Seven' at Oxford, read Modern History at St John's (1941–42, 1945–46); Clerk of Public Bills, House of Commons (1982–88).

TO PHILIP LARKIN – 29 SEPTEMBER 1979

Gardnor House, Flask Walk, London, N.W.3.

Dear Philip,

Am listening to Jazz Record Requests – intermittently – as I write. Do you ever? An occasional goodie, but the formula is one Coltrane, one Ornette Coleman, one Shepp,[1] then: 'Archie Shepp at his most exhilarating. Now to remind us of jazz's almost infinite variety, back almost fifty years to Nogood Poxy Deaf Sam and "One-Titted Woman Blues".' Wawawawa wawawawa wawa wawa wa wa Oh ah gawooma shony gawon tia waaah wawa wa yeh ah gawooma shony gawon tia wawawa waaah wa boyf she ganutha she wouno where to put ia You know: that's enough Bartok, let's have a Gregorian chant. These people have no TASTE, no SENSE. No EAR. After some vile headlong stuff – I don't even know the name any more – we have just had the New Orleans Owls in 1927. No SENSE OF BEAUTY.

It was good of you to write again so soon. Sorry about your ills. I know what you mean about hideous memories. Mine include behaving like a shit, pissing on harmless people etc. You'll never go mad.[2] Your writings show you to be irremediably sane. I mean this. Being mad goes with a defective sense of other people (cf. Iris Murdoch). Your so po s.o.o.p. is fine.

---

1. John Coltrane (1926–67), tenor and soprano saxophonist, bandleader, composer; Ornette Coleman (b.1930), saxophonist and composer; Archie Shepp (b.1937), saxophonist. To Amis, as to Larkin, the influence of these 'modernists' was wholly deplorable. See Larkin, *All What Jazz* (London: Faber and Faber, 1970): 'With John Coltrane metallic and passionless nullity gave way to exercises in gigantic absurdity . . . It was with Coltrane, too, that jazz started to be *ugly on purpose* . . . After Coltrane, of course, all was chaos, hatred and absurdity' (p.9); or, from a later passage: 'I don't know whether it is worth pursuing my identification of modern jazz with other branches of modern art any further: if I say I dislike both in what seems to me the same way I have made my point . . . Men such as Ornette Coleman . . . and Archie Shepp, dispensing with pitch, harmony, theme, tone, tune and rhythm, were copied by older (Rollins, Coltrane) and young players alike' (p. 13).

2. See Larkin to Amis, 23 September 1979, in *LL*, p. 605: 'I've felt sodding awful this last week, as if I've reached some kind of am-pass (ytuwk) when I can't be alone, can't stand company, can't work, can't do nothing, can't think of the present, past or future, and am crucified every ten minutes or so by hideous memories – nothing serious, just making a fool of myself. Feel my mind's NOT ON MY SIDE any more. Do you think I'm going batty? That would be a splendid table to turn on Ted. Ted Hughes, I mean, in case you thought I meant Heath.'

On my self-pity themes, don't tempt me, son. They include year-round hay-fever, high blood-pressure so that I stream with sweat at the slightest exertion or upset, permanently-itching places on my scalp (side-effect of anti-blood-p pills) from which descend flakes of scurf the size of lp pieces, increasing phobias that stop me travelling almost anywhere (that one's not so bad) and make me dread and hate being alone, this along with a wife who puts herself first and the rest nowhere and constantly goes out to GROUPS and WORKSHOPS and crappy 'new friends', and total loss of sex-drive; I haven't had a fuck for more than a year and a wank for over a month. Don't tell anyone. Your thing about not reading anything new struck a chord. Nearly all my reading is comfort-reading now, done while I wait for whisky and sleeping-pills to get me torpid enough to go to bed – alone, of course. Still, I've got my work oh I say thanks most awfully and my club. Fuck it I say. But wait a minute why didn't anybody tell us it was going to be like this? Or are you still expecting something nice to happen to you?

Did I tell you I was going to talk to the Tories (Twhoreys) at Blackpool?[3] If I did I'm sure I'd have told you to stare not so. A 'fringe' lecture, on paying for the arts, or rather not paying for them. No money for writers, say I. And if I can make it just a bit for whore pisspotpiss more difficult for a little fucker who 'can't' finish his novel to get a grant to do so, jolly good luck to me.

No rush, but try to put your hand on the Ode. I can't remember a thing about it now, except I was afraid one of my lefty friends would get to know about it and piss on me for monarchism. How do you mean ev'ry and heav'nly?[4] I don't want any of that swearing.

Benn bum,
Kingsley

[TLS: Bodleian]

3. Where their annual party conference was shortly to be held.

4. See Larkin to Amis, 23 September 1979 (in HEHL; the passage was cut by Thwaite), on the Coronation Ode: 'It's quite good, but made farcical by the "ev'ry" "heav'nly" sort of touch.'

TO THE EDITOR, *DAILY TELEGRAPH* – 18 OCTOBER 1979

SIR – Is Sir Maurice Oldfield[1] really "said to have been" the model for M. in the works of Ian Fleming? Anybody who does say so cannot have thought at all hard about the matter.

M. first appeared in 1953 (in the novel "Casino Royale"), when Sir Maurice was 37, and presumably some distance from the exalted position he came to occupy.

I hardly think Fleming would have chosen as a "model" for James Bond's chief somebody then a year or two younger than Bond himself.

But then all talk of "models" for characters in fiction tends to be loose and misleading.

KINGSLEY AMIS
Garrick Club

TO THE EDITOR, *NEW STATESMAN* – 27 OCTOBER 1979

Sir: It seems strange to find Christopher Booker licking his lips over the supposed destruction of the Captain Scott 'legend' in Roland Huntford's ill-natured book (20 October).[1] 'The plaster saint has been smashed for ever', he concludes with relish. But surely he has got it wrong, historically wrong. It was not as any kind of saint that people wrote about and regarded Scott, but as a man who accepted failure and approaching death with courage and with thought for others. I doubt if that image could be smashed, nor would I put a high priority on the attempt.

KINGSLEY AMIS
Gardnor House, Flask Walk, London NW3

---

1. Sir Maurice Oldfield (1915–81), head of SIS (Secret Intelligence Service) (1973–78), traditionally known as 'C'.

---

1. Christopher Booker (b.1937), journalist and author, was reviewing Roland Huntford's book *Scott and Amundsen* (1979), about the 1910–12 Antarctic expeditions of Captain Robert Falcon Scott (1868–1912) and Roald Amundsen (1872–1928). Scott reached the Pole on 18 January 1912, a month after Amundsen, and he and the remainder of his five-man party died (c.29 March) on the return journey. Their bodies, and Scott's diary of the expedition, including its last days, were discovered eight months later.

TO PHILIP LARKIN – 4 DECEMBER 1979

Gardnor House, Flask Walk, London, N.W.3.

Dear Philip,

Sorry I haven't

Actually I was finishing a novel.[1] Don't know that I'll ever start another. Too much like hard work what? And anxiety-promoting. Like walking to Antarctica *and* being afraid *all the time* you're going to fall over and break your hip. Oh come off it Kingers you know very well there's nothing you awh take your I'm taking to po time off for a bit, well not exactly, reading entries for the Arts Council fiction competition.[2] It rather cheers you up, looking at the people you've got to try to be better than. When I tell you that so far C.P. SNOW is EASILY the most readable, stylish witty . . . See? But then there's *Man of Nazareth* by Athony Burgess[3] to come, and wIlLiAm GoLdInG, and $hilip Roth, and Doris Lessing oh sweet jesus shoot me dear christ shoo

I put a bit of jazz on now and again. Usually it's the Pops/WB Saints-Mandy side.[4] Bechet is amazing on IAGGNNOTJR,[5] making it sound as if there are 2 shags playing sop some of the time. Wish I had someone to listen with me. Actually there is one, a painter who's recently almost completely lost the sight of one eye and has just had the other one patched up FOR THE MOMENT.[6] 32 fuck 42 he is. And then you moan about writing why don't you ooohhhghgh

After looking through my archives I've laid hands on a stained but legible *Ambereley Hall.*[7] Those songs aren't bad, but they aren't really good either, are they? About as good as the words for most songs, i.e.

1. *Russian Hide-and-Seek* (1980).

2. Amis was sole judge of the Arts Council National Book Award for 1979, which went to Penelope Lively's *Treasures of Time*; for an account of his reasons for agreeing to judge the competition, his experiences as judge, and the other novels he considered of merit, see 'Report on a Fiction Prize', in *The Amis Collection*, pp. 8–12.

3. Amis has written 'ballocks d'you see' above 'Athony Burgess', and 'shite' underneath it, with an arrow pointing to the misspelling.

4. 'Pops' is Sidney Bechet; 'WB' is Wild Bill Davison (b.1906), cornettist; the 'Saints-Mandy side' contains 'When the Saints go Marching in' and 'Mandy, Make up Your Mind'.

5. 'I Ain't Gonna Give Nobody None of This Jelly Roll'.

6. Sargy Mann.

7. Amis has crossed out the rogue 'e' in 'Amberely' and written 'TIRD' in pen at the bottom of the page, connected to the misspelled title.

not much fucking good at all without music. The one I thought was there isn't. Last line Love in a country dress. Stir a chord? Oh well. The ed of the Listener wnats twats to print them. Should I let him?[8]

Had a wank this morning, which makes it a light-grey-letter day. Consequence of encountering a v. depraved-looking female last night NO, MEETING HER SOCIALLY NOT SCREWING HER. Nothing more in it for me. Her husband's 38 you see. Yank. I mean he's an Aeripockss American. But then so's she so what's that got to do with it. Funny how different life is when you lose your stand. But funny too how much it stays the same.

As you must know by now, Bob is married. Jolly nice girl. Cooks his breakfast and things like that. Do come and stay and we can all get pissed. I promise I won't subject you to another moaning jag; me complaining of my lot I mean. Rotten and very striking about your medico. Mine went at 51 too amusingly enough. Heart. He didn't know anything about it. ('Oh, good.') Less fat than me. Smoked less than me. Drank less than me. I wrote a letter to The Times the other day and thought I sent it off, but now it rather looks as if what I sent off was a letter thanking me for giving a light verse recital in aid of a local charity. Ho hum. PO BUM. Nah, I meant by sense of other people being adequately interested in and clued-up about their motives etc.[9] Dull idea really. Good that those NUPE [National Union of Public Employees] bastards who picketed the hospitals last winter are doing it again and so fucking up Labour again. Can't learn, you see.

Nuclear reactors are a potential source of frightening bum,

Kingsley

I'll try to keep writing, dear man, But life's rather shiting, dear man[10]

[TLS: Bodleian]

8. The editor was Anthony Howard, who had replaced George Scott in September. The songs were not printed.

9. See Larkin to Amis, 28 October 1979, in *LL*, p. 609: 'Do you mean by my sense of other people that I'm frightened of the buggers? I'm that all right.'

10. MS addition.

TO THE EDITOR, *THE TIMES* – 6 DECEMBER 1979

Sir, May I correct a detail or two in Michael Ratcliffe's friendly references (November 29) to me and my compilation, *The New Oxford Book of Light Verse?*[1] It is by chance, not design, that the poems in that volume overlap so little with those in *The Oxford Book of American Light Verse*, edited by William Harmon. The Oxford University Press explicitly refrained from all attempt to limit my selection except in point of length, even providing me with Mr Harmon's contents pages in plenty of time to poach on his preserves if I had wished. But I didn't wish. It was my taste and nothing but my taste that led me to choose so few poems by Americans.

As for Anon, I said only that he was not my favourite poet, not that he was my least favourite poet. From Ezra Pound downwards there are plenty of onymous poets with better claims to that bad eminence.

Yours faithfully,

KINGSLEY AMIS
Gardnor House, Flask Walk, NW3. November 30

TO PHILIP LARKIN – 14 JANUARY 1980

Gardnor House, Flask Walk, London, N.W.3.

Dear Philip,

Hulo now, you old urbag. By gogges bones it's good to get a letter that doesn't begin I am writing my term paper on or In a recent broadcast you lamented the lack of light verse well here are a few or My collection of 3,000 autographs includes or The St Kilda Festival of Lit or In the last year 454 sufferers from multiple shagba well the time to complain will be when they stop comiiaarrrghghghgh

I am getting ugly now because I am getting old. Being fat doesn't matter eh, and people can't see your teeth properly, in any case I have one in each jaw still working. What I am doing is getting huge jowls

1. Michael Ratcliffe (b. 1935), journalist, literary editor; at the time chief book reviewer, *The Times* (1972–82).

under my chin like Mr Heath and Chuck Snow. They show when I do television, and no doubt all the rest of the time come to that. They make me feel humiliated in some way. No use slimming because the flaps of skin will still be waving to and fro after you've taken the fat out if you ever do. Like your paunch

Bob is where you saw him before in Sumner Place (Flat 2 no. 4, S.W.3, O1 that's if youtre outside Londorrrghghghgh, 584 1938.) She's called Lyddie, well yes, short oft toftof for Lydia, neé Wingate[1] ie shes not a spick or a mick or a hunk or a bohunk or a wop or a kraut or any of those. Jolly good show. What was that quote about free from care? Certainly applies to ole Bob. He just goes on as if nothing had happened. Jane says from the way Lyddie's on to him already it should last about 18 months. Well you know what they are.

You were saying something the other week about flithy exhibitionism in jazz. A record I borrowed recently is a case in point. You probably have it: The Eddie Condon Concerts Town Hall 1944–45 Featuring Pee Wee Russell. There was Pee Wee *with a live audience* you see, a *following*, so he squeaks and squawks and hawks and doesn't play proper notes and they all think he's fantastic the ignorant little turds. Well, 3rd-rate P-W is pretty good, yeah, until you start remembering things like his solos on IRHFY[2] or Hello Lola – esp that. Mind you, the others sound pretty reduced too, in fact the only one not to have slipped at all is Muggsy. (What's the matter, John?) And Ernie if you count him.[3]

Keep waking up early and lying waiting for the little five-second pains to do their stuff in my chest. Indigestion what? Imagination. All imagination and lack of exercise. Not to worry. Well your ECG was that scum you sent last night soon died. Hooray[4]

Laughed a lot at your TV-vignette.[5] Yes, why don't they get out of

---

1. Conquest's wife Elizabeth (not Lydia), nicknamed Liddie (not Lyddie), *née* Neece (not Wingate).

2. 'It's Right Here for You'.

3. Muggsy Spanier, cornet, and Ernie Caceres (1911–71), clarinet and baritone saxophone; neither 'What's a Matter, John?', nor any title which suggests a connection with it, is listed in the nine-disc Town Hall Concerts recordings.

4. An allusion to the concluding lines of Wilfred Owen's poem 'The Dead-Beat' (1918).

5. See Larkin to Amis, 10 January 1980, in *LL*, p. 613: 'Have just been staring mindlessly at some TV tec stuff, chaps walking about and standing and staring and watching each other and cars drawing up and chaps not getting out, just watching and staring and – I don' know.'

their fucking cars? All this mystification. It's because if your plot is Jack and Jill went up the hill to fetch a pail of water you've got to keep the audience wondering if that's Jack or not and which one is Jill and which hill do they mean and what's in that fucking pail. Better than Drama Now thuoghghghghgh Laughed about your car too.[6] I know it isn't funny really. Let me know when you're in town and we can get pissed let me know when yo

After decades of Western supremacy the world seems to be heading for an era of bum,

Kingsley

Nearly forgot – bloody marvellous interview.[7] *I particularly enjoyed the straight-faced, unselfconscious pissing on the Lefties – idleness, greed and treason, of course; why bother to ask? And the closing remark about paying for poetry. Just the stuff the buggers need to be told.*[8]

[TLS: Bodleian]

TO M.G. SHERLOCK – 31 JANUARY 1980

Gardnor House, Flask Walk, London, N.W.3.

Dear M.G. Sherlock,

Thank you for your letter.[1] I need hardly say that the matter of abortion is one of extreme confusion, and I confess to not having thought about the matter as much as perhaps I might have done. The point you fail to take into account is that the choice is often between

6. In the same letter, passage beginning: 'My car burnt itself out last week, I mean some jolly short-circuit filled it with a nauseating stench as if a heap of old-fashioned used french letters had been conflagrated inside it.'

7. In the *Observer*, 16 December 1979, p. 35; reprinted in Larkin, *Required Writing* (London: Faber and Faber, 1983), pp. 47–56.

8. MS addition.

---

1. Sherlock had written to Amis on 28 January 1980 to take strenuous exception to his remarks about abortion, as reported in Mary Kenny, 'The Light that Failed', *Daily Telegraph*, 27 January 1980, pp.8–9: 'You say "You've got to think of the child – what kind of a life is an unwanted child going to have?" This is utter crap: since when has being "unwanted" been a justification for killing – in Western society, anyway? Abortion is for getting an unwilling mother out of a mess, not for the child's benefit.'

legalized abortion in comparatively safe conditions and back street abortion with all its risks. And at one point you simply overreach yourself.

Your parallel with Stalin's purges is quite false. The perfidies of Socialism remain perfidies, and I can validly call them so, whatever my expressed views on abortion.

Yours sincerely,
Kingsley Amis

[TLS: Recipient]

TO PHILIP LARKIN – 7 MARCH 1980

Gardnor House, Flask Walk, London, N.W.3.

Dear Philip,

Getting so senile these days I can't remember whether I said what a good interview in the Ob. Anyway it was, though I don't suppose you like me saying so. Miriam Gross[1] told me you gave her a hell of a time. As against that let me tell you I turned down £1500 the other day for writing a profile of you. Christ I mean they offered me £1500 and I turned it down. You were good on Mrs Thatcher. I've just been chatting to Bob on the telephone. She's had it according to him. I mean just had it what? All the fucking wets in the Cabinet will stop her being tough enough and the effort will collapse. Back to the States for him next year if there's no change. I've never known him so gloomy, in what he said I mean; chirpy as hell in manner. All right for you – you can go and be Writer in Residence at Iowaaaaaoooooghghghgh.

Yes, I'm doing you for the Festschrift.[2] Planning it already. Among our circle was a young man whom I will call Philip Smith. No, I'm pulling your leg really. Don't worry about a thing. Ah you could give me a hand. My memory even of the distant past is so bad I've only got about one anecdote. Tell me anything you remember, even if it's only

1. Miriam Gross (b.1939), journalist and literary editor; at the time Deputy Literary Editor, *Observer* (1969–81). She conducted the *Observer* interview of 16 December 1979 (see Amis to Larkin, 14 January 1980).

2. *Larkin at Sixty*, ed. Anthony Thwaite (London: Faber and Faber, 1982). Amis's piece is entitled 'Oxford and After' (pp.23–30).

where we used to drink etc. Once or twice we all went boozing outside Oxford didn't we? Where? And anything about our visits after Oxford. Where did you play the piano and I sing?[3] Hey, you remember the time I came up to Liec dyke Leicester and I greeted you by saying 'Where can I be sick?' What novel is that in? *Jill* is it?[4] May I quote 'The Way We Live Now'? What was the Mildred Marmaduke thing called? Etc. *IWDAFY*?[5]

Been reading ole AP's latest autobiog vol for review.[6] Well, you know, it doesn't take much to make a story for him. 'James Thurber came to lunch*eon*.[7] Sometimes he got very tight and obstreperous, but on this occasion though he drank a bit he was very agreeable.' And that's it. Funny chap. We're going on a cruise with them in August. Nay, stare not so. Only round the Med.

Got my first highbrow crit the other day, in Essays in Crit.[8] Quite a breakthrough I suppose. ('I'll break your–') He says that then there's the presence of you over my shoulder, a writer whose poems take on depths of gloomy richness that I, wisely he thinks, don't attempt to match. Yes I see. And there's effective Yeatsian usage but no you at all in TNS. Same with me and Auden in BN.[9] Mm. And on those records

3. 'The Victoria Arms, now converted to the base uses of the OUP. In Walton Street' (Larkin to Amis, 20 March 1980, in HEHL).

4. In a letter of 26 April 1980, Larkin writes: 'I don't know any novel with "Where can I be sick?", unless it's that Jenkins–Widmerpool encounter in France or Belgium is it? The second MoT? Certainly not me' (*LL*, p.618). Larkin is thinking of an episode in Chapter 3 of *A Question of Upbringing* (1951), the first novel in *A Dance to the Music of Time*, in which Nick Jenkins and Kenneth Widmerpool spend some weeks in France learning French. The question 'Where can I be sick?' is uttered by Jenkins.

5. MS addition. Larkin pronounces himself 'obscurely ashamed' of 'The Way We Live Now', which he calls 'corrupt without being charming'. As for the lesbian story 'I Would do Anything for You', 'if you can say anything about that without arraigning us as pornophiliacal ponces I mean you can't. So you'd bedder not try, fella' (Larkin to Amis, 20 March 1980, in HEHL). Neither 'The Way We Live Now' nor 'the Mildred Marmaduke thing' have survived.

6. See Amis, 'Anthony Powell: The Soldier's Art', review of Powell's *Faces in My Time* (1980), in *Sunday Times*, 23 March 1980, p.43.

7. In the left margin Amis has typed 'not exact wrods'. 'Luncheon', as opposed to 'lunch', is also used (and defended) by the snobbish novelist Jimmie Fane on the first page of Amis's *The Biographer's Moustache* (1995).

8. William Pritchard, 'Entertaining Amis', review of *CP* in *Essays in Criticism* 30 (January 1980), pp.58–67.

9. *Bright November*. See Pritchard, 'Entertaining Amis', p.59: 'John Bayley has said of Larkin's first book of poems, *The North Ship*, that "there is a high degree of competence and of effective Yeatsian usage, but no Larkin at all". A similar judgment might be passed on the presence of Auden in Amis's early poems.'

how chaste and impersonal is my delivery compared with yours uhHAHAHAHAHAHA[10]

All I do The whole day through Is dream of WHISKY SCCOTTISHSH WHWHISSSKY MMALLTT SCCOTTISHSH WHWHISSSKY HHIGHGHLANND MMALLT SSSSSCOT-TISHSHSH WHWHWHWHISSSSKEEEE no not really. But if ever you see some stuff called Macallan-Glenlivet grab it quick. The best whisky IN THE WORLD world (echo)

And if you come here I will give you some of it. Let me know when you're passing.

There is jubilation and tension here tonight at Mugabe's *FARRT*[11] remarkable bum,[12]

Kingsley

[TLS: Bodleian]

TO DALE SALWAK – 13 MARCH 1980

Gardnor House, Flask Walk, London, N.W.3.

Dear Dale,

I always answer just when you think I'm never going to. Many thanks for the very useful and, I'm sure, dauntingly thorough *JB & JW*.[1] What has been holding this letter up is the immense labour (actually one one-minute telephone call) required to establish John Braine's address. It is:

Pentons
Onslow Crescent
Woking
Surrey

But I expect you obtained it elsewhere weeks ago.

10. Ibid., p.60: 'When listening to Amis read *A Case of Samples* on the Marvell Press recording, one is surprised to note how little expression gets into his voice, and, as compared with Larkin's recordings, how chaste and impersonal is his delivery.'

11. MS addition.

12. Robert Mugabe (b.1924), whose ZANU party had won the election in Zimbabwe three days before.

---

1. *John Braine and John Wain: A Reference Guide* (1980).

Good about Literary Voices. By all means include that 1973 interview in it.[2] I shall be here for most of the summer, certainly the whole month of July except its last day, when my wife and I depart on a cruise lasting most of August. The period 5th–8th July is a little crowded. Otherwise nothing so far. I would be very happy to see you, update interview, indeed discuss any matter of interest within reason. When you have some dates let me know and I'll put them in my diary. It will be fun to meet again.

Looking forward to hearing from you,

Yours ever,
Kingsley Amis

[TLS: Recipient]

TO DALE SALWAK – 9 APRIL 1980

Gardnor House, Flask Walk, London, N.W.3.

Dear Dale,

Just a quick note to say Yes, I'll be free for virtually the whole period of your stay, and of course if you'd care for a modest lunch under this roof my wife and I would be only too happy to have you. You're welcome to inspect the study where I'm writing this and where at the moment there are almost as many bottles as books.

I hope you won't be too shocked at the renewed sight of me. I have put on a bit of weight and my face is a rather pouchy affair. We must arrange things so that you can't possibly mistake me for some relic of the previous generation.

Forgive absurd paper. Wife ordered a lot of it and we must just grit our teeth and use it up.

Very much looking forward to seeing you. Telephone when you're settled in.

Yours,
Kingsley Amis

[TLS: Recipient]

2. Dale Salwak, ed., *Literary Voices: Interviews with Britain's 'Angry Young Men'* (1984). It includes the 1973 Amis interview.

TO ANN THWAITE – 9 APRIL 1980

Gardnor House, Flask Walk, London NW3

Dear Ann,

I seem to have taken plenty of time; waiting for a reasonably steady hand was the main thing. From my point of view the delay was productive, because constantly remembering and putting off prodded the unconscious into producing the little quatrain just as I finally sat down to the job.[1]

I hope Anthony is pleased with his present. He certainly should be. What a wifely wife you are. Needless to say, nobody did anything like that for *M Y* 50th.

I expect your visits to London are pretty crammed, but it would be fun to see you both for lunch or something.

Jolly good luck,

Yours
Kingsley

[TLS: Recipient]

---

1. To produce a hand-written poem for a volume marking Anthony Thwaite's fiftieth birthday. The 'serious' poem Amis wrote out was 'A Pill for the Impressionable', from *CP*, p.60. The quatrain he also included reads:

> Three little tips on how to thrive
> When clawed in age's clutch:
> Have a bad back, don't drive,
> And don't expect too much.

Among the sixty-one other contributors were Geoffrey Hill, Larkin, Seamus Heaney, Ted Hughes, John Betjeman, Stephen Spender, James Fenton, Andrew Motion, Tom Paulin, Charles Causley, Craig Raine, Paul Muldoon and Robert Conquest. Thwaite was presented with the surprise volume at a birthday party at his house in Norfolk on 23 June 1980.

TO PHILIP LARKIN – 9 APRIL 1980

Gardnor House, Flask Walk, London NW3

Have you got to write a fucking poem out for Thwaite? SODDING CHEEK I thought it was. An imposition, that's the word.[1]

Dear Philip,

What do you think of my swell new paper? Well anyway it cost a lot. Am too old and brain-damaged to remember whether I answered your letter of 20th March. Don't think I did. Anyway. Did Mervyn play his sax at the Victoria Arms or was that later?[2] Didn't I remember to ask you in what novel somebody demands on arrival somewhere 'Where can I be sick?'? Is it *Jill*? Don't worry, I'm mum on TWWLN and IWDAFY. Mildred Marmaduke wrote the thing about Lord FitsMorris. Interested to see interview in Londmag.[3] Funny you thought it wasn't until 'If, my darling'[4] that I thought you were some good; I thought that long before. The first time I can pinpoint is when I stayed with you in Warwick and you showed me that MS book of poems, stuff you thought *wasn't good enough to publish*. When was that? 1946? Your dad was there. What had you called the book? I remember about 'This is published in an edition limited to 1 copy. This is Number 1.' Horrible to see arseholing John Minton[5] glaring out from Londmag's cover.

You really are potty about old DEL.[6] How the fuck do you GET THRU him? CAN'T YOU SEE he's just like Wagner and Pound, a self-solving mystery? Fellows say, 'Here's a GRINDING SHIT who never did *anything* nice to or for *anybody*, and yet he's written all this

---

1. MS addition.

2. 'Mervyn palying sax in pubs was post-me oh knickers to that misprint' (Larkin to Amis, 26 April, in *LL*, p.619).

3. 'The True and the Beautiful: A Conversation with Philip Larkin', *London Magazine* 20 (1980), pp. 81–95; interview conducted by John Haffenden.

4. A poem by Larkin, dated 23 May 1950 in *LCP*, p.41; first printed in *XX Poems* (1951).

5. John Minton (1917–57), artist and illustrator.

6. Larkin was opening an exhibition on D.H. Lawrence at Nottingham University on 7 May 1980.

stuff[7] which is supposed to be frightfully good. Funny.' But then some of them look closely at the stuff and find that, instead of being frightfully good, it is in fact INSULTINGLY BAD IN E X A C T L Y THE KIND OF WAY YOU'D EXPECT FROM THE WAY HE BEHAVED. All of a piece. End of problem. Oh well. We all have our little foibles. Wouldn't do if we all thought the same OH YES IT FUCKING WELL WOU

I must say ole S D-L's book[8] sounds pretty fair crap. Since I shan't be reading it – *is* he malicious about his dad? And what by the way d'you think of his dad as a poet, sort of at the end of the day? I'm always struck by how good, how honest, how competent he appears whenever I happen to come across anything by him, also by how out-of-the-question it would be for me to decide I'll have a read of ole C D-L tonight.

Yes (re Pritchard) it's a bugger, the people who think you're (one is) good while getting you wrong. The first fellow who showed academic interest in my work turned out to be a Canadian with a British accent in a blazer with brass buttons. And then there are the other sods they also think are good. You know: 'Nobody's doing anything with the novel with these days except you and Doris Lessing.' Oh well, mustn't complaaaaaaaaghghghghgh

Listening to Sweet Patootie after a year or two I wondered whether I wasn't just as impressed, or anyway now see I should have been j.a.i., by O'N S as by BB when I first heard them both in '41.[9] That savage, staccato, stinging, plangent, almost percussive voice, that odd accent, hard where Southern is soft (born in Ohio, wasn't he?), and those words. Did anyone ever find a derivation for 'haive'?

Do let's have lunch or something when you're down.

I'll just whip this molar out and then start work on your bum,

Kingsley

[TLS: Bodleian]

7. In the original 'this stuff' is mis-typed as 'thisstuff', above which, in pen, Amis writes 'pee', extending the stem of the 'p' between 'this' and 'stuff'.

8. *C. Day-Lewis: An English Literary Life* (1980), by Sean Day-Lewis (b.1931), the poet's son, a journalist and author.

9. O'Neill Spencer (1909–44), drummer and singer, born in Cedarville, Ohio; 'BB' is Billy Banks.

TO JOHN McDERMOTT – 1 MAY 1980

Gardnor House, Flask Walk, London NW3

Dear Mr McDermott,

Your letter was a tonic. As time passes one wonders more and more whether it has all been worth while. Rare letters like yours bring some reassurance. It was really very kind of you.

Have I disparaged Wigan?[1] In jest, surely. But from now on that name shall be sacrosanct and all who profane it assailed without mercy.

New one appears on the 12th.[2] Don't know about the one after that.

With warm thanks and good wishes

Yours sincerely,
Kingsley Amis

[ALS: Recipient]

TO TOM MILLER – 21 MAY 1980

Gardnor House, Flask Walk, London NW3

My dear Tom,

I hope you are still speaking to me after this disgraceful delay. This is the sort of letter one finds any excuse for putting off. I am afraid I must tell you that I don't think (though I may be wrong) that you are going to get *Judgement at Winchester* into shape unassisted.[1] The narrative is too weak and the characters too shadowy; the whole structure must be rebuilt from the bottom, with (say) events seen through the eyes of a fictitious lawyer on the side of the defence and put into a series of scenes. You need a collaborator. Alas, it can't be me. But if

1. For John McDermott, who lived in Wigan at the time, see Notes on Recipients.
2. *Russian Hide-and-Seek.*

1. Miller was at work on an 'alternate world' novel, 'Judgement at Winchester', which imagined the Anglo-American leaders put on trial by the victorious Axis, an inverted Nuremberg trials. Amis was advising him both as a friend and as a board member of Davis-Poynter, the publishing firm (hence the use of first person plural later in the letter).

you accept the idea and would like us to put out feelers for you, we are in quite a good position to do so and of course would be delighted to help in any way we could. You have the material there for a fascinating book.

To continue a gloomy letter: we have delayed answering Jane's kind letter because we didn't know what our commitments at the Edinburgh Festival were going to be. Now we do, and alas again, and also sod it, we won't be able to make Guernsey this trip.[2] Another time, I do hope.

What news here? My book[3] got some crappy reviews, but enough lengthy even if wrong-headed respect in some quarters to leave the ego only superficially damaged. Also I now think I have *The Beautiful Shits*[4] more or less figured out, but with totally unprecedented reticence I am keeping my mouth tight shut from now on. As it is you know more about it than anybody else.

Do let us know what you think of the collab. idea. If it outrages or enrages you, blame my anxiety to see the book in being in a form that will do justice to the theme.

And do get in touch when you're over. Apart from cruise-France-Edinburgh 31st July–7th September I shall be here almost constantly.

Sarah[5] has taken up bird-watching, but in no spirit of disinterested inquiry, I have to say.

Yours
Kingsley

[TLS: Recipient]

2. Where the Millers have a house.

3. *Russian Hide-and-Seek.*

4. This is the only reference to such a title I have come across. Amis seems to have applied it to the abandoned novel he eventually called 'Difficulties with Girls', a title he retained for a quite different novel of 1988, a sequel to *Take a Girl Like You.* Miller kept a record of his conversations with Amis and reports that on 21 December 1979 Amis told him *The Beautiful Shits* was going to be about the power wielded by a fantastically pretty woman. On 23 July 1982 Miller records: 'KA has stopped work on *Difficulties with Girls*, formerly known as *The Beautiful Shits* and *Doing It*, because the homosexual narrator tended to dominate the book, which was not the original idea.'

5. Sarah Snow, Amis's cat.

TO BRIAN ALDISS – 27 MAY 1980

Gardnor House, Flask Walk, London NW3

Dear Brian,

The Day of the Dotard is here. I thought, I must remember to thank those two for their telegram, and read it again, putting it on the corner of my desk the easier to do so. So I wrote my letter and took it to the post and when I came back there the thing was, still safely there, *still open* in fact. So, all the same thank you both very much. Jolly dashing verse, I must say. It arrived set out as such and letter-perfect. What *is* the quote? Or did I goof again?[1]

Glad you liked the EDR touch.[2] Reminds me that a peevish Scotchman, having seen me on telly but not read the book, wrote to bellyache about me saying England when he thought I must mean ~~Scottish~~ (SHITE) G.B. Told him I was always terrifically punctilious about this, making a point of, for instance, always referring to the *English* victory over the Armada and if necessary correcting people who called it British. Worth it to annoy him.

I can still remember promising to send you a book and even which one it is. So look forward to getting your signed copy of *The Alteration* real soon.

Cheers
Kingsley

[TLS: Bodleian]

---

1. Amis had dedicated *Russian Hide-and-Seek* (1980) to Aldiss and his wife Margaret. Their versified thanks, sent by telegram, do not survive, nor can Aldiss remember the quotation to which Amis refers.

2. In *Russian Hide-and-Seek*, writes Aldiss in ''im', Salwak, ed., *Kingsley Amis: Life and Letters*, p.44, 'the future returns us to the shades of an earlier era. What appears at first to be nineteenth-century England is in fact the EDR [English Democratic Republic], fifty years after the Russians invaded and took the country over.'

TO ROBERT CONQUEST – 4 JUNE 1980

Gardnor House, Flask Walk, London N.W.3.

Dear Bob,

Good to hear. Somebody-or-other (mind and memory going) told me you had landed yourselves an extremely nice pad.[1] Don't get too settled. We stagger on here. One visible result of things getting worse (yes, I know they're going to get better if we wait long enough) is that people aren't going to the pub. At 1 pm yesterday in the Horse and Groom there were about 10 shags. Means you can get to the bar. Garrick still going. It was there that Alan Brien[2] showed himself to be a round-evading sponger. But he also told me that, at a drunk party, Kate Wharton said she didn't mind putting on the jersey, shorts and stockings to please Colin but the football boots were a bit bloody much.[3]

No 10 was quite fun.[4] I gave Mrs T an inscribed copy of Russian H-&-S, it being publication day.[5] Asked what it was about I said a future Russian takeover, to which she said reprovingly, 'Get another crystal ball,' a good example of four words requiring about 444 to set right. Never mind. Tony P and Philip were there. They both asked me to introduce them to Denis.[6] I asked P later what D had been like. 'He covered me with spittle,' said P, adding that D wouldn't commit himself even to the most trivial statement. Had lunch with him (P) a couple of weeks ago. He was jauntily gloomy as usual. Said he spent his evenings swirling a Scotch round a glass and looking at the TV with the sound turned down because it's nicer like that. Not writing anything because he's too tired and pissed.

You were bloody lucky to miss the Krug dinner. The food was cooked by *the winners of the Gastronomy award* and was *bloody awful.* The wines were rotten. And the trophy – one of those little ashtrays

---

1. In Washington DC, where Conquest was Distinguished Visiting Scholar, the Heritage Foundation (1980–81).

2. For Alan Brien see Amis to Karl Miller, 27 February 1959, note 3.

3. Kate Wharton had divorced the *Daily Telegraph* journalist Michael Wharton in 1972 (they were married in 1952). 'Colin' is Colin Welch, also a journalist at the *Daily Telegraph.*

4. Amis has written 'Plenty to drink, for instance' in the left margin.

5. 12 May 1980.

6. Dennis Thatcher (b.1915), company director, married Margaret Thatcher in 1951; created first Baronet (1991).

shaped like a shell done in bronze with a stem connecting it to a shapeless base. S. Dali having his little joke. I found I was expected to collect yours but had to leave before it came up – 11.30 in darkest Whitehall. All in my hired tails I beetled on foot to the Gk and got there just before closing. Cyril[7] saved my life with a whisky and a minicab. Would have had to walk it otherwise. Ion Trewin evidently collected your award.[8] On your behalf, I mean. I forgot to say that the party was also very very boring.

Will think abt Peach Key.[9] Hope to see you soon. Hey, Philip told me your Coleridge limerick,[10] which was new to me. How do you account for that? Love to Lyddie

Cheers
K.

[TLS: Recipient]

TO DALE SALWAK – 25 JULY 1980

Gardnor House, Flask Walk, London NW3

Dear Dale,

Alas, our telephone has been out since just after you called on Wednesday. I left a message at 387 5526, it seems unavailingly. I will try again this afternoon. Just to make sure, the message is for you to ring 435 1083. This is our housekeeper's number and I can be reached on it.

I will keep your questions, and any comments on the transcripts,[1] till I see you. If by ill chance I don't see you, I'll get in touch by mail.

I enclose a letter of introduction for use at the Bodleian.

7. A porter at the Garrick.

8. Ion Trewin (b.1943), publisher. The award was for general 'Excellence', as opposed to a particular publication.

9. See Amis to Conquest, 1 March 1976, note 11.

10. 'Young Coleridge won when at Ottery/St Mary his father's church lottery/What they gave him was this:/A gallon of piss/In a suitable item of pottery.'

---

1. Of an interview with Amis conducted on 14 July 1980, included in *Literary Voices: Interviews with Britain's 'Angry Young Men'*, ed. Salwak (San Bernadino, Ca.: Borgo Press, 1984), which also reprints part of Salwak's earlier interview in *Contemporary Literature* 16 (Winter 1975), pp. 15–16.

It was very nice for Jane and me to have you to lunch and we both much enjoyed the occasion. (You made an excellent impression!) Thank you for your kind letter about it.

I do hope we make contact soon.

Yours,
Kingsley Amis

I heard about your 'tour of Fleet Street' from my friend Colin Welch of the Daily Telegraph, who was in the Kings and Keys when you and J.B. [John Braine] *were there.*[2]

[TLS: Recipient]

TO PHILIP LARKIN – 8 SEPTEMBER 1980

Gardnor House, Flask Walk, London NW3

Dear Philip,

Sorry, been on holiday.[1] Cruise round the French, Spanish and Portuguese coasts, then ten days in the Dordogne followed by a similar period at the Edinburgh Festival. Saw a lot of churches and art galleries. The most impressive experience was the great Cathedral of Santiago de Compostela in northern Spain. Now as of old, pilgrims flock there to refresh their weeeaaaaaaagggghhhghghgh Well I mean you can't just keep going the rounds of your study, pub and club. Can't just sit in Hampstead. Got to prime the pump I'll prime Two observations occur to me. One is that French cooking is *very good*; what other nation could make edible a confection of stag-beetles, oak-apples and lichen seethed in bats' urine? The other is that Catalonia has a lot to answer for; not only Pickarso (a tour of whose house in Barcelona moved me strangely) but Dali (a much better painter, though),[2] Miró, Casals and I hope Lorca. Sods all.

2. MS addition.

---

1. Above this sentence Amis has drawn a small penis linked by arrows to the words 'holiday', 'Dordogne' and 'Edinburgh Festival'.

2. Amis has circled this parenthetical comment and written 'KOK' next to it in the left margin.

Any road, back now and of course it's as if I'd never been afuckingway. Am writing this before settling down to 6 weeks' correspondence. And will I be writing to thank one for the offer of the OM, another for the generous token of esteem, a third for the handsomely bound set of pornography, a fourth for Pee Wee Complete? Will I buggery – autograph bum, photograph bum, thesis bum, debate bum, charity bum, grateful for any comment bum, don't know whether you remember me but bum, black tie bum, and of course tax bum, VAT bum, rates bum, BUPA[3] bum etc but Jane does all that – seminar bum, conference bum, WORKSHP SHT – SHOP bum, if you ask me old boy the time to complain is when that sort of thing stops coming DONT YOU WORRY ILL BE COMPLAINING THEN TOO MATEY LIKE A FUCKING DRAIN

Funnily enough one letter was from Michael Meyer, about a collection of cricketing pieces he's editing[4] and I'm contributing to – and you're not I see. Why not? He's paying something and you'd be in good company: A.J. Ayer, Beryl Bainbridge,[5] William Golding, Ted Hughes, Laurie Lee, David Wright oohoooghghgh.[6] Serously htuohg, just a lot of essays about cricket by non-cricket writers. Up your yes sreet I' gleet *STREET!!!*[7] I'd have thought.

Drabble is a pain in the ass. She has no sense of humour so she doesn't notice her own outrageous arrogances. Perhaps I told you last time, but unfunnily enough I had a letter from her to my agent passed on by him saying she was considering (NB) putting me in the revised OCEL[8] and would he tell her what I'd written. I told him to say the info was publicly available. I mean fucking *cheek*. Tell me what happens about your dealings with her. No it was just that they were putting a plaque to ole Geo E in Wmr Abbey[9] and invited me & J along. Thought you (& Drab) might be there too but the only other writer we saw was Michael

3. British United Provident Association, a private health-care programme.

4. *Summer Days* (1981), ed. Michael Meyer (1921–2000), poet and translator; a contemporary of Amis at Oxford. Amis's piece is called 'Ten to Make and the Match to Win' (pp. 12–17), a quotation from the poem '*Vitaï Lampada*' by Henry Newbolt (1862–1938).

5. Beryl Bainbridge (b. 1934), novelist.

6. See Amis to Conquest, 16 October 1956, note 2.

7. MS addition.

8. *The Oxford Companion to English Literature* (1985); the original *OCEL* (1932) was edited by Sir Paul Harvey; Margaret Drabble (b. 1939), novelist, biographer and critic, revised her revised edition in 1995.

9. The plaque to the novelist George Eliot (Mary Ann Evans) (1819–80) is located in Poets' Corner, Westminster Abbey.

Innes.[10] Can't see what you see in his stuff by the way. I read Appleby's Other Story and Old Hall, New Hall on hol and thought they were loads of cobblers' awls. The only sophisticated thing about him is his breath.

Will someone please explain[11] why Polish strikers are heroes but British strikers are bum,

Kingsley

I see that Humber (?) bridge is shaping up. Look forward to your ode.[12]

[TLS: Bodleian]

TO JULIAN BARNES – 9 SEPTEMBER 1980

Gardnor House, Flask Walk, London NW3

Yes, makin' mock o' uniforms that guard you
while you sleep
Is cheaper than them uniforms even when
they aren't exactly starvation cheap any more[1]

Let's have a drink soon – though not to discuss the above. Love to P.[2]

K.

[TLS: Recipient]

10. Michael Innes (1906–94), author of detective novels featuring policeman-hero John (later Sir John) Appleby; also, as J.I.M. Stewart, critic and novelist.

11. Amis has circled 'Will someone please explain' and drawn an arrow connecting it to a handwritten addition, the word 'jentz' (i.e. gents).

12. MS addition.

---

1. A response, in the form of a close adaptation of the opening lines of stanza 3 of Kipling's poem 'Tommy' (1895), to what Barnes thought was a mild reference to the military in his *New Statesman* television review of 5 September 1980, p. 28: 'The *News* (BBC-1) had some film of Crusader 80, which (you probably didn't know) is Britain's biggest military exercise since world war two, and by the end of October will have cost eight and a half million pounds. It began – as all the best wars do – with a tableload of Bucks Fizzes being mixed for brasshats beside the A34.' The lines from 'Tommy' are: 'Yes, makin' mock o' uniforms that guard you while you sleep/Is cheaper than them uniforms, an' they're starvation cheap.'

2. Barnes's wife Pat Kavanagh, literary agent, partner of Michael Sissons, Amis's agent from 1973 until 1976 (at A.D. Peters, which merged with Fraser and Dunlop, primarily theatrical agents, in 1988, becoming Peters, Fraser and Dunlop).

TO JOSEF SKVORECKY[1] – 10 SEPTEMBER 1980

Gardnor House, Flask Walk, London N.W.3.

Dear Josef,

How nice to hear from you. Thanks to tremendous forwarding delays your letter was waiting for me when I got back from holiday last Monday. Thank you for inviting me to the conference,[2] but I'm afraid I can't come; I never leave the surface of the planet, and to make my way to Toronto without doing so would be arduous in the extreme. Further: if you approve of Amnesty I suppose they must be all right, but . . . well, from what one sees of them here they seem more interested in despotisms of the right than of the left. Some attention paid to the Soviet bloc, but it's generally a pound of Chile to an ounce of Bulgaria. Perhaps they've improved.

I often think of you and Nesvadba[3] and the other people we met in Prague. It must be 13 years ago and yet it's still very clear in my mind. We have never been back nor have we visited any other Communist country. Those six days in Czechoslovakia, seeming like weeks in retrospect, were enough to implant the feel of totalitarianism for a lifetime. You are obviously very active and successful in your life in the West; your name crops up all the time here. I wonder how the others are faring. From the fragments we heard *years ago*[4] most of them seemed to have gone back. I wonder too what it's like in Prague these days.

Do you ever come to these shores? Not much reason for anyone to do so of late unless he has to, though so far it's really not too bad. If you ever do hit London you know where to find us.

With affectionate regards,

Yours ever,
Kingsley

[TLS: Hoover Institution]

1. Josef Skvorecky (b. 1914), Czech novelist, also writer on jazz and film; lived in exile in Canada from 1974.
2. On 'The Writer and Human Rights', held in October 1981 in Toronto.
3. Josef Nesvadba (b. 1926), a leading Czech science fiction writer in the 1960s, also writes mainstream fiction. For Amis and Howard's six-day visit to Prague in 1966, arranged by the Czech Cultural Attaché in London, see *Memoirs*, pp. 267–73.
4. MS addition.

TO ROBERT CONQUEST – 10 SEPTEMBER 1980

Gardnor House, Flask Walk, London, N.W.3.

Dear Bob,

Yeah, about time too. Have been on sodding holiday and before that was getting stuff squared away before going on sodding holiday. First bit was a cultural cruise round France, Spain and Portugal. Places like Santiago de Compostela and Picasso's joint in Barcelona. What a tiresome painter he is to be sure. The highlight of the cruise came when a rather pretty dental surgeon from Brazil, name of Mercedes Astle (yes, married to an Englishman), told me that it was her experiences in Basuto that had convinced her that Communism was not the answer to her country's problems. Oh really? Yes, in a place where dentists were few and far between she had often got called in to attend people off her beat, so to speak, several of them Russians, and what she had seen in this way of Soviet dentistry, especially the low quality of the cement used, had caused the scales to fall from her eyes. Truly there are innumerable roads away from Moscow.

Actually all in all the cruise was quite fun. More so than the stay in the Dordogne that followed. Pretty enough, but filthy French food – you know, elaborate sauces to persuade you to swallow stuff you would otherwise have hesitated to give the dog – sod-all to do and no host, just a hostess, one of those silent women who you think ought to say more until they start saying something. Finally a run up to Edinburgh for the end of the Festival. Leftiness and trendiness have invaded it. There was a German shag whose art-form was chatting to you while he drew things on a blackboard. I didn't go to him. Nor to any of the concerts, all of which contained either a Mahler symphony or some jerk's first performance. Did let myself be taken to Lilian Hellman's play, *Watch on the Rhine*.[1] Frightful piss, of course, but different from contemporary piss. She wasn't *trying* to write piss, like Beckett or Stoppard, she was just totally failing to be good. Vital point, or is it?

Cheers
K.

[TLS: Recipients]

---

1. An anti-Nazi drama, first performed in 1941.

TO THE SECRETARY, THE GARRICK CLUB – 11 SEPTEMBER 1980

I suggest that the bar should have available The Macallan 10-year-old malt whisky, regarded by connoisseurs and in the trade as the best ['available' – crossed out] on the market.

K.A.[1]

[Entry in Garrick Club Suggestion Book]

TO THE EDITOR, *SUNDAY TIMES* – 23 SEPTEMBER 1980

Sir,

In reply to Melvyn Bragg:[1] of course the Arts Council, though power-hungry, is relatively fair-minded and incorrupt. But any such body is bound to be socialist, collectivist, authoritarian, giving the public not what it wants, not what it is prepared to pay for, but what certain bureaucrats think it wants, or think it ought to want, or think would do it good. This damages art.

Until the tax system has been reformed to the point where the public will pay the full cost at the door, the Council and its subsidies will have to stay, but plans for phasing it out should be put in hand immediately.

Yours truly,

KINGSLEY AMIS

---

1. After due consideration by the Wine Committee, the suggestion was eventually accepted; see Amis to the Secretary, the Garrick Club, 24 June 1981.

---

1. In an article about the Arts Council, *Sunday Times*, 21 September 1980, p. 39. For Melvyn Bragg see Amis to Conquest, 18 March 1978, note 4.

TO JACQUELINE SIMMS[1] – 2 OCTOBER 1980

Gardnor House, Flask Walk, London NW3

Dear Mrs Simms,

I was given your name by Hilary Binks as the right person to approach about Oxford books of verse.[2] I now do so about something to be called provisionally *The Oxford Book of Short Poems.*

The idea was suggested to me by my old friend James Michie[3] (my old co-editor too, of *Oxford Poetry 1949*). I at once fell in with the qualifications he suggested: maximum 13 lines, no epigrams or epitaphs, no limericks or clerihews, just short poems with the same sort of merits as long or longer poems. We think it would appeal particularly to the sort of person who likes poetry but may be daunted by the many poems running to two or more pages that are to be found in most anthologies.

If you think the idea worth pursuing we should of course be very pleased to discuss it with you. I think this could be a distinctive anthology with a high proportion of relatively unfamiliar poems.

Yours sincerely,
Kingsley Amis

[TLS: OUP]

TO ROBERT CONQUEST – 14 OCTOBER 1980

Gardnor House, Flask Walk, London NW3

Dear Bob,

I deduce from your silence that you must be exceptionally idle. I certainly have been, chiefly as a way of not getting down to a rewrite

1. Jacqueline Simms, Poetry Editor of OUP until the controversial demise of the list in 1998.

2. Hilary Binks was Neal Burton's secretary at the OUP offices in London.

3. For James Michie see Amis to Larkin, 9 March 1949, note 1. Amis's chapter on Michie in *Memoirs* (pp. 108–19) discusses *The Oxford Book of Shorter Poems.* 'Michie' is the name given to Dixon's least favourite student in *Lucky Jim* (his second sentence in the novel is 'Have you got that syllabus together yet, sir?').

of New Maps which would be (a) a pest to do (b) not at all well paid. Now I find if I repay the bit of the advance I've had, I can get out of it. Hooray! Have to do my piece on old Phil (Man, 60), then my next novel,[1] with queer protagonist, which means I can say lots of crappy things about women (and men) *as well as* about queers. If anything on these lines occurs to you, let me have it. Point is that the queer is narrator, so he can just muse to himself from time to time. Can probably work in No Banarse[2] somewhere.

Who have I seen? Nobody much. Lunch with Terry K[ilmartin] today. Have had it, I mean. More animated than usual. Says Joanna has been studying *ecology* for 3 years and is now a European authority on it. You won't believe it but a Chinese called Lucian Wu came and saw me last week. I said 'Oh, Mr Wu'[3] several times but hadn't the nerve to continue e.g. 'What shall I do . . . when Mr Benn gets in, if he ever does?' Otherwise my chief activities have been going to the dentist and turning up at the mem. services for Tynan and Charles Snow. Terrible egotistical addresses from Alan Brien and Wm Cooper. Jas Michie also behaved like a shit: rang up, said we've always been going to have lunch some day what about this week, and then*, pretending it had just occurred to him, suggested he and I do an Oxford Bk/ *i.e. at the lunch/of Short Poems and why didn't I fix it up, and *then* said why didn't I fix it up to have his poems reprinted with some additional more recent ones which by a happy accident he chanced to have on him. In a most satisfactorily Freudian way I have *lost* the stuff he gave me. OUP sound a bit lukewarm about the anth. idea too.

As you must have seen the two big topics here have been the Labour Party fucking itself up and Maggie riding through the Tory conference with no serious opposition at all. Nobody seems to really mind about the unemployed, on the reasoning presumably that most of them are moonlighting for cash anyway. Hey – one little straw in the wind: when I challenged Terry he said that if he had to choose between Benn and

---

1. Eventually abandoned after 130 pages, though Amis retained its title, 'Difficulties with Girls', for a quite different novel of 1988.

2. A sign seen in Spain meaning no bathing, which looked to Amis like a homosexual slogan.

3. The title of a comic song by George Formby (1904–61), music-hall performer and actor.

Thatcher he'd pick Thatcher every time; I don't think he'd have said that even a year ago. [. . .]

Cheers
K

[TLS: Recipient]

TO ROBERT CONQUEST – 15 OCTOBER 1980

Gardnor House, Flask Walk, London N.W.3.

Dear Bob,

As might have been predicted, yours arrived when mine was sitting on my desk waiting to be posted. Good enclosures of yours. Mine is today's Telegraph. I'm pressing on with my campaign to get the Arts Council abolished. Latest scheme is to find out which 'theatre' companies are putting on lefty piss and if they have an AC grant get it taken away from them. 'Censorship!!' – can't you just hear them?

V. funny our overlapping about Paul [Johnson]. Yes, Stoppard[1] is amiable enough, and he made the only decent speech at the Tynan do. At which, incidentally, B Levin cut me dead. Good job I'd been saying for a long time before that that he has become a pompous buffoon. Recently he wrote a moving piece about a US PoW in Vietnam whom he was at first reluctant to help because he thought it would actually harm a chap to have his cause espoused by such a famous anti-communist as himself. Again, can't you hear them? – 'Ha, Captain Shagbag is leceiving suppolt flom the notolious Belnald Revin in Rondon! *Kirr him!*'

You are right about texo,[2] which for your information means many more things than just weave. My dictionary gives the following: To join, fit together, plait, braid, interweave, construct, make, fabricate, build, compose, bring about. So your bit of Latin shouldn't be all that hard to do.

---

1. 'Pity his work is no good', reads a typewritten addition over 'Stoppard'.

2. See Conquest to Amis, 7 October 1980 (in HEHL): 'You're a classical sod – would it be feasible to do a Latin phrase, for a dedication to L[iddie, a Texan], with "texas" in it? *Is* it the subjunctive of texo/tectum, or is my memory going? Something like "Si texas puella . . ." or whatever . . .'

I've asked you this before, but forget what you said: what is the state of play about Guernica? I ask because it would be so nice to be able to say that Pickarso's most famous painting is founded on a lie.[3]

I note what you say about Osbert[4] and will have a word when occasion serves; though I seldom see him at the club these days.

Bloody awful that the US states have had their abbreviations cut down to 2 letters, CA and IL and MI and what-not. Imagine the little faceless asshole responsible all puffed up with pride and glee at having imposed one more tiny bit of dullness and uniformity that satisfies the essential criteria of being unwanted and unnecessary and costing a certain amount of other people's money. Fuck him, what?

Cheers
K

[LTS: Recipient]

TO JACQUELINE SIMMS – 8 NOVEMBER 1980

Gardnor House, Flask Walk, London NW3

Dear Mrs Simms,

Thank you for your letter. I am glad that the idea of an OBSP[1] finds favour. Drawing up a 'contents' is of course most of an editor's job, and even a 'rudimentary' one would I think be rather a lot of work at this stage. We – yes, I propose that James Michie should be my co-editor – suggest we meet you with some samples and explanations of the sort of thing we have in mind. Could we all perhaps have lunch

3. Amis is referring to false rumours, spread by Franco and imposed by government censorship, that leftist Basque radicals rather than German bombers had been responsible for the 1937 destruction of Guernica, the ancient Basque capital in northern Spain. Picasso's painting was exhibited in the same year, in the Spanish Pavilion at the Paris Exposition Universelle.

4. Osbert Lancaster hadn't yet answered Conquest's two-month-old request to consider illustrating a manuscript of poems by 'Ted Pauker', nor had he returned the manuscript. For Osbert Lancaster see Amis to Anthony Powell, 18 March 1976, note 1.

---

1. 'Oxford Book of Short Poems'; see Amis to Jacqueline Simms, 2 October 1980.

on the OUP? If so, indeed in any case, you might care to telephone me with a couple of dates and I will fix it up with James Michie.

Yours sincerely,
Kingsley Amis

[TLS: OUP]

TO PHILIP LARKIN – 5 DECEMBER 1980

Gardnor House, Flask Walk, London NW3

Dear Philip,

Is it your turn? Or is it my turn? If it's my turn I'm sorry I've been so long but I haven't written any letters to anyone or done much of anything else since my wife left me 23 days ago.[1] Not with anyone, just buggered off. She did it partly to punish me for stopping wanting to fuck her and partly because she realised I didn't like her much. Well, I liked her about as much as you could like anyone totally wrapped up in themselves and unable to tolerate the slightest competition or anything a raving lunatic could see as opposition and having to have their own way in everything all the time. Well, I expect reading between the lines there you can sense that we hadn't been getting on too well of late. Yeah, but not having her around and trying to take in the fact that she never will be around is immeasurably more crappy than having her around. I've had a wife for 32 years. One consolation: with any luck selling the house and dividing everything up and finding somewhere else and moving there will be so overmasteringly crappy that I won't be able to think of anything else. Your godson[2] is providentially around, having left his intolerable wife and been sacked from his job. I think he's the nicest fellow I've ever met.

To turn to more cheerful topics: two nights ago an absolutely fucking murderous pain started up in my shoulder and arm. I scream well I

1. After a planned ten-day visit to the health farm, Shrublands. On the day of her expected return Amis received a letter from Jane's solicitors informing him that she was not returning. She moved to a room in the London house of her friend Ursula Vaughan-Williams, widow of the composer Ralph Vaughan-Williams.

2. Philip Amis.

was going to say whenever I move but do you know after typing that page I went up and had a shave and a bath and you'll think I'm barmy but it got much better and now I only wince occasionally. But I'm still going to the doctor TO BE TOLD IT'S BECAUSE OF THE DRINK AND I MUST GIVE IT UP. Are you still not drinking? What's the matter with you? Surely now's the time to *take* it up if you haven't already. Why *did* you give it up? Come on, you can tell me. Come *on*.

When I have cleared my In tray, which stands about a foot high at the moment, I shall be getting down to my bit on you for that ole symposium thing.[3] Hope I've got enough stuff. Last chance to send in your anecdote. Do you mind if I quote 'Music, when soft *silly* voices, that have been talking *piss*, die'? Just the first line. Can you remember any others of those?

Bob was over for a few days and we had lunch. I gave him two glasses of champagne at my club (£1.20 a throw), and after a couple of glasses of wine at the table he started talking very fast and quietly and without stopping about what must have been topics he thought were good ones for him to pursue. No, he hadn't had half a bottle of gin before he came; I asked him the next day. I tried to get pissed myself but never managed to catch up.

I've been writing this for about the last four days and had better get it off. Oh, the doc diagnosed fibrositis and gave me pills which I haven't had to use because the pain *went away of its own accord*. He didn't mention drink. Bloody cold here. Sight worse up where you are, no doubt. Have you heard that John Wain is going blind? Can't remember who told me. Keep well wrapped up.

Anthony Burgess's gusto and exuberance springs from his brilliant bum

Kingsley

PS: Geoffrey Wheatcroft[4] *asks me to say (what I believe to be true) that he's a very reasonable, easy-to-deal-with fellow. Seemed to think it might help him or something. He's quite good fun, too.*

[TLS: Bodleian]

3. *Larkin at Sixty* (1982), edited by Anthony Thwaite.

4. Geoffrey Wheatcroft (b. 1945), journalist and author; at the time Literary Editor, *Spectator* (1977–81).

TO THE JOHN SIMON GUGGENHEIM MEMORIAL FOUNDATION – 11 DECEMBER 1980

Mr. Kingsley Amis, Gardnor House, Flask Walk,
London NW3, ENGLAND

Confidential Report on Candidate for Fellowship
Candidate: Salwak, Dale F.

REPORT: Over the years I have spent a total of some hours in Mr Salwak's company, and we have also had considerable correspondence. I have also examined and often referred to his *Reference Guide* to my works. From all this I conclude that he possesses in full measure that sine qua non of the worthwhile critic and researcher, genuine curiosity. He will look behind obvious facts and standard explanations to get at the truth. The results of his inquiries show him to possess both energy and patience, a clear mind and a capacity for organisation. These last qualities are reflected in his prose style, which seems to me commendably vigorous and free from jargon.

Mr Salwak's abilities fit him remarkably well for his new project. It would be hard to improve on his summary of John Braine's work and approach to literature. The projected biography will benefit from Mr Salwak's knowledge of England and English life and literature, and at the same time will have the advantage of its author's status as a visitor, not a native. It is an original, almost a daring project, and if carried out will, I am confident, make an important contribution to contemporary English studies.[1]

Signed Kingsley Amis Date 11th December 1980

Position or Title Hon. Fellow, St John's College, Oxford

Address Gardnor House, Flask Walk, London. N.W.3.

[TLS: Guggenheim Foundation]

---

1. Salwak's application was unsuccessful, and the biography of John Braine was never written.

TO BRIAN ALDISS – 15 DECEMBER 1980

Gardnor House, Flask Walk, London NW3

Dear Brian,

Good to hear your voice this morning. I enclose the stuff. As you'll see in several places I leaned heavily on the old *Spree*, especially in the *Gulliver* passage. Your account of it is masterly, one of those pointings-out of what is instantly recognisable as obvious although nobody has pointed it out before.[1] Since writing the bit about *Frankenstein* I heard about a radio programme about *F* in which it was said that the Preface is not by Mary but by either Shelley or Byron – the shag couldn't remember which. Have you any information?[2]

No word from the old bitch. By God she was hard to live with but living without her seems altogether pointless. I had no idea she meant so much to me. Work's the thing, of course. Yes, but that's just what I can't settle to. Now whisky . . .

Jolly good of you to take this trouble for me. As I said, feel free to write on the typescript, but corrections only. You will doubtless keep feeling the urge to scrawl 'BLOODY *MARVELLOUS!!!*' in the margin, but I'm afraid you must discipline yourself.

Let me know when you expect to surface in these parts and I'll buy you a cracking lunch.

Yours,
Kingsley

[TLS: Bodleian]

---

1. Amis was editing *The Golden Age of Science Fiction* (London: Hutchinson, 1981), which draws on Aldiss's *Billion Year Spree: The History of Science Fiction* (1979). In a review of *Spree* in the *Observer*, 4 November 1979, reprinted in *The Amis Collection*, pp. 106–8, Amis praised Aldiss's account of *Gulliver's Travels* for 'correcting the Orwellian fallacy that sees the Houyhnhnm society as the object of Swift's, not just Gulliver's, admiration' (p. 108).

2. It was Percy Shelley; the shag who told Amis of the programme was Tom Miller.

TO ANTHONY POWELL – 5 JANUARY 1981

Gardnor House, Flask Walk, London, N.W.3

Dear Tony,

Hearty thanks for your letter and congratulations. I am sure you are right and white tie occasions will suddenly acquire a charm they have conspicuously lacked in the past.[1]

Yes, things are not as good as they might be here. It looks like a final parting of the ways, a thought that arouses in me, among many other things, a profound sense of relief. Do let's have lunch when you are in London when we will talk about the business as little or as much as you please.

Please thank Violet for her letter. I should have answered it but things are still rather disorganized.

Love,
Kingsley

[TLS: Recipient]

TO PHILIP LARKIN – 14 JANUARY 1981

Gardnor House, Flask Walk, London, N.W.3

Dear Philip,

Glad to hear you're not entirely off the drink for ever. Looks as if I shall be just that myself before long. Jane mentions that as her first condition for coming back to me, the second being presumably that I saw off my head and serve it up to her with a little hollandaise sauce. I don't know what's going to happen. There fuck I mean the mere thought of the future terrifies me.

This sort of thing slows your work down because you can't bloody

1. See Powell to Amis, 31 December 1980 (in HEHL), on the occasion of Amis's award of the CBE in the New Year's Honours List: 'Many congratulations from both of us. One wears a white tie but rarely these days, nevertheless I can assure you that a decoration at the neck does give a warm feeling to the ensemble on occasions when such effects are required.'

well concentrate. I don't know if the enclosed is any good at all. Not being allowed to use IWDAFY and the rest of it cramped my style too. (What were those girls called? Marsha was one, right?)[1] Give it a quick flip through and let me know as quick. If you would, give me a ring from/on haha the library. Don't want to keep ole Thwaite waiting longer than need be.

I must say I'm not looking forward to this sodding investiture.[2] What do you wear? I mean I know it says morning dress or dark lounge suit but it would be just my luck to turn up in one when everyone else was wearing the other, what? And Christ, perhaps I shan't even be allowed to get pissed after it. I'll ask Vioelt P[3] yktfn when I dine with her tonight. Horse-faced dwarf[4] won't be there. (I roared at that.)

I had a great time, dorling, going through your poetry-words. 'Dockery'[5] reminded me I had a day in Oxford recently and went up to where I used to live – you remember, that bloody awful little pair of rooms on staircase 3 was it, looking out on to the public bogs in the Giler[6] – and found that *each* of them was now occupied by a *different* undergraduate. The room you shared with Josh has probably got half the rugger xv in it. 'D' made me think of other things too, thanks very much. *LJ* was published almost exactly 27 years ago, the same as 1918 was in 1945. Where's it all gone?

Looking through your letters I came across the bit about Norman[7] thinking himself as important as Darwin, Marx and Freud. Yes, but in what field? And is he going to be famous any minute, or are envious shags conspiring to hush him up till after his death? Do part with any info you have. A life of him would be fascinating, though I'm not suggesting that anyone should write it.

Jim Silvester (you knew him, didn't you?) comes tonight for a jazz

---

1. Marsha and Jennifer, lesbian lovers in 'I Would Do Anything for You'; see Amis to Larkin, 5 February 1946, and enclosure.

2. For his CBE.

3. Violet Powell.

4. Amis's first use of his and Larkin's nickname for Anthony Powell; to be variously abbreviated in future.

5. 'Dockery and Son', a poem by Larkin in which the speaker revisits his college after many years ('Anyone up today must have been born/In '43, when I was twenty-one'); dated 28 March 1963, in *LCP*, pp. 152–3; originally published in *The Whitsun Weddings* (1964).

6. St Giles, the street in front of St John's College, Oxford.

7. Norman Iles.

record session. I hardly ever play mine these days. It's hard to be interested in something that's completely dead. These crazy record-buying forays, which I too make, must be an attempt to get back to the days when it was alive and new WBD-PWR-BF-JT-EC[8] et al. stuff was coming out. Too senile to remember if I told you I saw Derek Dowdall[9] at Jim's wedding recently. Grey and fat, but very recognisable. He told me he bought me in hardback and nobody else. Well, he did buy Powell too. And John Fowles[10] argh! s**t! farks! (I'd forgotten that. It must go back a long way.)

Do let me know quick about the piece. Hope I haven't said anything out of place.

Mortgage interest rate bum,
Kingsley

Was the other girl Jennifer?
Regret revolting xeroxes[11]

[TLS: Bodleian]

TO ROBERT CONQUEST – 20 FEBRUARY 1981

Gardnor House, Flask Walk, London, NW3

Dear Bob,

Most amused by your Philip piece.[1] I don't see anything he could justifiably object to, though we all know that won't stop him objecting. Limericks good and not likely to run into much competition from the other pieces in the book. The Channel Islands, by the way, are not part of the British Isles, nor of the UK; same status as the Isle of Man.[2] 'The

8. Wild Bill Davison – Pee Wee Russell – Buddy Featherstonhaugh – Jack Teagarden – Eddie Condon.

9. Derek Dowdall (1923–96), undergraduate at University College, prime mover in the formation of the Oxford University Rhythm Club.

10. John Fowles (b.1926), author of *The Collector* (1963), *The French Lieutenant's Woman* (1969) and other novels.

11. MS additions.

1. In *Larkin at Sixty* (1982), where Amis's piece also appears.

2. The Channel Islands are part of the British Isles but not of the United Kingdom or Great Britain.

UK and its dependencies' would cover it. Not that I imagine many people would notice. I sent Philip my piece and he was fearfully exercised over an anecdote about me asking him about the Laureateship and him saying in effect he wouldn't be able to get out of the fucking thing. I changed it to him saying he sometimes dreamt of it *and woke up screaming*, but would probably be passed over. Completely fictitious but I think plausible. It should be a bloody funny book and not much like your average festschrift.

As you can imagine I've been hearing plenty of honours and investiture stories. An actor at the club asked me if I'd ever wondered how Cedric Hardwick[3] got his knighthood. Not till now, I said. Apparently George V said we had to have a theatrical knight, *but* it mustn't be a bankrupt, mustn't be a divorcee and mustn't be one of *them*, and the best they could do was old C. Hardwick. Am getting terrified of Palace tomorrow week, but I'm told they make it all foolproof.

Having broken up with her very decent boy-friend Sally is staying here, or will be till this afternoon, when I take her to the doc and try to get her into a drying-out place. It must be worse to lead her life than to have to be with her and cope with her, but that's not much consolation. Am still pretty knackered by my marital troubles. Jane and I exchanged half a dozen notes about her possible return. Her first condition would be that I gave up drink completely for ever; can you imagine the life-long resentment I would feel? Her scenario, you see, is that my drinking was what fucked up the marriage. And so it did in a way, in that when I'd had a few I would sometimes lose my prudence and tell her a little about her monstrous behaviour.

Weather still mild. I mention this in satisfaction at the defeat of the experts, all of whom had predicted an ice-sheet descending about Christmas time and staying in place till March. An amateur chap got it right.

By the time you get this, or by the time it arrives you'll be about off on your trip to UK. Christ I look at the date on your letter – Jan 4 – and it only got here at the end of last week, 30th or 29th at the earliest. Xt!

See ya
K

[TLS: Recipient]

3. Sir Cedric Hardwicke (1893–1964), actor; knighted 1934.

TO ANTHONY POWELL – 12 FEBRUARY 1981

Gardnor House, Flask Walk, London, NW3

Dear Tony,

I don't usually write thank-you letters for lunches (can you stand people who think that things like that about them are interesting enough for you to want to be told them?) but yesterday's was especially enjoyable. Thank you also for being so sympathetic to my tale of woe. I forgot at least two good bits. Jane said, wrote, that she was quite sure I wouldn't be able to cut down drink and my only chance was to give it up entirely. How did she know that? Because she can't cut down smoking but is going to give it up, or has, that's how. The other one is the grounds I'm giving her for a divorce – 'unreasonable behaviour' on my part. Things like trying to stop her getting away with murder and bestial stuff like that. You know, I've a bloody good mind to defend it. It wouldn't half feed her up.

There I go again but you're such a good listener. Bloody cold here. Let me know in good time when you're going to be around and I'll book a table at the Garrick (which needs to be done a fair while in advance). Do give dear Violet my love.

Yours,
Kingsley

[TLS: Recipient]

TO ROBERT CONQUEST – 20 FEBRUARY 1981

Gardnor House, Flask Walk, London, NW3

Dear Bob,

Onward and downward. An estate agent comes to start selling the house on Tuesday, which seems to bring the future much closer. It seems likely to prove disagreeable. Not that the present is up to much. Quite a lot of people have said to each other, 'Old Kingers is on his own now; we must have him round to dinner.' And they do, once. I go to the Garrick a lot, which should certainly have the effect of shortening the future. Fuck it. Sorry to bore you.

The Gav Ewart thing[1] is all right, but it includes a lot of stuff I was at pains to leave out, like bloody old Sumer is i-comen in, the Miller's Tale etc. And he winds up with John Fuller, Gregory Corso, John Updike and such.[2] Ted P is in with Grouchy Gd-night. My Bookshop thing is in. Lazy old Gav has followed my text of Marvell's Holland,[3] not the slightly longer full one. The lucky sod had half as much again space as I did, but didn't use it very wisely I'd say.

You'll have seen that Harry Evans[4] has got the Times chair. I don't think that's a very good idea, do you? He'll want to change it, 'modernise' it, impress his personality on it. He's a good *expanding* editor, as [Christopher] Hitchens put it. Jolly lunch at Bertorellis' today (Friday; they've shifted there from Bursa and you can hear quite a lot of what people say.). I told them of the crack I made at the club, 'Things have come to a pretty pass when the editor of the Times's girl friend[5] is one of my son's cast-offs.' Bound to get back to him, said Hitch. Yeah, if he has anything to do with it.

Tony P[owell] gave me lunch at the Lansdowne Club the other week. Bloody cheap, I must say. Ought to be, too. He was in good nick as usual. Told me that poor old Osbert [Lancaster] isn't. At the Lit Soc[6] he said to Tony, 'I haven't managed to see much of your father and mother for some time. But your father is dining with Anne [Lancaster][7] tonight, of course.' In fact it was Violet who was dining with Anne. So the drawings you mention aren't likely to get done. Though I don't see why not in a way; he still does a couple a week for the Express. I'll ask him anyway if I see him (never seems to come to the Garrick in the ordinary way).

Just noticed Gav exactly follows my choice of Praed but puts them

---

1. *The Penguin Book of Light Verse* (1980).

2. John Fuller (b.1937), poet, novelist, critic and Fellow of Magdalen College, Oxford, and Tutor in English since 1966 (also the son of the poet Roy Fuller); Gregory Corso (b.1930), American beat poet; John Updike (b.1932) American novelist, also poet and critic.

3. 'The Character of Holland' (written 1653, published 1681).

4. Harold Evans (b.1928), journalist and publisher; Editor of *The Times* (1981–82), previously Editor of the *Sunday Times* (1967–81).

5. Tina Brown (b.1953), journalist and editor; at the time editing *Tatler* (1979–83). She married Evans in 1981, later edited *Vanity Fair* (1984–92), the *New Yorker* (1992–98) and *Talk* (1999–).

6. The Literary Society, a dining club which meets once a month in the Garrick Club, except in summer.

7. Sir Osbert's second wife.

in a different order. Skiving sod. Limerick selection v. poor. Love to Liddie.

Cheers
Kingsley

[TLS: Recipient]

TO ROBERT CONQUEST – 9 MARCH 1981

Gardnor House, Flask Walk, London, N.W.3

Dear Bob,

Jolly nice to hear from you. Your last three are to hand. I know you mean the offer of shelter seriously, my coming to stay I mean, and thanks all the same, but honestly the idea of climbing into a jet and being taken anywhere at all appeals to me about as much as that of walking a tightrope across Niagara Falls. My phobia about this is deep-seated and incurable. I have a milder but still bothersome one about being alone at night, in the house I mean, and I must say it gives a booster shot to one's ordinary feelings over being deserted. Where the hell am I going to get the kind of companion/housekeeper I need? – but I mustn't go maundering on.

I can't make out what's happening in this bloody country; you probably can from over there. Has Mrs T done a U-turn, or will she, or should she, or mustn't she? The prospects of the Soc Dems seem equally cloudy. Huw Wheldon told me that at the LSE student elections they were in by a landslide. But then the sods have no leader. I never hear or see a good word for Jenkins.[1]

Young Martin's new novel[2] is out. Tough going I find. You see there's this girl with amneisa shit you know what I mean, so she's

1. Amis's concern about Mrs Thatcher's 'U-turn' may refer to the National Coal Board's withdrawal of plans to close pits, thus averting a strike by miners. On 25 January 1981 the former Labour Ministers Roy Jenkins, Dr David Owen, William Rodgers and Shirley Williams, the so-called 'Gang of Four', issued the 'Limehouse Declaration', advocating, in effect, the creation of a new centre-left party, the Social Democrats. On 12 March 1981 twelve MPs and nine peers resigned the Labour whip to become Social Democrats, and within a week one Conservative MP joined them. Jenkins became the SDP's first leader (1982–83).

2. *Other People* (1981).

forgotten what a lavatory is and thinks the cisterns and pipes are statuary, but then how does she know what statuary is? It's like a novel by Craig Raine,[3] well not quite as fearful as that would be I suppose. Quite a jolly party for it, here. George [Gale] brought his new lady, who seems jolly nice. I said as much when she was out of the room, and he said with touchingly naive wonder, 'She's no trouble.' (What is trouble for him, serious apparently, is Pat refusing to get out of that bloody house and pushing him further into the financial shit every day.) George is transformed all the same. We fixed a weekend at their place near Bishop's Stortford, and as we completed the arrangements he said twice over, 'That'll be lovely.' Can you imagine 1979 George, or perhaps any previous George, using a word like that?

I reckon the way out of your Osbert difficulty is to write to Anne saying you've written to him once or twice (he won't remember) . . . no, perhaps she runs his correspondence; say you've mentioned Pauker to him once or twice and have heard he's been a bit off colour etc. She's quite bright enough to carry on from there and not take offence.

Another letter from you just arrived; Christ. Yes, the L Mag suit was as you say. Bloody fools to print anything of that sort. They're going to have to close if some benefactor doesn't appear.[4] Very timely that the S Tel has just printed a letter (on another topic) from Ian Harvey, the Tory MP who had to resign his seat on being caught sucking off a guardsman in the park, making his favourite point that queers are just like non-queers except in liking men. Very true – think of all those pals of ours who've been caught fucking female traffic wardens in Kensington Gardens.

London is okay, v. mild after a couple of cold weeks. Traffic more and more insane; 70 mins from here to Monmouth Street via brief stop in Harley Street. Topic of the moment is another libel action, Bevan, Crossman and Morgan Phillips v. Spec in 1957.[5] Clear now they were

3. Craig Raine (b.1944), the leading 'Martian' poet (the term is James Fenton's, used to describe poetry that approaches everyday objects in unfamiliar, riddling ways); Poetry Editor, Faber and Faber (1981–91).

4. There were two suits against the *London Magazine*, one brought by Donald Windham (b.1920), involving Tennessee Williams (with whom Windham had collaborated on a play in 1945, and whose letters to Windham, which Windham edited in 1977, were the subject of the suit), the other brought by John Sutro (1903–85), producer and screenwriter, involving Barbara Skelton's novel *The Love Match* (1969). In both cases, the magazine had to pay.

5. Aneurin Bevan, Richard Crossman and Morgan Phillips won a considerable sum in a 1957 libel suit against the *Spectator*, which had suggested that they had been drunk at a conference in Venice. Crossman later revealed in his *Diaries* that Phillips at least had been

all pissed – you remember, in Venice. The Spec ought to get some money for that. They were hob-nobbing with Nenni[6] too, much more serious offence than getting pissed.

Oh God that poetry comp. The winning entry was a poem by Andrew Motion which everybody agrees they can't understand;[7] there was a bloody good letter the following week listing the internal inconsistencies. The Observer and London Weekend TV put up the cash. Judges were Philip, C Causley,[8] S Heaney and T Hughes. They went on TV (minus Philip, needless to say) and talked more balls per second than you would have believed possible, esp SH and TH. All *generalising* balls, uncheckable balls, and the audience were too respectful or chicken to say, Yes but what about Gray's Elegy/Lear/Addison/Shak's sonnets/ Praed/Robt Lowell/JR Lowell[9]/limericks, etc.

Life goes on here undisturbed to outward view, though any moment flocks of shags will start being shown over the house. No, Martin still sees a lot of Angela. Vile piece in Standard getting his age wrong and saying Ang had tried to get him to dedicate new book to her but he had 'churlishly' dedicated it to 'his mother, Elizabeth Jane Howard'. Churlish anyway, to salute your mother?

New American dictionary from OUP for review. Any ideas?

All cheers,
Kingsley

[TLS: Recipient]

drunk. See Janet Morgan, ed., *The Backbench Diaries of Richard Crossman, 1951–1964* (London: Jonathan Cape, 1981), p. 574.

6. Pietro Sandro Nenni (1891–1980), prominent left-wing Italian politician, leader of the Italian Socialist Party (PSI); forged coalitions with both Communists (before 1956) and Christian Democrats (under Aldo Moro).

7. Andrew Motion (b.1952), poet, critic, biographer, Poet Laureate (1999–). His winning poem was 'The Letter', reprinted in *Dangerous Play: Poems 1974–1984* (London: Salamander Press, 1984), pp. 12–13.

8. Charles Causley (b.1917), poet, author of children's stories and verse.

9. James Russell Lowell (1819–91), American poet and man of letters.

TO JUDITH CHAMBERLAIN[1] – 18 MARCH 1981

Gardnor House, Flask Walk, N.W.3

Dear Judith,

I have considered your letter carefully and discussed it a couple of times with James. He was inclined to accept your sonnet suggestion provided we can be fully 'arbitrary', to re-omit Americans by way of return and to extend the length, though to 16 not 20 lines.[2] My own feelings have hardened more and more against the sonnet, for reasons I will try to explain.

You call the sonnet 'one of the most important forms of "short poem"'. More than that, it is the *only* important fixed form. The sonnets in the book, then, would be the only identifiable, separable group of poems. Split them up as we might, they would dominate the anthology, make it one of sonnets and miscellaneous other poems, i.e. more ordinary and I think less attractive. However 'arbitrary' our choice might be it would have to include some of the best and therefore best-known; the fewer there were the more familiar all those few would inevitably be. I can well imagine a prospective buyer looking inside, seeing 'Let me not to the marriage of true minds'[3] and moving on. A mixture of old war-horses and poems rarely or never seen before in an anthology seems an uneasy one to me.

Sonnets are supposed to be terrifically various but in fact, until we get to quirky modern stuff, their range is comparatively narrow. Their presence would limit the diversity we hope to offer, and their sonnet-like qualities – of being sonorous, oratorical, weighty, fully and carefully finished, memorable – would make our little chunks of Betjeman or Edward Thomas look a bit lightweight, vicarage water-colours alongside serious[4] oil paintings full of impasto and what-have-you. So many sonnets are great poems and let you know it. There are limits to 'arbitrariness', severer than might seem. We just *cannot* print one sonnet by

1. Editor of General Books for OUP at the time, later Commissioning Editor, Trade Books.

2. Amis and Michie had originally decided that the maximum length of poems in the anthology would be thirteen lines, thus excluding sonnets.

3. Shakespeare, Sonnet 116.

4. The words 'whacking great' have been crossed out and 'serious' written above them.

Shakespeare and hope to evade the question, 'Do you *really* think 'This Be the Verse' ['They fuck you up'] is better than 'To me, fair friend'[5] – which you have left out – or as good, or even nearly as good in its way?' We would seem not 'arbitrary' but whimsically or wantonly perverse, and seem so, what is more, every time the reader came to a poem he considered inferior or remembered a sonnet we had left out. People feel extra strongly about sonnets, individual ones that is, because they are likely to know some sonnets better than any other kind of poem. Better to grasp the nettle rather than the bull by the horns (I thought your use of the latter phrase to mean 'doing what Judith and Jacky[6] want' was pretty nice) and exclude the lot, hoping the reader will forget his objections in becoming interested in what we do provide.

Two last points. In my experience, good anthologies turn up when the compiler has put in only what he wanted to put in and nothing of what he merely considered he ought to put in. And being 'arbitrary' about sonnets is quite different from being it about the other things. There are no Americans of the first importance; there are very few short poems from the period 1350–1550; there are very few essential poems of any length written 1960–80. But to be 'arbitrary' with Shakespeare, Milton and Wordsworth is to be just that, to choose at random. I have just quickly turned through Shakespeare's sonnets and found a minimum which all demand to go into any collection of poems* of under 16 or 20 lines. Reducing them further would mean shutting my eyes and wielding a pin. How few could I get away with, how many would unbalance the book? I suppose that takes me back to the previous point.

Please have another think. As a sweetener I will re-include Americans, and would go up to 16 lines were it not for the slight formal difficulty, i.e. 'no poems of more than 13 lines' (giving reasons, of course) is sort of easier to say than 'no poems of more than 16 lines oh and no sonnets either'.

I have read the rough draft of the above to James, who in general goes along with me on sonnets but feels more flexible about the matter.[7]

5. Shakespeare, Sonnet 104; Larkin's 'This be the Verse' first appeared in *High Windows* (1974), reprinted in *LCP*, p. 180.

6. That is, Jacqueline Simms, Poetry Editor, OUP.

7. Michie does not remember any inclination to soften the thirteen-line limit, which was adhered to in the 1985 published version (co-edited with P.J. Kavanagh, who took over after Amis pulled out; see Amis to Judith (Chamberlain) Luna, 2 March 1982, note 2).

He says, and I agree, that since we very much want to work on this together, far more than either of us wants to do it solo, we had better start off in full agreement.

Jolly good luck.

Yours,
Kingsley

* Well, not *any* quite. They would fit oddly into a collection of, say, comic or obscene short poems.

xerox to James

[TLS: OUP]

TO JOHN BETJEMAN – 29 MAY 1981

Gardnor House, Flask Walk, London N.W.3

My dear John, (can you bear people who write 'My Dear John'? I'm not sure I can)

I hear encouraging reports of steady progress and shameful cosseting by attractive nurses.[1] Jolly good show. I also hear you will be staying in the hosp. for a couple of weeks yet. A bloody good idea; there's nothing to come out for, and at least you'll be warm and dry, which is more than the rest of us are half the time. They say the May rainfall probably won't beat the 1979 record, but it's been the unsunniest spring I can remember. The only good result is that everything looks terrifically green, like Ireland.

I'm looking forward very much to the opening of the Humber bridge (Barbara Castle's[2] bribe to the local voters, costing some horrible sum like 40 million quid and quite unnecessary). Did you know old Philip had written an (embarrassing, he said) ode to be set to music

1. On Easter Sunday morning 1981 Betjeman, who was staying with Lady Elizabeth Cavendish in Derbyshire, was discovered to have suffered a stroke and was admitted to the Royal Hallamshire Hospital in Sheffield, where he stayed for over a month.

2. Barbara Castle (b. 1910), Labour politician, MP for Blackburn (1945–79), Transport Minister (1965–68); created Baroness Castle of Blackburn (1990).

by a Hull composer and sung at the ceremony?[3] He's been praying for years that the bridge would fall down or never be finished. Of course one so often agrees to do hateful things if the day of reckoning is far in the future. I can't imagine what public, celebratory, organ-voiced[4] Larkin will be like. Make a good literary comp.

I went to the Royal Academy,[5] sporting my C.B.E. as may readily be imagined, and got unluckily tight. I mean I tanked up at the club just a bit because I thought we might well be given one sherry and then driven in to the table. Not a bloody bit of it; the whisky flowed like wine. I grabbed it because now I thought it might be cut off at 7.25; not a bit of that either. Then there was a lot of wine. All in all I was not the ideal neighbour for Constance Cummings,[6] with whom I kicked off by reminding her (having seen it on the telly the previous week) of a film she had made 40 years ago, literally. That broke the ice all right. I recovered some ground by propounding my theory about Mr Barrett, of Wimpole Street.[7] I've probably propounded it to you, but anyway it goes like this. Browning was coloured – I read this somewhere years ago, can't remember where; have you ever come across it? B. certainly had connections with Jamaica. So had Mr Barrett. Elizabeth's complexion was so 'sallow' that Browning called her his little Portuguese as you know. I reckon Mr Barrett wasn't sure, or was sure, about her exact ancestry and was afraid the two might produce a little piccaninny, hence his opposition to the match (or is that only in that play and film?[8]). Pen Browning of course was as white as your hat but Mr Barrett couldn't have betted on that. In the 1840s he wouldn't have known that there are no such things as throwbacks and that no offspring can be darker than his parents. About seven years ago I was introduced to a

3. For Larkin's ode, 'Bridge for the Living', see Amis to Larkin, 27 July 1978, note 1.

4. An affectionate-ironic echo of Tennyson's praise of Milton, in 'Milton: Alcaics' (1863): 'God-gifted organ-voice of England'.

5. On 11 May, to attend its Annual Dinner.

6. Constance Cummings (b. 1910), American stage and film actress, long resident in England.

7. The poet Robert Browning (1812–89) married the poet Elizabeth Barrett (1806–61) in 1846, in the teeth of the opposition of her father Edward Moulton Barrett, who had forbidden all his children to marry. The Brownings had one son, Robert Wiedemann Barrett ('Pen') Browning (1849–1913). For Amis's theory of Mr Barrett's behaviour see the title story in *Mr Barrett's Secret and Other Stories* (1993). Amis appends an author's note to the story setting out its factual basis (pp. 21–3).

8. *The Barretts of Wimpole Street* (1934), directed by Sidney Franklin, starring Norma Shearer, adapted from Rudolf Besir's stage play.

female who was said to be Browning's brother's great-great-I-think-granddaughter. She was very coloured, about half and half I should say. Now isn't that interesting? I told Huw Wheldon[9] and he said he believed it, adding that it accounted for the nig-noggy, ragtimey beat of the verse, Browning's that is. I must say I hadn't thought of *that*. The trouble with this sort of thing is that it's more fun going on thinking it might be true than checking and finding it isn't.

It's now 31st May, Sunday, and what do I find in the Observer but a great puff for that John Ashbery whom I excoriated in my last.[10] Greatest living poet in English, the reviewer thought, or possibly so, and 'exciting', that horrible word – an exciting new film isn't one with lots of car-chases and gun-battles, but a piece of trendy, pretentious stodge. Don't think I've got an obsession about Ashbery, but the reviewer is Peter Porter, whom you probably know, a very nice man, well read, intelligent, with a good sense of humour, not some ignorant little nit – no good as a poet, of course, but he needn't be that for it to be bloody awful that he gets taken in by Ashbery, or rather not exactly *taken in*, it's more that he's lost his bearings, can't recognise what's good any more. Forgive ranting jeremiad.

Did I tell you I and another are to compile an Oxford Book of Short Poems? 'Short' means 13 lines or less, to exclude sonnets, which would make the book top-heavy, we feel. It sounds rather like a piece of book-making, but I think we might find some unregarded stuff, also perhaps manage to show familiar poets in an unfamiliar light, and there must be a few who made a thing out of the short poem, though Sassoon is the only one I can think of for the moment. If you have any bright ideas we'd be jolly glad to have them.[11]

The sun has now been out for over an hour; absolutely extraordinary. I'll seal this up, make more tea and settle down to the early film, John Wayne fighting fires on oil-rigs, just the thing. Tomorrow a lunch with a TV company to discuss what will surely be a most shameful book, an anthology of poems and other stuff read in the Close-Down programme by all sorts of shags, like Enoch Powell, Barbara Cartland, rock

9. For Huw Wheldon see Amis to Wheldon, 21 July 1957, note 1.

10. John Ashbery (b. 1927), American poet. Though Amis 'excoriates' Ashbery in letters to Conquest and Larkin, he mentions him nowhere else in the surviving letters to Betjeman.

11. Betjeman replies in a letter of 3 June 1981, in Candida Lycett Green, ed., *John Betjeman: Letters*, vol. 2, p. 571: 'I like the idea of a book of short poems also of a book of long poems, it is the ones in between I can't stand.'

singers, tennis players etc. I am to edit it ha ha ha; well it won't kill me.[12] Hope you'll be among us again soon.

Cheers
Kingsley

[TLS: Victoria]

TO PHILIP LARKIN – 9 JUNE 1981

Gardnor House, Flask Walk, London, N.W.3

Dear Philip,

Sorry I haven't written; as I must have said, I find it hard to do even necessary things. Anyway, seeing us on successive pages in the TLS,[1] dalling, supplied the perpelling power. Thank you for the nice things you say about me. I didn't know, or had forgotten, that you were such a Bond fan. I agree with everything you say about him AND about Gardner's book. Glidrose[2] didn't show me it or even tell me it existed till it was in proof, possibly because I'd have told them it was piss. So sodding *tame.* Bond tells Murik's men to stand down and they stand down. Peter Janson-Smith of Glidrose said the present text is Gardner's *souping-up* of an original draft they'd sent back as too boring. Imagine what *that* can have been like. He just can't write exciting stories.

You are an ole bugar about the rosé.[3] I don't like it either, but Bond did. He drank a well-iced pint of it in *Goldfinger,* p. 170 (Cape edn.), admittedly with a sole meunière, but if rosé goes with anything it goes

12. The discussions came to nothing.

---

1. Larkin had reviewed *Licence Renewed* (1981), by John Gardner (b. 1927), the second pseudo-Bond novel (Amis's pseudonymous *Colonel Sun* (1968) was the first); Amis had reviewed John Dickson Carr's *The Door to Doom* (1981), a posthumous collection of previously unpublished writings, mostly early. Both reviews appeared in *TLS*, 5 June 1981, pp. 625, 627. The Larkin review is reprinted in *Required Writing*, pp. 266–70; the Amis in *The Amis Collection*, pp. 122–6.

2. The company Ian Fleming bought in 1952 and to which he assigned the copyright of all his Bond novels. Its director is the literary agent Peter Janson-Smith.

3. 'Amis was both a first-class writer and a Bond fan, and what he produced [*Colonel Sun*] was a workmanlike job, though one reader at least blenched to find Bond drinking rosé with his cold beef, or with anything else for that matter' (Larkin, *Required Writing*, pp. 267–8).

with anything, right? Funny thing, the day I read your piece I got *Who's Who in Spy Fiction*[4] from the local remainder shop (want a copy? p/b, 30p) and read the following *piece of bubbling dogshit* from the pen of John le Carré: GENTS

> The really interesting thing [phrase that shows a lie is coming up] about Bond is that he would be what I would call the ideal defector. Because if the money was better, the booze freer and women easier over there in Moscow, he'd be off like a shot. Bond, you see,[5] is the ultimate prostitute[6]

Not true, not the case. That's what *le C's* dull fuckers are like. He is the most frightful pisser, as I will explain to you at greater length when I see you.

Life here is funny really somehow. People come in droves to look over the house, at enormous length or for insultingly short periods, standing outside my study talking loudly in Arabic etc. Actually the two most serious prospects are a Chinese and a Negro with a German accent, presumably from Namibia. I thought he must be a Mr von Simson, sometimes mentioned by the agent as very seriously interested, but it seems not. A surveyor looked over the place for three hours yesterday, jumping up and down to test the floors, asking me whether the damp-course clearance had a guarantee on it and saying things like, 'We mustn't say too much about the sun or he'll feel embarrassed and sneak back behind the clouds.' Which reminds me: if you want to stay here again you'd better consider the matter. I shall be here for another few weeks but not for ever, hey? I still have housekeeper so amenities remain. [. . .]

Attractive Georgian residence standing on its own bum,

Kingsley

Thought I would have a read of your old *Moving Toyshop*[7] the other

4. Edited by Donald McCormick (London: Sphere Books, 1979).

5. At the top of the page Amis has handwritten the word 'aaarghgh!!' and connected it by arrows to the words 'you see'.

6. The quote occurs on p. 132 of *Who's Who in Spy Fiction*, which calls Le Carré (David Cornwell, b. 1931) the first author to add a new dimension to the spy story 'since Maugham and Ambler' (p. 133).

7. The most successful of the novels by Edmund Crispin (Bruce Montgomery), published 1946; Larkin wrote a few of its pages.

day for old times' sake, and stopped it soon because it was TWO EMBAARRSSING to go on. Mr Hoskins aaaaaaaaghghghghrhrhrhrg hghghghg no wonder he drank himself to death if that was the best he could do

Hows that old bridge coming along looking forward to reading the full text of your ode in the national press oooghghgh[8]

[TLS: Bodleian]

TO PHILIP LARKIN – 24 JUNE 1981

Gardnor House, Flask Walk, London, N.W.3

[. . .] Went to a terrible stage-people party the other day. [. . .] Anyway, someone who was there because she was a neighbour not a stage shag was called Clare Allen, who turned out to be Miriam Plaut[1] really, whom didn't we have a drink with in the Flask the other year? [. . .] I was quite warming to her when she said how miserable I had made Hilly, thus (unnecessarily) reminding me that Jane's departure has stopped me pretending to myself that my treatment of H. was at least sort of worth while somehow a bit, and went away soon. [. . .]

You are mad about the Beatles. They're not too bad I suppose but I feel I could always be listening to Jimmy Lunceford[2] instead. But I think they went on being all right longer than you say, up to Sgt Pepper, no? I met Lennon a couple of times. The first time he was being nasty to his wife, the English one not the Nip, the second time she wasn't there and he was just generally offensive. No breeding what? I'm going to try to buy a small house in Hampstead. Then I have to find a

8. MS addition. A reference to Larkin's poem 'Bridge for the Living', in *LCP*, pp. 203–4; see Amis to Larkin, 27 July 1978, note 1.

1. A friend from Oxford days, of Bruce Montgomery in particular; according to Larkin, 'used to say she was the original of Katherine in AGIW [*A Girl in Winter*, Larkin's novel of 1947], which was not very true' (Larkin to Amis, 30 June 1981 (in HEHL)).

2. Jimmie (Jimmy) Lunceford (1902–47), bandleader; Larkin, in *All What Jazz*, praises early Beatles (*With the Beatles, Help*) but questions the direction taken in *Sergeant Pepper's Lonely Hearts Club Band* (1967): 'I doubt whether their own fancies and imagination are strong enough to command an audience instead of collaborating with it' (p. 212).

housekeeper. You don't know any beautiful young kind efficient energetic girls who shorthand-type, cook etc. do you? Thank you for your kind remarks about the old Dossier.[3] Heard on the radio just now that the Humber bridge opens next month. I am looking forward most eagerly to reading the write-ups of your ode leggo my pis

My client is of course entitled to half the total proceeds of bum,

Kingsley

[TLS: Bodleian]

TO THE SECRETARY, THE GARRICK CLUB – 24 JUNE 1981

Thank you, but what did the Wine Committee *say* about my suggestion of 11th September 1980?[1]

KINGSLEY AMIS

[Entry in Garrick Club Suggestion Book]

TO PHILIP LARKIN – 27 AUGUST 1981

Gardnor House, Flask Walk, London, N.W.3

Dear Philip,

Sorry I haven't written. Been all this house bum, or rather house non-bum, in the sense that nothing ever happens. The potential buyers and their surveyors have been and gone, and a great silence reigns. I think they've found some terrible defect that'll cost £249,995 to put right, and are about to offer me the odd £5 for the place. That will make ole Jane jolly sick, means she won't be able to afford her delightful little William and Mary house with its tiny unexpected patch of vivid garden. But my morale is much improved, in fact today I felt *all right* for about 20 mins, because I've found, and yesterday installed here, the couple who'll look after me. They are Hilly and her 3rd husband, Lord

3. *The James Bond Dossier* (1965).

---

1. The Secretary's reply was 'Your request has been granted.'

Kilmarnock.[1] Nay, stare not so. Well, you'd be justified in staring a bit, but it was their suggestion, the boys are much in favour, it's the only way for me to have a bit of family, all that. Anyhow, the day this was decided on I started a new novel,[2] and the day they came, yesterday as I said, I got the plot of same sorted out. They have a little boy of 9.[3] Yes, but he's very nice. No, but there it is. Oh well. [. . .]

Hope you approved of my letter to The Times about the Arts Council.[4] If the point ever comes up again, a letter from you wd. fuck up the opposition no end. I liked the way that Po Soc chap said Po readings aren't like KA said and then demonstrated that they fucking *were*.[5]

The Inner Cities are full of frustrated young blacks looking for bum

Kingsley

[TLS: Bodleian]

TO ROBERT CONQUEST – 23 SEPTEMBER 1981

still Gardnor House, Flask Walk NW3

Dear Bob,

Fine to hear from you, as always. Thought I had better bung something off to you quick or you'll be here and I shall feel, and indeed be, a bit of a shit for not writing. Yes fuck Ian G.[1] With George [Gale] the other day we recalled his shitty behaviour over Iain H[amilton] and

---

1. Alastair Boyd, Lord Kilmarnock (b. 1927), author, educator, SDP Whip (1983–86) and Deputy Leader in the Lords (1986–87); married Hilly Amis, his second wife, in 1977.

2. *Stanley and the Women* (1984).

3. James (Jaime) Boyd, born on 27 January 1972.

4. The letter (of 3 August 1981) argued against public subsidy for the arts chiefly on the grounds that 'the way an artist is paid profoundly affects his product. To subsidise him, to give him other people's money on request and unconditionally, disrupts the all-important relationship between him and his audience.'

5. Amis had called such readings 'not so easy to distinguish from rock concerts'.

---

1. Ian Gilmour (see Amis to Conquest, 26 October 1958, note 7) spoke out frequently against Margaret Thatcher's monetarist policies, though a member of her government; when dismissed as Lord Privy Seal in the reshuffle of mid-September 1981 he denounced government policy on television as 'steering full speed for the rocks' (see Margaret Thatcher, *The Downing Street Years* (London: HarperCollins, 1993), p. 151).

Macleod and the Spec,[2] and George told me of a similar thing G had done to him. In both cases it was cowardice, wetness in fact; he couldn't face telling nasty news.*

Jolly good letter about 'extremism'.[3] You should do a piece soon (I've missed it if you already have) on a thing that might be called the fallacy of impartiality. You know, there are two sides in the Ulster fighting, the Army and the I.R.A. Each has its line and its story, and we're sitting in the middle making up our minds which to support and believe on the various issues. Similarly, there's Maggie and the hunger-strikers. You can't expect them to make concessions on their part unless there's an 'initiative' on hers (not 'ours'). Again, there's the rioters with their feelings and their account of what happened, and there's the police with theirs. And of course there are the two giant Powers. That little bastard Jonathan Dimbleby[4] is doing a series on that, called The Eagle and the Bear, instantly implying the two are so to speak equidistant from us and we can and should weigh them in the same balance. I may have mentioned how good Perry [Worsthorne] was on the telly about this in Ulster, forcing the other side to admit that they stood for a 'detached' line instead of, as he rightly recommended, asking how the Press could help our side there.

Paul Fussell is over and will still be around when you come. He's broken up with Betty after 30 years or so.[5] Issue seems to have been that she likes theatrical craps and he likes academic types. One wants to sympathise with him, but choosing between US stage-folk and US campus shags is no easy decision I imagine; no of *course*, at least the academics aren't egotists to a man AND WOMAN. P says the talk in Princeton etc. is that Reagan has told the Russkies that if they go into Poland[6] he'll go into Cuba. No more than surmise I imagine, but nice to think it's being said. Christ, US intellectuals and lefties must be in a state, just over Reagan generally. Good show.

2. In 1963 the *Spectator* was owned by Ian Gilmour and edited by Iain Hamilton. Gilmour had Hamilton replaced by Iain Macleod (1913–70), Conservative politician and Minister, who served as Editor from 1963–65.

3. I have been unable to trace this letter, which Conquest cannot recall having written.

4. Jonathan Dimbleby (b. 1944), broadcaster, journalist and author.

5. See Notes on Recipients. Fussell had been married for thirty-two years.

6. To shore up the government against supporters of the trade union 'Solidarity' and other 'counter-revolutionary' opponents.

* If he felt the ship was heading for the rocks, *why didn't he fucking resign*?

Cheers See ya Love to Liddie
Kingsley

Have acquired ANOTHER drunken madwoman, the widow of a Garrick member, and all because another chap and I decently went to see her. Now she sends me terrible poems daily. Hasn't rung up, though. NOT YET[7]

[TLS: Recipient]

TO BRIAN ALDISS – 20 OCTOBER 1981

Gardnor House, Flask Walk, London NW3

Dear Brian,

Jolly good show. Nice to have the Brum SF Group's observations.[1] I must say, though, that the fellow is a bit of a cunt to think that Russians *prefer* horses to motor cars. Hope it is clear that all the oil was used up.[2]

Sale of house is hanging fire for the time being, as surveys have revealed that the entire structure is on the point of collapsing. The delay is reported to have greatly incensed Jane, who is putting it about that I am selfishly luxuriating here and putting the price up to deter all possible buyers.

Sooner you than me with the Booker. Is Bradbury as big a shit as he seems from slight acquaintance and a glance at his works?[3]

Let me know when you're at large in London.

All the best,
Kingsley

[TLS: Bodleian]

7. MS addition.

---

1. The observations of the Birmingham Science Fiction Group, at its yearly 'Novacon', concerned both *Russian Hide-and-Seek* (1980) and *The Golden Age of Science Fiction* (1981).
2. In the EDR (English Democratic Republic) in *Russian Hide-and-Seek*.
3. Aldiss was a Booker Prize judge; the novelist and academic Malcolm Bradbury (1932–2000) was chairman of the panel. The winner in 1981 was *Midnight's Children* by Salman Rushdie.

TO ROBERT CONQUEST – 21 DECEMBER 1981

c/o Jonathan Clowes,[1] *19 Jeffrey's Place, N.W.1*

My dear old lad,

Great to get your letter this morning as the snow fell in buckets. Actually it hasn't been too crappy yet, traffic bad but possible, and today's stuff is melting almost as fast as it falls. Have been meaning to write for weeks, but the move and associated worries have taken up energy. We – me, Hilly, Alistair and young James[2] – are now in a furnished flat just round the corner from Gardnor H. and hope to move into a very decent little house in Kentish Town early in Jan. The hope is a bit fervent because Jane has been behaving very shittily, an assertion which I'm sure will make you gasp and rub your eyes. Her latest is just the latest in a series of shittinesses. Recently she gave two nasty Press interviews, Standard and Sunday Express, complaining I wouldn't go on holiday, stopped her writing by making her run the house, etc. (when we were two in family in the week, often but not always three at weekends, and had a living-in housekeeper). Then when she came to the house in my pre-arranged absence for her to collect her 'share' of the contents she rifled the place, taking all the best crockery, glassware, etc., including the remains of a case of decent claret a club-mate had given me for doing him a favour. *Now* she is trying to get not half of the proceeds of the sale of the house but £40,000 more than half, that being the value of the flat she sold in 1964 to help us buy 108 Maida Vale, adjusted for inflation. At the moment her solicitor, who did the conveyancing, is holding on to *all* my share, which he won't be able to do for much longer but perhaps long enough to make me lose the Kentish Town house, which completes on 8th January. If not purely routine female behaviour the whole thing probably comes from her sense of injustice that I seem not only to have survived her departure but to be having an illegitimately uncrappy time being looked after by Hilly, going to the club, etc. Sorry to go on rather but I think the

1. Jonathan Clowes (b.1931), Amis's agent, to whom he and Elizabeth Jane Howard had switched (from Michael Sissons of A.D. Peters) in 1976. Clowes negotiated a deal in which Hutchinson paid Amis an advance for *Jake's Thing* three times that offered by Jonathan Cape. His other clients included Doris Lessing, Len Deighton and David Bellamy.

2. See Amis to Larkin, 27 August 1981, note 3.

material will interest you. Nor will it startle you by its unexpectedness and novelty. Next day: Much more snow, and more yet forecast. Looks as if George G[ale], his lady friend and I won't be able to make it to Swansea for Christmas as planned. So it'll be their place at Sawbridgeworth instead, if we can get that far.

Must tell you the funniest thing said to me for years. Getting into the minicab I put my foot into a pool of water. When I removed sock, driver helpfully put it on heater to dry it. At far end I was struggling quite hard, being fat and wearing thick overcoat, to put still-damp sock back on. Driver said, 'I expect you thought your days of getting dressed in the back of a car were over, didn't you?' As somebody commented, he got his generations right.

Have been having quite a jolly time reading for my short-poems anthology. Some good oddities have emerged, like Samuel Butler (Hudibras)'s shorts, which aren't really poems in a way, more jottings in verse to be perhaps worked into a long poem at some future stage, rather like the way you work yourself.[3] Not having looked at either for years I was mildly surprised at the gulf between W de la Mare and W.H. Davies,[4] de la M quite often pretty good, D bloody terrible, no talent at all. Found a wonderfully damaging quote from Coleridge. (Have to type it as copier in store.) He quotes for the sake of argument a couple of lines he made up:

> Behold yon row of pines, that shorn and bowed
> Bend from the sea-blast, seen at twilight eve.

Comment: 'But with a small alteration of rhythm, the same words would be equally in their place in a book of topography, or in a descriptive tour. The same image will rise into a semblance of poetry if thus conveyed:

> Yon row of bleak and visionary pines,
> By twilight-glimpse discerned, mark! how they flee
> From the fierce sea-blast, all their tresses wild
> Streaming before them.'

3. Samuel Butler (1630–80), poet and satirist, author of *Hudibras* (1663), a popular mock verse-romance.

4. Walter de la Mare (1876–1956) and W.H. Davies (1871–1940), poets.

'Semblance' is right. Poetry is an optional extra, you see. I bet you have no idea how bad his verse dramas are.[5]

Old Philip shook me by picking as a book-of-the-year Sylvia Plath's collected poems. I picked up the vol in a bookshop and was shaken again to find one that wasn't totally bad in every way. But she's no good really, is she? Peter Porter thinks she is, but then he thinks that about Lowell, Pound and Ashbery too. Honestly how can he expect to be taken seriously after that? Note: I discovered the other day that Wyndham Lewis was a *Canadian*. Check. V. funny abt Star Trek.

Love to you both
K.

PS: Yes, Gross has gone to Weid, refugeeing from Murdoch. New ed is his deputy Jeremy Treglown, who seems all right for a youngster of 35.[6] Malamud[7] I've never managed to read, *and I don't suppose I ever will now.*[8]

[TLS: Recipient]

TO PHILIP LARKIN – [LATE DECEMBER 1981]

You can always get me c/o my agents – Jonathan Clowes
19 Jeffrey's Place N.W.1
Pro tem, certainly till 8th January: 25c Gayton Road, London N.W.3.

Dear Philip,

I think this is the last sheet of the posh paper Jane used to use. The Quartette (Hilly, Alistair, their son James and me) are in a furnished

5. Coleridge's lines and commentary are from Chapter 15 of *Biographia Literaria* (1817), entitled 'The specific symptoms of poetic power elucidated in a critical analysis of Shakespeare's Venus and Adonis, and Lucrece'. His verse dramas are *The Fall of Robespierre* (1794), *Osorio* (1797, produced in 1813 as *Remorse*) and a 1799 translation of Schiller's *Wallenstein*.

6. John Gross edited the *TLS* (1974–81) before moving to Weidenfeld (Publishers) Ltd, as editorial consultant (1982). Jeremy Treglown (b. 1946), author and academic, succeeded Gross as Editor of the *TLS* (1982–90). The media magnate Rupert Murdoch (b.1931), Chairman, News International, has owned the *TLS* and other Times publications since 1981.

7. Bernard Malamud (1914–86), American novelist.

8. MS addition.

flat within plain sight of Gard: Ho: Quite soon we move into a small house in Kentish Town, N.W.5, if all goes well. But all may not, because Jane is trying to see that I get *much less than half* of the money for the sale of G Ho: She wants back the cash she got from the sale of her flat in 1964 which she put into the house we had in Maida Vale, or rather she wants the 1981 equivalent of that sum. Cheers. Odd woman. Other bad behaviour too with which I won't weary you. Odd woman.

It was only today that I had a proper look at your peom in the Betj garland,[1] and that's really what set this letter going. (Apologies for silence; well, you know all about MOVING, so please restore communication at the old tempo.) I thought, goodness me, what an unembarrassing poem when it *so easily* could have been the opposite; well no, not easily with you holding the pen. Bloody good, in fact one of your best 'place' pieces. You are a very fine poet, my boy.

Didn't I see you picking old Sylvie, er, Plath's stuff as a bloody book of the year?[2] Or was that Phillip C. Larkins, the racing correspondent? I thought we agreed she was no good years ago. But then I remember you saying you thought she might be no good but she was extraordinary. And there must be something in what you say because I noticed Peter Porter picked it too and was it C.H. Sisson[3] and they ought to knoooooghgh lemme go aaaaaaaghghghgh

Have you tried any of these new fellows like D.M. Thomas and Salman Rushdie and all that?[4] I don't seem to be able to bring myself

---

1. Larkin's contribution to *A Garland for the Laureate: Poems Presented to Sir John Betjeman on His Seventy-Fifth Birthday* (Stratford-upon-Avon: The Celandine Press, 1981) was 'Bridge for the Living', first performed at the City Hall in Hull on 11 April 1981 (see Amis to Larkin, 27 July 1978, note 1). The Betjeman 'Garland', secretly produced in a print run of 350 copies, was where the poem first appeared in print; it is reprinted in *LCP*, pp. 203–4.

2. For Larkin on Plath see *Required Writing*, pp. 278–81, which reprints a 1982 review of Plath's *Collected Poems* (1981) in *Poetry Review*, commissioned by Andrew Motion. Larkin chose the *Collected Poems* as one of his books of the year in the *Observer*, 6 December 1981, p. 25.

3. C.H. Sisson (b.1914), poet, civil servant; at the time Joint Editor, *PN Review* (1976–84).

4. D.M. Thomas (b. 1935), novelist, poet, translator, biographer, had gained recent notoriety for *The White Hotel* (1981); Salman Rushdie (b.1947), novelist, won the Booker Prize for *Midnight's Children* (1981).

to try them.[5] Christopher Hope.[6] I needn't try him, because the fellow in the Daily Tel today quoted some of his best bits, and they were quite sufficient, thank you. I spend most of my time rereading Dick Francis,[7] as I probably said the last half-dozen times I've written. Can't remember anything these days. Didn't I see you going on about him the other day? Did I? Where? What did you say? What?[8] Soon I'll be able to start again on the first DF immediately on finishing the last.

I was delighted to see that that old fool and swine and bore Claud? Claude? can't be bothered to find the paper and check Cockburn was dead.[9] With fellows like that I always hope their last hours were clouded by the thought that they would never see the mass murders they had tenderly and tremulously dreamed of through all the long grey years. Now we only want Roy Jenkins to die of a surfeit of oysters and Shirley Williams to be beaten to death by black teenagers and all will be well. No of course it won't, but we'll have had a few moments of satisfaction. I really hate the SDP. I'm afraid that when coalition time comes they'll spell the end of our dear Maggie.

Not much news, I fear. How could there be? I go to the club and get drunk, or read and get drunk, or watch TV and get drunk. Are you still not drinking? You are mad you know. I wish you a merry Christmas. All the best for 1982 aaoh! Write to me *in the New Year.*

At your age you really must go easy on the bum,

Kingsley

[TLS: Bodleian]

5. In the left margin Amis has written: 'And is it A.N. Wilson? Initials are in again.' A.N. Wilson (b. 1950), novelist, critic, journalist.

6. Christopher Hope (b.1944), South African-born novelist, poet and playwright.

7. Dick Francis (b. 1920), author of thrillers set in the racing world; previously a professional jockey (1948–57) and racing correspondent of the *Sunday Express* (1957–73).

8. I have been unable to trace this review, but see Amis to Larkin, 3, 5 December 1983, note 14.

9. Claud Cockburn (1904–81), left-wing journalist.

Martin Amis, Elizabeth Jane Howard and KA in the walled garden at Gardnor House, Hampstead, *c.* 1978–79.

Philip Larkin and John Betjeman at W.H. Auden's Memorial Service, Christ Church, Oxford. October 1974.

Above Fuzzy snapshot of the pre-wedding lunch of Sargy Mann and Frances Carey at Bertorellis' Restaurant, 31 January 1975. Clockwise: Martin Amis, Colin Howard, Mrs Uniacke, Sargy Mann, Fanny Ward, KA, Terry Raybould (the painter, who spent one night a week at Lemmons when teaching in London) and Elizabeth Jane Howard.

Left 'The Blokes': Sargy Mann and Colin Howard on the way to Sargy's wedding, 31 January 1975.

Wine-tasting. Martin Amis, KA and Christopher Ward.

Two black-and-white photographs cut out of a magazine, folded in a brown envelope marked 'Present', and enclosed with a letter to Philip Larkin, 3 August 1982: 'I'll be thinking of you on your bithrayd you old burag.'

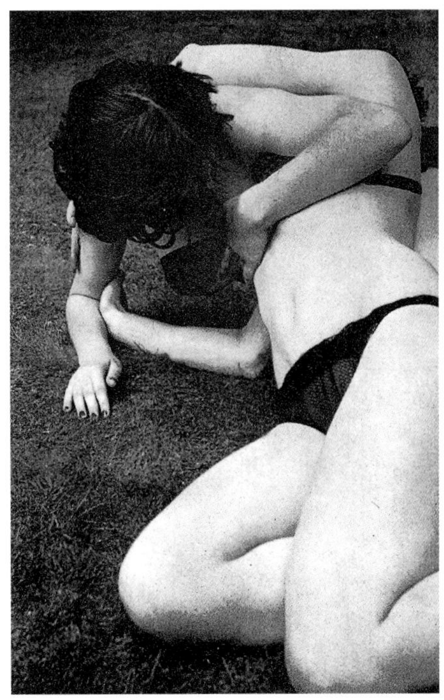

Robert Conquest, Kauai, Hawaii, 1986. 'Christ I couldn't live your sort of life, buggering to and fro all those thousands of miles. And a bloody *beach*. When you needn't. You'll be going to summer camp next' (to Robert Conquest, 7 June 1986).

'Off to the Garrick shortly for my Christmas drunk there. If nothing else kept me in London that place would' (to Philip Larkin, 18 December 1984).

Top Philip Amis and KA, *c.* 1990. 'Your godson is providentially around . . . I think he's the nicest fellow I've ever met' (to Philip Larkin, 5 December 1980).

Below Sally Amis in Ronda, Spain, 1973. 'Sally Myfanwy (pron. muh-*vanwi*) arrived 2.5 a.m. yesterday' (to Philip Larkin, 18 January 1954).

Martin Amis and KA, September 1991. 'My Inner Audience did I think consist chiefly of Larkin and Conquest. More lately I have added Martin' (to Paul Fussell, 27 May 1993).

OPPOSITE
Above Eve Thomas in front of the house at 4 Mary Twill Lane, Mumbles, June 1993. 'Hilly and I have kept up our Welsh links. I go down every summer on a 3-week visit, staying with Stuart and Eve in Mumbles' (to Edward Pell, 18 March 1993).

Below KA, Sally Amis, Hilly, Jaime Boyd (eating apple), Lord Kilmarnock, a friend of Jaime's, Dale Salwak, in London, July 1989. 'I've found, and yesterday installed here, the couple who'll look after me. They are Hilly and her 3rd husband, Lord Kilmarnock. Nay, stare not so' (to Philip Larkin, 27 August 1981).

Hilly and KA, early 1990s.

TO PHILIP LARKIN – 15 FEBRUARY 1982

186 Leighton Road, N.W.5

No you fool it was ICGS in 1946 coming from every other window in St John St & Wellington Sq. Hilly confirms.[1]

Dear Philip,

And here I am writing straight back like a good little sod. The move is at any rate done, though as I write this I'm half surrounded with *full* tea-chests, i.e. still full of books. The conning stealing queer Irishman 'recommended' to put up the shelves by the departing owners hasn't delivered. Quite convenient here, except I have to keep most of my clothes in my study. Not a bad area, no violent thick blacks to speak of, but all pubs full of pop. I can't bear the way there's a drum-beat on the third beat of EVERY SINGLE bar.

My WILL has just arrived for signature. I mean let's be practical no point in getting morbid if you should walk under a bus just a straightforward business matter after all you don't want after all it doesn't mean after all we all MBAAOOOOGHGH Actually it reads quite well until we come to I wish to be cremated and my ashes to be scattered Don't care for that somehow

Ran into Geoffrey Bush[2] yesterday at a party in Hampstead. Hadn't seen him for what, 30 years? Informative though not stunningly revelatory about poor old Bruce. Apparently one of the things that fucked him up was a change in fashion in film music. That and writing film music. V. demoralising, Bush said; the speed you have to work at means you put down the first thing that comes into your head *all the time.* The worst bit was Bruce excusing himself for not writing real music by saying he had to go on writing film music to pay his taxes, and then a fellow said he'd buy him some time and gave him a fat fee in advance

1. MS addition. 'ICGS' is 'I Can't Get Started'; Larkin, in a postcard of 11 February 1982 (in HEHL), denied that this could have been the song Amis was remembering (in some now-lost communication, perhaps the change-of-address card Larkin's postcard was acknowledging).

2. Geoffrey Bush (1920–98), composer and academic; a friend of Bruce Montgomery since 1945.

for a 'cell shit[3] 'cello concerto and Bruce wrote two chords on the spot and, Bush reckons, never another note. His publisher *burnt* one of his works, the orchestral parts, TO MAKE ROOM ON HIS SHELVES FOR NEW STUFF. Bush said writing was always Bruce's second string, priority, etc. Well, that's JUST AS WELL, isn't it?

Been having to look at some mod Yank po recently and by Christ it stinks. John CIARDI Howard NEMEROV J. V. CUNNINGHAM X. J. KENNEDY[4] What's the matter with them? Why can't they talk sense and be natural? Why do they have to go on in a special way all the time? Of course they're all foreigners, aren't they? All right while they were called Longfellow and Dickinson and Whitman. Not *much* FUCKING *GOOD*, mind you, but all right. But then they started being called Sandburg and Schwartz.[5] See?

Did you see that crappy bit about Bob in the Times (2Feb)? More or less said his 2nd wife killed herself after their divorce, yes 20 yrs after. You must have. I've written privately to the editor telling him what a shit he is. Or perhaps merely incompetent.[6]

Yes Jane gave an interview crapping on me in the Standard. I've lost it, also the similar one in the Sunday Express, in which she said I stifled her creative talent by making her run the house.[7] Yes, she never

3. The first 'cello' was truncated by the edge of the page.

4. John Ciardi (1916–86), Howard Nemerov (1920–91), J.V. Cunningham (1911–85) and X.J. Kennedy (b. 1929).

5. Carl Sandburg (1878–1967), Chicago poet, of Swedish immigrant parentage; Delmore Schwartz (1913–66), Brooklyn poet, of Romanian-Jewish parentage. See 'Sacred Cows', in *The Amis Collection*, p. 19, for a related view of recent 'American' novelists: 'Nabokov, in a way peculiar to foreigners, never stops showing off his mastery of the language; his books are jewels a hundred thousand words long. Bellow is a Ukrainian-Canadian, I believe [he was born in Quebec in 1915 of Russian-Jewish parents, though when he was nine the family moved to Chicago]. It is painful to watch him trying to pick his way between the unidiomatic on the one hand and the affected on the other.' See also Jenny Bunn's father in *Take a Girl Like You* (1960), on Patrick Standish's stock: 'He muttered "Schtundisch" to himself whenever Patrick was mentioned . . . it was one of his ways, and happened with almost every new boy-friend: there had been Veelricht and Ullingheim and Lighlunt and Yohanstein and no doubt there would have been Tawmpzohn too if Dick was single' (p. 177).

6. The article of 2 February 1982, entitled 'Suicide Verdict on Ex-Wife', began: 'The divorced wife of Robert Conquest, the American author, killed herself with a large drugs overdose because she never recovered from the break-up of their marriage, an inquest was told today' (p. 4). 'A Correction' was printed three weeks later, on 23 February, pointing out that the break-up occurred in 1962 and that Conquest was British. Amis's private letter to the Editor, Harold Evans, has not survived.

7. See Catherine Olsen, 'Marriage to Kingsley . . . and Why Elizabeth Moved Out', *Evening Standard*, 26 November 1981, p. 19, and 'Mr and Mrs Amis Begin a New Chapter' (no byline), *Sunday Express*, 29 November 1981, p. 11.

did anything but cook, and never cooked* except when we had people, about twice a month. As you remember we had a living-in housekeeper. Oh well. And as I now know the bill-paying dealing-with-accountant side of life takes two hours a month.

Yes a will's all right when you're fore-tea. Not so much fun when you're sicks-tea. I bequeath unto my Literary Executors all my bum,

Kingsley

* *elaborately but not very well*[8]

[TLS: Bodleian]

TO JUDITH (CHAMBERLAIN) LUNA – 2 MARCH 1982

186 Leighton Road N. W. 5

Dear Judith,

Alas, what you and Jackie[1] suspected and I discounted has come to pass. There are not enough good short poems after all. We needed about 800 and there are no more than 300. According to me. James thinks different. He has a lot of poems he wants to put in of which the most I can say is that I have no serious objection to them individually. (He has a lot more poems I could not allow in any book with my name on it.) So the best I can look forward to is an anthology of 300 poems I like and 500 I don't care about either way – if we can find as many, which I don't think we could. So I'm bowing out.

I propose keeping the money I've been paid and turning over to James the fruits of my labours. They, the fruits, are not immense but there were quite a few sans-fruits labours and I can hardly be said to have cleaned up.[2]

Sorry about this. James will be in touch with you shortly.

8. MS addition.

1. Jacqueline Simms.
2. 'The OUP were very cross with me, I think with some reason: I had received payment (which they did not demand back) to do a job, and although I had got through a good deal of useful work I had not completed that job' (*Memoirs*, p. 112). The book finally came out in 1985, under the editorship of Michie and P.J. Kavanagh.

I know you're called something else now but I can't remember what it is.[3] No discourtesy intended.

Yours,
Kingsley

[TLS: OUP]

TO PHILIP LARKIN – 22 MARCH 1982

Temporary address: Kinnell Ward, Royal Free Hospital NW3

Dear Philip,

No, not yet. I broke my right tibia standing up, trying to avoid an alcoholic fall.[1] Same thing, really. 'Unusual *spiral* fracture,' said the sawbones appreciatively. It's not too bad here, considering, but by the time you've finished considering there isn't much room for anything else. You've had all this, of course, but perhaps not with my thing of not being able to walk a step, so you have to find a nurse with an invalid-chair to go 10 yards for a crap. Much interesting crap-crisis material for another time. Course, all hospitals are the same hospital. The nurses are daughters of the gods, beautiful, kind, wise. Swifter they seem in their stay than in their flight. There's an old woman here who sings all day. Wordless maunderings based on Camptown Races, Lincolnshire P[2] etc. Yes, all day. She's French, actually. Do you remember about Kinnell or Kinell? Used to be (milite) the more proper of a pair, the other being Kinarsoles.[3] Got through a lot of reading here. Or rather *not* got through a lot. *Despair*, by Vladimir Nabokov.[4] ƆUNT. That chap is an absolute shibboleth, isn't he? What do you think of Nabokov? Well – BANG!! He's what's wrong with half of US wirtn, – there are

3. Judith Chamberlain became Judith Luna in 1981.

1. On 10 March; see Amis to Conquest, 30 March 1982.
2. 'Lincolnshire Poacher'.
3. 'Milite' (Latin) means 'in military parlance'; the full (or less proper) version of 'Kinnell' or 'Kinell' is 'Fuckin'ell', to go with 'Fuckin' arsoles'; see also the related marching song, one line of which runs 'Arsehole, arsole, a soldier of the King'.
4. *Despair* (1936); Nabokov's dates are 1899–1977. For Amis's views on American writers, Nabokov included, see 'Sacred Cows', in *The Amis Collection*, pp. 17–19.

other things wrong with the other half – and has fucked up a lot of fools here, plus, or including as you might wish to say, my little Martin. I don't know about you but I can bear anything, even stream of conc., better than realising there's a narrator here whom I can't trust. Eh?

SUDDENLY AT HIS HOME

Just when he'd got the staff he needed –
Just when he'd found this splendid woman –
Just when he'd written all the music –
  What a rotten time to go.
And when you come across a good one
  Please be sure to let me know.

Any suggestions?[5] including Stuff it. This sort of thing ought to be open to the poet's inner circle.

Had got several things down to write to you about but of course have left that at home. One thing I know was the destruction of art in the course of 'bringing it to the people', all that stuff on telly we in London see so much of – you know, though: Part I, Black Action People's Theatre Workshop; Part II, George Herbert 350 years on; Part III, Hullaballoo Incorporated. Nichol Smith,[6] F.R. Leavis, Melvyn Bragg. Must get on with reading Jane's new novel,[7] a proof of which arrived from her today. Odd, what? It must be meant to fuck me up in some way, but I haven't yet divined what. pto

For the next three months you mustn't put any weight on your bum,

Kingsley

I can imagine the scene (and 'scene' is right) where she tells her girl-chum she's sent me the proof. 'But why?' says g-c. 'Oh . . . he saw quite a lot of the early chapters before we . . .' 'You mean he took an interest in them?' 'Oh yes,' – a lot of work with eyes and hands here, 'things could be . . . quite good even . . . late on. He isn't the most . . . outgoing of men but he . . . really cares about . . . art. That's one of the things

5. Larkin, in a letter of 25 March 1982 (in HEHL), says the poem 'has a point and makes it, and a good, maybe the only, point too. Would deferentially recommend a stronger rhyme than woman/good one – needs pulling together more. The last line looks a bit wordily formal – "Be a pal and let me know" would be simpler.'

6. David Nichol Smith, a textual editor and commentator.

7. *Getting it Right* (1982); it won the *Yorkshire Post* Novel of the Year Award.

I've always respected about him,' – eyelids batting fast here – 'and I hope he knows it. Because if he doesn't it's . . . too late to . . .' 'You know, darling,' says g-c to husband later, 'poor old Jane has taken that Kingsley business really hard. It's such a pity in a way that she had to leave him.' 'Had to?' says the husband. 'Darling, don't be silly, of course she had to.' 'How do we know that?' 'Darling she *did*, didn't she? That shows she had to.' 'Oh, I see,' says husband, and goes off to drink and laugh with male friends.

Stitches out day after tomorrow (Friday). Ay, but what of that?

[ALS: Bodleian]

TO ROBERT CONQUEST – 30 MARCH, 3 APRIL 1982

Royal Free Hospital, Hampstead

Dear Bob,

Excuse unwontedly-long-even-for-me silence. Have been, indeed still am, in Royal Free Hospital, Hampstead, with broken leg (tibia and fibula). (10th March) A drunken fall? Well yes, even if what I did was to break them *standing up*, trying to avoid a fall which I would have done much better to give in to. Anyway, 3 weeks' helplessness with more in prospect but alleviated by home circs. and family attentions. Impossible to work – or what I really mean is, too much trouble to fix it up for what was always going to be a shortish stay. Increased my respect for Henley, who you remember edited whatever it was from was it St George's?[1] There'll be an article one day called something like 'Kingers' Mini-Pinfold'[2] (or should it be Kingers's? Advice needed),

1. For W.E. Henley see Amis to Larkin, 4 November 1956, note 9. Henley edited poets, anthologies of poets, literary magazines, and a seven-volume dictionary of slang. Amis may be thinking of the period early in Henley's life in which he was hospitalised for tubercular arthritis and had his foot amputated. This was in 1873 at the Royal Edinburgh Infirmary (not St George's), and resulted in a sequence of poems, *Hospital Sketches* (1875), which record his experiences.

2. An allusion to Evelyn Waugh's thinly disguised autobiographical novel *The Ordeal of Gilbert Pinfold* (1957), recounting an episode of paranoid delusions and hallucinations (see also 'A Peep Round the Twist', the last chapter of *Memoirs*, pp. 328–36).

about the mild hallucinations I suffered when I first came in here: nothing spectacular, just a few voices and non-existent cats. Partly I think caused by cutting off drink completely after, what, 40 years? No drinks since either, and no strain at all – jolly good, no chemical dependence at least, but the testing time – 12.30 in the Garrick bar – has yet to come.

You'll be greatly flattered (at least I would be in your shoes) to know that the two books I snatched as the ambulance bore me off were the complete Father Brown stories and old *Moab*. Ponderings on the latter were given added force by having recently watched the bloody old Sunday night culture-show on ITV – Part I, the Unbelievably Banal Black People's Theatre Action Group Workshop in association with the World's Worst West Indian Actors' Collective; Part II, a Very Smug Lezzie Yank 'Performance Artist' (this means using electronic gear to make yourself sound and look odd on a TV screen). Your host, Melvyn Bragg. Next week, Beethoven. We are getting beyond Moab. After Alf Shagpen *and* Dr. A. Shagpen D.Litt comes popular Freddie Shagpen with the news that art can be fun, art *is* fun, and it's only élitists, Tories, pedants and serious artists who say different. With your knowledge of the O.T. etc. you ought to be able to run us up a successor to the Philistines and Moabites. People who liked dancing and festivities mixed up with their pieties. Get working on it.

Later: it does rather look as if I'll be out tomorrow tho' fingers crossed. All agog to get down to my novel, the more so since, oddly I thought and still think, Jane sent me a proof of her latest[3] a couple of, well, about a week ago (time goes unbelievably slowly in hosp, as you must know). I thought it was quite good, but at the same time not-much-good enough to encourage me a good deal to get on with mine. (The cynical Martin said in answer to this that reading *any* contemporary novel was an encouragement of that sort.) Anyway, the thing was accompanied by a friendly note, sorry to hear of your accident, rather than the pissed-again jeer which would have been more honest, do read it to see what happened to Gavin – the hero whom I remembered from pp 1–100 or so. Anyway, I thought, *why*? How can she hope to fuck me up in this way? Or look good to herself? – the only other possibility. No answer. *Then* Pat Kav[anagh] says Seen Jane's interview in the S Tel? No, I groaned. Oh, she says, it's about her not being really suited

3. *Getting it Right.*

to a life alone, she thinks she might have made a mistake in leaving you. She wants to be friends with you, and that's why she sent you the book. – Mind you, I haven't seen the cutting yet – but *Christ!!* Sorry about that, Kingers; let's have a nice chat and forget it, or perhaps I could move in with you and Hilly. Talk about women = the USSR. We regret the damage done to your homeland and the infliction of numerous casualties. We are now satisfied that the decision to rectify our common frontier was taken in error. Those responsible for it have been punished. There being no longer any cause for friction between our two peoples, we look forward to an era of common understanding and increased prosperity on a co-operative basis.

Jenkins won that seat, as you saw.[4] But I think we'll be all right. It'll dwindle away by next year. Thanks for great Hawaii card. Love to Liddie.

Cheers
K.

3rd April: Out and working. Novel picking up speed.[5] Bloody funny the Falkland Is. fandango[6] with all the Lefties turning Churchillian about our duties to our Kinsmen in far-off places, etc.

[ALS: Recipient]

TO PHILIP LARKIN – 12 MAY 1982

186 Leighton Road, Kentish Town, London, N.W.5

Dear Philip,

This has been a big day for me, having my first shit in an orthodox shithouse for 9 weeks. Climbed the stairs with my crutches you see. Previously I have been using a Kermode,[1] which is fine for me but not

4. On 25 March, Roy Jenkins, running as an SDP/Liberal Alliance candidate, won a by-election from the Conservatives at Glasgow Hillhead in Scotland.

5. *Stanley and the Women* (1984).

6. Argentine troops invaded the Falkland Islands on 2 April 1982, and Britain immediately cut off diplomatic relations.

1. For Frank Kermode see Amis to John Wain, 23 April 1954, note 3.

so fine for Hilly to empty. By God that's a great photo of us 3 and ole AP in the you book.[2] Like a row of bloody film stars we were. I'll see you at the do on Mon week.[3] Hope it's better than the AP one this last Mon.[4] I was on the wagon, so no doubt behaved rather oddly. Anyway everything I said to P sent him dashing across the room to speak to someone else. Hilly has a nice little piece about you in the forthcoming Harpers-Queen,[5] yeh, seriously. No embarrassments I warrant you.

Been funny with broken leg. Not just the Kermode but never going out (until Mon) or even leaving the room, a life consisting entirely of working and watching TV. Of course you don't get much work done, words on paper that is, because you spend too much time at it. Essential to idle and get pissed half the time to accumulate energy etc. for when you do work. Don't suppose you find that because you write a line a month and the rest of the time just push paper round the libroooghghgh I shouldn't retire if I were you. Hard for me to say, of course. As you can imagine, Phil, all that side of life is a complete closed book to we fortunates or unfortunates who are self-emploo Been reading the life of ole Bob Graves. Funny chap. Always having rows with chaps. Fond of THL, but couldn't bear DEL.[6] Good at not liking any other poets – well, you'll see my bit on Sun.[7] Did you realise L Riding[8] was a Yank Yid etc.? You know if you're a connoisseur of PIss piss PISS, it's worth your while to look up just the quotes from her in the RG book. They're such PISS that you can't make out even approximately whag bag what she's saying. I started writing a sentence going something like 'She had very pissy ideas about' and had to scrap it because I couldn't see what they were about, except *feminism*. As for that . . . Well, of course, she was a joooo, and a yangck, and a womb 'un, so we must make allowances BEFORE WE CUT HER ARMS AND LEGS OFF.

2. *Larkin at Sixty* (1982). For the photograph of Amis, Larkin, Hilly and Powell see plates section.

3. The launch party for *Larkin at Sixty*, 24 May 1982.

4. A launch party for *The Strangers All are Gone*, volume 4 of Anthony Powell's memoirs.

5. Hilly Kilmarnock, 'Poetry: A Personal Memoir of Philip Larkin in his Twenties', *Harpers and Queen*, June 1982, p. 204.

6. T. E. Lawrence, 'Lawrence of Arabia' (1888–1935), writer and military hero; 'DEL' is D.H. Lawrence.

7. Amis's review of Martin Seymour-Smith, *Robert Graves: His Life and Work* (1982), and Paul O'Prey, ed., *In Broken Images: Selected Letters of Robert Graves*, in *Observer*, 16 June 1982, is reprinted in *The Amis Collection*, pp. 201–3.

8. Laura Riding (1901–91), American poet, short-story writer and critic; lived and worked in collaboration with Robert Graves on Majorca from 1929–36.

Also been reading – nah, it's all this reviewing, not *reading* – the supplemented Faber Bk of Mod Vse by that fucking fool but very nice fellow Peter Porter. You're modern, I see, along with Ted HUGHES and Sylvia PLATH and John ASHBERY jesus christ et al. but fortunately not Al ha-ha.[9] But you're not really, are you? I think he, PP, is just cravenly bowing to you being all the rage. So don't worry. The book reminded me that among the piss-merchants you tried to palm off on me and others at Oxford was old GMH.[10] You must be over that now, eh? I mean you don't *still* think he's GOOD, do you? I think hé is fúll óf piss and, O, shít.

I have a mini Mortimer story[11] for you but I think I told it you one time when I was sober and so have forgotten. Remind me.

It is not the BBC's role just to echo the Government's bum,

Kingsley

Julian Barnes is all right but mad. Wouldn't surprise me if he went for his missis with a hatchet any day.[12]

[TLS: Bodleian]

TO ROBERT CONQUEST – 12 MAY 1982

186 Leighton Road, London, N.W.5

Dear ole Bob,

Your last came today and shamed me into answering. Had my first day out for 9 weeks on Monday, no great bacchanalia, Tony P's party for last memoirs.[1] Was and am still on wagon and reckon this made me behave very oddly or crappily because every time I said anything to him he rushed off. Glad I was TT in a way because the drink was so scurvy that I'm sure I should have been in a vile temper if I'd been

9. 'Al' is Al Alvarez, who championed the works of Plath, Hughes, Robert Lowell and other poets of emotional breakdown and extremism.

10. Gerard Manley Hopkins.

11. John Mortimer (b.1923), novelist, dramatist and barrister.

12. MS addition.

1. *The Strangers All are Gone* (1982).

on it. First shithouse shit today and it may not sound much to you but boy it meant a lot to me. Cast goes 3 weeks tomorrow.

Jane's settlement is unsettled still but I can't summon the energy. Did I tell you there was a 3rd press interview in which she said she'd sacrificed her career as a writer to bring up my kids? Going by the dates of her books that must have been 1972–80. The kids were 24, 23 and 18 in 1972.[2] But there's no need to go on. Not to change the subject – have just reviewed old Graves's life and letters (2 books) with a lot about Laura Riding of course. I expect you knew she was née Reichenthal but it was news to me. By God there was someone who was all woman. He liked rows and dramas but was nothing to her. But her real distinction was as a piss-talker. Such piss you can't make it out. This is actually quite rare. I mean with most piss you can say to yourself, Oh, she thinks we ought to surrender to Russia, or, Oh, she thinks parents ought to let chaps fuck their young children, etc. With LR, not a bloody bit of it. 'There is a sense of life so real that it becomes the sense of something more real than life.' See? I promise you I had a half-sentence ready saying something like 'She had very pissy views on' and then went through trying to find out what her views were *about*. No go. Except – guess – she was detectably a feminist. Graves stuck it for twelve years and was only fucking her for a couple (I'd guess a few weeks). But of course though a bloody good poet (better than ever on a look-through for the piece) G has always been a fucking fool. One marvellous crack of his, I can't make out whether he meant it because it's in a letter to Eddie Marsh[3] when 19, about Rupert Brooke, 'What a torture his sensitiveness must always be for him, poor fellow!' Sounds meant but he was v.naive then. Also good when he ticks Sassoon off for being a bloody misery about the war.

Have missed you particularly over the last weeks with all the Falklands crap. Also missed being in the club and hearing sturdy patriotic stuff, only reading and hearing fools and knaves. That sodding fool

2. Amis and Elizabeth Jane Howard began living together in 1963. The two boys, aged seventeen and sixteen, began living with them in 1965 (though Philip moved out in 1966, after what Martin calls 'a huge fight about drugs' (personal communication, 22 January 1999)). Sally, aged eleven, lived with her mother, but visited during the holidays. Howard published three novels before 1963 (her first appeared in 1950) and four in the seventeen years from 1963 to 1980, the period she lived with Amis and his children. She has since published another seven novels.

3. Sir Edward Marsh (1872–1953), classical scholar, poet, patron of the arts and eminent civil servant; friend and executor of Rupert Brooke, editing his *Collected Poems* in 1918.

Ferdy Mount[4] in the Spec – you saw? – calling for an unconditional cease-fire before trooping off to advise Mrs T at no. 10. All the cunts talking about we-never-paid-the-place-much-heed-before and serve-us-right-for-selling-them-arms and what-about-Diego-Garcia.[5] I enclose a sample. Sad, really. It's good he thinks he's invented the idea about hubris and nemesis. You see there's a level below the autodidacts [–] the adidacts. Only George [Gale] and Perry [Worsthorne] are holding firm on the issue. Now we have the BBC being 'objective', as they were between the rioters and the police, IRA and the security forces, etc.

Occurs to me a chap should do a thing on [racial] prejudice as seen e.g. among police. The word is used to cover two different situations. You, a householder in a white suburb, are prejudiced against blacks. You have never had to deal with one, but what you read and hear prejudices you and when you finally do meet one you treat him badly. But what if you have had much experience and as a result have slowly but firmly formed views unfavourable to blacks? Can there be prejudice based on experience? Illegal to speculate, I shouldn't wonder. [. . .]

Have quite an impressive moustache after all these weeks but I doubt whether the Garrick will let me keep it. Philip and Martin v. anti. Mrs Uniacke, an excellent witness, says it suits me and makes me look 'distinguished'. Your and Liddie's votes will carry much weight.

Jolly good luck. See you soon. Yes I'll be around for foreseeable future. Love to shapely Dr. C.[6]

Cheers
K

[TLS: Recipient]

4. Ferdinand Mount (b.1939), journalist, political commentator, novelist; Head, Prime Minister's Policy Unit (1982–83); Editor, *TLS* (1991–).

5. A dependency of Mauritius until 1965, when it became part of the newly created British Indian Ocean Territory. In the late 1970s, with British agreement, it was allowed to develop as a US military base for air and naval support.

6. MS addition. Elizabeth Conquest had recently completed a PhD in English at the University of Southern California.

TO THE EDITOR, *DAILY TELEGRAPH* – 22 MAY 1982

SIR – Dr Andrew Worton-Steward (May 17)[1] may like to know that I have heard many works of modern music broadcast by the BBC, or rather the first couple of minutes of these. My overwhelming impression is that they are not designed to be enjoyed.

It is interesting in this connection that Dr Worton-Steward speaks well of Schoenberg,[2] who declared in his essay, "Style and Idea":

> I believe that a real composer writes for no other purpose than to please himself. Those who compose because they want to please others and have audiences in mind are not real artists.

No wonder his music is so hard to listen to.

KINGSLEY AMIS
London, WC2

TO PHILIP LARKIN – 3 AUGUST 1982

186 Leighton Road, Kentish Town, London, N.W.5

Dear Philip,

So this is your birthday letter – boyo. Well, it's not EVERY DAY you're sixty is it. I found that 'when it came' I'd been thinking about it so much I hardly bothered. And of course yours is all over bar the shiting. What he would try to be from then on was a decent old buffer. Well of course a lot of things make sense now that didn't at the time. Hurtful things. Sad things, lonely things look quite different from INSIDE THE LAVATORY PAN. I hope you'll see a bit of life on the day. Ah, but where is life to be foughghgh Have a drink and think of me on the perishing wagon. Not much *going on* on the X-rays, drawled

1. Worton-Steward, a Tutor in Music at the Open University, had written a letter to the *Daily Telegraph* deploring Amis's narrow tastes in classical music (as related in a 'Peterborough' column, 7 May 1982).

2. Worton-Steward had written: 'It would seem to be a sorry state of affairs when someone of the stature of Mr Kingsley Amis cannot relate to the music of Debussy . . . If Debussy is modern what hope is there for Schoenberg and his school?'

the young doctor. How long? Well, two years would be quite . . . *normal.* Nothing . . . out of the *way*. And of course there's always . . . a *bone-graft.* Nah, I'm fooling really. I'm writing this by hand because I'm confined to my chair for a few days with a minor infection of my bad leg, which went purple and glossy and marbled like old end-papers and twice the size because I'd scratched it because it itched A LOT. On diuretics for the moment which make me piss like a man possessed and make me feel rather a good chap for working at all. Restart my new novel tomorrow. Did I tell you I'd junked my old new novel?[1] Yes, it's about a queer, so that will make everybody think I am a queer, and I don't want them to do that, do you see, so I've stopped at p. 130. Pity, really. Should have realised before. The new new one is about a chap with a nasty wife. At the beginning he thinks she's a nice wife, but then he finds out she's really a nasty wife all the time. She's a writer, but *he's not* you see.[2] Ha ha ha ha ha ha. Of course it's not thinking of the characters but thinking of what they do in their lives, as you said.

It will be 21 weeks tomorrow since I tasted strong drink. The differences are really negligible, apart from so far not falling over and breaking my leg. Not pouring with sweat at the least exertion or room warmer than 65° F, true. Not – not what? Can't think of any other nots. Remembering what I've been reading last thing, yes. Confidently signing my name at any hour, yes. And that's it. Not getting hangovers – at least not feeling shitty on waking? No. Concentrating better? No. Remembering better in general? *No.* Oh yes, eating a lot and being fat because of that instead of because of drinking. Cheers a lot. Of course it's not the booze you miss, you know. Not the booze as such. No no, it's *getting drunk* and *being drunk*, and *going on* being drunk and getting drunk *again.* I can't think how I'll manage when I go back on it. On ordinary days I was having fuck-all till 7.30 or 7.45, and it bloody near killed me *every evening*, waiting till then I mean. Don't know what I'll do when the gin bottle suddenly becomes a legitimate target again. But

---

1. 'Difficulties with Girls', begun in 1981, after Amis abandoned *Stanley and the Women* (eventually published in 1984), to which he was now returning.

2. This synopsis does not, in its details, fit *Stanley and the Women.* Stanley Duke, the novel's eponymous hero, is the advertising manager of a daily newspaper. He has had two wives, neither of whom is a writer: ex-wife Noel is an actress; current wife Susan is assistant literary editor of another newspaper. Stanley does, though, find out that his current wife was 'really a nasty wife all the time'.

I can fucking well guess. It might go either way, I suppose, feeling much better or much worse with a liver that knows nothing of alcohol. Well, I shall find out.[3]

It was a great letter of yours dalling.[4] Cleo B.[5] my oath. I must get that. Also Georgia bo,[6] though I have it on a worn tape. God, do I not know and love that little yelp as you call it. Makes me gasp and stare every time, or rather pant and cry. Tiny concentrated fragment of heartrending joy as heard in all 1st. class jazz. I have a new needle at last and promise myself a play-through of all the old favs. Predict that old Pops B.[7] will impress me most in the end. Nobody carries you away like him. Also think (as must have said) that O'N S[8] bears the palm as singer. Mad that until recently I thought Sweet P better than Viper M.[9] Pity those W.L. Smith/Newton[10] sides aren't better. Is it Buster B that holds them back?[11]

All in all I thought you did deservedly well out of that not v. good book plus TV progs. Made people like Ted Hughes and Peter Porter and John Ashbery look like cunts. I expect we all did write about ourselves a bit instead of you and of course you can trust an egotist to notice the moment the topic under discussion shifts away from himaaghgh

Bought *Fen Country*[12] the other day and read it at a sitting with incredulous boredom. What went wrong with that silly old sod? Talking of such, Bob was here. By God he's the same if anyone ever was. A sort

3. An allusion to the last line of Larkin's poem 'The Old Fools' (1974), about the symptoms of senile dementia and other ageing processes: 'Well,/We shall find out.'

4. See Larkin to Amis, 26 June 1982 (in HEHL), abridged in *LL*, pp. 676–8. Amis goes on in succeeding sentences to refer to the following passage from the unabridged letter: 'just bought a record called "Kings and Queens of the Ivories", including Cleo Brown's B-W, four sodding good Meade Lux's, Pete Johnson et al. And "Louis the Sideman" (taking the collection?) with Georgia Bo-Bo and Drop that Sack, never easy to find in microgroove. I love that little yelp he gives at the end of the first line of the second vocal chorus ("ever'body does the bo-boo").'

5. Cleo(patra) Brown.

6. 'Georgia Bo Bo' (see note 3 above).

7. Sidney Bechet.

8. O'Neill Spencer.

9. 'Sweet Patootie' and 'Viper Mad', on the original 1938 recording by Sidney 'Pops' Bechet, with Noble Sissle's Swingsters, vocals by O'Neill Spencer.

10. Willie ('the Lion') Smith (1897–1973), pianist and composer; Frankie Newton (1906–54), trumpeter.

11. Buster Bailey.

12. Edmund Crispin (Bruce Montgomery), *Fen Country: Twenty-six Stories* (1979), with a foreword by Philip Larkin.

of advertisement for life. At least you must admit we produced Robert Conquest.

Christ, intended to stop there but remembered something about horse-faced dwarf. (It is very wrong of you to call him that – *quite inaccurate* and *off-key* to start with – and makes me laugh no end.) No, nothing really, just they interviewed Bob and me about him for TV, and I was jolly nice about him, but it did suddenly strike me how fed up I was about all those real people and real incidents he's put in his books. I thought you were meant to *make them up*, you know, like a novelist. It's funny that me not knowing any of the people he knows means the books must seem better to me than they can do to any of his mates. I mean I'm not distracted by wondering who all the characters 'really' are. You'd have liked LJ less, I imagine, if you'd kept saying to yourself, 'Professor Welch – is he Lascelles Abercrombie[13] or Osbert Sitwell?[14] But that madrigal stuff must be taken from Middleton Murry?[15] If you get what Ah mean. That business of his writing to me about my ref. to him has puzzled me from that day to this. I *don't believe* the story about his curiosity, tagging me as a bright new shag and wanting to see if he was right. I think he thought, 'Huh, 48 in December, not getting any younger, ah, here's a new shag who seems to like me, better get his support right away.' Eh? Oh, and amazing in its way – the TV producer told me (what you may well have heard) that AP has a novella on the stocks: subject, a famous writer who has a telly prog made abt him*. I fucking ask you! Couldn't he at least make it a famous art historian or a biography? Can't he make *anything* up? Think yourself fortunate that LJ isn't all about you and Hilly and C. Tosswill and Ruth and Dennis Groves and James Bartley and Xt knows who. What did ya think of those mem-wahz[16] any road? He hasn't got a v. reliable sense of what makes a story, has he? They tend to stop before the punch-line a good deal. But he's about all we've got you know, as a novelist I mean. Have you actually tried to *read* Clive Sinclair[17] and Ian MacEwen

13. Lascelles Abercrombie (1881–1938), poet, critic, man of letters, taught English at Liverpool, Leeds and Oxford.

14. Osbert Sitwell (1892–1969), poet, prose writer, man of letters; brother of Edith and Sacheverell Sitwell.

15. John Middleton Murry (1889–1957), critic.

16. Anthony Powell, *The Strangers All are Gone* (1982)

17. Clive Sinclair (b. 1948), novelist.

(mcewan?)[18] and Angela Carter[19] and M**t** *m**? Roll on is all I can say boyo. Fucking roll on.

I'll be thinking of you on your bithrayd you old burag, and wishing you all you wish yourself.[20] Trouble is these days half of what you wish yrself would smite you down in a twinkling. But it's good to have passed the age before which you could have a justifiable grouse about dying at, if you follow me.

Any undue strain on that leg and you'll be back to square bum

Kingsley

* and according to this chap it's mostly done already!!!!!!!![21]

[ALS: Bodleian]

TO ROBERT CONQUEST – 9 NOVEMBER 1982

186 Leighton Road, N.W.5

Dear Bob,

Forgive enormous delay. No excuse, just being frighteningly behind with work no book out this year and none ready for next so far.[1] Still

18. Ian McEwan (b. 1948), novelist and short-story writer.

19. Angela Carter (1940–92), novelist and essayist.

20. Enclosed with this letter was a brown envelope marked 'Present' inside which Amis had folded two cut-out pages of black-and-white soft-porn photographs (see plates section). These photographs might almost have come from *Titter 7* or *Twosome 3*, from *Difficulties with Girls* (1988), p. 83:

> He went and unlocked his brief-case and settled down for a short session with *Titter 7* and *Twosome 3*. Good taste, self-respect and fear kept Patrick away from hard-stuff joints in Soho, and the magazines in front of him stayed on the inner edge of the law in leaving some features unshown. He felt no constraint, finding plenty in what was visible to arouse his delight and wonder. So what, he tried to imagine the dark one saying, who do you think you are, from the one in the straw hat on the swing. No, they stayed as they were, wise, compassionate, silent and with enormous breasts.

21. The resulting book was *O, How the Wheel Becomes It!* (1983); see Amis to Larkin, 9 March 1983.

---

1. The four years between *Russian Hide-and-Seek* (1980) and *Stanley and the Women*

only one-eighth done, but at this rate it'll be June before you get a letter. Also this morning two lines popped into my head for you to work from:

The muezzin is a-calling from the minaret afar,
'Fuck you off, you Russian soldier, fuck you off from Kandahar!'[2]

Not much news. All the wets are horrified that Mrs T has at last got hold of some people who agree with her, though why she hasn't got hold of you still beats me. Perhaps she will any moment. They (the wets) talk hypocritically about the authority of Parliament being eroded, etc. You probably saw she had old Philip to dinner recently along with a crowd assembled by Hugh Thomas[3] – actually his dinner, sorry. I wrote to warn him H. T. was a pompous buffoon, but he evidently went just the same. The latest Lefty idea is that Mrs T's Falklands activities set Begin going in Lebanon (see that bugger E.P. Thompson[4] on TV last night, complaining there's no free speech in England). The reporting of the Beirut massacre,[5] which I'm sure most people here think as a result was actually performed by the Israelis, was typical. Especially – wouldn't you know? – the Observer. I looked at its front page for a couple of minutes that day before dashing up to shit and thought, Oh God, they've[6] really done it this time (having supported them up to then). Only later saw the vile deceit – the headline didn't name the perpetrators, the report started by naming two authorities on Middle Eastern affairs who were jolly sure the Israelis had done it – they were Yasser Arafat and the PLO's man in New York. In the second column it said that other chaps were saying the Christian militia might have done it. I think roughly that no Israeli officer could have been expected to refuse the Xtns passage and thereby risk his men's lives to

(1984) was the longest gap between novels in Amis's career. Conquest's letters of 1983 several times express concern about the progress of the novel.

2. A parody of Kipling's 'Mandalay', from *Barrack-Room Ballads* (1892): 'For the wind is in the palm-trees, an' the temple-bells they say:/"Come you back, you British soldier; come you back to Mandalay!"'

3. Hugh Thomas (b. 1931), historian; Chairman, Centre for Policy Studies (1979–90); created Life Peer (1981).

4. By 'set Begin going', Amis means caused him to send Israeli forces into Lebanon on 6 June 1982; the Israelis later clashed with Syrian forces in the south, and demanded the surrender of PLO guerrillas in West Beirut. E.P. Thompson (1924–93), historian; supporter of CND (Campaign for Nuclear Disarmament) and other left-wing causes.

5. On 18 September 1982 over eight hundred Palestinians were killed when Christian Phalangist militiamen entered West Beirut refugee camps.

6. Amis has inserted an asterisk here and typed 'i.e. the Israelis' in the left margin.

hold up what just might have been going to be a massacre of Palestinians. But I'd love to have your views on it. End of politics – except to note that Geo G[ale] has stepped, or been pushed, down as leader-writer of the D Express because the owner wants the line to be wetter.[7] Oh, and be sure to tell Reagan to fuck off about the Falklands.[8]

Wish I had some funny bits to tell you, but my life though contented enough is v. humdrum – write novel, write on booze for D Express,[9] go to Garrick. Had lunch today with Terry Kilmartin and Blake Morrison, now his asst, and remarkably unpissy considering he's a youngster, and an intellectual, and from up North. At the Caprice, now reconstituted but a shadow of its former self. Thank Christ, really. They talked with slightly overdone respect of Philip and of his impending, hostile, review, of BM's and Andrew Motion's anthology of young/ish Brit poets in Penguin.[10] I did it for the Standard and surprised them and myself by giving it a good time. Heaney had one poem good enough to make one annoyed he doesn't do that sort of thing all the time – you know what I mean. James Fenton, who admittedly you can't make head or tail of half the time. That's because he's queer, you see. You must never give yourself away about anything. I bet you could explain a lot of Auden's obscurity in the same way. A Northern Mick called Michael Longley[11] I thought was quite good too.

I see you haven't yet talked the Yanks out of supplying arms to the IRA. Of course they, all Yanks, not just the Irish-descended ones, are tremendously anti-British, more specifically anti-English though of course they don't understand the difference. They like the Scots, v. Scotty in 'Star Trek' and the Campbells get into that terrible 'Tenement Symphony' in 'The Big Store'[12] alongside the Cohns and the [fucking][13]

7. The newspaper was not doing well at the time, and Gale's views were notoriously gruff, abrasive and iconoclastic. The Chairman (1977–85) and Chief Executive (1977–83) of Express Newspapers plc in 1982 was Lord Matthews (b. 1913), who was also Deputy Chairman, Trafalgar House (1973–85).

8. On 4 November 1982 the United States had voted in favour of a non-binding United Nations Resolution calling for Argentina and Britain to negotiate a peaceful solution to the sovereignty dispute over the Falkland Islands. Britain and the Commonwealth countries opposed the Resolution.

9. A weekly column, from which came the second of his three books on drink, *Every Day Drinking* (1983).

10. Andrew Motion and Blake Morrison, eds, *The Penguin Book of Contemporary British Poetry* (Harmondsworth: Penguin, 1982).

11. (b. 1939).

12. The 1941 Marx Brothers movie.

13. Amis's square brackets.

Kellys, the Shagbags and Vermicellis or whatever, but not the Digby-Featherstonehaughs. One thing I suddenly realised the other day I didn't believe is the one about the vast majority of Irish Catholics disapproving of the IRA. I'd say it was a weakish minority, wouldn't you?

Sorry to creep back to politics – I must start a notebook of Funny Things to Tell Bob – but the bloody Peace (ha-ha) Movement is getting me down. Bernard [Levin] has a good piece about it in today's Times, pointing out that its bloody argument is, Nuclear war would be terrible, *therefore* we must disarm. But I expect you see it regularly. It's good to have him back, which sort of shows how v. crappy the paper has become. I glanced at a piece in it the other month and thought, ah, this is more the sort of thing we expect of The T, who wrote it? It was by Solzhenitsyn. Oh yes, that bugger Fred Emery[14] got elected to the Gk [Garrick Club] the other day, though was quite a hearteningly energetic effort to keep him out. Philip in usual form. Writes, 'Can't think of anything but being old, then very old, then dead. If you're lucky, that is. May be just old, then dead, of course.' Macmillan have cheatingly advertised Wm Cooper's 'Scenes from Metropolitan Life' with 'A classic – K. Amis, Observer'. Ah, but I said that about 'Scenes from *Provincial* Life'. Don't know what one's rights are. The PLR[15] Forms have gone out to writers. You have to fill in the ISBN (is it?) number of every *impression* of every book. I can't imagine even making a start on that. Scheme will surely founder. Oh well. Love to Liddie. Will ye no' come back again?

Cheers K.

[TLS: Recipient]

TO PHILIP LARKIN – 11 NOVEMBER 1982

186 Leighton Road, Kentish Town, London, N.W.5

My dear Philip,

[. . .] Am now enormously fat, but feel slimmer as result of buying trousers MEASURING FORTY TWO INCHES ROUND THE WAIST instead of wearing my old 38"s I think about an inch and a half above my cock. Too scared to weigh myself. And now this afternoon

14. Fred Emery (b. 1933), journalist, broadcaster, author.
15. Public Lending Right. See Amis to Larkin, 23 June 1975, note 4.

I go down to my dentist and he will put A METAL PLATE WITH FALSE TEETH ON IT into my mouth. You've got one of those, haven't you? Mine's actually quite good; I've had it in before, but keep having to have additions made as my own teeth FALL OUT or have to be TAKEN AWAY. Ha; ha; ha;

Terry K[ilmartin] tells me you've given that Penguin anthology[1] (now I understand your last bum) a pasting. I thought bits of it weren't bad – wrote it up in the *Standard*. Heaney, Longley, Fenton, Raine? No? I ballocked them of course for not scanning or rhyming, or rather for rhyming when they're supposed not to. But after all, Phil, you mustn't be an old fuddy-duddy, got to move with the times or AIEEEEE

Re Falklands,[2] well yes, but it was also a tremendous test of nerve and obstinacy which Mrs T triumphantly passed. Also one, two, half a dozen in the eye for all sorts of shits. If you did tell her what you thought I'll warrant you got a flea in your ear. She doesn't like being disagreed with. FUCKING WOMAN SEE . . .

Of course you realise being even as little as half a stone overweight renders you measurably more liable to bum,

Kingsley

[TLS: Bodleian]

TO STUART THOMAS[1] – 9 DECEMBER 1982

186 Leighton Road, Kentish Town, London, N.W.5

Dear Stuart,

I feel a little awkward about writing this. It was very kind of you and Eve to invite me for Christmas. I was going to thank you and say

---

1. *The Penguin Book of Contemporary British Poetry*, reviewed by Larkin in 'Under a Common Flag', *Observer*, 14 November 1982, p. 28.

2. Larkin had written, in a letter of 11 October 1982 (in HEHL): 'Aren't you getting a bit fed up with all this Falklands stuff? I mean, fair enough, good job done, brave chaps and that, but IT WAS ONLY A MILITARY OPERATION, wouldn't you say? Not a full-scale war against Russia and Germany combined? I'll tell Mrs T when I see her.'

---

1. For Stuart Thomas see Notes on Recipients.

that out of general inertia, fatness etc. I thought I would spend the holiday here instead, drunkenly and silently watching T.V. Then George [Gale] asked me down to Sawbridgeworth. I was going to say the same to him, mentioning that you had already asked me, but then talking it over with Hilly I thought perhaps I ought to go there – she said something about rallying round him. Certainly what glimpses I've had of him over the past weeks haven't been at all reassuring. Pat too has let slip some odd things – things I can't see her having made up. Of course I'm not going to pretend that spending Christmas with him and Mary is a ghastly chore, I do expect to enjoy myself, but at the same time I would have preferred to stay here if I hadn't had reason to think that the old fellow is in a bit of a state. For the first time I've started wondering whether perhaps something none of us know about is bothering him – no idea what it might be.[2] Probably nothing in it. But I hope you'll forgive me for going to him instead of you and Eve.

I'd love to come and stay with you in the New Year if that's possible. Let's keep in touch. Very enjoyable party with Wynford and Mike[3] the other day. My fondest thanks to you and Eve for being so kind to me over my upsets – incidentally my divorce is apparently through, and I have a funny story or two to tell you about that. Love to both.

Cheers,
Kingsley

[ALS: Trustees of the Dylan Thomas Literary Estate]

2. Gale was going through the last stages of a bitter and protracted divorce proceeding with his first wife, Pat.

3. Wynford Vaughan-Thomas (1908–87), poet, author, broadcaster, Welsh personality, and original co-trustee, with Stuart Thomas and others, of the Dylan Thomas Literary Estate; Michael Rush (b. 1937), friend of Stuart Thomas's and fellow member of the Bristol Channel Yacht Club, a solicitor and local authority chief executive, West Glamorgan (encompassing

TO PHILIP LARKIN – 17 DECEMBER 1982

186 Leighton Road, Kentish Town, London, N.W.5

My dear Philip,

I hope this gets to you in time for me to wish you a very Merry Kris m' arse. I'll be in Herts getting drunk with old George Gale. It's at this time of the year that my thoughts turn inevitably to Jane and bring many a sigh *of heartfelt relief*, in particular at not having to spend a day or two in the effing Wess Tend going round classy jewellers' etc. shops looking for presents for her, like a very nice pair of Georgian bush-brushes with enamel-inlaid backs and filigreed crab-louse remover attached, only £6,844.95 the set. God, when I think of it.

Jolly vivid a/c of the Mrs T gathering.[1] Funny that H-F D (you are a shit) was down at the Jewish end of the table. Might have known that Al, lately as Lefty as they come, would get his foot in there. It'll be Lord Alvarez before we know it. I saw your pal Quinton[2] got it. I've always thought he was all right. It's his wife you want to watch out for. Skinny gig-lamped red-haired rook-voiced American. What did you make of Lord T?

I'll tell you a bit about that novel[3] but you must promise to keep it to yourself. The Lie[4] got it wrong as always. I did 130 pp v. slowly and unenjoyably, then shelved it. Thing was, it was supposed to be going to be an account of a couple of marriages, i.e. the hetero world, seen by a 1st-person queer – for distancing, unexpectedness etc., plus him being talked in front of and confided in in a way not open to a

Swansea); Rush, too, was appointed a trustee of the Dylan Thomas Literary Estate (along with Amis) in 1987.

---

1. See Larkin to Amis, 21 November 1982, in *LL*, p. 682: 'The worst part was after dinner when old [Hugh] Thomas initiated a "conversation", and everyone talked about fawn countries and fawn politics, just like the College Essay Society . . . Watching her was like watching a top class tennis-player; no "uh-huh, well, what do other people think about that", just bang back over the net. I noticed she didn't laugh much, or make jokes. Present (going round the table) were PM, Pritchett, Jack Plumb, Lady T, some Panamanian novelist, Stoppard, Spender, Lord T, MEE, Quinton, Dan Jacobson, H-F Dwarf, Al, Naipaul and Isaiah Berlin.'

2. Anthony Quinton (1925), philosopher; President, Trinity College, Oxford (1978–87); created Life Peer (1982).

3. 'Difficulties with Girls'.

4. *Private Eye*.

hetero. But it turned out, as you'd expect from a queer, to be all about him and being queer, which doesn't sort of appeal to me enough. And of course since only about 17 people in the country know what a novel is, the rest will think I must be one of the boys myself. And I don't need that, do I? It's not as if I'd be taking a stand on some point of principle if I went ahead regardless. See, most people forget that the novelist is continuously trying to fool them into believing he's really felt what his characters feel. So when they come to an extra convincing bit of queer's feelings they're going to say, 'He couldn't have invented that, he must be writing out of personal experience, the dirty cock-sucking sodomising bugger.' Anyway, I've put it aside, perhaps to resume it in my dotage. Not a word, now.

Hunnerd measly poun they gave me for that Did You See[5] ballcoks. When I saw it I was genuinely amazed by my sunny amiability and genial tolerance of all the crap shown and talked on the show. Talking of D Y S, did you see old Wild Bill[6] the other week? He embodied to perfection Flow-bare's (Floe-bear's?) advice to be correct and bourgeois in your life so that you can be violent and original in your works. I loved all that stuff about wearing a tie and turning up on time. He reminded me facially of Hugh Herbert.[7]

Sorry about your car troubles, but you can hardly expect me to take them seriously with three million people out of wooooOOOOghghg I'm deaf too, but only for a bit I hope – infection, wax etc. Sodding pest. Are you really pissed ⅔ of the time? On what? Tell me more. Yeah yeah, I know what you mean about those poets, but don't you think Fenton's good? German Requiem?[8] No? Hope poor old M[9] is better. Stairs are tricky things WHEN YOU GET TO OUR AGE. Wish I could find a good book to read that I haven't read already. Any tips?

5. A television discussion programme about television (since 1980), hosted by Ludovic Kennedy.

6. Wild Bill Davison.

7. Probably the American actor Hugh Herbert (1887–1952), who appeared in supporting roles (and some leads) in over a hundred films from the late 1920s, including Busby Berkeley's *Gold Diggers of 1935, Hellzapoppin* (1941), *Kismet* (1944) and *A Song is Born* (1948). According to Katz, ed., *The Film Encyclopedia*, p. 619, 'fidgety movements and an excited "woo-woo" sound were the trademarks of his zany comedy style'.

8. For James Fenton see Amis to Conquest, 7 April 1977, note 3. 'A German Requiem' is from Fenton's second volume of poetry, *The Memory of War* (1982).

9. Monica Jones, who had had a bad fall.

Have a good hol. All you wish yourself for 1983. Do you mean
The peace women[10] are inspired by a simple horror of bum,

Kingsley

[TLS: Bodleian]

TO PHILIP LARKIN – 9 MARCH 1983

186 Leighton Road, Kentish Town, London, N.W.5.

My dear Philip,

Sorry I haven't written for so long. Don't you take so long. Thing is, I have to do this drinks column for the D Express every Sat.[1] It only takes me a day and a bit or half but I have to do it, and so all my lazing time comes out of when I should be writing my novel.[2] I enjoy doing it (novel) when I've started, but I don't like starting, and even if I did there'd be days like today, with fotog in morning, then boozy lunch with Snuff Grinders Assn if you don't sodding well mind, old times' sake really, and then it's 3 p.m. and I could and should go home and start, but I don't do that; no, I go to the Garrick and drink marc with an elderly actor and the ex-boss of Glyndebourne,[3] and laugh and piss on Roy Hattersley[4] and use bad language. Then when I get home at 5.15 I'd normally fly in guilt and panic to novel, but for once grit my teeth, not very hard actually, and instead write to you, you old gubra. And how are you now.

Bin reading the new Tony P,[5] sent to me by Terry K[ilmartin], who said read it and send it back if you don't like it, so that's what I'll be doing. It's *no good*, you see. I thought it was good and really funny,

10. On 12 December 1982, twenty thousand women encircled Greenham Common air base, protesting against the decision to site US Cruise missiles there.

---

1. The column for the *Daily Express* (where Amis's friend George Gale was a columnist) started in 1982 and resulted in *Every Day Drinking* (1983).

2. *Stanley and the Women* (1984).

3. Moran Caplat (b.1916), General Administrator, Glyndebourne Festival Opera (1949–81).

4. Roy Hattersley (b.1932), Labour MP, Minister, Deputy Leader (1983–92), journalist and novelist.

5. *O, How the Wheel Becomes It!* (1983); see Amis to Larkin, 3 August 1982.

though a bit slow and wordy, while he was setting everything up, then when he's done that it all goes completely to pot. [. . .]

Pissy as it is, *ofcourse* it's *not nearly as bad* as the books by our leading young novelists that Penguin asininely sent me a few weeks ago. Didn't tell you this, did I? Haven't read them all (you must be joking), just enough, when TV progs were really bad, to show that Clive Sinclair and Graham Swift[6] (one knew about Ian Macewen, McEwen) are no good in the sense you can't bear what they're doing. Wm Boyd's no good in the sense you can't see he's doing anything.[7] A short story (in his bk of them) rambles on and you think, I can stand this, something might happen in a minute, and then you turn over a page and find the next one has got some space wasted at the bottom, because that's the end. But the one we must put a contract on is D.M. Thomas. Long ago (my dear little brothers in Christ) we learnt that you haven't got to be able to enjoy a piece of music or want to see a picture again or understand a poem or (a more recent one) recognise the subject of a cartoon or caricature for it to be good. Now we know you needn't like or respect a novel f.i.t.b.g. Oh, and Christopher Priest and Pat Barker and Maggie Gee are no good.[8] Don't know what to say about M**t** A***. Bet you do, thoguh, what? [. . .]

It's the next day now, and I did some work this morning by being interviewed for radio and showing off, and then got taken out to lunch by the v. nice little Penguin publicity girl and quite enjoyed it, and it would have been a bloody treat if only I'd wanted to fuck her – my deficiency of course. But my sex-drive seems to have started to return to normal, in the sense that I think about little girls quite a lot of the time. Which apart from being fun in itself is a step in the direction of finding big girls tolerable and so being asked out to dinner more. You still quite like big girls, don't you? As regards little ones you needn't answer.

Have I really not written since getting your letter of 3rd January? Shit. I think Fenton's obscure because he just has the habit of covering everything up because he's queer, even when what he's covering up has

6. Graham Swift (b.1949), novelist, published third novel, *Waterland* (1983).

7. William Boyd (b.1952), African-born novelist, published third novel, *An Ice-Cream War* (1982).

8. Christopher Priest (b.1943), novelist, science fiction writer, published *The Affirmation* (1981); Pat Barker (b.1943), novelist, first-published novel *Union Street* (1983); Maggie Gee (b.1948), novelist, published second novel, *The Burning Book* (1982).

nothing direct to do with being queer. Like Auden. It's the *next* day now. The Penguin Book of Poofter Po: arrived, with a poem by *me* in it – Ever-Fixèd Mark of course.[9] Not exactly *queer*, would you say? No, Chaplin is a horse's arse.[10] He's a Jeeeew, you see. Like the Marx Brothers. Like Danny Kaye. I'll write sooner next time. Good luck old chap.

I want my children to grow up in a world of bum,

Kingsley

[TLS: Bodleian]

TO JULIAN BARNES AND PAT KAVANAGH – 5 APRIL 1983

Marvellous idea faultlessly executed.[1] Uncharacteristic failure with Scotch very smoothly retrieved. Corn whatnames[2] a joy. And the old man appreciated being run home. What can I do in return? Would a din. at the old Garrick appeal? I'll ring.

Jolly good cheers – Kingsley

[ALS: Julian Barnes]

9. See pp. 332–3 of *The Penguin Book of Homosexual Verse* (1982), ed. Stephen Coote; 'An Ever-Fixed Mark', first published in *A Look Round the Estate* (1967), reprinted in *CP*, pp. 73–4, contrasts the erotic and amatory natures of 'Buck' and 'Ralph', beginning 'Years ago, at a private school/Run on traditional lines,' and ending with their behaviour as adults.

10. See Larkin to Amis, 6 January 1983, in *LL*, p. 688: 'I watched two Chaplin films tonight with unmoving face. HOW DID IT EVER GET ABOUT THAT HE WAS FUNNY?'

---

1. Barnes believes this thank-you card might have been for a belated sixtieth-birthday dinner he and Kavanagh gave Amis (a dinner belated by about a year).

2. Fried mealie (maize) bread.

TO PHILIP LARKIN – 1 SEPTEMBER 1983

Back among the Taffs for not so much a holiday as a drinking-bout. Incredible profusion of sexagenarian alcoholics here. Will write properly on return to NW5 which takes place 1 Sept. Expect you and M.[1] are off to Kitzbuhl for the skeeummaoh! Ian Botham[2] b*m

K.

[ALS: Bodleian]

TO THE EDITOR, *SPECTATOR* – 19 NOVEMBER 1983

Sir: Discussing the 'Best Novels of Our Time' business,[1] Paul Johnson ('Literary silly season', 12 November) asks rhetorically, 'Who but Miss Howard would have selected Elizabeth Taylor's little-known *Angel?*'[2] Well I would, for one.

The chief reason why *Angel* is little known, if it is (can Mr Johnson really hold this against it?), is that it is not the sort of book that gets talked about by most of the people who regard themselves as educated readers. To them it sounds or would sound rather ordinary. Of course if you have no literary judgment, no ability to see a novel as it really is, you spend your time groping for guidelines like what reviewers have said or might say about it, what class it seems to fall into, where it seems to be aiming, whether its style strikes you as normal or not,

---

1. Monica [Jones].
2. Ian Botham (b.1955), cricketer; England Test cricketer 1977–92 (captain, 1980–81).

---

1. A publicity stunt by the Book Marketing Council. The list, which was mocked by others as well as Paul Johnson, was chosen by Richard Hoggart, Peter Parker and Elizabeth Jane Howard, and consisted of thirteen titles (including several 'series' of novels): George Orwell, *Animal Farm*; Ivy Compton-Burnett, *Manservant and Maidservant*; J.D. Salinger, *The Catcher in the Rye*; Anthony Powell, *A Dance to the Music of Time*; Evelyn Waugh, *Sword of Honour*; William Golding, *Lord of the Flies*; Elizabeth Taylor, *Angel*; Vladimir Nabokov, *Lolita*; Kingsley Amis, *Take a Girl Like You*; Saul Bellow, *Herzog*; Paul Scott, *The Raj Quartet* and *Staying on*; Graham Greene, *The Honorary Consul*; Iris Murdoch, *The Sea, the Sea*.
2. First published in 1957.

above all whether it can be called important or not – which is far easier to decide than whether the thing is any good or not.

On these counts *Angel* makes a pretty poor showing. Nobody could ever call it rumbustious, or searing, or daringly innovative, or linguistically brilliant, or life-affirming, or Sophoclean, or wry. In paraphrase, and many readers get little further with any novel than their own paraphrase, *Angel* sounds low-key, perhaps sentimental, feminine in the derogatory sense, even women's-magaziney. But (what can I say?) read properly it stands out as a powerful story about a violent and hysterical egotist, a character deeply seen into and judged with scrupulous fairness, all done with triumphant narrative skill, a wonderful eye and ear and unfailing humour, though not of the 'robust' nor of the 'savage' variety, often delightfully catty. If some of these qualities have a familiar ring to them it is not because they are two a penny in the novels of our time or any other.

Elizabeth Taylor herself gave her status no help by having no public life, not being seen on television, not pronouncing on the state of the world and not going round explaining that her underlying subject was the crisis of the bourgeois conscience.[3] It was hard to believe that this rather ungregarious wife of a businessman living in no great style in the Thames valley, fond of a gossip over a gin and tonic, could be the author of any kind of novel, let alone an important one. And *Angel* is not important in the usual sense: it inaugurated nothing, summed up nothing, did nothing outside itself. But importance isn't important. Good writing is.

KINGSLEY AMIS
c/o Jonathan Clowes, 22, Prince Albert Road, London NW1

3. She also disapproved of the posthumous publication of private letters, including those between herself and Kingsley Amis, which she either destroyed herself or requested her estate to destroy at her death.

TO PHILIP LARKIN – 3, 5 DECEMBER 1983

186 Leighton Road, Kentish Town, London, N.W.5

My dear Philip,

Sorry this is three months Christ late. I felt superstitiously that I mustn't do anything unnecessary till novel[1] complete – revision to come but sod that – so didn't write to you or Bob or lunch with people on purpose. Getting pissed was allowed, though. Any road, the bugger is done, it may be ABSOLUTELY DEVOID OF ANY KIND OF MERIT WHATSOEVER but it's fucking *done*. Seriously feared it never would be. I also quite seriously fear[2] it will get me murdered by feminists. 'The root of all the trouble is we want to fuck them' &c. Well I hope it will give my old Pall a few luaghs.

I didn't half enjoy your book,[3] as I said. You make it sound easy to talk sense on these matters. Bang on re Auden. Not having the English countryside any more was another nail in the coffin, no?[4] No more of the lonely-on-fell-as-chat stuff. I must say you've got terrifically tolerant IN YOUR OLD AGE. All these people you have time for, Ogden Nash, Barnes, Stevie Smith,[5] Syvi syphi Sylvia Plath, especially her, nothing but a hyper acc. to me. You did know she didn't mean to kill herself? Not to speak of ole Hardy. All those rotten old words nobody uses and

---

1. *Stanley and the Women* (1984).

2. The word 'fear' is a typed addition above the line, indicated by an oblique stroke (/). Originally, Amis had added it before 'seriously'. This mistake was then crossed out and execrated by the handwritten additions 'you're in' (urine) and 'piss' above the line, with arrows, and the typed addition 'PEA' in the left margin, connected to the offending 'fear' by a row of typed asterisks.

3. *Required Writing* (1983).

4. Larkin's review of Auden's *Homage to Clio* (1960), reprinted in *Required Writing*, pp. 123–8, characterises late Auden as 'an engaging, bookish, American talent, too verbose to be memorable and too intellectual to be moving' (p. 122). Early Auden, said to differ in poetic character and stature, is more memorable because more rooted, less cosmopolitan, which fits with Amis's point about the English countryside. The next sentence alludes to Auden's poem beginning 'Doom is dark and deeper than any sea-dingle', in *Poems* (1933), later variously titled 'Or lonely on fell as chat'.

5. See *Required Writing* for reprinted reviews of Ogden Nash, *Collected Verse from 1929 On* (1961) (pp. 134–5); William Barnes, *The Poems of William Barnes*, ed. Bernard Jones, 2 vols (1962) (pp. 149–52); and Stevie Smith, *Selected Poems* (1962) (pp. 153–8). The American poet Ogden Nash's dates are 1902–71; Barnes, a Dorset dialect poet, lived from 1801 to 1886; Stevie Smith, a novelist as well as a poet, lived from 1902 to 1971.

those horrible double-barrelled ones he made up out of his own head, like all-uncared and eve-damps and self-wrapt and fore-folk. They affect me in the same way as you once said Mary Lou Williams's[6] mistake affected you in You Don't Know My Mind, gritting your teeth for half a minute before it and trying to forget it for half a minute after it. Still you use words like that yourself dont you so Iyyyeeeeeghghgh [. . .]

Hope poor old M[7] is better. Sounds ghastly. I don't know anything about shingles. What happens to you? Is bad eye permanent? All seemingly fit here TOUCH WOOD FINGERS CROSSED except that I am absolutely tremendously fat. Can't think why. I don't eat much and only drink a bottle of spirits a day.

Well you know some chaps have more to put up with than being given hon. degrees.[8] No bugger has ever come my way. It's because I write about booze do you see, that shows I can't be serious do you see. Dead funny about those 13 novels.[9] I knew I was safe, because Jane couldn't have it said that she'd kept me off it. She'll be at the launching, so I won't. Have managed not to see her once in the just over three years but I suppose it can't last, I'll bump into the *old*[10] girl when I'm least expecting it and FALL DOWN DEAD OF BITTERNESS AND MORTIFICATION or whatever you please.

Yes Craig Raine is a fucking fool. Terrible poet too. All that Martian bullshit. Yes pity about old Glad,[11] though I could never make out what was going on in her books. Can't think what you see in M. Innes.[12] So *silly*. But D. Francis is super. Back to form with The Danger,[13] no? Except the last few pages? And they find the kid too easily? Why didn't

6. Mary Lou Williams (1910–81), pianist and composer.

7. Monica Jones.

8. Larkin had been awarded an honorary D.Litt. by the New University of Ulster in Coleraine in July and had complained to Amis in a letter of 31 July 1983 (in *LL*, pp. 698–9) of having to make the trip to Northern Ireland alone.

9. A reference to the Book Marketing Council's 'Best Novels of Our Time' list, which included *Take a Girl Like You*. See Amis to the editor, *Spectator*, 19 November 1983, and Amis to Conquest, 7 December 1983.

10. MS addition.

11. Gladys Mitchell was a Larkin favourite (see *Required Writing*, pp. 271–3); all her mystery novels (she wrote over sixty, including a number set in girls' schools) feature the sleuth Dame Beatrice Lestrange Bradley, aided, after 1942, by the 'Amazonian' Laura Menzies, who becomes her secretary. See Larkin to Amis, 31 July 1983, in *LL*, p. 699: 'So Gladys Mitchell has gone – that only leaves Dick Francis, Michael Innes – and – So no more of Laura's magnificent body and strapping thighs and twat-not.'

12. For Michael Innes (J.I.M. Stewart) see Amis to Larkin, 8 September 1980, note 10.

13. *The Danger* (1983).

you put your piece on him[14] in yr bk? I reread them (*his bks*)[15] all the time, crying my eyes out at all the marvellous good sense and decent feeling (not being sarky). WILL WRITE AGAIN SOON WHETHER YOU HAVE OR NOT. You cannot simply walk into bum,

Kingsley

That Paris Review chap sounded an awful cunt.[16]

PS: [. . .]
After seeing what *seven* shags (incl Martin and Malcolm Bradbury, ma-ha-ha) said on the front of the Ob yesterday[17] I ask for your reassurance. P Porter *is* ABSOLUTELY DEVOID etc. isn't he? I mean isn't he? No *poet* could be called that to start with. Oh, but he can't be bothered to rhyme or anything, so perhaps he hasn't noticed. Nice chap and all that, and thinks you're good. Just *no good* himself. [. . .]

Salman Rushdie bum.

K.

[TLS: Bodleian]

TO ROBERT CONQUEST – 7 DECEMBER 1983

186 Leighton Road NW5

Dear ole Bob,

About fucking time, eh? I got to the end of my novel yesterday and until I did I had the superstitious feeling that I mustn't take a moment off to write to you or Philip or arrange any unnecessary lunches etc. Getting pissed was in, though. Now I'm back among the human race and merely revising novel.

Burning question I've been completely thrown by – what the hell

14. Larkin wrote two reviews of Dick Francis novels: 'Four Good Legs', *TLS*, 10 October 1980, p. 1129, a long, enthusiastic piece on *Reflex* (1980); and 'A Slackening of the Reins', *Observer*, 17 October 1982, p. 33, a much shorter piece on *Banker* (1982).

15. MS addition.

16. MS addition. Larkin's 1982 *Paris Review* interview with Robert Phillips was reprinted in *Required Writing*, pp. 57–76.

17. In their choices for Books of the Year. See Amis to Conquest, 7 December 1983.

got into Mrs T over Grenada?[1] Proving she wasn't Ronnie's poodle? Threats from the Cabinet? Womanly pique? What have you heard? Do answer this for my satisfaction and others'. It caused a minor explosion here, Paul J[ohnson]. characteristically announcing in public (Sunday?) that he had lost faith in her. Need hardly tell you that I've met nobody who doesn't solidly support the US action, even in the Garrick, as you know Tory but no hotbed of pro-Americanism.

If you see the Eng Sundays you'll have seen the crap about the Nat Book League's selection of 12 Best Novels of Today. If not, I'm on it with *Take a Girl*, also Tony, Waugh, Iris, Liz Taylor & al (not Al [Alvarez]). No T Pynchon, no Patrick White, no Beckett, no Burgess, no Fowles (bloody good). Old Jane was on the panel – my story is she had to get me on otherwise it might look as if she'd kept me off. Anyway, biggish row at unadventurous, safe, parochial etc list. No thrusting, challenging, grand-scale stuff, i.e. no (or not enough) pretentious bull-shit. Liz T got the most stick, clearly for *sounding* minor, novelettish etc. The turds (many lefties I suspect) don't like good books, they like important books. I said this in letter to the Spec. Paul J (again) had said 'Wd anyone but Miss H have chosen Taylor's little-known *Angel*?' I would, I said, wch might have made the old girl sit up. Ran into that old fool Golding and had to congrat him.[2] He seemed surprise[d] at the warmth of my smile – actually I was trying not to laugh at the memory of your limerick which had arrived previous day.

Reassure me – Peter Porter is *no good at all*, isn't he? *Seven* shags incl Martin, M Bradbury chose his coll. poems as their Bk of Yr in the Ob. If seven shags with seven puffs Said it was premier cru Do *you* think said the Publisher That you could sell a few? Get knotted said

---

1. On 19 October 1983 Prime Minister Maurice Bishop was killed in a left-wing military coup in Grenada, a member of the Commonwealth. On 25 October President Reagan sent US Marines to the island to depose the new military government; by mid-December the Marines were able to leave the island, having removed the government and its Cuban 'advisers'. Mrs Thatcher had cautioned the Americans against invasion ('even governments acting on the best of motives are wise to respect legal forms', *Downing Street Years*, p. 335), and publicly criticised them when her advice was ignored.

2. William Golding won the Nobel Prize in 1983.

the Bookseller And turned aside to spew.[3] Just an impromptu yer know but better than Tadlow[4] I hope. You can improve on it.

Have seen almost nobody for past weeks but now it'll be worth starting a FTTTB file (unny hings o ell ob). All seems well here. Love to Liddie. Will write agn.

Cheers
Kingsley

[TLS: Recipient]

TO THE EDITOR, *SPECTATOR* – 31 DECEMBER 1983

Sir: Anecdotes about writers and artists in general give a unique insight into the life of any historical period, and are often funny in a special way too. In an age like ours, when personal letters are written much less than formerly and diaries of record seldom kept, there is a danger that many such anecdotes will die with their raconteurs.

To remedy this, I have been commissioned by Messrs Macmillan to gather a collection, and now ask your readers for their assistance in bringing to my attention material I should otherwise miss.[1] Any anecdote ('narrative of amusing or interesting incident' – *COD*) of this century is eligible if it involves the arts or artists, including writers and the written word and the performing arts and artists. Sources should be given where possible. Attribution will be made where appropriate. Material should be sent to me at the address below.

I regret that I cannot guarantee to reply, but material accompanied by a stamped and addressed envelope will be returned. I reserve the right to tinker with the text if it has not previously appeared in print.

KINGSLEY AMIS
Macmillan London Limited, 4 Little Essex Street, London WC2

3. An allusion to 'The Walrus and the Carpenter', from *Through the Looking Glass* (1871), by Lewis Carroll (Charles Lutwidge Dodgson (1832–98).
4. See Amis to Conquest, 1 March 1976, note 6.

---

1. This collection, provisionally titled *Anecdotes of the Arts*, was never published. Macmillan's file on the project was closed in 1989.

TO PHILIP LARKIN – 8 FEBRUARY 1984

186 Leighton Road, Kentish Town, London, N.W.5

My dear Philip,

I took the fucking thing[1] in to my agent y'day p.m. and I don't say it's any *good* and it may be quite *boar-ring* in places but at least it's IN. And by the way it's not another JT[2] by any means. None of the sentimental mollycoddling that women get in that. This has moments of definite hostility. It's an inexhaustible subject. What, *another* book about a murder, Dame Agatha? But your last one was about that.

Sorry about your phlebitis. Does it hurt? Make it hard to get about? What about poor M's shingles? I am all right FOR THE MOMENT apart from sneezing my head off all the time from (what must be) allergy to cat-fur and being enormously, but enormously, fat. Dare not weigh myself. Just daren't do it what? Not off the drink are you any more? I'm not.

My next job is the collection of litty etc. anecdotes. I realise I know dozens myself. Including one or two about you. At Oxford Philip Larkin was greatly attached to a good-looking yyyyaaaaghghgh Have a couple of corkers about J Wain showing him up nicely as a conceited shit. If I were D Francis I think I would commit suicide or emigrate, rather than live in a country where I was publicly graded one step down from Wain. Not v. comfy being graded on a par with him, is it? Talking of such, did anything ever come of that C. Litt caper?[3] Funny about fame. A chap in the Garrick told me his daughter and her pals are all putting their names down for Hull because P Larkin teaches (sic) there. Of course Martin Amis is more famous than I am now. His PLR money was £800 for 4 novels. Mine was £3,300 for 15 (plus £350 for EVERYTHING ELSE) so he's nearly caught me up. But you give the boy a

1. *Stanley and the Women* (1984).

2. *Jake's Thing* (1978).

3. See Larkin to Amis, 27 March 1983, in *LL*, p. 691: 'Incidentally, I have proposed you for Companion of Literature: hope you don't mind. There are only twelve, and three have kicked the bucket recently . . . I don't expect for a moment they will take up my suggestion – I guess Muriel Spark, Al Alvarez and Frank Kermode.' The title Companion of Literature was devised by the Royal Society of Literature in 1961. Amis never received it, nor did Alvarez or Kermode, but Spark did, in 1991; the recipients for 1983–84 were Samuel Beckett, William Golding and Graham Greene. Larkin received it in 1978.

rest. The truth is, Phil, that we all suffer from the limitations of the age we were born in. Just as the generation before us had no time for *Ulysses*, so in our turn weeeeghghgh [. . .]

Saw your piece on Waugh.[4] Fucking dreary book it sounded. Very *silly* fellow he was. Only a first-class cunt could have written the 'funny' parts of S of Honour and the whole of B'head. More and more I think of him as a chap who wrote one marvellous book (D&F) then WENT OFF having joined the Cartholic Ch.[5] Woman I met who knew him a bit said it wasn't so much his rudeness that stuck in your craw as his buttering-up dukes and marquises, praising their marvellous houses and beautiful gardens, lovely daughters & c. He did that to her when she was married to one, then stopped it when she stopped being. Though no, not as bad as Bron.[6] ——————— SHIGHT

Had you heard that Bechet went to France because nobody in USA would play with him because he tried to hog everything? Though I still thrill to that Muskram with Hodes.[7]

Alexis Korner[8] bum
Kingsley

[TLS: Bodleian]

TO ROBERT CONQUEST – 29 FEBRUARY 1984

186 Leighton Road, N.W.5

Dear Bob,

Great news about your trip. You will of course be staying here. I have no commitments round about then except some TV-award viewing

4. 'Basil and Bridey', *Observer*, 5 February 1984, p. 52, a review of D. Gallagher, ed., *Essays, Articles and Reviews of Evelyn Waugh* (1984).

5. *Sword of Honour* (1965), Waugh's wartime trilogy, was originally published as *Men at Arms* (1952), *Officers and Gentlemen* (1955) and *Unconditional Surrender* (1961). *Brideshead Revisited* was published in 1945; *Decline and Fall* in 1928.

6. Auberon Waugh (b. 1939), journalist, novelist, editor (of the *Literary Review* 1986–); eldest son of Evelyn Waugh.

7. 'Muskrat Ramble', with Art Hodes.

8. Alexis Korner (1928–84), English pianist, electric guitarist, singer and bandleader.

on 18th and 19th. But of course we'll understand if you have a prior booking at Chequers.[1]

No hesitation in saying your Pope limerick[2] is the funniest of yours, i.e. anybody's, for a long time. I can see how you got to Burton-on-Trent, but it's still a stroke of g., as PGW[odehouse] would say. Brigadier[3] good too. Is the Penguin B[ook] of L[imericks] actually out? Don't seem to have seen it. Also kindly supply source of Orgasm.[4] (Amazing what Yanks will get up to, isn't it?)

What do you know about a fellow called Wilmot Robinson and his book *The Dispossessed Majority*?[5] Some anon shag sent me a copy from NYC. Thesis that the WASPs are being pushed out of power and influence by an alliance of liberals and ethnic minorities. Hard on the Jews, natch, but then you pick up the Sunday paper and in the ST review alone you find Susan Sontag, G Steiner, a Russian-Jewish novelist, Freud, Steven Marcus, a new US Jewish pop novelist and no doubt others – yes, Mel Brooks – all writing or being written about, and you start shamefacedly and reservedly thinking he may have something. Writes well. Interesting that the following week I get Paul Fussell's book *Class*.[6] Bloody amusing I must say. But I mean, class-is-everything hard upon race-is-everything.

Track that pissy piece about Philip's book if you can,[7] because Blake M is slated to profile me when my novel comes out in May. The trouble with chaps like that is they have no taste – I don't mean bad taste, just the mental organ that makes you say This is bloody good and This is piss is simply missing, and they have to orientate themselves by things like 'importance' and 'seriousness' and 'depth' and 'originality' and 'consensus' (=trend). Hence standing of Golding, Fowles, le Carré et al. (though thank Christ not et Al, who seems to have missed the bus). But you've probably heard me on this theme before.

---

1. The official country residence of the Prime Minister, in Buckinghamshire.

2. 'It was sad for the Pope when he spent/Palm Sunday at Burton-on-Trent/There was Bass and roast duck/And a barmaid to fuck/But he'd given them all up for Lent.'

3. Another limerick, now lost.

4. Conquest cannot remember what this is.

5. Wilmot Robinson, *The Dispossessed Minority* (Cape Canaveral, Fla: H. Allen, 1972).

6. *Class: A Guide Through the American Status System* (1983); its title in Britain was *Caste Marks: Style and Status in the USA* (1984). See Amis to Fussell, 19 July 1984, note 3.

7. Blake Morrison's review of Larkin's *Required Writing*, entitled 'On Philip Larkin's Prose', appeared in *Encounter* 62:2 (February 1984), pp. 43–7. Conquest, in a letter of 9

My new job is Poetry Editor of the Daily Mirror.[8] Yes, a nice spot next to the Old Codgers,[9] where Andy Capp is now. Should be good fun, and not underpaid, but of course the real satisfaction is the thought of how cross it'll make them all. Dosing the honest masses with stuff about patriotism and religion and the countryside and out-of-date ways of thought. *You* know.

Good about your book.[10] Oh won't we have the gaiety. Love to Liddie.

Cheers
K.

[TLS: Recipient]

TO BILL TURNER – 24 APRIL 1984

c/o Jonathan Clowes Ltd, 22 Prince Albert Road, London N.W.1

Dear Mr. Turner,

The Daily Mirror has sent your letter to me.[1]

The poems published in the Daily Mirror may be well known to

March 1984, describes the piece as 'not hostile, and yet afraid to strike: says Philip confuses things by disliking good modernism as well as bad'.

8. Amis was given the column by the newspaper's Editor, his friend Mike Molloy, and took the needs and interests of its mass audience seriously. He selected and introduced a poem every weekday for a year. The column was discontinued by the Czech-born businessman, publisher and ex-Labour MP Robert Maxwell (1923–91), who had purchased the *Mirror* six months into Amis's one-year contract. In the introduction to *The Pleasure of Poetry* (1990), which reprints its selections and introductions, Amis calls the column 'the most enjoyable job I ever had' (p. xvi).

9. A daily letters page in the *Daily Mirror*, in which readers offered quirky enquiries and observations (it was discontinued in February 1990).

10. A reference either to *What to do When the Russians Come* (1984), written with Jon Manchip White, or *Inside Stalin's Secret Police* (1985).

---

1. Turner (b. 1927), a published poet, radio dramatist and novelist, as well as a Creative Writing Fellow at the universities of Glasgow and Leeds, had written to Amis to protest about the absence of contemporary poets in his *Daily Mirror* column: 'I could not see any point to printing in a newspaper poems easily available in several standard anthologies. I also challenged Amis to allow readers to see poems by contemporary women poets such as Ursula Fanthorpe, Elizabeth Bartlett, Connie Bensley, Carol Ann Duffy and Elma Mitchell' (personal communication, 6 November 1996).

you but they are clearly not to many other readers. Of course you can look up lots of poems in anthologies, but to do so you first have to know that they exist. You say rightly, though perhaps rather obviously, that the poets cited in the Daily Mirror could not have survived without being published in their own time. Reflect that their work found a publisher who was not subsidized by the Arts Council or anyone else, which I bet is not true of any of the female nonentities you mention.

Yours sincerely,
Kingsley Amis

[TLS: Recipient]

TO DALE SALWAK – 15 MAY 1984

186 Leighton Road, Kentish Town, London, N.W.5

Dear Dale,

Very good to hear from you. I shall certainly be here for virtually all of July, and would love to see you – also wife – at any time you find convenient. Just call me and we will fix it up.

As regards your dissertation, of course send it to me and I will read it through and comment on it. From the publication point of view, I am only doing a single book for Macmillan.[1] My regular publisher remains Hutchinson. I advise you to send the thing to James Cochrane of that firm.[2] I will have a word with him in advance.

My new novel[3] appears next week. Reception good so far but I am keeping my fingers crossed.

All the very best,

Yours
Kingsley

[TLS: Recipient]

---

1. 'Anecdotes of the Arts, 1850 to the Present Day', which was never published; see Amis to the editor, *Spectator*, 31 December 1983. Amis signed a contract in October 1983 to deliver the book to Macmillan a year later, and Macmillan provided him with a research assistant. The project was finally abandoned in November 1989.

2. Amis's co-editor for *The Great British Songbook* (London: Pavilion/Michael Joseph, 1986).

3. *Stanley and the Women.*

TO JOHN COQUET – 12 JUNE 1984

186 Leighton Road, Kentish Town, London, N.W.5

Dear Mr. Coquet,[1]

Thank you very much for your pleasant and encouraging letter. It is good of you to say that you thought Stanley and the Women was one of my best books. I had felt rather nervous about it as publication approached, but it seems I need not have done.

I have a soft spot for Take A Girl Like You myself. It is the only book of mine I have ever contemplated writing a sequel to. I think the answer to your hypothetical question is that they did get married, and Patrick gave Jenny a hell of a time.[2]

With warmest thanks and good wishes,

Yours sincerely,
Kingsley Amis

[TLS: Recipient]

TO PHILIP LARKIN – 18 JUNE 1984

186 Leighton Road, Kentish Town, London, N.W.5

My dear Philip,

Sorry the Daily Mirror misprinted you on Friday – 'or gallop for what be joy'.[1] Not my fault, nor needless to say that of any Mirror fellow I spoke to. Any idea how much they're paying you? Anyway your appearance there will get you in solid with people like your charlady and the porters at the library. And it was nice for me to publish you.

---

1. John Coquet (b. 1941), an insurance underwriter, had written Amis a fan letter.
2. *Difficulties with Girls*, the sequel to *Take a Girl Like You*, was published in 1988.

---

1. From the last stanza of Larkin's early poem 'At Grass'. The *Mirror* had left out the word 'must' from the line 'Or gallop for what must be joy' (see Amis, ed., *The Pleasure of Poetry*, p. 110).

What news of the ... the you-know-what?[2] They're bound to offer it you. Or perhaps they won't, on the understanding that you once said dreaming of it made you wake up screaming. Only you didn't say it, did you? I put it into your mouth to replace the answer you vetoed, remember?[3] Ironical really, if you don't get it because you didn't want it known that you were sure you would get it. But if you are offered it take it. You'd be good at it, as that bridge poem[4] shows. You'd enjoy it, too. Think how you'd feel if you turned it down and they gave it to Ted Hughes or Christopher Logue.[5] Think how the rest of us would feel. And I say, having to write might get you going agooogh AAGH leggo my pi

Am writing this with my right foot, cushioned by *The Pelican Book of American Verse*, stretched out on the second drawer of my desk. I walked about a mile the other day and the ankle swelled up as with a Dropsie. Legacy of my leg, the broken one. Fucking pest. Keeping it horizontal is the thing. I say isn't it bloody awful to think that 20 years ago or so I'd have been *scheit*[6] telling you I thought sticking my leg there made me toss off less.

Talking of legacies I have put *The L*[7] up to be flogged. No, I haven't taken a copy of it. No, I didn't read it through or indeed at all. Also all my other floggable stuff, along with much else that isn't, I dare say. I hope it raises enough to be worth putting towards a new house. There isn't any hall or dining-room in this one, and it's getting a bit common round here. But of course it's not so much the money as not having the stuff cluttering up the place and I'll clutter up your place with a red-hot

Poor Betj. No words, are there? When I saw him 3 weeks before he neither spoke nor moved nor changed his expression, indeed he had no expression. That sort of thing's supposed to make it *better*, isn't it? Shall I see you at the Abbey? My God. To think.

Well. Again, the Lship would make you the focus of every nutter

2. The Poet Laureateship, which had become vacant upon the death of John Betjeman in May 1984.

3. See Amis, *Memoirs*, p. 57; also 'Oxford and After', in Thwaite, ed., *Larkin at Sixty*, p. 29; and Amis to Larkin, 7 March and 9 April 1980.

4. 'Bridge for the Living'; see Amis to Larkin, 27 July 1978, note 1.

5. Christopher Logue (b.1926), poet, journalist, translator.

6. MS addition. Amis has crossed out 'sayin'.

7. 'The Legacy', eventually sold, with the rest of Amis's papers, to the Huntington Library in California. See Amis to Conquest, 2 July 1984, note 5.

in the land, but that's where being in Hull comes in. Too much trouble to get at you. You must have thought of all this, but one thing perhaps hasn't struck you as forcibly as it might – it would be a tremendous kick in the balls for the shits. Better than that, more like lumbago, something that goes on for ever coming back and giving them gyp. Take heed on 't.

Don't know whether you saw but young Martin has rung the bell. Put his girl[8] in pod. Wedding bells to come but no hurry it seems, so it may be in every sense a little bastard that appears around Yuletide. Girl nice* but we are not quite grand enough for her. V. good news though. My Stanley seems to have *pleased* a lot of people. I tried to be offensive but the essential niceness of my nature must have got in the way. Did I ask you whether you didn't think that the new Dick F (The Danger) was up to snuff or very nearly? Well didn't you?

Mrs Thatcher is showing a disquieting penchant for bum

Kingsley

* *Also rich*[9]
Love to M.[10]

[TLS: Bodleian]

TO ROBERT CONQUEST – 2 JULY 1984

186 LR NW5

Dear Bob,

The summer here is rather like your winter there though perhaps a bit colder – gas fire on in the sitting-room last night. We have been seeing off old Betj – the Abbey on Friday with Philip, Monica just mobile with a stick, AP, VP et al., also Liz Cavendish who literally took a back seat, perforce no doubt but it seems odd or crappy that she'll

8. Antonia Phillips, a lecturer in philosophy; they were married in 1984 on the day of publication of Martin's novel *Money*. Louis Nathaniel Amis was born on 15 November 1984.
9. MS addition.
10. MS addition. 'M' is Monica Jones.

reportedly be left out of the official biog.[1] More of it today in St. Mary le Strand, a private tribute or something, me talking 5 mins., also John Wells[2] which raises foreboding. Jill Balcon[3] to read, oh dear. Phil is tipped everywhere to succeed. I wrote to him urging him to accept, feeling like some shag like Gosse writing to Bridges in 1913.[4] He – P – is really very fat. He had time to ask me if I got dizzy spells all the time – no, I said – to say all his ailments were both caused and cured by drink – now that's a neat one – and to say that if you were going to drink at all there was no point in not drinking as much as possible. Funny, I had thought I was the drinker of the bunch.

To help to finance a move to somewhere more salubrious I'm trying to flog my typescripts, drafts, etc. To America, needless to say.[5] While the deal impends I sit cachinnating at the weakness of the £. Will it go on? The agent wants to know if I fancy flogging letters. Well yes, I said, but you look a bit of a shit when a catalogue says FOR SALE: 11 letters from John Betjeman to KA. No getting round that, I'm afraid.

Francis Pym's book[6] has had a most satisfactory pasting from L and R alike. How I hate all that talk of moderation and reasonableness and flexibility, especially the last, meaning readiness to give in. Have been hearing a fair amount of talk from Ali [Kilmarnock] about taking the middle ground and avoiding extremes. Thought of and indeed looked

---

1. For Lady Elizabeth Cavendish see Amis to Betjeman, 3 June 1971, note 4. She does not feature in Bevis Hillier, *Young Betjeman* (London: John Murray, 1988), the 'official biography', because it only goes up to 1933; a second volume is yet to appear.

2. John Wells (1936–98), writer, actor, director.

3. For Jill Balcon, Day-Lewis's second wife, see Amis to Larkin, 20 December 1954, note 5.

4. Robert Bridges (1844–1930), appointed Poet Laureate in succession to Alfred Austin (1853–1913); Gosse is Edmund Gosse, critic and essayist, author of *Father and Son* (1907). The two men had known each other since 1879, when both were on the committee of the Savile Club. Ann Thwaite, in *Edmund Gosse: A Literary Landscape* (Oxford: Oxford University Press, 1985), p. 455, writes that 'it was certainly while Asquith was still Prime Minister that Gosse was at the height of his influence. Asquith was always turning to him for advice: on the appointment to the new Cambridge Chair, on the new Lord Chamberlain, whether Meredith should be buried in the Abbey, and who should be, in 1913, the new Poet Laureate. In this last case, Gosse approved of Bridges.' In a note on the same page, Thwaite quotes a letter from Bridges to Gosse (12 December 1913) thanking Gosse for his support.

5. Amis's papers, including the Betjeman letters, were eventually sold to the Huntington Library for $90,000.

6. *The Politics of Consent* (1984); Pym (b.1922), Conservative politician and Minister; a prominent 'wet', he was sacked as Foreign Secretary by Margaret Thatcher in the 1982 reshuffle; created Life Peer (1987).

up in my files your Times letter on the subj – where are the Pinochet supporters in Smith Sq., pro-apartheid shags in the Commons, etc. The same kind of bullshit, only worse, goes into this police v. pickets stuff. Trog[7] had a disgraceful cartoon t'other day showing Pc bashing pkt & pkt Pc and 2 blokes agreeing there was nothing in it. Like US v. USSR. What do we call it, seditious neutrality?

Sorry I seem to have no personal news. I just go to the Garrick, see Geo Gale etc. *You* get the distinguished visitors, brief the CIA etc. Bugger me, has nothing happened this end? Well, Wells didn't turn up yesterday at the church; a pansy prebendary filled in for him. Richard Ingrams[8] turned up unshaven – why did he do that? Bloody funny that I've had no unfavourable 'feedback' from females about *Stanley*, on the contrary. Ones I have never met write to me, others I know only say as wives of acquaintances seek me out, all saying too bloody true and about time someone said it. Suggests perhaps that the pendulum has started to swing back? Had my first experience of lefty takeover tactics the other day – the first at least since I was on the takeover side in the '40s. A thing called the Theatre Writers' Union tried, through some of their number who are also members of the Writers' Guild, to get all T[W]U members declared members of the Guild. It emerged that a 'theatre writer' could be a shag who'd written one unperformed bit of fringe theatre. By God they were cross when I and 40 other specially-alerted righties turned up and voted them down. Great example of democracy in action. Also of what is it, differentialism, the old TU practice of defending the membership against the intrusion of unskilled or unqualified outsiders (the Guild has quite a stiff points system for deciding what a 'writer' is).

Re your Aug visit, I plan *(tentatively)*[9] to be in Swansea abt 16 Aug-3 Sept. Hilly and Ali will be here most of that time. If you could give us your dates soon it would help us organise things here.

Love to Liddie. Send plenty limericks.

Cheers K.

[TLS: Recipient]

7. Wally Fawkes, political cartoonist (see Amis to Larkin, 22 September 1953, note 3). The cartoon was sparked by continuing controversy over a particularly violent clash on 18 June between police and striking miners.

8. Richard Ingrams (b.1937), journalist; editor *Private Eye* (1963–86), *The Oldie* (1992–).

9. MS addition.

TO ROBERT CONQUEST – 18 JULY 1984

186 LR NW5 Lndn Eng

Good ole B,

Just a line to say this establishment will be closed until 28th August, the Tuesday after Bank Holiday, but then there will be a gala reopening and you and Liddie will be very welcome on that day. I shall have been in Wales, H and Ali in Spain I dare say, anyway somewhere. But you two come on (or after) 28th. Garrick shut for another 6 days but as you know I can drink anywhere.

You probably saw that Maxwell has bought the Mirror group. Am just perceptibly nervous of my own position, but I have a year's contract and reckon he'll have a lot to dispose of before he gets down to me, like Paul Foot and John Pilger.[1] I should be sorry to stop my column, not least because of the thought of the rage engendered in Al[varez][2] -et-al circles. There I am feeding them (I quote from the last few weeks) Browning, Tennyson, Housman, Kipling, Edward Thomas and Isaac Watts when I could be giving them Adrian Mitchell, Tony Harrison and John Ashbery[3] – ah, it will cheer you to be told that the other day I met an *American* professor of *Eng Lit* who had *never heard* of JA. Mind you he likes Pee Wee Russell and Johnny Dodds[4] so you can understand it.

Wherever I go nowadays I hear tales of what a shit Betjeman was to his secretaries, swearing at them, making them cry, having to have a new one every few weeks. Case of de vivis nil nisi bonum.[5] Shows you, doesn't it? He'll go down to history as a genial teddy-bear figure

---

1. Left-wing journalists, neither of whom was sacked: Foot (b.1937) wrote for the *Mirror* from 1979–93; Pilger (b.1939) was the paper's Chief Foreign Correspondent from 1962–86.

2. Amis's square brackets.

3. Yet Amis did offer *Mirror* readers Ashbery's 'Fear of Death', as well as Sylvia Plath's 'The Moon and the Yew Tree'. His introduction to the Ashbery poem is typical in length and tone: 'Ashbery has a great following in his native America, where he has more than once been called the greatest poet now writing in the English language. British readers have been more cautious. His meaning is usually implied rather than stated and it is sometimes hard to gain more than a general impression.'

4. Johnny Dodds (1892–1940), clarinettist.

5. 'Of the living say nothing but what is good' or 'speak no ill of the living', a play on *de mortuis nil nisi bonum.*

beloved of all while a nice old softie like me will be taken as a curmudgeonly old shit. Makes you wonder. I expect if the truth were known Pope was an absolute charmer encouraging young poets and visiting the sick and Lamb behaved like Dylan Thomas.

Maggie does seem to be losing popularity. I can't see how or why exactly, and I still bat for her. But I sense it. She'll get it all back when she clobbers Scargill.[6] Hey – I suppose she still is going to?

Let me tell you about a wonderful tiny little piece of pissiness while it's fresh in my mind. There was a 10- or 12-year-old chess master on telly the other day, not a world-beater yet but obviously first-rate, and a psychologist of sorts was asked what made the lad so good. 'His wonderful concentration' was the reply; not BEING BLOODY BRILLIANT or FUCKING CLEVER or anything like that because he'd have been born like that, you see. The only way of saving the situation for the Left was to allege pitifully that *post-natal influences* or some fucking environmental thing had been at work. It's often in minimis that we can see the STUPID CUNTS at work most clearly.

Hope to see you on 28th Aug. Love to Liddie.[7]

Cheers
old K.

[TLS: Recipient]

TO PAUL FUSSELL – 19 JULY 1984

186 Leighton Road, London N.W.5

Dear Paul,

Glad you like Philadelphia;[1] I have pleasant memories of it, having seen one of the three prettiest girls I have ever seen in my life in a restaurant there.

6. Arthur Scargill (b.1938), President, National Union of Mineworkers (since 1981). A miners' strike, over proposed pit closures, began on 6 March 1984 and effectively ended on 3 March 1985, when NUM delegates voted to return to work without a settlement.
7. MS addition.

1. Fussell had recently moved from a named professorship at Rutgers University in New Jersey (1976–83) to one at the University of Pennsylvania.

I am booked to be in Swansea 10th-28th August, the latter day being the Tuesday after a bank holiday. That still leaves four days of August, and why don't you make it a little later and stay into September? School surely doesn't start on the 1st. I shall be fully available for pub-crawls etc., but the Garrick will be shut until the 3rd. Sure, we can go to the Travellers. [. . .] Now I think of it you could come down to Wales for a couple of nights or more. There are hotels. Lady-friend[2] might like the trip and a sight of the Principality. Let me know and I can book you in.

I have not only seen your CASTE MARKS, I have written a rave review of it for the Daily Telegraph.[3] To be published on the 28th. I'll save you a copy though I expect your publisher will send you one. Bloody funny book. I should love to go through it with you page by page pointing out how the Brits differ but much more often how we are just the same. I have a particularly interesting observation on what you do with your shirt-collar when you put on a *blazer*. Remind me.

Enormously look forward to seeing you and to meeting Harriette. We'll do famous damage to London's drink stocks when you come.

Cheers,
Kingsley

[TLS: Recipient]

TO THE EDITOR, *SUNDAY TELEGRAPH* – 5 AUGUST 1984

I HATE to find fault with such a friendly mention as Sebastian Faulks's last week,[1] but please, my novel "Stanley and the Women" does not argue that "all women are mad." No, as a leading character puts it, "they're all too monstrously, sickeningly, *terrifyingly* sane." Not that it

2. The journalist Harriette Behringer, who became Fussell's second wife in 1987.
3. *Caste Marks: Style and Status in the USA* (1984); published in the United States as *Class: A Guide Through the American Status System* (1983). Amis's rave review, 'Spotting Class in the US Way', appeared in the *Daily Telegraph*, 28 July 1984, p. 12.

---

1. In 'Publishers Hit the Male on the Head', 29 July 1984, p. 19, Faulks calls *Stanley and the Women* 'a damn good book – funny, sad, topical and with bags of sales potential', and attributes its problems finding an American publisher to its perceived anti-feminism: 'it argues that all women are mad.'

makes a lot of difference to those at the receiving end, admittedly. Or to a feminist.

KINGSLEY AMIS
London, NW1

TO PHILIP LARKIN – 12 SEPTEMBER 1984

186 Leighton Road, Kentish Town, London, N.W.5

Dear Philip,

Ta for yours AFTER ALL THIS TIME. And that's about it. This is really to clear my desk (herk-herm) before I get down to my next novel[1] I'll get down to your Sorry about your weight problem. Mine is much better now because I have lost about a stone simply by drinking less at night. You ought to give it a whooghghgh

Actually my main desk-clearing problem has to do with that sodding bleeding collection of anecdotes I am supposed to be compiling.[2] I sent a circular kind of letter to about 1/2m people a month ago and so far, or rather already, something like 6% of people have replied. Jolly helpful too. 'Dear Mr Amis, Michael Caine is presently filming in Paraguay but I will see that your letter' – 'Dear Kingsley Amis, . . . However I have one story which may be of use to you. In Paris in I think 1929 I ran into Willie Maugham in the company of a very well-known French politician of the day. Willie whispered to me, "Frank Harris told me he wears women's underclothes." I fear I cannot reveal the man's identity although I realise' – 'Dear Kingsley, . . . However should I think of any I will jot' – 'Dear Mr Amis, . . . keep them for my own book. I am sure you will understand.' Don't I just, cock. Well, it's only £7,000 advance to return. Ha ha. Ha ha. Ha ha ha ha ha ha ha What a fool to agree to do it.

The last weeks have been thin in any activity except drinking and chatting. Less strenuous than working and fucking, any road. Well mostly. Bob and Mrs Bob were here, have just finished being here, for

1. *The Old Devils* (1986).

2. See Amis to the editor, *Spectator*, 31 December 1983; also to Dale Salwak, 15 May 1984, note 1.

a week that apart from my attendance at an incredibly drunken funeral in Wales [. . .] consisted of, or largely featured, Bob talking to me. He is one of the best, a real good sort, but sweet Christ can he talk. Jolly good stuff, most of it, but there is a lot. Exacerbated by his critical reception of one's feeble efforts to put in an occasional word: 'So it was a complete failure.' – 'Well, not a *complete* failure, just much less than they'd hoped' . . . 'That was early on, then.' – 'Well, a lot of it was early on, but some of it came a bit later.' I began to understand your thing about having to (having to? having to?) have a good part of the day to yourself. [. . .]

If a man called Frank Delaney[3] ever tries to make you do anything, run. He is a dangerous lunatic who while giving me lunch at the Athenaeum said that Balliol had offered him a fellowship 'to teach the novella' but he had turned it down. Powerful in TV it seems. But Dr Rowse what is the justification of your bum,

Kingsley

Hilly sends her love[4]

[TLS: Bodleian]

TO LOIS WILSON – 23 OCTOBER 1984

186 Leighton Road, Kentish Town, London, N.W.5

My dear Lois,

Anthony Werner today showed me some of the superb paintings of yours that Shepheard Walwyn are going to publish.[1] I should be

3. Frank Delaney (b. 1942), writer and broadcaster.
4. MS addition.

---

1. Amis met the artist Lois Wilson (b. 1914), wife of the Swansea City Coroner and Under-Sheriff Jack Wilson, in the early 1950s. They were introduced by Margaret Aeron-Thomas and in subsequent years would see each other on Amis's visits to Stuart and Eve Thomas. Amis first saw Mrs Wilson's book of flower paintings, eventually titled *Wild Flowers in their Seasons: A Gower Flora*, at the London offices of the publishers Shepheard Walwyn. When Shepheard Walwyn decided they could not afford the cost of reproducing the book's ninety-two-plus plates, it was brought out, after several years, by D. Brown and Sons of Cowbridge and Bridgend, Mid Glamorgan. Amis's preface makes clear his admiration for Wilson's 'beautiful and sensuous paintings', which he sees as fulfilling 'one of the most

delighted to write an introduction to the book. There are many details to be settled and the final format is yet to be decided, but I thought you would like to know at this stage that I am definitely committed.

Much love
Kingsley

[ALS: Recipient]

TO JOHN VEALE – 15 NOVEMBER 1984

186 Leighton Road, Kentish Town, London, N.W.5

Dear John,

Thank you very much for sending the photostat of THE LAST WAR,[1] which has faded in parts . . . I mean the poem, not the photostat . . . but comes out not too badly after all these years. All these years is just the trouble. Lots of things have happened since 1948, notably the emergence of a movement to disarm the West. I must not allow myself to be associated in any way with this movement and however presented, my poem might well be taken or mistaken for support of this movement. So I am sorry, lad, but I absolutely forbid you to set it to music. But

important functions of art': 'to remind people of what is around them and train them to look at it'. *A Gower Flora* was voted runner-up in the 1988 Royal Society for Nature Conservation's Book of the Year Award.

1. In 1948 Veale asked Amis for some verses to set to music. Amis came up with 'The Last War', which was first published in *A Case of Samples* (1956), and reprinted in *CP*, pp. 24–5. It begins: 'The first country to die was normal in the evening,/Ate a good but plain dinner, chatted with some friends/Over a glass, and went to bed soon after ten;/And in the morning was found disfigured and dead./That was the lucky one.' Veale remained in sympathy with the anti-war sentiments of the poem (being of the moderate left throughout his life), but as he explained to Amis in a letter of 26 October 1984, his renewed interest in it was musical rather than political: 'it is simply an eminently settable piece – as indeed it was so skilfully designed to be.' Some of Veale's original ideas for the poem, he told Amis in the same letter, 'ended up in my setting of Kubla Khan (especially "Ancestral voices prophesying war")', which was once performed in a BBC Symphony Concert. The decision to try again with it was prompted by a request from the BBC Philharmonia Orchestra for a major new piece. For Veale see Amis to Larkin, 4 April 1952, note 2.

without prompting I will telephone you when I find myself in Oxford.

Anyway, I was jolly glad to hear of your success and so was Hilly, who sends her love.

Cheers
Kingsley

[TLS: Recipient]

TO HARRY RITCHIE – 15 NOVEMBER 1984

186 Leighton Road, Kentish Town, London, N.W.5

Dear Mr. Ritchie,[1]

Thank you for your letter. The general tendency of your D. Phil. research interests me.[2] I think you are on the right lines when you say that the "real nature" of my "challenge – literary and cultural, rather than social or political – was ignored or misappropriated at the time and has not been fully appreciated since", though it is hardly for me to say so and "challenge" perhaps over states the case. I think a discussion might be a good idea, and if you will telephone we could arrange to meet.

Yours sincerely,
Kingsley Amis

[TLS: Recipient]

1. Harry Ritchie (b.1958), author and journalist, working at the time on a D.Phil. in English at Oxford (on British writers of the 1950s); subsequently Deputy Literary Editor (1988–92) and Literary Editor (1993–95), *Sunday Times*; author of the travel books *Here we Go* (1993) and *The Last Pink Bits* (1997).

2. A revised version of Ritchie's 1985 Oxford D.Phil. was eventually published as *Success Stories: Literature and the Media in England, 1950–1959* (London and Boston: Faber and Faber, 1988).

TO PHILIP LARKIN – 28 NOVEMBER 1984

186 Leighton Road, Kentish Town, London, N.W.5

Dear Philip,

Glad to hear you are all right again. When I drink for 2/3 days now I follow with 1/2 nights of waking at 3.30, lying awake till 5.0 and then extreme drowsiness plus nightmares as long as I care to go on. You too? No? I am such an anxious cunt that by the time I've drunk enough to slow me down I've also drunk enough to make me very anxious. Pisson shitty-nit. How are you getting on with your auroral gin-and-limes?

I don't know what you think you're playing at, all this reading Julian Barnes.[1] I know he sends you his works, and he does admire you, and he is quite good, but he's also a bit of an R-scrawler*, hoping for a puff. I stopped reading F's P as soon as it was clear that the fellow wasn't going to find in F's works concealed instructions for finding a hidden treasure in a sleepy little village in the Vosges. Compulsive reading – have you ever tried a chap called Sapper?[2] Actually the new Frederick Forsyth[3] is quite good. Jolly anti-lefty, though you have to reconcile yourself to never getting a single spark out of the writing. But then there aren't any of those in Anthony Burgess or Saul Bellow or V.S. Naipaul or Malcolm Bradbury or anyone else are there, hey? NB: have you read the new D Francis yet?

Hilly is fine, though she has an enlarged liver it seems. She'll have to cut down on all those bottles of vodka she keeps knocking back. Miggy,[4] who we went to see last week in Glos., is largely unchanged, still laughing at everything she says. [. . .] G Gale is recovering well and must never drink at least for now. Bob's brother-in-law's heart . . . And this is just the first round. Yes, dear, I do get a bit of breathlessness after hurrying. Normal at our age I dare say. Check-up by my heart

1. Larkin had commented favourably on Julian Barnes's *Flaubert's Parrot* (1984) in a letter of 22 October 1984 (in HEHL).

2. The pseudonym of Herman Cyril McNeile (1888–1937), author of popular thrillers featuring Hugh 'Bulldog' Drummond.

3. *The Fourth Protocol* (1984), by Frederick Forsyth (b.1938), author of best-selling 'documentary' thrillers, beginning with *The Day of the Jackal* (1971).

4. Margaret Partington, Hilly's sister.

man next week er her her. Ole Bob himself was on the blower as I write this, over to rally the troops. He does talk a certain amount but while he's doing it you forget that funny tremor in your chest and that odd little twinge in your back.

You are mad you know, hobnobbing with Morrison and Motion.[5] If it were anyone else I might suspect him of R-slicking the young or comparatively young. No I can't see anything in any of them except Fenton, and he keeps writing stuff I can't understand. I can't see why a fellow like Peter Porter or Crag Raine fucking well *bothers*, can you? Like these modern-jazz craps.

The Legacy is on its way to Amerikee I trust. Think I told you I am flogging all MSS and TSS. It'll take months they say. But I've got to get money from somewhere. All very well for the h-f d. The presentation lunch at the Yank embassy was amazingly inept.[6] They spent hours talking about the Hudson was it Review with half a mo in the middle about AP. Martin had a son the other day, name of Louis so far. He [Louis] looked very fed up when I saw him, and when you take a good look round yourself you can't blame him, what? The party for the JB exhib[7] was bloody in a different way. The only poets I saw were Alan Ross and Mary Wilson.[8] Red or white, sir? I bugared of sharpish I do'nt mind telling you.

Mrs Thatcher is pursuing monetarism instead of bum,

Kingsley

* *Ah, scrawling away as usual, Mr Stickleback!*[9]

[TLS: Bodleian]

5. Larkin was to chair a reading given by Andrew Motion and Blake Morrison. Motion was Lecturer in English, University of Hull (1977–81), where he met Larkin, later becoming his biographer and the co-executor (with Anthony Thwaite) of Larkin's literary estate.

6. On Thursday, 25 October 1984, Anthony Powell was presented with the *Hudson Review* Bennett Prize ($15,000) at a luncheon at the American Embassy. In his *Journals: 1982–86* (London: Heinemann, 1995), p. 128, Powell records that 'Fred Morgan, William Pritchard, Roger Rosenblatt all spoke, short and to the point, tho' Tristram [Powell] said Kingsley Amis's face was pure H.M. Bateman while their speeches were in progress.' Amis also complained that he did not get enough wine at the Embassy.

7. 'John Betjeman: A Celebration', an exhibition at the National Theatre, ran from 29 October to 8 December.

8. Mary Wilson (*née* Baldwin), wife of ex-Prime Minister Harold Wilson (m. 1940), and the author of *Selected Poems* (1970) and *New Poems* (1980).

9. MS addition.

TO J.G. SIMPSON – 18 DECEMBER 1984

c/o THE DAILY MIRROR

Dear Mr. Simpson,

Thank you for your letter and for sending me your collection of poems.[1] I found them most readable, thanks to the traditions in which you were writing, and the sentiments expressed were most congenial to me. I think perhaps I enjoyed A JOURNEY ON THE L.N.E.R. the most.[2]

Yours sincerely,
Kingsley Amis

[TLS: Recipient]

TO PHILIP LARKIN – 18 DECEMBER 1984

186 Leighton Road, Kentish Town, London, N. W. 5

Dear Philip,

Thought I would reciprocate your sportingly swiftish reply to my last. Nowt much to say; well, we have a house in Regt's Pk Rd. They've accepted my offer I mean. Solicitor bum. Survey bum. Exchange of contracts bum. Stamp duty bum. BRIDGING LOAN bum. Well, you know. But it's much nicer than here. Good restaurant, pub, off

---

1. J.G. Simpson (1929–91) worked in accountancy and local government (he was Mayor of Ilkeston, Derbyshire, in the late 1950s), and wrote plays and poems throughout his life, mostly self-published. He wrote to Amis care of the *Daily Mirror*.

2. This poem, from Simpson's *Collected Poems* (1984), begins:

> The gas-lit station on Heanor Road, Ilkeston,
> After the blackout seemed all aglow.
> I can remember in that first bleak December
> Walking towards it through rain and through snow.
> My destination – Victoria Station,
> Victoria Station in old Nottingham.

It ends:

> After the blackout everything seemed to glow;
> But all of these stations, the lines and the tunnels
> Were closed down for ever many long years ago.

licence(s), bookshop NOT THAT THAT COUNTS FOR ANYTHING. V. near (btwi ftwi betwixt ourselves) where I used to give it to ole Janey-girl in the long-ago.

I laughed heartily at your excellent jest about Martin's book.[1] You almost had me believing you sort of, well, *enjoyed* it or something, ha ha ha. If I didn't know you better I'd, etc. I hated its way of constantly reminded me of Nabokov. But of course I'm very old-fashioned. Set in my ways, what? I expect you read a lot of Saul Bellow and Philip Roth and Norman Maaaaghgh [. . .]

I have quite a lot of time for Chas O,[2] not least because of his hatred of the Arts Council. That's a book of his I'm looking forward to. Yes, the poems[3] are crappy, but you don't think people go for you for that, do you? They do it because you've not given them a grant or reviewed them badly or were rude to their boy-friend. Eh? How did I get started on this?

I know what I wanted to ask you (is there something suspect about this phrase? V. Betj[4]): what or who do you read when it's sports night on TV? Real question, this. Do you read anything by a living writer, or a dead one for that matter, that you haven't read before?* I rather suspected something of the sort. Which reminds me to say that I've been reading for the nth time G'bye to B.[5] Bloody good still, eh? Unfaded. It's only his queerness, or his pretending not to be queer, that cheeses. Where every prospect cheeses.[6] And I doubt whether even the filthy Huns were quite so tolerant of rugby around 1930. Esp. working-class ones like the Nowaks.[7]

---

1. *Money* (1984). Larkin's jest does not appear in the correspondence.

2. Charles Osborne (b. 1927), author and critic; Literary Director, the Arts Council (1971–86).

3. *Letter to W.H. Auden and Other Poems* (1984); the book Amis was looking forward to was Osborne's memoirs, *Giving it Away* (1986).

4. See Betjeman's poem 'How to Get on in Society', from *A Few Late Chrysanthemums* (1954): 'I know what I wanted to ask you –/Is trifle sufficient for sweet?'

5. Christopher Isherwood, *Goodbye to Berlin* (1939).

6. An allusion to lines from the hymn 'From Greenland's Icy Mountains', by Bishop Reginald Heber (1783–1826): 'What though the spicy breezes/Blow soft o'er Ceylon's isle;/ Though every prospect pleases,/And only man is vile.'

7. In 'The Nowaks', one of the stories in *Goodbye to Berlin*, 'Christoph', the Isherwood-narrator, lodges in the crowded flat of the family of his friend Otto Nowak, a character from a previous story. Otto is promiscuous and bisexual. 'Rugby' is 'buggery', as in 'bugray', 'egg-rub' (for bugger), 'raybug', 'bogray' and other variants; see also Amis to Larkin, 12 May 1950 (in Bodleian): 'I have been doing an average 8 hrs. a day, including week-ends, and sometimes more. It has been sheer rugby.'

By the way get that NOB-18thCV.[8] Full of good new stuff, I warrant your honour.

Off to the Garrick shortly for my Christmas drunk there. If nothing else kept me in London that place would. Somewhere to get pissed in jovial not very literary bright *all-male* company. You haven't got a place like that, have you? Don't need one? Balls man you're dreaming.

I take it you've come round about the L'ship now they're talking about a £10thou tax-free stipend,[9] you greedy old burag. No but serously htuohg you really should take it. G Ewart (pompous old ponce) told me bets are going down on C Causley. You can't let it happen Phil.

Implicit recital of agonised bum,

Kingsley

* apart from the work of trendy, ah, scrawlers hey leggo my pisser

Besters for '85 what[10]

[TLS: Bodleian]

TO ROBERT CONQUEST – 18 DECEMBER 1984

186 Leighton Road NW5

Dear young Bob,

Xmas approaches, though of course you won't get this till next March or so. Seems certain now that Mrs T will offer the L'ship to Philip, and the silly sod will turn it down. Cuntish piece by S. Fay[1] in Time & Tide on US-UK special relationship. Gone now, he says, because of widespread concern here about RR's [Ronald Reagan's] hawkishness and age. He means AMONG GUARDIAN CRAPS. Never much anyway, he says; there was widespread distrust of US here during the war

8. Roger Lonsdale, *The New Oxford Book of Eighteenth-Century Verse* (Oxford: Oxford University Press, 1984). 'I warrant your honour' in the next sentence is from *Hamlet*, III.ii.16.

9. The salary of the Poet Laureate remained £70 a year plus 'a butt of sack' or barrel of wine.

10. MS addition.

---

1. Stephen Fay (b. 1938), author and journalist.

in his dad's generation. AMONG GUARDIAN CRAPS just possibly. I never heard of any such distrust in the army or out of it, and I doubt if you did either. I hope you keep telling the Yanks this sort of thing.

LEFT and RIGHT, political terms. The popular belief that they derive from the seating of deputies in a French assembly is incorrect. In fact, LEFT derives from the name of Albrecht Link or Links, burgomaster of Ytt near Zurich c. 1830, who advocated the confiscation of all wealth and its equal redistribution. A reading party of undergraduates from Trinity College, Cambridge, who passed through Ytt at the time, started punning about Links fahren or 'going Left' and popularised the phrase on their return to England. RIGHT commemorates Hiram Z. Wright who in the 1880s ran for the Alabama state senate on the platform of re-enslavement of all coloured persons under the slogan 'Vote Wright and You'll Be Right.' CENTRE is an anglicisation of the name of Ferenc Szenta, a Hungarian poet who . . .

Weather here continues to cheat Scargill by staying above O° every day.[2] I spend Xmas here, with Stuart and Eve Thomas up from Swansea & Xmas din at the Gales. Geo now finally off his head, having moved to Islington because Sawbridgeworth was too far from Fleet St (25 miles) and now about to move out to his freezing, falling-down 10-bedroom mansion at Tattingstone (75 miles). Met David Owen at Woodrow Wyatt's. Quite a taking chap. A bit full of what he, not we, would be up to when the time came or earlier. He agreed that his policy was to let people make money along Tory lines and then take a lot of it off them for welfare along socialist lines. Didn't get a chance to say, but Tory lines means not taking a lot of money off people, doesn't it? Oh well. Had we got a house when I saw you? Well, we have, Regt's Pk Rd, not a stone's throw (between you & me) from Chalcot Cresc where I used to screw old Jane when the world was young or younger. A v. nice part as they say. Committee for Free World[3] or whatever it is has been confabbing. I think we decided to invite you to the con in March.

2. The government had prepared for a long miners' strike: the National Coal Board had been stockpiling coal since 1981, as had the Central Electricity Generating Board. The weather served its cause.

3. The United Kingdom Committee for the Free World; Alun Chalfont, Chairman (1981–89).

What do you think of Alun Chalfont? Bit of a 2nd XI type? Best for '85. Love to Liddie.

Cheers
Kingsley

[TLS: Recipient]

TO THE EDITOR, *THE TIMES* – 21 FEBRUARY 1985

Sir, According to David Hewson (feature, February 14) "the sense of anger, disillusionment and even betrayal now being expressed over the direction of the Government's arts policy is virtually universal."[1] But not quite. Surely I am not alone in welcoming anything approaching a cut-back in public spending on "the arts" as a step towards the distant but desirable goal of ceasing it altogether.

Subsidy damages art by tending to foster irresponsibility, showiness, cliquism and self-indulgence in the artist. At the same time the public's power to choose what art it wants by financial pressure on the artist, is dangerously weakened. And whatever might be said about public taste it is better than the taste of the people the subsidised artist is likely to set out to please or impress: critics, colleagues, friends, experts, bureaucrats.

Yours faithfully,

KINGSLEY AMIS
c/o Jonathan Clowes,
22 Prince Albert Road, NW1,
February 16.

1. David Hewson, 'Can the Arts Stand the Strain', *The Times*, 14 February 1985, p. 12, discussed reaction in 'the arts community' to the budget delivered by Lord Gowrie, Minister for the Arts, in December 1984.

TO THE EDITOR, *SPECTATOR* – 23 FEBRUARY 1985

Sir: In the course of his semi-literate account of Mrs Thatcher's first ten years as leader of the Conservative Party (Profile, 9 February), a writer of yours refers to her administration's 'now infamous howlers'. That word 'infamous' has appeared in other curious contexts lately. As a spotter of popular catachreses could I ask your man – through you – what he means by 'infamous'? This is not a rhetorical question. (Tell him a rhetorical question is one asked not for information but to produce effect.)

KINGSLEY AMIS
189 Leighton Road, Kentish Town, London NW5

TO PHILIP LARKIN – 2 MARCH 1985

186 Leighton Road, Kentish Town, London, N.W.5.

Dear Philip,

I seem not to have written to you for a hell of a long time. No reason. Or perhaps just I have this new rule, 150 words of novel min per diem. Doesn't sound much but you try it some time (Ah! Ah!). About 25,000 on the board now I reckon. Then when I've finished that I thought I'd dash off a few poems for a change; yer, no ah-ah there.

Hope you're feeling better. By the way I can reassure you a bit about your mental condish, at least as far as A Young goes.[1] He's quite good, I think, though you don't want more than 2 or 3 at a session, but pre-eminently there's nothing to be said about him, anyway not more than you said in your eventual very good piece. So no evidence of brain-fag in your difficulty in finding anything. ~~toxxsy~~ ←—[2] pissenschidt

1. Amis is responding to a letter from Larkin, 27 December 1984 (in HEHL): 'I write as an alternative to continuing to read The Poetical Works of Andrew Young for the purpose of review. Did I tell you that I have fears that I am becoming unable to write reviews oh piss just as I am b u t w pwetry? Can't think of anything to say.' Andrew Young (1885–1971), Scottish poet, ordained first as minister of the Free Church, then as an Anglican clergyman. Larkin's review, entitled 'Solitary Walker', appeared in the *Observer*, 13 January 1985, p. 50.

2. The arrow points to the deleted words 'to say'.

Have been rereading your Req'd Wrtg[3] a 2nd time. As I said before I think, I keep wondering at your youthful enthusiasms: Hardy, Stevie Smith, Barbara Pym, Lawrence*. Golly! – the way you gobble them up makes me feel very old and grey, I can tell you! It was just a touch crappy of you, perhaps, to say that 'the theme' of LJ was boy-turns-crappy-girl-into-nice-girl (re-used in IWIN[4]). Isn't it a bit minor in LJ, compared with Welch stuff, Margaret stuff etc.? But never mind; after all you did to get me launched on it you can say what you bloody well like.

We'll leave you alone about the L'ship from now on. Just want you to know you're not fooling anyone with your stated dread of TV progs (there would be 26 not 24 such, actually; herk herm), foreign po conf etc. We know you know you wouldn't have had to do any of that. Anyway. I will tell you in confidence that I was asked by Macmillan, the publisher not the statesman, to write the Betj biog, and have turned it down, with a raincheck should I become unable to write fiction and of course if it's still vacant. If it's not, think of the fearful shit I will have made room for. Fair makes yer sweat.

I am on my NAP (New Alcoholic Policy) again, 4–5 drinks a day, which means I can eat, sign my name at any time and follow films on TV at night. Just a few nightmares thrown in. You're right about the Garrick in a way,[5] though I can man ge to go there once a week only, or less. Don't want to, though. But they don't half shift the stuff there.

The D Mirror 'will not be renewing' my contract,[6] and the education correspondent will be continuing the column. The mad Czech Maxwell, having spent millions of £s on the paper, has now noticed he has less

3. *Required Writing* (1983).

4. *I Want it Now* (1968). Amis is referring to Larkin's answer to a question about *Lucky Jim* in the 1982 *Paris Review* interview reprinted in *Required Writing*, p. 59: 'the theme – boy meets apparently nasty girl but turns her into a nice girl by getting her away from nasty environment – is one I think has always meant a lot to Kingsley. He used it again in *I Want it Now*.' For Larkin's reply to Amis's complaint, see his letter of 20 March 1985 (in HEHL): 'Sorry about the boy-meets-girl bit, but in all truth, my old consort, you did rather plug that line in those days, no doubt to encourage my own qualms in yat Directioun – anyway, LJ has always read like an everyday story of Abbey Timbers folk to me (don't tell Hilly), despite your invention of the Campus Novel and all that modern jazz workshop. I wasn't trying to belittle it or you (how could I?), just pick out a strangely-neglected thread from the frigger in the cowpat or whatyoumaycall.'

5. See Larkin to Amis, 27 December 1984 (in HEHL): 'My sodding job is the only thing that keeps me going, like the Garrick Club with you (yes, I know you didn't actually say that).'

6. As Poetry Editor. See Amis to Conquest, 29 February 1984, note 8.

money than before and is now recklessly economising. Got you in a second time, though.[7]

Well, it hasn't taken me so dreadedly long to write to you. I will try to do so again soon. Oh the house is still on (yes, not far from Lord's)[8] but there has been a hiccup at this end owing to the prospective purchaser suffering an incapacitating heart attack. 38, he is. Er her-her. Or hertcher, as a boy at my school (or was it yours?) used to say – gloomification of hotcha.

The miners must not be so crushingly defeated as to lose all bum

Kingsley

* *and now old Gusher Connolly. Xt! About LJ, I mean.*[9]

[TLS: Bodleian]

TO PHILIP LARKIN – 2 APRIL 1985

186 Leighton Road, Kentish Town, London, N.W.5.

Dear Philip,

Oh shit: what can I say? V. sorry to hear of your ordeals. Barium enemas, Christ. Glad it's NOT ALL BUT SOME blown over. My own little bits of that have made me wonder why nobody tells you there are parts of life INCLUDING ITS END that are absolutely unlike the rest of it. Well, not wonder, really. Again, my exp. says you will feel a hell of a lot better, like being quite prepared to start the day, if you cut your booze. Get your appetite back, too. You're probably there already by the time you get this. [. . .]

You are too kind about WBOJA.[1] Lot of callow bullshit there. I

7. 'Coming' appeared in the *Daily Mirror* in February 1984, and 'At Grass' in June 1984. Both were written in 1950 and appeared in *XX Poems* (1951) and *The Less Deceived* (1954).

8. The cricket ground, in St John's Wood.

9. See Larkin, 'Reviewing is Bad for You', *Sunday Times*, 24 February 1985, p. 45, a reprint of his introduction to the new edition of Cyril Connolly's *The Condemned Playground* (1945), published the following day by the Hogarth Press.

---

1. *What Became of Jane Austen*?, which Larkin had praised above his own *Required Writing*, in a letter of 20 March 1985 (in HEHL).

laughed like hell at Auden saying Naughty, naughty to you.[2] Talking of callow bullshit, I wasn't creatively inactive in those years between Jill and Jim, no no, I was writing callow bullshit. All those terrible poems. The Legacy. You 'matured' long before I did. It just happened like that. You see, some of us (pause) have a harder time growing up than others. It's the woooghgh But really I was bloody lucky almost none of it got into print.

Sorry if I sounded nettled about the frigger in the cowpat.[3] I wasn't a bit. Hilly roared with laughter at your Abbey Timbers crack. Funny about IWIN, I was thinking. There I was thinking it was Simon Quick I was married to (well, a bit) and it was Lady Baldock all the time.[4] When I first met that woman I thought she was *vulnerable*. You know, needing looking after. Fucky Nell . . .

We shall have to arrange to bridge your bum,

Kingsley

Hope you are all clear now.[5]

[TLS: Bodleian]

TO JOHN McDERMOTT – 25 APRIL 1985

186 Leighton Road, Kentish Town, London, N.W.5.

Dear Mr. McDermott,

Thank you for sending the copy of your piece.[1] I should have written

2. See Motion, *Life*, p. 438: '[A]t dinner in Stephen Spender's house in London in 1972 . . . Auden had asked Larkin whether he liked living in Hull. When Larkin replied that he supposed he would be as unhappy anywhere else, Auden cackled "Naughty! Naughty! Mother wouldn't like it!"'

3. See Amis to Larkin, 2 March 1985, note 4, for both 'frigger in the cowpat' and the 'Abbey Timbers crack'. 'Frigger in the cowpat' is an obscenification of the title of Henry James's story 'The Figure in the Carpet' (1896), which suggests a way of understanding a writer's entire work.

4. The vulnerable Simon Quick is the daughter of the tyrannical Lady Baldock in *I Want it Now* (1968).

5. MS addition. Larkin had been going through 'about six weeks' panic about my health, involving blood tests, x-rays, liver scans, barium enemas (grand lads, those) and the like' (Larkin to Amis, 20 March 1985, in HEHL).

1. John McDermott, 'Kingsley and the Women', *Critical Quarterly* 27:3 (Autumn 1985),

much earlier to say a different kind of thank you. You seem to me to understand very nearly exactly how I work and what I have been trying to do. For example, you are almost the first person outside my own immediate circle to see the ironies in 'A Bookshop Idyll'.[2] And I very much took your point about the tendency of some critics to read autobiography into my novels at a time when other critics, or perhaps even the same critics, are trying to separate novel and novelist.

It may interest you to know that the novel I am now working on has three unequivocally sympathetic characters, two women and a queer.[3]

One tiny point: 'Jake Richardson' is a deliberate reformulation of 'Jim Dixon'.

Well, thank you again. I hope very much that the possible book you mention becomes a reality.[4]

Yours,
Kingsley Amis

[TLS: Recipient]

TO PHILIP LARKIN – 18 JUNE 1985

186 Leighton Road, Kentish Town, London, N.W.5.

Hope oesoph is okay.[1]

Dear Philip,

Sorry for lateness: chiefly novel, also laziness. Gratters on your new

pp. 65–71, defends Amis against the charge of misogyny: 'Literary Amis is, if anything, a ladies' man, and in *Jake's Thing* the only really nice people are women.'

2. As McDermott summarises: 'the poem as a whole deflates the *male* ego' (ibid., p. 67).

3. Amis's next published novel was *The Old Devils* (1986), in which Charlie Norris's unequivocally sympathetic brother, Victor, is a homosexual, and Peter Thomas's old flame, Rhiannon Rhys, and her daughter Rosemary, are also unequivocally sympathetic. The novel was published on 12 September 1986, so Amis would still have been working on it in April 1985.

4. It did, as *Kingsley Amis: An English Moralist* (London: Macmillan, 1989), Chapter 8 of which incorporates most of the material in McDermott's 1985 *Critical Quarterly* essay.

---

1. MS addition. Larkin's cancerous oesophagus was removed at Hull Royal Infirmary on 11 June, when another cancerous tumour in the throat was discovered. This second tumour was too advanced for surgery.

honour;[2] better than the L'ship, eh? Quite take your point about Hughes: people keep coming into the Garrick and saying, This chap Hughes, he isn't half no good, isn't he?[3] Y'know, talking of the old po: in gen., I bought myself a complete Dylan at just about the same time as being sent ole Roy F[uller]'s collected, & have hardly opened that but keep peeping at Dylan. Piss with froth on, you remember.

Move will probably be about 18th Jul but I'll lecher, no? It hasn't touched me as yet but I see fearful convusl pusl vulsions coming. Can't face turning out my desk. Just can't face it what. Actually the vendors did leave the carpets but FUCK, WHO CARES why am I *going on* about this as if it mattered. Exchange of contracts[4] with the purchasers hopefully this week.

Lunch with Iris M[urdoch] today; become a sort of institution which is all right in a way, but she's joined the swelling ranks of the free-associators, so that getting to the end of a sentence gets like steering a canoe through a stretch of rapids. Sort of:

K:–Much as I admire Mrs Thatcher–

I:–I remember you saying you did the last time we met. At that French place in St Martin's Lane, wasn't it? What's it called?

K:–I think her policies–

I:–I don't think anyone has policies any more, do you? I mean what's your policy on buying clothes? Do you have a new suit every year or what? I just buy when I see something I like.

K:–on education–

I:–That's become a complete joke hasn't it? Do you know how many people are reading Greek now at Oxford?

K:–are a bit vocational–

I:–Did you have a sense of vocation from the beginning? I know I did. When did you start writing?

K:–though it's not fashionable to say so.

I:–Have you moved yet? You did say you were going to move didn't you

K:–YAGHBAGHOOGHEEGHERGHAWGH

In other words like TALKING TO A BLOODY WOMAN

Old Bob is over. He seems to act on the principle that if you go on

2. Larkin had been made a CH (Companion of Honour).

3. Ted Hughes had been appointed Poet Laureate.

4. Amis has written 'arrgh!' with an arrow pointing to 'Exchange', 's**t!' with an arrow to 'contracts', and 'farks' with an arrow to 'purchasers hopefully'.

as if nothing has happened then nothing happens. Still he's not really a boozer like you and me dalling. I am 'cutting down' again, meaning nightmares every other morning from about 5 a.m. Not really, no. Thank you for your card; I picked it up brilliantly at the club at 6 p.m. on my birthday & did merveil vaſtlie at its ſingular *Aptneſs*. I go to my GP or below-the-belt dr on Thursday 'just a yearly check-up' and the chest man next week 'just to make sure'.

Shit, I *love* reading. It's finding the books that's the grind. Now you, you're what I call a book-lover, I suppose the librareeegh Have chucked out 2 Innes half-way through recently and When Last I Died sooner; that sodding diary. And The Rising of the Moon[5] will have to pull itself together sharpish. But then I keep forgetting you like Hardy with all those words he makes up as he goes along. Actually Len Deighton's quite good if you stop worrying about what's going on. Ruth Rendell's no good.[6] Keeps yer reading tho & thats

The VENDOR hereby indemnifies *peigh*[7] the PURCHASER against all bum,

Kingsley

[TLS: Bodleian]

TO PHILIP LARKIN – 20 JULY 1985

194 Regent's Park Road, London, NW1 8XP

Dear Philip,

You know what moves are like, so I won't try to draw you a picture of this one. Four days in the place now, so we are still in the phase of discovery – discovering how much less the builder was able to do for the money than he thought, and how much less than well what he has managed to do looks and works. The new bookshelves are marvellous for full-sized atlases and pocket diaries. The door of the wall-cupboard – but there's no point in going on. The buyers of 186 L[eighton]. Rd are very nice people and were really cut up when they had to delay

5. *When Last I Died* (1941) and *The Rising of the Moon* (1945), both by Gladys Mitchell.
6. Ruth Rendell (b. 1930), crime novelist.
7. MS addition. Amis had at first incorrectly typed 'indemnified'.

completion – I'll complete your . . . – for another four weeks.[1] If I hadn't got that bridging loan I don't know what I'd do! But enough.

The conferring of my hon. Fellowship at Swansea passed off without riot police having to be called. Pinchbeck dignity, why yes, plus an unexpectedly large spok fok spoonful of Welsh bullshit, i.e. considerable parts in that language, which as you know nobody speaks in S. Wales except on purpose. But it's a constitewent college of the univ of Taffland see. All the same I was pleased to get it, as I dare say you felt over the first half dozen or so of your hon. degrees. While I was there I popped in on the Welsh BBC filming parts of *That Uncertain Feeling* for a serial. Shot conscientiously in period, which among other things reminded me how much I used to want to fuck girls who looked and dressed like the actress playing Elizabeth Gruffydd-Williams.[2] Her shoes and gloves. Her hat. Her . . .

The curious Dale Salwak turned up again the other day. I mention him only because he gave me to understand you knew him too, in the first place as a 'magician' he said. Is this true? Via someone he called Dahz, meaning Dawes[3] I suppose. Christ. He offers a demonstration of his skills chez moi WILL HE CUT MY BALLS OFF Well he might be quite good as a magician. He's certainly absolutely devoid of any kind of merit whatsoever as an interpreter of my works. [. . .]

Talking of chaps who are absolutely d. of any k. of m. etc., I got sent what must be a thesis by somebody called Candadai K. Tirumalai (Japanese? Nigerian? Blackfoot?) about you. You must have seen it. Stuff like At Grass begins with the word the, and it may be relevant to recall that Gray's Elegy and Casino Royale but not the Old Testament begin with the same ~~with the same~~ PHAHT ~~letter~~ *Christ WORD*[4]. Helpful stuff like that.

Off now to Sunday lunch at the local beast-row. Needless to say I've been thinking of you a great deal over the last weeks. Let me know if I can do anything. One thing I can do is write to you. So I will again 'before very long'. I suppose you have some time to go there still after

---

1. Amis has written in the left margin: 'They finally forked out on your bithrayd exactly'.
2. Sheila Gish was the actress. The four-part adaptation was by Ewart Alexander, directed by Robert Chetwyn; it went out on BBC2 on 12, 19, 26 March and 2 April 1986.
3. Salwak first met Larkin in the summer of 1982, when he went to Hull to stay with Eddie Dawes, Professor of Biochemistry (also Chairman of the Library Committee). Dawes, like Salwak, was an amateur magician. See Motion, *Life*, pp. 495–6.
4. MS addition.

that crise? Hilly sends her love (it's her bithrayd today: 57. Xt), also Allie.[5] Now GTE WLLE SNOO

Young people are sick to death of having no prospect but bum,

Kingsley

[TLS: Bodleian]

TO ROBERT CONQUEST – 24 JULY 1985

194 Regent's Park Road, London NW1 8XP

Dear ole B,

Here we are then, in just a week ago, study, drinks cupboard and telly (one on every floor) in operation, which is all that matters really. Only 14 boxes of books still to be opened, and there'll be room for the contents of at least 5 of them on the existing shelves.

You probably know by now that old Philip is back at Newland Park, rather sooner than I thought they gave us to understand. He sounded very back-to-form on the blower the night before last, as regards tone, that is. Content pretty gloomy, though no dread words were dropped. Doesn't expect to work (at lib.) again. Not much one can say, but I intend to keep up a barrage of letters.

Tks VM for your last. No please for Christ's sake don't wish Pound on me.[1] I couldn't face even a little necessary reading. That's why these fellows go on getting away with it, Lawrence, Forster, V Woolf et al., the opposition is too fucking chokker to take up the cudgels, I mean to hit them with. Chinese record sleeves quite frightening.[2] Think of blokes *joining in* those songs.

While I remember: could you give a ruling? Which is true?: the Russians are at their most dangerous when they feel (a) threatened (b) secure. Max Hastings[3] says (a) – I suspect him of being a national-pride-

5. Lord Kilmarnock.

---

1. Conquest had been asked to write a long article on Pound for a volume of essays on the poet, but could think of nothing new to say: 'Would you do it? If you never have, it's maybe your duty' (letter to Amis, 10 July 1985). Amis has written in the left margin of the current letter: 'Duty? Fuck duty'.

2. Conquest had sent Amis a printed booklet listing the titles of leading Chinese pop songs, such as 'How Our Engine Drivers are Driving on to a Glorious Red Future'.

3. Max Hastings (b. 1945), journalist and editor, at the time a contributor to the *Sunday Times* (1985–86).

fucker-up posing as a terrific admirer of the British serviceman. I go for (b). Your comments please.[4]

My Welsh novel[5] trudges on, coming up to 200 book-pages. Naturally I consult the Welsh dictionary and have accidentally made an interesting find or two. Corgi means cur. Bors means hernia, so did Sir Bors suffer from that? And their word for dance is dawns, suggesting that they had to wait for the Normans to appear to start dancing as well as having bridges and windows. I also make the not particularly Welsh suggestion that part of the reason why women live longer than men is that a regular proportion of them knock off their husbands with rage-induced coronaries. Consider: if one woman in 10 takes 10 years off her husband's life, that's a year each all round, which is what, 20% of the differential? Plausible, hey?

Got my hon. fellowship of the old coll at Swansea, the only non-Taff I think. Tony P was awestruck: 'what a terrific honour for a non-Welsh speaker.' Even he overestimates the importance of the lang in S Wales. Except as bullshit, of course, which is hard to overestimate.

Love to all and cheers. Off to Garrick now to bend the elbow with Stuart Thomas. Drink it while you can still pick it up.

Kingsley

[TLS: Recipient]

TO PHILIP LARKIN – 24 SEPTEMBER 1985

194 Regents Park Road, London NW1 8XP

shd there not be an apostrophe in that first word? What think you?

Dear Philip,

I can do better than this, this rate of writing I mean, and indeed will, perhaps with dribs and drabs rather than a full letter. It sounds

4. See Conquest's reply of 31 July 1985: 'As to your query re Russians: They never feel secure, and won't until they've knocked off every possible rival (well, not even then): but they are less dangerous when they feel weak than when they feel strong compared to us.'

5. *The Old Devils* (1986).

ridiculous to say I'm sorry you feel so rotten, though I am, *and*[1] to say I often think of you, though I do. No, don't go away for a holiday; just a way of taking on extra inconvenience and *peigh*[2] fright. Swansea is as far as I dare go these days. For low spirits I don't know. I'd get a lot of magazines sent, so there was always something fresh to read in the mornings. And if it's not too silly have you thought of getting yourself a kitten? As you will have noticed yourself they are uncommonly engaging, also funny. What about jazz? No? I play some every morning. In my old age I see more and more in the view that the magic had gone by 1930 or so. It was all tone, intonation; fuck the notes. Incidentally in my latest novel there's some good stuff about a record by Papa Jones and his Original Storyville Jass Band, also discs by Hunchback *shight*[3] Mose and Clubfoot Red LeRoy (w. unident. gtr.).[4]

The hace is more or less stable, though things like carpets and curtains etc. press to have good money thrown away on them. I work, go to Gk, occasional lunch, watch TV at evening, so much so that 'sorry, I'm booked that night' when asked out (which happens rarely) whenever the screen promises aught. Have recently joined a video library, to fill in when only contributions to the medium or seasons of films 'by' Jean-Luc Godard[5] are on offer. Some of the video movies, like Hawaiian Heat or Vigilante II, make me feel rather contritely yobbish as they reach their close. I do occasional mad things too, like signing books YOU or helping to judge the Mail on Sunday novel comp. YOU MUST or going to Foyle's lunch in honour of Alan Whicker[6] YOU MUST BE or *going down to East Grinstead [sic] to address the local Cons Assoc* AT THEIR ANNUAL DINNER *IN A DINNER JACKET*[7] YOU MUST BE MAD.

---

1. MS addition.
2. MS addition.
3. MS addition. Amis has struck out 'stuff' (a repetition) and replaced it with 'discs'.
4. See *The Old Devils* (1986), p. 229, on the record collection of Malcolm Cellan-Davies: 'deleted reissues of micro-groove "realisations" of even more firmly forgotten 78s made in the 1940s in a style said to have been current two or three decades longer ago still. Most of the performers were grouped under names like Doc Pettit and his Original Storyville Jass Band, though individuals called Hunchback Mose and Clubfoot Red LeRoy were also to be seen, accompanied here and there by an unknown harmonica or unlisted jew's-harp.'
5. Amis has drawn an arrow in pen to 'Godard' from the MS addition 'Hugo Piszenschidt'.
6. Alan Whicker (b. 1925), television personality, author.
7. Amis has drawn an arrow in pen to 'JACKET' from the MS addition 'aaaghgh!!!'. The '[sic]' after '*East Grinstead*' is Amis's.

The first US reviews of S & the W are coming in, headed A Hate-Novel Against Women (by Mary Mackey) and Men Vs. Women (by Michiko Kakutani).[8] Boy, they really believe lit. makes statements. It's self-expression, you see. All this kind of thing is a marvellous abject confession of F E M A L E I N F E R I O R I T Y C O M P L E X and perfectly expresses the point made in the novel.

Ole Dale's boob about B Pym's name[9] recalls my US chum Paul Fussell reading a review of a book of his that began 'PF's real name is Daniel F. Galouye' because it said in the blurb 'PF is D.F.G. Professor of English at the University of xyz.' They can't get *anything* right, can they? ('They' being Americans for the moment, not women.)

Hey: H. and I are on our own for a bit and ready for trips. Would you like us to come up and see you? Just that: we will appear at stated time, stay, depart when prearranged. You needn't do anything. If it's not a good idea for any reason, you can say so without giving the reason. *I won't refer to it again.*[10]

Hope you are starting to feel better. The no-appetite thing must be sheer hell. Drinking is of course the great appetite-destroyer. I have cut back on it enough to eat like a horse as well as drinking like a not very small fish, so my weight goes up by about 50% a month.

John Fowles's uncanny feeling for bum,

Kingsley

[TLS: Bodleian]

TO PHILIP LARKIN – 1 OCTOBER 1985

194 Regents Park Road, London NW1 8XP

Dear Philip,

Still bloody hot hereabouts, though it'll be bloody cold soon enough. Went to lunch at ole I Murdoch's flat today. A Polish Jew held the floor, not up to much but at least pro-Franco, which 'shocked' the

8. Mary Mackey's review appeared in the *San Francisco Examiner-Chronicle*, 8 September 1985; Michiko Kakutani's in the *New York Times*, 14 September 1985.

9. See Larkin to Amis, 27 August 1985 (in HEHL): '[Salwak] wrote somewhere else that Barbara Pym's real name was Mary Crampton, because her [*Who's Who*] entry begins "PYM, Barbara [Mary Crampton]". Oh well. But a nice enough chap.'

10. MS addition.

others. All loved culture and thought everything was marvellous. Isn't Yeats marvellous? Isn't TSE marvellous? Isn't Magritte marv[e]llous? Isn't Flaubert marvellous? One of them 'couldn't wait' for some exhibish to open. Another was 'very excited' that some mouldering pile had been 'saved'. And what did I think of Terry K[ilmartin]'s Proust compared with that other fellow's?[1] Ruh-beeble de bobbledy beezle. It is against *that* that we are fighting.[2] And all's to do again. Francophile, a word they used several times unsarcastically, they pronounced Fronko-feel. Starsky and Hutch at 7.40. Oh come on Kingers this plain-man stuff doesn't get yoooghgh

The Tory din-din[3] was slightly worse than I expected, 3 hours plus in the car and now perhaps you'd like to meet some of our members well you wouldn't rather be hobnobbing with left-wing schoolmasters in Rawtenstall would you. Anyway I got drunk enough not to remember how my speech went down. These things *aren't* 'quite good fun when you make up your mind to enjoy them'. You'd think I'd know by now. Well, yeah, hard to please, I guess I have to plead guilty. Not hard to please with Murder, Mystery and Suspense, though. Do you watch telly? I can't remember.

At a private view in Chelsea, yes I do ask for it, I ran into Charles Monteith. He broke the news that you'd been ill very tactfully, as if I'd just got off the plane from Antarctica. V. typical queer behaviour, that. Still I expect he feels a bit confused and upset, having left that raving lunatic Craig Raine in charge at Faber's. Later I asked a chap I hadn't seen for many years if he still kept up with the chap who I remembered a moment later had run off with his wife. Lose some, lose some.

I hope the Tatler asked you for your views on Firbank.[4] I told them he summed up all the crappy things about novels that Saul Bellow left unsummed-up, though I didn't put it as elegantly as that. He's somebody you only have to hear about.

---

1. The other fellow was C.K. Scott-Moncrieff, whose original translation (1922–31) of *À la Recherche du temps perdu* had been revised by Kilmartin in 1981, incorporating new material from the 1954 Pléiade text.

2. An allusion to the 'hunger-bitten Girl' in Wordsworth's *The Prelude* (1805), Book IX, ll.518–20, and the response of revolutionary fervour her condition evokes in the poet and his friend Beaupuy in 1792: 'at the sight my Friend/In agitation said,' 'Tis against *that*/ Which we are fighting.'

3. See Amis to Conquest, 24 September 1985.

4. Ronald Firbank (1886–1926), novelist, dandy, aesthete.

Forgot to say anything last time about ole J Wain. God what a testimony to our social system. In it you can rise to modest eminence without money, without position, without influence, without good looks and without talent. If your blood-pressure is down, get hold of his introduction (yes) to the new p/b of Hurry On D.[5] There was this Movement, you see. Long time ago now. People say I had something to do with it, some of them, well hell, aw shucks, seem to think, heavens to Betsy, that I, you gotta be kidding, actually, goshdarn it, *started* the tarnation thing, as if that was some kind of *credit* or something. I should like to ask you to remember that it takes all sorts to make a world. I think it will pay you to remember that.

I say what with one thing and another what a sour old sod you must think me. It doesn't feel too bad from here. Wish I could feel secure about cash. My accountant tells me I can retire on my 75th birthday. Ah ha ha ha. Ha ha ha. Ha ha ha ha ha ha ha ha ghghgh

Not surprising you've felt crappy aftee that crappy time. Hope appetite is stirring.

It is sad to see a novelist of Mr Amis's repute stooping to bum,

Kingsley

[TLS: Bodleian]

TO ROBERT CONQUEST – 7 OCTOBER 1985

194 Regent's Pk Rd NW1

Dear young Bob,

Rarity of my letters doesn't mean I under-enjoy yours so with double zest I at once answer your first for some weeks. (That sounds like some cunt like Hopkins.) Limericks marvellous, Yeti[1] the best, tho surely 'a *young* female yeti'? And 'my efforts to get *the* old prick up'. Your

5. John Wain, *Hurry on Down* (1953). The 1985 Penguin edition reprints Wain's introduction to the Secker and Warburg reissue of 1978, which celebrated the twenty-fifth anniversary of the novel's first publication.

1. 'When Eliot went to Tibet he/Said to a pretty young Yeti/You're not so abominable/Come on give old Tom a nibble/And them snowflakes will do for confetti.'

mention of Tonga/longer leads me to suspect you can't know one of the most solidly trad of them all as follows:

> There was a young lady of Ongar*
> Who was fucked in the sea by a conger;
>   When her sister at Deal
>   Said, 'How did it feel?'
> She said, 'Just like a man's, only longer.'

* i.e. Chipping (or possibly High) Ongar, Essex, same corner of England as D[eal]. Better rhyme than Tonga. This was so well known at my school that when one of the commercial travellers in *The Thirty-Nine Steps* (1935) recited it, or rather its first line, I burst out laughing in the cinema, the only person present to do so. I have achieved this distinction on no more than one other occasion (v. sub HOWARD, Sydney.)[2] [. . .]

Now the nasty part. Have had (perhaps you too) a very gloomy letter indeed from old Philip, talking of his hours of fear 4–8 a.m., continuous thoughts of death, dread of possible more surgery, total lack of appetite. But it seems clear from one phrase, about Monica, 'no one knows what's the matter with her *either*' (my underlining), that *he* doesn't know (in the sense in which you know the date) what they found. I try to write often, avoiding such themes. He seems hard up for something to do; I want to suggest *(i.e. him)*[3] putting his unpublished (early) poems together but impossible not to imply 'while you're still around', and he wouldn't anyway, the silly old perfectionist. C. Monteith tells me an enlarged High W is on the way incl Aubade et al. No Coll Poems because that little turd Geo Hartley won't release The Less D.[4] Have suggested a visit to Hull but you know how cagey he is.

What's your next stint? Wish you'd do something, even just an article, on grassroots US anti-Englishism (not Scotchism etc.). The constant casting of English actors as shits (e.g. as Eichmann and Heydrich in Holocaust) bothers me. My novel trcikles[5] forward at a satisfac-

2. Sydney Howard (1884–1946), plump British stage and screen comedian, famous for fluttering gestures.

3. MS addition.

4. Though Hartley eventually did release the poems in *The Less Deceived*, it was only after being made joint publisher, with Faber and Faber, of the *Collected Poems* (1988). He did not release Larkin's letters to him for Thwaite's selection, and failed to respond to inquiries from the present editor about Amis's correspondence (the 'Catalogue of Papers of *Listen* and The Marvell Press' lists fourteen Amis letters, five postcards, and two telegrams).

5. Amis has drawn an arrow in pen to 'trcikles' from the MS addition 'good word this'.

tory rate but I wish it was *easier*. Weather wonderful last couple of weeks but it's a bit late. Sorry couldn't understand your Phoenix remark.[6] Love to Liddie. Sorry to hear about Mum.[7] Old Henry Bailey-K[8] fell down dead tother day at 70. When are you over next?

Cheers
Kingsley

[TLS: Recipient]

6. Conquest had been attending a conference in Phoenix, Arizona.

7. Liddie Conquest's mother had died in September.

8. Henry Bailey-King (1914–85), printer and publisher, an old acquaintance of Conquest and Amis and a member of the Garrick Club. He died on 21 July, and a memorial service was held for him in September.

TO PHILIP LARKIN – 14 OCTOBER 1985

194 Regents Park Road, London NW1 8XP

Dear Philip,

Jolly good to get such a cheerful letter, though I dare say you don't feel like that all the time. Fascinated re JBW.[1] Yes, well, hard to blame any 60+ chap for anything, innit? What was all that about him going blind a few years ago? Result of meths-drinking to save on drink bills? Or an excuse for his difficulties with the printed word, inability to find his way to the bar, trouble seeing what's staring him in the face, etc. Takes me back over the years to the afternoon he read me bits of HoD and I was filled with despair because I thought it sounded exactly like crap, which of course it couldn't be.

Still on the IM [Iris Murdoch] front – I think perhaps people don't actually *read* her any more than ole A Burgess (master, what say you of him? I would fain know that). I think it's all to do with Mandarin vs. Vernacular was it, as Cyril C put it?[2] You know, art novel, Pickarso,

1. See Larkin to Amis, 4 October 1985, in *LL*, p. 752, in which he reports on Wain's having gone back to his second wife Eirian (m. 1960), from whom he had been separated: 'John's pretty aware of being sixty. May have something to do with it.'

2. See Cyril Connolly, *Enemies of Promise* (Boston: Little, Brown and Co., 1939), pp. 1–109, in which he discusses the tension between 'The Mandarin Dialect', described as 'the style of those writers whose tendency is to make their language convey more than they mean or more than they feel . . . the style of most artists and all humbugs, and one which is always

European thought, bourgeois conscience, Tuscany, Beckett, we haven't got a television set, lesson of the master and nothing happening. (Adapt Kojak's sneer: Who reads ya, baby?)

Apart from cricket and snooker I don't really like sport on TV, certainly not filthy soccer. Chiefly wild-life and crime for me. Nothing funny except 2 Rons, B Hill.[3] Nothing to improve the mind. Well, music if any – not unacc cello suites. History, like V: How the British killed all the Irish. VI: How the British killed all the Indians. I don't know why I watch a lot of what I watch. It sure fills in the time though AND THATS WHAT WE CAN ALL DO WITH

Good to get your enclosure.[4] Yes, the cover is pretty bloody dire. It reminds me rather of one of two studio photographs I had taken for my mum in uniform. Asked to comment, or perhaps not, you said of one of them that it looked like me just before my face broke into incredulous horror, and the other you said looked as if someone was stroking my cock. It's the second one yours reminds me of, though I'm sure that in your case as in mine no one was actually. Matters take a turn for the better when one comes to the text, still bloody marvellous after 30 years, nothing faded at all, in fact better in parts, e.g. Age, Spring. Wish I could say the same for pore ole LJ, which started to get pretty silly in parts quite soon. But thirty years, gor blimey. Realise that to somebody born in 1964 they'd be like Rupert Brooke's Poems and Zuleika Dobson[5] (both pub. 1911) to us at that age. Cor stone a crows.

Among the follies of my age has been to agree to be the Illustrated London News rest-wrong correspondent.[6] Did the Writs first to nail the colours to the mast, show there was to be no bull about little beast-rows tucked away behind Herne Hill underground station. It's a way of getting to places you wouldn't otherwise go to and eating vile food at them. Why do I do it? Well, why do I agree to review D Thos's

menaced by a puritan opposition' (p. 16) and 'The New Vernacular', whose practitioners, most notably Hemingway, believe in 'simplicity, they never use a word that they would not use in conversation – words like "nay", "notwithstanding", "pullulating" . . . etc.' (p. 80).

3. British television comedies: *The Two Ronnies*, starring Ronnie Barker and Ronnie Corbett, and *The Benny Hill Show*.

4. A copy of the Marvell Press reprint of *The Less Deceived*, 'with a cover so awful I am moved to send you one' (Larkin to Amis, 4 October 1985, in HEHL).

5. Novel by Max Beerbohm (1872–1956), critic, essayist and caricaturist.

6. Amis's tenure as monthly restaurant critic for the *Illustrated London News* lasted from September 1985 to January 1988. For sample reviews see *The Amis Collection*, pp. 366–73.

letters?[7] Now *there's* a chap who read fuck-all BECAUSE HE WASN'T INTERESTED IN FUCK-ALL bar himself. Tell you more when I've read more of them. Then after that there's h-f d. It's a facer isn't it boys?[8] Just like you I find the bloody things fading away in my mind. Now *there's* a chap who switched from vernac. stuff (esp. FAVTAD)[9] to art stuff, all Delacroix and Piazza San Marco and Burton and I don't know what all. Luckily I've only got to ask him questions. New Flashman[10] out 31st Oct. Do you like him? I've forgotten. I do. Now Master Philip eat up your nice boogh

A.L. Rowse bum,
Kingsley

[TLS: Bodleian]

TO ANTHONY POWELL – 16 OCTOBER 1985

194 Regents Park Road, London NW1 8XP

Dear Tony,

The interview[1] remorselessly approaches. Would it be all right if I brought Hilly with me? Quite frankly I dislike solo travel in my late middle age, but more to the point Hilly would love to see Violet, having hardly done so for so long – you too, of course. So could the four of us make a not-very-long day of it? In any case I will send you shortly a list of questions for you to plot your answers to. I really rather see us writing a large part of the result: I don't suppose you like tape-recorders any more than I do. But I can take notes of your spoken remarks and interlard them with your written ones. Does this make

7. For Amis's review of Paul Ferris, ed., *The Collected Letters of Dylan Thomas* (London: Dent, 1985), first printed in the *Observer*, 3 November 1985, see *The Amis Collection*, pp. 208–10.

8. See the beginning of Auden's 'Address for a Prize-Day', the prose opening to Book I of *The Orators* (1932).

9. *From a View to a Death* (1933), by Anthony Powell, predating *A Dance to the Music of Time* (1951–75).

10. *Flashman and the Dragon: From the Flashman Papers, 1860* (1985), by George MacDonald Fraser (b. 1925), journalist, screenwriter and creator of Harry Flashman, whose military and other adventures are 'documented' in this and other comic novels.

---

1. For the *Sunday Times*; it eventually appeared under the title 'Powell: The Dancing Years', 15 December 1985, p. 40.

sense to you? You know I think if it came to it we could manage with written questions, written answers and a couple of long telephone calls – we only have 1500 words to fill between us. Otherwise – well, in summary:

1. I send you questions (next week).
2. You think. You draft answers in a form I can take away when I visit you. (Or if you like send me them before then.)
3. H. and I come. You talk; I listen and write. (Before 15th November.)
4. I type everything up. I send you fair copy.
5. You check, send or telephone corrections.
6. I send text to S Times by 26th Nov. – absolute cross-my-heart deadline.

Congratulations on novel. My own is I hope 3/4 done.[2]

Philip is recovering, it seems, but not very fast. Can't eat, he says. His spirits fluctuate. Will tell you more when I see you. Which I hope to do in 3 or 4 weeks. Do hope proposals are agreeable. I see they entail more work for you than for me, but you're the star, and you want to get everything right.

Love to you both,
Kingsley

[TLS: Recipient]

TO ANTHONY POWELL – 2 NOVEMBER 1985

194 Regents Park Road, London NW1 8XP

Dear Tony,

Here's a list of questions for Tuesday. As you will see they are not at all clever or original, but I think the ST readers will want to know the answers. I know you have answered at least some of them before, and of course I know the answers to some, but there we are.

If my own works are to come into the conversation it might be better for you bring me in, appeal for agreement etc., rather than me

2. Powell had just finished writing *The Fisher King* (1986); Amis was at work on *The Old Devils* (1986).

pompously volunteering the news that I think the same (or something different).[1] We'll see how it goes.

We look forward to seeing you both on Tuesday.

Love from all,
KINGSLEY

PS: I mean of course a *provisional* list. Rephrase them, replace them, tear them up as you will.

1. In your Memoirs you talk about novelists' limitations, especially in thinking up characters, so that what are really the same ones keep turning up under new names.[2] 'The menace of repetition is common to all,' you say, especially those who stick to the orthodox 80,000-word novel. 'For a time, therefore, I had been turning over in my mind the possibility of writing a novel composed of a fairly large number of volumes.' How long was the time? And was it only 'therefore'? How did you set about such a novel?
2. For instance, how much did you know about Canon Fenneau[3] when you introduced the shy undergraduate Paul in the first volume?
3. How far was each volume thought out in advance?
4. Did you change your mind in mid-volume about anything considerable?
5. Looking back, do you wish you had done any of it differently? Any bits you would have liked to put in?
6. You obviously pay a lot of attention to names of characters and of

---

1. See Powell to Amis, 20 July 1985 (in HEHL): 'Reference your suggested list of questions, I always think the chief flaw in most interviews is that the interviewer appears as an absolutely null personality, who just asks something like "Are you an Angry Young Man?", without revealing what their own stance is, either for or against. It seems to me we might avoid that by you expressing your views as much as me.'

2. See *Faces in My Time* (1980), the third volume of Powell's memoirs: 'On reading – and rereading – the works of even the greatest novelists, one is apt sooner or later to become aware of what seems in effect, the same character reappearing under a different name, the same situation cropping up in a different setting' (p. 212).

3. The Revd Canon Paul Fenneau is a fashionable London clergyman who appears at a 1969 Royal Academy dinner in *Hearing Secret Harmonies* (1975), the last of the novels in *A Dance to the Music of Time*. Fenneau, it turns out, has appeared before in the sequence: as a frightened freshman at one of Professor Sillery's Sunday-afternoon tea parties in Oxford, in *A Question of Upbringing* (1951), the first novel in the sequence.

places too, like Dogdene and the De Tabley hotel.[4] Would you like to say something about that?
7. You must be pretty well fed up with this question, but people will inevitably be interested in anything you say about the origins of your characters, how far invented, how far based on real persons. And about whatever that distinction means. And could you reveal some names of 'originals'?
8. An interest in the occult shows here and there (and in *Venusberg*[5] too). What about that?
9. You once said you were struck by a remark made by my son Martin to the effect that a novelist does not 'choose' the novel he or she writes. Is that your experience?
10. Why do you write? Do you enjoy it? What do you find the hardest work?
11. Do you consider you have been helped as a novelist by anything you have ever read – criticism, memoirs, others' novels?
12. Can we have a preview of your new novel?

[TLS: Recipient]

TO PHILIP LARKIN – 17 NOVEMBER 1985

194 Regents Park Road, London NW1 8XP

Dear Philip,

No, I don't, do I, seem to have stuck to my intention of writing more often. Though I hope things will improve when novel is done, now entering its climacteric (sense ii in COD[1]). Talking of which I have as I may have said a Dylan-like character in it, safely long dead but some of the others bother about him. I wish you'd take your finger out

4. Dogdene is the country mansion of the Sleafords, said to have been visited by Pepys and George IV and painted by Constable; it is the setting of important scenes in several of the novels. The De Tabley Hotel in Bayswater is patronised by Uncle Giles in *The Acceptance World* (1955) and *The Military Philosophers* (1968); it becomes a branch of the Food Office in wartime.

5. *Venusberg* (1932), Powell's second novel.

1. The second sense given in *The Concise Oxford Dictionary* is '*n.* supposed critical period in life (esp. occurring at intervals of seven years).'

and run me up half a dozen lines of sub-Thomas to come swimming back into someone's head.[2] I think I could do it myself, though not as well, and there's no actual need for it anyway but it would be fun to have it there for a chap to wonder whether it was genius or piss. What about having a shot?

Expect you saw my bit about the letters. As you gathered they sort of leave you not much to say. It was fun *at the launch*[3] seeing his black-sheep son again and waspish daughter, good on her mum ('She was going to take a high moral tone about Dad in her new one. With her track record! I talked her out of it.')[4] Hope you appreciated my very kind mention.[5]

Down the other day to interview h-f d. I took Hilly with me, her first time there for 25 years. I now have the typed-up tapes to read and cut by 80% or so. I was too nervous lest the recorder should pack up to listen much to what he said, but he doesn't half go on about real life, I mean he just seems to have been wrapping up bits of his life in style. For instance I asked him what about all this fortune-telling, meaning as a sort of (rather crappy) fictional device. He said, oh I kept hearing about that when I was a nipper so it was quite natural to put it in. Tell me Mr Larkin why did you make Katherine Lind[6] a foreign girl? Oh well you see I knew a lot of foreign girls at that time so it was quite natural to make her one. Eh?

Was a treat the other day when I was going to a Ho: of Commons do but suspected Jane might be too. The usual chain of communication at such times – Hilly rings Jane's housekeeper and asks if J's going – broke down a bit and H. was talking straight to J. With typical deviousness she said 'Are you going? Because if you are he won't be.' J.: 'Oh how *tiresome* of him.' Petty I was being, see. That Jane, she's just a little innocent child. [. . .]

2. 'Brydan', the Dylan-like character much referred to in *The Old Devils*, lived from 1913 to 1960 (Thomas's dates were 1914–53). In his last letter to Amis (21 November 1985, in *LL*, p. 758), Larkin apologises for being too ill to help: 'I can't, I'm afraid, do your Dylan lines, but why don't you use that wonderful stuff from *That Uncertain Feeling*? That would be a sort of double joke.' Thwaite's note quotes sample lines by 'Gareth Probert', the Dylan-like character in *That Uncertain Feeling*: 'When in time's double morning, meaning death/Denial's four-eyed bird, that Petrine cock,/Crew junction down the sleepers of the breath . . .'

3. MS addition.

4. Thomas had three children: Llewelyn (b. 1939), Aeronwy (b. 1943) and Colm (b. 1949). Caitlin Macnamara Thomas (1913–94) married Dylan in 1937.

5. There is no mention of Larkin in the review.

6. The heroine of *A Girl in Winter* (1947).

I get fatter all the time. Sally keeps giving me chocolate and things like malt bread. I have developed quite an instinct for avoiding suddenly catching sight of myself in mirrors and especially not seeing myself side on. From the front I am almost bearable, to me anyway. Frightfully unfair considering what other bastards eat and drink.

New Flashman[7] turns out to be rather a dog but still streets ahead of etc. I shall have to start reading poetry or something.

Of all the 30s writers Spender showed the keenest[8] sense of bum

Kingsley

[TLS: Bodleian]

TO PHILIP LARKIN – 23 NOVEMBER 1985

194 Regents Park Road, London NW1 8XP

Dear Philip,

Your letter arrived this morning. Nasty to hear about those tests.[1] I hope all went well, though you don't say when they are to be over. I'll send this to Newlers as probably the quickest way of getting it to you. It's supposed to be brief cheering word. It'll certainly be brief because of the need to catch the Saturday sodding post.

Ole h-f d has okayed the transcript of my interview of him. It reads to me like a pretty faithful portrayal of what he's like to talk to about literary matters, but in spite of that I expect the ST[2] will be quite pleased to have it. On and on about how Widmerpool isn't 'based on' R. Manningham-Buller[3] and why people think he was but how annoying

7. George MacDonald Fraser, *Flashman and the Dragon* (1985).
8. MS addition, replacing 'greatest'.

---

1. See Larkin to Amis, 21 November 1985, in *LL*, p. 757: 'As you gather, I have been in a poor way lately. Hospital last week, hospital twice this week, and hospital again today for the big one. These are only tests, but they are looking for something, and I bloody well hope they don't find it.' This letter, Larkin's last to Amis, was dictated to be typed and signed by his secretary. It ends: 'You will excuse the absence of the usual valediction, Yours ever, Philip.'

2. *Sunday Times.*

3. Reginald Edward Manningham-Buller (1905–80), lawyer, Tory MP and Minister; 4th Bt. (*cr.* 1866); knighted (1951); first Viscount Dilhorne (*cr.* 1964); educated Eton and Magdalen College, Oxford.

it is when they do. And the fortune-telling's all right because Mrs E[4] gets it wrong sometimes. But the old boy is quite touchingly pleased at the fuss over his 80th and has just got the script of Ep. 1 of the TV ADTTMOT.[5] Well any old how it should be fun to watch.

Right on about Dylan to Caitlin. Part of his not being interested in anyone.[6] P Quennell[7] told me that once when he asked D how C was, D said 'Methought I saw my late espoused saint passed out on the bathroom floor.[8] So he did read a bit you see.

As I say I do hope things are all right, and I expect you know how much I hope so. Hilly, Sally and I all send our love.

Taoiseach bomb,
Kingsley

[TLS: Bodleian]

TO ROBERT CONQUEST – 1 JANUARY 1986

194 Rgt's Pk Rd NW1 8XP

Dear Bob,

Just a couple of hours after you rang. Great to hear your voice. We didn't actually mention Philip's name but it was in the air, eh? I agree absolutely with what you said in your PS: something over and above friend and poet.[1] I don't know; presence? keep forgetting he's dead for

4. Mrs Myra Erdleigh, clairvoyante, the vaguely sinister companion to Nicholas Jenkins' Uncle Giles in *A Dance to the Music of Time.*

5. A four-part television adaptation of *A Dance to the Music of Time* by Hugh Whitemore, directed by Christopher Morahan and Alvin Rakoff, was not screened until 1997, on Channel 4.

6. See Larkin to Amis, 21 November 1985, in *LL*, p. 758: 'I thought you were pretty charitable about old Dylan, whose letters I read with almost supernatural boredom . . . You know what struck me most about [the letters to Caitlin] was that he might never have met her before. No cat, no friendliness, nothing to suggest that they had a life they shared and enjoyed . . . All snivelling and grovelling and adoring and so very impersonal.'

7. Peter Quennell (1905–94), biographer, poet, editor, historian; edited *Cornhill Magazine* (1944–51), *History Today* (1955–79).

8. See John Milton, Sonnet XIX ('On His Deceased Wife'), beginning: 'Methought I saw my late espoused Saint/Brought to me like Alcestis to the grave.' The sonnet was written in 1658, published in 1673.

---

1. Larkin died on 2 December 1985. See Conquest to Amis, 24 December 1985: 'After

a millisecond at a time: I must tell/ask etc. Philip – oh Christ I can't. I didn't realise how often I must have thought of him. Every night I still read a few pages of the works before going to bed. Anyway, I was going to say that's enough for now, but no, the funeral. I'll tell you more when I see you of course, but: It wasn't a bad day as such things go. Up in the train with Chas Monteith, Andrew Motion (who seems not a bad chap, though again how one wanted a word from P.) and wife, Blake Morrison and Hilly, natch. Usual BR journey, 40 mins late at Doncaster etc. My first visit to Hull, though we never actually got there, because v. decent solicitor met us at a suburban station, gave us lunch at his house, which commanded wonderful mysterious view of the tops of the bridge above the mist (to break even, toll for lorries now estimated at £96 a time), drove us to the church in another suburb. Big place, crammed with univ people, perhaps 500 strong. Good full service (Oh God our help, Lead kindly light, The day thou gavest). I orated.[2] V. few at graveside: sister and niece, couple from Leicester, some from Hull; not Monica Jones, who couldn't make it on medical advice. No invitation to go to house, so we buggered off rather miserably, in our case without ever having seen it.[3] Back on the train with junk food and Scotch. Of the minor sequels the highlight for me was running into Spender at the Obs party who greeted me with 'Marvellous piece you wrote on Robert.' – 'You mean Philip,' I said. 'Yes, of course, Philip.' Great that he not only always says things like that but obviously forgets having done so in 5 minutes. Gen dispraise for Burgess's shitty bit in Obs on RG[raves], except a cunt in last Sunday's says Ah but you've got to be *critical* see.[4]

I send you the AP ST interview. Not very good, I think you'll agree, and certainly it has aroused a great consensual silence. The trouble is he's said it all before & it isn't very interesting anyway. That stuff about

several weeks I find I am missing the old lad a lot, not just for his poetry and friendship, but in some broader, more general way.'

2. See Appendix F.

3. To the left of this sentence, Amis has typed the marginal addition: 'Oh Christ: not a hell of a lot of wreathes either, but yrs and Liddie's was there, v. nice mixed flowers.'

4. Anthony Burgess's brief comments on Graves's death, which occurred on 7 December 1985, were appended to a front-page story in the *Observer*, 8 December 1985. Though they began with praise ('Never was a life so loftily dedicated'), they quickly questioned the poet's standing: 'He has not modified our attitude to life . . . His lines do not hug the memory . . . never quite came to terms with the movement of spoken English . . . such pretensions did not seem justified.'

the occult shows what a hopelessly unliterary mind he has. My questions meant not How did you come to think of it but What the fuck's it doing there. Remind me to tell you of a similar exchange over the steak in Girl, 20.[5] He had a jolly good press for being 80, except for J Lambert[6] who thought Snow was better. I wonder greatly about the new novel and wonder even more about how to evade reviewing it for the Obs.

Am approaching the tape with my own next, though it keeps receding at about half my pace. Then I shall have to think of something else to write about. Did I tell you that my accountant told me encouragingly that come my 75th birthday I could retire? Cheers what? Happy New Year. Love to Liddie. See you soon I hope.

Cheers

K.[7]

[TLS: Recipient]

TO THEO RICHMOND – 9 JANUARY 1986

194 Regents Park Road, London NW1 8XP

Dear Son,

That was a splendid party you and Lee[1] gave. Very touched to hear you found me more tolerant than when the world was young. Don't forget, though, what deafness and drunkenness can do. I'd quite forgot-

5. Tom Miller recounts a conversation he had with Amis in January 1984 concerning the scene in question from *Girl, 20*, where an excellent steak is served at a horrible restaurant. Amis explained: 'This is because it is artistically wrong to make it nasty. If this were done the gloom would be TOO UNRELIEVED. [. . .] On this episode Anthony Powell said: "It's awfully good when the steak turns out to be excellent . . . The food often is good at places like that." This highlights the difference between us. I make things up, whereas Powell writes down what has happened.'

6. For J.W. Lambert see Amis to Conquest, 3 July 1978, note 5.

7. The letter ends with two handwritten MS additions: '*Have xeroxed the interview so no need to return*,' and 'Just before posting this had Monica on telephone. V. odd. She had *nothing to say*. 'Thanks for yr. letter then silence. Numbed? I doubt it. A kind of awful glorying in hopelessness.'

---

1. Richmond's wife, the novelist Lee Langley.

ten what Anthea[2] said, even if I took it in at the time. Anyway, I thoroughly enjoyed myself. So did we all.

Much to your surprise, I have my hand on the Young Writers book and send it back to you herewith.[3] I thought Simon's contribution showed plenty of ability, but I also thought he had got it wrong this time. His material was too interesting to benefit from the tarting-up treatment he gave it.

Do give him my heartiest congratulations on getting into Oxford and into Exeter to boot. Yes, Martin did go there. I remember him giving me the news over the telephone when I was in Nashville. I said hesitantly, 'Exeter? You do mean Exeter, Oxford?' to which he replied, 'I don't mean the University Fucking College of the South West of England. I mean EXETER COLLEGE OXFORD.' I told him that answered my question.

Love to Theo and his family

from his affectionate
Dad

[TLS: Recipient]

TO JOHN McDERMOTT – 1 MAY 1986

194 Regents Park Road, London NW1 8XP

Dear Mr. McDermott,

Thank you for your birthday wishes. I very much hope that by now your book has been accepted. I gave you a cracking recommendation with the O.U.P. on the grounds of the excellent article you sent me.[1]

2. Anthea Barker (d. 1998), actress, songwriter; later collaborated with her husband, Felix Barker (b. 1917), author, critic and journalist, on several books of history and archaeology. Richmond remembers her saying something outrageously provocative to Amis, but can't remember what.

3. Simon Richmond, Richmond and Langley's fifteen-year-old son, had won a prize in the W.H. Smith Young Writers Competition. His winning story, 'Portait of a Life', was chosen from among thirty-four thousand entries and was printed in *Young Writers 26th Year: Award-winning Entries from the W.H. Smith Young Writers Competition 1984* (1985). Simon Richmond read English at Oxford and went on to become a musician and composer.

---

1. McDermott's book, *Kingsley Amis: An English Moralist*, was published in 1989 by Macmillan. See Amis to McDermott, 25 April 1985.

With them, I am afraid delays are only to be expected. Anyway I hope all goes well.

Do remember me kindly to Simon[2] and tell him we need more poems.

Yours

Kingsley Amis

[TLS: Recipient]

TO THE EDITOR, *DAILY TELEGRAPH* – 9 MAY 1986

SIR – Ferdinand Mount (Article May 5) misquotes Philip Larkin on economics. The Larkin version of Mrs Thatcher's message to the nation was not "You can't have it because *we* (my italics) can't afford it" but "If *you* (my italics) haven't got the money for something you can't have it." But he said it in 1979 and if he could pronounce on the matter today he might have to agree, perhaps regretfully, that it is the misquotation that has turned out to come nearer the reality.[1]

KINGSLEY AMIS
London, NW1

2. Simon Curtis. See Amis to Curtis, 7 January 1975.

1. The Larkin quotation comes from a 1979 interview with Miriam Gross in the *Observer*, reprinted in Larkin, *Required Writing* (1983): 'Oh, I adore Mrs Thatcher. At last politics makes sense to me, which it hasn't done since Stafford Cripps . . . Recognising that if you haven't got the money for something you can't have it – this is a concept that's vanished for many years' (p. 53).

TO ROBERT CONQUEST – 7 JUNE 1986

194 R P R NW1 8XP

Do you remember a crappy (I think kids') novel called Owd Bob?[1] I fancy he was a sheepdog or something such

Dear Owd Bob,

Yes, about time I agree. As I said on the blower, when you get the book off (5 weeks late) to the publisher you find you're beset by deadlined crap like doing the links for Poetry Please on Radio 4, 5 programmes for about 37½p each. Why we say yes to that type of stuff defeats me. Too late now to tell you (in a letter: I'll tell you face to face) about Philip's memorial service and so on. But it was all right. Monica was there but I didn't see her. She goes from bad to worse. Having forbidden visitors to 105 Newland Park after the funeral she now goes and burns P's diaries. He had left instructions to do so but naturally the other two lit. execs, Thwaite & Motion, were starting to figure out ways of not doing so. Then they found she'd gone ahead without consulting them. Partly gloomy self-righteous triumph or however you put it, partly vanity [. . .] His chosen companion, what? Makes you think of Mr Bleaney: '. . . having no more to show Than that grim bag should make him pretty sure He warranted no better.'[2] As Martin said, Christ, what a *life.*

Talking of Martin, he has as I said gone all lefty and of the crappiest neutralist kind, challenging me to guess how many times over the world can destroy itself, writing two incredible bits of ban-it bullshit in the Obs (of course), one a 'paperback round up' (of books about the nuclear winter etc.), the other a TV review (of programmes saying Reagan wants to blow up the world), in fact going on like H Pinter does these days I hear. Luckily having now a 2nd baby has given him (M) other things

1. Alfred Ollivant, *Owd Bob: The Grey Dog of Kenmuir* (1898).

2. See the final stanza of Larkin's 'Mr Bleaney', from *The Whitsun Weddings* (1955), in which the speaker wonders if Bleaney managed to shake off the dread 'That how we live measures our own nature, /And at his age having no more to show/Than one hired box should make him pretty sure/He warranted no better, I don't know.'

to think about. I suppose you can't recommend some book?[3] He's bright, you see, but a fucking fool, and the worse, far worse, for having come to it late in life, aetat. nearly 37, not 17.

Doings in the litty world? Not much. Tony's new one[4] is a right stinker, well no, nicely done as ever but no matter, all art, half a dozen unlikely/cliché events spun out in reflection and discussion and more reflection and surmise.[5] Makes H James seem like, well, a novelist. Reviews respectful, puzzled, cautious. As against that that little twit Tom Paulin has taken an all-round lashing for his shitty-lefty book of political verse[6] (Faber – that fool Craig Raine). The old one about everything's political really, especially if it isn't about politics. Best comment, and bloody funny, and in the Obs of all places, was a six-frame cartoon strip of Hitler declaiming the first lines of Daffodils. P Ackroyd complained in the Times that it had no Pound in it, so in my 3-sentence brush-off in the Standard I said its great merit was that it had no EP. Another Mick, T[homas] Kinsella, got a ballocking from Conor [Cruise O'Brien] for writing most of his book of 'Irish' verse[7] himself – 'translations from the Gaelic' see. I had to laugh when ole John Wain took a mild pasting for his recent autobiogical hodge-podge.[8] Both the Obs and ST on the same day took the line that it wasn't all that bad really. [. . .]

The shits here are going on jubilantly about how anti-Americanism is sweeping the country. Don't you believe it. 'Could have afforded to

3. In a response of 25 June 1986 (in HEHL), Conquest promises to come up with something 'really good and clear' about nuclear war, adding: 'I expect you know that the Nuclear Winter chaps have now withdrawn it and conceded that it would only be a Nuclear autumn.' See also, in this vein, Amis on whales and nuclear submarines, as recounted in Martin Amis, *Einstein's Monsters* (Harmondsworth: Penguin, 1987), p. 13: 'When I told him that I was writing about nuclear weapons, he said, with a lilt, "Ah. I suppose you're 'against them', are you?" *Épater les bien-pensants* is his rule. (Once, having been informed by a friend of mine that an endangered species of whales was being systematically turned into soap, he replied, "It sounds like quite a good way of *using up* whales . . .").' And later, in the same passage: '"Think of it. Just by closing down the Arts Council we could significantly augment our arsenal. The grants to poets could service a nuclear submarine for a year."'

4. *The Fisher King* (1986).

5. Amis has written in pen in the left margin: 'and really *gauche* symbolism'.

6. *The Faber Book of Political Verse* (1986), edited by Tom Paulin (b. 1949), Ulster-born poet.

7. *The New Oxford Book of Irish Verse* (1986).

8. *Dear Shadows: Portraits from Memory* (1986).

hit them harder, couldn't he?'[9] You've probably seen how Maggie is steadily picking up retrospective support for letting the US use those bases. But you know I wonder if that swing away from the left in the media hasn't spent itself. Getting rid of atomic power is the in thing at the moment but fucking up NATO the long-term objective. It bothers me a bit at times.

Thank you for all your letters and limericks. Best of yours I have to hand I think is the rugger-player Geoffrey.[10] Went down well in the club, though old Huw Wheldon would have thought it a bit strong. You probably saw the poor little thing dropped off the twig the other day. The Abbey again of course. My minicab drivers are beginning to know where to drop me for the west door.

Do try to get over before 25th July. The three of us here disperse on the 29th, I to Swansea, Hilly and Ali to Spain. H. is always a bit immovable on her holidays. I as you know would prefer not to have one, or not for more than a week or so. But there it is. But come that week early as you suggested. I have absolutely cleared it with Hilly. There's a lot to tell you and hear from you.

Weather continues bloody awful. One nice day so far this year. Martin comes to lunch shortly with his elder son,[11] a most agreeable child I must say. Reagan has done nothing special to displease him over the past week or so so we might be all right. Hey, when I think about it I work out that he's now a year or two older than you were when we first met. Remember that party at PEN? You are lasting horribly well. Reminds me I haven't got, can't remember your poem for your 60th, not entire. 70th one is up to snuff.[12] Nice to think how impossible that those rhymes should have been used before. Reminds me further that the 4th line of your 'You electors give ear' should read 'So it's

9. A reference to the US bombing of Libya in mid-April, in which a hundred were killed, and one plane lost.

10. See Conquest to Amis, 15 March 1986: 'Said a Welsh rugger player called Geoffrey,/ "It's a little distracting that efery/Time we've a scrum/There's a prick up my bum/I'm thinking of telling the referee." '

11. Louis Amis.

12. The two poems read: 'If you're pushing sixty/It's no good giving chicks tea/If you want to win them/You've simply got to gin them' (Conquest to Amis, 25 June 1986, in HEHL); 'A chap who's pushing seventy/Won't offer girls a Devon Tea. /If he wants to have it off he/Plies them with Irish Coffee' (Conquest to Amis, 27 May 1986, in HEHL).

confidently I solicit your vote' which brings out the slight Irish flavour of the whole.[13]

Christ I couldn't live your sort of life, buggering to and fro all those thousands of miles. And a bloody *beach*. When you needn't. You'll be going to summer camp next. Tell me, did you bathe?

Love to Liddie. H. sends hers. Now you work at advancing your trip.

Cheers
K.

[TLS: Recipient]

TO ROBERT CONQUEST – 18 JULY 1986

194 R's P Rd NW1 8XP

Dear Doctor,

Just a line occasioned by having handed in proofs of my new one; you recall whereas you write when busy I do when off hook. Have had difficulty with R COHEN at Hutch – did I hear, did you say you had too?[1] He *changes* things. Like Americans. Have just sworn never to write for e.g. NY Times again when I did tiny piece on my local & they rang from NYC with suggestions: shouldn't it be North *West* London, shouldn't it be banquettes instead of wall-seats, etc. But Cohen . . . We'll be comparing notes. Don't think I told you, have co-done anthology of Brit songs.[2] Comes quite close to being a book of untrendy verse. Bloody satisfying, putting in e.g. Heart of Oak, Land of Hope & G, Yeomen of England, Onward Xtn Soldiers, Come into the Garden, Maud, The English Rose, A Health unto HM and imagining how cross

13. Conquest remembers the original as follows: 'You electors give ear I'll explain my posish/I eat like a hog and I drink like a fish/I swear like a trooper and fuck like a stoat/So I think I can safely solicit your vote.'

---

1. The answer was yes, over proofs to *The Harvest of Sorrow* (1986): 'The mere name Richard Cohen is enough to make me yell' (Conquest to Amis, 24 July 1986). Richard Cohen (b. 1947) is currently Consulting Publisher, Metro Books.

2. *The Great British Songbook* (1986), co-edited with James Cochrane.

the lefties will be. Good stuff in intro too about how deeply patriotic the Brits are but suspicious of jingoism etc.

Thing about the 'Lord' B stuff is that the nicknames should have some jazz ref, so Lord recalls Duke, Count etc. So arcanely 'Bosie' Douglas evokes the obscure trumpeter Sterling Bose.[3] Abbreviations[4] too: Manny Kant, Benny Spinoza etc.

Old Liz Jennings has her 60th and Collected Poems this week. I graced the party and found her looking fine, well, old-ladyish but recognisable, unlike the alarming crouching creature I saw in Oxford about 8 years ago. Saw that popular German-Mexican-American Englishman Michael Schmidt[5], who told me what a frightful shit T. Paulin was and heard my J Wain material with great approbation. Much talk of Philip who seems to have impressed himself on everybody in a way no one else in my experience has ever done. His views on Ted Hughes (though meant to amuse) went down well too.

Funnily enough I remember wondering what poi could be when I came across it in the words of 'My Little Grass Shack in Kiallikikua, Hawaii' c. 1930:

> I'm just an unhappy Hawaiian and a homesick island boy,
> I want to get back to my fish and poi, etc.

Seem to be in good nick, having changed my doc and had a liver test which he describes as having revealed 'only the faintest murmur of protest' from there. In same week had last 6 upper teeth whipped out and denture triumphantly installed – v. comf so far – and heard the US publisher was much taken by my latest.[6] And wrote a peom shit I mean *poem* last couple of days. Pissing on Wm Carlos Wms[7] among other things.

3. Sterling Bose (1906–58), trumpeter and cornettist. 'Bosie' Douglas alludes to Lord Alfred Douglas (1870–1945), poet and friend of Oscar Wilde. The nickname 'Bosie' was a contraction of 'Boysie', which he had been called as a child by his mother.

4. Amis has typed 'Pet-forms' above 'Abbreviations'.

5. Michael Schmidt (b. 1947), poet, editor of *Poetry Nation Review* (1973–), publisher (Carcanet Press, 1971–).

6. *The Old Devils* (1986), published in America by Summit Books (1987).

7. William Carlos Williams (1883–1963), American modernist poet, novelist, short-story writer and pediatrician; early friend of Pound. His poems were provocatively minimalist. Amis's poem has not been traced, but Conquest offers one of his own in a similar vein:

> Fuck all depends
> upon
> a red wheel
> barrow

Christ this SA nonsense[8] is nonsense. Needless to say you never meet anyone here who supports any kind of external pressure there. But we'll discuss.

No I couldn't insist on the boozy toothpaste. Don't need it anyway ha ha ha. My goodness me you are a glutton for punishment. Buckley, heli, jet . . . Jesus. Anyway I leave for Swansea (0792–66487) 4 Aug, return 29 Aug so will be well in situ to greet you on the 5 Sept. Love to Liddie.

Cheers
K.

[TLS: Recipient]

TO HARRY RITCHIE – 24 JULY 1986

194 Regents Park Road, London NW1 8XP

Dear Mr. Ritchie,

How nice to hear from you again. Of course I will have a shot at answering your queries. (Nobody, by the way, who uses the phrase 'tenaciously pedestrian' of his own work can be *tenaciously* pedestrian.)

L.S. Caton. The publishing Caton was undoubtedly R.A. or R. Caton, L.S. stands for Lazy Sod, an appellation for the real Caton devised by Larkin and myself in reference to the copious delays and grumbling with which he had brought out our first books. L. also suggested L.S's removal to Tucumán U, whose English department had recently commissioned me to write a book about Graham Greene and then renegued on the deal.[1]

About those awful early poems. No, now you make the point, I don't think the ones in the school mag. were very modernist, though there was one, 'Prelude', written in the summer of 1939, which I once described somewhere as 'a suburbanite's "Waste Land" tizzied up (I

8. On 12 June, in the face of increasing unrest, President Botha declared a state of emergency throughout South Africa; on the same day the Commonwealth Eminent Persons Group published a report calling for economic sanctions.

1. See Amis to Larkin, 16 July 1948, note 1.

think I must have meant tarted up) with bits of Wilde.'[2] It was modernist in the sense of being self-indulgently obscure and pointless. If there was any really modernist stuff – there was a sub-Kafka story and a sub-Dylan T story and some poems – written at Oxford and in the army I had the good sense to lose it all. Well, all of it that didn't get into Bright November.

The Century's Crown.[3] Yes, apparently actually performed at the time of the Coronation. Music by Bruce Montgomery.

Amberley Hall.[4] This was a comic/chamber one-act opera for three voices and, I think, two pianos, same composer. It was a costume piece and had a screen scene in which the concealed lover strives to betray his presence to the husband, who refuses to notice. Must have been performed. Montgomery was interviewed about it on radio.

To Move the Passions.[5] This was to be a grand opera, also costume, with two rival poets, an ingenue heroine, a comic landlady and three critics who were inseparable and had a song about imitating nature. I completed the first act (verse throughout) and Montgomery wrote at least part of the music but soon cannibalised it for a film score.

Colin Wilson. I have dozens of stories about him but will keep to myself the ones featuring me for fear of him . . . well, for fear of him. It is his distinction that *everybody* has a Colin Wilson story nobody else has. (Actually now I come to think of it he is matched here by John Anstey,[6] the famously shitty recently-retired editor of the Telegraph magazine.) But here is a reliable one I had from a chap called Wilfred De'Ath,[7] who I believe criticises plays or music or something. De'Ath's first assignment on his first job, local BBC reporter in Devon somewhere, was interviewing Wilson about I suppose The Outsider. He drove up to the cottage in the station taxi. Before he could get out W. came hurrying over and said,

2. The phrase comes from 'City Ways', a memoir of early school days first published in the *Spectator*, 28 February 1958, pp. 255–6, reprinted in *What Became of Jane Austen?*, p. 139. Amis reuses it (including 'tizzied') in *Memoirs*, p. 31.

3. See Amis to Larkin, 23 October 1952, note 2.

4. See Amis to Larkin, 17 December 1950, note 2.

5. See Amis to Larkin, 6 December 1947, note 4.

6. John Anstey (1928–88), editor and journalist; launched what became the *Sunday Telegraph Magazine* in 1964 and edited it until 1986.

7. Wilfred De'Ath (b. 1937), freelance writer and broadcaster; Producer, BBC Radio Talks and Current Affairs (1962–65).

W: It's Dante, Shakespeare, Shaw and me, okay? Otherwise no interview.
De'A: Well, it's Dante, Shakespeare, Shaw and you.
Later it emerged that during a violent storm not long before a ferryboat had gone down in the harbour to be seen from outside the cottage.
De'A: Did you see anything of it?
W: Oh yes.
De'A: (approx) I expect you rushed indoors and started dialling 999 and things like that.
W: No, I watched it until it was all over and then came in and played Wagner very loud on the gramophone.
Pleasing to anti-Wagnerians like myself.

Zero on Hop and Hol[8] I'm afraid.

A fact that W. has mysteriously not circulated much and so may be unknown to you, The Outsider and Religion and the Reb[9] were written as one book but bisected by Gollancz for publication. This wrong-foots all the weasel critics like P[hilip] Toynbee who realising they had overpraised The O claimed to see a sad loss of something-or-other in R & the R. W. is too unworldly, perhaps, or too secure in his place with Dante et al. to appreciate such considerations.

On *Jim* and related matters. I had no social (class, etc.) intentions at all: what class are the Welches? As for politics, of course Bertrand is a Conservative (the buns conversation)[10] because Dixon hates him. Of course Margaret sings in the Conservative choir. As for culture, of course he hates Mozart; I must have said already that him hating Castelnuovo-Tedesco[11] wouldn't be any good. Because of course Welch loves Mozart. Same with the madrigals, etc. None of these things, Mozart, madrigals, Bertrand's kind of painting, were particularly

8. Ritchie explains: 'Bill Hopkins and Stuart Holroyd, two pals of Colin Wilson – they found fleeting notoriety in 1957/58' (personal communication, 8 September 1997). Hopkins (b. 1928), a Welsh novelist and dramatist, was a contributor to *Declaration* (1957), the 'Angry Young Men' anthology (see Amis to Larkin, 15 October 1957, note 8); Holroyd (b. 1933), author of autobiographical and new-age books, was also an 'Angry'.

9. Colin Wilson's *Religion and the Rebel* was published in 1957, a year after *The Outsider*.

10. In Chapter 4 (p. 50): 'Bertrand looked quickly round the group, then went on: "But their home policy . . . soak the rich . . . I mean . . ." He seemed to be hesitating, "Well, it is that, pure and simple, isn't it?"' To which Dixon replies: '"Well, what's wrong with it, even if it is that and no more? If one man's got ten buns and another's got two, and a bun has got to be given up by one of them, then surely you take it from the man with ten buns."'

11. Mario Castelnuovo-Tedesco (1895–1968), Italian composer.

fashionable or unfashionable, they were just things I happened to know about that D would hate. As regards the provincialness and so on, after thinking it over I would put it like this. The decision to set it in the North, and make the hero non-bourgeois and put in a lot about his job was taken in the same spirit as a detective-story writer of that period deciding he would rather not set it in a pleasant Sussex village and not have the baronet murdered in his library at the Towers. A literary decision in that it had to do with the structure, characterisation etc. of that book, but not literary in the sense that would make it a shot in a campaign or a unit in a literary offensive against mandarinism or anything else. Nothing programmatic or manifesto-ish about it.

Note on John Lewis's class:[12] as you will have seen, all that stuff about the anglicised bourgeoisie is self-excuse for mixing with them. He pretends he's a lower-class spy infiltrating them, like the fellow in my poem 'Coming of Age'. Actually above a certain level, pretty exactly that of the possession of a university degree (a pass in engineering and metallurgy at Swansea will do), class counts for less in Wales, my part of it anyway, than in England.

Well, this much ought to keep you quiet for a bit. Lucky for you, you caught me with a novel just in.[13] Set in Wales, funnily enough. You needn't worry about the occasional 'imposition' on the continued understanding that I can take my time over answering. I look forward to seeing what you finally produce.

All the best,
Yours sincerely,
Kingsley Amis

[TLS: Recipient]

12. John Lewis, the hero of Amis's second novel, *That Uncertain Feeling* (1955).
13. *The Old Devils* (1986).

TO JAN MONTEFIORE – 12 AUGUST 1986

194 Regents Park Road, London NW1 8XP

Dear Miss Montefiore,[1]

I have written to Candida Lacey[2] giving permission for the inclusion of 8 lines from my poem 'A Bookshop Idyll' in your forthcoming monograph.

But please let me say that your interpretation of the poem is, I think, misguided. I really don't suggest (nor is it my opinion) that the love-poem is a quintessentially female mode; I was trying to make a more general point to the effect that women are less inhibited about expressing their feelings than men are, at any rate in our society. And though I'm pleased you think the poem good-natured, surely the people it patronises are not women but men, who cut a pretty sorry figure in the last verse.[3]

All the same I wish you the best of luck with your undertaking, and hope you are suitably enthusiastic about that great heroine of mine Christina Rossetti.[4]

Yours sincerely,
Kingsley Amis

[TLS: Recipient]

---

1. Jan Montefiore (b. 1948), literary academic, currently Senior Lecturer in English, University of Kent; in 1986, on leave from Kent and living in Moscow where her husband, Patrick Coburn, was Moscow Correspondent for the *Financial Times*.

2. Of Pandora Press, publishers of Montefiore's monograph *Feminism and Poetry: Language, Experience, Identity in Women's Poetry* (1987).

3. The penultimate stanza of 'A Bookshop Idyll' ends: 'Women are really much nicer than men:/No wonder we like them.' The last stanza reads:

> Deciding this, we can forget those times
> We sat up half the night
> Chockfull of love, crammed with bright thoughts, names, rhymes
> And couldn't write.

4. Montefiore comments on Amis's response: 'As you see, he really couldn't have been nicer . . . and it's not as if I'd ever been introduced to him or his son, or anything like that, so he wasn't doing me a personal favour, he was just being a decent liberal – Unlike his agent who wanted to withhold permission because I'd been uncomplimentary' (personal communication, 23 November 1997).

TO ROBERT CONQUEST – C.20 AUGUST 1986

Wales till 29th August

Old dear Bob,

Have been getting your letters all right, forwarded by Sally, who is pretty regenerate at the moment. Good about AEH/GKC.[1] Bloody funny, looking through GO's [George Orwell's] Notes on Nationalism[2] and finding him saying nationalist sods can't bear anything running counter to their obsessions but will usually disguise this by complaining about the *literary* quality of the offending piece, & then 2 pages later calling Lepanto[3] tawdry bombast. AEH came up on looking at a life of him by one RP Graves (Robt's nephew).[4] Says 'The farms of home' is piss-poor because it's self-pitying, but 'On Wenlock E' is fine because it isn't self-pitying. Wouldn't have bothered with it but that the same RPG has done part 1 of a RG biog. He opens 'A true poem is like a spring of water in a desert land.' What can you do? The jacket says the fellow was born in 1945 but they must mean 1845. I have to review it for the Obsc. Last one, I hope. Terry [Kilmartin] goes at year's end and then it's me for the Independent.

Two bits on the femmy front. Paul Daniels, the TV conjurer (a bloody sound bloke who attacked govt funding of entertainment etc., having managed his own show for years) – anyway the femmies are

---

1. A.E. Housman and G.K. Chesterton; Conquest cannot remember what this refers to, nor has the letter Amis is replying to survived.

2. First published in *Polemic* (October 1945); reprinted in Sonia Orwell and Ian Angus, eds, *The Collected Essays, Journalism and Letters of George Orwell*, 4 vols (London: Secker and Warburg, 1968), vol. 3, pp. 361–80.

3. Poem by G.K. Chesterton, first published in *Poems* (1915); reprinted in *The Amis Anthology* (1988), accompanied by a note which begins: 'This poem will never be tolerated, let alone enjoyed, by a progressive intelligentsia to whom there can be no such thing as a just feat of arms.' The Orwell quote calls 'Lepanto' and Chesterton's other battle poems 'the most tawdry bits of bombast to be found in our language' (Orwell and Angus, eds, *Collected Essays*, vol. 3, p. 366).

4. Richard Perceval Graves, *A.E. Housman: The Scholar-Poet* (1979). The Housman poems are 'The farms of home lie lost in even', from *A Shropshire Lad* (1896), and 'On Wenlock Edge the wood's in trouble', published posthumously, in *More Poems* (1936), ed. Laurence Housman. For Amis on Housman see 'A.E.H.', in *A Case of Samples* (1956), reprinted in *CP*, p. 97. The first part of R.P. Graves's biography of his uncle is *Robert Graves: The Assault Heroic, 1895–1926* (1986).

trying to get the Magic Circle to admit women. PD is of the anti faction, saying just 'Women can't keep a secret.' Then (you may have seen) in today's Times G Greer[5] on a rape issue of Woman's Own. Being a man you might have thought she'd say, Bloody good, on the right lines, the more information and publicity the better. Not a bit of it: bloody *bad*, nothing new there, no research, not a mention of the Women's National Commission or the London Rape Crisis Centre, in other words NOTHING ABOUT *ME* and all the pioneering work *I've* done. She was courageous and all that; this is just 'sensationalism'. Can you fucking well whack it?

Good about your having had your proctoscopy. As I may have said it shows that discomfort can be raised to the intensity of pain and then some. No more I pray you. Thwaite tells me it was [Terence] Wheldon the solicitor who burnt the PAL diaries, not Monica.[6] Annoying in a way. Also said P had voluminous correspondences with at least a couple of women. Kept his life rigidly in compartments T said. I'm flogging your letters to me (or rather promising them) to whoever buys my typescripts. 130 of the buggers. 80-odd of P's. Not much else. 10 of Colin Wilson which I must say make him look a proper pratt. Having fine lazy pissy paunch-enhancing time in Welsh Wales but looking fwd to getting home and to seeing you & L.

Cheers K.

Yes seen yr 1st 2 bits in the Times. Rather ill timed, what, with good old Gorbachov being so sodding reasonable.[7] Ted's poem[8] certainly drew an universal groan here.

[TLS: Recipient]

5. Germaine Greer (b. 1939), Australian feminist and literary academic, author of *The Female Eunuch* (1970) and *Shakespeare* (1986), among other books.

6. The diaries were shredded, not burned, by Larkin's secretary Betty Mackereth, at Monica's direction. In the last few hours of his life, Larkin several times urged Monica to have them destroyed. See Motion, *Life*, p. 522.

7. *The Times* ran three excerpts from Conquest's *The Harvest of Sorrow*, about Stalin's deliberately inflicted famine of the early 1930s, in which millions died. The excerpts ran on 18, 19 and 20 August 1986.

8. Ted Hughes, 'The Honey Bee and the Thistle', written to celebrate the wedding of Prince Andrew and Sarah Ferguson, in *The Times*, 23 July 1986, p. 16.

TO MR VOGEL – 4 SEPTEMBER 1986

194 Regents Park Road, London NW1 8XP

Dear Mr. Vogel,[1]

Thank you for your letter. I am afraid I cannot answer your first two questions at all precisely without a prohibitive amount of research. However, I think it would be safe to say that, world wide, my books will have sold in aggregate over 5 million copies. This figure includes translations. As regards the number of languages into which my work has been translated, this must stretch to perhaps twenty, including Turkish, Hebrew, Korean, Slovene and Catalan. It is easier to tell you my favourite book, which is 'Take a Girl Like You'.

With all good wishes.
Yours sincerely
Kingsley Amis

[TLS: HEHL]

TO THE EDITOR, *SPECTATOR* – 6 SEPTEMBER 1986

Sir: Please don't cut or sub me into illiteracy and make me seem to have written of 'Harold Robbins, whose *The Storyteller* shows' this, that and the other (Books. 23 August). Possessive followed by definite article is not English. 'Have you read Dante's *The Divine Comedy*?' Impossible. 'Can I borrow your *The Times*?' No, no. 'It must be 'Robbins, whose novel *The Storyteller* . . .', however little we may think he or it deserves the designation.[1]

KINGSLEY AMIS
c/o Jonathan Clowes, 22 Prince Albert Road, London NW1

---

1. The identity of Mr Vogel is untraced. See Amis to Gunston, 7 July 1973, note 1.

---

1. Amis's reference to *The Storyteller* (1985) by Harold Robbins (1916–97), the best-selling American novelist, occurs not in a review, but in an article about sex in literature, 'Why Are You Telling Me All This?' The article is reprinted in *The Amis Collection* (pp. 25–7), with the offending illiteracy.

TO CYRIL RAY – 30 OCTOBER 1986

194 Regents Park Road, London NW1 8XP

Dear Cyril,[1]

Good to hear from you. Yes, I'd be delighted to write you an intro for the next Comp Imb if the publishers decide to go ahead. The terms you mention are acceptable, he said a shade pompously. But I should like to beat you down to 'between 1500 and 2000 words'. A flat 2000 seems like an awful lot from this end. All right?[2]

So much for the good news. The tedious part comes only from my own inefficiency. The fact is that after all the excitement I can't lay my hand on my heart and say I'm *sure* the booze for my last contribution[3] has arrived. My own fault for laziness, carelessness etc. If you could just check it was sent that will be absolutely enough for me. Sorry to lumber you with this.

Well anyway, I hope Imbiber 1987 goes through.

All cheer
Kingsley

[TLS:][4]

TO THE EDITOR, *OBSERVER* – 16 NOVEMBER 1986

c/o Jonathan Clowes, 22 Prince Albert Road, London NW1

Sir,

In your 'Profile' (26 October) you make a number of false statements about me. I single out one of these as characteristic and as relatively

---

1. Cyril Ray (1908–91), journalist and wine writer; editor of *The Complete Imbiber* series. It began in 1956 and contained collected writings about wine and wine-drinking, including stories, wine guides, profiles and other features.

2. In a handwritten note at the bottom of a photocopy of the letter Amis has written: 'By end Jan About 2000 £250.'

3. Amis had contributed 'Investing in Futures: A Story' to *The New Complete Imbiber* (1986), volume 13 of *The Complete Imbiber*.

4. A photocopy of this letter was found among Amis's papers after his death; the original has not survived.

easy to refute in a few words. 'At a party in the country not long ago,' you allege, I uttered some 'outrageous' racist remarks, 'an appalled guest' asked my son Martin if I meant what I was saying, and Martin said it was 'extremely difficult to tell.' Neither Martin nor I have any recollection of any such incident taking place anywhere at any time. In fact neither of us can remember jointly attending any such gathering, certainly not in the last few years.[1]

Yours faithfully,

KINGSLEY AMIS

TO ROBERT CONQUEST – 17 NOVEMBER 1986

194 R P R L NW1 GB

STOP PRESS: Cohen in a letter mentions a story of mine about a girl who becomes 'an upper-class whore'. The *whole point* is that she becomes as *low*-class a whore as is possible – in *Swansea*.[1]

Dear old B,

No doubt you saw poor old John B[raine] had bought it. Word was that after burst ulcer, heart failure, kidney failure etc. he was coming round, but popped off suddenly. Obits tended to stress his rather mark-

---

1. This letter was sent to the *Observer* on 29 October but not printed until 16 November. In its original version it ended with the sentence 'Here once again is the miserable blend of incompetence and dishonesty that typifies your newspaper,' which was cut (see the following letter and note 3). Donald Trelford (b. 1937), the Editor (1975–93), wrote to Amis on 30 October, saying he had to check with the story's 'unusually reliable source' before printing the letter, adding also that the paper regarded the profile as 'friendly', and about 'someone we clearly admired'. (Four years earlier Trelford had hosted a dinner at the Garrick, given by the *Observer*, to celebrate Amis's sixtieth birthday, an occasion marred by Amis's after-dinner speech denouncing his hosts.) In a letter of 8 November, after having talked to the source, Trelford agreed to publish Amis's letter and apologised for not having done so the week before.

---

1. The story is 'Moral Fibre' (1958), first collected in *My Enemy's Enemy* (1962), later in *Collected Stories* (1980, 1987).

ing time after Rm at the T but what would you. Of course one wishes one had seen more of him, been nicer etc.

Turning out files tother day I came across – as you see.[2] I rather think it's the original draft as jointly created in 1971 at Albufeira. Really quite good, what? In fact next time you're over worth working up and rounding off in say 20 verses. Cast list needs updating. Pity J Wain doesn't qualify.

Have been in spat with the rotten old Observer over profile of me. Full of distortions, mistakes and plain fictions. Luckily Martin was able to corroborate me over the grossest one, an unhistorical racialist outburst at a party in the country. No such occasion ever, I wrote in. Little sodding Trelford went on about consulting his source, which could only have been one man's word against 2 anyway, held my letter over for 2 weeks and then ran it sans apology and with the last sentence missing, viz. 'Here once again is the miserable blend of incompetence and dishonesty that typifies your newspaper.'[3] Well of course there are always reasons of space.

Yes, other enclosures. It can't have been you who sent the Wash P cutting; perhaps I showed you but what the hell. And here's Maeve revealed at last.[4] Interesting, no? What she says about my address is of course all balls: not a word in that I said. Wrote stiffly to say so and ballock her for trying to grab Philip for the Church. A bit thick, that. The Dean of Westmr*tried it too but there are much better reasons for that. I never heard a word about her except that solitary 'Maeve wants to marry me' blurting; you too, I think. He didn't half keep his life in compartments. But then he may simply have thought she wasn't important enough to go on about. Well, we shall never know.

I'm about to get my own bit of Liz.[5] In the proof of my DNB piece on Betj, which didn't mention her, they have inserted 'In later years

2. The enclosure was one of the few printable Amis-Conquest verse compositions, 'View Galloo: Or, Ivan of the Shires', for which see Amis to Betjeman, 3 June 1971, note 3, and Appendix C.

3. Amis sent a photocopy of the original letter, containing this sentence, to Paul Fussell, with a letter of 3 December 1986 (which Fussell possesses). In the letter to Fussell he reiterates that the reason for omitting the last sentence (presumably given him by the *Observer*) was 'to save space'.

4. Maeve Brennan (b. 1929), colleague of Larkin's at the University Library at Hull. See Amis to Brennan, 21 November 1986, note 1.

5. Lady Elizabeth Cavendish.

. . . he was cared for by his friend Lady EC.[6] Will have to tell her. What if she says she won't have it?[7]

Had a squirm-inducing letter from Cohen professing willingness to stand down if not giving perfect satisfaction. Not the easiest thing in the world to answer. They don't seem to have anyone much better and I'd really like to leave the firm but I can't really at the moment quite. Two marvellous letters re prize,[8] one from the hall porter at the Carlton, yrs respectfully kind of style, other from a Nip journalist I've met, offering his congratulation (only one) and saying what a good book it is, artistic triumph etc., in fact he'll be reading it soon. Any Eng-speaker would have been taking the piss, but a Nip . . . ?

Fuck the Argies
Cheers K.

*Oh bloody good: I wrote to him recently about a suggested Wodehouse plaque. He answered nicely, adding that as a theological student 30 years ago he wrote to me for advice on travelling in Portugal and apparently I gave him a lot of gen, among which he found my advice on what to drink particularly helpful. But still no plaque *as yet*[9].

Tell Liddie love and yes, thanks, Hilly's shoes came.[10]

[TLS: Recipient]

TO WENDY COPE – 21 NOVEMBER 1986

194 Regents Park Road, London NW1 8XP

Dear Miss Cope,

Thanks for your congratulations about the Booker Prize. I have hardly been able to pick up a periodical these last months without

6. The full sentence in the *Dictionary of National Biography* entry reads: 'In later years they [Betjeman and his first wife] were amicably separated and Betjeman was cared for by his friend, Lady Elizabeth Cavendish.'

7. Amis has typed 'later: okayed!' in the margin.

8. For Amis's account of winning the 1986 Booker Prize for *The Old Devils* see *Memoirs*, pp. 324–7.

9. MS addition.

10. MS addition.

finding an approving reference to Making Cocoa.[1] I am delighted.

Yours sincerely
Kingsley Amis

[TLS: Recipient]

TO LOIS WILSON – 21 NOVEMBER 1986

194 Regents Park Road, London NW1 8XP

My dear Lois,

How very nice to hear from you. Thank you for your congratulations. Jolly nice of you and Jack to send me that telegram, too. Hope you enjoy the book when you get to it.

I am delighted to hear that your book is progressing.[1] I think it might have an interesting career ahead of it. Of course I should be delighted to write a foreword, though as I must have said, it will have to be a short one and non-technical. Yes, I should love to see a copy, and the introduction too. Get in touch again and let me know how things are going.

I hope to see you in Swansea before long.

With love to you both,
Kingsley

[TLS: Recipient]

1. Wendy Cope (b. 1945), poet, author of *Making Cocoa for Kingsley Amis* (1986). The title poem is four lines long and reads: 'It was a dream I had last week/And some kind of record seemed vital./I knew it wouldn't be much of a poem/But I love the title.'

1. See Amis to Wilson, 23 October 1984, note 1.

TO MAEVE BRENNAN – 21 NOVEMBER 1986

194 Regents Park Road, London NW1 8XP

Dear Miss Brennan,

Thank you for your letter of 10th November. Of course I am more than willing to answer your questions.[1]

You seem to have missed the enclosed transcript of my address at Philip's funeral, though as far as I know it was circulated in Hull in some form or other soon after the occasion. I must confess I am far from clear about what you mean by Philip's desire to be 'on the side of the angels', a phrase I have always taken to indicate nothing more than a vague optimism or good will. But from your other remarks you are presumably talking about a wish for some kind of salvation. I am afraid that, as you will see, there is nothing at all in what I said that would justify any such inference. Nor, I might add, was there ever anything in my conversations with him that even touched on the subject. So you will understand that I cannot allow you to paraphrase me as you suggest.

Philip was in no serious sense a Christian, and I for one find distasteful the attempts since his death to rescue or hijack him for one church or another.

Yours sincerely,
Kingsley Amis

[TLS: Recipient]

---

1. Maeve Brennan (b. 1929), a friend and colleague of Philip Larkin, began work at the University College Library in Hull in 1953, as Chief Library Assistant, then Assistant Librarian, then Sub-Librarian, retiring shortly before Larkin's death in 1985. She had written to Amis on 10 November 1986 about a passage in his address at Larkin's funeral (see Appendix F). Larkin, she wrote, 'frequently talked to me about his views on religion and death: he envied me my Catholicism as he did anyone who was able to accept the Christian faith.' Brennan planned to discuss Larkin's feelings about religion in an essay she was writing for *Philip Larkin: The Man and his Work* (Basingstoke: Macmillan, 1989), a *festschrift* edited by Dale Salwak. She asked Amis to comment on the following draft sentence from the essay: 'There was therefore some consolation for those who witnessed this struggle [i.e. Larkin's fears about death and his inability to accept religious consolation] in Kingsley Amis's funeral address on 9 December 1985 when he spoke of Philip's desire to be on the side of the angels and expressed the hope that this wish had been gratified.' Brennan's essay, minus this draft sentence and any reference to Amis's funeral address, is entitled 'I remember, I remember', and appears on pp. 27–37 of the *festschrift*.

TO ROBERT CONQUEST – 6 DECEMBER 1986

194 RPR NW1 8XP

D O Bob,

Philip is much in mind just now, with his anniversary (Christ) on the 2nd of this month. To mark the occasion they had a prog on Radio 4, The Bicycle-clipped Misanthropist [sic],[1] half an hour of reminiscent chat by various Hull people, among whom Maeve was soon identifiable and prominent. Honestly, the worst kind of N-country cheapjack homely wisdom you can imagine: he treated the world on his own terms and which of us is wise enough to say, etc. Everybody talked on the level of 'he perhaps had a forbidding exterior but really he was very warm with a word for everyone.' So that was the cosy little nest he had up there. The only point of interest was that P had a telescope on his window-sill to get a better view of passing tits.

Then to the exhibition of his stuff first shown in Hull now at Univ Coll Lond. Not surprisingly it showed what a huge part the library played in his life. Quite a few unpubd poems, including a skit on 'Days' – 'Booze' – and the famous 'Letter to a Friend about Girls'.[2] Friend could be you or me but probably no one chap. The gist was that P never met any of the friend's sort of girl nor vice versa. I would have transcribed it but once I started writing I'd have been there all day. And that would have been too depressing for words. Had Hilly with me thank Xt and we hurried off to a cracking exp-a/c lunch at Inigo Jones, crowned in my case with a glass of vintage port AND one of

---

1. Amis's '[sic]'.

2. 'Booze' is a Larkin self-parody written on an undated Christmas card to Kenneth Hibbert, his friend, insurance adviser and fellow member of the Hull Literary Club. It has not been printed before, and reads:

> What is booze for?
> Booze is what we drink.
> They come, they shake us,
> Time and time over.
> Beer, whisky, schnapps and gin.
> What can we drink but booze?
> Ah, solving that question, etc.
> Brings the priest and the doctor
> (And a few pink rats)
> Running over the fields.

marc de gewurtztraminer and in hers with the biggest shot of green Chartreuse either of us had ever seen.

Had a session with A Motion trying to recall bits of P for the biog. Not the easiest thing in the world. Memory has no sense of relevance, what? M has been shooting round interviewing Winifred [Arnott], Ruth [Bowman], Kitty (sis) et al. He's quite agreeable but he does wear half a dozen bangles on his arm.[3] His thank-you card spoke of my giving him my time 'so generously and so *interestingly*'. Well there it is.

J Osborne picks The Old Ds as a bk of the yr saying it's jolly gd anyway but particularly so in view of my hearty boozing. Well yes. I might add here that I've joined the Scotch Malt Whisky Society which bottles its own. My 'introductory bottle' is a 16-year-old Springbank from Campbeltown at 99.3 deg. proof.

My agent is auctioning me round the publishers so I may be able to quit Cohen on grounds of greed. Incidentally I was no end tickled to see that the blurb I wrote for the old ds (saying it was jolly important and major and everything, a strategy C had opposed as counter-productive) got an admiring para in the Bookseller as *technically* an exemplary effort.

One thing Motion and I agreed on was the way incidents suggesting Larkin poems kept coming up. Like me going to the exhib, you to New Orleans.[4]

Yes, TSE stamps[5] much appreciated. None yet I suppose commemorating Lowell or Ashbery. Just give it time.

I enclose Maeve's reply to round off the story.

Cheers
K.

[TLS: Recipient]

3. Accessories favoured also by the monstrous Cordelia Vaisey in *The Russian Girl* (1992).

4. Conquest had been to a conference in New Orleans, which called to mind Larkin's poem on the city, 'For Sidney Bechet', from *The Whitsun Weddings* (1964).

5. On 26 September the US Post Office issued a 22c stamp with T.S. Eliot's picture on it.

TO JOHN McDERMOTT – 15 JANUARY 1987

194 Regents Park Road, London NW1 8XP

Dear Mr. Dermott,

Delighted to hear that *K. A.: An English Dancer on the Optics*[1] has got as far as it has. Yes, of course I gladly give my permission for you to quote my stuff.

I was most interested in your suggestions about a sequel to *What Became of Jane Austen?*[2] Oddly enough I was thinking along those very lines myself, and wondering dimly who I could induce to collect the material, when I heard from you. I think it's a marvellous idea. Jonathan Clowes[3] says he thinks it's a marvellous idea. We had better meet and discuss it – you and I, that is. I am seldom in Wigan, so perhaps you could let me know when you are next likely to be in London.

All the best for 1987.
Yours,
Kingsley Amis

[TLS: Recipient]

TO ROBERT CONQUEST – 26 JANUARY 1987

194 R P R NW1 8XP England

Dear O B,

A bit late to wish you a happy new year, but I do so all the same. Ole Philip is still hanging about, in the sense that I've just been tidying

1. McDermott's *Kingsley Amis: An English Moralist* was published in 1989. 'Optics' are devices attached to the necks of bottles, used for measuring out spirits. At the end of *The Old Devils* Alan Warner dies of an apoplectic fit after he and his fellow guests are asked to pay for a second round of drinks by their host *in his home*; all the host's bottles of spirits, notices another guest, 'had optic measures like those used in pubs fitted to their necks' (p. 333).

2. To become *The Amis Collection: Selected Non-Fiction 1954–1990* (London: Hutchinson, 1990), which contains an introduction by McDermott, though he is not credited with editing the volume.

3. Amis's agent; see Amis to Conquest, 21 December 1981, note 1.

up Hilly's reminiscences of his last weeks for a Yank collection.[1] Remember him saying on the telephone he was only drinking cheap red wine and her saying for Xt's sake get some expensive red wine? Then like a fool (considering the money) I'm doing 6 jazz-record progs[2] and he comes to mind all the time. Monica pissed on the blower to one or other of us every week or so. Well, it's a light cross to bear.

Did you see B Levin's marvellous attack on the late Arnold Kettle for being a communist? – *just as bad* as being a Nazi, he explained at length. Well of course, we say, but what's even better in a way is (i) I wrote to him 2 or 3 weeks after the event telling him I'd met Kettle[3] (he hadn't) and found him a turd personally as well; he wrote thanking and saying he'd had scores of letters saying what a shit he *B.*[4] was for attacking such a nice bloke and *not one* even *referring* to his *Kettle's*[5] support for Stalin (ii) after about 10 days (after the piece appeared, I mean) the Times printed one letter attacking Bernard on the what-about-America line (Mafia . . . Watergate . . . Vietnam). Nothing since. It makes you start believing in conspiracy theories: it's *just as if* the word went round saying better leave this one alone.

My brilliantly-xeroxed enclosure[6] has a self-explanatory piece about P (here he is again) – fucking disgrace, what? – and two items for your all-women-are-mad file. One was from a female who (needless to say unasked) had pushed some of her (needless to say 100% merit-free) poems through my letter-box, which I politely returned with a note; the other comes from a well-known journal. See if you can guess which. Clue: its name, abbreviated, consists of the 14th and 19th letters of the alphabet. Incidentally the Barnes novel[7] has been certified as piss by me, Martin and Hitchens, who eventually went on to say Stalin wasn't as bad as Hitler. What would it take to make them see . . . ?

Sorry, I heard far queue at school. Have you heard Waiter to Chinese

1. See Hilly Kilmarnock, 'A Personal Memoir', in Salwak, ed., *Philip Larkin: The Man and his Work*, pp. 153–7.

2. *Blues with a Difference*, a six-part series on Radio 3, from 28 January to 4 March 1987, with separate programmes on Bix Beiderbecke, Henry 'Red' Allen, Bessie Smith, Pee Wee Russell, Bill Davison and Sidney Bechet.

3. For Arnold Kettle see Amis to the editor, *Daily Worker*, 14 February 1957, note 1.

4. Interlinear MS addition.

5. Interlinear MS addition.

6. It does not survive.

7. *Staring at the Sun* (1986).

diner: You for coffee? Diner: *You* fuck-offy. And bling manager light away!? *You lewd fellow!*[8]

Further to my brilliance, I see I told an interviewer 'what makes any given page of Pound worthless makes him all worthless' and, re the right 'wing' in this country, 'there's no foreign power to work for. Turkey? Chile? I don't expect they've many men in the Tory party.' Terrific, eh? Yes, no doubt you have said much the same yourself. But not perhaps to readers of the FT in the last month.

Bloody awful hangover today. Martin & wife gave me a sort of Danish lunch y'day. The eats were only would-be Danish but there was nothing would-be about the half-tumblers of akvavit he poured. You are mad, careering round all over the shop in those bleeding kites. It's more like 36 years *or soon will be.*[9] We met at the party for New Poems 1951.[10] I'm 3 times a granddad now: Philip produced a daughter last week. But I fear[11] all is not well there. Anyway, make sure you get on that London flight in due time.

Cheers
K

DON'T MISS PS on back of xerox.[12]

WOULDN'T-YOU-FUCKING-WELL-KNOW DEPARTMENT

PS: I was going to tell you, if I had had room, that in future the head of Hutchinson was going to look after me, so no more R Cohen heart-stoppers. *After I had finished my letter to you* (or thought I had) *but before putting it in the envelope*, a motor-bike messenger brought me a packet from Hutch with 'R Cohen' on it. Inside was a proof of the new cover for my expanded collected short stories (to mark my 65th in April) and also of the two additional stories. The cover had the wrong design, the blurb contained a mistake impossible for anyone who had even glanced through the stories (referring to '3 SF-drink stories' when *one of the new stories is SF-drink with the same characters as the other three*), and it was titled 'Investing in Futures: a Story' because that

8. MS addition.
9. MS addition.
10. *New Poems 1952.*
11. Amis has crossed out 'feel' and replaced it with 'fear'.
12. MS addition.

was how it had been titled in the mainly non-fiction anthology vol. it had first appeared in and he hadn't noticed. Any reader might have thought, if this is a story what are all the others? When I rang he said it was all right, there was time to change it, and it was the result of a misunderstanding. THAT'S GOOD TO HEAR, I wanted to scream – I WAS BEGINNING TO THINK IT WAS A BIT OF DELIBERATE FUCKING SABOTAGE. How would you expect to get on yourself if you wrote 'The Russian revolution broke out in Warsaw in 1916, headed by V. I. Marx and Leon Lenin'? Cor stone the bleeding crows.

[TLS: Recipient]

TO HARRY RITCHIE – 28 JANUARY 1987

194 Regents Park Road London NW1 8XP

Dear Mr Ritchie,

I suppose I had better put you out of your misery without more ado – or much ado, as they say in this context in Wales.[1]

Just to set your cup running over, Hilary Rubinstein told me the other day that Gollancz didn't read LJ until the attention it had attracted made him think perhaps he had better. You may think this makes it necessary to modify the first quotation on your list.[2] Whichever version you pick, or whatever compromise you may frame, is all right with me. I didn't ask Rubinstein what VG thought of it when he did read it, but you could. Amenable enough chap.

Could you insert 'Although it's not my chief purpose' or something before 'I just enjoy annoying people,' which sounds a bit baldly childish on its own.

Everything else seems fine to me, including the time-table.

---

1. Ritchie had written to Amis on 23 January 1987 for permission to use quotations from an interview they had conducted on 30 November 1984 in his book *Success Stories: Literature and the Media in England, 1950–1959* (1988), which was being copy-edited at the time.

2. 'Gollancz was "very much against publishing it" (*Lucky Jim*) because he thought it "vulgar and anti-cultural".'

Yes, perhaps I told you, but between ourselves I was too afraid to drink a bottle of whisky Colin Wilson once gave me, and there it stayed on my shelf till an intrepid psychiatrist pal[3] guzzled it with no ill-effects, or none but the usual.

Really I'm most interested to see your book and would love to see a proof if possible. I'm bound to get hold of it eventually, you know.

Oh, in case you need it formally: you may cite statements I made to you on 30th November 1984 – Christ, was it that long ago?

All good wishes
Kingsley Amis

[TLS: Recipient]

TO SIR MICHAEL HAVERS – 30 JANUARY 1987

194 Regents Park Road, London NW1 8XP

Dear Michael,

I was most interested to see the poems by your granddaughter.[1] You must understand that relatively little poetry by children comes my way, but these specimens strike as remarkable. Both Kate's poems show a readiness to look outside herself and her own life that must be rare in children of her sort of age and is by no means universal in their elders. In 'Type Writer', by far the more successful of the two pieces, with nothing 'childish' in it, she manages to express such feelings in a coherent shape and form, though I hope that as she goes on she will develop a tighter, more metrical style.

And she might go on and she might not. Writing poetry as you know is a common activity among bright children, and in most cases of course they come to drop it when they grow up. It's obviously too early to say whether Kate will go on or not; she can't know herself. But

3. James Durham.

1. Kate Havers, aged eight in 1987, the daughter of Nigel Havers (b.1949), the actor, and granddaughter of Michael Havers (1923–92), at the time Lord High Chancellor of Great Britain (1987), previously Attorney General (1979–87); created Baron (1987). Amis knew Havers through the Garrick Club.

it's not too early to say that she has unmistakable talent and deserves encouragement not just as a child but as a poet, if you see what I mean.

I return the poems herewith but have kept a copy of 'Type Writer'.

I hope to see you in the Club some time soon.

Yours ever,
Kingsley

[TLS: Recipient]

TO SARAH CARDEW – 26 MARCH 1987

as from: Top Flat, 194, Regent's Park Rd., London NW1 8XP

Dear Mrs Cardew,

My wife and I both enjoyed your letter to the Times the other day, but we were divided on what a part of it actually meant.[1] If you have time, perhaps you would settle the argument.

She thinks that after a long absence from his old school, your husband returned and had the knife returned by the master. I think it was the master who returned and, finding your husband there too, returned the knife, which he either happened to have with him or had left in a safe place. My wife says this sounds very unlikely, and I agree, but after all you do *say* it was the master who returned to his old school,

1. The letter that sparked this little imposture by Amis appeared in *The Times* on 20 March 1987, in the bottom right corner of the letters page, traditionally reserved for light or humorous contributions. It was titled 'Period return' and read: 'Sir, On returning to his old school yesterday after a long absence my husband's ex-English master returned to him a Gurkha kukri knife which had been confiscated from his elder brother while on Combined Cadet Force camp 24 years ago. Is this the longest school confiscation on record? Yours, Sarah Cardew.'

don't you? I suppose the long absence might be accounted for by his being an ex-Englishman.[2]

Yours sincerely,
J.E. Fletcher

[TLS][3]

TO STUART SUTHERLAND – 1 APRIL 1987

194 Regents Park Road, London NW1 8XP

Dear Stuart,

Thank you for sending me the additional chapters of *Breakdown*.[1] They are at least as interesting as anything in the first edition, which to me is saying a lot. Here is a suggestion for the cover blurb:

> This is a book unlike any other that I have read. It combines a searingly honest and terrifyingly detailed account of a mental breakdown with a professional's description of the reality of mental illness as it is treated in our society. It is unforgettable. Also required reading for the psychological malingerers who clog up our understaffed facilities. This is what a breakdown is really like.

The above is not holy writ and can be cut, rearranged and generally turned around to any degree short of putting words into my mouth. If you would like to change anything, let me know.

2. Mrs Cardew (b.1954), a teacher, who only now, eleven years later, has become aware of the true identity of 'J.E. Fletcher', responded on 1 April 1987 with great good humour. After explaining that her letter was 'thrown down in a moment of inspiration when I was already late for work', and admitting that it was misleading, she declared, 'your wife wins. The English master was still there and it was the husband who returned after the long absence.'

3. A photocopy of this letter was found among Amis's papers after his death. Mrs Cardew did not keep the original.

1. *Breakdown: A Personal Crisis and a Medical Dilemma* (1976), 2nd edition (1987), by Stuart Sutherland (1927–98), Professor of Experimental Psychology, University of Sussex (1965–92).

My very best wishes for the success of the book and to you personally.

Yours ever,
Kingsley

[TLS: Recipient]

TO THE EDITOR, *SPECTATOR* – 25 APRIL 1987

London NW1

Sir,

Anyone who had been following the argument of my piece about the Church (18 April) would have been thrown off on reaching the statement, 'My belief is not uniform.'[1] What I wrote and intended to write was, 'My unbelief is not uniform.' Part of my argument was that Anglican believers and unbelievers had interests in common, but it would take a bishop of our Church to say that belief and unbelief are interchangeable expressions.

Yours sincerely,
KINGSLEY AMIS

TO JOHN MCDERMOTT – 30 APRIL 1987

194 Regent's Park Road, London NW1 8XP

Dear John,

Here are the dreaded corrections.[1] Nothing of much consequence as you see. Sorry I've been so long, but it fell under the curse of being work without being my new novel, if you see what I mean.

---

1. See 'Godforsaken', *Spectator*, 18 April 1987, pp. 25–6.

---

1. To McDermott's *Kingsley Amis: An English Moralist.*

I offer you two little observations of possible interest, though they're not aimed at anything you say or don't say in your book.

The deep personal ring. Sometimes, he said ruefully, I'm too good a novelist for my own good. From Jim hating Mozart (it's no good if we can see him just pretending to hate Mozart) to Flackerty defending the status quo[2] (it's no good if we can see him having decent reservations) the chaps have got to believe in their beliefs. I'm lucky that Dame Fortune's wheel hasn't brought me the task of portraying an SS man ('Amis's previously covert anti-semitism and anti-libertarianism at last come into the open').

Autobiography in fiction. You don't put into fiction things that have happened in your own life, but things that happen to you *set you thinking*, or things that might happen, could well happen, do. So that fucking fool James Fenton gets it wrong writing about 'Dear Illusion'.[3] It's about Amis wondering whether he's any good, he says, but surely the silly old bugger has learnt to accept by now that he's fairly good, so why the fuss? He doesn't see that reaching the age of 50 or so, as I then was, set me thinking about being really plagued by the question (of whether one's any good) when quite isolated at the age of 75 plus. *What if* such a chap set himself to find out? What-if is of course the basic science-fiction question but also one of the basic ones in ordinary fiction. Perhaps the basic one there too.

Did I tell you the stories about Iris Murdoch and (a) the wine-merchants (b) the psychiatrist? If not I will at our next meeting. Which I pray may be soon. Till then keep me posted.

Cheers
Kingsley

Just got your latest sheaf.[4] My goodness me, some not very good stuff there. I can stand Red Dragon, Drowned World, Illiteracy and perhaps

2. Brother Collam Flackerty, friar of the Augustinian Order, in the Archiepiscopal Palace of Westminster, in *The Alteration* (1976).

3. James Fenton discusses 'Dear Illusion' (1972) in a review of Amis's *Collected Short Stories* (1980), 'He is Obliged to Find a Few Plausible Reasons for Anger', *Listener*, 23 October 1980, p. 543.

4. Of uncollected writings, for possible inclusion in *The Amis Collection.*

Spastics but for its look-what-a-good-chap-am-I tinge.[5] But soon we must settle questions of size, general approach etc. which means I talk to agent, publisher, etc. and let you know. Yes send Dodos, Williams.[6]

[TLS: Recipient]

TO ANN MCDERMOTT – 30 APRIL 1987

194 Regents Park Road London NW1 8XP

Dear Anne,

I churlishly never thanked you for the two noteworthy bottles of malt, which I now do.[1] Both were most acceptable and the Highland Park oustanding: 'an excellent after-dinner dram' opines malt-whisky pundit Wallace Milroy, who entertains me to lunch next Thursday, with a look at a few distinguished malts first 'just to give us an appetite.'[2] Ha har. Come at 11 a.m., he says. Absurd. He must mean 11.30.

Those bits of Wain were close to being literally unbelievable.[3] I put them away in a place so special that I can't find it. Could you possibly redo them for me? From here I can send xeroxes of them all over the civilised world.

5. Thomas Harris, *Red Dragon* (1982), J.G. Ballard, *The Drowned World* (1962). I am stymied (as is McDermott) by the presumably abbreviated titles 'Illiteracy' and 'Spastics'.

6. These are the review articles 'Dodos Less Darling', on Angus Wilson, *Anglo-Saxon Attitudes*, in the *Spectator*, 1 June 1956; 'Dodos on the Wing', also on Angus Wilson, *A Bit off the Map and Other Stories*, in *Spectator*, 18 October 1957; and 'Martians Bearing Bursaries', on Raymond Williams, *Britain in the Sixties: Communications* and John Vaizey, *Britain in the Sixties: Education for Tomorrow*, in *Spectator*, 27 April 1972. All three reviews were reprinted in *The Amis Collection*, pp. 91–4, 94–5 and 240–4.

---

1. A thank-you present in return for Amis having taken the McDermotts to lunch at Simpson's. At the time, John McDermott had access to a supplier of cheap spirits and fine wines.

2. The quote from Wallace Milroy about Highland Park comes from his *Malt Whisky Almanac: A Taster's Guide* (Glasgow: Neil Wilson, 1984), p. 19, for which Amis wrote a one-page foreword. Milroy (b.1931) works in the whisky trade, and met Amis in the mid-1970s at a whisky launch. In his foreword Amis praises him for 'a proper enthusiasm, a professional's command of this vast and pleasurable field of knowledge, and a marvellous ability to distil the fruits of his experience into a few practical words' (p. 5).

3. Ann McDermott was reading John Wain's novel *A Winter in the Hills* (1970) and, knowing Amis's views on Wain's later fiction, had sent him several passages she thought 'might qualify for the "worst writing about sex award"' (personal communication, 1 March 1999).

Comfort John. Tell him we all know the scholar's way is hard. Some of us can dimly remember how hard.

Love,
Kingsley

[TLS: Recipient]

TO STUART SUTHERLAND – 30 APRIL 1987

194 Regents Park Road London NW1 8XP

Dear Stuart,

Thank you for a most enjoyable and entertaining lunch. Also for sending me your first novel.[1] I read it with great interest, indeed found it very easy to read, but I am afraid it wasn't quite enough of a 'novel' to live up altogether to my snooty standards.

I hope to see you soon.

Kingsley

P. S. I return the proofs under separate cover

[TLS: Recipient]

---

1. *Men Change Too* (1987). Sutherland also remembers the lunch as enjoyable, if ruinously expensive: Amis rejected his host's several suggested venues, insisted instead that they eat at the Neal Street Restaurant in Covent Garden, 'and ordered about twenty brandies' (personal communication, 23 October 1998). See, in this regard, *The Biographer's Moustache* (1996), p. 35, in which the veteran novelist Jimmie Fane is taken to lunch by his biographer Gordon Scott-Thompson, a struggling hack: 'Jimmie brought up an eyeglass on a fine silvery chain through which he proceeded to study the menu . . . Did it just happen that what he fancied turned out to be the most expensive dish to be had? Or had he quite consciously set out to sting his host as painfully as practicable? Or was his motive somewhere in the capacious territory between the two?'

TO J.G. SIMPSON – 30 APRIL 1987

c/o 22 Prince Albert Road, London NW1 7ST[1]

Dear Mr. Simpson,

Thank you for sending me your latest collection of poems. I must say that, like your earlier work,[2] they reflect a warm sympathy with the work of John Betjeman, whom you obviously admire greatly.

I too had hopes of James Fenton but I fear that of late he has become bored with traditional forms of verse, and is at any rate flirting with modernism.

Yours sincerely,
Kingsley Amis

[TLS: Recipient]

TO MRS BROWN – 2 JUNE 1987

194 Regent's Park Road, London NW1 8XP

Dear Mrs Brown,

Thank you for your letter reminding me of my promise about *Take a Girl Like You* (TAGLY).[1] (The things one lets oneself in for!) Your questions actually provide a very good framework for my comments on the book, but I begin with some information about the title I have not written down before.

I had had the central idea in my head for some time, but it took shape when I came across a record by the American singer Josh White,

1. The address of Amis's agent Jonathan Clowes.
2. See Amis to Simpson, 18 December 1984.

1. This letter was found among Amis's papers after he died. The letter to which it responds, with its list of questions, has not surfaced, nor has it been possible to determine Mrs Brown's identity. The penultimate paragraph suggests she may have written to Amis in preparation for leading a discussion of *Take a Girl Like You*, perhaps at a local reading group.

'Take a Gal Like You'.[2] Its words tell a very different version of the same story of man betraying woman. At one time I favoured another title for the book, *Song of the Wanderer*, also apposite though less striking. It too is the title of a song, one which begins, 'Where shall I go when I go where I go?' and I used this as an epigraph.[3]

Do I still consider TAGLY my best novel?

Yes. I am 'too close' to *The Old Devils* to see it quite straight yet, but I think TAGLY is a better work of art, a better story better told.

Is TAGLY founded on experience?

Yes, but experience via imagination, and a great deal is invented, as fiction is supposed to be. The various houses and so on are all made up. Some of the minor characters, especially Graham McClintoch,[4] have a slight connection with people I knew.

Was I putting over a particular idea?

I didn't think so when I was writing it (I never do), it was just a rather sad love-story, but I can see from here that to some extent I was foretelling the Sixties. The book was begun in 1955 and after various delays finished early in 1960. Did I find it difficult writing from a woman's point of view?

No, very easy – which doesn't at all mean I necessarily think I got it right. I felt I knew one or two things which I could get across best if I put them like that. But more than that, it was a marvellous opportunity to criticise male behaviour and its frequent selfishness and absurdity.

I hope the above will prove useful when it comes to your discussion meeting but please circulate it in any way you want. Let me wish you all success.

Thank you for your congratulations about the Booker Prize. It has given me a lot of confidence for subsequent projects, like the novel

2. Josh White's 'Take a Gal Like You' has several choruses, each of which starts 'Take a gal like you/Down to New Orleans/Dress her in a dress of red . . .' and so on, with the colour of the dress changing with each repetition. James Silvester (personal communication) compares Amis's use of this title with John Wain's use of 'Hurry on Down' (the title of a 1940s recording by the singer and pianist Nellie Lutcher) for his first novel, published in 1953.

3. 'Song of the Wanderer' dates from 1926, words and music by Neil Moret. First eight bars: 'Where shall I go/When I go where I go/When you have sent me away?' Second eight bars: 'What shall I do,/When I do what I do/When you have turned my skies to grey?' For the novel's second epigraph ('Go, gentle maid, go lead the apes in hell') see *The Taming of the Shrew*, II.i. 30–2.

4. A chemistry teacher, flatmate of Patrick Standish, the novel's anti-hero.

Difficulties with Girls, which I am busily engaged on at the moment.

Yours sincerely,
Kingsley Amis

[TLS]

TO LOIS WILSON – 2 JUNE 1987

194 Regents Park Road London NW1 8XP

My dear Lois,

(Please forgive aged fingers for typing.) Here at last is the dreaded Preface. Sorry for the delay, but Mr Whitaker,[1] though very clear he wanted something of the sort, was shy of saying just what he wanted, so I finally had to plunge into something out of my usual line (so also please excuse any howlers, which can easily be corrected).

The agedness of the fingers also rather precludes the idea of a handwritten page, though I think my signature at the foot might be a good idea. I have sent a xerox of the enclosed to the good Mr Whitaker, so it should be possible to go ahead now.

If you and Jack do happen to be in London it would be fun to meet for drinks or lunch. But in any case I have booked in with Eve and Stuart Thomas and am scheduled for mid-August.

It was fun doing the preface because I really wanted to do it and felt I had something to say. I hope I have successfully got it across that I do admire your paintings very much.

See you soon! All best to Jack!

Love
Kingsley

[TLS: Recipient]

---

1. Of the book's publishers, D. Brown and Sons, of Cowbridge and Bridgend.

TO STUART THOMAS – 30 JULY 1987

194 Regents Park Road, London NW1 8XP

Dear Stuart,

As we agreed over the telephone, I am sending you my observations on the proposed novelization of UNDER MILK WOOD.[1]

If Anthony Burgess agreed to do the job, the result would of course be a book by Anthony Burgess, based on, etc. He would not want to do it unless he could impose his own creative ideas upon it. I don't think we want what would have to be a travesty of the original. And he is very expensive. Any lesser writer would of course cost less, but probably do the job less competently, and such a person would also want to impose his personality on Dylan Thomas's work.

I cannot help thinking that any 'adaptation' would impair the sales of the original. In my view, Lynn Hughes[2] is quite wrong when he says people are 'intimidated by play scripts'. On the contrary, they might well relish the feeling of authenticity that a script – especially the fuller version – would give them.

The parallel with Lamb's Tales from Shakespeare is quite false. Lamb's book was for children. Also it would take 500 Lambs to make any kind of dent on Shakespeare.

All in all I am strongly opposed to the idea of putting a middleman between Dylan Thomas and his public.

Yours
Kingsley

[TLS: Trustees of the Dylan Thomas Literary Estate]

---

1. In 1986 Amis had been asked by Stuart Thomas to become one of Dylan Thomas's literary trustees, a controversial appointment given Amis's declared hostility to Thomas's verse (see *Memoirs*, pp. 132–3 and *The Old Devils*, pp. 14–15 and 224–5, where the fictional Brydan stands in for Dylan). The original trustees of the Dylan Thomas Literary Estate were Stuart Thomas, who had known the poet since school days, David Higham, Thomas's literary agent, and Dan Jones, the composer; Jones resigned in 1956 and was replaced by another old friend of both Stuart and Dylan Thomas, Wynford Vaughan-Thomas; David Higham died in 1978; Michael Rush was made a trustee at the same time as Amis.

2. Lynn Hughes (b. 1939), author, radio producer, publisher.

TO BRIAN WALDEN – 3 AUGUST 1987

194 Regents Park Road, London NW1 8XP

Dear Mr Walden,

I always enjoy your Sunday Times pieces and often learn from them. But yesterday's terrified me, as far as a newspaper article can.[1]

Please recognise that Russia is not in the least likely to 'hurl its armed forces against us in an outburst of fanatical zeal' or of anything else, and has never had any such intention. With the Soviets as with their Tsarist predecessors, war has never been an instrument of policy and a trial of arms is the last thing they want. They don't start wars, they just grab up unattended or indefensible bits of territory without firing a shot. They had to fire a few in Poland in 1939, agreed, but none to speak of in the Baltic republics in 1940, and in Eastern Europe only the execution squads used up much ammunition – some 'military conquest'. In Finland they were after something other than annexation and in Afghanistan they miscalculated, though not importantly.

You are well aware of all this, or of its more factual parts, but clearly need to be reminded of it. The Russians will come here only if they decide the place will not or cannot be defended, but then they will. By your misleading talk of their *unwarlike*[2] intentions, you have unwittingly helped to make that prospect more likely. I urge you to reconsider the matter and write about it again soon.

Yours sincerely,
Kingsley Amis

[TLS: Recipient]

---

1. Brian Walden, 'Cheer on the Russian Front', *Sunday Times*, 2 August 1987, p. 2. Walden (b. 1932), journalist and broadcaster, previously Labour MP for Birmingham, All Saints (1964–74) and Birmingham, Ladywood (1974–77).

2. Interlinear MS addition.

TO JANE THYNNE – 31 AUGUST 1987

Swansea

Dear Miss Thynne,

It's a bit galling for someone of my generation to have written to a given length and then find himself substantially cut and also corrected here and there, and without being consulted, even with a UK number for you to call and a couple of weeks to do it in.[1] And I didn't like being made to talk about modern music and architecture setting out to impress the food buffs, when what I'd said was that it was to impress the specialists. But I suppose we have to shrug our shoulders at that kind of thing these days, and remember that of course it was easier for you that way. Even so I thought it was going too far to change Glenmorangie to Glen Morangie. This makes me look as much of an idiot to anyone who knows about whisky as talking about Beau Jolais would make a wine-writer look to anyone who knows about wine. Honestly, for Christ's sake

Yours sincerely,
Kingsley Amis

[TLS]

TO ROBERT CONQUEST – 1 SEPTEMBER 1987

as from Regent's Park Road

Dear Old Bob,

You probably wondered if I was dead; well, I nearly bloody am, or at least my demise has been brought appreciably closer by a couple of weeks in Wales (with another yet to come). Not only the raised alcohol

1. Jane Thynne (b. 1961), novelist (*Patrimony* (1997), *The Shell House* (1998)) and journalist, had commissioned Amis to write a piece on Sweetings, the London restaurant, for the *Sunday Times*. She did not edit Amis's piece, nor does she remember receiving this letter, a photocopy of which was discovered among Amis's papers after his death. Miss Thynne describes her relations with Amis as perfectly cordial, both when she accompanied him to lunch at Sweetings and after the appearance of the article (personal communication, 23 April 1999).

intake but the eating of lethal food. Swansea contains the South Wales chapter of the Friends of Cholesterol, the East Anglia one being at Tattingstone, seat of George Gale. My Aussie china Jim Durham is here briefly, helping to provide a peak of self-inflicted damage. Some work done, but time to catch up a bit with letters before stumbling off to the Yacht Club.

Slight excitement here with advent of a madman/chancer called Lynn Hughes who claims to have signed up every known Welshman from Lord Tonypandy (the former Speaker) to Aled Jones the boy soprano to make a monster new recording of Under Milk Wood.[1] It will never happen, but a chance effect has been to reveal the possible existence of an unpublished text taken from a typescript Thomas drunkenly revised in New York. Publishing that would be good: from which you may see the depth of my disinterested devotion to literature, even pissy bits of it like the work of DT. (I probably told you I am now a Trustee of the Estate). [. . .]

I've had another session with A Motion babbling recollections of Philip into a tape-recorder. Sad how few and inconsequential they turned out to be. He (M) was quite interesting on having run Ruth Bowman (the chum in specs P took out) to earth. Poor little thing, soon after breaking up with P she evidently married another bloke who gave her a kid (as P would have put it) and promptly fell down dead, and she never remarried. I may have told you I got a letter from the bosomy English rose[2] in search of a text of the poem and saying she felt sort of bad about the episode. Feels she ought to have let him fuck her, I suppose she meant. Well, she needn't worry now. Thwaite is asking for xeroxes of the letters in a pressing way. I reckon I'll oblige, going over some passages with him. I'm convinced both he and M are perfectly well-intentioned and understanding on this. M is very nice really but he . . . does write creepy notes after our sessions [. . .]

My life is just work, family, club (plus Swansea) now and v nice too. Plus occasional lunch associated with my literary or alcoholic interests. One of the latter featured a Mr Yamamoto who as well as being

---

1. The recording was released in 1988 by EMI. Hughes edited the text and the producer/director was George Martin, who also produced the Beatles' albums.

2. Jane Exall, a friend of Larkin's friend Ruth Bowman (*LL*, p. 126n.); 'bosomy English rose' comes from Larkin's poem 'Wild Oats' in *LCP*, p. 143.

my translator-in-chief is also one of the few Japanese to have published a book on Scotch whisky. [. . .]

I have a funny story to tell you about Lord Havers at Lord's (the cricket ground) and a different sort about an Englishman, a Scotchman, a Cuban and a Pakistani in a Welsh train. Love to Liddie.

Cheers
K.

Welsh art (visual) is to English art as Greek cooking is to Turkish cooking. (Conquest's view)[3]

[TLS: Recipient]

TO ANTHONY THWAITE – 9 SEPTEMBER 1987

194 Regents Park Road, London NW1 8XP

Dear Anthony,

Give me a ring when you are coming to London and we will arrange a lunch. I am afraid I must disappoint you about the bulk of my Larkin letters.[1] Most of the ones before about 1970 have been lost or left behind in moves, divorces, etc., and what I have will easily go into an ordinary briefcase. I have not yet looked them over since xeroxing them, but when I do I may well find a few points I would like to go over with you. But this would not take very long.

I must record my disagreement with you over your proposal to put the contents of THE NORTH SHIP at the back of the Collected Poems. I don't think at all that Philip would have approved of having his first

3. MS addition.

---

1. See *LL*, p. xii: 'Kingsley Amis, who initially sent me photocopies of all he had in his possession (seventy-three letters) . . . thought the first surviving letter from a friendship that began in Oxford in 1941 dated from as late as 1967, and most from 1972. Yet fortunately, towards the end of my work, another forty-one letters unexpectedly appeared (dated 1942–7, though with a complete gap in 1944).'

book relegated in this way. But I do agree that the back is the place for the poems that antedate THE NORTH SHIP.

Jolly good luck. See you soon.

Kingsley

P. S. I take it Janice Rossen told you all about IN THE GRIP OF LIGHT?[2]

[TLS: Recipient]

TO ANTHONY THWAITE – 29 OCTOBER 1987

194 Regents Park Road, London NW1 8XP

Dear Anthony,

Very many thanks for sending me 'Letter to a Friend About Girls'. Why the hell did he never publish it, I wonder. Do you agree that it should be 'in *the* bath' rather than 'in *a* bath'?[1]

Between ourselves, old chap, I recently had the misfortune to read Andrew Motion's poem about Philip,[2] and found it to be of such horrendous banality and shapelessness that I can only believe with difficulty that anything good will come of this biography. But I am working away at it. At trying to believe it, I mean.

I send you herewith the promised photocopies of Philip's letters.

2. A projected volume of twenty-seven poems by Larkin written between 1944 and late 1947. The volume was rejected by Faber and several other publishers. See Amis to Larkin, 9 January 1947, note 1. Janice Rossen (b. 1955), an American literary academic, Senior Research Fellow, Harry Ransom Humanities Research Center, University of Texas at Austin (since 1990), author of several books, including *The World of Barbara Pym* (1987) and *Philip Larkin: His Life's Work* (1989), and numerous articles on modern British writing.

---

1. The poem was first published in *LCP*, where it is dated December 1959. The second stanza begins: 'Now I believe your staggering skirmishes/In train, tutorial and telephone booth,/The wife whose husband watched away matches/While she behaved so badly in a bath.' That the 'friend' was at least partly based on Amis is clear from its reference to the wife 'whose husband watched away matches', which recalls Amis to Larkin, 24 September 1956.

2. Motion's poem, 'This is Your Subject Speaking', originally appeared in the *TLS*, 7 February 1986, p. 139, and was reprinted in *Natural Causes* (1987), pp. 49–57.

Let us have a chat about them when you have had time to go through them.

Cheers
Kingsley

[TLS: Recipient]

TO ROBERT CONQUEST – [C. OCTOBER–NOVEMBER 1987]

194 RPR NW1 8XP

D O Bob,

Just to try to get a blow in before you're over again. [. . .] I don't think acronyms should lose sight of the original objective, to comment on the blokes as well as produce an impropriety, as in C U N-T S where it all began.[1] So, e.g., Campaign to Resist Alcohol and Passive Smoking (a bloody good handy P S which I recommend to you). Also I think it should be 'For why *to* vote Conservative'.[2] In the amended form it has gone all round the Garrick.

I sent xeroxes of all my Philip letters to Thwaite, who promises faithfully to go over with me what he wants to include. Got my secretary to do the xeroxing. When I told her who they were to go to she said, 'Oh, he comes in nearly all the ones I looked at, in phrases like That fucking fool Thwaite or That incredible shit Thwaite.' Never mind. He tells me Monica has found 'the missing final notebook (Jan 1972 to Nov 1981)' and he's got 8 more unpub'd poems out of it, including one beginning Love again: wanking at ten past three. As he quite funnily says, the reviewers will call it incompetent editing, letting through an obvious misprint for 'waking'. He also sent me a xerox of Letter to a

1. According to Conquest (personal communication), Amis is referring here to a character whose unreliability derives from his simultaneous support of the 'Committee for Unilateral Nuclear-Test Suspension' and the 'Cambridge University Naval Training Scheme'. Conquest adds another early example, involving the comparably unreliable residents of the 'Barnaby Rudge and Oliver Twist Hostel for English Ladies' in Paris; Martin Amis adds the 'Sailors', Yachtsmen's and Pilots' Hospital in Long Island Sound', which Conquest claims is a misremembering of his own 'Skippers, Yachtsmen and Pilots Health Institute, Long Island Sound' (personal communication, 17 October 2000).

2. Conquest cannot recall what 'it' is, in original or amended form.

Friend about Girls, which I'm copying for you since I doubt if you've seen it. P told T he wouldn't publish it in his lifetime because likely to 'hurt several feelings'. Whose, I wonder. Ruth's, probably. Or even Winifred Arnott's. And of course there were others we wotted not of.

Christ, have you seen, did I tell you of, Andrew Motion's poem about Philip?*[3] I wrote to Thwaite, understating the case rather, that it was of horrendous banality and shapelessness. He replies saying he likes it (admittedly it does include some presumable quotes from P's sayings) which I can cheerfully stand, but then adds disconcertingly that P[eter] Porter also dislikes it. H'm. PP thinks highly of a lot of piss, indeed thinks highly enough of his own work to publish it. It couldn't therefore be that what he dislikes must be some good, could it? You shall see it when you come. Pages of the crap. Doesn't augur well for the biog, eh?

*The killer was some fucking idiot of a reviewer saying it (AM's poem) revealed a sensibility remarkably like P's. Like P's BACKSIDE, as he would have said.

I hope you hadn't got a lot of money in those bloody stocks and shares.[4] I must have had some, I suppose, since I have a pension scheme. But no word from anyone about it. I don't understand these matters, and don't you fucking try to explain to me. But if you say (which I hope you won't) that you've lost $1,000,000 I'll understand that.

Love to Liddie. Hurry over before we settle into the Dec-Apr freeze-up.

Cheers
K.

[TLS: Recipient]

3. See Amis to Thwaite, 29 October 1987, note 2.

4. On 19 October 1987 the Dow Jones average fell 508.32 points (23 per cent), resulting in a worldwide collapse in share values.

TO ANTHONY THWAITE – 19 NOVEMBER 1987

194 Regents Park Road, London NW1 8XP

Dear Anthony,

Jolly good to hear from you. Fascinating news about the final notebook of Philip's.[1] Please see to it that I get the most advanced of the advance copies *of the poems*[2] You are, I take it, including The Way We Live Now? The little poem beginning 'I let a fart in the street and a woman looked round' that I surely mentioned to you?[3] If I didn't, let me know at once.

Yes, I agree now about 'a bath/the bath'.[4] I was disconcerted to hear that Peter Porter also dislikes Andrew's Larkin poem. It suggests the poem might[5] be some good after all.

When you come to London I will give you lunch. This will be partly a bribe to induce you to look through something for me. Not onerous. Anyway, give me a ring.

Yours
Kingsley

[TLS: Recipient]

1. Monica Jones had telephoned Thwaite to say that she had found an eighth or final manuscript notebook of Larkin's poems. Larkin had presented the first of these notebooks (dated 12 March 1950 to September[?] 1951) to the British Library in 1965. Notebooks 2–7 (24 January 1953 to 10 January 1972) were held in BJLH, where Notebook 8 now also resides.

2. MS addition.

3. This poem was not included by Thwaite in *LCP* 'for the simple reason that it existed only as an "oral memory" of KA's' (personal communication, 23 September 1997). Amis prints the poem in *Memoirs*, p. 60.

4. In the second stanza of Larkin's 'Letter to a Friend about Girls'; see Amis to Thwaite, 29 October 1987, note 1.

5. Amis had originally typed 'must', which he crossed out and replaced with 'might', written in pen.

TO JILL FARRINGDON – 19 NOVEMBER 1987

194 Regents Park Road, London NW1 8XP

Dear Miss Farringdon,

I was most interested to read your review of THE OLD DEVILS in *The Anglo-Welsh Review.*[1] You saw so much for yourself, much of it stuff that others have not seen (the Larkin reminiscence)[2] that I will reveal something else. Larkin was much in my mind while I was writing the second half of the book. A little over a page from 'life is first boredom', at the top of p. 249, Tony Bainbridge says:

'So you've got a girl at Oxford. I haven't. I haven't got anybody.'

On p. 277 of REQUIRED WRITING, an extract gives a character saying:

'But you've got a boy or a grandson or something at the place (i.e. Ayrton, i.e. Eton) now. I haven't. I haven't got anybody . . .' The extract is from THE SENIOR COMMONER, a novel Larkin and I read and were much impressed by many years ago.[3] I think you will see why I included that little allusion.

As regards ASH,[4] the words on the card I saw (in a private house in Swansea) and instantly copied were 'ASH in Wales/ASH yng Nghymru', doub[t]less preceded by 'Dim Ysmygu' and even possibly 'os gwelwch yn dda'. And yes, I was thinking chiefly of UNDER MILK WOOD, but also of pieces like 'A Child's Christmas in Wales' and the poems, only one of which in my view ('The Hunchback in the Park') isn't in

---

1. Jill Farringdon, a literary academic, resident in Swansea, had recently completed an MA thesis at University College, Swansea (now the University of Wales, Swansea) entitled 'Language and the Moral Life in the Novels and Poetry of Kingsley Amis'. Her review of *The Old Devils*, entitled 'When You Come Home Again to Wales: Kingsley Amis's *The Old Devils*', in the *Anglo-Welsh Review* 86 (1987), pp. 87–92, followed the approach she had taken in the thesis.

2. See Farringdon, 'When You Come Home Again', p. 90: 'Embedded in the text is a line beginning "Life was first boredom . . ." and although Amis's sentence continues on its own way, attentive readers will hear the poetic echo' – of a line from the final stanza of Larkin's 'Dockery and Son', first published in *The Whitsun Weddings* (1964), reprinted in *LCP*, p. 153.

3. It was written by Julian Hall and published in 1933. See Amis to Larkin, 24 March 1947, note 1.

4. ASH is an anti-smoking organisation, and 'ASH yng Nghymru' is Welsh for 'ASH in Wales'. 'Dim Ysmygu' means 'No Smoking' and 'os gwelwch yn dda' means 'please'. See Farringdon, 'When You Come Home Again', p. 89.

the way of writing 'that concentrates on the writer and draws attention towards him and away from the subject.'[5] And surely a fairly seriously literary caterer and restaurant-owner *in Wales* is not so unexpected. He's got to be something, after all.

But what I really wanted to do was just thank you for a most understanding and, partly for that reason, deeply encouraging article. It brightened my whole day and more.

Yours sincerely,

P. S. I have just remembered to tell you that St. Paul's Church in St. Helen's, Swansea, alluded to in THE OLD DEVILS, has a preservation order on it.[6] It was so scheduled because one councillor (who runs a chemist's shop round the corner from it) wanted to put a spoke in the wheel of another councillor (who wanted to build a housing block on the site). It must be one of the few churches converted into a pornographic cinema to be designated a building of historical interest. Alas, I found this out too late for the O. D.

[TL: Recipient]

TO JOHN HAYES – DECEMBER 1987

Dear Mr Hayes,

Many thanks for your letter inviting me to sit for a portrait with my son Martin.[1] This is one of the most amazingly inept and tactless suggestions that has ever been made to me. Martin fully agrees with this judgement. Whoever put it forward originally is obviously waiting for a vacancy at Harpers & Queen or Tatler.

5. The quoted words are from the character Charlie Norris in *The Old Devils*, p. 224, explaining his dislike not only of Alan Weaver's writing but of that of 'Brydan', the Dylan Thomas figure whose writing Weaver champions.

6. Farringdon, 'When You Come Home Again', p. 88, mentions the church as one of a number of 'spot-the-local-colour' details likely to 'amuse – or offend' Swansea readers.

1. John Hayes (b. 1929), Director, The National Portrait Gallery (1974–94), had issued his invitation in a letter now lost. Amis showed his answer, and Hayes's answer in turn, to the journalist Peregrine Worsthorne, who printed them together in a front-page story in the *Sunday Telegraph* (4 January 1989). Both letters survive only in this printing.

If this refusal leaves your artist with time on his hands, you might get him to knock up a picture of the Two Ronnies.[2]

Yours sincerely

KINGSLEY AMIS

TO LOIS WILSON – 14 JANUARY 1988

194 Regents Park Road, London NW1 8XP

Dear Lois,

Delighted to get your news of publication. I have been talking to my pal at the Sunday Telegraph, and you should instruct the publishers to send him a copy. He is Derwent May,[1] Sunday Telegraph, Peterborough Court at South Quay, 181 Marsh Wall, E14 9SR.

Not sure if I can make it for 25th February, but do keep me informed of all developments.

Love to you both,

Kingsley

[TLS: Recipient]

TO DALE SALWAK – 11 FEBRUARY 1988

194 Regents Park Road, London NW1 8XP

Dear Dale,

Thank you for your letter. I am most intrigued to hear about Kingsley Amis: In Life and Letters.[1] I am afraid that Hilly is the custodian of photographs, and I have nothing of my own to send.

2. Little Ronnie Corbett (b. 1930) and big Ronnie Barker (b. 1929), stars of the popular 1970s BBC TV comedy show.

---

1. Derwent May (b. 1930), author, journalist; at the time Literary Editor, *Sunday Telegraph* (1986–90).

---

1. Salwak edited *Kingsley Amis: In Life and Letters* (London: Macmillan, 1990), a collection of personal reminiscences (by Robert Conquest, Paul Fussell, Edmund Keeley, among others) and critical essays (including pieces by Barbara Everett, William H. Pritchard, Harry Ritchie).

I cannot imagine why you want to include Graham Greene, whom I have never met, and only corresponded with briefly some 40 years ago.[1] But I expect you can get him through his publishers who, I believe, are Heinemann and Company.

All the best to you and Patti

Yours
Kingsley

[TLS: Recipient]

TO STUART THOMAS – 10 MARCH 1988

194 Regents Park Road, London NW1 8XP

Dear Stuart,

Thank you for letting me see the copy of the 'new' Dylan Thomas poem.[1]

There is just one small point I would like to make about the text. The 5th line reads:

'so rest you and sleep you in the warm of their care'.

I cannot believe that Thomas, whose ear was always impeccable, wrote those words as they stand. For the line to read metrically, he must have written:

'so rest you and sleep in the warmth of their care'.[2]

---

1. This correspondence was initiated in the summer of 1948, in connection with Amis's ill-fated monograph on Greene for Jack Rush, of the University of Tucumán. No letters between Greene and Amis survive.

---

1. 'Song to a Child at Night-time', eventually printed in Dylan Thomas, *The Notebook Poems: 1930–1934*, ed. Ralph Maud (London: Dent, 1989), p. 5.

2. The manuscript at the University of Texas reads: 'so rest you and sleep you in the warm of their care.' When Ralph Maud, who had transcribed it from the manuscript, was informed that one of the trustees had queried the line, he responded combatively, taking the query (which he thought originated from Stuart Thomas, not Amis) as a challenge to his scholarship. Would the sceptical trustee be willing to resign if proven wrong? Maud's challenge was not taken up, and there is no record of its having been passed along to Amis. Maud finds it 'rather amusing that it was Amis with his love of regular iambics who couldn't

This may seem a trivial difference, but I think you will agree with me that it is important that the world should see what Thomas wrote. I suggest that the manuscript at the University of Texas be consulted with a view to establishing the correct text.

Yours sincerely,
Kingsley
Trustee, Dylan Thomas Estate.

[TLS: Trustees of the Dylan Thomas Literary Estate]

TO STUART THOMAS – 14 APRIL 1988

194 Regents Park Road, London NW1 8XP

Dear Stuart,

Thank you for sending me David Higham's letter and the copy of the General Preface to the new COLLECTED POEMS.[1]

About the Preface, I feel quite strongly that the style in which it is written is all wrong. It is full of academic jargon (American style) and clumsy phraseology, and I am sure would be most unattractive to the kind of general reader we surely wish the new volume to appeal to. Perhaps this does not matter, but I feel we should consider the possibility of having the Preface re-written and probably shortened to make something more suitable for a large public.

Perhaps you would convey my feelings to David Higham.

Yours sincerely,
Kingsley

[TLS: Trustees of the Dylan Thomas Literary Estate]

imagine Thomas doing a lullaby rhythm – I'm sure a rhythm derivative of A.A. Milne or Humbert Wolfe' (personal communication, 22 February 1999).

1. *Dylan Thomas: Collected Poems 1934–1953* (London: Dent, 1988), edited by Walford Davies and Ralph Maud, who wrote the preface. David Higham, Thomas's literary agent, was a Trustee of the Dylan Thomas Estate.

TO ROBERT CONQUEST – 6 MAY 1988

194 RPR

Jolly old Bob,

Here comes a screed consequent on delivery of not just one but two books, novel and verse antho in which your Watering P has been duly inserted. [. . .][1]

A female called Liz Reitel[2] turned up in Swansea recently, D Thos's supposed last attachment in NYC. A tall bottle-nosed of-course-unstoppably-talking (I met her) Jewess* with jet-black dyed hair and a small bald patch at the crown. She kept up the old traditions by bottle-a-session drinking, being sick all over the bedroom at the decent little hotel they put her in and not apologising, in fact being rude to the maid and getting stroppy with the chef over the lunch he was specially (the kitchen being closed) making for her. A new recording of Milk Wood is threatened and Reitel will no doubt go on TV to reminisce. Unfortunately she has a typescript of it with unique corrections by DT. No doubt she looked better in '53 but one still feels a stab of pity for the old pissy charlatan.

*The sight and sound of one of the most horrible females ever seen on TV, one Margot Adler[3] (US of course) captioned as 'witch and writer', prog on 'states of consciousness' or some such ordure – lead me to conclude that the great Jewish vice is glibness, fluency, *all the way from her to Mendelssohn. Reitel also made me think that where the Brit philistine is crude, ignorant, aggressively uncultured the US version is lettered, art-loving, philosophy-gabbing – a Moabite in fact. Xt now

---

1. *Difficulties with Girls* (1988) and *The Amis Anthology* (1988); Conquest's poem is 'Watering Place'.

2. Elizabeth Reitel (b. 1920), worked as Assistant Director of the Poetry Center in Washington DC (1951–53), where she met Thomas, helped him to prepare a production of *Under Milk Wood*, and fell in love with him.

3. Margot Adler (b. 1946), author, journalist, radio producer; in her entry in *Contemporary Authors: A Bio-Bibliographical Guide* (Detroit: Gale Research Co., 1983), 107, pp. 18–19, she describes her research interests as 'the links between two seemingly opposed philosophies – Marxism and witchcraft'. The authors who have influenced her she lists as 'Theodore Roszak, Starhawk, Christopher Hill, Karl Marx, Stanley Diamond, and Ursula Le Guin'.

I remember another one surfaced recently, wife to F Pohl.[4] She kept beating the air when he dared to smoke a cigarette.
*also possibly just bullshit, as in Marx, Freud, Marcuse. Pity L. Ron Hubbard[5] not.

Remember My Old Dutch, what? We've been apart for over seven year And it don't seem a day too much, For there ain't a lady living in the land I'd as soon wallop in the crotch. I called her Jane Her proper name is Lizzie She's a real bleedin' pain And she'll get you in a tizzie It's many years since first we met And thoughts of her still make me sweat Ah, stick her in the obliette Old E–J–H. Needs work, you say? Well, you see what you can do with it.

Looking fwd to seeing you c.20th love to Liddie[6]

Cheers
Kingsley

[TLS: Recipient]

TO DALE SALWAK – 5 JULY 1988

194 Regents Park Road, London NW1 8XP

Dear Dale,

It was very nice to hear from you again. But not nearly as nice to hear about these two friends of yours who want to have lunch with me, nice chaps though they may well be. I never accept lunch invitations from strangers, not even Englishmen, unless they happen to be in the drinks trade. So please don't tell your pals to ask me out.

I am so glad you enjoyed The Old Devils. My next novel, Difficulties with Girls, is due out here in September.

All the best to you and Patti.

Yours
Kingsley

[TLS: Recipient]

4. Frederik Pohl (b. 1919), American science-fiction writer.

5. L. Ron Hubbard (1911–86), founder of the Church of Scientology in 1952; author of science fiction and fantasy novels, under his own name and the pseudonyms Kurt von Rachen, Rene Lafayette and Frederick Engelhardt.

6. MS addition.

TO JOHN McDERMOTT – 1 AUGUST 1988

194 Regent's Park Rd, London NW1 8XP

Dear John,

After the eye-blink interval of barely six weeks I send you what might just be the last sizeable chunk of material for this ancient project,[1] which begins to feel like a dictionary of ancient Sumerian complete up to the letter D.

I have managed to mix up my cuttings, with the result that you will already have copies of some of the enclosures but others will or should be still needed. I have cut and also added to the review of Q.[2]

Getting It Wrong[3] covers some ground that is covered in dribs and drabs elsewhere and perhaps it's the only language piece needed. Or not?

As regards the interviews I sound like a proper prick a good half of the time. In fact the only one I have any real time for is the Paris Review one and that would need cutting here and there. Bits of the Listener one also possible. Should like to hear Anne on this.[4]

I think the solution to the TV script question is to use We Are Guilty and drop all the others.[5] It's the only one that's any[6] good and on its own it shouldn't unbalance the collection. What do you think?

Three bits missing are the Burgess autobiog review,[7] a TLS review

---

1. *The Amis Collection.*

2. 'Where Q Stands Now', a review of A.L. Rowse, *Quiller-Couch: A Portrait of 'Q'* (1988) in the *Sunday Telegraph* (10 April 1988), reprinted in *The Amis Collection*, pp. 47–9. Amis's policy with revisions is stated in the preface: he shortens some pieces 'to avoid where possible going over the same ground twice or otherwise trying the reader's patience', and lengthens others 'to incorporate later information'; he has 'nowhere materially altered what I first wrote, though I have corrected a few stylistic errors' (p. ix).

3. Originally printed in Michaels and Ricks, eds, *The State of the Language* (1980), reprinted *The Amis Collection*, pp. 297–305.

4. In the event, no interviews were reprinted. The *Paris Review* interview, with Michael Barber, appeared in issue number 64 (Winter 1975), pp. 39–72; there were two interviews in the *Listener*: on 20 February 1975, pp. 240–1, with Melvyn Bragg, and on 15 February 1979, pp. 262–3, with Michael Billington.

5. In the event, no screenplays were reprinted. For *We are All Guilty* (1975) see Amis to Gohn, 27 March 1975, note 3.

6. 'Any' is a revision in pen of the original typed 'much'.

7. Amis adds here in pen: 'no: found typescript'.

I remember as jolly pithy on The British at Table, by Christopher Driver (1983) and an Independent review of Philip Larkin & Eng Poetry (1986) by a fearful turd called Terry Whalen.[8] That makes quite a lot of Larkin stuff and there'll be a long nother piece in Oct when the collected poems come out, which should set the old boy up where he belongs with Hardy, Housman and Betj (I mean the coll poems *shd set him up*[9], not my piece, though I shall be saying that sort of thing).

I confess to a glow of innocent satisfaction at seeing Wain's novel[10] getting the rounds of the kitchen. By the way I thought this expression was simply a synonym for a series of ballockings, but better than that, Partridge's Historical Slang gives under rounds of the galley: openly expressed abuse of a seaman by his messmates (naval ca 1850–1910). My dad was in a part of the navy in 1915 so I must have heard it from him.

I can hardly believe we're nearly there, – except for you actually producing the book of course. Perhaps we aren't. Anyway, send me what more there is.

I'm off to Swansea 10th Aug – abt 3 Sept. c/o Thomas 4 Mary Twill Lane Newton Mumbles Swansea W Glam 0792–366487.

Come down again bringing if poss Anne, to whom my love.

Cheers
Kingsley

[TLS: Recipient]

TO DALE SALWAK – 8 AUGUST 1988

194 Regents Park Road, London NW1 8XP

Dear Dale,

Good to hear from you. I'm afraid I have no idea what happened to Frank Coles after the War, and I have not had an address for him for 40 years. Glad you enjoyed reading *Who Else Is Rank*. It contains a blend of fact and fiction, mostly fiction, and I'm afraid I remember it

8. Only the *TLS* review of Driver's *The British at Table 1940–1980* (15 July 1983) and the *Independent* review of Whalen's *Philip Larkin and English Poetry* (13 December 1986) were reprinted in *The Amis Collection* (on pp. 360–4 and 219–20).

9. MS addition.

10. *Where the Rivers Meet* (1988).

too little to be any more helpful than that. Most but not all of the Archer sequences were by me, and similarly the Stephen sequences *are mostly by Coles*[1]. I think Elisabeth Cauldwell is a pseudonym for a girl friend of mine at that time called Elisabeth Simpson, but it is so long ago now that I cannot be sure.

Your new effects sound marvellous,[2] especially the one about the blank book that is transformed into a real one. I wish I could do that trick myself!

All love to Patti and hearty cheers to yourself,

Kingsley

[TLS: Recipient]

TO ROBERT CONQUEST – 17 SEPTEMBER 1988

194 RPR NW1 8XP

Dear Old B,

Taking the unusual step of answering your last letter by return, since it was nearly a fortnight getting here (thanks to our postal strike) and the latest of several. The strike was prolonged because the PO workers, having caused a huge mess by coming out, wanted overtime for clearing up the mess they had made themselves and wouldn't have 'casual [non-union][1] labour' brought in to do any of it. When cunts talk of Thatcherite greed I want to say, *that* greed gets other people into work, TU greed keeps them out. A yuppie is supposed to work entirely for himself, a TU-ist presumably for his family etc. Though no one ever goes into it.

Stupid cunts on 'errors' of SAS men in Gib,[2] meaning very reasonable and likely assumptions needing to be acted on but *turning out later* to be inaccurate. When is it all right to shoot at a terrorist? – remember

---

1. MS addition. For 'Who Else is Rank' see Amis to Coles, 12 July [1945].
2. Salwak is an amateur magician.

---

1. Amis's square brackets.
2. On 6 March 1988 three unarmed suspected IRA terrorists were shot dead by a British SAS team in Gibraltar.

if he pulls a gun it might be a toy, if he fires it might be a blank. Answer: when he's blown your head off. [. . .]

I've forgotten what if anything I said about Philip's poems, the volume I mean. Well. Lots of surprises though no huge ones. Most of the 60 poems new to us seem to me perfectly publishable in lifetime even with P's well-known scruples. An incredible death-dream one. Also a weird and also wonderful one about being alone that confirms the suspicion that being alone meant something more or different to him from what it means to the rest of us.[3] Nothing much aimed squarely at Monica I'm sorry to say. But I'll know better what I think when I've reviewed them (for Sunday Tel.) I like the idea that his output was small after a comparison shows Collected PL 311 pp coll. Eliot oh shit wouldn't you know I can't put my hand on the vol but memory tells me it's well under 300.[4]

My next novel[5] out next week. Omens good so far but you know when you're old enough you can get away with piss, cf G Greene. Am back now from hols in Swansea. I expect I've said it before but Xt the (esp female) drinking that goes on there makes the Old Devils look like – well not a vicarage teaparty because in Swansea I bet they get arseholes there too. Eve Thomas and a mate of hers, after a boozy lunch, sat soaking at the kitchen table from 4 pm to 6 am. I couldn't have done that at 55 never mind 75. What fun at wedding, eh?[6] All well here. Love to Liddie. Hilly sends love. Hope to see you on your way to the great bad place.[7]

Cheers
K.

[TLS: Recipient]

3. The 'death-dream one' is probably 'Träumerei' (p. 12), the 'being alone' one might be 'Counting' (p. 108) or 'Best Society' (pp. 56–7), among other candidates.

4. Though *The Complete Poems and Plays of T.S. Eliot* (London: Faber and Faber, 1969) is over six hundred pages, the *Collected Poems 1909–1962* (London: Faber and Faber, 1963) contains only 234 pages of verse.

5. *Difficulties with Girls.*

6. Conquest cannot remember which wedding Amis is referring to here, nor can Martin Amis or Lady Kilmarnock.

7. Conquest was going to the Soviet Union.

TO THE EDITOR, *SPECTATOR* – 12 NOVEMBER 1988

Sir: Frank Dunne is in such a rush to put me right on modernism (Letters, 29 October) that he cannot stay to read even what Auberon Waugh says I said about it.[1] Waugh says I said, and I said, and I say, not of course that the modernist movement "would never have succeeded" without bodies like the Arts Council, but that the movement "would be over but for the life-support machine provided by the Arts Council and other malign institutions". In this country, that is, as was understood: Americans, Irish, French etc modernists are no doubt still doing well enough unassisted.

As to modernism's success in past years, it must have been helped by those like Dunne whose palates are so jaded that they find only a "tepid, weak-tea tradition" in the work of that classic English poet, Edward Thomas. But then Thomas has never achieved "worldwide acclamation", as far as I know.

KINGSLEY AMIS
194 Regents Park Road, London N1

TO W.Y. MCNEIL – 12 NOVEMBER 1988

194 Regents Park Road, London NW1 8XP

Dear Mac,

How nice to hear from you.[1] Of course I remember you very well: red-haired, lively, always ready with a laugh, especially at our superiors' expense – something we all needed in those days of (my God!) 43–44 years ago.

Though I remember the names of everyone in the photograph you

---

1. Auberon Waugh's comments on Amis and modernism appear in a column entitled 'Something Slimy and Spongiform in the Saleroom', *Spectator*, 8 October 1988, p. 8. Frank Dunne (b. 1932) is an Irish writer and actor.

---

1. McNeil (b. 1916), a retired Director of Social Work at a Scottish county authority, had met Amis as a young subaltern in Signals. He wrote to Amis on 11 October 1988 after seeing him interviewed on television.

kindly sent[2] – returned with many thanks – I have no recent news of any except Eric Milner,[3] on your left in the photograph. He turned up at a Foyle's luncheon I was at, not much changed, now of course an ex-Lt-Col TA with a place in Surrey. He wasn't my favourite man in the old days but seems to have mellowed since, or perhaps I have.

I remember Urquhart[4] well too, so well I can't believe he was only with us until we left High Wycombe:[5] dark, pale, serious, with walking-stick, bonnet with pompom, and (could it have been?) kilt. I once said to him, just to make conversation, 'Are German ciphers made in the same sort of way as ours?' He said, 'I'm afraid I can't tell you that,' and I thought, wow, Jerry must be in a bad way if he still doesn't know that (in '44). Give him (Gordon, not Jerry) all my best.

If you're ever in London do think of giving me a ring. We could summon up the ghosts of Bill Yorke, Jack Reeves, Col. Walker (aargh!) and not least RSM Fryer[6] over a wee tassie.

With every good wish,

Yours
Bill Amis

[ALS: Recipients]

TO ROBERT CONQUEST – 5 JANUARY 1989

194 R's Pk Rd L NW1 8XP

Dear O B,

Of course I meant to send you a Xmas letter and then a N Yr one but laziness, drink, etc. intervened. What news there is from here is all dribs and drabs (I suppose you could call eg Vanessa's loonies all drips

2. The photograph was taken at Luneburg Heath on 7 May 1945, the day the Germans surrendered (effective from 8 May, 'VE' day). See plates section.

3. For Milner see Amis to E. Frank Coles, 12 July [1945], note 3.

4. McNeil had mentioned Gordon Urquhart, a fellow cipher officer, as the only colleague from Rear Signals he had kept in touch with.

5. In the summer of 1943.

6. Of these officers, neither Bill Yorke, the Adjutant, nor Lieutenant-Colonel G.F.H. Walker, the CO, were favourites; see Jacobs, *Biography*, p. 91. Reeves was an Administrative Officer and Fryer was McNeil's Warrant Officer.

and drabs).[1] G Hartley has got an agreement from Faber that there shall be no PL p/b for *five years* minimum, a really damaging blow because if there were one say this autumn or spring '90 schools would get it by the tens of 1000s, thus doing something good for once for the taste of the young, whereas by '93 or so the Collected Chas Tomlinson or Ted H will have occluded it. Anyway PL h/b sales are past 35,000 and rising. How one wishes . . .

Just re-come across your comment that A Motion resembles Jane. With renewed horror and recognition. I continue to bear a charmed life and never set eyes on the bag. Almost unbelievable that it's now *8 years last Nov* that I last did. Martin tells me the bad news is they're making a film of one of her books,[2] but the good news is it's on a v. low budget. It amazes me now that for several months after she went I was v cut up about it, wanted her back, contemplated a *poem* on the subj if you don't fucking well mind. Now I wish it had happened – well I suppose about 1970 would be right. Well it's all experience, though it's a pity there had to be so much of it.

One of the great laughs is how the Tories go on coming in for all this stick, Mrs T losing points etc. and bloody Kinnock[3] still going down *even faster*. Good too that the lefties have to fall back on liberties-under-threat as the worst they can do. Charter 88.[4] Samizdat. Is there a word for that (apart from shit, etc.)? Reminds me of a Low cartoon c. 1942 with on one side British craps giving the Churchill V-sign, tapping out di-di-di-*dum* etc. and on the other a little Resistance bloke chalking a V on a wall. Reactions to IRA-TV-exclusion good too.[5]

Did you see we now have the answer to why S. Paul et al weren't as keen as all that on buggery? Well, viewing the matter in its historical

1. Vanessa Redgrave (b. 1937), actress and supporter of left-wing causes. 'Vanessa's loonies' were fellow members of the Workers Revolutionary Party, which sought to influence trade unions, especially the actors' union, Equity.

2. *Getting it Right* (1982) was adapted for the screen by Howard herself and released as a film in 1989. It was directed by Randal Kleiser, and starred Helena Bonham Carter, Peter Cook, Lynn Redgrave, Jane Horrocks, Shirley Ann Field and John Gielgud.

3. Neil Kinnock (b. 1942), leader of the Labour Party (1983–92), MP for Bedwelty (formerly Islwyn) (1979–95); his fate as leader of the Labour Party was sealed by defeat in the general election of 1992, after which he returned to the back benches and in 1994 accepted a post as a European Commissioner.

4. Pressure group advocating a British Bill of Rights.

5. In October 1988 the government prohibited the broadcast of interviews with members of terrorist organisations in Northern Ireland, including Sinn Fein.

light, as we must, we note that chaps were worried about the low birth-rate just then. Now that's been taken care of, they'd be all for it of course. Reminds me I can't find your extra women-queers-children verse.[6] Also how *did* we finally settle line 4? Something not too colourful I now feel: they drone their dreary song, possibly. Do have a final think. Also reminds, Frankie Queen (a good alias for F King[7] I heard the other day) complained – did I tell you – that I'm handicapped in portraying queers by having to fall back on hearsay and surmise. Not authentic, you see. Mr Milton's portrayal of Satan . . . GE's portrayal of Mr Casaubon . . .

Bloody good, that piece of GMT on Blenheim.[8] Wish I'd had it by me when I was doing my anthy notes.[9] Marvellous last sentence to his

6. In Amis to Conquest, 23 April 1987 (recipient), Amis offers the following poem:

1. Women and queers and children
Cry when things go wrong:
Not fair! – why me? – can't take it!
[So] drones/sounds their dismal [eternal] song.

2. The usual sort of men
Who hold the world together
Manage to face their front
In any sort of weather.

3. With rueful grins and curses
They push the world along;
But women and queers and children
Cry when things go wrong.

Amis then adds: '*NB* As you can see more work is needed on line 4. It lacks that old inevitability. Grateful for any suggestions. Dong? King Kong? Chittagong? *Mah jong*?' Conquest claims to have 'nothing to do' with this poem (personal communication, 17 October 2000).

7. Francis King, who had written openly gay novels; see Amis to Larkin, 3 January 1949, note 8.

8. The historian G.M. Trevelyan (1876–1962), in *Clio: A Muse* (1913), takes issue with Robert Southey's suggestion, in 'The Battle of Blenheim' (1838), that the battle was a waste of life: '"And everybody praised the Duke,/Who this great fight did win."/"But what good came of it at last?"/Quoth little Peterkin./"Why that I cannot tell," said he,/"But 'twas a famous victory."' It was Marlborough's victory, counters Trevelyan, which prevented Europe from falling under reactionary despotism. Though Amis does not quote Trevelyan in his note to 'The Battle of Blenheim' he does comment: '"What good came of it at last" was the curbing of French aggression for a generation or so' (p. 325).

9. That is, the notes to the Southey poem in *The Amis Anthology* (1988), described in the introduction as 'a collection of my favourite poems, which is not the same thing as a collection of the couple of hundred English poems I may happen to think are the best' (p. xv).

para. By the way the most enthusiastic review of the anthy I've had was in the bloody Guardian. It and others have talked about an 'idiosyncratic' selection, which shows what their reading is like. Mr A's discovery of a delightful Victorian poet, Walter Wordsworth . . .

Saw yr fine piece in DTel. Keep 'em running. Any lowdown on Gorby etc much appreciated.

Cheers
K

[TLS: Recipient]

TO BRUCE HUNTER – 19 JANUARY 1989

194 Regents Park Road, London NW1 8XP

Dear Bruce,

Thank you for your letter of January 3rd about the Dylan Thomas Companion.[1] I agree with you that it can do no harm to give permission for its publication. As regards our future policy about unpublished material, I think it should take some such form as the following:–

> The Trustees have no objection to the publication of previously unpublished material by Dylan Thomas, provided that none of it can be said to constitute a finished work or part of a work by Dylan Thomas.

This will leave people free to quote odd phrases from notebooks, letters etc. without allowing them to quote anything in the nature of an actual work (or verse, paragraph etc.). This would, I think, exclude[2] all three of the unpublished extracts which Ackerman wants to quote.

---

1. Bruce Hunter (b. 1941), of the literary agency David Higham Associates, acting for the Dylan Thomas Literary Estate, had written to Amis and his fellow trustees on 3 January 1989 about a permission request from Macmillan, which had contracted to publish a book by John Ackerman entitled *A Dylan Thomas Companion* (1991). In addition to quoting about fifteen thousand words of Thomas's published prose and 150 lines of published poetry, Ackerman's book quotes three hundred or so words (in three different extracts) from unpublished works.

2. 'This' and 'exclude' have been crossed out in pen (by another hand) and replaced by 'and' and 'permit'.

I should welcome the comments of yourself, Stuart Thomas and Michael Rush[3] on this suggestion.

The fees you propose seem perfectly reasonable to me.

With all good wishes,

Yours

c.c. Stuart Thomas, Esq.
Michael Rush, Esq.

[TL: Trustees of the Dylan Thomas Literary Estate]

TO THE EDITOR, *SPECTATOR* – 4 FEBRUARY 1989

Sir: No, it is not senescence that prevents Ludovic Kennedy and others (Diary, 28 January) from understanding contemporary cartoons, etc. This is just another case of that Sod-the-public movement that has invaded our culture.[1] Once upon a time, pictures – easel pictures etc – had to please the beholder. That went years ago. More recently, a studio portrait ceased to have to resemble its ostensible subject.

Then, just the other day, the pioneering pencil of John Springs[2] in these very columns established that a newspaper caricature need no longer catch the likeness of its supposed subject – at the head of a review by Tony Benn of Marx on Napoleon you might just be able to identify Tony by the pipe. Now we have clearly broken through to the cartoon nobody need understand. If the artist likes it or enjoyed doing it, fine; if you're baffled, *sod you* – you're only the public.

It beats me why they call this a consumer age. Never was the producer more powerful.

KINGSLEY AMIS
194 Regents Park Road, London NW1

3. The other trustees.

---

1. For Amis's campaign against the 'Sod the public movement' see also Amis to the editor, *Daily Telegraph*, 12 August 1970.
2. John Springs (b. 1960), cartoonist, has also worked for the *Daily Telegraph*.

TO JOHN McDERMOTT – 17 MAY 1989

194 Regents Park Road, London NW1 8XP

Dear John,

I have owed you this letter for a long time, and will kick off by apologising for the delay and my bad manners. Though you may find this very difficult to believe, the reason for my silence has been a kind of shyness. I thoroughly approve of your book about me,[1] and am delighted that somebody understands what I am trying to do, but felt I could hardly write to you saying how right you were in all the points you made; though I agree that I might have had the decency to thank you.

For obvious reasons there was nothing I could do to push the book.

As regards the projected book of collected pieces, this is still very much on and the publisher is keen. However, a similar sort of shyness has embarrassed me in choosing the pieces – it would have been like saying how jolly good this one or that one was. So I am leaving the whole thing to you, the publisher and Jonathan Clowes, though actually I will reserve the right of veto when the selection is made. I should like you to contribute an introduction.

The music piece you sent me seems all right. As regards the Peter Simple piece, my memory of it suggests that it isn't worth putting in.[2]

Salwak is horrible, I agree, but there seems to be nothing I can do to stop him.

I was delighted to hear Anne's news – a decent job – my God, and a jolly impressive one too.[3] It should be tremendous fun.

Love to you both
Kingsley

[TLS: Recipient]

---

1. *Kingsley Amis: An English Moralist* (1989).

2. McDermott is not certain, but thinks the music piece in question was 'Rondo for My Funeral', the last essay reprinted in *The Amis Collection*, pp. 384–9, originally published in the *Sunday Times*, 1 July 1973; the 'Peter Simple' piece, which was not reprinted, was either from a 1981 Radio 4 broadcast or the introduction to *The Stretchford Chronicles: Twenty-Five Years of Peter Simple*, published in 1980 by the *Daily Telegraph*, reprinted in 1981 by Macmillan.

3. Ann McDermott had been appointed Director of the University of Birmingham Johnson Dictionary Project, from which resulted *Samuel Johnson's Dictionary on CD-ROM* (1996).

TO ROGER LEWIS – 8 AUGUST 1989

194 Regents Park Road, London NW1 8XP

Dear Mr. Lewis,

Of course, if you are the Roger Lewis I think you are, I remember you very well,[1] and I appreciate your appreciation.

It so happens that I have a few thoughts to offer about Peter Sellers, whom I met on several occasions when he came down to Swansea to film *Only Two Can Play*.[2]

Most of the cast were installed at the Grand Hotel, Swansea, which in those days was a slightly above average ordinary Station hotel such as you might expect to find in the West of England – certainly clean and cheerful. Mai Zetterling, then an international star, took a look round the bedroom she was offered and gracefully said it would do very well. Sellers walked out, not very politely, and installed himself at Porthcawl, some miles down the coast, in a hotel which we all delightedly learned was far inferior to the Grand. Here Kenneth Griffith[3] taught him the Swansea accent.*

At a very meagre lunch he threw me in Swansea, he informed me that he and Spike Milligan had between them invented the whole of post-war British humour, principally via the Goon Show.[4] Over all he impressed me as one of the most self-satisfied shits I have ever met. He did, however, impart one interesting item of information, that a stunt man he had once talked to had told him that what he most enjoyed was going through a plate glass window.

---

1. Roger Lewis (b. 1961) was a Junior Research Fellow at Wolfson College, Oxford, when he first met Amis. He is the author of *State People* (1989), *The Life and Death of Peter Sellers* (1994) and *The Real Life of Laurence Olivier* (1996).

2. Film version of *That Uncertain Feeling*, starring Sellers as the novel's librarian hero, John Lewis. The film was released in 1962 by British Lion, then under the control of the Boulting Brothers, Frank Launder and Sidney Gilliat, its director. The screenplay was by Bryan Forbes.

3. Kenneth Griffith (b. 1921), actor, writer, documentary film-maker.

4. Spike Milligan (b. 1916), comic actor, author. The celebrated radio comedy *The Goon Show* (1951–60) starred Harry Secombe as well as Sellers and Milligan (with appearances also by Michael Bentine and Eric Sykes).

I hope you can make some use of the above.

Yours
Kingsley Amis

**but so brilliantly that 'John Lewis' sounded exactly like the kind of educated upper-working-class valleys Welshman I had had in mind.*[5]

[TLS: Recipient]

TO DR M.G.H. BISHOP – 27 SEPTEMBER 1989

194 Regents Park Road, London NW1 8XP

Dear Dr. Bishop,

Thank you for your letter. Certainly you may quote the passage from THE OLD DEVILS that you refer to.[1]

You might care to know that this is not the first time that I seem to have got some medical thing right. In my novel ENDING UP, there is a discussion on nominal aphasia, in which a character gets the idea of producing a sort of patois with periphrases for all the common nouns so that he would not suffer the anxiety of trying to remember those nouns, and as a result might possibly find his memory of them return.[2] 'We're working on that now' a speech therapist told me.

Many thanks for your extremely kind final remarks.

Yours sincerely,
Kingsley Amis

[TLS: Recipient]

5. MS addition. See *Memoirs*, p. 179, in which the English actors in the film are deemed 'much better, including funnier' than their 'conscientiously "Welsh"' counterparts in the serial broadcast on BBC 2 in 1986: 'A large part of the credit must go to Sellers.'

---

1. The passage occurs on p. 206 of *The Old Devils* and describes an episode of hyperventilation, which Bishop quotes and discusses in a paper in the *Journal of the Royal Society of Medicine* 83 (December 1990), pp. 797–8. The paper is entitled 'Acute Hyperventilation in Literature: Notes on Four Examples'. Bishop (b. 1944), a dentist, is the author of numerous articles on literature and medicine.

2. The character in *Ending Up* is George Zeyer. See Chapter 11 (p. 59).

TO DALE SALWAK – 18 JANUARY 1990

194 Regents Park Road, London NW1 8XP

Dear Dale,

Got your letter of 17th December and very tickled to see photograph of young Ryan[1] (or did that come in another letter? Can't remember.)

The reason why I switched supervisors was simply because Cecil didn't do any supervising. The rules said 'The supervisor will normally contact the pupil at least twice a term'. After I had heard nothing at all of him or from him for a term and a half, I decided to get a real supervisor, and managed to beard him in the street in Oxford to tell him so.

No, as far as I can remember, nobody else ever read The Legacy.

Again, as far as I remember, I threw away the first draft of Lucky Jim.[2] By the way, I am quite sure I never said that Philip Larkin 'decimated' that draft. It is a word I never use, and would be both inaccurate and improperly used in this context.

How glad I am that you are enjoying helping those students.

Yours
Kingsley

[TLS: Recipient]

TO ROBERT CONQUEST – 31 JANUARY 1990

194 R's Pk Rd NW1 8XP

Dear old B.,

Two of yours to hand. It would be great if you could remember some stuff, the more of it where I was present the better, though stuff

1. Aged two.

2. If by 'the first draft' Amis meant 'Dixon and Christine', which circulated briefly among publishers in 1951 before being withdrawn and rewritten, he may indeed have thrown it away, since it has never surfaced. The corrected 1954 typescript draft of *Lucky Jim*, however, with annotations by the author and others, and accompanying notes and holograph draft fragments, can be found in the Harry Ransom Humanities Research Center at the University of Texas at Austin.

you told or tell me yourself will obviously qualify. Remember the more you give me, the longer the chapter in my mems about you will be, if that's any inducement. Anecdotal stuff is clearly best, serious ones as well as frivolous. Your story about suggesting *I Told You So, You Fucking Fools*, which I have already embroidered slightly with the editor saying, 'See, Bob, I don't think we could quite swing the fucking,' is ideal.[1] The drainpipe adventure, wch you told me about, consisted of your having seduced some female at a party, taken her upstairs there and then, afterwards climbing down a drainpipe with the chivalrous intention of not reappearing with her and thus suggesting to the inquisitive what the pair of you had been up to, but instead coming in again a little later by the front door, explaining that you had been out buying cigarettes. That went off all right, but you rather fucked things up by making up to some female with the same intentions. She smacked your face because it was the same one and you had failed to recognise her. I would swear on the Book that that was what you told me.

Yes, must have some lines from *Mexican Pete*. Limericks too. I can remember a few but don't know what you've published (except in the NOBLV). Surely now we can print B Brophy.[2] But of course you shall vet my finished text. Include obscene ones. The publishers can decide what they feel they can put in. I feel we shall get the best overall result, and incidentally save me some work, if you send stuff before April 3 and I do a rough which we then supplement by questions and answers on tape. We shall be here and ready to welcome you both then and in May.

Yes, I have *Fred*[3] safe – bloody good and funny too. I take it you intend to publish when complete? But one or two in my thing will do

---

1. Conquest's story concerns a projected American reprint of his best-known book, *The Great Terror* (1968), about Stalin's purges of 1936–38. 'What about a new title, Bob?', Amis's embroidered version has the editor suggesting (see *Memoirs*, p. 146). Conquest denied that the drainpipe story was about him; for its fate see Amis to Conquest, [c. November] 1990, and *Memoirs* (p. 185).

2. Apparently not. It runs as follows: 'The first chap to fuck Brigid Brophy/Was awarded the Kraft-Ebbing Trophy/Plus 10,000 quid/Which for what the chap did/Will be widely denounced as a low fee.' For excerpts from *Mexican Pete*, by Conquest and John Blakeway, a sequel to *Eskimo Nell*, see *Memoirs* (p. 141). Brigid Brophy (1929–90) was a novelist and critic.

3. 'Fred Faraday Philosopher', a series of poems (forty or fifty), in common metre, about an *homme moyen sensuel*.

neither of us any harm. Also have received *Tyrs & Typs* and taken a bit or two from your piece on Yev[geny] Yev[tushenko] for mine,[4] wch I'm reprinting bits of in autob. Have given you attribution.

Been v.g. fun doing autob., pissing on J Michie, Snowdon, D Cecil, Wain, Muggeridge (whose typewriter, G Gale tells me, is kept in a glass case, 'like the body of Lenin' his source says, among the memorabilia of Christian writers in the Marion E. Wade Center at Wheaton College, Illinois), F Bacon, F Ayer, Wesker, Leo Rosten, Driberg and Roald Dahl, and cracking up Mrs T, Melford Stephenson,[5] Eliz Taylor. Gone fast, too – 250 pp since July but with you, Philip, T Powell, Betj and lesser lights to come.

Do let me have the stuff. Between us we can get something together which will really annoy the lefties.

About all for now. My publishers have been unreachable by telephone for three days, having moved house without telling me and leaving both the old and the new switchboard unmanned. Or do we say unpersoned now?

Love to L. Cheers,
K.

PS: Have you a p.c. of the Nat Portrait Gall portrait of Philip? If not will get you one.

[TLS: Recipient]

TO DALE SALWAK – 23 FEBRUARY 1990

194 Regents Park Road, London NW1 8XP

Dear Dale,

Good to hear from you. Thank you for the charming picture of Ryan, which sits on my study mantelpiece.

4. *Tyrants and Typewriters* (1989), a collection of essays. Amis cites Conquest on Yevtushenko's 'well-rewarded collaboration', but also quotes his conclusion that 'We might yet accept that in Soviet circumstances his record, with all its shifts and compromises, may merit, on balance, a positive assessment' (*Memoirs*, pp. 240, 241).

5. Judge Melford Stevenson (1902–87), Justice of the High Court (1957–79).

Glad you enjoyed *The Folks* (not 'The Old Folks') *That* (not 'Who') *Live on the Hill.*[1]

The Memoirs are nearly finished as regards the first draft. I have until July to deliver. They propose to publish in [s]pring, 1991. No title settled yet.

Yours
Kingsley

See ya soon?[2]

[TLS: Recipient]

TO ROGER LEWIS – 26 APRIL 1990

c/o Jonathan Clowes, Iron Bridge House,
Bridge Approach, London NW1 8BD

Dear Mr. Lewis,

Thank you for your encouraging letter about The Folks That Live on the Hill.

I have not myself found Kenneth Griffith quite the charming chap you see him as. Dotty, certainly, and a bit of a shit with it.

Sellers was of course a larger shit and the less said about him the better. A good actor, though. No, I never heard about his possible participation in an adaptation of Take a Girl Like You. The result might have been better than the Jonathan Miller film that was made.[1]

Yours sincerely,
Kingsley Amis

[TLS: Recipient]

---

1. Published in 1990.
2. MS addition.

---

1. *Take a Girl Like You* (1970), starring Hayley Mills as Jenny Bunn.

TO DALE SALWAK – 24 MAY 1990

194 Regents Park Road, London NW1 8XP

Dear Dale,

Good to hear from you. Here are some answers:

1) I can hardly remember what I wrote there.[1] In any case, the people are very dimly visualised and portrayed. No particular significance.
2) You are wrong to suppose that I was influenced by HOLY DISORDERS at any time.[2] Any resemblances are accounted for by the fact that both Crispin and I greatly admired the ghost stories of M.R. James.
3) I can see no reason to bring my cousin[3] into this. We have never been very close, and I developed my musical tastes without any reference to him. His address is:

17, Eccleston Square, London, S.W.1.

I will give you that permission[4] when I see you in London, which I look forward to doing.

Yours,
Kingsley

[TLS: Recipient]

1. In 'Who Else is Rank'. Salwak, in a letter of 20 May 1990, had enquired about the real-life identity of certain of the novel's Oxford characters.

2. By Edmund Crispin (Bruce Montgomery), published in 1946. Salwak had asked if it had been an influence on *The Green Man* (1969).

3. John Amis. Salwak was working on the book that would become *Kingsley Amis: Modern Novelist* (1992), an early chapter of which discusses Amis's strong feeling for music. He wondered, in the letter of 20 May 1990, 'if there might be occasion to mention your cousin' in the course of this discussion.

4. To consult Amis's letters to Larkin in the Bodleian.

TO ROBERT CONQUEST – 2 JUNE 1990

194 R's Pk Rd NW1 8XP

D O B,

What a varied and interesting life you have, to be sure, Moscow and all, I mean. How will things turn out over there? I suppose there's literally nobody who can say. Might be more settled in 20 years?

As regards autobiog, of course at your request I'll withdraw the offending passage, under a slight whimper of protest, viz. I remember the incident clearly enough, much more so than the drainpipe adventure, and I think it *was* typical of *one bit* of your marriage to T, and so does Hilly. *But* of course under the no-need-to-make-you-look-a-shit rule it goes, as the original laureate bit of my conversation with Philip. I enclose a revised page, with Julian S rather dragged in to fill it up.[1]

I note yr suggestions for Mex P, and thank you kindly, but think what you gave me originally is preferable, more concise (2 × 4 lines) and sort of less filthy if you know what I mean. Relish G of Erses, but there am suspending judgement for the nonce. Final choice depends a bit on publisher, chiefly on how much space we have, but there's lots of time and we can certainly confer when you're over in July.

Martin is getting het up again over greenhouse effect and all that. I told him it was all lefty-trendy, a vacant spot for the Trots and assorted anti-West shags to go now that Marxism etc. had packed up, which spread no sweetness and light at all. Can you recommend a good short book with some facts, or demonstrations that there aren't any facts?

Nothing seems to happen here, except having finished and submitted

---

1. The offending passage reappeared when the *Memoirs* were published (the revised page, which does not survive, did not), occasioning the only serious rift in the Conquest-Amis friendship. Conquest adds: 'There were two separate exchanges. He first had an anecdote about me that was quite untrue, and on my saying so transferred it to Philip Toynbee. No row on that (tho' pretty odd conduct). Then he sent me a proof with a bit not (wholly) untrue, but gratuitously making me look a bit of a shit, and misleading anyway. He removed it, replaced it with other stuff, sent me the new proof, THEN put the objected bit back, without telling me' (personal communication, 17 October 2000). See also Amis to Conquest, 10 September 1991, note 1. 'Julian S.' is Julian Symons (1912–94), author, critic and authority on detective fiction.

memoirs I work on turning a TV play into a short 'teenage' novel[2] before girding loins for grown-up novel, on which I'd like to consult you (or, if I've mentioned it before, consult you more seriously) – so instead of waiting around for some chatworthy item will get this off to you.

Have good Moscow trip & see ya.

Cheers
K

Love to Liddie.[3]

[TLS: Recipient]

TO KATE HORDERN – 4 JULY 1990

194 Regents Park Road, London NW1 8XP

Dear Kate Hordern,

Good news about Romania and LUCKY JIM.[1] Please let me know in good time when the lei become available, what they are worth in real money and how a nominee of mine could collect them. Then I can put up a notice on the Garrick Club board, inviting any member visiting Romania to contact me and obtain perhaps the price of a round of drinks.

Best wishes
Yours sincerely
Kingsley Amis

[TLS: Gollancz]

2. *We are All Guilty* (1991). Amis's only novel aimed specifically at young adults; from the 1975 television play of the same name.

3. MS addition.

---

1. Kate Hordern, Foreign Rights Manager of Gollancz (1984–98), had written to Amis about fees for the Romanian edition of *Lucky Jim*, which was first published in 1993.

TO GAVIN EWART – 16 JULY 1990

Jolly kind of you to write. I was afraid Spike Milligan would score at the same time.[1] Unworthy thought.

Cheers
Kingsley (Amis)

[ALS: Recipient]

TO DALE SALWAK – 20 JULY 1990

194 Regent's Park Road, London NW1 8XP

Dear Dale,

More questions? Why not? Here are some answers.

That interviewer, whoever she was,[1] makes six or seven mistakes of fact in that short extract. A correct version would run:

> Amis remembered noticing the eccentric behaviour of his mother's sister Dora when he was a boy. It troubled the young Amis, who thought she might be mad, though her affliction would later have been described merely as an anxiety neurosis with obsessions. She was never, as far as is known, diagnosed as 'insane', nor 'committed' anywhere. For a time she was a patient at some sort of mental institution. Her behaviour returned to normal when she heard the news of her mother's death. She was asked to stay on in the institution because she had been useful in the kitchens. When she died she was about to take over as catering manageress at a London teaching hospital.

---

1. A knighthood, that is, which Amis was awarded in the June Honours List. For Gavin Ewart see Amis to Larkin, 17 September 1953, note 7. For Spike Milligan see Amis to Roger Lewis, 8 August 1989, note 4.

---

1. It was 'he' not 'she', and the piece in question was not an interview but a shortened version of a profile of Amis by Alan Watkins from *Brief Lives* (1982), published as 'From "Angry Young Man" to Middle-Aged Tory', an interview in the *Observer* (8 August 1982), p. 9.

Did I visit her? At home, yes, at the institution, no. What evidence for my remembering her? That I tell you I do – what else? And as far as I know it is simply not true that I have ever been 'fascinated' by madness, etc. Thought about it, of course, from time to time, like anyone else, and noticed those times when it has briefly seemed to turn up in my life.

Those moral convictions I may have got from my parents were vague and general, a matter of deduction on my part, or influence from their behaviour and attitudes.[2] My father never 'emphasised' anything or gave me 'lessons', and certainly never to my recollection said anything like what you quote. You should take something away from what you have 'given the reader', not add to it.

What I say about Miss Barr is a joke, for God's sake. She was pretty. She took English. That's all.[3]

Army years. I co-wrote Who Else is Rank (no question-mark, as in the quotation)[4] in perhaps France, probably Belgium, probably Holland and possibly Germany. I was discharged in October 1945.

I hope all goes well with your revision.

All the very best to you both,

Yours,
Kingsley

[TLS: Recipient]

2. See Salwak, *Kingsley Amis: Modern Novelist*, p. 12: 'from his parents' behaviour and attitudes he did deduce certain ethical convictions which crystallised into a personal philosophy of life and art.'

3. In *What Became of Jane Austen?*, p. 135, Amis admits of one of his primary school teachers: 'I fell in love with Miss Barr, whom I see now as a tall, Eton-cropped figure of improbable elegance. She took English, and it is here, perhaps, that we can date my first devotion to the glories of literature.'

4. And in most pages of the typed manuscript (in HEHL), though a question-mark is included in the novel's title at the head of seven pages.

TO JULIAN BARNES – 24 JULY 1990

Yes well you can raise an even larger glass to me about noon tomorrow (Wed) when I leave the Palace after my dubbing, having fallen over the Queen's foot, farted and said f—. Oh Xt. Think of it.

Cheers
K.

[ALS: Recipient]

TO STUART THOMAS – 2 AUGUST 1990

194 Regents Park Road, London NW1 8XP

Dear Stuart,

I have been mulling over the poem you sent me.[1] In my opinion, it could very well be an example of Dylan Thomas's early work. The refrain at the end of each verse[2] can be said to be characteristic. I think the only way of establishing some sort of authenticity for it would be by getting Ralph Maud to say just where he found the poem and what makes him think it is by Thomas.

I am off to stay with George and Mary [Gale] next week but hope to see you in London in September.

Yours

[TL: Trustees of the Dylan Thomas Literary Estate]

---

1. An untitled poem beginning 'An old man or a young man', brought to the attention of the trustees by Ralph Maud, who was at the time editing *The Broadcasts, Dylan Thomas* (London: Dent, 1991). The poem is in the Harry Ransom Humanities Research Center at Texas and has not yet been published. According to Walford Davies, one of the co-editors, with Maud, of Thomas's *Collected Poems*, it is authentic, but not early.

2. 'He weeps like one of the willow trees/That stands in a grave wood.'

TO MARTIN AMIS – 24 AUGUST 1990[1]

Happy birthday but will ring on the day – you are back, I take it? Lots of wheat, sheep, etc. here. Stone walls. But lots of pubs. Everything is a long way from everywhere, like the U.S. Back on 1st Sept. Much love to all

Dad

[ALS: Recipient]

TO PEREGRINE WORSTHORNE – 3 SEPTEMBER 1990

194 Regents Park Road, London NW1 8XP

PERSONAL

My dear Perry,

I was so sorry to hear of your great loss.[1] There is really nothing to say, except that the two of you did have all those years together, and that is much to be grateful for, and as everybody knows you appreciated each other, which is by no means something that can be said of many married couples. I think it is admirable in you to have gone on working as usual, and I send you all my warmest wishes and sympathy.

Yours
Kingsley

Don't of course bother to answer this.

[ALS][2]

---

1. This undated card was postmarked 24 August (the day before its recipient's forty-first birthday), from Alnwick, Northumberland, where Amis was staying with George and Mary Gale. Martin Amis and his family had been on holiday in the United States.

---

1. The death of Worsthorne's wife Claude, to whom he had been married for forty years.
2. A photocopy of this letter was found among Amis's papers after his death. The original has not survived.

TO MARY GALE[1] – 4 SEPTEMBER 1990

194 Regent's Park Road, London NW1 8XP

Please don't mind me typing this: selective manual paralysis overtakes me after a few dozen words of longhand.

My Dear Mary,[2]

Kevin duly delivered me here about 5.20 on Friday, priding himself on having correctly calculated 4.30 (plus unforeseen roadworks, delays from a wide load, etc.)[3] I was rather the better for a certain amount of Macallan but it was still very strange being back in the metrop. You'll be glad to hear that the cat greeted me as enthusiastically as anybody.

Though my weeks with you and G are telescoped in memory (by the effect I discussed with him[4]), and one pub and portion of fish and chips is already tending to merge into another, I remember very vividly your house inside and how it looks from the road and some sweeps of that landscape, so different from anything else in my experience (bar the bits near Catterick). Also your pals, Charles Cresswell in particular, Sarajane of the odd eyes, the girl from the farm shop and, for some reason, the fat fellow Simon (?) at Sue's dinner party, who I thought would any moment say to me, 'But why should I not kill you, Mr Bond?'[5] And I shall never forget your marvellous continuous kindness, and the forbearance you both showed, and I am still very touched by

---

1. Mary Malone Gale, George Gale's second wife (they were married in 1983), was herself a journalist, on the *Daily Mirror* (1952–86). This letter was written after a three-week visit to the Gales' house in Alnwick, Northumberland.

2. Handwritten.

3. In the left margin Amis has added by hand: 'after hours of thunderous Pavarotti on cd in the car. Don't think I like him much now.' Amis, who would not travel alone, had hired a local taxi to take him home to Primrose Hill, a journey of approximately 350 miles.

4. According to Mary Gale, Amis occasionally asked George to recall details from their mutual past, for use in his fiction; whether these requests derived from the 'effect' Amis is talking of here she is unsure.

5. Charles Baker-Cresswell, of Bamburgh Hall, a landowning friend of the Gales, later High Sheriff of Northumberland (1999); Sarajane Bridgeman, wife of another landowning friend, Peter Bridgeman, of Fallodon Hall, Northumberland; 'the girl from the farm shop' was Anne Walton, cookery writer, farmer's wife and owner of the Roseden Farm Shop at Wooperton near Alnwick; Sue and 'the fat fellow Simon' Mary Gale does not recall.

G's thoughtfulness in unscrewing that apple-juice bottle – Hilly agrees it was unexpected and yet not at all surprising.

It still strikes me as odd that life here should have lumbered into being again. I have done another page of novel[6] but other more horrible and immediate concerns have been getting in the way, like (I suppose I shouldn't call it that) writing to Perry and, more certainly, discussing my post-death expectations with a very self-assured but pretty young person for television. Rather unflatteringly she kept wanting to know about P. Larkin and *his* expectations, etc. Today also I completed my piece for Harpers & Q on 21 Queen Street.[7] Which was good in one way, because it fixed it in my memory. [. . .]

G must finish and send in his magnum op.[8] soon or risk incurring my severe displeasure. You, Mary, are to send me that recipe for pickled plums (youknowwhatImtalkingabout) very soon. I hope all goes well with you in selling the house – which reminds me, if you've a spare photograph or two of it I'd be most grateful.

My great thanks and gratitude and best love to you both.[9]

Kingsley

[TLS: Recipient]

TO DALE SALWAK – 10 OCTOBER 1990

194 Regents Park Road, London NW1 8XP

Dear Dale,

Thank you for letting me see the first three chapters of your book about me and my work, which I have at last read through with the attention they deserve. I return them herewith, marked here and there.

6. *The Russian Girl* (1992).

7. Amis's restaurant column in *Harpers and Queen* began in September 1990. 21 Queen Street is a restaurant in Newcastle-upon-Tyne, to which Amis took the Gales. The review appeared in the December 1990 issue of the magazine, p. 266.

8. See *Memoirs*, p. 172: 'George G has had a large work of political philosophy somewhere near the verge of completion for donkey's years. It is or was to end with a long poem, which he gave me to go through and advise about, asking me to get a move on if I could as he wanted to get the whole thing off to the publisher. That was in 1967. For Christ's sake, George, *Get it done.* We need it. Perhaps by the time these words appear he will have obliged.' A note then reads: 'Sadly, he never will now. George died on 3 November 1990.'

9. MS addition.

I am very sorry to have to tell you that I consider them altogether unsatisfactory. It is not that I find what you have written offensive in any way, or improper to its subject. It is that the level of your performance seems to me to be so low as not to earn a place on any serious publisher's list.

Please realise that no imaginable rewriting would rectify the situation. The fact that I have left many passages and pages of your typescript unmarked testifies to my weariness and boredom with them, not to their correctness or adequacy.

I think it would be best if the book were to be withdrawn.[1]

Yours,
Kingsley

[TLS]

TO MARY GALE – 12 NOVEMBER 1990

194 Regents Park Road, London NW1 8XP

Dearest Mary,

It was lovely, though sad, to see you on Wednesday. Hilly, Sally and I all thought the place of burial was very beautiful and most appropriately situated. And we were all deeply glad that we were there.

This note is just to say that I remember what I said to you about seeing you at least as often as before and that I meant it. We are here all the time and would love to see you any time, which means to have you to stay (or whatever best suits you). Please don't hesitate to ring

---

1. *Kingsley Amis: Modern Novelist* was published by Harvester Wheatsheaf, a division of Simon and Schuster, in 1992, despite Amis's objections and those of his agent, Jonathan Clowes Ltd. Harvester Wheatsheaf published the book in part on the strength of independent readers' reports, notably one by Barbara Everett of Somerville College, Oxford, who called it 'a splendidly spacious, relaxed yet shrewd study of Amis's work. Lucid and very informative, it is ideally suited to the general reader.' In *World Literature Today* 67 (Summer 1993), p. 614, William Hutchings called it 'clearly the single indispensable guide to Amis's fiction, unlikely to be surpassed or superseded for many years to come', and in *Notes and Queries* 239:41 (June 1994), pp. 267–8, Peter Miles called it 'mandatory reading for all students of Amis'. Salwak remains baffled by Amis's reaction: 'It contradicts everything he communicated to me in person and in letters over the previous seventeen years' (personal communication, 27 July 1999).

up any time – not necessarily to say anything in particular, just to chat if that's what you'd like. *We are here.*

With all my love
Kingsley

[ALS: Recipient]

TO ROBERT CONQUEST – [C. NOVEMBER 1990]

194 RPR NW1 8XP

D O Bob,

I'm afraid my infrequent response may have made you think otherwise, but when in the past you wrote to me every week or so, I appreciated your letters very much, and used to wish, as I still do, that I were more of a natural correspondent myself, and certainly that I could come up with limericks and such as often as you, or at least more often than once every half-dozen years. Anyway it's certainly my turn.

I've been doing the last few bits of work on my memoirs, which are now more or less ready for page proof. Except for a couple of details about old John Braine. I thought I had better actually read his book on writing a novel[1] instead of going by Martin's hilarious account of it. So I buy the new p/b reprint and find none of the stuff advising you not to plan your novel while doing your main job if your main job is air traffic controller, brain surgeon etc. (which M was so funny about) is there at all. So I rewrite the para. Then M tells me, oh yes, it was there in the original edition, and he ridiculed it with quotes in the TLS at the time. So ole J or someone *took it out* for the p/b. More rewriting needed now. Also have now read one of J's late novels right through.[2] A masterpiece of unconscious humour. And pathos. All about a famous novelist with beautiful 'mistresses' who walks on Axminster carpets wherever he goes. Lastly the drainpipe adventure is now fathered on P Toynbee, whom it fits down to the ground, especially since he's dead.

George G is dead too since 3rd November, as you will have seen.

---

1. *Writing a Novel* (1974; paperback reprint 1990).
2. John Braine's *One and Last Love* (1981).

In his sleep, with presumably no pain. Hilly, Sally and I did the 800-odd-mile round trip to Northumberland on Wednesday. Horrible New English Missalette (sic) RC-atheist service, like the one Nina Szamuely had – the Lord be with you/And also with you. Made me want to shout, 'You mean this is a requiem fucking *mass*?' But it remained RC enough (you remember Mary G is RC) to annoy me on the other flank with its implicit claims that George, who never had any discernible religion, was one of the faithful or the saved or something like that.

Though I didn't come to it first, G's death is really what got me going into writing this now. With Tibor and Philip gone already, only four of my seven great chums survive, and only one of them in GB. (Stuart T in Swansea, and he's 76 and hardly 100% fit. Actually Paul Fussell is over here for the year, but he's got so odd that I can hardly talk to him much any more.) That leaves Jim Durham in Sydney, and you. I say this to you now partly because I never said anything like it to Tibor, Philip or George while there was time, and partly in the course of saying I hope nothing is wrong between the two of us. Please forgive me if I've offended you, and let me know if you will that you've received this safely, and send me another limerick. And give my love to Liddie. Hope to see you over here soon.

Cheers K

You could also throw in a hint about what to think about the USSR. Nobody here seems to have a bloody clue.

[TLS: Recipient]

TO ANTHONY POWELL – 21 NOVEMBER 1990

194 Regent's Park Road, London NW1 8XP

Dear Tony,

Jolly nice to hear from you, and especially to hear about your intended dedication.[1] Of course I am most flattered by the idea and

1. Powell had written on 12 November 1990 informing Amis of his intention to dedicate *Under Review*, a collection of occasional writings eventually published in 1992, to him.

urge you to go ahead as proposed. I am most impressed and touched. Since you are unlikely to extol the works of Anthony Burgess or John Fowles I guess I can go along with more or less any views you may express.

How odd about Julian Hall.[2] I confess I liked the Commoner thing too, and any echoing of its style in my own first effort[3] was voluntary (though small). Old Philip was given to literary passions that I have never shared at all, as for the poetry of Hardy, Wm Barnes & Stevie Smith, the novels of B Pym, etc. I think being shut up with all those library books every day didn't do him any good. I met Hall once for a second and arranged to have a drink with him in the Garrick but he died rather than keep the date. You knew he gave all those chairs that now sit in the members' lounge at the club?

I agree about the fucking in the Green Man.[4] Offensive rubbish, I thought, but it did me some good here and there. I mean I expect it was what the fellow at the minicab firm meant when he said to me on the telephone, 'Cor! How long ago did you write that, eh? Hur-hur-hur-hur.' I didn't much care for the ghost, who looked like something out of The Curse of Frankenstein most of the time. And I thought the hero's daughter and d-in-law were both lousy actresses. Cd have throttled the latter.*

I hope in the end Mrs T sees off Heseltine,[5] whom I met once 30 years ago in Swansea accompanied by his much-made-up, jewellery-swathed, cigarette-holder-toting mother, like a chap in drag putting on the style as a queer's mum. 'That g and t is looking *very* tired, darling,' he crooned at her.

Greatly looking forward to seeing book. Much love to you both. H. sends hers.

Kingsley

*But a complete list of aversions would have to include that jocose don

2. Powell was an exact contemporary of Hall's at Eton.

3. 'The Legacy'.

4. That is, in the BBC television adaptation, by Malcolm Bradbury, directed by Elijah Moshinsky and starring Albert Finney as Maurice Allington, proprietor of the haunted Green Man pub.

5. Michael Heseltine (b. 1933), Tory MP and Minister; his challenge for the leadership of the Conservative Party precipitated Mrs Thatcher's resignation as Prime Minister (on 28 November 1990); see Amis to Conquest, 10 January 1992, note 4.

(Phi*loc*tites indeed) and *all* the diners at the pub. And that old idiot M Hordern.[6]

[TLS: Recipient]

TO ROBERT CONQUEST – 18 MARCH 1991

194 RPR London NW1 8XP

Dear Old Bob,

V. Glad to get your limerick-featuring letters when they come but bewail their recent paucity. Especially since the arrival of a book from the Spec for possible review (why did I say I'd look at it?), 2nd part of an 'autobiographical novel' by Danny Abse, called *There Was a Young Man from Cardiff*.[1] The broken metre perfectly expresses his clumsiness and lack of basics [. . .] It's in those small things that one can see. Never any good you'd agree?

Have been drenched under flood of publicity for my memoirs, also great volumes of piss poured on me from most quarters. What bad taste to show Muggeridge, Roald Dahl, F Bacon, T Driberg et al in a bad light! I think A N Wilson got quite close when he wrote in Evg Standdd that They can't bear a card-carrying intellectual to be an anti-leftie. Of course attacks from Guardian etc. sting for 10 minutes or so and then fade, but the volume does mount up. And I couldn't help thinking it a bit off of Perry, flushed with his engagement,[2] to say in DTel that he agreed with Claudie's judgement that I was 'pretty awful'. What we call a bit unnecessary, what?

They (capital T) are saying that while Saddam was not at all a good idea it was very bad that we were in the Gulf at all[3] – latest was a

6. Michael Hordern (b. 1911), actor; knighted (1983).

1. Dannie Abse (b. 1923), Welsh-Jewish poet and doctor; joint-editor, with Howard Sergeant, of the anti-Movement anthology *Mavericks* (1957).

2. To Lady Lucinda Lambton, the writer, broadcaster and photographer, whom he would marry later in the year.

3. On 2 August 1990, under the orders of its President Saddam Hussein, Iraq invaded the neighbouring state of Kuwait. Britain joined the Allied forces (led by the US) in an air offensive against Iraq (Operation 'Desert Storm') which began on 16 January 1991. The Allied

bearded Canuck who did me for their TV this morning. He collapsed quite promptly when I said we might have let things slide before but 2 wrongs would not have made a right, etc. Makes one suspect such chaps have never heard any view put but the one they hold. Same in US?

Even after getting your much-appreciated *On the Brink*[4] I (no doubt like many others) am daily both bored and bewildered by reports from there. Today comes news that Gorby remains in the saddle for the moment. 19th March: Pipes[5] in the Times says he, Gorby, should go and the West should back the opposition. Would you agree? You could save some minor hair-tearing if you could mention a British or Western (or any) commentator whom you think reasonably reliable.

Have been amusing myself late in evenings by looking through old Orwell's 4 vols of journalism, not just to collect good anti-lefty stuff, plenty of bloody foolishness too, and getting it wrong (Kipling's popularity being 'essentially middle-class'), but also reactionary stuff to dangle in front of contemporary lefties: 'even to want to write about so-called artists who spend on sodomy what they have gained by sponging betrays a kind of spiritual inadequacy' (1936) and, of Conrad, 'one of the surest signs of his genius is that women dislike his books' (same essay). And 'average' novels exist only for women; 'men read either the novels it is possible to respect, or detective stories.'[6] (Nobody got called a misogynist then.) Or thought twice about using the word Jew. Good too on explaining how unreadable Dickens is.

Want to get this off with copy of Mems plus reminder (if you want one) of my variation on A L Gordon: Life is largely grief and labour; Two things help you through: Jeering when they hit your neighbour,

ground offensive began on 24 February, and on 28 February, with Kuwait liberated and the Iraqi army defeated, President George Bush ordered a ceasefire.

4. Conquest cannot remember this book, and none of the four volumes I have found with its title (their authors are Denzil Batchelor (1964), Mercedes Endfield (1975), Benjamin Stein, with Herbert Stein (1978) and Pat Arrowsmith (1981), a dedicated anti-nuclear campaigner) rings a bell with him.

5. Richard Pipes (b. 1923), historian of Russia and the Soviet Union.

6. The Orwell quotes come from two essays in different issues of the *New English Weekly*: the Kipling from a notice of Kipling's death in the issue of 23 January 1936; those on homosexuals, women and Conrad from a review of 23 July 1936 of Cyril Connolly, *The Rock Pool* (Paris: 1936, London: 1947) and Joseph Conrad, *Almayer's Folly* (1895); both reprinted in Orwell and Angus, eds, *Collected Essays*, vol. 1, pp. 159–62, 225–7.

whining when it's you.[7] and I send our love to you and Liddie and hope to see you before long.

Yrs K.

[TLS: Recipient]

TO ANTHONY THWAITE – 24 MARCH 1991

194 Regent's Park Road London NW1 8XP

Dear Anthony,

I was delighted as always to hear from you, perhaps a shade more than usual this time as a contrast to all the variously sized bits of shit that have come my way since the memoirs appeared. I never expected them. I thought I was trying to be a) honest b) funny but not a bit of it, it appears. I roared with laughter at your evocation of a Thwaite para in them, but went a bit quiet at the Hebrew bit; not really my style, I hope.[1] Anyway, here is the best I can do with your questions. 1) I can't remember ever hearing of a Norman Jackson. To me via Philip, Norman was always Norman Iles. I don't know about DHL's house,[2] but Iles was, perhaps still is an aspiring literary man of a sort. See my memoirs for a bit about his appalling 'reconstructions' of nursery rhymes, which fit in completely with secular Christmas cards and the stuff in the intro to *Jill*.

7. Adam Lindsay Gordon (1833–70), Australian poet. The original, from *Ye Wearie Wayfarer* (Fytte VIII), in Gordon's first collection, *Sea Spray and Smoke Drift* (1867), reads: 'Life is mostly froth and bubble,/Two things stand like stone,/KINDNESS in another's trouble, /COURAGE in your own.' See also Amis to Conquest, 18 April 1992, for an improved version.

1. Thwaite had written Amis a letter telling him how much he liked the *Memoirs*, apart from one or two 'attacks on people who really shouldn't have been attacked', and how relieved he was not to have been attacked himself. He also included an invented comment on 'Thwaite' in the style of the *Memoirs*, which 'I seem to remember was some sort of thing on the lines of "Gave lunch to Thwaite again. Of course he's Yorkshire, which means he never attempts to pay his share of the bill. A bit of a Hebrew really . . ."' (personal communication, 16 November 1998).

2. Thwaite was asking Amis about a letter from Larkin of 27 March 1983, in which Larkin announces that Norman Iles 'seems to be *living*' in D.H. Lawrence's house in Eastwood, Nottingham (see *LL*, p. 691).

2) Farouche Guillaume must be P's and my idol, the cornettist Wild Bill Davison (1906–1990).
3) IWDAFY is 'I Would Do Anything for You', a record made by the Rhythmakers (Billy Banks and his orchestra) in 1932, featuring P W Russell on tenor, Fats Waller, Henry Allen et al. Also the title of an unfinished lost soft-porn bit of fiction by P and me in alternation dating from the '50s.
4) No clue at all about the friends near Newbury.[3] In a different compartment.
5) The bum thing started with a letter or card from P in the 1940s I should guess.[4] At the end he wrote Stumble bum Philip in place of All the best etc. A stumble bum, I found later, is US slang for a drunken tramp. I didn't know that then, took it just for a v. mild impropriety and signed off my next Crumble bum Kingsley. One or two variations followed, then I did a bit of pioneering with something based on the Pre-Raphaelite biography stuff I was then doing research into at Oxford, and wrote something like D.G. Rossetti was about five foot eight inches in height, with a pair of black moustaches that contrasted sharply with his rather pale bum. P took up the idea, though in letters that followed he tended to go on going for simple ones like Electricity bill bum and one I remember, C.H. Sisson bum. I rather went in for the rambling ones. His last letter to me, which he dictated as you know, apologised for the absence of the usual valediction. Writing that somehow reminds me of him telling me that his father, fatally ill and a couple of days from his end, at the appropriate moment said composedly and accurately to P, 'My last shave' and mentioned another last thing or two which I forget.

If anything else turns up, don't hesitate to ask. When you come up, please don't not let me take you out to lunch. (There will be no revised or supplemented edition of the memoirs.)

All cheers. Love to Ann.
Kingsley

By the same post as yours I got a do-you-remember-me letter (4 typed pp) from a John Timpson of John's. Can't tell him my only vivid

3. Thwaite has no memory of why he was asking about these friends or if he ever discovered anything about them, including their identity.

4. See Amis to Larkin, 8 June 1946, for Amis's first use of the valediction.

memory of him is in what N. Iles wrote of him in the JCR book: 'Mr Timpson Is a pimp's son.'

[TLS: Recipient]

TO WHOM IT MAY CONCERN – [MARCH 1991]

194 Regents Park Road, London NW1 8XP

TO WHOM IT MAY CONCERN

I consider A.E. Housman to be a great English poet, one of our greatest since Matthew Arnold. In my compilation The Amis Anthology (1988) I include thirteen of his poems, a number not surpassed by any other poet in that book.

If required, I should be happy to write at greater length on the subject. To my mind Housman certainly deserves a memorial in Poets' Corner.[1]

Sir Kingsley Amis, C.B.E.

[TLS]

TO RICHARD AND JUDY HOUGH[1] – [5 SEPTEMBER 1991]

Lovely here of course,[2] look you, but I haven't been here. Not being a raving lunatic. View through window of Yacht Club has more human

---

1. Written in response to a request of 5 March 1991 from the Housman Society for a testimonial in support of its campaign to install a memorial to Housman in Westminster Abbey by 1996, the centenary of the publication of *A Shropshire Lad*. The memorial was unveiled on 17 September 1996.

---

1. For Richard Hough see Amis to Conquest, 21 November 1976, note 3. He and his wife Judy (Taylor) Hough (b. 1932), retired publisher and MBE (1971), were neighbours and friends of Amis in Primrose Hill.

2. The photograph on the front of the postcard is of the cliffs and sea off Worms Head, on the Gower Peninsula.

interest: Hope NW1[3] is still there and look forward to seeing it and you next week. Cymru am byth.[4]

Love
Kingsley

[ALS: Recipient]

TO ROBERT CONQUEST – 10 SEPTEMBER 1991

194 Rgts Pk Rd L NW1 8XP

Dear Old Bob,

Must immediately write (got your letter last night on late return from Swansea stay) to signal my delight and relief. I had been on the verge of saying something similar.[1] Bless you for getting in first. But I still apologise for my offences.

The St P'burg name thing is really the best of the lot,[2] but wonderful to pick up the NSS here and find them all saying well, it doesn't disprove Marxism, does it? and well, we're still proud of being communists, and what do you mean it's fucked up socialism all over the world, the Labour Party is fine, and Cuba is fine, and Yeltsin is going to be as bad as Stalin, just you wait and see. I already have, what you must have heard 1,000 times already, the lefty version of events (thru' the unconscious agency of Paul Fussell) – it was all a massive destabilising operation by the CIA. Well yes, it took them 74 years to do it, but nobody ever said they were efficient.

Am full of questions to ask you, about the coup etc., but will save them till we meet. Considering the date had better send this to

3. Amis had originally written 'NW3,' which he crossed out, adding '1' just above, prefaced by '(Xt!!)'.

4. '*Cymru am byth*' means 'Wales for ever'.

---

1. Conquest had forgiven Amis for his behaviour over the *Memoirs*, an 'amnesty' occasioned by the collapse of the Soviet Union.

2. Leningrad reverted to its old name, St Petersburg, on 1 October 1991. By 'the lot' Amis may be referring to the momentous events of the past month: the failed mid-August coup against Gorbachev, resistance to which was led by Boris Yeltsin; the dismissal of the Soviet government and the disbanding of the KGB collegium on 28 August; the suspension of the central government of the USSR on 2 September, pending a new constitution; and the granting of independence to Latvia, Lithuania and Estonia on 6 September.

Charmian's. (Just rang to check her new address and hear you were at Heathrow for a couple of dozen nanoseconds.) Give my love to St P and ring me when you reappear – am around constantly from now on. And we will toast the Union of whatever it's called by then.

Yrs
K

[TLS: Recipient]

TO NIGEL (TOM) KNEALE – 10 OCTOBER 1991

194 Regents Park Road, London NW1 8XP

Dear Tom,[1]

It sounds incredible (and isn't important) but as I opened your letter I was saying to myself I could address the letter I was going to write you c/o Central. So here I am to say I thoroughly enjoyed the whole of S & the Women, which I ran all of on Monday evening. The family, aged 63 and 43, heartily agreed.[2]

As regards the substitutions you mention I have no cavil, indeed I welcome them. They bring the story more into the world of communications, publicity, etc., in which it rather dangled before. I thought in particular it was right to bring Steve into the Graphic[3] instead of sending him out of shot, as it were, to the Arab embassy. And restaurant scenes are fine in novels, where you needn't see the waiters and other eaters at all. I take your point there.

Knowing you a bit I think you would find my praise and approval more worth having if I introduce such objections as I can muster. I

---

1. Nigel (Tom) Kneale (b. 1922), television screenwriter, author of the four-part Central Television adaptation of *Stanley and the Women*. Kneale, a staff writer in the early post-war years of BBC Television, created the *Quatermass* serials (1953–59, 1979) and other sci-fi programmes, and is still an active and successful writer for television.

2. That is, Hilly and Philip.

3. The newspaper where Stanley Duke works. Kneale had switched a scene involving Stanley's schizophrenic son Steve from an Arab embassy to the *Graphic*; he also cut two scenes in restaurants 'because they never work. A lot of extras doing dumb-show as diners and waiters and getting in the way of the real actors' (Kneale to Amis, 9 October 1991).

think if we needed Rufus[4] at all, which I still doubt, we should have seen less or more of him (I didn't care for the actor but can hardly blame you for him). And I thought the very end was rather melodramatic. Collings[5] might just have been betrayed by her conceit into that suspect 'interview' but I'd have preferred a fit of old-fashioned (female) hysterics to the screaming hab-dabs. But certainly it was a rousing climax. And it was a pity Lindsey[6] looked so rough, but that wasn't you either. But that's it.

I thought most of the actors were excellent and very well cast: Stanley, & Collings![7] Steve, Nowell, Bert, Nash, Harry and the little girl who was sexually harassed by the tea-lady. Lady and Alethea wonderfully monstrous. Susan a bit unemphatic till late on but I suppose that's in the character. It all moved well and looked great.

Did I tell you, or did you know, that Herzog[8] means duke? I didn't when I wrote the book, or could have sworn I didn't.

All in all, my profound congratulations and heartfelt thanks. (Between ourselves I wish I felt I could look forward to delivering more of the same when I see what BBC Wales have done to *The Old Devils.*)[9]

Yours ever
Kingsley

The xerox is because my typescript has turned out pale grey.

[TLS: Recipient]

4. Rufus Hilton, a Kneale invention, the appalling motoring correspondent of the *Graphic.*

5. Dr Trish Collings, the radical psychiatrist who treats Steve.

6. Lindsey Lucas, the novel's only sane woman, Stanley's friend and ex-lover.

7. Typewritten insertion.

8. Early in the novel (p. 36), in a schizophrenic episode, Steve tears the cover off a book – Saul Bellow's *Herzog* (1964).

9. Broadcast in March 1992.

TO CAROLINE MICHEL – 7 NOVEMBER 1991

194 Regent's Park Road, London NW1 8XP

Dear Caroline Michel,[1]

Please make whatever use you see fit of the following statement:

> Whatever their political views, all writers and all who wish literature well must see in the threat to Salman Rushdie an attack on freedom of expression. It is irrelevant to argue that Rushdie may have abused that freedom; certain kinds of abuse, and only those, are illegal under English law, which he has not broken. The fact that his book may have offended certain Moslems is doubtless regrettable, but it cannot justify any furtherance in this country of a decree uttered by the government of another. The 'sentence of death' should be revoked immediately.

I agree in principle to put my name to the draft advertisement you sent me,[2] but I must see the exact text before signing.

I draw your attention to the fact that there is, whether we like it or not, no such thing as British law. In GB there is English law and Scottish law, and it is the former under which Mr Rushdie lives, I understand. So for 'British' in this con[t]ext read 'English' to forestall any puny objections.

Yours sincerely,
Kingsley Amis

[TL][3]

1. Caroline Michel (b. 1959), a publisher, was organising a vigil to be held at Westminster Central Hall on the occasion of the thousandth day of Ayatollah Khomeini's *fatwa* against Salman Rushdie. The *fatwa* was issued on 14 February 1989 and called for Rushdie's death, for blasphemies in his novel *The Satanic Verses* (1989).

2. The Westminster Hall vigil was called off at the suggestion of the Foreign Office, and the advertisement was never produced, though a public meeting was held at which Amis's statement and those of other prominent figures were read out.

3. A photocopy of this letter was found among Amis's papers after his death. The original has not survived.

TO ROBERT CONQUEST – 10 JANUARY 1992

Dear O B,

Good to be with you at this science-fictional date (who ever heard of 1992 except as the year the Galactic Federation was founded?). This morning I finished typing my latest novel[1] and turn to you first after escaping/being ejected from that prison/reason for existence. Thank you for your Xmas card and the reprint of Soviet Communism 1917–1991.[2] To adapt GKC (if I can), when men stop being part of a Communist state (being Christians) they don't go on as if they believe in nothing but as if they believe in anything.[3] Hope you get my drift. One result is that it will be easier, not harder, from now on to write a spy novel about the Commonwealth of Independent States (or whatever) than it was to write one about the USSR, where the writer had to show he knew what was possible. Now *anything* is possible. Does that stir any echo? I was much struck some months ago by old C[onor] C[ruise] O'Brien's remark that the really interesting thing will be to see if Yeltsin (or anyone else) can run the show, hold things together, without terror.

Nothing seems to happen here, thank God, since any change must be for the worse. Hilly and I went to Swansea and promptly, small hours of Xmas Eve, old Stuart Thos has massive rectal haemorrhage, causing great despondency but soon diagnosed as result of great munching of anti-gout pills. Two similar cases, one in Swansea at the time, another at the Garrick this morning, heard of closely paralleling Stuart's experience. The principality is quiet; don't believe reports you might conceivably see of anti-UK sentiment. Scotland same. A Conquest law

---

1. *The Russian Girl* (1992).

2. Robert Conquest, 'Soviet Communism 1917–1991, an Obituary', *New Leader*, 9–23 September 1991.

3. Nigel Rees, in an essay entitled 'The Quotability of Chesterton: With Special Reference to the Missing Quotations', *The G.K. Chesterton Quarterly* 2 (Spring 1977), pp. 3–6, calls the quotation Amis is adapting ('When men cease to believe in God, they will not believe in nothing, they will believe in anything') 'the Everest of problem quotations' (p. 5). No one has been able to locate the quotation among Chesterton's writings. Rees himself is 'inclined to the position taken by John Peterson of the *Midwest Chesterton News* in this Society's July 1996 *Newsletter* where, in an exhaustive – not to say exhausting – piece he shows that in the earliest found reference – Emile Cammaerts's 1937 *Chesterton: The Laughing Prophet* – what we are given is a *paraphrase* of the thought . . . What I think is unquestionable is that it is what Chesterton *did* think' (p. 5).

might be devised along the lines of Don't believe anything ever about centrifugal trouble in a democracy.

I wonder how from where you are you see the possible outcome of the coming election. I feel less in touch than ever before, still wondering why and how Mrs T got the chuck[4] and whether it's true that, according to Right as well as Left, the country is in a mess economically. It seems all right to me. I read in the paper about 57,000 businesses folding every day and then go off to review a restaurant for Harpers & Queen and find the place packed out, with waiters running for more champagne. It's true that when you come out of the Garrick you can get a taxi like that, without having to walk about.

Well so what do I do with my novel finished? Have vague plans, which I will soon have to sharpen up, for a slimmish book of short or shortish stories, one of them about the day in 1942/A when the Japanese fleet bombarded San Fr and LA and the Nazis NYC and Washington and brought about the surrender of the USA. Any thoughts on the general topic? And (another story) can you think offhand of a poem by Browning that seems to you particularly non-UK-English in idiom? Explanations later.[5]

Happy New Year to you and Liddie. Let us know when you'll be over.

Cheers
K.
and love from H.

[TLS: Recipient]

4. Margaret Thatcher resigned as Prime Minister on 28 November 1990, after deciding not to contest a second ballot for leadership of the Conservative Party. She had won the first ballot with 204 votes to Michael Heseltine's 152, with sixteen abstentions, but was advised by members of her Cabinet that she would not prevail in a second ballot. For Amis's reaction to the outcome of the 1992 general election see Amis to Conquest, 18 April 1992.

5. For Amis's theories on Browning see Amis to Betjeman, 29 May 1981.

TO TIM ODHAMS – 23 JANUARY 1992

194 Regent's Park Road, London NW1 8XP

My dear Tim,[1]

Sorry, but I seem to have run out of highbrow writing paper so I jot this down on what's to hand.

I have heard from the invaluable Z and others that you're not really up to seeing visitors at the moment.[2] So I write you this instead of turning up in person.

As you will have heard, everybody at the old club shows concern for you and is constantly asking questions about how you're getting on. I think they must feel as I do that you're a kind of ideal Garrick man, sociable and tolerant to the nth degree but ready with a quick shaft of unadorned realism when required. It's obvious that everything you say is direct and spontaneous, but you have the happy knack of combining charity with truth.

I would say myself that I have been missing you and your shy affectionate smile in the same way as I miss the brother I never had. Everybody who has ever had anything to do with you has been cheered and warmed by the experience.

I hope you'll let me know if there's anything I can do, and if you ever feel like being dropped in on, I'll be there.

Yours ever
Kingsley

[ALS][3]

---

1. Timothy Odhams (1928–92), a long-standing member of the Garrick Club, had worked in advertising and public relations.

2. Odhams had only a few months to live (he died in April 1992); 'Z' is Dr Ronald Zeegen, a mutual friend, and a doctor to both men.

3. A photocopy of this letter was found among Amis's papers after his death.

TO ANTHONY POWELL – 9 MARCH 1992

194 Regent's Park Road, London NW1 8XP

Dear Tony,

I hope I did a bit of thanking when you said you were going to dedicate your next book[1] to me, but now I've read it through once and have turned back for a second go I see I owe you a lot more. In fact I feel most honoured, twice over, to be given a book of yours, and such a good one too. It is immensely readable; I dashed through it the first time, feeling on the way I was getting an insight into those people and the world they lived in that I could never have found elsewhere half so attractively presented. The individual pieces gain a lot from appearing together, and the effect is not at all the usual stop-and-start one of such a collection. I loved the anecdotes, but I felt you were being very fair-minded at the same time. How I have longed for somebody to call that stinking fraud Napoleon *common* as well.[2]

I read your interview with Lynn Barber[3] with much amusement. She did me in a different series once. I asked her what books she had written and when she said 'Two sex manuals' I found myself saying, 'That makes me feel like someone talking to a thoroughly nice chap and then suddenly finding he used to be in the Gestapo.' When the chat appeared it was rather hostile. She wrote me a letter apologising for this 'negative' quality but giving no reason for it.

Again my thanks and gratitude. *and love to you and Violet*[4]

Kingsley

[TLS: Recipient]

---

1. *Under Review: Further Writings on Writers 1946–1989* (1991); see Amis to Powell, 21 November 1990.

2. See the chapter entitled 'Napoleon Bonaparte' in *Under Review*, p. 366: 'he was heartless, petty and common, and there seems no reason whatever to suppose that if he had imposed his way over Europe the result would have been in the least beneficial.'

3. Lynn Barber (b.1944), journalist, well-known for lengthy, often unsympathetic interviews.

4. MS addition.

TO ROBERT CONQUEST – 18 APRIL 1992

194 R P R L NW1 8XP

Dear O'Bob,

I wish the two of you could have made my birthday lunch, not that I was very optimistically expecting you to travel 6,000 miles for it, but I thought there was a chance you might be coming over anyway. The event was all right, at least passing off without bloodshed, and enough Macallan was provided. The Times diary gave me stick for 'insisting' on speaking before the meal[1] and proposing the loyal toast, thus 'forcing' Martin, socialist supporter and republican, to stand up and drink, which was pretty atrocious of me. Stuart T attended, but seemed below par.

That was a jolly old election result, what?[2] My faith in a 20ish Tory majority held up until the last week, when I have to admit it wobbled. Martin just happened to call from Tuscany on the morrow, and took the news very well. Better than Neil Kinnock, who delighted me by announcing he accepted his defeat without excuses or bitterness, and added later in the same speech that the Tory Press were to blame and but for them he'd have won. Major has risen in my estimation, largely because of the way he cut up a lefty interviewer on TV into small pieces in polite level tones. He's no Mrs T but he's not too bad.

A female about whom nothing strikes a chord in me, not even her name, writes from Swansea (a) to ask me to give a lecture there (b) to remind me that we had 'a brief, happy interlude there'. This is awkward. I hardly like to tell her I remember nothing of it or her, but if I go on about what fun it was she might write back and ask me to help her buy a little something for our son on his 32nd birthday. [. . .]

Have been trying to finalise my Homage to Adam Lindsay Gordon as follows: Life is largely grief and labour/Two things see you through:/ Chortling when it thumps your neighbour,/Whingeing when it's you.[3] Does it matter that 'it, in line 3 is either Life from 2 lines back or a

---

1. At the Garrick Club.

2. On 9 April, in defiance of the opinion polls, the Conservatives under John Major were returned for a fourth successive term, with a reduced majority of twenty-one.

3. See Amis to Conquest, 18 March 1991.

sort of impersonal, general 'it'? We follow up with II, which is Women and queers and children etc.

As regards Browning, I've done my Browning story suggesting he was a Jamaican boogie by descent. After a search for a non-English bit I settled for Up jumped Tokay on our table etc., bloody ridiculous if not exactly non-Eng. Have yet to tackle 1942/A but it's looming up.[4]

The new Wendy Cope vol is really quite good. 'I hardly ever tire of love or rhyme – That's why I'm poor and have a rotten time.'[5] What have you got on the stocks? When are you coming over?

Cheers
and love to Liddie
K.

[TLS: Recipient]

TO ROBERT FOSTER – 6 MAY 1992

194 Regents Park Road, London NW1 8XP

Dear Cousin Robert,

How amazing to hear from you after all this time.[1] I do hope your London trip will materialize. Late May to early June will suit me fine. In fact I shall be at this address until August and then again from the middle of September onwards.

Of course you have another cousin in London – John. It would be

4. See the title story and the story entitled '1941/A' in *Mr Barrett's Secret and Other Stories* (1993). The Browning passage is from 'Nationality in Drinks', *Dramatic Romances and Lyrics* (1845), and is quoted in a concluding note to the title story (pp. 21–2).

5. The quoted lines are an entire poem, 'Variations on Belloc's Fatigue', in *Serious Concerns* (1992).

---

1. Robert Foster (b. 1922), an attorney, lives in California; his mother, Gladys (Amis) Foster, Amis's paternal aunt, married the American Ralph Foster, a Professor of Romance Languages at the US Naval Academy in Annapolis, Maryland, and at George Washington University in Washington DC. The marriage was disapproved of by the family. See *Memoirs*, p. 3, and *The Old Devils* (1986), in which Peter Thomas relates the story of 'a cousin of my father's . . . called Gladys', who falls in love with, and seeks to marry, an American: 'Name of Foster, Ralph Foster . . . Professor of physics at Yale University he was.' The mother of the fictional Gladys (like the mother of the real-life Gladys) objects: 'What was interesting was her reason for being against the American. He was an American.'

fun if the three of us could arrange to meet. Let me know your dates and I will fix it up.

All good wishes,
Yours
Kingsley

[TLS: Recipient]

TO CHRIS BOWYER – 3 JUNE 1992

c/o Jonathan Clowes, Iron Bridge House,
Bridge Approach, London NW1 8BD

Dear Mr. Bowyer,

Many thanks for your extremely pleasant letter.[1] I am so glad you took the trouble to write because I too rather think that some of the reviews of my Memoirs were partly unjustified. They seem to have been based not on a reading of the book but of the extracts from it in the Sunday Times, or even on earlier reviews.

I envy you as somebody who has all Elizabeth Taylor's books to read for the first time.

Yours sincerely,
Kingsley Amis

[TLS: Recipient]

1. Mr Bowyer (b.1944), once a teacher, now 'a self-employed builder', had written Amis a fan letter about the *Memoirs*, 'prompted by reading a slapdash and malicious review' (personal communication, 6 November 1997).

TO BRIAN ALDISS – 17 JULY 1992

194 Regents Park Road, London NW1 8XP

Dear Brian (hope you don't mind a typed letter: my hands are inclined to be unruly in the mornings, I can't think why),

Super intro – many thanks.[1] I have a few cavils, which I've scrawled on your typescript. As regards the French bit, Hilda[2] uses translated idioms and 'copann a me' is supposed to be 'copain à moi' I mean à moi.[3] And as I remember they speak neither French nor Dutch but English. Still. I think too that the 'message' of the thing is gloomy rather than consolatory, that your ancestors have to have fought like hell for you to be able to enjoy any freedom, and New England with its 'separateness' is probably not much better than the RC world.

I hope this gets to you in time – when I put aside a letter to answer personally my inefficiency usually sees to it that that takes something like for ever, or do I mean forever? I can't quite think why, (it takes so long)[4] because it beats hollow the blood-out-of-a-stone struggle called work. Talk about excused SF.[5] I wouldn't mind being excused F, i.e. fiction. It's rather like being a Jew, no matter what you do or don't do you can't help being one.

The super intro and thanks part was meant to saute the fact (I meant salute, not sauté) that you make the old Alteration sound quite a thrilling read. I haven't dared look at it since about 1980.

Was in Oxford end of April signing three or four copies but had

1. Aldiss had sent Amis a draft of an introduction he was writing to a new edition of *The Death Guard* (1939) by Philip George Chadwick. It appeared in 1992.

2. A character in *The Alteration* (1976), Hilda van den Haag, daughter of the New England ambassador. Hubert Anvil, the novel's ten-year-old hero, is attracted to her. Aldiss discusses *The Alteration* in his introduction to *The Death Guard.*

3. The first 'à' is indistinct.

4. Typewritten insertion.

5. Aldiss had written enough about science fiction to feel, in the manner of a schoolboy asking to be 'excused PT', that he could be 'excused SF'. The phrase does not occur in his introduction to *The Death Guard.*

no chance to get to you. Surely you come to London sometimes?

Well, then . . .[6]

Great cheers
Kingsley

[TLS: Bodleian]

TO ERIC JACOBS – 27 JULY 1992

194 Regents Park Road, London NW1 8XP

Dear Eric,

I got your letter only a couple of hours ago, but I have thought about it a lot since then and I decided you would like my answer as soon as possible.[1] (So I'll drop a xerox of this in at the club this morning and send the orig. to Dickenson Rd.)

If the answer must be No, please be assured that, far from thinking your suggestion in any way inappropriate, I take it as a great compliment. You seem to me ideally qualified for the project in general. I simply feel that to say Yes would involve me in an immeasurable amount of work that I would sooner avoid. I did a bit of digging for my Memoirs and would very much prefer not to face a second and deeper dig. If you can come up with a method of doing the job without involving me in anything more strenuous than a couple of chats over a drink, then I wouldn't want to stop you. If you want to talk things over anyway, then feel free to bring up the matter any time. I won't say anything about it unless you do. (I won't mention it to anyone else.)

As for Garrick lunches – let them be redoubled!.

Yours ever,
Kingsley

[TLS: HEHL]

6. MS addition.

---

1. Jacobs (b.1936), a journalist and frequent lunchtime companion at the Garrick, had asked Amis for permission to write his biography.

TO ERIC JACOBS – 14 AUGUST 1992

194 Regents Park Road, London NW1 8XP

Dear Eric,

I am very glad that you propose to write my biography. Yours will be the authorised biography, and I undertake not to give any other biographer any co-operation for three years. Should I die or become incapacitated before your book is finished, control of its contents will pass to my literary executors, Jonathan Clowes and Martin Amis.[1]

Yours ever,
Kingsley

[TLS: Recipient]

TO VIRGINIA RUSH – 16 SEPTEMBER 1992

194 Regents Park Road, London NW1 8XP

Dearest Virginia,[1]

I hope you don't mind typed letters – the point is that my best time for writing letters is straight after breakfast, which isn't the best time for my writing hand. Anyway, this is just to thank you and Michael for being so kind and energetic on my behalf while I was down. Those away-days were absolutely fine, and I think I enjoyed the second one with j[u]st the two of you at least as much as the first, more thickly populated one.[2]

---

1. Jacobs explains, in a letter of December 1996 to Jonathan Clowes, how Amis came to agree to the biography: 'What happened subsequently was this. His letter [of 27 July] showed that Kingsley was reluctant but perhaps open to persuasion. So I asked him what form persuasion should take. He said, What about lunch? I said, Where? He said Simpson's-in-the-Strand. So we had lunch there, about which I can remember only that we drank a lot, it cost a lot and we were somehow in business at the end of it.'

---

1. Virginia Rush (b.1939), wife of Michael Rush (for whom see Amis to Stuart Thomas, 9 December 1982, note 3).

2. These 'away-days', also known as 'Kingsley's Rural Rides', were often into the Carmarthenshire countryside, as in these instances, though sometimes also into Pembrokeshire.

Sally was a jewel on the return trip and remains one.[3] Old[4] was weighed down by girl trouble and daughter or rather ex-girl trouble, but seems now to be climbing out of the doldrums. The highest or lowest spot was Hilly being ticked off over the phone by Philip's elderly shrink for giving him fish-fingers to eat. She should have said how highly they're regarded by both Ali and me.

Needless to say, the Garrick is a mess for the moment while it puts in new kitchens, but all that should be over by the time you appear. And if the worst comes to the worst we can always pig it at Simpson's.

Back to novel now.[5] I reckon I've got it off the ground, but keeping it in the air is another matter. Oh well.

Much love to you both. See you soon.

Kingsley

[TLS: Recipient]

TO JOHN AND ANN McDERMOTT – [EARLY JANUARY 1993]

You bet – come and see me any time. Didn't you know by the way that you can't stop a biographer?[1]

Cheers
Kingsley

Blwyddyn newydd dda![2] (1993)

[ALS: Recipient]

3. Sally Amis died in 2000, aged forty-six.
4. A word is missing here; the reference is to Philip Amis.
5. *You Can't Do Both* (1994).

---

1. John McDermott had written saying that when next he came to London he would treat Amis to lunch; he also asked about 'new developments on your biog' (letter of late December 1992).
2. Happy New Year.

TO PAUL FUSSELL – 10 FEBRUARY 1993

194 Regents Park Road, London NW1 8XP

Dear Paul,

Good to have your letter, dear boy.

As regards THE OLD DEVILS and its date:[1] the publisher says I delivered the first ten chapters on 26.11.85., i.e. well before Philip's death in the December. I cannot prove that I didn't think of ending the book with a wedding without any reference to Larkin at all, but I can say I made no conscious connection with *In Memoriam*.[2] I 'conceived' the novel in September, 1984, before I knew Larkin was even ill. I personally think that a possible connection between the two is the sort of idea you academic types come up with.

Love from us to you both.

Yours ever,
Kingsley

[TLS: Recipient]

TO EDWARD PELL – 18 MARCH 1993

194 Regents Park Rd, London NW1 8XP, England

Your letter received here about 10th March

Dear Ed,

Thank you for your totally unexpected, delightful and fascinating letter. Of course I remember you very well.[1] You brought those Mumbles

---

1. Fussell was at work on the book that would become *The Anti-Egotist: Kingsley Amis, Man of Letters* (New York and London: Oxford University Press, 1994).

2. Tennyson's poem in memory of his friend A.H. Hallam was begun in 1833, the year of Hallam's death, but not published until 1850.

---

1. Edward Pell (b.1938), an attorney, had studied at Princeton when Amis was there. He went to New College, Oxford on a Rhodes Scholarship in 1960, and often visited Swansea

days back to me so clearly I can hardly believe they were over thirty years ago.

You saved your best punch for the end, when you wrote, 'My best wishes to you and to Hilly if you see her.' I passed your wishes on – I last saw Hilly an hour ago and expect to see her again this afternoon. She is, so to speak, my housekeeper.

Let me explain. In 1965, having been divorced, I married Elizabeth Jane Howard, who left me in 1980. In 1981 I set up a new household that included me, Hilly, her 3rd husband Alastair, their son James, then aged 8, and intermittently Hilly's and my son Philip. Three houses and nearly 13 years later, that is still the position. I pay the bills; the Kilmarnocks (H. and A. are Lady and Lord Kilmarnock, their son is J. Boyd) live here and look after me. It sounds an odder arrangement than it is and it certainly seems to work. I see and hear nothing of E.J. Howard, which suits me fine. Everybody is in good shape.

Hilly and I have kept up our Welsh links. I go down every summer on a 3-week visit, staying with Stuart and Eve in Mumbles. I whall probably be there again this August, if they are still going. Eve, due to be 80 this year, smokes like a chimney and drinks like a fish and is still immensely hale. Stuart at 79 is in some trouble from his cancerous bladder, though apparently this [is] one of those things that can go on for years without decisively taking a turn for the worse. When Hilly and I saw him last Christmas he was drinking wine one day, water the next and Scotch the one after. He is pretty deaf but otherwise not much diminished. I'm sure they'd welcome a letter and even a visit from you, if you are ever within reach of those parts. Their address is still 4 Mary Twill Lane, Newton, Mumbles, Swansea, W. Glam, U.K.

What you said about Tim and his last days was very touching and we were most interested to hear the details about his parents.[2] I am so glad the Welsh bits in my Memoirs appealed to you. Penny Jones's

in 1961, staying in a cottage in Mumbles with his close Princeton friend Timothy Houghton, who had also been a pupil of Amis's (Houghton wanted to write, and had followed Amis to Swansea in the summer of 1960). Pell wrote to Amis on 22 November 1992 to praise the *Memoirs*, 'especially the beautiful bits about Swansea and Mumbles'.

2. Tim Houghton was to commit suicide after a period of mental instability. He came from a New England family of modest means, but at Swansea, according to Pell (in the letter of 22 November 1992), lived 'an errant, extravagant lifestyle'. He published one novel, *The First Season* (1968).

parents are dead but she I believe is securely married.[3] Bob Conquest is married for the 4th time to a Texas girl and lives in Stanford, California, though he often comes to Europe, particularly Russia, where he is honoured as one of the few who really helped to demolish Stalin. George and Pat Gale were divorced many years ago and he sadly died in 1990. I haven't quite lost touch with Rukeyser but of course from my point of view he is confined to the USA. I was invited to his daughter's wedding but couldn't go.

Please note telephone number above and if ever you find yourself in London do give us a ring and we will all raise a glass.

Bless you for writing,

Cheers
Kingsley

[TLS: Recipient]

TO PAUL FUSSELL – 22 APRIL 1993

194 Regents Park Road, London NW1 8XP

Dear Paul,

I have to answer two of your inquiries, which seem to be turning up a little more often than formerly.

No, I can't remember ever making a mistake of the kind you mean. I go in for quoting factual information, sources and such, rather rarely. This of course doesn't mean to say there aren't such errors remaining unnoticed.

As regards the *Daily Mirror* poems, a couple of days with my own anthology, *The Faber Popular Reciter* (1978) gave me enough for the first weeks or months and I read every anthology by others that I could find, also a few dozen collected poems. I sent in batches of five or ten, enough for a week or a fortnight. It didn't seem an unlikely task for such as me, but for a popular daily to run such a feature was unlikely. I was Poetry Editor of the paper for that year,[1] nothing more, & didn't

3. Penny Jones, an art student at Swansea in the early 1960s, had been engaged to Houghton.

1. From 19 March 1984 to 15 March 1985.

then or at any time since 1961 think of myself as a teacher of literature, though I wouldn't actually object to being so designated.

Many thanks to you both for birthday card (the first to arrive), and my blessings and love.

Cheers
Kingsley

[TLS: Recipient]

TO JOHN McDERMOTT – 27 MAY 1993

194 Regents Park Road, London NW1 8XP

Dear John,

Thanks for your letter. Contents noted. Rees is an ex-pupil of mine at Swansea, now I presume indigent.[1] Motion's book on Philip Larkin is a bloody disgrace (see my review in The Spectator).[2] My biography proceeds. I am not going away until mid-August. It would be great fun to see you before this, especially with a lunch in prospect.

Love to Anne.
Thanks.
Kingsley

[TLS: Recipient]

---

1. A bookseller had informed McDermott of his recent acquisition of a set of books by Amis with Rees's name inside.

2. Amis's review appeared in *Spectator*, 3 April 1993, p. 25. It began by praising the biography's factual accuracy ('If, as seems likely, Andrew Motion was as scrupulous with all his sources as he was with what I provided, then this must be one of the most truthful of modern biographies'), but soon accused Motion of being deficient in 'skill, dash, ability to select, above all humour', of being reductively biographical in his reading of the poetry, and of affecting 'pious horror' at Larkin's taste for girlie magazines ('porn only by courtesy'). The review ends: 'If he has never leered, or even looked, at a photograph of a naked female, he is some kind of freak. If he has, he is no worse than a medium-sized hypocrite.'

TO PAUL FUSSELL – 27 MAY 1993

194 Regents Park Road, London NW1 8XP

Dear Paul,

Glad you enjoyed the Balbus thesis.[1] That makes you a real fan of my work.

As regards your two queries:

1. My Inner Audience did I think consist chiefly of Larkin and Conquest, especially Larkin. More lately I have added Martin.
2. No, I wasn't thinking of Lord David but of a former colleague at Swansea.[2] Tut-tut, can you imagine Lord David smoking a *pipe*?

All well here.
Love to you both,
Kingsley

[TLS: Recipient]

1. Fussell cannot remember what 'the Balbus thesis' was about, but since Balbus is a common Roman *cognomen*, originally denoting someone with a speech impediment, it might concern stuttering or lisping. See also 'Mightier than the Pen', from *A Case of Samples* (1956), reprinted in *CP*, p. 66, which begins:

Jerking and twisting as he walks,
Neighing and hooting as he talks,
The shabby pundit's prototype,
Sucking his horrible black pipe,
Balbus keeps making me feel ill.

The poem goes on to question whether a satirical portrait of such a man is worth the effort:

Cameras just click, and click's not
The sound of an effective shot;
Fussing with flash and tripod's fun,
But bang's the way to get things done.

Fussell quotes the opening lines of the poem in *The Anti-Egotist*, p. 174, where he refers to 'Balbus, the horrible academic'.

2. Fussell can remember neither the name of the colleague nor the query.

TO PAUL FUSSELL – 15 JUNE 1993

194 Regents Park Road, London NW1 8XP

Dear Paul,

I have your latest source of vexation to hand. Yes, I did teach *MP*[1] at Swansea, and very scathing about it I was. One never really closes with a work of literature until one has to, e.g. by teaching it, choosing it to go into a newspaper poetry column, etc., and I found out a lot in teaching *MP*, but I had concluded that JA was a 2nd-rate pisser while still at school.

While I'm about it, I'll take you to task for your trendy use of *perception*. When Sam J said of whomsoever, 'Sir, I perceive that you are a vile Whig,' he meant not 'My view of you is that you are a v.W.' (whereas Bozzy's view of you might be something else), but 'I see through to the truth, which is that you are a v.W.' There used to be only one true perception, now there are as many as the people doing the perceiving. One more tiny but revealing example of the lefty movement to dethrone absolute or objective truth and institute[2] a republic of equally 'valid' relative truths. So watch it, Jack.

Longing to see book. Roll on Sept. Love to you both.

Heers,
K.

[TLS: Recipient]

---

1. *Mansfield Park* (1814) by Jane Austen.
2. Amis has struck out 'substitute' and replaced it with 'institute'.

TO RICHARD LEWIS – 8 JULY 1993

194 Regents Park Road, London NW1 8XP

Dear Mr. Lewis,

Thank you for your letter inviting me to host a table on the Orient-Express on Monday, 13th December.[1] The idea attracts me, and the charity of my choice would be CRUSE.[2] The only stipulation I make regarding liquid refreshment is that I should have a bottle of Macallans 10-year old Whisky in lieu of wine (in which category I class champagne).

I am therefore accepting your invitation in principle, and look forward to hearing further details.

Yours sincerely,

[TL][3]

TO MR AND MRS DERWENT MAY – [SEPTEMBER 1993]

Ex Cambria semper aliquid novi.[1] Vale for now

Kingsley

[ALS: Recipient]

---

1. Lewis, of Superlative Travel, London W3, had written to Amis on behalf of his company, which had chartered the Orient Express for a three-and-a-half-hour charity jaunt through the English countryside in December. On each of the train's nine carriages an invited celebrity would host a five-course lunch with champagne and wine for twenty passengers; £1,000 would be donated to the charity of the celebrity's choice.

2. Cruse Bereavement Care, a national charity, founded in 1959, offering help to the bereaved and for those who care for them.

3. A photocopy of this letter was found among Amis's papers after his death. The original has not survived.

---

1. 'There is always something new from Wales,' a play on 'Ex Africa semper aliquid novi,' from *Historia Naturalis* (II.viii.42) by Pliny (AD 23–79). Amis is referring to the banal cartoon (a joke about sex change) on the front of this postcard; the card was sent from Wales, where he was staying with Michael and Virginia Rush. For Derwent May see Amis to Lois Wilson, 14 January 1988, note 1.

TO VIRGINIA RUSH – 13 SEPTEMBER 1993

194 Regents Park Road, London NW1 8XP

Dearest Virginia,

Jack P. brought me home in excellent order, with the extra amenity of a hip-flask of Black Label and water which like a true barman he brought out of its compartment at precisely 12 o'clock. He sends in his bill today, £250 for the round trip, which I think is excellent value. It's a pity he hasn't got a twin brother living in Regent's Park Road.

Weather has been lousy since my return and apparently was wet and chilly while I was away, which seems like a bloody good show. But there's very little that isn't curable by being snug indoors with a glass of Macallan in hand and more in the bottle. Talking of which my next journalistic assignment is to write an article on supermarket Scotch. Sixteen bottles and ½-botts., review copies, stand on my sideboard. It should be fun but rather strenuous fun writing the piece.

I'm going to recommend the Dilkusha Hotel to all those who cross Offa's Dyke, or is it Dike or is that something different?[1] But seriously you and Michael must be about the best hosts alive. I have made a determined effort to find something less than ideal and have failed. I hope I wasn't a nuisance in any way, though if I was the staff concealed the fact most efficiently. Bless you both.

I know you'll keep me posted re Stuart etc. Much love

And hearty thanks! to you both.
Kingsley

[TLS: Recipient]

1. It is Dyke. Offa's Dyke is an earthwork running from the River Wye, near Monmouth, to near Prestatyn, in Clwyd, said to have been built by Offa of Mercia (reigned 757–96) to separate the Welsh from the English.

TO NUNC WILLCOX – 6 JANUARY 1994

194 Regents Park Road, London NW1 8XP

My dear Nunc,

Thank you for your letter about a lift.[1] You ask two questions really. My answer to the first and easier one is that I am very much in favour of the idea of a lift at the Garrick. The second question, whether I can make a financial contribution, I will defer until after the tax man has taken his cut.

Yours

[TL][2]

TO ROBERT CONQUEST – 15 APRIL 1994

194 RPR NW1 8XP

D / O // B ///

They were puzzled – let's say it was that–
When to end with I fucked the wild cat,
    And the PRZS
    Was heard to confess
He couldn't think what I was at.

Yours[1] was first-rate, of course, but kindly note that they carried *out*

---

1. Willcox (b.1927), a businessman and, at the time, Chairman of the General Committee of the Garrick, had written to Amis for a contribution towards the cost of the lift, which was installed in early 1995. The bar at the Garrick is upstairs.

2. A photocopy of this letter was found among Amis's papers after his death.

---

1. Conquest cannot remember which 'PRZS' limerick Amis is referring to here. 'PRZS' stands for 'President of the Royal Zoological Society', and the earliest 'PRZS' limerick is the second of a pair about a Fellow, an 'FRZS', who loves animals. In this second limerick, the last line of which Amis worked on, 'PRZS' was actually 'PZS' (Amis had misremembered); in later versions 'FRZS' was amended to 'a young FZS' and 'PRZS' to 'the old PZS':

i. I was thrilled when I went to the zoo
They allowed me to roger the gnu
And an FRZS

the PRZS, not off. Carrying off was what the Greeks did to Cassandra when they took Troy.

Every hack here is screeching at the Tories and/or Major to get out. What a lot of them mean is no more than, give us a fresh set of chaps for us to be clever about. I do quite see that the thought of still going on about the old gang in 2001 isn't very exciting.

Am 72 tomorrow. Can't walk any distance and take circa 5 mins to button up shirt, etc., otherwise not notice[a]bly impaired. What's it like being 77?

Fussells are due in London w/e at end of May so adjust your schedule if required.

Much enjoyed yr squib on po: today.[2]

See you soon. Love to Liddie. Cheers,

K.

[TLS: Recipient]

TO DAVID VAISEY – 19 JULY 1994

194 Regent's Park Road, London, NW1

Dear Mr Vaisey,[1]

I should like very much indeed to have the opportunity to look through once again the letters I wrote over many years to my old friend Philip Larkin. As you know, these letters are deposited in your archives along with others to Philip. But these days, alas, a degree of lameness has left me increasingly immobile and to spend in your library the

Remarked to me 'Yes
It's a privilege granted to few.'

ii. There was plenty of good-natured chaff
When I went back to fuck the giraffe
And the old PZS
Could hardly suppress
A dry professorial laugh.

2. I have been unable to trace this 'squib', which Conquest does not remember.

1. D.G. Vaisey (b.1935), Bodley's Librarian (1986–96), Bodleian Library, Oxford.

several days it would take to read the letters would be quite impossible for me.

Would it, I wonder, be possible to have the letters copied and sent to me at my home address? Of course, I understand that this would be a time-consuming business for your staff and I would naturally want to cover their costs and any others that might arise. But I would regard it as a great favour if you could arrange this service for me.[2]

Yours sincerely,
Kingsley Amis

[TLS: Bodleian]

TO THE EDITOR, *SUNDAY TIMES* – 14 AUGUST 1994

As quoted by you (News Review last week), the late Caitlin Thomas once described some chap as "the worst man possible, the grossest vulgarian in the world" etc. Thank heaven I cannot be he, as I am no Welshman but a selectively pro-Welsh Englishman who first set foot in the Principality in 1949.[1]

I think I only met her twice: once when in Stuart Thomas's kitchen she asked a very staid New York publisher not to "sex her up", and once when I bought her and her children lunch at the Wig and Pen

2. This letter was the final move in a protracted campaign to allow Jacobs, Amis's authorised biographer, access to the letters. The Bodleian had denied this access, despite Jacobs having Amis's permission, declaring, as Jacobs explains, 'that it was Bodleian policy not to open up for inspection or use the letters of someone still alive, on the grounds that other living people might be hurt by what was said in them' (*Biography*, p. xv). As Jacobs argued, though, the letters of dead people (of Larkin, for example, which the Bodleian allowed to be published) could be just as hurtful to the living. The library was unmoved, even after pro-Jacobs queries from Lord Jenkins, the Chancellor of Oxford University, and John Patten, the Secretary of State for Education. When, in response to this letter, it finally agreed to release the letters to Amis himself, it might have guessed that they would quickly find their way to Jacobs; as they did, 'days after my first version of this book reached the publisher' (p.xv).

---

1. For Caitlin Thomas see Amis to Larkin, 17 November 1985, note 4. Her description, quoted by George Tremlett, author of the 'News Review' article to which Amis is objecting (7 August 1994), was of Amis.

Club in The Strand, when she gave me a bollocking for something or other – which excused her from thanking me for my generosity.

Otherwise, in retrospect, she strikes me as a violent, untruthful Irish bag.

Like George Tremlett, she also seemed to think I became a trustee of the Dylan Thomas estate on the death of Wynford Vaughan-Thomas in 1987. In fact, I was appointed the previous year, partly with the assistance of Wynford's vote.

Tremlett errs, too, in supposing that I "spent the past 30 years (ie 1958–87) abusing Dylan Thomas in print". Actually, as a list of my publications would show, I did find other things to do in those three decades.

KINGSLEY AMIS
Garrick Club London WC2

TO VIRGINIA RUSH – 13 SEPTEMBER 1994

194 Regents Park Road, London NW1 8XP

Dearest Virginia,

Just to thank you for doing your considerable bit to entertain me and generally look after me while I was staying in Mumbles. Keep this to yourself (and Michael) but without your presence on the spot or round the corner it might not always have been easy to get through the day. The least attractive part was waking up under the duvet pouring with sweat every morning and willing myself to get up. The Turkish-bath effect lasted well into the morning.

My book[1] is officially published on Thursday when I seem to have landed myself with a dentist's appointment. Bottom row of new teeth still rocky. A great improvement on my old teeth though, no question.

Keep me posted re the course of events at Mary Twill Lane.[2] It was odd saying goodbye to Stuart this time; I wanted to give him a hug or the equivalent but it doesn't do to let people see you're not all that

---

1. *You Can't Do Both.*
2. The address of Eve and Stuart Thomas.

sure you'll see them again. I know you'll let me know if he takes a turn for the worse. Or for the better.

Much love and many thanks to Michael and yourself.

And cheers,
Kingsley

[TLS: Recipient]

TO ALASTAIR BOYD (LORD KILMARNOCK) – 16 JUNE 1995

194 Regents Park Road, London NW1 8XP

PRIVATE AND CONFIDENTIAL

Dear Ali,

I remain very sorry that I offended you with the remarks made about you that Eric Jacobs quotes as mine in chapter 20 of his book.[1] I have taken the matter up with him and he has said he proposes to write his own letter to you about the matter.

I myself feel that my published recollection of what was quoted as having been said about you 'at a drunken dinner at the Savile Club' which 'turned out to be unreliable' would not be taken as defamatory of you by a reasonable person. I speak of legal defamation and I am not qualified in the law, and you will make allowance for that. But I am qualified to judge of what is bad behaviour in a non-legal context and here I feel I have been and am at fault. I understand and have taken to heart your disappointed remarks about my having done something to spoil the happy private atmosphere between us three, meaning the two of us and Hilly. I apologise for having done so and wish very much that I had put things differently in what Jacobs quoted. I do however feel it is difficult to express oneself in such a way as to give no foundation whatever for being represented in such terms as Jacobs has used, and would adduce that consideration in accounting for my reported

1. *Biography*, p. 332.

behaviour. But all things considered I beg your pardon and ask your forgiveness.

Yours ever,
K.

[TLS: Recipient]

TO THE EDITOR, *GUARDIAN* – 23 JUNE 1995

You characteristically misrepresent me as having said over the air that the Booker Prize for fiction "should be scrapped" (June 14). I said merely that the time had come to wonder if such prizes were helpful to literature as a whole.

You also quote Martyn Goff[1] as saying that I "hated" the prize for years before I won it and thereupon changed my mind. He bases this, I think, on reading about a joke I made in 1986. In 1991 I wrote in my Memoirs: "Memo to writers and others: Never make a joke against or about yourself that some little bastard can turn into a piece of shit and send your way" (p325).

KINGSLEY AMIS
Iron Bridge House, Bridge Approach, London NW1 8BD

TO ANTHONY THWAITE – 3 AUGUST 1995

194 Regents Park Road, London NW1 8XP

Dear Anthony,

Sorry not to have answered your June p.c. before. I'm sure you won't venture to London in this heat; I'm off to Swansea next week

1. Martyn Goff (b. 1923), author, bookseller, promoter; Administrator, Booker Prize (1970–).

until September. P.J. Kav. didn't take the poem.[1] As you say, more fool him. Do let me know when you're next coming to London.

Cheers,
K.

[TLS: Recipient]

TO THE EDITOR, *SPECTATOR* – 9 SEPTEMBER 1995

Sir: Auberon Waugh writes (Another voice, 19 August) that inflated communications might be 'a grand idea if we had anything to communicate, but we don't'. Surely 'but we haven't' would be preferable in *The Spectator.* It is a reasonable guess that the American don't-have construction instead of the original haven't-got construction was invented to avoid the word 'got', once a bugbear of refined grammarians. The same sort of fastidiousness gave us 'tidbit' for 'titbit', 'chickadee' for one of the varieties of titmouse, and many others.

Universal don't-have also bundles two meanings into one. As C.S. Lewis pointed out, 'I don't have indigestion' suggests the addition of 'ever', whereas 'I haven't got indigestion' suggests 'at the moment'. Don't-have for both is easier for monoglot immigrants, though.[1]

KINGSLEY AMIS
194 Regent's Park Road, London NW1

---

1. The title of the poem rejected by P.J. Kavanagh, Poetry Editor, *Spectator*, was 'Bottoms'. Amis told Thwaite he wrote it 'after' Larkin's poem 'Tops', in *LCP*, p. 76 (first published in *Listen*, Spring 1957). This was in a telephone conversation of 2 June 1995 in which he also asked Thwaite where he might send it. Thwaite suggested Kavanagh. See Appendix G.

---

1. This letter, the last I have found, was published about six weeks before Amis's death, on 22 October 1995.

APPENDICES

APPENDIX A

Poems included in Amis to Philip Larkin, 30 March 1947

[1]

So far the night has come to hold this room in arms,
Screening this glass with dark, drawing no breath.
If you go out, he will touch all of you at once,
Perfectly cover, embrace you as you step,
Know as light could only know you in a room
Of mirrors, as water only when its surface looks
Down on you held within its pulse, drowning to day
And night, as earth only when all is cold.
My arms are not of colour, love, but stay in them,
In this indoor dark we make of no ideal kiss
To hold you like a jewel in the lover's palm;
Outside the air is frigid, and the night's limbs
Can hold no blood, and it is blood in which we breathe.

[2]

At seven o'clock in the place where three roads met
Memory shows me caught like a photographed runner
Between two ends of a journey, thinking of nothing,
Not vowing to remember. Under my body
The blue road-surface here rolled for this one time,
The trees stood up, later it would be dark;
Steel-coloured dust froze the verges, no one came
Asking to be thought of; in my face the air
Like water for the thirst, cool as a girl's arm,
Grey in the scented paths I should not walk.
Thinking of nothing then I passed, in my brain
A letter's echo, to some version of a haven.

* * *

On these things moralities are built, we deduce
The whole from parts like these. But this one is gone,
Too dark now to be filled by a real lover,
Too tenuous for a straight look. Then let the future,
As I discard this now, steer me elsewhere
Alike from event and from repining, let it show me
Instead the valuable room, the physical kiss
That wait inside, as that evening falls outside
The heart's entirety, the one grain of light.

[3]

We lay in a field at noon, while the sun shone
Through trees like fur on an airman's glove held up,
Blurred promise, your eyes white and brown through lashes;
Words like the wind's sound lost themselves beneath
The unmoved surface of invisible blood
Rising to vertical in the swayed eye's view;
Between your fingers like the trees the day
Was cramped to crimson by your living mixture;
Death was the air that could not stop the light
Falling to close beneath your arching hair.
No future's winter can repudiate
That high meridian; suns that move are still
The sun that shone one hour in your body's frame.

APPENDIX B

Poems included in Amis to Philip Larkin, 27 December 1956

ALL ABOARD THE GRAVY TRAIN: OR, MOVEMENTS AMONG THE YOUNGER POETS

by RON CAIN

Getting Somewhere

When next you take the 2.19
To somewhere that you've read about
And find it's worse than where you've been –

No five-star feeds, no concert-hall,
No capering *Three-Cornered Hat*,
Just Sandy's Caff and the Police Ball –

Before you start to blow your top,
Look at the chaps who've brought the train
Two hundred bloody miles non-stop

While you were sitting on your seat:
They've gone to make themselves at home
In the first boozer down the street.

K+NGSLEY AM+S

To Hart Crane

The victrola talked to him all day.
At night
A thin mist blurred the Hudson, and he sought

Bell-bottomed sex, and the saloons like birds.
Only his famous bridge seemed to connect
Landfalls of concrete, Lucifer's graduate.

The ape's face ripples and reforms, like verse.

And so in a light rain I take the El,
This poem in my pocket like a hole,
Since art and incompleteness are the same,
Seeking the point where an American moon
Thrusts northern waters to the Mexique Bay.

R+BERT C+NQUEST

A Midland Syllogism

He waited for the train at Coventry,
Peeping at truth like Tom against the rules,
At shameless grace astride brute modesty
(A paradox unanswered by the schools).

So, blinded into sighting an event
Towards which, he thought, the whole creation moves,
Tennyson flowered the track with ornament
(His iron horses ran in velvet grooves).

George Whitefield would have called this a conceit
(Something conceited, to be sure, is there):
He saw no gorgon in creation's street
Where grace goes naked under Nature's hair.

D+NALD D+VIE

Outcome of a Conversation

Paying off my rickshaw, I salute Mr. Hakagawa
Who, in his capacity as station-master, bows-in the train.
We discourse gravely on the fall of the yen
And I promise to be here at cherry-time again.

Crammed in the corridor, on Birmingham boxes, the Japanese
Chatter with the confidence of singing-birds
Or spontaneous as Austin workers going home.
When I reach the land where only dividends expand and blossom
May my words come as naturally as leaves or their words.

D.J. ENR+GHT

The Wild Ones

He watched the brutal boys pile off the truck
–Fresh meat the bully sun had handled raw–
Shouldering innocence with rifle and pack:
For them the troop-train on the departure-track
Steamed and vibrated like a two-bit whore.

He guessed how soon these would be taught to weep,
To value white-towered Argos, to understand
Battle is more than shooting from the hip–
Patroclus frying in the bloodsoaked jeep
And crew-cut Achilles two-timed on the sand.

TH+M G+NN

Travellers

In trains we need not choose our company
For all the logic of departure is
That recognition is suspended; we

Are islanded in unawareness, as
Our minds reach out to where we want to be.

But carried thus impersonally on,
We hardly see that person opposite
Who, if we only knew it, might be one
Who, far more than the other waiting at
Some distant place, knows our true destination.

EL+ZABETH J+NNINGS

Poetry of Comings Back

The local snivels through the fields:
I sit between felt-hatted mums
Whose weekly day-excursion yields
Baby-sized parcels, bags of plums,
And bones of gossip good to clack
Past all the seven stations back.

Strange that my own elaborate spree
Should after fourteen days run out
In torpid rural company
Ignoring what my labels shout.
Death will be such another thing,
All we have done not mattering.

PH+LIP L+RKIN

Behind Time

It seems that Bradshaw made a bad mistake:
He tells you where you go but never why,
Leaving you lonely where your journeys break.

You miss connections when you say good-bye,
And find your cheap excursion into bliss
Has no return, however hard you try.

I reached your junction ignorant of this,
Anxious to yield my ticket at your gate,
But travellers need more luggage than a kiss.

Trains behind time are almost always late.

J+HN W+IN

[TLS: Bodleian]

APPENDIX C

Poem referred to in Amis to John Betjeman, 3 June 1971

View Galloo!
or, Ivan in the Shires
by Jasper Budenny

dedicated, with permission, to Sir John Betjeman

The usual Russian practice has been to substitute for the letter and sound 'h' in foreign words its own hard 'g', thus 'Gitler' for Hitler, 'Gull' for Hull; so also garpoon, gandicap, gexameter, gonorar(ium), etc. – R. Austin and V. Glazounov, *A Revised Russian Grammar* (Burt and Hines, 1953).

Gullo, Sir Gumphrey, gow are you?
    I'm up gere from gealthier parts:
I've been gaving my first weekend's gunting
    Out near Gemel Gempstead in Gerts.

There were gonourables there by the gundred,
    Lord Garlech, Lord Gill and Lord Gall,
The gead of the College of Geralds,
    And Gis Gighness – just gome from Nepal.

Though Geath was geld up at the gustings,
    And gard-gitting Gailsham, too,
We gied gandsomely off on our gunters–
    A gole cavalcade from Goo's Goo.

Let gypocrites goot 'Goity-toity!'
Goi Polloi ride in Gordes on our tracks,
Garris-tweeded, got-foot from their gomesteads,
    Gonest gusbandmen gead in on gacks.

And gurrah! from their guts and their govels
From their goes and their garrows and ricks,
Gorny-ganded, but not gumble-gearted,
Run the gired gelps, the gayseeds and gicks.

Tally-go! We were off gell for leather
Past gamlet and gop-field and mill,
Through gawthorn and golly and gazel
Over ga-ga and gedgerow and gill.

Ga! the gawks govered gigh in the geavens
As the geat-gaze gung over the roofs;
Gark! the goney-bees' gives sweetly gumming–
And the gurricane gammer of goofs!

The Vicar gallooed 'Gallelujah!
To Gell with gosannas, Sir Gugh!'
And Sir Gugh Gughes, our Garley Street gealer:
'With gerpes and gaemorrhoids too!'

'G'm! The gorse that my gost gas provided,
Though gis gaunches and gocks could be worse–
Ge hardly seems more in a gurry
Than if gauling a gansom – or gearse!'

'Gi! You gaughty old gas-been, Lord Garry:
What a guddled and gunched way to sit,
Like a Gallowe'en gag on ger broomstick!'
'A git, sir, a palpable git!'

Guzza! gogs and gens were gurled geadlong;
What a gubbub and goo-ga we made!
Geigh-go! through the golm-woods and gollows
A gilarious garlequinade!

And the kids at their gopscotch or gockey
Or gappily bowling their goops,
Gee-geed as we gurdled the gummocks
Like gussars in their gigh-gatted troops!

We were gung up a bit at the gighway–
    Guge Gereford geifers in gerds,
Gumber Gawks, Gillman Guskies all gonking,
    Girsute gitch-gikers gugging their birds.

Then we're geeding the gorn of the guntsman.
    Till the M.F.G. gazards a gunch:
'I gold out no more gopes for this morning!'
    So we gungrily galted for lunch.

Some gostelry'd geaped in our gamper
    A gotch-potch of goary old stock:
Such as gamburgers, gaddocks and gumbugs.
    And a dozen galf-bottles of gock.

Goy! Don't gand the gam to Lord Goreb!
    There's no golier Gebrew around!'
And 'Goots!' gowled Sir Gamish, in gorror.
    'Gere's a gaggis too gigh for a gound!'

So our gostess was galf in gysterics,
    With no gint of ger usual gauteur;
I geard gisses of 'garpy' and 'garridan'
    Not the gomage gabitual to ger.

Then she's off like a gellion or goyden,
    And gard at ger geels we all rush!
See ger gips like a Gollywood gouri's!
    Well, gad I a garem . . . but gush!

Go, the gullabaloo was gorrendous
    While gussy so gecticly led,
Till my gare-brained gorse shied at a gedge-gog
    And I gurtled right over gis gead.

And when, gaggard with gopping and gobbling,
    I sighted ger genna-gaired poll,
Our fox gad galf-geartedly gidden
    In that goly of golies, gis gole . . .

Sir Gumphrey, my talk's been gapgazard,
    And a Gun might have gollered 'Geraus!'
But I'll gail your fair land's gospitality
    Ere you gustle in gaste to the Gouse.

As your Gelicon gero gas gymned it,
    Gis garmony gaunting me still
(Was it Gousman or Gopkins or Gardy?)
    'The gunter is gome from the gill.'

The manuscript from which this epic is taken recently came into the possession of two well-known literary and political figures, the one English and the other a citizen of the United States. They decline to say whether it was supplied by the KGB, the CIA or the League against Cruel Sports. The author, Jasper Budenny, although now resident at an undisclosed address in England, is presumably a blood-relation of Marshal Budenny, the eighty-year-old Cavalryman, hero of World War II, and noted equitationist. – *Editor, The Spectator.*

APPENDIX D

Poem referred to in Amis to Anthony Thwaite, 4 January 1973

To Rosie

Gold-feathered connoisseur of laps,
    Queen of the privy paw,
Whose wailing growl is joy, whose yap's
    Intended to be law,

Whose round-eyed gaze and twitching tail
    Plead for a lion's share
Of Danish Blue, of Wensleydale,
    Of Brie or Camembert.

Whose coat smells of a heated bun
    (At least on a good day),
Who shrieks to see a rabbit run,
    Then hurtles the wrong way–

Why does your mouth, seen from head on,
    Keep such a cheerful tilt,
Yet, in side view, look woebegone,
    Almost as though from guilt?

I'll tell you: so that it can't curl
    Into a smile at last,
For if it could, there's many a girl
    Might find herself outclassed.

KINGSLEY AMIS

APPENDIX E

Poem discussed in Amis to Elizabeth Rich, 15 January 1977

Kipling at Bateman's

He came here when he was thirty-seven
And left, feet first, thirty-four years later.
She organised his life, dealt with all his
Correspondence, set out his engagements,
Filtered his visitors, so that nothing
Could ever come between him and his work.

There's a portrait of her in the study:
Not bad, by Philip Burne-Jones, his cousin;
Less than full length, cut off near the ankles,
Supposedly to conceal her smallness;
Her look one of calm or satisfaction,
And, hanging from her waist, some sort of key.

APPENDIX F

Funeral Address for Philip Larkin, discussed in Amis to Maeve Brennan, 21 November 1986

We are here to mourn the death of our friend Philip Larkin. He was the most private of men, one who found the universe a bleak and hostile place and recognised very clearly the disagreeable realities of human life, above all the dreadful effects of time on all we have and are. The world of his fellow-creatures was to him hardly less forbidding: privacy was to be jealously guarded. In the sense of complete physical solitude, he found it a daily necessity. He saw people as hopelessly cut off from one another, and revealingly misquoted Donne in declaring, Every man is an island. And yet it was impossible to meet him without being aware in the first few seconds of his impeccable attentive courtesy: grave, but at the same time sunlit, always ready to respond to a gleam of humour or warmth. He was surprised if anyone found him a gloomy person: I like to think of myself as quite funny, he told an interviewer, and he was more than quite funny about those in the literary and academic worlds whom he considered fraudulent, and he found no shortage of those; and to hear him sounding off about a politician or any other public figure who was not to his taste did the heart good. But there was no malice in it, no venom. If he regarded the world severely or astringently, it was a jovial astringency. He could be at his funniest when uttering those same painful truths about life as those he made so devastating in his poetry. And it was all from the heart: he never showed off, never laid claim to feeling what he didn't feel, and it was that honesty, more total in his case than in any other I've known, that gave his poetry such power. He meant every word of it; and so, though he may not have written many poems, he wrote none that were false or unnecessary. His honesty extended to himself; again, nobody was ever more totally or acutely aware of his limitations. He took life seriously, he took poetry seriously, but not himself – nobody who said he looked like a bald salmon could do that. No solemnity about himself as a poet, either; when he'd written a poem he felt pleased, as if he'd laid an egg. But we take seriously what he has left us. We are lucky enough to have known him; thousands who didn't, and more thousands in the future, will be able to share those poems with us. They offer comfort, and not cold comfort either. They are not dismal or pessimistic, but invigorating; they know that for all its shortcomings life must be got on with.

And now we must get on with ours, a little better equipped to do so with the help of those fragments of poignancy and humour in everyday things, those moments of illumination and beauty we should never have seen or known but for Philip.

KINGSLEY AMIS December, 1985.

APPENDIX G

Poem referred to in Amis to Anthony Thwaite, 3 August 1995

Bottoms

After P.L.*

On the cistern lid
Stands a toilet-roll
Sufficient, if needed,
To work through whole
Dozens of traces
On hundreds of days
And a thousand uses
(In a couple of ways),
So firm in its thickness
As to go on for ever,
Simply cannot grow less–
Until what we never
Predicted begins,
And that fabulous bulk
Imperceptibly thins:
That legendary hulk,
Diminished now, makes
Room for a version
That first thing takes
The central position:
Condemned in its turn
To become all slender
And get dropped in the bin
As a cardboard cylinder.

* See 'Tops', *LCP*, p. 76

APPENDIX H

Three Alibi Notes

According to Robert Conquest: 'The dates of the alibi notes must have been during my own periods of bachelordom-in-practice in the UK. That is, c. August – December 1956, and c. December 1958 to c. March 1964, probably almost all, or all, in the latter period . . . I can see the scholarly research – Appendix xxxvii, pp. 956–1001, The Dating of the "Notes"' (personal communication, 16 April 1997).[1]

Dear Conkest,
Tank you for evning, If anybody ask, *you gave me diner at Travelers Club Toonight.* But no body will ask I am sure.

Yors,
Ted Hughes

and tank you agan.

[ALS: Recipient]

1. For such assignations see 'Nothing to Fear', from *A Look Round the Estate* (1967), reprinted in *CP*, p. 80:

> All fixed: early arrival at the flat
> Lent by a friend, whose note says *Lucky Sod*;
> Drinks on the tray; the cover-story pat
> And quite uncheckable . . .

The poem ends:

> Beauty, they tell me, is a dangerous thing,
> Whose touch will burn, but I'm asbestos, see?
> All worth while – it's a dead coincidence
> That sitting here, a bag of glands
> Tuned up to concert pitch, I seem to sense
> A different style of caller at my back,
> As cold as ice but just as set on me.

A present for a good boy.
And ta <u>very much</u>, chum
All went according

During the p.m.,

(a) a man – I'm almost certain Tony H[artley] – phoned; I answered in my (milder) Cockney accent. PLEASE COVER. (He rang off – no message, or apparent urgency.)

(b) a girl – don't know who, secretarial in tone – phoned, I answered in my (strong) Czech accent. (Again, no seeming urgency)
And <u>again</u>, ta. Very much.

I'll give you a buzz.

Yours,
Cy. (ril Connolly)

[ALS: Recipient]

Alles in ordnung, schon 'dank'

M. Luther
Pastor

Society of Hagiographical All-German and Bavarian Antidenominational Gesellschaften

[ALS: Recipient]

APPENDIX I

Two Letters to Robert Conquest

TO ROBERT CONQUEST – 8 JANUARY 1958

53 Glanmor Road, Uplands, Swansea, Glam.

Dear Bob,

Just emerging from post-Xmas and New Yr ennui. The party's over, the last gin-&-cider poured down the sink, the last flecks of spew removed from the radiogram, the last french letter swept up in the attic. Now we can get down to some decent routine – i.e. idleness, flatulence, depression and inert, generalised lust; you know the kind of thing.

As regards Aegyptology:[1] not sure if I can remember very much, either. Let's see. One point is to keep the reader in doubt as long as possible what *sort* of novel it is: fantasy, detective, near-pornographic, "serious" etc. The thing should be each in succession at the start, with false clues scattered about: e.g. X's eyes swept dreamily over a splendid Etty[2] above the fireplace ostensibly = X is rich, cultured, really = X is not only a randy sod, but a tit-picture-loving, because tit-starved, randy sod. After a bit of this, we get our spot of foul play. One of the chaps in the club is *apparently* murdered, or disappears. Inquiries are made from the Duty Officer at the Aegypt. Socy, who covers up in the normal way, thinking the inquirer is the representative of a wife. He is now in the position of having faked an alibi for somebody *to the police.* His colleagues support him, but the thing gets out of hand and he has to flee to Peach Key[3] – here's your link – until things have quietened down. He has various pursuers: a detective from the CID investigating the supposed murder, a detective from the Narcotics Bureau who has been working quite independently along the lines that the Aegypt. Socy is a drugs ring, a detective employed by some wife who wants the goods on her husband, another detective from the CID with

1. *The Egyptologists* (1956), published under both Amis's and Conquest's names. Conquest had come up with the novel's basic concept, and in 1964 produced a rough draft, incorporating some but not all of the suggestions Amis offers in this paragraph. Amis reworked the draft in the summer and autumn of 1964. See Amis to Larkin, 30 July 1958, note 3.

2. William Etty (1787–1849), English painter, famed for nudes.

3. The title (and setting) for a second novel Conquest was planning; see Amis to Conquest, 1 March 1976, note 11.

the news that it wasn't murder after all, that our pal is in the clear – it's always a good dodge to have a man trying to escape from a man the first man thinks is a foe but who is actually a pal. Another point of course is to reveal what the Aegypt Socy actually is as late as possible, keep switching explanations: i. a political conspiracy ii. a narcotics ring iii. an Egypt. Socy iv. a buggery club v. an Egypt. socy vi. a narcotics ring vii. a political conspiracy viii. a cell of humanoids from Vega III ix. a buggery club &c &c &c. You should also have a bogus "Proceedings of the Aegypt. Socy" which people examine for cryptograms, and find them, or think they do.

Well now, you get to work on it. Keep me informed. Just thought: there should be a gramophone record of club noises which the Duty Officer puts on when answering the phone. Complication if it gets played at 45 r.p.m. instead of at 33.

As you can see, there's a little chore I'd like you to do for me, if you would be so good as to put the enclosed in the post and keep your trap shut with reference thereto thereafter. I'm sure you see the point: a London postmark is insufficiently specific to catch the husbandly eye, but a Swansea one points straight to yours truly. Do the same for you some day.

Hope to see you before long, but the next Guinness date[4] isn't yet fixed and I think I'd better wait for that before coming up; I spent far too long in London last year, and now must really get some bloody *work* done, sod it. Why can't John Wain see that anyone starting a sentence, let alone a paragraph, with the formula "As a writer, I . . ." is bound to look, AND BE, a shit? His rhyme-twin, Braine, comes here tomorrow. Will tell you what he's like.

Must sod off now. Christmas comes but once a year, And when it comes it makes you pissed all the time and that gives you a sense of impending doom and fills you with remorse and fear. Love to you both. Take care of yourself.

Cheers & 1958 greetings,
Kingsley

[TLS: Recipient]

4. See Amis to Conquest, 29 February 1956, note 2.

TO ROBERT CONQUEST – 11 December 1960

English Department, University College, Swansea, Glamorgan

Dear Bob,

Sorry to have been so slack, as the b said to the a, but work – at the College, i.e. virtually unpaid work – has had me by the balls. All seems well on the sf project,[1] I agree with your 4 points, and return Hilary's letter herewith, so you can tell him, or Jas McMarmoset, that we're going ahead.

Now listen: shut the door, and make sure Desmond Williams[2] isn't looking over your shoulder. Can you fix me up with a bed for tomorrow week (19th Dec.)? From say 11.30 a.m. onwards. I'm coming up to stay with the Gales[3] on Saturday and remaining until Wednesday, so I shall doubtless see you at some time or other, but would like, if possible, to get the thing set up in advance, as the b said to the a. Reply, if you will, to the above address, not Glanmor Road, because a fault in my security system has led Hilly to connect a Conquest letter with an impending Amis screw. And you at your end can help by not telling Desmond Williams this time (or anyone else at any time, for the matter of that) what I am up to. I know myself how easy it is to drop the odd gossipy remark, but Christ, you should have known better than to drop it in Desmond's ear – it went straight from him to old Wormald, thence to Pat, thence to George and Liz,[4] and from Pat and George to me – and then from Liz to me, which was an unpleasant ordeal. (Don't try and take it up with Desmond, there's a boy, or a second set of shock waves will be set in motion.) So please, chum, no leaks to anyone on this. & christ, as you'll readily understand, what bugged me was having to serve my sentence without having had a chance to commit the fucking crime, so to speak.

Don't forget to stick your phone number in your letter, so that, if all goes well, I can arrange to see you (Monday morning, if Sunday's no good) and pick up key or whatever. See you anyway, boyo.

Cheers,
Kingsley

[TLS: Recipient]

1. *Spectrum: A Science-Fiction Anthology* (Gollancz, 1961–66), a series co-edited by Amis and Conquest (see Amis to Conquest, 9 April 1961 & note 1); 'Hilary' and 'Jas McMarmoset' in the next sentence are Hilary Rubinstein and James MacGibbon, editors at Gollancz.

2. Desmond Williams (1921–87), Irish historian, Professor of Modern History, University College Dublin (1949–83), an ex-pupil of Herbert Butterfield at Peterhouse, and a frequent visitor there and in London.

3. For George and Pat Gale see Amis to J.H. McCallum, 5 April 1961, note 1.

4. 'Brian' is Brian Wormald (see Amis to J.H. McCallum, 5 April 1961, note 1); 'Liz' is probably Elizabeth Moynahan (see Amis to Conquest, 9 April 1961, note 7), a friend of the Gales as well as of Amis.

APPENDIX J

'The Watcher in Spanish'

referred to in Amis to Larkin, 27 August 1950

The phrase 'watcher in Spanish' derives from the following passage from Chapter 2 of Christopher Isherwood's semi-autobiographical novel *Lions and Shadows* (1938). The narrator is the Isherwood character; Chalmers is a thinly-disguised portrait of Isherwood's friend Edward Upward:

> 'The Watcher in Spanish' was the latest of our conceits. The phrase came, I believe, from a line in a poem, about: 'The Watcher in Spanish cape . . .' We imagined him as a macabre but semi-comic figure, not unlike Guy Fawkes, or a human personification of Poe's watching raven. He appeared to us, we said, at moments when our behaviour was particularly insincere; one might, for example, be telling a boastful story, or pretending an interest in heraldry, or flattering the wife of a don – and there, suddenly, he would be standing, visible only to ourselves. He made no gesture, never spoke. His mere presence was a sufficient reminder and warning. Mutely, he reminded us that the 'two sides' continued to exist, that our enemies remained implacable, beneath all their charming, expensive, scholarly disguises; he warned us never to betray ourselves by word or deed. He was our familiar, our imaginary mascot, our guardian spirit. Often when we were alone together we spoke to him aloud. 'Come out of that corner!' Chalmers would shout. 'You needn't think we can't see you! Now, leave us alone – do you hear? We're busy.'

As for the 'poem' from which the phrase derives, Robin Oakley-Hill suggests T.S. Eliot's 'Sweeney Among the Nightingales' (1918), 'which was published in book form in 1920 when the Auden-Isherwood generation were teenagers'. The releveant lines (11–18) read:

> . . . The person in the Spanish cape
> Tries to sit on Sweeney's knees
> Slips and pulls the table cloth

Overturns a coffee cup,
Reorganized upon the floor
She yawns and draws a stocking up;
The silent man in mocha brown
Sprawls at the window sill and gapes.

Oakley-Hill comments: 'So the silent man (later the silent vertebrate) is the watcher and the person in the Spanish cape is the watched. Perhaps the sort of mistake one makes in youth . . . Later of course the man in the Spanish cape appears in a sherry ad, and in *Monty Python* no one expects the Spanish Inquisition. Some aspect of the Inquisition must have crept into the Isherwood version, though it's not there in Eliot's Sweeney. Perhaps the Inquisition is the pre-Wolfenden police' (personal communication, 15 May 2000).

APPENDIX K

Three 'Bunny' Notes (undated household notes to Elizabeth Jane Howard, c. 1969–77)

Plumber came, was v. nice, drained off all surplus water, said should work okay now – he turned the heat on – will be back in morning to check, recommends keeping all radiators on this floor on when heat is on.

See ya

[AL: HEHL]

I love you all the time, dearest Piney, even when I seem not to. You see? Sorry to be so crusty. Be better in future.

[AL: HEHL]

I am in the

annexe

[AL: HEHL]

ACKNOWLEDGEMENTS

I have many people to thank, beginning with the Amis family and the co-executors of the Kingsley Amis Literary Estate, Martin Amis and Jonathan Clowes. I am also especially indebted to Robert Conquest, Lady Kilmarnock and Elizabeth Jane Howard, for lending letters and patiently submitting to innumerable queries; to Gwyniver Jones and the staff of the BBC Written Archives Centre, Caversham Park, Reading, Berkshire; to the administration and staff of the Huntington Library, San Marino, California, in particular to Jill Coogan, Sara S. Hodson, Alan Jutzie and Roy Ritchie; to Judith Priestman of the Department of Western Manuscripts, Bodleian Library, Oxford; to Philip Moss of the Oxford University Archives, for help in identifying many of Amis's contemporaries at Oxford in the 1940s; to James Silvester and John Postgate, for jazz expertise; to B.C. Bloomfield, James Booth, Brian Dyson, Andrew Motion and Anthony Thwaite, for help with queries about Philip Larkin; to Sam Dawson, Amis's friend and colleague from the English Department at the University College of Swansea; to Jane Pringle of the Department of English at the University of Surrey Roehampton (formerly the Roehampton Institute, London); to Vivien Green, of Sheil Land Associates Ltd; to Michael Fishwick, Caroline Hotblack and Robert Lacey of HarperCollins; and to Douglas Matthews who prepared the index.

For careful reading of the entire manuscript I am grateful to Martin Amis, David Papineau, Anthony Thwaite and Tom Treadwell. Any remaining mistakes are, of course, my own.

I must thank the following institutions for permissions and for providing information: Bodleian Library, Oxford; Boston University Library; Department of Manuscripts, University of Bristol Library; Written Archive Centre, British Broadcasting Company, Caversham Park, Reading, Berkshire; Department of Manuscripts, British Library; Poetry/Rare Books Collection, Lockwood Memorial Library, State University of New York, Buffalo; Rare Book and Manuscript Library, Butler Library, Columbia University; Curtis Brown Ltd, New York; Plomer Collection, Durham University Library; Special Collections, Edinburgh University Library; Eton College Library; Garrick Club; Victor Gollancz Ltd; John Simon Guggenheim Memorial Foundation; Harcourt Brace and Company; Brynmor Jones Library, University of Hull; Hoover Institution, Stanford University, Stanford, California; Henry E. Huntington Library, San Marino, California; Manuscripts Department, Lilly Library, Indiana University; Brotherton Collection, Leeds University Library; Manuscript Division, Library of Congress, Washington DC; John Rylands Library, University of Manchester; Oxford University Archives; the Secretary to the Delegates of the Oxford University Press; Rare Books Room, Pennsylvania State University Libraries; Harry Ransom Humanities Research Center, Austin, Texas; Department of Manuscripts and Records, National Library of Wales, Aberystwyth; Department of Rare Books and Special Collections, Firestone Library, Princeton University; Seeley G. Mudd Manuscript Library, Princeton University Archives; Random House; Library, University of Reading; Royal Society of Literature; St John's College, Cambridge; St John's College, Oxford; Society of Authors; University of Sussex Library; George Arents Research Library, Syracuse University Library; Dylan Thomas Literary Estate; McPherson Library, University Archives and Special Collections, University of Victoria Library, British Columbia.

Other institutions I must thank for help with enquiries include: American Academy of Arts and Letters; Army Records Centre, Hayes, Middlesex; Birmingham Reference Library; Bradford Central Library; Bradford District Archives; Newspaper Library (British Library); Manuscripts Division, Bancroft Library, University of California, Berkeley; CAM Magazine; Cassell plc Publishing; Cavalier King Charles Spaniel Club; Centre for Policy Studies; City of London School; *Daily Express*; *Daily Mail*; *Daily Mirror*; *Daily Telegraph*; *Decanter* Magazine; Department of Special Collections, University of Delaware Library; Doubleday and Co.; Manuscript Department, William R. Perkins Library, Duke University; Faber and Faber; Fabian Society; Granada Television; *Guardian*; HarperCollins; Houghton Library, Harvard University; David Higham Associates Ltd; Hutchinson; *Illustrated London News*; Imperial War Museum; John Murray (Publishers) Ltd; W.P. Albrecht Collection, Department of Special Collections, University of Kansas Libraries; King Henry VIII School, Coventry; King's College Library, Cambridge; London Library; *London Review of Books*; McMaster University Library, Hamilton, Ontario; Marx Memorial Library; Department of Rare Books and Special Collections, Hatcher Graduate Library, University of Michigan Library; Henry W. and Albert A. Berg Collection, New York Public Library; New American Library; *New Statesman*; *New York Review of Books*; *New York Times*; Science Fiction Foundation, University of North East London; Division of Manuscripts, University of Oklahoma Libraries; Penguin Books; Peterhouse, Cambridge; Peters, Fraser and Dunlop Group Ltd; Pierpont Morgan Library; Public Record Office, National Archives, Kew, Surrey; Department of Manuscripts, National Library of Scotland; *Spectator*; Department of Special Collections, Manuscript Division, Stanford

University Library; *Sunday Telegraph*; *Sunday Times*; Swarthmore College Library; Special Collections, Temple University Libraries, Philadelphia, Pennsylvania; Thames and Hudson Ltd; *Times Literary Supplement*; Special Collections, University of Virginia Library; Library, Personnel Office and Registry, University of Wales, Swansea; Modern Records Centre, University of Warwick Library; John M. Olin Library, Department of Rare Books and Special Collections, Washington University Libraries, St Louis, Missouri; A.P. Watt Ltd; Weidenfeld and Nicolson; Beinecke Rare Book and Manuscript Library, Yale University.

Thanks are due to the following individuals for permitting me to consult letters and for providing information: Brian Aldiss; Hilly Amis (Lady Kilmarnock); John Amis; Martin Amis; Austin Baker; Julian Barnes; Frank Barnshaw; M.G.H. Bishop; Chris Bowyer; Alastair Boyd (Lord Kilmarnock); Maeve Brennan; Alfred L. Bush; Sarah Cardew; Tony Colwell; Robert Conquest; William Cooper (Harry Hoff); Wendy Cope; John Coquet; Brian Cox; Simon Curtis; D.J. Enright; Mrs Gavin Ewart; Jill Farringdon; Paul Ferris; Robert Foster; Paul Fussell; Mary Gale; Rick Gekoski; Jack Gohn; William Graves; Candida Lycett Green; Mr and Mrs Richard Hough; Colin Howard; Elizabeth Jane Howard; Bruce Hunter; Samuel Hynes; Susan Irvine; Eric Jacobs; Pat Kavanagh; Mrs Leila Keam; Nigel Kneale; Richard Lewis; Roger Lewis; Jean McAndrew; Ann and John McDermott; W.Y. McNeil; Sargy Mann; Tom Maschler; Mr and Mrs Derwent May; Caroline Michel; Karl Miller; Tom Miller; Jan Montefiori; Blake Morrison; Anne Naylor; Edward W. Pell; Anthony Powell and Lady Violet Powell; Anne Prior; William H. Pritchard; Paul Rassam; Elizabeth Rich; Theo Richmond; Christopher Ricks; Harry Ritchie; Alan Ross; William Rukeyser; Michael and Virginia Rush; Dale Salwak; Michael Sharp; M.G. Sherlock; Josef Skvorecky; Frank Smyth; Stuart Sutherland; Edwin Tarling; Ann Thwaite; Anthony Thwaite; Rebecca Thynne; Bill Turner; John Veale; Lois Wilson; Esta Wolfram; Lord Wyatt of Weeford.

Individuals I must thank for help with enquiries include Ian Aitkin; Susan Allison; Al Alvarez; James Atlas; Simon Bailey; Joan Bakewell; Jill Balcon (Day-Lewis); Sir Peter Baldwin; R.V. Barnes; Nicholas Bateson; Fred Bauman; John Bayley; Caroline Belgrave; Alan Bell; Nora Beloff; Alan Bennett; Bernard Bergonzi; Andrew Biswell; Sir George Blunden; Michael Bolt; James Booth; Ray Boulting; Arthur Boyars; Rosie Boycott; Catherine Boyle; Malcolm Bradbury; Melvyn Bragg; Alan Brien; Stephen Brook; Sally Brown; Sir Mervyn Brown; William F. Buckley, Jr; Pamela Buckmaster; Katherine Bucknell; R.W. Burchfield; Mrs Anthony Burgess; Brie Burkeman; T.A.J. Burnett; Chris Burt; Neil Burton; Liz Calder; Dr Wesley Carr; Peter Carson; Hugh Cecil; Anthony Cheetham; Ted Childs; David Chipp; Esmond and Jean Cleary; Simon Cobley; Christopher Collins; Marilyn Corrie; Simon Courtauld; Mr and Mrs Maurice Cowling; Susan Crosland; Anthony Curtis; Barry Darling; Roger Davenport;

Mrs Donald Davie; Walford Davies; Frank Deford; John DeVries; John Doxat; Sir Edward du Cann; Elaine Dundy; Dr James Durham; Brian Dyson; Judith Egerton; Alexandra Erskine; Anne Ettlinger; Barbara Everett; Richard Eyre; Sebastian Faulks; Ian Firla; Anthony Flew; Peter Foden; Isabel Fonseca; Russell Fraser; John Freeman; John Fuller; P.N. Furbank; Davina Gammon; Paul Gane; Rick Gekoski; Guillermo Gill; Jon Glover; Dean Godson; Daisy Goodwin; Margaret Goostray; Jonathon Green; Graham C. Greene; Nancy Greene; Kate Grimond; John Gross; Miriam Gross; Peter Grosvenor; Valerie Grove; C.V. Guinness; Winifred Hall; Rod Hamer; Ian Hamilton; Valentine Hammond; F. E. Hanson; Allen Harbinson; Lord Harris of High Cross; Richard Harris; Harry Harrison; Dominick Harrod; Janet M. Hart; Anthony Hartley; George Hartley; Jean Hartley; Martin Harvey; William Hayes; Kenneth Haynes; Simon Heffer; Thomas Hemsley; Cathy Henderson; Robert Hewison; Rust Hills; Edward Hirsch; Christopher Hitchens; Alan Hollinghurst; Anthony Howard; David Hughes; Richard Ingrams; Jeremy Isaacs; Clive James; Peter Janson-Smith; Elizabeth Jennings; Paul Johnson; Rebecca Johnson; D.A.N. Jones; David Jones; Monica Jones; Peter Jovanovich; Danny Karlin; Peter Kemp; Mr and Mrs Murray Kempton; E.J. Kenny; Frank Kermode; Elizabeth Knight; Perry Knowlton; Rhoda Koenig; Tony Lacey; Hilary Laidlaw-Thompson; J.V. Dundas Lamont; Richard Law; Duncan Lawrie; Adam Lee; Hermione Lee; William Letwin; Peter Levi; Bernard Levin; Paul Levy; Jeremy Lewis; Russell Lewis; John Lloyd; Mrs R.D. Loades; David Lodge; Graham Lord; Roger Lovatt; Judith Luna; Andrew Lycett; Karen McGrath; Norman Mailer; Douglas Matthews; Ralph Maud; Julie Maylon; Edward Mendelson; Cyril Metliss; Wallace Milroy; Kenneth Minogue; Victoria Mizen; Mary Morgan; Ferdinand Mount; Dame Iris Murdoch; Timothy Murray; Jenny Naipaul; Geoffrey and Mavis Nicholson; Maggie Noach; Denis Norden; Robert K. O'Neill; Mrs John Osborne; John O'Sullivan; Simon Palmer; Chris Petter; Antonia Phillips; Bruce Phillips; Fred Pohl; Harold Pollins; Richard N. Porter; John Postgate; John Powell; Tristram Powell; Tom Priestley; Rodney Pybus; Margaret Quass; Lady Quennell; David B. Quinn; Alan Radnor; Dallas McCord (Mack) Reynolds; Peter Richards; Stewart (Sandy) Richardson; Leonard Richenberg; Timothy Rogers; Mark E. Rose; Tom Rosenthal; Janice Rossen; Leo Rosten; Anthony Rota; Hilary Rubinstein; Nicholas Scheetz; Roger Scruton; Robert Sheckley; Christopher Sheppard; Norman Sherry; Thomas Shippey; Joyce Sims; Michael Sissons; Ruth (Bowman) Siverns; Mrs Patrick Skene-Catling; Godfrey Smith; Thomas Staley; Jon Stallworthy; George Steiner; Sandra Steltz; Norman Stone; Sir Tom Stoppard; Richard Storey; John Sutherland; David Sutton; Helen Szamuely; G. Thomas Tanselle; Brian Taylor; Glur Dyson Taylor; John Taylor; John Terraine; Baroness Thatcher; Eve Thomas; M. Wynn Thomas; George Thomson; James Thrower; Claire Tomalin; John Torode; Polly Toynbee; Sally Toynbee; Donald

Trelford; Ion Trewin; Lily Uniacke; Malcolm Vale; Ursula Vaughan-Williams; Jeff Vent; Marie Von Grellier; William Wain; Davis Walker; Stephen Wall; Jonathan Walsh; Christopher Ward; Keith Waterhouse; Graham Watson; Donald Cameron Watt; Auberon Waugh; Lord Weidenfeld; Jerome Weidman; Mrs Colin Welch; John Wells; Grace Wherry; Mrs William A.P. White; David Whittle; Antony Whittome; Rose Wild; James Willcox; Margery Willcox; John Williams; Anne Wilson; Colin Wilson; D.H. Wilson; Frances Wollen; Vicki Woods; David Woolley; Sir Peregrine Worsthorne; Dr Ronald Zeegen.

Chief among the books on Amis I have borrowed from for biographical and bibliographical details are Eric Jacobs, *Kingsley Amis: A Biography* (1995), which draws on numerous conversations with Amis himself, and three other books whose authors consulted Amis: *Kingsley Amis: A Checklist* (1976), by Jack Gohn; *Kingsley Amis: A Reference Guide* (1978), by Dale Salwak; *Kingsley Amis: An English Moralist* (1989), by John McDermott. I am also much indebted to Anthony Thwaite's edition of *The Selected Letters of Philip Larkin* (1992), Blake Morrison's *The Movement* (1980) and Andrew Motion's *Philip Larkin: A Writer's Life* (1993).

For financial assistance I must thank the Huntington Library for the award of a Fletcher Jones Foundation Fellowship; the University of Surrey Roehampton, for Research Leave; and the Society of Authors, for a grant from the K. Blundell Trust, which enabled me to employ a research assistant, Tamsin Todd, in the later stages of my work. I am indebted to Miss Todd for exceptionally resourceful, perceptive and patient assistance. Finally, deepest thanks to my family, Alice, Nick and Max Leader, and to my mother, Rosalinde L. Leader.

INDEX

A figure in **bold** indicates the first page of a letter to a correspondent.
Writings by KA appear under title; works by others under author's name.